Utah Geological Association
Publication 28

GEOLOGY of UTAH'S PARKS and MONUMENTS

Douglas A. Sprinkel, Senior Editor
Thomas C. Chidsey, Jr., Co-editor
Paul B. Anderson, Co-editor

Utah Geological Association
P.O. Box 520100
Salt Lake City, Utah 84152-0100

Millennium Field Conference

CREDITS

Cover photograph:
Trail through Bryce Canyon National Park
Photo Courtesy of Utah Travel Council

Title page photograph:
Goblin Valley State Park
Photo Courtesy of Utah Division of Parks and Recreation

Back cover photographs:
A collection of Utah's Parks and Monuments
Photos Courtesy of Utah Travel Council
and Utah Division of Parks and Recreation

Cover design and desktop publishing:
Vicky Clarke, Graphic Designer
Salt Lake City, Utah

Printing by:
Publishers Press, Salt Lake City, Utah

ISBN
0-9702571-0-4

CONTRIBUTORS

The Utah Geological Association gratefully acknowledges and thanks the following organizations and companies for their financial support. Their support provided the funding to allow this book to be printed in color.

National Park Service

Utah Travel Council

Utah Division of Parks and Recreation
Department of Natural Resources

Rocky Mountain Section Foundation,
American Association of Petroleum Geologists

Bureau of Land Management

Sinclair Oil Corporation

Ashley National Forest

Flying J Oil & Gas Inc.
(Subsidary of Flying J Inc)

U.S. Geological Survey

URS Corporation

Utah Geological Survey

Cedar Breaks National Monument
Photo courtesy of the Utah Travel Council

CONTENTS

PARK HISTORY

NATIONAL PARKS

NATIONAL MONUMENTS

NATIONAL RECREATION AREAS

STATE PARKS

COMPANION VOLUME

2000 Utah Geological Association
Publication 29 (compact disc)

Geologic Road, Trail, and Lake Guides to Utah's Parks and Monuments

Paul B. Anderson, Editor
Douglas A. Sprinkel, Co-editor

Includes Interactive E-document of an Invertebrate Fossil Inventory, Grand Staircase-Escalante National Monument.

Available publications of the

UTAH GEOLOGICAL ASSOCIATION

These publications are for sale at 1594 W. North Temple, Salt Lake City, Utah. To order, write to NATURAL RESOURCES MAP AND BOOKSTORE, P.O. Box 146100, Salt Lake City, Utah 84114-6100. Orders also are accepted by telephone—call (888) UTAHMAP or (801) 537-3320—or by fax (801) 537-3395.

UTAH GEOLOGICAL ASSOCIATION

www.utahgeology.org

2000 OFFICERS/UGA BOARD

President . . . . Thomas C. Chidsey, Jr. . . . . . . Utah Geological Survey
Program Chairperson . . . . Grant C. Willis . . . . Utah Geological Survey
Treasurer . . . . Dale Schreck . . . . Flying J Oil and Gas Inc.
Secretary . . . . Mark R. Milligan . . . . Utah Geological Survey
President-Elect . . . . Marv Brittenham . . . . Flying J Oil and Gas Inc.
Past-President . . . . Michael V. Lowe . . . . Utah Geological Survey
Newsletter Editor . . . . Don Harris . . . . Sinclair Oil Corporation

MILLENNIUM TOUR COMMITTEE

Chair . . . . Douglas A. Sprinkel . . . . Utah Geological Survey
Coordinator – Moab . . . . Thomas C. Chidsey, Jr. . . . . . . Utah Geological Survey
Coordinator – Wasatch Front . . . . Kathy Morrow . . . . Utah Parks and Recreation
Coordinator – Vernal . . . . Jason Blake . . . . Independent
Coordinator – St. George . . . . Craig D. Morgan . . . . Utah Geological Survey
National Park Coordinator . . . . Tim Connors . . . . National Park Service
Teacher Coordinator . . . . Sandy Eldredge . . . . Utah Geological Survey
Transportation . . . . Roger Bon . . . . Utah Geological Survey
Registration . . . . Roger Bon . . . . Utah Geological Survey

MILLENNIUM TOUR LEADERS

Moab Tour . . . . Hellmut H. Doelling . . . . Utah Geological Survey
                                               Thomas C. Chidsey, Jr. . . . . . . Utah Geological Survey
Wasatch Front Tour . . . . Grant C. Willis . . . . Utah Geological Survey
                                               Julie Willis . . . . Independent
                                               W. Adolph Yonkee . . . . Weber State University
St. George Tour . . . . Robert F. Biek . . . . Utah Geological Survey
                                               Grant C. Willis . . . . Utah Geological Survey
                                               Michael D. Hylland . . . . Utah Geological Survey
                                               Hellmut H. Doelling . . . . Utah Geological Survey

Green River Outlook, Canyonlands National Park
Photo courtesy of the Utah Travel Council

PRESIDENT'S MESSAGE

Welcome to Utah's Parks and Monuments!

Each year millions of people from around the world visit the classic displays of geology in Utah's many national and state parks, monuments, and recreation areas. To celebrate the new millennium and the 30th anniversary of the Utah Geological Association (UGA), I am pleased to present this Millennium Guidebook to not only the geologist, but the geo-hobbyist, earth science teacher, student, hiker, or anyone with an interest in the geology of Utah's spectacular parks.

"The landscape everywhere . . . is of rock–cliffs of rock, tables of rock, plateaus of rock, terraces of rock, crags of rock–ten thousand strangely carved forms; rocks everywhere," are the words penned by Major John Wesley Powell on July 17, 1869, describing what is now part of Canyonlands National Park. The rest of Utah's parks and monuments have rocks everywhere too–with ages ranging from Precambrian to Pleistocene. These parks have faults, folds, mountains, canyons, arches, caves, volcanoes, and dinosaurs. There is something for everyone in Utah's parks and monuments, and the Millennium Guidebook contains general geology papers on 25 parks and monuments. These include all five national parks, six national monuments, the Glen Canyon and Flaming Gorge National Recreation Areas, ten geologic-based state parks, and Monument Valley Tribal Park, as well as eight topical papers.

The Millennium Guidebook is dedicated to Fred "Pete" Peterson of the U.S. Geological Survey and a long-standing member of UGA. Fred is recognized for his many contributions to the understanding of the geology of Utah's parks and monuments, particularly the Jurassic stratigraphy of the Colorado Plateau.

Many organizations made generous financial contributions in support of this book which allowed us to print it in color and keep the price affordable. I would like to thank all the authors who donated literally months of time and used their expertise to produce the fine papers in this special guidebook. Many authors even contributed multiple papers and road logs! I thank Paul B. Anderson for his dedicated work as Co-Editor and author, and for his outstanding marketing efforts. Finally, I would like to thank Douglas A. Sprinkel, Senior Editor, for the absolutely incredible job in organizing, reviewing, tracking, financial soliciting, writing, and marketing that was required to complete this book.

The objective of the UGA is "the increase and diffusion of geological knowledge and encouragement of public appreciation . . . of geologic science." I sincerely hope you find the UGA Millennium Guidebook useful as you visit and explore the geologic wonders of Utah's parks and monument.

Thomas C. Chidsey, Jr.
President

Devil's Playground, Grand Staircase-Escalante National Monument
Photo by Douglas A. Sprinkel

EDITOR'S COMMENTS

For decades, geologists have come to Utah to study the geology of this state and to explore for a variety of geologic resources—and Utah does have wealth of geologic resources. Of those, the well-exposed geology itself may be the most important resource that Utah has to offer to future generations of geologists and people interested in geology. Simply put, Utah has some of the most spectacular examples of classic geology found anywhere in the world! The geologic examples that are studied from here are used in the classroom as well as the corporate boardrooms. Some of the best of Utah geology are showcased in Utah's many national and state parks, monuments, and recreation areas. Places such as Arches, Bryce, Canyonlands, and Zion are well known for their grand geology and geologic vistas. But other parks such as Capitol Reef, Dinosaur, Goblin Valley, and Snow Canyon are equal in geologic majesty to their more visited counterparts. Visitors to Utah's parks and monuments are captivated by the variety of plants and wildlife that call the parks home. However, it is the landscape, the cliffs and canyons, and the odd rock formations—in a word the geology—that leaves the visitor awestruck.

The parks and monuments of Utah include rocks of all ages; from Archean high-grade metamorphic rocks of Antelope Island State Park and Flaming Gorge National Recreation Area to the recent basalt flows in Zion National Park and Snow Canyon State Park. Common to many parks in Utah is the scenic and memorable Jurassic section. Jurassic rocks form the shear red and white sandstone cliffs of the Navajo Sandstone that embrace Zion National Park to the world class dinosaur bone deposits of the Morrison Formation in Dinosaur National Monument. Even Utah's centennial license plate displays Jurassic rocks in the rendition of Delicate Arch, an arch formed in the Entrada Sandstone and Curtis Formation in Arches National Park. The parks also preserve some of the best examples of structural geology, sedimentary and geomorphic features, and paleontological resources.

To celebrate Utah's geologic parks during the millennium year, the UGA is proud to publish this year's guidebook, "Geology of Utah's Parks and Monuments." This guidebook contains articles on each national parks, monument, and recreation area in Utah, as well as 10 state parks and the only designated geological area in Utah. In addition, the guidebook includes eight topical articles on research in and around the parks.

As senior editor, I thank all of the authors who contributed to this guidebook. Their willingness and enthusiasm to share their geologic expertise is evident in their articles and have made this a truly unique guidebook. I also thank the organizations and companies who financially contributed toward the publication of this guidebook and provided the means to print it in color. Finally, I thank my co-editors who were instrumental in completing this ambitious project.

Douglas A. Sprinkel
Senior Editor

In Memoriam

Wendy Virginia Romney Hassibe

1940 - 1999

Wendy Virginia Romney Hassibe dedicated her life to serving and improving the customer service given to the general public, geologists, and professionals who needed maps, documents, and information on parks, public land, and U.S. Geological Survey (USGS) information. She joined the Utah Geological Association in 1974 and served as newsletter editor for many years. Sadly, Wendy passed away on March 11, 1999, shortly after her retirement from her beloved profession. While her presence will be missed by many of those who knew her, her commitment, dedication, and concern for serving the needs of the public lives on in the work of those whom she influenced.

Wendy led her professional life with the USGS where she began in the Salt Lake City Office in 1967 as an information specialist, providing maps guidance and information to those interested in her beloved west. In 1987 she moved to Reston, Virginia where she managed the entire network of Information Services at USGS Headquarters. She concluded her career in Denver, Colorado leading a team of specialists charged with the task of re-engineering USGS services as a part of the National Performance Review and Reinvention Initiative, directed by the office of Vice President, Al Gore. She was responsible for improving, streamlining, and updating many of the information services that directed maps, brochures, and information to people across the country. Wendy was known and honored for her organizational and leadership skills; she was recognized by the office of the Vice President with the Golden Hammer award for her successful efforts at re-inventing government. Wendy will be remembered for her love of the west, commitment to excellence, and love of her family.

—Kim Hassibe

Geology of Utah's Parks and Monuments
2000 Utah Geological Association Publication 28
D.A. Sprinkel, T.C. Chidsey, Jr., and P.B. Anderson, editors

Dedication to Fred "Pete" Peterson

by Christine E. Turner

Those of us who know Pete Peterson (O.K., so perhaps his proper name is Fred, but everyone knows him as "Pete") know that it is a singular treat as a geologist to ride along as a passenger with him anywhere on the Colorado Plateau. If you want to know what formations form the landscape coming into view, what depositional environments they include, how they correlate with other areas on the Plateau, or perhaps how a certain formation name changed historically—he is more than happy to share his extensive knowledge. During the course of a distinguished career at the U.S. Geological Survey (USGS), he has become the quintessential field geologist who knows everything worth knowing about the Colorado Plateau. His special fascination has been with the Mesozoic, most particularly the Jurassic, but just spring almost anything on him, and be astonished by his repertoire of geologic insights.

It is befitting that a volume about the geology of Utah's parks and monuments is dedicated to Pete. He has contributed significantly to our understanding of the geology of many national parks, particularly in Utah. He also got his first taste of geology and the first thought of becoming a geologist during a visit as an Illinois teenager to Rocky Mountain National Park during a summer jaunt across the country with two of his friends. As they stood breathing in the fresh mountain air and overlooking the magnificent glacial topography, one of his companions said, "Wouldn't it be neat to be a geologist, and learn more

Figure 1. *Plane table mapping in the Gunsight Butte quadrangle, southern Kaiparowits region, Utah. Navajo Point is just above the alidade and Navajo Mountain is shrouded in clouds in the distance, August 1967. Note the trademark "red kerchief" in Pete's back pocket.*

Figure 2. Four Colorado Plateau geologists at the type locality of the Cow Springs Member of the Entrada Sandstone. From left are Jim Wright, Pete Peterson, Larry Craig, and Jack Strobell, September 25, 1965.

about those rocks?" The comment, and the possibilities, made a lasting impression. Two of the three young boys from Illinois (including Pete) went on to become geologists.

He didn't know at first how that dream would be realized. After being drafted and doing a tour of duty in the army, he had the means, as a beneficiary of the G.I. Bill, to go to college and begin a lifelong affair with geology. In his junior year at San Diego State University, and with Professor Baylor Brooks' encouragement, he took the exam for employment with the USGS. He passed, and, upon graduation, was offered a job with the Conservation Division of the USGS in Farmington, New Mexico in 1960.

Between mostly summer stints at the USGS in Farmington, and graduate work at Oregon State and then Stanford University, Pete found time to visit not only the Cretaceous rocks of the San Juan basin that were the focus of his coal studies, but also all of the fascinating sedimentary rocks in the surrounding region. On weekends, he loaded his '55 Chevy with sleeping gear, canned food, and all of the maps and guidebooks of the Four Corners Geological Society and the state surveys, with only a plastic sheet for a rain cover should an evening storm visit him at his campsite out under the open sky. Baling wire was the "duct tape" of the day, serving to hold his car together as he coaxed it over the unpaved roads of the Navajo reservation.

After shifting from the San Juan basin to the Kaiparowits Plateau to work with Harry Waldrop and Whitey (H.D.) Zeller, Pete made his first major contribution to the geology of the Colorado Plateau in what was to become his Ph.D. dissertation. He hiked, and packed in by horseback, to some of the most remote regions of southern Utah — the deeply incised canyons in the northeastern part of the Kaiparowits Plateau — and documented the

structural control of coal accumulations in the Upper Cretaceous Straight Cliffs Formation in the Kaiparowits basin, which is now part of the Grand Staircase-Escalante National Monument. He demonstrated that shoreface sandstones stacked vertically over or near the crests of paleoanticlines and that the coal accumulated to greater thicknesses in the adjacent and shoreward synclines. Not only was this an interesting discovery, it provided a geologic model for more accurately assessing the coal resources of the region. He continued studying the Upper Cretaceous for many years, "walking out" the outcrops along steep mesas, and working with Bill Cobban, the legendary Cretaceous ammonite specialist, to unravel the stratigraphic and age relationships. This work led to publications that contained major revisions in the Cretaceous stratigraphy between the Kaiparowits, Henry Mountains and Black Mesa basins, and the Wasatch Plateau (Peterson and Kirk, 1977; Peterson and others, 1980).

Pete's mapping of the Kaiparowits country also meant that he became familiar with Jurassic rocks down to the Glen Canyon Group, and his introduction to the Jurassic became a lasting and ongoing love affair. He had an opportunity to delve more deeply into the Jurassic, as he was called upon to map the lower Glen Canyon area in 1963, just as the water was beginning to rise behind Glen Canyon Dam. He mapped from Wahweap marina to Rainbow Bridge National Monument in what is now the Glen Canyon National Recreation Area. Seeing so much rock over so much territory gave him an intimate knowledge of the rocks that comprise the landscape. When the "submarine sand wave" craze hit the field of sedimentology in the early 1970s, and the Navajo Sandstone was incorrectly reinterpreted as marine in origin, Pete's meticulous documentation of what were clearly subaerial sedimentary structures in the formation helped to quickly re-establish the eolian interpretation of the Navajo. At the same time that he was mapping in the Glen Canyon area, he was also working on his dissertation in the Kaiparowits region. This double duty meant that he sometimes would put in a six-month field season, trying to keep ahead of the water as it rose behind the dam.

In addition to the Navajo, Pete was keenly interested in all of the great sand seas that dominated the Colorado Plateau region during much of the Mesozoic era. He was interested in the often subtle unconformities that held the key to the regional stratigraphy, at a time (the mid-1970s) that pre-dated the current emphasis on sequence stratigraphy, a time when emphasis was more on facies analysis than on gaps in the rock record. George Pipiringos, who was tracing regional unconformities from Wyoming down into Utah, could carry his early Middle Jurassic "chert pebble unconformity" as far south as the Waterpocket fold, in Capitol Reef National Park. He was perplexed by the Kaiparowits region, where he couldn't find the unconformity. Pete located this surface in a seemingly unlikely place – within the upper part of the Navajo Sandstone. Recognition of this unconformity led to reinterpretation of

Figure 3. Camp site deep in the Kaiparowits country with (L-R) Whitey Zeller, his field assistant Pete Alvey, and Pete Peterson, summer, 1972.

the regional correlations of Lower and Middle Jurassic strata and definition of a new unit — the Page Sandstone — named by him for classic exposures in the Glen Canyon National Recreation Area.

Recognizing the importance of regional unconformities, Pete extended his studies of Lower and Middle Jurassic rocks throughout southeastern Utah, and refined the stratigraphy of this interval in several national parks, including Zion, Capitol Reef, and Arches. The new information led to publication of a classic USGS Professional Paper with George Pipiringos (Peterson and Pipiringos, 1979). At the same time, he meticulously gathered cross-bedding dip-vector data from all of the units he studied, both fluvial and eolian. He didn't realize how valuable this information would be until much later, when he received a call from Judy Parrish, a well-known paleoclimatologist. Judy asked, "Do you have any cross-bedding data from Mesozoic eolian strata on the Colorado Plateau." Pete replied, "Which ones do you want?" to which Judy responded, "Which ones do you have?" Pete answered, "All of them." Judy said that she would be right over! The two of them then collaborated on a landmark paper, in which they combined the eolian data sets with paleogeographic reconstructions and climate models to reconstruct the movement of continents through climatic belts with time (Parrish and Peterson, 1988). They were able to explain the shift in prevailing wind directions from Middle to Late Jurassic time as a northward shift in the position of the North American continent into a different climatic belt. Pete also contributed to an important paper with Ron Blakey and Gary Kocurek on the major ergs (eolian sand seas) of Western North America (Blakey and others, 1988).

In the 1970s, a boom in the uranium industry resulted in renewed interest in the Colorado Plateau, home of significant uranium deposits. Pete's expertise in the Jurassic was now well known, and he was asked to transfer from the Conservation Division to the Geologic Division of the

U.S. Geological Survey to join the Branch of Uranium and Thorium Resources. He focussed his efforts on the Morrison Formation and, in addition to turning his interest to uranium ore genesis, continued to improve our understanding of the stratigraphy and sedimentology of the Jurassic. He was keenly aware that good geology starts with the stratigraphic and sedimentologic framework, and that detailed geochemical studies are only meaningful when tied to that framework. His detailed studies of the Morrison resulted in recognition of a new basal unit—the Tidwell Member, which he named. Recognition of the unconformity that separates the lithologically similar Tidwell Member and underlying Summerville resolved some long-standing problems related to the Summerville Formation in the Grand Staircase-Escalante region and the Capitol Reef area. At the same time, he sorted out relationships between a sandstone unit in the Glen Canyon National Recreation Area and the Summerville, and named it the Romana Sandstone, which forms massive cliffs that loom majestically over Lake Powell (Peterson, 1988).

Pete then focused his attention on the Salt Wash Member of the Morrison Formation in the Henry Mountains area of southeastern Utah, the unit that hosts the uranium ore. Detailed analysis of the member led him to recognize that paleosynclines controlled the distribution of grey lacustrine mudstones, that, in turn, played a role in uranium ore genesis (Peterson, 1980). This was a significant breakthrough in the understanding of ore distribution in the Morrison Formation. He wrote his famous "quivering craton" paper based on the idea that movement along minor structures influenced fluvial sedimentation patterns in the Colorado Plateau region (Peterson, 1984).

Meanwhile, his studies of the Lower Jurassic Glen Canyon Group (Wingate Sandstone, Kayenta and Moenave Formations, and Navajo Sandstone) took him into Zion, Capitol Reef, and Canyonlands National Parks, and Colorado National Monument. This group of rocks took on added significance when news filtered back from a meeting of workers in the Triassic-Jurassic rift basins of the eastern U.S. Two prominent eastern geologists, based on the newly revised ages in the rift basins and the probable correlations to the Colorado Plateau, believed that the Glen Canyon Group ought to be Early Jurassic rather than largely Late Triassic in age. The Triassic age of the Glen Canyon Group had been based on vertebrate remains, and the Triassic-Jurassic boundary was thought to be well up in the Navajo Sandstone. Curious to learn how he could help resolve the discrepancy, Pete called Bruce Cornet, one of the eastern geologists, and discussed the problem. Bruce, a palynologist, suggested that a palynomorph-bearing sample, collected from somewhere low in the Glen Canyon Group, would go a long way toward solving the problem. From his decades of field experience on the Plateau, Pete knew exactly where to go to find the rocks that would yield palynomorphs. Too excited to wait for spring, he stopped over in the Arizona strip country on the

Figure 4. Pete Peterson and Christine Turner searching for microfossils in the Tidwell Member of the Morrison Formation at Ladder Canyon, near Grand Junction, Colorado, August 27, 1992.

way to San Diego for Christmas, and did a little field work in the brisk winter weather. He collected samples from the Moenave Formation and sent them immediately to Bruce. Bruce, also unable to contain his excitement, ran the samples instantly, identified Early Jurassic palynomorphs in the samples, and confirmed that the Glen Canyon Group was Jurassic rather than largely Triassic in age (Peterson and Pipiringos, 1979)!

Pete's most recent research endeavor, in cooperation with the National Park Service, was to help bring together and oversee a team of geologists to study the Morrison Formation as an "extinct ecosystem." He worked with Dan Chure and Christine Turner to develop an integrated research effort. Because of his extensive knowledge of the Morrison, he was able to extend the regional framework from the Colorado Plateau to northern Montana, which provided the regional stratigraphic framework for proper stratigraphic placement of all samples collected by the various specialists. The work involved Morrison exposures in and between numerous National Park Service units, including Dinosaur National Monument, Arches National Park, Capitol Reef National Park, Grand Staircase-Escalante National Monument, Glen Canyon National Recreation Area, Hovenweep National Monument, Colorado National Monument, Black Canyon of the Gunnison National Recreation Area, Curecanti National Recreation Area, Bighorn Canyon National Recreation Area, Yellowstone National Park, and Glacier National Park. A consequence of this integrated research effort is that the Morrison is now one of the most completely studied terrestrial deposits in the U.S.

Pete has retired from the USGS, but only to have more time to continue his efforts to learn more geology and to unravel more of the mysteries held in the rock record. Last summer, Pete joined two Canadian Jurassic experts, Terry Poulton and James White, to determine how the Morrison correlates with the Upper Jurassic in Canada. He is now able to tie the terrestrial and marine deposits of the Morrison and related rocks in Montana to the correlative marine sequences of Canada. He is currently co-editing a volume from the research results of the Morrison extinct ecosystem study.

Pete is admired by all who know him, yet remains a quiet, unassuming field geologist, who prefers to spend time in the field and helping others (students, Park Service personnel, the U.S.G.S., other agencies, and the public) enjoy the mysteries of the magnificent strata of the Colorado Plateau. The only dust on his boots is the outdoor kind that comes from tromping around where he is most at home – on the mesas and in the canyons of his beloved Colorado Plateau.

REFERENCES

Blakey, R.C., Peterson, Fred, and Kocurek, Gary, 1988, Late Paleozoic and Mesozoic ergs of western North America: Sedimentary Geology, v. 56, no. 1/4, p. 3-126.

Parrish, J.T., and Peterson, Fred, 1988, Wind directions predicted from global circulation models and wind directions determined from eolian sandstones of the Western Interior of the United States—a comparison: Sedimentary Geology, v. 56, no. 1/4, p. 261-282.

Peterson, Fred, 1980, Sedimentology of the uranium-bearing Salt Wash Member and Tidwell unit of the Morrison Formation in the Henry and Kaiparowits basins, Utah, *in* Picard, M.D., editor, Henry Mountains symposium: Utah Geological Association Publication 8, p. 305-322.

Peterson, Fred, 1984, Fluvial sedimentation on a quivering craton—influence of slight crustal movements on fluvial processes, Upper Jurassic Morrison Formation, western Colorado Plateau: Sedimentary Geology, v. 38, nos. 1-4, p. 1-29.

Peterson, Fred, 1988, Stratigraphy and nomenclature of Middle and Upper Jurassic rocks in the western Colorado Plateau, Utah and Arizona: U.S. Geological Survey Bulletin 1633-B, p. 13-56.

Peterson, Fred, and Kirk, A.R., 1977, Correlation of the Cretaceous rocks in the San Juan, Black Mesa, Kaiparowits, and Henry Basins, southern Colorado Plateau: New Mexico Geological Society Guidebook, 28th Field Conference, San Juan Basin III, p. 167-178.

Peterson, Fred, and Pipiringos, G.N., 1979, Stratigraphic relationships of the Navajo Sandstone to Middle Jurassic formations, southern Utah and northern Arizona: U.S. Geological Survey Professional Paper 1035-B, p. B1-B43.

Peterson, Fred, Ryder, R.T., and Law, B.E., 1980, Stratigraphy, sedimentology, and regional relationships of the Cretaceous System in the Henry Mountains region, Utah, *in* Picard, M.D. editor, Henry Mountains symposium: Utah Geological Association Publication 8, p. 151-170.

Geology of Utah's Parks and Monuments
2000 Utah Geological Association Publication 28
D.A. Sprinkel, T.C. Chidsey, Jr., and P.B. Anderson, editors

Overview of the National Park System in Utah

Tim Connors[1]

THE MISSION OF THE NATIONAL PARK SERVICE

The National Park Service (NPS) preserves, unimpaired, the natural and cultural resources and values of the national park system for the enjoyment, education, and inspiration of this and future generations. The National Park Service cooperates with partners to extend the benefits of natural and cultural resource conservation and outdoor recreation throughout this country and the world.

President Wilson created the National Park Service on August 25, 1916, to protect the existing national parks and monuments (approximately 35) that were then managed under the Department of the Interior. At that time Utah already had national monuments proclaimed for Dinosaur, Natural Bridges, Rainbow Bridge, and the present day Zion National Park. Legislation governing the Park Service is termed the **"Organic Act"** and states the following:

> **"the Service thus established shall promote and regulate the use of the Federal areas known as national parks, monuments and reservations ...by such means and measures as conform to the fundamental purpose of the said parks, monuments and reservations, which purpose is to conserve the scenery and the natural and historic objects and the wild life therein and to provide for the enjoyment of the same in such manner and by such means as will leave them unimpaired for the enjoyment of future generations."**

Today, the number of National Park Service units has dramatically increased to 375 areas covering more than 83 million acres in 49 States, the District of Columbia, American Samoa, Guam, Puerto Rico, Saipan, and the Virgin Islands. Yellowstone became the **world's** first national park in 1872 "as a public park or pleasuring-ground for the benefit and enjoyment of the people" and was placed "under exclusive control of the Secretary of the Interior." Other agencies have managed national parks and monuments over the years including the War Department, the Forest Service, and the Bureau of Land Management.

National parks can only be designated by acts of Congress, but national monuments can be created by presidential proclamation using the **Antiquities Act of 1906**, if these lands are already under federal jurisdiction.

NATIONAL PARK SERVICE NOMENCLATURE

The National Park Service administrates lands designated as national parks, monuments, recreational areas, preserves, seashores, lakeshores, riverways, historic sites, memorials, and battlefield parks. The national parks, monuments, preserves, seashores, lakeshores, or riverways are usually set aside because they contain significant natural resources (land or water) and contain magnificent "scenery" that is usually indicative of scientific importance. They may also include natural features such as forest, grassland, tundra, desert, estuary, or river systems. These parks may contain "windows" on the past for a view of geological history, imposing landforms such as mountains, mesas, thermal areas, and caverns. Finally, they may be habitats of abundant or rare wildlife and plantlife.

Generally, a **national park** contains a variety of resources and encompasses large land or water areas to help provide adequate protection of the resources. A **national monument** is intended to preserve at least one nationally significant resource. It is usually smaller than a national park and lacks its diversity of attractions. Historical areas are customarily preserved or restored to reflect their appearance during the period of their greatest historical significance. In recent years, **national historic site** has been the title most commonly applied by Congress in authorizing the addition of such areas to the National Park System. Originally, **national recreation areas** in the National Park System were units surrounding reservoirs impounded by dams built by other federal agencies. The National Park

---

[1]*National Park Service, Geologic Resources Division, Denver, CO 80225*

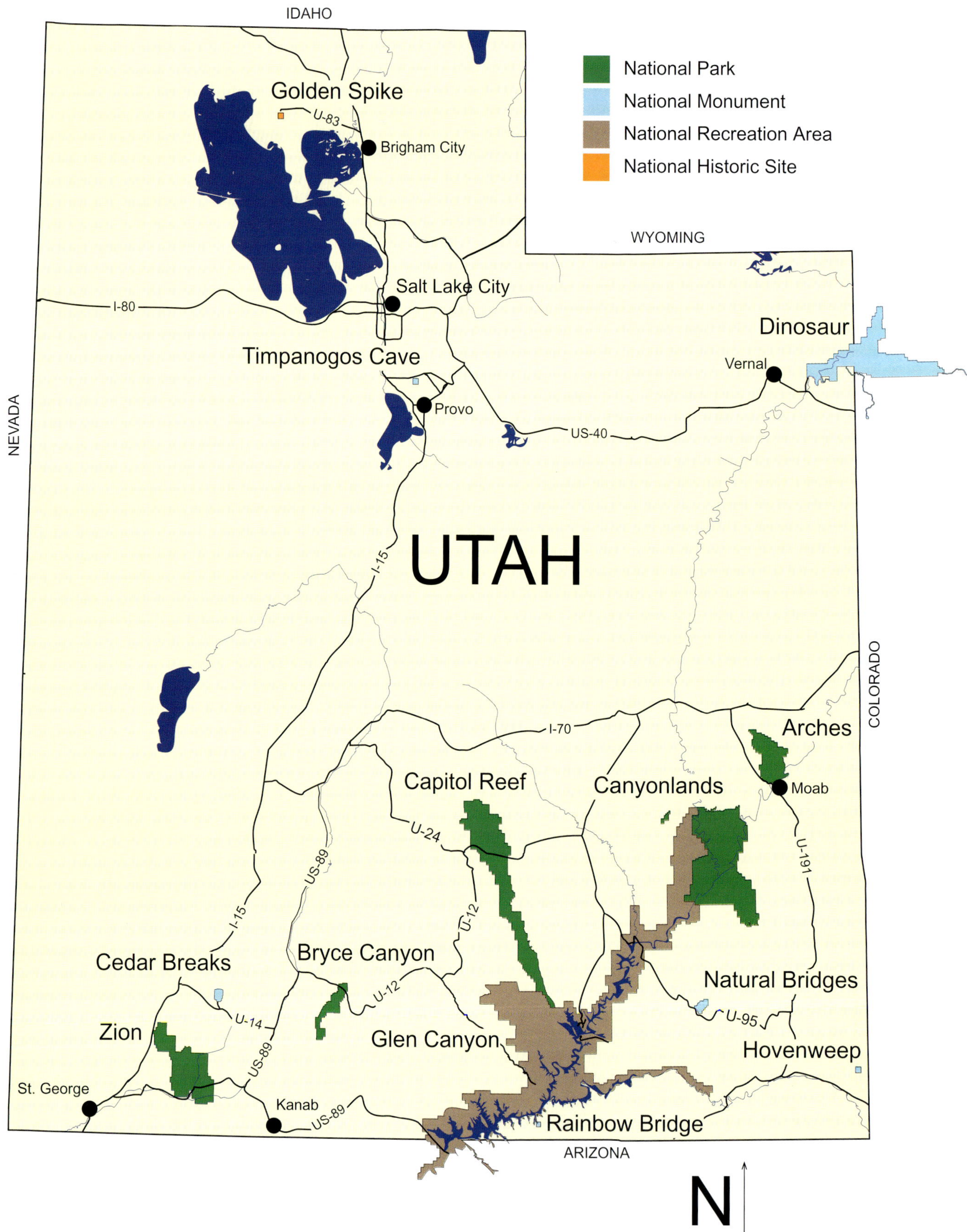

Figure 1. Map showing the National Park System units in Utah.

Table 1. Information on the national parks and recreation area in Utah administered by the National Park Service.

Park Information[1]	Established	Boundary Changes	Size
Arches National Park P.O. Box 907 Moab, UT 84532-0907 435-259-8161 http://www.nps.gov/arch	• NM April 12, 1929 • NP November 12, 1971.	• November 25, 1938 • July 22, 1960 • January 20, 1969 • October 30, 1998	<u>79,978.98 acres</u> Federal: 76,673.01 Nonfederal: 3,305.97
Bryce Canyon National Park Bryce Canyon, UT 84717-0001 435-834-5322 http://www.nps.gov/brca	• NM June 8, 1923 • renamed and redesignated Utah NP June 7,1924 • renamed Bryce Canyon NP February 25, 1928	• May 12, 1928 • June 13, 1930 • January 5, 1931 • February 17, 1931 • May 4, 1931 • March 7, 1942	<u>35,835.08 acres</u> Federal: 35,832.58 Nonfederal: 2.50
Canyonlands National Park 2282 S. West Resource Blvd. Moab, UT 84532 435-259-7164 http://www.nps.gov/cany	• NP September 12, 1964	• November 12, 1971	<u>337,597.83 acres</u> Federal: 337,570.43 Nonfederal 27.40
Capitol Reef National Park H.C. 70, Box 15 Torrey, UT 84775-9602 435-425-3791 http://www.nps.gov/care	• NM August 2, 1937 • NP December 18, 1971	• July 2, 1958 • January 20, 1969 • December 18, 1971	<u>244,392.26 acres</u> Federal: 243,559.87 Nonfederal: 832.39
Glen Canyon National Recreation Area P.O. Box 1507 Page, AZ 86040-1507 520-608-6200 http://www.nps.gov/glca	• administered under cooperative agreements with the Bureau of Reclamation and U.S. Dept. of the Interior April 18, 1958 and September 17, 1965. • NRA October 27, 1972	• January 3, 1975	<u>1,254,306.19 acres</u> Federal: 1,252,246.01 Nonfederal. 2,060.18
Zion National Park Springdale, UT 84767-1099 435-772-3256 http://www.nps.gov/zion	• Originally named Mukuntuweap NM July 31, 1909 • incorporated in Zion NM March 18, 1918 • NP November 19, 1919 • Separate Zion NM January 22, 1937; incorporated in park July 11, 1956.	• June 13, 1930 • June 3, 1941 • February 20, 1960 • October 21, 1976 • November 12, 1996.	<u>146,592.31 acres</u> Federal: 143,035.07 Nonfederal: 3,557.24

Service manages many of these areas under cooperative agreements. The concept of recreational areas has grown to encompass other lands and waters set aside for recreational use by acts of Congress and now include major areas in urban centers. There are also national recreation areas outside the National Park System that are administered by the U.S. Forest Service.

Unique Features of Utah's Park Units

Utah contains five national parks, six national monuments, one national recreation area, and one national historic site administrated by the NPS. This guidebook includes articles on all of the National Park System units except Hovenweep National Monument and Golden Spike National Historic Site (figure 1). Below is a brief description of each unit administered by the National Park Service in Utah. Additional information is summarized in tables 1 and 2.

Arches National Park contains one of the largest concentrations of natural sandstone arches in the world. The arches and numerous other extraordinary geologic features, such as spires, pinnacles, pedestals, and balanced rocks, are highlighted in striking foreground and background views created by contrasting colors, landforms, and textures.

At **Bryce Canyon National Park**, erosion has shaped colorful Tertiary Claron limestone, sandstone, and mudstone beds into thousands of spires, fins, pinnacles, and mazes. Collectively called "hoodoos," these colorful and whimsi-

Table 2. Information on the national monuments in Utah administered by the National Park Service.

Park Information[1]	Established	Boundary Changes	Size
Cedar Breaks National Monument 2390 W. Hwy. 56 #11 Cedar City, UT 84720-2606 435-586-9451 http://www.nps.gov/cebr	• NM August 22, 1933	• March 7, 1942 • June 30,1961	<u>6,154.60 acres</u> all Federal
Dinosaur National Monument 4545 E. Highway 40 Dinosaur, CO 81610-9724 970-374-3000 http://www.nps.gov/dino	• NM October 4, 1915	• July 14, 1938 • September 8, 1960 • February 21, 1963 • October 9, 1964 • November 10, 1978	<u>210,844.02 acres</u> Federal: 206,256.24 Nonfederal: 4,587.78
Golden Spike National Historic Site P.O. Box 897 Brigham City, UT 84302-0897 435-471-2209 http://www.nps.gov/gosp	• NHS April 2, 1957 • officially authorized under NPS administration July 30, 1965	• July 30, 1965 • September 8, 1980	<u>2,735.28 acres</u> Federal: 2,203.20 Nonfederal: 532.08
Hovenweep National Monument McElmo Route Cortez, CO 81321-8901 435-459-4344 http://www.nps.gov/hove	• NM March 2, 1923.	• April 26, 1951 • November 20, 1952 • April 6, 1956	<u>784.93 acres</u> all federal
Natural Bridges National Monument P.O. Box 1 Lake Powell, UT 84533-0101 435-692-1234 http://www.nps.gov/nabr	• NM April 16,1908.	• April 16, 1908 • September 25, 1909 • February 11, 1916 • August 14, 1962	<u>7,636.49 acres</u> all federal
Rainbow Bridge National Monument c/o Glen Canyon NRA P.O. Box 1507 Page, AZ 86040-1507 520-608-8200 http://www.nps.gov/rabr	• NM May 30,1910	None to date	<u>160 acres</u> all federal
Timpanogos Cave National Monument R.R. 3, Box 200 American Fork, UT 84003-9803 801-756-5239 http://www.nps.gov/tica	• NM October 14,1922 • transferred from Forest Service to NPS August 10, 1933.	None to date	<u>250 acres</u> all federal

cal formations stand in horseshoe-shaped amphitheaters along the eastern edge of the Paunsaugunt Plateau in southern Utah.

Geologic processes have played the most important part in shaping the desert ecosystem of **Canyonlands National Park**. The arid climate and sparse vegetation allow the exposure of large expanses of bare rock, while the deep canyons of the Colorado and Green Rivers reveal 300 million years of geologic history.

Capitol Reef National Park preserves the dominating Waterpocket Fold, an uplifted area of highly colored sedimentary layers known to geologists as a monocline. The 100-mile-long Waterpocket Fold extends from nearby Thousand Lakes Mountain to the Colorado River (now Lake Powell). Capitol Reef National Park was established to protect this grand and colorful geologic feature, as well as the historical and cultural history that abounds in the area. The name of the park is partly derived from Navajo Sandstone, which weathered into large, light-colored domes that reminded visitors of capitol rotundas.

At **Cedar Breaks National Monument**, a huge natural amphitheater has been eroded out of the variegated Pink Cliffs of the Claron Formation near Cedar City, Utah. Millions of years of sedimentation, uplift, and erosion have created a deep canyon of rock walls, fins, spires, and columns, that spans some three miles, and is over 2,000 feet deep. The rim of the canyon is over 10,000 feet above sea level, and is forested with islands of Englemann spruce, subalpine fir and aspen; separated by broad meadows of brilliant summertime wild flowers.

The quarry at **Dinosaur National Monument** is the single most important Jurassic dinosaur paleontological site to be found anywhere. The monument also has a nearly complete stratigraphic record that is well exposed in the spectacular canyons of the monument cut by the Yampa and Green Rivers.

Glen Canyon National Recreation Area offers unparalleled opportunities for water-based and backcountry recreation. The recreation area stretches hundreds of miles from Lees Ferry in Arizona to the Orange Cliffs of southern Utah, encompassing scenic vistas, geologic wonders, and a panorama of human history. Additionally, the controversy surrounding the construction of Glen Canyon Dam and the creation of Lake Powell contributed to the birth of the modern day environmental movement.

At **Golden Spike National Historic Site**, completion of the world's first transcontinental railroad was celebrated here where the Central Pacific and Union Pacific Railroads met on May 10, 1869.

Hovenweep National Monument protects some of the finest examples of ancient stone architecture in the southwest. The inhabitants of Hovenweep were part of the large farming culture which occupied the Four Corners region of Utah, Colorado, New Mexico, and Arizona from about 500 B.C. until nearly A.D. 1300. These peoples also constructed the cliff dwellings in nearby Mesa Verde National Park. The monument is noted for its solitude, clear skies, and undeveloped, natural character.

Natural Bridges National Monument was the first NPS unit established in Utah. The pinyon and juniper covered mesa is bisected by deep canyons, exposing the Permian Cedar Mesa Sandstone. Where meandering streams cut through sandstone walls, three large natural bridges formed. Sipapu and Kachina Bridges are the world's second and third largest natural bridges. Owachomo, while smaller, is only nine feet thick.

Rainbow Bridge National Monument contains the world's largest natural bridge, rising 290 feet above the floor of Bridge Canyon. The span has undoubtedly inspired people throughout time--from the neighboring American Indian tribes who consider Rainbow Bridge sacred, to the 300,000 people from around the world who visit it each year. Once remote and difficult to reach, the bridge is now accessible by boat from Lake Powell.

Timpanogos Cave National Monument sits high in the Wasatch Mountains. The cave system consists of three spectacularly decorated caverns. Each cavern has unique colors and formations. Helictites and anthodites are just a few of the many dazzling formations to be found in the many chambers. As visitors climb to the cave entrance, on a hike gaining over 1,000 feet in elevation, they are offered incredible views of American Fork Canyon.

Protected within **Zion National Park** is a spectacular cliff-and-canyon landscape and wilderness full of the unexpected including the world's largest arch - Kolob Arch - with a span that measures 310 feet. Mesozoic rocks dominate the scenery and younger volcanic flows attest to the active tectonics of the region.

Wasatch Mountain State Park
Photo by Alan Day

Geology of Utah's Parks and Monuments
2000 Utah Geological Association Publication 28
D.A. Sprinkel, T.C. Chidsey, Jr., and P.B. Anderson, editors

Overview of Utah's State Parks

Courtland C. Nelson[1]

Each year, thousands of visitors walk the red rock mesa that is Dead Horse Point State Park and gaze at a labyrinth of canyons far below. Many wonder at the shifting arcs of crescent-shaped dunes or sift the fine, salmon-colored grains at Coral Pink Sand Dunes State Park. Others choose to wander through a canyon of weathered gnomes at Goblin Valley State Park. They, like most of us, marvel at the sheer cliff walls, colors, and shapes, knowing very little about the phenomena creating such incredible natural beauty.

Utah's state parks, along with all the beauty and natural resources within them, belong to the citizens of Utah. And it is the responsibility of the Division of Utah State Parks and Recreation to provide access to, protect, and interpret the cultural, historical, and natural resources within our parks.

The importance of creating recreation areas was realized early in Utah's history. The first formal Utah state park agency was established in 1925 and given authority by the Utah legislature to accept gifts of land or money for state parks. Later, in 1957, the legislature created the Utah State Park and Recreation Commission and instructed the agency not only to acquire parks, but to develop parks and recreation areas, while preserving their scenic, natural, and historical resources.

As the number of parks increased, recreational programs were also added, with the boating program in 1959, followed by winter and summer off-highway vehicle programs. In July 1967, the commission became a division within the Department of Natural Resources.

Utah's state park system began with four heritage sites, which hosted an estimated 350,000 visitors in 1957. Today, Utah State Parks and Recreation manages 44 recreation areas comprising 95,000 acres of land and more than 1 million surface acres of water, enjoyed by nearly 7 million visitors annually.

This book highlights 10 of Utah's 44 state parks, with

histories as unique and varied as the resources within them.

Antelope Island State Park

Antelope Island was named by John C. Fremont in October 1843 when he wrote in his journal, "We found water and several bands of antelope. Some of these were killed and in grateful supply of food the antelope furnished, I gave the name of the island." In addition to antelope, herds of bison, mule deer, and bighorn sheep roam free on this island, the largest on the Great Salt Lake. Antelope Island State Park opened to the public in 1969 when the north 2,000 acres of the island were acquired by the state. In 1981, the remaining 44,000 acres of the island were purchased and are now accessible by a backcountry trail system.

Coral Pink Sand Dunes State Park

Coral Pink Sand Dunes was just one area included on a list of potential parks in the 1959 final report by the Utah State Park and Recreation Commission. Because of its unique beauty and dunes of a color not found any place in the world, the Commission recommended early action be taken to develop the area into a state park. Land for Coral Pink Sand Dunes State Park was purchased from the Bureau of Land Management (BLM) and the park opened to the public in April 1963. Today, 3,730 acres of dunes are a playground for more than 160,000 visitors each year.

Dead Horse Point State Park

Perhaps the most spectacular state park, Dead Horse Point was a popular attraction for many years before it became an official state park. Tourists and sightseers braved the long, rutted, dirt road to the Point. In the late 1800s, cowboys ranged cattle through the area and used the Point as a natural corral for capturing wild horses. These wild horses might be responsible for giving the point its name, as local legend suggests horses corralled too long on the Point, died of thirst. San Juan County purchased 628 acres from the BLM and donated it to the Utah State

[1]*Director, Division of Utah State Parks and Recreation*
Utah Department of Natural Resources
Salt Lake City, UT 84114-6100

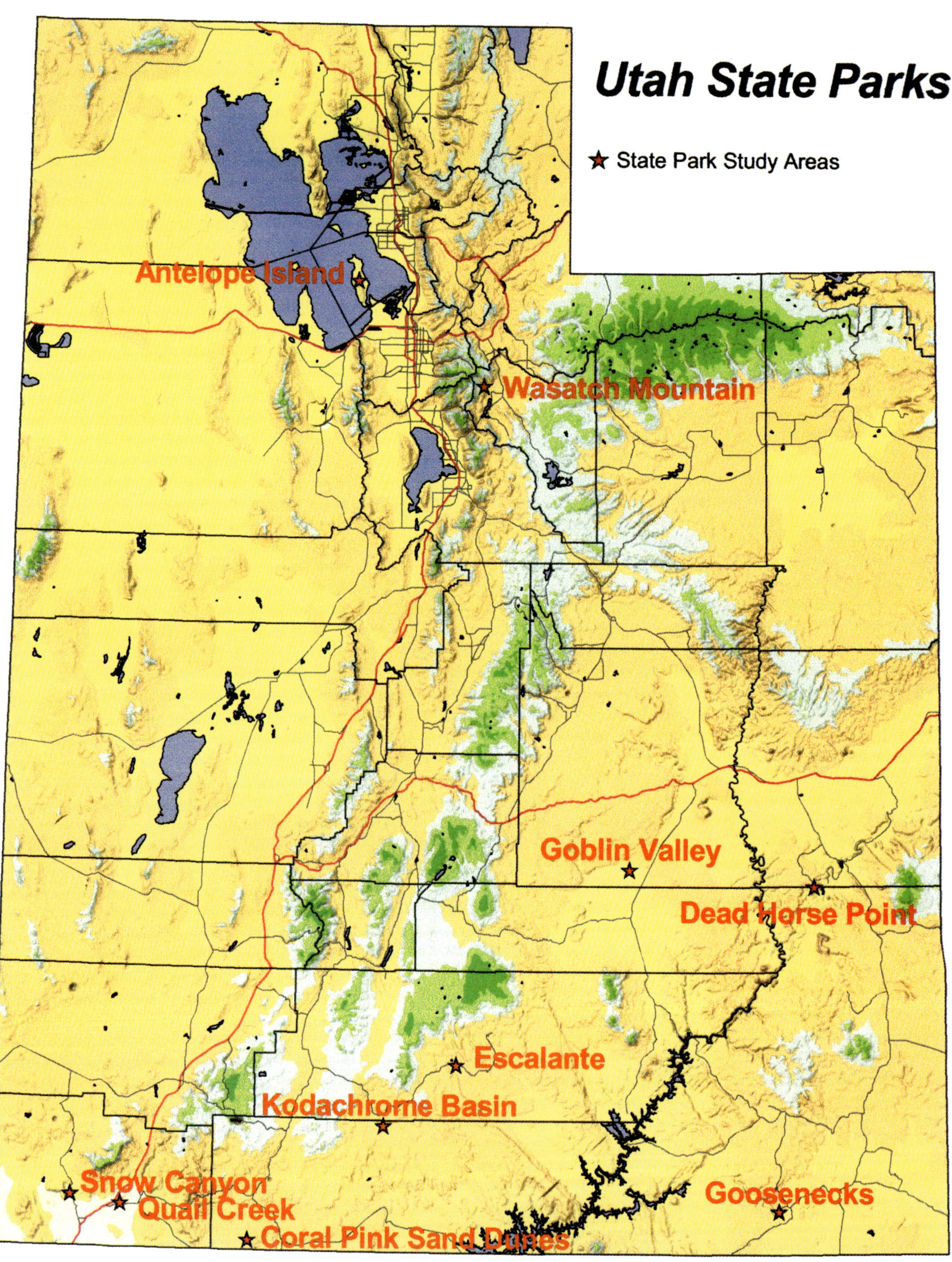

Utah State Parks
State Park Study Areas
Antelope Island
Wasatch Mountain
Goblin Valley
Dead Horse Point
Escalante
Kodachrome Basin
Snow Canyon
Quail Creek
Coral Pink Sand Dunes
Goosenecks

Park and Recreation Commission in July 1959. Dead Horse Point State Park was dedicated and opened to the public in December that same year. Since then, the park has grown in size from its original 628 acres to more than 5,300.

Escalante State Park

In 1963, the Utah State Park and Recreation Commission purchased 949 acres from the BLM to create the Escalante Petrified Forest State Reserve to protect the abundance of petrified wood and develop the area for recreation. Additional land was purchased later, increasing the size of the area to 1,784 acres. In 1975, this state reserve was developed into a state park and was renamed Escalante State Park in 1986. Built on the shore of Wide Hollow Reservoir, today the park offers fishing, boating, swimming, in addition to its nature trails through the petrified forest.

Goblin Valley State Park

At the southern tip of the San Rafael Reef lies a strange landscape of eroded sandstone formations known today as goblins. In 1949, Art Chaffin photographed and explored this area, which he named Mushroom Valley. Goblin Valley and its surrounding area have seen a varied and colorful history. During the 1800s, cattlemen and outlaws roamed the desert in search of adequate feed and secure hideouts.

In 1954, the state of Utah acquired the property to protect it from vandalism, and gave the area the official name of Goblin Valley. Dedicated in 1974, Goblin Valley State Park has seen an increase in visitation and acreage with nearly 70,000 touring the 3,000-acre park in 1999.

Goosenecks State Park

Goosenecks State Park is an incredible scenic overlook, providing views of the spires of Monument Valley and the meandering San Juan River. Walking the rim, visitors may see kayaks and rafts on the chocolate-colored waters of the river, some 1,000 feet below. The tiny, 10-acre Goosenecks State Park was acquired from the BLM in 1962 and opened to the public that same year.

Kodachrome Basin State Park

Originally, Kodachrome Basin was known as Thorley's pasture after a local cattle rancher of that time. It was in 1963 when the Bryce Lions Club persuaded the state of Utah to set aside 2,241 acres as a state reserve because of the area's unique beauty and geologic structures. In 1984, members of a National Geographic expedition exploring the area named it Kodachrome Basin due to spectacular colors of the rocks and cliffs.

Quail Creek State Park

Quail Creek Reservoir was completed in 1985 to provide irrigation and culinary water to the thirsty Washington County area. The land on which the park is located is leased from the BLM as part of the Recreation and Public Purposes Act. More than 350,000 visitors each year enjoy some of the warmest waters of the state at Quail Creek State Park.

Snow Canyon State Park

Though discovered in the early 1850s by cowboys searching for lost cattle, Snow Canyon was named after Lorenzo and Erastus Snow, prominent early pioneer leaders. Petroglyphs, artifacts, and structural remnants also reveal the ancient Anasazi culture inhabited this region between 1250 to 400 A.D. Snow Canyon State Park offers 6,000-acres of spectacular sandstone and lava rock.

Wasatch Mountain State Park

With two 18-hole golf courses, a web of snowmobile trails, and miles of cross-country ski tracks, equestrian, hiking, and biking trails, Wasatch Mountain State Park is the most developed state park in Utah. Wasatch Mountain was recognized in the 1959 final report by the Utah Park and Recreation Commission as an important recreation asset. The more than 22,000 acres that make up today's Wasatch Mountain State Park were acquired from the BLM, state school lands, and private landowners.

Summary Comments

Over the past few years, Utah State Parks and Recreation has focused less on acquisition and more on education. Personal watercraft and off-highway vehicle education programs were developed to protect public safety and natural resources. Our Junior Ranger program aims to educate children about geology, flora, fauna, and outdoor ethics. And most recently, interpretive ranger positions were added to help educate visitors about the natural, historical, and cultural resources within our state parks.

Through this book, the editors intend to educate and interpret the geology of our state parks. We believe through education, we can protect our parks, and the natural resources found within them, for future generations.

GEOLOGIC TIME SCALE

(after Hansen, 1991)

Subdivisions (and their symbols)				Age estimates of boundaries in mega-annum (Ma) [1]	Other age estimates [1,5]	Age and stage names commonly used in Utah [1,6]
Eon or Eonothem	Era or Erathem	Period, System, Subperiod, Subsystem	Epoch or Series			
Phanerozoic [2]	Cenozoic [2] (Cz)	Quaternary [2] (Q)	Holocene	0.010	0.01	
			Pleistocene	1.6 (1.6 - 1.9)	1.6	
		Tertiary (T) — Neogene [2] Subperiod or Subsystem	Pliocene	5 (4.9 - 5.3)	5.3	66.4
			Miocene	24 (23 - 26)	23.7	Maastrichtian 74.5 (4)
		Tertiary (T) — Paleogene [2] Subperiod or Subsystem	Oligocene	38 (34 - 38)	36.6	Campanian 84.0 (4.5)
			Eocene	55 (54 - 56)	57.8	Santonian 87.5 (4.5)
			Paleocene	66 (63 - 66)	66.4	Coniacian 88.5 (2.5)
	Mesozoic [2] (Mz)	Cretaceous (K)	Late / Upper	96 (95 - 97)	97.5	Turonian 91 (2.5) / Cenomanian 97.5 (2.5)
			Early / Lower	138 (135 - 141)	144	Albian 113 (4)
		Jurassic (J)	Late / Upper		163 (15)	Aptian 119 (9)
			Middle / Middle		187 (34)	Neocomian 144 (5)
			Early / Lower	205 (200 - 215)	208 (18)	
		Triassic (℞)	Late / Upper		230 (22)	
			Middle / Middle		240 (22)	
			Early / Lower	~240	245 (20)	Ochoan 250
	Paleozoic [2] (Pz)	Permian (P)	Late / Upper		258	Guadalupian 255 / Leonardian 270
			Early / Lower	290 (290 - 305)	286 (12)	Wolfcampian 275 / 290
		Pennsylvanian (℗)	Late / Upper			Virgilian / Missourian / Desmoinesian 310
			Middle / Middle			
			Early / Lower	~330	320	Atokan / Morrowan
		Mississippian (M)	Late / Upper			
			Early / Lower	360 (360 - 365)	360 (10)	Chesterian 330 / 340
		Devonian (D)	Late / Upper		374 (18)	Meramecian / Osagean
			Middle / Middle		387 (28)	Kinderhookian
			Early / Lower	410 (405 - 415)	408 (12)	365
		Silurian (S)	Late / Upper			
			Middle / Middle		421 (12)	
			Early / Lower	435 (435 - 440)	438 (12)	
		Ordovician (O)	Late / Upper		458 (16)	
			Middle / Middle		478 (16)	
			Early / Lower	500 (495 - 510)	505 (32)	
		Cambrian (Є)	Late / Upper		523 (36)	
			Middle / Middle		540 (28)	
			Early / Lower	~570 [3]	570	
Proterozoic (P)	Late Proterozoic (Z)	None defined		900	900	
	Middle Proterozoic (Y)	None defined		1600	1600	
	Early Proterozoic (X)	None defined		2500	2500	
Archean (A)	Late Archean (W)	None defined		3000	3000	
	Middle Archean (V)	None defined		3400	3400	
	Early Archean (U)	None defined		3800 ?	3800 ?	
	pre-Archean (pA) [4]					

[1]Ranges reflect uncertainties of isotopic and biostratigraphic age assignments. Age boundaries not closely bracketed by existing date shown by -. Decay constants and isotopic ratios are cited in Steiger and Jager (1977). Designation m.y. used for an interval of time.

[2]Modifiers (lower, middle, upper or early, middle, late) when used with these items are informal divisions of the larger units; the first letter of the modifier is lowercase.

[3]Rocks older than 570 Ma also called Precambrian (pC), a time term without specific rank.

[4]Informal term without specific rank.

[5]From Palmer (1983) uncertainty in parentheses.

[6]Cretaceous from Palmer (1983); Mississippian, Pennsylvanian, and Permian from Cosuna Chart (Hintze, 1985).

Hansen, W.R., 1991, Suggestions to authors of reports of the United States Geological Survey (7th edition): Washington, D.C., U.S. Geological Survey, 289 p.

Geology of Utah's Parks and Monuments
2000 Utah Geological Association Publication 28
D.A. Sprinkel, T.C. Chidsey, Jr., and P.B. Anderson, editors

Geology of Arches National Park, Grand County, Utah

Hellmut H. Doelling[1]

ABSTRACT

Arches National Park, located in east-central Utah, is a 74,000-acre park with the greatest concentration of rock arches in the world. Most are formed in three geologic formations: ascending, the Dewey Bridge Member of the Carmel Formation, the Slick Rock Member of the Entrada Sandstone, and the Moab Member of the Curtis Formation. The arches were formed by a unique set of circumstances involving Middle Pennsylvanian to Late Triassic salt tectonics, Middle Pennsylvanian to Late Cretaceous sedimentation, Tertiary folding and faulting, and Quaternary erosion and salt dissolution.

Arches National Park is located in the heart of the fault-and-fold belt of the Pennsylvanian Paradox basin. The most important structural feature is the Salt Valley-Cache Valley salt wall or diapir. The salt wall formed from Middle Pennsylvanian to Late Triassic time and was covered with sediment laid down in Late Triassic to Late Cretaceous time. Thereafter, the area was folded and faulted, probably during Early Tertiary time. The axes of the anticlines were superimposed over the northwest-trending salt walls of the Paradox fault-and-fold belt. Many of the brittle sandstone formations were fractured (jointed) during the folding. Tertiary faults paralleled and displaced the salt walls. With the uplift of the Colorado Plateau, beginning in Late Tertiary time and continuing to the present, the Colorado River and its tributaries eroded the sedimentary formations and formed deep canyons, slopes, and cliffs. The formations formed either cliffs or slopes according to their erosional resistance. After erosion cut down deep enough, ground water reached the upper parts of the region's salt walls, including those of the Salt Valley-Cache Valley feature, and dissolved salt. The ensuing collapse created graben-valleys that overlie the salt walls today. Brittle hard sandstones "rolled over" into the salt-dissolution valleys or grabens and were eroded into thin fins along their previously formed, now-opened joints. Weathering then attacked weak horizontal zones such as formational boundaries, bedding planes, and soft partings, forming alcoves and arches in and through the fins.

Hence, most arches are located along the rims of the salt valleys where the favorable formations begin to "roll over" and collapse into the grabens. Each trail and road along the rims of the Salt Valley-Cache Valley graben provides access to several arches, especially in the Devils Garden area. Delicate Arch, developed at the contact between the Entrada and Curtis Formations, is the most famous, and is located on the north rim of the Cache Valley portion of the salt wall. The Fiery Furnace is a well-developed area of stone fins that form a colorful maze of narrow passageways.

INTRODUCTION

Arches National Park is located in east-central Utah just north of the town of Moab (figure 1). Physiographically it is located in the Colorado Plateaus Province, and geologically it is located in the fold-and-fault belt of the Paradox basin. The Colorado River flows along the south boundary of the national park. This very important river and its tributaries have carved the strata into the beautiful and spectacular canyons that surround Arches National Park. Arches National Park was so dedicated based on unique geologic phenomena, and the views that delight, please, inspire, and provide enjoyment to the visitor are of a geologic nature. Desert plants, wildlife, and cryptobiotic soils are nicely displayed in the park, but are not unique to the park and are present throughout the Colorado Plateaus.

The rock strata and geologic structure in the park favor the making of rock arches, and indeed the area has the greatest concentration of these features in the world (Stevens and McCarrick, 1988) (figure 2). Although most people visit the park to see these arches, it is also a show-

[1]*Utah Geological Survey, Salt Lake City, UT 84114-6100*

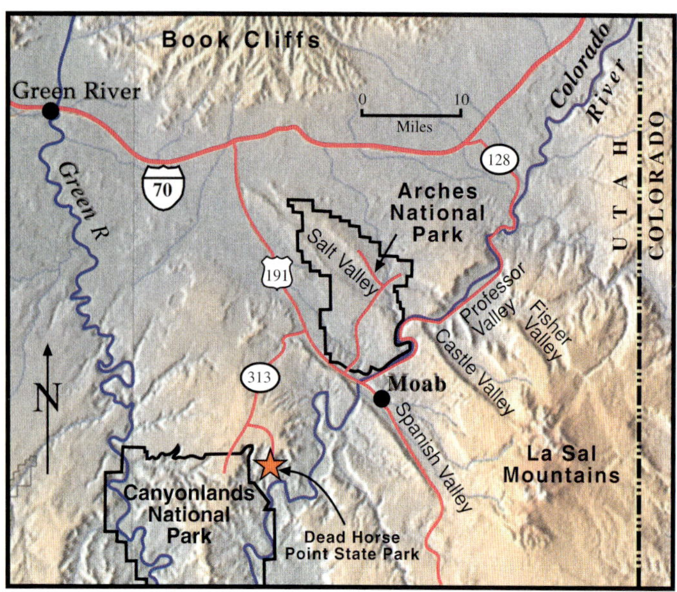

Figure 1. *Index map to Arches National Park showing surrounding towns and parks.*

case for salt anticlines. Thick layers of salt underlie much of the park, and dissolution of the salt in recent geologic history has contributed to the formation of the rock arches. There is an old saying, "You can't see the forest for the trees." This is certainly true in Arches National Park. Many visitors go from arch to arch, but fail to see the magnificent displays of geologic structure that formed the arches. It is hoped that this paper will give the visitor a further appreciation of why this is a national park.

The area was first established as a national monument in 1929 after several prominent visitors and locals recommended it for inclusion into the National Park system. At first it consisted of two sections totaling only 4,520 acres. These were the Windows and Devils Garden sections. The Windows section included a narrow band between Balanced Rock and Salt Wash and included the Garden of Eden, Elephant Butte, Double Arch, Cove of Caves, North Window, South Window, and Turret Arch (figure 3). The Devils Garden section extended northwestward from the Fiery Furnace to Dark Angel. Additions and some subtractions to the total area of the monument were made in 1938, 1960, and 1969. It was made a National Park by an act of Congress in 1971, and now has an area of 74,234 acres.

Figure 2. *Delicate Arch is the best known rock arch in the world and is the symbol for Arches National Park. This free-standing arch is located on the north rim of Cache Valley. The base and pedestals are Slick Rock Member of the Entrada Sandstone. The upper part or bridge is Moab Member of the Curtis Formation.*

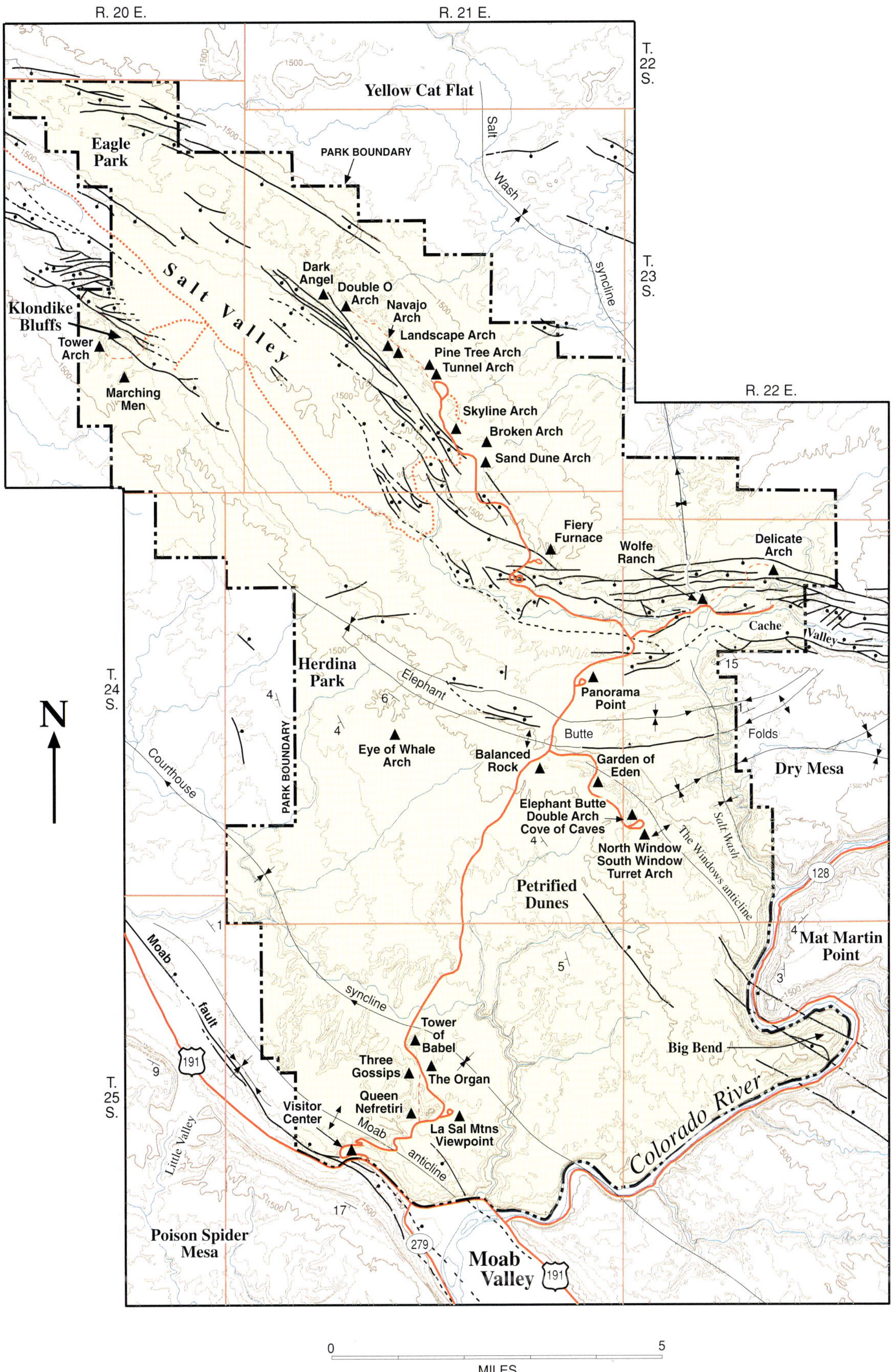

Figure 3. Structures and features map of Arches National Park.

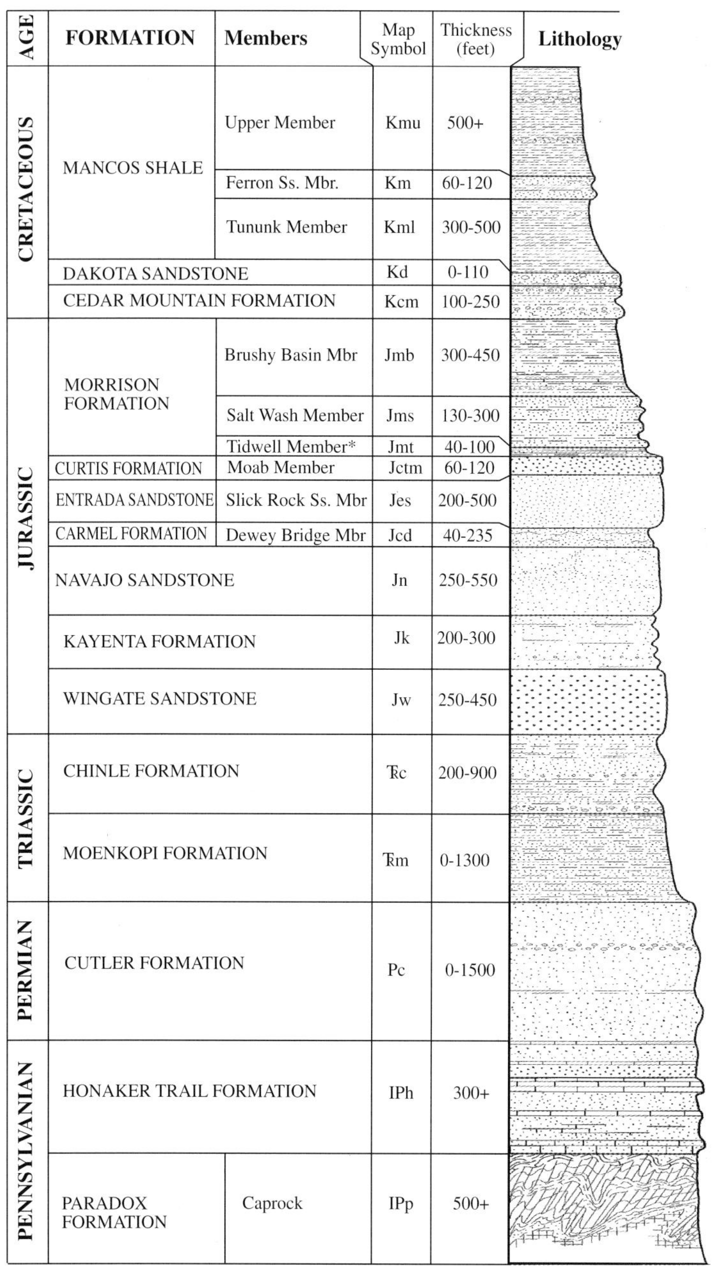

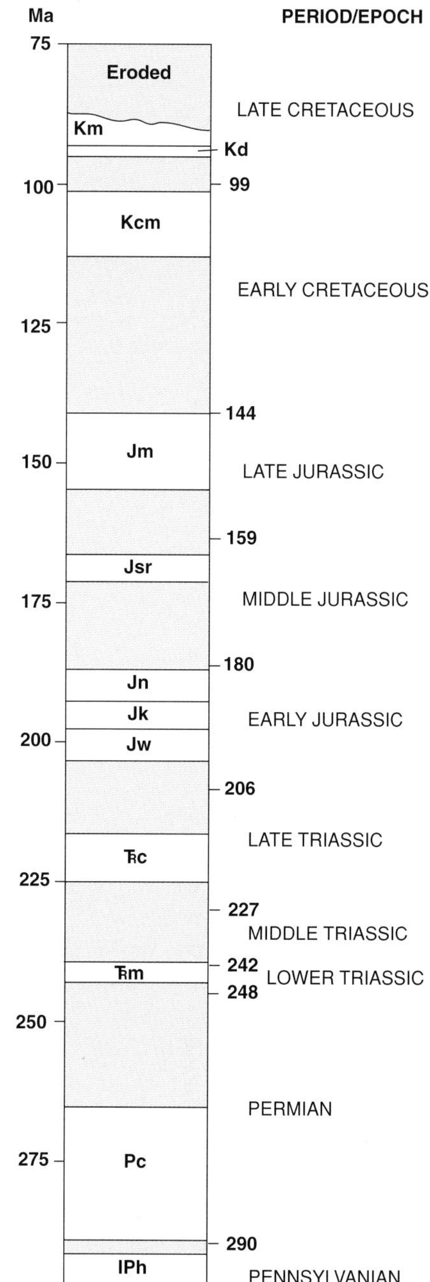

* Includes a thin section of the Summerville Formation at the base, that is generally less than 10 feet thick.

Figure 4. Formations and ages of rocks in Arches National Park. Lithologic column, left, relates formations and members to thickness and outcrop habit. The correlation diagram, right, relates formations and members to time and age of deposition. Gray areas indicate when rocks were not deposited (or were deposited and subsequently eroded). In the correlation diagram, Jm includes all members of the Morrison Formation. The San Rafael Group (Jsr) includes the Summerville, Curtis, Entrada, and Carmel Formations as shown in the lithologic column. Ma (millions of years ago) shows the time intervals when the formations were deposited.

The first comprehensive geologic study of the area was made by Carle H. Dane as part of his Ph.D. dissertation at Yale University. Other geologic studies and maps of Arches National Park have been produced by Lohman (1975), Dyer (1983), and Doelling (1985, 1988). An excellent treatise on arch formation, types of arches, and numbers of arches in the park is given in Stevens and McCarrick (1988).

STRATIGRAPHY

Consolidated sedimentary rock formations exposed within Arches National Park range in age from Middle Pennsylvanian to Late Cretaceous (figure 4 and 5). These rocks were laid down intermittently from 300 to 85 million years ago. Older rocks are present at depth, but are not exposed in the park. Additionally, unconsolidated deposits of sand, silt, gravel, and clay found in various mixtures that are the products of the current erosional regime; they are temporary deposits of wind, water, and gravity.

Thickness of the exposed formations varies considerably across the Arches N.P. area, but averages about 5,100 feet. The rock formations are the products of several depositional environments. Some of the earliest and latest were laid down under marine conditions; those in between were laid down in terrestrial environments as dunes, channel and overbank deposits, beach and tidal-flat deposits, and in other environments.

Pennsylvanian Rocks

Paradox Formation (IPp)

The oldest rocks exposed in Arches National Park are Pennsylvanian in age (figure 4). These were laid down cyclically in a restricted embayment of an ocean that lay to the west. Evaporation of the bay's sea water precipitated salt. Because salt is very soluble, none remains exposed at the surface today. Drill holes in nearby Moab Valley pass through 500 feet of unconsolidated basin fill and 400 feet of Paradox Formation residuum before reaching the first salt bed. Paradox Formation residuum is called caprock by geologists and consists of contorted gray shale, carbonaceous shale, gypsum beds, and thin limestone beds. Basically caprock consists of the Paradox Formation minus its salt.

Geologists have discovered that the salt in the Paradox Formation was deposited in 29 cycles, most of which are not present in any one place (Hite, 1961). A cycle began when fresh sea water flowed into the embayment from the sea that lay to the west. The bay was then cut off from open ocean circulation. Suspended sediments, which later formed shales, siltstones, and sandstones, were first laid down in the bottom of the bay. Then evaporation concentrated its dissolved chemicals. Limestone was precipitated, followed by gypsum, and then salts such as halite (common table salt), carnallite (potash- and magnesium-bearing salt), and sylvite (potassium chloride). These are mined near Dead Horse Point by pumping fresh water into the salt beds to dissolve the salt, followed by pumping the brine back to the surface. This brine is then evaporated in ponds to extract valuable potash salts used in agriculture as fertilizer. Such salt underlies large areas of Arches. In some places, such as under Salt Valley, Cache Valley, and Moab Valley, the Paradox Formation is more than 10,000 feet thick. In other areas the Paradox Formation is much thinner and devoid of salt. In the areas where the Paradox Formation is very thick, it is not uncommon to have single salt beds more than 900 feet thick. The insoluble rock layers between the salt beds are known as marker beds to geologists who drill into the formation to discover petroleum, potash salts, and other commodities. Oil and gas are extracted from the Paradox Formation in areas near the park.

The visitor will not see salt in the Paradox Formation exposures in Arches National Park. The nearest salt bed is 400 to 600 feet beneath Paradox Formation surface exposures. Caprock crops out in the middle of Salt Valley, west of Devils Garden, and is visible along the Klondike Bluffs access road (figures 3 and 5). The gravel road starts at the paved road about 3/4 of a mile south of the Devils Garden trailhead loop. It descends into Salt Valley and follows Salt Valley Wash for a distance. Good exposures of caprock are present along the sides of the wash, and contorted thin limestone, gray shale, and other insoluble rock are well displayed. Eventually the road rises out of the wash onto a larger exposure of caprock veneered with reworked white gypsum.

Honaker Trail Formation (IPh)

The Honaker Trail Formation overlies the Paradox Formation in the Arches National Park subsurface. By Late Pennsylvanian time, the water in the basin or bay in which the Paradox Formation was deposited, circulated with the open ocean to the west and salts were no longer deposited. A mountain range (Uncompahgre mountains) rose several miles east of the park along a major fault. Rocks older than the Paradox Formation were gradually eroded from the rising mountain range. Deposits near the mountains were laid down subaerially as alluvial fans. The more distant deposits, including those under most of the park, were deposited as offshore sand in the shallow ocean. The sand lenses intertongued with lime deposits which precipitated from the seawater. When the mountain range rose at an accelerated rate, the sand tongues extended farther to the southwest and when it rose more slowly, limestones were more commonly deposited.

Limestone and sandstone are the most common rock types in the Honaker Trail Formation in the area of Arches National Park The limestones are generally gray, thin to medium bedded, cherty, argillaceous (contain clay minerals), and fossiliferous. The beds commonly weather to hackly surfaces and to nodular shapes. They are resistant, forming ledges and cliffs. Fossils include brachiopods, horn corals, bryozoa, and crinoids. A few trilobites and numerous fusulinids date the uppermost beds as Virgilian in age (latest Pennsylvanian). The sandstones are brown, white, yellow gray, red, maroon, and lavender, fine to medium grained, mostly well sorted, and in beds that are medium to massive. Some are subarkosic (they contain a percentage of feldspar and dark minerals in addition to quartz); others are micaceous. The sandstones are also mostly resistant, forming ledges and cliffs. The Honaker Trail Formation also contains a few shale and siltstone beds.

The thickness of the Honaker Trail Formation is highly variable and is estimated to vary between 0 and 2,200 feet in the park area. It is thin or missing over areas where the Paradox Formation is very thick. It is exceptionally thick where the Paradox Formation contains no salt. The Honaker Trail Formation has only one exposure in Arches, but more than 600 feet are visible across the park boundary southwest of the visitor center (Doelling and others,

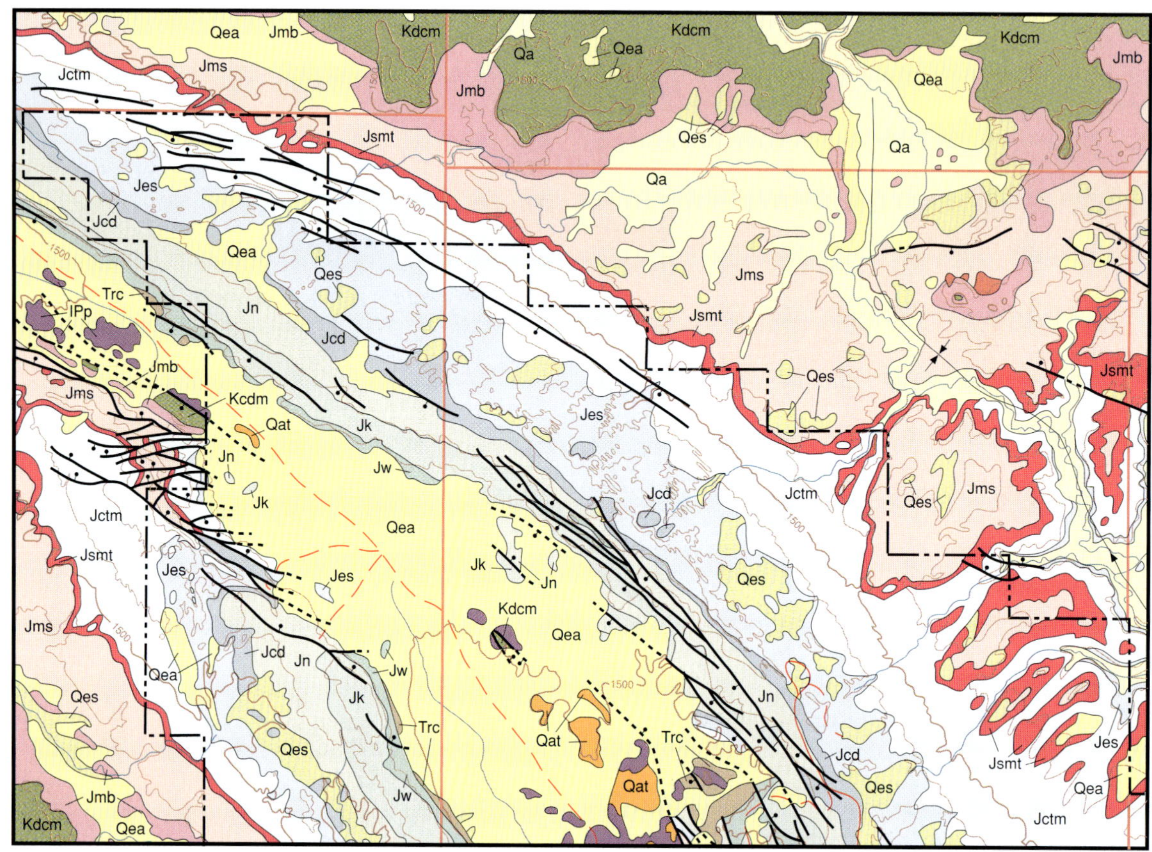

GEOLOGIC MAP OF ARCHES NATIONAL PARK,
GRAND COUNTY, UTAH, NORTH PART

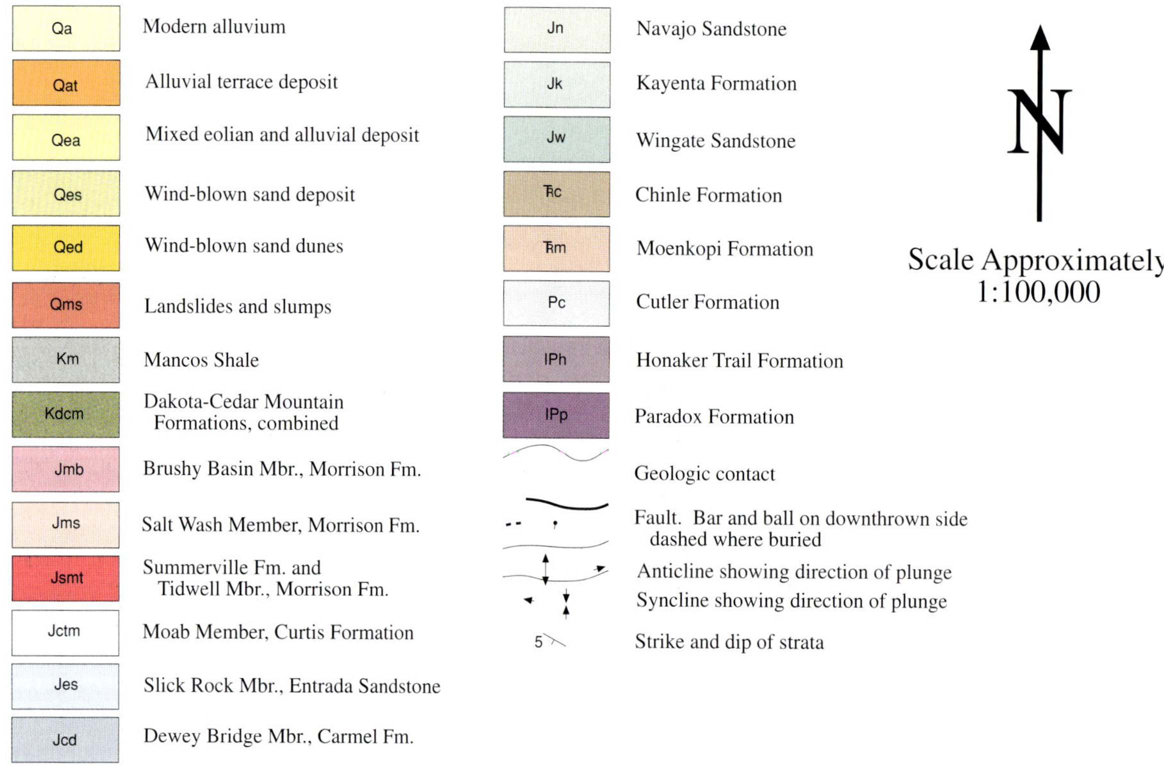

Figure 5. Geologic maps of Arches National Park, north and south parts.

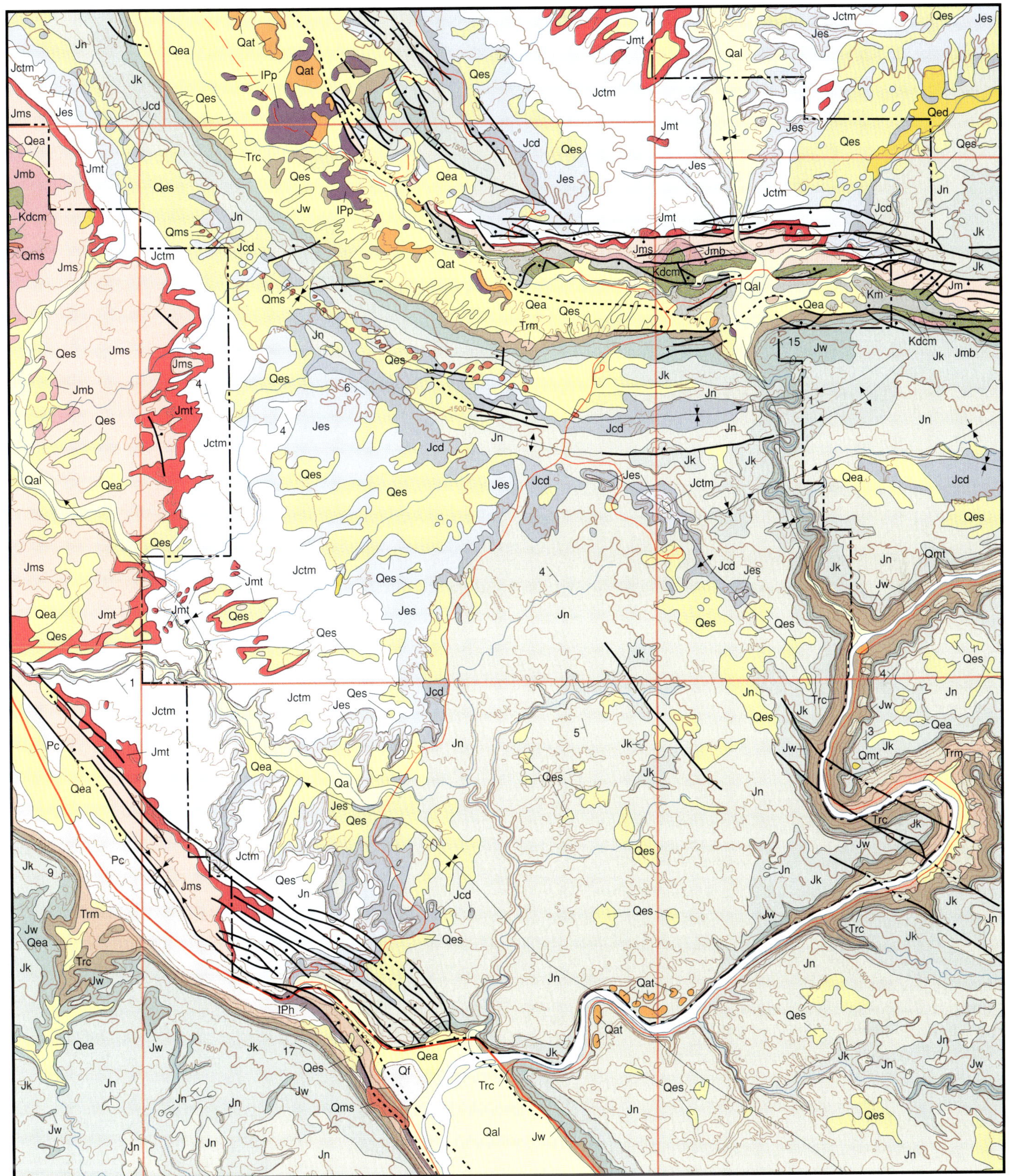

GEOLOGIC MAP OF ARCHES NATIONAL PARK, GRAND COUNTY, UTAH. SOUTH PART
SCALE 1:100,000

1995) (figure 5). The strenuous hike to the bench above U.S. Highway 191 and the railroad, opposite the visitor center, is a worthwhile enterprise. The limestones at the bench level are abundantly fossiliferous. The Honaker Trail Formation is locally missing above the Paradox Formation caprock outcrops in Salt Valley.

Permian Rocks

Cutler Formation (Pc)

The Cutler Formation unconformably overlies the Honaker Trail Formation. During Cutler time the Uncompahgre mountains rose rapidly in relation to geologic time. Alluvial fans at the foot of the mountains extended much farther southwestward, and only in the lower part of this formation are thin limestones found. By this Early Permian time the older Paleozoic rocks had been mostly eroded from the mountains, and erosion was attacking Proterozoic feldspar-rich granitic rocks.

The Cutler Formation that underlies the national park consists of interbedded red-brown to orange brown, mostly fine-grained, subarkosic to quartzose sandstone and red-purple arkosic sandstone and conglomeratic sandstone. Arkoses are sandstones containing significant percentages of feldspars; they indicate a relatively short transport distance from the mountain source. The red brown to orange-brown, subarkosic to quartzose sandstone is mostly fine to medium grained, moderately well sorted, commonly micaceous, and displays tabular-planar cross-bedding and horizontal bedding. The red-purple arkosic rocks are poorly sorted and are medium to coarse grained. These arkosic beds are commonly trough cross-bedded and have cut-and-fill structures. The conglomeratic sandstones contain granitic or gneissic pebbles and cobbles commonly as much as two inches in diameter, and contain abundant visible mica and feldspar grains. The red-brown to red-orange sandstones are generally more resistant than the red-purple arkosic sandstones and conglomeratic sandstone. A few siltstone and limestone beds are present in the lower part of the Cutler Formation where some of the sandstone beds are mottled to a nearly white color. The siltstone beds are generally purple, red, or green, are thin bedded, and form slopes. The limestone is light gray, thin to medium bedded, and ledge forming. These limestone beds commonly contain fossil fragments. The lower part of the Cutler Formation that contains the limestone, mottled sandstone, and siltstone beds was formerly divided into a separate geologic unit known as the Rico Formation (McKnight, 1940).

The Cutler Formation is not exposed in the park. It is missing over the thick salt that underlies Salt Valley and Cache Valley. It is exposed in the walls of Poison Spider Mesa on the southwest side of U.S. Highway 191 (figure 3). At the head of Little Valley the formation is 1,100 feet thick and it pinches out at the southwest margin of Moab Valley, just a little south of the covered tailings pond (Qf on the geologic map, figure 5). It is also missing over most of the thick Paradox Formation salt that underlies Moab Valley. Beneath the park, the Cutler Formation probably ranges in thickness from 0 to 1,500 feet or more.

Triassic Rocks

Moenkopi Formation (Ŕm)

The Moenkopi Formation unconformably overlies the Cutler Formation. The contact or boundary between the underlying Cutler and overlying Moenkopi can be discerned by a change from the red-brown, orange-brown, or red-purple of the Cutler Formation to the "chocolate" brown of the Moenkopi Formation. The unconformity between the two formations is locally slightly angular. It represents a significant time interval (see correlation diagram, figure 4), of at least 20 million years. More sediment may have been deposited on the Cutler Formation, but was eroded off before the Moenkopi Formation was deposited. The Uncompahgre mountains to the east were still actively eroding when Moenkopi beds were deposited, and outcrops along the Colorado River near the Big Bend are coarse grained and arkosic. The formation is a sequence of redbeds deposited in fluvial, mudflat, sabkha, and shallow marine environments (Stewart and others, 1972a; Dubiel, 1994). The open ocean lay to the west and the surface upon which the Moenkopi was deposited was quite flat. Many of the beds are ripple marked, attesting to the fact that water played an important part in the deposition of the formation.

The Moenkopi Formation, as exposed in Arches National Park and in surrounding areas, consists of three parts; a lower steep slope, a middle ledge former, and an upper steep slope. Locally, at the base of the formation, a thin basal conglomerate containing quartz, feldspar, and chert is present. The lower steep slope consists of interbedded medium-"chocolate"-brown silty sandstone, sandy mudstone, fissile siltstone, and shale. The bedding is indistinct, thin, and relatively continuous. The sandstone and siltstone are micaceous and the ripple marks are particularly common in the thin bedded, fine-grained sandstone beds. This lower unit is called the Tenderfoot Member of the Moenkopi Formation (Shoemaker and Newman, 1959). The mostly thin beds of the lower steep slope become progressively thicker upsection and eventually form distinct ledges. Except for the thicker bedding, the ledge-forming rock retains the same descriptive elements as the slope-forming rock. This ledgy part of the Moenkopi Formation is called the Ali Baba Member. The change to the upper steep slope is abrupt. The upper steep slope has thin to fissile beds and is a light-"chocolate"-brown rather than a medium-"chocolate"-brown. This upper steep slope is called the Sewemup Member (pronounced sew-em-up). In the Big Bend area the Moenkopi has a thin upper member known as the Pariott Member. It is ledge-forming and consists mainly of red-brown to lavender, fine- to medium-grained sandstone interbedded with "chocolate" brown, orange-brown, and red siltstone, mudstone, and shale. Some of the Pariott Member beds resemble the overlying Chinle Formation.

In Arches National Park the upper part of the Moenkopi Formation is exposed at the Big Bend of the Colorado River and in scattered outcrops along the south margin of Salt Valley extending from Salt Wash eastward for about four miles figure 5. A complete outcrop of the formation is present on the cliff wall below Poison Spider Mesa southwest of U.S. Highway 191. Like the Cutler Formation, the Moenkopi is thin or missing over areas of thick Paradox Formation salt and is abnormally thick elsewhere. The outcrop southwest of the visitor center thins southeastward from about 340 feet and pinches out adjacent to Moab Valley just south of the park area. The formation is very thick in some drill holes in and adjacent to the park and is estimated to be 0 to 1,300 feet thick in the park area.

Chinle Formation (Ṟc)

The Chinle Formation unconformably overlies the Moenkopi Formation. The contact between the underlying Moenkopi and overlying Chinle can be discerned by a change from the light-"chocolate"-brown slope of the upper steep slope of the Moenkopi to the red and commonly ledgy slopes of the Chinle Formation. The contact ranges from a disconformity to an easily recognizable angular unconformity. Commonly there is a thin white or light-pink-gray ledge at the base of the Chinle overlain by a mottled sandstone and conglomerate unit that is called the lower Chinle (not mapped on figure 5). The white ledge is a marker that is easily seen on most cliff faces.

The lower Chinle is a package of light-green-gray, orange-pink, and pale-red-brown, interbedded sandstone, conglomerate, siltstone, and mudstone. The rocks are commonly mottled white, light gray, red, purple, yellow, orange, and red brown. Sandy units form thin to massive ledges and cliffs separated by narrow steep slopes of mudstone and siltstone. The sandstone is fine to coarse grained and conglomeratic. The quartz grains making up the rock are poorly to moderately sorted and subangular to rounded. Subordinate quantities of chert and feldspar grains are present as well. The mottled rocks are considered to be paleosols (ancient soils) and contain networks of vertical tubular features suggestive of fossilized root systems (Doelling and Ross, 1998). The root casts are generally filled with mudstone and siltstone and a color alteration halo is present around each root trace. Calcareous and cherty nodules are also commonly present.

The upper Chinle is unconformably separated from the lower. Locally the upper member can be subdivided into a lower slope-forming unit, a middle ledge-forming unit, and an upper slope forming unit. The lower slope consists of gray-red and green-gray interbedded siltstone, mudstone, and sandstone. It commonly contains thin discontinuous ledges of sandstone and brown conglomeratic sandstone. The bedding is indistinct. Siltstone and mudstone are commonly micaceous and break up into rectangular fragments. The sandstones are fine to medium grained with ripple laminations and small-scale crossbeds. Conglomeratic sandstone is intraformational, calcareous, and forms lenses with scoured bases. The middle ledge consists of brown-gray, green gray, and red-brown conglomeratic sandstone and sandstone interbedded with red-brown siltstone and mudstone. The strata are in thick to massive ledges separated by thin slopes of siltstone and mudstone. The conglomeratic sandstone commonly contains petrified wood. The uppermost ledge of the middle ledge-forming unit is informally named the Black Ledge (Stewart and others, 1972b). In some places the middle ledge-forming unit is not well developed and not discernible, especially east of the park. The upper slope-forming unit is similar to the lower. However, near the top are 3 to 35 feet of light-brown to red-orange, very fine to fine-grained sandstone. These beds are mostly horizontally laminated and thick bedded. Faint cross-bedding is locally present. These sandstone beds are interbedded with pale-red to red-brown siltstone and mudstone. The sandstones are thought to be eolian (wind-blown) sand sheets deposited prior to the advance of the overlying Wingate Sandstone erg (sand-dune area) (Blakey and Gubitosa, 1983; Dubiel and others, 1989).

In the park, exposures of the Chinle Formation are found along the south and southwest margins of Salt Valley and in the Colorado River canyon below Mat Martin Point and around the Big Bend, and extending downstream for a few miles (figures 3 and 5). Outcrops are also found on the cliff below Poison Spider Mesa southwest of Moab Valley along U.S. Highway 191. Opposite Mat Martin Point the lower Chinle is 380 feet thick and is separated from the nearly 400 foot upper Chinle by an angular unconformity. In Salt Valley and Cache Valley, Chinle exposures are thin and locally directly overlie the Paradox Formation caprock. There the Chinle is 200 to 250 feet thick. The middle ledge former is not well developed and the lower member is very thin. Southwest of U.S. Highway 191 the Chinle Formation varies along the outcrop from 280 to 400 feet thick. Like the Moenkopi, Cutler, and Honaker Trail Formations, the unit is thin over the thicker salt of the Paradox Formation and thick where the Paradox Formation contains little or no salt. The Chinle Formation probably ranges from 200 to 900 feet in thickness in the Arches area. Most of the Chinle was deposited on the floodplains of rivers (Blakey and Gubitosa, 1983). The ledgy sandstones and conglomerates represent old stream channels and the siltstones and mudstones represent overbank or floodplain deposits.

Jurassic Rocks

Wingate Sandstone (Jw)

The contact between the Chinle Formation and Wingate Sandstone is disconformable, and is generally an abrupt change from a red slope former to a red-brown vertical massive cliff stained with desert varnish. The Wingate Sandstone is one of the easiest formations to recognize in the Arches area except where it has been damaged by salt-dissolution collapse. The formation is consolidated eolian sand in a massive, very resistant unit with nearly no partings or bedding planes. The Wingate normally erodes as slabs of rock are undercut and separate from the main mass of the cliff along vertical fractures that extend through the formation. The Chinle below is less resistant. As this supporting material for the cliff is gradually removed by erosion, these large slabs fall onto the Chinle and Moenkopi slope below, breaking up as rock fall. Such rock-fall events occur regularly in the Arches National Park area.

The upper surface of the Wingate is generally a broad plateau with unimpressive dry washes or shallow swales. During and shortly after torrential summer rainstorms, the water in normally dry washes flows over the edges of the cliff as magnificent waterfalls onto the Chinle slopes below. In contrast to typically massive cliffs, the Wingate is shattered along the flanks of many parts of the salt valleys, forming a very ledgy and blocky orange-brown cliff.

The Wingate is a relatively homogeneous unit of gray-orange to gray-orange-pink and moderate-orange-pink to pale-red-brown sandstone. The sandstone contains mostly quartz grains, some feldspar, traces of chert, and accessory minerals (Lohman, 1965). The grains are moderately to well sorted and subangular to rounded. Many of the quartz grains are frosted, suggesting eolian transport. The sandstone is calcareous and siliceous and commonly stained with iron oxides. The unit usually weathers to shades of red brown over which dark-brown and black stains of desert varnish are common. Close examination of the cliff surface reveals both flat beds and high-angle cross-bedding.

Outcrops of the Wingate Sandstone in the Arches area line the canyon of the Colorado River eastward from about a mile east of the Courthouse syncline, the canyon of Salt Wash south of Cache Valley, both sides of Moab Valley, the cliff southwest of U.S. Highway 191 below the rim of Poison Spider Mesa, and the south and southwest sides of Salt Valley and Cache Valley (figures 3 and 5). The Wingate Sandstone is 250 to 450 feet thick and averages 300 feet in the area. It was deposited in an erg (sand-dune desert).

Kayenta Formation (Jk)

Deposition was nearly continuous from Wingate time to Kayenta time. The change represents a gradual change in climate and depositional environment (Blakey, 1994). In some places the top few inches to a foot of the Wingate is bleached white, over which the thick to massive fluvial sandstones of the Kayenta are found. Locally the contact is erosional with scouring and cut and-fill features. Some geologists believe the contact is unconformable and others that it is gradational and conformable. The amount of time elapsed between the deposition of the Wingate Sandstone and the Kayenta Formation was probably relatively short. Where the Wingate is mostly red-brown on weathered surfaces, the Kayenta beds are more red or pale purple, lithologically more heterogeneous, and contain fluvial sedimentary features. In many places the contact is difficult to identify. Generally, the contact is placed where the vertical cliff of the Wingate is replaced by the thick ledges of the Kayenta Formation.

The Kayenta Formation commonly forms ledgy bare-rock surfaces and consists mostly of stream-deposited sandstone lenses, with subordinate interbeds of eolian (wind-blown) sandstone, intraformational conglomerate, siltstone, and shale. The appearance of the unit as a whole is primarily reddish, but individual lenses and beds vary considerably; some are purple, lavender, red, tan, orange, and white. Most of the sandstone lenses are moderate orange pink and the finer grained deposits are dark red brown to gray red. Sandstone in the Kayenta Formation shows both high-angle and low-angle cross-bedding. Some beds and lenses display channeling, current ripple marks, and rare slump features. The sand grains are mostly quartz, but mica and subordinate quantities of dark minerals and feldspar are commonly present. Most sandstone is fine to medium grained, but locally it is more coarse. Siltstone, shale, and intraformational conglomerate beds are more common in the upper half of the formation.

The Kayenta Formation invariably caps the Wingate cliffs. In some cases it forms a bench, such as on Poison Spider Mesa. Locally drainages on the benches have cut deeply into the overlying rocks to expose the Wingate Sandstone. The Kayenta Formation is 200 to 300 feet thick in the Arches area.

Navajo Sandstone (Jn)

The contact between the Kayenta Formation and Navajo Sandstone is intertonguing and is locally difficult to place. Thick eolian sandstones near the top of the Kayenta are similar to sandstone in the Navajo and are thought to intertongue laterally into the Navajo Sandstone. Generally, the contact is placed where the dominantly fluvial red or lavender rocks of the Kayenta are replaced by light-brown or light-gray eolian rocks of the Navajo Sandstone. The Navajo Sandstone trademark is its high-angle cross-bedding. These are generally etched out by weathering processes and form the basis for the Petrified Dunes area of the park. Where it forms the bench above the deep canyons of the Colorado River and its tributaries, it is generally exposed as bare rock surfaces. Locally some thin patches of self-derived sand fill hollows in its surface.

The Navajo Sandstone is a mostly orange to light-gray, mostly fine-grained, generally well sorted, massive sandstone. However, medium to coarse grains of quartz are common along cross-bed laminae. It is cemented with calcite and quartz. Even though the Navajo is a well-cemented cliff former, the sandstone is somewhat friable in hand specimen. The sandstone is divided into cross-bed sets, generally 15 to 25 feet thick. Between the set boundaries the cross-bedding dips up to 35 degrees. Set boundaries are generally planar surfaces that are thought to represent former water table surfaces. Apparently, loose dry sand in dunes above the water table was blown off, while the more coherent wet sand below the water table was preserved. The processes was repeated as the deposits before the next layer of dune sand accumulated above this set boundary. As the deposits subsided the water table rose to a new level and the process was repeated. Locally, gray to pink-gray, thin, hard, lenticular lacustrine limestone is also found in the unit, and is interpreted to have developed in oases, playas, or interdune lakes (Stokes, 1991) when the water table rose above the sand surface. Laterally these limestones grade into calcareous reddish siltstones that eventually become set boundaries. Stokes (1991) reported the presence of petrified wood in the vicinity of such deposits. Limestone beds locally contain small nodules of authigenic jasper (red chert). The limestone outcrops commonly form a resistant bench covered with a dark sandy or rubbly soil.

The Navajo Sandstone forms the bench on much of the area east and northeast of Moab Valley and in the park between the Great Wall and the Big Bend of the Colorado River between Cache Valley and the Colorado River (figure 5). The formation is 200 to 550 feet thick in the Arches area. The variation in thickness is not surprising inasmuch as its upper surface is a regional unconformity.

Carmel Formation

Dewey Bridge Member (Jcd): The nomenclature given to this unit in this publication varies from that in the past literature, including that of my own (Doelling, 1985 and 1988). Dane (1935), who first studied the Arches National Park region in detail, assigned this unit to the Carmel Formation. Later investigators proposed a change consistent with lithological criteria (Wright, and others 1962; Lohman, 1965). The suggested name for this unit was the Dewey Bridge Member of the Entrada Sandstone and assignment to the Entrada was based on the fact that these reddish beds are mostly sandstone whereas the Carmel Formation contains limestone, gypsum, and other rock types. Nevertheless, the Carmel Formation in the San Rafael Swell, to the west, is clearly continuous with the beds in Arches and is therefore of the same age. Dewey Bridge-like rocks are found in Carmel outcrops in the Swell interbedded with limestone and gypsum and hence there has been some confusion. Therefore, I suggest returning to Dane's (1935) original assignment, retaining the Dewey Bridge as a member of the Carmel Formation rather than as a member of the Entrada Formation. The change is presented here as a suggestion. Collaborators and I propose to present this argument formally in a later publication.

The contact between the Navajo Sandstone and the Dewey Bridge Member has been named the J-2 regional unconformity (Pipiringos and O'Sullivan, 1978). Broad relief is displayed along the contact and the lower part of the Dewey Bridge Member fills low areas in the Navajo Sand-

Figure 6. *Balanced Rock. This landmark has a Carmel Formation base that supports a bulb of the smoother weathering Slick Rock Member of the Entrada Sandstone.*

stone. Generally, planar or flat-bedded sandstones of the Dewey Bridge Member cover the surface of the high-angled cross-bedded Navajo. The weathered coloration of the lower Dewey Bridge is commonly the same as that for the Navajo Sandstone. However, much angular white chert is present immediately above the contact in the Dewey Bridge Member. I have traced limestone beds eastward into western Grand County where they are replaced by sandstone. The lower part of the Dewey Bridge Member may be the Page Sandstone of Peterson and Pipiringos (1979), which intertongues with and replaces the lower members of the Carmel Formation in central and southern Utah.

In the Arches National Park area the Dewey Bridge Member may be divided into two subunits (not divided on figure 5). The lower part is dominated by yellow-gray, planar-bedded, fine-grained sandstone. The beds are generally medium to thick and resistant. In some areas the lower unit is color banded with pink to red-brown sandstones between the dominantly yellow-gray beds. The upper unit is mostly a red-brown, muddy, mostly fine-grained silty sandstone with irregular contorted to "lumpy" bedding (figure 6). It generally forms a slope or a red-brown to "chocolate"-brown recess between the lower unit and the overlying Slick Rock Member of the Entrada Sandstone.

The lower unit is 15 to 85 feet thick and the upper unit is 60 to 157 feet thick in the Arches area; the entire member varies from 70 to 200 feet, thinning roughly eastward. The member is thin where the Navajo Sandstone is thick. The member is about 90 feet thick at the Garden of Eden, 139 feet thick at Klondike Bluffs, and about 104 feet thick near the Visitor Center. The Dewey Bridge Member of the Carmel Formation is interpreted to have been deposited on broad tidal flats marginal to a shallow sea (Carmel sea) which lay to the west (Wright and others, 1962). It forms

Figure 7. Skyline Arch. The opening is 71 feet wide and 33.5 feet high. The arch is formed along a parting in the Slick Rock Member of the Entrada Sandstone.

Figure 8. Joints in the Moab Member of the Curtis Formation on the northeast flank of the Salt Valley anticline. Red-orange scabs to left are Summerville Formation and Tidwell Member of the Morrison Formation. The canyon in the upper right exposes the the upper part of the Slickrock Member of the Entrada Sandstone.

the pedestal of Balanced Rock and the base of The Windows arches. The park highway follows the Dewey Bridge outcrop to Courthouse Towers and again along the base of The Great Wall. The pavement also extends along the Dewey Bridge Member outcrop northward from the Fiery Furnace.

Entrada Sandstone

Slick Rock Member (Jes): The Slick Rock Member of the Entrada Sandstone overlies the Dewey Bridge Member of the Carmel Formation. The contact is generally sharp, but locally extraordinarily irregular. In some cases the Slick Rock Member intertongues with the Dewey Bridge. Near the Visitor Center the Dewey Bridge appears to be angularly planed off by the Slick Rock Member, but this is attributed to soft-sediment deformation in the Dewey Bridge. In nearby areas to the east (not in the park), the Slick Rock contact is arch-like, with thin pedestals of Slick Rock making contact with the lower unit of the Dewey Bridge, and the "arch" area being filled with the red-brown to "chocolate"-brown sandstone of the upper unit. Dane (1935) described the contact as an invasion of the Carmel Formation by dikes or irregular masses of the overlying Entrada Sandstone. He noted that the deformation is not wholly plastic; that the contact is locally cut by small faults that extend upward into the Slick Rock for short distances and then die out.

The Slick Rock Member of the Entrada Sandstone is a massive, well-indurated, red-orange or brown, very fine to fine-grained sandstone containing sparse and scattered medium to coarse grains. The sand grains are held together with calcite and iron-oxide cement. It commonly weathers to form smooth cliffs and bare-rock slopes. Parts of the member are distinctly cross stratified (eolian deposition), other parts are planar bedded. Small holes are commonly aligned along cross-bed laminae. In most places it is striped or banded in color. In some cases the

banding is hardly noticed, in others it is pronounced. Locally pronounced indentations paralleling the banding are present in the Slick Rock Member.

The Slick Rock Member of the Entrada Sandstone is perhaps the most important geologic unit in Arches National Park. Most of the arches in the park are positioned along its lower and upper contacts and along the indentures in the middle of the unit (figure 7). It is found above the red-brown or "chocolate"-brown marker of the Dewey Bridge Member, making up the vertical cliffs of The Courthouse Towers and The Great Wall. It makes up the fins of the Fiery Furnace and the area northeast of Salt Valley where it is cut by numerous closely spaced vertical fractures called joints (figures 8 and 9). Where the Slick Rock is not exposed as a cliff, fin, or arch, the outcrop band is covered or partly covered by large irregular fields of self-derived wind-blown sand (figure 5). It was deposited in a dune field in a back-beach area. The Slick Rock Member is normally 200 to 350 feet thick within Arches National Park.

Curtis Formation

Moab Member (Jctm): The nomenclature given to this unit in this publication varies from that in the past literature, including that of my own (Doelling, 1985 and 1988). Dane (1935) included this unit as the Moab Sandstone Member of the Entrada. McKnight (1940) noticed the Moab Member pinching out into the Curtis Formation west of the park and believed the Moab to be a tongue of the Entrada Sandstone that extends into the Curtis. However, to the west, the Entrada is separated from the Curtis Formation by a regional unconformity that Pipiringos and O'Sullivan (1978) named the J-3 unconformity. I believe this unconformity continues eastward between the Slick Rock and Moab sandstones and that the Moab Member is not a tongue of the Entrada Sandstone. I have identified this unconformity as far east as the Colorado state line

Figure 9. Entrada Sandstone fins. Joints at "roll overs" open and form fins along Salt Valley graben rims. Weakly cemented partings in fins can then weather into arches.

(Doelling and Morgan, 1996; Willis and others, 1996) and throughout the area of the Moab and La Sal 30' x 60' quadrangles (Doelling, 1993; Doelling, in press). The change from normal Curtis Formation lithology into the Moab Member is abrupt; from areas west of Arches, Curtis Formation rock types continue eastward under the sandstone Moab Member into the Arches area and are exposed in the northern part of the park.

The unconformable contact between the Moab Member and Slick Rock Member of the Entrada Sandstone is sharp. In the north part of the park, near Eagle Park, about 25 feet of recess forming Curtis-like beds (brown, thin-bedded, silty, fine-grained, slope- or recess-forming sandstone) are found above the plane of the unconformity, followed by typical Moab Member. In the central park area the contact is a reddish indenture of siltstone. In the south park area the contact is a subtle line above which banding, typical of the Slick Rock Member, is not present and above which the white or gray-white Moab Member is present. Cross-beds in the Slick Rock Member are truncated at the line.

The Moab Member of the Curtis Formation is a conspicuous, resistant sandstone that forms a capping surface on many of the Entrada Sandstone cliffs. It is mostly a pale-orange, gray-orange, pale-yellow-brown, or light-gray, fine-to medium-grained, calcareous, massive, cliff-forming sandstone that weathers white or light gray. The sandstone is typically well indurated, exhibits low angle cross-stratification, and is generally highly jointed in outcrop. The sandstone resembles the Navajo in color, cementation, and in the differential etching of cross-bed laminae.

The Moab Member forms the upper part of Delicate Arch; the Slick Rock Member forms the pedestals (figure 2). Moab member outcrops form bare-rock sloping jointed benches on each side of Salt Valley. These northwest-trending jointed benches present spectacular views from an airplane (figure 8). Outcrops may also be observed on the Delicate Arch hike. The thickness of the Moab ranges from 60 to 120 feet in the park.

Morrison Formation

<u>**Summerville Formation and Tidwell Member, undifferentiated (Jsmt):**</u> The unit overlying the Moab Member of the Curtis Formation is a relatively thin red-bed marker unit. Dane (1935) and McKnight (1940) called this interval the Summerville Formation and appear to have correlated it with beds present in the San Rafael Swell to the west. Later O'Sullivan (1980, 1981) indicated that there were actually two units represented here that were separated by the J-5 unconformity of Pipiringos and O'Sullivan (1978). In fact, the lower part of this thin red-bed marker unit correlates with the Summerville Formation and the upper and dominant part of the marker in the Arches area is the Tidwell Member of the Morrison Formation. Because they are both relatively thin, the Summerville Formation and the Tidwell Member of the Morrison Formation have been mapped as one unit on figure 5. With a little practice, however, they are easily divisible in the field.

The Summerville Formation consists of thin- to medium-bedded, light-tan to brown, ledgy sandstone and slope-forming red sandy siltstone that forms a steep slope. A zone of yellow-gray reworked sandstone is generally present at the base of the Summerville. Locally, dinosaur footprints can be identified in this reworked horizon (Lockley, 1991). A prominent thin- to medium-bedded, blocky to platy, ripple-marked sandstone ledge commonly marks the top of the formation. The Summerville Formation is non-calcareous. The contact between the Summerville and the Morrison Formations is placed at the base of thin gray limestone beds or maroon to lavender siltstone of the Tidwell Member of the Morrison Formation, all of which are calcareous. Most of the Tidwell consists of red, maroon, lavender, or light-gray weathering siltstone. Discontinuous beds of light-gray limestone are interspersed throughout the siltstone, but are more common at the base and top of the unit. In many places in Arches, large, mostly white chert concretions are found immediately above the lowermost limestone bed. Some of these concretions are as much as 6 feet in diameter and a few contain irregular red and brown patches of jasper. The origin of these very large chert concretions is puzzling. The Tidwell forms a more gentle slope than the Summerville Formation beneath it. The Summerville and the Tidwell commonly appear in a recess between the resistant Moab Member below and the ledgy conglomeratic sandstones of the Salt Wash Member of the Morrison Formation above.

The Summerville Formation is only 6 to about 20 feet thick in the park, thinning southward and thickening in all other directions. Along the Delicate Arch trail it is about 15 feet thick and on the Moab anticline northwest of the visitor center it is only 6 feet thick. The Tidwell Member ranges from 25 to 50 feet in thickness. The Summerville Formation is a delta deposit that was laid down marginal to a shallow sea lying to the west (McKnight, 1940). The

Tidwell was probably deposited in a nearly flat area as a fluvial overbank and associated lakes deposit. The red-bed unit is exposed far down on each side of the Salt Valley salt anticline, near the axis of the Moab anticline, and in down-faulted blocks on the north side of Cache Valley on both sides of Salt Wash (figures 3 and 5).

Salt Wash Member (Jms): The contact of the Tidwell Member with the overlying Salt Wash Member is gradational and locally intertonguing. It is generally placed below the first significant thick, light-gray, yellow-gray, or light-brown sandstone lens or bed of the Salt Wash Member. The Salt Wash is a bench and cliff-forming unit of sandstone and muddy siltstone. I call it a "messy" sandstone because large broken pieces of sandstone beds and lenses are littered about the outcrops, breaking apart as the softer siltstones between the lenses are eroded away and no longer give support.

The Salt Wash Member is composed of 25 to 40 percent sandstone lenses alternating with 60 to 75 percent red and green muddy siltstone. The sandstone lenses form ledges that range from 2 to 20 feet thick; most are 2 to 4 feet thick, however sandstone lens thickness generally increases up-section with a corresponding decrease in the muddy silt-stone intervals. Typically, there are six or seven thick, vertically stacked sandstone lenses in the Salt Wash Member. The sandstone is cross-bedded, fine to coarse grained, moderately to poorly sorted, and calcareous. The sand grains are dominantly quartz. The muddy siltstones are red, green-gray, maroon, and lavender. Thin limestone beds and nodules are locally present in the Salt Wash muddy siltstones.

Outcrops of the Salt Wash Member are present along the western and northeastern park boundaries. A band of tilted Salt Wash outcrops is present in fault slices in Cache Valley and eastern Salt Valley. Locally dinosaur bone and fragments of petrified wood have been found in the member. The Salt Wash Member is a fluvial deposit laid down as channel deposits in an anastomosing braided river system. The muddy siltstones are considered overbank deposits. The Salt Wash Member ranges from 130 to 300 feet thick in the park, and averages about 180 feet thick.

Brushy Basin Member (Jmb): The upper contact of the Salt Wash Member is placed at the top of the interval dominated by light-gray sandstone lenses, below dark-colored conglomeratic sandstone lenses or brightly colored-banded or bright-green mudstone of the Brushy Basin Member. The Salt Wash sandstones are mostly quartzose whereas the sandstone or conglomeratic sandstone lenses in the Brushy Basin Member are lithic, that is, are composed of fragments of other rocks. Sand is more common in Brushy Basin mudstone than in Salt Wash mudstone, which is dominantly siltstone. This member is dominated by mudstone and forms smooth variegated or green slopes with few ledges.

The member is predominantly silty and clayey mudstone and muddy sandstone interbedded with a few local conglomeratic sandstone lenses. The steep-sloped outcrops may be banded in various shades of maroon, green, gray, and lavender. To the southeast they are a bright green. Most of the rock is indistinctly bedded, and has a high-clay content as is evident from "popcorn" weathered surfaces. Many of the mudstones are probably decomposed volcanic tuff beds. The sandstone is commonly cross-bedded, coarse grained to gritty, with local pebble-stone and conglomerate lenses. About 75 percent of the Brushy Basin is mudstone. The sandstone and conglomerate lenses are generally found near the base of the unit.

Because of the clay content, the Brushy Basin Member is prone to landsliding and its outcrops are generally replete with slumps. The member is 300 to 450 feet thick in the park. Dinosaur bone and petrified wood are locally found in the member. It was partly deposited on a broad flood plain dotted with small lakes and partly in a larger lake known as Lake To'odichi (Peterson and Turner, 1987). It is thought that the bright green Brushy Basin sediments were deposited subaqueously and that the variegated, maroon, and banded deposits were deposited terrestrially.

Cretaceous Rocks

Cedar Mountain Formation and Dakota Sandstone, undifferentiated (Kdcm)

The upper contact of the Brushy Basin Member of the Morrison Formation is an unconformity. It is placed at the base of a persistent cliff-forming sandstone about 10 to 30 feet thick at the top of the brightly banded or bright green slope of the Brushy Basin. Above this cliff forming sandstone the Cedar Mountain Formation is much like the Brushy Basin Member in composition and weathering habit. However, the slope is not as bright, and has a more pastel or dull coloration.

The lower Cedar Mountain Formation sandstone unit is mostly light to dark brown, weathering to a darker hue. The grain size varies between fine, medium, coarse, gritty, and conglomeratic. The mudstone is silty and contains sandstone intervals. Locally, nodular gray or brown limestone is present containing sporadic chert nodules. Also, the sandstone intervals become resistant and form ledges much like the one at the base, and many are lithified to quartzite. They become so well indurated that the rock breaks across the sand grains rather than around them. The Cedar Mountain generally has less clay in it than the Brushy Basin Member of the Morrison Formation.

Cedar Mountain Formation outcrops in Arches National Park are mostly confined to the tilted fault blocks in Cache and Salt Valleys, especially around the Wolfe Ranch house where Salt Wash crosses Cache Valley. More extensive outcrop areas are between U.S. Highway 191 and the park boundary to the west, and north of the north park boundary. The formation is 100 to 250 feet thick in the park area, but most sections are only 100 to 150 feet thick. Because its outcrop band is thin in Cache and Salt Valley and the Dakota Sandstone is even thinner, they are com-

Figure 10. View southward down Salt Valley and into Arches National Park. Valley area is filled with mixed alluvium and eolium overlying basin fill that buries collapsed bedrock. Mounds of rock in valley have commonly been lowered as much as 3,000 feet due to the removal of salt by dissolution at depth. The light unit along the left rim is the Navajo Sandstone.

bined on the geologic map (Kdcm). The Cedar Mountain locally contains scattered fossils such as ostracodes, protistids, and snails. White petrified wood, especially in the lower cliff former, is locally relatively abundant. Dinosaur bones have also been found in this unit (Kirkland and others, 1999). In local areas, chalcedony fragments abundantly weather out of the formation. The Cedar Mountain Formation was deposited in an environment similar to that in which the Brushy Basin Member of the Morrison Formation was deposited.

The contact between the Cedar Mountain Formation and the Dakota Sandstone is also an unconformity. It is placed at the base of a white claystone or a yellow-gray to brown sandstone, conglomeratic sandstone, and conglomerate of the Dakota Sandstone.

The Dakota Sandstone is a heterogeneous unit containing white siliceous claystone and limestone, carbonaceous shale, thin coaly seams, yellow-gray conglomeratic sandstone, gray slope forming shale, and yellow-brown and yellow-gray sandstone. To the east the unit contains a lower sandstone or conglomerate, a middle shale and coaly sequence, and an upper sandstone (Willis and others, 1996). To the west the unit becomes discontinuous and is locally missing (Doelling, 1993). In the Arches area, in Salt and Cache Valleys, the yellow-gray conglomeratic sandstone lithology is the most obvious.

Except for the Salt and Cache Valley outcrops, the Dakota is not present in the park. In Salt and Cache Valley it is exposed as a steeply dipping orange or brown hogback immediately north of the highway leading to Wolfe Ranch and the parking area to the Delicate Arch overlook. The Dakota Sandstone is 0 to 110 feet thick in the region. In the Salt and Cache Valley outcrops the unit is typically 20 to 80 feet thick. The Dakota was deposited on a broad coastal plain and in lagoons in front of an advancing Mancos Sea (western interior seaway) that inundated the area thereafter (Molenaar and Cobban, 1991).

Mancos Shale (Km)

The youngest bedrock unit in Arches National Park is the Mancos Shale. The contact with the Dakota Sandstone is gradational over a narrow interval. The unit is a slope former, but contains thin sandstone layers that commonly form slight ledges. The most prominent of these is the Ferron Sandstone Member (not divided on figure 5).

The Mancos Shale is mostly medium-gray fissile shale that forms a soft slope. Most of the shale is slightly calcareous. The lower part of the Mancos in Cache and Salt Valleys corresponds to the Tununk Shale Member. Near the top of the Tununk the rock becomes sandy and grades into the Ferron Sandstone Member. The sandy character of the Ferron makes it more resistant and gives it a darker brown-gray color. In Cache Valley the Ferron forms low ridges and rounded hills. Most of the Ferron is platy or

Figure 11. Unconsolidated Quaternary deposits that have been deformed because of dissolution collapse. The white layers are volcanic ashes that have yielded Pleistocene ages.

thin-bedded, brown-gray, very fine grained sandstone, but in the middle it consists of dark-gray and black carbonaceous shale. Overlying the Ferron are shales assigned to the Blue Gate Member of the Mancos. These rocks are like the Tununk Shale Member, but may be slightly lighter in color.

In the park, outcrops are confined to Cache and Salt Valleys where they are folded and perhaps attenuated by faulting. The Tununk may be 100 to 400 feet thick, the Ferron is 90 to 120 feet thick, and the uneroded Blue Gate is no greater than 500 feet thick. The unit is fossiliferous. Zones of mostly shellfish (pelecypods) can be found immediately above the Dakota Sandstone and at the top of the Ferron Member. Molenaar and Cobban (1991) indicated that the Mancos was deposited in a shallow sea; the Ferron Member in a shallow shoaling sea.

QUATERNARY DEPOSITS

Modern Alluvium (Qa)

Alluvium is found along modern stream channels and consist of mixtures of sand, silt, gravel, and clay derived from upstream source areas. Alluvial deposits along the Colorado River carry cobbles of igneous rocks from the La Sal Mountains and gneisses from the Uncompahgre Highland area to the east. Some of the deposits have been laid down in washes that are dry most of the year but that drain relatively large areas. Flash floods in the washes carry in new materials a few times a year to only once in several years. Most deposits are less than 25 feet thick and mostly Holocene in age; but the alluvium in the north part of Moab Valley is very thick and its lower parts may be Pleistocene in age. There and perhaps where Salt Wash crosses Cache Valley, salt is probably being dissolved at depth; resulting subsidence allows for the thicker accumulations of alluvium (basin-fill deposits) (figure 11). Alluvium in Moab Valley is several hundred feet thick.

Terrace Gravel Deposits (Qat)

These alluvial deposits are 80 or more feet above modern stream and wash channels. They consist of the same materials as found in the modern channels. Those along the Colorado River contain small flakes and flour-sized particles of gold (too fine and sparse to mine profitably). Those in the middle of Salt Valley were laid down in an ancient stream that no longer flows in the valley; the deposits contain cobbles eroded from the Book Cliffs many miles to the north. These deposits are generally less than 15 feet thick.

Mixed Eolian and Alluvial Deposits (Qea)

These are complex unconsolidated deposits with lenses of basin-fill alluvium, channel deposits, overbank deposits, and wind-blown sand sheets. They consist mostly of sand, silt, gravel, and clay deposits. Some of these deposits are relatively old (Pleistocene) and have well-developed caliche horizons. They are mostly less than 25 feet thick, but in Salt Valley they are several hundred feet thick because salt was being dissolved when the sediment accumulated (figures 10 and 11). Some deposits in Salt Valley are enriched with gypsum derived from the local outcrops of the Paradox Formation caprock. Some have interbedded layers of Pleistocene volcanic ash. Two of the ash layers are named and have well-known ages. These are the Bishop ash, and Lava Creek B ash which were deposited 730,000 and 610,000 years ago derived from volcanos in California and Yellowstone National Park (Colman and others, 1988). Some of these thicker deposits have been folded into synclines and anticlines, due to collapse as salt beds beneath them have been dissolved away (figure 11).

Eolian Sand (Qes, Qed)

Wind-blown sand commonly fills hollows on sandstone deposits, especially on the Slick Rock Member of the Entrada Sandstone. Others accumulate in protected places as the sand is blown across the area by the prevailing wind. Long fingers of such sand cover mixed eolian and alluvial (Qea) deposits in Salt Valley. In some areas the sand accumulates in dunes.

Landslide Deposits (Qms)

These are blocks and slumps of bedrock that have detached and slid from outcrops. Landsliding occurs when fine-grained clayey bed rock outcrops are subjected to cycles of wet weather. The bentonite-bearing Morrison Formation produces most landslides, especially the Brushy Basin Member. Numerous small old landslides and slumps dot the area of the Elephant Butte folds. The source of these slides is perplexing since the closest bedrock containing these materials is now several miles away.

STRUCTURAL HISTORY AND GEOLOGY

Regionally, Arches National Park is positioned in an

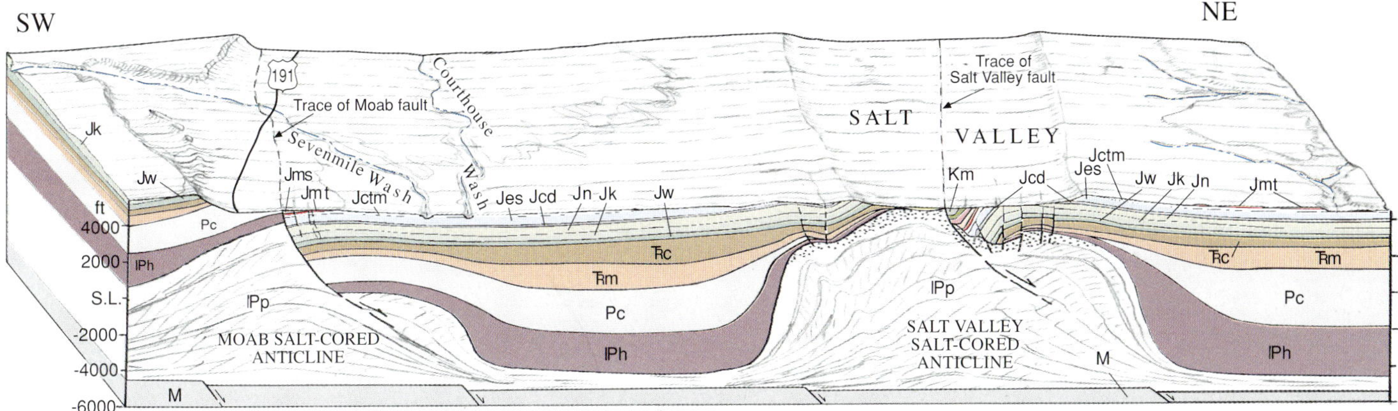

Figure 12. Cross-sectional block diagram of the Arches National Park area drawn approximately to scale. Unit (formational) symbols correspond to those shown on figures 3 and 5.

area where the rock formations dip gently northward. Superimposed over this regional dip are several structural features formed by tectonic forces (conditions prevalent in the earth's crust) or by salt movement or dissolution. By some interpretations the formation of the rock arches in the park is due to a unique set of geologic phenomena and conditions. For geologists, arches are only one of the many fantastically displayed geologic features of the park.

Salt Deposition and Movement

About 300 million years ago much of southeast Utah and southwest Colorado subsided to form a basin (Paradox basin) that was a shallow embayment of an open ocean that lay to the west. The basin collapsed as mostly northwest-trending normal faults were intermittently activated. As the basin subsided evaporitic sediments were deposited on the ocean floor because the climate of the basin area was hot and dry and there was minor freshwater input. These evaporites consisted of gypsum, and sodium-, potassium-, and magnesium-bearing salts. Salts have a low specific gravity and after being covered and confined by heavier sediments have a tendency to be squeezed upward. Under pressure, the plastic salt forced its way upward along lines of weakness, such as faults. The salt moved upward toward the surface as enormous salt walls (salt-cored anticlines) parallel to the faults. The sediments deposited in the subsiding basin as the salt rose were laid down thinly over, and thickly in the areas between the rising salt walls (figure 12). This process continued for 75 million years. Such salt walls are present beneath Salt, Cache, and Moab Valleys. The Paradox Formation is nearly devoid of salt between the salt walls, the salt having been squeezed out of it.

Overlying rock formations between the salt walls are commonly several times their normal thicknesses, and are thin or missing over the tops of the salt walls (figure 12). Drill holes indicate the sides of the salt walls are mostly very steep, in some places overhanging. The salt walls are about two miles high (more than 10,000 feet) and the rocks marginal to them are commonly brecciated, upturned, and

display numerous angular unconformities. One of the better of these unconformities is displayed just west of Mat Martin Point in the canyon of the Colorado River. Rocks of the lower unit of the Chinle Formation were tilted as salt rose, then planed off by erosion, and then covered by the upper unit of the Chinle Formation. The presence of such unconformities have been confirmed in all formations between the salt-bearing Paradox Formation and the Chinle Formation. Each unconformity registers a time when the subsurface faults were active and salt moved. Fault activity ceased during the time the upper unit of the Chinle Formation was deposited. In Salt, Cache, and Moab Valleys, the Chinle is the first formation that covers the salt-bearing beds.

Jurassic and Cretaceous Sedimentation

The area intermittently received additional sediments during the remainder of the Mesozoic Era as described in the stratigraphy section and as shown on figure 4. The area continued to lie near sea level, receiving continental deposition during Early Cretaceous time and marine deposition during Late Cretaceous time (Hintze, 1988). Because there are no younger bedrock units present than the Upper Cretaceous Mancos Shale in the park, there is no rock record of geologic events that happened in the interval between 80 and 15 million years ago.

Late Cretaceous-Early Tertiary Folding and Faulting

Based on evidence from surrounding areas, the rocks in the park were faulted and folded during the Late Cretaceous and early Tertiary and the La Sal Mountains granitic (intrusive igneous) rocks were intruded into a salt wall south of Arches National Park about 29 million years ago. Relatively large-sized uplifts and basins developed in the Colorado Plateau region after the withdrawal of the Late Cretaceous western interior seaway (Mancos Sea). These developments are generally assigned to the Laramide orogeny (Hintze, 1988). The Uinta Basin developed to the north and another basin developed along the west margin

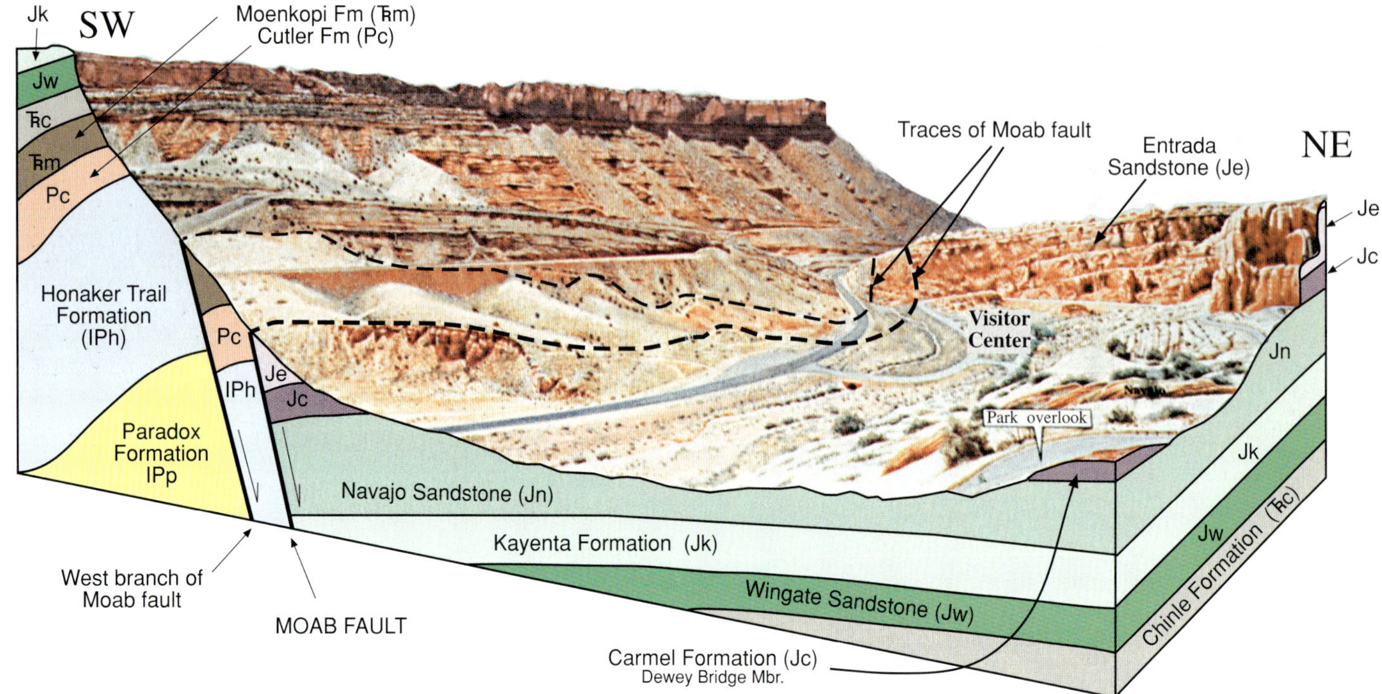

Figure 13. The Moab fault has a total displacement of 2,400 feet across the fault zone. The dashed lines show the approximate traces of the fault. Note the position of the Wingate Sandstone near the top of the cliff to the left with respect to the dark-green layer (also Wingate Sandstone) on the right side of the diagram.

of the Colorado Plateaus in the Wasatch Plateau area. The Circle Cliffs, San Rafael Swell, Monument upwarp, and Uncompahgre Plateau represent the uplifts. Smaller basins may have developed between the uplifts. The Arches area lies between the Uinta Basin to the north and the Monument upwarp to the south and the regional dip in the park is 2 to 4 degrees northward. The Uinta Basin continued to receive sediments until about 35 million years ago.

Smaller gentle, mostly northwest-trending anticlines and synclines developed on this regional slope. In the Arches area, anticlinal axes are superimposed directly over the Salt Valley and the Moab Valley salt walls. Hence, the anticlines are salt cored (figure 12). The Moab anticline continues northwest of Moab Valley for about 6 miles, plunging and gradually dying out. The axis of the Salt Valley anticline ceases to follow the underlying salt wall southeast of the Fiery Furnace and continues as The Windows anticline for about 4 miles before dying out (figure 3). The flanks of these anticlines generally dip from 4 to 17 degrees. No Late Cretaceous-early Tertiary fold follows the east-west-trending Cache Valley salt wall. The Courthouse syncline lies between the Moab and Salt Valley-The Windows anticlines, and the Salt Wash syncline lies to the east of the Salt Valley-The Windows anticline. The Salt Wash syncline crosses Cache Valley perpendicularly along a north-south trend.

Major Tertiary normal faults are associated with each of the salt walls. Drill holes have shown that the Moab fault north of Moab Valley cuts through and parallels the middle of the 2-mile wide Moab Valley salt wall (figures 12

and 13). The downthrown block is on the northeast side. At the visitor center the Honaker Trail Formation is abutted against the Entrada Sandstone, indicating a displacement of 2,400 feet (Doelling and others, 1995) across the Moab fault. The fault has two branches that are easily discernible from the visitor center. A thin slice of Moenkopi Formation separates the Honaker Trail Formation from the Entrada Sandstone. A similar, but less obvious fault cuts the middle of the salt wall under Salt and Cache Valleys. Where traceable it is shown as a dotted (buried) fault line on the geologic map (figure 5). On one side of the fault, cupolas of Paradox Formation caprock are covered by the upper Chinle Formation. On the other side are deeply collapsed Mesozoic rocks. The displacement on this fault is not discernible because the rocks on the northeast side of the fault have been intensely deformed by later salt dissolution events (see cross section, figure 12). It is unclear how normal faults, which indicate extension of the earth's crust, are related to anticlines and synclines (folding), which indicate compression of the earth's crust. The timing of these events also remains unclear, except that they occurred between about 80 and 15 million years ago.

Jointing

The brittle sandstone formations of the park are generally highly jointed (figure 8). Joints are parallel fractures that cut rocks in sets. For the most part they subparallel the northwest trends of the salt anticlines, but locally they do not. At the south end of the Fiery Furnace (figure 14) the joints are truncated by east-west faults along which the

Figure 14. Aerial view toward the Fiery Furnace. Notice how the joints in the Entrada Sandstone terminate against collapsed rock as Salt Valley turns to trend east-west and join with Cache Valley. The light biscuit board surface areas are the Moab Member of the Curtis Formation.

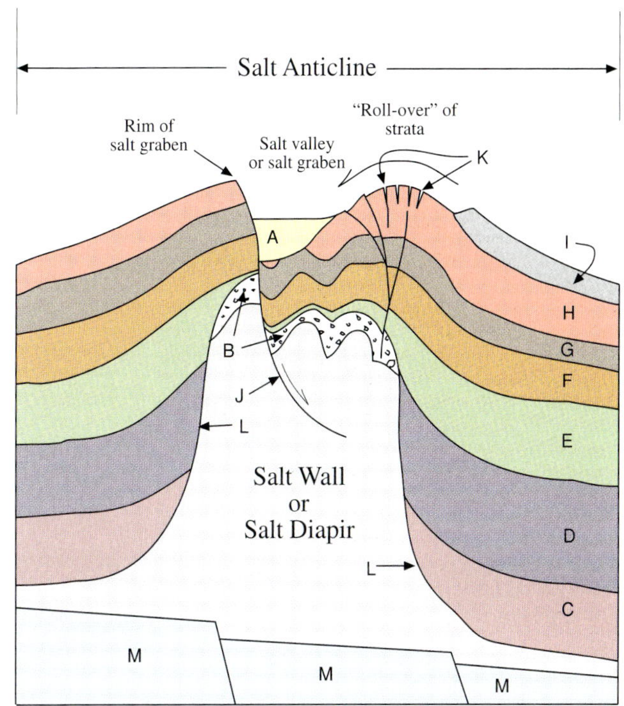

Figure 15. Cartoon diagram of a salt wall. See text in salt structure section for explanations.

rocks have collapsed. Joints are especially noticeable between the Devils Garden and the Fiery Furnace. In the park, the rock between the nearly vertical joint fractures are called fins (figure 9). It is assumed that the fins formed in response to the folding event(s) in Late Cretaceous-early Tertiary time. A discussion of the jointing in Arches National Park is found in Dyer (1983), Cruikshank (1993), and in Cruikshank and Aydin (1993).

A swarm of northwest-trending normal faults subparallel the Moab anticline northwest of Moab Valley. These are essentially joints along which there has been vertical movement because the rocks (figure 5) are too brittle to bend sharply. These joints generally dip toward the Moab anticlinal axis and are thought to have formed in response to its formation in Late Cretaceous-early Tertiary time.

Late Tertiary-Quaternary Regional Uplift and Salt Dissolution

Most investigators believe that the Colorado Plateaus area began rising in elevation about 15 million years ago (Hunt, 1956; Lucchitta, 1979; and Fleming, 1994). Erosion gradually stripped away overlying rock formations; the detritus being carried to the sea by the Colorado River and its tributaries. Locally fine-grained formations that sealed the salt walls from fresh ground water were stripped away. Joints and faults provided the plumbing for the fresh water to reach and dissolve salt in the upper parts of the salt walls. The depth to which the salt could be dissolved was controlled by the water table, which in turn was controlled by the depth to which the ancestral Colorado River and its tributaries had eroded canyons. As dissolution progressed, graben valleys developed over the salt walls and gradually widened. Rocks on top of the salt wall were undermined and collapsed into the graben valleys along fractures that opened parallel to the valleys. Collapse may also have caused these overlying rocks to "roll over" from the anticlinal limb; each fault successive-

ly tilting the rocks more steeply valleyward (figure 15). Therefore, secondary anticlines developed along the valley margins. Seismic and drilling data have shown that Moab Valley has widened to where the sides of the salt wall are nearly under the bounding cliffs of the valley. However, the salt wall that is continuous between Salt and Cache Valleys is wider than the width of the current graben, showing that dissolution and collapse have not progressed as far in those areas (figure 12).

Although evidence for dissolution is clearly evident in the graben areas over the salt walls, and caprock is present under the basin fill of the valleys, some investigators feel that the roll-overs are mostly due to extension along the major normal faults that cut the salt walls (Ge and others, 1996; Ferrill and Morris, 1997). Faults that cut salt are soon healed by salt recrystallization at depth and it is difficult to imagine propagating a fault through two miles of salt. The roll-over deformation in the extensional model requires that the normal faults are listric; that is, they curve and become less high-angled at depth within the salt (figure 16). These listric faults are thought to die out in the salt. It may well be that both mechanisms (dissolution of salt and crustal extension) are important in the Arches National Park area. Many questions involving timing of events remain to be answered.

The rocks preserved in the grabens give some indication when the activity took place. The youngest consolidated rock unit exposed in Salt and Cache Valleys is the Mancos Shale. The Mancos Shale has been completely removed from park areas not affected by salt dissolution or crustal extension. Comparing the displacement between rocks exposed on Dry Mesa against those collapsed into

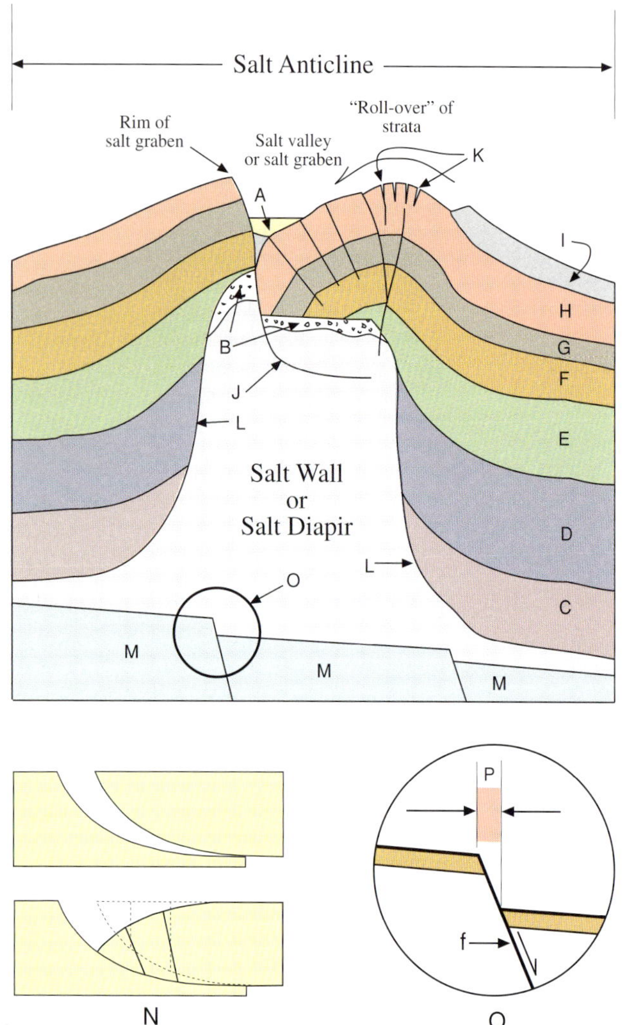

Figure 16. Alternative explanation for the deformational features in salt valley or salt graben rims overlying salt walls as suggested by Ferrill and Morris (1997). See text in salt structures section for explanations.

Cache Valley, the maximum amount of dissolution may be as much as 2,800 feet. However, a Late Cretaceous-early Tertiary fault is present and suspected of producing some of the displacement by extension. Synclines have developed where Mesozoic rocks overlie Paradox Formation caprock in the valleys. Where participating rocks are brittle, the synclinal axes are sharp and the troughs are v-shaped rather than u-shaped. Salt dissolution continues into present time, but is controlled by the depth to which the Colorado River allows fresh water to reach the salt, which in turn depends on the depth to which the river has dug its canyon. The Elephant Butte folds are a series of synclines and anticlines that have developed on the south flank of Salt and Cache Valleys. These may indicate the presence of salt under this flank of the Salt Valley anticline. The anticlines and synclines in this belt are v-shaped. Many other structural phenomena are well displayed in Arches National Park, but it would take too much space to describe them all.

UNIQUE GEOLOGY

Understanding the geologic events that have shaped the landforms will greatly enhance the enjoyment and add another dimension to the geology at its best. Arches National Park administers and protects an area with the greatest concentration of natural rock arches in the world. Many rock arches are present in surrounding areas and in other parts of the world, but Stevens and McCarrick (1988) indicate there are more than 500 of them in the park. According to Stevens and McCarrick (1988) a rock arch by definition must have a light-opening of at least 3 feet or about a meter. Otherwise it is just a small hole in the rock. Salt and Cache Valleys are showcases for salt-anticline features. There are a few other areas in the world displaying salt-tectonic and salt-dissolution features, but few have these features enhanced by colorful Mesozoic strata. Also, a dry climate prevails so that rocks and features are not masked by heavy vegetation and deep soils.

Arches and Fins

Closely spaced joints (parallel fractures) in the brittle rocks exposed in Arches National Park with associated soft bedding-plane partings, indentations, and thin soft-rock layers favor the formation of alcoves, arches, and fins (figure 17). The best place to visualize arch formation is between The Fiery Furnace and Dark Angel (figure 3). There, the brittle Entrada Sandstone, in the northeast flank of the Salt Valley anticline, is cut by joints subparalleling the salt-cored anticline. The rocks "roll over" to accommodate the collapse of sandstone formations into the anticlinal graben along the valley rim. At the "roll over" the joints have opened and allow erosion to occur at a more rapid rate. Generally, loose sand accumulates between the fins; the sand holds slightly acidic rainwater against the fin walls by surface tension and capillary action. The natural cement holding the sand grains in the sandstone of the fins together in the sandstone of the fins is largely calcareous and dissolves in the slightly acidic water. The action is favored along more weakly cemented rock found along bedding-plane partings and indentations. Eventually, a horizontal crevice is opened through the fin along one of these weak planes. Stresses develop in the overlying rock because of gravity since the weight of the rock over the crevice is now supported only by the limbs of the newly formed arch. Generally, fractures develop and blocks of rock drop from the arch (upward stoping) until the classical arch form is developed. This action is responsible for Stevens and McCarrick's (1988) free-standing and cliff-wall arches. Free-standing arches form in isolated fins or in thin walls projecting from cliff faces. Cliff-wall arches develop short distances behind the faces of cliffs. Alcoves are large arch-shaped recesses that have not yet eroded through a fin.

Larger, more massive arches develop in thicker sandstone fins or walls. Generally these require a soft base such as afforded by the Dewey Bridge Member of the

Figure 17. Alcoves in The Windows Section.

Carmel Formation. The best examples are in The Windows Section. Relatively thin buttes of the Slick Rock Member of the Entrada Sandstone and underlying Dewey Bridge Member rest on the Navajo Sandstone along the crest of The Windows anticline. The darker hued Dewey Bridge is eroded into recesses and alcoves below the massive Slick Rock Entrada. Recesses and alcoves eroding from the opposite side of the thin butte eventually break through to form a light opening. After eroding through the rock, stresses develop in the rocks above the opening, causing the rock to fracture. Fragments of rock above the initial opening fall to enlarge the arch. These arches are more massive because the original wall is thick and more massive to begin with. Large arches commonly develop where a relatively thin rock wall or fin forms a prominence along a cliff face.

Pothole arches develop as running flood waters swirl to form potholes near a cliff face. A pothole gradually drills downward until it finds a soft parting. An alcove developing in a cliff face by eroding this soft parting eventually connects with the pothole to form the arch.

Jug-handle arches are crevice arches that form along vertical joint surfaces. Since their openings are largely vertical rather than horizontal, and since they are less affected by gravity, jug handle arches do not widen much.

Geologically, massive hard brittle sandstones jointed by folding activity, resting on or containing soft layers or partings, and located near salt-cored anticlines undergoing dissolution, and a dry climate, favor the formation of arches. Rarely do all these phenomena occur in one place, but they do in Arches National Park

Salt Structures

Salt anticlines and collapse structures are some of the most unique features in Arches National Park, though they are less visible than the arches. Salt walls underlies Salt Valley, Cache Valley, and the Moab anticline in Arches. I have already discussed the formation of salt walls in the Paradox basin in the Structural History and Geology section. Figures 12, 15, and 16 show cross sections of salt-cored anticlines, anticlines cored with thickened salt. Unfortunately, visitors can only view what is at the surface. It would be extremely exciting if overlying and adjacent strata were stripped away, revealing a wall of salt 2 miles high, as much as 3 to 4 miles wide, and 70 miles long!

Figure 15 is a diagrammatic cartoon of a salt-cored anticline. A is alluvial fill or basin fill of unconsolidated sand, silt, and gravel. Normally, alluvial deposits in the park area are thin because of the erosional regime of the Colorado Plateau. Such deposits laid down by rivers and washes in channels and on banks are soon moved farther downstream during floods. However, because salt is slowly dissolved at the top of the salt wall, the overlying rock collapses and subsides to form a basin or graben that can accumulate thick layers of alluvium (figures 10 and 11). Since rivers and streams are controlled by regional base level, this alluvium is protected and accumulates as the basin deepens. B in figure 15 is caprock, which consists of the insoluble residue at the top of a salt wall left behind when the salt dissolves.

C through I represent bedrock strata. The salt was intermittently squeezed toward low-confining pressure areas (normal faults) and into units C athrough E. The bedrock and salt margins, L, were commonly brecciated. Adjacent bedrock strata thin rapidly toward the salt wall along multiple unconformities, indicating that salt movement was intermittent and contemporaneous with their deposition. M represents strata beneath the salt-bearing formation that are not affected by diapirism. Normal faults cut these underlying rocks, indicating extension of the Earth's crust, which helped make space for the salt walls.

Bedrock strata are generally deposited in horizontal position. However, they dip away from Moab and Salt Valleys, indicating that, though collapsed in the middle, these structures are true anticlines. At least one major normal fault, J, parallels the axes of these salt-cored anticlines. This fault displaces bedrock, units F through I, that was deposited over the top of the salt wall. The fault is thought to die out at depth in the salt. Salt, being highly mobile, would tend to heal itself and to absorb the displacement in the salt wall.

Some salt dissolution may have occurred while the salt was intruded into units C through E. All strata, including the salt wall, subsided as units F through I were laid down. Recent uplift has allowed fresh water, capable of dissolving salt, to reach the top of the salt walls. The removal of salt has provided space into which overlying strata have collapsed. On rims without displacing faults, these strata simply "roll over" or sag into the valley. When the rocks sagged, the upper surfaces stretched, and joints, K, opened to favor the formation of arches and fins. Collapsed strata and associated faults are readily observable in the graben areas, especially along the trail to Delicate Arch. Moab Valley is another graben valley overlying a salt wall. This valley is abruptly terminated along the south boundary of Arches National Park. North of that boundary, strata are arched over the Moab anticline and no graben valley has yet formed (figure 5). However, many low-displacement faults are present paralleling the crest of the anticline indicating that collapse may be starting. Faults and joints such as these are the conduits that conduct the fresh water to the top of the salt wall to begin salt dissolution.

Figure 16 is a diagrammatic cartoon illustrating an alternative mechanism for creating the features associated with a salt valley graben area (Ge and others, 1996; Ferrill and Morris, 1997). Here the "roll over" on one side the valley or graben is caused entirely by extension of the Earth's crust. Circle O is enlarged below to show how a normal fault allows for extension of the crust. As the fault f moves, the fault block that moves down relative to the other slips down a ramp. The orange bed is displaced and shifted a distance P (pink area between horizontal arrows) which represents a horizontal extension of the crust. Since the deep faults, which cut M, do not propagate well through salt, this extension is accommodated higher up by a listric fault, a fault which becomes horizontal at depth in the salt. This is illustrated by block diagrams N. Overlying strata E through H are pulled apart and collapse along faults and joints (which open) to form a "roll over." Caprock, B, at the top of the salt wall, was wholly formed by dissolution as the salt wall was rising.

The structural features along the salt valleys are probably due to a combination of the two mechanisms. Clearly, many of the deformational features in the graben or graben rims are the result of salt dissolution. However, dissolution alone may not account for the all of the deformational features that are present.

LOCATION AND DESCRIPTION OF CLASSIC GEOLOGICAL SITES WITHIN THE PARK

(see figure 3 for location)

1. Delicate Arch (figure 2). This world-famous arch is located on the north side of Cache Valley. A 1-1/2 mile trail extends to the arch from a paved road and parking lot (Wolfe Ranch area) where Salt Wash crosses the valley. The trail starts in the Salt Wash Member of the Morrison Formation and crosses several faults. Geologic formations and members exposed along the trail include the reddish to lavender Tidwell Member of the Morrison Formation with its large hackly white chert nodules, the red-brown Summerville Formation, the massive light-colored and well-jointed Moab Member of the Curtis Formation, and the orange-brown smooth-weathering Slick Rock Member of the Entrada Sandstone (figure 5). Delicate Arch is freestanding and has a horizontal span of about 32 feet and a vertical span of 46 feet. The top of the arch is about 52 feet over the base. The plane of weakness in this arch is the contact between the Moab Member and the Slick Rock Member.

Figure 18. Top to bottom, Elephant Butte, Petrified Dunes, Tower Arch, and Landscape Arch.

2. Landscape Arch (figure 18). In terms of span, this arch is the largest in the park. The opening is 306 feet wide and more than 88 feet high. It can be seen by walking about a mile north of a parking lot in the south part of Devils Garden. It is entirely within a fin of the Slick Rock Member (Jes). It is classified a free-standing arch, but originally began as a cliff-wall arch. In just the last few years, blocks of rock have broken and fallen from the underside of the span, indicating that this arch will soon (hundreds of years?) collapse by natural processes. Its demise may be precipitated by an earthquake.

3. The Windows Section. The most massive arches, called windows, are found in this part of Arches National Park. These are mostly free-standing arches formed in a wall of the Slick Rock Member underlain by the Dewey Bridge Member. The well-known arches in The Windows Section include the Parade of Elephants (figure 17), North Window, South Window, and Turret Arch. This is also a good place to see alcoves (Cove of Caves, figure 17) and the nature of the softer Dewey Bridge Member of the Carmel Formation (Garden of Eden).

4. Balanced Rock (figure 6). This well-known and central landmark in Arches National Park consists of a huge orange-brown bulb of the Slick Rock Member resting on a narrow dark-brown pedestal of the Dewey Bridge Member. This is a good place to familiarize yourself with these two important geologic members.

5. Park Avenue. This short trail is about 0.8 miles in length in the area of the Courthouse Towers. The trail begins between two high monoliths of the Slick Rock Member of the Entrada Sandstone underlain with the Dewey Bridge Member of the Carmel Formation. Along the way are the bust of Queen Nefretiri, Popsicle Rock (figure 19), the Three Gossips, and the Organ. All this can be seen by staying on the highway, but by taking the hike many beautiful "nooks and crannies" are observable, which would be missed from the highway. At the end of the hike is an incipient arch, known as Baby Arch.

6. Devils Garden. This area of fins extends from the Fiery Furnace northward to Dark Angel along the northeast rim of Salt Valley. Many arches have developed in this region, the more well-known being Sand Dune Arch, Broken Arch, Skyline Arch (figure 7), Tunnel Arch, Pine Tree Arch, Landscape Arch (figure 18), Navajo Arch, and Double O Arch. The longest maintained trail in the park gives access to many of these arches. The full trail is 7.2 miles round trip. Stevens and McCarrick (1988) reported the presence of 123 arches in the Devils Garden area; most are free standing and cliff-wall arches.

7. The Great Wall. This wall of Entrada Sandstone parallels the highway from about a mile north of the Tower of Babel to Balanced Rock. Several arches are hidden along this wall, especially pothole arches. The wall has a length of about four miles.

8. Klondike Bluffs. This is an area of fins and exposures of the Entrada Sandstone on the southeast rim of the Salt Valley anticline. The most famous arch at Klondike

Figure 19. Upper left and right show the bust of Queen Nefretiri and "Popsicle Rock," respectively, as seen along Park Avenue. Lower left, a group of hikers in the Fiery Furnace

Bluffs is Tower Arch (figure 18). This is also the site of the Marching Men, another interesting erosional feature.

9. Moab fault (figure 13). This is a normal fault that displaces the Moab salt wall as much as 2,400 feet. In the vicinity of the visitor center it consists of two branches. The high cliff southwest of the Visitor Center exposes rocks much older than the rocks exposed to the northeast. Nicely developed slickensides are present on the upthrown block of the west branch in the Honaker Trail Formation west of the Visitor Center.

10. Fiery Furnace (figure 14). This is a maze-like labyrinth between Entrada Sandstone fins at the south end of Devils Garden. The maze is so complex that a trail guide is usually required. Some spaces between fins are so narrow that sunlight does not reach the bottom. The hike locally requires the use of hands and feet to scramble up and through narrow cracks and along narrow ledges above drop-offs. Also present are former arches that have collapsed.

11. Cache Valley. Salt Valley and Cache Valley are parts of the same salt wall. Whereas the salt wall under Salt Valley trends northwest, that under Cache Valley trends east-west (figure 3). Much of Cache Valley is east of the park boundary, but perhaps it should have been in-

Figure 20. The La Sal Mountains from a viewpoint in Arches National Park. The igneous rock in the North and South parts of these mountains were intruded into salt.

cluded. It is the best place to view and study the effects of dissolution collapse. Whereas the collapsed rocks of Salt Valley are commonly covered with unconsolidated Quaternary deposits, those in Cache Valley are hardly buried at all. A dirt road extends eastward from the Delicate Arch viewpoint parking area and affords access to this beautiful valley. One can hike all the way to the Colorado River (six strenuous miles one way), seeing innumerable interesting geologic features related to dissolution collapse along the way. Don't forget your camera.

12. Elephant Butte folds. The dissolution collapse has just begun on the crest of the Salt Valley-Cache Valley salt-cored anticline. Several paralleling anticlines and synclines have developed (figure 3) on the southwest and south sides of these valleys. The synclines are V-shaped and the anticlines between them are linear and sharp, as one might expect when rocks collapse into voids left by the removal of salt at depth. The fold areas will eventually become a part of the Salt Valley-Cache Valley graben. Lining the axial areas of the synclines are numerous debris piles of Morrison and Cedar Mountain Formation rocks left behind when their cliffs were still near the valley rims. These cliffs have now been eroded back several miles. The main paved road crosses these folds between Balanced Rock and Panorama Point.

13. Petrified Dunes (figure 18). Most of the area east of the Great Wall exposes outcrops of bare-rock Navajo Sandstone. The Navajo was deposited in a great sand-dune desert rivaling the Sahara Desert. The formation is characterized by sweeping high-angle cross-beds truncated by set boundaries. Now cemented into solid rock, these ancient dunes have been eroded into rounded domes called petrified dunes or frozen dunes.

14. La Sal Mountains (figure 20). Though not in Arches National Park, the views of the La Sal Mountains from the park are spectacular. About 29 million years ago, hot magma rising from deep within the earth intruded under layers of sedimentary rock, forming laccoliths (domed shaped intrusions that wedged between, and bowed layered rock upward). The mountains are the erosional remnants of these laccoliths. They are high because the igneous rock is much more resistant to weathering and erosion than the sedimentary rock (Doelling, 1993; M.L. Ross, Utah Geological Survey, unpublished data, 1996).

ACKNOWLEDGEMENTS

I wish to thank Grant C. Willis and Douglas A. Sprinkel for carefully reviewing this document and providing excellent suggestions for its improvement. I wish to acknowledge the Utah Geological Survey for giving me the opportunity to work in such a challenging and inspiring area for so many years.

REFERENCES

Blakey, R.C., 1994, Paleogeographic and tectonic controls on some Lower and Middle Jurassic erg deposits, Colorado Plateau, *in* Caputo, M.V., Peterson, J.A., and Franczyk, K.J., editors, Mesozoic systems of the Rocky Mountain region, USA: Society for Sedimentary Geology, Rocky Mountain Section, p. 273-298.

Blakey, R.C., and Gubitosa, R., 1983, Late Triassic paleogeography and depositional history of the Chinle Formation, southern Utah and northern Arizona, *in* Reynolds, M.W., and Dolly, E.D., editors, Mesozoic paleogeography of the west-central United States: Society of Economic Paleontologists and Mineralogists, Rocky Mountain Paleogeography Symposium 2, p. 57-76.

Colman, S.M., Choquette, A.F., and Hawkins, F.F., 1988, Physical, soil, and paleomagnetic stratigraphy of the upper Cenozoic sediments in Fisher Valley, southeastern Utah: U.S. Geological Survey Bulletin 1686, 33p.

Cruikshank, K.M., 1993, Fracture patterns associated with

Salt Valley anticline: Stanford, California, Stanford University Proceedings of the Rock Fracture Project, v. IV, 10 p.

Cruikshank, K.M., and Aydin, Atilla, 1993, Joint patterns in Entrada Sandstone, southwest limb of Salt Valley anticline, Arches National Park, Utah, USA: Stanford, California, Stanford University, 25 p.

Dane, C.H., 1935, Geology of the Salt Valley anticline and adjacent areas, Grand County, Utah: U.S. Geological Survey Bulletin 863, 184 p.

Doelling, H.H., 1985, Geologic map of Arches National Park and vicinity, Grand County, Utah: Utah Geological and Mineral Survey Map 74, 15 p., scale 1:50,000.

Doelling, H.H., 1988, Geology of Salt Valley anticline and Arches National Park, Grand County, Utah, in Salt deformation of the Paradox region, [Utah]: Utah Geological and Mineral Survey Bulletin 122, p. 7-58.

Doelling, H.H., 1993, Interim geologic map of the Moab 30' x 60' quadrangle, Grand County, Utah and Mesa County, Colorado: Utah Geological Survey Open-File Report 187, scale 1:100,000.

Doelling, H.H., (compiler), in press, Interim geologic map of the La Sal 30' x 60' quadrangle, San Juan County, Utah and Montrose and San Miguel Counties, Colorado: Utah Geological Survey, scale 1:100,000.

Doelling, H.H., and Morgan, C.D., 1996, Interim geologic map of the Merrimac Butte quadrangle, Grand County, Utah: Utah Geological Survey Open-File Report 338, 81 p., scale 1:24,000.

Doelling, H.H., and Ross, M.L., 1998, Geologic map of the Big Bend quadrangle, Grand County, Utah: Utah Geological Survey Map 171, 29 p., scale 1:24,000.

Doelling, H.H., Ross, M.L, and Mulvey, W.E., 1995, Interim geologic map of the Moab quadrangle, Grand County, Utah: Utah Geological Survey Open-File Report 322, 100 p., scale 1:24,000.

Dubiel, R.F., 1994, Triassic deposystems, paleogeography, and paleoclimate of the western interior, in Caputo, M.V., Peterson, J.A., and Franczyk, K.J., editors, Mesozoic systems of the Rocky Mountain region, USA: Society for Sedimentary Geology, Rocky Mountain section, p. 133-168.

Dubiel, R.F., Good, S.C., and Parrish, J.M., 1989, Sedimentology and paleontology of the Upper Triassic Chinle Formation: The Mountain Geologist, v. 26, no. 4, p. 113-126.

Dyer, J.R., 1983, Jointing in sandstones, Arches National Park, Utah: Stanford, Stanford University, Ph.D. dissertaion, 202 p.

Ferrill, D.A., and Morris, A.P., 1997, Geometric considerations of deformation above curved normal faults and salt evacuation surfaces: The Leading Edge, p. 1,129-1,133.

Fleming, R.F., 1994, Cretaceous pollen in Pliocene rocks: Implications for Pliocene climate in the southwestern United States: Geology, v. 22, p. 787-790.

Foxford, K.A., Garden, I.R., Guscott, S.C., Burley, S.D.,

Lewis, J.J., Walsh, J.J., and Watterson, J., 1996, The field geology of the Moab fault, in Huffman, A.C., Jr., Lund, W.R., and Godwin, L.H., editors, Geology and resources of the Paradox basin: Utah Geological Association and Four Corners Geological Society Guidebook 25, p. 265-283.

Ge, Hongxing, Jackson, M.P., and Vendeville, B.C., 1996, Extensional origin of breached Paradox diapirs, Utah and Colorado: Field observations and scaled physical models, in Huffman, A.C., Jr., Lund, W.R., and Godwin, L.H., editors, Geology and resources of the Paradox basin: Utah Geological Association and Four Corners Geological Society Guidebook 25, p. 285-293.

Hintze, L.F., 1988 (rev. 1993), Geologic history of Utah: Brigham Young University Studies Special Publication 7, 202 p.

Hite, R.J., 1961, Potash-bearing evaporite cycles in the salt anticlines of the Paradox basin, Colorado and Utah: U.S. Geological Survey Professional Paper 424D, p. D136-D138.

Hunt, C.B., 1956, Cenozoic geology of the Colorado Plateau: U.S. Geological Survey Professional Paper 279, 99 p.

Kirkland, J.I., Cifelli, R.L., Britt, B.B., Burge, D.L., DeCourten, F.L., Eaton, J.G., and Parrish, J.M., 1999, Distribution of vertebrate faunas in the Cedar Mountain Formation, east-central Utah, in Gillette, D.D., editor, Vertebrate Paleontology of Utah: Utah Geological Survey Miscellaneous Publication 99-1, p. 201-217.

Lockley, M.G., 1991, The Moab megatracksite: A preliminary description and discussion of millions of Middle Jurassic tracks in eastern Utah, in Averett, W.R., editor, Dinosaur quarries and tracksites tour, western Colorado and eastern Utah: Grand Junction Geological Society, Grand Junction, Colorado, p. 59-65.

Lohman, S.W., 1965, Geology and artesian water supply Grand Junction area, Colorado: U.S. Geological Survey Professional Paper 451, 149 p.

Lohman, S.W., 1975, The geologic story of Arches National Park: U.S. Geological Survey Bulletin 1393, 113 p.

Lucchitta, Ivo, 1979, Late Cenozoic uplift of the southwestern Colorado Plateau and adjacent Colorado River region: Tectonophysics, v. 61, p. 63-95.

McKnight, E.T., 1940, Geology of the area between Green and Colorado Rivers, Grand and San Juan Counties, Utah: U.S. Geological Survey Bulletin 908, 147 p.

Molenaar, C.M., and Cobban, W.A., 1991, Middle Cretaceous stratigraphy on the south and east sides of the Uinta Basin, northeastern Utah and northwestern Colorado: U.S. Geological Survey Bulletin 1787-P, 34 p.

O'Sullivan, R.B., 1980, Stratigraphic sections of Middle Jurassic San Rafael Group and related rocks from the Green River to the Moab area in east-central Utah: U.S. Geological Survey Map MF-1247.

—1981, Stratigraphic sections of Middle Jurassic San Rafael Group and related rocks from Salt Valley to Dewey Bridge in east-central Utah: U.S. Geological

Survey Oil and Gas Investigations Chart OC-113.

Peterson, Fred, and Pipiringos, G.N., 1979, Stratigraphic relations of the Navajo Sandstone to Middle Jurassic formations, southern Utah and northern Arizona: U.S. Geological Survey Professional Paper 1035-B, 43 p.

Peterson, Fred, and Turner-Peterson, C.E., 1987, The Morrison Formation of the Colorado Plateau: Recent advances in sedimentology, stratigraphy, and paleotectonics: Hunteria, v. 2, no. 1, 18 p.

Pipiringos, G.N., and O'Sullivan, R.B., 1978, Principal unconformities in Triassic and Jurassic rocks, western interior United States--a preliminary survey: U.S. Geological Survey Professional Paper 1035-A, 29 p.

Shoemaker, E.M., and Newman, W.L., 1959, Moenkopi Formation (Triassic? and Triassic) in salt anticline region, Colorado and Utah: American Association of Petroleum Geologists Bulletin, v. 43, no. 8, p. 1835-1851.

Stevens, D.J., and McCarrick, J.E., 1988, The arches of Arches National Park--a comprehensive study: Moab and Orem, Utah, Mainstay Publishing, 169 p.

Stewart, J.H., Poole, F.G., and Wilson, R.F., 1972a, Stratigraphy and origin of the Triassic Moenkopi Formation and related strata in the Colorado Plateau region: U.S. Geological Survey Professional Paper 691, 191 p.

—1972b, Stratigraphy and origin of the Triassic Chinle Formation and related strata in the Colorado Plateau region: U.S. Geological Survey Professional Paper 690, 336 p.

Stokes, W.L., 1991, Petrified mini-forests of the Navajo Sandstone, east-central Utah: Utah Geological Survey, Survey Notes, v. 25, no. 1, p. 14-19.

Willis, G.C., Doelling, H.H., and Ross, M.L., 1996, Geologic map of the Agate quadrangle, Grand County, Utah: Utah Geological Survey Map 168, 34 p., scale 1:24,000.

Wright, J.C., Shawe, D.R., and Lohman, S.W., 1962, Definition of members of Jurassic Entrada Sandstone in east-central Utah and west-central Colorado: American Association of Petroleum Geologists Bulletin, v. 46, no. 11, p. 2,057-2,070.

Geology of Utah's Parks and Monuments
2000 Utah Geological Association Publication 28
D.A. Sprinkel, T.C. Chidsey, Jr., and P.B. Anderson, editors

Geology of Bryce Canyon National Park, Utah

George H. Davis[1] *and Gayle L. Pollock*[2]

ABSTRACT

Bryce Canyon National Park lies along the high eastern escarpment of the Paunsaugunt Plateau in the Colorado Plateau region of southern Utah. Its extraordinary geological character is expressed by thousands of rock chimneys (hoodoos) that occupy amphitheater-like alcoves in the Pink Cliffs, whose bedrock host is Claron Formation of Eocene age. The specific location and geologic attributes of Bryce Canyon National Park reflect the geo-historical interplay of (1) deposition of colorful Mesozoic and Cenozoic marine and nonmarine sedimentary rock layers in the Colorado Plateau foreland; (2) multiple faulting of the sedimentary rock column during Laramide (90 to 50 Ma, that is, 90 to 50 million years *before present*), early Miocene (25 to 20 Ma), and Basin and Range (15 Ma to present) deformations; and (3) the erosional sculpting of the Pink Cliffs by the headwater tributaries of the Paria drainage system. The interrelationships of these three factors are quite unique, and thus it is not surprising that Bryce Canyon is one of a kind.

INTRODUCTION

Bryce Canyon National Park (referred to herein as "the Park") lies near the eastern margin of the High Plateaus province of the Colorado Plateau (figure 1). Its dramatic landscapes adorn the precipitous eastern escarpment of the Paunsaugunt Plateau (figure 2). The Park is 56.2 square miles (36,010 acres) in area and resides within an elevation range of 7,600 to 9,100 feet (2,300 to 2,760 m) above sea level. To arrive at the Rim of Bryce Canyon, visitors drive up and onto the broad flat-topped surface of the Paunsaugunt Plateau (from either west or east) along Scenic Highway 12 (figure 3), turn south from Highway 12 onto Utah 63, and travel three miles to reach the Park entrance. Visitors to the Park are greeted by a surreal lithic canvas, unique in its expression of texture, color, and depth. The textural elegance resides in the landscape of hoodoos, that is, rock chimneys, each projecting skyward and commonly marked by gravity-defying balancing acts executed by the capstones. The hoodoos occupy a series of huge natural amphitheater-like alcoves (a few hundred feet deep and wide), carved into sedimentary rocks. Within the alcoves are a fantastic array of pinnacles, windowed

Figure 1. Location map of Bryce Canyon National Park in relation to the geographic setting of the Colorado Plateau and surrounding geologic provinces. Adapted from DeCourten (1994).

---

[1] *Department of Geosciences, University of Arizona, Tucson, AZ 85721*
[2] *Bryce Canyon Natural History Association, Bryce Canyon National Park, UT 84717-0002*

Figure 2. (A) View of the colorful and textured landscape of Bryce Canyon National Park. (B) Cleopatra rock-sculpture "walking" along the Queens Garden Trail. Photographs by G.H. Davis.

walls, pedestals, fins, and spires. The sensational color is the pink of the lower member of the host rock, the Claron Formation, deposited approximately 60 to 40 million years ago. The incredible depth of the canvas is in reality the *distances* encaptured. Visitors come expecting a canyon, and instead find promontories, amphitheaters, and long views, for strictly speaking there is no canyon at all. Such a misallocation of the term "canyon" is forgivable in a country where canyons abound.

Herbert Gregory mapped the geology of the Paunsaugunt Plateau, and his descriptions of the distinctive landscape of Bryce Canyon National Park are marvelous: "From the bottoms of the alcoves cut into the Pink Cliffs rise spires and ridges, and many of them are filled to the brim with literally hundreds of towers, needles, cathedrals, narrow mesas, and myriads of fantastic figures that stand alone or are grouped about buttresses of the enclosing walls, which themselves are decorated with windows and niches of many shapes" (Gregory, 1951, p. 103).

THOSE WHO CAME BEFORE

It would have been thrilling to have earned a look at the Bryce Canyon region well before the first roads or good trails were established. Native Americans first occupied the Colorado Plateau 12,000 years ago, but left little to tell of their activities on the Paunsaugunt Plateau. Paiutes were living throughout the region when the first Euro-Americans arrived in southern Utah. The Paiutes "recognized the rock walls of the Bryce Canyon area as the ruins of a great city, buried in red mud and now partly excavated, the work of Shin-awav, a Paiute demigod of great power" (Gregory, 1951, p. 17). In fact, an elderly Paiute gave this account to Gregory (1951, p. 17): "Before there were any Indians, the To-whon-an-ung-wa lived in that place. There were many of them. They were of many kinds—birds, animals, lizards, and such things—but they looked like people. They were not people; they had power to make themselves look that way. Because they were bad Shin-awav turned them all into rocks; some standing in rows, some sitting down, some holding on to others. You can see their faces, with paint on them just as they were before they became rocks. The name of that place is Angka-ku-wass-a-wits [meaning, 'red-painted faces']." Other Paiutes apparently called Bryce "Unka-timpe-wa-wince-pock-ich," meaning 'red rock standing like men in a bowl-shaped recess.'"

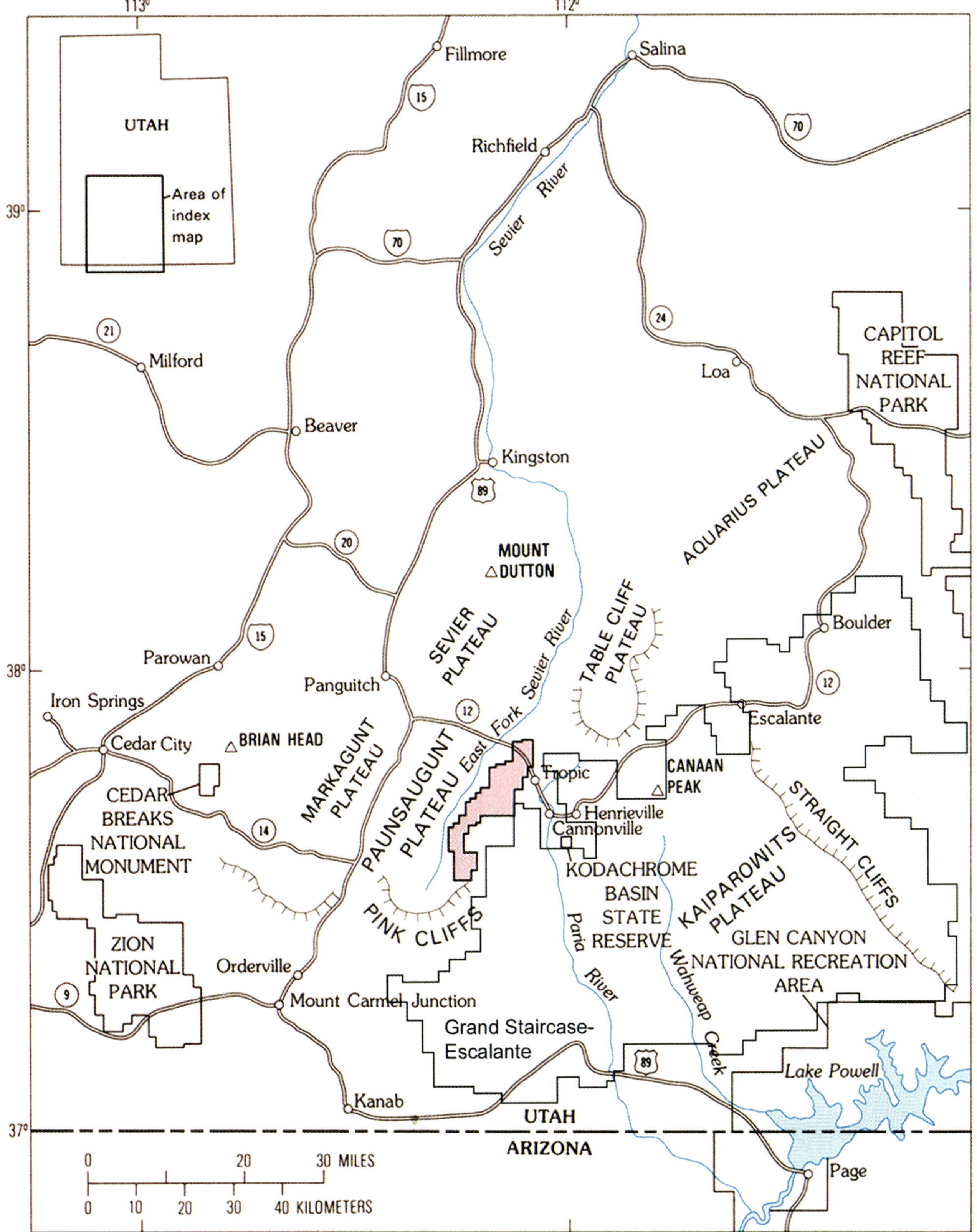

Figure 3. Location map of Bryce Canyon National Park within the Paunsaugunt Plateau region. From Bowers (1991).

John Wesley Powell, famous for his geographic and geological exploration of the Grand Canyon via "running" the Colorado River, tackled the exploration of this region between 1868 and 1879. His brother-in-law, Almon Thompson, was in charge of topographic mapping. In 1872 Almon and his men passed close to Bryce Canyon. In the very first written description of the Pink Cliffs, Thompson (1875) observed: "…the south end of the table-

Figure 4. View of the Pink Cliffs of Paunsaugunt Plateau, viewed from the east in morning light. Photograph by G.H. Davis.

land known as the Pauns-agunt Plateau rose to an altitude which we determined to be 3,295 feet above our camp, or about 9,200 feet above sea level. The eastern boundary of this plateau is a line of cliffs, having a general trend N. 45° E. These cliffs show in the distance a beautiful pink color, and for the upper 2,000 feet, present bold, perpendicular faces, with here and there steep rocky slopes" (figure 4).

In 1872 Lt. W.L. Marshall, Edwin E. Howell, and Grove Karl Gilbert constructed reconnaissance topographic maps of the region in the course of the Wheeler Survey (1870-1876) (Wheeler, 1874, 1875). Marshall mapped the rim of the Paunsaugunt Plateau, as well as the head of the Paria Valley (Gregory, 1951, p. 6).   Gregory (1951, p. 6) mentions that a pencil drawing by John E. Weyss, reproduced in the reports of the Wheeler Survey, is the first known illustration of the strikingly picturesque erosion remnants of Bryce Canyon National Park.

Clarence E. Dutton, best known for his literary publications on his geological exploration of the Grand Canyon and the High Plateaus, came into the Paunsaugunt region during the period 1875-77, after the work of the Wheeler Survey was completed. Dutton (1880) wrote: "The Paunsaugunt …is exceedingly simple in its structure and presents very little matter for special remark." And yet he had much to say about the landscape: "The glory of all this rock work is seen in the Pink Cliffs, the exposed edges of the lower Eocene strata. The resemblances to strict architectural forms are often startling. The upper tier of the vast amphitheater is one mighty colonnade. Standing obelisks, prostrate columns, shattered capitals, panels, niches, buttresses, repetitions of symmetrical forms, all bring vividly before the mind suggestions of the work of giant hands, a race of genii once rearing temples of rock, but now chained up in a spell of enchantment, while their structures are falling in ruins through centuries of decay." Dutton honored the Paiute's original naming of many of the landscape features, including Paunsaugunt (home of the beavers), Paria (muddy water), Panguitch (fish), and Yovimpa (point of pines).

The Paiutes themselves left, gradually, as emissaries of the Church of Jesus Christ of Latter-Day Saints (Mormons) established many small communities throughout Utah. Ebenezer Bryce helped settle southwestern Utah and northern Arizona. No visitor to the Park leaves without having heard Ebenezer's assessment of Bryce Canyon: "hell of a place to lose a cow." In 1916, Reuben C. (Ruby) Syrett brought his family to southern Utah, establishing a ranch near the present site of Ruby's Inn (near the intersection of Highways 12 and 63) (figure 3). A few weeks after his arrival, Ruby was told about "the canyon called Bryce," and he and his family made a Sunday visit to the canyon rim. They were so impressed by what they saw that they spread the word about the canyon's beauties, and became hosts to visitors who wanted to see it. By 1919 Ruby Syrett had obtained permission from the state to build a lodge, which he named the "Tourist Rest." He built it near the brink of Bryce Canyon. On June 8, 1923, President Warren G. Harding proclaimed part of the area as Bryce Canyon National Monument. Ruby then moved the "Tourist Rest" to the location of his ranch and named it "Ruby's Inn," which thrives today. In 1924, legislation was passed to establish the area as a National Park, but it was not until February 25, 1928, that the area was officially established "Bryce Canyon National Park."

REGIONAL GEOLOGIC SETTING OF BRYCE CANYON NATIONAL PARK

Bryce Canyon National Park is situated in the Colorado Plateau tectonic province (figure 1). The Colorado Plateau today stands high, with minimum elevations of 4000 feet (1,200 meters) and with maximum elevations of 11,000 feet (3,333 meters). In many locations marine beds of Cretaceous age (as young as 75 million years) reside at elevations of 7,000-9,000 feet (2,120 – 2,730 meters).

It was John Wesley Powell's contribution to divide the mountainous western United States into three physiographic provinces: the Park Province, the Plateau Province, and the Great Basin Province (Stegner, 1954). The Park Province, to the east of the Colorado Plateau, is referred to today as the Rocky Mountains (figure 1), an array of mighty tectonic uplifts produced by strong horizontal compression of the western United States during the *Laramide* deformation between approximately 90 and 50 million years ago. The uplifts were achieved by major thrust faulting involving thousands of feet of displacement. In contrast, the Great Basin Province, to the west, is today referred to tectonically as the Basin and Range Province (figure 1). It represents a region that was profoundly extended (that is, stretched) between approximately 30 million years ago to present. The extension, as much as 100 percent, resulted in the topographic lowering of an originally much higher region, and was achieved through large faults that now separate isolated ranges from isolated basins. Geologists speak of this as the *Basin and Range* deformation.

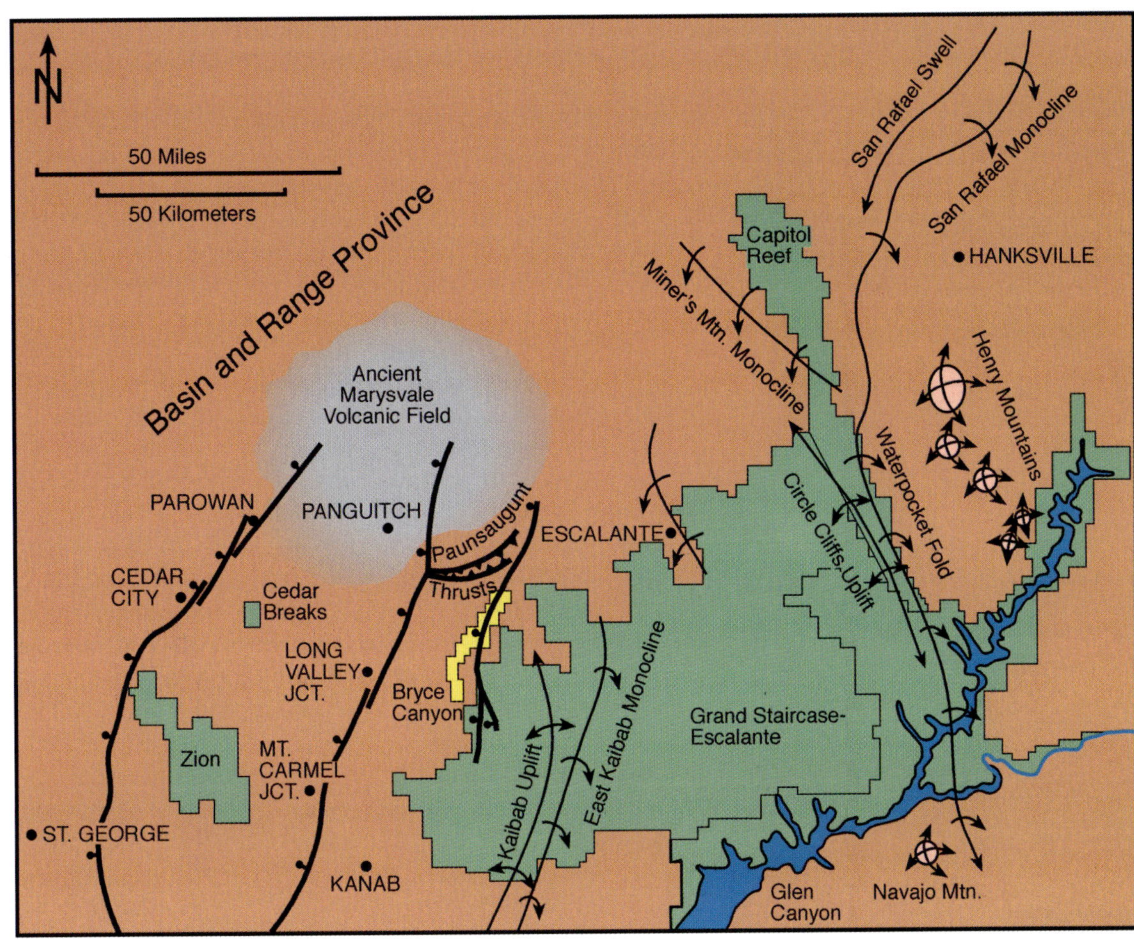

Figure 5. Map of the major structures in the Colorado Plateau region of southern Utah.

The Plateau Province, now referred to as the Colorado Plateau (figure 1), shows the mild effects of both the older compression and the younger extension (Kelley, 1955; Kelley and Clinton, 1960; Davis, 1999) and yet rocks in the Colorado Plateau largely escaped deformation, as evidenced by the vast regional exposures of continuous, flat-lying sedimentary formations. Yet, there are significant exceptions, in the form of the Laramide uplifts of the Colorado Plateau (Kelley, 1955; Kelley and Clinton, 1960; Davis, 1978, 1999). The major uplifts in Utah are the Kaibab uplift, the Circle Cliffs uplift, the San Rafael swell, and the northern part of the Monument uplift (figure 5). Each is a broad, elongate arch of sedimentary strata (more than 100 miles (167 km) long and 20 to 40 miles (33 to 66 km) wide. The uplifts are asymmetrical, with one flank (by far the longest) very gently dipping, and the other marked by a profound fold, called a monocline. Colorado Plateau monoclines represent an abrupt bending of the rocks above a fault, which is usually hidden, that is, "blind" (figure 6A). In effect, the fault offset at depth is expressed as folding higher up. Monoclines are big, with displacements typically in terms of hundreds to thousands of feet. The Laramide uplift closest to Bryce Canyon National Park is the Kaibab uplift, to the east and south (Davis, 1999; Tindall and Davis, 1999) (figure 5) . In fact, Bryce Canyon National Park lies on the west flank of the Kaibab uplift, which was first discovered, described, and

named by John Wesley Powell. Tindall (2000) describes the east flank of this structure in this same volume. Her article serves as a useful guide for those who wish to appreciate the geology exposed along the Cockscomb Road between Highway 89 and Cannonville (figure 3).

The Colorado Plateau did not escape Basin and Range deformation. In particular there are two major Basin and Range faults in the Colorado Plateau near Bryce. These faults are important to the geological story of the Bryce Canyon National Park, for they control the margins of the Paunsaugunt Plateau, within which Park resides. The Sevier fault marks the western margin of the Paunsaugunt Plateau, and the Paunsaugunt fault controls the eastern margin (figure 5). Both of these faults trend north-northeast, dip steeply to the west-northwest, and drop rocks down to the west. Fault offsets are on the order of 2,000 feet (600 meters). They are *normal* faults (figure 6B), the kind of faults that extend or stretch the crust; in contrast to thrust faults (figure 6C), which shorten and thicken the crust. Gilbert (1875) first recognized the Sevier fault, which he and Gregory (1951) referred to as the Sevier Valley fault. On the other hand, Gilbert (1875) and Howell (1875) passed through the region without recognizing the presence of the Paunsaugunt fault, for this fault is not faithfully reflected in the topography. It was Dutton (1880) who discovered the Paunsaugunt fault. It appears on his maps, where he refers to the east escarpment of the Pink

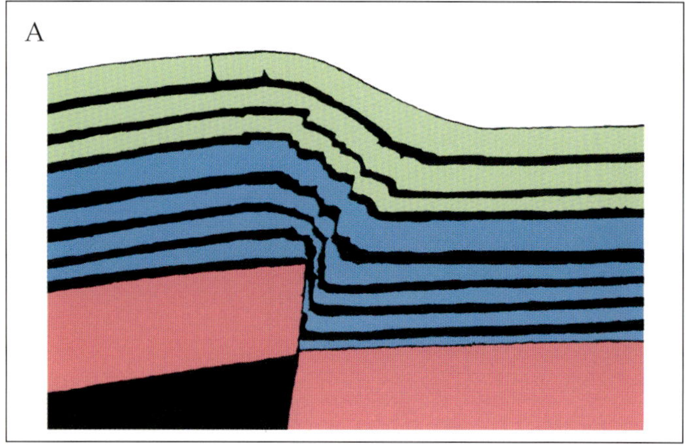

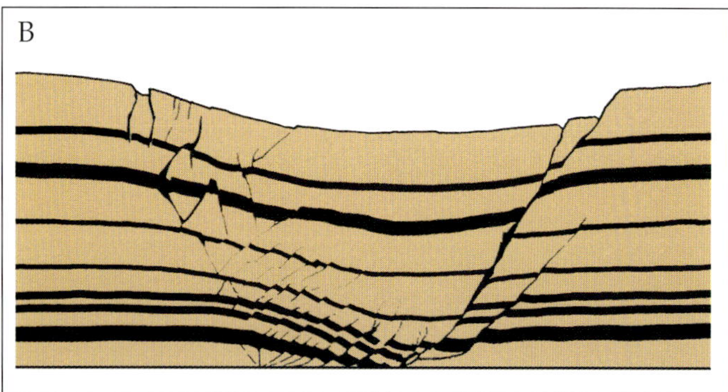

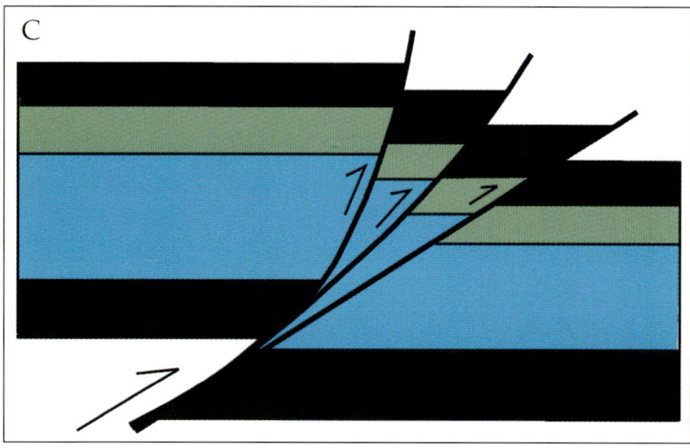

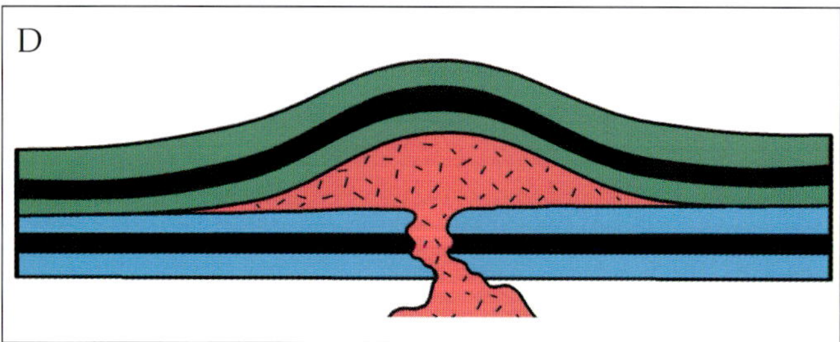

Figure 6. Four important kinds of structures in the Colorado Plateau. (A) Monoclines, which are huge, abrupt folds in otherwise horizontal sedimentary layers. Folding reflects faulting at depth. (From Davis, 1978). Monoclines are formed in compression. (B) Normal faults, which form as a result of extension. Modified from Cloos (1968). (C) Thrust faults, which form as a result of compression. Modified from Dahlstrom (1969). (D) Laccoliths, which are very large mushroom-shaped (flat-bottomed, dome-topped) igneous intrusions that dome and thus tilt the overlying sedimentary cover rocks.

Cliffs as a "cliff of erosion," with the "Paunsaugunt fault" identified east of the cliffs, trending north-northeast.

Dutton (1880) actually placed the western boundary of the Colorado Plateau at the location of the Paunsaugunt fault, and ascribed the region between the Paunsaugunt and Hurricane faults to the High Plateaus (figures 1 and 5), which can be thought of as a transitional tectonic province between the Colorado Plateau and the Basin and Range (figure 1). It is a sensible interpretation, and one that places Bryce Canyon National Park in the easternmost part of the High Plateaus.

In addition to Laramide and Basin and Range structures, the Colorado Plateau has structures attributable to a *mid-Tertiary* deformation (30 to 20 Ma). In the Basin and Range Province to the west and south of the Colorado Plateau, mid-Tertiary deformation was marked by profound extensional stretching of the crust by means of faulting and shearing. This stretching was accompanied by vast outpourings of ash flows and by other volcanic phenomena. The mid-Tertiary deformation left its mark on the Colorado Plateau as well, in the form of *igneous* geology. One expression is the voluminous Marysvale volcanic field, located in the region northwest of Bryce Canyon National Park (figure 5). Between 30 and 20 million years ago the Marysvale region was a site of profound volcanism, much of it explosive, expressed in the form of numerous composite volcanoes, some of which may have been 15,000 feet (4,545 m) in height. From the volcanic centers issued lava flows and ash deposits that spread out over many thousands of square miles, accumulating to great thicknesses. Yet another expression of mid-Tertiary magmatism is preserved in the Henry Mountains, located in southeastern Utah (figure 5). The Henry Mountains consist of five domal mountains, each cored by igneous rock (Gilbert, 1877). The magma that formed the igneous rock ascended upward from great depth and ultimately, at shallow levels of the crust, spread out along the bedding within the sedimentary rock cover, and then domed the overlying sedimentary layers, in places to radically steep angles (figure 6D). Gilbert coined the term "laccolith" for the enormous dome-topped, flat-bottomed igneous bodies that created the Henry Mountains (figure 6D). Furthermore, he was the first to suggest that the volcanism of the Marysvale volcanic field and the laccoliths of the Henry Mountains were of the same age and of a common tectonic origin. There are laccoliths in the Marysvale volcanic field as well!

LOCAL GEOGRAPHIC SETTING OF BRYCE CANYON NATIONAL PARK

Bryce Canyon National Park occupies the easternmost margin of the Paunsaugunt Plateau (figure 7), a plateau which is 20 miles (33 km) long and 10 miles (16.5 km) wide, residing at an average elevation of 8,200 feet (2,485 m). Tilted gently northward, the Plateau's highest elevation, about 9,105 feet (2,760 m), lies at Rainbow Point at the

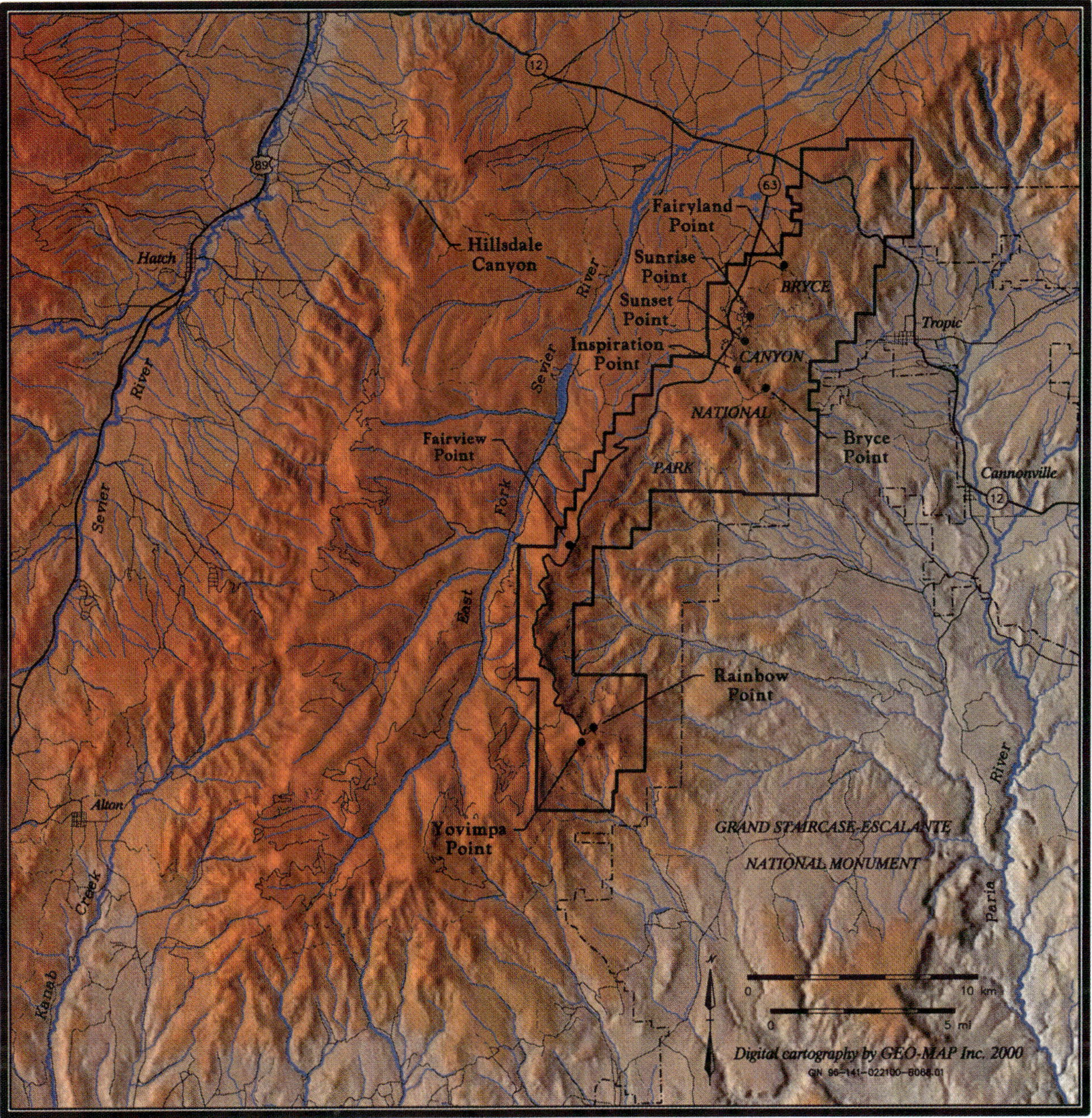

Figure 7. Digital topographic image of the Paunsaugunt Plateau region, including Bryce Canyon National Park. Courtesy of GeoMap, Inc., Tucson, Arizona.

southernmost rim of the Paunsaugunt Plateau. The Plateau surface is flatland with broad, shallow valleys (Gregory, 1951). The base of the Pink Cliffs, which rim the Paunsaugunt Plateau, reside at an elevation of 7000 feet (2,120 m), rising toward the south and dropping toward the north because of regional tilt of the strata. From there the land falls in a series of ridges and valleys to a general elevation of 6,000 feet (1820 m).

As surprising as it may seem, a river flows northward directly down the center of the Paunsaugunt Plateau (figure 7). It is the East Fork of the Sevier River whose headwater tributaries are at the southern end of the Plateau itself. Far to the north, the waters of the East Fork of the Sevier River join the main course of the Sevier, which emp-

ties out into the Great Basin. The Tropic Ditch, hand-dug by Mormon settlers from Cannonville, taps into the East Fork of the Sevier River and transports water eastward through Water Canyon and then on to the Tropic Valley (figure 7). Part of the source for the Sevier River is the runoff which drains westward off of the western margin of the Paunsaugunt Plateau.

Utah Highway 12 follows Red Canyon and is the access route to Bryce Canyon National Park from the west. The headwaters of Kanab Creek originate high on the southwest rim of the Paunsaugunt Plateau (figure 7), and these waters eventually feed into the Colorado River by way of the Virgin River system, the North Fork of which cuts the main canyon through Zion National Park. Precipitation that flows off of the southeastern and eastern margins of the Paunsaugunt Plateau feed the Paria River, which links up with the Colorado River near the Grand Canyon (figure 7).

Bowers (1991, p. 1) emphasized that the Paunsaugunt Plateau forms the western side of the Paria Amphitheater, sometimes called the Tropic Amphitheater, which is bounded on the northeast and east by the Table Cliff Plateau and the Kaiparowits Plateau, respectively. The Paria Amphitheater is the headwaters region of the Paria drainage system, the northwesternmost tributaries of which have worked like fingers eroding into what is now Bryce Canyon National Park.

There are a number of scenic overlooks in Bryce Canyon National Park that can be reached along Utah Highway 63. The most popular vistas include Fairyland Point, Sunrise Point, Sunset Point, Inspiration Point, Bryce Point, Paria View, Fairview Point, Natural Bridge, Rainbow Point, and Yovimpa Point (figure 7).

There are of course wonderful hiking trails in Bryce Canyon National Park (figure 7). The Rim Trail connects Fairyland Point, Sunrise Point, Sunset Point, and Bryce Point. The Under-The-Rim Trail traverses the entire distance between Bryce Point and Rainbow Point. The most popular and accessible trails for hikers who wish to go below the Rim into the alcoves and then return to the top wind their ways through the splendor of Bryce Canyon, Campbell Canyon, and Fairyland Canyon. Fairyland Loop Trail arcs around Boat Mesa between Fairyland Points and Sunrise Point. The Queens Garden Trail links Sunrise and Sunset Points. The Navajo Loop Trail access is Sunset Point. The Peekaboo Loop Trail, a horse trail open to hikers as well, connects the Navajo Loop Trail with Bryce Point.

THE STRATIGRAPHY

The sedimentary rock layers within Bryce Canyon and the surrounding region are alive with distinctive colors and textures. In fact, the world-renowned stratigraphy of the Bryce Canyon region is among the most photographed anywhere on Earth. Some of the thickest and strongest layers within the stratigraphic column define the Grand Staircase of southern Utah and northern Arizona. Dutton (1880, p. ix) called attention to the so called 'grand staircase" in the preface to his famous report on the geology of the High Plateaus of Utah: the "cliffs are bold escarpments hundreds and thousands of feet in altitude – *grand steps* by which the region is terraced." (figures 8 and 9).

Bryce Canyon National Park occupies the Pink Cliffs, the top riser in the Grand Staircase. The rock is Claron Formation, most of which is of Eocene age. Yet from several vantage points in Bryce Canyon National Park it is possible to see the land descending southward down the staircase: from the Pink Cliffs (Claron Formation, Eocene), to the Grey Cliffs (Straight Cliffs and Wahweap Formations, Upper Cretaceous), to the White Cliffs (Navajo

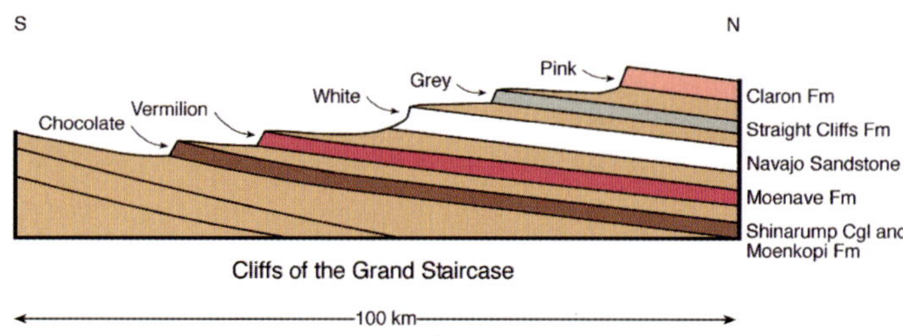

Figure 8. Schematic cross section showing the Grand Staircase, as defined and described by Dutton (1880). Modified from Davis (1999).

Sandstone, Jurassic), to the Vermilion Cliffs (Moenave Formation, Jurassic), and finally to the Chocolate Cliffs (Moenkopi Formation and Shinarump Conglomerate, Triassic) (figures 8 and 9). Gregory noted that the inclination of strata on Paunsaugunt Plateau, including all of these cliffs, reveals a regional dip of 0.5° to 3°, mainly northward to northeastward (figure 8). The result is a series of broad and gently north-dipping plateaus, and ledgy, cliffy south-facing escarpments.

Building upon Dutton's (1880) initial work, Gregory began working in the 1920s in the Kaiparowits Region east of Bryce Canyon National Park, where he began to lay the formal stratigraphic framework for the area (figure 9). From east to west these formations and names were extended to Zion National Park and in 1951 to Bryce Canyon National Park. Bowers (1991) provides an excellent summary of lithologies and thicknesses for each of the formations as seen within or adjacent to Bryce Canyon National Park.

Jurassic Formations

The Navajo Sandstone is a 'signature' rock formation in the Colorado Plateau, primarily because of its great thickness, its beautiful hue (white and/or reddish-brown), and the giant cross-bedding textures it possess (figure 9). The cross-bedding reflects deposition of the Navajo Sandstone in a vast desert adjacent to a seaway, sloping in the direction the wind was blowing some 200 million years ago. Beneath Bryce Canyon National Park, the Navajo Sandstone is at least 1,500 feet (454 m) thick! It forms the White Cliffs section of the famous Grand Staircase (figure 8) of southern Utah.

Overlying the Navajo Sandstone is the Carmel Formation, of Middle Jurassic age (figure 9). Composed mainly of red siltstones, mudstones, and evaporites, it was deposited primarily in a very shallow marine environment, within a seaway that moved southward into Utah all the way from Canada. Near Bryce Canyon National Park it is 925 feet (280 m) thick. Additional redbeds of Middle Jurassic age overlie the Carmel Formation, and these represent deposition in both eolian and subaqueous environments. These are the rocks of the Entrada Formation (figure 9). The Entrada Formation is beautifully exposed in Kodachrome Basin State Park, east of Cannonville, Utah (figure 7).

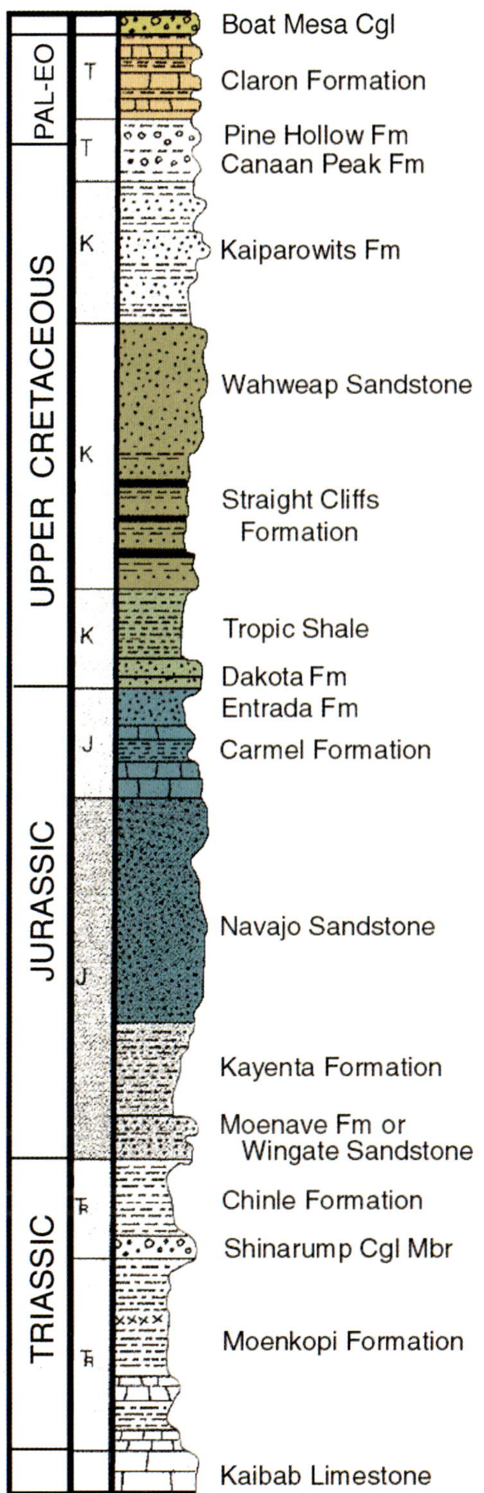

Figure 9. Stratigraphic column for southern Utah. After Hintze (1980; 1988, p. 193-194).

Though not shown in figure 9, there is an often overlooked formation at the very top of the Jurassic in the vicinity of Bryce Canyon National Park: the Henrieville Sandstone (Upper Jurassic). It was named for rocks exposed near the local community of Henrieville, Utah, 20 miles (36 km) east of Bryce Canyon. The Henrieville For-

mation forms a white to cream-colored sandstone cliff. It was deposited predominately in fluvial and eolian environments.

Upper Cretaceous Formations

Big changes took place between the Jurassic and Upper Cretaceous periods. The region shifted from one of predominantly nonmarine deposition (eolian and fluvial) to marine. The giant Cretaceous Seaway swept into the interior of North America from the south, from the Gulf of Mexico all the way into Utah. North America as we know it today was divided into two "island" masses: in the east the Appalachian Mountains, and in the west the Sevier Mountains. During the Cretaceous the Sevier orogenic belt was active and rising along a north-south stretch that included western Utah and eastern Nevada. The shoreline between the Cretaceous Seaway and the Sevier landmass moved back and forth close to Bryce Canyon National Park, leaving a record of marine, nonmarine, and intertidal deposition. Though the marine Cretaceous sedimentary rocks of the Bryce Canyon region look drab grey and dull (the Grey Cliffs are Cretaceous!), they are rich in fossils. For example, straight shelled and coiled ammonites are found in abundance in one of the marine units, the Tropic Shale (figure 9), sharks teeth are found in the lower portion of the Straight Cliffs Formation (figure 9), and yet there are parts of formations (for example, the Wahweap Formation, figure 9) that represent near-shore, on-land conditions and contain the remains of large vertebrate dinosaurs, principally hadrosaurs.

The lowermost Upper Cretaceous rock formation in the Bryce Canyon region is the Dakota Formation (figure 9). It marks the arrival of the seaway, and is deposited unconformably on the Jurassic. As thick as 300 feet (91 m), it was deposited in ever-changing environments, including lagoonal, near shore marine, marine, fluvial, and lacustrine. Thus it is composed of sandstone, siltstone, and some conglomerate. Oyster beds with millions of fossils are found within the Dakota Formation, as is abundant petrified wood. Coal is also present and represents part of the vast coastal swamps that formed along the margin of the late Cretaceous Seaway.

Overlying the Dakota Formation is the Tropic Shale, named by Gregory and Moore (1931) for outcrops around the small community of Tropic at the foot of Bryce Canyon (figures 3 and 9). The Tropic Shale forms the largely unvegetated, badland landscapes in the Tropic Valley that can be seen from Bryce Canyon. It is black and dark grey in color, not nearly as striking as the more colorful formations in the region, but it is perhaps the most fossil rich of any in the region. It represents the maximum transgression of the Late Cretaceous Seaway into Utah and is nearly 1,000 feet (303 m) thick in the Paria Amphitheater.

An abrupt change occurs above the Tropic Shale, for the overlying Straight Cliffs Formation (figure 9) forms nearly unscaleable cliffs and escarpments of whitish to yellow-grey sandstones, with relatively thin interbedded shales and mudstones. The Straight Cliffs Formation is subdivided into four members, which include from oldest to youngest: the Tibbet Canyon, Smoky Hollow, John Henry, and the Drip Tank. At Bryce Canyon National Park only three of the members are present: the Tibbet Canyon, Smoky Hollow, and the John Henry. The Tibbet Canyon Member is predominately a cliff-forming sandstone that rests conformably on the Tropic Shale. It was deposited in shallow marine and near-shore environments and represents the final retreat of the Cretaceous Seaway as it withdrew to the east and into the interior of North America. The Smoky Hollow Member consists of shales and sandstones with two distinguishable coaly or carbonaceous mudstone marker beds serving as the break between the Tibbet Canyon. This member was deposited in coastal swamps and lagoonal environments on the margin of the retreating Cretaceous Seaway. The John Henry Member represents the thickest member of the Straight Cliffs Formation in the Bryce Canyon region. It is characterized by a series of alternating shales and sandstones with vast amounts of coal in several zones that extend throughout the region. This member was deposited in a variety of environments that include coastal swamps, fluvial, and lagoonal. In the Escalante area there are several marine tongues of sandstone that represent the last incursions of the late Cretaceous Seaway into the region. Thickness of the Straight Cliffs Formation in the Bryce Canyon region is as great as 1700 feet (515 m).

Overlying the Straight Cliffs Formation is the Wahweap Formation (figure 9), which forms a portion of the Grey Cliffs section of the Grand Staircase (figure 8). Named by Gregory and Moore (1931), it consists of a series of sandstones and shales deposited mainly in fluvial environments and containing a rich record of vertebrate fauna. Its thickness near Bryce Canyon ranges up to 700 feet (212 m).

Uppermost Cretaceous strata overlie the Wahweap Formation, and these are the grey sandstones and mudstones of the Kaiparowits Formation (figure 9), also named by Gregory and Moore (1931). Though hundreds of feet thick in some parts of the region, the Kaiparowits Formation is very thin (up to 100 feet [33 meters]) near Bryce Canyon. The Kaiparowits Formation was deposited in fluvial, flood plain and lacustrine environments.

Tertiary Formations

Two formations (the Canaan Peak and Pine Hollow Formations, figure 9), as young as Paleocene, represent a tiny restricted record of the transition from Cretaceous to Tertiary, but are not exposed in the Bryce Canyon area. Fundamentally they are sandstones and conglomerates representing stream and river deposition, and the emergence of high topography along uplifts such as the Kaibab. But normally the Upper Cretaceous is overlain directly, though unconformably, by the Claron Formation, expressed as the Pink Cliffs (figures 8 and 9). This is the formation that gives luster to Bryce Canyon. At the time of

Gregory's (1951) mapping, the Claron Formation was called the Wasatch Formation.

At Bryce Canyon National Park, the Claron Formation is Eocene in age, but regionally it ranges in age from Paleocene to middle Oligocene. Two members can be distinguished: the Pink Member (up to 700 feet thick [212 m]), which is found throughout the park and is home to the most well developed hoodoo terrain; and the White Member (up to 300 feet [91 m]), which is found only at the highest elevations of the Paunsaugunt Plateau, especially south of Sunset Point (figure 7). In the northern portion of the Park the White Member has been eliminated by erosion. The basal part of the Claron Formation is composed primarily of siltstone, sandstone, and conglomerate, and records the transition from a predominantly fluvial and intermontane environment to deltaic and lacustrine environments (Goldstrand, 1990).

Evidence for fluvial deposition within the Claron Formation is clearly seen in Red Canyon along Utah Highway 12, where channel conglomerates are well preserved. Goldstrand (1990, 1991, and 1992), who studied the Claron Formation in detail, pictures a depositional environment in which meandering streams flowed sluggishly on broad, nearly featureless plains. From time to time (perhaps averaging once every 1,000 years) there were awesome flood events in which the rivers overflowed their natural levees, spreading fine silt and mud over large expanses. Between flood events these overbank deposits became deeply weathered. The soils supported abundant plant growth, and the deep roots of the plants thoroughly churned and disturbed the muds and silts into which they descended. An oxidizing environment ensured that the iron in the muds and silts would assume the form of hematite, contributing the pink and red hues. It is these disturbed silts and muds that make up much of the Pink Member of the Claron Formation. In contrast, much of the White Member of the Claron Formation is composed of limestone, with interbedded siltstone, and represents deposition in shallow, expansive lakes. Conditions for life must have been poor, for there are very few fossils in the White Member of the Claron Formation, mainly freshwater snails and clams. Perhaps the lakes were akin to the modern Lake Titicaca in the high plateau region (Altiplano) of Bolivia and Peru, South America. This region may be a modern analogue for the Laramide setting of western North America.

Not much overlies the Claron Formation at Bryce Canyon National Park. But worth mentioning is the Conglomerate at Boat Mesa, which is Oligocene or Miocene in age (figure 9). It is mainly a conglomerate with minor sandstones and lacustrine limestones (Bowers, 1991). This formation primarily represents fluvial and overbank deposits. Its thickness is less than 100 feet (30 m). Above Boat Mesa Conglomerate are minor gravels, the Sevier River gravels, which represent Pliocene-Pleistocene valley-fill deposits by the ancestral Sevier River drainage system.

GEOLOGIC MAPPING OF BRYCE CANYON NATIONAL PARK

The geology of Bryce Canyon National Park was first mapped comprehensively by Gregory (1951, Plate I, scale of 1:62,500) as a part of his overall mapping of the Paunsaugunt Plateau (figure 10). Gregory's (1951) geologic mapping (figure 10) covered all of the Paunsaugunt Plateau. Major normal faults bound the Plateau on both the west and east, the Sevier and Paunsaugunt faults, both of Basin and Range origin. Each of these faults trends N5° to 15°E. They dip to the west and down-fault the strata by 2,000 feet (600 m) on the west. The other significant fault structures that Gregory (1951) mapped on the Paunsaugunt Plateau are the two east-west trending faults at the northern end of the Paunsaugunt Plateau. These bound Johnson Bench north and south (figure 10). The southernmost of these is the Ruby's Inn fault; the northernmost fault is the Pine Hills fault. These two faults demarcate an east-west trending swath of Upper Cretaceous rocks, separated both to the north and south by Claron Formation (Eocene).

The highest elevations of the Paunsaugunt Plateau are capped by Claron Formation (Eocene). Trending north-south down the middle of the Paunsaugunt Plateau is a narrow strip of Upper Cretaceous strata, exposed because of deeper erosion along the East Fork of the Sevier River (figure 10). The East Fork has cut all of the way through the Claron Formation, revealing the Cretaceous rocks on which the Claron Formation rests. Similarly, Upper Cretaceous rocks are exposed along the western and eastern flanks of the Paunsaugunt Plateau. On the western margin of the Paunsaugunt Plateau, these Upper Cretaceous rocks are cut off abruptly to the west by the Sevier fault (figure 10). To the west of the Sevier fault is Claron Formation, brought down to this level approximately 2,000 feet (606 m) by the faulting. On the eastern margin of the Paunsaugunt Plateau, these Upper Cretaceous strata are cut off abruptly to the east by the Paunsaugunt fault (figure 10). To the east of the Paunsaugunt fault are yet older rocks, mainly Jurassic in age.

Gregory (1951) mapped Quaternary basalt flows at the south end of the Paunsaugunt Plateau, the largest of which was erupted several thousand years ago at Bald Knoll and flowed south-southeast for a distance of 7 miles (11.6 km) (figure 10). Basalt flows also were mapped by Gregory (1951) both north and south of Red Canyon along the Sevier fault. Though mapped by Gregory (1951) as "Quaternary," basalt at Red Canyon is actually Miocene (Hintze, 1988). The Sevier fault cuts and displaces one of the flows in the Red Canyon area. With few exceptions, the formations within the area mapped by Gregory (1951) are essentially flat-lying, though in detail the rocks dip 0.5° to 3° north or northeastward. The exceptions are quite revealing, and these will be described in the section on "Structural Geology."

Later Bowers (1991) of the U.S. Geological Survey

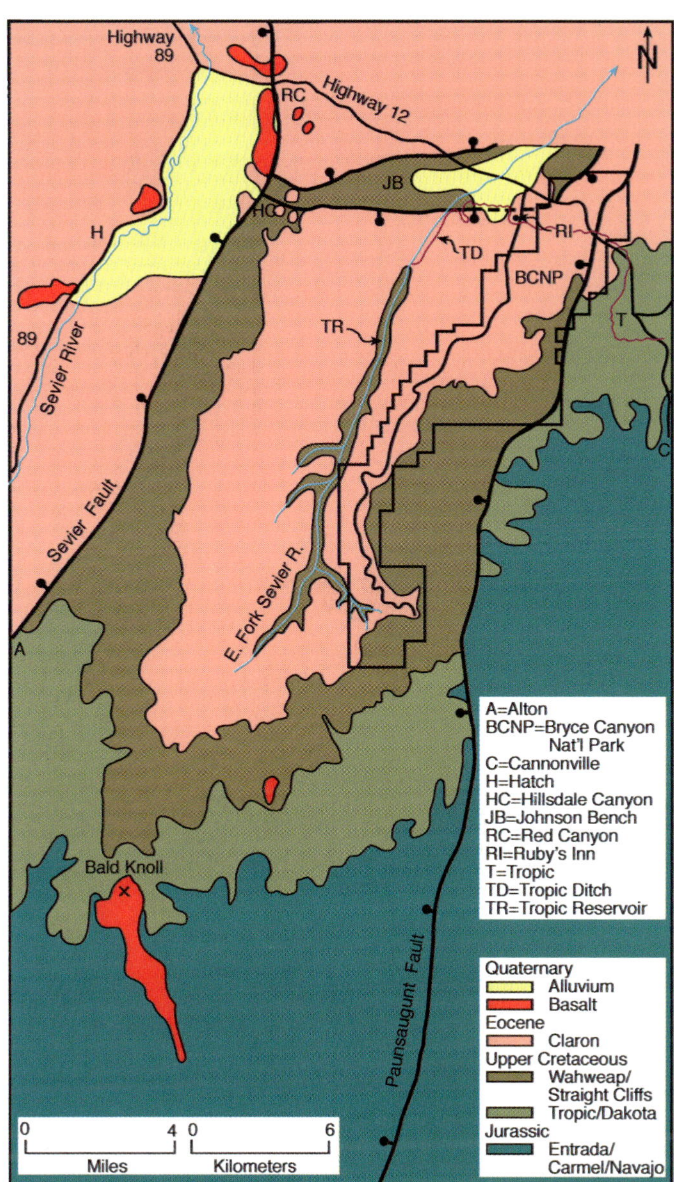

Figure 10. Simplified version of Gregory's (1951) geologic map of Paunsaugunt Plateau.

mapped Bryce Canyon National Park and vicinity more recently and at a closer scale than Gregory, namely 1:24,000 (figure 11). The most notable structural geologic addition to the mapping by Gregory and Bowers came through the mid-1980s discovery and subsequent findings (Davis and Krantz, 1986; Lundin, 1987, 1989; Merle and others, 1993) that the east-west-trending faults in the northern part of the Paunsaugunt Plateau are low-dipping mid-Tertiary thrust faults, and not Basin and Range normal faults as previously interpreted. Results of this work, especially the mapping by Lundin (1987, 1989), were incorporated into the mapping by Bowers (1991), and created a whole new chapter in the geological history of Bryce Canyon National Park.

Bowers' (1991) map (figure 11) includes all of Bryce Canyon National Park, and in fact spills out beyond the

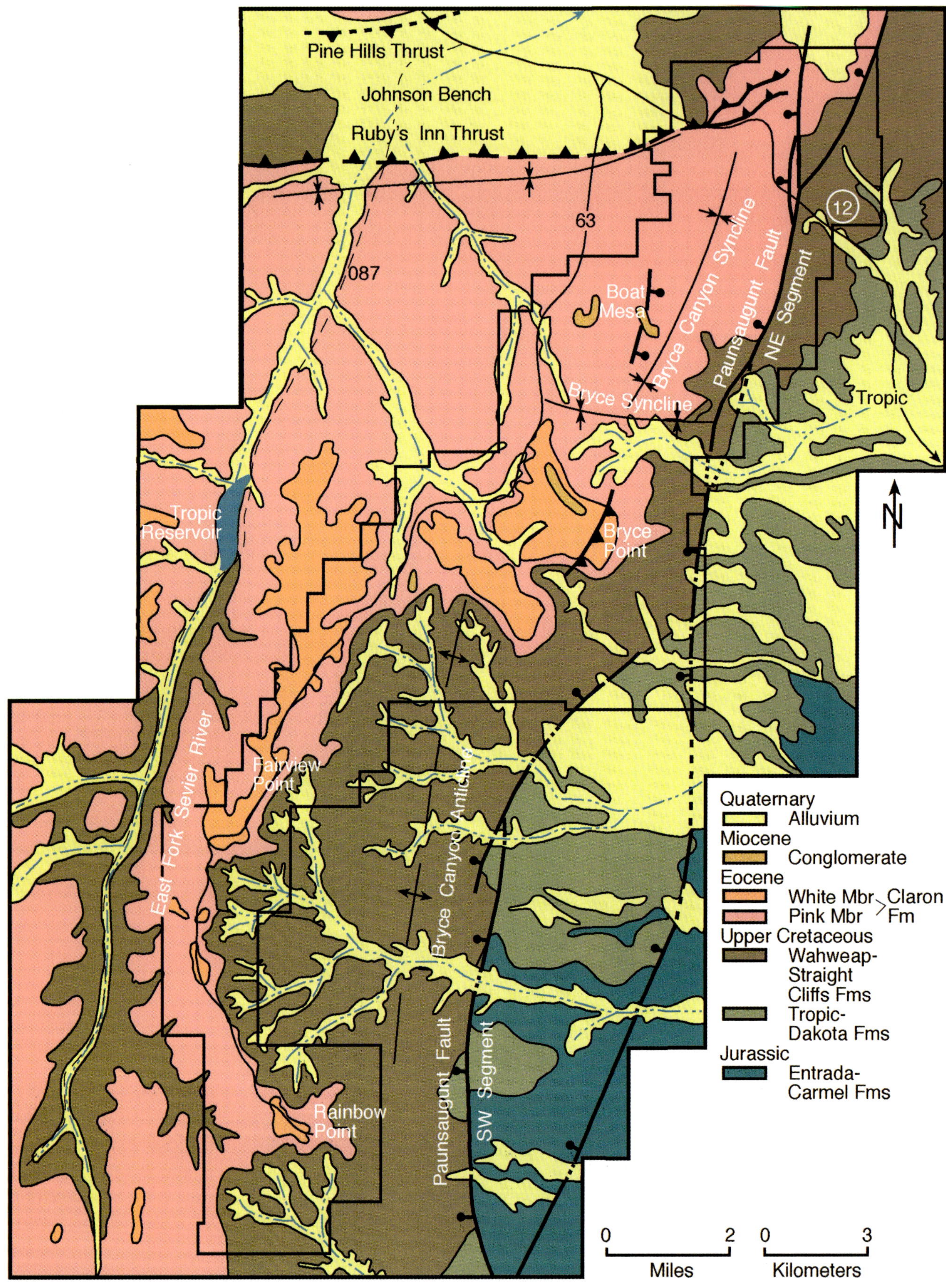

Figure 11. Simplified version of Bowers' (1991) geologic map of Bryce Canyon National Park and vicinity.

Park boundaries. The distribution of rock formations in Bryce Canyon National Park and surroundings as mapped by Bowers (1991) is divisible into four sectors (figure 11): (I) The top of the Paunsaugunt Plateau is capped by the Claron Formation. The Pink Member dominates, while the White Member caps only the highest elevations. The Upper Cretaceous rocks, which immediately underlie the lower member of the Claron Formation, are exposed on the top of the Paunsaugunt Plateau only along the East Fork of the Sevier River. The formation represented there is Wahweap Formation. (II) Johnson Bench is largely covered by Quaternary alluvium, but bedrock is exposed through the alluvium in the form of the upper member of the Straight Cliffs Formation (figure 11). The Ruby's Inn and Pine Hills faults, with associated folds, crop out along the margins of Johnson Bench. (III) Below the Rim, the southwest segment of the Paunsaugunt fault zone separates Upper Cretaceous rocks on the west (Wahweap and Straight Cliffs Formations) from Upper Cretaceous (Tropic Shale and Dakota Formation) and Jurassic rocks (Entrada and Carmel Formations) on the east (figure 11). (IV) The northeast segment of the Paunsaugunt fault zone separates Eocene Claron Formation on the west from Upper Cretaceous rocks (Straight Cliffs Formation and Tropic Shale) on the east (figure 11). The youngest bedrock formations in the map area are conglomerates and sandstones found in patchy distribution in sector IV, namely the Sevier River gravels and Boat Mesa Conglomerate.

The splendid alcove amphitheaters of Bryce Canyon National Park are primarily located in sector III, bounded on the north by the Ruby's Inn fault, on the east by the northeastern segment of the Paunsaugunt fault, on the south by the 'stepover' from the northeast segment to the southwest segment of the Paunsaugunt fault, and on the west by the eastern Rim of the Paunsaugunt Plateau (figure 11). This area represents the home of "hoodoo landscape" and is the only broad 'below-the-Rim' expanse of Claron Formation in the Paunsaugunt Plateau. Its location here is the result of the fault patterns and associated displacements in combination with the overall gentle northward dip of the Grand Staircase.

STRUCTURAL GEOLOGY

Basin and Range Faults

Sevier Fault

The youngest faults in Bryce Canyon National Park and vicinity are Basin and Range faults, namely the Sevier and Paunsaugunt faults (figures 5 and 10). There is a marvelous exposure of the Sevier fault on the north side of Utah Highway 12 at the entrance to Red Canyon (figure 10). It is located where the cliffs and ridges of the Pink Member of the Claron Formation on the east suddenly give way to a broad open valley (the Sevier River valley). Basalt is down-faulted on the west against the Pink Mem-

Figure 12. North-directed photograph of the Sevier fault as exposed at the mouth of Red Canyon. Quaternary basalt (black) on the left (west) has been down-faulted against Eocene Claron Formation (pink) on the right (east). Photograph by G.H. Davis.

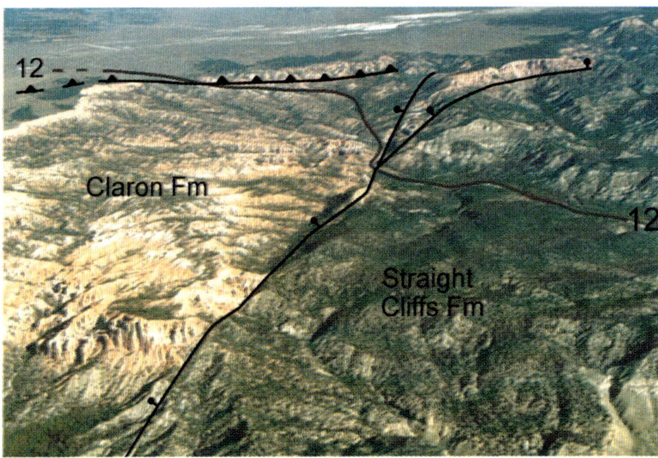

Figure 13. North-northwest-directed oblique aerial view of the Paunsaugunt fault. Its location is conspicuous, for it separates pink rocks on the west from grey rocks on the east. Pink rocks are Claron Formation (Eocene); grey rocks are Straight Cliffs Formation (Upper Cretaceous). The locations of Utah Highway 12, the Paunsaugunt fault, and the Ruby's Inn thrust have been traced on this photograph. Photograph courtesy of Kurt Constenius.

ber of the Claron Formation on the east (figure 12). The dip of the fault is approximately 70° westward. The basalt flow is estimated to be 12 million years old (Miocene), and has been offset 200 feet (60 m).

The beautiful Sunset Cliffs, which form the western escarpment of the Paunsaugunt Plateau south of Red Canyon, owe their expression to the Sevier fault (figure 7). The Sevier fault is located at the base of the cliffs. The fault zone strikes N30°E over a long distance, and has accommodated at least 2,000 feet (600 m) of down-to-the-west offset. The age of the Sevier fault is late Tertiary to Holocene (Anderson and Miller, 1979; Smith and Arabasz, 1991).

The Paunsaugunt Fault

The Paunsaugunt fault has its most dramatic expression when viewed from the air (figure 13), for it separates

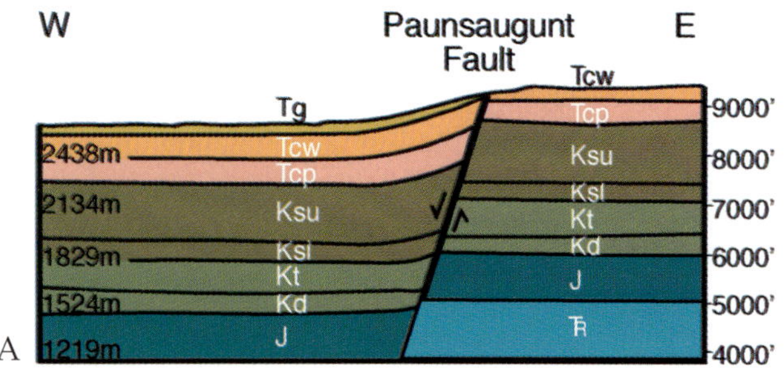
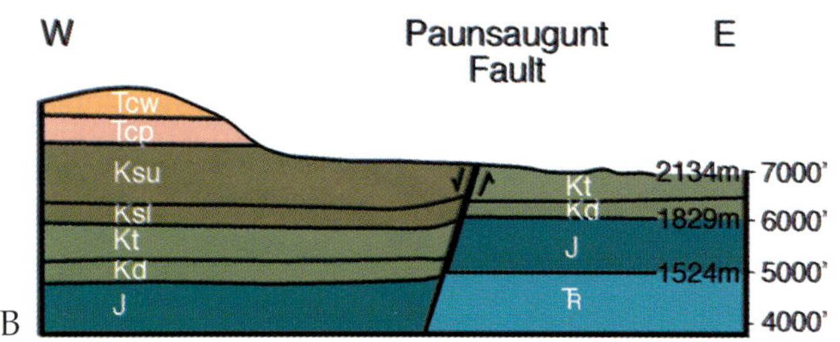

Figure 14. (A) Schematic cross section showing offset along the Paunsaugunt fault. (B) Diagram showing the effects of subsequent erosion by headwaters of tributaries to the Paria River. The net result of faulting followed by erosion is the creation of a landscape in which the down-dropped western block stands higher topographically than the eastern block. Topography and structure are thus "inverted."

Figure 15. Northeast-directed photograph across Bryce Canyon (foreground) toward Table Cliff (background). The Pink Member of the Claron Formation occupies both sites, even though the Claron Formation of Table Cliff lies 2,000 feet (600 m) higher than that in Bryce Canyon. The discrepancy is due to the effect of Paunsaugunt faulting. The actual location of the fault trace is immediately beyond Sinking Ship, which is the zone of tilted strata in the middle ground. Photograph by G.H. Davis.

the colorful Pink Member of the Claron Formation (on the west) from the drab grey expression of the Straight Cliffs Formation (on the east). The abrupt change in color signifies the location of the trace of the fault, which trends N20°E, on average. The Paunsaugunt fault dips westward, just like the Sevier fault. What is difficult to envision is the *sense* of offset along the Paunsaugunt fault, for topography and structure are "inverted." In other words, the higher topography is on the relatively down-dropped fault block, and the lower topography is on the relatively uplifted fault block. Because the higher topography along the rim of the Paunsaugunt Plateau lies west of the fault, whereas the lower topography lies to the east, it is tempting to imagine that the fault accommodated a *down-to-the-east* movement. Not so! The Pink Member of the Claron Formation (Eocene) stratigraphically *overlies* the Lower Member of the Straight Cliffs Formation (Upper Cretaceous) (figure 9), and thus the faulting must be *down-to-the-west* in order to bring these to formations into juxaposition (figure 14A). The fault offset is nearly 2,000 feet (600 meters). It is the nature of the subsequent erosion of the faulted geologic column that creates the opposite impression (figure 14B). A reminder of the true sense of displacement is always available to visitors to the Park. Standing on the Pink Member of the Claron Formation at the rim of the Park (west of the Paunsaugunt fault) at an elevation of 8,500 feet (2,576 m), one can look northeastward to the Table Cliff Plateau (east of the fault) and see the Pink Member at an elevation of 10,230 feet (3,100 m) (figure 15). The Claron Formation of the Paunsaugunt

Plateau was originally at the same elevation as that of the Claron Formation on the Table Cliff Plateau

The most convenient place to actually view the Paunsaugunt fault is along Utah Highway 12 (figure 16). There the fault abruptly separates grey Straight Cliffs Formation on the right (east) from the Pink Member of the Claron Formation on the left (west). The condition of the rock in the fault zone is highly sheared, fractured, and broken, with clay-rich gouge representing extreme grinding and powdering of the rock. Movement indicators, such as fault grooves and scratches, reveal that the west block moved nearly directly down the dip of the fault surface. Similar exposures of the Paunsaugunt fault can be seen in the cliffs to the south of Highway 12, where the grey Cretaceous rocks "cling" to the underside of pink Eocene rocks.

To see the very best exposure of the Paunsaugunt fault requires some serious hiking (figure 17). The location is Campbell Canyon near the Sinking Ship. Gregory (1951) may have been the first geologist to document this exposure, and he includes a photograph of it in his professional paper (Gregory, 1951, figure 38, p. 76). The exposure is stunning, capturing the sharp juxtaposition between Cretaceous and Eocene strata. The fault at this location is inclined approximately 70° westward.

The Paunsaugunt fault is more difficult to spot from the Rim of Bryce Canyon National Park, and yet "the Sinking Ship" provides a reference (figure 15). Sinking Ship is a large westward-tilted block of Claron Formation, and it shows up strikingly from most vistas because all the rest of the Claron Formation in sight is essentially flat-lying. The Sinking Ship lies immediately west of the Paunsaugunt fault, and its tilt is attributable to "drag" on the fault (figure 18).

The age of the Paunsaugunt fault is probably about the

Figure 16. *North-directed photograph of exposure of the Paunsaugunt fault at a location just north of Utah Highway 12. The trace of the fault is evident, separating Claron Formation (pink) on the west from Straight Cliffs Formation (grey) on the east. Photograph by G.H. Davis.*

Figure 17. *North-directed photograph of the exposure which Gregory (1951) presents as figure 38, p. 76, in his U.S. Geological Survey Professional Paper. Location is Campbell Canyon, near the Sinking Ship. Claron Formation (pink) on the west (left) is down-dropped 2,000 feet (600 m) against Straight Cliffs Formation (grey) on the east (right). The fault separating the two formations dips steeply westward. Photograph by G.H. Davis.*

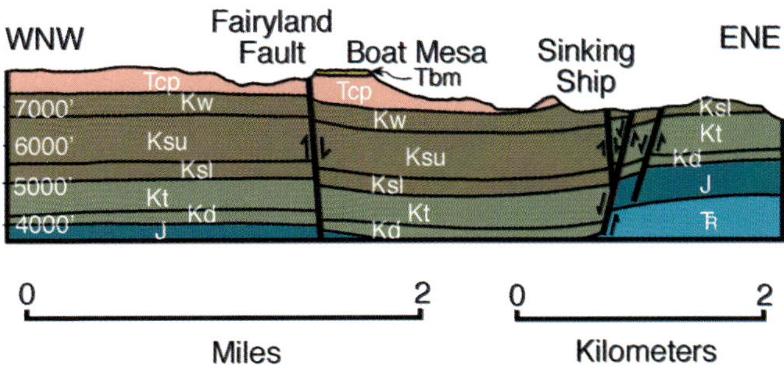

Figure 18. *Cross section illustrating the relationship of the "Sinking Ship" to the Paunsaugunt fault. Sinking Ship represents a localized bending of the strata as the Claron Formation was down-dropped relative to the older strata on the east. Modified from Bowers (1991).*

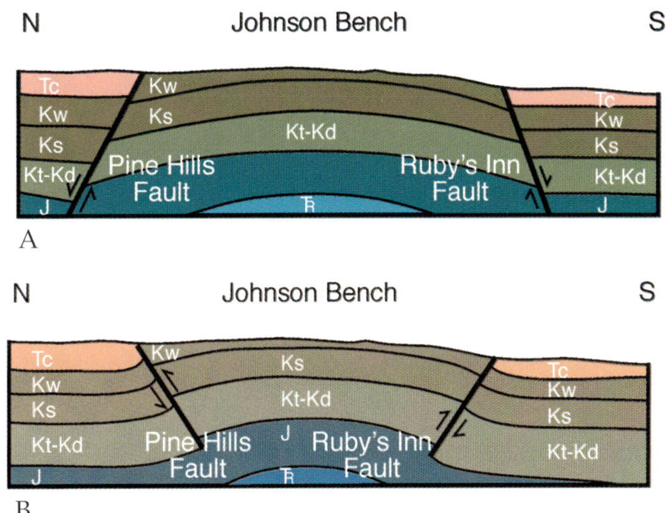

Figure 19. *(A) Cross-sectional diagram showing Gregory's (1951) interpretation of the Ruby's Inn fault and Pine Hills fault as normal faults, with Johnson Bench an uplifted "horst" block. Gregory (1951) interpreted the Ruby's Inn fault to be steeply south dipping, and the Pine Hills fault to be steeply north dipping. (B) Reinterpretation of these faults as thrust faults (Davis and Krantz,1986). The Ruby's Inn thrust dips north and places Cretaceous rocks on top of Eocene rocks. The Pine Hills thrust dips south and similarly places Cretaceous rocks on top of Eocene rocks.*

same as that of the Sevier fault: late Tertiary to Holocene (Anderson and Miller, 1979; Smith and Arabasz, 1991). The youngest formations cut by the Paunsaugunt fault are about 20 million years old, and therefore there is no stratigraphic basis to sharply constrain the age of the faulting.

The Bryce Canyon Syncline

Midway between the trace of the Paunsaugunt fault and the Rim of Bryce Canyon National Park is the previously unnamed "Bryce Canyon syncline." It was mapped by Bowers (1991) (figure 11), and trends parallel to the Paunsaugunt fault. The Bryce Canyon syncline can be recognized easily because strata to the east of it dip gently westward, and strata to the west of it dip gently eastward. Claron Formation is affected by the folding, and thus the syncline is younger than the Bryce Canyon anticline, perhaps forming as a response to drag on the Basin and Range Paunsaugunt fault (DeCourten, 1994). The syncline can

best be seen by looking north-northeast from either Bryce Point or Inspiration Point.

Mid-Tertiary Thrust Fault System

The "Paunsaugunt thrust system" (Merle and others, 1993) is the other significant structural presence in Bryce Canyon National Park and vicinity. Its expression is much more subtle, and its geology much more complex, than that of the Basin and Range faults. This partly explains why the Paunsaugunt thrust system was *ostensibly* not recognized until the mid-1980s (Davis and Krantz, 1986). The chief elements of this system are Ruby's Inn fault and the Pine Hills fault, the east-west-trending faults that demarcate the south and north boundaries of Johnson Bench. Gregory (1951) mapped these as normal faults (figure 10), inferring that the Ruby's Inn fault dips south and the Pine Hills fault dips north (figure 19A). Davis and Krantz

Figure 20. Photograph of the expression of a splay of the Ruby's Inn thrust fault, at a location north of Utah Highway 12. The Claron Formation is smoothly polished, and grooved. Some of the Claron Formation is broken and crushed. Photographs by G.H. Davis.

(1986), however, determined that the Ruby's Inn fault dips north and that the Pine Hills fault dips south, in the manner depicted in figure 19B. Indeed, these faults are thrust faults that place older rocks (Cretaceous in age) on top of the younger rocks (Eocene in age). The age of the faulting is post-middle Eocene, for the faults cut and displace the Claron Formation. However, the faulting pre-dates Basin and Range deformation, because the Ruby's Inn thrust is truncated and offset by the Sevier fault (figure 10). Thus the faulting is post Eocene, pre-Basin and Range in age, that is, mid-Tertiary (early Miocene, 25 to 20 Ma) (Davis, 1999).

Lundin's (1987, 1989) mapping resulted in discovery of magnificent outcrop exposures of faulting just north of Utah Highway 12. Beneath overhanging ledges of Claron Formation there are smooth, polished, striated and grooved fault surfaces (figure 20). The directions of the fault grooves and slickenlines yield the direction of fault movement, which near Utah Highway 12 is to the S 10° E.

At the very northern end of Bryce Canyon National Park, immediately south of Utah Highway 12, there is an uncanny exposure of the Ruby's Inn thrust. It is preserved in a tall hoodoo (figure 21), with a capstone of Upper Cretaceous rock that rests in fault contact on Claron Formation. Thrusting placed Upper Cretaceous Straight Cliffs Formation atop Eocene Claron Formation. Subsequent erosion created the hoodoo, which preserves a tiny remnant of the fault relationship. Moreover, on a larger scale, the Claron Formation directly beneath the Ruby's Inn thrust at this location is folded into a large overturned syncline, creating steeply tilted bedding in Claron Formation. This fold is represented on Bowers' (1991) geologic map (figure 11).

Following the Davis and Krantz (1986) announcement of the "discovery" of thrusting in the Claron Formation, Chevron geologist Frank Royse informed Davis and Lundin that Chevron had discovered the thrusting back in

Figure 21. (A) South-directed view of a hoodoo at north end of Bryce Canyon National Park, just south of Utah Highway 12. The caprock of this hoodoo is Upper Cretaceous Straight Cliffs Formation, which is in thrust fault contact with the underlying Claron Formation. Note steep dip of bedding in Claron Formation in background. (B) Northeast-directed view showing the hoodoo, with Highway 12 in the background. The thrust is traced on the photograph. Photographs by G.H. Davis.

the mid-1950s! Royse shared Chevron's drilling and seismic data, which then became the "control" for cross sections published by Lundin (1989) (figure 22). The subsurface information revealed that the Ruby's Inn fault *flattens*

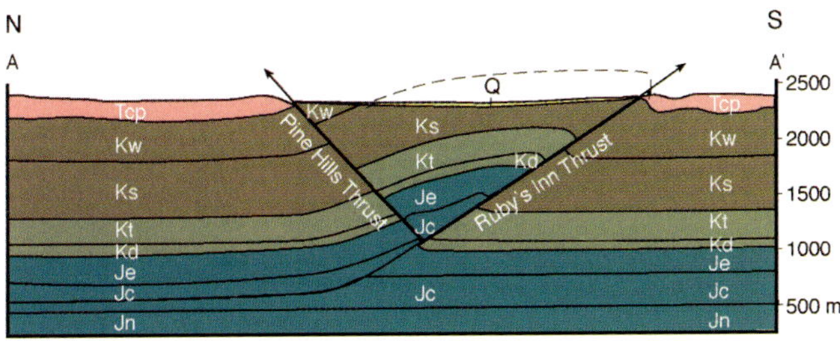

Figure 22. Cross section of the Rubys Inn and Pine Hills faults, based on observations by Davis and Krantz (1986), mapping by Lundin (1987, 1989), and subsurface data courtesy of Chevron, Inc. (Lundin, 1989). Note how the faults flatten into the Carmel Formation (Jurassic), which is rich in mechanically weak evaporites (salt, gypsum, anhydrite). After Lundin (1989).

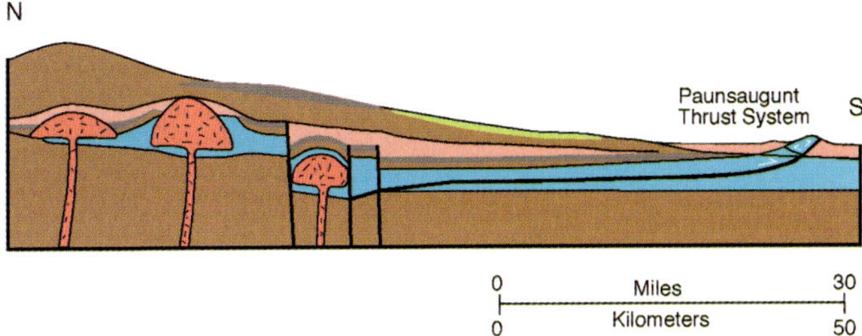

Figure 23. Diagrammatic cross section showing the collapse and spreading of the Marysvale volcanic field, and its relationship to the Paunsaugunt thrust system near Bryce Canyon National Park. Modified from Davis (1999).

into evaporites (that is, salt, gypsum, anhydrite) of the Carmel Formation (Jurassic), the formation just above the Navajo Sandstone of the White Cliffs. The fault proved to be a classic thrust fault (figure 6C).

The total trace length of the Paunsaugunt thrust system is at least 60 miles (100 km), extending well west of the trace of the Sevier fault, and extending northeast of Bryce Canyon National Park several tens of miles (figure 5). The direction of fault movement is divergent, to the southeast, south, and south-southwest, with magnitude of movement on the order of 3,000 to 5,000 feet (900 – 1,500 m). The arcuate thrust system itself is concave to the northwest, wrapping around the southernmost part of the Marysvale volcanic field of early Miocene age (figure 5). The thrusting appears to have resulted from the collapse and spreading the Marysvale volcanic field during the period 25 to 20 million years before present (Davis and Rowley, 1993; Merle and others, 1993). Volcanoes have the capacity to spread and collapse under their own weight, just like Mt. Etna is spreading and collapsing today (Borgia and others, 1992). Spreading is especially common if the volcanic edifice is built atop mechanically soft rock, such as the Carmel Formation. Part of the spreading and collapse of the Marysvale volcanic field may have been favored by the emplacement of laccoliths (figure 6D) which domed the Claron Formation near the southeast margin of the volcanic field north of Panguitch. Doming and lateral spreading may have increased gravitational potential, leading to huge landslides at the earth's surface. At a deeper level, the gravitational spreading and collapse was accommodated by the low-angle thrusts that flatten into the Carmel Formation evaporites. Thrusts broke out along the Ruby's Inn thrust zone; backthrusts also formed, such as the Pine Hills thrust fault (figure 23).

Laramide Deformation

The deposition of the Claron Formation postdates Laramide compressional deformation, and thus evidence for the Laramide deformation must be found in rocks older than the Claron. It seems probable that the Jurassic and Cretaceous strata in Bryce Canyon National Park were impacted by Laramide compressive stresses, for the Kaibab uplift, itself of Laramide origin, lies so close (figure 5). Evidence for Laramide shortening can be seen in the form of the Bryce Canyon anticline (figure 11), mapped by Bowers (1991) in the southern half of the Park within Cretaceous strata. It trends approximately N10°E, essentially parallel to the trace of the Paunsaugunt fault. The Bryce Canyon anticline is a very gentle fold, with limb dips no greater than 5°. It would hardly seem to be an important fold, except for the fact that there is clear stratigraphic evidence that this fold was on the rise in the Late Cretaceous time: namely, all of the Kaiparowits and Wahweap Formations and some of the underlying Straight Cliffs Formation were removed by erosion along the very crest of the fold, prior to the deposition of the Claron Formation (Bowers, 1991). Thus the crest of the fold is marked by an angular unconformity between Upper Cretaceous rocks below and Eocene rocks above.

The presence of the Laramide Bryce Canyon anticline, which lies so close to the Basin-and-Range Paunsaugunt fault, raises the possibility that the Paunsaugunt fault might originally have been created during the Laramide. The ancestral Paunsaugunt fault may have originated in the Laramide as a high-angle thrust fault, and then it was reactivated during Basin and Range deformation as a normal fault.

GEOLOGIC HISTORY OF BRYCE CANYON NATIONAL PARK

It is useful now to step back and try to reconstruct the geological history of Bryce Canyon National Park. Though the emphasis is on what happened from Triassic to today, the Precambrian and Paleozoic should not be forgotten. They deeply underlie the Mesozoic and Cenozoic stratigraphy of the Bryce Canyon region, and represent the foundation upon which the colorful High Plateaus stratigraphy was deposited. Moreover, as can be confirmed by exposures in the Grand Canyon, the East Kaibab monocline is underlain by an ancient Precambrian fault zone which, in the Laramide, was reactivated to help accommo-

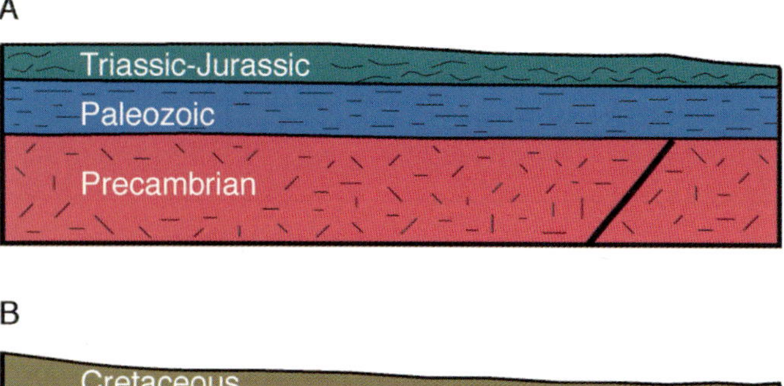
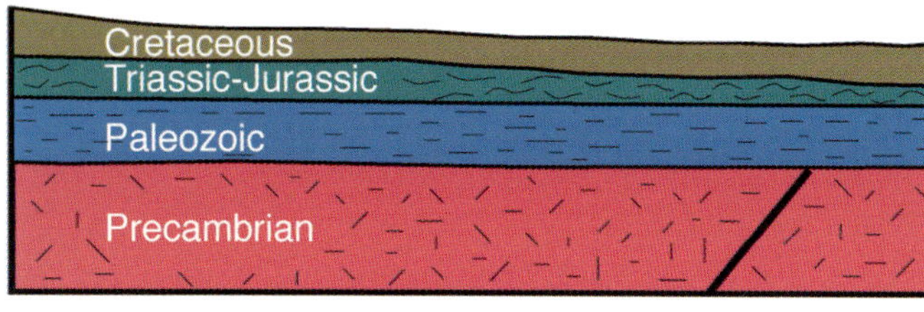
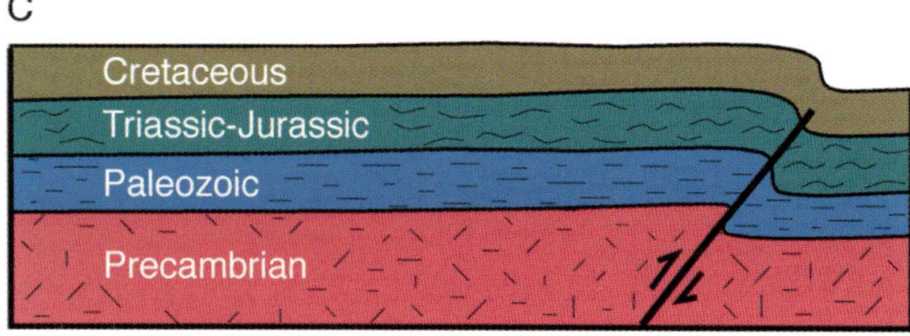
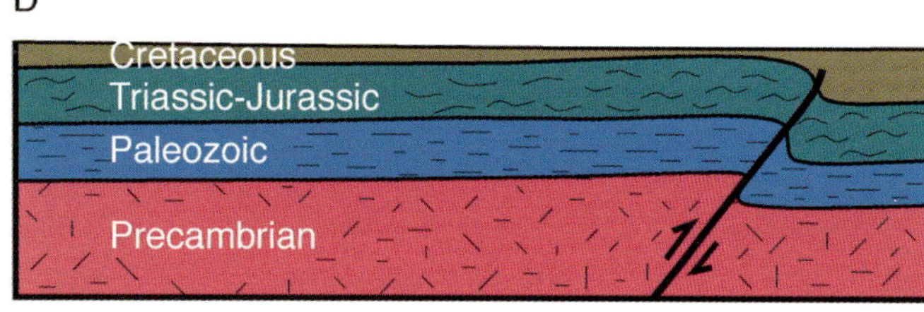
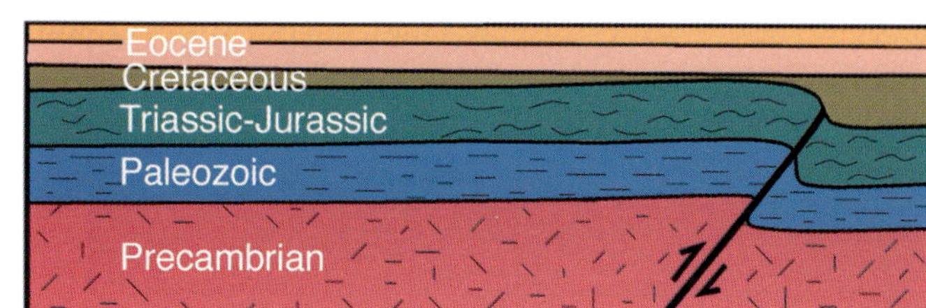
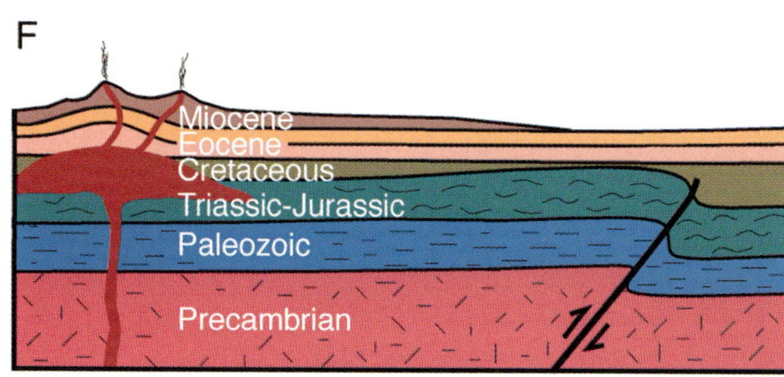
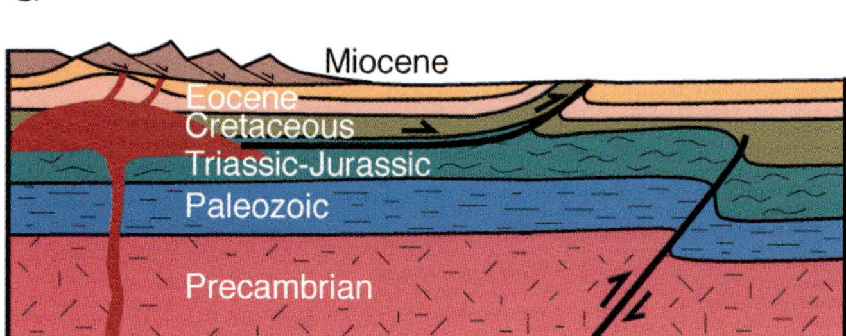
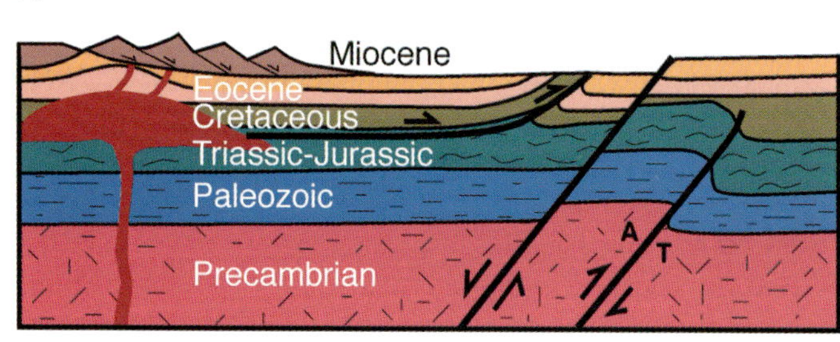
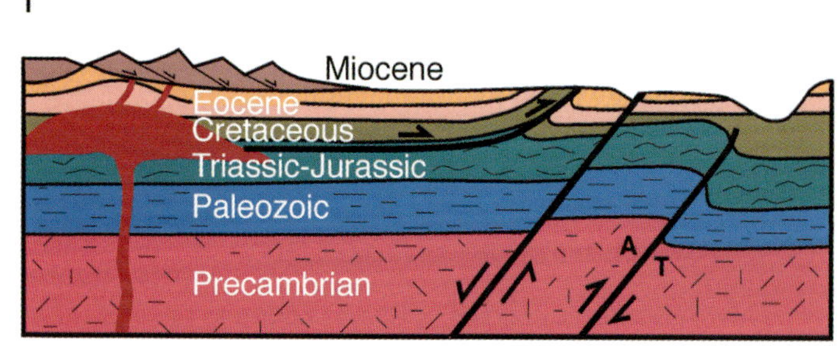

Figure 24. Sequential diagrams showing the geological evolution of the Bryce Canyon National Park region. (A) Deposition of dominantly nonmarine river and dune siltstones and sandstones during the Triassic and Jurassic. (B) Deposition of dominantly marine/nearshore sandstone, siltstone, and peat deposits in Upper Cretaceous, followed by influx of sandstones and conglomerates from the highlands to the west in uppermost Cretaceous time. (C) Laramide compressional deformation and the formation of the Kaibab uplift. During this time the Colorado Plateau region became elevated. (D) Beveling of the Kaibab uplift by erosion, followed by (E) deposition of nonmarine river deposits of siltstones, sandstones, and conglomerates (Pink Member of the Claron Formation); then followed by nonmarine lake deposition of limestone (White Member of Claron Formation). (F) Outpouring of Marysvale volcanics, including lava flows and ash flows, in early Miocene time. (G) Mid-Tertiary tectonic collapse of the Marysvale volcanic field, and formation of the Ruby's Inn and the Pine Hills thrust faults. (H) Basin and Range faulting, creating the Sevier and Paunsaugunt normal faults. (I) Development of alcove amphitheathers and hoodoos by headward erosion of the Paria River drainage system.

date the formation of the Kaibab uplift.

Triassic-Cretaceous Sedimentation

During the Triassic and Jurassic periods a red-and-white bedrock stratigraphy developed, composed of continental siltstones, sandstones, and mudstones primarily deposited in ancient river systems, mudflats, and dune systems (figure 24A). These are the rocks exposed in the Chocolate Cliffs (Moenkopi Formation and Shinarump Conglomerate), the Vermilion Cliffs (Moenave/Wingate and Kayenta Formations), and the White Cliffs (Navajo Sandstone) (figure 8). Where not deformed these resistant rock formations give rise to the extensive plateau and mesa exposures of flat-lying, colorful stratigraphy. In Cretaceous time there was a shift, such that depositional environments changed from dominantly nonmarine to dominantly marine (figure 24B). Thus Upper Cretaceous, dominantly marine strata were deposited (Dakota, Tropic and Straight Cliffs Formations).

Laramide Deformation

The initiation of Laramide deformation is recorded in an influx from the west of uppermost Cretaceous and earliest Cenozoic sediments in the form of non-marine conglomerates and sandstones (figure 24B). The sediments were shed from the Sevier mountains to the west, rising in response to compressional thrust faulting; and from uplifts, such as the Kaibab, rising within the Colorado Plateau proper. Erosional debris was transported by streams eastward into the Paunsaugunt region to form the sandstones of the Wahweap and Kaiparowits Formations, and the conglomerates of the Canaan Peak and Pine Hollow Formations.

The overall effect of this Laramide mountain building was to lift gradually the Colorado Plateau region, possibly to its present elevations. As evidence for this, absolutely no marine sediments have been deposited in the Colorado Plateau region since latest Cretaceous time. Major structures produced during the Laramide include the Kaibab uplift (figure 24C), on whose western, gently dipping flank Bryce Canyon National Park is perched.

The Bryce Canyon anticline formed during the Laramide as well. We know from modern examples today that fold structures form at depth in association with earthquakes generated along faults. The close spatial proximity of the Bryce Canyon anticline and the Paunsaugunt fault suggests that the Paunsaugunt fault may occupy a site of Laramide faulting, the ancestral Paunsaugunt fault.

The Laramide to Mid-Eocene Interval

Following Laramide deformation there was a period of quiescence during which the Kaibab uplift (including the East Kaibab monocline) became beveled along a horizontal erosion surface (figure 24D). It was atop this surface of erosion that the Claron Formation was deposited in Eocene time. The sediments of the Claron Formation were deposited in rivers, streams, and lakes (figure 24E).

From Mid-Eocene to Today

Following deposition of the Claron Formation some 50 million years ago, there were nearly 25 million years of quiescence, ultimately interrupted by the eruptions that created the Marysvale volcanic field, northwest of Bryce Canyon National Park (figure 24F). The closest flows and ashfalls come within less than 20 miles (33 km) of Bryce Canyon. They probably covered Bryce Canyon and were later removed by erosion. Approximately 20 million years ago, the southern part of the Marysvale volcanic field collapsed and spread under its own weight. Its foundation gave way because of the weakness of the evaporites of the Carmel Formation (Jurassic), less than 5,000 feet (1,500 m) below the surface. One of the structural expressions of this collapse was the formation of the Ruby's Inn thrust, which resulted in the folding and faulting of the Claron Formation in Bryce Canyon National Park (figure 24G). Another expression is the Bryce syncline, which trends east-west, perpendicular to the thrust motion.

Since 20 million years ago, the only sediments to be deposited were gravels, which crop out from place to place. Whether the Boat Mesa Conglomerate formed at this time, or earlier, is not known for certain. At 15 million years before present, Basin and Range extensional faulting began (figure 24H). This extended the Bryce Canyon region in an east-west direction, and produced (or perhaps reactivated) the Sevier and Paunsaugunt faults. In fact, both of these may be active today, even though earthquakes are few and far between.

CREATION OF THE PRESENT LANDSCAPE

Opening of the Gulf of California

With the geology fundamentally in place, an event was needed to begin the process that would generate the distinctive Bryce Canyon landscape. This event was the opening of the Gulf of California (the Sea of Cortez), which began about 5 to 10 million years ago. It did so when the continental fragment now known as the Baha Peninsula progressively rifted away northwestward from Mexico. As this occurred the ancestral Colorado River began to spill toward the mouth of the Gulf of California. This "shortcut" route to the sea induced terrific downcutting of the Colorado River and its tributaries. This is why the Colorado Plateau region of northern Arizona and southern Utah is everywhere marked by deep canyons along its major drainages, and by narrow "slot canyons" along parts of its many lesser drainages. Historically geologists have tended to interpret canyon downcutting as a testimony to uplift of the Colorado Plateau, concluding that wholesale uplift of the Colorado Plateau took place in the past 10 million years. We prefer the interpretation that the Colorado Plateau region was uplifted in the Laramide, and that it held its elevation during canyon downcutting by the Colorado River and its major tributaries. Indeed, the Basin and Range Province, which was higher than the Colorado Plateau at the end of the Laramide, foundered and collapsed away from the Colorado Plateau during the past 15 million years.

Headward Erosion During Canyon Cutting

As the Grand Canyon began to form as a result of entrenchment of the Colorado River, major tributaries to the Colorado River, including the Paria River, received the signal to do likewise. The Paria cut headward (northward) towards what is now Bryce Canyon National Park (figure 7). Creation of the amphitheater alcoves and hoodoo landscape in the Claron Formation of Bryce Canyon and surroundings was favored by this headward erosion. Tributaries within the Paria drainage system worked their way north-northwestward toward the Paria (or Tropic) amphitheater (figure 7) through easily eroded Jurassic and Cretaceous formations immediately east of the Paunsaugunt fault. Major tributaries to the Paria River eventually carved through the Paunsaugunt fault and entered into the soft rocks of Upper Cretaceous age (for example, Tropic Shale) west of the fault from below (figure 24I). In effect, the headward-working drainages of the Paria River system encroached upon the Claron Formation from a low-elevation topographic vantage on the east, thereby enhancing the formation of the narrow gullies leading westward to alcove amphitheaters (Davis, 1999, p.25).

Gregory (1951, p. 79, figure 42) constructed a marvelous block diagram which depicts this landscape development (figure 25). He emphasized that the streams on top of the Paunsaugunt Plateau contribute nothing to the development of the alcoves, for the streams flow away from the rim. "The sculpturing agents are the snow and the rain that fall directly into the canyon and the frost and atmospheric acids. The transporting agents are intermittent and ephemeral streams of short length" (Gregory, 1951, p. 103).

Creation of the Bryce Canyon Landscape

The geologic, climatic, and topographic situation is simply perfect for creating the alcoves and the hoodoo landscape of Bryce Canyon National Park. The geologic ingredients are several. If the Pink Member of the Claron Formation were entirely a soft and completely homogeneous rock, no hoodoos would have formed. The Pink Member would simply have weathered and eroded into rounded muddy hills. However, within the Pink Member of the Claron Formation there are relatively thin horizontal resistant beds (mainly composed of limestone and conglomerate), spaced from several feet to several tens of feet, which act like struts and provide a modicum of strength and stability. Remnant survivors of these resistant beds eventually become the capstones that are so commonly seen at the heads of hoodoos, tending to protect the softer

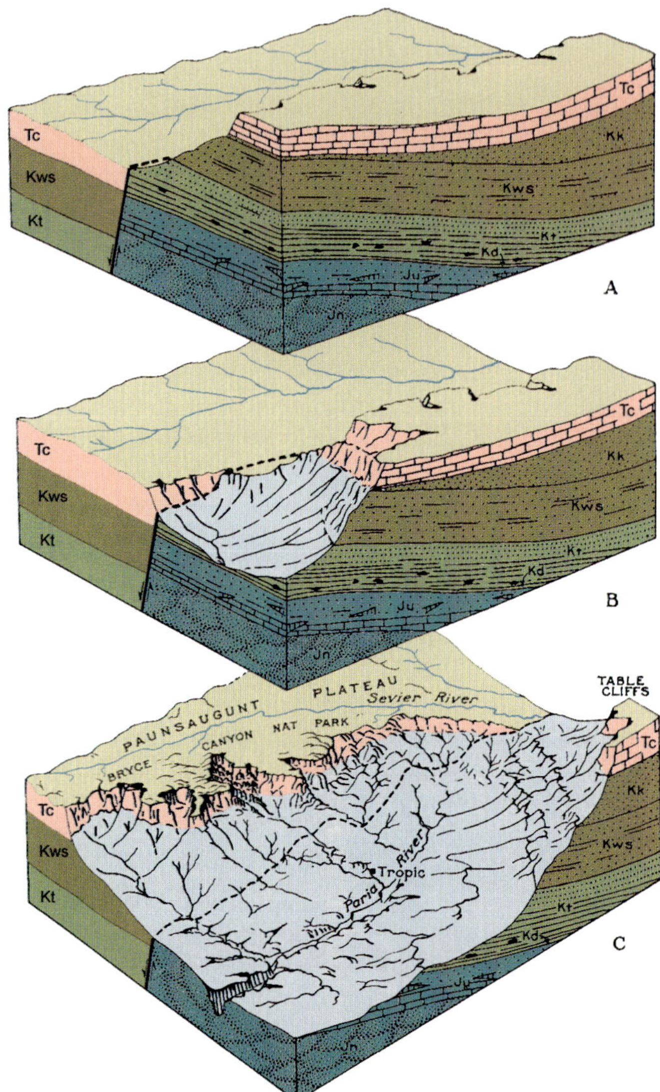

Figure 25. Block diagrams from Gregory (1951, p. 79, figure 42), illustrating the progressive development of the landscape at Bryce Canyon.

bodies beneath.

A second geologic ingredient essential to the hoodoo-forming process is the presence of nearly vertical fractures (called "joints") that break the cohesion of bedrock. Joints are ubiquitous in rocks and form in tension as a mechanism to relieve built-up tectonic or burial stresses. Joints in sedimentary rocks, such as the Claron Formation, typically are expressed in any region by two or more sets, each marked by a distinctive and characteristic orientation. Those in Bryce Canyon tend to be oriented northwest and northeast (DeCourten, 1994). As a result, the joints crisscross one another in intersecting grid-like patterns. The spacing between joints of any one set also tends to be systematic, related to the elastic stiffness and the thickness of the rock layer in which they occur. Joint spacing within the Pink Member of the Claron Formation typically might range from one foot to several feet, with orientations nearly perpendicular to bedding. Once a joint develops, it never goes away, like a crack in a wall or the foundation of a home.

Yet a third geologic ingredient is the presence of outcrop-scale fault surfaces (especially the thrust faults) that formed during the mid-Tertiary deformation. These are conspicuous in the northernmost part of the Park, for example along Fairyland Trail. Faults are distinguishable from joints in that faulting is accompanied by shearing motions whereas jointing is accompanied by tensional opening. But, once formed, both joints and faults enhance weathering in that they each represent conduits for surface waters and ground water. Water, especially when transformed into a weak acid (carbonic acid) through contact with atmosphere, can damage bedrock both physically and chemically, thus accelerating erosional demise.

Climatic ingredients are indispensable in the shaping of the landscape of Bryce Canyon National Park. First, there is ample precipitation to impact weathering and erosion: approximately 16 inches (400 cm) per year on the Paunsaugunt Plateau, in sharp contrast to the 10 inches (254 cm) per year down in the adjacent desert basins of the Paria Amphitheater. Second, though the winter nights at high elevation are commonly marked by subfreezing temperatures, the high-elevation solar radiation of winter days typically lifts the temperatures above freezing. As a consequence, Bryce Canyon is marked by an unusually large number of freeze-thaw cycles per year. The freeze-thaw action "works" jointed rock and faulted rock, causing it to break up. The freeze-thaw action is especially effective at fracture intersections, where joints and faults criss-cross one another. Corners of blocks are the first to go. A third ingredient is the torrential summer rains, especially those experienced in the wettest month, August (DeCorten, 1994). The run-off can quickly remove the season's freeze-thaw rock debris, and create a rilling and gullying of the hillslopes.

Finally, there are topographic ingredients. The first of these is the eastern Rim escarpment of the Paunsaugunt Plateau, which actually slopes westward and away from the amphitheaters. Thus, as Gregory (1951) emphasized, rain that hits the plateau flows to the East Fork of the Sevier River instead of flowing into the amphitheaters. The Rim, therefore, is a passive topographic feature which retreats back (westward). The rate of retreat is estimated to be 4 feet (1.2 m) per century (DeCourten, 1994), which would produce 7 miles (12 km) of cliff retreat in a million years! Cliff retreat permits the amphitheaters to enlarge and to become more scalloped (DeCourten, 1994).

A second topographic ingredient is the presence of oversteepened slopes. Such oversteepening sets the stage for mass wasting, including rock falls and landsliding. Animals, including humans, accelerate mass wasting of the slopes, but the prime mover is the undercutting action of intermittent streams, which periodically fill during torrential rains and scour the toes of the slopes that converge to the gully. If a slope is at its maximum angle of repose, any such scouring will render it unstable. Stability is again

Figure 26. A hoodoo which reveals the presence of thrust faults and related fractures. Height is 35 feet (11 m). Photograph by G.H. Davis.

achieved by mass movements of materials. Because the walls of gullies tend to be so steep, there are times when the debris entering the gullies (due to the landsliding for example) is too much to handle, but there are other times when torrential downpours clean out the gullies by high-velocity floods.

Thus the circumstances of geology, climate, and topography are the fundamental controlling factors for landscape evolution, and the sculpting action itself is achieved through several dynamic processes, including freeze-thaw within cracks; gullying and rilling by the downslope runoff of water; gravity-induced mass wasting achieved by soil creep, rock falls, and landsliding; chemical dissolution by weakly acidic waters; and wind abrasion. These dynamic processes, with the exception of mass wasting mechanisms, "pick at" the fundamental rock architecture in the same way that an archeologist patiently but incisively exhumes artifacts with small brushes and sharp dental tools. Small wonder that the resulting bedrock landscape lays bare the intricate details of bedding and fracturing, as well as the differential resistance to erosion of strong versus weak lithologies. We might imagine that

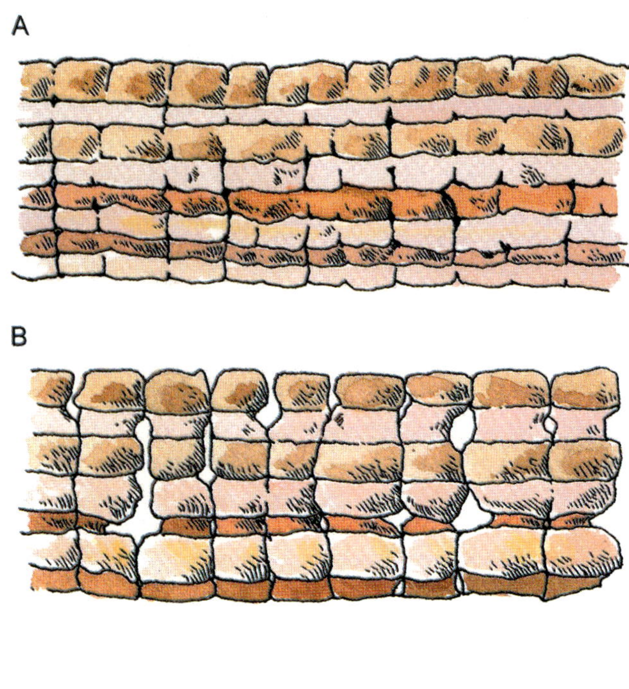

Figure 27. Origin of hoodoos, as depicted in an illustration in De-Courten (1994, p. 76). Weathering and erosion of fins is most effective along the near-vertical joints, and thus joint locations become widened, setting the stage for the creation of the hoodoos. The resistant rock layers within the Pink Member of the Claron Formation give the formation some integrity, and remnants of such layers ultimately serve as capstones on the tops of hoodoos.

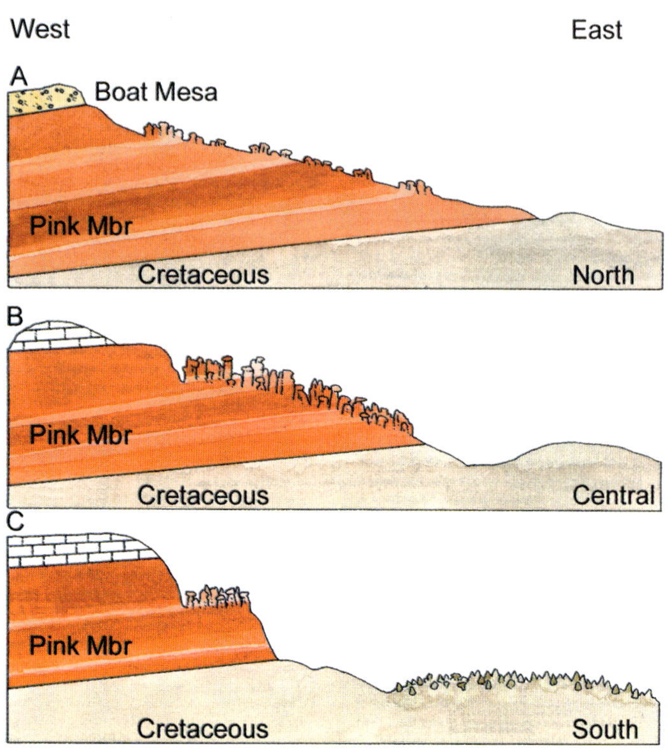

Figure 28. Diagrams from DeCourten (1994, p. 74) that reveal the differences in maturity of the landscape within different parts of Bryce Canyon National Park. See text.

the caprocks on hoodoos bring the erosional process into slow-motion, permitting a combination of processes to enhance the geometric expressions of all of the weaknesses – bedding, jointing, and faulting, in particular. Although most hoodoos subscribe to the same general appearance, no two are exactly the same, because no two have exactly the same internal structure, and no two have been subjected to the same set of processes working at exactly the same rates. For example, the effects of outcrop-scale thrust faulting on hoodoo development is apparent at vistas closest to the trace of the Ruby's Inn thrust. The compressive deformation associated with the thrusting created thousands of minor fault surfaces within the rocks, especially low-dipping thrust surfaces and steeply dipping strike-slip surfaces. These are commonly quite obvious on the flanks of many hoodoos, where their expression has been enhanced by weathering and erosion (figure 26).

The evolution of the landscape, especially the hoodoos, is illustrated in figure 27. The combination of weathering and erosional processes tends to create narrow walls, sometimes fins, which can become breached to form windows or natural arches. Continuous weathering and erosion of the fins and walls results in a gradual separating of pillars of rocks, and some of these emerge into the form of hoodoos (figure 27). Then as emphasized by De-Courten (1994, p. 75), the very processes that created the hoodoos eventually destroy them: "erosion is both their creator and, eventually, their executioner."

The influence of duration of weathering and erosion on a particular tract of bedrock is quite clear in the Park (figure 28) (DeCourten, 1994). Northward- and westward-eroding tributaries of the Paria River system first penetrated the southern end of the Park. Only later did they encroached upon the northern reaches of the Park. That this is so is revealed in the systematic variation in landscape development of Bryce Canyon National Park (figure 28). The southern reaches are the most deeply eroded, and feature broad exposures of Cretaceous rocks in the floors of canyons. Clusters of surviving hoodoos occupy relatively small areas. In contrast the northern reaches are least eroded, with well developed though incipient hoodoo landscapes few and far between. The central sector – Bryce Canyon! - is "just right," featuring extensive, well-developed hoodoos.

We might conclude that if Bryce Canyon National

Figure 29. A walk down Wall Street kindles the imagination. Photograph by G.H. Davis.

Park had been established 3 million years ago, different vistas may have been chosen, and the lodge may have been built much farther south than where it resides today. Perhaps we will simply allow our imaginations to consider this possibility, as well as the whole scenario of the geologic evolution of Bryce Canyon National Park (figure 29). For indeed, Bryce landscapes stimulate the imagination!

ACKNOWLEDGMENTS

We wish to thank Susie Gillatt for her skillful rendering of our illustrations for this chapter. We also acknowledge the digital topographic image (figure 7) rendered by GeoMap, Inc. The Bryce Canyon Natural History Association supported most of the costs of preparation of the illustrations, and for this we are very appreciative. The manuscript benefited greatly from reviews by Sarah Tindall, Steve Reynolds, Doug Sprinkel, and Tom Chidsey.

REFERENCES

Anderson, L.W., and Miller, D.G., 1979, Age and extent of Quaternary faulting in Utah [abs.]: Geological Society of America Abstracts with Programs, v. 11, no. 3, p. 66.

Borgia, A., Ferrari, L., and Pasquara, G.P., 1992, Importance of gravitational spreading in the tectonic and volcanic evolution of Mount Etna: Nature, v. 357, p. 231-235.

Bowers, W.E., 1991, Geology of Bryce Canyon National Park and vicinity, Utah. U.S. Geological Survey Map I-2108, scale 1:24,000.

Cloos, E., 1968, Experimental analysis of Gulf Coast fracture patterns: American Association of Petroleum Geologists Bulletin, v. 52, p. 420-444.

Dahlstrom, D.C.A., 1969, Balanced cross sections: Canadian Journal of Earth Sciences, v. 6, p. 743-757.

Davis, G.H., 1978, The monocline fold pattern of the Colorado Plateau, *in* Matthews, V., editor, Laramide folding associated with basement block faulting in the western U. S.: Geological Society of America Memoir 151, p. 215-233.

—1999, Structural geology of the Colorado Plateau region of southern Utah, with special emphasis on deformation bands: Geological Society of America Special Paper 342, 157 p.

Davis, G.H., and Krantz, R.W., 1986, Post-Laramide thrust faults in the Claron Formation, Bryce Canyon National Park, Utah [abs.]: Geological Society of America Abstracts with Programs, v. 18, p. 98.

Davis, G.H., and Rowley, P., 1993, Miocene thrusting, gravity sliding, and near-surface batholithic emplacement, Marysvale volcanic field, southwestern Utah: EOS (Transactions, American Geophysical Union), v. 77, no. 46, p. F641-642.

DeCourten, Frank, 1994, Shadows of time -- the geology of Bryce Canyon National Park: Bryce Canyon Natural History Association, Bryce Canyon, Utah, 128p.

Dutton, C.E., 1880, Report on the geology of the High Plateaus of Utah: U.S. Geographic and Geological Survey of the Rocky Mountain region (Powell), 307 p.

Engdahl, E.R., and Rinehart, W.A., 1991, Seismicity map of North America project, *in* Slemmons, D.B., Engdahl, E.R., Zoback, M.D., and Blackwell, D.D., editors, Neotectonics of North America: Boulder, Geological Society of America, p. 21-27.

Gilbert, G.K., 1875, U. S. Geographic and Geological Surveys West of 100th Meridian (Wheeler Survey Report), v. 3.

—1877, Report on the geology of the Henry Mountains: U.S. Geographic and Geologic Survey of the Rocky Mountains region, 170 p.

Goldstrand, P.M., 1990, Stratigraphy and paleogeography of Late Cretaceous and Early Tertiary rocks of southwest Utah: Utah Geological and Mineral Survey Miscellaneous Publication MP90-2, 58p.

—1991, Tectonostratigraphy, petrology, and paleogeography of Upper Cretaceous to Eocene rocks of southwest Utah: Reno, University of Nevada, Ph.D dissertation, 205 p.

—1992, Evolution of Late Cretaceous and Early Tertiary

basins of southwest Utah based on clastic petrology: Journal of Sedimentary Petrology, v. 62, no. 3, p. 495-507.

Gregory, H.E., 1951, The geology and geography of the Paunsaugunt region, Utah: U.S. Geological Survey Professional Paper 226, 116 p.

Gregory, H.E., and Moore, R.C., 1931, The Kaiparowits region, a geographical and geologic reconnaissance of parts of Utah and Arizona: U.S. Geological Survey Professional paper 164, 161p.

Hintze, L.F., 1980, Geologic map of Utah: Salt Lake City, Utah Geological and Mineral Survey, scale 1:500,000.

—1988, Geologic history of Utah: Brigham Young University Geology Studies Special Publication 7, 203 p.

Howell, E.E., 1875, Report on the geology of portions of Utah, Nevada, Arizona, and New Mexico examined in 1872 and 1873: U. S. Geographic and Geological Surveys West of 100th Meridian (Wheeler), v. 3, p. 227-301.

Kelley, V.C., 1955, Monoclines of the Colorado Plateau: Geological Society of America Bulletin, v. 66, p. 789-804.

Kelley, V.C., and Clinton, N.J., 1960, Fracture systems and tectonic elements of the Colorado Plateau: University of New Mexico Publications in Geology, no. 6, 104 p.

Lundin, E. R., 1987, Thrusting of the Claron Formation, the Bryce Canyon region, Utah: Tucson, The University of Arizona, M.S. thesis, 51p.

—1989, Thrusting of the Claron Formation, the Bryce Canyon region, Utah: Geological Society of America Bulletin, v. 101, p. 1038-1050.

Merle, O.R., Davis, G.H., Nickelsen, R.P., and Gourlay, P.A., 1993, Relation of thin-skinned thrusting of Colorado Plateau strata in southwestern Utah to Cenozoic magmatism: Geological Society of America Bulletin, v. 1050, p. 387-398.

Smith, R.B., and Arabasz, W.J., 1991, Seismicity of the Intermountain Seismic Belt, *in* Slemmons, D.B., Engdahl, E.R., Zoback, M.D., and Blackwell, D.D., editors, Neotectonics of North America: Boulder, Geological Society of America, p. 185-228.

Stegner, W., 1954, Beyond the hundredth meridian - John Wesley Powell and the second opening of the West: New York, Penguin Books, 438 p.

Thompson, A.H., 1875, Report on a trip to the mouth of the Dirty Devil River [in 1872], *in* Powell, J.W., Exploration of the Colorado River of the West and its tributaries explored in 1869, 1870, 1871, and 1872, p. 133-145.

Tindall, S.E., and Davis, G.H., 1999, Monocline development by oblique-slip fault-propagation folding -- the East Kaibab monocline, Colorado Plateau, Utah: Journal of Structural Geology, v. 21, p. 1303-1320.

Wheeler, G.M., 1874, U.S. Geographical and Geological Exploration and Surveys West of 100th Meridian, Geological Atlas, sheets 56, 67 p.

Wheeler, G.M., 1875, U.S. Geographical and Geological Exploration and Surveys West of 100th Meridian, v. 3.

Geology of Utah's Parks and Monuments
2000 Utah Geological Association Publication 28
D.A. Sprinkel, T.C. Chidsey, Jr., and P.B. Anderson, editors

Geology of Canyonlands National Park, Utah

Donald L. Baars[1]

ABSTRACT

Canyonlands National Park lies astride the broad, northerly plunging nose of the Monument upwarp above the western flank of the Paradox basin. Rocks of Middle Pennsylvanian through Jurassic age comprise the magnificent scenery of this rugged desert landscape. Structural features seen at the surface today result from Laramide and younger rejuvenation of preexisting fracture patterns of Precambrian age, complicated by the presence of salt of the Middle Pennsylvanian Paradox Formation at shallow depths.

The oldest rocks exposed in the park are gypsum and related black shale and dolomite of the Akah cycle of the Paradox Formation that crops out at the mouth of Gypsum Canyon in Cataract Canyon. The Paradox evaporites thicken eastward from this thin exposure to more than 3,000 feet of evaporites, including considerable proportions of salt, near Moab, Utah, just east of the park boundary. Above the Paradox Formation, the Late Pennsylvanian Honaker Trail and Elephant Canyon Formations are exposed in the ledgy cliffs of Cataract Canyon and its deeper tributary canyons. The Elephant Canyon Formation interfingers with redbeds of the Halgaito Shale in lower Cataract Canyon.

Rocks of Lower Permian age consist of the Cedar Mesa Sandstone and the overlying Organ Rock Shale, both of which grade eastward across Canyonlands National Park into arkosic clastic rocks of the Cutler Formation. The red arkosic Cutler sandstone beds were derived from the Uncompahgre uplift of the Ancestral Rocky Mountains that lay to the east in Pennsylvanian-Permian time, and the Cedar Mesa lightcolored sandstone was derived from the northwest and deposited in coastal environments. Overlying the Organ Rock Shale in northern Canyonlands, west of the Colorado River, is the White Rim Sandstone, the eastern and shoreward equivalent of the Toroweap Formation.

Mesozoic time is represented by the dark brown intertidal deposits of the Moenkopi Formation of Early Triassic age and, above a regional disconformity, the varicolored Chinle Formation of Late Triassic age, with its prominent basal Moss Back Member. Rocks of Jurassic age consist of majestic cliffs of the Wingate Sandstone, the ledgy thinner bedded cliffs of the Kayenta Formation, and the rounded white knobs and ridges of the Navajo Sandstone. Rocks of younger Jurassic formations have been removed from the park by recent erosion.

Spectacular views of northern Canyonlands are readily accessible from Dead Horse Point Utah State Park, Grand View Point and Green River Overlook in the Island in the Sky District of Canyonlands National Park. All viewpoints are from the lower Kayenta Formation above awesome cliffs of the Wingate Sandstone. From Dead Horse Point and Grand View Point, the scene is looking southward across the Colorado River into rugged terrain eroded from rocks of Permian age, with the La Sal and Abajo laccolithic mountains visible in the distance. From Green River Overlook, one can see into The Maze District, with its Land of Standing Rocks, and Elaterite Basin toward the southwest across rocks of Permian through Jurassic age; the Henry Mountains are in the distance.

In The Needles District of the park, grotesquely eroded buttes, spires, and "toadstool" pedestals dominate the countryside, eroded from complex fractures, largely from salt subsidence, in the Cedar Mesa Sandstone. Color banding in the rocks is due to the interfingering of the white Cedar Mesa Sandstone and the red Cutler arkose across The Needles District. Just to the west is The Grabens, which have formed from collapse of overlying rocks into groundwater-leached Paradox salt, with downdip extension by gravity gliding on top of the salt toward Cataract Canyon and the Meander anticline.

Intricate erosional patterns in the Cedar Mesa Sandstone dominate The Maze District of Canyonlands National Park west of the Colorado River. Nearby, a well-preserved offshore bar (some argue eolian [wind] sand buildup) in the White Rim Sandstone provides an exposure of a classical stratigraphic trap for petroleum in Elaterite Basin.

[1]*Grand Junction, CO 81504*

Salt-related structures that occur across Canyonlands National Park are of lesser size and significance than the giant salt-intruded anticlines in the heart of the Paradox basin east of the park; for example, the Moab Valley and Salt Valley salt-intruded structures. Three prominent gypsum plugs are exposed in Cataract Canyon along a more extensive structural trend known as the Meander anticline. Flowage into the gypsum plugs was no doubt enhanced by the present of salt, although the depositional thickness of salt in the area was minimal. The course of the Colorado River closely follows a deep-seated, well-documented basement fracture zone, the Colorado or Cataract lineament, above which the river wanders about the crest of the Meander anticline. The sharp, but relatively minor surface anticline was probably formed by flowage of salt along the basement fracture zone.

The origin of Upheaval Dome has been highly controversial for decades. The more plausible theories of its origin regard either salt flowage or meteorite impact. As late as 1999, two papers were published by respected workers. One explanation regards the magnificent structure as a pinched-off salt-piercement dome, while the other contends that a meteorite hit the surface here at about the end of the Cretaceous Period. Both give convincing arguments. Controversies in Canyonlands country geology continue.

INTRODUCTION

Canyonlands National Park lies in the heart of the Paradox basin, consequently geologic and topographic features seen at the surface today ultimately owe their origin to a considerable thickness of salt at depth. In the heart of the park, the salt occurs at relatively shallow depths in the subsurface, causing widespread collapse of the overlying sedimentary rocks across much of the region, punctuated by occasional salt diapirs and salt bulged anticlines. The resulting fracture patterns in the sedimentary cover, and ensuing erosional processes, localize myriad crags and spires, gullies and canyons:

> *"... The landscape everywhere, away from the river, is of rock -- cliffs of rock; plateaus of rock; terraces of rock; crags of rock --Ten thousand strangley carved forms. Rocks everywhere..." (Powell, 1875).*

The layered rocks exposed in Canyonlands are the result of both marine and non-marine deposition from Middle Pennsylvanian through Jurassic time, an interval of some 250 million years. The oldest, the Paradox Formation of Middle Pennsylvanian age, is exposed in Cataract Canyon, the foci of the park. This formation contains the bedded salt, so important to the final magnificent scenery. The Paradox Formation is overlain by marine limestone and interbedded clastic rocks of the later Pennsylvanian Honaker Trail and Elephant Canyon Formations, seen only in the walls of Cataract Canyon and its deeper tributaries. Above these relatively dull-colored strata, and exposed widely across the region, are colorful sandstone and mudstone deposits of Permian through Jurassic age (figure 1). The Wingate Sandstone and its little complimentary protective cap of lower beds of the Kayenta Formation, both of Early Jurassic age, make up the formidable cliffs that stand guard over the inner canyon country (Baars, 1993).

The primary factor that controlled deformation of these strata are deep-seated fractures in the Precambrian basement that formed somewhere around 1.7 to 1.6 billion years ago. The continental-scale basement fractures are believed to be wrench fault zones, much like the San Andreas fault zone in southern California, that were reacti-

vated repeatedly throughout Paleozoic and Mesozoic times (figure 2). The culmination of structural deformation of this basic framework came in Late Cretaceous and Early Tertiary time during the Laramide orogeny. The Laramide episode of mountain-building created the classic geologic structures seen today across the entire Colorado Plateau Province, once again jostling the ancient basement structural fabric. Finally, the intense erosional processes associated with the Green and Colorado river systems have sculpted the fairyland we see today.

The geologic story behind the magnicent scenery of Canyonlands National Park is one of complex interactions between structural forces and sedimentation over unbelievable eons of geologic time.

Figure 1. Along the White Rim, Canyonlands National Park. The White Rim Sandstone caps the ledges above the Organ Rock/upper Cutler red beds (both Permian in age) in the foreground. Storm clouds mask the La Sal Mountains in the distance.

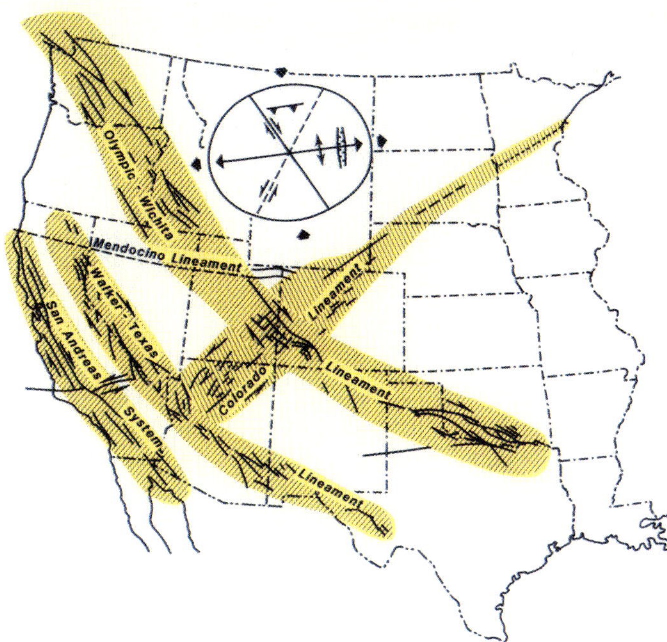

Figure 2. Regional map showing the major basement structural linea-ments that control the structural fabric of the Colorado Plateau. The strain elipsoid is oriented to coincide with the northwest-trending lin-eaments. Modified after Baars (1993).

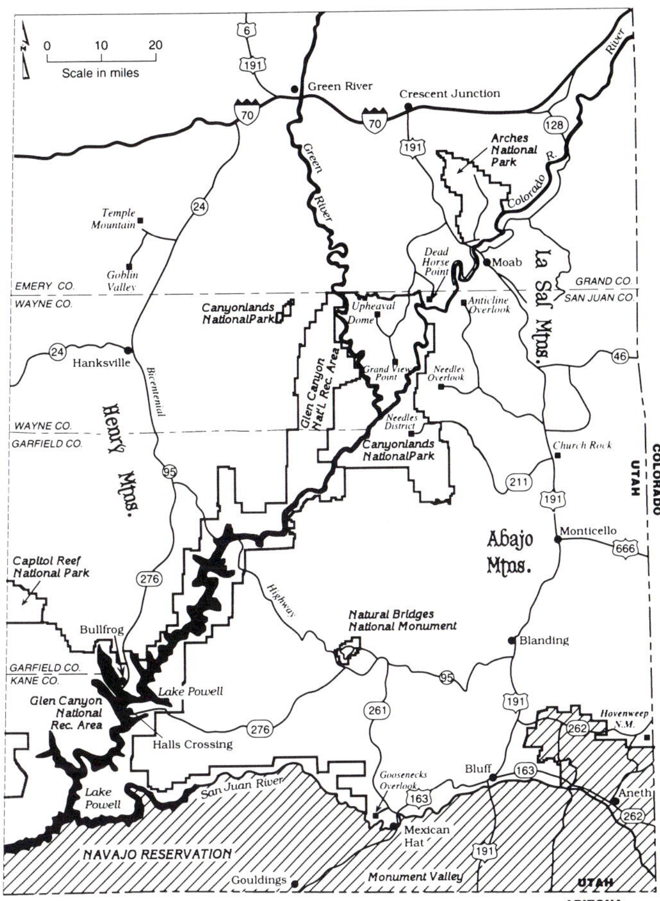

Figure 3. Regional index map showing the location of Canyonlands National Park relative to other geographic locations in the Four Cor-ners area.

Note: Originally, Canyonlands National Park was proposed to be a much larger geographic entity than was finally approved by Congress. Because petroleum and uranium exploration was still active at the time, along with grazing, there was opposition to the proposed boundaries. Consequently, a smaller skeleton National Park was designated by Congress in 1964 as "...only the heartland of this extraordinary area... the very minimum area which a true park should embrace." In 1999 the Su-perintendent's Office of Canyonlands National Park pro-posed "completion" of the park to extend the boundaries essentially rim-to-rim, using the massive Wingate Sand-stone façade as more natural boundaries for esthetic and operational purposes. As the extension of the boundaries for park "completion" has not been approved as of this writing, I have described areas that may be eventually in-cluded in Canyonlands National Park, but have shown the present boundaries on the index maps (figures 3 and 4).

STRATIGRAPHY

Pre-Pennsylvanian Strata

Rocks older than Middle Pennsylvanian age occur in the subsurface, but are nowhere exposed in Canyonlands National Park. The older Paleozoic and Precambrian rocks are known from deep drilling in the vicinity of the park, but are only exposed on the Colorado Plateau Province in the Grand Canyon, the San Juan Mountains, and the Uinta Mountains on the borders of the province. The ancient metamorphic basement rocks are also exposed on the Un-compahgre uplift, particulary at Colorado National Mon-

ument. Where rocks of Precambrian age have been pene-trated in deep drill holes in the vicinity of Canyonlands, they everywhere consist of pink, coarse-grained granite.

The **Cambrian System** is well represented deep be-neath Canyonlands National Park. The section is much like that of Grand Canyon, consisting of a basal transgres-sive sandstone, overlain by offshore marine mudstone and siltstone beds, and topped with rather thick carbonate rocks. The total section thickens toward the west. Forma-tion names used vary according to the petroleum geolo-gists who gather subsurface data. The lower sandstone section is usually called the Ignacio Formation, for expo-sures in the San Juan Mountains, the Tapeats Sandstone for Grand Canyon outcrops, or the Tintic Quartzite for the central Utah equivalent. The middle shale unit is usually referred to as the Bright Angel Shale, as it differs little from Grand Canyon exposures. The upper carbonate rocks are sometimes called the Muav Limestone, but more often Maxwell Limestone and Lynch Dolomite, for they resem-ble the central Utah section to a greater extent.

A regional unconformity tops the Cambrian interval, as rocks of Late Devonian age rest directly on the Late Cambrian. There are no known occurrences of strata of Ordovician, Silurian, or Early Devonian age anywhere on the Colorado Plateau Province.

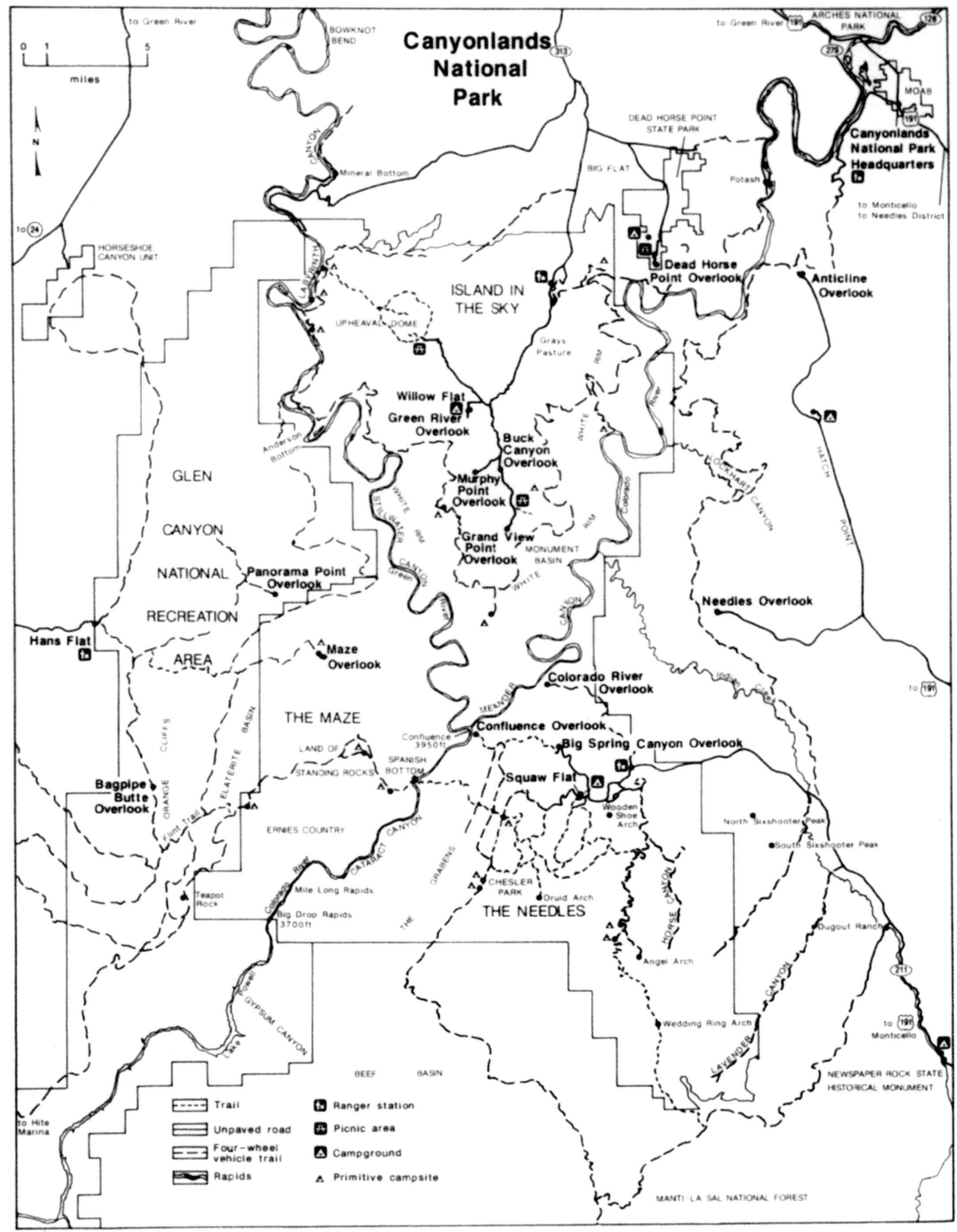

Figure 4. Index map showing localities discussed in this paper in and near Canyonlands National Park. From Baars (1989).

The **Devonian System** consists of three formations of Late Devonian age. The lower unit, the Aneth Formation, is a dark-colored, dense dolomite that occurs in the Four Corners area. It was named for the Aneth Trading Post in a cored interval in the Shell Oil Company No. 1 Bluff (NW1/4NE1/4 section 32, T. 39 S., R. 23 E.) well. The core contained the fossil remains of Late Devonian fish plates. Due to sparse drilling in the vicinity of Canyonlands National Park, the stratigraphic relationships are debateable north of about Monticello, Utah. It is probably present throughout the Canyonlands region, but the relationships are vague.

Overlying the Aneth Formation is a light-colored quartzite bed named the McCracken Member of the Elbert Formation, also designated in the Shell No. 1 Bluff well and named for McCracken Mesa. It is rather extensive in the Four Corners and San Juan Mountains region, but the McCracken Member only occurs in a few scattered wells drilled to the north. The McCracken is almost friable and produced oil at Lisbon oil field, south of Moab; however, it is not known to occur in the immediate vicinity of Canyonlands National Park. Instead, sandy dolomite marks the base of the Elbert Formation in Canyonlands. The upper member of the Elbert Formation consists regionally of platy, thin-bedded dolomite and apple-green shale interbeds, deposited in widespread intertidal mud-flats. The formation typically contains mud cracks, salt casts, and stromatolitic interbeds, attesting to a mudflat origin. Rocks assigned to the Elbert Formation in the Canyonlands region are thicker and contain more massive dolomite beds toward the northwest.

A generally dark-brown, massive, marine limestone, the Ouray Limestone, gradationally overlies the Elbert Formation. Although named in the San Juan Mountains near Ouray, Colorado, the distinctive limestone is widespread in occurrence in the subsurface of the eastern Colorado Plateau, including the Canyonlands region. The Ouray contains a distinctive assemblage of fossil brachiopods, typified by *Paurorhyncha endlichi*, that paleontologists consider to be latest Devonian in age. Endothyrid foraminifera have been reported from drill holes in the vicinity of Lisbon Valley. They occur near the top of the formation, and indicate an Early Mississippian (Kinderhookian) age. This may indicate that the Ouray Limestone was deposited across the temporal boundary, at least in the eastern Canyonlands country (Baars, 1966).

An important sequence of limestone and dolomite mark the **Mississippian System** throughout the Colorado Plateau. The massive carbonate formation was formerly called the Leadville Limestone for exposures in the nearby San Juan Mountains. More recently, and perhaps more appropriately, it has been called the Redwall Limestone for its similarities to extensive exposures in the Grand Canyon. The Redwall Limestone varies in thickness from about 400 to 500 feet beneath Canyonlands National Park.

The Redwall Limestone consists of two significant members in Canyonlands. The lower half of the formation consists of massive dolomite that is usually porous. Deep drilling has shown that the porosity in the lower member consistantly contains nothing but salt water. McKee (1963) documented a regional erosional unconformity that occurs at the middle of the Redwall Limestone in the Grand Canyon. Detailed studies of cores taken from deep wells in the Canyonlands region reveal a thin layer of limestone pebble conglomerate at the same horizon, indicating that the unconformity is, indeed, of regional importance. The lower member is probably of Early Mississippian (Kinderhookian) age, based on endothyrid foraminifera found in a few localities (Baars, 1966).

The upper member of the Redwall in Canyonlands is generally a massive limestone, although dolomitization may be important locally. Rather common endothyrids found in the member indicate a late Lower Mississippian (Osagean) age. The member is normally a dense, gray-colored micrite (lime mud) deposit. At selected localities along the high side of the major basement fault blocks, crinoidal bioherms (Walsortian banks) are common. They consist of thickened deposits of lime mud with large proportions of fossil crinoidal debris, with some bryozoa and brachiopods present. Where the crinoidal banks have been dolomitized, the lime mud has changed to a saccharoidal (sugary) texture and the crinoidal debris has been leached by the dolomitization process. The leached crinoids provide ample porosity, and the saccharoidal texture provides good interconnection of the pores, to produce excellent reservoir rocks for petroleum. The Lisbon oil field has produced over 50 million barrels of high-quality oil from both the Redwall limestone and the Devonian McCracken Sandstone since its discovery by Pure Oil Company in 1960 (Smouse, 1993; Utah Division of Oil, Gas and Mining, 2000). Gas injection recovery practices have precluded the need for pumps in the field. Several other smaller fields are present along the basement structural trend that produced from similar crinoidal bank deposits. One important abandoned oil field near the Canyonlands National Park northern boundary is the Big Flat field, near the intersection of the Island in the Sky and Dead Horse Point roads. Drill pipe collapse through the overlying salt section caused the premature abandonment of the field.

A thick red soil mantle, the Molas Formation, caps the Mississippian section across most of the Colorado Plateau and Southern Rocky Mountains Provinces. The lateritic soil developed during deep weathering of the Mississippian carbonate rocks in a humid, tropical climate that lasted through Late Mississippian and Early Pennsylvanian time. The widespread red mudstone is a product of paleokarst development that formed caves and mud-filled channels at the post-Redwall erosional surface. Where it has not been removed by the reworking of Pennsylvanian marine erosion, the Molas Formation forms a protective seal for underlying petroleum reservoirs.

Pennsylvanian Time

The relative quiescence of earlier Paleozoic time was

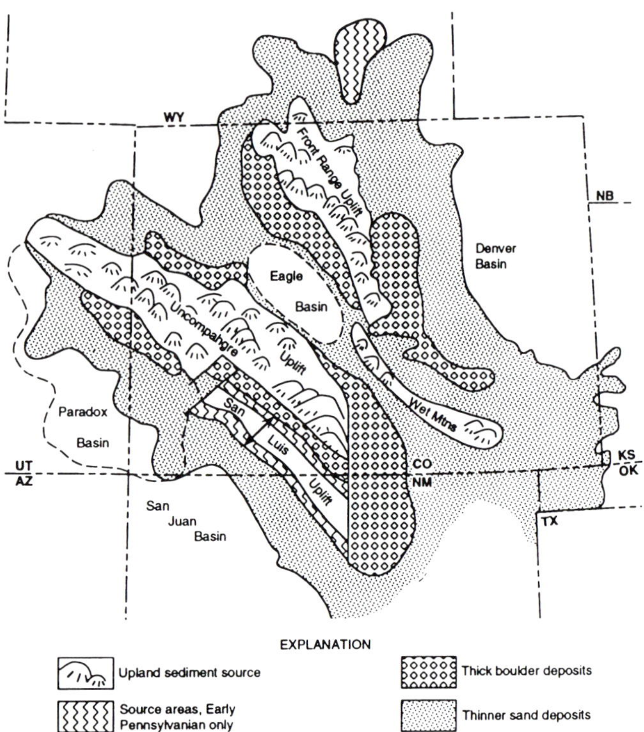

Figure 5. *The Ancestral Rocky Mountains as they appeared in Middle Pennsylvanian time, and the regional distribution of course sediments derived from the uplifts.*

Figure 6. *The maximum extent of salt in the Paradox Formation (Middle Pennsylvanian) is shown in light green, with the salt-intruded anticlines shown in dark green. Isopachous contours of gross salt thickness are in black. Major faults and anticlinal structures are shown in gray. From Baars and Stevenson (1982).*

drastically altered during Early Pennsylvanian time. The Ancestral Rocky Mountains of western Colorado begin to rise along pre-existing basement fault zones, forming significant highland areas from which untold cubic miles of arkosic sediments were derived (figure 5). Accompanying the rise of the Uncompahgre uplift segment of the Ancestral Rockies, vast amounts of arkosic sand and gravel were being deposited by streams along the eastern margin of the rapidly sagging Paradox basin. Extensive movement of northwest-trending wrench faults, and compensatory movement along northeast-trending conjugate faults, caused significant extension across the region now known as the Paradox basin. As a result, a deep, elongate depression formed, extending from the Four Corners area northwestward to about Price, Utah. As deep-water stagnation of seawater within the down-faulted extensional basin developed and salt began to accumulate on the sea floor, the Paradox evaporite basin began to form.

Sedimentation during Pennsylvanian and Early Permian times was cyclic on a global scale. It is widely believed that the cyclicity was caused by episodic glaciation in the polar regions. Sedimentation in the Paradox basin was no exception. Along the marginal shelves of the evaporite basin, cyclic alternation of marine limestone, sandstone, and shale predominate in the lower Pinkerton Trail and upper Honaker Trail Formations of the Hermosa Group. Several cycles of largely limestone, that are grossly equivalent to salt cycles of the Paradox Formation in the deep basin, are productive of oil and gas. These cycles have been given formal designations, named for oil fields

where each is productive. Baars and Stevenson (1982) proposed that these pay zones be designated as formal "stages" in the Desmoinesian Series, as they are time-stratigraphic units. From bottom to top, the Middle Pennsylvanian oil zones are: the Barker Creek, Akah, Desert Creek, and Ismay stages. More or less equivalent evaporites of the regionally intervening Paradox Formation were deposited in some 29 cycles in the deep basin center. The evaporite cycles were punctuated by thinner "black shale" (actually sapropelic dolomite) beds that would become prolific source beds for petroleum. The salt cycles have been numbered from top to bottom, Bed 1 through Bed 29, by Hite (1960).

Distribution of the salt cycles began in the central basin, spread laterally with time to maximum extent at mid-Middle Pennsylvanian (mid-Desmoinesian) time in the Akah cycle, and then individual cycles of salt deposits began to retreat toward the northwestern terminus of the basin. By the end of Middle Pennsylvanian time, salt deposition ended, and marine limestone and interbedded clastic rocks of the Honaker Trail Formation buried the entire basin.

It is a widely accepted interpretation that individual salt beds were deposited in relatively deep, highly saline seawater. During highstands of sea level, normal marine water could enter the Paradox basin across the shallow structural margins of the basin, depositing widespread black shale beds. As sea level lowered, seawater in the basin stagnated and intense evaporation occurred in the

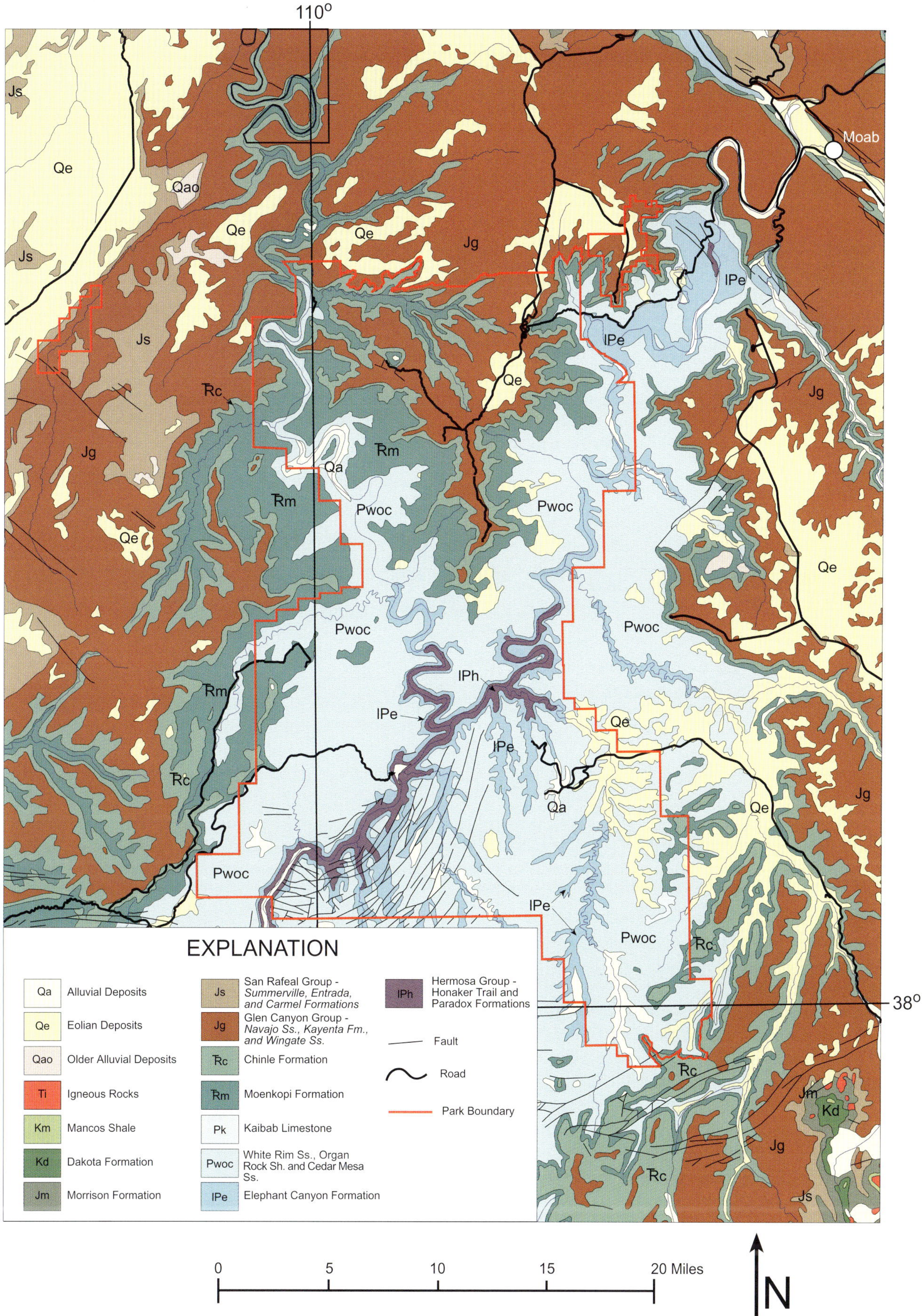

Figure 7. Geologic map of Canyonlands National Park and surrounding areas. Modified from Hintze (1980) and Hintze and others, (2000).

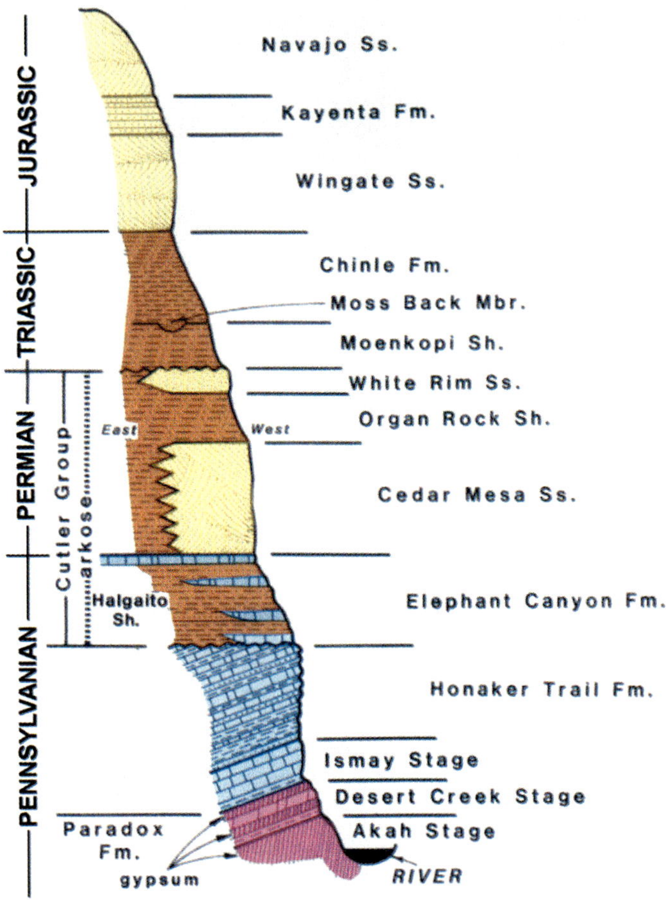

Figure 8. *Stratigraphic column of exposed rocks in Canyonlands National Park.*

Figure 9. *View of the canyon walls along the Colorado River near the head of Cataract Canyon in the heart of Canyonlands National Park. The ledgy cliffs in the lower two-thirds of the canyon wall are composed of interbedded limestone, sandstone, and shale of the Pennsylvanian Honaker Trail and Elephant Canyon Formations. The massive cliff at the skyline is the Permian Cedar Mesa Sandstone.*

highly arid climate. Brine formed at the surface of the stagnant sea and sank to the bottom as intense evaporation progressed. The resulting dense brine could not pass across the basin threshholds, as in-flowing seawater created a hydrodynamic barrier. Salt hoppers sinking through the deep brine layers then "seeded" salt deposition in the deep water of the basin.

Thickness of the gross salt section varies from zero at the Four Corners and mouth of Gypsum Canyon in Cataract Canyon to well over 4,000 feet in the heart of the basin (figure 6 on p. 50). It is impossible to estimate the depositional thickness of salt that may have accumulated in the eastern, deepest part of the Paradox basin. There, prior to Late Pennsylvanian time, salt had begun to flow into salt-piercement anticlines along the large, rejuvenated basement fault blocks, and the resulting thicknesses vary widely. Thickness of salt varies from zero along the high fault blocks underlying the southwest flanks Moab and Paradox Valley salt anticlines, to about 15,000 feet in the core of Paradox Valley as determined by drill holes.

West of the large salt anticlines in Canyonlands National Park, depositional thickness of the salt section varies from zero at the mouth of Gypsum Canyon to about 3,500 feet at the Moab salt anticline. Thickness of gross salt section is difficult to determine accurately even there, for salt flowage has bulged overlying strata to produce such anticlinal structures as Cane Creek anticline and Shafer dome (see Doelling and Chidsey, this volume), and, debatably, the Meander anticline.

Exposed Paleozoic Rocks

The oldest rocks that are exposed in Canyonlands National Park occur at, and near, the mouth of Gypsum Canyon near the southern park boundary (figure 7). There, about 400 feet of gypsum, with smaller amounts of dolomite and black shale, in the Akah cycle of the Paradox Formation, occur in the canyon bottom. Karst brecciation in the gypsum suggests that some salt had been present in the layer prior to erosional exposure. This appears to be near the depositional edge of salt in the Akah cycle, which is the cycle of maximum geographic extend of salt deposition. Salt in this cycle thickens to the east and northeast toward the basin center, as other salt cycles appear above and below. The evaporitic facies of the Desert Creek cycle overlies the Akah gypsum in the higher canyon walls, which is in turn overlain by the carbonate facies of the Ismay cycle and the high walls of Honaker Trail Formation (figure 8).

Gray, ledgy cliffs of cyclically alternating limestone,

sandstone, and shale of the Honaker Trail Formation comprise the bulk of the walls of Cataract Canyon upstream from Gypsum Canyon to near the Confluence of the Green and Colorado Rivers (figure 9). The dominantly marine section contains numerous fossil brachiopods, crinoids, bryozoa, corals, pelecypods, and gastropods. Commonly occuring fusulinids date the formation as Middle Pennsylvanian (middle Desmoinesian) to lower Late Pennsylvanian (upper Missourian) in age. The result of these exposures is rugged, often impassable, steep canyon walls more than a 1,000 feet high. It has been said that the internal stratigraphic relationships within the Honaker Trail are "layer cake" in nature. That is far from the truth, however, as detailed stratigraphic studies indicate the presence of numerous scoured surfaces and individual bed pinchouts within the beautiful exposures. The Honaker Trail Formation interfingers with evaporites of the Paradox Formation in the lower part, but overlies the Paradox evaporites in the upper parts throughout Canyonlands National Park and across the Paradox basin.

The Elephant Canyon Controversy

A regional erosional unconformity occurs at the top of the Missourian Honaker Trail Formation that extends from Canyonlands northwestward onto the San Rafael Swell, and beyond. There is some local angular discordance at the erosional surface near the Confluence of the Green and Colorado Rivers in the heart of Canyonlands National Park. As the unconformity is difficult to visualize from vertical aerial photos, its existence has been disputed. However, the widespread nature of the erosional surface and the distribution of the largely marine rock sequence above, indicate that the rocks were deposited in a separate basin that formed to the northwest of the Paradox basin (Baars, 1987a).

The younger section of alternating, largely marine, limestone, sandstone and shale, much like the underlying Honaker Trail Formation, was named the Elephant Canyon Formation by Baars (1962). Originally, available fusulinid determinations indicated a Lower Permian (Wolfcampian) age for the formation. Several years later, Amoco paleontologists re-examined the fusulinids and determined that they were of latest Pennsylvanian (Virgilian) age.

This was complicated further when Russian paleontologists proposed an "official" base of the Permian System, the Asselian Series in the Ural Mountains of Russia, to be considerably higher and younger in age to that in common use by American paleontologists (Davydov and others, 1995). The base of the Asselian Series is now placed at the base of the fusulinid Zone of *Pseudoschwagerina* (Davydov and others, 1995), and the conodont Zone of *Streptognathodus isolatus* (Chernykh and Ritter, 1997). Consequently, Ross and Ross (1994, 1998) have since proposed a new youngest Pennsylvanian series, named the Bursumian, for that extended interval between the widely recognized Virgilian (Late Pennsylvanian) and Wolf-

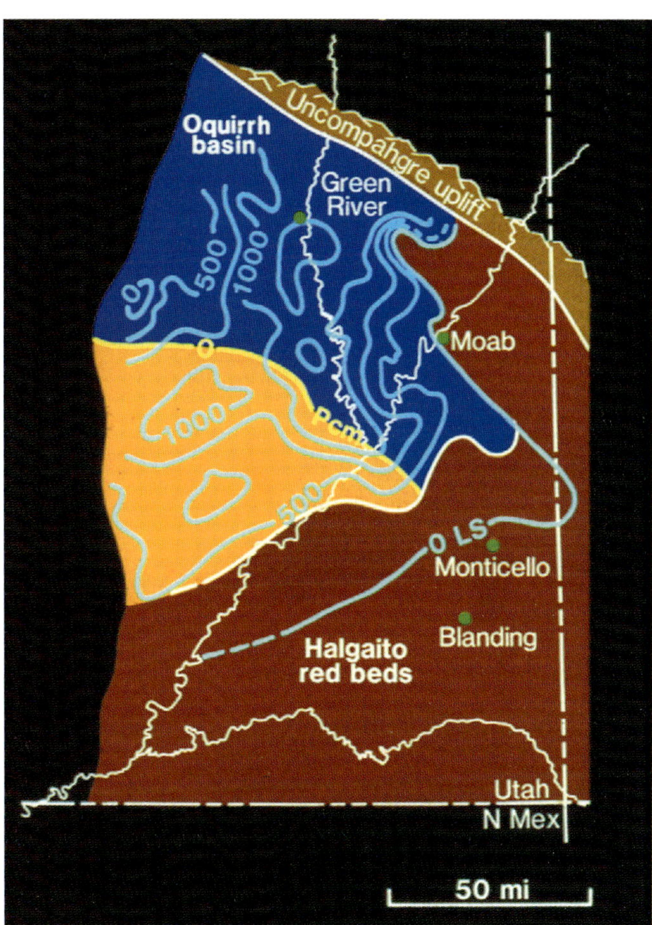

Figure 10. Isopach and facies map of the latest Pennsylvanian Elephant Canyon Formation. The blue area represents the presence of deposits of marine sediments, the yellow pattern is the partially equivalent Cedar Mesa Sandstone and the brown represents red beds of the equivalent Halgaito and undifferentiated Cutler Formations. Modified after Baars (1987a).

campian (Early Permian) Series.

The Elephant Canyon Formation grades southward along Cataract Canyon into the red beds of the Halgaito Shale. The facies change, although not apparent from distant views, is most pronounced between Gypsum Canyon and Dark Canyon. Both facies are now considered to be of Virgilian to Bursumian age, both Late Pennsylvanian (figure 10).

In the subsurface west and northwest of Canyonlands National Park, the upper Elephant Canyon Formation interfingers with the Cedar Mesa Sandstone (Baars, 1987a). As the upper Elephant Canyon fauna includes the fusulinid genus *Pseudoschwagerina*, in the cored General Petroleum 45-5-G well (section 5, T. 24 S., R. 15 E.), the upper Elephant Canyon and the Cedar Mesa Sandstone are now considered to be Wolfcampian (Asselian), or Early Permian in age.

The Permian System

Now that the Pennsylvanian-Permian boundary has been established internationally at the base of the *Pseudoschwagerina fusulinid* zone, sedimentary rocks of

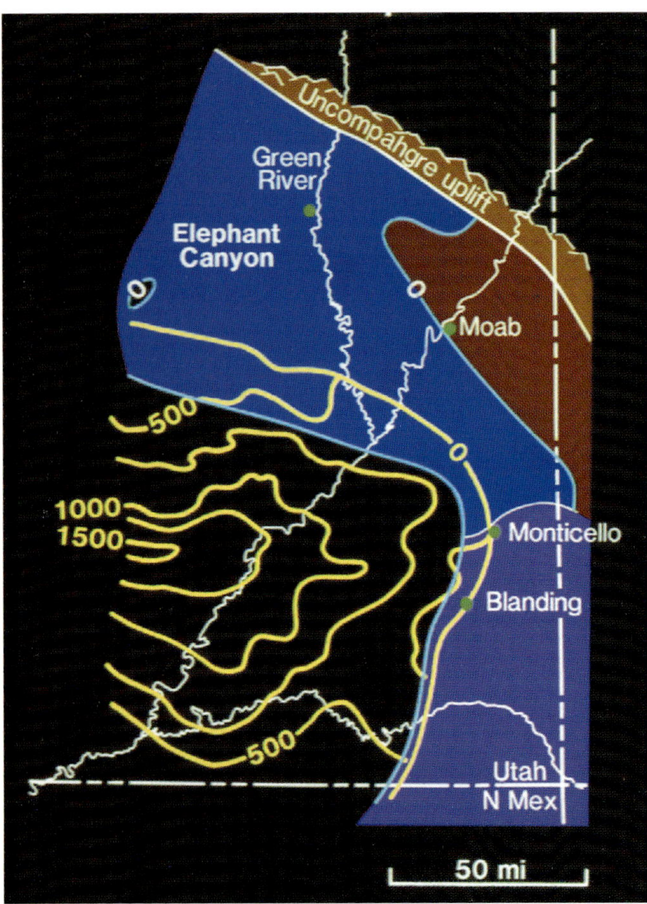

Figure 11. *Map showing the distribution of the Cedar Mesa Sandstone (yellow contours), the equivalent marine facies (blue), and gypsiferous facies (purple). Modified after Baars (1987a).*

Figure 12. *Eastern portion of Monument Basin from near the White Rim Trail, with the Abajo Mountains in the distance. The butte in the right upper middleground is capped by the thin White Rim Sandstone overlying red beds of the upper Cutler Formation (Organ Rock equivalent), all of Permian age. Thin white beds of sandstone in the foreground are distal interbeds of Cedar Mesa Sandstone, interfingering with arkosic red beds of the undifferentiated Cutler Formation.*

Canyonlands National Park require age revisions. As noted above, the lower Elephant Canyon Formation, as seen in Canyonlands National Park, and the equivalent Halgaito Shale, are considered to be Late Pennsylvanian in age. The Cedar Mesa Sandstone is now believed to be of Early Permian (Wolfcampian) age. Thus, the Cedar Mesa Sandstone, Organ Rock Shale, and White Rim Sandstone constitute the Permian System in Canyonlands National Park.

The **Cedar Mesa Sandstone** is a thick, cliff-forming sandstone that is seen as formidable cliffs at the top of the canyon walls in Cataract Canyon. It typically consists of numerous thick sets of highly cross-bedded, light-colored sandstone that is fine grained and well sorted. The Cedar Mesa attains a thickness of about 1,500 feet southwest of Canyonlands National Park (figure 11). Numerous red sandstone interbeds occur in The Needles District, where the Cedar Mesa interfingers with arkosic sandstone beds of the undifferentiated Cutler Formation.

Originally the Cedar Mesa Sandstone was believed to be wind-blown in origin, due to the large-scale cross-bedding found throughout the formation. Baars (1962) reported that the formation had a shallow marine origin based on the character of the cross-bedding, ripples, and convolute bedding. Fossil foraminifera, rare crinoid ossi-

cles, and occasional glauconite grains found in the sandstone gave further credence to the interpretation. Many modern workers again support the wind-blown origin. Fluctuating shorelines of Early Permian time, as seen in the subsurface to the west and northwest of Canyonlands, where marine rocks of the upper Elephant Canyon interfinger with sandstone beds of the Cedar Mesa, suggest that neither interpretation is totally correct. Some sets of cross-bedding are, without question, eolian; some alternating beds are shallow marine in origin. Horizontal surfaces between the bedding sets indicate exposure to weathering at times of shoreline withdrawal. A solution consistent with the available evidence is that the Cedar Mesa Sandstone as a coastal accumulation at or near a fluctuating shoreline. The same relationships occur between the age equivalent Pakoon Formation and the Esplanade Sandstone in western Grand Canyon (George Billingsley, written communication, 2000).

A spectacular facies change occurs in the Cedar Mesa Sandstone a short distance east of Cataract Canyon in Canyonlands National Park. There, long eastward-extending tongues of the light-colored Cedar Mesa Sand-

Figure 13. View from near the western end of the "River Road" near its junction with Shafer Trail. Note the vehicle on the road in the foreground for scale. The lower red beds are in the Organ Rock Shale (upper Cutler Formation), capped by ledges of the light-colored sandstone of the White Rim Sandstone. Above the White Rim are ledgy brown beds of the Moenkopi Formation (Lower Triassic), a thin ledge of Moss Back Member may be seen at the base of the upper slopes and ledges of the Chinle Formation (Upper Triassic), and the high cliffs are in the Lower Jurassic Wingate Sandstone, with its typical thin remnant of Kayenta Formation at the skyline.

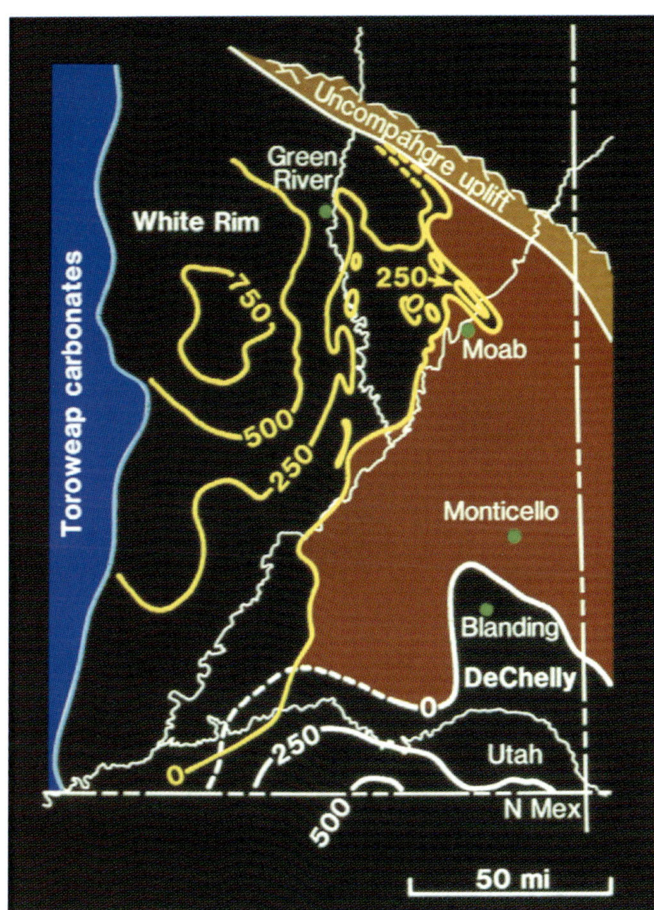

Figure 14. Regional isopach map of the White Rim Sandstone of Permian (Leonardian) age shown by yellow contours. The blue pattern to the west represents the equivalent marine strata of the Toroweap Formation. The white contours in the Four Corners area are of the slightly older DeChelly Sandstone of the Monument Valley region.

stone interfinger with equally long tongues of fluvial (river) red beds of the Cutler Formation. The banded appearance of this interfingering relationship is evident in The Needles District, and is best observed from a low-flying airplane. To the west, in Cataract Canyon, the section is entirely composed of nearly white sandstone cliffs; to the east of Salt Creek, the section is entirely of reddish brown Cutler arkose. Through The Needles District, color banding from the facies change is the rule. The facies change extends south along the eastern flank of the Monument upwarp to the Lime Ridge monocline (between Bluff and Mexican Hat) where the sandstone facies changes abruptly eastward into gypsiferous pink mudstone and siltstone of apparently lagoonal origin. A similar facies change occurs in the Virgin River Gorge of southwestern Utah (George Billingsley, written communication, 2000).

Overlying the Cedar Mesa Sandstone are red beds of the **Organ Rock Shale**. Although not a true shale in Canyonlands, the formation is found beneath the White Rim bench as a soft-weathering unit between the Cedar Mesa below and the cliff-forming White Rim Sandstone above. As is apparent along the river road from Potash westward across Canyonlands, the Organ Rock grades westward from coarse arkose of the fluviatile Cutler Formation into finer-grained and less resistant steeply slope-forming sedimentary rocks near the Confluence (figure 12). Farther afield, westward and southwestward from the Uncompahgre uplift source area, the Organ Rock becomes a mudstone/shale sequence as seen on upper Lake Powell. The Organ Rock Shale forms the slopes beneath the cliffs and buttes of DeChelly Sandstone in Monument Valley, and is the Hermit Shale in Grand Canyon.

At the apparent top of the Permian sequence in northwestern Canyonlands National Park is a light-colored cliff, the White Rim Sandstone, that forms prominent benches and terraces high above the Colorado and Green Rivers (figure 13). The **White Rim Sandstone** thickens markedly toward the northwest across Canyonlands, from a pinchout beneath Dead Horse Point to some 200 feet where it goes into the subsurface beneath the Green River (figure 14). There are no exposures of the White Rim Sandstone

Figure 15. *The eastern flank of the "Elaterite bar" developed in the White Rim Sandstone in Elaterite Basin west of the Green and Colorado Rivers. The sloping sandstone in the foreground is the depositional top of the White Rim Sandstone. The light gray and tawny-colored mudstone and siltstone above the White Rim surface is pre-Moenkopi red beds, here bleached by the lighter petroleum fractions of oil present in the White Rim Sandstone. The angular unconformity below the Moenkopi surface is visible in the upper right of the photograph.*

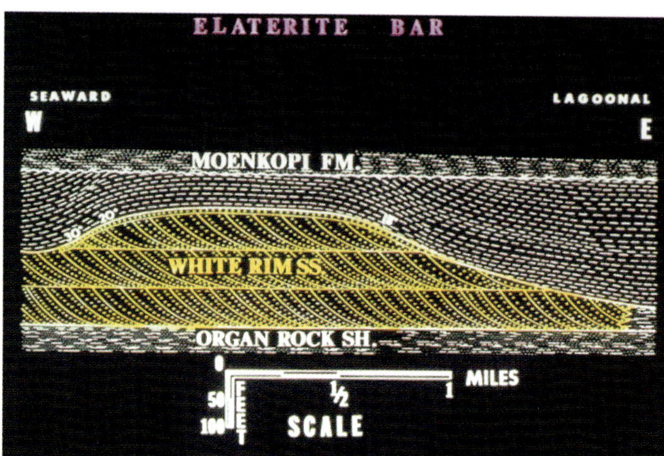

Figure 16. *Diagramatic cross section through the "Elaterite bar," illustrating the features seen in figure 15.*

east of the Colorado River in Canyonlands National Park. Horizontally bedded White Rim occurs east of the river, only in and near White Canyon to the south. Perhaps the coincidence of the eastern pinchout at the river is because of paleotopography caused by early salt flowage on the Meander anticline.

Like the Cedar Mesa Sandstone, the White Rim is considered by many to be entirely of windblown (eolian) origin. A detailed study of the formation by Baars and Seager (1970) revealed that the formation is of a nearshore marine origin in western exposures in Elaterite Basin (figure 15), grading eastward into shoreline eolian deposits at the foot of Shafer Trail beneath Dead Horse Point. As interpreted by this author, the White Rim Sandstone is an offshore bar in Elaterite Basin, a barrier bar at the head of Stillwater Canyon on the Green River at Mile 36 (Baars, 1987b), with beach and windblown deposits near the foot of Shafer Trail. Thus, it represents an expected landward gradation of facies along the eastern limits of the marine Toroweap Formation.

Thin red beds drape across the bedding surface at the edges of the White Rim Sandstone along the flanks of the Elaterite Basin offshore bar (figure 16) and the Stillwater Canyon barrier bar. The red beds are in turn truncated by an angular unconformity, apparently beneath the Triassic Moenkopi Formation (figure 17). As the rippled bedding at the top of the White Rim Sandstone is beautifully preserved, the red beds must have been deposited shortly after the White Rim (Toroweap) sea withdrew to the west (see figure 14). The red beds are stripped from the top of the sand bars by the erosional surface. These relationships

Figure 17. *The angular unconformity seen midway up the lower cliffs in the right half of the photograph occurs in red beds above the top of the White Rim Sandstone (not seen here), and below the lower Moenkopi Formation in lower Labyrinth Canyon on the Green River. Just down river from this point, an interpreted barrier bar in the White Rim Sandstone is exposed at the head of Stillwater Canyon. The draping lower beds seen here are along the eastern flank of the barrier bar. The high cliffs to the left consist of the Wingate Sandstone, with its capping beds of the Kayenta Formation.*

indicate that the red beds are of Permian age, and should not be considered basal Moenkopi. The isolated sections of red beds may be fluvial equivalents of the Kaibab Formation to the west, or an unnamed, previously unrecognized unit (Baars and Seager, 1970).

No rocks of Late Permian age are known to occur anywhere on the Colorado Plateau. Marine deposits of Late Permian age are found west of the Wasatch line in western Utah and far to the south in the Guadalupe "reef" trends in west Texas and southern New Mexico. The Colorado Plateau Province was left high and dry to the east and north of these seaways. Any continental sediments that may have been deposited on the Plateau did not survive the severe erosion that formed the post-Permian regional unconformity.

Rocks of Triassic Age

The Triassic **Moenkopi Formation** occurs directly above a regional erosional unconformity. Confusing stratigraphic relationships in the White Canyon area, south of Canyonlands National Park, and west of the Green River, leave some doubt as to the placement of the unconformity regarding the Hoskinnini Member of the Moenkopi in that region. The Hoskinnini Member, as defined, overlies the DeChelly Sandstone west of Monument Valley. The DeChelly Sandstone, however, grades rapidly northward into sandy red beds near Piute Farms on the San Juan River. Both the DeChelly red beds and the Hoskinnini can be traced physically northward into White Canyon, where the combined unit is mapped as Hoskinnini overlying the White Rim Sandstone; actually, a stratigraphic impossibility. Then there are the red beds that drape across the sand buildups of Elaterite Basin and along the Green River. Are these in the Hoskinnini Member? If so, is the Hoskinnini Member Permian or Triassic?

The Moenkopi Formation in Canyonlands National Park consists of dark brown mudstone and siltstone that contain myriad sedimentary structures characteristic of tidal mud flat deposition. Small-scale ripples, dessication cracks, rain drop impressions, and burrows typify bedding surfaces. These are so well preserved that the rock is used widely for decorative stone in walkways and rock walls throughout the region. The formation is responsible for broad terraces and slopes above the more resistant Permian rocks throughout the park (figure 18). The formation here averages about 600 feet in thickness. The entire formation grades westward into marine deposits along the western border of the Colorado Plateau.

The top of the Moenkopi Formation is scarred by erosional features, especially channels, sometimes cut rather deeply into the upper surface. Stream sand and gravel of the **Moss Back Member of the Chinle Formation** commonly in-fill the paleotopography on the eroded surface throughout Canyonlands. Because of the sporadic nature of the erosional depressions, the distribution of the Moss Back Member is irregular and spotty. Similar, but somewhat older, occurrences of stream deposits on the regional disconformity occur south of Canyonlands National Park, from White Canyon and North Wash southward, where it is named the Shinarump Conglomerate Member of the Chinle Formation. In both cases, the basal fluvial deposits form low cliffs and benches that mark the base of the Chinle Formation. The Moss Back and Shinarump Conglomerate Members contain significant amounts of uranium in Canyonlands, where they were heavily prospected and mined in previous years. The uranium ores occur mostly in point bar river deposits in association with fossil plant debris.

Upper members of the Chinle Formation consist of, in ascending order, the mudstone member (Petrified Forest), the "black ledge member," and the upper siltstone member (Church Rock) (Molenaar, 1987). Pastel colors pre-

Figure 18. The "Airport Tower" along the White Rim Trail, Canyonlands National Park. The bench in the foreground is on top of the White Rim Sandstone. The low bluffs in the middleground are the Moenkopi Formation, with the Chinle Formation exposed in the slopes beneath the buttes. The cliffs in the background and the pinnacles consist of the Wingate Sandstone and the Kayenta Formation, capped by lower beds of the Navajo Sandstone.

dominate and vary widely in the slope-forming members (figure 18). Fine-grained sandstone and siltstone cliffs of the "black ledge member," heavily stained with desert varnish, are conspicuous midway up the formation in Canyonlands. The formation is about 500 feet thick in Canyonlands. The Petrified Forest Member contains bentonite, which makes dirt roads treacherous when wet. Upper members of the Chinle Formation form broad slopes beneath the Wingate Sandstone cliffs that surround Canyonlands National Park, and are often heavily masked by debris fallen from the cliffs.

Jurassic Deserts

Rocks of Early Jurassic age belong to the **Glen Canyon Group** in Canyonlands National Park. The group consists of the lower Wingate Sandstone, the middle Kayenta Formation and the upper Navajo Sandstone. Near-vertical cliffs of Wingate Sandstone, capped by thin remnants of the Kayenta Formation, form the nearly impenetrable walls surrounding all but the southern limits of the park. A recent proposal to "complete" Canyonlands National Park by expansion of the boundaries to the Wingate façade, would create an entity with natural topographic

Figure 19. Dead Horse Point from the Colorado River. The entire section from the Elephant Canyon through the Kayenta Formation is beautifully exposed here.

and geologic integrity. The foreboding cliffs are only crossed by roads where rivers and major tributaries breach the cliffs, or where trails and primitive roads were literally blasted from the bare rock.

The **Wingate Sandstone** forms massive, usually brown cliffs that are seen in detail to be highly cross-stratified. The formation is generally believed to be of a windblown origin, but what appears to be fluvial bedding occurs in some localities. The cliffs are unbroken, with little or no evidence of individual bedding surfaces apparent in distant views of the outcrop. Thin, highly resistant beds of the lower Kayenta Formation invariably cap the Wingate cliffs (figure 19). Although the Wingate Sandstone was originally believed to be of Late Triassic age, palynological studies and regional stratigraphic relationships reveal that it is of Early Jurassic age (Peterson and Pipiringos, 1979). The formation is between 300 and 400 feet thick in Canyonlands, although it thins drastically to less than 100 feet across salt-bulged structures such as the Cane Creek anticline. The desert sandstone, actually the Lukachukai Member of the Wingate Sandstone, directly overlies the basal Jurassic (J-0) unconformity of Pipiringos and O'Sullivan (1978). The regional distribution across the Colorado Plateau of the unconformities within the Jurassic System was recognized by Pipiringos and O'Sullivan (1978), who designated each by code. J-0 occurs at the base of the

Lukachukai Member of the Wingate Sandstone, J-2 occurs at the top of the Navajo Sandstone, J-3 is at the top of the Entrada Sandstone and J-5 is at the base of the Morrison Formation.

The **Kayenta Formation** is a fluvial (river) sandstone that forms low purplish cliffs and ledges above the massive Wingate cliffs. Outcrops almost universally display classic cut-and-fill deposits typical of fluvial deposition. Roads and trails are readily built along the very resistant benches eroded from the formation, especially obvious at the head of Shafer Trail in the Island in the Sky District of Canyonlands National Park. Bedding surfaces are well known for their display of dinosaur tracks and trails throughout the areas of exposure. The Kayenta Formation typically thickens in synclines formed by salt withdrawal, and thins against the salt-intruded structures.

Overlying the ledgy cliffs of the Kayenta Formation are generally rounded, nearly white cliffs and erosional mounds of the **Navajo Sandstone**. Exposures of the Navajo everywhere show spectacular, large-scale cross-beds typical of classic windblown sand accumulations. Magnificent exposures of Navajo Sandstone abound on the Kayenta-capped plateaus surounding Dead Horse Point and the Island in the Sky District of Canyonlands National Park. The J-2 erosional surface is not apparent within Canyonlands, as the top of the Navajo is not exposed within the park boundaries.

The **San Rafael Group** overlies the J-2 unconformity, although the group is not exposed anywhere within Canyonlands National Park boundaries. Where it is preserved near the park, as along State Highway 313 leading into Dead Horse Point and the Island in the Sky District, the group consists of the lower Carmel Formation and the upper Entrada Sandstone. Terminology is confused in this region because the Carmel was re-designated the Dewey Bridge Member of the Entrada Sandstone for simplicity in mapping Arches National Park. The Carmel/Dewey Bridge is easily distinguished, where exposed, by crinkly thin red beds above the Navajo Sandstone and below the massive sandstone cliffs of the Slickrock Member of the Entrada Sandstone in the Moab region.

The Entrada Sandstone consists of the lower Slickrock Member (above the Carmel/Dewey Bridge) and the Moab Tongue, a light-colored sandstone with minor cross-bedding, that occurs above a prominent horizontal bedding plane. The Slickrock Member hosts myriad natural arches in nearby Arches National Park. Rocks of the Salt Wash Member of the Morrison Formation unconformably overlie the Entrada in that region.

STRUCTURAL GEOLOGY

Canyonlands National Park lies astride the northplunging nose of the Monument upwarp. The north-south trending anticlinal structure extends some 100 miles from near Kayenta, Arizona to the area between Canyonlands National Park and Green River, Utah. It is about 60 miles

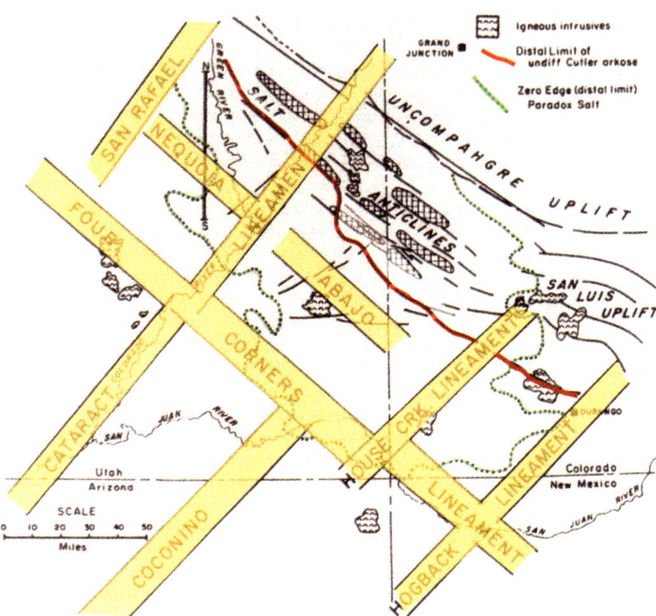

Figure 20. Generalized map showing the relationships between basement lineaments of the eastern Colorado Plateau and the distribution of salt-related features. The distal limit of salt deposition is shown in green; the limits of coarse-grained Cutler arkose is shown in red. Note that the general course of the Colorado River follows the Cataract (Colorado) lineament. Modified after Stevenson and Baars (1987).

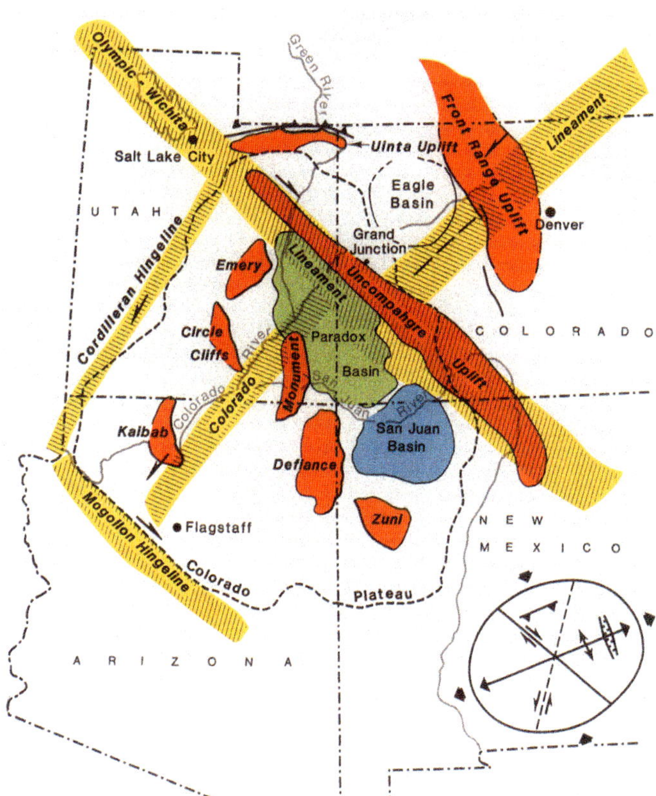

Figure 21. Generalized map showing the relationship of the Colorado Plateau, and its major structural features, to continental-scale basement fracture zones. From Baars and Stevenson (1982).

wide from Comb Ridge on the east to Lake Powell on the west, with some 6,000 feet of structural relief at Elk Ridge. The structure is a complex anticlinal feature south of the Abajo Mountains and the Four Corners lineament in White Canyon, consisting of several anticlines and synclines scattered across the broad asymmetrical arch (figure 6). To the north, however, the Monument upwarp is a large, uncomplicated anticline that plunges regionally northward under Canyonlands National Park. Fracture patterns along the plunging axis of the broad fold, and their effects on the underlying Paradox salt, have created unique topographic features in both The Needles District and along the White Rim in the Island in the Sky District. Other structural features, such as The Grabens, Meander anticline, Shafer Dome, Cane Creek anticline, and the major salt-intruded anticlines east of the park, are related to the presence of salt at depth throughout the park.

Although the broad structure of the Monument upwarp is a Laramide feature, it and the smaller structures in and near Canyonlands National Park are localized by basement fracture zones that originated in Precambrian time (figure 20). Basement faults occur in northwest- and northeast-oriented patterns throughout the region (Baars and others, 1995). The major salt-intruded anticlines of the eastern Paradox basin lie along basement faults of considerable magnitude that trend northwesterly, as does the greater Paradox basin. Other northwest-trending faults of lesser magnitude form smaller salt-thickened anticlines in parts of Canyonlands; the Cane Creek anticline northeast of the park is a prominent example.

An important northeast-trending fault zone underlies the general course of the Colorado River from near Grand Junction, Colorado to eastern Grand Canyon (figure 21). The basement fault zone was recognized by Case and Joesting (1972) as a result of geophysical studies of the region by the U.S. Geological Survey. They called it the "Colorado lineament" for its position beneath the general course of the river. Later, Warner (1978) included the basement fault with numerous other northeasterly basement faults that occur in a broad band some 50 miles wide, and called the entire fault zone the "Colorado lineament." Because of the possible confusion resulting from these designations, it was renamed the "Cataract lineament" by Stevenson and Baars (1987). Regardless of the name, the Colorado River generally follows the fractured zone in surface rocks above the basement fault zone across Canyonlands. Minor recurrent seismic activity along the basement fracture zone was documented by Wong and others (1987) in their study of earthquake activity along the Meander anticline for the Woodward-Clyde Paradox basin search for suitable nuclear waste disposal sites.

Anticlines Along the Colorado River Trend

There are conflicting opinions concerning anticlines along the Colorado River trend (Case and Joesting, 1972; Huntoon, 1982; Baars, 1993). In general these are: (1) development of anticlines was due to basement vs. salt

Figure 22. Promell dome, a prominent gypsum plug, is obvious at the mouth of Lower Red Lake Canyon in Spanish (Cataract) Bottom on the Colorado River. The jumbled mass in the middle of the photograph is a contorted mass of gypsum, black shale, and dolomite brought up from the Paradox Formation at shallow depth. The sedimentary rocks dipping away from the gypsum core consist of the upper Honaker Trail and Elephant Canyon Formations, capped on the left with cliffs of Cedar Mesa Sandstone.

Figure 23. The first appearance of the Meander anticline along the Colorado River in Canyonlands National Park. The rocks exposed here are in the Elephant Canyon and lower Cutler Formations.

movement, (2) the relationship of the surface structure to the basement lineament is incidental, and (3) the structure has virtually nothing to do with salt flowage. Several structural features in and near Canyonlands National Park mark the course of the "Cataract lineament." Three gypsum plugs, circular pipes formed by salt and gypsum intrusion, occur in the depths of Cataract Canyon along the basement lineament and the southwestern extension of the "Meander anticline." The first gypsum plug is an obvious intrusive feature at the mouth of Red Lake Canyon in Spanish Bottom (or Cataract Bottom) at the head of the infamous series of rapids in Cataract Canyon (figure 22). The enclosing sedimentary rocks are punched upward by a mass of highly contorted gypsum and black shale, named "Prommel dome." A second similar gypsum plug, "Harrison dome," occurs in Tilted Park about 4 miles downstream where tar seeps sometimes mar the beach in low water stages. A third is "Crum dome"at the mouth of an unnamed canyon at Mile 206.9 (Baars, 1987b). All were named for prominent geologists who studied the region in the early days. All occur along a northeast-trending anticlinal feature known as Meander anticline.

From about "Crum dome," a low relief but sharp-crested anticline, the "Meander anticline," extends upstream to the northeast along the course of the Colorado River (figure 23). It is commonly believed that erosion of the canyon by the river unloaded the underlying salt, causing it to flow upward beneath the river. Many have observed that the narrow anticline follows the meandering course of the river. Canyon cutting may have enhanced the structure in the last few millennia. In fact, if studied in detail, the canyon meanders about the crest of the struc-

ture, rather than the structure meandering with the river. And the course of the river generally follows the basement lineament, which in turn controls the location of the salt-flowage structure, just as in the large salt anticlines to the east.

The deep-seated basement discontinuity beneath the course of the Colorado River in Canyonlands was first noted by Case and Joesting (1972) as a result of geophysical studies of the region by the U.S. Geological Survey. The feature is also prominent in detailed aeromagnetic studies (Parker Gay, verbal communication, 1992), and is still rather weakly active as basement adjustments seen in earthquake studies by Wong and others (1987). Several other northeast-trending structural lineaments in and near Canyonlands were documented by Hite (1975). Although the presence of this particular basement structure, and any associated salt flowage, has not been documented by drilling, many others in the Paradox basin have been (see Baars and Stevenson, 1982).

A great many geologists working on the Colorado Plateau place the blame on the origin of all structures onto the Laramide and younger orogenies, as that is about all that is seen at the surface. They don't take into account what has happened prior to that great structural episode. In fact, it has been shown by numerous geologists that the "peculiar" orientation of regional structures in the province has been inherited from the Precambrian basement structural fabric that has been repeatedly rejuvenated throughout Phanerozoic time. (Note the documentation of minor modern earthquakes along the Cataract [Colorado] lineament by Wong and others, 1987.) It is clear to many that the Laramide orogeny merely rejuvenated and enhanced basement fault patterns. Any structural analysis must consider the entire tectonic history of an area to fully understand the present features seen at the surface today.

Farther upstream, where the depositional thickness of Paradox salt is much greater, the Colorado River wanders

Figure 24. The gentle crest of Shafer Dome as it appears along the "River Road" near Shafer Canyon. The gently arched surface in the middle of the photograph is on the "Shafer lime," the top-most limestone of the Elephant Canyon Formation.

Figure 26. Aerial view of parts of Cataract Canyon and The Grabens, looking south from above the Confluence of the Green and Colorado Rivers.

Figure 25. Aerial view of the Cane Creek anticline's northwesterly plunging nose, view looking to the northeast. All visible strata thin markedly across the salt-thickened structure, verifying the continued growth on the structure through Permian to Jurassic time.

from the Permian Cutler Formation up through the Jurassic Wingate Sandstone thin dramatically across the crest of the anticline, providing detailed documentation of the time and extent of salt flowage.

The Grabens

In The Needles District of Canyonlands National Park, prominent topographic features related to the presence of salt at depth are spectacular. The Needles complex of pinnacles was formed by weathering along the complex fracture pattern formed at the crest of the plunging Monument upwarp. The presence of salt at depth probably enhanced the extensional fracture system, widening individual fractures to the weathering process. Interfingering of the light-colored Cedar Mesa Sandstone with the reddish Cutler arkose caused the color-banding that adds much to the beauty.

Down the western flank of the Monument upwarp, immediately west of the axial region, the fracture system is enhanced and down-dip gravity gliding of surface rocks above the salt form huge slump blocks known as "The Grabens" (figure 26). These are actually a complex system of horsts and grabens that extends from near the crest of the uplift westward and down-dip to Cataract Canyon (McGill and Stromquist, 1975). Dissolution of the salt by groundwater has no doubt played a large role in forming the faulted complex by collapse of overlying strata. Gravity gliding of the collapse blocks down the regional dip to the west has obviously caused the extensional fault system to form. Salt flowage into the Meander anticline along the river has certainly been important, perhaps to initiate gravity gliding, but the existence of the canyon itself undercuts the system down-dip, causing continued movement of the slump blocks toward, and into, Cataract Canyon (figure 27). Gravity gliding is active today, as seen by huge slump blocks forming the walls of Cataract Canyon and constricting the course of the river to form the

in and out of Shafer dome (figure 24). This much larger salt-bulged anticline, lying directly below Dead Horse Point, trends generally northeastward along the Cataract lineament. The salt flowage that formed the anticline was documented by the old Midwest Exploration Company J.H. Shafer No. 1 well, (SE1/4SE1/4 section 16, T. 27 S., R. 20 E.) drilled in 1926-27.

The Cane Creek anticline, a few miles to the northeast of Shafer Dome, developed along the more prominent northwesterly basement fracture zone (figure 25). During the early days of mining potash salt from the Paradox Formation at a depth of about 2,000 feet in Cane Creek anticline, miners found that the salt section was highly contorted due obviously to salt flowage. The complexity and expense of underground mining of such disturbed strata led to the solution mining process that is now underway. In this case, it is readily obvious that all stratigraphic units

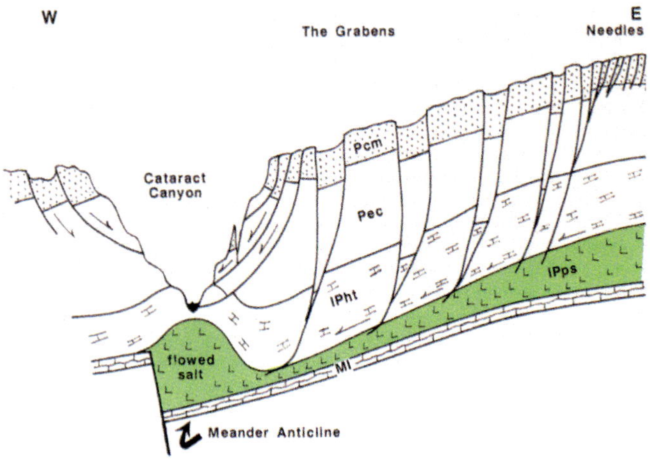

Figure 27. Diagrammatic cross section through The Grabens in The Needles District of Canyonlands National Park. Strata from the Honaker Trail (IPht), Elephant Canyon (Pec), and Cedar Mesa (Pcm) Formations are highly fractured by collapse and gliding on top of the Paradox salt (IPps), shown in green, down-dip into Cataract Canyon and the Meander anticline. The Mississippian Leadville Limestone (Ml) lies below the Paradox salt. Modified after Baars (1989).

Figure 28. Aerial view of Upheaval Dome, looking toward the north. The outer light-colored ring of rocks is the Navajo Sandstone, the next brown ring is the Kayenta Formation, with the reddish-colored inner cliffs of the Wingate Sandstone. The core of the prominent dome is composed of the Chinle Formation and the bleached Moenkopi Formation, with pierced sandstone dikes of the White Rim Sandstone in the very apex of the structure. Is this a meteorite impact feature, or a pinched-off salt dome?

infamous rapids. Fissures along individual faults within The Grabens are widening at a measurable pace today, as the land glides on the salt surface quietly toward the canyon.

Upheaval Dome

One of the most spectacular topographic features in Canyonlands National Park is Upheaval Dome, located in the Island in the Sky District (figure 28). The origin of the sharply up-turned structure has been under debate for generations. In the early days, numerous studies have attributed its origin variously to meteorite impact (Boone and Albritton, 1938), cryptovolcanic activity (Bucher, 1936), or salt penetration (Harrison, 1927). Geophysical studies suggest that the structure is a gravity low and a magnetic high (Joesting and others, 1967), yet both characteristics are of such minor degree as to essentially eliminate either salt flowage or volcanic intrusion as the cause. A recent seismic line found "little or no salt" at depth.

The late Gene Shoemaker was involved in mapping Upheaval Dome for the U.S. Geological Survey in the 1950s. Early on he thought that the feature was a classic salt dome. Others, especially petroleum geologists from the Gulf Coast region, believed that it is an exposed example of a classic Gulf Coast salt dome. After all, there is salt at depth regionally, there are other salt-intruded anticlines in the vicinity, there is a well-defined rim syncline surrounding the structure, and some evidence indicates that it has a long growth history. Then Mattox (1975) examined the evidence for various possible origins in detail and concluded that Upheaval Dome is indeed a salt dome.

Then in the early 1980s, Gene Shoemaker and his co-workers, with a thorough knowledge of planetary geology, declared the structure to be unquestionably formed by me-

teorite impact (Shoemaker and Herkenhoff, 1983, 1984). A paper published recently by Kreins and others (1999) revealed the results of detailed mapping that show, without doubt, that Upheaval Dome is indeed an impact structure. This interpretation is further advanced by Huntoon (this volume).

Almost simultaneously, five geologists from the Bureau of Economic Geology, University of Texas, and Exxon Production Research Company, published the results of a detailed re-study of Upheaval Dome (Jackson and others, 1998). They presented convincing evidence, through detailed mapping, that the fracture patterns and continued growth of the structure, at least through Jurassic time, required long-term, continuous growth from salt rising from depth. To explain the lack of salt beneath the structure today, they postulated that the diapir flowed salt onto the surface in Chinle Formation through Navajo Sandstone time, and then the salt blob was pinched off, the flowed salt having since been eroded away. Another mechanism to cause a salt pinch-off would be that the mother source of salt was depleted in the late development of the structure.

So now what? One camp proved that Upheaval Dome is unquestionably a meteorite impact structure. Another has convincingly proven that the structure is a pinched-off salt dome. Who are we to believe? It seems that "we find what we are looking for." This is not a case where "further research is needed." Upheaval Dome has been sufficiently trampled by dedicated geologists. What is needed is an unbiased interpretation of the many well-documented structural features, studied in detail by both factions that are found in the field. In the meantime, as always, the solution to the problem is subject to one's personal bias.

CLASSIC GEOLOGICAL SITES

Island in the Sky District

Northern Canyonlands National Park is referred to as the Island in the Sky District (figure 4). The primary points of interest are overviews of Canyonlands from viewpoints above the Wingate-Kayenta cliffs, and Upheaval Dome. Of course, when visiting the Island in the Sky District, Dead Horse Point State Park should not be bypassed enroute (see Doelling and Chidsey, this volume).

Grand View Point in the Island in the Sky District is similar to Dead Horse Point, in that the grand view is of the western parts of Canyonlands National Park and the proposed extended boundaries. The La Sal Mountains to the east and the Abajo Mountains to the south, are laccolithic intrusive igneous ranges that form prominent geographic landmarks. Monument Basin lies directly below the Wingate-Kayenta cliffs, intricately eroded from the White Rim Sandstone into red beds of the Organ Rock--equivalent Cutler Formation (see figure 12). White Rim Trail is visible around the margin of Monument Basin, with straight scars of seismic lines shot in the 1950s still visible across the White Rim bench. The Needles District is visible in the middle distance to the south, with the Cedar Mesa-Cutler interfingering visible in clear weather conditions. Junction Butte is to the right (west), lying between the Green and Colorado Rivers near the Confluence, and displaying good exposures of the Triassic rocks beneath the Wingate Sandstone cliffs.

A broad vista of western Canyonlands National Park is provided at the **Green River Overlook** nearby to the west. White Rim Trail is seen wandering across the White Rim bench immediately below, with the Green River visible beyond. The White Rim Sandstone is noticeably thicker here than seen from the previous viewpoints. The skyline to the west across the Green River consists of the Orange Cliffs of Wingate Sandstone, with Ecker Butte and Elaterite Butte forming spires capped by Wingate Sandstone beneath the western cliffs, all within Glen Canyon National Recreation Area and within the proposed extended park boundaries. Beneath Elaterite Butte is Elaterite Basin with its legendary tar seeps in the White Rim Sandstone. Just to the east, on the light-colored bench of the Cedar Mesa Sandstone, is The Maze District and the Land of Standing Rocks between Elaterite Butte and Cataract Canyon.

Upheaval Dome is a short distance by road (12 miles) from the Green River Overlook, and a must stop on any tour of the Island in the Sky District. From the picnic ground at the foot of the dome, a short, but steep, rocky trail leads up to the rim and viewpoint into the heart of Upheaval Dome. The overlook is on top of the Wingate Sandstone cliffs, with the Kayenta Formation forming the racetrack low rim around the structure. The crags in the depths of the eroded dome are sandstone dikes from the White Rim Sandstone below.   Here the Moenkopi sur-

rounding the sandstone dikes is a tawney color due to bleaching of the usually reddish-brown mudstone by the seepage of natural gas from the White Rim Sandstone. For a discussion of the origin of Upheaval Dome, see a summary in this paper and more details in Huntoon (this volume).

Shafer Trail

Not for the faint of heart, the way down from the Island in the Sky is **Shafer Trail**, a tortuous dirt road that winds its way down the majestic cliffs that guard inner Canyonlands National Park. The route was no doubt originally an Indian trail, later used by cattlemen. In the 1950s, the Atomic Energy Commission "improved" the trail for the hardy uranium explorers in order to facilitate their search along the exposures of the Moss Back Member of the Chinle Formation below the Wingate cliffs.

Shafer Trail begins a short distance east of the Visitor Center and follows ledges in the Kayenta Formation precariously perched atop the Wingate cliffs. At the first obvious switchback, where the road descends into the top of the Wingate Sandstone, one is strongly advised to shift into low gear to avoid brake fires. Through sharp, rocky hairpin turns, the road descends the magnificent(?) cliff and then passes down-section through the upper varicolored members of the Chinle Formation and the ledge-forming Moss Back Member. Near the base of the steep grade, the chocolate brown Moenkopi Formation, with myriad sedimentary structures of tidal flat origin, rests atop the light-colored bench on the White Rim Sandstone (figure 13).

A close inspection of the White Rim Sandstone reveals that well-developed eolian dune sand rests on horizontal, crinkly beds of similar sandstone. The upper dune sand is of obvious origin, but the lower crinkly beds could be interpreted to be either beach deposits or horizontal wind-blown interdune layers. Either interpretation leads to the conclusion that one has reached the White Rim, or Toroweap, shoreline. The formation pinches out a short distance to the east beneath Dead Horse Point, and is not present south of the Colorado River canyon.

At the foot of Shafer Trail, at the top of the White Rim Sandstone, there is an obvious junction. The road ahead is the White Rim Trail that proceeds along the prominent bench on top of the White Rim Sandstone. The bench follows alongside the Colorado River to near the Confluence and then turns northward above the Green River to Mineral Bottom and the Horsethief Trail. Four-wheel-drive vehicles are a must for parts of the trail, and it is best to allow two days for the long trip.

Turn left at the road junction and descend down-section through the White Rim Sandstone into Shafer Canyon, carved from the arkosic Cutler Formation. A high-clearance vehicle is strongly recommended, and four-wheel-drive works even better. The road and the wash lead to a prominent limestone bench-maker called locally the "Shafer lime." This is the topmost limestone of the Elephant Canyon Formation of latest Pennsylvanian age, and forms the caprock for the inner canyon of the Colorado River below. From here the road crosses Shafer Dome, a salt-bulged anticline, passes the brilliant blue evaporation ponds of the potash mining operation, and crosses the Cane Creek anticline into Potash, the operating mill. There, surprisingly, the road is abruptly paved for the trip across the salt-withdrawal syncline to Moab.

The Needles District

Southern Canyonlands National Park, south and east of the Colorado River, is known as **The Needles District**. The region is approached by driving south from Moab on U.S. Highway 191 to the junction with State Highway 211. The road heads west, crosses the Shay graben near Newspaper Rock, and then proceeds mainly along Indian Creek to the park entrance. The massive cliffs above the road are the Wingate Sandstone overlying the Chinle and Moenkopi slope-forming formations. Finally, the road crosses down-section through the Moss Back Member and the Moenkopi Formation into the reddish-brown, arkosic Cutler Formation.

The picturesque needles are carved by erosion along a complex fracture system in the Cedar Mesa Sandstone. Color banding in the spires is due to the interfingering of the light-colored Cedar Mesa Sandstone from the northwest with the reddish-colored fluvial sandstone tongues of the Cutler Formation to the east. The erosional patterns and the banded bedding is well diplayed around the Visitor Center and Squaw Flat campground. A short, but scenic, drive by dirt road west from the campground provides further views of the rugged topography and colorful rocks before reaching a picnic area at Elephant Hill. Travel from there into The Grabens and Chesler Park is necessarily by high-clearance, four-wheel-drive vehicles only.

The Grabens consist of a series of linear horsts and grabens formed by extension in the Cedar Mesa Sandstone as the surface rocks glide down-dip toward Cataract Canyon on top of the Paradox salt (figures 26 and 27) (McGill and Stromquist, 1975). The surface slumping is active today, so beware of widening fractures along the graben-horst interfaces. Exit from The Needles District is by the way we entered.

The Maze District

One can't get there from here! But there are three ways to try. The first, and perhaps most difficult, is to go to Spanish Bottom (Cataract Bottom) by boat, and make the rather arduous climb up the trail on the west side of the canyon wall. From the top, in the Doll House, exploration of **The Maze** is restricted to foot traffic.

A second approach can be even worse. From State Highway 24, the route from Green River to Hanksville west of Canyonlands, take the dirt road heading east from near the Goblin Valley turnoff to Hans Flat (46 miles), then to French Spring, the Bagpipe Butte Overlook, and the

Figure 29. *The Maze and the "Land of Standing Rock" from near Elaterite Butte, west of the Green and Colorado Rivers in Canyonlands National Park. Light-colored rocks seen in The Maze are intricately carved gullies and canyons in the Cedar Mesa Sandstone. The spires on the distant horizon are erosional remnants of the Organ Rock Shale, all Permian in age.*

head of Flint Trail. The long, dusty drive makes the river trip to Spanish Bottom more desireable. Then lookout! Flint Trail is another terrifying descent down the Wingate and Chinle cliffs, much like Shafer Trail, but steeper with sharper switchbacks and bare rock road surface. The gravel road topping was washed out by a torrential rain storm in 1964, and as of my last trip, it had not been replaced. Flint Trail ends at Flint Flat, a bench on the Moss Back Member of the Chinle Formation. From there, a road to the right goes south toward Teapot Rock and the road into The Maze and the Land of Standing Rocks. Turn left and one descends down-section through the Moss Back Member and the Moenkopi Formation into Elaterite Basin. These roads can be treacherous when wet, making four-wheel-drive vehicles a must down from the top of Flint Trail.

The recommended route into The Maze District is from the Hite Marina on Lake Powell, north on another dirt road heading toward Teapot Rock, The Maze, and Elaterite Basin. The road begins from State Highway 95, west of Blanding and southeast of Hanksville, between the bridges across the Colorado and Dirty Devil Rivers across from the Hite Airport. The turnoff is easy to miss, but a search for a dirt road heading north between the bridges will be successful. This is another long, dusty, and sometimes rough drive that basically follows along the Organ Rock-Cedar Mesa contact. The Organ Rock Shale and the overlying White Rim Sandstone provide scenic views to the west of topographic features such as The Sewing Machine.

As the road approaches Teapot Rock, a turn to the right leads to The Land of Standing Rocks at the head of The Maze (figure 29). The "standing rocks" are erosional pillars of Organ Rock Shale rising above the Cedar Mesa Sandstone plateau. The Maze is an area of intricate canyons carved down into the Cedar Mesa Sandstone. Exploring The Maze on foot is fascinating and sometimes confusing because of the tortuous canyon complex.

The road ahead at Teapot Rock crosses the base of the butte eroded from the White Rim Sandstone, repleat with petroliferous saturation of the sandstone at the southern terminus of the Elaterite sand bar (figure 15). The road proceeds up the steep slope of the Moenkopi Formation to the top of the Moss Back Member of the Chinle Formation on Flint Flat. This stretch of road is treacherous when wet, and four-wheel-drive is necessary. Crossing Flint Flat and passing the foot of Flint Trail, the road again descends steeply through the Moss Back Member and Moenkopi Formation. Before starting the steep descent, it is wise to check the road ahead for washouts before putting the vehicle in jeapardy.

At the base of the Moenkopi slope, the road follows a shallow valley alongside the west flank of the Elaterite sand bar in the White Rim Sandstone. The surface expression of the "offshore bar" is obvious, as the mound represents the upper surface of the bar as it appeared in Middle Permian time. Arroyos cutting at right angles through the bar allow easy access to interior sedimentary structures that constitute the original core of the feature. Small dribbly tar seeps are common in the arroyo walls. Large-scale cross-bedding within the bar is capped by thin-bedded caprock displaying large-scale oscillation ripples. The capping layers cross the top of the mound, with the oscillation ripples becoming smaller as the top of the bar, and shallower water, is approached. It has been suggested that the cross-bedded inner sandstone represents eolian bedding in the White Rim Sandstone, and that the rippled surface layers are the reworked top of sand dunes by nearshore water of the Kaibab Formation. This interpretation is highly debatable, as there is no direct evidence to support a two-part history. The cross-bedding is unlike eolian bedding, and the rippled surface most likely resulted from the stagnation and withdrawal of the Toroweap (White Rim) sea (Baars and Seager, 1970).

The road eventually crosses the top of the sand bar, alongside a much-eroded landing strip of the 1950s, and descends the eastern flank of the bar. Here one can again appreciate the original shape of the "offshore bar," and the rippled caprock as the ripples enlarge down-slope into deeper water shoreward from the bar. A short distance beyond the east slope of the White Rim bar, a shallow wash to the right of the road, not quite visible from the road, is floored with an impressive tar seep. Indeed, the presence of the offshore bar in the White Rim Sandstone and the nearby up-dip pinchout of the formation, provide an unexcelled example of a classic stratigraphic oil trap.

Above the edge of the sandstone mound, bleached red beds drape across the rounded feature, and in turn are beveled by erosion beneath red beds of the Moenkopi Formation. The bleaching is obviously the result of petroliferous seepage from the tar-saturated White Rim Sandstone below. The zone of bleaching closely follows the sloping surface of the sandstone mound, and the discoloration grades laterally into red beds away from the mounded surface. As the rippled top of the sand bar is beautifully preserved from erosion of Late Permian time, it is believed that the White Rim Sandstone was almost immediately buried by the capping red beds that must be of Middle Permian, rather than Triassic, age (Baars and Seager, 1970).

Elaterite Basin and its intriguing story of Permian deposition within the White Rim Sandstone are presently within Glen Canyon National Recreation Area. The proposal to expand the boundaries of Canyonlands National Park will include the preserved offshore bar and its classic stratigraphic oil trap.

Similar draping and bleached red beds occur above the barrier bar in the White Rim Sandstone at the head of Stillwater Canyon on the Green River. There, however, water-formed cross-bedding is capped by eolian sedimentary structures within the White Rim, all capped by the bleached red beds.

ACKNOWLEDGMENTS

Critical reviews by Peter W. Huntoon and George Billingsley greatly improved an earlier version of the manuscript, and were appreciated. Extensive editorial revisions by Doug Sprinkel and Tom Chidsey are greatly appreciated. Renate Baars contributed much to the drafting of the illustrations, especially coloring of existing drawings.

REFERENCES

Baars, D.L., 1962, Permian System of the Colorado Plateau: American Association of Petroleum Geologists Bulletin, v. 46, p. 149-218.

—1966, Pre-Pennsylvanian paleotectonics--key to basin evolution and petroleum occurrences in the Paradox Basin, Utah and Colorado: American Association of Petroleum Geologists Bulletin, v. 50, p. 2082-2111.

—1987a, The Elephant Canyon Formation revisited, in Campbell, J.A., editor, Geology of Cataract Canyon and Vicinity: Four Corners Geological Society Guidebook, p. 81-90.

—1987b, Cataract Canyon via the Green or Colorado Rivers, a river runner's guide: Evergreen, Colorado, Cañon Publishers Ltd., p. 1-80.

—1989, Canyonlands Country: Grand Junction, Colorado, Cañon Publishers, Ltd., 140 p.

—1993, Canyonlands Country: Salt Lake City, Utah, University of Utah Press, 138 p.

Baars, D.L., and Seager, W.R., 1970, Stratigraphic control of petroleum in the White Rim Sandstone (Permian) in and near Canyonlands National Park, Utah: American Association of Petroleum Geologists Bulletin, v. 54, p. 709-718.

Baars, D.L., and Stevenson, G.M., 1982, Subtle stratigraphic traps in Paleozoic rocks of Paradox basin, *in* Halbouty, M.T., editor, The deliberate search for the subtle trap: American Association of Petroleum Geologists Memoir 32, p. 131-158.

Baars, D.L., Thomas, W.A., Drahovzal, J.A., and Gerhard, L.C., 1995, Preliminary investigations of basement tectonic fabric of the conterminous USA: Basement Tectonics 10, p. 149-158.

Boone, J.D., and Albritton, C.C., Jr., 1938, Established and supposed examples of meteoritic craters and structures: Field and Laboratory, v. 6, p. 44-56.

Bucher, W.H., 1936, Cryptovolcanic structures in the United States: International Geological Congress, 16th, Washington, D.C., Report , v. 2, p. 1055-1084.

Case, J.E., and Joesting, H.R., 1972, Regional geophysical investigations in the central Colorado Plateau: U.S. Geological Survey Professional Paper 736, 31 p.

Chernykh, V.V., and Ritter, S.M., 1997, *Streptognathodus* (Conodonta) succession at the proposed Carboniferous-Permian boundary stratotype section, Aidaralash Creek, northern Kazakhstan: Journal of Paleontology, v. 71, p. 459-474.

Davydov, V.I., Glenister, B.F., Spinosa, C., Ritter, S.M., Chernykh, V.V., Wardlaw, B.W., and Snyder, W.S., 1995, Proposal of Aidaralash as GSSP for the base of the Permian System: Permophyles, no. 26, p. 1-9.

Harrison, T.S., 1927, Stratigraphic results of a reconnaissance in western Colorado and eastern Utah: American Association of Petroleum Geologists Bulletin, v. 11, p. 111-133.

Hintze, L.F., 1980, Geologic map of Utah: Utah Geological and Mineral Survey, scale 1:500,000.

Hintze, L.F., Willis, G.C., Laes, D.Y.M., Sprinkel, D.A., and Brown, K.D., 2000, Digital geologic map of Utah: Utah Geological Survey Map 179DM, scale 1:500,000.

Hite, R.J., 1960, Stratigraphy of the saline facies of the Paradox Member of the Hermosa Formation of southeastern Utah and southwestern Colorado: Four Corners Geological Society 3rd Field Conference Guidebook, p. 86-89.

Hite, R.J., 1975, An unusual northeast trending fracture zone and its relation to basement wrench faulting in the northern Paradox basin, Utah and Colorado, *in* Fassett, J.E., editor, Canyonlands country: Four Corners Geological Society Guidebook, p. 217-224.

Huntoon, P.W., 1982, The Meander anticline, Canyonlands, Utah--an unloading structure resulting from horizontal gliding on salt: Geological Society of America Bulletin, v. 93, p. 941-950.

Huntoon, P.W., Billingsley, G.H., Jr., and Breed, W.J., 1982, Geologic map of Canyonlands National Park and vicinity, Utah: Canyonlands Natural History Association, 1 sheet, scale 1:62,500.

Jackson, M.P.A., Schultz-Ela, D.D., Hudec, M.R., Watson, L.A., and Porter, M.L., 1998, Structure and evolution of Upheaval Dome--a pinched-off salt diapir: Geological Society of America Bulletin, v. 110, p. 1547-1573.

Joesting, H.R., Case, J.E., Plouff, D., 1967, Regional geophysical investigations of the Moab-Needles area, Utah: U.S. Geological Survey Professional Paper 516-C, 21 p.

Kreins, B.J., Shoemaker, E.M., and Herkenhoff, K.E., 1999, Geology of the Upheaval Dome impact structure: Journal of Geophysical Research, v. 104, no. E8, p. 18,867-18,887.

Mattox, R.B., 1975, Upheaval Dome, a possible salt dome in the Paradox Basin, Utah, *in* Fassett, J.E., editor, Canyonlands country: Four Corners Geological Society Guidebook, p. 225-234.

McGill, G.E., and Stromquist, A.W., 1975, Origin of Graben in The Needles District, Canyonlands National Park, Utah: Four Corners Geological Society 8th Field Conference Guidebook, p. 235-243.

McKee, E.D., 1963, Nomenclature for lithologic subdivision of the Mississippian Redwall Limestone, Arizona: U.S. Geological Survey Professional Paper 475-C, p. C21-C22.

Molenaar, C.M., 1987, Mesozoic rocks of Canyonlands Country, *in* Campbell, J.A., editor, Geology of Cataract Canyon and vicinity: Four Corners Geological Society Guidebook, p. 19-24.

Peterson, Fred, and Pipiringos, G.N., 1979, Stratigraphic relations of the Navajo Sandstone to Middle Jurassic formations, southern Utah and northern Arizona: U.S. Geological Survey Professional Paper 1035-B, 43 p.

Pipiringos, G.N., and O'Sullivan, R.B., 1978, Principal unconformities in Triassic and Jurassic rocks, western interior United States--a preliminary survey: U.S. Geological Survey Professional Paper 1035-A, 29 p.

Powell, J.W., 1875, Exploration of the Colorado River of the west and its tributaries: U.S. Government Printing Office, Washington, D.C., p. 3-145.

Ross, C.A., and Ross, J.R.P., 1994, The need for a Bursumian Stage, uppermost Carboniferous, North America: Permophyles, v. 24, p. 3-6.

—1998, Bursumian Stage, uppermost Carboniferous of Midcontinent and southwestern North America: Carboniferous Newsletter, v. 16, p. 40-42.

Shoemaker, E.M., and Herkenhoff, K.E., 1983, Impact origin of Upheaval Dome, UT [abs.]: Eos (Transactions American Geophysical Union), v. 44, p. 747.

—1984, Upheaval Dome impact structure [abs.]: Houston, Lunar and Planetary Science XV, 15th Lunar and Planetary Institute, Abstracts, part 2, p. 778-779.

Smouse, DeForrest, 1993, Lisbon field, *in* Hill, B.G., and Bereskin, S.R., editors, Oil and gas fields of Utah: Utah Geological Association Publication 22, non-paginated.

Stevenson, G.M., and Baars, D.L., 1987, The Paradox, a pull-apart basin of Pennsylvanian age: *in* Campbell, J.A. editor, Geology of Cataract Canyon and vicinity: Four Corners Geological Society Guidebook, p. 31-50.

Utah Division of Oil, Gas and Mining, 2000, December 1999 oil and gas production report: Utah Division of Oil, Gas and Mining, non-paginated.

Warner, L.A., 1978, The Colorado lineament--a Middle Precambrian wrench fault system: Geological Society of America Bulletin, v. 89, p. 161-171.

Wong, I.G., Humphrey, J.R., Kollmann, A.C., Munden, B.B., and Wright, D.D., 1987, Earthquake activity in and around Canyonlands National Park, Utah: Four Corners Geological Society 10th Field Conference Guidebook, p. 51-58.

Capitol Reef National Park
Photo courtesy of the Utah Travel Council

Geology of Utah's Parks and Monuments
2000 Utah Geological Association Publication 28
D.A. Sprinkel, T.C. Chidsey, Jr., and P.B. Anderson, editors

Geology of Capitol Reef National Park, Utah

Thomas H. Morris[1], Vicky Wood Manning[1], and Scott M. Ritter[1]

ABSTRACT

Capitol Reef National Park envelops a nearly 100-mile-long fold in the uppermost sedimentary rocks of the Earth's crust. This monoclinal flexure is called the Waterpocket Fold.

The bedrock strata exposed in the Waterpocket Fold area range in age from Permian to Tertiary and represent a wide variety of ancient environments including open marine, parallic (nearshore), fluvial (river), lacustrine (lake), and ergs (sandy deserts). Structural features including folds, fractures, and faults are evidence of the major tectonic events of the past. Together the bedrock strata and structural features depict the ever-changing paleogeography and climatic conditions that existed in Utah and western North America during the past 275 million years. This geologic history indicates that western North America moved from a low latitude, passive margin tectonic setting in the Permian to an active, convergent margin setting at middle latitudes by Late Cretaceous time. In the process, the Capitol Reef area experienced orogenic (mountain building) events in a variety of styles. Later, two stages of volcanism from the late Oligocene to early Miocene and again in the Pliocene, covered much of the folded strata in the area.

Mechanical and chemical erosion of the Waterpocket Fold has provided the numerous arches, bridges, monoliths, cathedrals, slot canyons, strike valleys, massive landslides, and other geomorphic features seen in the park. The erosive process exposes views of other interesting geologic features such as igneous dikes and sills, gypsum domes, oyster reefs, petrified logs, dinosaur bones, bentonitic hills, and unusual soft-sediment deformational features. An understanding of the geologic processes that created the landforms and vistas of the park will enhance the visitor's appreciation of this desert wonderland called Capitol Reef National Park.

INTRODUCTION

The Name of the Park

Capitol Reef National Park derives its name from the numerous rounded "domes" of rock that were created by headward stream erosion, downcutting, slope retreat, and natural weathering of the cross-bedded Jurassic Navajo Sandstone. Many of these dome-shaped outcrops are similar in shape to the rotundas of capitol buildings (figure 1). The term "reef" was applied by early geographers and pioneers when first exploring the West to impassable areas of rock, derived from their background as maritime sailors. Hence, geographical "reefs" of the Colorado Plateau are not ancient marine reefs but are simply barriers to travel.

The park owes its existence to a long fold in the upper

Figure 1. Westward view of Navajo Dome along Highway 24. Navajo Dome is one of many dome-shaped features created by mechanical and chemical weathering of the Jurassic Navajo Sandstone.

[1] *Department of Geology, Brigham Young University, Provo, UT 84602*

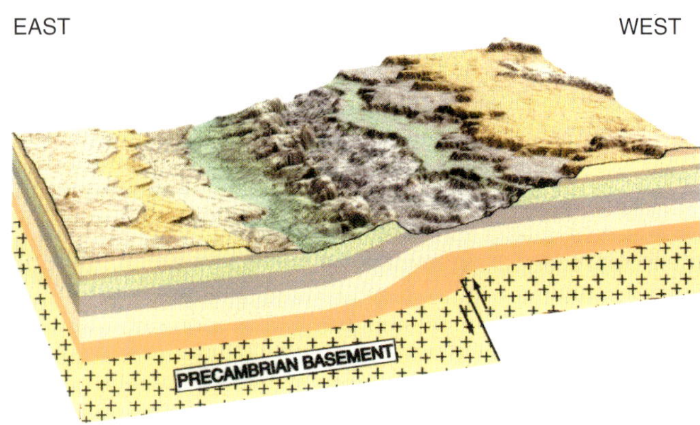

Figure 2. Block diagram of a monocline. Brittle Precambrian basement rocks rupture (creating a fault scarp) due to compressional forces. Overlying ductile sedimentary strata drape the fault scarp creating a monocline. Monoclines are characteristic features of the Colorado Plateau. Note the erosional profile of the folded sedimentary strata (modified from Tasa Graphics).

sedimentary strata of the Earth's crust. Geologists call this type of fold a monocline (see discussion below). The name of the monocline at Capitol Reef is the Waterpocket Fold. Waterpocket refers to the holes, pots, and pockets sculpted into the bedrock by erosional processes. These pockets, which temporarily store water from rain or snow were an important source of water for ancient peoples and early pioneers.

Geology of the Park

The centerpiece of Capitol Reef National Park is the Waterpocket Fold, a nearly 100-mile- long monoclinal flexure in the Earth's upper crust. A monocline is defined as a local steepening or "kink" in otherwise uniformly horizontal, flat rock. Monoclines are characteristic structural features of the Colorado Plateau, a major geologic province of North America.

The Waterpocket Fold was produced by the collision of the North America plate and the Pacific Ocean plate during Late Cretaceous and early Tertiary time. Tectonic stresses translated far inland from the collision zone resulted in differential uplift of the Capitol Reef area. Precambrian basement rocks west of the park were uplifted along a major fault zone nearly 7,000 feet higher than their counterparts in the eastern portion of the park. Overlying sedimentary rocks responded more passively without major faulting although fracture systems did develop. The overlying sedimentary pile deformed in a more ductile fashion, passively draping the growing irregularity (figure 2). As a result, flat-lying strata forming the topographically high mesas west of the park bend sharply downward along the axis of the Waterpocket Fold before flattening again deep in the subsurface below Caineville (figure 3).

Uplift was accompanied by erosion. Thousands of feet of Late Paleozoic and Mesozoic strata were stripped from the region by erosional processes. Differential erosion laid bare the structure of the Waterpocket Fold and

created the spectrum of desert landforms for which Capitol Reef is famous. Over 10,000 feet of variegated strata, ranging from Permian to Tertiary in age, are exposed within the park boundaries (figures 4 and 5). These tell a 275 million year-long story of changing environments and changing landscapes, of which the present-day desert ecosystem is only the latest chapter.

The enchantment of Capitol Reef National Park, located in the red rocks country of south- central Utah (figure 3), results from its vastness, scenic vistas, and geologic variety. There is an unparalleled array of landforms – arches, natural bridges, slot canyons, monoliths, cathedrals, and hogbacks – carved into colorful sedimentary strata of the Waterpocket Fold, one of the longest continuously exposed monoclines in the world. Add to this a wealth of more subtle geologic features such as classic strike valleys, dikes and sills, intrusive gypsum domes, massive landslides, oyster reefs, petrified logs, dinosaur bones, bentonitic hills, unusual soft-sediment deformational features, and one can begin to appreciate the allure of Utah's fifth national park.

Serenity and oneness with nature can easily be achieved at Capitol Reef National Park. The visitor who ventures off the road and into the back country will be rewarded with unforgettable memories of its geology, solitude, and beauty.

STRATIGRAPHY

Figure 4 illustrates the succession of sedimentary strata exposed in Capitol Reef National Park. Figure 5 shows their geographic distribution. Seventeen formations range in age from Permian in the west to Cretaceous in the east portions of the park. The distinguishing characteristics and depositional environments of these formations are discussed below.

Permian System

Cutler Group

The Cutler Group is composed of (in ascending order) the Elephant Canyon Formation, Cedar Mesa Sandstone, Organ Rock Shale, and White Rim Sandstone throughout most of southeastern Utah. At Capitol Reef National Park, however, only the sandstone formations are represented: rivers have not eroded deeply enough to expose limestones and arkosic sandstones of the Elephant Canyon Formation and the Organ Rock Shale pinches out east of the park. Where the Organ Rock Shale is missing, quartzose sandstones of the White Rim Sandstone cannot be readily distinguished from those of the underlying Cedar Mesa Sandstone. Therefore, on figure 5, the Cutler Group is mapped as a single stratigraphic entity.

The Cutler Group is best exposed along the walls of the Fremont River and other incised drainages (for example, the Goosenecks at site #9 of figure 3) in the western portion of the park (figure 5). Steep, inaccessible cliffs of

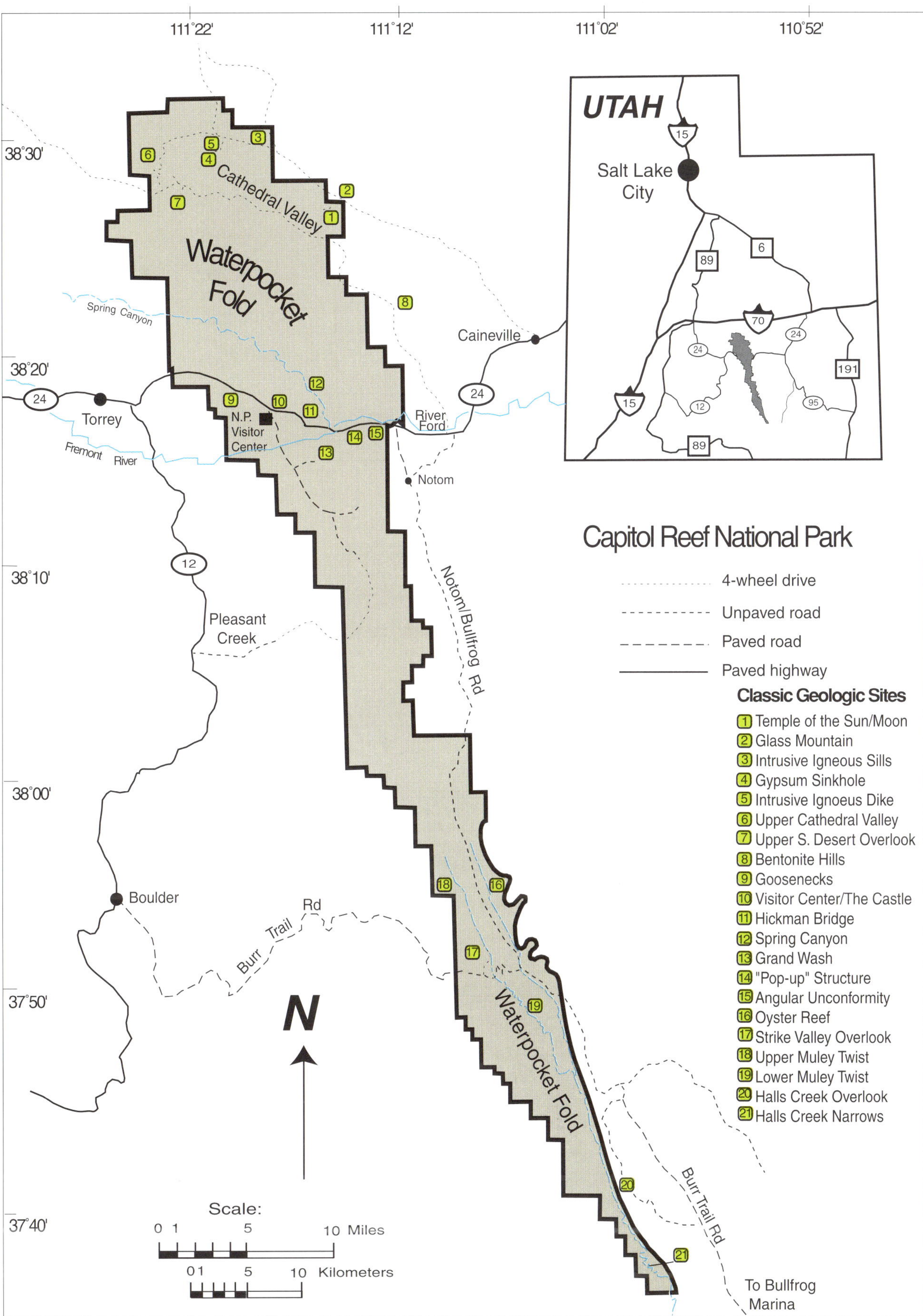

Figure 3. Location map of Capitol Reef National Park, south-central Utah. Numbers are locations of classic geologic sites (see text discussion on classic geologic sites).

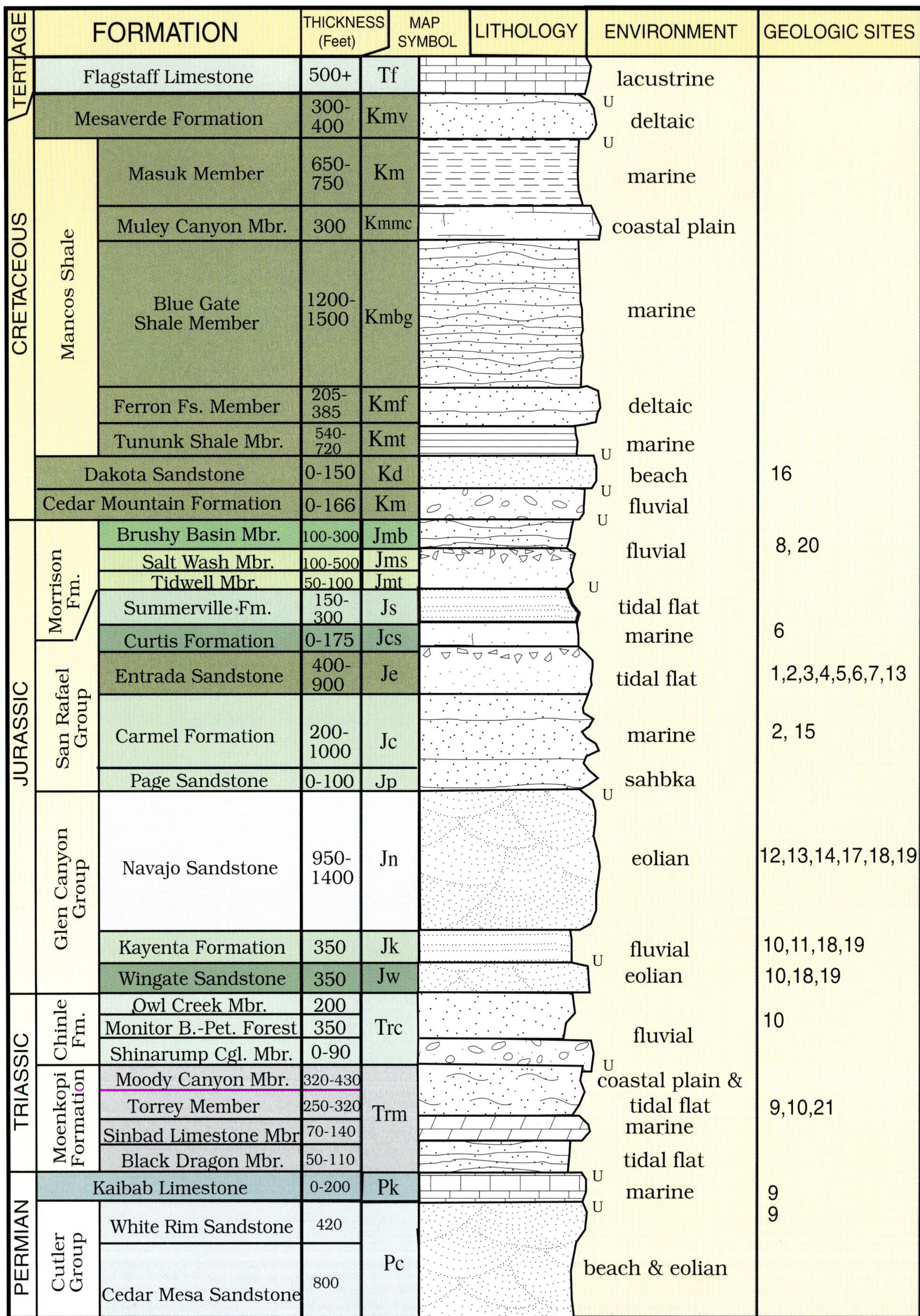

Figure 4. Stratigraphic column illustrating the age, group-formation-member names, thickness, lithology, depositional environment, and stop numbers of classic geological features (refer to figure 3 and discussion of classic geologic sites). U = unconformity.

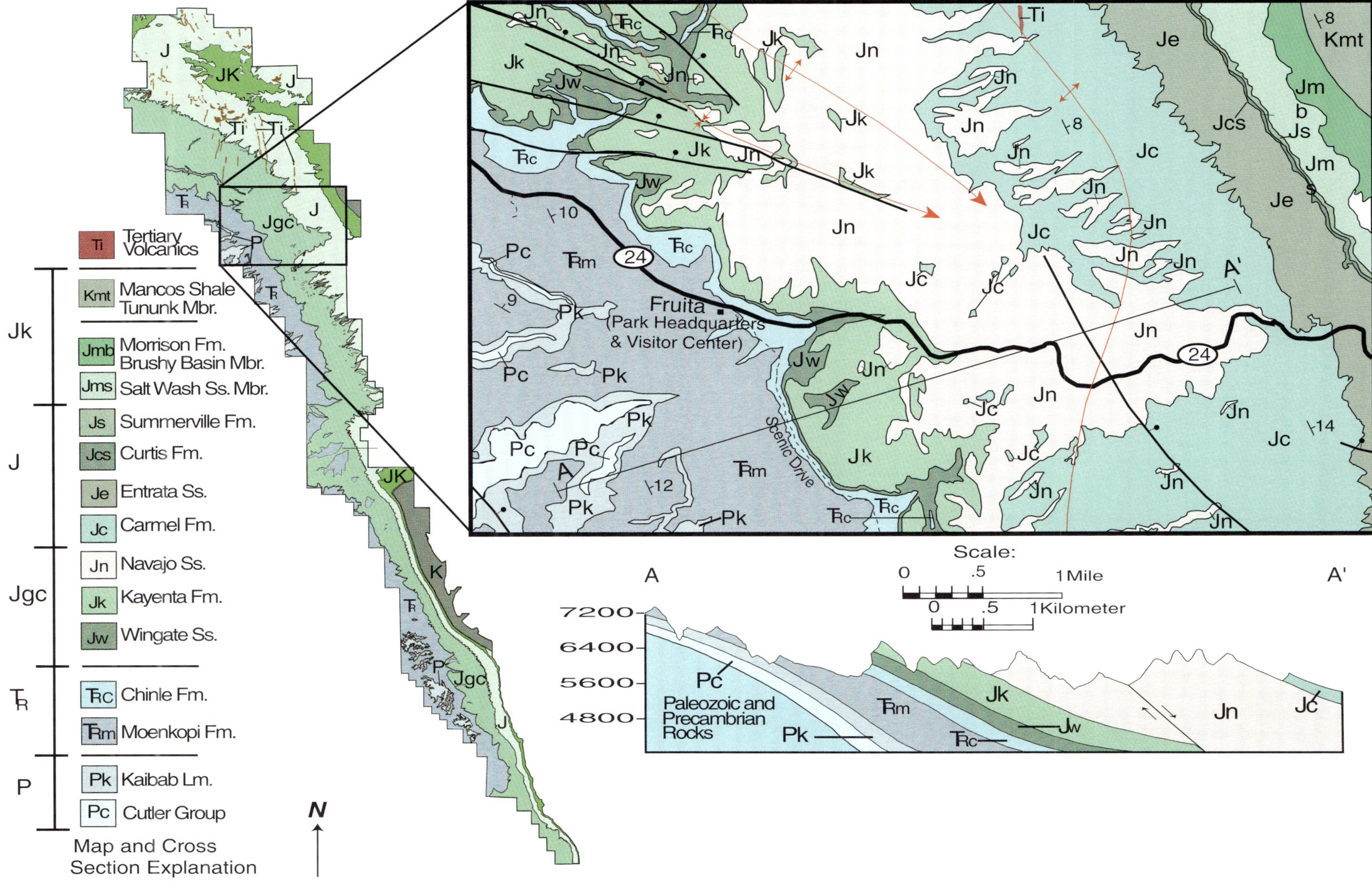

Figure 5. Bedrock geologic map of Capitol Reef National Park grouped by geologic age (for example Jgc = Jurassic Glen Canyon Group); inset map and cross section is by age and formation. Vertical exaggeration of cross section (x3) illustrates the structure of Waterpocket Fold (Modified from Billingsley and others, 1987).

light-yellow to gray, cross-bedded sandstones characterize the Cutler Group in these outcrops. Cutler sandstones, reach a thickness of 800 feet and are comprised of well-rounded, moderately well-sorted sand grains that range in size from very fine- to medium-grained. Individual cross-bed sets in the upper part of the Cutler (White Rim Sandstone) range from 5 to 75 feet in thickness, with most foresets (inclined dune bedding) dipping from 20 to 25 degrees southeast (Mitchell, 1985).

Cross-bedded and rounded grains in the Cutler Group indicate deposition under eolian conditions. However, oscillation ripples and marine trace fossils suggest that some parts of the Cutler were deposited subaqueously. Kamola and Chan (1986) and Cole and others (1996) conclude that the White Rim and Cedar Mesa Sandstones were formed in a coastal dune complex subjected to periodic marine flooding.

Kaibab Limestone

Like the Cutler Group, the Kaibab Limestone is exposed only in the deeper canyons along the western margin of Capitol Reef National Park. Although well exposed, the 200-foot-thick Kaibab Limestone forms steep cliffs that make it relatively inaccessible. Lithologically the Kaibab Limestone is comprised of light gray to white, cherty dolostone, with thin sandstone and siltstone interbeds particularly in the lower half of the formation. Thin limestone beds contain the disarticulated and fragmented remains of several invertebrate fossils including brachiopods, pelecypods, gastropods, crinoids, and bryozoans. Among the few identifiable fossils are the Permian brachiopods *Neospirifer pseudocameratus* (typically found in the upper 50 feet) and *Dictyoclostus bassi*, which occurs in the lower part of the formation (Smith and others, 1963). The middle and upper portions of the Kaibab contain rubbly silcretes and calcretes (siliceous and calcitic paleosols, respectively) that developed during episodes of intermittent subaerial exposure.

The mixture of oolitic dolostone, fine-grained sandstone, and fossiliferous limestone indicates that the Kaibab Limestone was deposited under normal to marginal marine conditions. This formation represents the last in the long series of shallow seas that covered Capitol Reef throughout most of the Paleozoic Era. Withdrawal of the sea by Middle Permian time exposed the Kaibab Limestone to subaerial erosion. Channels reaching 100 feet in depth were scoured into the limestone surface during this period of exposure (Stewart and other, 1959).

Triassic System

The Triassic System at Capitol Reef encompasses the Moenkopi Formation of Lower Triassic age and the Chinle Formation of Upper Triassic age. These two formations are separated by an erosional unconformity representing all of Middle Triassic time (approximately six million years).

Moenkopi Formation

The Moenkopi Formation welcomes visitors approaching Capitol Reef from the west on Highway 24. Chocolate-colored shales, siltstones, and sandstones of the Moenkopi Formation underlie the gullied flatlands traversed by Highway 24 from the west entrance to Park Headquarters at Fruita. Distinctly bedded shales and siltstones of the uppermost Moenkopi Formation form the lower slopes of the prominent, west-facing Waterpocket escarpment and the lower portions of such features as the Egyptian Temple and Twin Rocks, which are located along Highway 24 (watch for road signs).

The Moenkopi Formation is divided into four members at Capitol Reef. In ascending order, these are the Black Dragon, Sinbad Limestone, Torrey, and Moody Canyon Members. The Black Dragon comprises 50 to 110 feet of reddish, slope-forming conglomerate, siltstone, and sandstone. Conglomerates at the base of the member contain abundant angular chert clasts derived from erosion of the underlying Kaibab Limestone. Ripple marks and mudcracks are common on bedding planes in the upper part of the member, as are thin interbeds of dolostone and limestone with sparse marine fossils. These features indicate deposition under coastal plain and tidal flat conditions.

The Sinbad Limestone (70 to 140 feet) is readily distinguished from other members of the Moenkopi on the basis of its yellowish color and carbonate lithology. It is composed of fossiliferous to muddy limestone and dolostone with subordinate amounts of siltstone and sandstone. Oolitic layers, composed of tiny carbonate spheres, are characteristic of the lower part. Sinbad carbonates are generally thin-bedded to laminated, but small-scale trough cross-bedding occurs locally. Identifiable fossils include the inarticulate brachiopod *Lingula* and the ammonite cephalopod *Meekoceras* (Stewart and others, 1959). The latter indicates an Early Triassic age for the member and permits correlation with the Timpoweap and Thaynes beds of southern and northern Utah, respectively. The Sinbad was deposited during a relatively short-lived incursion of the ocean across Capitol Reef during Early Triassic time.

Upon retreat of the Sinbad sea, tidal flat conditions returned to Capitol Reef as reflected in the redbeds of the Torrey and Moody Canyon Members. These members are most readily distinguished on the basis of their weathering profile. The Torrey comprises a 250-to 320-foot- thick, ledgy sequence above the Sinbad Limestone. The overlying Moody Canyon grades from slope-forming beds at the base to cliff-forming beds at the top.

The Torrey Member is composed of reddish-brown to chocolate colored siltstone and fine-grained sandstone with rare interbeds of mud-pebble conglomerate, sandy dolomite, dolomitic limestone, and claystone (Mitchell, 1985). Sandstones exhibit both horizontal bedding and low angle cross-bedding. Finer grained beds contain ripple marks and mudcracks. The Torrey Member is well known for its large reptile and amphibian trackways. Three-toed swim tracks can be found on freshly fallen blocks. Smaller amphibian tracks and halite crystal casts are scattered throughout the upper portion of the member.

The Moody Canyon Member comprises two informal members, a lower slope-forming unit (200 to 300 feet) and an upper cliff-forming unit. The lower unit is comprised of horizontally laminated, reddish-brown siltstones that weather to an earthy slope. Few if any ripple-laminated interbeds are present. By contrast, 30 to 50 percent of silt-stones in the upper member are ripple laminated. Stewart and others (1972b) placed the contact at the gradational transition from structureless or horizontally laminated silt-stones below to ripple-laminated siltstones above. The rippled siltstones are relatively resistant to erosion and form the distinctly bedded, reddish-orange cliffs at the base of the Waterpocket escarpment. The upper cliff-form-ing unit is particularly well exposed in the lower part of the Egyptian Temple and at Chimney Rock at the western part of the park along Highway 24.

Chinle Formation

The Chinle Formation extends over most of the Col-orado Plateau region. At Capitol Reef it comprises four members; the Shinarump Conglomerate Member, Monitor Butte, Petrified Forest, and Owl Rock. These members form the purple and orange slopes beneath the Wingate cliffs along the entire extent of the west-facing Waterpock-et escarpment.

The Shinarump Conglomerate Member is discontinu-ous in Capitol Reef National Park. Near the west entrance it fills broad channels eroded into the top of the Moenkopi Formation and attains a thickness of 90 feet (Dubiel, 1987). Farther east (for example the Castle; site #10 of figure 3) it is completely absent and the Monitor Butte rests directly (unconformably) upon redbeds of the Moenkopi Forma-tion. The Shinarump is comprised of white to yellowish gray, fine- to coarse-grained, friable sandstone with lenses and interbeds of conglomerate and conglomeratic sand-stone. Pebbles and granules are characteristically com-prised of quartz, quartzite, and chert. Siltstone and clay-stone clasts derived from erosion of the underlying Moenkopi Formation are common in the lower part of the member. Much of the Shinarump displays low- to high-angle cross-stratification and some tabular cross-bedding. The Shinarump weathers into a prominent white cliff and forms the caprock for such features as the Egyptian Tem-ple, Twin Rocks, and Chimney Rock. Stewart and others (1972a) concluded that the Shinarump was deposited by a complex stream system that flowed across southeastern Utah at the beginning of the Late Triassic. Bedforms and grain sizes indicate relatively high velocity streams typical of a braided-fluvial system.

The Monitor Butte is the most heterogeneous member of the Chinle Formation (Dubiel, 1987). Its distinct light purplish-gray color makes it readily traceable along the lower to middle slopes of the Waterpocket escarpment. It consists primarily of slope-forming bentonitic claystones and clayey sandstones with interbeds and lenses of cross-bedded sandstone and carbonate nodules. Bentonitic clays derived from alteration of admixed volcanic ash pro-duce a characteristic frothy or crumbly crust on surfaces underlain by the Monitor Butte. Lungfish burrows meas-uring 5 inches in diameter and 5 feet in length were re-ported from this member by Dubiel (1987). Other fossils include petrified plant remains. Dubiel concluded that this member was deposited in response to northward progra-dation of a fluvial-deltaic system into a large marsh or lake.

Reddish-orange bentonitic siltstones and clayey sand-stones overlying the Monitor Butte are assigned to the Pet-rified Forest Member of the Chinle. The contact is placed at the change from purplish-gray, structureless clayey sandstones below to reddish-orange, cross-bedded silt-stones and fine-grained sandstones above. The lower 150 to 200 feet weathers to gullied slopes. The upper part is capped by a regionally persistent, cross-bedded sandstone known as the "Capitol Reef bed," and forms a prominent cliff or ledge. Quartz is the dominant sandstone con-stituent although green mica and feldspar are common in some beds. Dubiel (1987) reported abundant tetrapod re-mains, lungfish toothplates, and coprolites in addition to marine snails and bivalves in this member. Carbonate nod-ules, developed during episodes of exposure and soil gen-esis, are characteristic of certain horizons. Within the Capi-tol Reef area, the Petrified Forest represents deposition under fluvial conditions. Dubiel (1987) determined that the trough cross-bedded sandstones of the "Capitol Reef bed" were formed in high sinuosity river channels that flowed across the region during Late Triassic time. Incor-poration of ashes erupted from nearby volcanoes pro-duced the bentonites typical of the Monitor Butte and Pet-rified Forest Members.

The Owl Rock Member, the uppermost member of the Chinle Formation (150 to 200 feet), is comprised of slope-forming orange and purple mudstones, siltstones, and fine-grained sandstones with characteristic 1- to 10-foot-thick interbeds of mottled pink to green limestone. Unlike typical Chinle Formation mudstones, those of the Owl Rock are not bentonitic. Limestones are micritic with a knobby texture resulting from coalescence of carbonate nodules. Large cyclindrical burrows and ostracodes are the most common fossils in the limestones. Spectacular dessication cracks, reaching widths of up to 4 inches and depths of 3 feet occur at the very top of the member. These mudcracks are filled with sandstones of the overlying Wingate Sandstone. The Owl Rock comprises the littered slopes that directly underlie the Wingate Sandstone cliffs on the west-facing escarpment of the Waterpocket Fold. It has been interpreted as a lacustrine (lake) deposit (Dubiel, 1987).

Jurassic System

Glen Canyon Group

Many of the distinctive arches, domes, and slot canyons of Capitol Reef National Park are carved into the sandstones of the Glen Canyon Group. The tripartite group (Wingate Sandstone, Kayenta Formation, and Navajo Sandstone) ranges from 1,500 to 2,700 feet in thickness and forms the backbone of the Waterpocket Fold. Although the lowest part of the Glen Canyon Group (Wingate Sandstone) was originally assigned to the Triassic System, recent palynological (pollen) studies place the group entirely within the lower part of the Jurassic System (Hintze, 1993). Hence, the Triassic-Jurassic boundary coincides with the erosional unconformity between the Chinle Formation and Wingate Sandstone.

Wingate Sandstone: The 350-foot-thick basal member of the Glen Canyon Group consists of well-rounded, fine-grained, quartzose sandstone with large-scale, low- to high-angle trough cross-sets. Cross-bed orientations suggests a general southeastern transport of sand under eolian (wind blown) conditions (Stewart and others, 1959). Massive sandstones of the Wingate Sandstone cap the western escarpment of the Waterpocket Fold and form such features as the Castle and Fruita Cliffs. Weathered iron oxide cements produce its characterisitic salmon color.

Kayenta Formation: Sandstones of the 350-foot-thick Kayenta Formation reflect a change from eolian to fluvial (river) deposition. Instead of forming massive cliffs, the Kayenta Formation weathers into a series of low cliffs, ledges, and recessive slopes. The contact between the Wingate Sandstone and Kayenta Formation is gradational, and owing to the similarities in grain size and color, is difficult to discern in many areas. The contact is best exposed along the Fremont River, 100 feet west of the Highway 24 at mile marker 82.

The Kayenta Formation is divided into three units on the basis of weathering features; a lower ledge, a middle cliff, and an upper slope. The lower and middle units are composed of very fine-grained sandstone, whereas the upper unit contains a higher percentage of siltstone. Clay-pebble conglomerate and traces of interbedded mudstone and limestone occur throughout the formation as do horizontal and small-scale lenticular and tabular cross-beds. Fluvial cross-beds in the Kayenta Formation are small (a few feet in thickness) compared to the sweeping eolian cross- beds of the subjacent Wingate and superjacent Navajo Sandstones. Kayenta Formation sandstones are also distinguished by the higher relative abundance of horizontal trunction planes. Paleocurrent studies by Friz (1980) indicate that rivers responsible for deposition of the Kayenta Formation flowed in a general westward to southwestward direction. The transition to fluvial conditions reflects a period of climatic change during which the

Figure 6. Entrada Sandstone in Upper Cathedral Valley weathers into monoliths or cathedrals. Note that the most distal cathedral is capped by gray sandstones of the slightly more resistant Curtis Formation.

Wingate Sandstone erg was reworked by river currents.

Navajo Sandstone: A return to arid, wind blown conditions resulted in deposition of 800 to 1,100 feet of cross-bedded, sand dune deposits known as the Navajo Sandstone. The contact with the underlying Kayenta is gradational and conformable. The Navajo Sandstone is composed of well- rounded, frosted quartz grains. Sandstones are generally very fine to fine-grained with medium- sized grains occuring in some beds. White, tan, and light reddish-brown hues prevail. Trademark large-scale (60 feet), high-angle, trough cross-beds attest to the presence of Sahara-like sand dunes during Early Jurassic time (see Chan and Archer in this volume). Slumped and contorted cross-beds occur in the upper and middle portions of the formation within the park. Differential weathering of the Navajo forms massive white to reddish-brown cliffs, monoliths and domes, such as Capitol and Navajo Domes.

San Rafael Group

The spectacular scenery of Cathedral Valley (figure 6 and site #'s 1-6 of figure 3) and a portion of the subdued splendor of the Strike Valleys (figure 7 and site #'s 16 and 17 of figure 3) are sculpted from rocks of the San Rafael Group. This group, consisting of the Page, Carmel, Entrada, Curtis, and Summerville Formations represents a spectrum of interbedded restricted marine to marginal marine strata deposited in response to frequent, short-lived sea level changes that affected the Capitol Reef area during Middle and Late Jurassic time. The San Rafael Group is separated from the underlying Glen Canyon Group by a regionally traceable erosion surface.

Page Sandstone: The Page Sandstone ranges from 0 to 100 feet in thickness. It is composed of the Harris Wash, Judd Hollow, and Thousand Pocket Members. These members developed in sabkha-like (an environment of deposition above high tide on an arid coastal plain) conditions as marine waters flooded portions of the Navajo Sandstone erg. At mile marker 86.5 above the falls of the Fremont River,

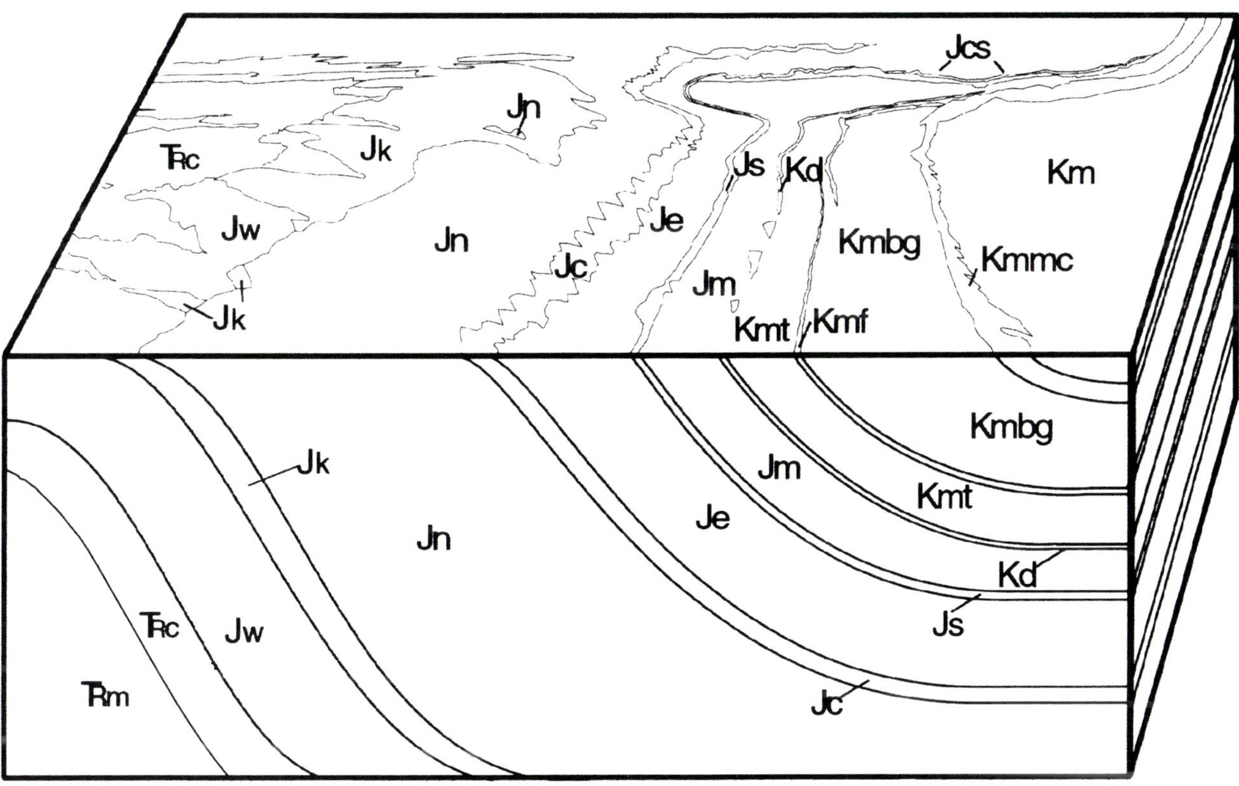

Figure 7. Aerial photograph (looking north), and interpreted surface and subsurface geology on the east flank of Capitol Reef National Park. Stratigraphic units are progressively older to the west. Note the prominent strike valleys and roll of the Waterpocket Fold monocline (photo courtesy of W.K. Hamblin).

the Judd Hollow Member forms a red cliff. Trough cross-bedded sandstones above this cliff belong to the Thousand Pockets Member.

Carmel Formation: The Carmel Formation comprises from 200 to 1,000 feet of evenly bedded sandstone, siltstone, mudstone, fossiliferous limestone, and gypsum. Whitish-gray limestones and gypsums alternate with reddish-brown siltstones and sandstones to produce a distinctive banded appearance. The Carmel Formation has been stripped from the subjacent Navajo and Page Sandstones along much of the crest of the Waterpocket Fold, although erosional remnants cap many of the Navajo domes and in places produce the whimsical scenery. The Carmel Formation is most readily seen in the reddish to reddish-brown "flatirons" or triangular-shaped spurs that form the eastern rampart of the Waterpocket Fold. Complex interbedding of quartzose sandstones and siltstones with fossil-bearing limestone (mostly marine bivalves and ammonoids) and chickenwire gypsum attest to a period of intermittent marine flooding and evaporation.

Entrada Sandstone: The regionally extensive Entrada Sandstone contributes to the scenery of several national parks and monuments in Utah: it forms the trademark landforms at Arches National Park and the ghostly figured "hoodoos" at Goblin Valley State Park. At Capitol Reef it forms the majestic monoliths and cathedrals of Cathedral Valley (figure 6). The Entrada Sandstone ranges from 400 to 900 feet in thickness and is characterized by a distinct, but gradual change from slope-forming, flat-bedded siltstones in the southern portion of the park to slope- and cliff-forming, cross-bedded sandstone and siltstones in the north. It maintains an earthy red to reddish-orange color throughout. Although the Entrada Sandstone represents eolian deposition in eastern Utah, at Capitol Reef, tidal flat conditions seem to have prevailed during Entrada time.

Curtis Formation: The fourth member of the San Rafael Group, the Curtis Formation thins from a maximum of 175 feet in the northern part of Capitol Reef to a feather edge in the south where it is locally absent. The Curtis Formation is comprised of uniformly light grayish-green sandstone and siltstone with thin intercalated beds of sandy limestone. Sandstones are fine grained with calcite cement and glauconite, a dull green iron- and potassium-bearing silicate mineral that forms only in marine environments where sedimentation rates are fairly low. Monoliths and cathedrals in the northern part of the park owe their existence to the presence of this resistant shallow marine layer which forms the light-colored caprock of many such landforms.

Summerville Formation: This 50-to 250-foot-thick formation is composed of thin-bedded, reddish-brown siltstones and mudstones alternating with less frequent beds of greenish-gray limestone and sandstone. Primary gypsum beds ranging from 1 to 28 feet in thickness are observable, as are secondary gypsum veinlets. Mudcracks, ripple marks, and inch-scale cross- bedding indicate tidal flat conditions during Summerville time. In the Strike Valley, the Summerville Formation is poorly exposed. In Cathedral Valley it forms the reddish slopes above the Curtis Formation caprock.

Morrison Formation

The Late Jurassic Morrison Formation is world renowned for its wealth of dinosaur bones and uranium. At Capitol Reef the formation is subdivided into three members, the Tidwell, the Salt Wash and Brushy Basin. A thin section of the Tidwell Member (50 to 100 feet) may exist in Capitol Reef although it is difficult to recognize. Turner and Peterson (1998) suggest that the Tidwell in southeastern Utah is gypsiferous and was deposited in hypersaline lagoons. The Tidwell Member in other areas of the Colorado Plateau is composed of lacustrine deposits of limestone and mudstone.

The lithologically diverse Salt Wash Member (100 to 500 feet) consists of interbedded claystone, mudstone, siltstone, sandstone, and pebble conglomerate. Slope-forming claystones and mudstones are chiefly gray in color, but can locally display a spectrum of reds, browns, yellows, and greens. Laterally discontinuous lenses of cross-bedded sandstone and conglomerate form ledges and small cliffs. Sandstones are fine- to medium-grained with moderate sorting. Conglomeratic pebbles are mainly chert with minor amounts of quartzite and silicified limestone.

The overlying Brushy Basin Member (200 to 350 feet) comprises variegated claystone, mudstone, and siltstone with only minor amounts of sandstone and conglomerate. The boundary between the two members of the Morrison is somewhat arbitrary, but is generally placed at the level where sandstones and conglomerates become less abundant upwards. Another key to distinguishing the Salt Wash and Brushy Basin is the surface texture of the shale slopes. Brushy Basin clays contain a large percentage of smectite, a family of swelling clays that dry to a crumbly "popcorn" surface. In Utah and Western Colorado the Brushy Basin Member contains several major dinosaur quarries. The Brushy Basin is superbly exposed in the Bentonite Hills (figure 8).

Sedimentologists have long recognized the fluvial (meandering stream and flood plain) nature of the Salt Wash Member. Petersen and Roylance (1982) interpreted a lacustrine and fluvial-deltaic origin for the Brushy Basin. More or less complete dinosaur skeletons occur in lake-floor and flood-plain clays. Disarticulated bones and teeth are more common in higher energy channel sandstones.

Cretaceous System

Cedar Mountain Formation

The oldest Cretaceous rocks at Capitol Reef are assigned to the Cedar Mountain Formation (0 to 166 feet). This formation consists of variegated, slope-forming mudstones and sandstones similar to those of the underlying

Figure 8. The colorfully barren Bentonite Hills are composed of smectitic clays of the Brushy Basin Member of the Morrison Formation. These clays swell when wetted and crack upon drying, creating the popcorn-like weathered surface seen in the foreground.

Morrison Formation. North and east of Capitol Reef, the Morrison-Cedar Mountain boundary is placed at the base of a 73-foot-thick, cliff- forming conglomerate, dubbed the Buckhorn Conglomerate Member of the Cedar Mountain Formation. At Capitol Reef, the fluvial Buckhorn is nearly absent, making distinction between the Morrison and Cedar Mountain Formations somewhat tenuous. Peterson and others (1980) indicate that the relatively more pastel shades of the Cedar Mountain Formation are helpful, but not completely reliable, in distinguishing the two formations. Sedimentary features along with freshwater mollusks, freshwater ostracodes, fish scales, dinosaur bones, charophytes, pollen, and the fern *Tempskya* indicate deposition under continental fluvial conditions during the Early Cretaceous (Peterson and others, 1980).

Dakota Sandstone

The Dakota Sandstone (0 to 150 feet) marks the initiation of the Western Interior seaway, an inland ocean that covered eastern Utah during much of Cretaceous time. As the area subsided in response to thrust faulting in western Utah, marine waters encroached across the area, draping the eroded top of the Cedar Mountain Formation with a blanket of high energy, nearshore sandstones. The Dakota Sandstone consists of very fine to fine-grained, tan to brownish-gray, quartzose sandstone with thin interbeds of coal, carbonaceous shale, and conglomerate that weather to small cliffs and hogbacks. Horizontal and cross-stratified beds are both common. Sandstones in the lower part of the Dakota Sandstone contain petrified wood whereas those in the upper Dakota Sandstone yield specimens of the marine bivalves *Pycnodonte newberryi* and *Corbula* sp. This succession of fossils indicates a transition from marine shoreface to open marine conditions as flooding progressed (Peterson and others, 1980).

Mancos Shale

The Mancos Shale consists of the Tununk Shale, Ferron Sandstone, Blue Gate Shale, Muley Canyon, and Masuk Members. These form a series of parallel strike valleys and subdued hogbacks on the east flank of the Waterpocket Fold (figure 7).

The Tununk Member (40 to 720 feet) is composed of bluish-gray bentonitic shale that erodes into gullied slopes. Interbeds of mudstone, siltstone, and very fine-grained sandstone are common. Bluish shales of the Tununk produce the scenery at Blue Desert just southeast of Cathedral Valley. Tununk fossils include cephalopods, fish scales, and bivalves indicating deposition in open marine conditions.

The Ferron Sandstone (205 to 385 feet) consists of cliff-forming, middle to lower shoreface (shelf) sandstones with hummocky to low-angle, cross-stratification. Oscillation ripples and ball-and-pillow structures are common in some sandstone beds (Peterson and others, 1980). *Ophiomorpha* (trace fossil) and *Inoceramus* (marine bivalve) characterize the lower part of the member. To the north, the Ferron Sandstone contains coal seams. The Ferron Sandstone has been well studied by petroleum geologists because it was deposited by fluvial- and wave- dominated deltas and provides a useful model. Worldwide, delta systems are often prolific provinces for oil.

Bentonitic clays, siltstones, and sparse limestones above the Ferron Sandstone are assigned to the Blue Gate Shale. This 1,200-to 1,500-foot-thick member weathers to gullied slopes resembling those of the Tununk Shale. Like the Tununk, it reflects sedimentation in open marine conditions. The presence of *Clioscaphites vermiformis* and *C. choteauensis* (planktonic foraminifera) in the upper Blue Gate indicate an Upper Cretaceous age for the member.

Eastward progradation of the shoreline across the Capitol Reef area resulted in deposition of the evenly bedded, fine-grained sandstones and carbonaceous shales of the Muley Canyon Member (300 to 400 feet). Coal beds in the upper Muley Canyon indicate a transition up-section from marine shoreface to continental coastal plain deposits.

The Masuk Member (650 to 750 feet) consists of slope-forming, yellowish-gray to bluish- gray mudstones and cliff-forming, cross-bedded and ripple cross-laminated sandstones. Fossils include gastropods, bivalves, turtles, crocodiles, and ceratopsian dinosaurs (Peterson and others, 1980). Deposition of the Masuk represents fluctuation between shallow marine and non-marine (primarily coastal plain) environments.

Mesaverde Formation

The Mesaverde Formation (300 to 400 feet) consists of light-brown to dark-gray sandstone with shale interbeds. It forms cliffs in the extreme southeastern corner of the park. Sandstones are thick-bedded and cross-stratified. Pebble conglomerates occur in the upper part of the

Mesaverde Formation, otherwise fine-grained textures prevail. The Mesaverde Formation represents the eastward progradation of barrier beaches and deltas into the Western Interior seaway.

Tertiary System

Flagstaff Limestone

The 500-foot-thick Flagstaff Limestone is the youngest sedimentary formation in the vicinity (slightly NW of the park boundary) of Capitol Reef National Park. It consists of lacustrine (lake) limestone, sandstone, siltstone, claystone, and conglomerate. Locally, tuffaceous beds rival limestone beds in abundance (Smith and others, 1963). The latter display a range of rock types including sandy limestones and limestone pebble conglomerates. Fossils recovered from the Flagstaff include fresh-water ostracodes (*Metacypris* sp. and *Paracypris* sp.), algae (*Chlorellopsis coloniata*), and gastropods.

STRUCTURAL GEOLOGY

Capitol Reef National Park contains numerous examples of large-scale structures including folds (for example monoclines, synclines, and anticlines), fractures, and faults. As mentioned, these features are created by tectonic forces as Earth's crustal plates interact. This interaction stresses the rocks of the crust, causing them to strain or deform. The resulting deformation, whether brittle or plastic, depends upon the type of rock, the heat and pressure conditions of the rock, and the amount of time the force is allowed to work on the rock.

Geologists use stratigraphic and cross-cutting relations to unravel the relative succession of deformational events. The geologist can infer much about the geologic history of an area within its global context. The following is a summary of the geologic history of Capitol Reef National Park based on these inferences.

Tectonics and Geologic History

Plate tectonics, the unifying theory of the Earth sciences, has played a major role in the development of structural features as well as the stratigraphy observable in Capitol Reef National Park. Rocks of the Cutler Group (approximately 290 to 250 million years old), the oldest rocks of the park, record the history of western North America when the western portion of the continent was a passive margin. This passive tectonic setting is comparable to the west coast of Africa today, an area where interaction with other tectonic plates is lacking. During the Permian, California had not fully accreted (been added onto) to the continent. Utah, occasionally covered by shallow marine waters, was part of the continental shelf. Also, the North American continent was in a lower latitudinal position. To reconstruct its position at approximately 290 million years ago, one would have to drop it approximately to the equator and rotate it slightly clockwise (it was ro-

tating counterclockwise and moving northward during the Permian; Scotese, 1999). Approximately 275 million years ago, Utah was located near 10 degrees north latitude. The climatic setting would have been in or near a dry, high atmospheric pressure climatic belt such as the Sahara Desert of today. Under this paleogeographic and climatic setting, southern Utah experienced desert-like conditions but due to its relatively low elevation was occasionally inundated by shallow marine seaways. This depositional and climatic setting created the rocks of the Cutler Group and the Kaibab Limestone.

The coastal plain setting prevailed through the Triassic (250 to 206 million years ago) although climatic conditions changed, bringing more moisture to Utah. This was a time when Utah was again very close to the equator (Scotese, 1999). This, combined with changing paleogeographic and paleoceanographic conditions, created more tropical climates. Under these conditions, the tidal flat setting of the Moenkopi Formation and then the lacustrine and coastal plain settings of the Chinle Formation were created.

In the Jurassic (206 to 144 million years ago), the North American continental plate was moving northward and rotating slightly clockwise bringing Utah out of tropical latitudes and back into the dry, high pressure climatic belt. Dry, continental conditions prevailed through much of the Jurassic creating the eolian ergs so prominent in the Glen Canyon Group. Cross-bedding within sandstones of the Wingate and Navajo Sandstones suggest southernly transport from northerly winds. Paleogeographic reconstructions show little change in the north-south orientation of the continent during the Jurassic, relative to its present position (Scotese, 1999). Therefore, the ancient wind direction must also have been largely north to south, suggesting different atmospheric circulation than is seen today within the trade wind belt of 10 to 30 degrees north latitude (see Chan and Archer in this volume). Younger Jurassic rocks of the Page, Carmel, Entrada, Curtis, and Summerville indicate coastal plain, sabkha, and tidal flat conditions, possibly indicating a shift of the continent out of the dry, high pressure trade wind belt. During Morrison time, fluvial and lacustrine conditions prevailed, indicating wetter conditions. Evidence suggests that severe drought conditions were occasionally experienced (Richmond and Morris, 1996). Tectonism southwest of Utah probably became more active at this time, creating highlands which shed sediments to the northeast.

With the convergence (collision) of the North American continental plate and the Farallon oceanic plate on the western edge of North America during the Cretaceous Period (144 to 65 million years ago), the passive margin tectonic setting ceased. Western North America became very active tectonically. In western Utah and Nevada, sedimentary strata detached from underlying Precambrian basement rocks and were pushed eastward due to plate convergence. The sedimentary strata stacked up (overthrust) along the length of central Utah and throughout much of western North America. This mountain building event is called the Sevier orogeny. Geologists call this type of mountain building "thin-skinned" tectonics because it primarily involves the sedimentary strata that overlie thick Precambrian basement rocks of the crust. In Utah, this overthrust belt built a high mountain range whose weight isostatically depressed the Earth's crust. The isostatic depression created a topographic low east of the Sevier overthrust belt. Eastern Utah and much of central North America became a relatively low area called a foreland basin. The ocean transgressed this isostatically depressed low area. This seaway covered the continent from central Utah to Minnesota and from the Gulf of Mexico to the Arctic Ocean.

The transgressive rise of this ocean is recorded in the rocks of the Dakota Sandstone (approximately 100 to 94 million years ago; Hintze, 1993) which are interpreted to represent depositional systems of nearshore transgressive environments. The Western Interior seaway then filled the broad foreland basin. In Utah, normal marine shales were deposited, producing the Mancos Shale (approximately 94 to 85 million years ago). Occasionally, relative sea level fell and the western shoreline migrated eastward depositing nearshore marine sandstones of the Ferron and Muley Canyon Members. Parallic and alluvial sediments were then deposited in the area until approximately 58 million years ago.

The tectonic style changed in Utah during the latest Cretaceous and early Tertiary (approximately 70 to 50 million years ago), probably in association with different rates of convergence and angles of subduction (or dive) of the Farallon oceanic plate beneath the North American continental plate. The overthrust belt was subdued by erosion. While the Western Interior seaway was shrinking due to infilling and uplift, plate convergence continued. The tectonic compressive regime in eastern Utah now involved basement rocks. This tectonic style is called "thick-skinned" because it involves a thicker section of the Earth's crust. Geologists called this younger tectonic event the Laramide orogeny (in reference to mountains and structures near Laramie, Wyoming). High-angle normal and reverse faults in the metamorphic rocks of the Precambrian basement caused the overlying ductile sedimentary rocks to fold over the fault scarps in a draping fashion (figures 2 and 7). This process created the Waterpocket Fold, which is just one of many classic monoclines characteristic of the Colorado Plateau. Within the Waterpocket Fold, secondary anticlinal and synclinal folds as well as faults developed. Erosion of the folded rocks exposed older rocks to the west and younger rocks to the east (figure 5).

An intermontane basin (within the mountains) started to develop in eastern Utah at approximately the same time as the creation of the Waterpocket Fold (Stanley and Collinson, 1979). This basin abutted the Uinta Mountains to the north and the remnants of the Sevier orogeny to the west. A large lake, called Lake Uinta, developed within

Figure 9. Vertical igneous dike (arrows) cutting horizontal beds of the Jurassic Entrada Sandstone in Cathedral Valley just north of the Gypsum Sinkhole (stop #5 of figure 3). These dikes represent the roots of a former volcanic field. A thin alteration zone can be seen adjacent to the dike at the skyline. Where the Entrada is eroded the dikes form cockscomb or hogback ridges. View is to the southeast.

the basin by fluvial drainage from both the north and south (Morris and others, 1991). Lacustrine sedimentation continued in the basin from approximately 58 to 35 million years ago, creating the Flagstaff Limestone and Green River Formation. Just south of the Uinta Mountains, sediment accumulation within this lake was more than 9,000 feet thick. However, preserved time equivalent rocks near Capitol Reef are only 200 feet thick (Nelson, 1989).

Composite volcanoes covered the pre-existing area just west of the park from approximately 25 to 20 million years ago (Nelson and Davidson, 1998). The entire rock succession was then uplifted which likely produced regional fracture sets. Approximately 4.6 to 3.7 million years ago another volcanic field covered the northern quarter of the park (Delaney and Gartner, 1997). However, with continued uplift and associated erosion of the area over the past several million years, only the deeper roots of this volcanic field are preserved. The remnants of this field are evidenced by the intrusive igneous dikes, sills, and diatremes (breccia-filled volcanic pipe formed from a gaseous explosion) preserved in the northern quarter of the park (figure 9).

The Black Boulders of Capitol Reef National Park

In the final stages of the geologic history, Quaternary sediment derived from the basalt-rich bedrock of Boulder Mountain and Thousand Lake Mountain to the west, was deposited on top of the folded and eroded strata by alluvial, debris-flow, and possibly glacial processes. Over time, the finer-grained material was washed (winnowed) away by rain and water and transported off of the resistant bedrock surfaces. In many places, only the large rounded black basaltic boulders remain perched on the bedrock. To date, erosional forces have removed up to 7,000 feet of Tertiary and Mesozoic strata to expose the present outcrops.

LOCATION AND DESCRIPTION OF CLASSIC GEOLOGIC SITES

Classic geologic features can be observed in a number of places along three routes in Capitol Reef National Park: (1) Cathedral Valley Loop, (2) Highway 24 west to east transect, and (3) the Notom-Bullfrog Road. Sites where these features can be viewed are discussed in this section and referenced to the index map (figure 3). The stratigraphic unit in which the feature is developed is listed within the stratigraphic column (figure 4).

Cathedral Valley Loop

A. Cathedrals and Monoliths of Cathedral Valley

Cathedral Valley is located in the northern portion of the park and is accessible only by high clearance and/or four-wheel drive vehicles. In this area, bedrock dips very gently (3 to 5 degrees) to the northeast. Erosion within the nonresistant red-orange mudstone, siltstone, and fine-grained sandstone of the Entrada Sandstone forms the topographic depression known as Cathedral Valley. Numerous isolated, freestanding masses of rock known as monoliths are found within these topographic valleys. Monoliths resembling religious edifices are referred to as cathedrals or temples. Temple of the Sun and Temple of the Moon (site #1 of figure 3; figure 10) are outstanding examples of monoliths. Cathedrals in Upper Cathedral Valley (site #6 of figure 3; figure 11), also rise in splendor above the valley floor. Monoliths are occasionally capped by slightly more resistant gray-green sandstones of the Curtis Formation. In a number of places, the southwest wall of the valley displays closely spaced rock towers. These towers are the precursors to monoliths/cathedrals. Over time, continued headward erosion by streams and rivers and associated downcutting and slope retreat, will strand these towers and create monoliths.

Monoliths and cathedral-like towers are created by accelerated erosion along fractures in the rock. Fracture sets commonly intersect at high angles creating a conjugate fracture system. Water penetrates the formation along the fracture system and, through a combination of mechanical and chemical weathering processes, erodes the fractured rock. This leaves unfractured areas of free-standing rock. Some areas of the Entrada have been capped by particularly resistant or thick beds of Curtis Formation. The resistant caprock can also protect the underlying rock from erosion. It is the combination of these two processes that have contributed to the formation of the monoliths of Cathedral Valley.

B. Glass Mountain and Gypsum Sinkhole

Figure 10. Photograph (looking south) of Glass Mountain (foreground), Temple of the Sun, and Temple of the Moon (background - left center of photo: stop #1 of figure 3). Glass Mountain is composed of large selenite crystals that were pushed upward as a plug or diapir from the underlying Carmel Formation. Temples of the Sun and Moon are monoliths within the Entrada Sandstone.

Figure 11. Northwest view of upper Cathedral Valley. The light gray caprock on the monoliths in the valley center (left edge of photo) is Jurassic Curtis Formation which overlies the Entrada Sandstone. The red mudstone, siltstone, and sandstone of the Jurassic Summerville Formation overlie the Curtis. Above the Summerville and on the skyline are the light-colored sandstones of the Salt Wash Member of the Morrison Formation (see figure 4).

Glass Mountain and Gypsum Sinkhole are located within Cathedral Valley in the northern portion of the park (sites #2 and #4 of figure 3, respectively). Both of these features developed from a relatively thick layer of the mineral gypsum that was precipitated from evaporating seawater during the deposition of the Carmel Formation approximately 165 million years ago (Hintze, 1993). When enough sediment and rock buried the layer of gypsum, it became unstable and began to flow and plastically deform. In areas of lower pressure, possibly created by faults and fractures in the overlying rock column, the gypsum flowed upward as small domes or plugs into the overlying Entrada Sandstone. Glass Mountain, which rises more than 10 feet above the valley floor, is the surface expression of one of these plugs (figure 10). Glass Mountain displays the clear, colorless variety of gypsum called selenite.

Gypsum Sinkhole, located approximately 7 miles to the northwest of Glass Mountain, is thought to result from dissolution of a different gypsum plug. Because gypsum is readily soluble, ground water carried the dissolved gypsum away from the area through subsurface fractures, leaving behind the gaping "hole" in the valley floor.

C. Dikes and Sills

In the area just north of the Gypsum Sinkhole, spectacular, resistant dark gray igneous dikes intruded into the erodible red-orange sandstones of the Entrada (site #5 of figure 3; figure 9). Gartner (1986) interpreted these dikes and sills as part of a larger basaltic dike complex that extends out of the park to the north and into the San Rafael Swell. The dike complex represents the shallow feeder system of a 4.6 to 3.7 million year old volcanic field that was subsequently eroded away (Delaney and Gartner, 1997).

Dikes intrude at high angles to the essentially horizontally bedded sedimentary rocks, and are sometimes associated with horizontal sills. Sills in Cathedral Valley are tabular sheets of intrusive igneous rock parallel to sedimentary bedding. World-class sills can be seen on steep west-facing hillsides adjacent to the road just a few miles to the east of the Gypsum Sinkhole turnoff (site #3 of figure 3). A diatreme is exposed adjacent to the walking path on a west facing pillar of rock at the Upper South Desert Overlook (site #7 of figure 3).

D. Bentonite Hills

The Bentonite Hills are located to the east of North Blue Flats just outside of Capitol Reef National Park. The best view of these variegated-colored hills is approximately 9 miles north of the River Ford (Fremont River crossing). These barren and rounded hills are primarily developed within the Brushy Basin Member of the Morrison Formation (site #8 of figure 3, figure 8). A significant component of this member of the Morrison Formation is a group of clay minerals known as smectites. Smectitic clays are derived from the alteration of volcanic glass and from weathered primary silicate minerals. The abundance of the smectitic clays in the Morrison suggests that volcanism was an active process in the area during Morrison time. Smectitic clays are considered swelling clays because they expand each time they are wetted, and contract each time they are dried. This creates the highly "cracked" or "popcorn" nature of the land surface and allows the Brushy Basin to erode relatively rapidly creating the rounded hills.

The Morrison Formation is recognized worldwide for its abundant and diverse Jurassic-age dinosaur fauna. To the astute observer, bones within this formation can be seen in and around the park. The reader is reminded that it is illegal to collect any fossil, mineral, or rock material

Figure 12. Petrified (silicified) log within the Morrison Formation near the Bentonite Hills (stop #8 of figure 3).

within the park. Within the Morrison Formation at Bentonite Hills, a number of large petrified logs are observable (figure 12). Dinosaur bones and petrified logs are evidence that a terrestrial environment existed when the Morrison was deposited. Recent work suggests that at times, the normally humid, wet conditions were interrupted by large-scale, cataclysmic drought (Richmond and Morris, 1998). During times of drought dinosaurs gathered at the shrinking watering holes and died, thereby creating concentrated accumulations of bones such as those at Dry Mesa Dinosuar Quarry located 250 miles east of Capitol Reef in western Colorado.

Highway 24: West to East Transect

E. "The Goosenecks" at Sulfur Creek

The "Goosenecks" at Sulfur Creek, located approximately 2.2 of miles west of the Visitor's Center, are aptly named because the stream channel and associated steep-walled canyon can be seen to curve or meander similar to the neck of a goose (site #9 of figure 3). The "Goosenecks" is a classic example of a superposed meandering stream. The meandering drainage pattern originally developed on relatively flat-lying rocks during Paleocene/Eocene time. The older, underlying strata had previously been folded. Through time, the drainage system eroded through the flat-lying rocks into the underlying folded rocks. Its meandering pattern was superposed on the underlying folded rocks.

The canyon floor at the Goosenecks exposes some of the oldest rocks in Capitol Reef National Park. The rocks are Permian age and are part of the 250 to 290 million-year-old Cutler Group. The sandstones of the Cutler Group were deposited in a coastal dune complex that was occasionally reworked by marine incursions as the adjacent seaway transgressed the land (Kamola and Chan, 1986; Cole and others, 1996). Overlying formations include the Kaibab Limestone, and then the Black Dragon, Sinbad Limestone, Torrey, and Moody Canyon Members of the

Figure 13. View of "the Castle" from the Visitors Center parking lot (stop #10 of figure 3). The red rock at the lower part of the photo is the Moody Canyon Member of the Triassic Moenkopi Formation (Trm). The Shinarump Conglomerate, the basal member of the Triassic Chinle Formation, normally overlies the Moody Canyon but is absent at this locality. Ascending up section is the gray and purple beds of the Monitor Butte Member of the Chinle, the slope-forming red siltstone and sandstone of the Petrified Forest Member with the resistant "Capitol Reef bed" capping this member (ledge in the middle of the slope). The upper slope is composed of mudstone, siltstone, and fine sandstone of the Owl Creek Member of the Chinle Formation (Trc). "The Castle" is created within fractured Jurassic Wingate Sandstone (Jw). Overlying the Wingate is the Jurassic Kayenta Formation (on skyline, Jk).

Moenkopi Formation, respectively. The Kaibab Limestone is a chert-rich carbonate deposit that exhibits evidence of many marine transgressions and regressions. The Moenkopi was deposited as a broad, coastal tidal flat that was infrequently inundated by marine waters.

F. Visitor Center/ "The Castle"

The Visitor Center of Capitol Reef (mile marker 79.4 of Highway 24) offers visitors an abundance of information relative to the geology and cultural history of the area (site #10 of figure 4). One of the outstanding features within the Visitor Center is the physiographic model displayed in the main room. This model accurately depicts the Waterpocket Fold and its myriad of landforms. Before exploring the park, the visitor would be well served by taking a few moments to study this model and pose questions to the friendly staff.

Looking north across Highway 24 from the Visitor Center parking lot, a set of vertical fractures in the sandstone wall forms the picturesque "Castle" (figure 13). This geomorphic feature developed within the Wingate Sandstone, a well-indurated eolian sandstone of early Jurassic age (Hintze, 1993). It became fractured during uplift of the Colorado Plateau which began approximately 20 million years ago. Erosion by running water in the form of stream downcutting and slope retreat has created the cliff faces. Slope retreat was especially active in the easily eroded, mudstones and siltstones of the underlying Chinle Forma-

tion. The erosion of the Chinle effectively undercut the vertical cliffs of the Wingate. Mechanical (ice wedging) and chemical (solution) weathering processes have accentuated the fractures evident on the walls of "the Castle."

Fruita, which encompasses the Visitors Center and the campground area, sits at the contact of the Moenkopi and Chinle Formations. The variegated colors of the Chinle can be observed by looking east at the escarpment across the road from the camping area. The easily eroded mudstone and siltstone beds of the Chinle Formation retreated northeastward off of the underlying Moenkopi siltstone and sandstone, creating the relatively flat area around Fruita and the campground. Note that the basal Shinarump Member of the Chinle Formation, which is a relatively resistant coarse-grained sandstone, is missing in the outcrop east of the campground. This member has been interpreted to represent a braided river deposit that was sourced from highlands to the southwest of the Grand Canyon. In the Fruita area, this ancient braidplain was beginning to thin and feather out. At the west edge of the park along Highway 24, the Shinarump pinches and swells up to 40 feet thick as seen at Twin Rocks (composed of Shinarump). West of Torrey, where the Fremont River crosses Highway 24, the Shinarump is approximately 70 feet thick.

G. Arches/Bridges

Capitol Reef National Park has a number of natural arches and bridges, the most accessible of which is Hickman Bridge. The trailhead to Hickman Bridge can be accessed directly from Highway 24 at mile marker 81.8 (site #11 of figure 3). Stratigraphically, Hickman Bridge is within the Kayenta Formation of the Jurassic Glen Canyon Group. Brimhall Double Bridge, which can be viewed from Halls Overlook (site #20 of figure 3), and Saddle Arch (near Upper Muley Twist Canyon) are also spectacular displays of these natural landforms. The development of bridges and arches is due to the interaction of differential erosion (erosion rates vary between less resistant and more resistant rocks), fractures, and ground water. The details of arch and bridge formation are discussed in this volume under Arches National Park (Doelling, this volume). The effort of a prepared hiker is often rewarded by obtaining postcard-quality photos of these bridges/ arches.

H. Capitol Dome/Navajo Dome

Capitol Dome and Navajo Dome, two of the more spectacular and easily observed domes in the park, can be viewed from a number of places along Highway 24 between the Hickman Bridge turnout (mile marker 81.8) and Grand Wash (mile marker 84.3; figure 1). Capitol Dome is located just west of Navajo Dome and can be viewed at the Hickman Bridge turnout. These and numerous rounded "domes" of rock have been created by headward erosion, downcutting, slope retreat, and weathering of the crossbedded Navajo Sandstone. Capitol Dome derives its name from its similarity to the rotundas of capitol buildings.

Figure 14. Honeycomb weathering in large-scale, high-angle trough cross-stratified dune sets of the Jurassic Navajo Sandstone in Spring Canyon (stop #12 of figure 3). View is to the south. Location is approximately 0.5 miles up-canyon from the confluence of Spring Canyon and the Fremont River.

Figure 15. Recumbent folds (outlined in lower center above dark desert varnish) and a flower or pop-up structure (outlined above recumbent fold and slightly left) indicating slumping and soft-sediment deformation in the Jurassic Navajo Sandstone erg. Soft-sediment deformation is common in the upper part of the Navajo within this area of the park. Outcrop is located at mile marker 86.2 along Highway 24. Note that lamina at the lower left edge of photo (above road level) are not involved in the folding. View is to the southeast.

I. Cavernous Weathering

Park visitors will observe cavernous weathering features along the base of sandstone faces throughout the park and along Highway 24 (site #12 of figure 3; figure 14). The lattice-work of small pockets in the sandstone walls are called "stone lace" or "honeycomb" weathering. Larger caverns are referred to as alcoves. Most of the pockets are irregularly oblong to hemispherical in shape. Some individual pockets have depths as much as two to three times the opening diameter and may branch internally to form several chambers (Mustoe, 1983).

Caverns are the result of chemical and mechanical weathering, in which grains and flakes of rock are loosened so as to enlarge hollows and recesses (Jackson, 1997). Granular disintegration may be due to hydration and dehydration. Mustoe (1983) in his study of cavernous weathering at Capitol Reef found different soluble minerals in the quartz-rich cement. As these minerals freeze and thaw, they loosen the surrounding grains making them subject to wind, water, and bioerosion. This process is accelerated in areas that are often damp and do not have a protective coat of desert varnish (a ferro-manganese residual on rock faces). The damp areas of sandstone walls, frequently found in dark slot canyons and at the bases of sandstone cliff faces, can absorb salt from underlying formations. This process makes the rock more susceptible to cavernous weathering.

J. Slot Canyons

The park visitor will have a variety of choices when it comes to traversing narrow, steep-walled canyons. These "slot" canyons allow one to experience yet another aspect of Capitol Reef National Park. The confined nature of the canyons allows the hiker to experience a world of rock texture and cool shade. The visitor should take note of weather conditions before traversing slot canyons as lives have been lost due to thunderstorm-induced flash floods. Stop at the Visitor Center for weather, road, and hiking conditions before venturing into any of these canyons.

Some favorite canyon hikes include Spring Canyon (one to two days), Grand Wash (half day), Upper and Lower Muley Twist Canyons (long day or overnight hikes), and Halls Creek Narrows (overnight hike) (see site #12 of figure 3 and figure 14, and sites 13, 18, 19 and 21 of figure 3, respectively). Most of the slot canyons in the park are sculpted into the thick Navajo Sandstone. As the area of the Waterpocket Fold was uplifted and the overlying flat layered rocks were eroded away, the dipping strata of the Waterpocket Fold allowed water to run off rapidly. Erosion along fractures focused the energy of the erosive water and created a myriad of beautiful steep-walled canyons.

K. Soft-Sediment Deformation

Soft-sediment deformation can be observed in outcrops of the Navajo Sandstone between mile marker 86.2 and 87 on Highway 24. Soft-sediment deformation occurs when unconsolidated sediments become contorted. The movement of the soft-sediment can result from gravitational forces, changes in ground water, or earthquakes.

One type of soft-sediment deformation is convolute bedding. This is described as lamina sets that are highly contorted, yet bounded above and below by noncontorted lamina (Jackson, 1997). On the southeast vertical wall at mile marker 86.2, one can observe recumbent folds and a flower (or pop-up) structure (site #14 of figure 3; figure 15). These structures were created by compressional and translational forces when lamina sets were still unconsoli-

Figure 16. "The Elf's Toe," a soft-sediment deformational feature, can be viewed by looking one third of the way up the west wall of Spring Canyon approximately 1.5 miles up-canyon from its confluence with the Fremont River (stop #12 of figure 3). For scale note geologist along the brush line. This feature is found stratigraphically lower in the Navajo Sandstone than are the features observed in figure 15.

Figure 17. Angular unconformity at mile marker 87.5 along Highway 24 (stop #15 of figure 3). This unconformity (white arrow) places gently dipping Quaternary alluvium over more steeply dipping Jurassic beds of the Carmel Formation (Jc; right center of photo) and Entrada Sandstone (Je; red beds at left middle edge of photo). Note the dark basaltic boulders and cobbles within and above the Quaternary alluvium (black arrow).

dated. The structures suggest that semi-cohesive lamina sets moved downward and laterally. Close observation reveals that there is a basal surface on which the contorted lamina sets detached and slid. This surface is finer grained than the host sandstone and is largely composed of silt- and clay-size particles. We suggest that this surface became wetted either by a rising ground water table associated with the transgressing Carmel Sea and/or associated climatic change, or by percolation of meteoric precipitation from above. In either case, water "greased" the silt- and clay-size particles of the basal surface which allowed gravity to pull the overlying dune sediments downward. Seismic triggering of this movement is also possible.

Another spectacular example of large-scale soft-sediment deformation is located approximately 1.5 miles up-canyon from the confluence of Spring Canyon and the Fremont River (site #12 of figure 3, figure 16). One must look one third of the way up the west wall of the canyon to observe this feature. The authors have called this unique curl within the Navajo Sandstone "The Elf's Toe." It was created by downslope movement (landslide-like movement) when the sand was cohesive, but not lithified. The downslope movement probably pushed a pile of sediment ahead of the toe. The pile may have acted as an abutment which in association with possible fluid expulsion, caused the up-slope bedsets of the toe to curl. The gradient of the basal surface of this structure does not seem to have been as high relative to the flower structure outcrop. Soft- sediment deformation, in the shape of a "sea lion," can also be observed closer to the canyon floor on the same wall.

L. Unconformities

The sedimentary strata of Capitol Reef National Park contain numerous unconformities. Unconformities are defined as substantial breaks or gaps of time in the geologic record. This implies that there was a significant amount of time between the adjacent beds where either there was no sedimentation or there was substantial erosion, or both. If an angular relationship exists between the two adjacent rock units, one can infer that the underlying strata were tectonically tilted previous to the deposition of the overlying beds. This type of unconformity is called an angular unconformity.

A particularly striking angular unconformity is found at mile marker 87.5 along Highway 24 (site #15 of figure 3; figure 17). On the southeast vertical outcrop, highly dipping beds of Carmel Formation and Entrada Sandstone terminate upward against more gently dipping Quaternary deposits of basalt-rich alluvium (black cobble and gravel clasts). The contact of these two units represents more than 100 million years of Earth history that has been eroded away.

The relationship between the two units helps geologists interpret the timing of the tectonic forces that created the Waterpocket Fold. Paleozoic and Mesozoic sediments (Permian through Cretaceous in the park) were deposited, buried, and lithified. They were then folded during the Laramide orogeny approximately 70 to 50 million years ago. Tertiary lacustrine (lake) sediments then onlapped and covered the folded strata from approximately 58 to 35 million years ago (Franczyk and others, 1991). Some of the oldest lacustrine sediments may have been involved in the Laramide folding. Composite volcanoes then covered the area just west of the park from approximately 25 to 20 million years ago (Nelson and Davidson, 1998). The entire rock succession was then uplifted allowing erosional forces to remove up to 7,000 feet of strata before exposing the present outcrops. Quaternary alluvium and debris flows, sourced from the basalt- rich bedrock of Boulder Mountain and Thousand Lake Mountain to the west, were deposited on top of the folded and eroded strata (figure 17). Over time, the finer-grained portions of this material has been transported off of the resistant bedrock surfaces.

Figure 18. Southwest view of Halls Creek Overlook looking toward the Circle Cliffs. The Red Slide is visible in the left center of the photo and fills much of the Entrada Sandstone strike valley. The dark, shadow-covered cliff face at the crest of the Waterpocket Fold is the Jurassic Wingate Sandstone (Jw; right center on skyline of photo).

The larger, black basalt boulders perched on the bedrock around the park are the remnants of this process.

Notom-Bullfrog Road

M. Oyster Reef

A few yards east of the road approximately 24 miles from the turnoff of Highway 24, one can observe large oyster shells incorporated within the Dakota Sandstone (site #16 of figure 3). Again, park visitors are reminded that collection of fossil material is illegal without a scientific research permit whether inside the national park or outside of the park in Bureau of Land Management areas. The concentration and accumulation of the oysters occurred when the Western Interior seaway started to transgress (or flood) the continent in the Late Cretaceous. At its peak, this seaway covered an area from central Utah to Minnesota and from the Gulf of Mexico to the Arctic Ocean. As the sea transgressed the land, brackish water oysters were concentrated in relatively high energy depositional environments such as the beach. For this and other reasons, the Dakota Sandstone has been interpreted to represent a marine foreshore and shoreface sandstone.

N. Strike Valleys

The Notom-Bullfrog Road runs north-south and parallels the length of the Waterpocket Fold on its east side (figure 3). The road essentially runs within strike valleys of upper Jurassic and Cretaceous age rocks (figure 7). Strike valleys form when tilted sedimentary rocks differentially erode. The harder, more resistant strata develop into ridges, sometimes referred to as hogbacks. The softer, less resistant strata form the valleys, where roads are often constructed. With a high clearance vehicle, one can obtain the best view of the park's strike valleys by driving and walking to the Strike Valley Overlook (site #17 of figure 3).

O. Landslides

Halls Creek Overlook is located approximately 49 miles from Highway 24 on the Notom-Bullfrog Road (site #20 of figure 3). The overlook provides a vantage point from which the visitor may observe a number of geological features. To the north is a stunning view of strike valleys. To the west one can observe Brimhall Double Bridge. Hiking to these bridges is possible via a 2.4-mile trail across the strike valley developed primarily on the Entrada Sandstone. To the southwest one can view the Circle Cliffs and see essentially a cross section of the Waterpocket Fold (figure 18). Erosion of the Glen Canyon Group exposes variegated redbeds of the Moenkopi and Chinle at the crest of the fold.

To the south and spilling out of the higher ridges of the fold into the Entrada strike valley, one can observe the Red Slide, a large landslide/mudslide that is composed of material primarily from the Moenkopi Formation. The Moenkopi Formation, in the Circle Cliffs area, is exposed at the topographic crest of the Waterpocket Fold. The fold is essentially an anticline, with rocks dipping both to the east and to the west of the crest. Red Slide formed when the Moody Canyon Member of the Moenkopi Formation slid on the more sand-rich Torrey Member. In the Quaternary, climatic conditions may have provided much more precipitation than at present to southern Utah. Under these wet conditions the exposed mudstones became soaked. The added weight of water and the reduced friction between layers of rock due to the water, caused the mudstone to become unstable and slide downslope by the force of gravity. It is likely that the Torrey Member was a bit more coherent than the Moody Canyon and acted as a detachment surface over which the wetted Moody Canyon slid. Once in motion, the landslide material flowed eastward over the flanks of the fold. It traveled over successively younger rock until its motion ceased in an Entrada-cored strike valley.

ACKNOWLEDGMENTS

The authors wish to thank Ken Hamblin for aerial photos and numerous consultations relative to the development of landforms at Capitol Reef. Craig Lybbert, a good friend and die-hard backpacker, came upon the Elf's Toe, realized it was strange, and brought a photo of it to the senior author. His enthusiasm and astute observational skills embellished our love of the park. Our colleague Steve Nelson helped us understand the volcanic history of the area. Allyson Mathis of the National Park Service provided insights into the unique aspects of the park and helped review the paper. Thanks to all involved in the National Park Service sponsored field trip and scoping meeting at Capitol Reef held in the September of 1999. Tom Clark, also of the National Park Service, provided us with insights and access to the park and to camping facilities when they were needed. The readability of the manuscript was improved by two reviewers. Thanks again to

Tom Clark (National Park Service) for his review of the manuscript and especially Margie Chan (University of Utah) for her most thorough review of the manuscript. Lastly, thanks to editors Tom Chidsey and Doug Sprinkel for allowing us to write about a park that we love and one that continues to fascinate us.

REFERENCES

Billingsley, G.H., Huntoon, P.W., and Breed, W.J., 1987, Geologic map of Capitol Reef National Park and vicinity, Emery, Garfield, Millard, and Wayne Counties, Utah: Utah Geological and Mineral Survey, map 87, scale 1:62,500.

Cole, R.D., Moore, G.E., Trevena, A.S., Armin, R.A., and Morton, M.P., 1996, Lithofacies definition in Cutler and Honaker Trail Formations, northeastern Paradox basin, *in* Huffman, A.C Jr., Lund, W.R., and Godwin, L.H., editors, Geology and resources of the Paradox basin: Utah Geological Association Publication 25, p. 161-172.

Delaney, P.T., and Gartner, A.E., 1997, Physical processes of shallow mafic dike emplacement near the San Rafael Swell, Utah: Geological Society of America Bulletin, v. 109, no. 9, p. 1177-1192.

Dubiel, R.F., 1987, Sedimentology of the Upper Triassic Chinle Formation, Southeastern, Utah: Boulder, Colorado, University of Colorado, Ph. D. dissertation, 132 p.

Franczyk, K.J., Hanley, J.H., Pitman, J.K., and Nichols, D.J., 1991, Paleocene depositional systems in the western Roan Cliffs, Utah, *in* Chidsey, T.C Jr., editor, Geology of east-central Utah: Utah Geological Association Publication 19, p. 111-139.

Friz, D.R., 1980, Paleocurrent directions in Late Triassic (?) Kayenta Formation, Capitol Reef National Park, Utah, *in* Picard, M.D., editor, Henry Mountain Symposium, Utah Geological Association Publicaton 8, p. 123-150.

Gartner, A.E., 1986, Geometry, emplacement history, petrography, and chemistry of a basaltic intrusive complex, San Rafael and Capitol Reef areas, Utah: U.S. Geological Survey Open-File Report 86-61, 112 p.

Hintze, L.F., 1993, Geologic History of Utah: Brigham Young University Geology Studies Special Publication 7, 45-49p.

Jackson, J.A., 1997, Glossary of Geology, Fourth Edition: American Geological Institute, p. 769.

Kamola, D.L., and Chan, M.A., 1986, Coastal dune facies, Permian Cutler Formation (White Rim Sandstone), Capitol Reef National Park area, southern Utah: Sedimentary Geology, v. 56, p. 341-356.

Mitchell, G.C., 1985, The Permian-Triassic stratigraphy of the northwest Paradox basin area, Emery, Garfield, and Wayne Counties, Utah: The Mountain Geologist, v. 22, no 4, p. 149-163.

Morris, T.H., Richmond, D.R., and Marino, J.E., 1991, The Paleocene/Eocene Colton Formation: a fluvial-domi-nated lacustrine deltaic system, Roan Cliffs, Utah, *in* Chidsey, T.C., Jr., editor, Geology of east-central Utah: Utah Geological Association Publication 19, p. 129-139.

Mustoe, G.E., 1983, Cavernous weathering in the Capitol Reef Desert, Utah: Earth Surface Processes and Landforms, New York, John Wiley and Sons Ltd., v. 8, p. 517- 526.

Nelson, S.T., and Davidson, J.P., 1998, Laccolith complexes of southeastern Utah time of emplacement and tectonic setting- workshop Proceedings: U.S. Geological Survey Bulletin 2158, p. 85-100.

Nelson, S.T., 1989, Geologic map of the Geyser Peak Quadrangle, Wayne and Sevier Counties, Utah: Utah Geological and Mineral Survey Map 114, 18 p., 2 plates, scale 1:24,000.

Petersen, L.M., and Roylance, M.M., 1982, Stratigraphy and depositional environments of the Upper Jurassic Morrison Formation near Capitol Reef National Park, Utah, *in* Hamblin, K.W., Gardner, C.M., editors, Brigham Young University Geology Studies, v. 29, pt. 2, p. 1-12.

Petersen, Fred, Ryder, R.T., and Law, B.E., 1980, Stratigraphy, sedimentology, and regional relationships of the Cretaceous System in the Henry Mountains region, Utah, *in* Picard, M.D., editor, Henry Mountains Symposium: Utah Geological Association Publicaton 8, p. 151-170.

Richmond, D.R., and Morris, T.H., 1998, Stratigraphy and cataclysmic deposition of the Dry Mesa Dinosaur Quarry, Mesa Country, Colorado, in Carpenter, K., Chure, D.J., and Kirkland, J.I., The Upper Jurassic Morrison Formation: An Interdisciplinary Study, Modern Geology, v. 22, pt. 1, p. 121-144.

Scotese, C.R., 1999, PALEOMAP animations: 1999 PALEOMAP project, compact disc.

Smith, F.J., Jr., Huff, L.C., Hinrichs, E.N., and Luedke, R.G., 1963, Geology of the Capitol Reef Area, Wayne and Garfield Counties, Utah: U.S. Geological Survey Professional Paper 102, p. 1-98.

Stanley, K.O., and Collinson, J.W., 1979, Depositional history of Paleocene-Eocene Flagstaff Limestone and coeval rocks, central Utah: American Association of Petroleum Geologists Bulletin, v. 63, p. 331-323.

Stewart, J.H., Poole, F.G., and Wilson, R.F., 1972a, Stratigraphy and origin of the Chinle Formation and related Upper Triassic strata in the Colorado Plateau region with a section on sedimentary petrology by R.A. Cadigan *and on* conglomerate studies by William Thordarson, H.F. Albee, and J.H. Stewart: U.S. Geological Survey Professional Paper 690, p. 336.

—1972b, Stratigraphy and origin of the Triassic Moenkopi Formation and related strata in the Colorado Plateau region with a section on sedimentary petrology Cadigan: U.S. Geological Survey Professional Paper 691, p. 195.

Stewart, J.H., Williams, G.A., Albee, H.F., and Raup, O.B.,

1959, Stratigraphy of Triassic and associated formations in part of the Colorado Plateau region: U.S. Geological Survey Bulletin p. 487-573.

Turner, C.E. and Peterson, Fred, 1998, Late Jurassic ecosystem reconstruction during deposition of the Morrison Formation and related beds in the western interior of the United States: U.S. Geological Survey, The Morrison Extinct Ecosystems Project, report to National Park Service.

The Watchman, Zion National Park
Photo courtesy of the Utah Travel Council

Geology of Utah's Parks and Monuments
2000 Utah Geological Association Publication 28
D.A. Sprinkel, T.C. Chidsey, Jr., and P.B. Anderson, editors

Geology of Zion National Park, Utah

Robert F. Biek[1], Grant C. Willis[1], Michael D. Hylland[1], and Hellmut H. Doelling[1]

ABSTRACT

The cliffs and mesas of Zion National Park are carved from nearly 7,000 feet (2,130 m) of colorful sedimentary strata ranging in age from the Early Permian Toroweap Formation to newly recognized late Early Cretaceous strata. These rocks provide a record of changing environmental conditions through 275 million years of geologic time. Fossils and other clues in the rocks tell us that they were deposited in a variety of shallow-marine, coastal-sabkha, tidal-flat, coastal-plain, sand-desert, river, and lake environments. Perhaps the most famous of all are the immense ancient sand dunes of the Navajo Sandstone, seen in the great, sweeping cross-beds of the canyon walls. Zion National Park owes much of its character to the Navajo Sandstone, which here attains its maximum thickness of about 2,200 feet (671 m).

The rocks of Zion National Park are tilted gently to the northeast as part of a large structural block - bounded on the east by the Sevier fault zone and on the west by the Hurricane fault zone - at the western margin of the Colorado Plateau. Although the structure of the main part of the park is relatively simple, exceptionally well-developed joints are largely responsible for the orientation of the existing canyon network. In the Kolob Canyons portion of the park, these rocks are folded into the Kanarra anticline, where beds on the east limb of the anticline are duplicated by back-thrust faults of the Taylor Creek fault zone.

Zion National Park is a window through which we can view and comprehend these stories entombed in ancient layers of rock, but above all, it is a monument to erosion. The canyons of Zion National Park represent an early stage in the erosion of the Kolob Terrace, which rises high above the Hurricane Cliffs. Erosion of this structural block by the Virgin River and its tributaries began with headward erosion of the first fault scarps on the Hurricane fault zone, which probably first moved in the Pliocene, at least several million years ago. Several times over about the past 1.5 million years, basaltic lava flowed down and blocked the Virgin River and some of its tributaries, and many of the flows now form classic examples of inverted topography. The flows also provide unique control on the erosive history of Zion National Park and vicinity, and demonstrate that most of Zion Canyon was carved within the past 2 million years. Landslides and lava flows have periodically blocked the canyons of Zion National Park, forming small lakes and ponds. Lacustrine deposits associated with at least 14 lakes are known in the park, and they provide a record of more recent environmental changes.

Zion National Park is replete with classic geologic sites and informative exposures, from the scale of a small outcrop to an entire canyon network. We offer a necessarily incomplete list of two dozen of these sites.

INTRODUCTION

Zion National Park is best known for Zion Canyon, a narrow chasm whose sheer walls of Navajo Sandstone tower 2,000 feet (610 m) above the canyon floor. The canyon is a narrow slot in its upper reaches, but widens considerably below "The Narrows" where it cuts into less resistant beds of the underlying Kayenta and Moenave Formations. The canyon walls are adorned with blind arches and alcoves of every description; with hanging valleys, some with waterfalls, that record differential erosion along the Virgin River and its tributaries; and with colorful surficial stains derived from seeps, desert varnish, and the red mudstones of the overlying Temple Cap Formation. The flat canyon floor records the evolution of river terraces and of a large landslide-dammed lake.

It's hard to imagine that Zion National Park has much more to offer, yet the geologic cross section exposed in Zion Canyon represents just a sliver of the larger history collectively recorded in the Kolob Canyons portion of the

---

[1]*Utah Geological Survey, Salt Lake City, UT 84114-6100*

Figure 1. View east to the southwest part of Zion National Park. The West Temple is on the skyline at right.

park, in areas high above the rim of Zion Canyon, and in the southern part of the park (figure 1). Sedimentary strata as old as the Early Permian Toroweap and Kaibab Formations are exposed in the Hurricane Cliffs near the Kolob Canyons. The Early Triassic Moenkopi Formation and the Late Triassic Chinle Formation form east-dipping cuestas near there as well, and are also found in the mesas of the southern part of the park. The great cliffs of Navajo Sandstone are capped by Temple Cap, Carmel, and, farther back from the rim, Cretaceous strata. Nearly 7,000 feet (2,130 m) of sedimentary strata is exposed at Zion National Park, and these rocks, stacked layer upon layer, provide a record of changing environmental conditions through 275 million years of geologic time.

Zion National Park is readily accessible via Interstate 15 and Utah Highway 9 in eastern Washington County, in the southwestern corner of the state (figure 2). The park

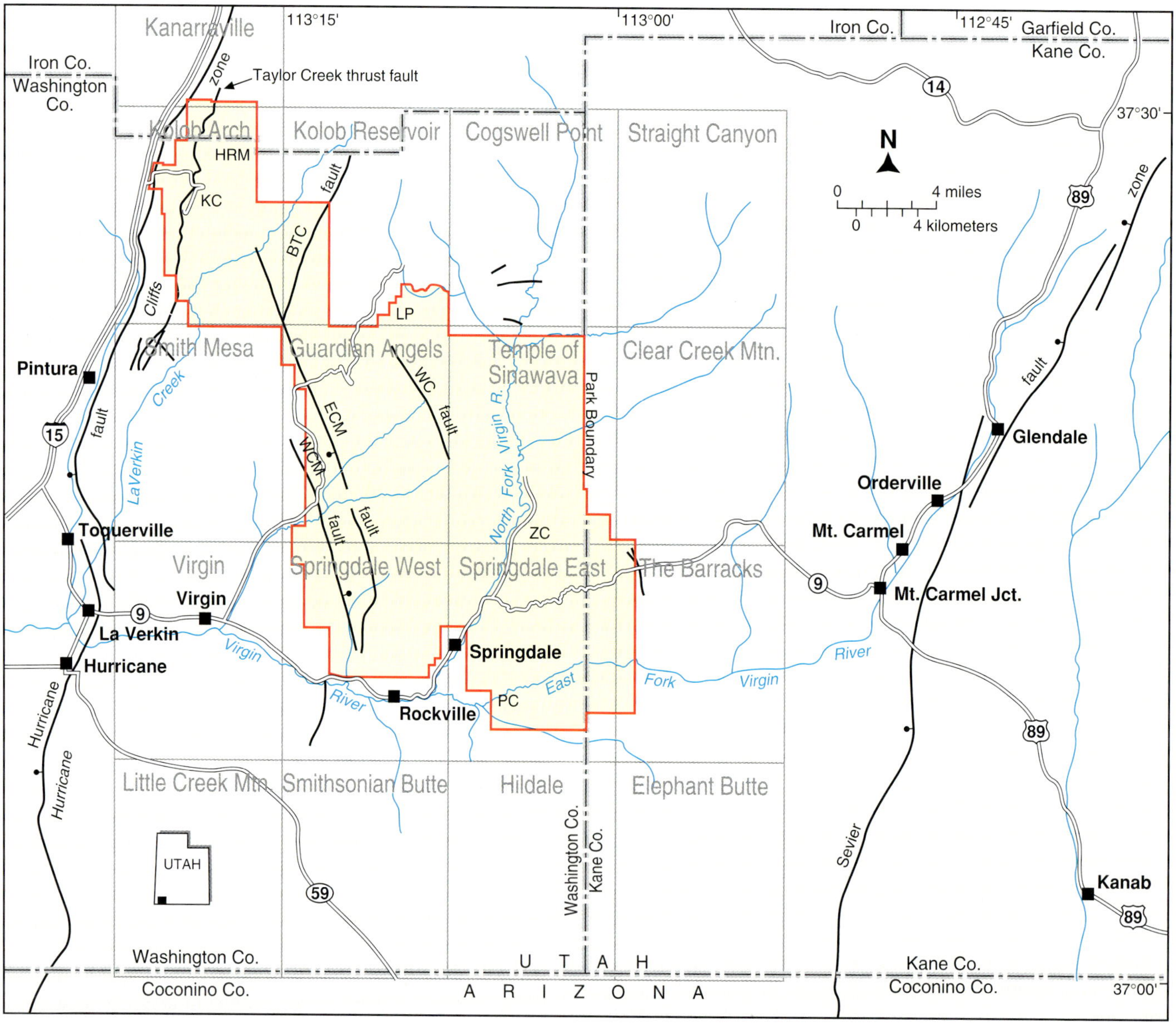

Figure 2. Location of Zion National Park showing USGS 7.5' quadrangles. BTC = Bear Trap Canyon, ECM = East Cougar Mountain, HRM = Horse Ranch Mountain, KC = Kolob Canyons, LP = Lava Point, PC = Parunuweap Canyon, WCM = West Cougar Mountain, WC = Wildcat Mountain, ZC = Zion Canyon.

ranges in elevation from about 3,700 feet (1,220 m) near Grafton to 8,726 feet (2,659 m) at Horse Ranch Mountain, and so encompasses several climatic zones, ranging from the dry Sonoran climate of the Virgin River lowlands to the cool Ponderosa forests of the Upper Kolob Plateau. Little snow falls in Zion Canyon, but snow accumulates on the higher plateaus, closing the road to Lava Point during the winter months.

Untold numbers of geologists have studied the rocks and sediments of Zion National Park, and the geology outlined here draws heavily on their collective efforts. Some of these reports are cited in the following text, while a more complete list of references will be available in our reports and geologic maps (in progress) of the Clear Creek Mountain, Cogswell Point, Kolob Arch, Kolob Reservoir, Springdale East, Springdale West, Temple of Sinawava, and The Guardian Angels 7.5' quadrangles in which the park lies (figure 2). Gregory (1950) reviewed the early exploration of the region and is generally credited with producing the first detailed geologic account and map (at a scale of 1:125,000) of the Zion National Park region. Hamilton (1978) produced a 1:31,680-scale geologic map of the park and subsequently wrote a popular account of the park's geology (Hamilton, 1995). In 1996, under a Utah Geological Survey/National Park Service cooperative project, we began mapping the geology of the park and surrounding area at a scale of 1:24,000.

Regional Setting

Zion National Park lies at the western margin of the Colorado Plateau, near the transition zone between the Colorado Plateau and Basin and Range physiographic provinces. The Colorado Plateau province is a relatively coherent and tectonically stable region underlain by generally horizontal sedimentary strata that are locally disrupted by early Tertiary Laramide basement-block uplifts, Oligocene/Miocene igneous intrusions, and late Tertiary to Quaternary basalt flows. The Basin and Range Province is characterized by thinned crust and roughly east-west extensional tectonics, with block faulting and widespread igneous activity. Both provinces have experienced broad, regional uplift. The transition zone is characterized by sedimentary strata and structures common to both physiographic provinces.

In southwestern Utah, the transition zone and western Colorado Plateau include several major down-to-the-west normal fault zones that step down from the Colorado Plateau to the Basin and Range Province. Zion National Park lies on an intermediate structural block bounded on the west by the Hurricane fault zone and on the east by the Sevier fault zone (figure 2). The bulk of the park is carved from sedimentary strata that dip gently northeast, and, although prominently jointed, are little complicated by faults. This area, however, also roughly coincides with the leading edge of the Sevier orogeny, the middle Mesozoic to early Tertiary compressional event that gives the park one of its two most prominent structural features - the Kanar-

ra anticline in the Kolob Canyons area (figure 2). The anticline is complicated by the Taylor Creek thrust fault, which duplicates strata on the east limb of the anticline. The Hurricane fault zone, the other major structural feature in the park, also in the Kolob Canyons area, is an active, north-trending, west-dipping normal fault that displays significant Quaternary offset.

GEOLOGIC HISTORY

The Bedrock History of Zion National Park

Natural wonders abound in Zion National Park, but for most visitors it is the landscape itself, and the colorful, nearly horizontal layers of rock from which it is carved, that first attracts one's attention. These sedimentary rocks, stacked layer upon layer, provide a record of changing environmental conditions through 275 million years of geologic time (figure 3). The rocks of Zion National Park were deposited in a variety of shallow-marine, tidal-flat, sabkha, sand-desert, coastal-plain, river, and lake environments reminiscent of the modern Caribbean Sea, Gulf Coast coastal plain, Sahara desert, and coastal Arabian Peninsula, among other places. These changing depositional environments are a direct result of almost imperceptibly slow plate tectonic movements. Over this enormous span of time, Utah, as part of North America, drifted northward from a position about 10 degrees north of the equator, moving through 27 degrees of latitude and several climatic belts (see, Scotese, 1999, for web address).

Both the oldest and youngest sedimentary bedrock formations in Zion National Park are in the Kolob Canyons portion of the park (figures 4, 5 and 6; appendix 1). The oldest geologic formation, the shallow-marine limestone of the Early Permian Toroweap Formation, is exposed at the base of the Hurricane Cliffs, in the east limb of the Kanarra anticline. Strata become progressively younger eastward across the limb of the anticline to Horse Ranch Mountain, where the youngest sedimentary rocks in the park—Cretaceous strata deposited in a basin in front of the ancestral Sevier orogenic belt—are exposed. Nearly 7,000 feet (2,130 m) of Permian to Cretaceous sedimentary strata lie between these two formations, including the Navajo Sandstone for which the park is justly famous. Basalt flows from several vents in and near the park provide unique control on volcanic, erosive, and fault movement histories. Landslide and lake deposits throughout the park attest to more recent environmental changes and the ever-present erosion of the canyons of Zion National Park.

Permian

At Zion National Park, Permian time is represented by sedimentary strata that accumulated on the western margin of the great supercontinent Pangea, which was flanked farther west by a complex island arc assemblage. The Early Permian Toroweap and Kaibab Formations were de-

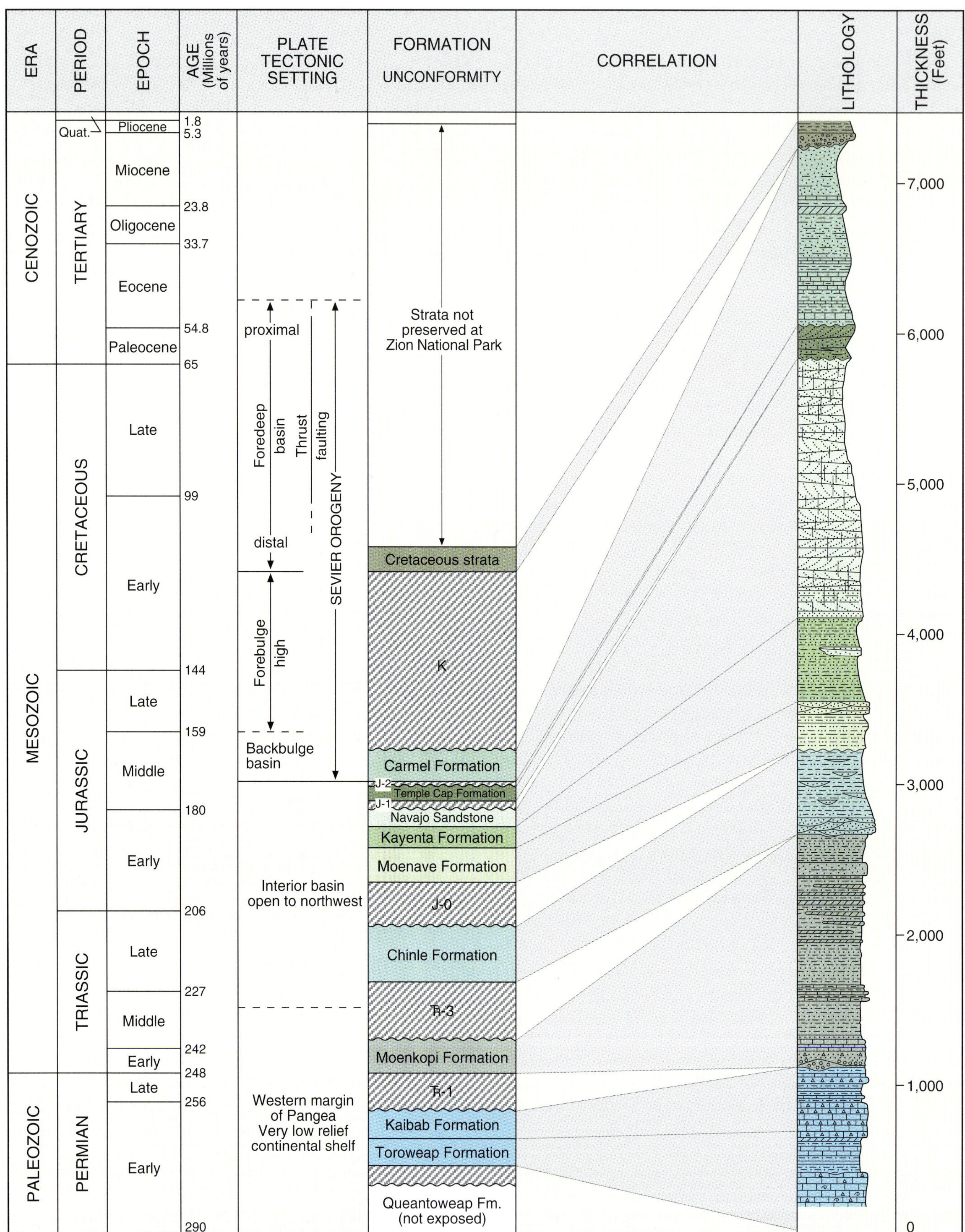

Figure 3. *Summary chart showing geologic history of sedimentary bedrock formations of Zion National Park. Formations of Cretaceous to late Tertiary age total several thousand feet thick immediately outside the park, but were removed by erosion from the park itself. This erosion is directly tied to the uplift of the Colorado Plateau, which occured principally in the Late Cretaceous to early Eocene. Unconformity designations from Pipiringos and O'Sullivan (1978).*

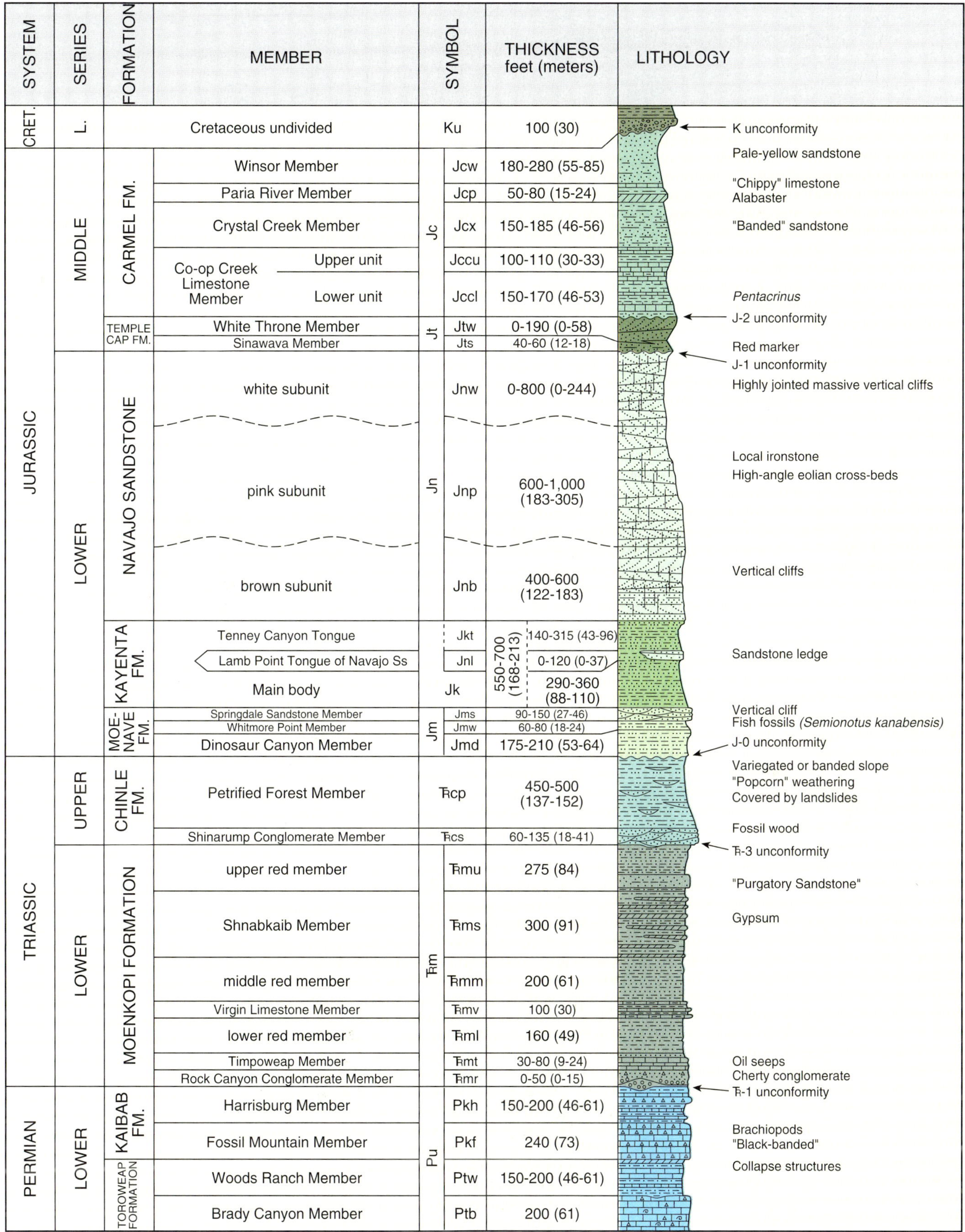

Figure 4. Lithologic column showing rock units present in Zion National Park.

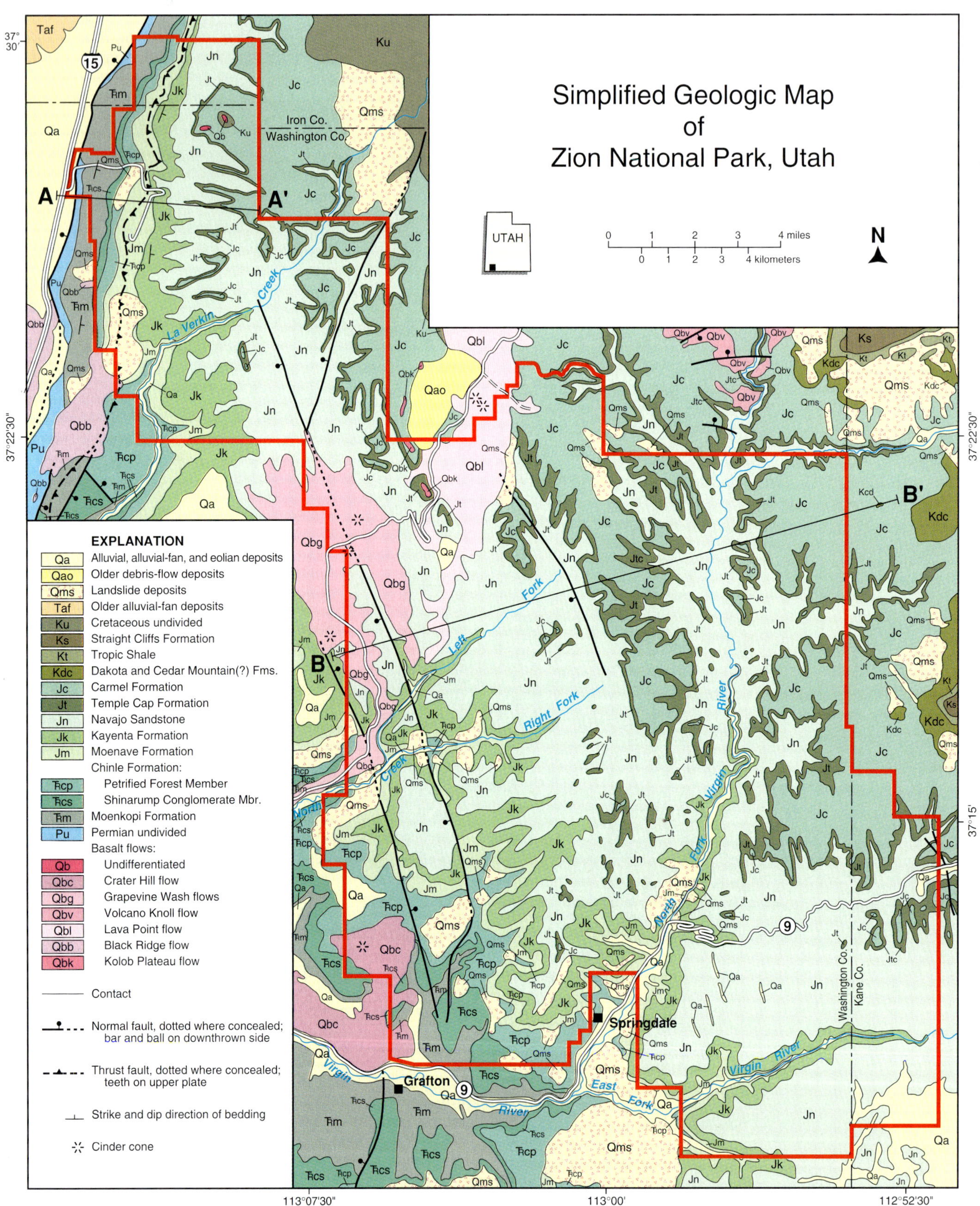

Figure 5. *Simplified geologic map of Zion National Park. Compiled and simplified from Cook (1960), Doelling and Davis (1989), and the authors' mapping. Cross sections A–A' and B–B' shown on figure 6.*

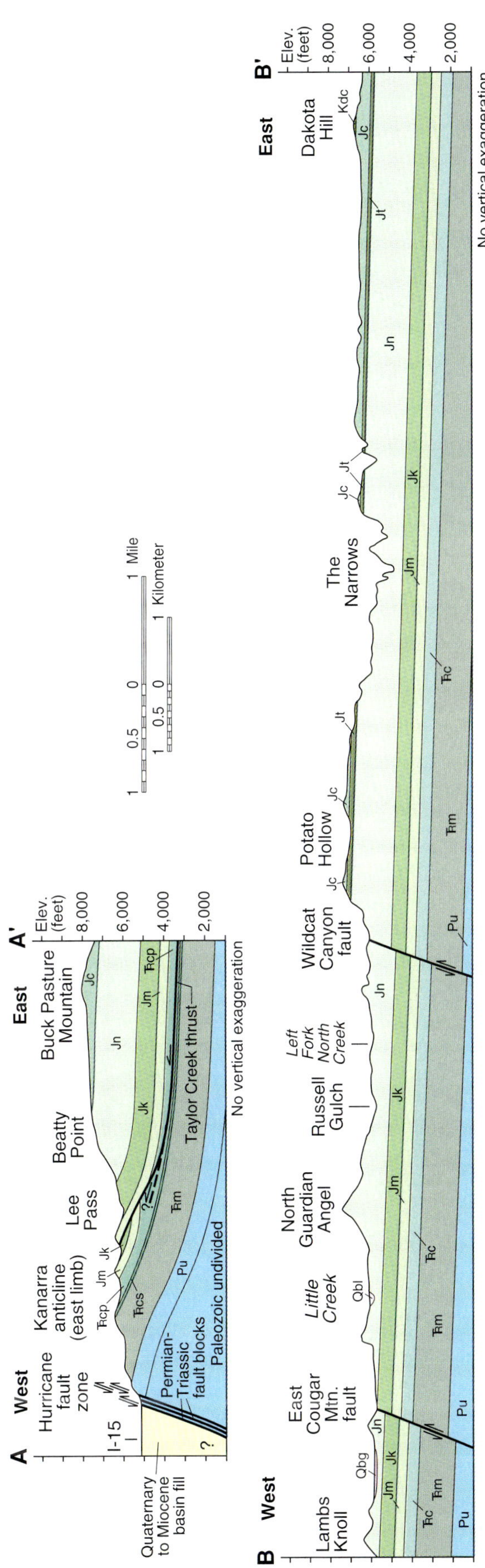

Figure 6. Simplified geologic cross sections of Zion National Park. No vertical exaggeration, but scales differ from map. See figure 5 for cross section locations.

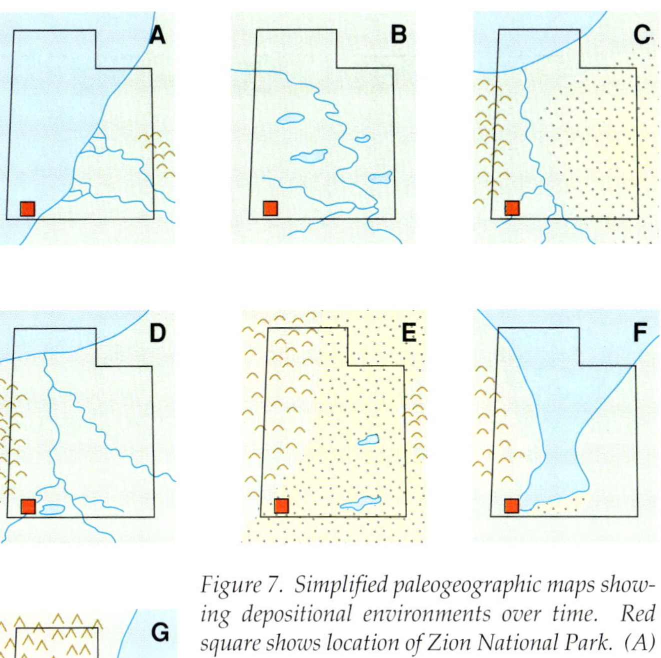

Figure 7. Simplified paleogeographic maps showing depositional environments over time. Red square shows location of Zion National Park. (A) Early Permian Toroweap and Kaibab Formations to Early Triassic Moenkopi Formation; (B) Late Triassic Chinle Formation; (C) Early Jurassic Moenave Formation; (D) Early Jurassic Kayenta Formation; (E) Early Jurassic Navajo Sandstone; (F) Middle Jurassic Temple Cap and Carmel Formations; and (G) middle Cretaceous strata. Modified from DeCourten (1998).

posited when southwestern Utah lay just north of the equator, at the Pangean margin, alternately inundated by warm, shallow seas and exposed as broad coastal sabkhas (sabkhas are broad, very flat surfaces near sea level with very high evaporation rates, such as in some parts of the Arabian Penninsula) (figure 7A). The park includes just two short segments of the Hurricane Cliffs where the Kaibab Formation and the underlying Toroweap Formation are found, but these beds are widely exposed in the Hurricane Cliffs both to the north and south of the park. Near the Kolob Canyons Visitor Center, these strata are highly faulted and altered along the Hurricane fault zone; several uranium prospects are located in Kaibab strata just south of the park boundary.

The Toroweap Formation includes three members, the Seligman, Brady Canyon, and Woods Ranch Members, but only the uppermost part of the Brady Canyon Member and the Woods Ranch Member are exposed in the park. Limestone, cherty limestone, and gypsiferous siltstone of the formation record a major west-to-east shallow-marine transgression, highstand, and regression (McKee, 1938; Rawson and Turner-Peterson, 1979; Nielson, 1981, 1986; Sorauf and Billingsley, 1991). The similar rocks of the Kaibab Formation are grouped into two members, the Fossil Mountain Member and the overlying Harrisburg Member, that record the last major Permian transgression in southwest Utah (Nielson, 1981; Sorauf and Billingsly,

Figure 8. View of southwest side of Hurricane Mesa showing Moenkopi strata (Ʀml, Ʀmv, Ʀmm, Ʀms, Ʀmu) and the cliff-forming Shinarump Conglomerate Member (Ʀcs) of the Chinle Formation.

1991). The warm, shallow-marine nature of these limestones is revealed by fossil brachiopods, sponge spicules, disarticulated corals, crinoids, and bryozoans.

The upper contact of the Harrisburg Member is an erosional unconformity that spans 10 to 20 million years during Late Permian and Early Triassic time (Nielson, 1981, 1991; Sorauf and Billingsley, 1991). This is the TR-1 unconformity of Pipiringos and O'Sullivan (1978), the first regional unconformity of the Triassic Period in the western U.S. In Zion National Park, erosion associated with the Permian-Triassic unconformity has locally incised several tens of feet into the upper part of the Harrisburg Member.

Triassic

The Moenkopi Formation of southwestern Utah, with its alternating reddish-brown, white, and gray layers, documents renewed sedimentation along the western margin of Pangea. The Moenkopi Formation consists of three transgressive members (the Timpoweap, Virgin Limestone, and Shnabkaib Members), each of which is overlain by an informally named regressive red-bed member (the lower, middle, and upper red members, respectively) (figure 8); the Rock Canyon Conglomerate Member locally forms the base of the Moenkopi Formation (Reeside and Bassler, 1921; Stewart and others, 1972; Dubiel, 1994). These members record a complicated series of shallow-marine transgressions and regressions across a very gently sloping continental shelf, where sea level changes of several feet translated into shoreline changes of many miles (Dubiel, 1994). The Moenkopi Formation is exposed atop the Hurricane Cliffs and in fault-bounded blocks along the Hurricane fault zone in the Kolob Canyons area, and in the lower reaches of Coalpits Wash and Huber Wash in the southwest corner of the park.

Perhaps the most interesting part of the Moenkopi Formation is its basal member, the Rock Canyon Conglomerate. It consists of two main rock types: a rounded pebble and cobble conglomerate found in paleovalleys, and a widespread, but thin, regolithic breccia. The clasts

are chert and minor limestone derived exclusively from Harrisburg Member strata. These deposits are restricted to paleochannels that are up to several tens of feet deep and are characterized by low-angle cross-stratification. Channels as much as 200 feet (61 m) deep are known in the St. George area (Higgins, 1997). Rock Canyon Conglomerate breccia deposits are poorly developed at Zion National Park, but are found over paleotopographic high areas between channel-form conglomerates. These deposits consist of both clast- and matrix-supported breccias that contain well-cemented, angular, pebble- to cobble-size chert and limestone clasts derived from in-situ weathering of the underlying Harrisburg Member of the Kaibab Formation (Nielson, 1991).

The Timpoweap and Virgin Limestone Members of the Moenkopi Formation form eastward-thinning wedges of shallow-marine limestone and mudstone that thicken from east to west across the former continental shelf of southwestern Utah. The Shnabkaib Member also thickens westward, but its abundant gypsum and interbedded mudstone indicates deposition in a restricted marine environment with complex water-table fluctuations (Lambert, 1984). Conversely, the red bed members thin to the west, away from the former continental margin. Common ripple marks and other features indicate that they were deposited in tidal-flat and coastal-plain environments (Stewart and others, 1972).

In southwestern Utah, the TR-3 regional unconformity (Pipiringos and O'Sullivan, 1978) separates Early Triassic (Moenkopi Formation) and Late Triassic (Chinle Formation) rocks and marks a change from mostly shallow-marine to continental sedimentation. Thus by the Late Triassic, Utah was part of a large interior basin drained by north- and northwest-flowing rivers that deposited the colorful layers of the Chinle Formation (figure 7B). The Chinle Formation of southwestern Utah consists of the Shinarump Conglomerate and the Petrified Forest Members; sandstones locally present at the base of the Petrified Forest Member may belong to a distal, unmapped facies of the Monitor Butte Member (Doelling and Davis, 1989). The Shinarump Conglomerate forms a prominent east-dipping cuesta in the Kolob Canyons area, and forms bold mesas, including Rockville Bench, in the southwest part of the park (figure 9). The overlying Petrified Forest Member is commonly covered by landslide deposits, but where well exposed, it displays bright, variegated mudstone slopes.

The sandstone, pebbly sandstone, and pebbly conglomerate of the Shinarump Conglomerate was deposited principally in braided-stream channels by north- and northwest-flowing streams, whereas the Petrified Forest Member was deposited in flood plains, lakes, and high-sinuosity stream channels in a low, forested basin (Stewart and others, 1972; Dubiel, 1994). Amphibians, reptiles - including the crocodile-like phytosaur - freshwater clams, snails, ostracods, and fish made their home on this once vast, coastal lowland, and petrified conifer trees are com-

Figure 9. View north into Zion Canyon from the radio towers southeast of Rockville. The Shinarump Conglomerate (Ŧcs) forms the prominent mesa in the lower left, above which is Petrified Forest strata (Ŧcp) mostly covered by landslides (Qms) and pediment gravels (Qap). The Petrified Forest Member is overlain by ledges of the Dinosaur Canyon (Jmd) and slopes of the Whitmore Point (Jmw) Members, above which is the prominent cliff of Springdale Sandstone (Jms). The Kayenta Formation (Jk) forms a steep slope mostly covered by talus below the massive cliffs of the Navajo Sandstone (Jn). Note the high pediment surface (Qap) at the eastern base of Mt. Kinesava.

mon in Chinle strata; fossil cycads, ferns, and horsetails are also known (Stewart and others, 1972; Blakey and others, 1993; Dubiel, 1994; DeCourten, 1998). Abundant bentonitic mudstone, which swells when wet and shrinks when dry (giving weathered surfaces a "popcorn" appearance), was derived from volcanic ash that drifted in from an island arc to the west. These mudstones are notoriously susceptible to landslides and have caused numerous building foundation problems in southwest Utah. Ancient soil horizons (paleosols) are common in the Petrified Forest Member and are noted for their mottled beds and limestone nodules. The upper contact of the Petrified Forest Member is the J-0 unconformity and represents a gap of about 10 million years during the Late Triassic and Early Jurassic (Pipiringos and O'Sullivan, 1978).

Jurassic

The interior basin setting that characterized the Late Triassic persisted into the Early Jurassic with deposition of the Moenave Formation in a variety of river, lake, and flood-plain environments (Clemmensen and others, 1989; Blakey, 1994; Peterson, 1994) (figure 7C). The Moenave Formation forms a distinctive, three-part sequence in the Kolob Canyons area, in the lower reaches of Zion and Parunuweap Canyons, and in the southwest part of the park. In ascending order, it is divided into the slope-forming Dinosaur Canyon and Whitmore Point Members, overlain by the cliff-forming Springdale Sandstone Member (figure 9).

If the Dinosaur Canyon Member is noted for its uniformity - mostly reddish-brown, thin- bedded, very fine- to fine-grained sandstone and silty sandstone - the Whitmore Point Member must be known for its variety. The Whitmore Point contains similar sandstone and siltstone as the Dinosaur Canyon, but also contains reddish-purple

to greenish-gray mudstone and claystone and thin dolomitic limestone beds. The limestones are bioturbated and contain small, moderate-reddish-brown chert nodules and blebs, poorly preserved and contorted algal structures, and locally abundant fossil fish scales and bones of *Semionotus kanabensis* (Hesse, 1935; Schaeffer and Dunkle, 1950). The fish fossils were originally thought to be restricted to the Triassic and so conflicted with palynomorphs from the Whitmore Point Member that indicate the unit is Early Jurassic (latest Sinemurian to earliest Pliensbachian) (Peterson and others, 1977; Imlay, 1980). Olsen and Padian (1986) later found that *Semionotus kanabensis* is not age diagnostic, which resolved the long-standing debate on the Early Jurassic age of the Moenave, Kayenta and Navajo Formations. Recently discovered dinosaur tracks in correlative beds near St. George also confirm an Early Jurasic age for the lower Moenave Formation in southwest Utah (James Kirkland, Utah Geological Survey, verbal communication, March 30, 2000).

The Springdale Sandstone Member forms the first significant cliff below the Navajo Sandstone, except for the less prominent Lamb Point Tongue of the Navajo Sandstone in the southeast part of the park. It forms a prominent cliff in the lower reaches of Zion and Parunuweap Canyons and the southwest part of the park, and an east-dipping cuesta repeated by thrust faults in the Kolob Canyons area. Because the Springdale was deposited principally in river channels, it contains thin, discontinuous lenses of intraformational conglomerate, with mudstone and siltstone rip-up clasts and poorly preserved, petrified and carbonized fossil plant remains. Similar channel deposits near Leeds, just west of the park, were the primary ore horizons of the Silver Reef mining district (Proctor and Shirts, 1991).

The Kayenta Formation was deposited in river, distal

Figure 10. View west from the Canyon Overlook above The Great Arch. The Kayenta Formation (Jk) forms slopes covered by talus above the Springdale Sandstone Member of the Moenave Formation (Jms) and below the Navajo Sandstone (Jn). Utah Highway 9 climbs up landslide deposits (Qms) developed in the Kayenta Formation.

river/playa, and minor lake environments (Blakey, 1994; Peterson, 1994) (figure 7D). It forms a deep-red, steep slope between cliffs of the Springdale Sandstone below and the Navajo Sandstone above, but its outcrop belt is commonly covered by talus derived from itself and the Navajo Sandstone (figure 10). In Zion and Parunuweap Canyons, an eolian (wind blown) sandstone known as the Lamb Point Tongue of the Navajo Sandstone forms a ledge about one-third of the way down from the base of the Navajo. Thus, in eastern exposures, the lower two-thirds of the Kayenta are designated the main body of the Kayenta Formation. The upper third is known as the Tenney Canyon Tongue. The Lamb Point Tongue pinches out westward so that the Kayenta Formation is undivided in the Kolob Canyons and most of the Guardian Angels parts of the park. In southwest Utah, the Kayenta is probably best known for its dinosaur tracks, some of which are found near the Subway on the Left Fork of North Creek.

As plate motions continued to move North America northward, and as mountains in Nevada and California created a rain shadow (see, Scotese, 1999, for web address), Utah entered the arid, low-latitude climatic belt. Vast dune fields similar to the modern Sahara eventually overwhelmed the Kayenta playas, leaving behind the Navajo Sandstone, part of the world's largest coastal and inland paleodune field (Blakey and others, 1988; Blakey, 1994; Peterson, 1994) (figure 7E). This transition is wonderfully recorded in strata that enclose the gradational contact between the Kayenta Formation and Navajo Sandstone. During this transitional time, the area was a sabkha, a broad, flat evaporation pan with a high water table. As sand was blown onto the sabkha, it adhered to the wet surface. Crinkle bedding and salt casts formed through the growth of evaporite minerals (Tuesink, 1989; Sansom, 1992). Eventually, the sabkha was overtaken by the windblown sand, but the water table remained high. This led

to the formation of planar sandstone beds in the lower Navajo as dry sand was blown away and wet sand remained behind. With time, large sand dunes eventually formed. The great, sweeping cross-beds of these sand dunes are preserved in the middle and upper parts of the Navajo Sandstone, where uncommon planar sandstone and limestone beds provide a record of widely scattered oases. A good example of such oasis deposits can be seen along the Canyon Overlook Trail.

The Early Jurassic Navajo Sandstone is renown for its uniformity and great thickness, locally exceeding 2,000 feet (610 m). It consists of moderately well-cemented, well-rounded, frosted, fine- to medium-grained quartz grains and weathers to bold, rounded cliffs. The Navajo is characterized by large-scale cross-beds; rare convoluted cross-beds represent slumping of sand dunes near widely scattered oases. The sand was probably recycled from Paleozoic and Triassic sandstone to the north in Montana, and perhaps as far away as Alberta, Canada, in addition to being reworked from more local sources (Peterson, 1988).

Though lithologically the Navajo Sandstone is remarkably uniform from bottom to top, it is locally divided into three informal subunits based on color. In ascending order, these are the brown, pink, and white subunits. The brown Navajo is cliff-forming, probably because it is slightly more strongly cemented by iron oxide; hanging valleys tend to form at the top of this subunit. The pink subunit appears to be more uniformly stained by iron oxides (hematite) and may reflect the unaltered color of the Navajo. The pink subunit is somewhat porous and friable, but in places, iron mineralization or cementation is very pronounced, and sheets, concretions, and nodules of ironstone litter the outcrops. Ironstone may contain less than 1 percent to about 20 percent iron oxide. The white subunit forms the highest cliffs of the Navajo Sandstone in Zion National Park and is exemplified by the Great White Throne. The white color is due to a change in the oxidation state of the iron minerals that help to cement the sandstone, from the original iron oxide (hematite) cement of the pink subunit to hydrated iron oxide (limonite) of the white subunit. The top of the white subunit is locally stained red by runoff from the mudstone and siltstone of the overlying Sinawava Member of the Temple Cap Formation, giving rise to descriptions of blood dripping from the highest prominences or altars of the park (such as the Altar of Sacrifice). The color units are not valid in a stratigraphic sense and were formed by post-depositional alteration of cement in the sandstone by ground-water and possibly hydrocarbon movement through the rock. The boundaries between these subunits are irregular, rise and fall across cross-bed sets, and are difficult to discern except from a distance. The white subunit disappears in western exposures.

The top of the Navajo Sandstone forms a remarkably flat surface, the J-1 unconformity (Pipiringos and O'Sullivan, 1978). Over short distances, little relief is noticeable along the contact, but when extended over several miles, the relief may be as much as several hundred feet. This is

Gregory and Moore (1931)	Gregory (1933)	Baker & others (1936)	Gregory (1948, 1950)	Wright & Dickey (1963a, b)	Cashion (1967)	Thompson and Stokes (1970)	Doelling and Davis (1989), and this report
Morrison(?) Formation	Undifferentiated Jurassic(?)	Curtis Formation	Winsor Formation	Carmel Formation	Winsor Member	Winsor Member	Winsor Member
Summerville(?) Formation							
			Curtis Formation		Gypsiferous member	Paria River Member	Paria River Member
Carmel Formation		Entrada Sandstone	Entrada Sandstone		Banded member	Crystal Creek Member	Crystal Creek Member
	Carmel Formation	Carmel Formation	Carmel Formation		Limestone member	Kolob Limestone Member	Co-op Creek Limestone Member

Figure 11. *History of nomenclature of the Carmel Formation in the Zion National Park area.*

believed to account for differences in the total Navajo thickness, which ranges from 1,800 to 2,200 feet (550-670 m) in the park. The lower part of the Temple Cap Formation, named for beds that cap the West Temple (figure 1), marks a brief respite in desert conditions, when rising warm shallow seas in the Utah-Idaho trough beveled the top of the Navajo Sandstone, leaving behind red mudstone of the Sinawava Member (figure 7F). Wind-blown sand dunes of the White Throne Member herald a similarly brief return to desert conditions of a coastal dune field (Blakey, 1994; Peterson, 1994). The White Throne Member thins westward and pinches out near the Hurricane fault; only the Sinawava Member, which thickens westward, is present in the Kolob Canyons area. Like the Navajo Sandstone, the top of the White Throne Member was beveled flat by encroaching seas, forming the J-2 unconformity of Pipiringos and O'Sullivan (1978).

By Middle Jurassic time, deformation associated with the subduction of the Farallon oceanic plate in the California area spread eastward into western Utah. These eastward-directed compressional forces created the Sevier thrust system, which consists of, from west to east, a thrust belt, a foredeep basin, a forebulge, and a back-bulge basin (see, for example, Willis, 1999). Each of these four parts of the thrust system migrated eastward through the park area over time, and each created unique environments of deposition or erosion. The Carmel Formation, for example, was deposited in a shallow inland sea of the back-bulge basin (figure 7F), the first clear record of the effects of the Sevier orogeny in southwestern Utah. Due to rapidly changing conditions in the basin, the Carmel of southwestern Utah has many different rock types and a complicated history of nomenclature (figure 11). As presently mapped, the Carmel consists of four members in the Zion National Park area. In ascending order, these are the Co-op Creek Limestone, Crystal Creek, Paria River, and Winsor Members. Although widely exposed on the Upper Kolob Plateau north and east of the park, the Winsor Member is not exposed within the main part of Zion National

Park; ongoing mapping will determine if it is present in the Kolob Canyons and Lava Point areas. In southwestern Utah, the Middle Jurassic Carmel Formation forms an eastward-thickening wedge preserved beneath the Cretaceous (K) regional unconformity of Pipiringos and O'Sullivan (1978) (Imlay, 1980).

The limestone beds of the Co-op Creek are gray and many are fossiliferous, containing abundant pelecypods, gastropods, and *Pentacrinus* sp. (star-shaped) crinoid columnals. The resistant, upper surface of the Co-op Creek forms a plateau veneered by a relatively thin layer of unconsolidated reddish-brown loess and residual Crystal Creek sediments. The Crystal Creek Member is only preserved in the northeast corner of Zion National Park, near Lava Point and north of Orderville Canyon; ongoing mapping will determine if this unit is present atop the Upper Kolob Plateau in the Kolob Canyons portion of the park. Like the Crystal Creek Member, the Paria River Member is only preserved in the northeast part of the park, although it is widely exposed to the north and east of the park on the Upper Kolob Plateau. There, the lower three-quarters of the member consists of ledge- and cliff-forming alabaster gypsum with few thin mudstone or sandstone interbeds. The upper part of the member consists of ledge-forming, thin-bedded, platy- or chippy-weathering micritic and argillaceous limestone with few poorly preserved fossil pelecypods, ostracodes, and *Pentacrinus* sp. crinoid columnals. Preliminary mapping north of the Lava Point area suggests that the gypsum may pinch out to the west and that the member there consists mostly of thin-bedded limestone.

Cretaceous

By late Middle Jurassic time, the back-bulge basin had migrated eastward, and most of Utah was a forebulge high, a broad, gentle uplift that was high enough in southwestern Utah to undergo a prolonged period of modest erosion; thus, there are no rocks of late Middle Jurassic to middle Early Cretaceous age preserved in southwestern

Figure 12. View north of the Taylor Creek thrust fault. Two main splays of the back thrust result in three east-dipping sections of the Moenave Formation. Springdale Sandstone (Jms) and Shinarump Conglomerate (Ʀcs).

Utah (figure 3). By late Early Cretaceous time, the first coarse synorogenic sediments, represented by pebbly conglomerate, sandstone, and mudstone of the youngest bedrock formation in Zion National Park, were deposited in the foredeep basin (figure 7G). Within the park, these rocks are limited to exposures at the top of Horse Ranch Mountain, in the Kolob Canyons area. Younger foredeep basin strata—including alluvial-fan and alluvial-plain sediments that grade into coastal plain, marginal marine, and marine deposits—total several thousand feet in thickness immediately north and east of the park. The rocks in the park were mapped by Hamilton (1978) as the early Late Cretaceous (Cenomanian) Dakota Formation, consisting of pebble to cobble conglomerate and tan sandstone totaling approximately 100 feet (30 m) thick. However, recent palynological data from mudstones that overlie these beds in areas immediately east of Zion National Park indicate that they are no younger than late Albian (late Early Cretaceous) (Utah Geological Survey unpublished data; see also Doelling and Davis, 1989; Doelling and others, Geology of Grand Staircase-Escalante National Monument, this volume). Thus, either the basal Dakota in the Zion National Park area is older than it is elsewhere in southern Utah, or it may represent previously unrecognized Cedar Mountain Formation, a lithologically similar unit considered to be mostly of late Early Cretaceous age (Tschudy and others, 1984; Kirkland and others, 1997, 1999).

As thrust faulting of the Sevier orogenic belt encroached on southwestern Utah, strata were folded into the Kanarra anticline (and, farther southwest, into the colinear Virgin anticline), probably in Late Cretaceous to late Paleocene time, about 70 to 55 million years ago. The Kanarra anticline extends nearly 40 miles (64 km) from near Toquerville to near Cedar City (figure 2). Only the east limb of the Kanarra anticline is conspicuous within Zion National Park, although parts of the crest of the fold are present at the mouths of Taylor Creek and Camp Creek.

Beds on the east limb generally dip from 20 to 35 degrees east and shallow abruptly as they pass under the great cliffs of Navajo Sandstone (figure 6). The west limb of the fold, and in places the crest and part of the fold's east limb, has been sheared off by the Hurricane fault zone along a line roughly parallel with the fold axis. Kurie (1966) reported 5,000 feet (1,524 m) of relief on the anticline. The fold was named by Gregory and Williams (1947), and has also been called the Pintura fold (Gardner, 1941; Neighbor, 1952; Stewart and Taylor, 1996; Hurlow, 1998).

The east limb of the Kanarra anticline is complicated by the Taylor Creek thrust-fault zone (figure 12). This fault zone consists of one principal and several lesser, east-dipping back thrusts that are subparallel to bedding and that repeat Jurassic strata on the fold's east flank. The thrust-fault zone is best illustrated by repetition of the resistant, cliff-forming Springdale Sandstone Member of the Moenave Formation. Smaller back thrusts locally displace Kayenta, Chinle, Moenkopi, and Kaibab strata. Kurie (1966) reported about 2,000 feet (610 m) of vertical and 2,500 feet (762 m) of horizontal displacement on the Taylor Creek thrust. Fault drag and small folds along the length of the thrust zone in the Kolob Canyons area clearly demonstrate westward-directed compression associated with these back thrusts. These relatively small thrust faults, and the Kanarra and Virgin anticlines, generally parallel regional structures related to Sevier compression, and are thus interpreted to be Sevier-age structures that formed during the Late Cretaceous to early Tertiary (Higgins and Willis, 1995; Biek, 1997, 1998; Willis, 1999). The faults formed early during the folding of the Kanarra anticline and were later rotated to steep east dips with final folding of the anticline.

Tertiary

Tertiary-age sedimentary and volcanic rocks once covered Zion National Park, and while they are still widespread to the north, they have been removed by erosion from the park itself. The Paleocene fluvial and lacustrine sedimentary rocks of the Claron Formation form the basal Tertiary unit throughout much of southwest Utah, and are wonderfully exposed at Cedar Breaks National Monument and Bryce Canyon National Park. During Oligocene and early Miocene time, explosive andesitic volcanism dominated areas immediately to the west and north, doubtless covering the park with several hundred feet of welded tuff since eroded away. The Pine Valley laccolith was emplaced just west of the park in the early Miocene, about 21 million years ago, as molten rock from deep within the earth moved upward into shallow overlying sedimentary rocks. There it spread out like the cap of a mushroom and crystallized into what is one of the largest such intrusions in the world. Granite-like boulders of the Pine Valley quartz monzonite can be seen in older debris-flow deposits on the Upper Kolob Plateau.

Faulting In and Near Zion National Park

During the late Cretaceous to early Eocene, around 75 to 50 million years ago, the Colorado Plateau began to rise from its position near sea level due to complex interaction between the North American plate and various oceanic plates on the western margin of North America (see, for example, Graf and others, 1987). Later, as the Basin and Range began to collapse and extend westward, the western margin of the Colorado Plateau was broken into a series of large blocks bounded by the Hurricane, Sevier, Paunsaugunt, and other faults. Zion National Park lies on an intermediate structural block, bounded on the east by the Sevier fault zone, and on the west by the Hurricane fault zone.

The Hurricane fault zone is a major, active, steeply west-dipping normal fault that stretches at least 155 miles (250 km) from south of the Grand Canyon northward to Cedar City. Stewart and Taylor (1996) defined a fault-segment boundary just north of Toquerville, thus dividing the Hurricane fault zone into the Ash Creek segment to the north and the Anderson Junction segment to the south. Only two short lengths of the Ash Creek segment are in Zion National Park, at the mouths of Taylor Creek and Camp Creek. At both localities, Permian Harrisburg and Triassic lower Moenkopi strata on the upthrown side display prominent fault drag and are in fault contact with basin-fill deposits on the downthrown side. Tectonic displacements along the fault zone are about 3,600 feet (1,098 m) and 4,900 feet (1,494 m) at the latitudes of St. George and Toquerville, respectively (Anderson and Christenson, 1989). Lund and Everitt (1998) determined an average slip rate for part of the Ash Creek segment near the Kolob Canyons area of about 16 inches/1,000 years (0.39 m/1,000 yr) since about 900,000 years ago. The average slip rate over the past 350,000 years on the Anderson Junction segment near Hurricane is about one-half that amount (Biek, 1998).

The age of first movement on the Hurricane fault zone is unknown, but based on a constant displacement rate determined from offset Quaternary basalts, Stewart and Taylor (1996) postulated that it may have begun as early as late Miocene or early Pliocene, about 11 to 5 million years ago. This estimate, however, is based on total stratigraphic separation and not tectonic displacement and may thus yield an inappropriately old age for initiation of faulting. In addition, it is unlikely that the rate of displacement has been constant over time. Anderson and Mehnert (1979) and Anderson and Christenson (1989) consider the Hurricane fault zone to be a late Pliocene to Quaternary feature (formed within about the past 3 million years).

Other faults in the Zion area include the East and West Cougar Mountain faults, the Wildcat Canyon fault, the Bear Trap Canyon fault, and the comparatively small Scoggins Wash faults (figure 2). The East and West Cougar Mountain faults are parallel, northwest-trending, steeply dipping normal faults in the southwest part of Zion National Park. They have opposite displacement, and together form a graben. However, the east fault has more displacement than the west fault, such that overall, the fault set produces down-to-the-west displacement. The maximum displacement on the larger East Cougar Mountain fault is about 750 feet (229 m) near Coalpits Wash. The timing of movement on the faults is poorly constrained. Both faults trend beneath, but do not offset, the 250,000-year-old Grapevine Wash basalt flows, and the youngest rock displaced by the faults is Jurassic. However, the faults are extensional in nature and we assume they are related to Basin and Range extension.

The Wildcat Canyon fault is a high-angle fault that trends northwest, parallel to the Cougar Mountain faults. Displacement of Temple Cap and Carmel strata in Wildcat Canyon reveals up to 180 feet (55 m) of down-to-the-east offset. The fault does not displace the 1.0 million year old Lava Point flow to the north, and is probably contemporaneous with the East and West Cougar Mountain faults. The Bear Trap Canyon fault is a high-angle, steeply west-dipping normal fault that trends northeast in the Kolob Canyons portion of the park. Hamilton (1995) reported more than 900 feet (274 m) of displacement on this fault.

Although there are few faults in Zion National Park, joints are exceptionally well developed, and by channeling runoff, they are largely responsible for the orientation of the existing canyon network. Joints are simple cracks in bedrock, natural fractures with no significant displacement of the adjacent blocks. They are particularly prominent in the Navajo Sandstone. The most prominent joints in the park are north-northwest-trending, nearly vertical and widely spaced joints (see shaded-relief base of figure 20). Many joints in the Navajo Sandstone exhibit crushed or sheared zones, known as deformation band shear zones, indicative of small-scale displacement (Davis, 1999). These joints formed as the result of two diametrically opposite types of crustal stresses: (1) relaxation of compressive stresses that the rocks were subject to during the middle Mesozoic to early Tertiary Sevier orogeny, and

(2) tensile stresses that the rocks have been subject to during late Cenozoic Basin and Range extension. Some joints, termed exfoliation joints, form roughly parallel to rock faces as a result of erosional unloading. Short surficial joints, such as those at Checkerboard Mesa, are attributed to local expansion and contraction of the rock due to changes in temperature and moisture.

The Recent History of Zion National Park

At first glance, it may seem that Zion National Park is all bare rock. However, surficial deposits, including basalt flows and cinder cones, are surprisingly abundant and varied and together they reveal a great deal about the recent erosional history of the park. Six main types of surficial sedimentary deposits, with many variations, are common in the park: alluvium, colluvium and residuum, talus, eolian (windblown) deposits, mass-movement deposits (including landslides and debris flows), and lacustrine or basin-fill deposits. Spring tufa deposits are also present, but rare. Because of its scale and simplification, most surficial deposits are not shown on figure 5. Only certain alluvial, lacustrine, and mass-movement deposits are described below. Several basaltic lava flows and cinder cones stand in stark contrast to the surrounding redrock scenery.

Older Debris-Flow Deposits

One of the more interesting surficial deposits are older debris-flow deposits that are widespread in the vicinity of Kolob Reservoir and west of Home Valley Knoll, just north of Zion National Park. The southernmost extent of these deposits barely reaches into the park immediately west of Little Creek Sinks on the Upper Kolob Plateau. Similar deposits farther north, east of Cedar City, were described by Averitt (1962, 1964) and Anderson and Mehnert (1979). These deposits weather to poorly exposed, vegetated slopes and are characterized by huge igneous boulders derived from the Pine Valley Mountains, somewhat smaller boulders of Cretaceous sandstone, cobbles and small boulders derived from the Carmel Formation, and rounded pebbles and small cobbles of Precambrian and Cambrian quartzite. Except for the rounded quartzite, most clasts are subangular to subrounded. Reconnaissance mapping near Kolob Reservoir has revealed Pine Valley clasts up to 24 feet (7.3 m) long, 22 feet (6.7 m) wide, and an estimated 12 feet (3.7 m) thick; clasts with long dimensions of 9 to 15 feet (3-5 m) are common. As also noted by Anderson and Mehnert (1979), the great size of common clasts, and the general lack of sorting and distinct bedding, suggests that the material was transported by debris flow and not by stream flow.

At Little Creek Sinks and west of Home Valley Knoll, the deposits are covered in part by angular blocks of basalt, but it is not clear whether the basalt is incorporated into the debris-flow deposits or simply represents a lag left behind from erosion of the 1.4-million-year-old basalt-capped ridge that trends south from Little Creek Peak. At

Kolob Reservoir, uncommon subrounded basalt boulders are clearly incorporated into the debris-flow deposits.

Anderson and Mehnert (1979) clearly established a westerly source for similar debris-flow deposits east of Cedar City. The debris-flow deposits near Kolob Reservoir lie about 16 miles (26 km) northeast of the Pine Valley Mountains, but outcrops of Pine Valley igneous rocks are present in small fault blocks along the Hurricane fault zone both to the north and south of the Kolob Canyons Visitor Center, and they are believed to underlie at least part of the New Harmony basin (Kurie, 1966; Hurlow, 1998). The debris-flow deposits thus reflect east or northeast transport of at least 10 miles (16 km) and possibly as much as about 16 miles (26 km). Anderson and Mehnert (1979) were only able to constrain the age of those deposits as younger than about 20 million years and older than about 1 million years. However, basalt boulders in the deposits at Kolob Reservoir suggests they are only a few million years old. Mapping in the Kolob Reservoir quadrangle (in progress) may help to narrow the age of these deposits and their relationship to the basalt flows, which is important because a westerly source implies that the Hurricane fault zone was not a significant topographic barrier at the time of deposition.

Basalt Flows and Cinder Cones

Zion National Park is within the Western Grand Canyon basaltic field, which extends across the southwest portion of the Colorado Plateau and adjacent transition zone in southwestern Utah, northern Arizona, and easternmost Nevada. Within the field are hundreds of widely scattered late Tertiary and Quaternary basaltic cinder cones and lava flows (Hamblin, 1963, 1970; Best and Brimhall, 1970, 1974; Best and others, 1980; Smith and others, 1999). Most basaltic flows are less than 7 million years old and the youngest is less than 500 years old. The Zion National Park flows are part of a cluster of young flows in southwestern Utah that are all less than 2.4 million years old (Willis and Higgins, 1996; Biek, 1998; Willis and others, 1999). The Zion flows range in age from about 1.4 million years to an estimated 100,000 years old (unpublished UGS data) (figure 13).

Parts of six lava flows are within the park (figure 5). Two major source areas are also within the park, whereas several flows originated at vents outside the park to the north and west. The flows are typically 10 to 40 feet (3-12 m) thick, but reach thicknesses of several hundred feet where they filled canyons. The flows are classified as basalt, trachybasalt, basaltic trachyandesite, and basaltic andesite on the total alkali versus silica (TAS) diagram of LeBas and others (1986) (though not all the flows are true basalt, we here refer to them collectively as "basalt" for simplicity) (figure 14). In hand sample the basalts are medium to dark gray, and weather dark grayish brown to black. They are phenocryst poor, with scattered small white plagioclase, and common tiny dark-greenish-brown olivine and black pyroxene phenocrysts.

BASALT FLOW	AGE	SOURCE
Crater Hill	100,000 years, estimated	Crater Hill
Grapevine Wash	0.22 ± 0.03 to 0.31 ± 0.02 Ma	Firepit and Spendlove Knolls and smaller vents
Black Ridge	0.84 ± 0.03 to 0.88 ± 0.05 Ma[1]	Pintura area
Lava Point	1.0 to 1.1 million years[2]	Home Valley Knoll
Kolob Plateau	1.44 ± 0.04 Ma	unknown
Horse Ranch Mountain	> 1.0 million years, estimated	unknown

Figure 13. Ages of basalt flows in Zion National Park. Ages from (1) Lund and Everitt (1998), (2) Best and others (1980) and unpublished UGS data; all others UGS unpublished data.

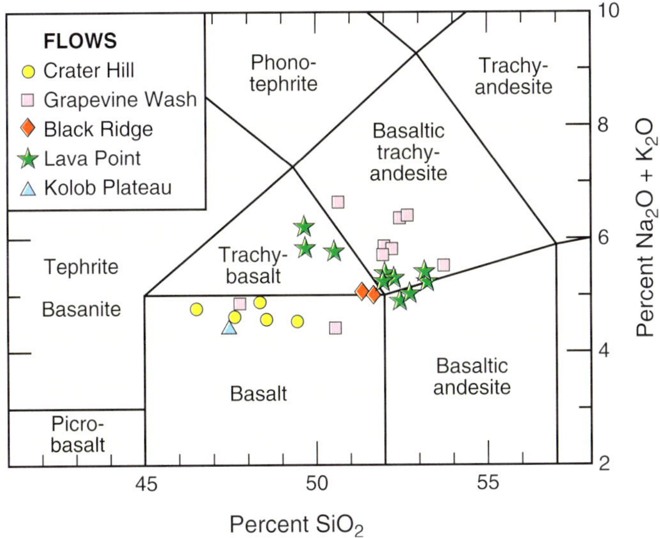

Figure 14. Geochemical classification of basaltic rocks in Zion National Park using the scheme of LeBas and others (1986).

Sanchez (1995) and Smith and others (1999) showed that most basaltic volcanoes in the Hurricane area (figure 2) are monocyclic, meaning that each vent produced only one eruptive cycle -- in other words, the volcano erupted during a single phase that lasted less than about 100 years, and then went extinct. Subsequent eruptions formed new volcanoes in different locations. There is some structural control on the location of vents, as magma tends to migrate upward in structurally weakened zones, such as along faults and major deep-seated joints. These concepts hold true for the Zion National Park flows as well, where it appears that each vent produced only one eruptive phase, vents cluster in some areas, and vents are aligned along fault zones.

In addition to providing a striking contrast to the redrock scenery, the flows provide important insight into the uplift and erosional history of the Zion area over the past two million years. Because each flow was emplaced in a "geologic instant," flowed up to 10 or more miles (16 km) across the landscape, and is resistant to erosion, the flow provides a "snapshot" of the landforms that existed at that time. Southwest Utah is an area of regional uplift in which erosion is cutting ever deeper into the bedrock. Thus, incision in soft sedimentary rocks along the flow margins has gradually isolated the resistant basalt (which flowed down canyons and valley floors) as elevated surfaces capping ridges; older flows stand at higher elevations above adjacent major drainages than do younger flows. These basalt-capped ridges are called "inverted valleys" (see, for example, Hamblin, 1970, 1987). When the age of the flow is known, a downcutting rate for the area can be calculated. This information has been particularly useful in deciphering the history of the spectacular canyons of Zion National Park. The flows had other impacts as well. In some areas, they dammed rivers and streams, forming lakes and ponds. In other areas, they deflected streams, causing them to carve new canyons.

The Crater Hill flow is one of the more interesting flows in the park (figure 15). Our recent mapping shows that the flow represents a single (monocyclic) eruption at the Crater Hill cinder cone in the southwest corner of the park, rather than a long, multi-event eruptive history proposed by Nielson (1977) and Downing (2000). It is located near the West Cougar Mountain fault, and the volcano plumbing may have developed along weaker rocks in the fault zone. The lava flowed into, and overflowed, the canyons of ancestral Scoggins and Coalpits Washes. It then flowed southward into the ancestral Virgin River where it ponded and flowed westward along the river channel for about 5 miles (8 km). The Crater Hill flow was one of the more voluminous lava flows in the area – a water well drilled through the distal end of the flow over the ancestral Virgin River channel penetrated over 400 feet (122 m) of continuous basalt (Fred Johnson, Virgin, Utah,

Figure 15. Aerial photograph of the Crater Hill basalt flow. Utah Highway 9 and the Virgin River are at the bottom of the photo; north is up. Reduced from full-color, 1:20,000-scale Bureau of Land Management photos UT94EC, 3-85-6 and 3-85-8 taken June 22, 1994.

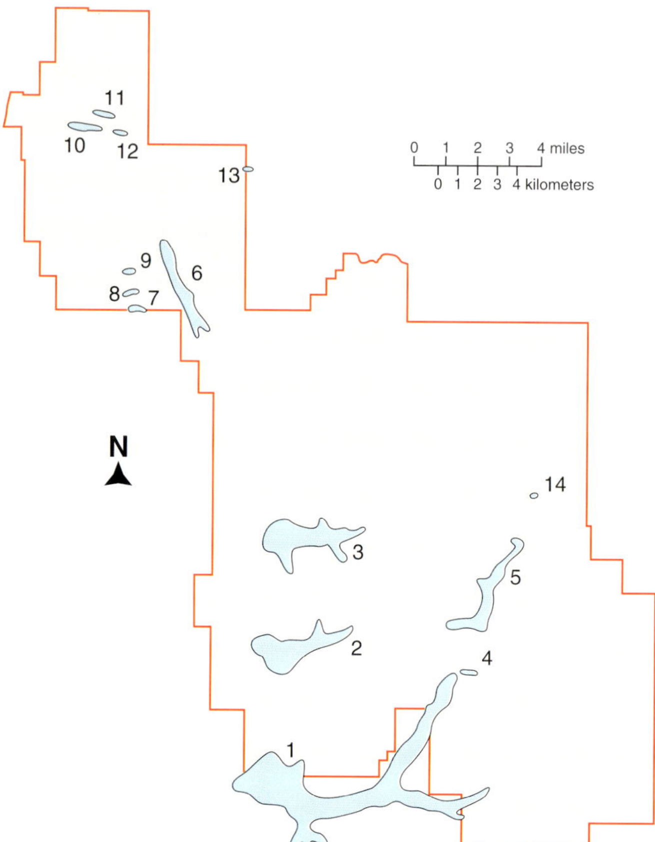

Figure 16. Approximate extent of Quaternary lakes of Zion National Park. Pleistocene, lava- dammed lakes include : (1) Lake Grafton, (2) Coalpits Lake, and (3) Trail Canyon Lake (slide-dammed in a later stage). Holocene lakes include: (4) Pine Creek Lake, (5) Sentinel Lake, (6) Hop Valley Lake, (7) Smith Creek Lake, (8) Cane Creek Lake, (9) Current Creek Lake, (10) Paria Lake, and (11) Middle Fork Taylor Creek Lake. Existing slide-dammed lakes include: (12) Beatty Lake, (13) Potamogeton (Chasm) Lake, and (14) Mystery Lake. With the exception of Lake Grafton and Sentinel Lake, most lakes in the park probably held water only during brief wet periods and were probably more like bogs or broad alluvial plains. Other lakes likely existed in the past, but evidence of their existence has been removed by erosion. Modified from Hamilton (1995).

verbal communication, 1997), a tremendous thickness for flows in the area. The top of the flow has huge frozen pressure ridges and giant rafted blocks of basalt, also indicative of a large-volume flow. The largest rafted block is near the southern top edge of the flow about 2 miles (3.2 km) west of Coalpits Wash. This rafted block is so large that Nielson (1977) proposed it as a separate vent. The Crater Hill flow has not yet been reliably dated, but based on the downcutting rate of 1,300 feet per million years (396 m/my) determined from the Lava Point flow at the high mesa northeast of Virgin, we estimate this flow is about 100,000 years old. Coalpits Lake and Lake Grafton, described below, were impounded behind this flow.

Lacustrine Deposits and Prehistorical Landslides

Because of the impounding effects of landslides and lava flows, the canyons of Zion National Park have periodically held small lakes and ephemeral ponds. Sedi-

ments that accumulate behind such dams commonly contain invertebrate fossils, pollen, and even buried stumps and other plant remains indicative of environmental conditions at the time of sedimentation. Lacustrine deposits associated with at least 14 lakes are known in the park (figure 16). The largest of these lakes was Lake Grafton, whose existence was first proposed by Threet (1958) and whose lake sediments were first identified by Hamilton (undated, 1995). Lake Grafton formed about 100,000 years ago when the Crater Hill basalt flow blocked the Virgin River near the ghost town of Grafton. Sediments associated with this lake, mineralized with gypsum and interlayered with volcanic cinders, are just outside the park boundary near Grafton. Lake Grafton probably covered about 10 square miles (26 km^2) and may have reached upstream to the Visitor Center area, but erosion has removed most sediments associated with this lake and no lake de-

Figure 17. Landslide deposits (Qms) in the Right Fork Canyon of North Creek, below cliffs of Navajo Sandstone (Jn) (view looking west; Pine Valley Mountains in distance). Light-colored lacustrine sand (Qls) overlies part of the landslide deposits. Discontinuous exposures of the Springdale Sandstone Member of the Moenave Formation (Jms) are present beneath the landslide deposits west of the East Cougar Mountain fault.

posits are known within the park boundary.

Coalpits Lake: Coalpits Lake formed contemporaneously with Lake Grafton when the Crater Hill basalt flow blocked ancestral Coalpits Wash just east of Crater Hill (Threet, 1958; Hamilton, 1978, 1979, undated, 1995). The basalt abutted a landslide complex developed principally in Petrified Forest strata on the south side of the wash. The maximum depth of the lake may have been about 110 feet (33 m), its length may have been 2 miles (3.2 km), and its width may have been a half mile (0.8 km). Hamilton (undated) measured three sections in the lake deposits. The bed of the lake is locally lined with about 5 to 20 feet (1.5-6 m) of dark-gray and yellow sand- to pebble-size cinders, overlain by yellowish to orange sand, with few clay and limestone beds. Most of the lake deposits rest on older landslide deposits. The highest lake deposits we could find are at an elevation of 4,360 feet (1,329 m). After the basin filled with sediments, the deposits were capped by a gravelly mantle. Eventually, ancestral Coalpits Wash shifted onto the adjacent landslide and cut a new drainage. Much of the lake and gravelly deposits have been removed by erosion. Given the rarity of fine-grained, deep-water lake clays and evidence for at least periodic subaerial exposure, as well as lack of a large upstream drainage basin, Coalpits Lake likely was not full of water for extended periods of time. Hamilton (1979, undated, 1995) reported tracks of insects and a variety of other invertebrates, a camel, and a large bird from these deposits.

Trail Canyon Lake: A lake occupied the area of the confluence of Trail Canyon and the Right Fork of North Creek at least once, and probably twice, during Pleistocene time. The most recent lake resulted from the damming of Right Fork by a large landslide involving the Kayenta Formation

on the north side of Right Fork, just west of the East Cougar Mountain fault. The upstream part of the landslide deposits are locally overlain by sediments deposited in a lake that formed behind the landslide dam (figure 17). These sediments consist of sand, silt, clay, marl, and minor limestone, and contain a variety of fossils, including snails, fish vertebrae, and a bison thoracic vertebra (Hamilton, 1979).

Prior to the existence of the landslide-dammed lake, Right Fork was blocked by the Grapevine Wash basalt flow, which erupted from vents near the Firepit and Spendlove Knolls volcanic cones to the north. Erosional remnants of this flow are present in the lower Right Fork canyon. Right Fork was undoubtedly dammed by the basalt, creating a lake that would have occupied part of the Right Fork canyon for a period of time until the dam was breached and stream flow was re-established. Hamilton (1979) interpreted the lacustrine deposits in the Right Fork canyon below an elevation of 4,600 feet (1,400 m) as possibly being associated with a basalt-dammed lake, based on the elevation of the erosional remnants of the basalt flow and a tentative correlation of volcaniclastic sediments with the Spendlove Knoll vent (Hamilton, undated).

Sentinel Lake: Sentinel Lake formed upstream of the Sand Bench landslide in Zion Canyon (Grater, 1945; Hamilton, 1995). The Sand Bench landslide is actually a huge collapsed wall or fin of Navajo Sandstone that formed between two closely spaced joints on the east side of The Sentinel. The lake stretched from the Court of the Patriarchs upstream nearly to the Temple of Sinawava. The lake was at least 200 feet (61 m) deep in its early stages, and unlike other Quaternary lakes in Zion National Park, was probably full of water year round. Assuming a lake level of 4,400 feet (1,341 m), the elevation of the highest preserved deep-water lake deposits, the lake would have covered Zion Lodge with at least 125 feet (38 m) of water. Sentinel Lake lacustrine deposits consist of thin, horizontal, alternating layers of gray clay and yellow sand, and are well exposed in several side canyons, including Birch canyon and the canyon southwest of Zion Lodge. The alternating layers may be varves, reflecting annual accumulations of sediment, or they may reflect individual, large storm events. They are overlain by several tens of feet of yellowish sand that may represent lake-margin deposits. The Virgin River has since eroded away at least 200 feet (61 m) of lake sediments. Throughout most of the canyon, the lacustrine deposits are concealed beneath younger alluvial deposits of the Virgin River. The Virgin River still has to cut through at least 70 feet (21 m) of lake and landslide deposits before it re-establishes its pre-Sand Bench landslide profile.

Radiocarbon ages on plant material from a drill hole near the base of the deposits at the Court of the Patriarchs show that the lake was present at least 6,200 to 8,000 years ago (UGS unpublished data), and Hamilton (1979, 1995) reported a radiocarbon age of 3,600 ± 400 yr B.P. (before

Figure 18. View north down Hop Valley from the Hop Valley Trail. Deposits of Hop Valley Lake may be as much as 350 feet (107 m) thick in this valley. On skyline, note planar upper surface of the Navajo Sandstone, the J-1 unconformity.

Figure 19. Peat associated with Hop Valley Lake deposits, which yielded a radiocarbon age of 2,640 ± 60 yr B.P., exposed at the south end of Hop Valley.

present) for the upper part of the lake deposits along a dry fork of Birch Creek at the Court of the Patriarchs. It is unknown whether these lake deposits reflect one or more episodes of lake formation.

Hop Valley Lake: Hop Valley Lake is the youngest of the large, landslide-dammed paleolakes of Zion National Park. The lake formed when a large landslide dammed the outlet to Hop Valley. The landslide broke away along a series of joints in the Navajo and Kayenta Formations that trend northwest, parallel to Hop Valley and the East Cougar Mountain fault. We estimate the lake sediments, which form a flat valley floor that slopes gently north, to be up to 250 to 350 feet (76-107 m) thick. They are dissected by stream erosion, creating terraces about 40 feet (12 m) high at the south end of the lake and about 15 feet (5 m) high at the north end. The gentle northward slope of the terraces probably reflects the original northward slope of sandy lake or deltaic deposits. The effect is an altogether enchanting valley seldom seen by visitors to the park (figure 18).

Eardley (1966) obtained a radiocarbon age of 670 ± 200 yr B.P. on wood collected at the north end of the lake deposits, about 15 feet (5 m) below the elevation of maximum fill. We dated a peat deposit exposed in a stream bank at the southwest end of the reservoir first reported by Hamilton (1995) (figure 19). This peat bed yielded a radiocarbon age of 2,640 ± 60 yr B.P., and may reflect the accumulation of organic debris blown by prevailing winds to the south end of the lake shortly after the lake's formation. Alternately and more likely, Hop Valley Lake may never have filled completely during its initial stages, such that these peat deposits may reflect deposition sometime during the middle of the lake cycle, once part of the valley had filled with sediment. Regardless, the age of 2,640 ± 60 yr B.P. establishes a minimum age for the lake's formation.

Smaller Lakes: Deposits of several smaller lakes or ephemeral ponds are known in Zion National Park (figure 16). Because they are small and located in small catchment basins, most if not all of these "lakes" probably held water only during brief wet periods; most were probably more like bogs or broad alluvial plains. Three lakes still exist in the park: Beatty Lake and Mystery Lake, which hold water only during brief wet periods, and Potamogeton (Chasm) Lake. Many of these small lakes and lake deposits are discussed in the accompanying road and trail logs, and by Hamilton (undated, 1995).

Historical Landslides in Zion Canyon

Landsliding has occurred periodically in recent decades in the stretch of Zion Canyon located beneath The Sentinel. These landslides involved the ancient landslide material of Sand Bench (see Sentinel Lake discussion), and were triggered partly as a result of continuing erosion and oversteepening of the 600-foot-high (180 m) face of Sand Bench by the North Fork of the Virgin River. Two relatively major landslides were documented in the early 1900s, one in 1923 and the other in 1941 (Grater, 1945). In

1992, a landslide may have been triggered in Zion Canyon by the M_L (local magnitude) 5.8 St. George earthquake, which had an epicenter about 30 miles (48 km) southwest of Zion Canyon (Solomon, 1995). This earthquake also triggered a large landslide just outside of the park boundary in Springdale (Black and others, 1995; Jibson and Harp, 1996).

The most recent significant landslide in Zion Canyon was in 1995. On April 12 at about 9:00 p.m., a slide occurred in the lower face of Sand Bench. The landslide dammed the North Fork of the Virgin River, forming a pond about 20 feet (6 m) deep (Solomon, 1995). The ponded water eventually overtopped the landslide dam. No flooding occurred downstream, but the river eroded the east bank and washed out a 600-foot (180-m) section of Zion Canyon Scenic Drive. More than 300 people were stranded upstream at Zion Lodge until the morning of April 14, when a temporary access road was opened on the east side of the river. The 1995 landslide mass was roughly 500 feet (150 m) long and 150 feet (45 m) wide, and involved approximately 110,000 cubic yards (84,000 m^3) of material (Solomon, 1995). The likely cause of the landslide was elevated pore pressures and reduced cohesion within the landslide mass due to excessive precipitation during the preceding months. Zion National Park weather records showed the amount of precipitation in March 1995 was 5.73 inches (14.55 cm), over twice the average precipitation for that month, and precipitation for the water year through April 14 was 189 percent of average in the southwestern Utah region (Solomon, 1995).

Formation of the Canyons of Zion National Park

Zion National Park is a window through which we can view and comprehend the geologic history entombed in its ancient layers of rock, but above all, it is a monument to erosion. After the Colorado Plateau rose from its position near sea level, its western margin was broken into a series of large blocks bounded by the Hurricane, Sevier, Paunsaugunt, and other faults. Zion National Park lies on an intermediate structural block, bounded on the east by the Sevier fault zone, and on the west by the Hurricane fault zone. Over time, movement on these faults displaced the Zion and adjacent blocks thousands of feet and tilted the mostly flat-lying rocks gently to the northeast. Streams eroded thousands of feet of strata from the Zion block. Erosion was more rapid near the steep, western fault escarpment, which created west-draining canyons along the west edge of the fault block.

In fact, Zion National Park owes its existence to the Hurricane fault zone. Headward erosion by the Virgin River and its tributaries carved the canyons of Zion National Park. The Virgin River is normally a small, placid stream, not difficult to wade across, and it is hard to imagine that it could erode such an immense canyon as Zion. But the river has a relatively steep average gradient of about 71 feet per mile (13 m/km) through Zion National Park and it carries away more than 1 million tons of rock waste each year (Eardley and Schaack, 1991). During the period 1926 to 1997, the average annual discharge of the North Fork of the Virgin River near Springdale was 102 cubic feet per second (cfs) (2.9 m^3/sec), but with a tremendous range of peak flows from 20 to 9,150 cfs (0.6-256 m^3/sec); downstream at Virgin, a 65-year record shows an average of 206 cfs (5.8 m^3/sec) with peak flows ranging from 22 to 22,800 cfs (0.6-638 m^3/sec) (U.S. Geological Survey, 1999, for website). Sandberg and Sultz (1985) reported that for the 1970 water year at Virgin, the total suspended sediment load for the year was 1,334,781 tons (1,210,646 metric tons), which is representative for a moderately wet year at the site. This is an average of 3,657 tons (3,317 metric tons) per day -- 366 dump truck loads every day. However, such averages skew our understanding of the erosional processes in the arid southwest. During large floods, the Virgin River can transport more sand, silt, and gravel than during an entire year of normal flow. And although the Virgin River may appear clear much of the time, it is always carrying fine suspended silt. Fed by the more abundant rain and snowmelt of the Pleistocene, average sediment transport was probably greater still during the past two million years.

Two dominant erosional processes have combined to form the canyons of Zion National Park: downcutting and canyon widening. Nowhere is downcutting more apparent than at The Narrows at the head of Zion Canyon. For about 10 miles (16 km) beyond the end of the Zion Canyon Scenic Drive, the North Fork of the Virgin River flows through a spectacular gorge cut into the Navajo Sandstone. The relatively homogeneous Navajo Sandstone is soft enough to be readily eroded but strong enough to stand in tall, vertical cliffs. In places, the gorge is just 16 feet (5 m) wide at the bottom of a 1,000-foot-deep (305 m) slot. The Virgin River truly acts like a moving ribbon of sandpaper where it cuts through The Narrows.

Canyon widening is an important process below the Navajo Sandstone. The relatively soft and thin-bedded siltstone, sandstone, and mudstone of the Kayenta Formation is more easily eroded than the overlying Navajo Sandstone. As the Kayenta is eroded and slips away in landslides, the great cliffs of Navajo Sandstone are undermined and, despite their inherent strength, they eventually break away. Rock falls and landslides are thus an important part of the canyon widening process. Seeps at the contact of permeable Navajo and impermeable Kayenta strata, and joints in the Navajo itself, facilitate undermining and collapse of Navajo strata.

One of the questions that has long intrigued both geologists and visitors to the park is "How long did it take to form Zion Canyon?" Fortunately, there is some evidence in the rock record to answer that question. At the high mesa northeast of Virgin, a remnant of the 1.0 million-year-old Lava Point basalt flow caps the mesa about 1,300 feet (396 m) above the Virgin River. The Lava Point flow, which erupted from the Home Valley Knoll high on the Upper Kolob Plateau to the north, flowed down the ancestral North Creek, which was probably graded to the Virgin River at the time. Thus, we know that in the vicinity of Virgin, the Virgin River has cut down about 1,300 feet (396 m) in the past 1 million years, yielding an average rate of erosion of 1.3 feet per 1,000 years (40 cm/1,000 yr). By projecting the ancestral Virgin River upstream, we find that 1 million years ago Zion Canyon was only about one-half as deep as it is today in the vicinity of Zion Lodge, exposing only the upper half of what was to become The Great White Throne. The Narrows, as we know them today, had not yet begun to form, although similar narrows probably existed downstream in the Navajo Sandstone where the river had not yet cut down into Kayenta strata. No other definitive evidence is available for determining long-term erosion rates of Zion Canyon, but if we use the simplistic assumption of constant incision rates over time, the upper half of Zion Canyon was carved between about 1 and 2 million years ago. Data are admittedly sparse, but given one well-dated control point and assuming constant average erosion rates, approximately 2 million years is required for the formation of Zion Canyon below the level of the Carmel Formation. A canyon similar to the modern Zion Canyon probably existed in the vicinity of Virgin and Rockville 2 million years ago.

The geologic history of Zion National Park is one of ancient landscapes, of the plate tectonic framework upon which these landscapes evolved, and of the erosive power of everyday storms that over time have stripped away much of the rock to yield a fascinating cross section of strata at Zion National Park. Popular narrative histories of these units and the erosional development of Zion National Park are available in Gregory (1956), Crawford (1988), Harris and Tuttle (1990), Eardley and Schaack (1991), Hintze (1993), Hamilton (1995), and DeCourten (1998).

CLASSIC GEOLOGIC SITES

Zion National Park is replete with classic geologic sites and informative exposures, from the scale of a single outcrop to an entire canyon. To a geologist's eyes, the surrounding area is no less fascinating. Everywhere one looks, the layered rocks, lava flows, and younger sediments are part of a larger, fascinating geologic history. Any list of such classic features is thus necessarily incomplete. The two dozen features described below simply illustrate some of our favorite geologic sites that can be seen in the park. The sites are numbered to correspond with figure 20, and many of the sites are described in more detail in the cited road and trail logs.

1. The Springdale Landslide

The Springdale landslide, located just outside the south park entrance on the west side of Utah Highway 9, is an old landslide complex that has probably moved many times. It was triggered again by the September 2,

1992, magnitude (M_L) 5.8 St. George earthquake. The 1992 landslide involved 18 million cubic yards (14 million m^3) of material, consisting mostly of the Moenave Formation sliding on weak claystone of the Petrified Forest Member of the Chinle Formation, and underwent about 33 feet (10 m) of primarily translational movement (Black and others, 1995; Jibson and Harp, 1996). Landslide movement resulted in the destruction of three homes and two water tanks within the slide area, disruption of utility lines, and closure of Utah Highway 9. (Utah Highway 9, LaVerkin to Zion Canyon road log, Stop 4.)

2. The Watchman Overlook

The Watchman Overlook provides an excellent view of the bedrock units exposed in Zion Canyon, from the resistant bench of Shinarump Conglomerate at the mouth of Zion Canyon to the gray limestones of the Carmel Formation high above the cliffs of Navajo Sandstone. It also offers a view of landslides, joints, pediments, debris flows, and river terraces that help to outline the erosional history of Zion Canyon. (The Watchman Trail log.)

3. Zion-Mt. Carmel Highway Tunnel

In the vicinity of The Great Arch, the Zion-Mt. Carmel Highway passes through a 1.1-mile-long (1.8 km) tunnel cut just a few feet back from the face of the south wall of Pine Creek canyon. The tunnel, which was completed in 1930, was drilled and blasted through the lower 260 feet (80 m) of the Navajo Sandstone. It cost a little over $1,000,000 and was the first million-dollar mile of highway construction in U.S. history. (Utah Highway 9, Zion Canyon to Mt. Carmel Junction road log, mile 3.2.)

4. Joints Along Zion-Mt. Carmel Highway

Much of the spectacular, cliffy landscape of Zion National Park is due to weathering and erosion of the Navajo Sandstone along near-vertical fractures, or joints. The most prominent set of joints are north-northwest-trending, nearly vertical, relatively widely spaced fractures that control the orientation and alignment of side canyons in the eastern part of the park; excellent examples can be seen from the Zion-Mt. Carmel highway (figure 20). (Utah Highway 9, Zion Canyon to Mt. Carmel Junction road log, Stops 2 and 3.)

5. Checkerboard Mesa

Checkerboard Mesa derives its name from the checkerboard pattern of roughly perpendicular sets of grooves that are so well developed in the Navajo Sandstone here (figure 21). The nearly horizontal grooves are a result of differential weathering along layers of coarse sand that coincide with eolian bedding sets. The vertical grooves appear to be shallow fractures that probably result from local expansion and contraction of the rock surface due to changes in temperature and moisture. (Utah Highway 9, Zion Canyon to Mt. Carmel Junction road log, Stop 5.)

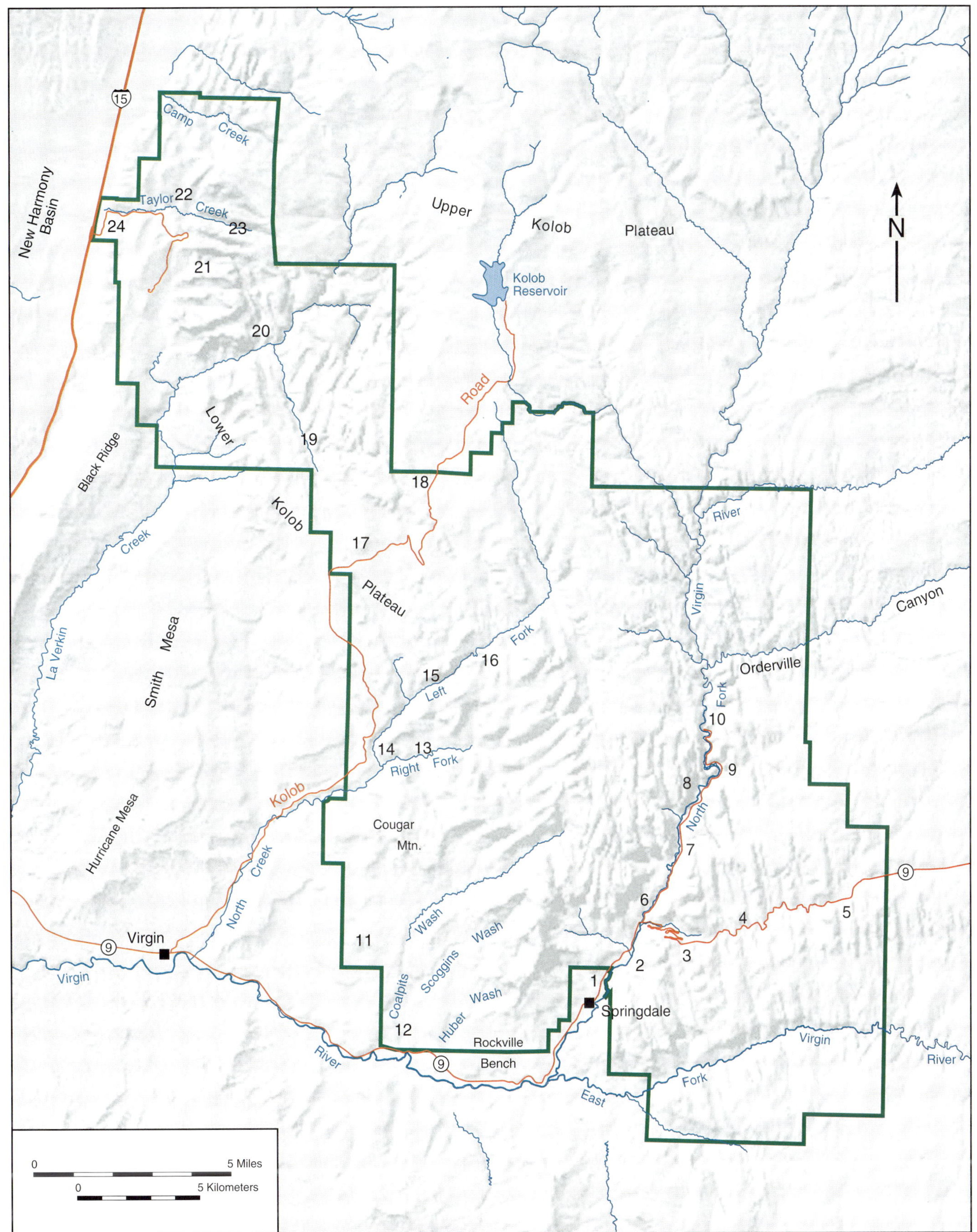

Figure 20. Locations of selected classic geologic sites in Zion National Park. Numbers are keyed to discussions in text. The north to northwest alignment of canyons in the southeast part of the park is controlled by joints.

Figure 21. View south to Checkerboard Mesa.

Figure 22. View east to hanging valley just north of Nagunt Mesa, in the Kolob Canyons portion of the park.

6. Sand Bench Landslide

The Sand Bench landslide is actually a huge collapsed wall or fin of Navajo Sandstone that formed between two closely spaced joints. The collapsed rock blocked Zion Canyon just east of The Sentinel, creating Sentinel Lake, about 7,000 years ago. The Virgin River has ever since been eroding the eastern part of the landslide, creating an oversteepened, unstable slope that intermittently slides. In historical times, smaller slides have dammed the Virgin River in 1923, 1941, and most recently in 1995. When the Sand Bench collapse occurred, the Virgin River was at least 70 feet (21 m) lower in elevation than it is today. (Zion Canyon Scenic Drive road log, Stop 2; Sand Bench Trail log.)

7. Sentinel Lake

Sentinel Lake formed upstream from the Sand Bench landslide, stretching from the Court of the Patriarchs on the south, upstream nearly to the Temple of Sinawava. The lake was at least 200 feet (61 m) deep in its early stages, and unlike other Quaternary lakes in Zion National Park, was probably full of water year round. Horizontal lake sediments can be seen from the southern part of the Emerald Pools Trail near the river footbridge, and

along the first part of the Sand Bench Trail. (Zion Canyon Scenic Drive road log, Stop 3; Sand Bench and Emerald Pools Trail logs.)

8. Hanging Valleys

The rims of the main canyons in Zion National Park are scalloped by shallow tributary valleys. These tributary valleys, whose floors are high above the floors of the main valleys, are alluvial hanging valleys (figure 22). Larger rivers such as the North and East Forks of the Virgin River have more erosive energy than the smaller, typically ephemeral tributary streams, and therefore cut down at a more rapid rate. This leaves the floors of the tributary valleys "hanging" above the floors of the main canyons. During and after rainstorms, waterfalls cascade from the mouths of the larger hanging valleys.

9. Weeping Rock

Weeping Rock is a picturesque alcove near the base of the Navajo Sandstone, below the mouth of Echo Canyon. Infiltration of surface runoff in Echo Canyon concentrates ground water directly beneath the canyon. Downward movement of the ground water is impeded by the rela-

Figure 23. View north up The Narrows.

Figure 24. Dinosaur tracks along the Left Fork trail. Note hat for scale.

tively impermeable Kayenta Formation, which forces the ground water to flow laterally toward the cliff face and ultimately seep out of the rock. The seeping ground water drips from the ceiling of the alcove and provides year-round moisture for a lush hanging garden. The water is also alkaline, so that the springs deposit tufa (calcium carbonate). (Zion Canyon Scenic Drive road log, Stop 6.)

10. The Narrows of Zion Canyon

For about 10 miles (16 km) beyond the north end of Zion Canyon Scenic Drive, the North Fork of the Virgin River flows through a spectacular gorge cut deeply into the Navajo Sandstone (figure 23). Relatively rapid down-cutting by the river through the more-or-less homogeneous Navajo Sandstone has resulted in a narrow, steep-walled canyon. The canyon is most impressive at The Narrows, in the vicinity of its confluence with Orderville Canyon, where it reaches a minimum width of about 16 feet (5 m) at the bottom of a 1,000-foot-deep (300 m) slot. (Zion Canyon Scenic Drive road log, Stop 8.)

11. Crater Hill Flow and Cinder Cone

The Crater Hill cinder cone, north-northwest of Grafton, is the largest cinder cone in the park. It marks the vent of the Crater Hill flow, one of the more voluminous flows in southwestern Utah (figure 15). The basalt flowed southward into Coalpits and Scoggins Washes, and then into the ancestral Virgin River valley where it accumulated to a depth of over 400 feet (122 m). Pressure ridges, which form concentric rings, and large rafted blocks of basalt are "frozen" into the upper surface of the flow. The flow blocked the Virgin River, forming Lake Grafton, and Coalpits and Scoggins Washes, forming Coalpits Lake. (Utah Highway 9 - LaVerkin to Zion Canyon, mile 7.4 to 12.3 and Stop 3.)

12. Coalpits Wash

Coalpits Wash is a small drainage in the southwest part of the park that has a long, interesting geologic history, much of which can be viewed by a hike up the wash.

Features visible along lower Coalpits Wash include the ancient basalt-plugged channel of the Virgin River, post-basalt gravels of the Virgin River, a major debris-flow plug, and several young terraces cut by the rapidly adjusting stream. In the upper Coalpits Wash area, near the head of the basalt flow, a group of huge chaotic basalt boulders is evidence of undercutting and collapse of the flow into the new wash. (Utah Highway 9 - LaVerkin to Zion Canyon, Stop 3.)

13. Trail Canyon Lake

Just upstream from its confluence with the Left Fork, the Right Fork of North Creek was dammed during Pleistocene time by the Grapevine Wash basalt flow and later by a large landslide involving the Kayenta Formation. The landslide deposits are locally overlain by sediments deposited in a lake that formed upstream of the landslide (figure 17). Hamilton (1979, 1995) reported that these lake sediments contain a variety of fossils including snails, fish vertebrae, and a bison thoracic vertebra. (Kolob Road - Virgin to Lava Point, Stop 2.)

14. Basalt Stack at Left Fork North Creek

The Grapevine Wash flows erupted from a group of vents on the Lower Kolob Plateau at and near Spendlove and Firepit Knolls. These flows moved southward around sandstone knobs and eventually cascaded into North Creek. There, at least 17 cooling units stacked up to form a spectacular basalt plug at least 450 feet (137 m) thick. Both the base and top of the stacked basalt yielded $^{40}Ar/^{39}Ar$ radiometric ages of about 270,000 years, showing that the entire stack is from one or more closely spaced eruptions. The best place to view the stack is by hiking a short distance east on the Grapevine Springs Trail. (Kolob Road - Virgin to Lava Point, Stop 3.)

15. Dinosaur Tracks at Left Fork North Creek

A large fallen boulder of Kayenta Formation sandstone is covered with three-toed dinosaur tracks (figure 24) about 0.5 miles (0.8 km) up Left Fork on the popular

Subway hiking trail. Stokes and Bruhn (1960) reported that the tracks are of a large bipedal tridactyl.

16. Subway

The Subway is aptly named for a narrow canyon eroded in lower transitional strata of the Navajo Sandstone on the Left Fork of North Creek. The Subway formed along a thin siltstone parting, which enabled the lower canyon walls to erode faster than those above. The result is a canyon wide and rounded at the bottom and narrow and steep-walled at the top, much like an upside-down keyhole. During periods of low flow, the stream flows on the floor of the Subway along a series of joints, clearly illustrating the influence of joints on the development of many canyons in Zion National Park. (Kolob Road - Virgin to Lava Point, Stop 5.)

17. Firepit and Spendlove Knolls

Two nearly perfectly conical cinder cones are located near the Kolob Road in the west-central part of the park. The cones cover at least two of the vents of the Grapevine Wash basalt flows; other, smaller cinder cones are present in the same area south and west of these two cones. Spendlove Knoll yielded an $^{40}Ar/^{39}Ar$ age of 0.22 ± 0.03 Ma, and Firepit Knoll an age of 0.29 ± 0.02 Ma (unpublished UGS data).

18. Old Debris-Flow Deposits

Old debris-flow deposits characterized by huge igneous boulders derived from the Pine Valley Mountains are found west of Little Creek Sinks (Qao on figure 5), and to the north on the Upper Kolob Plateau. The deposits contain boulders up to 24 feet (7.3 m) long, 22 feet (6.7 m) wide, and an estimated 12 feet (3.7 m) thick that reflect east or northeast transport of at least 10 miles (16 km) and possibly as much as 16 miles (26 km). Their presence on the Upper Kolob Plateau implies that the Hurricane fault zone was not a significant topographic barrier at the time of deposition.

19. Hop Valley

Hop Valley is a seldom visited, but immensely beautiful valley in the Kolob Canyons portion of the park (figure 18). The narrow, vertical-walled valley formed along the north end of the East Cougar Mountain fault. Sometime prior to 2,640 ± 60 yr B.P., a large landslide dammed the mouth of Hop Valley, creating Hop Valley Lake, the youngest of the large, landslide-dammed paleolakes of Zion National Park. Lake sediments, which form an enchanting flat valley floor that slopes gently north, may be as much as 350 feet (107 m) thick. (Hop Valley Trail log.)

20. Kolob Arch

Kolob Arch, located just north of LaVerkin Creek in the Kolob Canyons portion of Zion National Park, has a span of 310 feet (94.5 m), a window height of 330 feet (101 m), and a thickness of 80 feet (24 m) and is billed as the

Figure 25. View east-southeast to the Finger Canyons of the Kolob. Road cuts along the Kolob Canyons Scenic Drive are visible in the Hurricane Cliffs at the right side of the photo.

world's longest natural arch (Blake, 1984; Hamilton, 1995). The arch formed in the middle part of the massively cross-bedded Navajo Sandstone, and it appears to be related to north-northwest-trending joints, and possibly exfoliation joints, that are parallel to the East Cougar Mountain fault. (Timber Creek Trail and Kolob Arch log, Stop 8.)

21. Finger Canyons of the Kolob

The Finger Canyons of the Kolob are aptly named for a series of west-trending canyons eroded into the edge of the Upper Kolob Plateau (figure 25). The canyons formed along a series of west-trending joints that bound large monoliths of little-jointed Navajo Sandstone. In many respects, each canyon is like a miniature Zion Canyon, broad at the mouth where erodible, pre-Navajo strata are exposed, but narrowing to a slot in its upper reaches. (Kolob Canyons Scenic Drive, Stop 6.)

22. Taylor Creek Thrust Fault Zone

The Taylor Creek thrust fault zone consists of one principal and several lesser east-dipping thrust faults that duplicate Moenave strata on the east flank of the Kanarra anticline (figure 12). The faults are Sevier-age back thrusts that formed during the Late Cretaceous to early Tertiary. (Kolob Canyons Scenic Drive, Stop 6; Middle Fork Taylor Creek Trail, Stops 3, 4, and 5.)

23. Double Arch Alcove

Double Arch Alcove consists of two blind arches, or alcoves, formed in the massively cross-bedded Navajo Sandstone. The two arches illustrate two different methods of arch formation: the lower one controlled by spring sapping and lateral stream migration, the upper one by joints (figure 26). Although located on the north-facing wall of the Middle Fork of Taylor Creek, reflected light bathes the arches with a rich, reddish-orange light. (Middle Fork Taylor Creek Trail, Stop 8.)

24. Hurricane Fault Zone

More than anything else, Zion National Park owes its

Figure 26. *Double Arch Alcove, at the end of the Middle Fork Taylor Creek Trail. Inset shows blind arch high above the lower alcove.*

existence to the Hurricane fault zone, a major, active, steeply west-dipping normal fault that stretches at least 155 miles (250 km) from south of the Grand Canyon northward to Cedar City. Tectonic displacement along the fault zone at the latitude of the southern boundary of the park is about 3,600 feet (1,098 m) (Anderson and Christenson, 1989), and this relative uplift of the eastern block, which includes Zion National Park, has contributed greatly to the erosive power of streams draining the Kolob Terrace. Two short segments of the fault zone are contained within the park, at Taylor Creek and Camp Creek.

ACKNOWLEDGMENTS

Funding for recent geologic mapping in the park by the authors was provided by the Utah Geological Survey (UGS) and a grant from the National Park Service. The UGS graciously allowed the authors the opportunity to pull together this recent work in the form of a paper and road and trail logs. Once again, Jim Parker (UGS) turned our crude drawings into superb illustrations. Paul Anderson (consulting geologist), Tom Chidsey (UGS), and Doug Sprinkel (UGS) provided constructive reviews of the manuscript. We appreciate the assistance of Laird Naylor (formerly with the National Park Service [NPS] and now Bureau of Land Management) and Dave Sharrow (NPS) during this mapping project.

REFERENCES

References of general interest are bolded.

Agenbroad, L.D., Mead, J.I., and Anderson, R.S., 1993, Quaternary paleoenvironmental studies of the Colorado Plateau, year II: Flagstaff, Northern Arizona University, unpublished report for National Park Service contract RMR-R91-0176.

am Ende, B.A., 1991, Depositional environments, palynology, and age of the Dakota Formation, south-central Utah, in Nations, J.D., and Eaton, J.G., editors, Stratigraphy, depositional environments, and sedimentary tectonics of the western margin, Cretaceous Western Interior Seaway: Geological Society of America Special Paper 260, p. 65-83.

Anderson, R.E., and Christenson, G.E., 1989, Quaternary faults, folds, and selected volcanic features in the Cedar City 1° x 2° quadrangle, Utah: Utah Geological and Mineral Survey Miscellaneous Publication 89-6, 29 p., scale 1:250,000.

Anderson, R.E., and Mehnert, H.H., 1979, Reinterpretation of the history of the Hurricane fault in Utah, in Newman, G.W., and Goode, H.D., editors, 1979 Basin and Range Symposium: Rocky Mountain Association of Geologists, p. 145-165.

Averitt, Paul, 1962, Geology and coal resources of the Cedar Mountain quadrangle, Iron County, Utah: U.S. Geological Survey Professional Paper 389, 72 p.

—1964, Table of post Cretaceous geologic events along the Hurricane fault near Cedar City, Iron County, Utah: Geological Society of America Bulletin, v. 75, p. 901-908.

Baker, A.A., Dane, C.H., and Reeside, J.B., Jr., 1936, Correlation of the Jurassic formations of parts of Utah, Arizona, New Mexico, and Colorado: U.S. Geological Survey Professional Paper 183, 66 p.

Best, M.G., and Brimhall, W.H., 1970, Late Cenozoic basalt types in the western Grand Canyon region, in Hamblin, W.K., and Best, M.G., The western Grand Canyon district: Guidebook to the Geology of Utah, no. 23, p. 57-74.

—1974, Late Cenozoic alkalic basaltic magmas in the western Colorado Plateaus and the Basin and Range transition zone, U.S.A., and their bearing on mantle dynamics: Geological Society of America Bulletin, v. 85, no. 11, p. 1,677-1,690.

Best, M.G., McKee, E.H., and Damon, P.E., 1980, Space-time-composition patterns of late Cenozoic mafic volcanism, southwestern Utah and adjoining areas: American Journal of Science, v. 280, p. 1,035-1,050.

Biek, R.F., 1997, Interim geologic map of the Harrisburg Junction quadrangle, Washington County, Utah: Utah Geological Survey Open-File Report 353, 124 p., scale 1:24,000.

—1998, Interim geologic map of the Hurricane quadrangle, Washington County, Utah: Utah Geological Survey Open-File Report 361, 161 p., scale 1:24,000.

Black, B.D., Mulvey, W.E., Lowe, M., and Solomon, B.J., 1995, Geologic effects, *in* Christenson, G.E., editor, The September 2, 1992 M_L 5.8 St. George earthquake, Washington County, Utah: Utah Geological Survey Circular 88, p. 2-11.

Blake, R.H., 1984, Measuring the span of the great arch at Zion National Park, Kolob section: unpublished 16-page report on file at the Zion National Park library.

Blakey, R.C., 1994, Paleogeographic and tectonic controls on some Lower and Middle Jurassic erg deposits, Colorado Plateau, *in* Caputo, M.V., Peterson, J.A., and Franczyk, K.J., editors, Mesozoic systems of the Rocky Mountain region, USA: Denver, Colorado, Rocky Mountain Section of the Society for Sedimentary Geology, p. 273-298.

Blakey, R.C., Basham, E.L., and Cook, M.J., 1993, Early and Middle Triassic paleogeography of the Colorado Plateau and vicinity, *in* Morales, M., editor, Aspects of Mesozoic geology and paleontology of the Colorado Plateau: Museum of Northern Arizona Bulletin 59, p. 13-26.

Blakey, R.C., Peterson, Fred, Caputo, M.V., Geesman, R.C., and Voorhees, B.J., 1983, Paleogeography of Middle Jurassic continental, shoreline, and shallow marine sedimentation, southern Utah, *in* Reynolds, M.W., and Dolley, E.D., editors, Mesozoic paleogeography of west-central United States: Rocky Mountain Section of Society of Economic Paleontologists and Mineralogists, p. 77-100.

Blakey, R.C., Peterson, Fred, and Kocurek, Gary, 1988, Synthesis of late Paleozoic and Mesozoic eolian deposits of the Western Interior of the United States: Sedimentary Geology, v. 56, p. 3-125.

Cashion, W.B., 1967, Carmel Formation of the Zion Park region, southwestern Utah - a review: U.S. Geological Survey Bulletin 1244-J, 9 p.

Clemmensen, L.B., Olsen, H., and Blakey, R.C., 1989, Erg-margin deposits in the Lower Jurassic Moenave Formation and Wingate Sandstone, southern Utah: Geological Society of America Bulletin, v. 101, p. 759-773.

Cook, E.F., 1960, Geologic atlas of Utah - Washington County: Utah Geological and Mineral Survey Bulletin 70, 119 p., scale 1:125,000.

Crawford, J.L., 1988, Zion National Park - towers of stone: Zion Natural History Association, 47 p.

Davis, G.H., 1999, Structural geology of the Colorado Plateau region of southern Utah with special emphasis on deformation bands: Geological Society of America Special Paper 342, 168 p.

DeCourten, Frank, 1998, Dinosaurs of Utah: Salt Lake City, University of Utah Press, 300 p.

Doelling, H.H., and Davis, F.D., 1989, The geology of Kane County, Utah - geology, mineral resources, geologic hazards: Utah Geological and Mineral Survey Bulletin 124, 192 p., 10 plates, scale 1:100,000.

Downing, R.F., 2000, Imaging the mantle in southwestern Utah using geochemistry and geographic information systems: Las Vegas, University of Nevada, M.S. thesis, 128 p.

Dubiel, R.F., 1994, Triassic deposystems, paleogeography, and paleoclimate of the Western Interior, *in* Caputo, M.V., Peterson, J.A., and Franczyk, K.J., editors, Mesozoic systems of the Rocky Mountain region, USA: Rocky Mountain Section of Society of Economic Paleontologists and Mineralogists, p. 133-168.

Eardley, A.J., 1966, Rates of denudation in the High Plateaus of southwestern Utah: Geological Society of America Bulletin, v. 77, p. 777-780.

Eardley, A.J., and Schaack, J.W., 1991, Zion - the story behind the scenery: Las Vegas, Nevada, KC Publications, 46 p.

Gardner, L.S., 1941, The Hurricane fault in southwestern Utah and northwestern Arizona: American Journal of Science, v. 239, p. 241-260.

Graf, D.L., Hereford, Richard, Laity, Julie, and Young, R.A., Colorado Plateau, *in* Graf, W.L., editor, Geomorphic systems of North America: Boulder, Colorado, Geological Society of America, Centennial Special v. 2, p. 259-302.

Grater, R.K., 1945, Landslide in Zion Canyon, Zion National Park, Utah: Journal of Geology, v. 53, no. 2, p. 116-124.

Gregory, H.E., 1933, Colorado Plateau region: 16th International Geological Congress, Guidebook 18, 38 p.

—1948, Geology and geography of central Kane County, Utah: Geological Society of America Bulletin, v. 59, no. 3, p. 211-248.

—1950, Geology and geography of the Zion Park region, Utah and Arizona: U.S. Geological Survey Professional Paper 220, 200 p.

—1956, A geologic and geographic sketch of Zion National Park: Zion-Bryce Natural History Association, 36 p.

Gregory, H.E., and Moore, R.C., 1931, The Kaiparowits region, a geographic and geologic reconnaissance of parts of Utah and Arizona: U.S. Geological Survey Professional Paper 164, 161 p.

Gregory, H.E., and Williams, N.C., 1947, Zion National Monument, Utah: Geological Society of America Bulletin, v. 58, p. 211-244.

Hamblin, W.K., 1963, Late Cenozoic basalts of the St. George basin, Utah, *in* Heylmun, E.B., editor, Guidebook to the geology of southwestern Utah: Intermountain Association of Petroleum Geologists 12th Annual Field Conference, p. 84-89.

—1970, Late Cenozoic basalt flows of the western Grand Canyon, *in* Hamblin, W.K., and Best, M.G., editors, The western Grand Canyon district: Utah Geological Society Guidebook to the Geology of Utah, no. 23, p. 21-38.

—1987, Late Cenozoic volcanism in the St. George basin, Utah, *in* Beus, S.S., editor, Geological Society of America centennial field guide - volume 2, Rocky Mountain section: Geological Society of America, p. 291-294.

Hamilton, W.L., 1978 (revised 1987), Geological map of Zion National Park, Utah: Zion Natural History Association, scale 1:31,680.

—1979, Holocene and Pleistocene lakes in Zion National Park, Utah, *in* Linn, R.M., editor, Proceedings of the First Conference on Scientific Research in the National Parks, 1977 New Orleans Conference, NPS-AIBS, DOI-NPS Transactions and Proceedings, ser. 5., p. 835-844.

—undated, Quaternary ponds and lakes in Zion National Park, Utah: unpublished 42-page report on file at the Zion National Park library.

—1995, The sculpturing of Zion: Springdale, Utah, Zion Natural History Association, 132 p.

Harris, A.G., and Tuttle, Esther, 1990, Geology of National Parks - 4th edition: Dubuque, Iowa, Kendall/Hunt Publishing Company, 652 p.

Hereford, Richard, Jacoby, G.C., and McCord, V.A.S., 1996, Late Holocene alluvial geomorphology of the Virgin River in the Zion National Park area, southwest Utah: Geological Society of America Special Paper 310, 41 p.

Hesse, C.J., 1935, *Semionotus* cf *gigas* from the Triassic of Zion Park, Utah: American Journal of Science, 5th series, v. 29, p. 526-531.

Hevly, R.H., 1979, Pollen studies of ancient lake sediments in Zion National Park, Utah, *in* Linn, R.M., editor, Proceedings of the First Conference on Scientific Research in the National Parks, v. 2, NPS-AIBS, DOI-NPS Transactions and Proceedings, ser. 5., p. 151-158.

Higgins, J.M., 1997, Interim geologic map of the White Hills quadrangle, Washington County, Utah: Utah Geological Survey Open-File Report 352, 94 p., scale 1:24,000.

Higgins, J.M., and Willis, G.C., 1995, Interim geologic map of the St. George quadrangle, Washington County, Utah: Utah Geological Survey Open-File Report 323, 114 p., scale 1:24,000.

Hintze, L.F., 1993, Geologic history of Utah: Brigham Young University Geology Studies Special Publication 7, 202 p.

Hurlow, H.A., 1998, The geology of the central Virgin River basin, southwestern Utah, and its relation to ground-water conditions: Utah Geological Survey Water-Resources Bulletin 26, 53 p., 6 plates, various scales.

Imlay, R.W., 1980, Jurassic paleobiogeography of the con-terminous United States in its continental setting: U.S. Geological Survey Professional Paper 1062, 134 p.

Jibson, R.W., and Harp, E.L., 1996, The Springdale, Utah landslide - an extraordinary event: Environmental & Engineering Geoscience, v. 2, no. 2, p. 137-150.

Kauffman, E.G., 1977, Geological and biological overview - Western Interior Cretaceous basin: The Mountain Geologist, v. 14, p. 75-99.

Kirkland, J.I., Britt, Brooks, Burge, D.L., Carpenter, Ken, Cifelli, Richard, DeCourten, Frank, Eaton, Jeffrey, Hasiotis, Steve, and Lawton, Tim, 1997, Lower to middle Cretaceous dinosaur faunas of the central Colorado Plateau - a key to understanding 35 million years of tectonics, sedimentology, evolution and biogeography, *in* Link, P.K., and Kowallis, B.J., editors, Mesozoic to Recent geology of Utah: Brigham Young University Geology Studies, v. 42, pt. 2, p. 69-103.

Kirkland, J.I., Cifelli, R.L., Britt, B.B., Burge, D.L., DeCourten, F.L., Eaton, J.G., and Parrish, J.M., 1999, Distribution of vertebrate faunas in the Cedar Mountain Formation, east-central Utah, *in* Gillette, D.D., editor, Vertebrate paleontology in Utah: Utah Geological Survey Miscellaneous Publication 99-1, p. 201-217.

Kurie, A.E., 1966, Recurrent structural disturbance of the Colorado Plateau margin near Zion National Park, Utah: Geological Society of America Bulletin, v. 77, p. 867-872.

Lambert, R.E., 1984, Shnabkaib Member of the Moenkopi Formation: Depositional environment and stratigraphy near Virgin, Washington County, Utah: Brigham Young University Geology Studies, v. 31, pt. 1, p. 47-65.

LeBas, M.J., LeMaitre, R.W., Streckeisen, A., and Zanettin, B., 1986, A chemical classification of volcanic rocks based on the total alkali-silica diagram: Journal of Petrology, v. 27, p. 745-750.

Lund, W.R., and Everitt, B.L., 1998, Reconnaissance paleoseismic investigation of the Hurricane fault in southwestern Utah, including the Ash Creek section and most of the Anderson Junction section, *in* Pearthree, P.A., Lund, W.R., Stenner, H.D., and Everitt, B.L., Paleoseismic investigations of the Hurricane fault in southwestern Utah and northwestern Arizona, Final Project Report: U.S. Geological Survey, National Earthquake Hazards Reduction Program, p. 8-48.

McKee, E.D., 1938, The environment and history of the Toroweap and Kaibab Formations of northern Arizona and southern Utah: Carnegie Institute of Washington Publication 492, 268 p.

Neighbor, F., 1952, Geology of the Pintura structure, Washington County, Utah: Utah Geological Society, Guidebook to the geology of Utah, no. 7, p. 79-80.

Nielson, R.L., 1977, The geomorphic evolution of the Crater Hill volcanic field of Zion National Park: Brigham Young University Geology Studies, v. 24, pt. 1, p. 55-70.

—1981, Depositional environment of the Toroweap and

Kaibab Formations of southwestern Utah: Salt Lake City, University of Utah, Ph.D. dissertation, 495 p.

—1986, The Toroweap and Kaibab Formations, southwestern Utah, *in* Griffen, D.T., and Phillips, W.R., editors, Thrusting and extensional structures and mineralization in the Beaver Dam Mountains, southwestern Utah: Utah Geological Association Publication 15, p. 37-53.

—1991, Petrology, sedimentology and stratigraphic implications of the Rock Canyon Conglomerate, southwestern Utah: Utah Geological Survey Miscellaneous Publication 91-7, 65 p.

Nielson, R.L., and Johnson, J.L., 1979, The Timpoweap Member of the Moenkopi Formation, Timpoweap Canyon, Utah: Utah Geology, v. 6, no. 1, p. 17-27.

Olsen, P.E., and Padian, Kevin, 1986, Earliest records of Batrachopus from the southwestern United States, and a revision of some Early Mesozoic crocodylomorph ichnogenera, *in* Padian, Kevin, editor, The beginning of the age of dinosaurs - faunal changes across the Triassic-Jurassic boundary: Cambridge University Press, p. 260-273.

Peterson, Fred, 1988, Pennsylvanian to Jurassic eolian transportation systems in the western United States, in Kocurek, Gary, editor, Late Paleozoic and Mesozoic eolian deposits of the western interior of the United States: Sedimentary Geology, v. 56, p. 207-260.

—1994, Sand dunes, sabkhas, streams, and shallow seas - Jurassic paleogeography in the southern part of the Western Interior Basin, *in* Caputo, M.V., Peterson, J.A., and Franczyk, K.J., editors, Mesozoic systems of the Rocky Mountain region, USA: Denver, Colorado, Rocky Mountain Section of the Society for Sedimentary Geology, p. 233-272.

Peterson, Fred, Cornet, Bruce, Turner-Peterson, C.E., 1977, New data on the stratigraphy and age of the Glen Canyon Group (Triassic and Jurassic) in southern Utah and northern Arizona [abs.]: Geological Society of America Abstracts with Programs, v. 9, no. 6, p. 755.

Peterson, Fred, and Pipiringos, G.N., 1979, Stratigraphic relations of the Navajo Sandstone to Middle Jurassic formations, southern Utah and northern Arizona: U.S. Geological Survey Professional Paper 1035-B, 43 p.

Pipiringos, G.N., and O'Sullivan, R.B., 1978, Principal unconformities in Triassic and Jurassic rocks, western Interior United States - a preliminary survey: U.S. Geological Survey Professional Paper 1035-A, 29 p.

Proctor, P.D., and Shirts, M.A., 1991, Silver, sinners and saints - a history of old Silver Reef, Utah: Provo, Utah, Paulmar, Inc., 224 p.

Rawson, R.R., and Turner-Peterson, C.E., 1979, Marine-carbonate, sabkha, and eolian facies transitions within the Permian Toroweap Formation, northern Arizona, *in* Baars, D.L., editor, Permianland: Four Corners Geological Society Guidebook, 9th Field Conference, p. 87-99.

Reeside, J.B., Jr., and Bassler, Harvey, 1921, Stratigraphic sections in southwestern Utah and northwestern Arizona: U.S. Geological Survey Professional Paper 129-D, p. 53-77.

Sanchez, Alexander, 1995, Mafic volcanism in the Colorado Plateau/Basin-and-Range transition zone, Hurricane, Utah: Las Vegas, University of Nevada, M.S. thesis, 92 p., scale 1:52,000.

Sandburg, G.W., and Sultz, L.G., 1985, Reconnaissance of the quality of surface water in the upper Virgin River basin, Utah, Arizona, and Nevada, 1981-1982: Utah Department of Natural Resources, Division of Water Rights, Technical Publication No. 83, 69 p.

Sansom, P.J., 1992, Sedimentology of the Navajo Sandstone, southern Utah, USA: Oxford, England, Department of Earth Sciences and Wolfson College, Ph.D. dissertation, 291 p.

Schaeffer, B., and Dunkle, D.H., 1950, A semionotid fish from the Chinle Formation, with consideration of its relationships: American Museum Novitates, no. 1457, p. 1-29.

Scotese, C.R., 1999, PALEOMAP animations: 1999 PALEOMAP project, www.scotese.com.

Smith, E.I., Sanchez, Alexander, Walker, J.D., and Wang, Kefa, 1999, Geochemistry of mafic magmas in the Hurricane volcanic field, Utah - implications for small- and large-scale chemical variability of the lithospheric mantle: The Journal of Geology, v. 107, p. 43-448.

Solomon, B.J., 1995, Geologic reconnaissance of the Zion Canyon landslide of April 12, 1995, Zion National Park, Washington County, Utah, *in* Mayes, B.H., compiler, Technical reports for 1994-1995, Applied Geology Program: Utah Geological Survey Report of Investigation 228, p. 74-79.

Sorauf, J.E., and Billingsly, G.H., 1991, Members of the Toroweap and Kaibab Formations, Lower Permian, northern Arizona and southwestern Utah: The Mountain Geologist, v. 28, no. 1, p. 9-24.

Stewart, J.H., Poole, F.G., and Wilson, R.F., 1972, Stratigraphy and origin of the Triassic Moenkopi Formation and related strata in the Colorado Plateau region, with a section on sedimentary petrology by R.A. Cadigan: U.S. Geological Survey Professional Paper 691, 195 p., scale 1:2,500,000.

Stewart, M.E., and Taylor, W.J., 1996, Structural analysis and fault segment boundary identification along the Hurricane fault in southwestern Utah: Journal of Structural Geology, v. 18, p. 1017-1,029.

Stokes, W.L., and Bruhn, A.F., 1960, Dinosaur tracks from Zion National Park and vicinity, *in* Harrison, G.L., editor, Proceedings of the Utah Academy of Sciences, Arts, and Letters, p. 75-76.

Thompson, A.E., and Stokes, W.L., 1970, Stratigraphy of the San Rafael Group, southwest and south-central Utah: Utah Geological and Mineralogical Survey Bulletin 87, 50 p.

Threet, R.L., 1958, Crater Hill lava flow, Zion National Park, Utah: Geological Society of America Bulletin, v.

69, p. 1,065-1,070.

Tschudy, R.H., Tschudy, B.D., and Craig, L.C., 1984, Palynological evaluation of Cedar Mountain and Burro Canyon Formations, Colorado Plateau: U.S. Geological Survey Professional Paper 1281, 24 p., 9 plates.

Tuesink, M.F., 1989, Depositional analysis of an eolian-fluvial environment - the intertonguing of the Kayenta Formation and Navajo Sandstone (Jurassic) in southwestern Utah: Flagstaff, Northern Arizona University, M.S. thesis,189 p.

U.S. Geological Survey, 1998, Streamflow in Utah: U.S. Geological Survey website www.water.usgs.gov/ infores/streamflow.html.

Willis, G.C., 1999, The Utah thrust system - an overview, *in* Spangler, L.E., and Allen, C.J., editors, Geology of northern Utah and vicinity: Utah Geological Association Publication 27, p. 1-9.

Willis, G.C., Biek, R.F., and Higgins, J.M., 1999, New ^{40}Ar/^{39}Ar ages of basalt flows in the lower Virgin River basin of southwest Utah - implications for volcanic, faulting, and downcutting histories [abs.]: Geological Society of America Abstracts with Programs, v. 33, no. 4, p. A-61.

Willis, G.C., and Higgins, J.M., 1996, Interim geologic map of the Washington quadrangle, Washington County, Utah: Utah Geological Survey Open-File Report 324, 108 p., scale 1:24,000.

Wright, J.C., and Dickey, D.D., 1963a, Relations of the Navajo and Carmel Formations in southwest Utah and adjoining Arizona, *in* Geological Survey research 1962, Short papers on geology, hydrology, and topography: U.S. Geological Survey Professional Paper 450-E, p. E63-E67.

—1963b, Block diagram of the San Rafael Group and underlying strata in Utah and part of Colorado: U.S. Geological Survey Oil and Gas Investigations Chart OC-63.

Appendix 1. *Bedrock units of Zion National Park with selected references.* (1) *Kauffman, 1977; Tschudy and others, 1984; am Ende, 1991.* (2) *Imlay, 1980; Blakey and others, 1983.* (3) *Blakey, 1994; Peterson, 1994.* (4) *Tuesink, 1989; Sansom, 1992.* (5) *Clemmensen and others, 1989; DeCourten, 1998.* (6) *Stewart and others, 1972; Dubiel, 1994.* (7) *DeCourten, 1998.* (8) *Dubiel, 1994.* (9) *Lambert, 1984.* (10) *Nielson and Johnson, 1979; Dubiel, 1994.* (11) *Nielson, 1991.* (12) *McKee, 1938; Nielson, 1986, Sorauf and Billingsley, 1991.* (13) *McKee, 1938, Rawson-Turner Peterson, 1979; Nielson, 1986.*

NAME		DOMINANT ROCK TYPE	DEPOSITIONAL ENVIRONMENT	REMARKS
Cretaceous rocks		Pebble to cobble conglomerate and tan sandstone	River and alluvial plain[1]	Only lowermost strata preserved in park at Horse Ranch Mountain, but widely exposed to north and east
Carmel Formation	Winsor Member	Yellowish-gray to reddish-brown, fine- to medium-grained sandstone; minor siltstone and pebbly sandstone	Broad sandy mudflat along northward regressing inland sea[2]	Poorly cemented, forms slopes
Carmel Formation	Paria River Member	Ledge- and cliff-forming alabaster gypsum overlain by thin-bedded argillaceous limestone; gypsum pinches out westward	Restricted shallow marine; limestone represents southward transgression of sea[2]	Gypsum forms prominent cliff up to 60 feet (18 m) high; limestone is platy or chippy weathering
Carmel Formation	Crystal Creek Member	Reddish-brown, fine-grained sandstone and siltstone	Coastal sabkha and tidal flat, sea regressive northward[2]	Poorly cemented, forms reddish slopes
Carmel Formation	Co-op Creek Limestone Member	Gray micritic limestone and calcareous shale; local crinoid columnals (*Pentacrinus*), pelecypods, gastropods	Shallow marine, sea transgressive southward[2]	Lower part forms slopes, upper part cliffs; upper surface forms plateau
Temple Cap Fm.	White Throne Member	Yellowish-brown, fine- to medium-grained sandstone much like the Navajo Sandstone	Coastal eolian dunes[3]	Cliff former; pinches out westward between Zion Canyon and Kolob Canyons
Temple Cap Fm.	Sinawava Member	Reddish-brown, fine-grained sandstone, siltstone, and mudstone	Coastal sabkha and tidal flat[3]	Forms narrow, vegetated slope above Navajo Sandstone
Navajo Sandstone		Fine- to medium-grained sandstone with large-scale cross-beds; grains are rounded and frosted quartz; uncommon planar interdune deposits; includes basal transition zone	Vast eolian dune field of arid west coast tropical desert; basal part represents sabkha deposits[3,4]	Forms sheer cliffs; color changes due to post-depositional alteration of cement by ground water and possibly hydrocarbon migration through the rock
Kayenta Formation	Tenney Canyon Tongue of Kayenta Fm	Similar to main body Kayenta but becomes sandier upward	Distal river and playa[3,4]	Similar to main body Kayenta
Kayenta Formation	Lamb Point Tongue of Navajo Sandstone	Similar to Navajo Sandstone	Eolian dune field[3,4]	Records interfingering of Navajo sand desert and Kayenta river/playa sediments; pinches out westward
Kayenta Formation	Main body Kayenta	Reddish-brown, thin- to very thick-bedded siltstone, fine-grained sandstone, and mudstone; uncommon thin dolomite beds	River, distal river/playa, minor lake[3,4]	Forms ledgy slopes commonly covered by talus

	NAME	DOMINANT ROCK TYPE	DEPOSITIONAL ENVIRONMENT	REMARKS
Moenave Formation	Springdale Sandstone Member	Yellowish-gray to pale-pink, medium- to very thick-bedded, fine- to medium-grained sandstone; thin mudstone interbeds and intraformational conglomerate lenses	Braided stream and minor flood plain[3,5]	Forms bold cliff; contains local petrified and carbonized plant remains
Moenave Formation	Whitmore Point Member	Varicolored mudstone; lesser reddish-brown, very fine- to fine-grained sandstone and siltstone; few thin dolomitic limestone beds	Lake and flood plain[3,5]	Forms poorly exposed but brightly colored slopes; locally contains fossil fish scales
Moenave Formation	Dinosaur Canyon Member	Reddish-brown, thin-bedded, very fine- to fine-grained sandstone, silty sandstone, and lesser siltstone and mudstone	River and flood plain[3,5]	Forms ledgy slopes
Chinle Formation	Petrified Forest Member	Brilliantly variegated mudstone and claystone; lesser siltstone, sandstone, pebbly sandstone; common paleosols, limestone nodules, and petrified wood	Flood plain, lake, and high-sinuosity streams[6,7]	Forms poorly exposed slopes widely involved in landslides; abundant swelling bentonitic mudstone
Chinle Formation	Shinarump Conglomerate Member	Tan to light-gray, thick to very thick-bedded, medium- to coarse-grained sandstone and pebbly sandstone; clasts are quartz, quartzite, and chert; common petrified wood	Braided streams that flowed north and northwest[6,7]	Forms prominent cliff; commonly stained by iron-manganese oxides to form "picture stone"
Moenkopi Formation	upper red member	Reddish-brown, thin- to medium-bedded siltstone, mudstone, and very fine- to fine-grained sandstone	Tidal flat and coastal plain[6]	Slope and ledge former
Moenkopi Formation	Shnabkaib Member	Reddish-brown, thin-bedded mudstone and siltstone and white to greenish-gray, thin to thick gypsum beds; minor thin dolomite beds	Tidal flat, coastal sabkha, and restricted shallow marine[9]	Forms banded red and white ledgy slopes
Moenkopi Formation	middle red member	Like lower red member but with several thick gypsum beds near base	Tidal flat and coastal plain[6]	Forms slopes
Moenkopi Formation	Virgin Limestone Member	Yellowish-gray to light-gray, finely to coarsely crystalline limestone and interbedded gray mudstone; locally common crinoid, gastropod, and brachiopod fossils	Shallow marine[8]	Forms three limestone ledges separated by mudstone slopes
Moenkopi Formation	lower red member	Reddish-brown, thin-bedded mudstone and siltstone	Tidal flat and coastal plain[6]	Stratigraphically lowest red-bed interval exposed in park
Moenkopi Formation	Timpoweap Member	Brownish-gray, thin- to thick-bedded limestone and cherty limestone; upper part includes yellowish-brown, very fine-grained sandstone and siltstone	Shallow marine[10]	Cliff former; rough weathering due to disseminated chert blebs

	NAME	DOMINANT ROCK TYPE	DEPOSITIONAL ENVIRONMENT	REMARKS
Kaibab Formation	Rock Canyon Conglomerate Member	Brownish-gray pebble and cobble conglomerate and thin regolithic breccia; clasts are reworked from Harrisburg strata	River channel and in-situ weathering (regolith)[11]	Locally deposited over irregular surface of TR-1 regional unconformity
Kaibab Formation	Harrisburg Member	Gray, thin- to thick-bedded limestone, cherty limestone, and siltstone	Shallow marine and coastal sabkha[12]	Forms ledgy slopes; irregular bedding and local intraformational breccia due to gypsum dissolution
Kaibab Formation	Fossil Mountain Member	Gray, thick- to very thick-bedded fossiliferous limestone and cherty limestone	Shallow marine[12]	Forms "black banded" cliffs due to abundant black chert
Toroweap Formation	Woods Ranch Member	Gray, thin- to thick-bedded limestone, cherty limestone, and minor gypsiferous siltstone	Shallow marine and coastal sabkha[13]	Forms slopes
Toroweap Formation	Brady Canyon Member	Gray, thick- to very thick-bedded limestone and cherty limestone similar to Fossil Mountain strata	Shallow marine[13]	Forms cliffs

Geology of Utah's Parks and Monuments
2000 Utah Geological Association Publication 28
D.A. Sprinkel, T.C. Chidsey, Jr., and P.B. Anderson, editors

Geology of Cedar Breaks
National Monument, Utah

Stanley C. Hatfield[1], Peter D. Rowley[1], Edward G. Sable[2], David J. Maxwell[1],
Bryant V. Cox[1], Matthew D. McKell[1], and David E. Kiel[1]

ABSTRACT

Cedar Breaks National Monument is located high on the western rim of the Markagunt Plateau of the Colorado Plateau physiographic province, with spectacular views westward into the Basin and Range province. Tourists are drawn to this small monument partly because of its high, pine-covered elevations and partly because, just below the rim, amphitheaters of colorful red, orange, and white, fluvial and lacustrine strata of the Claron Formation (Eocene and Paleocene) have been eroded into spectacular hoodoos, cliffs, and related landforms. The rocks of the monument dip gently eastward and range from marine rocks of the Upper Cretaceous Straight Cliffs Formation and overlying fluvial rocks of the Upper Cretaceous and Paleocene(?) Wahweap Sandstone/Grand Castle Formation, all well below the rim, to poorly exposed rocks of the Brian Head Formation (Oligocene and Eocene) and Markagunt Megabreccia (Miocene), at and above the rim. Excellent exposures of these two younger units, however, as well as Oligocene and Miocene regional ash-flow sheets derived from far to the west in the Great Basin, occur on Brian Head and Blowhard Mountain adjacent to the monument. These post-Claron rocks bespeak a more complicated and fascinating geologic story than the simple east-dipping plateau might suggest. For their story includes massive gravity sliding, with shear planes in incompetent, tuffaceous fluvial and lacustrine rocks of the Brian Head Formation, that resulted in deposition of the Markagunt Megabreccia over large parts of the Markagunt Plateau. Starting about 10 million years ago, the plateau has been uplifted along basin-range faults, including the Hurricane fault zone. Erosion of the east-dipping rock of the fault scarp has caused the plateau rim to retreat eastward several miles, and this process continues today.

INTRODUCTION

Cedar Breaks National Monument is located 18 miles east of Cedar City, Utah, on the western edge of the Markagunt Plateau (figure 1). Geologically and in terms of physiography, Cedar Breaks is very similar to its better known neighbor 40 miles to the east, Bryce Canyon National Park. There are important and distinctive differences between the two parks, however. Both are located in the High Plateaus transition zone between the Basin and Range province to the west and the Colorado Plateau province to the east and therefore share geologic characteristics of each. In both, weathering and erosion of the Tertiary Claron Formation have exposed picturesque pink, orange, and white cliffs in impressive natural amphitheaters (figure 2). Also for both, younger Tertiary volcanic rocks of the huge Marysvale volcanic field (Rowley and others, 1979, 1998, in press; Cunningham and others, 1983; Steven and others, 1984, 1990) are exposed just to the

Figure 1. Location map of Cedar Breaks National Monument, Utah. Stars with labels that refer to field trip indicate road log route on compact disc (UGA Publication 29).

[1]Southern Utah University, Cedar City, Utah 84720
[2]U.S. Geological Survey, Denver, Colorado 80225

Figure 2. Photograph, looking east-northeast, showing the general scenery of Cedar Breaks National Monument. Most rocks shown belong to the red and white members of the Claron Formation. Brian Head peak is on the right horizon.

north. The geologic map and cross section are given as figures 3 and 4. Cedar Breaks is much higher topographically (about 11,000 feet elevation) so that its erosional landforms have been modified to a greater extent by glacial and periglacial processes. Cedar Breaks also was overrun by massive gravity slides resulting in the spectacular and enigmatic Markagunt Megabreccia. Although the Markagunt Plateau is technically the westernmost segment of the Colorado Plateau in this part of Utah, many of the rock units found at Cedar Breaks are better exposed in the Great Basin subprovince of the Basin and Range province to the west, again evidence of the transitional nature of the geologic setting.

In this paper we discuss the geology of Cedar Breaks National Monument, noting both the obvious characteristics as well as some of the lesser known geologic aspects. Although less publicized and probably not as well understood, these more obscure details are an important part of the geologic picture at Cedar Breaks and provide important clues to the geologic history of the area. Despite the apparent simplicity of the exposed rock units, Cedar Breaks National Monument has experienced a complicated and interesting geologic past.

STRATIGRAPHY

The names and interpretations of some of the stratigraphic units in the Cedar Breaks area have lacked consensus among workers. Rock units are shown on the stratigraphic column (figure 5) and described below, from oldest to youngest.

Straight Cliffs Formation (Upper Cretaceous)

The Straight Cliffs Formation is poorly exposed in the western part of Cedar Breaks National Monument. Moore and Nealey (1993) assigned these rocks to an upper, 1,200-feet-thick Straight Cliffs unit of soft, predominantly light-gray, yellowish-gray, light-yellowish-brown, reddish-brown, and brownish-gray mudstone containing thin beds of lenticular, fine- to medium-grained sandstone. It contains fossil wood and plant fragments and is mostly of continental origin. To the west, in Cedar (Coal Creek) Canyon, a lower unit consists of gray cliffs of marine shoreline sandstone interbedded with thin units of fossiliferous oyster-bearing limestone and coal. Based on studies north of Cedar Breaks National Monument, Goldstrand and Mullett (1997) correlated beds at the same and

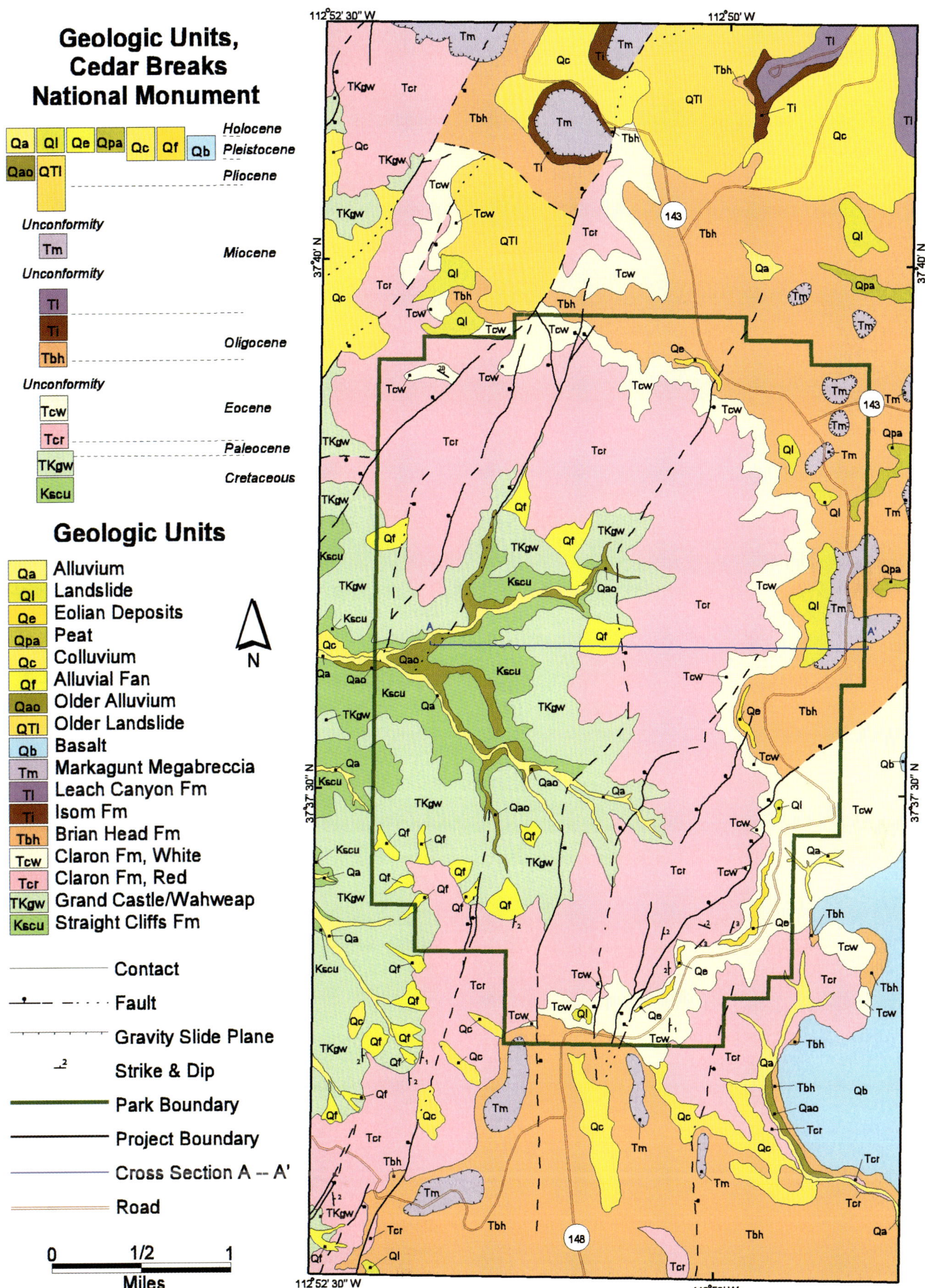

Figure 3. Geologic map of Cedar Breaks National Monument and vicinity.

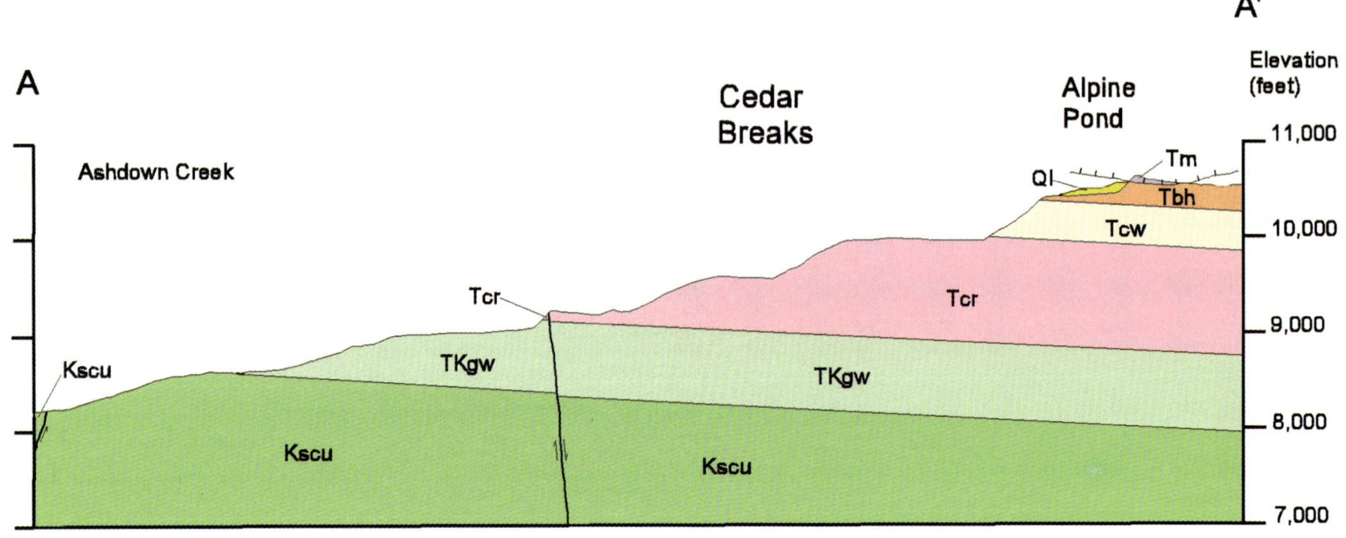

Figure 4. Geologic cross section through Cedar Breaks National Monument.

older stratigraphic interval with the mostly continental Cretaceous Iron Springs Formation of the Basin and Range. On the basis of lithology, they suggested that the Straight Cliffs, however, should be applied to the rocks south of Cedar Breaks. Based on regional mapping, E.G. Sable (unpublished data, 1993) has, in fact, recognized the uppermost unit of the Straight Cliffs Formation, the Drip Tank Member, south of the monument; in this report, therefore, we use the name Straight Cliffs rather than Iron Springs for rocks of this interval. Eaton and others (1999) K-Ar (potassium-argon) dated two ash beds in the area, one of 86.7 million years (Ma) in the upper Straight Cliffs Formation in Cedar Canyon west of the monument and the other 83.0 Ma in the upper Iron Springs Formation in Parowan Canyon north of the monument. They concluded that both formations represent two adjacent local basins of distinct rock types, the boundary between which was near Cedar Breaks, in the lower part of the mostly non-marine foreland basin of the Sevier deformational event to the west. The lower unit of the Straight Cliffs may represent shoreline transgression from the east.

Wahweap Sandstone (Upper Cretaceous)/ Grand Castle Formation (Paleocene? and Upper Cretaceous)

In and near the western part of Cedar Breaks National Monument, a unit overlying the Straight Cliffs has been interpreted on the basis of incomplete geologic mapping (Moore and Nealey, 1993; E.G. Sable, unpublished data, 1993) and of measured sections (Goldstrand, 1991; Goldstrand and Mullett, 1997) as either the Wahweap Sandstone and overlying Kaiparowits(?) Formation (both Upper Cretaceous) or the Grand Castle Formation (Paleocene). The Wahweap Sandstone consists of poorly exposed, interbedded soft, variegated, mostly brownish

gray, olive-brown, and reddish-brown mudstone, and subordinate amounts of gray, black, and grayish-orange, locally cross-bedded, clayey, fine-grained, lenticular, thin-bedded sandstone and lesser siltstone (Moore and Nealey, 1993). Sandstone is the dominant rock type only in the upper part of the formation. The unit locally contains carbonized fossil wood, leaf impressions, and spherical calcareous, limonitic concretions, and thin bedding to laminated trough cross-bedding, locally recording penecontemporaneous deformation. The Wahweap, probably mostly of fluvial origin, is about 1,000 feet thick.

Moore and Nealey (1993) designated 200 feet of fluvial rocks sandwiched between the Wahweap and Claron Formations as the Kaiparowits(?) Formation. They described the lower part of the unit as poorly exposed, friable, light-gray to light-yellowish-gray, cross-bedded sandstone that locally is interbedded with the underlying Wahweap Sandstone. Its upper part is a ledge of yellowish-brown, orange-gray, and white "salt-and-pepper," poorly to moderately sorted, angular, fine- to coarse-grained, cross-bedded, argillaceous, cherty sandstone and small-pebble mudstone conglomerate. This sandstone ledge locally contains pelecypods, fossil wood, and vertebrate fossils. More likely these 200 feet of strata should be designated Wahweap Sandstone (Nichols, 1997). Alternatively, as noted by Sable and Maldonado (1997a), subsequent work in the Cedar Breaks area suggests that these and older rocks might be correlated with the Grand Castle Formation of Goldstrand (1990, 1991, 1994) and Goldstrand and Mullett (1997). The Grand Castle was described by these workers as mostly an orthoquartzite sandstone and conglomerate unit that is about 650 feet thick in the western part of the monument; as such, it also would include much of the Wahweap of Moore and Nealey (1993). Goldstrand and Mullett (1997) considered it to be of Paleocene age on the basis of lithologic correlation with rocks of the Canaan

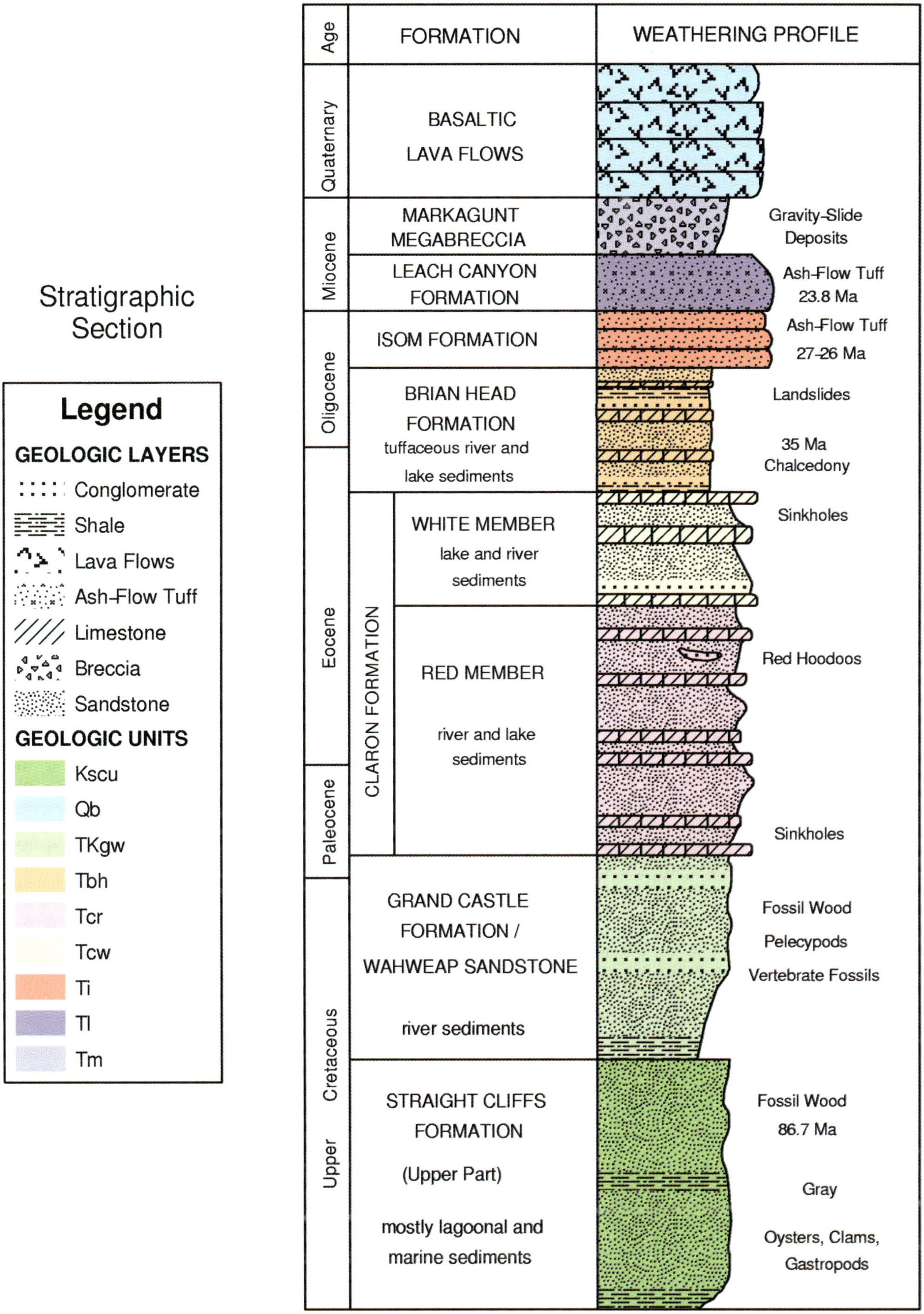

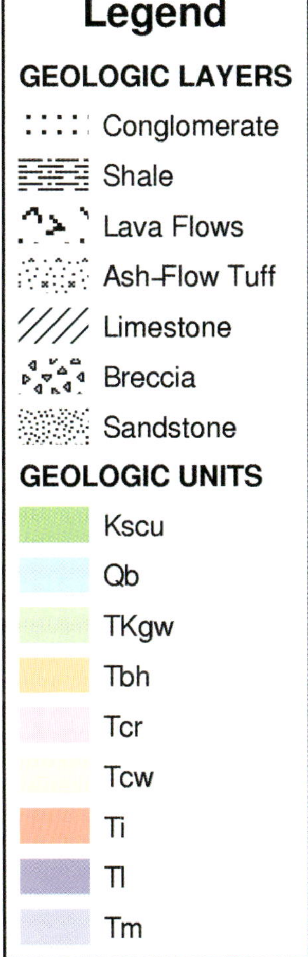

Figure 5. Stratigraphic column of rock units in and near Cedar Breaks National Monument.

Peak and Pine Hollow Formations (Bowers, 1972) in the Table Cliff region 50 miles to the east. Goldstrand and Mullett (1997) interpreted the unit to postdate, and represent the erosion of, thrust sheets of the Sevier orogeny in southwestern Utah and to predate later Laramide deformation in the Colorado Plateau. Nichols (1997), however, suggested on the basis of pollen samples that the Grand Castle in and near Cedar Breaks is Late Cretaceous and only the uppermost 80 feet of the unit, where no pollen samples were collected, might be Paleocene. Until more conclusive stratigraphic evidence is known in the area, we map the unit as Wahweap Sandstone/Grand Castle Formation and consider it to be of Late Cretaceous and Paleocene(?) age.

Claron Formation (Eocene and Paleocene)

The source of the spectacular scenery at Cedar Breaks National Monument and Bryce Canyon National Park is the succession of red, orange, and white fluvial and lacustrine beds of the Claron Formation. These strata generally erode to spectacular cliffs and hoodoos (figure 2). This poorly fossiliferous unit consists of alternating beds of sandy limestone and calcareous sandstone, with subordinate calcareous mudstone and minor conglomerate. Previously assigned informally to the Wasatch Formation (Richardson, 1909; Gregory and Moore, 1931; Gregory, 1951) of southwestern Wyoming, the rocks were recognized by Mackin (1947) to require a locally defined formation name. He proposed the name Claron Formation, which had been applied by Leith and Harder (1908) to lithologically similar rocks in the Iron Springs mining district 10 miles west of Cedar City. Gregory (1951) was the first to subdivide the Wasatch (Claron) Formation into two informal members, a lower red member and an upper white member. In the Cedar Breaks area, the red member consists of alternating beds of pink, red, and reddish-orange, resistant, thick-bedded, argillaceous, sandy micritic limestone, mostly reddish-tan and pink, resistant, thick-bedded, locally cross-bedded sandstone, and red and pink, soft, silty mudstone, as well as minor lenticular, gray, pink, and reddish-tan, resistant conglomerate and conglomeritic sandstone (Moore and Nealey, 1993). The limestone commonly contains thin, branching veinlets of sparry calcite that presumably represent algal filaments and vertical burrow fillings; it also locally contains stylolites, solution features including sinkholes, and rare pelecypod and gastropod fossils. The base of the formation is considered by Moore and Nealey (1993) to be a 65-feet-thick limestone bed that contains shallow caves and local springs. Although the formation has been widely recognized to be of fluvial and lacustrine origin, Mullett and others (1988a, 1988b) and Mullett (1989) proposed that the Claron, and notably the red Claron, has been modified by soil-forming (pedogenetic) processes and by bioturbation after its original deposition and that many of the limestone beds are caliche beds formed during these processes. Schneider (1967) measured a section of the red member of

about 1,000 feet thick in Cedar Breaks National Monument, although in a reinterpretation of the stratigraphy in that section, Sable and Maldonado (1997a) preferred a thickness of about 1,300 feet there.

The base of the white member in the Cedar Breaks National Monument is drawn at the base of a conspicuous 40-feet-high cliff of white and light-orange, micritic limestone. It is overlain in the monument by mostly soft, yellowish-gray to light-brown, interbedded mudstone and fine- to medium-grained sandstone (Moore and Nealey, 1993). The uppermost bed is a distinctive, 43-feet-high cliff of white, light-yellowish-gray, and light-orange, micritic limestone; this bed contains veinlets and vugs of sparry calcite and, in the basal part, is locally replaced by chalcedony (Moore and Nealey, 1993). This caps the impressive, west-facing scarp making up the rim of the central Markagunt Plateau. In the monument, the white member is about 360 feet thick. The age of the Claron is poorly constrained, partly because the soil-forming processes noted by Mullett (1989) have obliterated many of the beds and fossils, and the few invertebrate fossils recovered are not diagnostic, although suggestive of an Eocene age (Gregory, 1951). Fossil insects were recovered by Bown and others (1997) from the Claron, but these fossils provide no specific information about the age of the rocks. Goldstrand (1994), however, found palynomorph (spores and pollen) fossils in basal Claron rocks from the eastern Pine Valley Mountains (30 miles southwest of the monument) that indicate a Paleocene age for this part of the section, and a fission-track date of 50 Ma from strata just below Claron beds in the Table Cliff Plateau (50 miles east of the monument) indicates that there the basal Claron is Eocene. Goldstrand (1990) also collected gastropod fossils from the lower part of the Claron that resemble those of Paleocene to Eocene in the Flagstaff Formation of central Utah studied by LaRocque (1960).

Brian Head Formation (Oligocene and Eocene)

The Brian Head Formation consists of mostly light-gray, soft continental sedimentary rocks. The name Brian Head Formation was first proposed by Gregory (1944) for a thick sequence of sedimentary and volcanic rocks that overlie the red member of the Claron Formation in the Cedar Breaks and adjacent areas. In Gregory's later work (for example, Gregory, 1951), he excluded the current white member of the Claron from the Brian Head Formation. Anderson and Rowley (1975) abandoned use of the formation in part because the stratigraphy of the rocks was poorly defined and contradictory and in part because the rocks that Gregory included in the upper part of his unit represented the distal edges of many of the regional volcanic units derived from the southern Marysvale volcanic field and Great Basin. Mullett and others (1988a) and Mullett (1989) noted a regional unconformity at the top of the Claron Formation; in places all of the white member and the upper part of the red member were removed by erosion. Long-term field work in and near the Markagunt

Plateau by J.J. Anderson, Florian Maldonado, and E.G. Sable identified a widely exposed sequence of tuffaceous and nontuffaceous fluvial and lacustrine sedimentary rocks and tuffs, at least 300 feet thick, resting above this unconformity and below the regional ash-flow volcanic sequence. Based on mapping in the Red Hills west of the Markagunt Plateau, Maldonado and others (1990) used the term "sedimentary and volcanic rocks of the Red Hills" for these rocks. Anderson (1993), however, reintroduced the name Brian Head Formation for that sequence because the best exposures are on the slopes of Brian Head. He noted that the base of the unit is a conglomerate that is overlain by non-tuffaceous red and gray sandstone, then in turn by tuffaceous sedimentary rocks, including interbedded, thin-bedded, "salt-and-pepper" (the "pepper" being igneous minerals, lithic fragments, and chert) fluvial and eolian sandstone, conglomerate, shale, ash-flow and airfall tuff, and white limestone beds that contain root casts, burrow fillings, clay of volcanic origin, and amoeboid masses of varicolored replacement chalcedony. The unit is generally soft and poorly exposed, and its high percentage of volcanogenic clay makes it structurally incompetent and prone to Quaternary landsliding.

Sable and Maldonado (1997a) provided a detailed discussion and type section of the redefined Brian Head Formation, which they estimated at as much as 700 feet thick in the High Plateaus and adjacent Great Basin. They divided it into three poorly exposed units: (1) a lower thin-bedded unit of soft, reddish-brown, pink, and reddish-orange, nontuffaceous sandstone and conglomerate, with subordinate siltstone, claystone, and micritic limestone; (2) a thick soft middle unit of thin-bedded, gray, greenish-gray, and yellowish-gray, bioturbated beds of volcaniclastic clayey sandstone, conglomeratic sandstone (containing pebbles and cobbles in its upper part that include ash-flow tuff), claystone, micritic limestone (commonly replaced by chalcedony), and airfall tuff; and (3) an upper, mostly resistant, heterogeneous unit (not present in the Brian Head area) of volcanic mudflow breccia, immature volcanic sandstone and conglomerate, mafic lava flows, and local ash-flow tuff. In some places, basal beds of the lower unit occur in channels cut into the white member of the Claron in the southern part of Cedar Breaks National Monument; the rest of the lower unit, as well as the middle unit above it, is exposed on the slopes of Brian Head. We also map it underlying part of Blowhard Mountain just southwest of the monument, although little more is exposed here besides a pink, biotite-bearing sandstone and underlying small-pebble conglomerate located just west of the communication site on Blowhard Mountain.

The lower unit of the Brian Head Formation (redefined) was suggested by Sable and Maldonado (1997a) to be late Eocene on the basis of a vertebrate fauna (Eaton and Hutchison, 1995) from rocks 30 miles east of the monument that were considered to be correlative with the lower unit. Feist and others (1997) suggested a maximum age of middle Eocene for basal parts of rocks correlated

with the Brian Head on the basis of a charophyte fossil flora collected from the southern Sevier Plateau 35 miles east-northeast of the monument. Fleck and others (1975, sample R-4) reported a K-Ar date of 31.9 Ma for a local ash-flow tuff interbedded within rocks correlated with the Brian Head Formation (Anderson and Kurlich, 1989). Maldonado (1995) published K-Ar dates of 34.2 and 26.3 Ma and ^{40}Ar/^{39}Ar (argon-argon) dates of 33.7 and 33.0 Ma from a sample of a local ash-flow tuff within rocks of the Brian Head Formation in the Red Hills 15 miles northwest of Cedar Breaks. Sable and Maldonado (1997a) reported a ^{40}Ar/^{39}Ar date of 34.99 Ma from a sample of tuffaceous sandstone 65 feet above the base of the Brian Head along U.S. Highway 89 about 20 miles east of the monument. The Wah Wah Springs and Isom Formation (see below), which are regional ash-flow tuffs of western derivation, are intertongued with limestone beds in the southeastern Bull Valley Mountains (50 miles southwest of Cedar Breaks). The limestone beds may correlate with the Brian Head Formation (see Rowley and others, 1994). The Wah Wah Springs Formation also is overlain by 10 feet of sandstone of Brian Head lithology just southeast of Brian Head peak. Sable and Maldonado (1997a), in their redefinition of the Brian Head Formation, placed the upper contact of the Brian Head at the base of these outcrops of Wah Wah Springs.

The Wah Wah Springs Formation (Oligocene), which belongs to the Needles Range Group, is not shown on the map but it is exposed several miles east of the mapped area. The formation is a regional ash-flow tuff that is derived from the Indian Peak caldera complex at the Utah-Nevada border (Best and others, 1989a, 1989b), 60 miles to the west-northwest. The tuff is a distinctive resistant, gray and pink, crystal-rich (as much as 40 percent phenocrysts), moderately welded, dacite ash-flow tuff that occurs near the base of the volcanic section over wide areas of southern Nevada and southwestern Utah. Its eastern extent is the southwestern High Plateaus (Mackin, 1960; Anderson and Rowley, 1975; Steven and others, 1990; Rowley and others, 1998, in press). This includes the area just north and northeast of Cedar Breaks National Monument, where it appears to have pinched out against higher topography to the north and east (Rowley and others, 1978). In the central Markagunt Plateau, some of this topography consisted of south-tilted fault blocks uplifted along west-northwest-striking faults in the northern Markagunt Plateau (Anderson, 1993). A 10-foot-thick ash-flow tuff of the formation from Lowder Creek, about 2 miles southeast of Brian Head, rests on Brian Head Formation about 9 feet below the Isom Formation. A sample of the Wah Wah Springs was dated by K-Ar methods at 32.4, 30.4, and 29.1 Ma (Rowley and others, 1994). Published K-Ar dates of the Wah Wah Springs Formation average 29.5 Ma (Best and others, 1989a, 1989b) but later unpublished ^{40}Ar/^{39}Ar dates suggest a somewhat older age (M.G. Best, written communication, 1993).

Isom Formation (Oligocene)

The Isom Formation of the Needles Range Group is a regional ash-flow tuff sequence probably also derived from the Indian Peak caldera complex (Best and others, 1989a). Cooling units of the Isom are distinctive, resistant, reddish-brown to dark-gray, crystal-poor (about 3 to 15 percent phenocrysts), densely welded, trachytic ash-flow tuffs that are spread over large parts of southern Nevada and southwestern Utah. The eastern extent of Isom tuffs is the Markagunt Plateau (Mackin, 1960; Anderson and Rowley, 1975), where it consists of three members, the lower Blue Meadows Tuff Member that is found only in the Markagunt Plateau, the widespread Baldhills Tuff Member that locally is about 650 feet thick and widely distributed on the Markagunt Plateau, and the upper Hole-in-the-Wall Tuff Member whose eastern extent is west and north of Cedar City. The Baldhills Tuff Member is exposed just below the top of Brian Head. It forms at least three cooling units totaling about 80 feet thick and consists of dark-gray, black, and brick-red tuff containing linear vesicles and local breccia. As with the Wah Wah Springs Formation, the two members of the Isom in the Markagunt Plateau pinch out northward against tilt blocks uplifted along west-northwest-striking faults (Anderson, 1993). The Blue Meadows Tuff Member has a K-Ar date of 25.9 Ma (Fleck and others, 1975; sample R-7). The Baldhills Tuff Member has an average K-Ar age of 25.7 Ma, but two ^{40}Ar/^{39}Ar dates are older, about 27 Ma (Rowley and others, 1994).

Leach Canyon Formation and Younger Rocks (Miocene)

The Leach Canyon Formation is a regional ash-flow tuff sequence whose source is not known but is centered on, and may represent an old phase of, the Caliente caldera complex of Nevada/Utah (Williams, 1967; Rowley and others, 1995), 60 miles to the west. Cooling units of the Leach Canyon are distinctive, resistant, light-tan, crystal-poor (10 to 20 percent phenocrysts), moderately to poorly welded, rhyolite ash-flow tuffs that are spread over large parts of southern Nevada and southwestern Utah. The tuff is characterized by sparse but omnipresent brownish-red rhyolite lithic clasts, rounded gas cavities lined with yellow vapor-phase minerals, and--especially in near-source areas--abundant white collapsed pumice fragments. The eastern extent of Leach Canyon tuffs is in the Markagunt Plateau (Mackin, 1960; Williams, 1967; Anderson and Rowley, 1975). The Leach Canyon caps Brian Head, where it is a simple cooling unit containing a salmon-colored, poorly welded, basal zone as thick as 16 feet, a resistant, platy, dark-brown and black vitrophyre (glass) zone as thick as 23 feet, and a tan devitrified upper zone as thick as 46 feet. K-Ar dates of the Leach Canyon are summarized by Rowley and others (1994); the most likely age is 23.8 Ma based on preliminary ^{40}Ar/^{39}Ar dates (Best and others, 1993).

Two other post-Isom units, the Bear Valley and Mount Dutton Formations, are here mentioned, even though they are exposed more than 5 miles north and northeast of Cedar Breaks National Monument. The older of these is the Bear Valley Formation (Anderson, 1971), consisting of a lower cross-bedded eolian sandstone with a large percentage of airfall tuff and an upper unit of mafic lava flows and rhyolite ash-flow tuff that are the product of local volcanism north and northeast of the monument. Two samples of the volcanic rocks yielded K-Ar dates, 24.6 Ma from an airfall tuff (Fleck and others, 1975; sample R-10) and 24.5 Ma from an ash-flow tuff (Fleck and others, 1975; sample R-9). The Bear Valley Formation may largely postdate the Leach Canyon, but the two formations are not exposed in the same area; therefore lower parts of the Bear Valley may also predate the Leach Canyon (Anderson, 1993). Like the Isom Formation, the distribution of the Bear Valley is partly controlled by west-northwest-striking faults, such that thickest sequences of sandstone and volcanic rocks are from pooling in graben areas among the fault blocks (Anderson, 1965, 1971, 1993). The other post-Isom unit, which overlies the Bear Valley and older units, is the Mount Dutton Formation (Anderson and Rowley, 1975; Rowley and others, 1998, in press). This is a sequence of volcanic mudflow breccia that thickens considerably northward and is derived from local clustered stratovolcanoes of the southern Marysvale volcanic field.

Markagunt Megabreccia (Miocene)

The Markagunt Megabreccia is a mostly poorly exposed, structurally chaotic assemblage of angular clasts and broken masses of older rock units that is spread over the crest of the northern and central Markagunt Plateau (Sable and Anderson, 1985; Anderson, 1993; Sable and Maldonado, 1997b). The rock units involved in the assemblage are the Brian Head, Wah Wah Springs, Isom, Bear Valley, and Mount Dutton Formations. Most commonly these rock masses are house- to city-block-sized, in a matrix of sheared and folded rocks of the same units, but some masses are as large as 1 square mile. Generally the megabreccia rests on undeformed rocks belonging to the white member of the Claron, the Baldhills Tuff Member of the Isom, or the Leach Canyon Formation, but in some places it rests on undeformed Bear Valley or Mount Dutton Formations. Northerly-striking slickensides on low-angle surfaces locally underlie the Megabrecccia. Anderson (1993) proposed a type locality of the unit, at least 500 feet thick, along Utah State Highway 143 just east of Panguitch Lake, which is 10 miles east of the monument; here various aspects of the unit can be seen. The age of the Markagunt Megabreccia is suggested to be about 22 to 20 Ma (Anderson, 1993; Sable and Maldonado, 1997b).

The Markagunt Megabreccia overlies the Leach Canyon Formation at Sidney Peaks, 2 miles east-northeast of Brian Head. Eroded and surficially reworked remnants of the Markagunt Megabreccia underlie many parts of Cedar Breaks Monument and surrounding areas. These

Figure 6. Large angular boulder of the Baldhills Tuff Member of the Isom Formation, deposited as part of the Markagunt Megabreccia, just north of the southern boundary of the monument.

remnants take the form of isolated angular boulders as long as 16 feet, nearly all composed of the Baldhills Member, but locally of the distinctive chalcedony that replaces limestone in the Brian Head Formation. Many large blocks occur along the main highway, including one just north of the southern boundary of the monument (figure 6) and another just south of the parking area for the trail to Alpine Pond. The boulders also cap the ridge of Blowhard Mountain, just southeast of the monument, where they were mapped by Moore and Nealey (1993) as "breccia" that they considered to be Pleistocene and late Tertiary.

Two units post-date the Markagunt Breccia but are not shown on the geologic map because they are exposed in the Panguitch Lake area. The first consists of beds of poorly to moderately consolidated, gray and tan, stream conglomerate and sandstone, about 15 to 100 feet thick, that rest in angular unconformity on the Markagunt Megabreccia (Anderson, 1993). This deposit in turn is overlain by the second unit, a local ash-flow tuff named the Haycock Mountain Tuff (Miocene), remnants of which are exposed in only a half dozen places. The tuff is a resistant, tan, crystal-poor, poorly welded, rhyolite ash-flow tuff that nowhere exceeds 50 feet thick (Anderson, 1993). The tuff, in fact, lithologically and petrographically resembles the local ash-flow tuffs of the Bear Valley Formation, which are exposed in, and clearly erupted from, the same general area. Probably all, in fact, are part of the same sequence of local eruptions, although by definition they are now placed in different stratigraphic units (Anderson, 1993; J.J. Anderson, verbal communication, 1999). In other words, the old products (in the Bear Valley Formation) of this sequence predate the formation of the Markagunt Megabreccia, whereas the young products (Haycock Mountain Tuff) postdate it (Anderson, 1993; J.J. Anderson, verbal communication, 1999). Rowley and others (1994) and Sable and Maldonado (1997b) reported several K-Ar and ^{40}Ar/^{39}Ar dates from a unit they correlated with the Haycock Mountain Tuff; these consist of dates of 24.23 and 22.3 Ma from

one sample and of 24.8, 24.3, 23.86, and 22.8 Ma from another sample. These samples, however, are from a deformed ash-flow tuff that we here interpret to be one of the older (Bear Valley) products of the rhyolitic ash-flow eruptions. The Haycock Mountain Tuff, as does the Leach Canyon Formation and the ash-flow tuffs in the Bear Valley Formation, contains subequal amounts of quartz, sanidine, and plagioclase, with minor biotite. This mineralogy (the most common for ash-flow tuffs), as well as the isotopic dates given above, led Sable and Maldonado (1997b) to suggest that the Haycock Mountain Tuff is actually the Leach Canyon Formation. However, the Leach Canyon always contains sparse and small but distinctive red rhyolite lithic clasts and the Haycock Mountain Tuff always contains abundant, large, distinctive basalt lithic clasts. We interpret that the two tuffs are separate units. A ^{40}Ar/^{39}Ar date of a sample from the type locality of the Haycock Mountain Tuff is 22.75 ± 0.12 Ma (E.G. Sable, unpublished data, 2000). This substantiates the interpretation of Anderson that the Haycock Mountain is not correlative with the Leach Canyon and constrains the age of the Markagunt Megabreccia at less than 22.75 Ma.

Basaltic Lava Flows (Quaternary)

Resistant, black and gray, vesicular, generally crystal-poor, basaltic lava flows, flow breccia, dikes, and cinder cones are present just east of Cedar Breaks National Monument (Moore and Nealey, 1993). Most of these rocks are likely Pleistocene, but some flows farther east are unvegetated and likely are Holocene. Native American legends are reported to refer to "smoking hills" in the Panguitch Lake area, east of the Monument (E.G. Sable, unpublished data, 1999).

Surficial Deposits (Quaternary)

Surficial deposits in and near Cedar Breaks (Moore and Nealey, 1993) include Pleistocene glacial deposits, represented by two or more probable terminal moraines and knob-and-kettle topography in Sidney Valley (Castle Creek drainage) 5 miles east-southeast of Brian Head (E.G. Sable, unpublished mapping, 1995). Pleistocene and Holocene landslide deposits, especially in the Brian Head Formation, are common. Alpine Pond, for example, sits in a depression made by a landslide; the landslide scarp above the pond exposes about 50 feet of Isom blocks (belonging to the Markagunt Megabreccia; see the road log). Pleistocene and Holocene colluvium, alluvial fans, and alluvium are common. Pleistocene and Holocene bog deposits, including peat, occur in and near the monument. Holocene vegetated eolian dunes occur just east of the Cedar Breaks rim.

STRUCTURAL GEOLOGY

The Markagunt Plateau is a tilted fault block that dips a few degrees eastward. Uplift and tilting took place along faults of the Hurricane fault zone, the main trace of which is along the western base of the plateau scarp, such as on the eastern outskirts of Cedar City (Averitt and Threet, 1973). The Hurricane fault zone is one of the major range-front fault zones in Utah, with normal-fault displacement of at least 10,000 feet in the Cedar City area, as indicated by geophysical gravity data that show this thickness of basin-fill deposits beneath Cedar City (Cook and Hardman, 1967). The Hurricane fault marks the boundary between the relatively undeformed Colorado Plateau to the east and the greatly deformed Great Basin to the west. The Markagunt Plateau, however, is one of many plateaus (the High Plateaus subprovince of the Colorado Plateau) in a structural transition zone between the Colorado Plateau and the Great Basin. Amount of fault displacement and number of faults decreases eastward across the High Plateaus to the main part of the Colorado Plateau.

The normal faults along which the Markagunt Plateau was uplifted belong to the late Cenozoic basin-range episode of deformation (Christiansen and Lipman, 1972; Anderson and Rowley, 1975; Anderson and others, 1983; Anderson, 1989). This episode, the youngest major deformational event in the area, is responsible for the present topography. The basin-range episode is named, in fact, for the topography now seen in the Great Basin, consisting of north-trending ranges and intervening basins. In the Cedar City area, basin-range faulting appears to date to the last 10 million years, based on K-Ar dating of basalt lava flows within the basin-fill deposits (Best and others, 1980; Anderson, 1989); the oldest of these basalts is about 10 Ma. Some faulting along the Hurricane and nearby faults is continuing, as indicated by recent seismicity (the largest quake being 5.9 M_L (local magnitude), near the town of Washington, Utah in September 1992). Fault scarps of Quaternary age occur along the Hurricane fault zone but none have large displacement. The age of basin-range faulting has been well constrained in the Kingston Canyon area of the High Plateaus, about 40 miles northeast of the monument. Here the main offset along the Sevier fault zone, along which the gently east-tilted Sevier Plateau was uplifted at least 6,500 feet, took place after 8 Ma based on K-Ar dates on the youngest bed deposited before uplift and tilting, and before 5 Ma based on K-Ar dates on the oldest rocks deposited after uplift and tilting (Rowley and others, 1981). The only evidence in Cedar Breaks National Monument of basin-range faults are many north- to north-northeast-striking faults of generally less than 100 feet of displacement. Several are visible from observation sites at Cedar Breaks.

Emplacement of the Markagunt Megabreccia

The origin of the Markagunt Megabreccia is speculative. Probably it originated as gravity slides, the slip surfaces of which were stratigraphically controlled (Anderson, 1993; Maldonado and others, 1990, 1992; Maldonado, 1995). The main slip surfaces were within the Brian Head Formation, which was lithologically and structurally unstable because of its high content of volcanic ash and its poor lithification. The Bear Valley Formation also is largely incompetent for the same reasons and thus contained slip surfaces, and other surfaces were in the mudflow breccia of the Mount Dutton Formation. These three units are currently structurally incompetent; they may have been more so during gravity sliding because then the three rock units were less lithified than today.

Moore and Nealey (1993) measured a thickness of 130 feet of exposed breccia at Blowhard Mountain. Breccia deposits to the east and south of Blowhard Mountain were estimated to be 5 to 30 feet thick and were interpreted to be an unconsolidated residual mantle. They proposed that at Blowhard Mountain, the base of the deposit includes an alluvial boulder gravel as much as 15 feet thick that partly fills a paleovalley cut in the underlying red member of the Claron. We include this boulder gravel in the basal Brian Head Formation. Moore (1992) and Moore and Nealey (1993) concluded that the breccia formed from repeated landsliding or gravity sliding during and following tectonic uplift of the Markagunt Plateau. A problem with a landslide origin is that only Brian Head rises topographically above the breccia in the area and Brian Head is 6 miles from Blowhard Mountain, seemingly too far for a typical landslide to move. Even if slides moved that far, they would have carried clasts from outcrops of Leach Canyon Formation at Brian Head; Leach Canyon clasts, however, do not occur in the breccia, even though its rocks are as resistant as Isom Formation. Furthermore, the Baldhills Isom blocks scattered in and near the monument are rarely represented in the bedrock Baldhills Isom cooling units exposed just below the Leach Canyon Formation on Brian Head peak; the Isom bedrock units on Brian Head are lithologically different from most of the blocks. We suggest, in contrast, that the gravel channel and some of the overlying unexposed deposits on Blowhard Mountain represent the basal strata of the Brian Head Formation, which in turn is overlain by deposits of the Markagunt Mebabreccia. The presence of Brian Head Formation is intuitively required because it is the most common bearer of the shear planes along which the Megabreccia slid. Evidence in favor of this idea that the Markagunt Megabreccia once covered Cedar Breaks National Monument, Blowhard Mountain, and areas at least several miles farther south is the nature of many Isom Baldhills clasts. A sizeable percentage of these clasts are internally brecciated, then relithified by silicification or devitrification; they are resistant and they ring to the hammer (figure 7). Such resistant, yet internally broken clasts of moderately to densely welded ash-flow tuff, including the Isom and Leach Canyon Formations, are a characteristic feature of the 20-Ma gravity slides in and south of the Iron Springs mining district (for example, Rowley and others, 1989; Blank and others, 1992; Hacker and others, 1996; Hacker, 1998).

The hummocky topography on the "breccia" that Moore (1992) and Moore and Nealey (1993) observed may be due at least in part to the surficial processes they sug-

Figure 7. Internally brecciated angular block of the Baldhills Tuff Member of the Isom Formation, from the top of Blowhard Mountain.

gested, namely Pleistocene icefield processes and local landslides. They may also have been due to small glaciers. Another surficial process is formation of abundant sinkholes recognized and mapped by Moore and Nealey (1993) in the underlying white and red members of the Claron. Sinkholes probably were unusually well developed because of the high levels of ground water and surface water during and following the local Pleistocene glaciation of the Cedar Breaks area (Laird Naylor, Bureau of Land Management, and G.C. Willis, Utah Geological Survey, verbal communication, 1999). Some of these sinkholes break through overlying Quaternary basalt flows that rest on the Claron, as in The Craters area about a half mile southeast of the monument (Moore and Nealey, 1993). It is even possible that most of the deposits of Markagunt Megabreccia were lowered from a higher-level surface by sapping and dissolution of Claron limestone.

The direct causes of the sliding are poorly known. Anderson (1993) suggested that the slides moved both northward off a large structural uplift in the central Markagunt Plateau and southward down the dip slopes of tilted fault blocks that developed along west-northwest-striking faults in the northern Markagunt Plateau. He suggested that these faults began to form before eruption of the Wah Wah Springs Formation and continued through deposition of the Bear Valley Formation. In regards to the structural uplift scenario, he suggested that such uplift might have been due to doming above a large batholith, whose location in the northern Markagunt is surmised from the presence of widespread likely cupolas (Anderson and Rowley, 1975) and whose southward extent into the central Markagunt Plateau is indicated by geophysical studies (Blank and Kucks, 1989; Blank and others, 1998). Sable and Maldonado (1997b) attributed the Megabreccia to sliding off a structural dome caused by emplacement of the Iron Peak laccolith and possible related intrusive bodies located about 15 miles north-northeast of Cedar Breaks National Monument. They noted a radial pattern to the slickensides

on bedrock surfaces that underlie the Megabreccia that points to mapped exposures of the laccolith, and they cited other southward movement indicators for the Megabreccia. These slickensides, however, also point to the tilt blocks mapped by Anderson (1993).

The Markagunt Megabreccia is one of several large structurally emplaced units in the southern High Plateaus and Red Hills. A structural feature probably related to emplacement of the Markagunt Megabreccia is the 22.5- to 20-Ma low-angle Red Hills shear zone (Maldonado and others, 1990, 1992, 1994, 1997; Maldonado, 1995) that is also present in the western Markagunt Plateau. Another allocthonous unit composed of 30 to 20 Ma shallow-depth thrust faulted sheets was mapped on the southeastern side of the Marysvale volcanic field (Davis and Krantz, 1986; Lundin, 1989; Bowers, 1990; Nickelsen and Merle, 1991; Merle and others, 1993; Davis, 1999). Davis and Rowley (1993) and Davis (1999) attributed the thrusts to radial southward outward thrusting, the sole of which bottomed in incompetent evaporite beds of the Jurassic Carmel Formation (Lundin, 1989) caused by the weight of the Marysvale volcanic field. Further support for this interpretation comes from Davis (1999), who recorded deformation bands in areas of the Markagunt Plateau along State Highway 14 south of Cedar Breaks and in a broad arc continuing eastward, concentric with the southern Marysvale field. Davis (1999) proposed a "two-tiered model" of the spreading and collapse of the Marysvale field, in which rocks above the Carmel Formation moved as a thrust sheet mostly in the subsurface, whereas the Markagunt Megabreccia moved as a gravity slide at the surface.

GEOLOGIC HISTORY

The story of Cedar Breaks National Monument began in the Late Cretaceous, when the lower member of the Straight Cliffs Formation, of near-shore, mostly shallow marine origin, was deposited east of the Sevier deformational belt that consisted of mostly eastward-verging thrust faults. Plants as well as invertebrate and vertebrate animals were abundant in the oceans and along the shorelines. Dinosaur fossils have been discovered in nearby areas in the Cretaceous rock sequence. With uplift, continental (mostly fluvial) deposition resulted in strata of the upper member of the Straight Cliffs, the Wahweap Sandstone (Upper Cretaceous), and the Grand Castle Formation (Upper Cretaceous and Paleocene?). Following Sevier deformation, the Claron Formation (Paleocene and Eocene) was laid down in large stable basins containing mostly well aerated (oxidizing) lakes and streams. The resulting beds were modified by soil-forming processes, including caliche deposition, after they were deposited. The overlying lake and stream deposits of the Brian Head Formation (Eocene and Oligocene) were deposited in basins similar to those of the white part of the Claron. Extensive volcanoes in areas to the west and north and, after about 32 Ma from the Marysvale volcanic field to the north, contributed tuffaceous material to the sediments of the middle parts of the Brian Head Formation (Rowley and others, 1994).

Eventually, the continental deposits in the area were completely inundated by volcanic material, beginning with emplacement of the Wah Wah Springs Formation (30 Ma; Oligocene), an enormous ash-flow sheet derived from western sources. The Isom Formation (27 Ma; Oligocene) and the Leach Canyon Formation (24 Ma; Miocene), made up of ash-flow tuffs of nearly the same extent as the Wah Wah Springs, also spread to the Brian Head area. They also were derived from the West. The landscape at the time was dominated by volcanic landforms. Featureless ash-flow plains, dotted by large calderas, were the main landform to the west, whereas the Marysvale volcanic field, whose southern margin is just north of the monument, consisted mostly of stratovolcano complexes and, later, calderas. Volcanic mudflow breccia of the Mount Dutton Formation are the product of clustered stratovolcanoes, and ash-flow tuff from local centers in the southern Marysvale field eventually overran the Leach Canyon Formation.

Some of the landscape of the time, however, formed by uplift along strike-slip and normal faults that coincided with volcanism. Closer to Cedar Breaks, the north-striking faults of the ancestral Hurricane fault zone probably were active at the time, for this boundary marking the western edge of the Colorado Plateau has had a long, although subtle, history of movement. East-striking transverse zones west and north of the area likely also were active (Rowley, 1998). Uplift of the Colorado Plateau may have begun before, and continued after, emplacement of the Wah Wah Springs Formation (Rowley and others, 1978). West-northwest-striking faults just to the north of Cedar Breaks were active by 26 Ma (Anderson, 1971; Anderson and Rowley, 1975). Deep grabens produced by these faults were filled by the Bear Valley Formation, in part an eolian sandstone derived from the west, as well as by ash-flow units. By 22 to 20 Ma, the Markagunt Megabreccia was emplaced as giant gravity-slide sheets or shallow thrust sheets in and north of the monument. These sheets were in the form of large rock masses that, in the Cedar Breaks area, moved southward along subhorizontal shear planes in incompetent rock units (Brian Head, Bear Valley, and Mount Dutton Formations). Several hypotheses for the origin and mechanism for gravity sliding have been advanced. Movement may have been down dip slopes of fault blocks created by the west-northwest-striking faults or dip slopes created by uplift along plutons or a batholith north of the monument (Anderson, 1993; Sable and Maldonado, 1997b). Alternatively, sliding may have been a surface effect of movement along outward-directed thrusts (Davis and Krantz, 1986; Lundin, 1989) that are especially prominent on the southern side of the Marysvale volcanic field and appear to be due to collapse and shearing within incompetent beds in the Jurassic Carmel Formation, under the weight of the volcanic field (Davis and

Rowley, 1993; Merle and others, 1993; Davis, 1999).

By about 20 Ma, the basin-range extensional tectonic episode began. Most basin-range faulting, however, appears to have started about 10 Ma. The main result of the episode was the development of the Great Basin to the west, but at this time the Hurricane fault zone also underwent its latest episode of faulting, and the other High Plateaus also were blocked out. This episode of extensional deformation, characterized by normal faulting, continues into the present. The Markagunt Plateau was uplifted to its current height or more, and dramatic erosion created the current features of Cedar Breaks. This erosion of the western edge of the scarp has caused it already to retreat several miles eastward, in the direction of the dip of the beds, and what we see now represents an instant of geologic time. The highest parts of the plateau, in the Cedar Breaks area, contained standing snow fields and probably local valley glaciers during the Pleistocene, and underwent other forms of mass wasting by landslides, soil creep, and sinkholes continuing to the present. In the future, the rim will be eroded farther eastward and what we see now will slowly disappear.

GEOLOGIC UNIQUENESS OF THE MONUMENT

Cedar Breaks National Monument is best known for its multicolored rocks that are displayed as cliffs, spires, pinnacles, and other shapes carved by erosion and weathering of the Claron Formation on the western edge of the Markagunt Plateau. Running water is often cited as the primary agent that created the features in Cedar Breaks National Monument, but physical weathering and mass wasting have sculpted the finer details of the scenery. Headward erosion of the Ashdown Creek drainage is generally responsible for the current location of the monument at the abrupt plateau edge or "breaks," a term used by pioneers and settlers to describe an area where higher altitudes descend rapidly, or "break" to a lower altitude (Harris and others, 1997). However, alternate freezing and thawing of water along joints (mechanical weathering) as well as chemical dissolution of the rock units of the Claron Formation have carved out the intricate shapes found in the rock layers at Cedar Breaks. Once weakened and loosened by the intense weathering, the force of gravity moves the sediment downslope along with the aid of water in the form of sheetwash and gully flooding. In many parts of the Claron Formation, solution resulting from chemical weathering has produced caves in the limestone beds and resulting surface sinkholes by collapse of the caves.

The varied colors of the Claron Formation are yet another characteristic which contributes to the unique appearance of Cedar Breaks. The difference between the darker orange and red units, as compared to the lighter white or gray units, may be due to greater oxidation in the source terrains in and surrounding the depositional basin. While little definitive work has been done to determine the exact coloring agents in the rock layers, they are believed to be due to various iron and manganese compounds.

Another distinctive feature at Cedar Breaks National Monument is its location in the transition zone between the Basin and Range and Colorado Plateau. Cedar Breaks provides one of the most spectacular places in all of southern Utah to view the Basin and Range landscape to the west while standing on a plateau of nearly flat-lying rock layers, much like the rest of the Colorado Plateau. The variety of volcanic and sedimentary rock units derived from various source areas are further evidence of the transitional nature of the geology in the monument. Finally, an additional, but relatively inconspicuous feature at Cedar Breaks is the Markagunt Megabreccia. The presence of the megabreccia has resulted in the numerous large boulders scattered throughout the park and more importantly allows us to infer that a significant structural event occurred in the geologic history of the region that affected much larger areas of the Markagunt Plateau.

ACKNOWLEDGMENTS

We are grateful to J.J. Anderson for field tours of the Markagunt Megabrecia and for insights into its origin that led directly to our interpretations. Most of the geologic mapping was done in the 1980s and 1990s by E.G. Sable and D.W. Moore of the U.S. Geological Survey. D.W. Moore of the U.S. Geological Survey provided unpublished data and digital files of the geology of parts of the monument area. Steve Robinson and Tom Henry of Cedar Breaks National Monument gave many forms of help, including the loan of aerial photos. Laird Naylor (Bureau of Land Management) and G.C. Willis (Utah Geological Survey) helped us interpret the geology of the monument. Partial funding to Southern Utah University for the geologic mapping and for the creation of digital files was provided by the National Park Service, coordinated by Bruce Heise, Joseph Gregson, and Timothy Connors. We thank J.J. Anderson, R.E. Blackett, and D.W. Moore for technical review of the manuscript.

REFERENCES

Anderson, J.J., 1965, Geology of northern Markagunt Plateau, Utah: Austin, University of Texas, unpublished Ph.D. dissertation, 194 p.

—1971, Geology of the southwestern High Plateaus of Utah—Bear Valley Formation, an Oligocene-Miocene volcanic arenite: Geological Society of America Bulletin, v. 82, no. 5, p. 1179-1205.

—1993, The Markagunt Megabreccia—large Miocene gravity slides mantling the northern Markagunt Plateau, southwestern Utah: Utah Geological Survey Miscellaneous Publication 93-2, 37 p.

Anderson, J.J., and Kurlich, R.A., III, 1989, Post-Claron Formation, pre-regional ash-flow tuff early Tertiary stratigraphy of the southern High Plateaus of Utah [abs.]: Geological Society of America Abstracts with Programs, v. 21, no. 5, p. 50.

Anderson, J.J., and Rowley, P.D., 1975, Cenozoic stratigraphy of the southwestern High Plateaus of Utah, *in* Anderson, J.J., Rowley, P.D., Fleck, R.J., and Nairn, A.E.M., editors, Cenozoic geology of southwestern High Plateaus of Utah: Geological Society of America Special Paper 160, p. 1-52.

Anderson, R.E., 1989, Tectonic evolution of the Intermontane System, Basin and Range, Colorado Plateau, and High Lava Plains, Chapter 10, *in* Pakiser, L.C., and Mooney, W.D., editors, Geophysical framework of the continental United States: Geological Society of America Memoir 172, p. 163-176.

Anderson, R.E., Zoback, M.L., and Thompson, G.A., 1983, Implications of selected subsurface data on the structural form and evolution of some basins in the northern Basin and Ranger province, Nevada and Utah: Geological Society of America Bulletin, v. 94, p. 1055-1072.

Averitt, Paul, and Threet, R.L., 1973, Geologic map of the Cedar City quadrangle, Iron County, Utah: U.S. Geological Survey Geologic Quadrangle Map GQ-1120, scale 1:24,000.

Best, M.G., Christiansen, E.H., and Blank, R.H., Jr., 1989a, Oligocene caldera complex and calc-alkaline tuffs and lavas of the Indian Peak volcanic field, Nevada and Utah: Geological Society of America Bulletin, v. 101, no. 8, p. 1076-1090.

Best, M.G., Christiansen, E.H., Deino, A.L., Gromme, C.S., McKee, E.H., and Noble, D.C., 1989b, Excursion 3A—Eocene through Miocene volcanism in the Great Basin of the western United States: New Mexico Bureau of Mines and Mineral Resources Memoir 47, p. 91-133.

Best, M.G., McKee, E.H., and Damon, P.E., 1980, Space-time-composition patterns of late Cenozoic mafic volcanism, southwestern Utah and adjoining areas: American Journal of Science, v. 280, no. 12, p. 1035-1050.

Best, M.G., Scott, R.B., Rowley, P.D., Swadley, W C, Anderson, R.E., Gromme, C.S., Harding, A.E., Deino, A.L., Christiansen, E.H., Tingey, D.G., and Sullivan, K.R., 1993, Oligocene-Miocene caldera complexes, ash-flow sheets, and tectonism in the central and southeastern Great Basin, *in* Lahren, M.M., Texler, J.H., Jr., and Spinosa, Claude, editors, Crustal evolution of the Great Basin and Sierra Nevada: Field Trip Guide, Geological Society of America, Cordilleran and Rocky Mountain Sections Meeting, p. 285-311.

Blank, H.R., Butler, W.C., and Saltus, R.W., 1998, Neogene uplift and radial collapse of the Colorado Plateau—regional implications of gravity and aeromagnetic data, *in* Friedman, J.D., and Huffman, A.C., Jr., coordinators, Laccolith complexes of southeastern Utah—time of emplacement and tectonic setting—workshop Proceedings: U.S. Geological Survey Bulletin 2158, p. 9-32.

Blank, H.R., and Kucks, R.P., 1989, Preliminary aeromagnetic, gravity, and generalized geologic maps of the USGS Basin and Range-Colorado Plateau transition zone study area in southwestern Utah, southeastern Nevada, and northwestern Arizona (the "BARCO" project): U.S. Geological Survey Open-File Report 89-432, 16 p., scale 1:250,000.

Blank, H.R., Rowley, P.D, and Hacker, D.B., 1992, Miocene monzonite intrusions and associated megabreccias of the Iron Axis region, southwestern Utah, *in* Wilson, J.R., editor, Field guide to geologic excursions in Utah and adjacent areas of Nevada, Idaho, and Wyoming: Utah Geological Survey Miscellaneous Publication 92-3, p. 399-420.

Bowers, W.E., 1972, The Canaan Peak, Pine Hollow, and Wasatch Formations in the Table Cliff region, Garfield County, Utah: U.S. Geological Survey Bulletin 1331-B, 39 p.

—1990, Geologic map of Bryce Canyon National Park and vicinity, southwestern Utah: U.S. Geological Survey Miscellaneous Investigations Series Map I-2108, 15 p., scale 1:24,000.

Bown, T.M., Hasiotis, S.T., Genise, J.F., Maldonado, Florian, and Brouwers, E.M., 1997, Trace fossils of Hymenoptera and other insects, and paleoenvironments of the Claron Formation (Paleocene and Eocene), southwestern Utah, *in* Maldonado, Florian, and Nealey, L.D., editors, Geologic studies in the Basin and Range—Colorado Plateau transition in southeastern Nevada, southwestern Utah, and northwestern Arizona, 1995: U.S. Geological Survey Bulletin 2153, p. 41-58.

Christiansen, R.L., and Lipman, P.W., 1972, Cenozoic volcanism and plate tectonic evolution of the western United States—II. Late Cenozoic: Royal Society of London Philosophical Transactions (A), v. 271, p. 249-284.

Cook, K.L., and Hardman, Elwood, 1967, Regional gravity survey of the Hurricane fault area and Iron Springs district, Utah: Geological Society of America Bulletin, v. 78, no. 9, p. 1063-1076.

Cunningham, C.G., Steven, T.A., Rowley, P.D., Glassgold, L.B., and Anderson, J.J., 1983, Geologic map of the Tushar Mountains and adjoining areas, Marysvale volcanic field, Utah: U.S. Geological Survey Miscellaneous Investigations Series Map I-1430-A, scale 1:50,000.

Davis, G.H., 1999, Structural geology of the Colorado Plateau region of southern Utah, with special emphasis on deformation bands: Geological Society of America Special Paper 342, 157 p.

Davis, G.H., and Krantz, R.W., 1986, Post-"Laramide" thrust faults in the Claron Formation, Bryce Canyon National Park, Utah [abs.]: Geological Society of America Abstracts with Programs, v. 18, no. 5, p. 98.

Davis, G.H., and Rowley, P.D., 1993, Miocene thrusting, gravity sliding, and near-surface batholithic emplacement, Marysvale volcanic field, southwestern Utah [abs.]: EOS, v. 74, no. 43, p. 647.

Eaton, J.G., and Hutchison, J.H., 1995, A late Eocene fauna from undescribed strata overlying the Claron Formation, Sevier Plateau, southwestern Utah [abs.]: Geological Society of America Abstracts with Programs, v. 27, no. 4, p. 10.

Eaton, J.G., Maldonado, Florian, and McIntosh, W.C., 1999, New radiometric dates from Upper Cretaceous rocks of the Markagunt Plateau, southwestern Utah, and their bearing on subsidence histories [abs.]: Geological Society of America Abstracts with Programs, v. 31, no. 4, p. A-11.

Feist, Monique, Eaton, J.G., Brouwers, E.M., and Maldonado, Florian, 1997, Significance of charophytes from the lower Tertiary variegated and volcaniclastic units, Brian Head Formation, Casto Canyon area, southern Sevier Plateau, southwestern Utah, *in* Maldonado, Florian, and Nealey, L.D., editors, Geologic studies in the Basin and Range—Colorado Plateau transition in southeastern Nevada, southwestern Utah, and northwestern Arizona, 1995: U.S. Geological Survey Bulletin 2153, p. 27-39.

Fleck, R.J., Anderson, J.J., and Rowley, P.D., 1975, Chronology of mid-Tertiary volcanism in High Plateaus region of Utah, *in* Anderson, J.J., Rowley, P.D., Fleck, R.J., and Nairn, A.E.M., editors, Cenozoic geology of southwestern High Plateaus of Utah: Geological Society of America Special Paper 160, p. 53-62.

Goldstrand, P.M., 1990, Stratigraphy and paleogeography of Late Cretaceous and Paleogene rocks of southwest Utah: Utah Geological and Mineral Survey Miscellaneous Publication 90-2, 58 p.

—1991, Tectonostratigraphy, petrology, and paleogeography of Upper Cretaceous to Eocene rocks of southwest Utah: Reno, University of Nevada, Ph.D. dissertation, 205 p.

—1994, Tectonic development of Upper Cretaceous to Eocene strata of southwestern Utah: Geological Society of America Bulletin, v. 106, no. 1, p. 145-154.

Goldstrand, P.M., and Mullett, D.J., 1997, The Paleocene Grand Castle Formation—a new formation on the Markagunt Plateau of southwestern Utah, *in* Maldonado, Florian, and Nealey, L.D., editors, Geologic studies in the Basin and Range—Colorado Plateau transition in southeastern Nevada, southwestern Utah, and northwestern Arizona, 1995: U.S. Geological Survey Bulletin 2153, p. 59-78.

Gregory, H.E., 1944, Geologic observations in the upper Sevier River Valley, Utah: American Journal of Science, v. 242, no. 4, p. 577-606.

—1951, The geology and geography of the Paunsaugunt region, Utah: U.S. Geological Survey Professional Paper 226, 116 p.

Gregory, H.E., and Moore, R.C., 1931, The Kaiparowits region, a geographic and geologic reconnaissance of parts of Utah and Arizona: U.S. Geological Survey

Professional Paper 164, 161 p.

Hacker, D.B., 1998, Catastrophic gravity sliding and volcanism associated with the growth of laccoliths—examples from early Miocene hypabyssal intrusions of the Iron Axis magmatic province, Pine Valley Mountains, southwest Utah: Kent, Ohio, Kent State University, Ph.D. dissertation, 258 p.

Hacker, D.B., Rowley, P.D., Blank, H.R., and Snee, L.W., 1996, Early Miocene catastrophic gravity sliding and volcanism associated with intrusions of the southern Iron Axis region, southwest Utah [abs.]: Geological Society of America Abstracts with Programs, v. 28, no. 7, p. A511.

Harris, A.G., Tuttle, Esther, and Tuttle, S.D., 1997, Geology of the National Parks, 5th edition: Dubuque, Iowa, Kendall/Hunt Publishing Company, 758 p.

LaRocque, A., 1960, Molluscan faunas of the Flagstaff Formation of central Utah: Geological Society of America Memoir 78, 100 p.

Leith, C.K., and Harder, E.C., 1908, The iron ores of the Iron Springs district, southern Utah: U.S. Geological Survey Bulletin 338, 102 p.

Lundin, E.R., 1989, Thrusting of the Claron Formation, Bryce Canyon region, Utah: Geological Society of America Bulletin, v. 101, no. 8, p. 1038-1050.

Mackin, J.H., 1947, Some structural features of the intrusions in the Iron Springs district: Utah Geological Society Guidebook 2, 62 p.

—1960, Structural significance of Tertiary volcanic rocks in southwestern Utah: American Journal of Science, v. 258, no. 2, p. 81-131.

Maldonado, Florian, 1995, Decoupling of mid-Tertiary rocks, Red Hills-western Markagunt Plateau, southwestern Utah, *in* Scott, R.B., and Swadley, W. C., editors, Geologic studies in the Basin and Range—Colorado Plateau transition in southeastern Nevada, southwestern Utah, and northwestern Arizona, 1992: U.S. Geological Survey Bulletin 2056, p. 233-254.

Maldonado, Florian, Sable, E.G., and Anderson, J.J., 1990, Shallow detachment of mid-Tertiary rocks, Red Hills (Basin and Range), with implications for a regional detachment zone in the adjacent Markagunt Plateau (Colorado Plateau), southwestern Utah [abs.]: Geological Society of America Abstracts with Programs, v. 22, no. 3, p. 94.

—1992, Evidence of a Tertiary low-angle shear zone, Red Hills, with implications for a regional shear zone in the adjacent Colorado Plateau, *in* Harty, K.M., editor, Engineering and environmental geology of southwestern Utah: Utah Geological Association Publication 21, p. 315-323.

Maldonado, Florian, Sable, E.G., and Nealey, L.D., 1994, Evolution of Cenozoic structures, western Markagunt Plateau, southwestern Utah, *in* Blackett, R.E., and Moore, J.N., editors, Cenozoic geology and geothermal systems of southwestern Utah: Utah Geological Association Publication 23, p. 105-116,

—1997, Cenozoic low-angle faults, thrust faults, and anastomosing high-angle faults, western Markagunt Plateau, southwestern Utah, *in* Maldonado, Florian, and Nealey, L.D., editors, Geologic studies in the Basin and Range—Colorado Plateau transition in southeastern Nevada, southwestern Utah, and northwestern Arizona, 1995: U.S. Geological Survey Bulletin 2153, p. 125-150.

Merle, O.R., Davis, G.H., Nickelsen, R.P., and Gourlay, P.A., 1993, Relation of thin-skinned thrusting of Colorado Plateau strata in southwestern Utah to Cenozoic magmatism: Geological Society of America Bulletin, v. 105, no. 4, p. 387-398.

Moore, D.W., 1992, Origin of breccia of the Isom Formation near Cedar Breaks National Monument, Markagunt Plateau, southwestern Utah [abs.]: Geological Society of America Abstracts with Programs, v. 24, no. 6, p. 54.

Moore, D.W., and Nealey, L.D., 1993, Preliminary geologic map of Navajo Lake quadrangle, Kane and Iron Counties, Utah: U.S. Geological Survey Open-File Report 93-190, 20 p., scale 1:24,000.

Mullett, D.J., 1989, Interpreting the early Tertiary Claron Formation of southern Utah [abs.]: Geological Society of America Abstracts with Programs, v.21, no. 5, p. 120.

Mullett, D.J., Wells, N.A., and Anderson, J.J., 1988a, Early Cenozoic deposition in the Cedar-Bryce depocenter—certainties, uncertainties, and comparisons with other Flagstaff-Green River basins [abs.]: Geological Society of America Abstracts with Programs, v. 20, no. 3, p. 217.

—1988b, Unusually intense pedogenic modification of the Paleocene-Eocene Claron Formation of southwestern Utah [abs.]: Geological Society of America Abstracts with Programs, v. 20, no. 5, p. 382.

Nickelsen, R.P., and Merle, Olivier, 1991, Structural evolution at the tip line of a mid-Tertiary compressional event in southwestern Utah [abs.]: Geological Society of America Abstracts with Programs, v. 23, no. 1, p. 109.

Nichols, D.J., 1997, Palynology and ages of some Upper Cretaceous formations in the Markagunt and northwestern Kaiparowits Plateaus, southwestern Utah, *in* Maldonado, Florian, and Nealey, L.D., editors, Geologic studies in the Basin and Range—Colorado Plateau transition in southeastern Nevada, southwestern Utah, and northwestern Arizona, 1995: U.S. Geological Survey Bulletin 2153, p. 81-106.

Richardson, G.B., 1909, The Harmony, Colob, and Kanab coal fields, southern Utah: U.S. Geological Survey Bulletin 341-C, p. 379-400.

Rowley, P.D., 1998, Cenozoic transverse zones and igneous belts in the Great Basin, western United States--their tectonic and economic implications, *in* Faulds, J.E., and Stewart, J.H., editors, Accommodation zones and transfer zones--the regional segmentation of the Basin and Range province: Geological Society of America Special Paper 323, p. 195-228.

Rowley, P.D., Anderson, J.J., Williams, P.L., and Fleck, R.J., 1978, Age of structural differentiation between the Colorado Plateaus and Basin and Range provinces in southwestern Utah: Geology, v. 6, no. 1, p. 51-55.

Rowley, P.D., Cunningham, C.G., Steven, T.A., Mehnert, H.H., and Naeser, C.W., 1998, Cenozoic igneous and tectonic setting of the Marysvale volcanic field, and its relation to other igneous centers in Utah and Nevada, *in* Friedman, J.D., and Huffman, A.C., Jr., coordinators, Laccolith complexes of southeastern Utah—time of emplacement and tectonic setting—workshop proceedings: U.S. Geological Survey Bulletin 2158, p. 167-202.

Rowley, P.D., Cunningham, C.G., Steven, T.A., Workman, J.B., Anderson, J.J., and Theissen, K.M., in press, Digital geologic map of the central Marysvale volcanic field, southwestern Utah: U.S. Geological Survey Investigation Series Map I-2645-A, scale 1:100,000.

Rowley, P.D., McKee, E.H., and Blank, H.R., Jr., 1989, Miocene gravity slides resulting from emplacement of the Iron Mountain pluton, southern Iron Springs mining district, Iron County, Utah [abs.]: EOS, v. 70, no. 43, p. 1309.

Rowley, P.D., Mehnert, H.H., Naeser, C.W., Snee, L.W., Cunningham, C.G., Steven, T.A., Anderson, J.J., Sable, E.G., and Anderson, R.E., 1994, Isotopic ages and stratigraphy of Cenozoic rocks of the Marysvale volcanic field and adjacent areas, west-central Utah: U.S. Geological Survey Bulletin 2071, 35 p.

Rowley, P.D., Nealey, L.D., Unruh, D.M., Snee, L.W., Mehnert, H.H., Anderson, R.E., and Gromme, C.S., 1995, Stratigraphy of Miocene ash-flow tuffs in and near the Caliente caldera complex, southeastern Nevada and southwestern Utah, *in* Scott, R.B., and Swadley, W.C., editors, Geologic studies in the Basin and Range—Colorado Plateau transition in southeastern Nevada, southwestern Utah, and northwestern Arizona, 1992: U.S. Geological Survey Bulletin 2056, p.43-88.

Rowley, P.D., Steven, T.A., Anderson, J.J., and Cunningham, C.G., 1979, Cenozoic stratigraphic and structural framework of southwestern Utah: U.S. Geological Survey Professional Paper 1149, 22 p.

Rowley, P.D., Steven, T.A., and Mehnert, H.H., 1981, Origin and structural implications of upper Miocene rhyolites in Kingston Canyon, Piute County, Utah: Geological Society of America Bulletin, pt. I, v. 92, no. 8, p. 590-602.

Sable, E.G., and Anderson, J.J., 1985, Tertiary tectonic slide megabreccia, Markagunt Plateau, southwestern Utah [abs.]: Geological Society of America Abstracts with Programs, v. 17, no. 4, p. 263.

Sable, E.G., and Maldonado, Florian, 1997a, The Brian Head Formation (revised) and selected Tertiary sedimentary rock units, Markagunt Plateau and adjacent areas, southwestern Utah, *in* Maldonado, Florian, and Nealey, L.D., editors, Geologic studies in the Basin and Range—Colorado Plateau transition in southeastern Nevada, southwestern Utah, and northwestern Arizona, 1995: U.S. Geological Survey Bulletin 2153, p. 5-26.

Sable, E.G., and Maldonado, Florian, 1997b, Breccias and megabreccias, Markagunt Plateau, southwestern Utah—Origin, age, and transport directions, *in* Maldonado, Florian, and Nealey, L.D., editors, Geologic studies in the Basin and Range—Colorado Plateau transition in southeastern Nevada, southwestern Utah, and northwestern Arizona, 1995: U.S. Geological Survey Bulletin 2153, p. 151-176.

Schneider, M.C., 1967, Early Tertiary continental sediments of central and south-central Utah: Brigham Young University Geology Studies, v. 14, p. 143-194.

Steven, T.A., Morris, H.T., and Rowley, P.D., 1990, Geologic map of the Richfield 1° x 2° quadrangle, west-central Utah: U.S. Geological Survey Miscellaneous Investigations Series Map I-1901, scale 1:250,000.

Steven, T.A., Rowley, P.D., and Cunningham, C.G., 1984, Calderas of the Marysvale volcanic field, west central Utah: Journal of Geophysical Research, v. 89, no. B10, p. 8751-8764.

Williams, P.L., 1967, Stratigraphy and petrography of the Quichapa Group, southwestern Utah and southeastern Nevada: Seattle, University of Washington, Ph.D. dissertation, 182 p.

Geology of Utah's Parks and Monuments
2000 Utah Geological Association Publication 28
D.A. Sprinkel, T.C. Chidsey, Jr., and P.B. Anderson, editors

Geology and Paleontology of Dinosaur National Monument, Utah-Colorado

Joe D. Gregson[1] and Dan J. Chure[2]

ABSTRACT

Dinosaur National Monument preserves a true treasure trove of unique geological and paleontological resources. Originally a modest preserve set aside to protect the remaining fossils at Dinosaur Quarry after years of excavation by the Carnegie Museum of Natural History and others, the monument was later expanded to include the magnificent canyon country that the Green and Yampa Rivers have carved into the faults and folds of the southeastern Uinta Arch. The Uinta Arch and many of Dinosaur's faults and folds represent classic and enigmatic east- and northeast-trending structures that formed during the Laramide orogeny about 70 to 40 million years ago. Indeed, geologic deformation and subsequent erosion in the Dinosaur area have exposed a great thickness of sedimentary rocks that represent a complex geologic history and one of the most complete stratigraphic records found anywhere in the National Park System. From towering canyon walls and spires of Paleozoic sandstone to Mesozoic hogbacks and strike valleys, the preserved wealth of Dinosaur's sedimentary strata are well displayed. This unique combination of stratigraphy, structure, and erosion make Dinosaur a world-class site for the study of paleontology and paleoecology. In addition to the historical discoveries at Dinosaur Quarry, recent research and discoveries in the Morrison and Cedar Mountain formations are shedding new light on the dinosaurs and the ecological systems in which they lived.

INTRODUCTION

Although Dinosaur National Monument is best known for its world-class fossil locality at Dinosaur Quarry, the spectacular canyons cut by the Green and Yampa Rivers expose rock strata and structures that record over a billion years of Earth's history. The Dinosaur area lies near the eastern end of the Uinta Mountains, which are one of only a few enigmatic east-west trending mountain ranges in the western United States. The Uinta Mountains are the topographic expression of a regional-scale anticline or arch, known as the Uinta arch (figure 1), with its many related folds and faults exposed in Dinosaur's sheer-walled canyons (figure 2). Most of the folding and faulting accompanied the mountain-building event known as the Laramide orogeny about 70 to 40 million years ago (Ma). Since Laramide time, the deformed and uplifted rocks have been worn down and covered, further tilted and subsided in places, as well as weathered and eroded into the current plateau- and canyon-dominated landscape that we see today. Far more than just shaping the landscape, the geologic processes of faulting, folding, weathering, and erosion have also exposed famously fossiliferous rock units, such as the Morrison and Cedar Mountain Formations (figure 3). Indeed, the wealth of dinosaur fossils found in the Morrison Formation at Dinosaur Quarry really do make Dinosaur National Monument the real Jurassic Park. From algal globules that grew more than a billion years ago (Ga) and Jurassic dinosaurs to remains of shallow seas and eroded mountains, Dinosaur's rocks and sediments record a rich variety of ancient flora, fauna, and geologic events. Written in the rocks for millennia, the ancient drama of Dinosaur reveals epic geologic stories ranging from monotonous ages to awesome catastrophes—for anyone willing to listen.

STRATIGRAPHY

From Split Mountain to Lodore Canyon and the Yampa Plateau, everywhere one looks in the Dinosaur area, layers of rock (strata) are spectacularly displayed. Relative to the geologic time scale, Dinosaur National Monument has one of the most complete stratigraphic columns exposed within the National Park System (figure 3; Hansen, 1977b). Almost all rock outcrops in and near

[1]*National Park Service, Fort Collins, CO 80525*
[2]*Dinosaur National Monument, Dinosaur, CO 81610*

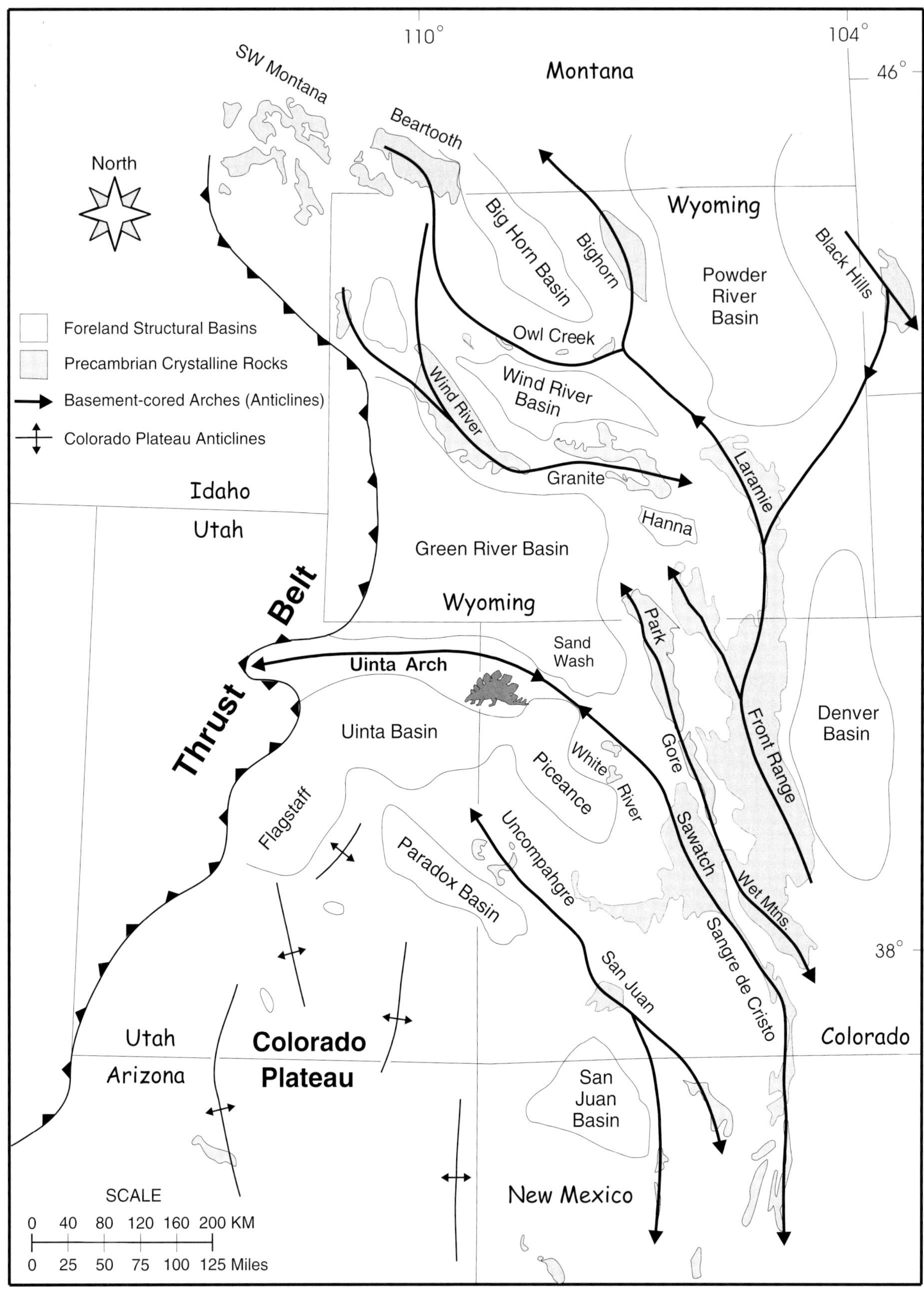

Figure 1. Tectonic map of the Laramide foreland (modified from Gregson and Erslev, 1997) illustrating the anastomosing nature of the basement-cored arches (regional-scale anticlines) and spatial relationships with the adjacent thrust belt, Colorado Plateau, and North American craton. The location of Dinosaur National Monument relative to the Uinta Arch is indicated by the stegosaurus icon.

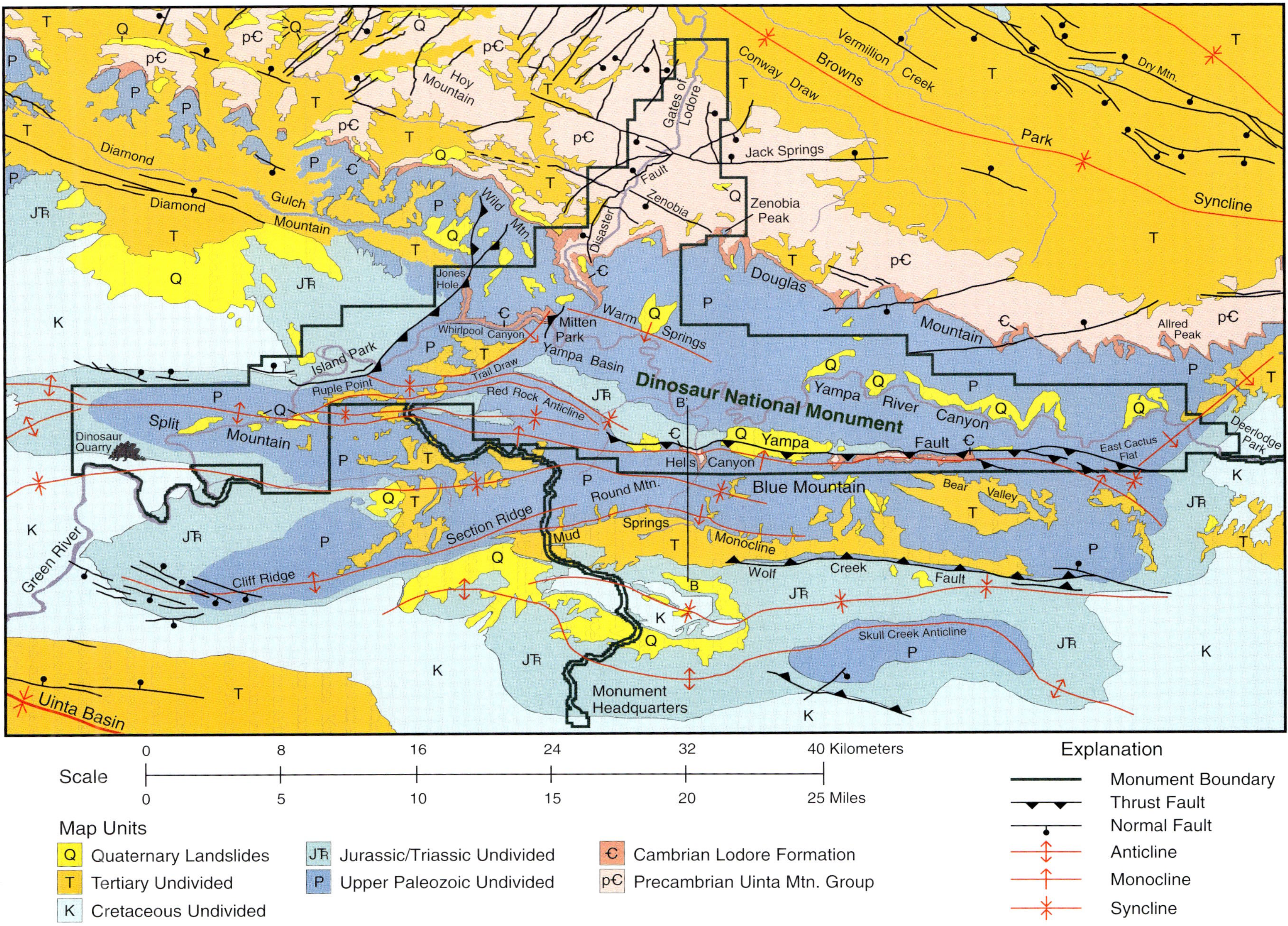

Figure 2. Geologic map generalized after Rowley and others (1985) and Hansen and others (1983). Many surficial units not shown. See the section on STRATIGRAPHY, figure 3, as well as the geologic maps referenced above and in the text for more detailed rock unit descriptions. Cross section B-B' across Mud Springs Monocline and Yampa Fault is illustrated in figure 6.

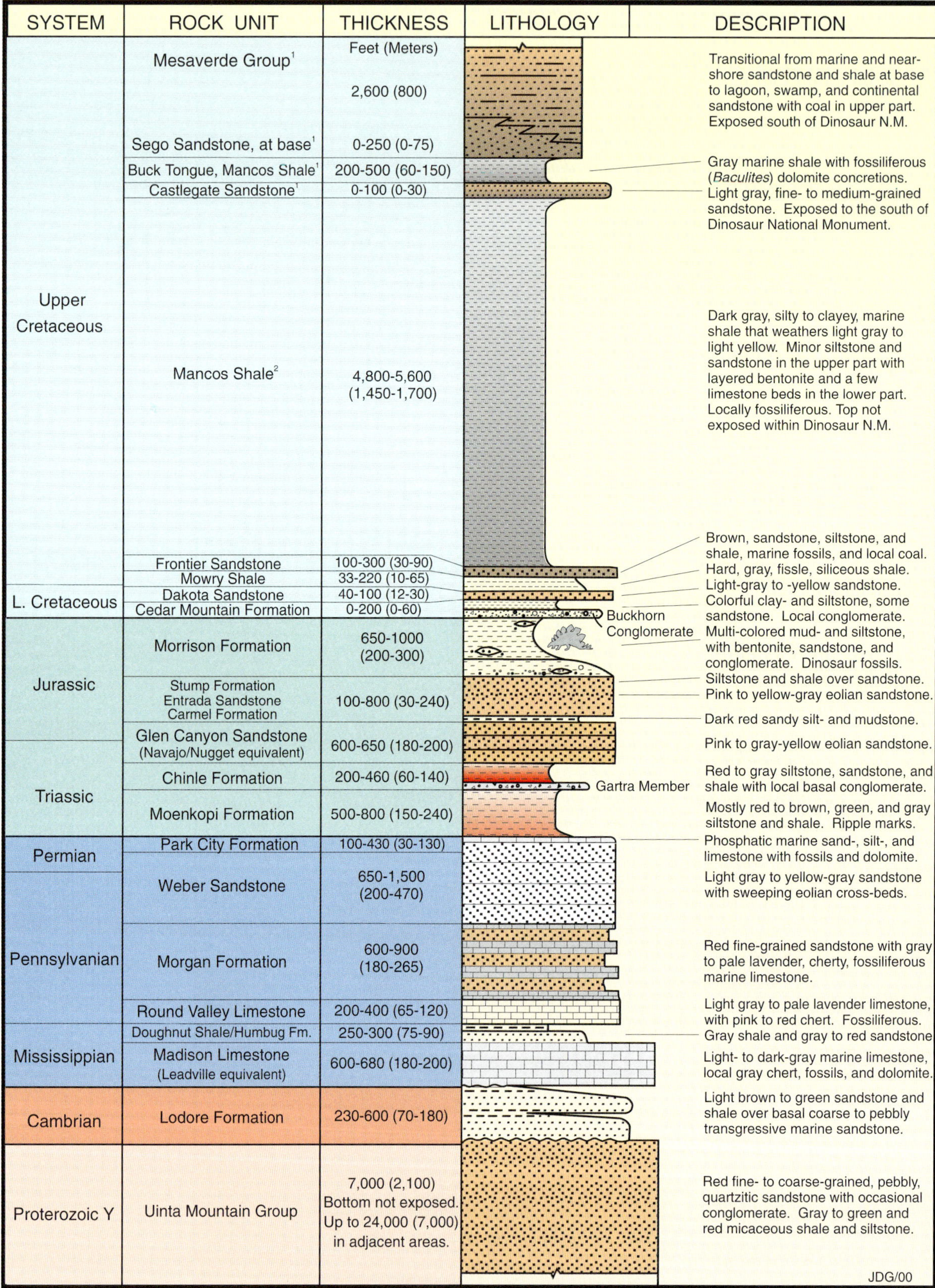

SYSTEM	ROCK UNIT	THICKNESS	LITHOLOGY	DESCRIPTION
Upper Cretaceous	Mesaverde Group[1]	Feet (Meters) 2,600 (800)		Transitional from marine and near-shore sandstone and shale at base to lagoon, swamp, and continental sandstone with coal in upper part. Exposed south of Dinosaur N.M.
	Sego Sandstone, at base[1]	0-250 (0-75)		
	Buck Tongue, Mancos Shale[1]	200-500 (60-150)		Gray marine shale with fossiliferous (*Baculites*) dolomite concretions.
	Castlegate Sandstone[1]	0-100 (0-30)		Light gray, fine- to medium-grained sandstone. Exposed to the south of Dinosaur National Monument.
	Mancos Shale[2]	4,800-5,600 (1,450-1,700)		Dark gray, silty to clayey, marine shale that weathers light gray to light yellow. Minor siltstone and sandstone in the upper part with layered bentonite and a few limestone beds in the lower part. Locally fossiliferous. Top not exposed within Dinosaur N.M.
L. Cretaceous	Frontier Sandstone	100-300 (30-90)		Brown, sandstone, siltstone, and shale, marine fossils, and local coal.
	Mowry Shale	33-220 (10-65)		Hard, gray, fissle, siliceous shale.
	Dakota Sandstone	40-100 (12-30)		Light-gray to -yellow sandstone.
	Cedar Mountain Formation	0-200 (0-60)	Buckhorn Conglomerate	Colorful clay- and siltstone, some sandstone. Local conglomerate.
Jurassic	Morrison Formation	650-1000 (200-300)		Multi-colored mud- and siltstone, with bentonite, sandstone, and conglomerate. Dinosaur fossils.
	Stump Formation / Entrada Sandstone / Carmel Formation	100-800 (30-240)		Siltstone and shale over sandstone. Pink to yellow-gray eolian sandstone. Dark red sandy silt- and mudstone.
	Glen Canyon Sandstone (Navajo/Nugget equivalent)	600-650 (180-200)		Pink to gray-yellow eolian sandstone.
Triassic	Chinle Formation	200-460 (60-140)	Gartra Member	Red to gray siltstone, sandstone, and shale with local basal conglomerate.
	Moenkopi Formation	500-800 (150-240)		Mostly red to brown, green, and gray siltstone and shale. Ripple marks.
Permian	Park City Formation	100-430 (30-130)		Phosphatic marine sand-, silt-, and limestone with fossils and dolomite.
	Weber Sandstone	650-1,500 (200-470)		Light gray to yellow-gray sandstone with sweeping eolian cross-beds.
Pennsylvanian	Morgan Formation	600-900 (180-265)		Red fine-grained sandstone with gray to pale lavender, cherty, fossiliferous marine limestone.
	Round Valley Limestone	200-400 (65-120)		Light gray to pale lavender limestone, with pink to red chert. Fossiliferous.
Mississippian	Doughnut Shale/Humbug Fm.	250-300 (75-90)		Gray shale and gray to red sandstone
	Madison Limestone (Leadville equivalent)	600-680 (180-200)		Light- to dark-gray marine limestone, local gray chert, fossils, and dolomite.
Cambrian	Lodore Formation	230-600 (70-180)		Light brown to green sandstone and shale over basal coarse to pebbly transgressive marine sandstone.
Proterozoic Y	Uinta Mountain Group	7,000 (2,100) Bottom not exposed. Up to 24,000 (7,000) in adjacent areas.		Red fine- to coarse-grained, pebbly, quartzitic sandstone with occasional conglomerate. Gray to green and red micaceous shale and siltstone.

Figure 3. Pre-Cenozoic stratigraphic column for the Dinosaur National Monument area (modified from Gregson and Erslev, 1997) based on Rowley and others (1985), Hansen and others (1983), and other geologic maps referenced in text.
[1]*Exposed in the monument.* [2]*Not completely exposed in the monument.*

Dinosaur are sedimentary, and they range in age from the late Precambrian (about 1 Ga) to Miocene (about 25 to 10 Ma) to recent surficial deposits (Hansen and others, 1983; Hansen, 1986a, 1986b). With the exception of the Ordovician(?), Silurian, and Devonian, all of the periods of the geologic time scale are represented (Untermann and Untermann, 1954). In their own way, the strata in the monument contain the rhymes and verses that compliment similar vignettes of geologic history found in other rock outcrops throughout the west. The following sections work their way upward through the geologic systems that are on display at Dinosaur and provide brief snapshots of the sediments and geologic history preserved in the area.

Uinta Mountain Group (Middle and Late Precambrian)

Deposited about 1.1 Ga (Hansen and others, 1983), the red sedimentary rocks of the Uinta Mountain Group are the oldest strata exposed in the monument. The maximum thickness of the Uinta Mountain Group studied within the Uinta Mountains is more than 24,000 feet (about 7,000 m), but only about the upper 7,000 feet (2,100 m) are exposed in Dinosaur National Monument (Hansen, 1996). The red Uinta Mountain rocks crop out in the central and northern sections of the monument where faulting and erosion have sculpted the strata that dip gently southward off the crest of the Uinta arch. The most prominent outcrops are in the Canyon of Lodore, but erosion along the Yampa and Mitten Park faults expose the Uinta Mountain Group along the north side of Blue Mountain and in Whirlpool Canyon, respectively (Hansen and others, 1983).

The Uinta Mountain Group in the Dinosaur National Monument area consists predominantly of ancient quartz sandstone that is so well cemented with silica that it forms sedimentary quartzite (sometimes called orthoquartzite). The Uinta Mountain Group sandstones are commonly interbedded with siltstones and gray, pale olive green, and red micaceous shales that are thick enough in the Canyon of Lodore to be mapped as separate units (Hansen and others, 1983). The sandstones are mostly light- to dark-red, medium- to coarse-grained or pebbly with cross-beds that suggest fluvial origin. The red and gray shales are interbedded with siltstones, and fine- to coarse-grained sandstones (Hansen and others, 1983). Similar shales in the Uinta Mountain Group near Manila, Utah have yielded specimens of *Chuaria*, which are probably fossilized algal globules that have been flattened into disks a fraction of an inch (a few millimeters) across (Hansen, 1996). *Chuaria* were first studied and named by C.D. Walcott in the Precambrian-age Chuar Shale of the Grand Canyon.

After deposition of the Uinta Mountain Group, there was a period of erosion and sedimentary hiatus in Dinosaur area that lasted several hundred million years until Late Cambrian time. The nature of this great unconformity was described well by Hansen (1977b, see map references for place name locations):

"Floaters on the Green River in Lodore Canyon can view the entire Paleozoic section between Alcove Brook and Echo Park. At the base of this section, near Alcove Brook, the Lodore Formation rests on the Uinta Mountain Group with an angular unconformity of about 2 to 3 degrees. This relationship is more obvious from the canyon rim than from the river. The dip of the Lodore Formation is slightly steeper than that of the underlying Uinta Mountain Group, indicating that the group was first tilted northward a few degrees and then was truncated by erosion before the Lodore was deposited. The present southerly dip of the whole section was caused by the uplift of the Uinta Mountains in Cretaceous time."

"In detail, the unconformity at the base of the Lodore is very uneven, having a local relief of several tens of meters [scores of feet]. The Lodore Formation was deposited along the strand of an expanding seaway, and, as the ancient shoreline yielded slowly to the onslaught of the waves, eroded remnants of the Uinta Mountain Group persisted offshore as stacks, skerries, and reefs. Although the barren landscape was totally devoid of life, small creatures flourished in the sea, especially marine worms and brachiopods, less commonly trilobites, and, of course, the ubiquitous seaweeds and other primitive marine plants."

Lodore Formation (Upper Cambrian)

Although commonly buff colored, much younger, and less well cemented outcrops of the Lodore Formation (about 525 to 505 Ma) generally resemble the interbedded sandstones and shales of the Uinta Mountain Group. The thickness of the Lodore Formation ranges from about 230 feet (70 m) at Blue Mountain to about 600 feet (180 m) in Lodore Canyon near Rippling Brook (Hansen, 1977b; Hansen and others, 1983, see map references for place name locations). The type locality for the Lodore Formation is near Limestone Draw in the lower reach of Lodore Canyon about 2.5 miles (4 km) upstream from Echo Park (Hansen, 1996). Also similar to the Uinta rocks, the Lodore crops out in and near the canyons of Dinosaur National Monument due to local faulting and erosion into the gently dipping southern limb of the Uinta arch.

In its thickest sections, the uppermost 50 feet (15 m) of the Lodore Formation is a light-brown to greenish-gray, ledge-forming sandstone, overlying pink to tan to pale-greenish gray glauconitic, slope-forming shale and dolomite interbedded with tan to light-green sandstone as much as 165 feet thick (50 meters)(Hansen, 1977b). The basal rocks of the Lodore are as much as 280 feet (85 m) thick and consist of variegated pink to gray to light-green, medium- to coarse-grained, cross-bedded, and somewhat friable sandstone. The lower sandstone is locally quartzitic and contains numerous gray quartz pebbles

(Hansen, 1977b).

The pale-green shales of the Lodore Formation gain their color from the mineral glauconite which is a dull-green, amorphous, micaceous mineral that is somewhat similar to clay and often forms in warm, shallow, marine waters. In addition to glauconitic shales, the Lodore Formation contains numerous trace fossils. Rare body fossils, such as trilobites, have been found only at Jones Hole (Hansen, 1996).

After deposition of the Lodore strata, the Dinosaur area experienced another period of erosion and a hiatus of over a hundred million years until early in the Mississippian time. Hansen (1977b) also described this unconformity:

"After the Lodore was deposited, the sea withdrew, and non-marine conditions lasted for the millions of years of the Ordovician, Silurian, and Devonian Periods. During this long time interval, the area must have stood only slightly above sea level, because the unconformity between the Mississippian and the Cambrian rocks is scarcely discernible, even though it represents a hiatus of perhaps 155 million years."

Intrusive Dike
(Upper Cambrian or Lower Ordovician)

During the latest Cambrian through Devonian sedimentary hiatus, the only dike found in Dinosaur National Monument was emplaced into the Uinta Mountain Group strata. The dike is known from a single exposure within a small ravine in the Canyon of Lodore about 0.4 miles (0.55 km) upriver from Pot Creek (Hansen and others, 1982, 1983, see map references for place name locations). A rubidium-strontium radiometric age indicates intrusion about 483+/-29 Ma shortly after deposition of the Lodore Formation during the Late Cambrian or Early Ordovician. The dike is up to 75 feet (23 m) thick with a depth of emplacement of about 4,000 feet (1,200 m), which is the depth below the top of the Lodore Formation (Hansen and others, 1982, 1983).

The dike rock has been described by Hansen and others (1982, 1983) as leucitite or tephritic leucitite (in the terminology of Rittman, 1952) based on chemical composition, but the rock contains no mineralogically identified leucite. Hansen and others (1982, 1983) describe the dike as medium dark gray, slightly brownish, and generally microcrystalline with a few larger crystals of potash feldspar (sanidine) about 0.04 inch (1 mm) long. The ground mass is crowded with disseminated hematite, rutile, and anatase. Thin amygdaloidal zones (small mineral-filled voids or vesicles) occur parallel to dike walls, and very fine-grained black dikelets cut the main dike. The south border of the dike, and the adjacent wall rock are highly sheared from Laramide and/or late Miocene faulting (Hansen and others, 1982, 1983). For more detailed infor-

mation on mineralogy and genesis of the dike, see Hansen and others (1982) and Hansen (1996).

Hansen (1977b) reported that unrecognized Devonian (about 360 to 400 Ma) strata might exist at the top of the Cambrian rocks in the canyons of Lodore and Jones Hole where irregularly bedded gray sandstone, resembling the Chaffee Formation of central Colorado, crops out at the top of the Lodore Formation. After the early Paleozoic hiatus, fossils and other organic remains indicate that the overlying strata accumulated in predominantly marine or marginal marine environments.

Madison Limestone (Lower Mississippian)

The Madison Limestone and its correlatives throughout the west (the Leadville, Redwall, Pahasapa Limestones; about 350 to 340 Ma) mark an extensive interior sea that reached from the present day Arctic Ocean to the Gulf of Mexico. The Madison Limestone is about 600 to 680 feet (180-200 m) thick and characteristically forms resistant, jagged cliffs and dip slopes in many locations in the Dinosaur area (Hansen and others, 1982, 1983; Rowley, Dyni, and others, 1979; Rowley, Kinney, and others, 1979; Rowley and others, 1985).

The Madison Limestone generally consists of light- to dark-gray, fine- to medium-grained, thick and unevenly bedded, cherty limestone and dolomitic limestone that is sparsely fossiliferous. In contrast with the pink or red Pennsylvanian cherts, Madison chert is mostly light gray (Hansen and others, 1982, 1983; Rowley, Dyni, and others, 1979; Rowley, Kinney, and others, 1979; Rowley and others, 1985). Although sparsely fossiliferous, the Madison contains corals, echinoderms, brachiopods, bivalves, and gastropods that indicate a shallow marine environment in Early Mississippian time (Hansen and others, 1982, 1983; Rowley, Dyni, and others, 1979; Rowley, Kinney, and others, 1979; Rowley and others, 1985).

Humbug Formation (Upper Mississippian)

The Humbug Formation and Doughnut Shale (about 340 to 320 Ma) form colorful hard and soft beds that are quite distinctive from the gray beds of the Round Valley and Madison limestones above and below. The combined thickness of the Humbug and Doughnut is about 250 to 300 feet (75-90 m) (Hansen and others, 1983; Rowley and others, 1985).

The Humbug Formation generally consists of light-gray to red, fine- to very fine grained sandstone interbedded with light-gray limestone and red to black shale with hematitic sandstone at the top locally (Hansen and others, 1983). The Humbug Formation was deposited under varied but predominantly near-shore marine conditions (Rowley and Hansen, 1979a, 1979b). In most areas of Dinosaur National Monument, Humbug forms ledgy slopes and appears to truncate the underlying Madison Limestone (Hansen and others, 1983; Rowley and others, 1985).

Doughnut Shale (Upper Mississippian)

Although mostly marine, traces of coal have been found in Doughnut Shale. The presence of coal within the predominantly dark-gray, clayey shales suggest relatively brief intervals of non-marine conditions and fresh- or brackish-water in vegetation-rich swamps. However, in other areas, the Doughnut Shale contains marine fossils such as brachiopods and fish (Hansen and others, 1983; Rowley, Dyni, and others, 1979; Rowley, Kinney, and others, 1979; Rowley and others, 1985).

In general, the Doughnut Shale is predominantly a dark-gray, clayey shale that becomes more red toward its base. The Doughnut Shale is an important unit because it becomes plastic when wet, making it prone to landslides (Hansen and others, 1983; Rowley and others, 1985).

Round Valley Limestone (Lower Pennsylvanian)

The Round Valley Limestone marks the return of a marine environment to the Dinosaur National Monument area during Early Pennsylvanian time about 310 Ma. The Round Valley strata are well exposed in many areas of the monument and form gray ledgy slopes and/or multi-tiered cliffs ranging in thickness from about 200 to 300 feet (65-90 m) at Split Mountain to about 400 feet (120 m) at the head of Yampa Canyon (Hansen and others, 1983; Rowley, Dyni, and others, 1979; Rowley, Kinney, and others, 1979; Rowley and others, 1985).

The Round Valley Limestone is generally light-gray to pale-lavender, fine-grained, and thick-bedded with thin partings of gray to red shale. In contrast to the gray chert and sparse fossils in the older Madison Limestone, the Round Valley contains pink to red chert in nodules, irregular masses, and fossil replacements. In addition, numerous fossil brachiopods, bryozoans, echinoderms (especially crinoid columnals), and mollusks have been found in the limestone (Hansen and others, 1983; Rowley, Dyni, and others, 1979; Rowley, Kinney, and others, 1979; Rowley and others, 1985).

Morgan Formation (Middle Pennsylvanian)

Pennsylvanian rocks, including the Morgan Formation and overlying Weber Sandstone, make up some of the most spectacular rock outcrops in Dinosaur National Monument. The Morgan Formation (about 300 Ma) is well exposed in the middle reach of the Yampa Canyon, the lower reach of Lodore Canyon, and the limbs of Split Mountain anticline, where it forms beautiful red cliffs and lower gray slopes in Split Mountain Canyon. In addition, the Weber and the upper Morgan are beautifully displayed in the sheer northeast face of Warm Springs Cliff which rises to a height of 1,700 feet (515 m) in one of the most impressive landmarks in the eastern Uinta Mountains (Hansen, 1977b, see map reference for place name locations). Generally ranging from about 600 to 900 feet (190-265 m) thick, the Morgan was deposited mostly as beach and near-shore sediments in a shallow, intermittently marine environment, as indicated by abundant fossil bryozoans, brachiopods, echinoderms, fusulinids, and other invertebrates (Hansen and others, 1980, 1983; Rowley, Dyni, and others, 1979; Rowley, Kinney, and others, 1979; Rowley and others, 1985).

The lower member of the Morgan Formation consists of predominantly light-gray to red and green shale and siltstone with interbedded gray sandstone and gray to lavender fossiliferous limestone. The lower Morgan forms slopes, is commonly mantled with colluvium, and is slide prone. Although contacts with adjacent units are poorly exposed, the lower unit is about 130 feet (40 m) thick at Split Mountain and 300 feet (90 m) thick at both Hells Canyon and the head of Yampa Canyon (Hansen and others, 1980, 1983; Rowley, Dyni, and others, 1979; Rowley, Kinney, and others, 1979; Rowley and others, 1985).

The upper member of the Morgan Formation is predominantly red, fine-grained, cross- to planar-bedded to massive, well-cemented sandstone and gray to pale-lavender, cherty, fossiliferous marine limestone occurring in individual beds from several feet thick (Hansen and others, 1980, 1983; Rowley, Dyni, and others, 1979; Rowley, Kinney, and others, 1979; Rowley and others, 1985). The chert in the Morgan limestones is pink to dark red. Locally, some of the sandstone is gray and resembles the Weber Sandstone (Hansen and others, 1980, 1983; Rowley, Dyni, and others, 1979; Rowley, Kinney, and others, 1979; Rowley and others, 1985). The contact between the Morgan and Weber is generally placed at the top of the uppermost limestone or red sandstone, but is generally poorly exposed and is indefinite where well exposed. The upper Morgan has a total thickness of about 575 feet (175 m) at Split Mountain and 500 feet (150 m) at the east end of Yampa Canyon (Hansen and others, 1980, 1983; Rowley, Dyni, and others, 1979; Rowley, Kinney, and others, 1979; Rowley and others, 1985).

Weber Sandstone (Middle Pennsylvanian to Lower Permian)

The Weber Sandstone (about 300 to 275 Ma) conformably overlies the Morgan Formation. In Dinosaur National Monument, the Weber Sandstone ranges in thickness from about 650 to 1,500 feet (200-470 m) and forms some of the most notable landforms in the area (Hansen and others, 1980, 1983; Rowley, Dyni, and others, 1979; Rowley, Kinney, and others, 1979; Rowley and others, 1985). Indeed, as one approaches Dinosaur National Monument from the south, the steep-sided prominences of Cliff Ridge and Split Mountain provide classic exposures of the light-colored Weber strata. The Weber Sandstone also mantles much of the massive Blue Mountain highland and makes up many canyon walls and rims throughout the monument, especially within the Yampa Canyon area. Steamboat Rock and Jennie Lind Rock are good examples of monoliths eroded out of the Weber Sandstone (Hansen and others, 1980, 1983; Rowley, Dyni, and others, 1979; Rowley, Kinney, and others, 1979; Rowley and others, 1985, see map references for place name locations). South of the monument, the Weber Sandstone is economically important as the primary reservoir rock within the giant Rangely oil field. Many geologists have studied the Weber outcrops in the Dinosaur area to gain understanding of the sandstone's petrology and stratigraphic associations.

The Weber Sandstone consists mostly of fine- to very fine grained, well-cemented quartz sand. It is generally tan or cream colored to light or yellowish gray. Very thick, sweeping cross-beds indicate mostly eolian deposition in a beach and sand dune environment (Hansen and others, 1980, 1983; Rowley, Dyni, and others, 1979; Rowley, Kinney, and others, 1979; Rowley and others, 1985). Soft-sediment deformation is well displayed in many Weber outcrops. Locally, interlayered limestone beds contain fossil fusulinids, corals, and brachiopods that indicate a close marine association (Hansen and others, 1980, 1983; Rowley, Dyni, and others, 1979; Rowley, Kinney, and others, 1979; Rowley and others, 1985). The upper Weber Sandstone is assigned a Lower Permian (Wolfcampian) age based on foraminifera found in the Split Mountain area (Bissell, 1964; Bissell and Childs, 1958).

Park City Formation (Lower Permian)

The Permian Park City Formation (about 250 Ma) consists of gray resistant beds overlain by softer gray and yellow beds. Although the softer strata erode more easily, the resistant beds commonly form protective caps on top of the Weber Sandstone, especially along the flanks of Split Mountain and Blue Mountain, and atop mesas such as Jenny Lind Rock. The Park City strata reach as much as 430 feet (130 m) in thickness (W.R. Hansen, written communication, 2000). At Dinosaur, the Park City Formation correlates with parts of the Phosphoria Formation and Park City Group of Wyoming, Idaho, Utah, and Nevada (Hansen and others, 1980, 1983; Maughan, 1979; Rowley, Dyni, and others, 1979; Rowley, Kinney, and others, 1979; Rowley and others, 1985). Although more distinctive west of Dinosaur, the strata include non-phosphatic rocks of the Franson Member of the Park City Formation, and a lower unit correlated with the Meade Peak Phosphatic Shale Member of the Phosphoria Formation. Rich deposits of phosphate rock, which accumulate where mineral-rich, cold bottom marine waters well up into warmer zones or currents, are mined for the production of fertilizer in the Brush Creek area northwest of Dinosaur National Monument (Hansen and others, 1980, 1983; Maughan, 1979; Rowley, Dyni, and others, 1979; Rowley, Kinney, and others, 1979; Rowley and others, 1985).

In more detail, the Park City consists of resistant, light-gray, light-yellow, and tan sandstone; sandy-cherty limestone, dolomite, claystone, and phosphatic shale that are overlain by soft, light-gray, light-green, light-yellow, and red, siltstone, sandstone, dolomite, limestone, and shale. Especially in the western part of the Dinosaur area, the

strata contain marine bivalves, gastropods, scaphopods, cephalopods, and brachiopods (Hansen and others, 1980, 1983; Rowley, Dyni, and others, 1979; Rowley, Kinney, and others, 1979; Rowley and others, 1985).

Moenkopi Formation (Lower Triassic)

The redbeds of the Moenkopi Formation (about 220 Ma) are generally less resistant to erosion than most of the underlying formations and hence form the floors of many strike valleys in the Dinosaur area. Moenkopi strike valleys partially enclose Split Mountain and the south flank of Blue Mountain, forming intermittent drainages in such places as Red Wash, Cottonwood Wash, and Disappointment Draw. The Moenkopi Formation ranges in thickness from 550 feet (170 m) at Disappointment Draw to 800 feet (240 m) at Split Mountain (Hansen and others, 1980, 1983; Rowley, Dyni, and others, 1979; Rowley, Kinney, and others, 1979; Rowley and others, 1985, see map references for place name locations).

The Moenkopi Formation consists chiefly of soft, red to vari-colored brown, green, and gray shale, mudstone, siltstone, and fine-grained sandstone. Light-gray gypsiferous siltstone and shale predominate near the base and ripple marks are common in some beds (Hansen and others, 1980, 1983; Rowley, Dyni, and others, 1979; Rowley, Kinney, and others, 1979; Rowley and others, 1985). Fossils are sparse in the Lower Triassic redbeds; only a few reptile tracks and marine mollusks have been identified. The Moenkopi was deposited mostly in a near-shore continental (possibly tidal flat) to marine environment where gypsum precipitated in times of high aridity (Hansen and others, 1980, 1983; Rowley, Dyni, and others, 1979; Rowley, Kinney, and others, 1979; Rowley and others, 1985).

Chinle Formation (Upper Triassic)

The Chinle Formation is easily divided into a discontinuous basal conglomeratic sandstone, the Gartra Member, and an overlying main body of redbeds. The Gartra commonly forms cliffs, benches, caprocks, and hogbacks, but the main body of the Chinle erodes easily into slopes and narrow strike valleys similar to those in the underlying Moenkopi Formation (Hansen and others, 1980, 1983; Rowley, Dyni, and others, 1979; Rowley, Kinney, and others, 1979; Rowley and others, 1985). Chinle strike valleys also ring the mountains and the eroded folds of the Dinosaur area. The Chinle Formation ranges in thickness from about 200 to 460 feet (60-140 m), and the basal unconformity truncates and channels the underlying Moenkopi Formation (Hansen and others, 1980, 1983; Rowley, Dyni, and others, 1979; Rowley, Kinney, and others, 1979; Rowley and others, 1985). The maximum thickness of the Gartra Member is about 100 feet (30 m) but is locally discontinuous. The Chinle strata generally thicken westward toward the Wasatch Mountains and southward in the Colorado Plateau province (Hansen and others, 1980, 1983; Rowley, Dyni, and others, 1979; Rowley, Kinney, and others, 1979; Rowley and others, 1985).

The main body of the Chinle consists chiefly of red to occasionally gray, siltstone, shale, sandstone, and conglomerate deposited in streams and lakes (Hansen and others, 1980, 1983; Rowley, Dyni, and others, 1979; Rowley, Kinney, and others, 1979; Rowley and others, 1985). Distinctive ocher or mustard-colored beds in the lower part of the section correlate with similar rocks of the Popo Agie Formation in Wyoming (W.R. Hansen, written communication, 2000). The basal Gartra Member is pale-yellowish gray to tan to pink, coarse-grained to conglomeratic sandstone that generally is thickly bedded to cross-bedded. The Gartra was deposited by streams and rivers (Hansen and others, 1980, 1983; Rowley, Dyni, and others, 1979; Rowley, Kinney, and others, 1979; Rowley and others, 1985). Although sparsely fossiliferous, the Chinle contains scattered remains of reptiles, amphibians, mollusks, and petrified wood (Hansen and others, 1980, 1983; Rowley, Dyni, and others, 1979; Rowley, Kinney, and others, 1979; Rowley and others, 1985).

Glen Canyon Sandstone (Lower Jurassic)

The Glen Canyon Sandstone (about 200 Ma) forms the massive, light-colored, strike ridges, and prominent hogbacks and questas flanking Split Mountain and the south side of Blue Mountain (Hansen and others, 1980, 1983; Rowley, Dyni, and others, 1979; Rowley, Kinney, and others, 1979; Rowley and others, 1985). The Glen Canyon strata range in thickness from about 600 to 650 feet (180-200 m) and preserve the remnant sand dunes of an extensive sand sea or erg that once covered the whole region. The formation is broadly correlative with the Nugget and Navajo Sandstones in adjacent areas and the entire Glen Canyon Group to the south (Hansen and others, 1980, 1983; Rowley, Dyni, and others, 1979; Rowley, Kinney, and others, 1979; Rowley and others, 1985).

The Glen Canyon is mostly pink to light-gray or grayish-yellow, fine- to medium-grained, quartz sandstone (Hansen and others, 1980, 1983; Rowley, Dyni, and others, 1979; Rowley, Kinney, and others, 1979; Rowley and others, 1985). The sandstone is barren of fossils but displays elegant sweeping cross-beds as a reminder of its eolian (wind-deposited) origin. Eolian cross-bedding diminishes and flat bedding increases towards the base (Hansen and others, 1980, 1983; Rowley, Dyni, and others, 1979; Rowley, Kinney, and others, 1979; Rowley and others, 1985).

Carmel Formation (Middle Jurassic)

The Carmel Formation (about 155 Ma), generally forms a narrow ribbon of subdued, easily eroded red rocks that separate the underlying Glen Canyon Sandstone from the overlying Entrada Sandstone. Thin Carmel strike valleys show up well around the sides of Split Mountain and the south side of Blue Mountain (Hansen and others, 1980, 1983; Rowley, Dyni, and others, 1979; Rowley, Kinney, and others, 1979; Rowley and others, 1985). The Carmel thick-

ens westward and pinches out toward the east, ranging from about 130 feet (40 m) thick near Island Park, about 110 feet (33 m) thick south of Cub Creek, to about 60 feet (19 m) thick at Plug Hat Rock. It disappears entirely near Skull Creek, Colorado, and its stratigraphic position is marked by an erosional surface or unconformity (Hansen and others, 1980, 1983; Rowley, Dyni, and others, 1979; Rowley, Kinney, and others, 1979; Rowley and others, 1985, see map references for place name locations).

Carmel rocks are chiefly medium- to dark-red. The soft strata include thin- to medium-bedded sandy shale, fine- to medium-grained sandstone, siltstone, and mudstone (Hansen and others, 1980, 1983; Rowley, Dyni, and others, 1979; Rowley, Kinney, and others, 1979; Rowley and others, 1985). Locally, the Carmel contains thin beds of light-yellow sandstone and light-gray gypsum, as well as purplish-red and gray laminated siltstone and shale at the top. Generally, the Carmel accumulated in freely circulating, shallow marine water, but local areas became restricted enough at times to cause stagnation, evaporation, and precipitation of gypsum (Hansen and others, 1980, 1983; Rowley, Dyni, and others, 1979; Rowley, Kinney, and others, 1979; Rowley and others, 1985). Fossil bivalves, echinoderms, and gastropods collected from the Carmel in the eastern Uinta Mountains indicate a shallow marine depositional environment (Hansen and others, 1980, 1983; Rowley, Dyni, and others, 1979; Rowley, Kinney, and others, 1979; Rowley and others, 1985).

Entrada Sandstone (Middle Jurassic)

Although somewhat less indurated than the Glen Canyon Sandstone, the Entrada (about 150 Ma) resembles the Glen Canyon and locally displays sweeping cross-beds that mark its eolian origin (Hansen and others, 1980, 1983; Rowley, Dyni, and others, 1979; Rowley, Kinney, and others, 1979; Rowley and others, 1985). Separated from the Glen Canyon by the thin red Carmel Formation in the western part of the monument, Entrada outcrops are generally more subdued. However, in Island Park, the Entrada forms a long line of vertical cliffs. The formation thins unevenly eastward from about 165 feet (50 m) at Dinosaur Quarry to some 120 feet (37 m) at Plug Hat Rock to only 40 feet (12 m) near Deerlodge Park (Hansen and others, 1980, 1983; Rowley, Dyni, and others, 1979; Rowley, Kinney, and others, 1979; Rowley and others, 1985).

The Entrada Sandstone is pink, gray, or buff to light-green, fine- to medium-grained quartz sandstone that is medium to thick bedded and cross-bedded (Hansen and others, 1980, 1983; Rowley, Dyni, and others, 1979; Rowley, Kinney, and others, 1979; Rowley and others, 1985). Although less conspicuous than in the Glen Canyon, the Entrada cross-beds indicate mostly eolian deposition with the sandy sediment reworked locally by marine waters during temporary advances of the sea. The Entrada is not fossiliferous in the Dinosaur area (Hansen and others, 1980, 1983; Rowley, Dyni, and others, 1979; Rowley, Kinney, and others, 1979; Rowley and others, 1985).

Stump Formation (Middle and Upper Jurassic)

In contrast to the underlying eolian Entrada Sandstone, both the resistant gray Curtis Member (Middle Jurassic, about 175 Ma) and the overlying soft olive-green Redwater Member of the Stump Formation (Upper Jurassic, about 150 Ma) are marine deposits (Hansen and others, 1980, 1983; Rowley, Dyni, and others, 1979; Rowley, Kinney, and others, 1979; Rowley and others, 1985). The Curtis Member forms ledgy outcrops that thin from about 50 to 100 feet (15-30 m) in the western part of monument to about 23 feet (7 m) at Deerlodge Park. The Redwater Member generally forms slopes and also thins from about 130 feet (40 m) in the western part of the monument to 70 to 90 feet (22-27 m) in the east (Hansen and others, 1980, 1983; Rowley, Dyni, and others, 1979; Rowley, Kinney, and others, 1979; Rowley and others, 1985).

The Curtis Member consists of light-gray to light-greenish-gray, thin- to medium-bedded, cross-bedded, medium- to coarse-grained sandstone that is locally ripple marked and fossiliferous (Hansen and others, 1980, 1983; Rowley, Dyni, and others, 1979; Rowley, Kinney, and others, 1979; Rowley and others, 1985). The soft Redwater Member is light-green to olive-green, fissile, glauconitic siltstone and shale with sparse interbeds of tan, lavender, or greenish-gray cross-bedded, glauconitic, oolitic fossiliferous limestone and sandstone (Hansen and others, 1980, 1983; Rowley, Dyni, and others, 1979; Rowley, Kinney, and others, 1979; Rowley and others, 1985). Both members of the Stump Formation contain fossils. The Curtis yields only sparse bivalves and furrowed traces of bottom crawlers, but in contrast, the Redwater is locally rich with brachiopods, bivalves, echinoderms, and cephalopods, especially belemnites (Hansen and others, 1980, 1983; Rowley, Dyni, and others, 1979; Rowley, Kinney, and others, 1979; Rowley and others, 1985).

Morrison Formation (Upper Jurassic)

Because of its wealth of dinosaur fossils, the soft gray and multi-colored Morrison Formation (about 145 Ma) is among the most famous rock formations in the world. Deposited during the time of the dinosaurs and now exposed in strike valleys and low ridges, the Morrison contains the sedimentary record of the real Jurassic Park. Indeed, Dinosaur National Monument was originally created to preserve and protect the remains of the dinosaur-rich bed at Dinosaur Quarry, Utah. Dinosaur Quarry was discovered in 1909 by paleontologist Earl Douglass of the Carnegie Museum, Pittsburgh, and many dinosaur fossils were discovered and exhumed from 1909 to 1923 (Rowley, Kinney, and others, 1979). As the quarry advanced, the excavation reached a length of 400 feet (120 m) and a depth of 60 feet (20 m). Partial or complete fossil skeletons from about 300 individual dinosaurs (14 species), crocodiles, freshwater turtles, freshwater bivalves, and silicified wood were recovered from the site (Rowley, Kinney, and others, 1979). Fossil charophytes and ostracods lived in freshwater Mor-

rison lakes or ponds (Hansen and others, 1980, 1983; Rowley, Dyni, and others, 1979; Rowley, Kinney, and others, 1979; Rowley and others, 1985). In addition to the rich fossil resources of Dinosaur Quarry, the Morrison outcrops that ring much of the monument provide potential for other significant paleontological discoveries, including mammalian remains (see PALEONTOLOGY section of this paper).

In the Dinosaur area, Morrison strata range in thickness from about 650 to 1000 feet (200-300 m). The rocks consist of soft olive-gray, light-gray, red, light-purple, and bluish-gray bentonitic shale, claystone, and siltstone with locally interbedded, fine- to coarse-grained lenticular cross-bedded sandstone (Hansen and others, 1980, 1983; Rowley, Dyni, and others, 1979; Rowley, Kinney, and others, 1979; Rowley and others, 1985). Mudstone and marlstone predominate in the upper Morrison, but the lower part contains more abundant fissile shale and includes local conglomerate and limestone. A friable (crumbly) gray sandstone, about 50 feet (15 m) thick or more, commonly occurs at the base of the unit (Hansen and others, 1980, 1983; Rowley, Dyni, and others, 1979; Rowley, Kinney, and others, 1979; Rowley and others, 1985). This sandstone correlates with part of the Sundance Formation (Upper Jurassic) of Wyoming and north-central Colorado. The Morrison contact with the underlying Stump Formation is poorly exposed and only approximately located on published maps (Hansen and others, 1980, 1983; Rowley, Dyni, and others, 1979; Rowley, Kinney, and others, 1979; Rowley and others, 1985).

The Morrison Formation was deposited entirely within a continental environment. Lenticular cross-bedded sandstones indicate alluvium deposited by streams and rivers (Hansen and others, 1980, 1983; Rowley, Dyni, and others, 1979; Rowley, Kinney, and others, 1979; Rowley and others, 1985). Shales and mudrocks indicate alluvial overbank flood deposits and shallow lakes. Bentonite beds record episodic volcanic ash falls from distant volcanoes to the west. The famous dinosaur quarry bed represents low-flow and storm deposits in bars and the channel of an eastward-flowing river (Hansen and others, 1980, 1983; Rowley, Dyni, and others, 1979; Rowley, Kinney, and others, 1979; Rowley and others, 1985). Recent work by Christine Turner, Fred Peterson, and others (verbal communication, 1999; Turner and Peterson, 1998) shows that the Morrison ecosystem was more arid with more ephemeral stream flows than previously hypothesized. Indeed, drought stricken species may have been caught up and buried periodically in the river bed by dry season flash floods. For more detailed information on the geology of the Morrison and its ecosystem, please refer to Bilbey (1973, 1992, 1998), Bilbey and others (1974), Bowman and others (1986), Kowallis (1986), Kowallis and others (1991), Turner and others (1997), Carpenter and others (1998), Kowallis and others (1998), and Peterson and Turner (1998).

Cedar Mountain Formation
(Lower Cretaceous)

The Cedar Mountain Formation (about 120 Ma) is lithologically very similar to the underlying Morrison Formation, and where the discontinuous Buckhorn Conglomerate is missing, the two are not readily separable at most map scales (Hansen and others, 1980, 1983; Rowley, Dyni, and others, 1979; Rowley, Kinney, and others, 1979; Rowley and others, 1985). In the Dinosaur area, the Cedar Mountain and Morrison erode together into strike valleys and low ridges that occasionally are separated by a hogback of Buckhorn Conglomerate. The Cedar Mountain strata generally range from about 100 to 200 feet (30-60 m) thick but locally are discontinuous (Hansen and others, 1980, 1983; Rowley, Dyni, and others, 1979; Rowley, Kinney, and others, 1979; Rowley and others, 1985).

The Buckhorn Conglomerate Member consists of resistant light- to medium-gray or brown, cross-bedded small-pebble (dark chert) conglomerate and coarse-grained sandstone (Hansen and others, 1980, 1983; Rowley, Dyni, and others, 1979; Rowley, Kinney, and others, 1979; Rowley and others, 1985). In the Dinosaur Quarry area, the Buckhorn is about 50 feet (16 m) thick. As with the Morrison, the conglomerates and mudrocks indicate deposition in streams, rivers, and lakes in a continental environment (Hansen and others, 1980, 1983; Rowley, Dyni, and others, 1979; Rowley, Kinney, and others, 1979; Rowley and others, 1985). Although not as intensely studied and quarried as the Morrison, the Cedar Mountain has yielded vertebrate fossils within Dinosaur National Monument, including sauropod dinosaur remains. In addition, the Cedar Mountain outcrops that flank Split Mountain and Blue Mountain provide largely untapped resources for new Lower Cretaceous-age fossil discoveries, including small mammals.

Dakota Sandstone (Lower Cretaceous)

The Dakota Sandstone (about 110 Ma) is genetically related and commonly mapped with the Mowry Shale (Lower Cretaceous) and Frontier Sandstone (Upper Cretaceous) (Hansen and others, 1980, 1983; Rowley, Dyni, and others, 1979; Rowley, Kinney, and others, 1979; Rowley and others, 1985; U.S. Geological Survey, 1999). Generally speaking, the Dakota represents shoreline beach and fluvial deposits of the transgressing Mancos Sea (the Cretaceous Western Interior Sea), and the Mowry Shale accumulated after the marine flooding covered the area. The overlying Frontier Sandstone accumulated as offshore sandbars, as deltas, and as swamp deposits at and near the shoreline. The thick overlying Mancos Shale marks deeper marine flooding in the region.

The Dakota generally crops out in the Dinosaur area as a resistant hogback of light-colored sandstone flanking the folds of Split Mountain and Blue Mountain. Indeed, the Dakota hogback continues almost unbroken for more than 40 miles (50 km) along the north side of U.S. Highway 40. In contrast to its significant topographic expression, the Dakota varies in thickness from about 40 to 100 feet (12-30 m) and averages only about 50 feet (15 m) near Dinosaur Quarry (Hansen and others, 1980, 1983; Rowley, Dyni, and others, 1979; Rowley, Kinney, and others, 1979; Rowley and others, 1985).

The Dakota strata are generally light-gray, white, and light-yellow, cross-bedded, medium- to coarse-grained to pebbly sandstone and minor pebble conglomerate with subordinate black and dark-gray carbonaceous shale. Other Dakota sediments include sparse black and red chert grains, white shell fragments, and petrified wood in some locations (Hansen and others, 1980, 1983; Rowley, Dyni, and others, 1979; Rowley, Kinney, and others, 1979; Rowley and others, 1985).

Mowry Shale (Lower Cretaceous)

The gray Mowry Shale (about 110 to 100 Ma) generally forms a narrow strike valley between the underlying Dakota Sandstone and the overlying Frontier Sandstone, which forms the outermost prominent hogback flanking Split Mountain and Blue Mountain. The Mowry strata range in thickness from 220 feet (65 m) in western part of the Dinosaur area to only about 33 feet (10 m) in eastern part. Near Dinosaur Quarry, it is about 125 feet (38 m) thick (Hansen and others, 1980, 1983; Rowley and others, 1985).

The Mowry Shale is fissile, dark-gray and siliceous shale that weathers to silvery-gray. In addition, the Mowry contains beds of bentonite that are characterized by an abundance of swelling clays. Although it is commonly covered by colluvium from the overlying Frontier Sandstone, its presence is marked by silver-gray shale chips in the soil. The Mowry is a marine deposit, and it contains abundant fish scales, less common fish bones, and occasional ammonites, bivalves, and shark teeth (Hansen and others, 1980, 1983; Rowley, Dyni, and others, 1979; Rowley, Kinney, and others, 1979; Rowley and others, 1985).

Frontier Sandstone (Upper Cretaceous)

The Frontier Sandstone (about 100 Ma) overlies the Mowry Shale and is informally divided into lower and upper parts. In the western Dinosaur area, the lower and upper Frontier are separated by a medial shale as much as 50 feet (15 m) thick (Hansen and others, 1980, 1983; Rowley, Dyni, and others, 1979; Rowley, Kinney, and others, 1979; Rowley and others, 1985; U.S. Geological Survey, 1999). The upper part forms hogbacks and flatirons, whereas the lower unit forms slopes and saddles. Well displayed in the outermost ridges flanking Split Mountain and southern Blue Mountain, bold outcrops of Dakota-Mowry-Frontier rocks form the picturesque double hogbacks near Dinosaur Quarry and Monument Headquarters. In the eastern Uinta Mountains, the Frontier Sandstone ranges in thickness from about 115 to 300 feet (35-90 m). Near Dinosaur Quarry, the lower part is 80 feet (24 m) thick and the upper part is 145 feet (44 m) thick (Untermann and Untermann, 1968). Near Deerlodge Park, the lower part is 130 feet (40 m) thick, and the upper part is 80 feet thick (24 m) (Hansen and others, 1980, 1983; Rowley, Dyni, and others, 1979; Rowley, Kinney, and others, 1979; Rowley and others, 1985).

The lower part of the Frontier is dark-gray, fossiliferous, calcareous shale, silty shale, and siltstone that weathers light yellowish gray (Hansen and others, 1980, 1983; Rowley and others, 1985). It contains fossil bivalves, ammonites, gastropods, and petrified wood deposited near the shoreline in marine and swampy environments. In contrast, the upper part of the Frontier is generally light-brown to light-greenish-gray, thin-bedded to massive, fine-grained calcareous sandstone that is locally cross-bedded and ripple marked. It contains abundant fossil worm burrows and coal (Hansen and others, 1980, 1983; Rowley, Dyni, and others, 1979; Rowley, Kinney, and others, 1979; Rowley and others, 1985).

Mancos Shale (Upper Cretaceous)

The Mancos Shale (about 100 to 80 Ma) is not completely exposed anywhere within Dinosaur National Monument (Hansen and others, 1980, 1983; Rowley and others, 1985; U.S. Geological Survey, 1999). However, several incomplete exposures of the lower Mancos crop out above the underlying Frontier Sandstone near Dinosaur Quarry. In most areas, the eroded Mancos strata form sparsely vegetated badlands, low slopes, and hummocky valley bottoms. The broad lowlands and badlands near Deerlodge Park and around Split Mountain and Cliff Ridge are representative Mancos Shale landforms. The soft gray shales and swelling bentonitic clays make the Mancos especially susceptible to landslides, and roads across the formation are commonly rough and hummocky (Hansen and others, 1980, 1983; Rowley and others, 1985). Although a complete stratigraphic section is not in the monument, the Mancos is about 5,000 feet (1,500 m) thick in the adjacent Jensen area south of Dinosaur Quarry and about 5,660 feet (1,700 meters) thick near Elk Springs east of the monument (Hansen and others, 1980, 1983; Rowley, Dyni, and others, 1979; Rowley, Kinney, and others, 1979; Rowley and others, 1985).

The Mancos is typically dark-gray, silty to clayey, calcareous or expansive shale that weathers light gray to light yellow. Subordinate siltstone and sandstone occur in the upper half (Hansen and others, 1980, 1983; Rowley, Dyni, and others, 1979; Rowley, Kinney, and others, 1979; Rowley and others, 1985). Layered bentonite and a few thin beds of limestone and a basal sandstone are found in the lower part. The Mancos is locally fossiliferous and contains a wide variety of marine fauna. Preserved mollusks, especially certain bivalves such as Inoceramus, and ammonite cephalopods called baculites provide important index fossils that geologists use to subdivide the formation throughout the western interior. Other marine fossils in the Mancos include protozoans, brachiopods, bryozoans, echinoderms, and trace fossils (Hansen and others, 1980, 1983; Rowley, Dyni, and others, 1979; Rowley, Kinney, and others, 1979; Rowley and others, 1985).

Bishop Conglomerate (Oligocene)

By Oligocene time, upland areas had been beveled by streams and mantled with gravel derived from the crest of the range. Indeed, an extensive pediment, the Gilbert Peak erosion surface, formed a graded slope from the high Uinta uplands to the floor of the adjacent basins (Hansen and others, 1980, 1983; Hansen, 1986a; Rowley and others, 1985). Remnants of the Gilbert Peak surface are preserved in the Dinosaur area on Ruple Point and the Yampa Plateau.

The Bishop Conglomerate (about 29 Ma) must have once blanketed the extensive Gilbert Peak erosion surface, extending up all the major valleys and filling in around the high peaks and ridges of the Uinta Mountains (Hansen and others, 1980, 1983; Hansen, 1986a; Rowley, Dyni, and others, 1979; Rowley and others, 1985). The Bishop strata crop out in many areas of Dinosaur National Monument including on Blue Mountain, the Yampa Plateau, Ruple Ridge, the trail to Harpers Corner, near Jones Hole, and the drainages of Diamond Gulch and Pot Creek (Hansen, 1986a). The Bishop Conglomerate ranges in thickness from about 500 feet (150 m) near Jones Hole to about 200 feet (60 m) along the road and trail to Harpers Corner and on Klauson Pasture near the head of Yampa Canyon. The Bishop is very thin in places due to post-Bishop erosion (Hansen and others, 1980, 1983; Hansen, 1986a; Rowley, Dyni, and others, 1979; Rowley and others, 1985).

The Bishop Conglomerate is generally very light gray to pinkish-gray to tan, very poorly sorted, loosely cemented, pebbly-cobbly-bouldery conglomerate and coarse-grained sandstone (Hansen and others, 1980, 1983; Rowley, Dyni, and others, 1979; Rowley, Kinney, and others, 1979; Rowley and others, 1985). The generally sub-angular to subrounded boulders (some greater than 6 feet [2 m]) and gravel are derived chiefly from Paleozoic limestones and the Precambrian Uinta Mountain Group. Pebbles of red chert are common. The Bishop contains light-gray hornblende-biotite tuff at Diamond Mountain (K/Ar age about 29 Ma; Hansen, 1986a), Yampa Plateau, and along Mud Springs Draw south of Round Top Mountain (Hansen and others, 1980, 1983; Rowley, Dyni, and others, 1979; Rowley, Kinney, and others, 1979; Rowley and others, 1985). For a more detailed description of the genesis and distribution of the Bishop Conglomerate and Gilbert Peak erosion surface, please refer to Hansen (1986a).

Browns Park Formation (Miocene)

After deposition of the Oligocene Bishop Conglomerate, subsidence in the eastern Uinta Mountains formed an east-southeast trending topographic and structural trough into which the Browns Park Formation (about 15 to 10 Ma) accumulated (Hansen, 1986a). Within the subsided trough east of the monument in the area between Elk Springs and Maybell, Colorado, the Browns Park strata overlie the Bishop Conglomerate topographically and stratigraphically. However, in the Browns Park valley itself and regionally in the Uinta Mountains, Bishop remnants cap mesas and benches at higher elevations than the Browns Park rocks (Hansen, 1986a).

The only exposures of the Browns Park Formation within Dinosaur National Monument are found north of the Gates of Lodore in the broad east-west valley of Browns Park, the type locality of the unit (Powell, 1876). Indeed, anyone visiting or embarking on a raft trip from the Gates of Lodore will have to travel across a significant portion of the Browns Park outcrop to reach their embarkation point. As a continuous body, the formation extends from about 10 miles west of the Utah-Colorado state line north of Dinosaur to the Elk Springs and Maybell areas in Colorado and attains a thickness of about 1,600 feet (490 m) (Dyni, 1968; Hansen, 1986a).

The lithology of the Browns Park Formation is highly varied but consists mostly of sandstones and unconsolidated, ashy tuffs (commonly intermixed) with minor chert, limestone, siltstone, conglomerate, and mudstone (Hansen 1965, 1986a; Hansen and others, 1983; Rowley and others, 1985). The volcanic ash-derived sediments are generally rhyolitic, light-gray to white, cross-bedded to massive, vitric (glassy) tuffs deposited by airfall and reworked by wind and streams. Earthy tuffs were deposited in lakes. Some lake clays contain diatoms and sparse ostracods (Hansen, 1986a). In addition, the sandstone is mostly light colored to white, friable (crumbly), and commonly tuffaceous, with bedding ranging from fluvial (stream deposited) in the west to widespread lacustrine (lake deposited) to eolian (wind deposited) in the east (Hansen, 1986a). Although most of the non-volcanic sediments were locally derived, the source of the tuffs is largely unknown. However, explosive volcanic activity was wide spread in the western United States during Miocene time (Hansen, 1986a). For a more detailed description of the genesis and distribution of the Browns Park Formation, please refer to Hansen (1986a).

Surficial Deposits (Pleistocene and Holocene)

Overshadowed by monumental outcrops of bedrock, surficial deposits (about 1 Ma to recent) are produced by the same processes that formed and continue to shape the rugged canyon country landscape. Indeed, the processes of weathering, erosion, and sedimentation contribute to formation of soil, talus, landslides, debris flows, slumps, and a variety of alluvial (stream), lacustrine (lake), and eolian (wind) features that are constantly shaping the surface of the earth. Both spectacular landforms and inconspicuous surficial deposits are greatly affected by the physical properties and physiographic setting of the associated bedrock (Hansen, 1977b). For example, resistant bedrock commonly erodes into steep slopes where both talus and landslide deposits may accumulate. Talus accumulates chiefly below cliff faces of hard, brittle bedrock, whereas landslide deposits result from significant volumes of rock detaching along weak zones and sliding downhill in large mass movements (Hansen, 1977b).

Most landslides in the Dinosaur area are rooted in weak shale units of the Lodore, Doughnut, Morgan, Morrison, and Mancos Formations, and many examples may be seen within the monument (figure 2; Rowley and others, 1979). In Yampa Canyon, extensive landslide deposits resulted after the river undercut and removed support of the lower member of the Morgan Formation. Recent erosion has cut gullies through these slide deposits down to the Round Valley Limestone bedrock (Rowley, Dyni, and others, 1979). Downstream at Warm Springs Cedars, landsliding also resulted from the Yampa River undercutting the Morgan Formation. Subsequent gullying in Warm Springs Draw and Iron Mine Draw exposed both the Round Valley Limestone bedrock and excellent sectional views of the slide (Hansen, 1977b). Many other landslides have developed along the Yampa River canyon and elsewhere in the Dinosaur area where erosion has cut into the lower member of the Morgan Formation (Rowley and others, 1979). For example, the road into Jones Hole from Diamond Mountain crosses a large active landslide on the south side of Diamond Gulch, where both the Morgan strata and toe of the slide are under almost continuous attack by stream erosion in the gulch (Hansen, 1977a; W.R. Hansen, U.S. Geological Survey, written communication, 2000). Landslides in Split Mountain Canyon also occurred after the Green River undercut and removed the support of the lower Morgan and Doughnut Shale (Rowley and Hansen; 1979a, 1979b). Other large landslides mantle the steep front of the Yampa fault and fold near Hells Canyon (Hansen and others, 1983). East of Hells Canyon, a complex landslide involves several rock units. The western section of this slide carried boulders and rock debris from the Madison, Humbug, Round Valley, and Morgan Formations for hundreds of feet. Farther east in the same slide, displaced blocks of Glen Canyon Sandstone are large enough to resemble bedrock outcrops. Although mostly inactive, some parts of the slide are still potentially active, especially in the central section near The Seeps (Hansen and Carrara, 1980). In addition to displacements along steep terrain, strata that contain muddy sediments and swelling clays commonly fail over large areas of gentle slope and dip. An impressive example occurs in the huge landslide deposit south of Buckwater Ridge on Blue Mountain. In this area, the exposed Morrison Formation has failed and moved down-slope over a wide area. Where the Dinosaur National Monument road crosses the slide, continued movement and swelling bentonite clays have caused rough and hummocky pavement and localized slumping of the roadbase (Rowley and Hansen, 1979a).

In addition to landslides, debris flows play a major

role in the geomorphologic development of the Dinosaur landscape, especially in the deep river canyons and side canyons. Indeed, almost all of the rapids found in the Green and Yampa River canyons are at the toes of debris fans created by debris flows dumping their muddy masses of boulders and unsorted sediment into the streams (Hansen, 1977b). The size of the fans, and commonly the associated rapids, are generally proportional to the drainage area of the tributary canyon complex, and the resulting deposits may be greatly influenced by one large flash flood event. For example, the large Warm Springs rapid at the mouth of Warm Springs Draw on the Yampa River about 4 miles upstream from its confluence with the Green River was formed June 10, 1965 when a flash flood deposited a huge amount of bouldery debris into the river (Hansen, 1977b). Sudden storms, flash floods, and debris flows are common events in the Dinosaur area, and anyone camping on debris fans in the canyons should be aware of their dangerous potential, especially during inclement weather (Hansen, 1977b, 1996).

Debris fans in the canyons commonly alter the course of the river by forcing the stream against the opposite bank and undercutting the adjacent strata. Once a cliff is undercut, huge blocks of dislodged rock often tumble into the channel (another hazard for boaters and campers!) and contribute debris to the rapids (Hansen, 1977b). In addition to rock falls, talus cones commonly accumulate at the foot of steep, undercut cliff faces.

Although the greatest quantity of alluvial (stream related) sediment in the Dinosaur area comes from ephemeral side streams (streams that only flow seasonally or after a rain), both the Green River and Yampa River transport and deposit large quantities of sand and gravel (Rowley and Hansen, 1979b). Since the completion of Flaming Gorge dam in the 1960s, the Green River transports much less sediment than in the past and can be observed mixing its clear waters with those of the muddy Yampa at their confluence in Echo Park. Most of the rivers' alluvium is confined to the river channels and adjacent flood plains, and since most of the deposits are occasionally inundated, campers should be aware of the potential flooding hazard (Rowley and Hansen, 1979b). Geologic maps of the Dinosaur area often depict extensive alluvial deposits, debris fans, alluvial fans (fan-shaped surfaces of stream deposits), and pediments (where streams and tributaries form coalescing surfaces of erosion) as separate surficial units. Pediments generally form where erosion has beveled the underlying rock into a graded surface, such as the small Holocene pediments mapped on the Mancos Shale at Deerlodge Park and the Morrison Formation in the vicinity of Daniels Ranch south of Split Mountain (Rowley and Hansen, 1979b).

In addition to alluvial deposits, eolian (wind related) deposits are common in the Dinosaur area. Eolian sand deposits occur mostly as partly vegetated dunes resting on a friable (crumbly) source, such as the Glen Canyon Sandstone. Other dunes are common along the river banks where wind has reworked flood plain alluvium, beaches, and bars (Rowley and Hansen, 1979a, 1979b; Hansen, 1996).

STRUCTURAL GEOLOGY

Dinosaur National Monument is near the eastern end of the Uinta Mountains which are the eroded topographic expression of the regional-scale Uinta anticline or arch (figure 1; Hansen, 1957, 1965; 1986a; Erslev, 1993; Gregson and Erslev, 1997). The Uinta anticline is one of many uplifted areas (structural arches) that formed during the Laramide orogeny in the Rocky Mountain foreland province from about 70 to 40 Ma (Perry and others, 1992). The Rocky Mountain foreland is generally defined as the region east of the Cordilleran thrust belt (Powers, 1982; also called the Sevier, Idaho-Wyoming, and Western thrust or overthrust belt by various authors) where structural deformation involved basement rocks (figure 1; Gries, 1983). In map view (and structurally), the central Rocky Mountain foreland consists of a series of anastomosing (branching and rejoining) structural arches (very large anticlines or uplifts) with an average trend toward the northwest (figure 1; Erslev, 1993). However, the Laramide trends vary greatly and range from east-west (Uinta, Granite, and Owl Creek arches) to more north-south (Front Range, Park-Gore Range, Rock Springs, and Douglas Creek arches). Although the average Laramide compression and shortening directions were probably oriented northeast-southwest (Brown, 1988; Erslev, 1993), local variations due to pre-existing structures, crustal boundaries, and interactions among structures are still poorly understood. In the Uinta arch, the combination of trend, pre-existing structure, and structural interaction makes understanding its origin a challenge as well.

The Uinta arch extends into the Cordilleran (Sevier) thrust belt on the west and is bounded by Laramide thrust faults on the north, northeast, and south (figure 4). The Uinta arch consists of western and eastern elongate domes whose culminations roughly coincide with the north-south trending Moxa arch and Rock Springs/Douglas Creek arches (Hansen, 1957, 1965, 1986b). In the western Uintas, the Cottonwood uplift and Wasatch fault effectively truncate the mountain range, but the anticlinal axis of the Uinta arch may extend westward through the Wasatch Range to the Oquirrh Mountains in the Basin and Range Province (Hansen, 1957, 1986b; Ritzma, 1969). Also in the western Uintas, recent work has linked the Sevier-age Charlston-Nebo thrust with faulting under the southwestern Uinta arch (Constenius and Mueller, 1996), and other studies have linked the Hogsback thrust with the North Flank fault zone on the northwest side of the arch (Bradley and Bruhn, 1988; Bryant and Nichols, 1988). In contrast, the surface expression of the eastern Uinta arch axis disappears under the Miocene fill of the Browns Park Formation but probably continues eastward through the Cross and Juniper Mountains pop-up structures that expose the

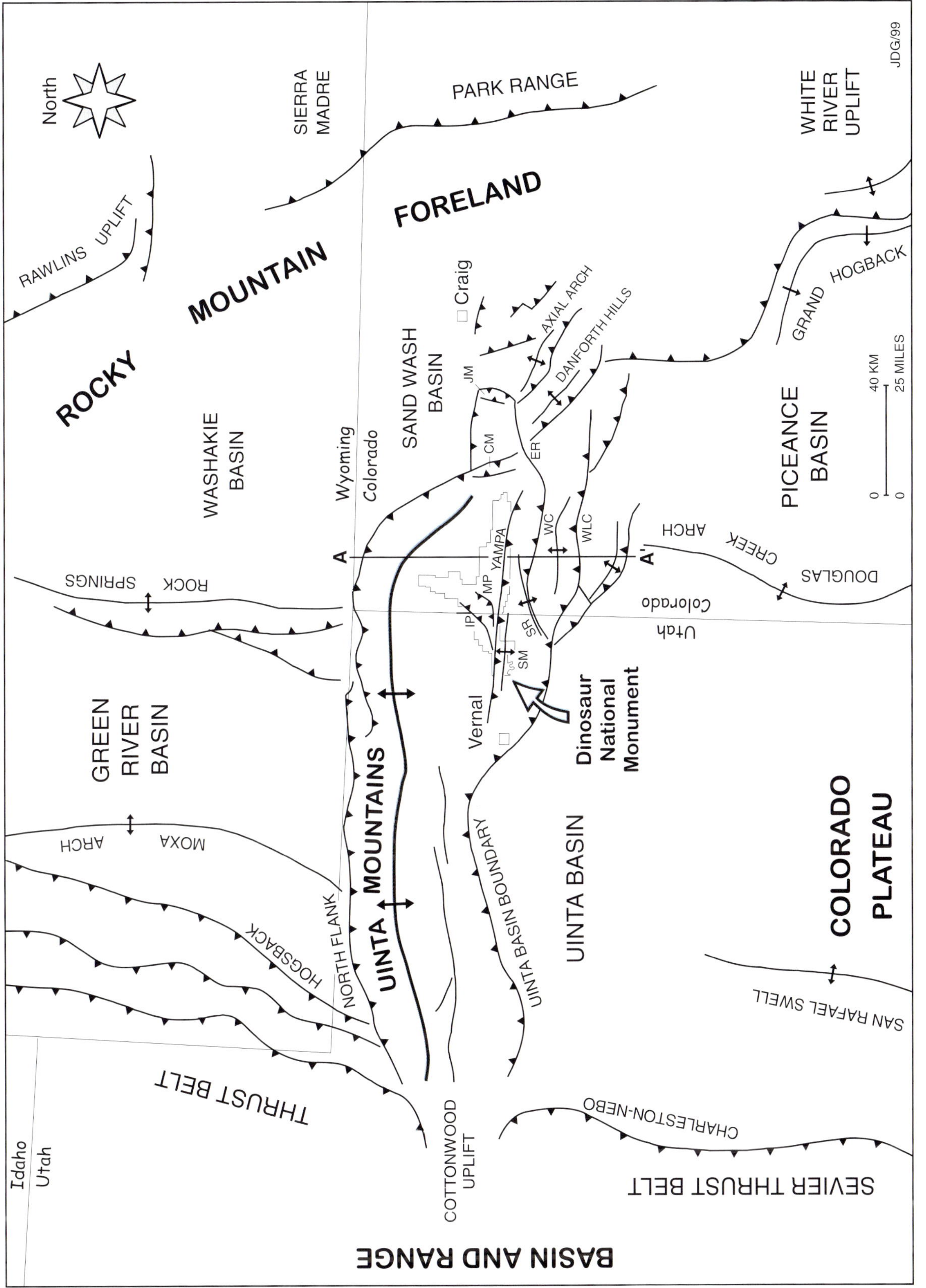

Figure 4. Structure map of the Uinta Mountains area (modified from Gries, 1983; Rowley and others, 1985; Stone 1986a; Morel and others, 1986; Gregson and Erslev, 1997). Features marked on the map include Island Park (IP), Mitten Park (MP), Split Mountain (SM), Section Ridge (SR), Wolf Creek (WC), Willow Creek (WLC), Cross Mountain (CM), Elk Ridge (ER), and Juniper Mountain (JM). Section A-A' is illustrated in figure 5 (Hansen, 1986b; Gregson and Erslev, 1997).

Eastern Uinta Arch

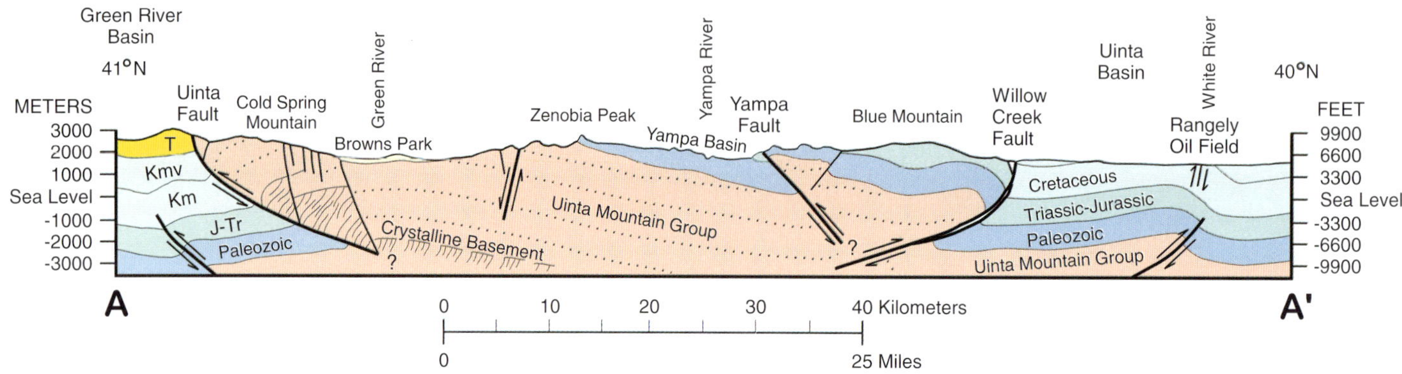

Figure 5. *Generalized geologic section A-A' shown in figure 4 (modified from Hansen, 1986b; Gregson and Erslev, 1997). The section is across the eastern Uinta Mountains along longitude 108° 52' 30" showing the structural relief between the Uinta Arch and the Green River Basin to the north and the Uinta Basin to the south.*

Late Precambrian Uinta Mountain Group strata (figure 4; Hansen, 1957, 1986b; Ritzma, 1969, Stone 1986b). The eastern Uinta arch aligns with the White River Uplift southeast of Juniper Mountain in the Danforth Hills/Axial arches (Hansen, 1986b), but these structures display a southwest vergence direction opposite the Uinta thrust margin adjacent to the Sand Wash Basin (figure 4; Gregson and Erslev, 1997).

Structural Development of the Uinta Arch

The Uinta arch coincides with an east-trending, Late Precambrian (Middle and Upper Proterozoic, about 1.16 Ga) sedimentary trough that accommodated 23,000 to 35,000 feet (7,000-10,700 m) of Uinta Mountain Group sediments (Hansen, 1957, 1986b; Stone, 1993a). After deposition and consolidation of the sediments, the strata were tilted northward and beveled by erosion before the Upper Cambrian Lodore Formation was deposited on an angular unconformity over the Uinta Mountain Group (Hansen, 1986b; Stone, 1993a). However, the lack of deformation in Cambrian through Cretaceous strata indicates that the Uinta area west of the White River Uplift was mostly tectonically quiescent (except for localized faulting and dike intrusion) until major structural inversion in the Laramide orogeny (figure 5; Hansen, 1986b). The coincidence of the late Precambrian basin with later Laramide structures has been documented through surface outcrop, seismic, and well data, but the total extent of the Uinta paleobasin is not well defined (Hansen, 1986b; Stone, 1986c, 1993a). In addition, south and east of Dinosaur, seismic and well data indicate that Precambrian Uinta Mountain Group rocks are preserved in the hanging walls of Laramide thrusts in the Axial, Beaver Creek, and Rangely anticlines but not in the footwalls, suggesting that these structures may be inverted Uinta paleobasin-bounding faults (Stone, 1986b, 1993a; Morel and others, 1986; Richard, 1986; J. Lowell, 1995, verbal communication). Thinning of Pennsylvanian strata in the hanging walls indicate that initial inversion of

Precambrian extensional structures occurred on the Axial and Beaver Creek thrusts during the Ancestral Rocky Mountain orogeny (Stone, 1986b; Morel and others, 1986). Similarly, other nearby seismic and drill hole data also show that Pennsylvanian-age structures were reactivated during the Laramide (Stone, 1986c, 1993a; Morel and others, 1986). Although deformation related to the Ancestral Rocky Mountain orogeny did not extend westward into the Dinosaur area and Uinta Mountains, its effect on sedimentation is well reflected in the rock record (for example, the Weber Sandstone).

During Late Cretaceous through Early Tertiary time, crustal contraction inverted the ancient Uinta paleobasin and formed the Uinta arch with 7 to 8 miles (11-13 km) of structural relief relative to surrounding basins (figure 5; Sales, 1971) with the greatest structural relief in the eastern Uinta arch (Ritzma, 1969; Hansen, 1986b). In general, the geometry of Laramide structures on the north, south, and east flanks of the Uinta arch combined with the impingement and merging of the Cordilleran thrust belt to the west suggests that both Sevier and Laramide deformation contributed to the arch's development (Armstrong and Oriel, 1986; Bradley and Bruhn, 1988; Bryant and Nichols, 1988; Gregson, 1994; Constenius and Mueller, 1996; Gregson and Erslev, 1997). This idea is also supported by paleostress analyses from the Eastern Uinta Mountains (Gregson, 1994; Gregson and Erslev, 1997).

During and after uplift of the Uinta arch, erosion was unroofing the structure and providing sediment into the surrounding basins. As discussed in other sections, Laramide structures in the eastern Uinta Mountains underlie the Gilbert Peak erosion surface, an angular unconformity under the Oligocene Bishop Conglomerate (Hansen, 1986a, 1986b). Subsequent structural development in the Eastern Uinta Mountains is evidenced by offsets of the Gilbert Peak unconformity and Bishop strata which indicate post-Laramide regional northeastward tilting, subsidence, and the formation of the Browns Park basin (Hansen, 1986a, 1986b).

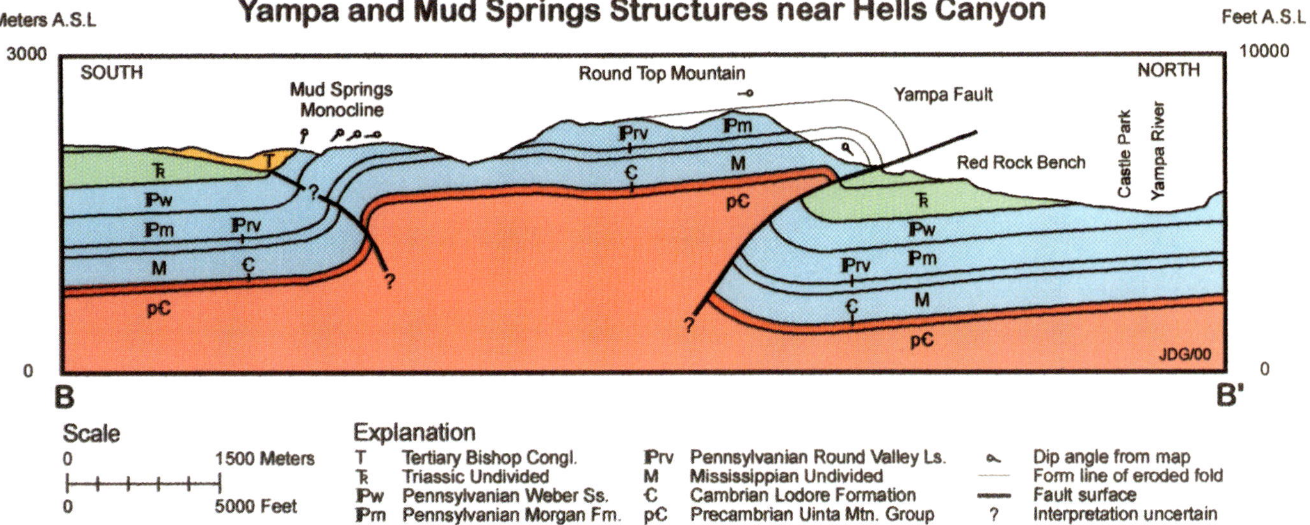

Figure 6. Geologic cross section B-B' shown in figure 2 (subsurface interpretation after Hansen, 1986b; Hansen and Rowley, 1980a; and Stone, 1993a). The section is drawn along a north-south line about 0.5 mile (0.8 km) west of Hells Canyon (Hansen and Rowley, 1980a).

Major Structural Features in the Dinosaur Area

Faults and folds in Dinosaur National Monument are essentially "piggy-back" features located in the hanging wall of the Uinta Basin boundary fault (Stone, 1993a). However, the faults bounding the south side of Blue Mountain (Wolf Creek, Willow Creek, Skull Creek faults) may actually be splays of the Uinta Basin boundary. In many ways, the structure exposed in the Dinosaur area mimics the greater structure of the Uinta arch and the Rocky Mountain foreland as a whole. In map view, the faults and folds form a complex anastomosing (branching and rejoining) pattern (figure 4; Gregson and Erslev, 1997). In addition, most of the Laramide faults are generally thrust faults—many of which dip toward one another and must somehow intersect at depth, but that relationship is not well understood (figures 5 and 6; Hansen, 1986b). Although the faults in Dinosaur National Monument have limited exposures and generally pass laterally or vertically into monoclines, most may be easily inferred under the adjacent structural folds (Hansen, 1986b). Overall, the Dinosaur area contains some of the best exposures of Laramide-age faults and folds found within the Rocky Mountains. Figure 7 illustrates the rugged structural topography that is reflected in the surface of the Weber Sandstone in the central part of Dinosaur National Monument. Although not depicting the underlying faults, the three-dimensional (3-D) surface model in figure 7 displays the complex relationships among the structures in Dinosaur National Monument and the structural influence on surface topography and landforms quite well (Gregson, 1994; Gregson and Erslev, 1997).

The Yampa fault and fold forms the longest continuous structural feature within Dinosaur National Monument (figures 2 and 4). The greater Yampa structure extends from near Elk Springs on the east, bounds the north side of the Blue Mountain highland, and trends westward into the Split Mountain anticline (Hansen and Carrara, 1980). The Yampa fault is discontinuously exposed across the Hells Canyon, Tanks Peak, Haystack Rock, and Indian Water Canyon quadrangles, but a classic thrust fault trace is displayed in the walls of Hells Canyon (figure 6, Hansen and others, 1983). At Hells Canyon, the Yampa fault dips about 20 degrees south and placed the uppermost Uinta Mountain Group over the Triassic Chinle Formation (Hansen 1986b). According to Hansen and Rowley (1980a), the strata are offset vertically (stratigraphic throw) about 5,000 feet (1,500 m) and the slip on the fault surface is about 8,000 feet (2,400 m). The folding in both the hanging and footwalls of the Yampa fault appears to be quite concentric (figure 6; Hansen, 1986b). The Yampa fault splays and passes into the Yampa monocline and Ruple Point-Red Rock anticline about 3.5 miles (5.5 km) west of Hells Canyon (figure 2; Hansen and others, 1983).

The Mitten Park and Island Park faults combine to form the northeast-trending "pop-up" structure that visitors often unknowingly traverse when driving to Harpers Corner. On the northwest side of this structure, the Island Park fault is discontinuously exposed for over 12.5 miles (20 km) from its junction with the Split Mountain structure until it splays and dies out northeast of Jones Hole (Hansen and others, 1983). According to Hansen (1986b), the dip of the Island Park fault ranges from about 20 degrees at Sage Creek near Whirlpool Canyon to as much as 75 degrees at Jones Hole, only 3 miles (5 km) to the northeast. Similarly, the Mitten Park fault and fold bound the southeastern side of the "pop-up." From the viewpoint at the end of the Harpers Corner trail, the Mitten Park fault is well displayed above the northeast bank of the Green River. Although its trace and 50 degree dip are well exposed along the Green River at the head of Whirlpool

Weber Sandstone Structure in the Blue Mountain - Yampa Basin Area

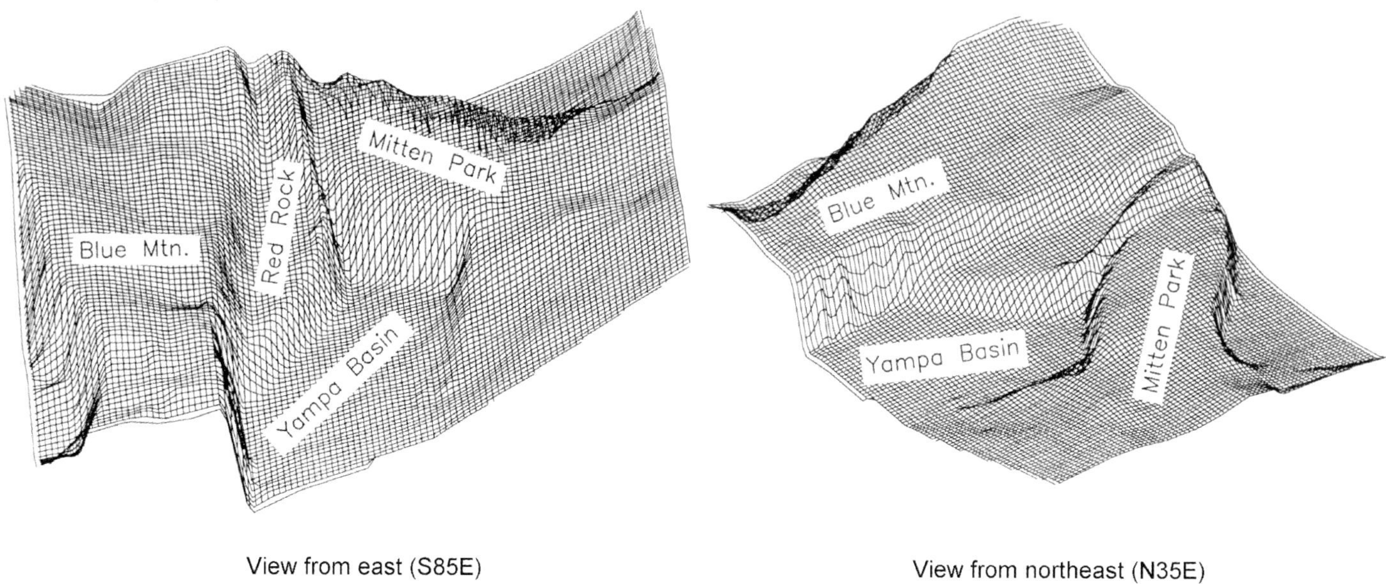

Figure 7. Structure surface plots on top of the Weber Sandstone illustrating the complex folding associated with the faults underlying the central Blue Mountain, Mitten Park, Red Rock, and Yampa Basin areas. Fault traces, such as the Yampa fault, are not shown. Much of the surface topography in this area reflects the underlying structural control quite well.

Canyon, the fault disappears toward the northeast after intersecting the Warm Springs monocline (figure 2; Hansen and others, 1983; Hansen, 1986b). In the opposite direction, the Mitten Park fault passes into the Mitten Park monocline which intersects the Yampa structure about 5 miles (8 km) to the southwest (Hansen and others, 1983). Folding in the footwall of the Mitten Park fault also appears to be quite concentric (Hansen, 1986b).

The Yampa basin is a compressional trap door structure that is bounded by the Warm Springs monocline on the north, the Mitten Park fault and monocline on the west, and the Yampa fault and Red Rock anticline on the south (figure 2; Hansen and others, 1983). The broad Yampa bench and surrounding highlands form the topographic expression of the Yampa basin as seen from overlooks on the Harpers Corner road. The 3-D structural surface diagram (figure 7) displays the Yampa basin quite well.

The Red Rock-Ruple Point anticline forms a tight angular fold where it intersects with the Mitten Park monocline (figure 7). This kink-like fold geometry is quite different from other nearby concentric folds. The geometry of the fold probably relates to crowding between the Mitten Park and Red Rock structures and the interaction of the underlying faults, but the kinematics (deformation processes) are still not well understood. Nevertheless, the Red Rock-Ruple Point anticline is a classic structure where visitors can observe and contemplate its origin themselves. Viewpoints along the Harpers Corner road and just north of the Echo Park turnoff provide views and ac-

cess to the anticline.

When visitors drive along U.S. Highway 40 or approach Dinosaur Quarry from the south, the awe-inspiring hogbacks and flatirons of Split Mountain and Cliff Ridge (Section Ridge anticline) dominate the scene. Although the underlying faults are not exposed at the surface, the sheer magnitude of these structures with their carapace of Weber Sandstone is spectacular to behold. The sharp amplitudes and steep dips of the anticlines caused some geologists in the past to hypothesize steep to vertical faults under the folds (for example, Stearns, 1971), but as noted earlier, seismic, drill hole, and cross section data show that similar structures are contractional and generally underlain by thrust faults (Berg, 1962; Lowell, 1983; Stone, 1986a). A published seismic section across the west end of the Split Mountain anticline illustrates the underlying thrust faults quite well (Stone, 1993a).

This discussion of major structures has focused on the Laramide-age deformation that dominates in the Dinosaur area. However, after culmination of Laramide orogeny and formation of the Gilbert Peak erosion surface in the Oligocene, general subsidence and other more minor deformations occurred throughout the Uinta Mountains that commonly involved the earlier Laramide structures (Powell, 1876; Hansen 1965, 1986a, 1986b). Indeed, John Wesley Powell generally deduced as much in 1876! Miocene and later deformation of the Uinta range has been interpreted as a consequence of a north down, south up rotation, as indicated by tilted erosion surfaces (Hansen, 1986a; 1986b). Most of the post-Laramide deformation preceded deposition of the Browns Park Formation, but local offsets observed in the Browns Park strata reflect even later deformation (figure 2; Hansen 1986a, 1986b). In the Dinosaur area, structure contours drawn on the Gilbert Peak erosion surface under the Bishop Conglomerate indicate post-Bishop movement on the Yampa and Island Park faults (Hansen, 1986a). For more detailed descriptions of the post-Laramide tectonics and structure, please refer to the Hansen (1986a).

GEOLOGIC HISTORY

The historical geology of the Dinosaur National Monument can be traced back more than 2.5 billion years to a time when the Uinta area was at or near an east-trending continental margin defined by the ancient rocks of the Wyoming province (Hills and Houston, 1979; Condie, 1982; Hansen, 1986b; Stone, 1993a). By about 1.8 Ga, additional crust had accreted onto the proto-North American continent to the south of the Uinta area (Condie, 1982). The major tectonic contact that separates the Archean-age Wyoming province from the Proterozoic-age rocks to the south is often referred to as the Wyoming shear zone or the Cheyenne suture (Condie, 1982; Stone, 1993a). At least two other major crustal masses accreted to the proto-North American continent before the end of Precambrian time (Condie, 1982), but by about 1.1 Ga, the Uinta region was east of a north-trending rifted continental margin. The red sediments of the Uinta Mountain Group accumulated in a long linear basin or trough that probably formed as a failed arm of a rift (an aulacogen) beginning about 1.5 Ga (Sears and others, 1982; Stone, 1993a). After deposition and lithification of thousands of feet of sediments, the Uinta Mountain Group strata were uplifted, tilted northeastward, and beveled by erosion before deposition of the Cambrian Lodore Formation (Hansen, 1986b; 1996, figure 10).

Minor tectonic activity continued in the Uinta region during the early Paleozoic as evidenced by displacements of the Lodore Formation along the Disaster fault (figure 2) and shearing observed in an Ordovician-age dike (Hansen, 1986b). The area must have remained relatively high during the Ordovician to Devonian sedimentary hiatus, but the Uinta region was tectonically quiescent for the remainder of the Paleozoic and much of the Mesozoic. However, continued subsidence in the area of the Uinta trough allowed accumulation of some 10,000 feet (about 3,000 m) of Mississippian through Jurassic sediments (figure 3; Hansen, 1986b). As the area remained low and exhibited little relief throughout the Paleozoic, the sea repeatedly transgressed and withdrew across the area (as discussed here in the Stratigraphy section). Although deformation related to the Ancestral Rocky Mountain orogeny has not been recognized in the Dinosaur area, late Paleozoic and early Mesozoic sedimentation was greatly affected by the proximity of the mountainous highlands to the southeast. Sometimes called the Colorado orogeny for

the extensive deformation (Front Range, Uncompahgre, and Apishapa highlands) and sedimentation (Maroon, Minturn, Cutler, and Fountain Formations) that occurred in that state, the Pennsylvanian-Permian tectonic event also formed structures of great relief in Utah (Paradox and Oquirrh basins), Arizona (Zuni uplift and Pedrogosa basin), New Mexico (San Luis uplift and Delaware basin), Oklahoma (Anadarko basin), and west Texas (Central Basin platform and Midland basin) as well (Peterson and Smith, 1986; Kluth, 1986). In the Dinosaur area, the great thickness of the Morgan Formation and Weber Sandstone accumulated in the Uinta trough during Pennsylvanian and Permian time. To the west, enormously thick deposits accumulated in the southern Wasatch region where temporally equivalent rocks (for example, the Oquirrh Group) are many thousands of feet thick.

During the Mesozoic Era, continental depositional environments became more extensive and are reflected in the strata of the redbeds (Moenkopi and Chinle), the eolian (wind derived) sandstones (Glen Canyon and Entrada), and the fluvial/lacustrine deposits (Morrison and Cedar Mountain)(Hansen and others, 1980, 1983; Rowley, Dyni, and others, 1979; Rowley, Kinney, and others, 1979; Rowley and others, 1985). However, the sea still influenced many formations (Carmel and Stump), and by Cretaceous time, marine and marginal marine conditions again dominated the sedimentary environments. During Cretaceous time, the Mancos or Pierre Sea transgressed across the western interior of North America in response to crustal loading by the Cordilleran thrust belt which probably extended the length of the continent (Cole, 1987). The loading of the east-directed thrusts (west of Dinosaur) depressed the crust to the east and created a continental scale foreland basin that the Mancos Sea occupied for several million years. As the sea transgressed, shoreface and nearshore sediments accumulated (Dakota, Mowry, Frontier), but as the thrust belt loading became greater, the seaway became deeper and the muds of the Mancos Shale were deposited. Finally in the Late Cretaceous, as the thrust belt highlands encroached on the western margin of the seaway, sedimentation overpowered the sea, and multiple cycles of bar, beach, lagoon, and swamp deposits prograded eastward into the Mancos basin (Mesaverde Group and equivalents). Also in the Late Cretaceous, basement-involved structures began forming within the western foreland basin, and as the structures grew into uplifts and subbasins, the last great seaway of the western interior regressed from the continent.

From its subsea beginning in the Late Cretaceous, the Laramide orogeny evolved into a complex set of highlands (arches) and basins that formed in the foreland east of the Cordilleran (Sevier-Wyoming) thrust belt. Many of the arches, such as the Uinta, Wind River, and Sawatch, grew into immense mountain ranges (figure 1), whereas, others were merely ridges within the intermontane basins (for example, Douglas Creek, Rock Springs, and Moxa arches; figure 4). Deformation in the Laramide foreland overlapped for a time with thrusting in the Sevier-Wyoming belt to the west, but the relationship between the two is still not well understood. However, as discussed in the STRUCTURE section, the development of the Uinta arch overlapped both the Sevier and Laramide events in space as well as in time, and both must have influenced its development. Contraction across the old rift basin inverted the subsided structure and uplifted the Uinta Mountain Group and underlying Precambrian rocks well above much younger strata in the surrounding basins. Similarly, Laramide compression reactivated other existing structures in the foreland, but multiple new ones formed as well.

As Laramide foreland arches became positive features, erosion and sedimentation began almost simultaneously. Indeed, the timing and evolution of the Laramide structures are reflected in the sedimentary sequences and fossils, especially pollen, deposited in the adjacent basins (Perry and others, 1992). In general, Laramide structures were initiated and grew in stature from west to east, but most have long and complex histories (Perry and others, 1992). The Uinta arch separated the greater Green River and Uinta basins to the north and south respectively (figure 1), where great lakes, generally referred to as the Green River lakes, existed during the Eocene Epoch. North and south of the arch, Uinta rivers and streams flowed into Lake Gosiute and Lake Uinta, respectively. In general, coarse boulders and gravel were deposited near the mountain front (Fort Union and Wasatch Formations) with finer sand and silt traveling farther out into the basins (Wasatch and Green River Formations). In the lakes, fine calcareous and organic-rich muds accumulated in thick deposits that are known today as marlstone and oil shale (the Green River Formation). However, none of these strata crop out in the Dinosaur area, and if ever there, they have since been removed by erosion (Hansen and others, 1980, 1983; Hansen, 1986a; Rowley, Dyni, and others, 1979; Rowley, Kinney, and others, 1979; Rowley and others, 1985).

Laramide deformation had ceased by Oligocene time and upland areas had been beveled by streams and mantled with gravel derived from the crest of the range. An extensive pediment (the Gilbert Peak erosion surface) formed a graded slope from the high Uinta uplands to the floors of the adjacent basins that in turn was covered by the Bishop Conglomerate (Hansen, 1986a, 1986b). After the tectonic quiescence during Oligocene time, Miocene and later deformation resulted in subsidence and a north down, south up rotation of the Uinta range and the formation of the Browns Park basin (figure 2; Hansen, 1986a, 1986b). Post Oligocene deformation also occurred in the Dinosaur area, mostly along existing structures (Hansen, 1986a).

Initial development of the Green and Yampa River drainages began after deposition of the Bishop Conglomerate and evolved steadily during and after deposition of the Browns Park Formation (Hansen, 1986a). According to Hansen (1986a):

The Browns Park Formation continued to accumulate in Browns Park [basin] until the old valley was overtopped at the site of Lodore Canyon in late Miocene or early Pliocene time... Drainage that had flowed toward the downwarp at the east end of the Uintas now spilled south toward the Uinta Basin... superimposing itself into the underlying older rocks, where it ultimately cut its canyons..., [and] eventually capturing all the runoff of the Green River Basin.

In addition, the ancestral Yampa River flowed into the easternmost Dinosaur area and deposited the basal conglomerate of the Browns Park Formation (Hansen, 1986a). Although not well understood, the eastern Browns Park area subsequently became a stilling basin until further tectonic subsidence or the spillover of the Green River into Lodore Canyon rejuvenated the drainage system (Hansen, 1986a). More recently in middle Pleistocene time, the drainage system captured the Green River from its ancestral easterly coarse across the Rock Springs uplift in Wyoming (Hansen, 1986a). Canyon profiles and river terraces indicate that re-entrenchment of the Green River continued after initial canyon development due to regional uplift or changes in river discharge (Hansen, 1986a). Indeed, continuing entrenchment of the modern Green and Yampa Rivers maintains the spectacular canyons and drainage base levels that dominate the landscape and sedimentation that visitors see today. For more detailed information about Dinosaur's Neogene historical geology, please refer to Hansen (1986a).

UNIQUE GEOLOGIC FEATURES

Dinosaur Quarry

On August 17, 1909, Dr. Earl Douglass of the Carnegie Museum of Natural History, Pittsburgh, PA., climbed to the top of a sandstone bed north of the sleepy hamlet of Jensen, Utah. There, he saw 8 tail vertebrae of *Apatosaurus* projecting out of the ground, still articulated just as when they were in the living animal. Douglass recorded his elation in his diary (Cooley and others, 1982):

At last in the top of the ledge where a softer overlying [sandstone] bed forms a divide--a kind of saddle--I saw eight of the tail bones of a Brontosaurus in exact position. It was a beautiful sight. Part of the ledge had weathered away out and the beautifully petrified centra lay on the ground. It is by far the best dinosaur prospect I have ever found. The part exposed is worth preserving anyway.

And with those words, work began on what would turn out to be one of the greatest dinosaur quarries ever found, one containing the remains of over 400 individuals, and ultimately to the creation of Dinosaur National Monument in 1915. For more information about the history of Dinosaur Quarry, please refer to the PALEONTOLOGY section below and to the paleontology summary paper by Santucci in this volume.

Dinosaur's Canyons

The canyons of the Green and Yampa Rivers are two of the great river gorges of western North America. Both canyons are spectacular landforms, but each has its own unique character. On the Green River, the Canyon of Lodore cuts through the red rocks of the Uinta Mountain Group for most of its length beneath cliffs 2,000 feet (600 m) high, whereas awe-inspiring exposures of the Weber Sandstone dominate the precipitous walls of Yampa Canyon (figure 2). Indeed, one of the most awesome landforms in Dinosaur National Monument is what river runners call the Grand Overhang, an undercut, overhanging cliff 1,100 feet (330 m) high that exposes the full thickness of the Weber Sandstone (Hansen and Carrara, 1980; Hansen, 1996). The cliff is within the deeply entrenched gooseneck meanders of the Yampa River below Harding Hole (Hansen, 1996). In contrast to the more ancient rocks of the Canyon of Lodore, the oldest rocks exposed in the walls of Yampa Canyon belong to the Madison Limestone (Hansen and Carrara, 1980).

Split Mountain Canyon, Whirlpool Canyon, and Jones Hole are also unique, spectacular canyons. As its name implies, the Green River "splits" the mountain and exposes a unique cross sectional perspective of the Split Mountain anticline. In addition, the Green River drops an average of 19.3 feet per mile (3.7 m per km) through Split Mountain, the greatest of any of Dinosaur's canyons (Hansen, 1996). Whirlpool Canyon cuts through the uplifted Mitten Park structural block as well as the Mitten Park and Island Park faults (figure 2; Hansen and others, 1983). High in the walls of Whirlpool Canyon, the Uinta Mountain Group grandly displays a rugged contact with the overlying Lodore Sandstone where "fossil sea stacks" up to about 185 feet (55 m) high were buried by the sediments of the Cambrian Lodore sea more than 500 Ma (Hansen, 1996; W.R. Hansen, written communication, 2000). Further downstream is Jones Hole, an extended, steep-walled canyon, that becomes Diamond Gulch on upstream. About 4 miles (6.5 km) above its confluence with the Green River in Whirlpool Canyon (figure 2), the clear and cold Jones Creek emerges abruptly from openings in the Round Valley Limestone (Hansen, 1996). From the Jones Creek springs down to its confluence with Ely Creek, a smaller tributary stream and canyon, upper Jones Hole trends along the Island Park fault trace which is locally visible in the canyon walls. Southwest of the Ely Creek confluence, one can climb the fault trace where Cambrian-age Lodore strata are placed against Pennsylvanian-age rocks.

Weber Sandstone

Just as in Yampa Canyon, the Weber Sandstone forms towering landforms almost everywhere it is exposed. Per-

haps the best known Weber outcrop of all is Steamboat Rock, an enormous sandstone monolith more than a mile long that towers 1,010 feet (320 m) above the Green River (Hansen, 1996). Steamboat Rock was formed by erosion on the inner side of an entrenched meander that also carved the outer canyon walls of Echo Park, which was named by John Wesley Powell and his crew on June 18, 1869, more than 130 years ago (Powell, 1876). In addition to monoliths, such as Steamboat and Jenny Lind Rocks, the thick Weber Sandstone forms the wonderful array of hogbacks, flatirons, and box canyons partly enveloping Split Mountain and the south side of Blue Mountain (figure 2). The Weber strata are also the primary reservoir rocks of the giant Rangely Oil Field south of Blue Mountain, and petroleum geologists have studied the classic Weber outcrops to better understand the field's characteristics.

CLASSIC GEOLOGICAL SITES

Type Localities

Type localities are the areas of exposed strata where rock formations are first definitively described and documented by geologists. Type localities for two formations are found within or near Dinosaur National Monument. The Lodore Formation is named for its type locality at the southern end of Lodore Canyon near Limestone Draw about 2.5 miles (4 km) upstream from Echo Park and the confluence of the Green and Yampa Rivers (Hansen, 1996). The formation was first named the Lodore Group by Powell in 1876 (Powell, 1876; U.S. Geological Survey, 1999). Similarly, the type locality of the Browns Park Formation is in Brown's Park, Colorado and Utah. The name Brown's Park Formation was also first used by John Wesley Powell in 1876 (Powell, 1876; U.S. Geological Survey, 1999).

Laramide Structures

The Dinosaur area contains some of the best exposures of Laramide-age faults and folds found anywhere within the Rocky Mountains. Fault types range from high-angle normal to classic low-angle thrusts, and fold shapes range from classic cylindrical to quite angular and kink-like. For example, thrust faults exposed at Hells Canyon and Mitten Park are clearly associated with well-exposed, cylindrically-folded strata (Hansen, 1986b). However, only a few miles southwest of the Mitten Park fault outcrop, the Ruple Point-Red Rock anticline is tightly folded into a kink-like angular structure (Hansen, 1986b; Gregson, 1994; Gregson and Erslev, 1997). Indeed, analyses of Dinosaur's structures as well as their shapes and orientations have supported a variety of tectonic theories and models through the years (Berg, 1962; Sales, 1968, 1969; Stearns, 1971; Stone 1975; Chapin and Cather, 1983; Gries, 1983; Brown, 1988; Hamilton, 1988; Erslev, 1993; Gregson, 1994; Gregson and Erslev, 1997). Although a comprehensive analysis of tectonic theories for the genesis and evolution of the Laramide orogeny is beyond the scope of this paper, the classic exposures of Laramide-age structures in Dinosaur National Monument will continue to provide a unique outdoor laboratory to test current and future tectonic hypotheses and theories for years to come.

PALEONTOLOGY

Dinosaur National Monument has a rich and diverse fossil record that extends over a half-billion years, but not all of that record is well understood. Even after 90 years of excavation, Dinosaur's sedimentary rocks continue to yield spectacular fossils that astound the public and scientific community. The general paleontology and many of the invertebrate fossils are discussed in Santucci (this volume) and in the preceding section on STRATIGRAPHY. This section focuses on the important Mesozoic vertebrate and plant fossils that have been discovered during the last 20 years.

Although Precambrian fossil algal globules called Chuaria occur in the Uinta Mountain Group in other areas (Hansen, 1996), no fossils are known from the Precambrian rocks in the monument. However, during this era of life's history, most organisms lacked external and internal hard parts, and thus their fossils are rare even on a global scale. Therefore, fossils of Precambrian age are unknown in the monument.

The Paleozoic-age marine rocks displayed in the Dinosaur area are also widespread in the western United States, and marine invertebrates are common in many of the formations. The major taxonomic groups that occur in these strata are summarized in Santucci (this volume) and in the STRATIGRAPHY section of this paper. Although somewhat dated, Untermann and Untermann (1954) contains the best tabulation of Paleozoic-age genera and species from the Dinosaur area.

Vertebrate Fossils in Mesozoic Rocks

The Mesozoic-age sedimentary rocks exposed in Dinosaur were deposited in a mixture of marine and terrestrial environments. As noted for the Paleozoic-age marine formations, please see Untermann and Untermann (1954) for the best tabulation of Mesozoic-age invertebrate fossils.

Early Triassic Fossils: Trackways through Time

No vertebrate fossils have been discovered in the Moenkopi Formation (Lower Triassic). However, Lockley and others (1990) reported that a few impressions that appeared to be vertebrate tracks were observed in rocks along with burrows called *Scoyenia*, an invertebrate trail that often occurs with vertebrate tracks.

As in the Moenkopi, vertebrate body fossils are rare in the Chinle Formation (Upper Triassic). However, a dermal scute and bone fragments of the crocodile-like phytosaurs and unidentified reptile teeth have been found in a few sites. In contrast to the sparse record of body fossils, vertebrate trackways are common in the Chinle. Fourteen localities have been identified and documented in the mon-

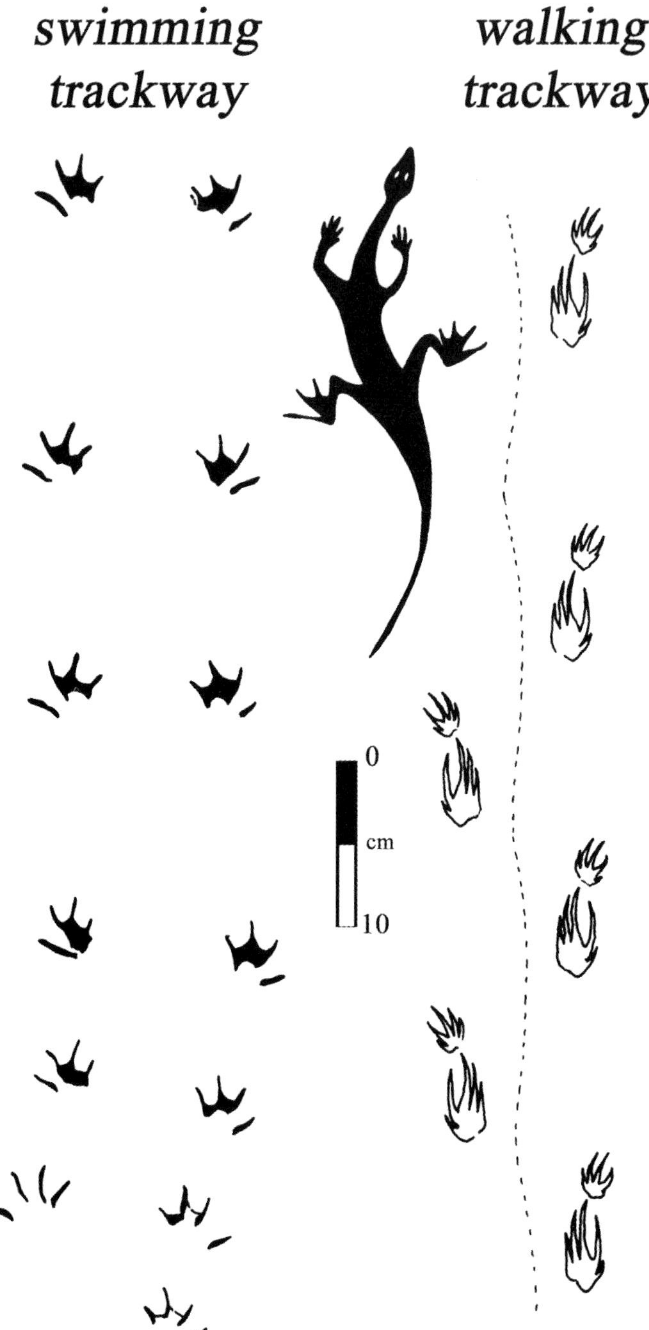

Figure 8.   Swimming and walking trackways of Gwyneddichnium *from the Late Triassic. Swimming trackway (DINO 15006) from Dinosaur National Monument, Utah. Walking trackway from Vermillion Creek area, Moffat County, Colorado. Silhouette of* Tanytrachleos, *probably trackmaker, in center. Note splayed toes and webbing in swimming trackway (from Lockley and Hunt 1995).*

ument along with several others just outside its boundaries (Lockley and others, 1992). Fossil tracks known as *Rhynchosauroides* may have originated from a lizard or a lizard-like sphenodontids. *Gwyneddichnium* (figure 8) is possibly the track of the aquatic reptile *Tanytrachelus*, and *Apatopus* may be the track of a trilophosaurian reptile. *Brachycheirotherium* probably represents the track of a quadrupedal, heavily armored aetosaur reptile. Two trackways are suggestive of phytosaurs. Dinosaurs are most likely represented by *Agialopus*, the trace of a small, bipedal animal. A single track seems to have been made by a synapsid, a group of mammal-like reptiles. Invertebrate tracks include those of horseshoe crabs (*Kouphichnium*) and conchostracans (*Isopodichnus*).

Gwyneddichnium is known from the eastern and the western United States. Many of these tracks represent an animal walking on land or along the shoreline of a lake. However, a *Gwyneddichnium* trackway in Dinosaur was made by a swimming animal (figure 8). Preserved on a ripple marked surface, the tracks indicate only contact of the hindlimbs with the sediment. The toes were splayed, and the impressions indicate a web of skin between the toes. This trackway displays the first known case of a vertebrate ichnogenus (a species group defined from fossil tracks) with a combination of both walking and swimming trackways (Lockley and others, 1992; Lockley and Hunt, 1995).

The Chinle Formation in the Dinosaur area is an excellent example of the importance of the long-neglected study of tracks and trails known as ichnology. The ichnological record from the monument documents the presence of a diverse fauna of terrestrial and semiaquatic vertebrates from the beginning of the age of dinosaurs--a story of ancient life that is virtually unknown from fossilized bones. The ancient Triassic scene is further documented by a number of multiple trackways found in sites adjacent to the monument. This wealth of fossil tracks are attributed to aetosaurs (*Brachycheirotherium* tracks), herbivorous prosauropod dinosaurs (*Tetrasauropus* and *Pseudotetrasauropus* tracks), small carnivorous dinosaurs (*Grallator* tracks), small arthropods (*Scoyenia*, Pterichnus), conchostracans (*Isopodichnus, Acripes*), beetles (*Bifurcalapes*), worms (*Cochlichnus*), and invertebrate traces of unknown origin (*Treptichnus*) (Lockley and others 1992). In addition, the track data contribute information beyond a simple list of icthno-taxa. Lockley and others (1992) and Lockley and Hunt (1995) analyzed the data to estimate the relative abundance of various members of the fauna.

Early and Middle Jurassic Fossils: More Trails through Time

Vertebrate fossils, including dinosaurs, are known from the Glen Canyon Sandstone and equivalent formations (Lower Jurassic) elsewhere in the southwestern United States, but no such remains have been found in Dinosaur. However, as in the Chinle Formation, the fossil track record provides important information on the vertebrate fauna and the age of these rocks.

Tracks have been reported from red playa lake sediments about 33 feet (11 m) above the base of the Glen Canyon Sandstone (Lockley and others, 1992). One of these tracks is attributed to *Brachycheirotherium*, an index track for a Late Triassic age (Haubold, 1986; Lockley and Hunt 1995). Although many geologists believe that the Glen Canyon is only Lower Jurassic in age, these tracks

suggest that the lower part of the sandstone may be Triassic and that the Triassic-Jurassic boundary could be within the Glen Canyon Sandstone (Lockley and others, 1992).

Tracks have been found also at six other levels in the Glen Canyon of Dinosaur, but the principal track-bearing horizons are within 50 feet (15 m) of the top of the sandstone unit. The higher sites represent a minimum of 125 trackways with exposures extending nearly 0.6 mile (1 km) along strike. The dominant track (*Otozoum*) probably indicates a prosauropod. Small- to moderate-sized carnivorous dinosaur tracks (*Anchisauripus sillimani*, and unidentified members of the *Grallator-Anchisauripus-Eubrontes* complex) also occur (Lockley and others, 1993). These tracks are generally associated with horizontally bedded, sometimes ripple marked, brown to red stained, often heavily dinoturbated units between eolian cross-bedded units. Lockley and others (1993) interpreted that the tracks were made in interdunal areas that were periodically wet and that during those wet times, dinosaurs were fairly active.

Although no vertebrate fossils have been found in the Carmel Formation (Middle Jurassic) of the monument, Lockley and others (1998) and Lockley and Hunt (1995) identified at least 60 trackways of small to medium size theropod dinosaurs (*Carmelopodous untermannorum*) and swimming traces of crocodilians from nearby Carmel exposures.

About 63 miles (100 km) to the southwest of the monument, Lockley (1991) and Lockley and Hunt (1995) documented a vast "dinosaur freeway" in the top layers of the Entrada Formation (Middle Jurassic) near Moab, Utah. The total estimated number of tracks preserved in the horizon ranges from 1 billion to 10 billion. The majority of the tracks were made by theropods. However, despite field work by Lockley and his field crews in the Dinosaur area, this Entrada trackway does not extend into the monument.

Vertebrates are almost unknown from the marine Stump Formation (Middle and Upper Jurassic) in the monument and surrounding area, except for partial remains of 3 ichthyosaurs, probably in the genus *Opthalmosaurus* (Chure, 1993).

The Real Jurassic Park: The Morrison Formation

The Late Jurassic Morrison Formation contains the most significant vertebrate fossils in Dinosaur National Monument. The areal extent of the Morrison Formation is about 40,000,000 square miles (100,000,000 km^2) in the Western Interior (Dodson and others, 1980a, 1980b). Indeed, the Morrison is among the most productive dinosaur fossil resources in the world. Even after more than 150 years of geological and paleontological exploration, the Morrison Formation continues to be a focus of study and discovery (Carpenter and others, 1998). The most exhaustive list of fauna and flora from the Morrison (table 1) is in Chure and others (1998), although new taxa have been described since then.

Table 1. Vertebrate fauna of the Morrison Formation of Dinosaur National Monument. Only the names of taxa considered valid are listed, synonyms are not included.

REPTILIA

Dinosauria
    Theropoda
        Allosaurus fragilis
        Allosaurus jinmadseni
        Ceratosaurus sp.
        Torvosaurus tanneri
        Koparion douglassi
        unnamed ?troodontid
        ?Marshosaurus bicentesimus
    Sauropoda
        Apatosaurus louisae
        Barosaurus lentus
        Camarasaurus lentus
        Diplodocus longus
    Ornithopoda
        Camptosaurus medius
        Dryosaurus altus
    Stegosauria
        Stegosaurus sp.
Crocodilia
        Goniopholis sp.
        Hoplosuchus kayi
        "Fruitachampsa" sp.
        unidentified eutrettauranosuchid
Choristodera
        Cteniogenys sp.
Lacertilia (lizards)
        Dorsetisaurus sp.
        Paramacellodus sp.
        Schilleria utahensis
Sphenodontia (lizard-like diapsid reptiles)
        Opisthias rarus

MAMMALIA

Triconodonta
        Triconolestes curvicuspis
        unidentified triconodontian
Multituberculata
        Ctenacodon laticeps
        C. serratus
        Ctenacodon n. sp.
        Glirodon grandis
        Psalodon n. sp.
Symmetrodontia
        unidentiied spalacotheriid
Dryolestoidea
        Amblotherium gracilis
        A. debilis
        Dryolestes priscus
        Herpetarius arcuatus
        Araeodon intermissus
        Euthlastus cordiformis

AMPHIBIA

Anura (frogs and toads)
        Rhadinosteus parvus
        cf. *Enneabatrachus hechti*
        unidentified ?discoglossid
        Unidentified genus and species A
        Unidentified genus and species B
Urodela (salamanders)
        Two new undescribed genera of
        slamanders

OSTEICHTHYES

Dipnoi (lungfish)
        Ceratodus guentheri
Pycndontiformes
        Unidentified pycnodontid

The Carnegie Dinosaur Quarry

The discovery of the Carnegie Quarry marks one of the most important events in the history of vertebrate paleontology. Although the history of the excavations and development of the in-situ Dinosaur Quarry exhibit have been summarized several times (Gilmore, 1924, 1936a, 1936b; White, 1964; Brown, 1937; Good and others, 1958; Colbert, 1968; McIntosh, 1977; Cooley and others, 1982; Chure and McIntosh, 1990; Mehls, 1990; Elder, 1999; Santucci, this volume), none of these publications covers the history in depth. This is unfortunate, because the holographic and photographic documentation about the quarry is particularly rich.

The number of fossil dinosaur bones recovered from the Carnegie Quarry exceeds those from any other containing Jurassic vertebrates. Although few of the skeletons belonged to new species, most specimens belonged to previously known genera and species. However, the Dinosaur Quarry fossils were (and remain to this day) the best preserved and most complete specimens known of those taxa.

Morrison Fossils Outside Dinosaur Quarry but Inside the Monument

From the 1950s through the 1980s, the emphasis of the paleontology program in the monument focused on the development of the in-situ (in place) dinosaur exhibit in that part of the Carnegie Quarry enclosed within the monument's visitor center. However, by the early 1990s, 1,500

Figure 9. The spectacular skull of a new species of <u>Allosaurus</u> (DINO 11541), collected from the Morrison Formation in the backcountry of Dinosaur National Monument.

Figure 10. Side view of the front part of the skull of the type specimen (DINO 10822) of the multituberculate mammal <u>Glirodon grandis</u> from the Morrison Formation of Dinosaur National Monument. Note that scale bar is in millimeters!

bones had been exposed in the main bone-bearing layer, and attention shifted to the rich Morrison exposures elsewhere in the monument. Several reasons influenced this shift in emphasis. First, workers had exposed most of the layer inside the visitor center. Secondly, the great abundance of fossil material from the Carnegie Quarry is biased with large vertebrates, especially dinosaurs. From a scientific, resource management, and interpretive standpoint, understanding the Upper Jurassic ecosystem of the Morrison Formation required looking at other sites that favored the preservation of the smaller contemporaries of the dinosaur. Discoveries from this change of emphasis continue through the time of this writing and show no sign of abating. Indeed, Dinosaur's small-vertebrate faunal record is as rich and diverse as that of the large dinosaurs.

New Taxa

Type specimens of several dinosaurs have been discovered: *Allosaurus jimmadseni* (Chure, 2000), *Apatosaurus louisae* (Holland, 1916), *Camarasaurus annae* (Ellinger, 1950), *Diplodocus hayi* (Holland, 1924a), *Koparion douglassi* (Chure, 1994), and *Uintasaurus douglassi* (Holland, 1924b), crocodilians: *Hoplosuchus kayi* (Gilmore, 1926), lizards: *Schilleria utahensis* (Evans and Chure, 1999), turtles: *Deinochelys whitei* (Gaffney, 1979), *Glyptops utahensis* (Gilmore, 1916), frogs: *Rhadinosteus parvus* (Henrici, 1998a), salamanders: (two new genera currently under study), and mammals: *Glirodon grandis* (figure 10; Engelmann and Callison, 1999) and *Triconolestes curvicuspis* (Engelmann and Callison, 1998).

The Dinosaur Nursery: Eggs, Embryos, and Juveniles

Although not as numerous as fossils from some sites, the monument contains a rich record of dinosaurian nestlings. Recently, Bray and Hirsch (1998) described four different types of dinosaur eggshell fragments. Chure and others (1994) described an embryo of the herbivorous dinosaur *Camptosaurus*, which represents the most complete dinosaur embryo yet found in the Jurassic rocks of North America.

The number of juvenile dinosaur fossils is greater from the Carnegie Quarry than from any other Morrison quarry: *Apatosaurus* (Berman and McIntosh, 1978), *Camarasaurus lentus* (Gilmore, 1925a), *Deinochelys whitei* (Gaffney, 1979), *Diplodocus* (Holland, 1924a), *Dryosaurus altus* (Gilmore, 1925b; Carpenter, 1994, 2000), *Glyptops plicatulus* (Gaffney, 1979), and *Stegosaurus* (Galton, 1982a, 1982b).

Skulls

Skulls rank among the rarest and most sought after dinosaur fossils. Skulls often separate from the rest of the skeleton, and the annals of vertebrate paleontology are filled with such "headless wonders." However, against these odds, 13 complete or fairly complete skulls were recovered from the Carnegie Quarry: *Allosaurus* (Madsen, 1976; 2 skulls), *Apatosaurus* (Berman and McIntosh, 1978, the first and only skull known for this genus), *Camarasaurus* (Gilmore 1925a; Madsen and others, 1995; 5 skulls), *Dryosaurus* (Gilmore, 1925b; Carpenter, 1994, 2000; 2 skulls), and *Diplodocus* (Holland, 1924a; 3 skulls). Work outside of Dinosaur Quarry also has yielded skulls of dinosaurs: *Allosaurus* (figure 9; Chure, 2000; 1 skull), sphenodonts: ?*Opisthias* (Fraser and Wu, 1998, 3 skulls under study), lizards: *Paramacellodus* (Evans and Chure, 1998a, 1998b, 1999), *Schilleria* (Evans and Chure, 1999; 1 skull of each), frogs: *Rhadinosteus parvus* (Henrici, 1998a; several skulls), salamanders: (2 skulls, under study), and mammals: *Glirodon grandis* (figure 10; Englemann and Callison, 1999; 1 skull).

Complete Skeletons

Approximately 20 skeletons from the Carnegie Quarry are complete enough to be mounted, although not all have been mounted. Skeletons from Dinosaur Quarry are on display at the Carnegie Museum of Natural History (McGinnis, 1982), Denver Museum of Natural History (Markman, 1961), United States National Museum (Gilmore, 1932), University of Nebraska at Lincoln (Griesener and others, 1976), American Museum of Natural History, and the Museum of Paleontology at the University of Michigan. The juvenile *Camarasaurus lentus* (Gilmore, 1925a) is the most complete sauropod dinosaur skeleton ever found and was the first sauropod skeleton complete enough to allow a skeletal restoration based on a single specimen. In addition to physiologic restoration, fossilized bones also relate information about dinosaurian pathology and disease. Evidently, dinosaurs suffered sickness, and sometimes those diseases left traces in their skeletons (Blumberg and Sokoloff, 1961; Moodie, 1923, 1925; Rothschild, 1990; Rothschild and Berman, 1991; Rothschild and Martin, 1992).

Paleobotany

Historically, plant fossils have been rare in the Late Jurassic Morrison Formation of Dinosaur. Although the paleontologic record of the monument's ancient flora is increasing, plant macrofossils remain poorly known, consisting of gymnosperms: *Czekanowskia* (Ash, 1994), ?*Auricarioxylon* (D.J. Chure, personal observation), and *Behuninia* short shoots (D.J. Chure, personal observation), ginkgophytes (D.J. Chure, personal observation), cycadophytes: *Carpolithus* and *Jensensispermum* (D.J. Chure, personal observation), charophytes (green algae; Schudack and others, 1998), and a wide variety of undescribed seeds. In contrast, fossil pollen and spores in the Morrison are much more abundant than plant macrofossils and provide a better understanding of the flora. However, only a preliminary analysis has been completed yet (Litwin and others, 1998).

Fossils in Cretaceous Rocks

Only recently, paleontologists have started work in the Early Cretaceous rocks of Dinosaur, but already, the fossil discoveries have been spectacular. From the Cedar Mountain Formation (Lower Cretaceous), the fragmentary remains of a small deinonychid are under study, but it is already clear that the fossil is not a juvenile *Utahraptor*. Also from the Cedar Mountain, a magnificently preserved sauropod skull, articulated with neck vertebrae, marks one of the most important sauropod fossils found anywhere in Cretaceous rocks. This specimen, currently under study, will provide important data for understanding the evolution of sauropods and the interrelationships of the various families of this group of dinosaurs. In contrast to the discoveries in the Cedar Mountain, no vertebrate fossils have been recovered yet from the Dakota Sandstone in the monument.

Although isolated fish scales are common in the Mowry Shale (Lower Cretaceous), preliminary excavations in two sites in Dinosaur have revealed shark teeth, skull material of ichthyodectiform osteichthyians, ammonites, and angiosperm leaves (Stewart and others, 1994). Additional excavations are expected to uncover more fossil remains. Although not as fossiliferous as the underlying Mowry, isolated shark teeth from the Frontier Sandstone (Upper Cretaceous) in Dinosaur have been re-trieved from ant mounds. Overlying the Frontier, the Mancos Shale is rich with invertebrate fossils. However, no vertebrate fossils have been recovered from the Mancos in the monument.

Other Reading

The REFERENCES section lists many popular articles and books about Dinosaur National Monument's paleontology and geology (Gilmore, 1936b; Hamilton, 1961; White, 1967; Hansen, 1969, 1996; Untermann and Untermann, 1969; Keller, 1973; Colbert, 1977; McIntosh, 1977; West and Chure, 1984; Averett, 1987; Chure, 1987, 1991; E.P.W., 1987; Schaffer, 1987; Chure and McIntosh, 1990; Chure and Hoops, 1997; Elder and others, 1997; Henrici, 1997; DeCourten, 1998; Santucci, this volume;).

ACKNOWLEDGEMENTS

The summary of the geology in and around Dinosaur National Monument leans heavily on the quality work of many geologists, especially Wallace R. Hansen and his colleagues from the U.S. Geological Survey. Earlier geologists who contributed significantly to our knowledge of Dinosaur's geology include John Wesley Powell and Earl Douglass as well as G.E. and B.P. Untermann, whose contributions still assist with understanding the area's geology and paleontology today. Special thanks are extended to Wallace Hansen, Steve Fryer, Vince Santucci, and Elizabeth Rockwell for their timely reviews and comments that made this paper more accurate, informative, and understandable. Steve Fryer digitized the geologic units for the map in figure 2.

REFERENCES

Armstrong, F.C., and Oriel, S.S., 1986, Tectonic development of the Idaho-Wyoming thrust belt, *in* Peterson, J.A., editor, Paleotectonics and sedimentation in the Rocky Mountain region, United States: American Association of Petroleum Geologists Memoir 41, p. 240-279.

Ash, S.R., 1994, First occurrence of *Czekanowskia* (Gymnospermae, Czekanowskiales) in the United States: Review of Palaeobotany and Palynology, v. 81, p. 129-140.

Averett, W.R., 1987, Paleontology and geology of the Dinosaur Triangle: Museum of Western Colorado Field-trip Guidebook, 162 p.

Berg, R.R., 1962, Mountain flank thrusting in Rocky Mountain foreland, Wyoming and Colorado: American Association of Petroleum Geologists Bulletin, v. 46, no. 11, p. 2019-2032.

Bilbey, S.A., 1973, Petrology and geochemistry of the Morrison Formation, Dinosaur Quarry quadrangle, Utah: Logan, Utah State University, M.S. thesis, 103 p.

—1992, Stratigraphy and sedimentary petrology of the Upper Jurassic - Lower Cretaceous rocks at Cleveland-

Lloyd Dinosaur Quarry with a comparison to the Dinosaur National Monument Quarry, Utah: Salt Lake City, University of Utah, Ph.D. dissertation, 295 p.

Bilbey, S.A., Kerns, R.L., and Bowman, J.T., 1974, Petrology of the Morrison Formation, Dinosaur Quarry quadrangle, Utah: Utah Geological and Mineral Survey, Special Studies 48, 15 p.

Bissell, H.J., 1964, Lithology and petrography of the Weber Formation in Utah and Colorado, *in* Sabatka, E.F., editor, Guidebook to the geology and mineral resources of the Uinta Basin, Utah's hydrocarbon storehouse: 13th Annual Field Conference, Intermountain Association Petroleum Geologists, p. 68-91.

Bissell, H.J., and Childs, O.E., 1958, The Weber Formation of Utah and Colorado, *in* Curtis, Bruce, and Wamer, H.L., editors, Symposium on Pennsylvanian rocks of Colorado and adjacent areas: Rocky Mountain Association of Geologists, p. 26-30.

Blumberg, B.S., and Sokoloff, L., 1961, Coalescence of caudal vertebrae in the giant dinosaur *Diplodocus:* Arthritis and Rheumatism, v. 4, p. 592-601.

Bowman, S.A., Bowman, J.T., and Drake, R.E., 1986, Interpretation of the Morrison Formation as a time-transgressive unit [abs.]: Fourth North American Paleontological Convention, Programs with Abstracts, p. A5.

Bradley, M.D., and Bruhn, R.L., 1988, Structural interactions between the Uinta arch and the overthrust belt, north-central Utah; implications of strain trajectories and displacement modeling, *in* Schmidt, C.J. and Perry, W.J., Jr., editors, Interaction of the Rocky Mountain foreland and the Cordilleran thrust belt: Geological Society of America Memoir 171, p. 431-445.

Bray, E., and Hirsch, K.F., 1998, Eggshell from the Upper Jurassic Morrison Formation, *in* Carpenter, K., Chure, D.J., and Kirkland, J.I., editors, The Morrison Formation—an interdisciplinary approach: Modern Geology, v. 23, nos. 1-4, p. 219-240.

Britt, B.B., 1987, The major characters of *Torvosaurus* and a report of its occurrence at Dinosaur National Monument: Journal of Vertebrate Paleontology, v. 7 (supplement to no. 3), p. 12A.

Brown, B., 1937, Dinosaurs on parade: Natural History, v. 40, p. 505-513.

Brown, W.G., 1988, Deformational style of Laramide uplifts in the Wyoming foreland, *in* Schmidt, C.J. and Perry, W.J., Jr., editors, Interaction of the Rocky Mountain foreland and the Cordilleran thrust belt: Geological Society of America Memoir 171, p. 1-26.

Bryant, Bruce, and Nichols, D.J., 1988, Late Mesozoic and early Tertiary reactivation of an ancient crustal boundary along the Uinta trend and its interaction with the Sever orogenic belt, *in* Schmidt, C.J., and Perry, W.J., Jr., editors, Interaction of the Rocky Mountain foreland and the Cordilleran thrust belt: Geological Society of America Memoir 171, p. 411-430.

Carpenter, K., 1994, Baby *Dryosaurus* from the Upper Jurassic Morrison Formation of Dinosaur National Monument, *in* Carpenter, K., Hirsch, K.F., and Horner, J.R., editors, dinosaur eggs and babies: New York City, Cambridge University Press, p. 287-297.

—2000, Eggs, nests, and baby dinosaurs—a look at dinosaur reproduction: Indiana University Press, 336 p.

Carpenter, K., Chure, D.J., and Kirkland, J.I., editors, 1998, The Upper Jurassic Morrison Formation—an interdisciplinary study: Modern Geology, v. 23, nos. 1-4, pt. I, 533 p., part II, 537 p.

Chapin, C.E., and Cather, S.M., 1983, Eocene tectonics and sedimentation in the Colorado Plateau - Rocky Mountain area, *in* Lowell, J.D., editor, Rocky Mountain foreland basins and uplifts: Rocky Mountain Association of Geologists Guidebook, p. 33-56.

Chure, D.J., 1987, Dinosaur National Monument: a window on the past, *in* Averett, W.R., editor, Geology and paleontology of the Dinosaur Triangle: Grand Junction, Museum of Western Colorado, p. 75-77.

—1991, Dinosaur National Monument — an educational resource: Cultural Resources Management Bulletin, National Park Service, v. 14, no. 3, p. 1, 3, 7.

—1992a, The flora and non-dinosaurian fauna of the Morrison Formation: how rare is it? [abs.]: Geological Society of America, Abstracts with Programs, v. 24, no. 6, p. 5.

—1992b, Lepidosaurian reptiles from the Brushy Basin Member of the Morrison Formation (Upper Jurassic) of Dinosaur National Monument, Utah and Colorado, USA: Journal of Vertebrate Paleontology, v. 12, supplement to no. 3, p. 24A.

—1993, The first record of ichthyosaurs from Utah: Brigham Young University Geology Studies, v. 39, p. 65-69.

—1994, *Koparion douglassi*, a new dinosaur from the Morrison Formation (Upper Jurassic) of Dinosaur National Monument; the oldest troodontid (Theropoda: Maniraptora): Brigham Young University Geology Studies, v. 40, pt. 1, p. 11-15.

—2000, A new species of *Allosaurus* from the Morrison Formation, Dinosaur National Monument (UT-CO) and a revision of the Theropod Family Allosauridae: New York City, Columbia University, Ph.D. dissertation, 1200 p.

— in press 2000a, The wrist of *Allosaurus* (Saurischia: Theropoda), with observations on the carpus in theropods—the origin of birds: New Haven, Yale University Press.

— in press 2000b, On the orbit of theropod dinosaurs: Gaia, Special Volume on Aspects of Theropod Paleobiology, Lisbon, Portugal.

Chure, D.J., Britt, B.B., and Madsen, J.H., 1997, A new specimen of *Marshosaurus bicentesimus* (Theropoda) from the Morrison Formation (Late Jurassic) of Dinosaur National Monument: Journal of Vertebrate Paleontology, v. 17, supplement to no. 3, p. 38A.

Chure, D.J., Carpenter, K., Litwin, R.J., Hasiotis, S.T., and Evanoff, Emmett, 1998, The flora and fauna of the

Morrison Formation, *in* Carpenter, K., Chure, D.J., and Kirkland, J.I., editors, The Upper Jurassic Morrison Formation—an interdisciplinary study: Modern Geology, v. 24, nos. 1-4, p. 507-537.

Chure, D.J., and Engelmann, G.F., 1989, The fauna of the Morrison Formation in Dinosaur National Monument, *in* Flynn, J.J., editor, Mesozoic/Cenozoic vertebrate paleontology—classic localities, contemporary approaches: 28th International Geological Congress, Field Trip Guidebook T322, p. 8-14.

Chure, D.J., Engelmann, G.F., and Madsen, S.K., 1989, Non-mammalian microvertebrates from the Morrison Formation (Upper Jurassic, Kimmeridgian) of Dinosaur National Monument, Utah-Colorado, USA: Journal of Vertebrate Paleontology, v. 9, supplement to no. 3, p. 16A-17A.

Chure, D.J., and Hoops, H.H., 1997, Clones, bones, and interpretive groans, interpreting dinosaurs in the face of an entertainment megahit, *in* Johnston, M., and McChristal, J., editors, Partners in paleontology—protecting our fossil heritage: Proceedings of the Fourth Conference of Fossil Resources, Natural Resources Report NPS/NRFLFO/NRR-97/01, National Park Service, Denver, p. 46-49.

Chure, D.J., Kirkland, J.I., and Sheetz, R.D., 1993, Embryos, hatchlings, juveniles, and adults of the ornithopod dinosaur *Dryosaurus* from the Late Jurassic Morrison Formation: Journal of Vertebrate Paleontology, v. 13, supplement to no. 3, p. 29A-30A.

Chure, D.J., Madsen, J.H., and Britt, B.B., 1993, New data of theropod dinosaurs from the late Jurassic Morrison Formation: Journal of Vertebrate Paleontology, v. 3, supplement to no. 3, 30A.

Chure, D. J., and McIntosh, J.S., 1990, Stranger in a strange land: a brief history of the paleontological operations at Dinosaur National Monument: Earth Sciences History, v. 9, no. 1, p. 34-40.

Chure, D.J., Turner, C.E., and Peterson, Fred, 1994, An embryo of *Camptosaurus* from the Brushy Basin Member (Early to Middle Tithonian) of the Morrison Formation in Dinosaur National Monument, *in* Carpenter, K., Hirsch, K.F., and Horner, J.R., editors, Dinosaur eggs and babies: New York City, Cambridge University Press, p. 298-311

Colbert, E.H., 1968, Men and dinosaurs: Dutton, New York, 283 p. (reprinted: 1984 The Great Dinosaur Hunters and Their Discoveries: Dover Press).

Colbert, E.H., 1977, The year of the dinosaur: New York, Charles Scribner's Sons, 171 p.

Cole, R.D., 1987, Cretaceous rocks of the Dinosaur Triangle, *in* Averett, W.R., editor, Paleontology and geology of the Dinosaur Triangle: Museum of Western Colorado Guidebook, p. 21-35.

Condie, K.C., 1982, Plate-tectonics model for Proterozoic continental accretion in the southwestern United States: Geology, v. 10, p. 37-42.

Constenius, K.N., and Mueller, R.E., 1996, The Uinta allochthon—an element of the Sevier thrust belt? [abs.]: Geological Society of America Annual Convention, Abstracts with Programs, v. 28, no. 7.

Cooley, E.L., Dye, D.L., and Ward, N.W., 1982, Register of the papers of Earl Douglass (1862-1931): Register 27, Manuscripts Collection (MS 196), Special Collections Department, University of Utah Libraries, Salt Lake City, Utah, 111 p.

Cullins, H.L., 1968, Geologic map of the Banty Point quadrangle, Rio Blanco County, Colorado: U.S. Geological Survey Geologic Quadrangle Map GQ-703, scale 1:24,000.

—1969, Geologic map of the Mellen Hill quadrangle, Rio Blanco and Moffat Counties, Colorado: U.S. Geological Survey Geologic Quadrangle Map GQ-835, scale 1:24,000.

—1971, Geologic map of the Rangely quadrangle, Rio Blanco and Moffat Counties, Colorado: U.S. Geological Survey Geologic Quadrangle Map GQ-903, scale 1:24,000.

DeCourten, F., 1998, Dinosaurs of Utah: Salt Lake City, University of Utah Press, 300 p.

Dickinson, W.R., Klute, M.A., Hayes, M.J., Janecke, S.U., Lundin, E.R., McKittrick, M.A., and Olivares, M.D., 1988, Paleogeographic and paleotectonic setting of Laramide sedimentary basins in the central Rocky Mountain region: Geological Society of America Bulletin, v. 100, p. 1023-1039.

Dodson, P., Behrensmeyer, A.K., and Bakker, R.T., 1980a, Taphonomy of the Morrison Formation (Kimmeridgian-Portlandian) and Cloverly Formation (Aptian-Albian) of the western United States: Memoires de la Societe geologique de France (N.S.), v. 59, no. 139, p. 87-94.

Dodson, P., Behrensmeyer, A.K., Bakker, R.T., and McIntosh, J.S., 1980b, Taphonomy and paleoecology of the dinosaur beds of the Jurassic Morrison Formation: Paleobiology, v. 6, no. 2, p. 208-232.

Dyni, J.R., 1968, Geologic map of the Elk Springs quadrangle, Moffat County, Colorado: U.S. Geological Survey Geologic Quadrangle Map GQ-702, scale 1:62,500.

Elder, A.S., 1999, The history of Dinosaur National Monument's Douglass Quarry—the Park Service years, *in* Gillette, D.D., editor, Vertebrate paleontology in Utah: Utah Geological Survey Miscellaneous Publication 99-1, p. 71-76.

Elder, A.S., Madsen, S.K., and Chure, D.J., 1997, Yes Virginia, you can do large scale excavation in a National Park, with spectacular result, *in* Johnston, M., and McChristal, J., editors, Partners in paleontology—protecting our fossil heritage: Proceedings of the Fourth Conference of Fossil Resources, Natural Resources Report NPS/NRFLFO/NRR-97/01, Natural Resource Information Division, National Park Service, Denver, p. 58-61.

Ellinger, T.U.H., 1950, *Camarasaurus annae* — a new American sauropod dinosaur: American Naturalist, v. 84, p.

225-228.

Engelmann, G.F., and Callison, George, 1998, Mammalian faunas of the Morrison Formation, *in* Carpenter, K., Chure, D.J., and Kirkland, J.I., editors, The Morrison Symposium: An Interdisciplinary Approach: Modern Geology v. 23, no. 1-4, p. 343-380.

—1999, *Glirodon grandis*, a new multituberculate mammal from the Upper Jurassic Morrison Formation, *in* Gillette, D.D., editor, Vertebrate Paleontology in Utah: Utah Geological Survey, Miscellaneous Publication 99-1, p.163-177.

Engelmann, G.F., and Chure, D.J., 1992, Diversity and distribution of fossil vertebrates in the Jurassic Morrison Formation of Dinosaur National Monument [abs.]: Geological Society of America, Abstracts with Programs, v. 24, no. 6, p. 9.

Engelmann, G.F., Chure, D.J., and Madsen, S.K., 1989, A mammalian fauna from the Jurassic Morrison Formation of Dinosaur National Monument: Journal of Vertebrate Paleontology, v. 9, supplement to no. 3, p. 19A.

Engelmann, G.F., Greenwald, N.S., Callison, George, and Chure, D.J., 1990, Cranial and dental morphology of a Late Jurassic multituberculate mammal from the Morrison Formation: Journal of Vertebrate Paleontology, v. 10, supplement to no. 3, p. 22A.

E.P.W., 1987, On the duplication of dinosaurs: Rubber Development v. 40, no. 2, p. 32-35

Erslev, E.A., 1993, Laramide basement tectonics, *in* Schmidt, C.J., Chase, R.B. and Erslev, E.A., editors, Laramide basement deformation in the Rocky Mountain foreland of the western United States: Geological Society of America Special Paper 280, p. 339-358.

Evans, S.E., and Chure, D.J., 1998a, Morrison lizards: structure, relationships, and biogeography, *in* Carpenter, K., Chure, D.J., and Kirkland, J.I., editors, The Upper Jurassic Morrison Formation—an interdisciplinary study: Modern Geology, v. 24, no. 1-4, p. 35-48.

—1998b, Paramacellodid lizard skulls from the Jurassic Morrison Formation at Dinosaur National Monument, Utah: Journal of Vertebrate Paleontology, v. 18, no. 1, p. 99-114.

—1999, Upper Jurassic lizards from the Morrison Formation of Dinosaur National Monument, UT, *in* Gillette, D.D., editor, Vertebrate paleontology in Utah: Utah Geological Survey Miscellaneous Publication 99-1, p. 151-159.

Fiorillo, A.R., 1994, Time resolution at Carnegie Quarry (Morrison Formation: Dinosaur National Monument) —implications for dinosaur paleobiology: University of Wyoming Contributions to Geology, v. 30, p. 149-156.

Fraser, N.C., and Wu, X.-C., 1998, Sphenodontians from the Brushy Basin Member, *in* Carpenter, K., Chure, D.J., and Kirkland, J.I., editors, The Morrison symposium—an interdisciplinary approach: Modern Geology, v. 23, no. 1-4, p. 17-34.

Gaffney, E.S., 1979, The Jurassic turtles of North America: Bulletin of the American Museum of Natural History, v. 162, p. 91-135.

Galton, P.M., 1977a, The ornithopod dinosaur *Dryosaurus* and a Laurasia-Gondwanaland connection in the Upper Jurassic: Nature, v. 268, p. 230-232.

—1977b, The Upper Jurassic dinosaur *Dryosaurus* and a Laurasia-Gondwanaland connection: Milwaukee Public Museum Special Publication in Biology and Geology, no. 2, p. 41-54.

—1982a, A juvenile stegosaurian dinosaur *"Astrodon pusillus"* from the Upper Jurassic of Portugal, with comments on Upper Jurassic and Lower Cretaceous biogeography: Journal of Vertebrate Paleontology, v. 1, no. 3/4, p. 245-256 (for 1981).

—1982b, Juveniles of the stegosaurian dinosaur *Stegosaurus* from the Upper Jurassic of North America: Journal of Vertebrate Paleontology, v. 2, no. 1, p. 47-62.

Galton, P.M., and Jensen, J.A., 1973a, Small bones of the hypsilophodontid dinosaur *Dryosaurus altus* from the Upper Jurassic of Colorado: Great Basin Naturalist, v. 33, no. 2, p. 129-132.

—1973b, Skeleton of a hypsilophodontid dinosaur (*Nanosaurus rex*) from the Upper Jurassic of Utah: Brigham Young University Geology Studies, v. 2, part 4, p. 137-157

Gilmore, C.W., 1916, Description of a new species of tortoise from the Jurassic of Utah: Annals of the Carnegie Museum, v. X, p. 7-12, plates I-II.

—1924, Expedition to the Dinosaur National Monument: Smithsonian Miscellaneous Collection, v. LXXVI, p. 12-16.

—1925a, A nearly complete articulated skeleton of Camarasaurus, a saurischian dinosaur from the Dinosaur National Monument, Utah: Memoirs of the Carnegie Museum, v. X, no. 3, p. 347-384, plates XIII-XVII.

—1925b, Osteology of ornithopodous dinosaurs from the Dinosaur National Monument, Utah: Memoirs of the Carnegie Museum, v. X, p. 385-409.

—1926, A new aetosaurian reptile from the Morrison Formation of Utah: Annals of the Carnegie Museum, v. XVI, no. 2, p. 326-342, plate XXVII.

—1932, On a newly mounted skeleton of *Diplodocus* in the United States National Museum: Proceedings of the United States National Museum, Article 18, 21 p.

—1936a, Osteology of *Apatosaurus* with special reference to specimens in the Carnegie Museum: Memoirs of the Carnegie Museum, v. XI, p. 175-300.

—1936b, The great dinosaurs of the Carnegie Museum: Section of Vertebrate Paleontology, Pamphlet no. 2, 14 p.

Good, J.M., White, T.E., and Stucker, G., 1958, The Dinosaur Quarry: National Park Service, Washington, D.C., 47 p.

Gregson, J.D., 1994, North-northwest shortening across Laramide structures in the southeastern Uinta Mountains, Colorado and Utah: Colorado State University, M.S. thesis, 147 p.

Gregson, J.D., and Erslev, E.A., 1994, Heterogeneous Laramide deformation in Rocky Mountain foreland arches [abs.]: American Association of Petroleum Geologists Annual Convention Official Program, v. 3, p. 158.

—1996; Heterogeneous Laramide deformation in the Uinta Mountains, Colorado and Utah [abs.]: Geological Society of America Annual Convention, Abstracts with Programs, v. 28, no. 7.

—1997, Heterogeneous Laramide deformation in the Uinta Mountains, Colorado and Utah, *in* Hoak, T.E., Blomquist, P.K., and Klawitter, A.L., editors, Fractured reservoirs—characterization and modeling: Rocky Mountain Association of Geologists Guidebook, p. 137-154.

Gries, Robbie 1983, North-south compression of Rocky Mountain foreland structures, *in* Lowell, J.D., editor, Rocky Mountain foreland basins and uplifts: Rocky Mountain Association of Geologists Guidebook, p. 9-32.

Hamilton, D.L., 1961, Dinosaur National Monument — a unique, in-pace exhibit: Museum News, v. 39, no. 6, p. 20-23.

Hamilton, W.B., 1988, Laramide crustal shortening, *in* Schmidt, C.J. and Perry, W.J., Jr., editors, Interaction of the Rocky Mountain foreland and the Cordilleran thrust belt: Geological Society of America Memoir 171, p. 27-39.

Hansen, W.R., 1955, Geology of the Flaming Gorge quadrangle, Utah-Wyoming: U.S. Geological Survey Geologic Quadrangle Map GQ-75, scale 1:24,000.

—1957, Structural features of the Uinta arch (Colorado-Utah): Intermountain Association of Petroleum Geologists Guidebook, 8th Annual Field Conference, p. 48-52.

—1965, Geology of the Flaming Gorge area, Utah-Colorado-Wyoming: U.S. Geological Survey Professional Paper 490, 196 p.

—1969, The geologic story of the Uinta Mountains: U.S. Geological Survey Bulletin 1291, 144 p.

—1977a, Geologic map of the Jones Hole quadrangle, Uintah County, Utah, and Moffat County, Colorado: U.S. Geological Survey Geologic Quadrangle Map GQ-1401, scale 1:24,000.

—1977b, Geologic map of the Canyon of Lodore South quadrangle, Moffat County, Colorado: U.S. Geological Survey Geologic Quadrangle Map GQ-1403, scale 1:24,000.

—1978, Geologic map of the Zenobia Peak quadrangle, Moffat County, Colorado: U.S. Geological Survey Geologic Quadrangle Map GQ-1408, scale 1:24,000.

—1986a, Neogene tectonics and geomorphology of the eastern Uinta Mountains in Utah, Colorado, and Wyoming: U.S. Geological Survey Professional Paper 1356, 78 p.

—1986b, History of faulting in the eastern Uinta Mountains, Colorado and Utah, *in* Stone, D.S., editor, New interpretations of northwest Colorado geology: Rocky Mountain Association of Geologists, p. 229-246.

—1996, Dinosaur's restless rivers and craggy canyon walls: Vernal, Dinosaur Nature Association, 103 p.

Hansen, W.R., and Carrara, P.E., 1980, Geologic Map of the Tanks Peak quadrangle, Moffat County, Colorado: U.S. Geological Survey Geologic Quadrangle Map GQ-1534, scale 1:24,000.

Hansen, W.R., Carrara, P.E., and Rowley, P.D., 1980, Geologic map of the Haystack Rock quadrangle, Moffat County, Colorado: U.S. Geological Survey Geologic Quadrangle Map GQ-1535, scale 1:24,000.

—1981, Geologic map of the Crouse Reservoir quadrangle, Uintah and Daggett Counties, Utah: U.S. Geological Survey Geologic Quadrangle Map GQ-1554, scale 1:24,000.

—1982, Geologic map of the Canyon of Lodore North quadrangle, Moffat County, Colorado: U.S. Geological Survey Geologic Quadrangle Map GQ-1568, scale 1:24,000.

Hansen, W.R., and Rowley, P.D., 1980a, Geologic map of the Hells Canyon quadrangle, Moffat County, Colorado: U.S. Geological Survey Geologic Quadrangle Map GQ-1536, scale 1:24,000.

—1980b, Geologic map of the Stuntz Reservoir quadrangle, Utah-Colorado: U.S. Geological Survey Geologic Quadrangle Map GQ-1530, scale 1:24,000.

—1991, Geologic map of the Hoy Mountain quadrangle, Daggett and Uintah Counties, Utah and Moffat County, Colorado: U.S. Geological Survey Geologic Quadrangle Map GQ-1695, scale 1:24,000.

Hansen, W.R., Rowley, P.D., and Carrara, P.E., 1983, Geologic map of Dinosaur National Monument and vicinity, Utah and Colorado: U.S. Geological Survey Miscellaneous Investigations Series Map I-1407, scale 1:50,000.

Haubold, H., 1986, Archosaur footprints at the terrestrial Triassic-Jurassic transition, *in* Padian, K., editor, The beginning of the age of dinosaurs: Cambridge University Press, p. 189-201.

Henrici, A.C., 1997, The frog fauna from the Late Jurassic Morrison Formation at the Rainbow Park Microsite, Utah: Journal of Vertebrate Paleontology, v. 17, supplement to no. 3, p. 52A.

—1998a, A new pipoid anuran from the Late Jurassic Morrison Formation at Dinosaur National Monument, Utah: Journal of Vertebrate Paleontology, v. 18, no. 2, p. 321-332.

—1998b, New anurans from the Rainbow Park microsite, Dinosaur National Monument, *in* Carpenter, K., Chure, D.J., and Kirkland, J.I., editors, The Upper Jurassic Morrison Formation—an interdisciplinary study: Modern Geology, v. 23, no. 1-4, p. 1-16.

Hills, F.A., and Houston, R.S., 1979, Early Proterozoic tectonics of the central Rocky Mountains, North America: University of Wyoming Contributions to Geology, v. 17, no. 2, p. 89-109.

Hintze, L.F., 1988, Geologic history of Utah: Brigham Young University Geology Studies, Special Publication 7, 202 p.

Holland, J.W., 1915, Heads and tails—a few notes relating to sauropod dinosaurs: Annals of the Carnegie Museum, v. IX, p. 273-278.

—1916, Skeletons of *Diplodocus* and *Apatosaurus* in the Carnegie Museum of Natural History: Geological Society of America Bulletin, v. 38, p. 153.

—1924a, The skull of *Diplodocus:* Memoirs of the Carnegie Museum, v. IX, p. 379-403.

—1924b, Description of the type of *Uintasaurus douglassi:* Annals of the Carnegie Museum, v. XV, p. 119-138.

Hubert, J.F., and Chure, D.J., 1992, Taphonomy of an *Allosaurus* quarry in deposits of a late Jurassic braided river with a gravel-sand bedload, Salt Wash Member of the Morrison Formation, Dinosaur National Monument, Utah, *in* Wilson, J.R., editor, Field guide to geologic excursions in Utah and adjacent areas of Nevada, Idaho, and Wyoming: Geological Society of America, Rocky Mountain Region Section, Utah Geological Survey Miscellaneous Publication 92-3, p. 373-382.

—1995, From bone tissue to fossil bone in Jurassic dinosaurs at Dinosaur National Monument [abs.]: Geological Society of America, Northeastern Section, Abstracts with Programs, p. 56.

Hubert, J.F., Panish, P.T., Chure, D.J., and Prostak, K.S., 1996, Chemistry, microstructure, petrology, and diagenetic model of Jurassic dinosaur bones, Dinosaur National Monument, Utah: Journal of Sedimentary Research, v. 66, no. 3, p. 531-547.

Johnson, R.C., and Finn, T.M., 1986, Cretaceous through Holocene history of the Douglas Creek arch, Colorado and Utah, *in* Stone, D.S., editor, New interpretations of northwest Colorado geology: Rocky Mountain Association of Geologists, p. 77-96.

Jones, R., McDonald, G.H., and Chure, D.J., 1998a, Hot horses and topless theropods—using radiological surveying to locate subsurface Jurassic to Pliocene fossil vertebrates: Journal of Vertebrate Paleontology, v. 18, supplement to no. 3, p. 54A.

—1998b, Using radiological surveying instruments to locate subsurface fossil vertebrate remains, *in* Martin, J.E., Hogenson, J.W., and Benton, Rachel, editors, Partners preserving our past, preserving our future: Dakoterra, Museum of Geology, South Dakota School of Mines; v. 5, p. 84-90.

Jones, R., and Chure, D.J., in press [2000], The recapitation of a Late Jurassic theropod dinosaur—successful application of radiological surveying for locating subsurface fossilized bone: Gaia, Special Volume on Aspects of Theropod Paleobiology.

Kinney, D.M., 1951, Geology of the Uinta River and Brush Creek-Diamond Mountain areas, Duchesne and Uintah Counties, Utah: U.S. Geological Survey Oil and Gas Investigations Map OM-123, scale 1:63,360.

—1955, Geology of the Uinta River-Brush Creek area, Duchesne and Uintah Counties, Utah: U.S. Geological Survey Bulletin 1007, 185 p.

Kluth, C.F., 1986, Plate tectonics of the Ancestral Rocky Mountains, *in* Peterson, J.A., editor, Paleotectonics and sedimentation in the Rocky Mountain region, United States: American Association of Petroleum Geologists Memoir 41, p. 353-369.

Kowallis, B.J., 1986, Fission track dating of bentonites and bentonitic mudstones from the Morrison Formation, Utah and Colorado: Fourth North American Paleontological Convention, Boulder, Colorado, p. A26.

Kowallis, B.J., Christiansen, E.H., and Deino, A.L. 1991, Age of the Brushy Basin Member of the Morrison Formation, Colorado Plateau, western USA: Cretaceous Research v. 12, p. 483-493.

Kowallis, B.J., Christiansen, E.H., Deino, A.L., Peterson, Fred, Turner, C.E., Obradovich, J.D., and Kunk, M., 1998, The age of the Morrison Formation, Utah and Colorado, *in* Carpenter, K., Chure, D.J., and Kirkland, J.I., editors, The Morrison symposium—an interdisciplinary approach: Modern Geology, v. 22, no. 1-4, p. 235-260.

Laws, R., Hasiotis, S.T., Fiorillo, A.R., Chure, D.J., Breithaupt, B.H., and Horner, J.R., 1996, The demise of a Jurassic dinosaur after death — three cheers for the dermestid beetle [abs.]: Geological Society of America Annual Meeting, Abstracts with Programs, p. A299.

Litwin, R.J., Turner, C.E., and Peterson, Fred, 1998, Palynological evidence on the age of the Morrison Formation, Western Interior U.S., *in* Carpenter, K., Chure, D.J., and Kirkland, J.I., editors, The Morrison symposium—an interdisciplinary approach: Modern Geology, v. 22, no. 1-4, p. 297-320.

Lockley, M.G., 1991, The Moab megatracksite: a preliminary description and discussion of millions of Middle Jurassic tracks in eastern Utah, *in* Averett, W.R., editor, Paleontology and geology of the Dinosaur Triangle: Grand Junction, Museum of Western Colorado, p. 59-65.

Lockley, M.G., Conrad, K.L., Paquette, Marc, and Hamblin, A.L., 1992, Late Triassic vertebrate tracks in the Dinosaur National Monument area, *in* Wilson, J.R, editor, Field guide to geologic excursions in Utah and adjacent areas of Nevada, Idaho, and Wyoming: Geological Society of America, Rocky Mountain Region Section, Utah Geological Survey, Miscellaneous Publication 92-3, p. 383-391.

Lockley, M.G., Conrad, K.L., Paquette, Marc, Greben, R., Forney, G., and Farlow, J.O., 1993, Distribution and significance of Mesozoic vertebrate trace fossils in Dinosaur National Monument: Second Annual Report (for period July 1, 1991-June 30 1992) to Dinosaur National Monument (Contract # CA-1463-5-001), 21 p.

Lockley, M.G., Fleming, R.F., and Conrad, K.L., 1990, Distribution and significance of Mesozoic vertebrate trace fossils in Dinosaur National Monument: First Semi-Annual Report to National Park Service, Contract

PX1200-0-C809.

Lockley, M.G., and Hunt, A.P., 1995, Dinosaur tracks and other fossil footprints of the Western United States: New York City, Columbia University Press, 338 pp.

Lockley, M.G., Hunt, A.P., Paquette, Marc, Bilbey, S.A., and Hamblin, A.L., 1998, Dinosaur tracks from the Carmel Formation, northeastern Utah—implications for Middle Jurassic paleoecology: Ichnos, v. 5, p. 255-267.

Lowell, J.D., 1983, Foreland deformation, *in* J.D, Lowell, editor, Rocky Mountain foreland basins and uplifts: Rocky Mountain Association of Geologists Guidebook, p. 1-8.

Madsen, J.H., 1976, *Allosaurus fragilis*—a revised osteology: Utah Geological and Mineral Survey Bulletin 109, 163 p.

Madsen, J.H., McIntosh, J.S., and Berman, D.S., 1995, Skull and atlas-axis complex of the Upper Jurassic sauropod *Camarasaurus* Cope (Reptilia: Saurischia): Bulletin of the Carnegie Museum of Natural History, v. 31, 115 p.

Markman, H.C., 1961, Fossils: a story of rocks and their record of prehistoric life: Fourth Edition, Denver, Denver Museum of Natural History, 96 p.

Maughan, E.K., 1979, Petroleum source rock evaluation of the Permian Park City Group in the northeastern Great Basin, Utah, Nevada, and Idaho, *in* Newman, G.W. and Goode, H.D., editors, Basin and Range Symposium: Rocky Mountain Association of Geologists - Utah Geological Association, p. 523-530.

McGinnis, H., 1982, Carnegie's Dinosaurs: Carnegie Museum of Natural History, 119 p.

McIntosh, J.S., 1977, Dinosaur National Monument: Phoenix, Constellation Press, 40 p.

—1981, Annotated catalogue of the dinosaurs (Reptilia: Archosauria) in the collections of the Carnegie Museum of Natural History: Bulletin of the Carnegie Museum of Natural History, no. 18, 67 p.

—1990a, Species determination in sauropod dinosaurs with tentative suggestions for their classification, *in* Carpenter, K. and Currie, P.J., editors, Dinosaur systematics—approaches and perspectives: Cambridge University Press, p. 53-69.

—1990b, Sauropoda, *in* Weishampel, D.B., Dodson, P., and Osmolska, H., editors, 1990, The Dinosauria: University of California Press, 733 p.

McIntosh, J.S. and Berman, D.S., 1975, Description of the palate and lower jaw of *Diplodocus* (Reptilia: Saurischia) with remarks on the nature of the skull of *Apatosaurus:* Journal of Paleontology, v. 49, no. 1, p. 187-199.

McKay, E.J., 1974, Geologic map of the Lone Mountain quadrangle, Moffat County, Colorado: U.S. Geological Survey Geologic Quadrangle Map GQ-1144, scale 1:62,500.

McKay, E.J. and Bergin, M.J., 1974, Geologic map of the Maybell quadrangle, Moffat County, Colorado: U.S. Geological Survey Geologic Quadrangle Map GQ-1145, scale 1:62,500.

Mehls, S.F., 1990, Dinosaur National Monument: a study of the evolution of private sector - public sector support of science in the West: Forest and Conservation History, v. 34. no. 2, p. 76-81.

Molzer, P.C., and Erslev, E.A., 1995, Oblique convergence during northeast-southwest Laramide compression along the east-west Owl Creek and Casper Mountain arches, central Wyoming: American Association of Petroleum Geologists Bulletin, v. 79, no. 9, p. 1377-1394.

Moodie, R.L., 1923, Paleopathology: Urbana, University of Illinois Press, 567 p.

—1925, The Antiquity of Disease: University of Chicago Science Series, 147 p.

Morel, J.A., Bursk, P.H., and Dlouhy, D.L., 1986, An interpretation of the subsurface structural style of the Beaver Creek Anticline, Moffat and Routt Counties, Colorado, *in* Stone, D.S., editor, New interpretations of northwest Colorado geology: Rocky Mountain Association of Geologists Guidebook, p. 195-202.

Pagnac, D., and Chure, D.J., 1997, Rare sauropod elements from the Carnegie Quarry (Morrison Formation) Dinosaur National Monument: Journal of Vertebrate Paleontology, v. 17, supplement to no. 3, p. 68A.

Perry, W.J., Jr., Nichols, D.J., Dyman, T.S., and Haley, C.J., 1992, Sequential Laramide deformation of the Rocky Mountain foreland of southwestern Montana, Wyoming, and north-central Colorado: U.S. Geological Survey Bulletin 2012, 14 p.

Peterson, Fred, and Turner, C.E., 1998, Stratigraphy of the Ralston Creek Formations and Morrison Formations (Upper Jurassic) near Denver, Colorado, *in* Carpenter, K., Chure, D.J., and Kirkland, J.I., editors, 1998, The Morrison symposium—an interdisciplinary approach: Modern Geology, v. 22, nos. 1-4, p. 3-38.

Peterson, J.A., and Smith, D.L., 1986, Rocky Mountain paleogeography through geologic time, *in* Peterson, J.A., editor, Paleotectonics and sedimentation in the Rocky Mountain Region, United States: American Association of Petroleum Geologists Memori 41, p. 3-19.

Powell, J.W., 1876, Report on the geology of the eastern portion of the Uinta Mountains and a region of country adjacent thereto: U.S. Geological and Geophysical Survey of the Territories (Powell), 218 p.

—1895 (1961), The exploration of the Colorado River and its canyons (original title: Canyons of the Colorado): Reprinted and excerpted by Dover Publications (Flood and Vincent), New York, 400 p.

Powers, R.B., editor, 1983, Geologic studies of the Cordilleran thrust belt: Rocky Mountain Association of Geologists Guidebook, 976 p., 22 plates.

—1986, The Willow Creek fault, eastern Uinta Mountains—geologic analysis of a foreland subthrust play, *in* Stone, D.S., editor, New interpretations of northwest Colorado geology: Rocky Mountain Association of Geologists Guidebook, p. 183-190.

Richard, J.J., 1986, Interpretation of a seismic section across the Danforth Hills Anticline (Maudlin Gulch) and

Axial arch in northwest Colorado, *in* Stone, D.S., editor, New interpretations of northwest Colorado geology: Rocky Mountain Association of Geologists Guidebook, p. 191-195.

Rittman, Alfred, 1952, Nomenclature of volcanic rocks—proposed for the use in the catalogue of volcanoes, and the key-tables for the determination of volcanic rocks: Bulletin Volcanologique, series 2, v. 12, p.75-102.

Ritzma, H.R., 1969, Tectonic resume, Uinta Mountains, *in* Lindsey, J.B., editor, Geologic guidebook of the Uinta Mountains: Intermountain Association of Geologists, p. 57-63.

—1971, Faulting on the north flank of the Uinta Mountains, Utah and Colorado, *in* Renfro, A.R., editor, Wyoming tectonics symposium, 23rd Field Conference, Wyoming Geological Association, p. 145-150.

Rothschild, B.M., 1990, Radiologic assessment of osteoarthritis in Dinosaur: Annals of the Carnegie Museum, v. 59, no. 4, p. 295-301.

Rothschild, B.M., and Berman, D.S., 1991, Fusion of caudal vertebrae in Late Jurassic sauropods: Journal of Vertebrate Paleontology, v. 11, no. 1, p. 29-26.

Rothschild, B.M., and Martin, L.D., 1992, Paleopathology: Disease in the fossil record: Ann Arbor, CRC Press, 386 p.

Rowley, P.D., Dyni, J.R., Hansen, W.R., and Pipiringos, G.N., 1979, Geologic map of the Indian Water Canyon quadrangle, Moffat County, Colorado: U.S. Geological Survey Geologic Quadrangle Map GQ-1516, scale 1:24,000.

Rowley, P.D., and Hansen, W.R., 1979a, Geologic map of the Plug Hat Rock quadrangle, Moffat County, Colorado: U.S. Geological Survey Geologic Quadrangle Map GQ-1514, scale 1:24,000.

—1979b, Geologic map of the Split Mountain quadrangle, Uintah County, Utah: U.S. Geological Survey Geologic Quadrangle Map GQ-1515, scale 1:24,000.

Rowley, P.D., Hansen, W.R., and Carrara, P.E., 1981, Geologic map of the Island Park quadrangle, Uintah County, Utah: U.S. Geological Survey Geologic Quadrangle Map GQ-1560, scale 1:24,000.

Rowley, P.D., Hansen, W.R., Tweto, Ogden, and Carrara, P.E., 1985, Geologic map of the Vernal 1° X 2° quadrangle, Colorado, Utah, and Wyoming: U.S. Geological Survey Map Miscellaneous Investigations Series I-1526, scale 1:250,000.

Rowley, P.D., Kinney, D.M., and Hansen, W.R., 1979, Geologic map of the Dinosaur Quarry quadrangle, Uintah County, Utah: U.S. Geological Survey Geologic Quadrangle Map GQ-1513, scale 1:24,000.

Sales, J.K., 1968, Crustal mechanics of Cordilleran foreland deformation—a regional and scale model approach: American Association of Petroleum Geologists Bulletin, v. 52, no. 10, p. 2016-2044.

—1969, Regional tectonic setting and mechanics of origin of the Uinta Uplift, *in* Lindsey, J.B., editor, Geologic guidebook of the Uinta Mountains: Intermountain Association of Geologists, p. 65-78.

—1971, Structure of the northern margin of the Green River Basin, Wyoming, *in* Renfro, A.R., editor, Wyoming tectonics symposium, 23rd Field Conference, Wyoming Geological Association, p. 85-102.

Schaffer, Ann, 1987, Dinosaur National Monument: paleontology in the public eye, *in* Averett, W.R., editor, Paleontology and geology of the Dinosaur Triangle: Grand Junction, Museum of Western Colorado, p. 115-118.

Schudack, M., Turner, C.E., and Peterson, Fred, 1998, Biostratigraphy, paleoecology, and biogeography of charophytes and ostracodes from the Upper Jurassic Morrison Formation, Western Interior, USA, *in* Carpenter, K., Chure, D.J., and Kirkland, J.I., editors, The Morrison Formation—an interdisciplinary approach: Modern Geology, v. 22, nos. 1-4, p. 379-414.

Sears, J.W., Graff, P.J., and Holden, G.S., 1982, Tectonic evolution of lower Proterozoic rocks, Uinta Mountains, Utah and Colorado: Geological Society of America Bulletin, v. 93, p. 990-997.

Stearns, D.W., 1971, Mechanisms of drape folding in the Wyoming Province, *in* Renfro, A.R., editor, Wyoming tectonics symposium: 23rd Field Conference, Wyoming Geological Association, p. 125-143.

Stewart, J.D., Bilbey, S.A., Chure, D.J., and Madsen, S.K., 1994, Vertebrate fauna of the Mowry Shale (Cenomanien) in northeastern Utah: Journal of Vertebrate Paleontology, v. 14, supplement to no. 3, p. 47A.

Stokes, W.L., 1986, Geology of Utah: Utah Museum of Natural History, Occasional Paper Number 6, 280 p.

Stone, D.S., 1975, A dynamic analysis of subsurface structure in northwestern Colorado, *in* Bolyard, D.W., editor, Deep drilling frontiers of the central Rocky Mountains, Rocky Mountain Association of Geologists Guidebook, p. 33-40.

—editor, 1986a, New interpretations of northwest Colorado geology: Rocky Mountain Association of Geologists Guidebook.

—1986b, Seismic and borehole evidence for important pre-Laramide faulting along the Axial arch in northwest Colorado, *in* Stone, D.S., editor, New interpretations of northwest Colorado geology: Rocky Mountain Association of Geologists Guidebook, p. 19-36.

—1986c, Geology of the Wilson Creek Field, Rio Blanco County, Colorado, *in* Stone, D.S., editor, New interpretations of northwest Colorado geology: Rocky Mountain Association of Geologists Guidebook, p. 229-246.

—1993a, Tectonic evolution of the Uinta Mountains: palinspastic restoration of a structural cross section along longitude 109° 15′, Utah: Utah Geological Survey Miscellaneous Publication 93-8, 19 p., 3 plates.

—1993b, Basement-involved thrust-generated folds as seismically imaged in the subsurface of the Rocky Mountain foreland, *in* Schmidt, C.J., Chase, R.B., and Erslev, E.A., editors, 1993, Laramide basement deformation in the Rocky Mountain foreland of the western

United States: Geological Society of America Special Paper 280, p. 271-317.

Turner, C.E., and Peterson, Fred, 1993, Fluvial sedimentology of the Carnegie Quarry, Upper Jurassic Morrison Formation, Dinosaur National Monument, Utah: Journal of Vertebrate Paleontology, v.13, supplement to no. 3, p. 60A.

—1998, The Morrison Formation extinct ecosystems project—final report: National Park Service/United States Geological Survey Interagency Agreement No. 1443-IA-1200-94-003, 594 p.

Turner, C.E., Peterson, Fred, and Chure, D.J., 1997, Upper Jurassic Morrison Formation at Dinosaur National Monument, Utah and Colorado—the geologic setting for vertebrate paleontological resources, *in* Johnston, M., and McChristal, J., editors, 1997, Partners in paleontology—protecting our fossil heritage: Proceedings of the Fourth Conference of Fossil Resources, Natural Resources Report NPS/NRFLFO/NRR-97/01, National Park Service, p. 186-188.

U.S. Geological Survey, 1959-1973, Geology of the Permian rocks in the western phosphate field: U.S. Geological Survey Professional Paper 313 (in parts A-F by several authors).

U.S. Geological Survey, 1999, GEOLEX - The National Geologic Map Database Geologic Names Lexicon: http://ngmdb.usgs.gov/Geolex/geolex_home.html.

Untermann, G.E., and Untermann, B.R., 1954, Geology of Dinosaur National Monument and vicinity, Utah-Colorado: Utah Geological and Mineralogical Survey Bulletin 42, 227 p.

—1965, Geologic map of the Dinosaur National Monument, Colorado-Utah: Dinosaur Nature Association - Utah Geological and Mineralogical Survey Map no. 22, scale 1:62,500.

—1968, Geology of Uintah County: Utah Geological and Mineralogical Survey Bulletin, 72, 98 p.

—1969a, A popular guide to the geology of Dinosaur National Monument: Jensen, Dinosaur Nature Association, 126 p.

—1969b, Geology of the Uinta Mountain Area, Utah-Colorado, *in* Lindsey, J.B., editor, Geologic guidebook of the Uinta Mountains: Intermountain Association of Geologists, p. 79-86.

West, Linda, and Chure, D.J., 1984, Dinosaur—the Dinosaur National Monument Quarry: Jensen, Dinosaur Nature Association, 40 p.

White, T.E., 1958, The braincase of *Camarasaurus lentus*: Journal of Paleontology, v.32, no. 3, p. 477-494.

—1964, The Dinosaur Quarry, *in* Sabatka, E.F., editor, 1964, Guidebook to the geology and mineral resources of the Uinta Basin: Intermountain Association of Petroleum Geologists, Eighth Annual Field Conference, p. 21-28.

—1967, Dinosaurs at home: New York City, Vantage Press, 232 p.

Geology of Utah's Parks and Monuments
2000 Utah Geological Association Publication 28
D.A. Sprinkel, T.C. Chidsey, Jr., and P.B. Anderson, editors

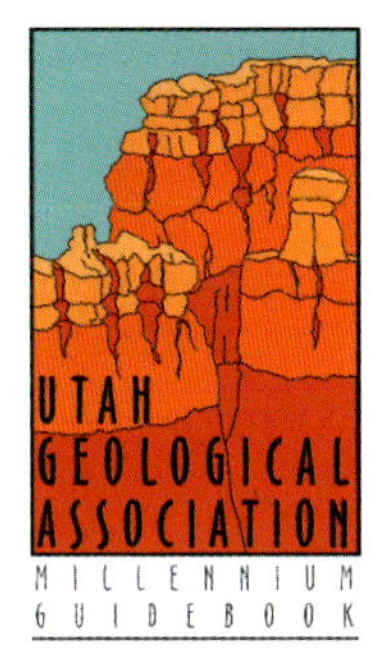

Geology of Grand Staircase-Escalante National Monument, Utah

Hellmut H. Doelling[1], Robert E. Blackett[1], Alden H. Hamblin[2], J. Douglas Powell[3], and Gayle L. Pollock[4]

ABSTRACT

The 1.9-million-acre Grand Staircase-Escalante National Monument was created September 18, 1996 by President Clinton and was the first national monument to be placed under the management of the U.S. Bureau of Land Management. Located in southern Utah, the monument contains an array of geological, paleontological, historic, archaeological, and biological resources. It lies in a remote area comprised of canyons, plateaus, mesas, and cliffs set in an environment of colorful geologic formations.

The monument is surrounded by several national and state parks, a primitive area, and a national recreation area. It can be divided into three geographical sections: from west to east these are the Grand Staircase, Kaiparowits Basin, and Escalante Canyons sections. Rock formations exposed in these sections range in age from Permian to Cretaceous comprising more than 200 million years of Earth's history. Structurally, these rocks dip gently northward, and are deformed by mostly north-south-trending faults, anticlines, synclines, and monoclines.

The monument area contains known coal, oil and gas, and mineral resources and potential resources which are generally undeveloped because market areas are distant and because ways of transporting the commodities out of the region have never been in place. As a national monument, the area will provide many future opportunities to study a region of remarkably well-exposed geology.

INTRODUCTION

Grand Staircase-Escalante National Monument was established by presidential proclamation on September 18, 1996 to protect an array of geological, paleontological, historic, archaeological, and biological resources. Following the creation of the monument, Congress passed the Utah Schools and Land Exchange Act, which transferred ownership of all trust lands administered by the Utah School and Institutional Trust Lands Administration (SITLA) (176,699 acres) and trust mineral interests (24,000) acres within the monument boundaries, to the Federal Government. In exchange for these interests, and other lands and interests within national parks and monuments in Utah, the State of Utah received title to federal lands elsewhere, mineral royalties from other federal lands in Utah, and a one-time cash payment. It is the first national monument managed by the U.S. Bureau of Land Management (BLM), incorporating the principles of the Federal Land Policy and Management Act (FLPMA). The proclamation governs how the provisions of FLPMA will be applied within the monument. FLPMA directs the BLM to manage public land on the basis of multiple use and in a manner that will protect the quality of scientific, scenic, historic, ecological, environmental, air and atmospheric, water resources, and archaeological resources (U.S. Department of Interior, 2000).

The monument covers about 1.9 million acres of land in south-central Utah (figure 1). About 68 percent of the monument is in Kane County, while the remaining 32 percent is in Garfield County. Conversely, about 49 percent of Kane County and 18 percent of Garfield County lie within the monument boundaries. The monument is primarily surrounded on three sides by national forest and national park lands, as well as other BLM administered lands to the south and west. Kodachrome State Park also adjoins the monument near Cannonville. For more information on monument management and use restrictions, the reader should refer to the approved management plan (U.S. Department of Interior, 2000)

[1]*Utah Geological Survey, Salt Lake City, UT 84114-6100*
[2]*Fremont Indian State Park and Museum, Sevier, UT 84766*
[3]*Grand Staircase-Escalante National Monument, Kanab, UT 84741*
[4]*Bryce Canyon National History Association, Bryce Canyon National Park, UT 84717-0002*

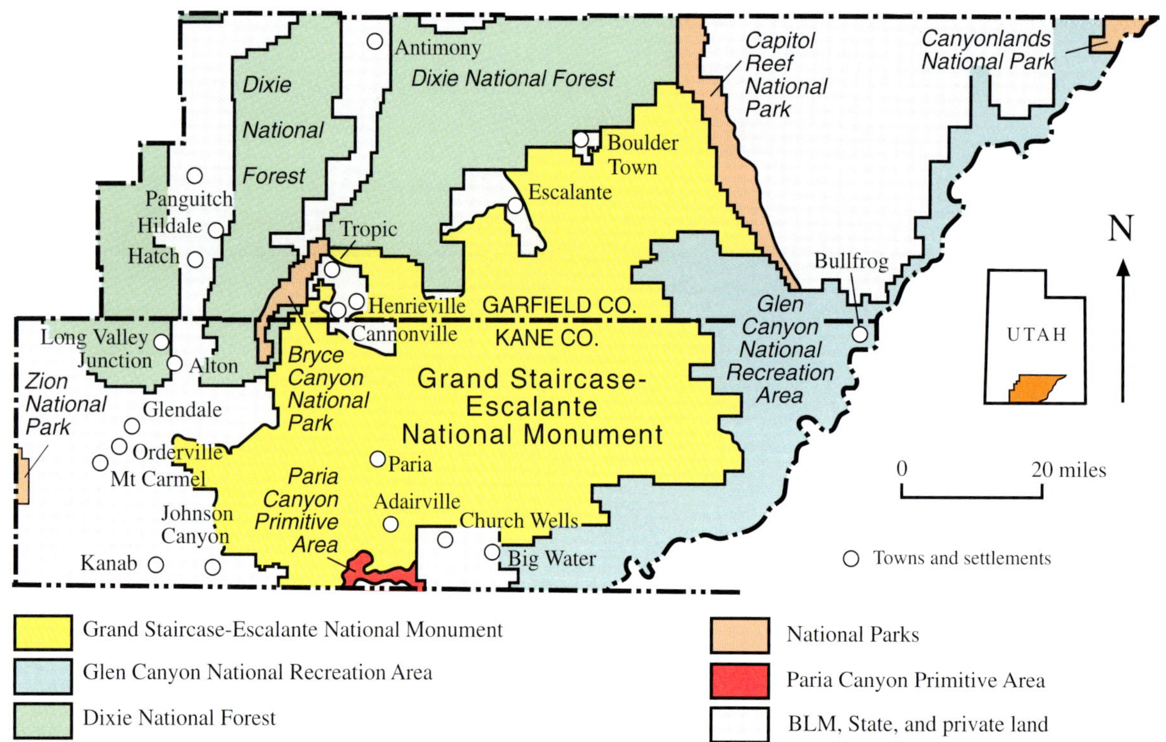

Figure 1. Index map for Grand Staircase-Escalante National Monument in Garfield and Kane Counties, Utah. The 1.9-million-acre monument is encircled by national parks, a national recreation area, a primitive area, and a national forest. Four state parks, Coral Pink Sand Dunes, Kodachrome, Escalante Petrified Forest, and Anasazi Indian Village State Parks are also in the area, west of Kanab, near Cannonville, near Escalante, and near Boulder Town, respectively.

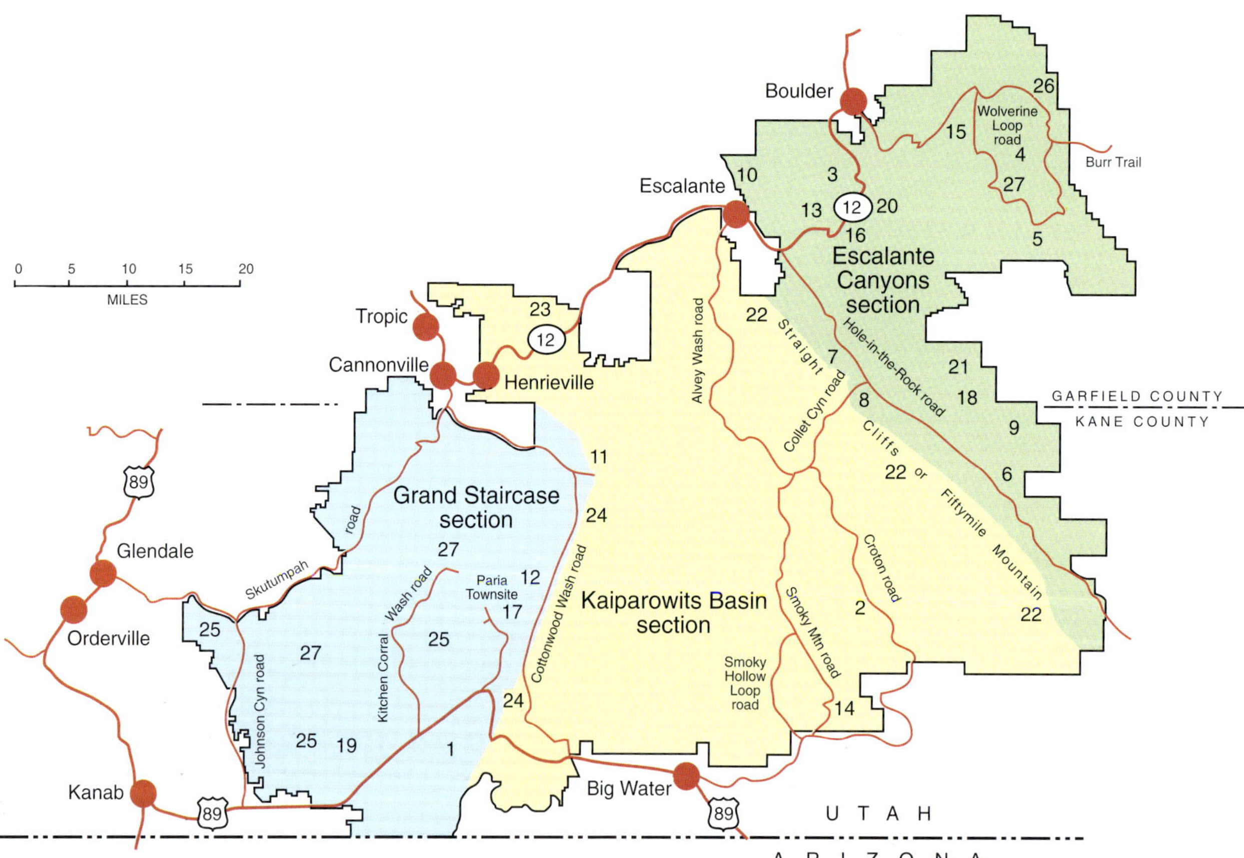

Figure 2. Map showing the locations of the classic geologic sites (numbers) within Grand Staircase-Escalante National Monument in southern Utah. See text for descriptions of these sites. Also, the Grand Staircase section is shown in blue, the Kaiparowits Basin section in yellow, and the Escalante Canyons section in green.

GEOGRAPHY

Grand Staircase-Escalante National Monument is located within the Colorado Plateau physiographic province, near its western margin. It is bordered by the gateway communities of Boulder, Escalante, Henrieville, Cannonville, Tropic, Glendale, Kanab, and Big Water (figures 1 and 2). Annual precipitation in the region varies from about six inches at the lowest altitudes near Lake Powell (4,000 ft), to about 25 inches at the highest altitudes near Canaan Peak (9,280 ft). The variations in altitude and precipitation produce three climatic zones: upland, semi-desert, and desert. At the highest altitudes, precipitation falls primarily during the winter. The majority of precipitation in the semi-desert and desert areas occurs during the summer months.

The monument may be divided into three broad areas: from west to east these are the Grand Staircase, Kaiparowits Basin, and Escalante Canyons sections (figure 2). **The Grand Staircase section** is a broad feature that encompasses the western third of the monument, and consists of a series of topographic benches and cliffs that, as its name implies, step progressively up in elevation from south to north. The risers correspond to cliffs and the steps correspond to the benches, terraces, or plateaus in the staircase (figure 3). The bottom of the staircase commences at the top of the Kaibab uplift, which correlates with and is in the same stratigraphic position as the highest bench of the Grand Canyon in Arizona. The first riser above this bench is the Chocolate Cliffs, which are not well developed in the Grand Staircase section and consists of the Upper Red Member of the Lower Triassic Moenkopi Formation capped by the Upper Triassic Shinarump Member of the Chinle Formation. Descriptions of these formations are given in the stratigraphy section of this paper. Discontinuous Shinarump outcrops explain why this riser is not well developed in the monument. The next step is known as the Shinarump Flats. This bench is mostly developed on top of the hard Shinarump Member and the overlying soft Petrified Forest Member of the Chinle Formation. The Vermilion Cliffs form the next riser, which is well developed in the monument. The cliffs are made up of the resistant red sandstone beds of the Lower Jurassic Moenave and Kayenta Formations. The Wygaret Terrace forms the next step and includes the soft upper part of the Kayenta and the lower parts of the Lower Jurassic Navajo Sandstone. The imposing White Cliffs form the next riser and consist of the upper part of the Navajo Sandstone and the Middle Jurassic Co-op Creek Limestone Member of the Carmel Formation. The bench on this riser is the Skutumpah Terrace built on the remaining soft parts of the Carmel Formation and the overlying Entrada Sandstone. The Gray Cliffs are a series of low cliffs formed by hard Cretaceous sandstone beds. Several benches have formed between these cliffs in the softer shales and sandstones of the Tropic, Straight Cliffs, Wahweap, and Kaiparowits Formations. The final riser, mostly north and west of the monument, in Dixie National Forest and Bryce Canyon National Park, is formed by the Pink Cliffs. The Pink Cliffs consist of lower Tertiary limestones and marls that are sculpted into the beautiful natural features found in Bryce Canyon. The cliffs culminate as the Paunsaugunt Plateau, which is the uppermost bench or step of the Grand Staircase.

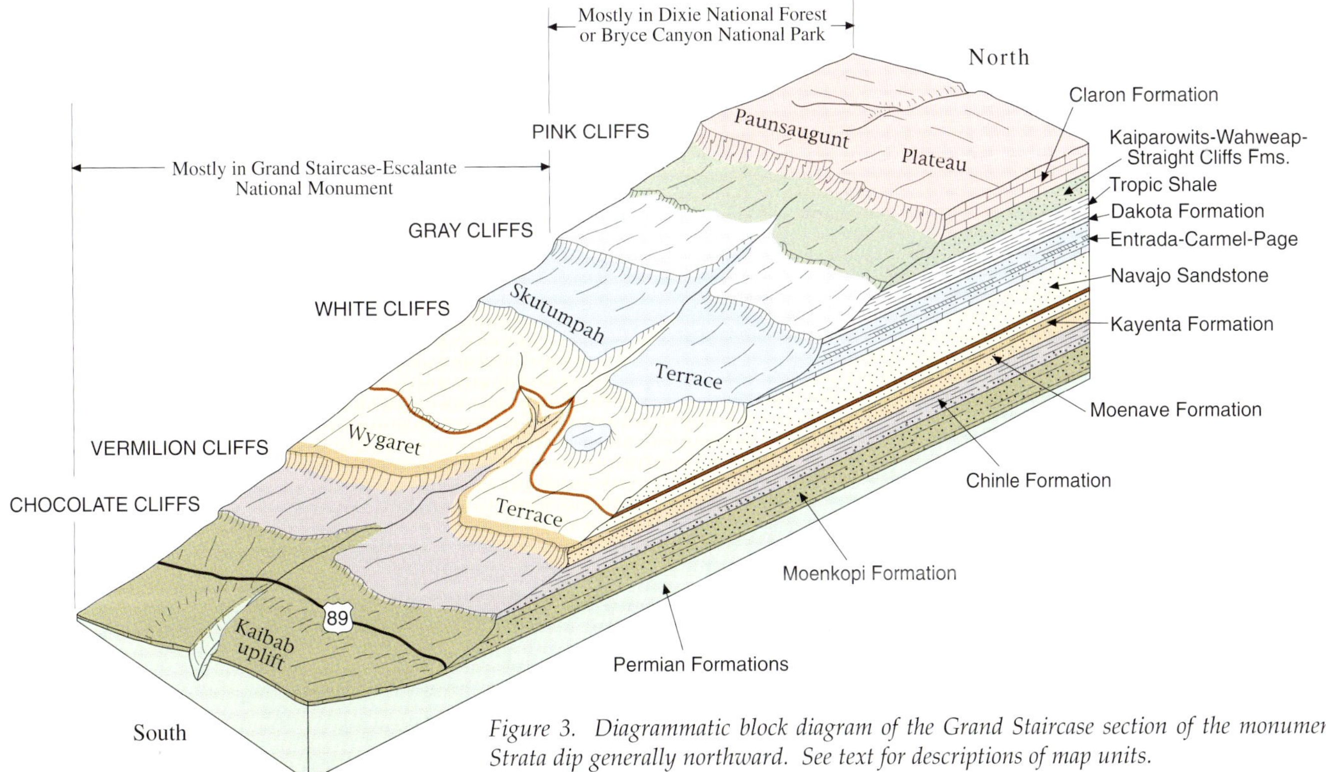

Figure 3. Diagrammatic block diagram of the Grand Staircase section of the monument. Strata dip generally northward. See text for descriptions of map units.

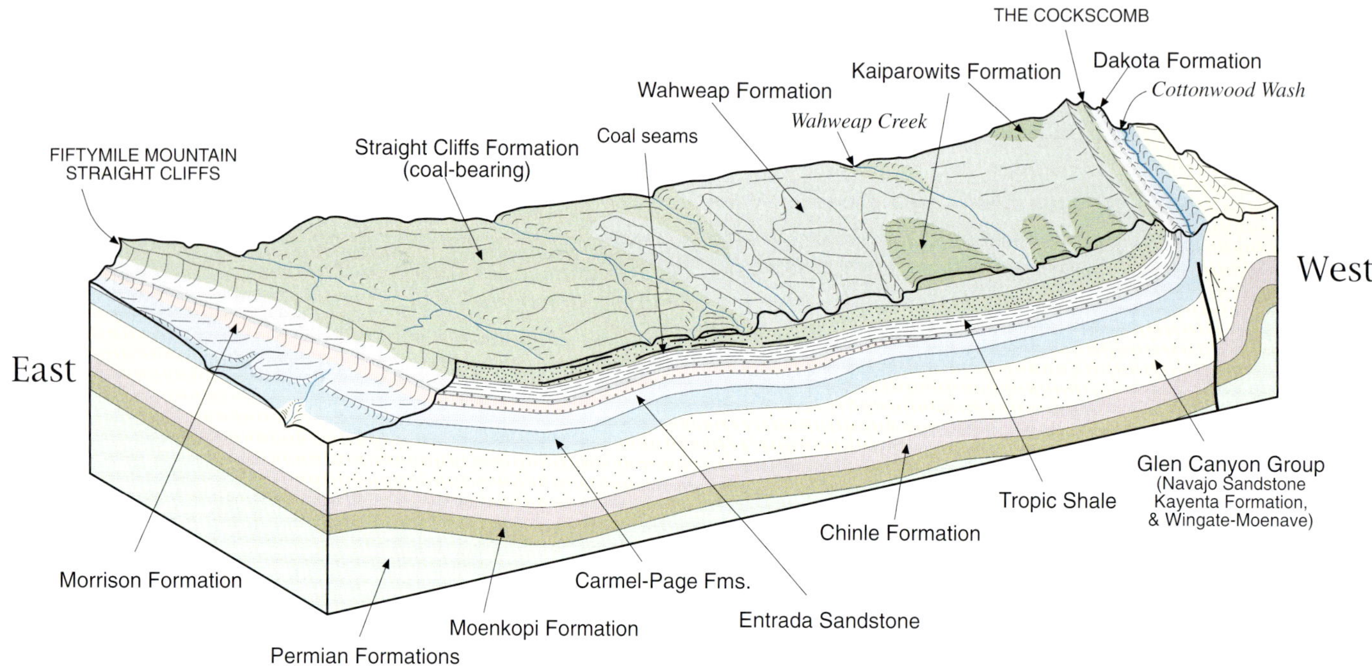

Figure 4. Diagrammatic block diagram and east-west cross section across the Kaiparowits Basin section of the monument. View is from the north looking south. The deepest part of the basin is aligned north-south along Wahweap Creek. The strata dip generally northward, but north-south-trending anticlines and synclines warp the block. The Straight Cliffs mark the east boundary and the Cockscomb marks the west boundary of the section.

The boundary between the Grand Staircase and Kaiparowits Basin sections is The Cockscomb, a series of hogbacks along the East Kaibab monocline, where strata are folded sharply downward to the east. The Cockscomb trends approximately N. 20° E. from the Arizona border to Grosvenor Arch (No. 11 on figure 2) as a sharp fold in the strata. Dips diminish and become more gentle as the trend wraps northwesterly north of the towns of Henrieville, Cannonville, and Tropic. The character of rocks stratigraphically higher than the Tropic Shale is like that in most of the Kaiparowits Basin section and should be considered a part of that section.

The Kaiparowits Basin section is centrally situated in the monument and is mostly exemplified by the Kaiparowits Plateau. Doelling and Davis (1989) described this section as "a series of plateaus, buttes, and mesas carved in Cretaceous rocks that reflect the structures of the underlying geologic strata." The Kaiparowits Basin covers about 1,650 square miles in the central part of the monument (figure 4). The feature is a broad structural basin; however, the topographic expression is that of a northward-tilted, highly dissected plateau that has been modified by generally north-south-trending folds. The Aquarius and Table Cliff plateaus lie northward and topographically above the Kaiparowits Plateau.

The Kaiparowits Plateau is bounded by the base of the Cretaceous strata (Hettinger and others, 1996) or the base of the Dakota Formation. The Straight Cliffs form a prominent escarpment that rises 1,100 feet or more and extends for more than 50 miles northwest to southeast above the Dakota and Tropic Formations. The cliffs roughly mark

the plateau's east boundary with the Escalante Canyons section of the monument. Some Jurassic strata are exposed in the Kaiparowits Basin section of the monument, along its southern boundary, below the Cretaceous cliffs. These Jurassic rocks have a "Canyonlands" character and, indeed, make up the canyonlands above Glen Canyon of the Colorado River.

The Escalante Canyons section provides a web of multi-hued, steep, narrow canyons and "slickrock," sculpted in the drainage basin of the Escalante River (figure 5). The section is bounded on the southwest by the Straight Cliffs, on the north by the Aquarius Plateau and Boulder Mountain, on the east by the Waterpocket Fold, and on the south by Glen Canyon of the Colorado River. The Escalante Canyons section can be subdivided into two landscapes based on physiography: Escalante canyons and benchlands, and the Circle Cliffs uplift. The latter is a large doubly plunging anticline, the core of which is eroded into a large kidney-shaped physiographic basin surrounded by the imposing vertical cliffs of the Wingate Sandstone.

CLASSIC GEOLOGIC SITES WITHIN THE MONUMENT

This 1.9-million-acre monument in colorful southern Utah undoubtedly has thousands of sites to excite not only professionals in geology, archaeology, botany, zoology, and paleontology, but also any visitor with an eye for the unusual and beautiful features of nature. Nowhere else in the world are the rocks and geologic features so well ex-

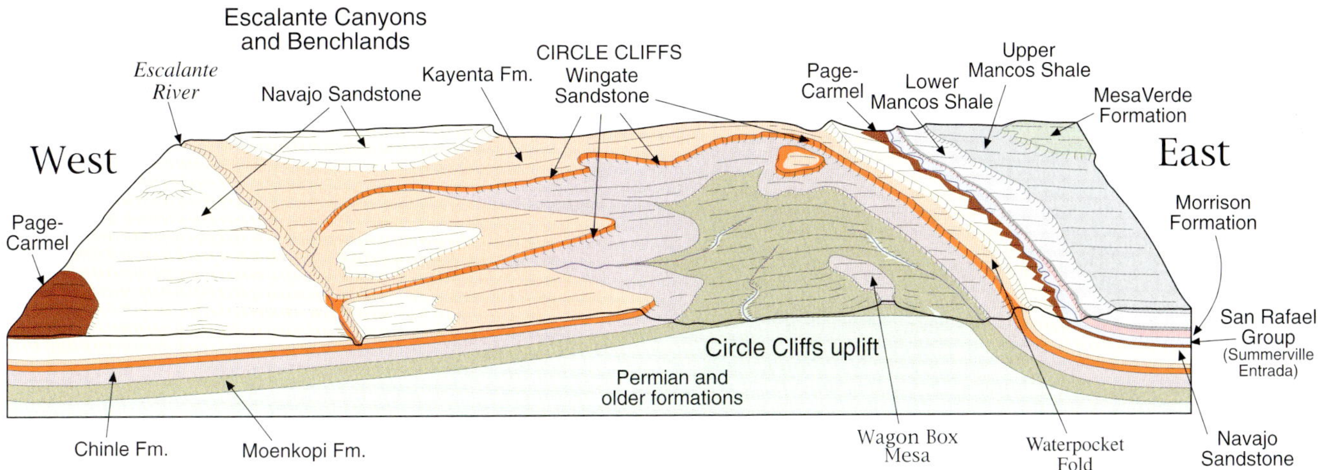

Figure 5. Diagrammatic block diagram across the Escalante Canyons section of the monument. This section consists of two parts. To the west are Glen Canyon Group bench and canyonlands incised by the Escalante River and its tributaries. To the east is the Circle Cliffs uplift, a large doubly plunging, north-south-trending anticline that exposes a fossil oil field in its core. The steeply dipping Waterpocket Fold makes up the east boundary of the uplift and is in Capitol Reef National Park.

posed, so brilliantly colored, and so excitingly displayed. The area is large enough to allow for many new discoveries to be made; certainly to allow for rediscoveries and re-evaluations of geologic features, processes, and theories, whether in the scale of the microscopic or in scales of the vast panoramas that will unfold before you. In an area of this size, not all classic sites can be mentioned because of space constraints. The list below is small compared to what is available for those who will leave their autos, ATVs, and bicycles behind, and venture into the back-country on their own.

The approximate locations of the following classic geologic sites are shown by number on figure 2. They are alphabetically arranged below. Larger scale maps, available from local monument/BLM offices and at the Utah Geological Survey offices in Salt Lake City, will help guide you to these features.

Access descriptions given here are general, and some roads may not be open to the public. Visitors will need to check with Grand Staircase-Escalante National Monument offices, contact stations, and visitor centers in local communities to verify available access routes to these sites.

1. **Buckskin Gulch and the Kaibab uplift**: Buckskin Gulch, a continuation of Kitchen Corral Wash, forms a deep gash through Buckskin Mountain at the north end of the Kaibab uplift in the Grand Staircase section of the monument (figure 6). This gash exposes the oldest rocks (Permian) of the monument: (ascending) the Hermit Shale, Coconino Sandstone, Toroweap Formation, and Kaibab Limestone. The Early Triassic Timpoweap Member of the Moenkopi Formation forms a carapace on top of this section which appears as a "whaleback" from U.S. Highway 89. U.S. Highway 89 makes a loop around the uplift, avoiding the inclines of Buckskin Mountain. Access to the top of the deep gash is provided by following a side road (high-centered vehicles only) off the House Rock Valley

Figure 6. Aerial view of Kaibab Gulch with the Vermilion and White Cliffs in the background. Kaibab Gulch is a cut through Buckskin Mountain and exposes the oldest (Permian) rocks in the Grand Staircase section of the monument.

Figure 7. Lower Calf Creek Falls in the Escalante Canyons section of the monument.

3. **Calf Creek Falls**: Calf Creek is a south-flowing tributary of the Escalante River (Escalante Canyons section) that heads on Boulder Mountain. It has carved a deep canyon into the Navajo Sandstone and the Kayenta Formation, being controlled along a shallow syncline. Two exquisitely beautiful and high waterfalls have formed in the monument and are known as Upper and Lower Calf Creek Falls. Figure 7 gives a view of Lower Calf Creek Falls. Calf Creek forms only one of the many spectacular tributary canyons of the Escalante River. A two-mile hike up the canyon from a campsite off State Road 12 provides access to the base of the lower falls. A view of the upper falls can be obtained by hiking a trail that extends west from State Road 12 a few miles north of the campsite.

4. **Circle Cliffs breached anticline**: Remnants of a large oil field can be seen in the rocks of the Circle Cliffs area (Escalante Canyons section). Oil and gas became trapped in this area after the rocks were deformed or folded into this broad, northwest-southeast elongate dome. As erosion cut through the surface of the dome and into the oil and gas reservoir, the lighter, more volatile fractions of the oil vented to the atmosphere. Left behind were only the heavier, more viscous residues such as heavy bitumen or tar, which saturated the sandstones (tar sands) of the Torrey and Moody Canyon Members of the Triassic Moenkopi Formation. Fractures formed during the folding process, as seen in the Jurassic Wingate Sandstone, probably contributed to the movement of oil and gas into the Moenkopi Formation from Pennsylvanian and Permian source rocks. The 300-foot-high Wingate Sandstone cliffs surround the deeply eroded center of the Circle Cliffs anticline, giving the feature its name (figure 31). Drive the Wolverine loop road to see the tar sands, cliffs, and other features of the anticline.

5. **Colt Mesa mines**: These mines are found at the base of a very thick channel of the Shinarump Member of the Chinle Formation in the south part of the Circle Cliffs area in the Escalante Canyons section of the monument. These mines were opened in the early 1970s for the purpose of producing copper. The ore deposits were quite rich but small and, in addition to copper, contained silver, molybdenum, and cobalt. These mines are highly interesting because the ore minerals are brightly colored and the ore horizon is easily identifiable so that anyone can begin to understand ore emplacement processes. Similar processes were important in the emplacement of the Colorado Plateau uranium ores, which helped usher in the "Atomic Age." The ore horizon here is a massive, medium-grained sandstone with tiny bits of coal interspersed throughout. The ore is in pods in the lower 6 feet of this sandstone where blue and green copper minerals coat, cement, and, in some cases, replace the sand grains. Minerals that have been identified at this property include chalcopyrite, pyrite, malachite, bornite, chalcocite, and erythrite. Access to the mines is along a road extending south from the Wolverine loop road. Visitors will need to walk about 1/4-

road, which extends southward from U.S. Highway 89 just before the highway cuts eastward through the Cockscomb. Hiking through Buckskin Gulch is also worthwhile.

2. **Burning Hills**: This area of reddened and baked rocks is found in the southeastern Kaiparowits Plateau (Kaiparowits Basin section). Here, as coal beds were exhumed by erosion, coal fires were ignited by spontaneous combustion as heat was generated by the oxidation of coal in the atmosphere. The coal was reduced to ash, reducing the volume by more than 90 percent. The overlying rocks collapsed into the space, being fractured in the process. Cracks formed by the collapse propagated to the surface and allowed more oxygen to reach additional coal below the surface, keeping the fires going. The encasing rocks were baked during the burning; shales were altered to varicolored brick and sandstone and iron impurities were oxidized to give a reddened color. Several fires still burn in this area. They are best recognized in the winter, when steam and gases condense at the surface. Even in the summer, however, a strong creosote smell exudes from cracks in the ground. The Burning Hills can be seen from the Croton road (No. 2 on figure 2).

Figure 9. Death Hollow, aerial view looking southeast shows deeply entrenched stream channel within Jurassic Navajo Sandstone.

Figure 8. Dinosaur tracks in the Escalante Member of the Entrada Sandstone near Twentymile Wash in the Escalante Canyons section of the monument.

mile from a pullout to the mine site.

6. **Dance Hall Rock**: This prominent monolith within the Gunsight Butte Member of the Entrada Sandstone is located roughly 40 miles southeast of Escalante along the Hole-in-the-Rock Road (Escalante Canyons section). While the Hole-in-the-Rock trail was being forged in 1879, Mormon pioneers camped at Fortymile Spring and held meetings and dances in the shelter of the stage-like erosional feature of the Entrada Sandstone known as Dance Hall Rock. The site was designated a National Historical Site by the U.S. Department of the Interior in 1970. The Hole-in-the-Rock trail was constructed to provide access from Escalante to areas on the opposite side of the Colorado and San Juan Rivers in southeast Utah. The pioneering effort to forge the road, negotiate the sheer cliffs, and to cross the Colorado with wagons and livestock and settle southeast Utah is considered one of the more interesting pioneering achievements in western history. The Gunsight Butte Member of the Entrada Sandstone has a very irregular contact with the upper part of the Carmel Formation in this area. In some places the smooth, rounded, orange-brown sandstone of the Gunsight Butte Member appears

to have "sunk" deeply into the bedded Carmel Formation.

7. **Devils Garden**: At Devils Garden, Mother Nature has sculpted the Entrada Sandstone into goblins, stone babies, monuments, and delicate arches to delight the beholder (figure 24). The features are formed along the contact of the Gunsight Butte and Cannonville Members of the Entrada Sandstone and are accessible along a short side road extending west from the Hole-in-the-Rock Road (Escalante Canyons section). Some of the features are bizarre and visitors have commonly attached their own informal nomenclature to them. When you visit the "garden" have fun doing the same.

8. **Entrada track site**: Normally devoid of fossils, the Escalante Member of the Entrada Sandstone at this site displays approximately 250 tracks of as many as 30 individual dinosaurs (Escalante Canyons section). Most are three-toed tracks of bipedal (two-legged) carnivorous dinosaurs. The site also has a trackway of a quadrupedal (four-legged) sauropod dinosaur (herbivorous) which appears to have left tail drag marks (figure 8).

9. **Escalante Canyons**: Erosion of the Colorado Plateau has resulted in the sculpting of a series of deep magnificent canyons in the Escalante Canyons section of the monument. In mid-Tertiary time (before 15 million years ago), Utah's surface was a little above sea level. To the present that 15-million-year-old surface would have been elevated as much as 15,000 feet had erosion not started to attack the uplift. The ancestral Colorado River and its tributaries have irregularly cut into the rocks of the region leaving high plateaus (some at over 10,000 feet above sea level), cliffs, benches, and deep canyons. A stream eroding a hard rock formation cuts a deep canyon because it cannot erode fast enough to keep up with the rate of uplift. When a stream erodes a soft rock it can form wider valleys. In order to do so it meanders across its valley floor eventually widening the valley. These meanders may become entrenched into harder rocks after the softer rock above is re-

Figure 10. Grosvenor arch is a double free-standing feature cut in the Henrieville Sandstone, Cedar Mountain Formation, and lower part of the Dakota Formation in the Grand Staircase section of the monument.

moved below the stream bed. The Glen Canyon Group of rocks, which consist of the Wingate Sandstone, Kayenta Formation, and Navajo Sandstone, are relatively hard and so the tributaries of the Escalante River have cut deep canyons. Locally meanders have been entrenched into the harder rock. The stream may locally be able to erode across loops in the meanders to form rincons after entrenching has taken place, adding interest to the canyons. Locally, natural arches and bridges are encountered in the canyons. Figure 9 shows Death Hollow, a tributary to the Escalante River.

The upper reaches of these canyons are in the monument; the lower and deeper canyons are found in the Glen Canyon Recreation Area. Access for hiking these canyons is from the monument. Favorite canyons accessible from the Hole-in-the-Rock Road include Harris Wash, Twenty-five Mile Wash, Coyote Gulch, Hurricane Wash, Fortymile Gulch, and Sooner Gulch. The upper reaches of the Escalante River, together with the lower canyons of Death Hollow, Sand Creek, Calf Creek, and Boulder Creek are accessible from State Road 12. The Wolverine Loop road and the Burr Trail road provide access to the canyons of Deer Creek, The Gulch, Wolverine Creek, and Death Hollow (figure 9).

10. **Escalante monocline**: The Escalante monocline is a sharp flexure predominantly involving the Jurassic Navajo Sandstone (Escalante Canyons section). This monocline folds strata down to the west and trends N. 30° W. A nice view of this feature can be seen north of the Escalante High School or the Escalante cemetery, east of town, along State Road 12. The Pine Creek road, which extends northward from Escalante, parallels the monocline and offers corresponding views. Most overlying rocks have been stripped off the Navajo Sandstone, which helps to accentuate the flexure. As viewed from high above the town of Escalante (figure 30) the dark rocks in the background, on the Aquarius Plateau and Boulder Mountain (beyond the monument boundary), are mostly Tertiary welded tuffs (volcanic rocks). The Escalante monocline is the steep west limb of the Escalante anticline, the axis of which lies to the east. Anticlines are geologic structures that may trap oil and gas. The north end of the Escalante anticline, beyond the monument boundary, is known to contain carbon dioxide resources.

11. **Grosvenor Arch**: Grosvenor Arch was named after Gilbert C. Grosvenor, the founder of the National Geographic Society. The arch is located near the east boundary of the Grand Staircase section of the monument and is

easily reached along the Cottonwood Wash road about 10 miles east of Kodachrome State Park (Grand Staircase section). It is a double free-standing arch cut in the Henrieville Sandstone, the Cedar Mountain Formation, and the Dakota Sandstone. The unconformities that divide these formations are plainly visible in the arch (figure 10).

12. **Hackberry Canyon:** The Early Jurassic Navajo Sandstone is exposed at the confluence of Cottonwood Wash and Hackberry Canyon. One of the premier hiking locations in the Grand Staircase-Escalante National Monument, Hackberry Canyon offers spectacular views of the Upper Triassic Chinle Formation and overlying Lower Jurassic Moenave, Kayenta, and Navajo Sandstone Formations (figure 11).

13. **Head-of-the-Rocks**: Located along State Highway 12, about 10 miles east of the town of Escalante, Head-of-the-Rocks overlook provides visitors with breathtaking vistas of the terrain typified in the Escalante Canyons section of the monument. The exposed rocks here are mostly of the Lower Jurassic Navajo Sandstone which exhibits large-scale, high-angle cross-bedding. The Navajo Sandstone is believed to represent a coastal to inland dune field by most geologists. Some workers have suggested that the Navajo and equivalent rocks may have been the largest recorded dune field in Earth's history, extending from southern Nevada through Utah into southwest Wyoming.

14. **Kelly Grade**: The Kelly Grade is part of the roadway extending from Escalante to Big Water across the Kaiparowits Plateau (Kaiparowits Basin section). Coal developers, finding themselves in a very remote area in the southern part of the plateau, hired the Kelly Construction Company of Escalante to extend the road from the top of Smoky Mountain, down to the bench below to get access to Glen Canyon City (Big Water) and the then-new Highway 89 extending from Kanab, Utah to Page, Arizona. They were drilling for coal on Smoky Mountain and the way back to Escalante was four or more hours. So in the early 1960s, Kelly took his bulldozer and "pushed" a road down the steep cliff that is still in use today. The top of the Kelly Grade provides a spectacular vista of Lake Powell and all the land below the plateau. The road is narrow and "scary" and eventually uses an old landslide to get down, but passes through the John Henry, Smoky Hollow, and Tibbet Canyon Members of the Straight Cliffs Formation and the Tropic Shale on the way down. A landslide, brightly colored by clinker, is passed on the way down, which is worth the drive on its own. See the discussion about "clinker" in the section on the John Henry Member of the Straight Cliffs Formation. The section of road along which the Kelly Grade is found is known as the Smoky Mountain road.

15. **Land of the Sleeping Rainbow**: Outcrops of the varicolored Petrified Forest Member of the Chinle Formation ring the Circle Cliffs area of the Escalante Canyons section below the Wingate Cliffs. These are especially beautiful

Figure 11. A hiker in Hackberry Canyon. This canyon is located just west of the Cockscomb and is a popular hiking area.

and enchanting as one emerges from Long Canyon into the Circle Cliffs area traveling toward the Waterpocket Fold from Boulder on the Burr Trail road. The name is an interpretation of how the American Indians of the region appreciated these vistas.

16. **Moqui marbles**: Moqui marbles are particularly common in the Navajo Sandstone. It is believed that these ironstone concretions formed near the water table during deposition as iron-froth-coated air bubbles in water-saturated sand. Moqui marbles are abundant in the Spencer Flat area in the Escalante Canyons section of the monument. Collecting Moqui marbles from monument lands is not permitted.

17. **Paria area**: Like the Land of the Sleeping Rainbow, this area is special because of the brightly banded outcrops of the Petrified Forest Member of the Chinle Formation in the Grand Staircase section (figure 19). However, this area is also special for views of the Vermilion Cliffs, steeply dipping Moenkopi strata, channels of the Shinarump Member of the Chinle Formation, faults, the flood plain of the Paria River, the ghost town of Pahreah, Shurtz Gorge, and the movie set (now dismantled) for the film, "The Outlaw Josie Wales," which starred Clint Eastwood. Some regard

Figure 12. *The Straight Cliffs extend for fifty miles from Escalante to the Colorado River broken only by the mouths of two canyons. The Straight Cliffs are mostly lenses of beach sand in the Straight Cliffs Formation.*

this as the most sublime geologic area in the world.

18. **Peek-A-Boo Gulch**: Narrow slot canyons have been carved into Navajo Sandstone benches by small washes as influenced by joints. During summer monsoon storms, these slot canyons flood with sediment-laden waters which further scour the walls and drill potholes. Peek-A-Boo Gulch and Spooky Gulch are two of the more popular slot canyons within the monument. They are located about 25 miles down the Hole-in-the-Rock Road in the Escalante Canyons section.

19. **Petrified Hollow**: Petrified Hollow is located east of Kanab below the Vermilion Cliffs of the Grand Staircase section of the monument near the Paunsaugunt fault. Petrified wood occurs in the Petrified Forest and Monitor Butte Members of the Chinle Formation. Though collecting is no longer allowed, it was a popular rock-hounding area for many years.

20. **Phipps Arch**: Set in the Navajo Sandstone, this arch stands above Phipps Canyon. Over time the erosive forces of gravity, ice, wind, and water cut this arch through a narrow ridgeline. This arch is located not far downstream from the place where State Road 12 crosses the Escalante River near its confluence with Calf Creek in the Escalante Canyons section.

21. **Sand dunes at Little Egypt**: Wind-blown sand collects as dunes in the Little Egypt area in the Escalante Canyons section.   Here, Mesozoic eolian sandstones undergo weathering, erosion, and redeposition to form an active dune field. The source of sand is the Entrada Sandstone. Generally sandy areas are ubiquitous on Entrada outcrops.

22. **Straight Cliffs**: Forming a nearly continuous escarpment for more than 50 miles along the eastern edge of the Kaiparowits Plateau (Kaiparowits Basin section), the Straight Cliffs present a series of stacked marine sandstone layers within the Straight Cliffs Formation. These sandstone layers were probably barrier islands during the Late Cretaceous nearly 90 million years ago. Behind these bar-

rier islands swamps formed that favored the creation of the thick coal beds seen in the Kaiparowits Plateau area. Today, the Straight Cliffs closely follow an ancient shoreline of the Late Cretaceous Western Interior Seaway. Another name for the Straight Cliffs is Fiftymile Mountain. Between Escalante and the Colorado River, a distance of 50 miles, only two canyons break the otherwise straight line of cliffs (figure 12).

23. **The Blues**: The Kaiparowits Formation is an Upper Cretaceous unit that was deposited very thickly in the Kaiparowits Basin section of the monument. It forms outstanding "badlands" topography in the area just south of Powell Point. The gray or gray-blue Kaiparowits Formation is about 2,500 feet thick at the BLM viewpoint along State Road 12. The viewpoint overlooks a nearly complete section of the formation, where it is not covered by vegetation or other debris to mar the view. Known for its abundant fossil record, the Kaiparowits Formation has yielded specimens of small mammals, sharks, crocodiles, turtles, hadrosaurs, theropods, and ankylosaurs.

24. **The Cockscomb**: This feature is the physiographic display of the East Kaibab monocline. This sharp flexure of the earth's crust is the boundary between the Kaiparowits Basin section and the Grand Staircase section of the monument; it extends 35 miles from the Arizona border northward into Garfield County.   The rock strata dip abruptly eastward at angles ranging from 15 degrees to slightly overturned, with an average dip of 40 to 60 degrees in the steepest part of the flexure (figure 29). Rocks on the east side of this flexure have been displaced downward as much as 5,000 feet. The landforms along the monocline consist chiefly of a series of closely spaced hogbacks and strike valleys. Because of the steep folding, the rocks have been locally faulted and attenuated and appear to be thinner than they were originally deposited. The Cottonwood Wash road parallels the feature.

25. **Vermilion Cliffs**: The Jurassic Moenave and Kayenta Formations combine to form the massive Vermilion Cliffs,

Figure 13. View of part of a 90-foot petrified tree trunk in the Wolverine area in the Circle Cliffs.

a riser or step of the Grand Staircase. In the monument, they can be seen north of U.S. Highway 89 from Johnson Canyon to the Cockscomb, but essentially extend along the Utah-Arizona boundary from Washington County, Utah to the Colorado River at Lees Ferry. Iron-oxide cement gives these formations their brilliant color for which they are so well known.

26. **White Canyon Flat tar seep**: Most of the tar exposed in the Circle Cliffs breached anticline is in the Moenkopi Formation, but locally, some is found in sandstone channels of the Shinarump Member of the Chinle Formation. Located along the east edge of the monument (Escalante Canyons section) at White Canyon Flat, tar drips from sandstone pore spaces in the summer. The oil originally filled the bottom of the Shinarump channel and was probably derived from the same source as that in the Moenkopi Formation.

27. **White Cliffs**: The Jurassic Navajo Sandstone is often described as a fossilized desert because of its eolian origin. In the Grand Staircase section, the 1,800-foot-thick Navajo consists of three parts, based on post-depositional groundwater coloring action. The lower part is brown and cliff-forming. The middle part is pink and forms both cliffs and slopes. The upper part is white and forms a magnificent 500- to 600-foot cliff or riser of the Grand Staircase called

the White Cliffs (figure 20). The White Cliffs are a line of cliffs extending from Zion National Park eastward to the Cockscomb and lie above the Vermilion Cliffs. Take a short drive north of U.S. Highway 89 on the Kitchen Corral Wash road through the Vermilion Cliffs to get excellent views of the White Cliffs.

28. **Wolverine petrified wood area**: The Wolverine petrified wood area is located in the Circle Cliffs (Escalante Canyons section).   The Petrified Forest Member of the Chinle Formation contains numerous petrified logs, at least one of which measures 6 feet in diameter and is nearly 90 feet long (figure 13). The logs represent conifer trees covered by volcanic-ash-derived stream sediments. Silica from the ash replaced much of the original organic matter in the logs during the process of petrifaction. *Araucarioxylon* and *Woodworthia* are the most common plants represented by the petrified wood.

HISTORY

Geologic

Nearly 270 million years of geologic history is revealed in the exposed rocks and paleontology of the monument (Baars, 1972; Hintze, 1988). The oldest rocks record a time when the North American plate was situated such that the equator angled northeasterly from southern California and across the southeast corner of Utah. The area was a marginal marine lowland of streams, flood plains, and tidal flats. The sea lay to the west, but it occasionally spread eastward across the area, depositing limestone beds containing diverse shells, sponges, and other fossils between the red beds of sandstone and mudstone that were being deposited on adjacent lowlands. The Hermit Shale, Toroweap Formation, Kaibab Limestone and Moenkopi Formation (Blakey and others, 1993; Blakey, 1996), which crop out in the Circle Cliffs and at Buckskin Mountain, record the events of the first 35 million years of exposed geologic history in the monument. A missing record of nearly 20 million years separates the last record of the Permian Period from the Triassic Period in the monument (figure 14). Evidence for climatic regimes, environments of deposition, and other paleohistoric data are available only from the rocks that we currently see in the monument, or only 43 percent of the 270-million-year interval.

One might ask what happened during the remaining 57 percent of time. Strata may have been deposited only to be eroded before the next sequence was laid down. They may have been deposited or eroded in environments that differ from those recorded in the rocks that are present. Unfortunately the missing intervals are generally not recorded in neighboring localities; the events that affected the monument affected the region similarly. Nevertheless there is a wealth of information found in the 43 percent of the rocks that are present and much information remains to be gleaned from them.

The Upper or Late Triassic-age rocks in the Circle Cliffs section have remarkable specimens of petrified wood, including logs exceeding 90 feet in length. These logs represent conifer trees that were left as driftwood on river flood plains. Cellular organic tissues were replaced by silica derived from volcanic ashes which were deposited as part of the Chinle Formation (Dubiel, 1994). Fossils of other kinds of plants, fish, amphibians, and reptiles, tracks of early dinosaurs, and freshwater clam and gastropod shells also give hints about the environment and life in the monument during Late Triassic time (Foster and others, 1999).

Following the Late Triassic, and a period of 5 to 6 million years of non-deposition and erosion, sand was deposited during Early Jurassic time (208 to 187 million years ago). In the Escalante Canyons section this sand was initially deposited in a sand-dune desert (Wingate Sandstone). The desert environment changed for a time and streams deposited sand in channels and overbank deposits on flood plains (Kayenta Formation). The desert climate returned and sand was again deposited in a huge area of sand dunes (Navajo Sandstone). In the Grand Staircase section, Lower Jurassic tidal flats (lower Moenave Formation) gradually changed to flood plains (upper Moenave and Kayenta Formations), and finally ended in a wind-blown sand environment (Navajo Sandstone). These

Lower or Early Jurassic-age rocks form the Vermilion and White Cliffs in the Grand Staircase section and make up the walls of the canyon and tributary canyons of the Escalante River. Many people consider these Lower Jurassic rocks to be the most interesting and scenic of the monument. Though generally devoid of fossils, these rocks commonly exhibit tracks of small to medium-sized dinosaurs (Hamblin, 1998).

Middle Jurassic time in the monument is mostly represented by the Carmel and Entrada Formations. The Carmel was deposited near the south margin of a shallow sea that advanced into the area from the north. Carmel limestones contain marine mollusks, brachiopods, crinoids, coral, and algae. Desert sand dunes (beach and back-beach sands of the Entrada Sandstone) were deposited on Carmel sediments and limestones in the wake of the retreating Carmel sea. Another 3 to 5 million years elapsed between the time the Entrada sands were deposited and Upper Jurassic Morrison Formation sediments were laid down. In the Escalante Canyons section, the Morrison was deposited by northeast-flowing streams. The sluggish meandering and anastomosing streams of Morrison time developed broad flood plains. Dinosaurs roamed the monument in profusion and "sloshed" across the streams and through the ponds and lakes that developed on the flood plain.

Late Jurassic to early Tertiary compressive forces in the Earth's crust formed high mountain ranges in western Utah and eastern Nevada which peaked in the Late Cretaceous. This mountain-building event is known as the Sevier orogeny. Simultaneously, an epicontinental sea spread to the foot of these mountains and inundated the monument area. The sea covered most of the interior of the North American continent from the Arctic Ocean to the Gulf of Mexico, dividing the continent into two parts. At its maximum extent the sea stretched to the Cedar City area in southwest Utah, west of the monument. Sediments, provided by the erosion of the Sevier mountains, were carried eastward by rivers and streams to the sea. Dakota Formation sediments were deposited in coastal areas ahead of the encroaching sea. The Tropic Shale represents the muds deposited at the bottom of the sea, and the Straight Cliffs, Wahweap, and Kaiparowits Formations represent sediments deposited on a piedmont belt between the mountains and the sea after the sea retreated east of the monument area. The west part of the monument area was elevated before sediments were deposited during the transgressive and regressive stages of the epicontinental sea. In the west part of the monument all Upper Jurassic and a good part of the Middle Jurassic rocks were removed by erosion before the Cretaceous sediments were deposited (see figure 14).

The thickness, continuity, and broad temporal distribution of the Kaiparowits Plateau stratigraphy provide opportunities to study the paleontology of Late Cretaceous time. Significant fossils, including marine and brackish-water mollusks, turtles, crocodilians, lizards, di-

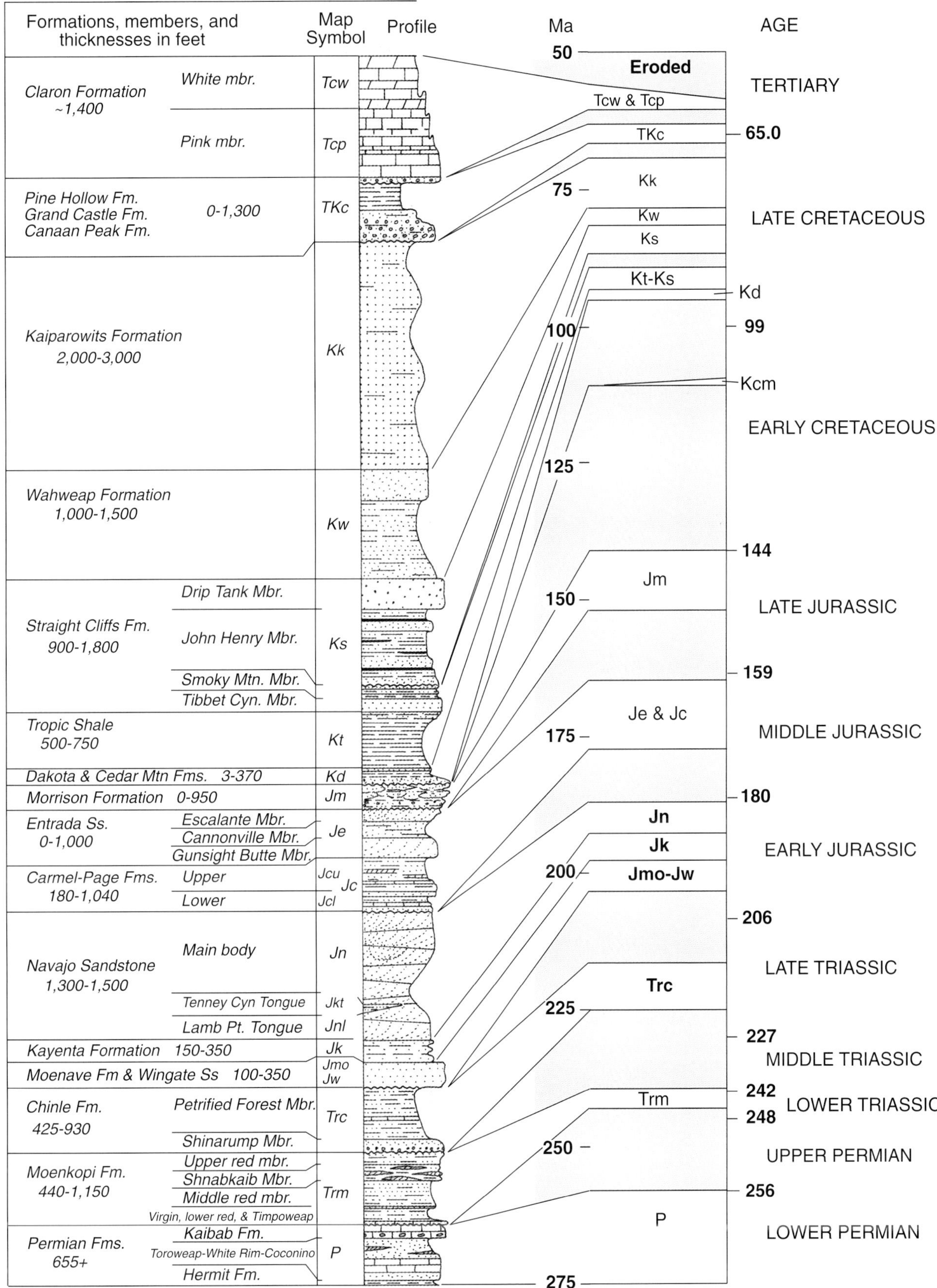

Figure 14. Age, thickness and names of formations and members of geologic units exposed in the Grand Staircase-Escalante National Monument. Symbols are those used on the geologic maps shown in figures 7, 8, and 9. Profile-lithology plot shows true relative thickness (averages) as compared with geologic time. Gray areas denote time with missing rock records. Je includes Romana Mesa Sandstone and Henrieville Formation. Ma stands for millions of years ago. Numbers between period designations indicate age of time boundary.

nosaurs, fish, and mammals have been recovered from the Dakota Formation, Tropic Shale, Straight Cliffs, Wahweap, and Kaiparowits Formations. These formations provide evidence of a diverse terrestrial vertebrate fauna, especially for mammals and dinosaurs, in the 20 million years after the retreat of the epicontinental sea. This sequence of rocks in the monument contains one of the best and most continuous records of Late Cretaceous terrestrial life in the world (Kirkland and others, 1998; Eaton and others, 1999). The research on these strata is still in its earliest stages.

The Canaan Peak Formation straddles the boundary between Cretaceous and Tertiary time. Dinosaurs became extinct during its deposition and changes in depositional environments followed. The Sevier mountains to the west were gradually removed by erosion by early Tertiary time and several large lakes occupied areas extending from southwestern Wyoming to southwestern Utah. The Claron Formation, which forms the Pink Cliffs at Powell Point and Bryce Canyon National Park, was deposited in a lake which covered much of the monument area.

Much volcanic activity took place in central Utah in middle Tertiary time. Today, volcanic rocks cap the Aquarius Plateau and Boulder Mountain north of the monument, but volcanic boulders litter benches in the north part of the Escalante Canyons section. All during the middle Tertiary Utah and surrounding areas lay at low elevations, not far above sea level. A general rise of the landscape and tectonic activity (faulting) occurred in latest Tertiary time and continues into the present. The Colorado Plateau uplift began about 15 million years ago. In western Utah the uplift was accompanied by faulting brought on by crustal extension (stretching). This faulting formed grabens, horsts, and tilted fault blocks that form the north-south-trending basins and ranges in western Utah and Nevada. The monument is located at the east edge of this basin-and-range faulting. The Johnson Canyon and Paunsaugunt faults are the easternmost of the basin and range faults. Although detailed fault and seismic studies are necessary, the Johnson Canyon and Paunsaugunt faults may be active and may relate to small earth tremors and earthquakes that have been experienced in the area (Doelling and Davis, 1989; University of Utah Seismology Catalog, 1986). The Grand Canyon uplift occurred simultaneously with the Colorado Plateau uplift and its specific effect extends into the monument area as the Kaibab uplift (McKee & McKee, 1972; Lucchitta, 1972).

The Colorado Plateau is still rising. The Colorado River and its tributaries cut deep canyons into the landscape and into the colorful formations deposited in late Paleozoic and Mesozoic time. The basin-and-range faults continue to move and affect the Grand Staircase section of the monument. The unconsolidated fluvial and wind-blown deposits that are temporarily lodged in the hollows of the eroding formations, and on their way to the ocean, hold the secrets of the events of the last few million years and hold most of the evidence of human habitation for the last few thousand years.

Cultural

Archaeologists have divided the cultural history of the monument into six generalized periods. They are the Paleo-Indian period (11,500-9,000 years ago), Archaic period (9,000-2,000 years ago), Early Agricultural period (2,000-1,500 years ago), Formative period (1,500-700 years ago), Late Prehistoric-Protohistoric period (700-150 years ago), and the Historic period (150-0 years ago) (Spangler and Metcalf, in preparation).

The Paleo-Indian period began at the Pleistocene-Holocene boundary or at the end of the last Ice Age. The inhabitants of this time period hunted big game animals such as mammoth, bison, camel, and horse. Evidence of their existence has been found throughout the Colorado Plateau region in the form of large Clovis and Folsom spear points.

The Archaic period began after post-Pleistocene warming was complete and many of the larger mammals had become extinct. These inhabitants adapted to a gathering and small-game hunting way of life.

In the Early Agricultural period, corn and squash farming was introduced into the region and by 1,200 years ago became the dominant means of making a living.

The Formative period is the most obvious and studied cultural period in the monument area. The inhabitants constructed more permanent storage facilities and dwellings, they made pottery, and the population reached a high level. Formative people were farmers and small-game hunters as were those of the two previous periods. Two different groups of people were present at this time: the Fremont culture in the northeast part and the Anasazi culture in the southwest part of the monument.

During the Late Prehistoric period, between 1300 and 1500 A.D., both Anasazi and Fremont cultures left the region, most likely because of extended periods of drought (Gieb and others, 1999).

The first written accounts of native American cultures in this region were made by Fathers Dominguez and Escalante as they passed through the region on a Spanish expedition in 1776. Their accounts describe the inhabitants of the Protohistoric period. These explorers noted an Indian culture that was later named the Southern Paiute culture. No other explorers ventured near the monument until Mormon settlers began colonizing southern Utah in the 1850s.

The last and most recent period, known as the Historic period, commences with the Mormon colonization of southern Utah. Journals of these settlers described the Southern Paiute Indians as nomadic people that moved with the seasons to maximize their hunting and gathering activities. This time period coincides with the great western expansion of the United States of America. In the years that followed, several famous surveyors and explorers traveled through the monument region. These include Jacob Hamblin, John Wesley Powell, Almon H. Thompson, Clarence Dutton, G.M. Wheeler, and G.K. Gilbert. In the

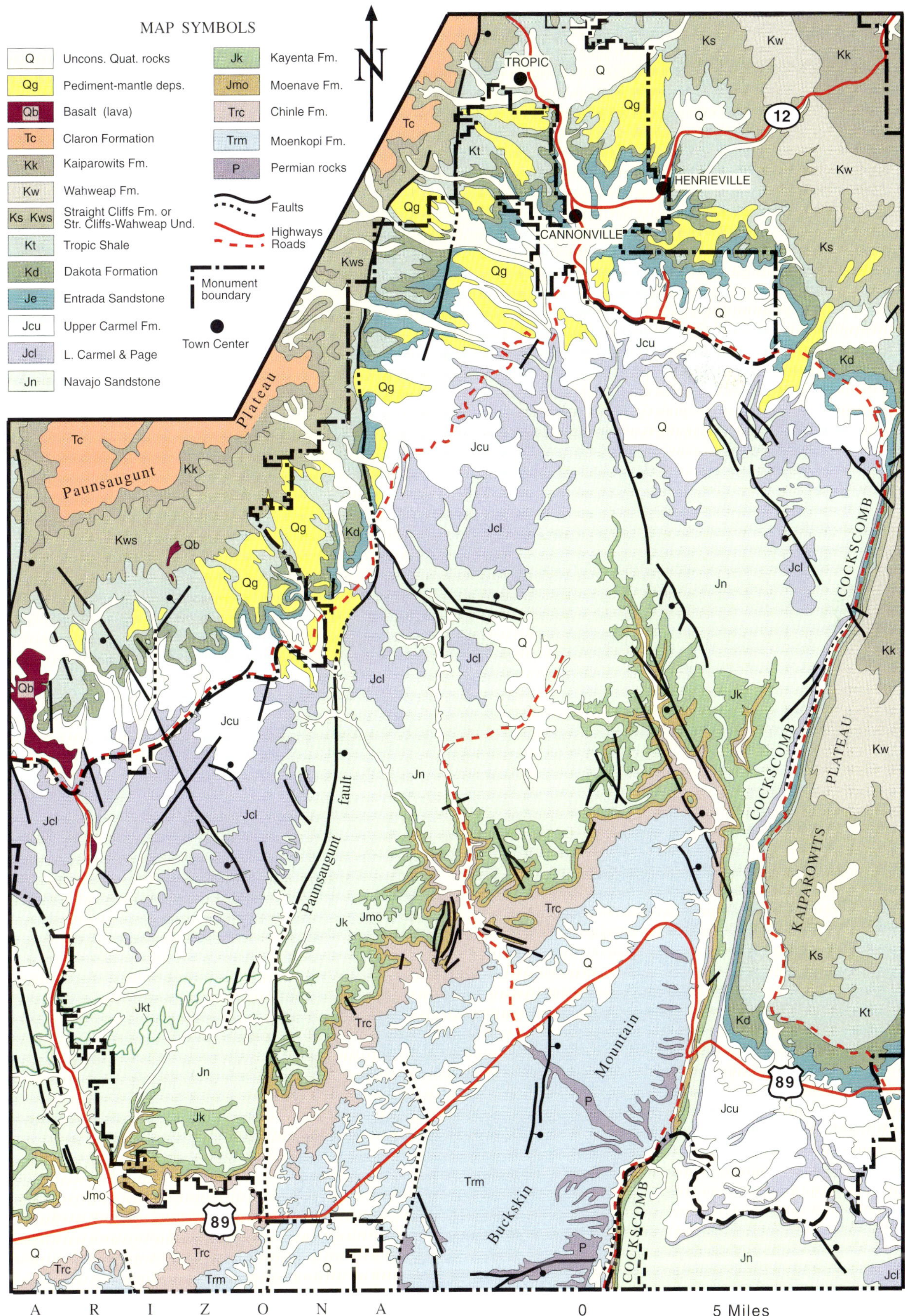

Figure 15. Generalized geologic map of the Grand Staircase section of the monument. The "Grand Staircase" is named for a series of cliffs. The lowermost Chocolate Cliffs are aligned along the Moenkopi-Chinle (Trm-Trc) contact. The Vermilion Cliffs are aligned along the Moenave-Kayenta (Jmo-Jk) outcrops; the White Cliffs are aligned along the upper third of the Navajo Sandstone (Jn); the Gray Cliffs are here aligned along the Dakota Formation (Kd), and the highest Pink Cliffs are aligned just above the Kaiparowits-Claron (Kk-Tc) contact. See text for descriptions of map units.

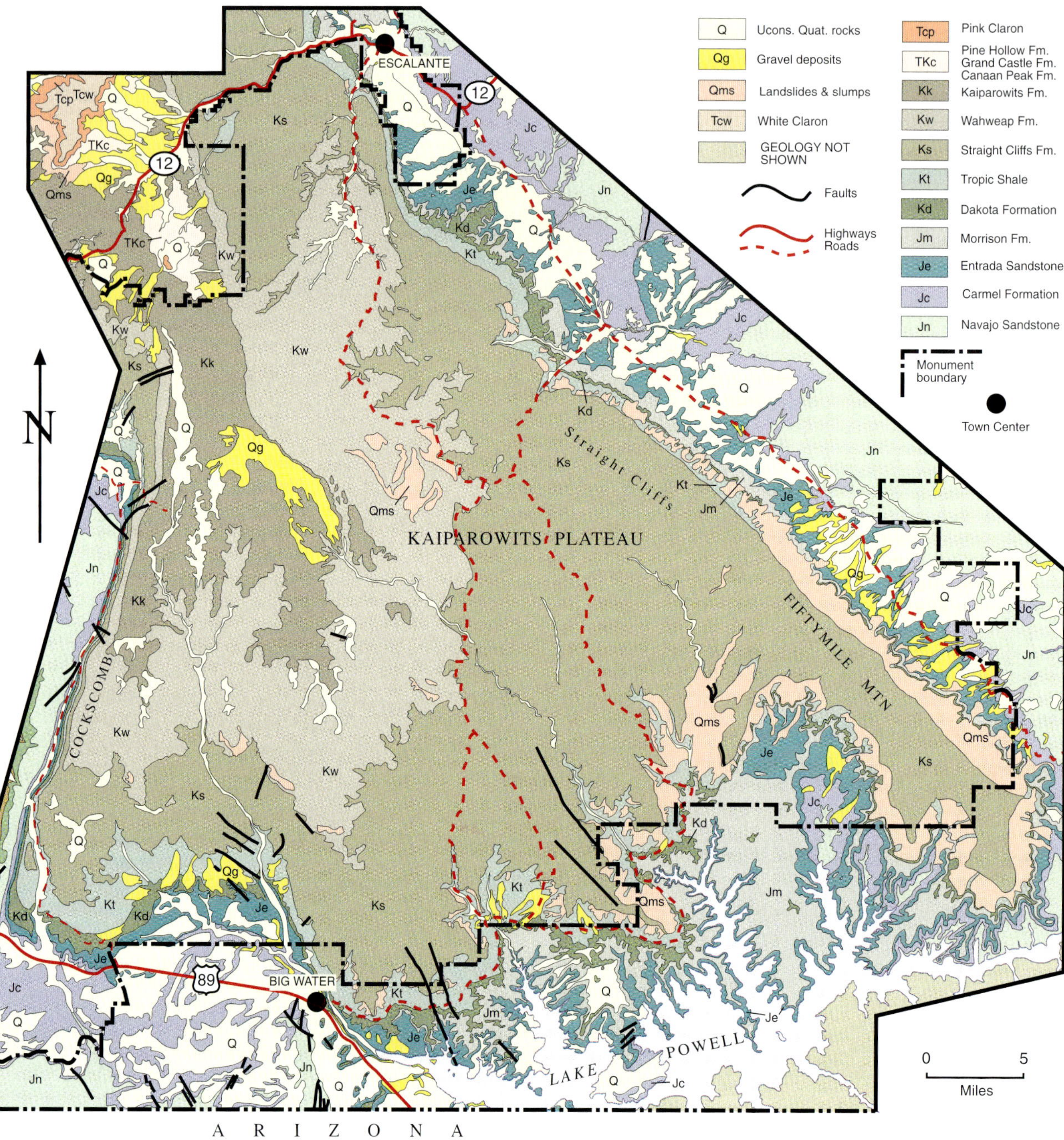

Figure 16. *Generalized geologic map of the Kaiparowits Basin section of the monument. This section represents a large structural basin, but is topographically high. Part of the Escalante Canyons section is represented northeast of Fiftymile Mountain. See text for descriptions of map units.*

early 1900s, H.E. Gregory began the first detailed geologic study of the region. In more recent times, the lure of precious metals, oil, gas, coal, uranium, and other minerals drew prospectors, miners, and energy companies into the region that produced more detailed reports on the geology, natural resources, and unique sites of the region. Due to its harsh and remote character, the monument area was one of the last places in the continental U.S. to be mapped. Today, the area is largely unpopulated except for the small and scattered communities found along the edges of the monument (Cassity and Truman, in preparation).

STRATIGRAPHY AND PALEONTOLOGY

Bedrock exposed in the monument ranges in age from Early Permian to Late Cretaceous. Precambrian, Cambrian, Devonian, Mississippian and Pennsylvanian rocks are present in the subsurface. Additionally, there are several types of unconsolidated deposits ranging in age from late Tertiary to Holocene. Since the area is presently one of active erosion, the unconsolidated deposits are geologically temporary, but important with respect to geologic hazards, environmental issues, and human habitation patterns.

The monument is large, a little over 70 miles from its southernmost point to its northernmost point and about 82

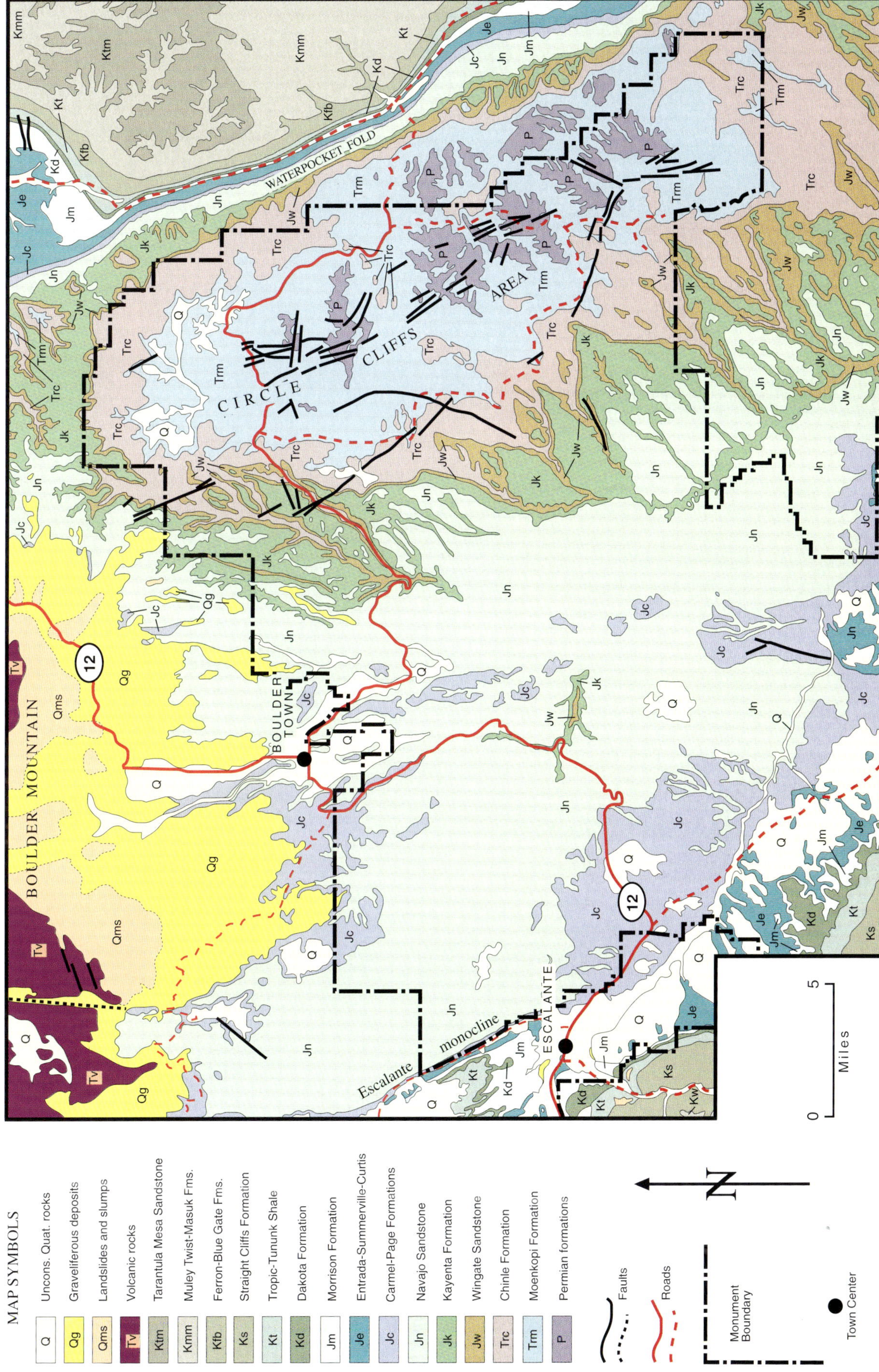

Figure 17. *Generalized geologic map of the Escalante Canyons section of the monument. This section is comprised of two parts: the Circle Cliffs area to the east which abuts against the Waterpocket Fold (Capitol Reef National Park) and the Bench-and-Canyonlands area to the west, dominated by Navajo Sandstone benches. See text for descriptions of map units.*

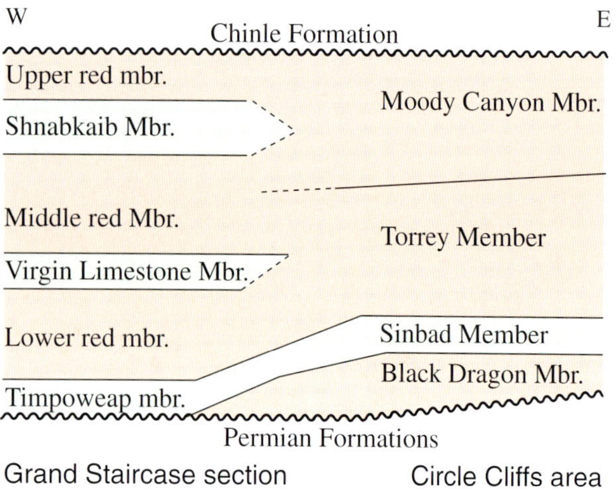

Figure 18. Correlation of the Moenkopi Formation members between the Grand Staircase section and Circle Cliffs area. Green-colored members represent marine encroachments from the west; pink-colored members are red-bed deposits. The Moenkopi thickens westward.

miles from its westernmost point to its easternmost point. Some of the geologic formations undergo significant facies and other changes over these distances. Exposed strata in the Grand Staircase section total from 6,000 to 7,000 feet and range from Permian to Cretaceous in age. Exposed strata in the Kaiparowits Basin section also total from 6,000 to 7,000 feet, but range in age from Middle Jurassic to latest Cretaceous, with a much thicker Cretaceous section. Exposed strata in the Escalante Canyons section total 4,500 to 5,500 feet and range in age from Permian to Late Jurassic. A list of units is given on figure 14 and are shown on the geologic maps, figures 15 to 17.

Permian Rocks (P)

Permian rocks are the oldest rocks exposed in the monument. Outcrops are present in Buckskin Gulch and in adjacent canyons associated with the Kaibab uplift in the Grand Staircase section and are present in scattered places in the core of the Circle Cliffs uplift in the Escalante Canyons section. In the Kaibab uplift the (ascending) Hermit Shale, Coconino Sandstone, Toroweap Formation, and Kaibab Limestone are exposed; in the Escalante section-Circle Cliffs uplift the White Rim Sandstone and the Kaibab Formation are exposed.

Hermit Shale

Only the upper 55 feet of the Hermit Shale is exposed in Buckskin Gulch. The Hermit is red silty sandstone, siltstone, micaceous shale, claystone, and minor dolomite. It correlates with the Organ Rock Shale in eastern Utah, which may underlie the White Rim Sandstone in the Circle Cliffs area. Wells indicate the Hermit-Organ Rock ranges from 100 to 600 feet thick, thickening southward under the monument. The unit was deposited partly in a fluvial environment and partly in a tidal-flat environment. As yet no fossils have been found in the Hermit Shale within the monument. Fossils from the Hermit Shale out-

side the monument include land plants, insects, amphibian footprints, and worm trails (Gillette and Hayden, 1997).

Coconino Sandstone

Less than 64 feet of Coconino Sandstone is present above the Hermit Shale in Buckskin Gulch. There it consists of alternating beds of arenaceous limestone and irregularly bedded fine-grained buff sandstone. The limestones contain poorly preserved marine fossils. At the Grand Canyon it is 330 to 350 feet thick and is a uniform fine-grained, cross-bedded, white to light-gray sandstone with siliceous cement. At Buckskin Gulch it probably interfingers with the lower part of the Brady Canyon Member of the Toroweap Formation. Drill holes indicate it is present only in the south half of Kane County. The Coconino is probably a near-shore deposit grading southward into a beach sand.

Toroweap Formation-White Rim Sandstone

The Toroweap Formation can be divided into two members in Buckskin Gulch: a lower 90-foot section of cliff-forming, cherty, fossiliferous limestone interbedded with calcareous sandstone and 175 feet of slope-forming, mostly yellow preceded by mostly gray to red, very fine and medium-grained (bimodal) gypsiferous sandstone. The upper beds locally contain gypsum, marl or travertine, and intraformational conglomerate. The lower cliff-former is known as the Brady Canyon Member and the upper slope-former is known as the Woods Ranch Member. The Toroweap was deposited in and adjacent to a shallow sea and represents a single marine transgressive and regressive cycle (McKee, 1938).

The oldest exposed geologic unit in the Circle Cliffs uplift is the White Rim Sandstone. There it can be divided into two units. The lower unit, of which up to 108 feet is exposed, is white quartzose cross-stratified sandstone of eolian origin. The grains are very fine to fine, subangular to angular, and are mostly siliceously cemented. The lower unit intertongues with the upper. The upper unit is thin to thick planar-bedded and is 65 to 155 feet thick. It consists of pale-yellow to yellow-brown dolomitic sandstone with a few sandy dolomite beds. Grains are very fine to fine and subrounded to rounded. Some beds contain poorly preserved fossils such as fragments of gastropods and pelecypods. It is assumed that these beds were laid down as a transgressive marine deposit as Permian seas encroached eastward. The White Rim Sandstone in the Circle Cliffs area is a resistant unit.

The Toroweap Formation and White Rim Sandstone grade into each other under the Kaiparowits Basin section. Logs of oil-test wells west of the basin recognize only the Toroweap Formation. Logs of oil-test-wells in the basin generally give thicknesses for the Toroweap or for both the Toroweap and White Rim. East of Fiftymile Mountain, in the Escalante section of the monument, only White Rim thicknesses are reported.

Kaibab Formation

The Kaibab Formation is present under most of the monument, but generally thickens westward. In the Kaibab uplift it is about 160 to 280 feet thick, but the Circle Cliffs outcrops (in the Escalante Canyons section) are at most 60 feet thick. In the Circle Cliffs area the Kaibab is a thin-bedded, light-yellow dolomite. It is absent in the southern part of the Circle Cliffs, where it may have been removed by Late Permian and Early Triassic erosion rather than by just pinching out to the east. The Kaibab has been encountered in oil-test wells east of the monument.

In the Circle Cliffs area the Kaibab is a very fine to fine-grained, oolitic, porous dolomite. Interbedded are a few partings of green glauconitic feldspathic sandstone. It erodes to ledgy slopes and the upper beds contain small quartz geodes, stringers of gray chert, and gray chert nodules and fragments. Locally the beds contain fossils with fossil hash as much as 6 inches thick. The hash includes crinoid columnals, pelecypods, gastropods, productid brachiopods and various spines and spicules (Davidson, 1967).

In the Kaibab uplift (in the Grand Staircase section), the Kaibab Formation can be divided into two members. The lower Fossil Mountain Member is 140 to 200 feet of massive cliff-forming, fossiliferous, cherty gray limestone and calcareous, commonly cherty, well-indurated fine-grained sandstone. The chert is found as nodules, in beds, and in irregular bodies. White spheroidal chert is most distinctive. Some beds are quite fossiliferous, containing a wide variety of marine fossils including branched and fenestellid-type bryozoans, rugosid corals, crinoids, brachiopods and the sponge *Actinoceolia* (Foster and others, 1999).

The upper Harrisburg Member is 15 to 80 feet thick. Beds in the upper member are medium to thick bedded and unfossiliferous. The lower part of the upper member is mostly cherty limestone. Toward the top, sandstone beds become numerous. The unit is capped by a hackly weathering blocky gray limestone bed. The upper half of the bed displays vertical tubes filled with brown, rough-weathering, sandy chert (bioturbation features?). The Fossil Mountain Member was deposited in an advancing sea and the Harrisburg Member in a retreating sea.

Triassic Rocks

Moenkopi Formation (Trm)

The Lower Triassic Moenkopi Formation is divisible into four to six members in the monument. In the Grand Staircase section the members are (ascending) Timpoweap, Lower Red, Virgin Limestone, Middle Red, Shnabkaib, and Upper Red. In the Escalante Canyons section the members are (ascending) Black Dragon, Sinbad, Torrey, and Moody Canyon. A Black Dragon equivalent may not be present in the Grand Staircase section. The Timpoweap Member correlates in time with the Sinbad Member, while the Lower Red, Virgin Limestone and Middle Red Members correlate with the Torrey Member. The Shnabkaib and Upper Red Members correlate with the Moody Canyon Member (Blakey, 1974). In the Grand Staircase section, the Moenkopi Formation ranges from 910 to 1,150 feet in thickness. In the Escalante Canyons section, the Moenkopi ranges from 440 to 730 feet in thickness.

The Moenkopi Formation is bounded above and below by regional unconformities. The lower boundary may be described as a disconformity of low relief. The upper boundary is also a disconformity, but locally, channels of the overlying Shinarump Member have cut deeply into the Moody Canyon and Upper Red Members. Moenkopi Formation member relationships are shown on figure 18 (Blakey, 1974).

Fossils from the Moenkopi are a mix of terrestrial and marine taxa. They include plants, crinoids, brachiopods, gastropods, bivalves, ammonoids, nautiloids, arthropods, fish, reptiles, labyrinthodont amphibians, and reptile footprints (Gillette and Hayden, 1997). Reptile tracks are known from a number of localities in both the Grand Staircase and Escalante Canyons sections of the monument (see Hamblin, this volume). Horseshoe crab tracks have been found in the Circle Cliffs area (Foster and others, 1999).

Black Dragon Member: The Black Dragon Member is exposed in the north Circle Cliffs area in the Escalante Canyons section of the monument where it ranges up to 40 feet in thickness. It is not present in the area south of the Burr Trail road. Typically the member consists of laminated to very thin-bedded siltstone and silty sandstone. It is locally ripple marked and intercalated with thin-bedded, very fine-grained, micaceous sandstone. Commonly the base of the member contains chert or quartz pebbles and locally chert-pebble conglomerate. It forms a steep slope and weathers flaggy or earthy. Locally, some gypsum may be found in this unit. It is thought that the unit was deposited on a mudflat or tidal flat and in associated lagoons (Blakey, 1974).

In the Grand Staircase section, the Timpoweap Member rests directly on the Harrisburg Member of the Kaibab Formation. In a short gulley being eroded into the side of the steep flank of the Kaibab uplift, a very thin section of tan and red sandy siltstone is found between the top of the Kaibab and normal Timpoweap Member beds, which may correlate with the Black Dragon Member.

Sinbad Member - Timpoweap Member: The Sinbad Member overlies the Black Dragon Member in the Circle Cliffs area in the Escalante Canyons section of the monument. The Sinbad Member is up to 55 feet thick in the Circle Cliffs area, thickening to the northwest. It is missing in the southeast part of the Circle Cliffs, but its outcrops extend a little farther southeastward than those of the Black Dragon Member. On the Kaibab uplift (Buckskin Mountain) the Timpoweap Member forms a thin but resistant 20- to 50-foot carapace over the uplift whaleback.

In the Circle Cliffs area the Sinbad Member consists of

yellow-gray to pale-orange-brown weathering limestone, dolomite, and calcareous siltstone. The beds are thin, weather platy, and form bench-forming ledges. It intertongues with the Black Dragon Member below and the Torrey Member above. Some limestone beds are fossiliferous, containing mostly poorly preserved pelecypods and gastropods. The Meekoceras zone has been correlated into the Sinbad-Timpoweap Members, but no truly recognizable cephalopods have yet been found so far in either unit in the monument (Davidson, 1967; Blakey, 1974).

At Buckskin Mountain, the Timpoweap Member consists of highly resistant carbonate rocks, sandstone, chert breccia, and siltstone. Some of the sandstones are pebbly. The overall color is light brown to yellow gray and the individual beds are thin to thick bedded and blocky. The upper half is more resistant than the lower part. The contact between the Kaibab and Timpoweap is difficult to discern, but the Timpoweap is generally slightly darker than the very light Kaibab Formation beds. The Sinbad-Timpoweap Member was deposited in a marine environment representing a transgression that extended the farthest east in the Moenkopi depositional basin. The thin, even beds in the Circle Cliffs might indicate quiet water deposition, whereas the chert breccias in the Timpoweap might indicate deposition in more turbulent waters.

Lower red member: The lower red member of the Moenkopi laps onto the lower parts of the Kaibab uplift whaleback, where it is 140 to 220 feet thick, thickening westward. It consists of red to chocolate-brown, interbedded and thin-bedded siltstone and fine-grained sandstone. The unit is earthy weathering and forms slopes with slight ledges. The sandstones are silty, arkosic, and micaceous. The ledges weather platy and display abundant ripple marks. The lower red member was deposited on a tidal flat traversed by meandering streams (Irwin, 1976). It correlates with the lower part of the Torrey Member in the Circle Cliffs area.

Virgin Limestone Member: The Lower Red Member is overlain by the Virgin Limestone Member around the Kaibab uplift south of Paria. The unit is only 10 to 30 feet thick, and thickens to the west. It is conspicuous because it is ledge forming. It consists of interbedded yellow-brown sandstone, siltstone, and limestone. The limestone, a minor constituent here, is very sandy and grades into calcareous sandstone in eastern sections. The pinchout of the Virgin Limestone Member probably is not far to the east of Buckskin Mountain. It is not fossiliferous in the monument where it marks the eastern limit of a Moenkopi marine incursion. The Virgin Limestone Member correlates with part of the Torrey Member in the Circle Cliffs area.

Torrey Member: The Torrey Member overlies the Sinbad Member in the Circle Cliffs uplift in the Escalante Canyons section of the monument. There it is 240 to 310 feet thick and like the other members in the uplift, thickens north-

westerly. The very fine to fine-grained sandstone and silty sandstone forms thin- to medium-bedded ledges, cliffs, and slopes. The slope-forming constituents are generally quite micaceous and the ledge formers display ripple marks, load casts, drag structures, and even animal trails. A few mud-pebble conglomerate lenses and mudstone lenses are also present in the unit. The color of the member ranges from pale red-brown to gray red where not saturated with tarry hydrocarbons. Locally hydrocarbons have bleached the Torrey Member, making it pale yellow-brown to gray and even black, according to the degree of saturation.

The Torrey Member correlates with the Lower Red Member, Virgin Limestone Member, and lower part of the Middle Red Member in the Grand Staircase section of the monument. The Torrey Member was deposited in a deltaic and shoreline environment. The upper contact with the Moody Canyon Member is intertonguing to gradational and sometimes difficult to place.

Middle red member: The middle red member overlies the Virgin Limestone Member in the area between the Vermilion Cliffs and the Kaibab uplift in the Grand Staircase section of the monument. Much of it is covered by Quaternary unconsolidated deposits (alluvium and colluvium). It is the thickest of the Moenkopi members in this section and the least resistant to erosion. Its soft and slope-forming nature has induced many of the local drainages to flow along its strike. It is 280 to 400 feet thick and probably thickens westward.

The middle red member consists of interbedded medium-brown to chocolate-brown mudstone and siltstone and light-brown, tan, or gray-green, fine-grained silty sandstone. Many of the beds are criss-crossed with gypsum veinlets. The more resistant thin-bedded sandstones are commonly rippled. The amount of gypsum in the member increases upward. It was probably deposited in mudflat and tidal flat environments. Blakey (1974) correlated the lower middle red member with the upper part of the Torrey Member and the upper part of the middle red member with the lower part of the Moody Canyon Member in the Circle Cliffs uplift.

Shnabkaib Member: The Shnabkaib Member overlies the middle red member in the area between the Vermilion Cliffs and Kaibab uplift in the Grand Staircase section of the monument. There it is 150 to 250 feet thick, thickening westward. It is a ledge- and slope-forming unit consisting of ledges of white to light green silty gypsum and light-brown very fine-grained sandstone and slopes of earthy weathering very fine-grained sandstone and red and green-gray siltstone. The lower contact is placed just under the first thick gypsum bed and the upper just above the uppermost thick gypsum bed.

The Shnabkaib was probably deposited in restricted embayments of a sea surrounded by low tidal-flat and mud-flat areas. The open sea lay to the west and encroached eastward from time to time, carrying in a fresh supply of calcium and sulfate ions needed to precipitate the gypsum.

Upper red member: The upper red member is the uppermost member of the Moenkopi Formation and overlies the gypsiferous Shnabkaib Member in the area between the Vermilion Cliffs and the Kaibab uplift in the Grand Staircase section. It is 90 to 180 feet thick, thickening to the west. It is a dark chocolate-brown to red-brown unit. The lower half forms a steep slope and the upper half weathers into ledges. The chocolate-brown ledge- and cliff-forming characteristic at the top of the member, coupled with the overlying cliff-forming Shinarump Member of the Chinle Formation form the **Chocolate Cliffs** riser of the Grand Staircase. However, the Chocolate Cliffs are better developed to the west, between the Hurricane and Paunsaugunt faults on the Arizona strip. In the monument, the Shinarump is discontinuous and does not form a conspicuous and continuous line of cliffs.

The upper red member is composed of interbedded siltstone and sandstone. The siltstones are dark chocolate brown to red brown, micaceous and sandy, and shaly to thin bedded. The sandstones are light brown to red brown, very fine grained, micaceous, and calcareous. The principal ledges are medium to thick bedded but weather blocky, platy, or shaly. As in most Moenkopi members, many sandstone beds are ripple marked and mud cracked. The upper red member is mainly a tidal flat deposit.

Moody Canyon Member: The Moody Canyon Member is 200 to 330 feet thick in the Circle Cliffs uplift area of the Escalante Canyons section, thickening to the west. It is mostly a slope former composed of red-brown interbedded siltstone and mudstone. Dolomite, gypsum, and sandstone are minor constituents. It is finely to poorly laminated to thin bedded, but is generally earthy weathering. The Moody Canyon Member correlates with the upper red member, Shnabkaib Member, and upper half of the middle red member in the Grand Staircase section of the monument. The Moody Canyon is believed to have been deposited in shallow quiet water, such as in ponds or lagoons on a tidal flat (Blakey, 1974).

Chinle Formation (Trc)

The Upper Triassic Chinle Formation in the Colorado Plateau consists of several members, some of which are present in the monument. The most well-known of these are the Shinarump and Petrified Forest Members. All the members (ascending) include the Temple Mountain, Shinarump, Monitor Butte, Moss Back, Petrified Forest, Owl Rock, and Church Rock Members. These members are not present in every location, and for the newcomer, may be difficult to differentiate. The simplest subdivision of the Chinle is into its lower ledge-forming and upper slope-forming parts.

The Chinle is a lithologically heterogeneous unit composed of varying amounts of fluvial and lacustrine interbedded sandstone, mudstone, claystone, siltstone, limestone, gritstone, and conglomerate. It is 500 to 930 feet thick in the Grand Staircase section of the monument and 425 to 750 feet thick in the Circle Cliffs area. There are no detectable thickness trends in the monument and changes in thickness of 150 feet or more are common across short distances.

The most abundant fossil in the Chinle Formation is petrified wood (see Petrified Forest Member discussion), mostly the wood of conifers, ferns, and cycads. Others include bivalves, fish, labyrinthodont amphibians, phytosaurs, dinosaurs, and dinosaur tracks. Discoveries of vertebrate skeletal material has been sparse in the monument area, but vertebrates are well represented by fossil tracks (Hamblin, this volume).

Temple Mountain Member: This member has only been recognized in the Circle Cliffs area of the monument. There it is up to 50 feet thick, averaging 15 to 20 feet thick. It forms slopes and ledges between the Moody Canyon Member of the Moenkopi Formation and the resistant cliff-forming sandstones of the Shinarump Member. It rests on an erosional surface at the top of the Moenkopi Formation that exhibits an average of two feet of relief.

The most distinctive thing about the Temple Mountain Member is its mottled appearance. The dominant colors are maroon and white, but yellows, reds, purples, and blacks are common. It is a paleosol (ancient soil) and vertical bleachings probably represent root casts. It consists of well-cemented siltstone containing scattered medium and coarse angular grains of quartz. Considerable amounts of dark minerals, notably tourmaline, are present, indicating the source of the siltstone was not the Moenkopi Formation. It is mostly a fluvial deposit that was highly weathered before the Shinarump and later sediments were deposited.

Shinarump Member: The Shinarump Member of the Chinle Formation is primarily a stream-channel deposit. Streams meandered northwestward across an old Moenkopi surface where local thick soils had developed. The streams locally cut deep channels into this surface. The Shinarump Member is found mostly southwest of the Henry Mountains and does not correlate with basal members of the Chinle in the Paradox basin (Moab area). In the Kanab to St. George area, the Shinarump becomes a blanket stream deposit. During Chinle time, southwest Utah may have been an area of interior drainage, with the Shinarump streams depositing their loads of suspended materials over a broad flat that had developed on the old Moenkopi surface. The Shinarump has been recognized both in the Circle Cliffs area in the Escalante Canyons section and in the Paria area of the Grand Staircase section of the monument. In both places it is discontinuous. In the Paria area, it is channel-form and, in the vicinity of the old Paria movie set, rests in scours directly on the top of the upper red member of the Moenkopi Formation. There is generally a few feet of bleached Moenkopi beneath the channel. The Grand Staircase section Shinarump is up to

Figure 19. Gingham Skirts Butte in the Paria area, Grand Staircase section. The colorful banded Petrified Forest Member of the Chinle Formation is breathtaking to the beholder. Similar color is also displayed in the Circle Cliffs area, Escalante Canyons section, in the Petrified Forest Member.

155 feet thick and averages 55 feet. In the Circle Cliffs area the Shinarump was deposited in channels and as a blanket deposit. Some of the larger and deeper channels of this member have cut through the Temple Mountain Member into the Moody Canyon Member of the Moenkopi. Larger Shinarump channels in the Circle Cliffs, such as those preserved in the Stud Horse Peaks, are as much as 190 feet deep and as much as 8,000 feet wide. In the Circle Cliffs area the flow direction of the ancient paleo-rivers that deposited the Shinarump Member was primarily from the southeast to the northwest.

In the Paria area the Shinarump Member consists of very pale orange, gray orange, yellow gray, or very light gray sandstone and conglomeratic sandstone and some partings of green or gray mudstone. It is lenticular and massive, cliff forming, well cemented, with cobbles as much as 3 inches in diameter. The cementing material is commonly calcareous. Conglomeratic sandstones contain scattered fragments of petrified wood. The sandstone is quartzose, mostly medium to coarse grained, and trough cross-bedded. In the Circle Cliffs area the Shinarump can be subdivided into three units. There is a lower interbedded, medium-grained, very thick bedded sandstone; an intermediate interlayered, thin-bedded sandstone, siltstone, and mudstone and an upper poorly sorted, slabby, thin- to thick-bedded sandstone. The colors are the same as in the Paria area. The sandstone is feldspathic and composed of quartz, feldspar, kaolin, and flakes of muscovite and biotite. The grains are poorly sorted and cemented with kaolin. Fragmentary plant material and small uranium-copper deposits have been found in the Shinarump Member in the Circle Cliffs area.

Monitor Butte Member: The Monitor Butte Member overlies the Shinarump Member in the monument and intertongues with its neighbors above and below. It forms ledgy slopes and is commonly included with the Shinarump because of its dominant gray coloration. The member may be up to 185 feet thick in the Paria River area with most sections averaging 60 to 70 feet. In the Circle Cliffs area it is 100 to 200 feet thick.

In the Paria area it is light-colored sandstone with interbeds of gray silty mudstone or siltstone. The sandstones are thin bedded to massive, fine to medium grained and some are gritty and pebbly. Toward the top of the member, mudstone, sandstone, nodular-weathering brown limestone and gritty conglomeratic sandstone are complexly interbedded and highly lenticular. Generally the unit becomes less resistant, but more coarsely grained upward. It locally contains abundant petrified wood in the form of logs, branches, and fragments. North of the Paria cemetery it contains carbonaceous shales and coal beds.

In the Circle Cliffs area the Monitor Butte Member is a green-gray bentonitic mudstone interlensed with gray sandstone and brown conglomerate. The mudstone consists of a mixture of bentonitic claystone, silty claystone, and clay-rich siltstone. The sandstone beds are gray to light brown, very lenticular, moderately to well sorted, very fine grained to fine grained, micaceous, and are locally conglomeratic. The sandstone and conglomerate beds contain scattered petrified wood fragments. Generally, sandstone beds are more common in areas overlying channels of the Shinarump Member, indicating that stream courses established by Shinarump streams were maintained during Monitor Butte time.

Monitor Butte sediments were deposited on the flood plains of streams. Locally lakes and ponds developed on these plains, which were lined with abundant vegetation. Vegetal matter accumulated in long-lived lakes, forming peat bogs and eventually coal.

Petrified Forest Member: Whereas the lower three members of the Chinle Formation generally form cliffs or ledgy slopes, the upper three members generally form slopes, steep slopes, and higher in the section, ledgy slopes. These three members are the Petrified Forest, Owl Rock, and Church Rock Members. The most conspicuous characteristic of the Petrified Forest Member is its bright coloration (figure 19). It displays a spectacular variety of color, usually differentiated in bands, that on a sunny day have inspired such names as The Land of the Sleeping Rainbow, Gingham Skirts Butte, and Calico Peak. The beauty of the member is partly blemished by the fact that this unit contains abundant swelling clays and is, therefore, extremely prone to slope and foundation failures. Numerous landslides in the region are rooted in this member. In developed areas the member is known as the "blue clay." Houses built upon it and not firmly anchored in something more "solid," suffer structural damage as walls and foundations settle differentially, brick walls develop cracks, and the like. Piping is another problem. Roads built upon it commonly develop chuck holes deep and large enough to swallow tires and small vehicles. The beautiful coloration invites hikers to walk upon it, but the steep slopes are hard and unyielding in dry weather and more slippery than ice after a rain.

In the Grand Staircase section of the monument, the Petrified Forest Member is the first formation beneath the Vermilion Cliffs. In the Escalante Canyons section the member is exposed beneath the Circle Cliffs (Wingate Sandstone), although not directly beneath. In the Circle Cliffs area the Owl Rock and Church Rock Members overlie the Petrified Forest Member beneath the Wingate Sandstone cliffs. Perhaps the best place to observe the Petrified Forest Member in the Grand Staircase section is on the approach to the old Paria town site at Gingham Skirts Butte and, in the Escalante Canyons section, at the head of Long Canyon at The Land of the Sleeping Rainbow. In the Grand Staircase section the Petrified Forest Member is also exposed in Hackberry Canyon.

The Petrified Forest Member is mainly bentonitic mudstone, friable muddy sandstone, and minor conglomerate. A small amount of brown- or nodular-weathering limestone is also present. Bentonite, or montmorillonite, is a type of clay produced from the decomposition (devitrification) of volcanic ash. It swells dramatically when wet. Bentonitic character can be recognized by peculiar "popcorn" surfaces of outcrops. The bentonitic character seems to disappear in the upper parts of some sections. It is common to have the normal steep colorful slope replaced by a hummocky landslide surface on which angular boulders and fragments of overlying sandstone formations "swim."

The Petrified Forest Member was deposited on a fluvial plain largely as overbank deposits. The plain was dotted with lakes and ponds. At times, as the sediments accumulated, volcanic ash settled on the plain, which was altered to clay and locally into siliceous brown nodules. Local layers in the Petrified Forest Member contain abundant fossil wood. In the Circle Cliffs area, silicified logs as much as 6 feet in diameter and 90 feet in length have been found. The petrified wood was locally mined in the Grand Staircase section of the monument (before the monument was established). These logs are brightly colored and were avidly sought by collectors for cutting and polishing. A half-inch slab of a log with a diameter of 9 inches, polished to a high sheen, could be purchased in a Berlin, Germany rock shop for $2,000 in 1990. Remember that collecting is forbidden in the monument. The unit has been aptly named.

Owl Rock Member: The Owl Rock Member was identified by Davidson (1967) in the Circle Cliffs area as overlying the Petrified Forest Member. It crops out in the steep slope formed by the three upper units of the Chinle Formation. It is 150 to 250 feet thick. Some investigators indicated they believe that the less bentonitic upper part of the Petrified Forest Member near the Paria ghost town is correlative with the Owl Rock Member (Stewart and others, 1972; Blakey 1974).

The Owl Rock Member is composed of thin lenticular beds of green limestone interbedded with red, brown, and green-gray sandstone and mudstone. The limestone beds are hard and resistant, generally forming ledges. Whereas the Petrified Forest Member contains abundant bentonitic mudstone, this unit contains much less. It too was deposited in a fluvial environment on a plain dotted with lakes.

Church Rock Member: In eastern Utah the Church Rock Member consists of red-brown to orange-brown sandstone and silty sandstone. Some of the upper sandstones are resistant and blocky weathering. About 15 to 25 feet of such sandstones underlie the vertical cliff of the Wingate Sand-

Figure 20. A part of the White Cliffs in the Grand Staircase section of the monument. The upper white part of the Navajo Sandstone is capped by a thin layer of Co-op Creek Limestone Member of the Carmel Formation.

Figure 21. Wilsey Hollow and Mollies Nipple, erosional forms in the Navajo Sandstone in the Grand Staircase section.

stone in the Circle Cliffs area. The sandstone is fine to medium grained, massive to thick bedded, and it is cross-stratified on a small scale. The sediments were deposited in lakes and by streams on an alluvial plain that sloped away from the Uncompahgre uplift in eastern Utah during Late Triassic time (Stewart and others, 1972).

Jurassic Rocks

Lower, Middle, and Upper Jurassic rocks are exposed in the monument; the formations of each series are separated by significant regional unconformities (Pipiringos and O'Sullivan, 1978), shown as wavy lines on the litho-logic profile, figure 14. Lower Jurassic formations include (ascending) the Wingate Sandstone-Moenave Formation, Kayenta Formation, and Navajo Sandstone. These are sometimes combined as the **Glen Canyon Group**. Middle Jurassic formations include (ascending) the Page Sandstone, Carmel Formation, Entrada Sandstone, Henrieville Sandstone, and Romana Mesa Sandstone that are sometimes combined as the **San Rafael Group**. Upper Jurassic rocks consist of members of the Morrison Formation.

Erosion beneath a regional unconformity at the base of the Cretaceous rocks has successively cut out Upper and Middle Jurassic units down to the Carmel Formation from the east to the west. Relationship and facies changes in the Middle Jurassic formations are evident across the monument.

Wingate Sandstone - Moenave Formation (Jw-Jmo)

The name "Circle Cliffs" originated from the bounding rim of Wingate Sandstone cliffs that encircle this area (figure 31). The Wingate Sandstone forms prominent, massive, vertical cliffs; locally, joints pass from the top to the bottom of the 230- to 350-foot cliff. At times a slab made up of the entire thickness of the formation crashes

and disintegrates into rubbly rock fall at its base. Parting surfaces are rare in the unit. Close examination, however, reveals the presence of large-scale cross-beds and cross-bed sets.

The sandstone is orange brown, very fine to fine grained, very well sorted, and quartzose. In many parts of the Circle Cliffs area, the Wingate Sandstone is yellow-gray, presumably reduced by hydrocarbons. It is commonly moderately to well cemented with carbonate. The beds are planar and trough cross-bedded in sets 40 to 60 feet thick. Nevertheless, the bed and set boundaries are not selectively weathered or eroded more than the rock between them, thus maintaining the smooth cliff face. The Wingate Sandstone was deposited in eolian (sand dune) and sabhka environments. Few fossils have been found in the Wingate Sandstone. A single dinosaur track site is present in the Circle Cliffs area. This site exhibits about 10 Gralator-type tracks, five of which form a trackway (Hamblin, this volume).

The Wingate Sandstone is not recognizable in the Grand Staircase section of the monument, and is replaced by the laterally equivalent Moenave Formation. The two formations intertongue in the subsurface of the Kaiparow-its Basin, and a tongue of the Wingate persists under the Moenave for a considerable distance westward. Some of the lower sandstones in the Moenave Formation in the Grand Staircase section are reminiscent of the Wingate. The Moenave is divisible into (ascending) the Dinosaur Canyon Member and Springdale Sandstone Member. West of Johnson Canyon, a third member appears between the Dinosaur Canyon and the Springdale (Whitmore Point Member). The Whitmore Point Member is not recognizable in the monument.

Dinosaur Canyon Member: The Dinosaur Canyon Member forms the **lower part of the Vermilion Cliffs** and varies in thickness from 100 to 220 feet in the Grand Staircase Section of the monument. The member forms steep slopes, ledgy slopes, and cliffs.

Figure 22. Etched-out cross-beds in the Navajo Sandstone on the benches in the Escalante Canyons section.

This member is mostly red-orange to red-brown siltstone with lesser amounts of red, very fine grained sandstone, claystone, and conglomerate. The percentage of sandstone and coarse siltstone increases to the northeast. These form thin to thick tabular beds, ledges, and cliffs. The finer constituents form laminae to very thin beds and steep slopes. The Dinosaur Canyon was deposited on a lake-covered flood plain and mud-flat dominated environment on which a few small rivers flowed. Fossils found in the monument include fish remains and vertebrate dinosaur tracks (Foster and others, 1999).

Springdale Sandstone Member: The Springdale Sandstone Member is a red-brown to orange-brown cliff former that forms the **middle part of the Vermilion Cliffs** and is about 100 to 230 feet thick in the Grand Staircase section of the monument. It commonly exhibits a yellow-gray upper surface at its contact with the Kayenta Formation that is a few inches to a foot thick.

The Springdale is mostly fine- to very fine grained and consists of relatively uniform, lenticular, overlapping beds of cross-bedded sandstone. Partings and thin beds of siltstone and claystone separate the thick to massive beds. Locally, it contains intraformational conglomerate lenses of claystone pellets and angular fragments of siltstone in a quartz sand matrix. The sandstone exhibits trough cross-stratification, ripple marks and mud-cracked surfaces.

The environment of deposition was similar to that for the Dinosaur Canyon Member in the Grand Staircase section.

Kayenta Formation (Jk, Jkt)

This unit forms the **upper part of the Vermilion Cliffs** and the surface of part of the Wygaret Terrace in the Grand Staircase section of the monument. In the Escalante Canyons section, the Kayenta is a bench former. Many mesas and buttes held up by the Wingate Sandstone are capped by this ledgy formation. Whereas underlying and overlying formations are massive, commonly smooth-weathering sandstones, the Kayenta forms thick ledges of sandstone. This ledgy habit contrasts conspicuously with the smooth cliffs of the Wingate, Navajo, and Moenave. It is 150 to 350 feet thick in the Escalante Canyons section and 190 to 340 feet thick in the Grand Staircase section.

Red, brown, lavender, and purple are the colors most commonly used to describe this formation, but some individual beds are light yellow, buff, and gray, though they are commonly stained from the red-browns and dark purple-reds of the majority of beds. The Kayenta is a succession of lenticular, mostly medium grained, fluvially cross-bedded, thick-bedded sandstone with thinner red interbeds of siltstone and mudstone, subordinate thin to medium beds of gray or lavender-gray limestone, and thin to thick beds of intraformational pebble conglomerate.

The environment of deposition of the Kayenta Formation is dominantly fluvial, but lacustrine and eolian beds are interbedded, notably in the upper part of the unit. Dinosaur tracks are locally common in the Kayenta Formation. Other fossils occurring in the monument include petrified wood and undiagnostic vertebrate bone fragments.

The upper part of the Kayenta intertongues with the Navajo Sandstone. Usually the tongues are insignificant; that is, they cannot be reliably correlated over long distances. However, significant intertonguing is present west of the Paunsaugunt fault in the Grand Staircase section. Here a tongue of the Kayenta extends eastward into the Navajo Sandstone, pinching out just before reaching the Paunsaugunt fault. That part of the Kayenta participating in the tongue is called the Tenney Canyon Tongue. That part of the Navajo Sandstone beneath the Tenney Canyon Tongue is called the Lamb Point Tongue of the Navajo Sandstone.

Lamb Point Tongue of the Navajo Sandstone (Jnl): This tongue is typically like the main body or upper part of the Navajo Sandstone. It is white, tan, or gray eolian cross-bedded cliff-forming sandstone with minor thin, red-brown siltstone and gray limestone. It is 250 to 350 feet thick in the monument.

Lamb Point sandstone is mostly fine to medium grained with mostly rounded to subrounded frosted quartzose grains. A small quantity of chert and feldspar grains are also present. Carbonate cementation is loose and irregular so that the rock may be quite friable. It is an excellent aquifer and wells in it supply the culinary water for Kanab and Fredonia. The Lamb Point Tongue exhibits thick cross-bed sets (as much as 25 feet thick) and cross-bed angles locally exceed 36 degrees. Toward the top the cross-beds are commonly contorted.

Like the Navajo, the Lamb Point Tongue represents windblown sand converted to rock. High water tables during time of deposition account for the minor, thin, red-brown siltstone and gray limestone beds and partings.

Tenney Canyon Tongue of the Kayenta Formation (Jkt): This tongue of red-brown siltstone, mudstone, and fine-grained sandstone forms either a ledgy slope or a recess between the main body of the Navajo Sandstone and the Lamb Point Tongue between Johnson Canyon and the Paunsaugunt fault in the Grand Staircase section of the monument. Near the Paunsaugunt fault it grades into the eolian beds of the Navajo Sandstone, but the red-brown color persists to the canyon of the Paria River. It is up to 80 feet thick in the monument. It locally contains a thin gray limestone bed. Like the main body of the Kayenta Formation the Tenney Canyon Tongue is a fluvial deposit. Because it is so thin it is shown as a dark green line on the geologic map (figure 15).

Navajo Sandstone (Jn)

The Navajo Sandstone is an easily recognized and prominent unit in Grand Staircase-Escalante National Monument and is present in both the Escalante Canyons and Grand Staircase sections. It is a massive cliff former and **its upper part forms the White Cliffs riser** of the Grand Staircase (figure 20). It generally forms bare-rock outcrops with high-angle cross-beds. It is 1,300 to 1,500 feet thick in the Grand Staircase section and is 1,100 to 1,300 feet thick in the Escalante Canyons section. It generally thickens from east to west.

The Navajo is a light-colored, fine- to medium-grained, massive sandstone. It displays an elaborate array of high-angle cross-beds (figure 22) and forms cliffs, domes, monuments, and other bizarre erosional forms (figure 21). Locally, thin lenses of limestone, dolomite, or dark-red sandy mudstone are also present. Where it does not form cliffs or monuments, its hollows are commonly filled with sand. The light coloration of the Navajo has been described with almost every color; white, tan, buff, salmon, pink, vermilion, brown, red, yellow, cream, orange, and gray. Hematitic cement produces the red colors, limonite the yellows, and ferrous iron minerals the browns and local greens. Most of the grains are subrounded to well rounded, well sorted, frosted, and quartzose. Much of the Navajo is lightly cemented and friable. The upper part, however, is better cemented, either with silica or carbonate cement and is more likely to form cliffs. Cross-beds are in sets as much as 35 feet thick. Locally, and especially near the base (especially in the Lamb Point Tongue), the Navajo includes massive horizontal or planar beds.

The Navajo is dominantly an eolian deposit laid down in dunes above a shallow water table. The thin limestones, dolomites, and dark-red sandy mudstones were deposited in oases, playas, or ponds. As the sands subsided, the water table surface rose and wind commonly blew away sand above it to form a set boundary before the next dune was deposited over it. One might imagine ridges of wandering dunes over a damp surface during Navajo time. Locally, both in the Grand Staircase and Escalante Canyons sections, a thick iron scum or froth accumulated on the tops of the water tables. During diagenesis these hardened to form ironstone sheets within the sandstone. Locally these occur as disk, ball, and dumb-bell forms. At Spencer Flat (No. 16 on figure 2), they occur as spheres known as "Moqui marbles." It is assumed that air bubbles were forced upward to the water table where an iron scum had accumulated and formed a froth of bubbles. These spheres contain only loose or friable sand in the centers which falls out when the ironstone concretion is broken (Doelling, 1968). Between Hackberry Canyon and Cottonwood Wash (just west of the Cockscomb) iron sheets have been deformed to produce bizarre shapes. Ironstone is also quite common northeast of The Swags at the end of the Kitchen Corral Wash road. Only vertebrate tracks have been found in the Navajo Sandstone: a few on dune faces, most on the thin limestones.

The top of the Navajo Sandstone is a major regional unconformity. In the Grand Staircase section it is overlain by the Co-op Creek Limestone Member of the Carmel Formation. In the Escalante Canyons section it is overlain by the Page Sandstone. In the Escalante Canyons section the lowermost Page may look much like the Navajo Sandstone and is difficult to separate from it. The contact may appear to be a simple set boundary near the top of the Navajo. The base of the Page locally contains angular fragments of chert. Also the Page is generally slightly darker than the Navajo Sandstone. This unconformity (J-2 unconformity of Pipiringos and O'Sullivan, 1978) at the top of the Navajo Sandstone appears to be a flat surface, but undulates with wide amplitude and accounts for differences in the thickness of the Navajo of up to 200 feet or more.

Page Sandstone and Carmel Formation (Jc, Jcl, Jcu)

The Page Sandstone and Carmel Formation intertongue and undergo facies changes from west to east across the monument (figure 23). The Carmel Formation to the west contains marine rocks that intertongue with terrestrial rocks eastward. The Page Sandstone represents beach, back-beach, and dune deposits on the landward side of Carmel deposition. The Carmel sea transgressed southward from Canada in a north-south-trending embayment that terminated in northern Arizona. Rocks exposed in the monument were deposited along the east margin of that embayment. Generally, the rocks thin from west to east.

In the Grand Staircase section the following members and tongues are exposed: (ascending) Co-op Creek Limestone Member, Crystal Creek Member, Thousand Pockets Tongue of the Page Sandstone, Paria River Member, and Winsor Member. The lower two members of the Carmel Formation become very thin east of the East Kaibab monocline (The Cockscomb) where they are combined into one unit known as the Judd Hollow Tongue of the Carmel Formation. Limestone persists in the Judd Hollow Tongue for a few miles beneath the Kaiparowits basin and represents the easternmost extension of the Co-op Creek transgression of the Carmel sea. Thereafter the sea regressed leaving the Crystal Creek Member followed by the Thousand Pockets Tongue of the Page Sandstone in its wake. The Co-op Creek Limestone, Crystal Creek, and Thousand Pockets Tongue units are grouped into the Jcl unit shown on the geologic map (figure 15). On the other two geologic maps (figures 16, 17) the Carmel and Page are mapped as an undivided unit (Jc). A second major transgression followed to deposit the Paria River Member. The sea spread eastward across and beyond the monument area and its deposits are characterized by thin platy limestone and gypsum beds. Though widespread, the sea was very shallow, and was commonly cut off from open-sea circulation. A very gradual retreat of the sea is represented in the Winsor Member, which was also deposited across the entire monument area. Thompson and Stokes (1970) differentiated the Wiggler Wash Member as the youngest member of the Carmel Formation, but we believe this member is a gypsum-bearing facies of the Winsor. The type Wiggler Wash Member has gypsum beds near the top of the Carmel Formation, but gypsum beds can be found region-

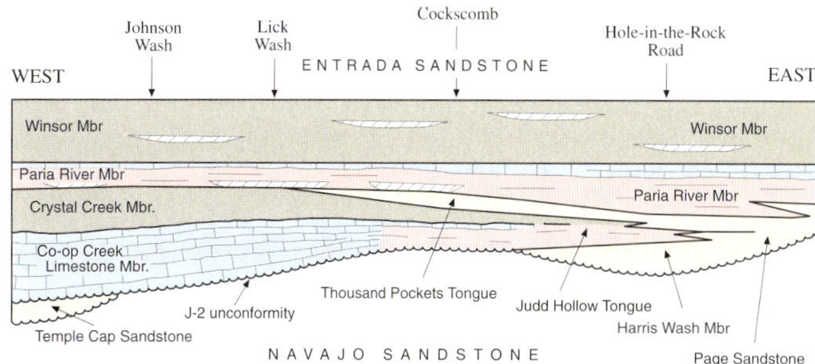

Figure 23. Diagram showing Carmel-Page relationships from west to east across the Grand Staircase-Escalante National Monument.

ally at any level within the Winsor Member.

The Page Sandstone was deposited concurrently with the Carmel Formation east of the Co-op Creek transgression of the Carmel sea and was deposited over much of the monument area prior to the Paria River transgression. East of the monument the Paria River Member grades into Page Sandstone lithologies as does the lower part of the Winsor. The Carmel Formation and Page Sandstone are both exposed along the boundary of the Kaiparowits Basin and Escalante Canyons sections of the monument and subparallel the Hole-in-the Rock road in the Escalante Canyons section. They are eroded from the Circle Cliffs uplift and crop out again in the Waterpocket Fold (Capitol Reef National Park), east of the monument. There the following members are exposed: (ascending) Harris Wash Member of the Page Sandstone, Judd Hollow Tongue of the Carmel Formation, Thousand Pockets Tongue of the Page Sandstone, and Paria River and Winsor Members of the Carmel Formation.

Harris Wash Member (Page Sandstone): This member rests upon the Navajo Sandstone in outcrops that subparallel the Hole-in-the-Rock Road on the east side of the Straight Cliffs (Fiftymile Mountain). It is not present in the Grand Staircase section of the monument. It has the appearance of the Navajo Sandstone, commonly displays high-angle eolian-type cross-stratification in sets 7 to 22 feet thick, and is a massive cliff former.

The contact at the base of the Page Sandstone, the J-2 unconformity of Pipiringos and O'Sullivan (1978), is not a set boundary, but an erosional surface, above which angular bits and pieces of chert are commonly found. The relief on this unconformity may be as much as 70 feet, but is hardly noticeable because the distance between troughs and highs is considerable. The Harris Wash Member is commonly slightly darker in color than the Navajo below and locally contains red-brown, lenticular, very fine grained silty sandstone reminiscent of regressive Carmel Formation deposits. The member is 50 to 120 feet thick along Hole-in-the-Rock Road and is not present on the west side of the Kaiparowits Basin section. The Harris Wash Tongue is mostly light-brown to light-gray, very fine to fine-grained sandstone. It is porous and slightly calcareous.

Co-op Creek Limestone Member (Carmel Formation):
The Co-op Creek Limestone Member crops out in the Grand Staircase section of the monument on the Skutumpah Terrace. There it is 35 to 170 feet thick, becoming thicker westward. In the Cockscomb area it may locally be thinner than 35 feet and attenuated. The Co-op Creek Limestone Member forms steep slopes with ledges near the top and bottom. The steep slopes are generally littered with plates, chips, and pencils of limestone.

The Co-op Creek Limestone Member consists of light-gray limestone and olive-gray calcareous shale. Although beds are thin to thick bedded, most are thin bedded. Medium and thick beds are encountered near the base and near the top of the member. Red siltstones and sandstones and even conglomerate may crop out at the base and correspond to the Gypsum Springs Member of the Twin Creek Limestone as found in northern Utah. A few thin gypsum beds have been noted in the Bull Valley Gorge area (Grand Staircase section) above the thin red siltstones near the base of the member. The thicker bedded, ledgier parts of the member are locally fossiliferous and contain pelecypods, gastropods, and the star-shaped crinoid stem, *Pentacrinus*.

Crystal Creek Member (Carmel Formation): This brown-banded silty sandstone forms earthy slopes. The banding is best displayed in steep slopes and fresh road cuts. Like the Co-op Creek Limestone Member, it becomes very thin eastward and becomes part of the Judd Hollow Tongue along the eastern edge of the Grand Staircase Section of the monument. The unit ranges from about 10 to 70 feet and reaches a maximum of about 180 feet west of Kanab. Its outcrop band lies above the Co-op Creek Limestone Member on the Skutumpah Terrace, continuing across the Paria amphitheater to the Cockscomb. It is generally only 10 to 15 feet thick in the Cockscomb area.

The Crystal Creek Member is mostly a silty, very fine grained, friable, poorly cemented sandstone and sandy siltstone. Gypsum is the usual cementing material. Locally, a thin gypsum bed may crop out or a thin bed of coarse-grained sandstone may be present. It is overlain by the Thousand Pockets Tongue of the Page Sandstone east of Lick Wash on the Skutumpah Terrace. It is overlain by gypsum of the Paria River Member west of Lick Wash.

Judd Hollow Tongue (Carmel Formation): Along the Cockscomb the Judd Hollow Tongue is 30 to 60 feet thick, and forms a prominent reddish recess of sandstone, siltstone, and silty limestone, between the Navajo Sandstone and the Thousand Pockets Tongue of the Page Sandstone. Some of the thinner sections may represent thinning due to attenuation along the steeply dipping East Kaibab monocline. A persistent 10- to 15-foot-thick reddish recess above the Judd Hollow may represent another thin Carmel tongue in the lower part of the Thousand Pockets Tongue. Along Hole-in-the-Rock Road, it consists of interbedded ledgy sandstones and reddish silty sandstone 15 to 40 feet thick. This appears to be a zone of inter-

tonguing between the red calcareous sandstones of the Judd Hollow and the yellow-gray sandstones of the Page.

Thousand Pockets Tongue (Page Sandstone): This tongue of sandstone first appears at Lick Wash in the Grand Staircase section, thickens eastward, and in outcrop is thickest along the Cockscomb. It is present, but thin, along the Hole-in-the-Rock Road, at the boundary between the Kaiparowits and Escalante Canyons sections of the monument. It is up to 200 feet thick, including thin Carmel tongues that may appear between its upper and lower contacts.

The Thousand Pockets Tongue is yellow-gray to gray-white, fine- to medium-grained quartzose sandstone that exhibits eolian-type, high-angle cross-bedding. It is mostly massive and cliff or ledge forming. Grains are generally subrounded and well sorted. It is friable and yellow gray in exposures from Lick Wash into the Tropic Amphitheater; it is better cemented and gray-white in eastern sections. South of the Kodachrome State Park area, it is locally (near Rock Springs Canyon) mineralized and coated or disseminated with copper and lead minerals.

Paria River Member: The Paria River Member is a transgressive deposit of the Carmel sea. Although it has far wider distribution than the lower Co-op Creek transgression, and crops out both in the Kaiparowits Basin and Grand Staircase sections, its limestone beds are considerably thinner than that of the Co-op Creek Limestone Member. It reaches a maximum thickness of about 280 feet in West Cove in the southern part of the Cockscomb area. There the upper limestone is completely replaced by a massive yellow-gray resistant beach-sand deposit. The member may be as little as 100 feet thick near the west boundary of the monument; from there it thickens easterly to the area of the Cockscomb, and then thins again, and is only 50 to 100 feet thick along the Hole-in-the-Rock Road.

The member consists of red or red-brown interbedded silty sandstone and sandy siltstone near the base and white or lavender chippy to platy, very thin bedded limestone at the top. The limestone locally contains poorly preserved pelecypods and gastropods and is locally sandy. In the west a very thick, white, massive alabaster gypsum bed lies at the base. This basal gypsum bed is not present in the Cockscomb area and eastward. On the Skutumpah Terrace patches of the 10- to 20-foot-thick basal gypsum bed are present. At Averett Canyon on the west side of the Tropic amphitheater the patchy nature of the gypsum is well illustrated. A thick bed is present on one side of the canyon and is completely missing on the other.

Winsor Member: This member is a steep slope-forming, earthy-weathering unit reminiscent of the Crystal Creek Member beneath it. It is mostly light to medium brown, but yellows are common, especially in the west part of the monument. West of Lick Wash, in the Grand Staircase section of the monument, it is unconformably overlain by the coal-bearing Dakota Formation. To the east of Lick Wash it is conformably overlain by various facies of the Entrada Sandstone. It varies in thickness from about 110 to 320 feet. It is probably 250 feet thick along the west monument boundary. It thickens gradually to the Cockscomb where it reaches maximum thickness, and then thins eastward. Near Fiftymile Point at the south end of the Straight Cliffs, it is only 120 feet thick.

The Winsor Member is mostly light- to medium-brown, very fine to medium-grained sandstone that weathers to an earthy slope. To the east it contains thin to medium beds of varicolored gypsum and gypsiferous sandstones that are gray green. These gypsum beds weather blocky and have locally been extracted to make small sculptings for indoor use. The coloration in the gypsum exhibits pinks, browns, greens, and less commonly blues in thin laminae. Unfortunately, in the open, the gypsum weathers and breaks apart along these thin laminae. Bedding is indistinct in western exposures; to the east a few resistant ledges develop in the member, and together with the gypsum beds, give a good sense of the stratification. The gypsum beds can and do appear at any level within the member.

The Carmel-Entrada contact is thought to be conformable. In most places it is sharp and placed beneath the smooth-weathering (slickrim), bare-rock Entrada outcrop. Locally the contact is uneven because of post-depositional deformation. Especially along the Hole-in-the Rock road, large bodies of the Entrada have "sunk" deeply into the Winsor Member. Winsor strata around these large bodies of Entrada Sandstone are deformed.

Entrada Sandstone (Je)

The Entrada outcrops begin at Lick Wash in the west part of the Grand Staircase section of the monument and extend eastward. West of Lick Wash the Entrada was removed by erosion prior to Cretaceous deposition. East of Lick Wash, on the Skutumpah Terrace extending around the Tropic amphitheater and down the Cockscomb on the west margin of the Kaiparowits Plateau, the Entrada is overlain by the Dakota Sandstone. Between Cannonville and Butler Valley in the Tropic amphitheater, the Entrada is capped by the Henrieville Sandstone, which some investigators believe is merely a hardening at the top of the Entrada Sandstone (Bowers, 1975, 1983). On the southeast and east sides of the Kaiparowits Plateau, the Entrada is overlain by the Romana Mesa Sandstone and Morrison Formation, respectively. The Morrison and Romana Mesa Sandstone are also cut out by the same unconformity that cuts out the Entrada west of Lick Wash. This is evident a few miles east of Big Water along the south margin of the Kaiparowits Plateau. The Entrada was deposited in environments similar to those that deposited the Carmel Formation in its terrestrial environments: tidal flat, sabhka, beach, and back-beach deposits.

The Entrada Sandstone is divisible into three parts: (ascending) the Gunsight Butte, Cannonville, and Es-

Figure 24. *Two Devils Garden goblins with the Straight Cliffs in the background. The goblins form in the Entrada Sandstone at the contact between the Gunsight Butte and Cannonville Members.*

calante Members. The Escalante Member is only present in the north half of the monument, along the north edge of Kane County and in Garfield County.

Gunsight Butte Member: The lower member of the Entrada Sandstone is a typical "slickrim" sandstone. It weathers into cliffs and rounded bare-rock smooth-weathering outcrops. The color along the Hole-in-the-Rock Road and in the Tropic amphitheater is orange-brown to red orange. Along the south half of the Cockscomb it is yellow gray and in West Cove has a red band in it. It locally forms very picturesque and conspicuous erosional forms. These include Dance-Hall Rock, Sooner Rocks, Cave Point, and Lone Rock. It is up to 450 feet thick. Along the Hole-in-the-Rock Road it is 200 to 450 feet thick with the thickest sections to the south. Along the Cockscomb the member is 150 to 280 feet thick, but is locally attenuated and faulted out. In the Tropic amphitheater the member is 200 to 300 feet thick.

The Gunsight Butte Member is very fine to fine-grained and silty sandstone that contains sparse medium to coarse, frosted, subrounded to rounded grains of pink and gray quartz. Like the Navajo Sandstone, it exhibits large-scale eolian cross-bedding, but weathers to smooth surfaces. Thin lenses of somewhat darker mudstone interrupt the otherwise massive unit. Much of it is covered by sandy surficial deposits that are largely derived from it (see figures 15, 16, and 17).

The Gunsight Butte Member is a wind-blown deposit probably laid down in dunes. The upper contact with the Cannonville is represented by a change from resistant bare-rock outcrops to bedded, earthy-weathering, slope-forming sandstone. In areas where the "slickrim" is orange-brown, a yellow-gray sandstone overlies it, above which the Entrada becomes earthy weathering. The top of the Gunsight Butte Member locally forms goblins and other interesting erosional forms as is displayed in the Devils Garden along the Hole-in-the-Rock road about 17 miles southeast of Escalante (figure 24).

Cannonville Member: The middle or Cannonville Member of the Entrada Sandstone generally forms a steep slope and is banded. In the Tropic amphitheater it displays a yellow-white color with faint red bands. This persists along the Cockscomb. In the area between Escalante and Cat Pasture along the Hole-in-the-Rock Road, the member is prominently banded in shades of brown or red brown. Here large areas of Cannonville outcrop are covered with unconsolidated sandy Quaternary deposits. Between Cat Pasture and Fiftymile Point, the Cannonville Member changes into a medium red-brown, medium to thick-bedded ledgy unit that commonly stands in a cliff above the rounded "slickrim" Gunsight Butte Member. The Cannonville Member is generally 200 to 400 feet thick, but may be only 60 to 80 feet thick along the south edge of the Kaiparowits Plateau. West of Cannonville it thins and is eventually cut out by the sub-Cretaceous unconformity.

The Cannonville Member of the Entrada Sandstone consists of interbedded very fine grained sandstone, silty sandstone, and siltstone. Medium-grained sandstones, some gritty and with a few pebbles, are found in the upper two-thirds of the Cannonville Member. Also deep-red-brown, purple-weathering siltstones are found at widely spaced intervals. At the base is a persistent yellow-gray cliff-forming sandstone.

In the Little Valley area, in the Escalante Canyons section, between Harris Wash and Twentyfive Mile Wash, the banded earthy-weathering nature of the Cannonville Member is well displayed. Here many pipe-like features are present and are quite resistant. One monolithic pipe forms a monument about 40 feet high.

Escalante Member: The upper member forms rounded bare-rock sandstone outcrops and displays high-angle eolian cross-stratification. The upper part is resistant and cliff forming. The lower part is earthy as is the Cannonville Member. It is, however, not banded and mostly yellow-gray to gray-white in color. Tafoni are common in the Escalante Member and is the scientific term for holes lined up along cross-bed striae. Davidson (1967) called these "bird-hole" solution cavities. We prefer "stonepecker" holes (like woodpecker holes) and do not believe they are solution cavities. Our theory is that air "bubbles" lodged in the rock when it was being cemented by ground water prevented the sand from being cemented inside the "bubbles." When erosion cuts into these ancient "bubbles," the sand merely falls out. The member is up to 300 feet thick on the east side of the Straight Cliffs, thickening to the north. It is not identifiable south of Cat Pasture. In the northern part of the Cockscomb and in the east half of the Tropic amphitheater it is up to 40 feet thick (not including the Henrieville Sandstone), and is mostly a slope-forming, earthy-weathering sandstone.

The Escalante Member is mostly fine grained and massive sandstone. The lower half is very friable and forms earthy slopes and ridges. The upper half exhibits rounded to cliffy bare-rock outcrops. The member is calcareous. Dinosaur tracks are locally present in the Escalante Member (figure 8). One site contains over 250. Most are the tracks of bipedal, tridactyl theropod dinosaurs; two are of quadrupedal dinosaurs and include indications of tail drags.

The upper contact of the Escalante Member is abrupt east of Fiftymile Mountain and is taken where the resistant massive yellow-gray sandstone changes to the red-brown siltstone slope at the base of the Tidwell Member of the Morrison Formation. This contact is presumed to be unconformable, but little relief is evident. In the Cockscomb and Tropic amphitheater it is mostly overlain by the Henrieville Sandstone.

Romana Mesa Sandstone

The Romana Mesa Sandstone crops out unconformably below the Morrison Formation and above the Entrada Sandstone along the south and east margins of the Kaiparowits Plateau. It is up to 135 feet thick in the monument. It starts as a feather edge at Cat Pasture and thickens to the south. In the cliffs along the southeast margin of the Kaiparowits Plateau, it looks much like the Entrada Sandstone, except that its color is much lighter.

The rock is mainly gray-yellow-green to yellow-gray, very fine to fine-grained sandstone that normally stands as a cliff. Thin to medium beds of red friable sandstone are commonly found at the base. Locally the sandstones are bioturbated. The Romana Mesa Sandstone correlates with the Cow Springs Sandstone in Arizona and may intertongue with the Summerville Formation as exposed to the east. It is combined with the Entrada Sandstone (Je) on the geologic map of the Kaiparowits basin section (figure 16).

Henrieville Sandstone

The Henrieville Sandstone crops out in the northeast corner of the Tropic amphitheater between Henrieville and the Cockscomb and is best recognized at Grosvenor Arch of which it forms the pedestals (No. 11 on figure 2 and figure 10). It is generally cliff forming and yellow gray in overall color. It ranges from a feather edge to 234 feet in thickness.

It consists of very fine grained, well-sorted sandstone that is slightly calcareous, porous, and thick bedded to massive. Locally coarse grains of sand are present. It is a cliff former, but locally forms steep slopes. The lower part is planar bedded and the upper part is cross-bedded. Cross-bed sets become thicker upward in the unit. In addition to sandstone, the lower part contains a few siltstone, claystone, and shale beds.

The lower contact with the Entrada Sandstone is wavy and sharp. The upper contact at Grosvenor Arch is a regional unconformity and is also wavy and sharp. Some investigators believe the Henrieville Sandstone is a hardening at the top of the Entrada Sandstone and should be included with that unit (Bowers, 1975, 1983). The Henrieville started out as a fluvially deposited unit and then reverted to an eolian-deposited unit. It is combined with the Entrada Sandstone (Je) on the geologic maps, figures 15 and 16.

Morrison Formation (Jm)

The Upper Jurassic Morrison Formation consists of three members: (ascending) the Tidwell Member, Salt Wash Member, and Brushy Basin Member. In the monument the Morrison is exposed along the east and south margins of the Kaiparowits Plateau. To the west it is cut out by the sub-Cretaceous regional unconformity. Hence, in the Grand Staircase section, no Morrison rocks are exposed and Cretaceous rocks rest directly on the Middle Jurassic Carmel or Entrada Formations.

Tidwell Member: These rocks form a red slope or recess between resistant Salt Wash Member ledges above and resistant cliff-forming sandstones below from Cat Pasture northward to Boulder Mountain (Escalante Canyons section). It is up to 150 feet thick. The outcrop band is quite conspicuous in the vicinity of the town of Escalante.

The member consists of light-colored, fine-grained, ledgy sandstone beds, and red, purple, brown, and green mudstones and siltstones. A few gritstones are also present. The member is strongly calcareous.

Thompson and Stokes (1970) considered the member to be a facies of the Summerville Formation and called it the White Point Member. Doelling also continued to assign these beds to the Summerville Formation (Doelling and Davis, 1989), but has since "changed his mind" after extensive new field mapping. The presence of Morrison-like gritstones in the member and its calcareous nature helped convince him that these beds belong with the Morrison Formation. Zeller and Stephens (1973) assigned these rocks to a lower member of the Morrison Formation. Peterson (personal communication, 1987) believed the beds should be assigned to the Tidwell Member. The beds were deposited in a fluvial environment, on a flood plain dotted with numerous lakes and ponds.

Salt Wash Member: This ledge- and cliff-former ranges up to 700 feet thick in the monument. The member is a heterogeneous complex of sandstone, conglomerate, and mudstone that becomes thicker and has a greater percentage of coarse clastics to the south. It is not present in the Grand Staircase section, being cut out by the sub-Cretaceous regional unconformity, as previously noted.

It is generally a gray, yellow-gray, yellow-brown, lenticular, quartzose sandstone interbedded with conglomeratic sandstone, conglomerate, and red and green silty mudstone. Average grain size increases to the south. The composition is 90 percent quartz; the remainder is chert and milky feldspar. Sandstone and conglomerate exhibit trough cross-bedding and have been deposited as lenses. The mudstones form recesses or slopes and overlying lenses of sandstone commonly break up into large pieces producing a "messy" outcrop.

The Salt Wash Member was deposited in an anasto-mosing system of braided rivers and streams. Stream-channel deposits are more abundant than the overbank mudstones. The streams flowed from south to north as attested by the greater percentage of lenticular sandstones and conglomerates and the coarser average grain size to the south. Locally, petrified wood is common in the member, some being of polishable quality. Channels in the vicinity of Cat Pasture are mineralized with uranium minerals, but in quantities that rate them as "low grade." Regionally, the Salt Wash Member is famous for its dinosaur fossils, but only bone fragments have been found in the monument. Foster and others (1999) report finding a crocodile tooth, two possible sauropod track sites, and evidence for a possible fossil termite nest.

Brushy Basin Member: This bentonitic slope former is present only along the northeast edge of the Kaiparowits Plateau. It is characterized by variegated colors and the dominance of mudstone over channel sandstones and conglomerates. The Brushy Basin is somewhat inconsistent in thickness because its upper contact with the Dakota Sandstone is unconformable, but it probably also thickens northward at the expense of the Salt Wash Member. Outcrops range in thickness from 0 to about 100 feet.

The Brushy Basin Member consists mostly of red, purple, gray, yellow, green, and white mudstone that is silty, sandy, or clayey with subordinate medium- to coarse-grained and sometimes pebbly sandstone and nodular gray-brown limestone. The mudstones commonly contain much swelling clay that weathers to produce a "popcorn-" like surface on the rounded hills and badlands it forms.

The Brushy Basin Member was deposited fluvially, mostly as overbank deposits and as accompanying lacustrine deposits. It locally contains petrified wood (especially in sandstones) and contains rare dinosaur bone.

Cretaceous Rocks

Cretaceous rocks in the Grand Staircase-Escalante National Monument are mostly limited to the Kaiparowits Basin section. Cretaceous outcrops are present north of the Grand Staircase section and are in Dixie National Forest, in Bryce Canyon National Park, and in Capitol Reef National Park east of the Escalante Canyons section of the monument. In the Kaiparowits section Cretaceous rocks are 5,000 to 6,000 feet thick and were deposited in marine, mixed continental and marine, and continental environments. During this time mountains developed in western Utah and the Western Interior Seaway transgressed and regressed into and out of the monument area.

Cedar Mountain Formation

This formation is the only Early Cretaceous deposit found in the monument. It is discontinuous and found in scattered outcrops, "lodged" between two unconformities along the south margin of the Kaiparowits Plateau, along the Cockscomb, and around the Tropic amphitheater. The outcrops generally consists of resistant conglomeratic

Figure 25. John Henry Member beds in the Kaiparowits Basin section of the monument. A coal bed is commonly found above each thick sandstone bed.

sandstone. Outcrops are up to 50 feet thick, but generally less than 25 feet thick. Because the Cedar Mountain Formation is discontinuous and thin it is included with the Dakota Formation (Kd) on the geologic maps, figures 15 and 16.

The unit crops out as interbedded conglomerate, pebbly sandstone, and sandstone with minor amounts of siltstone and mudstone. Not all of these lithologies are everywhere present. It generally forms ledges or combines with other cliff-forming units above and below. The clasts consist of chert, quartzite, silicified limestone, feldspathic sandstone, and petrified wood and are subrounded to subangular. The rock is generally slightly calcareous. The sandstones are mostly poorly sorted and fine to coarse grained. Sandstone and conglomeratic sandstone commonly exhibit trough cross-bedding and the unit is thought to be of fluvial origin.

The best place to see the Cedar Mountain Formation is at Grosvenor Arch, where it is exposed near the top of this landmark between the two unconformities (figure 10). Pollen found in mudstone partings generally point to an Aptian-Albian (Early Cretaceous) age for these rocks (Doelling and Davis, 1989). Cedar Mountain Formation outcrops were considered to be a part of the Dakota Formation by earlier workers.

Dakota Formation (Kd)

The Dakota Formation crops out around the edges of the Kaiparowits Plateau, and continues westerly around the Tropic amphitheater and along the south margin of the Paunsaugunt Plateau north of the Grand Staircase section of the monument. It generally appears as a medium-gray slope overlain by a resistant cap of sandstone, although locally it has a basal brown sandstone ledge. Thin coal beds are present around the Kaiparowits Plateau, which thicken along the south margin of the Paunsaugunt Plateau. The lower medium-gray slope is 3 to 240 feet thick, thickening to the west. The upper resistant cap is up to 80 feet

thick.

The lower member, previously called the middle member by workers who included the Cedar Mountain Formation as their lower member (Peterson, 1969a), consists of interbedded mudstone and shale, sandstone, carbonaceous mudstone, claystone, coal, and conglomerate. The mudstone and shale are gray to nearly black, brown, and olive gray, and shaly to laminated. Mudstone is composed of silty and sandy clay; the clay includes kaolinite, illite, and montmorillonite. Sandstone is orange, yellow gray, and gray. It is mostly fine to fine grained with a few medium- and coarse-grained beds, with subangular, moderately sorted grains. The sandstone beds are thin to thick bedded, calcareous, lenticular and cross-stratified, and resistant, forming ledges between the mudstone slopes. Coal beds surrounding the Kaiparowits Plateau are generally thin, mostly less than 2 feet thick, but locally thicken to 6 or more feet. Nevertheless, some of these coal beds were exploited by early settlers.

The upper member is mostly discontinuous fossiliferous marine sandstone and mudstone with minor shale, carbonaceous mudstone, and coal. The sandstone is yellow, orange gray, or brown in color, ledgy, and forms a hard caprock on top of the formation. It forms the base of the Gray Cliffs north of the Grand Staircase section along the south margin of the Paunsaugunt Plateau. The upper member commonly consists of one or two sandstone ledges, each 5 to 20 feet thick, separated by mudstone and an upper coal zone. Coal beds in the upper member around the Kaiparowits Plateau are also thin, mostly less than 2 feet thick, but locally thicken to 6 feet or more. However, south of the Paunsaugunt Plateau coal beds as much as 16 feet thick are present.

The Dakota Formation is called the Dakota Sandstone in most parts of Utah. However, Lawrence (1965) redefined the Dakota in southern Utah as the coal-bearing beds between the sub-Cretaceous unconformity and the marine Tropic Shale above. Excepting the basal part we now believe is Cedar Mountain Formation, it is the transgressive deposit of the Western Interior Seaway. The lower part of our Dakota Formation shows fluvial influence, but the upper parts become strongly marine in character. The upper ledges of the Dakota are very fossiliferous and commonly include *Ostrea* and *Exogyra* coquinas. The upper Dakota grades into the Tropic Shale.

Tropic Shale (Kt)

The Tropic Shale represents the westernmost deposit of the Western Interior Seaway in Utah. It extended as far west as Cedar City, where "pure" marine shales thin and intertongue with nearshore sandstone and beach sandstone deposits. In the monument area it is exposed around the edge of the Kaiparowits Plateau and ranges from 500 to 750 feet thick. It forms a gray slope commonly covered with mass movement (landslide and slump) deposits.

The Tropic Shale is a thinly laminated to thin-bedded mudstone and shale unit with lesser amounts of sandstone, bentonitic claystone, siltstone, and limestone. The mudstone and claystone are often nodular and chunky when fresh, but shaly and earthy when weathered. Toward the top the Tropic commonly becomes quite sandy and thin interbeds of yellow-gray, very fine grained calcareous sandstone make their appearance, changing the overall color from drab gray to yellow gray.

The muds were deposited on the floor of a shallow sea that had transgressed westward from the midcontinent area. The Tropic is locally fossiliferous and contains key cephalopod faunas that date the unit as Cenomanian-Turonian (Late Cretaceous).

Straight Cliffs Formation (Ks)

The Straight Cliffs Formation was initially named the Straight Cliffs Sandstone by Gregory and Moore (1931) for exposures along the Straight Cliffs (Fiftymile Mountain) on the east side of the Kaiparowits Plateau. Peterson and Waldrop (1965) suggested calling the unit a formation, since the unit contains many rock types other than sandstone. Peterson (1969b) divided the formation into members which are: (ascending) the Tibbet Canyon, Smoky Hollow, John Henry, and Drip Tank Members, named after various geographic features in the Kaiparowits Plateau. The entire formation is 900 to 1,800 feet thick in the Kaiparowits Basin section of the monument; the thicker sections are found in the Kaiparowits syncline.

Tibbet Canyon Member: The lowermost member of the Straight Cliffs Formation is a cliff-forming sandstone that crops out above the Tropic Shale all around the margin of the Kaiparowits Plateau. These outcrops locally extend deeply into canyons that cut into the plateau. The member probably ranges in thickness between 70 and 185 feet.

It is mostly yellow-gray to moderate-brown sandstone that coarsens upward. Sorting is poor to moderate in the lower half of the member and the upper half is moderately to well sorted. Gray mudstone and siltstone partings are common in the lower part. The sandstone is calcareous, cross-bedded and thin to thick bedded. Thick beds are more common in the upper part. The lower contact with the Tropic Shale is gradational and is placed at the top of the first medium or thick sandstone bed of the Tibbet Canyon Member.

The member was deposited in beach and shallow-water marine environments. It is locally fossiliferous, containing pelecypods, rare cephalopods, shark teeth, and trace fossils. The unit is locally bioturbated.

Smoky Hollow Member: This is a ledge- and cliff-forming unit of sandstone, gray shale, mudstone and very thin coal. In the northern part of the Kaiparowits Plateau it is difficult to separate from the Tibbet Canyon Member. Several geologic maps show it combined with the Tibbet Canyon and called the lower member of the Straight Cliffs Formation. The Smoky Hollow Member ranges from 25 to 230 feet in thickness.

Sandstone beds of this member are very fine to medium grained, poorly to moderately sorted, cross-bedded and resistant. Mudstone beds are bentonitic, olive gray, and slope forming. Coal, where present, is generally found in the lower part of the member, associated with dark-gray carbonaceous mudstone and thin-bedded sandstone. Near the top is a peculiar white or light-gray, cross-bedded sandstone bed that is about 25 feet thick, fine to coarse grained, poorly sorted, and commonly includes pebbly sandstone.

The Tibbet Canyon and Smoky Hollow Members represent a regressive phase of the Western Interior Seaway and probably correlate with the Ferron Sandstone Member of the Mancos Shale in central Utah. The Smoky Hollow beds were deposited in a variety of nearshore continental environments in lagoons and on flood plains.

John Henry Member: The John Henry Member is a slope- and ledge-forming unit of sandstone, mudstone, carbonaceous mudstone, and coal. It crops out over a large part of the Kaiparowits Basin section of the monument. It ranges in thickness from 590 to 1,100 feet. It is thinner over anticlines and thickens easterly to some extent. It unconformably overlies the Smoky Hollow Member and interfingers with the overlying Drip Tank Member.

The member is dominated by thick-bedded to massive, cliff-forming, yellow-gray to yellow-brown sandstone with interbeds of gray mudstone, thin, friable to blocky sandstone beds, and thin limestone beds (figure 25). The resistant sandstone is mostly fine to medium grained, poorly to moderately sorted, and calcareous. It is commonly cross-bedded. Some of the sandstones, especially to the east, contain significant quantities of titanium and zirconium minerals. Identified minerals in some of the beach deposits include zircon, magnetite, ilmenite, rutile, quartz, calcite, monazite, garnet, sphene, hematite, and anatase (Peterson, 1969b). Locally these minerals may constitute 25 percent of the sand grains in the rock.

Two major coal zones are found in the member and are known as the Christensen-Henderson zone and the Alvey zone. All coal zones are dominated by mudstone, carbonaceous mudstone and shale, claystone, and contain relatively thick coal beds. Kaiparowits Plateau coal beds are commonly 20 feet or more in thickness. The Alvey coal zone is found high in the member and is similar lithologically to the Christensen-Henderson zone. The Alvey coal zone is better developed in the east part of the Kaiparowits Plateau.

The John Henry Member was deposited in lagoons, deltas, and in fluvial environments. Beach sands are also present in the eastern part of the Kaiparowits Plateau. The member exhibits many interesting features attendant with the coal. Natural coal fires are common on the plateau and tend to redden and bake the surrounding non-combustible rocks. Shales and clays are baked into brick in a variety of colors that "clink" when walked upon or are struck with a rock hammer. Hence this material is called "clinker" in the coal-mining industry. Some of the rock has melted and some has metamorphosed under the intense heat of the fires. Fossil oysters and fragments of woody plants have locally been burned black and red in the "clinker."

Drip Tank Member: The highest member of the Straight Cliffs Formation is a prominent cliff-former. Upper surfaces or benches of the Kaiparowits Plateau are commonly developed on the Drip Tank Member. It is 140 to 550 feet thick and probably thickens to the west.

It is mostly yellow-brown to yellow-gray, fine- to medium-grained, poorly sorted, cross-bedded, lenticular sandstone in medium to thick beds. It contains mudstone partings and local pebble conglomerate lenses. Conglomerate becomes more common to the north and west.

The Drip Tank Member is a fluvial deposit. Abundant low-and high-angle, medium-scale trough cross-beds, and cut-and-fill structures all attest to this. Rare petrified wood and vertebrate bone fragments are found in the Drip Tank Member in the monument area.

Wahweap Formation (Kw)

The Wahweap Formation is divisible into a lower, mostly slope-forming unit and an upper, mostly cliff-forming unit. The lower member has generally receded from the cliffy edge of the Drip Tank Member of the Straight Cliffs Formation and intertongues with it and the upper member. The Wahweap Formation is 1,000 to 1,500 feet thick in the Kaiparowits Plateau. The lower slope-forming unit is 800 to 1,100 feet thick and the upper cliff-forming unit is 200 to 400 feet thick.

This formation is composed of interbedded mudstone, claystone, siltstone, resistant and non-resistant sandstone, and conglomerate. In the lower unit slope-forming rocks dominate and in the upper unit resistant rocks dominate. Sandstones are fine to coarse grained, with fairly well sorted, subangular grains. The resistant cliff-forming sandstones are yellow gray and the friable sandstones are yellow, orange, or brown. Both are calcareous. Bedding is medium to massive. Claystone, mudstone, and siltstone are various shades of gray.

The Wahweap Formation is locally fossiliferous and contains petrified wood, vertebrate teeth and bones, and gastropods. These are more common in the upper resistant sandstones. It was deposited under continental conditions in flood plain, fluvial, and lacustrine environments.

Kaiparowits Formation (Kk)

The Kaiparowits Formation is a drab-gray, olive-gray, or green-gray, slope-forming and badlands-forming unit composed of subarkosic sandstone. The sandstone is muddy and gives the appearance of being finer grained. It is best displayed at The Blues (No. 23 on figure 2) where the unit is 2,000 to 3,000 feet thick.

The subarkosic sandstone is mostly very fine to fine grained, and in detail, poorly sorted with a salt-and-pepper appearance. It is weakly cemented with calcite. The grains are mostly quartz, with orthoclase, albite, biotite,

Figure 26. Toreva-type landslide along the Kelly Grade at the south end of the Kaiparowits Plateau. Colors in the landslide material are due to "clinker," shales and sandstones baked by coal that has burned in place in the Straight Cliffs Formation above.

calcite, gypsum, clay, iron, and bits of coal or charcoal. The bedding is poorly defined to lenticular; lenses rarely exceed five feet in thickness. Very thin partings and beds of siltstone and mudstone are also present. A few beds of nodular-weathering brown, green, white, or gray sandy limestone and lime silt are present.

This formation was probably deposited in freshwater or brackish-water lakes and on a subsiding alluvial plain. There are scattered fossils that include freshwater snails, vertebrate bones, and plant fossils (dicotyledons and cycads) (Lohrengel, 1969).

Formations Visible From the monument (TKc, Tcp, Tcw)

The Kaiparowits Formation is unconformably overlain by Upper Cretaceous and Tertiary units that are nicely visible from The Blues viewpoints. These include the Canaan Peak, Grand Castle, Pine Hollow, and Claron Formations. The Canaan Peak and Grand Castle Formations are locally as much as 900 feet thick, the Pine Hollow Formation is locally as much as 400 feet thick, and the Claron Formation may be as much as 1,400 feet thick. The lower three formations (TKc) have only been recognized in the area of Canaan Peak, Powell Point, and the Table Cliff Plateau (Goldstrand and Mullett, 1995) northwest of the Kaiparowits Basin section. The Claron Formation is generally divisible into at least two units: a lower pink unit (Tcp) and an upper white unit (Tcw). The lower pink unit forms the Pink Cliffs north of the Grand Staircase section of the monument where it is sometimes called the "Bryce Canyon Formation."

The Canaan Peak Formation consists of light-brown or gray conglomerate, sandstone, and lenticular mudstone. The rounded cobbles and small boulders in the unit are of quartzite, chert, and dense porphyritic igneous rocks. The formation makes steep gravel-covered slopes. The Pine Hollow Formation consists of gray to red calcareous silt-

Figure 27. A hoodoo rock (demoiselle) on the Tropic Shale along the margin of the Kaiparowits Plateau. Soft shale is protected from erosion by the large boulder that has fallen from sandstone cliffs. Locally whole families of hoodoos are present, especially along the southeast margins of the plateau.

stone, mudstone, and claystone that forms steep, poorly exposed slopes. The pink member of the Claron Formation consists mostly of pink, pale-orange, light-gray, and white limestone that is irregularly to indistinctly bedded to massive. It weathers into the Pink Cliffs that are sculptured into columns, spires, minarets, castles, and other interesting forms. The white member consists of mostly white clastic to microcrystalline limestone, also indistinctly to irregularly bedded, that commonly forms cliffs. It is locally dolomitic.

The four formations have unconformable contacts with one another and were deposited in fluvial and lacustrine environments. The Claron Formation was deposited at the south end of a large lake that covered central Utah during the Paleocene.

Volcanic Rocks

The Aquarius Plateau and Boulder Mountain are capped with volcanic tuffs and basaltic andesite mostly of Oligocene or Miocene age. Tertiary volcanic bedrock units are not exposed in the monument, but large boulders of basaltic andesite are scattered on many of the benches in the Escalante Canyons section of the monument as volcanic terrace alluvium. These were probably deposited on the benches by ancient streams that headed in the highlands. The rock consists of dark-gray to black, vesicular, and porphyritic lava.

Unconsolidated Deposits (Q, Qg, Qms)

Because of the small scale of the accompanying geologic maps (figures 15, 16, and 17), only three divisions are given for the Quaternary unconsolidated deposits. Only the larger deposits are shown on the maps; myriads of smaller areas were omitted. Unconsolidated deposits marked with a Q are deposits of a general nature and are deposits of sand and smaller grain sizes. The Qg designation is given to larger surfaces containing gravel, especially pediment-mantle and terrace deposits. The Qms designation is restricted to larger landslide, slump, and related deposits.

Alluvium

Alluvium is gravel, sand, silt, clay, and other detrital material deposited by running water. If deposited by rivers, streams, or intermittent washes in channels it is called **channel alluvium**. Most channels in the monument are dry washes except during periods of flash flooding brought on by torrential summer rainfall. Some washes fill to as much as 10 feet in depth and move boulders the size of small houses. Generally the floods are only a few feet deep, but have no trouble moving boulders a few feet in diameter. Walk down a few of the larger washes in the monument and you will find evidence of the sizes of materials that can be moved and deposited in the channels. When the volume of water exceeds that which the channel can handle it floods its valley depositing finer grained materials called **overbank or flood plain alluvium**.

In time, streams and washes cut deep valleys or canyons in the rock. As they do so their older deposits are commonly found stranded on benches. Streams meander and commonly abandon earlier channels. These older deposits are known as **terrace alluvium**. Along the larger and longer lived rivers, terrace alluvium is found at several levels above and up to several hundred feet above the present channel level.

The debris carried by washes and streams is dropped when the water velocity is decreased, such as at the mouths of canyons along mountain or cliff fronts. The deposit develops a fan shape with the apex at the point where the stream gradient first diminishes. Such landforms are called **alluvial fans**. The most recent deposits lie high on the fan surface. The next flood will choose a lower path on which to deposit its load and so the drainage swings back and forth over the fan surface gradually building it up. If the cliff or mountain front is long, a series of fans may be built up and coalesce to form a **bajada**.

In time, cliffs and mountains retreat because of erosion. Washes and streams may then cut into and through older fans or bajadas. Older fans become dissected and their remnants are then found on the benches between drainages. The bedrock surfaces eroded in the foothills below the cliffs and mountain fronts are pediments (piedmonts) and the deposits that the streams leave on them are **pediment-mantle alluvium**. Alluvial deposits are found in all sections of the monument.

Mixed Eolian and Alluvial Deposits

Streams may meander across a plain developed on benches formed at the top of a relatively hard sedimentary formation. Until the streams can cut through or deeply into this hard underlying formation, alluvium is deposited on the bench in shallow hollows and is temporarily held up from moving downstream. The alluvium may fill these hollows and eventually bury all the rocks. Such alluvium may remain on these benches a considerable length of time. Wind may redistribute its finer constituents (fine sand and silt) and bring in sand from outside of the area, depositing it in sheets on top of the alluvium. These wind-blown deposits may then be covered or mixed by more alluvium, as during wet climatic cycles. Soil may also develop on the surfaces. As part of soil development, a white caliche layer may slowly develop a few feet below the surface. Examples of mixed eolian and alluvial deposits are common on benches beneath the Straight Cliffs (Fiftymile Mountain) and at the base of the Vermilion Cliffs in the Grand Staircase section of the monument.

Eolian (wind-blown) Deposits

Most sandstone beds in the monument are friable and weather to produce loose sand. Such sand is blown by wind to fill shallow hollows in bedrock or to accumulate on the lee sides of cliffs and other impediments. Some sandstone units produce much sand and are commonly covered with wind-blown sand either in sheets or in dunes. In the monument the Entrada Sandstone provides the sand that produces the largest of these deposits. These deposits are most evident left and right of the Hole-in-the-Rock Road. Some of these sheets and dunes are stabilized and no longer move, being held in place by vegetation. Others are active deposits that migrate from one place to another.

Landslides and Slumps

Clay-bearing formations such as the Chinle Formation and Tropic Shale are commonly covered with self-derived landslide debris and slumps. The Petrified Forest Member of the Chinle is conducive to slumping, especially in the Circle Cliffs area, where it contains more clay than in other areas. The Tropic Shale contains much bentonitic clay along Fiftymile Mountain and along the south margin of the Kaiparowits Plateau (figure 26). It too is covered with talus and landslide debris. In places the Tropic has

"oozed" down the cliff formed by the Dakota Formation, Morrison Formation, and Entrada Sandstone.

Undercutting produced by the weathering of soft slope-forming units causes vertical cracks to open in the hard cliffs above them. During wet years moisture enters these cracks and eventually reaches permeable and porous material found above or below the clay beds. The water then moves toward the outcrops through the permeable strata, wetting the adjacent clay. Weight above the wet slippery clay causes the overlying rocks to slide, rotate, or slump. Landsliding is the normal way clay-rich rocks are eroded.

The landslides and slumps attendant to the Tropic Shale are some of the largest landslide complexes in the world and are best displayed at the southeast end of Fiftymile Mountain. The poorly sorted jumble of rock material is commonly interestingly eroded to form hoodoo rocks (figure 27). Hoodoo rocks or pedestal rocks are formed when a large boulder rests on easily eroded finer grained landslide debris. The boulder protects the finer grained materials directly beneath it from removal or weathering during rainstorms. Eventually the boulder sits on a pedestal of the finer grained material. In some places whole families of hoodoos delight the sightseer.

Talus and Rock Fall

Rock fall consists of large chunks of rock that become dislodged from escarpments (cliffs and ledges) and drop or roll to more level areas below. Talus is the name given to conical deposits that form at the base of escarpments and is a mixture of rock fall and finer constituents. Talus and rock-fall deposits are ubiquitous in the monument.

STRUCTURAL GEOLOGY

Generally, structural geologic features seen today within the monument region result from two phases (or styles) of deformation. Many of the folds that we see today in the Kaiparowits and Circle Cliffs regions began during the latter part of the Mesozoic (Jurassic-Cretaceous); initiated during the Sevier orogeny and later modified as compression of the region continued through the Laramide event (Cretaceous-Tertiary). During mid-Tertiary, uplift of the Colorado Plateau was accompanied by basin and range extension which affected the western portions of the monument region resulting in the development of the Sevier and Paunsaugunt faults. The uplift of the Kaibab region and folding along the East Kaibab monocline accompanied initial formation of the Grand Canyon starting about 15 million years ago.

Grand Staircase Section

All strata in the Grand Staircase section of the monument dip gently (mostly 2 to 4 degrees) northward in a homocline that is warped and faulted (figures 3 and 12). Hence, the oldest rocks are generally exposed to the south and the youngest to the north. The strata are cut by many

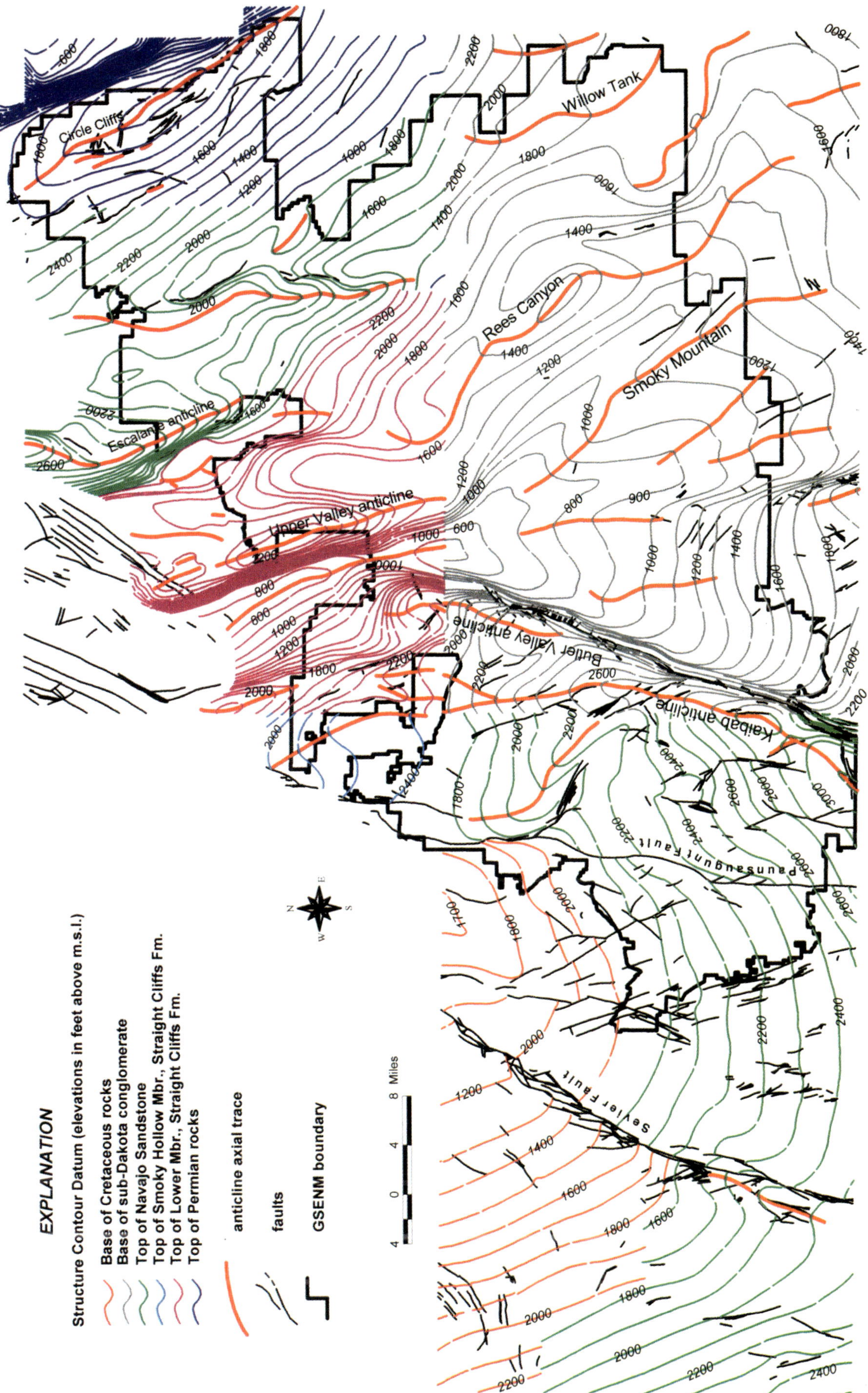

Figure 28. Structure contour map of Grand Staircase-Escalante National Monument.

Figure 29. The Cockscomb is the physiographic expression of the East Kaibab monocline which forms the boundary between the Kaiparowits Basin and Grand Staircase sections of the monument. Ribs of harder formations are found between slope-forming softer units.

normal faults with displacements ranging to about 800 feet (figure 15).

The **Paunsaugunt fault,** which extends from Arizona northward into central Utah, is the most significant of the Grand Staircase section faults (see geologic map, figure 15). The fault is a high-angle normal fault, and the up-thrown block is to the east. The displacement decreases southward from about 800 feet near Willis Creek to less than 100 feet near Deer Spring Point. From there to the Arizona border it increases again to approximately 500 feet. The fault plane dips at various angles from 45° E. as a reverse fault to 45° W. Differential erosion of bedrock near the fault has resulted in reverse topography. Because west-side strata generally stand higher in elevation than the east side the outcrops of older rocks are exposed farther north on the upthrown block (figure 28). The northern segment, outside the monument, shows evidence for surface rupture during Quaternary time, but movement along the southern segment during Quaternary is not apparent (Hecker, 1991).

The **Johnson Canyon faults** are present along the west margin of the monument. These faults may be active, however, to date, associated earthquakes have registered very low magnitude on local seismographs (University of Utah Seismology Catalog, 1986). Seismologists have not determined a link between movement on the Johnson Canyon faults and local earthquakes.

Two major faults (**Paria River faults**), 3/4 to 1/4 mile apart, occur on each side of the Paria River just north of the abandoned Paria townsite. These form a graben or down-dropped block, the river generally flowing between them. Each exhibits a maximum displacement of about 250 feet. It is assumed these faults are not tectonic in origin, are shallow and die out not far beneath the surface. The strata on each side of the canyon is thought to be moving riverward due to gravity-induced sliding.

The **Kaibab uplift** is present in the southeast corner of the section. It is expressed as a positive topographic feature known as Buckskin Mountain. The uplift is most easily recognized traveling southward along U.S. Highway 89 between the Paria turnoff and the deep cut through the Cockscomb as a whaleback. The uplift is connected and synchronous with the Grand Canyon uplift in Arizona. The axis of the uplift trends roughly north-south and is known as the **Kaibab anticline**. This anticline extends north to south completely across the monument, generally plunging northward. In the Buckskin Mountain part of the anticline, the east boundary of the uplift or east limb of the anticline (East Kaibab monocline as expressed by the Cockscomb) is steeply dipping and locally overturned.

North of U.S. Highway 89, the Kaibab anticline is very subtle and gentle on both flanks. There it is bounded on the west by the **Paria River syncline** and on the east by the **Hackberry Canyon syncline,** which are also gentle, generally north-south-trending folds.

The east boundary of the Grand Staircase section is the Cockscomb, the topographic expression of the **East Kaibab monocline** (figure 29). It trends north-northeast from the south boundary of the monument nearly to the north boundary and is paralleled by the Cottonwood Wash road. The rock strata dip abruptly eastward at angles ranging from 15 degrees to slightly overturned. The structural relief across the monocline is about 5,000 feet to the south and decreases gradually to the north end of the monument near Butler Valley. Locally, the monocline is faulted and strata are attenuated. It is the most magnificent structural feature in all of Grand Staircase-Escalante National Monument.

Kaiparowits Basin Section

Like the Grand Staircase section, strata in the Kaiparowits Basin section dip gently northward. Because of the displacement on the East Kaibab monocline, Cretaceous outcrops shift southward and dominate the Kaiparowits Basin section. The strata are composed of alternating hard and soft units as in the Grand Staircase section, but the cliffs are all subdivisions of the Gray Cliffs part of the Grand Staircase. Superimposed on the north-dipping homocline are several north-south-trending anticlines and synclines (figure 4). Most of these have gentle limbs, but a few form monoclines.

Figure 30. The Escalante monocline looking north toward Boulder Mountain.

The Kaiparowits Basin section is a structural basin topographically expressed as a high plateau. The deepest part of the basin lies westward near the East Kaibab monocline. The strata gradually rise eastward. The Cretaceous rocks are cut off by erosion along Fiftymile Mountain (Straight Cliffs). West to east, from the East Kaibab monocline to the Straight Cliffs, the principal folds in the basin include the **Coyote Creek-Blue Wash-Table Cliff syncline** (deepest part of the Kaiparowits Basin), **Tommy Canyon anticline, Wahweap syncline, Nipple Bench anticline, Warm Creek syncline, Smoky Mountain anticline, Last Chance syncline, Upper Valley anticline, Alvey Wash syncline, Rees Canyon anticline,** and **Croton syncline**. Fewer of these folds are present to the north where the plateau-basin is narrower. The folds radiate out southward like the plications of a fan. Folds to the west trend southwesterly; folds to the east generally trend southeasterly.

Escalante Canyons Section

The boundary between the Escalante Canyons and Kaiparowits Basin sections of the monument is placed at the base of Fiftymile Mountain (Straight Cliffs). The dominant structural feature of the Escalante Canyons section is the **Circle Cliffs uplift** (figure 5). It has a gentle southwest limb that extends from the Hole-in-the-Rock Road east-northeast to the axis of the uplift. The east limb of the uplift is the Waterpocket Fold, another steeply dipping monocline like the East Kaibab monocline. The **Waterpocket Fold**, however, is in Capitol Reef National Park. The core of the Circle Cliffs uplift is lined by the prominent vertical and magnificent red-brown or orange-brown cliffs of the

Wingate Sandstone. These cliffs "circle" the uplift and are the basis for its name. The core of the uplift exposes Permian and Triassic rocks. The **Escalante monocline** is a north-northwest-trending feature north of the town of Escalante that dips to the west (figure 30).

Several anticlines and synclines are superimposed on the gentle west limb of the uplift. These include the **Collet anticline** and **Red Breaks syncline** to the north, and the **Hurricane Wash syncline, Bridge anticline**, and **Fiftymile Creek syncline** to the south. The Escalante River and its tributaries have cut deep canyons into the gentle west limb that are favorites for hikers. These deep canyons are the basis for the name of the Escalante Canyons section of the monument.

GEOLOGIC RESOURCES

Mineral, oil and gas, coal and other geologic resources are found within Grand Staircase-Escalante National Monument. At the time the monument was created, many thousands of acres of oil and gas leases, coal leases, and mining claims were still valid. Here we discuss the geology of these resources as part of the natural scientific endowment of the monument.

Coal

The Kaiparowits coal field is mostly based on coals found in the Cretaceous Straight Cliffs Formation in the Kaiparowits Basin section of the monument. Thin coal beds are also found in the Cretaceous Dakota Formation. The Straight Cliffs coals were first mined by settlers near Escalante in the late 1800s. Coal studies were initiated by Gregory and Moore (1931). All mining in the coal field ceased in the early 1960s as the local market converted to the use of petroleum products for heating purposes. Only 37,000 short tons were produced during the production history of the coal field (Doelling, 1972; Jahanbani, 1997). Energy companies became interested in developing the resource in the early 1960s to produce electrical energy. Coal leases were obtained by 23 separate companies (Doelling and Graham, 1972). Hundreds of coal test holes were drilled as plans were made to build a 5,000 megawatt coal-fired power plant on Nipple Bench on the Kaiparowits Plateau. Plans were scaled back in the early 1970s to a 3,000 megawatt plant to be built on Fourmile Bench and were eventually dropped altogether because of economic and environmental concerns. One coal company in the Kaiparowits area was actively working to get a mine started when the monument was created.

In the 1960s and 1970s coal drilling and exploration efforts by industry, the U.S. Geological Survey, and the Utah Geological Survey showed that the Kaiparowits Plateau was underlain by thick beds of high-volatile C bituminous coal with heating values averaging 11,000 Btu/lb and sulfur contents averaging less than 1 percent. Estimates of the original coal resource in place in the plateau range from 62 billion short tons (Hettinger and others, 1996) to 15.2 billion tons (Doelling and Graham, 1972). The overburden above coal beds in the Kaiparowits Plateau dictates that the coal would need to be extracted in underground mines. Most of the Kaiparowits coal field is contained within a northwest-trending, 15- to 18-mile-wide band within the John Henry Member of the Straight Cliffs Formation. Coal is found in nearly horizontal to gently dipping seams that have undergone little folding. Very little has been mined in the past, however, because of the remote location of the coal field, the small local market, and environmental concerns. It is, however, the largest relatively untapped coal resource in the lower 48 states.

Coal is also found in the Alton coal field which partly extends into the Grand Staircase section of the monument. The coal in the monument is found in the Dakota Formation and was locally mined by ranchers in the early days. West of the monument the coal is very thick and stripminable. However, in the monument the Dakota coal beds are generally thin and contain more sulfur and ash than the Kaiparowits coals.

Coal remains an important scientific resource in the monument. The public can see what a natural coal outcrop looks like, how coal burns and oxidizes along outcrop (Burning Hills), the nature of roof and floor rocks, and many other aspects of coal geology. Scientists can study the processes involved in coal-producing environments and better understand the problems that coal producers face. It is a place where the public can learn to understand the geology of coal and its place in the geologic world.

Petroleum

The geology of the monument and surrounding region are favorable for the accumulation of oil and gas. Howev-

Figure 31. View eastward across the north end of the Circle Cliffs area from Boulder Mountain. The Circle Cliffs get their name from the nearly vertical cliffs formed by the Wingate Sandstone. The Henry Mountains are in the background.

er, the only commercial quantities of oil within the boundaries of the monument are at the Upper Valley field near Canaan Peak. To date 48 wildcat (exploratory) wells have been drilled within the confines of the monument. All of these wells have been capped and abandoned. The number of wells drilled indicates the geologic favorability of the area and the presence of encouraging oil shows.

Anticlines are favorable structures to explore for oil and gas and there are many in the monument. Petroleum generally collects in the elevated areas of reservoir rocks above formation water. Wildcat wells in the monument have mostly been drilled along the anticlinal axes. The anticlinal theory of oil accumulation generally assumes a water table under oil to be level. However, the oil of the Upper Valley anticline was discovered in its steep western flank where the oil-water contact is tilted westward. Apparently, a flood of carbon dioxide, other non-hydrocarbon gasses, and deep ground water drove the oil from the axis into the flank of the anticline (Utah Geological Survey, 1998). Because the flanks of other anticlines in the region have not been thoroughly tested through drilling, some workers believe the monument area may contain undiscovered oil and gas resources.

The Upper Valley oil field was discovered in 1964 by Tenneco, and has since produced nearly 26 million barrels of oil, mostly from the Permian Kaibab Limestone. Citation Oil & Gas Corporation currently operates 22 production wells and 11 water injection wells within the field. Five of the production wells and two injection wells are located in the monument. Production from the wells in the monument represents about 27 percent of the total field production. It is estimated that the total production of the field will amount to about 30 million barrels of oil.

Petroleum has also been discovered at the surface as tar and seeps in the core of the Circle Cliffs uplift or anticline. This oil is asphaltic. The Circle Cliffs anticline would have been a giant oil field had it been discovered before the oil-bearing reservoir rocks had been exposed by erosion. Lighter constituents of the oil have long since evaporated, leaving only the heavier petroleum residues. These residues and the rock in which they are found are called tar sands. They are mostly in the Triassic Moenkopi Formation, but tar sands have also been found in the Shinarump Member of the Chinle Formation. The technology for producing gasoline and other usable products from tar sands is available, but the process is much more expensive than producing oil from wells.

The Circle Cliffs area is a good place to visualize oil reservoirs. Good reservoir rocks have pore spaces or openings between the sand and mineral grains. These spaces are commonly filled with water, oil, or gas. When buried at great depth, rocks are commonly under great pressure and the oil rises when tapped by wells. Drilling through confining impermeable rock allows man to produce and make use of these commodities.

Recently oil companies have developed new concepts in their efforts to discover petroleum resources. The concept that Precambrian rocks might serve as reservoir rocks has been tested in the monument. Conoco, Inc., completed the most recent wildcat well within the monument in November, 1997 on a former SITLA lease on the Rees Canyon anticline in the Kaiparowits Plateau. The well was completed to a depth of 11,911 feet, reportedly encountering shows of natural gas and non-flammable gas (D.A. Sprinkel, verbal communication, November 1999). The well was plugged and abandoned because of subeconomic quantities of natural gas.

Minerals

Various types of metallic mineral deposits are known within the monument. Most are small and of low grade. Manganese was mined in the 1940s from the Petrified Forest Member of the Chinle Formation in the Grand Staircase section because this metal was on the critical list during World War II. Total production was about 300 to 400 tons of ore containing about 40 percent manganese (Buranek, 1945). Manganese is also found in small areas within the Page and Carmel Formations near the Hole-in-the-Rock Road (Doelling, 1975).

Uranium associated with vanadium or copper is present within the Moenkopi, Chinle, and Morrison Formations. The Chinle and Moenkopi-hosted occurrences are in the Circle Cliffs uplift area and along the Cockscomb on the east side of the Kaibab uplift. These deposits are found on the bottoms and sides of paleochannels in the Shinarump Member of the Chinle Formation. Mineralization has locally extended into and bleached the Moenkopi Formation below.

Gold was reported in Permian to Jurassic sedimentary rocks across much of southern Utah, particularly in the Chinle and Moenkopi Formations (Butler and others, 1920). Lawson (1913) reported several early unsuccessful attempts to mine the gold in the Chinle Formation near the ghost town of Paria by hydraulic methods.

The Carmel Formation and Page Sandstone are locally mineralized in the Tropic Amphitheater area in the north part of the Grand Staircase section. Lead, silver, and copper have been found in above-normal quantities. A little lead was produced in the 1930s by grinding sandstone in an *arrastre* at the Rock Spring deposit near Kodachrome basin (Doelling and Davis, 1989). An *arrastre* is a primitive device in which sandstone ore is ground by placing the ore between two hard millstones, the upper being rotated by a mule or ass walking around in a circle. The ground sandstone is then washed through a sluice box to concentrate the heavier ore particles.

A number of heavy-mineral fossil placer deposits containing titanium and zirconium minerals are present in the John Henry Member of the Straight Cliffs Formation in the Kaiparowits Plateau. The deposits occur in a belt extending southward from Dave Canyon, a few miles south of Escalante, to Sunday Canyon, near the south end of the monument. At least 14 fossil beach placers have been identified that contain variable amounts of ilmenite, zircon, monazite, magnetite, rutile, and silicates (Gloyn and others, 1997).

ACKNOWLEDGMENTS

The writers thank D.A. Sprinkel, G.C. Willis, and Michael Hylland for carefully reviewing this document. We also thank Grand Staircase-Escalante National Monument, the Bureau of Land Management, and the Utah Geological Survey for their encouragement and support in preparing this document, enabling us to use data generated for those organizations.

REFERENCES

Baars, D.L., 1972, Red Rock Country - The geological history of the Colorado Plateau: Doubleday, Garden City, New York, 264 p.

Blakey, R.C., 1974, Stratigraphic and depositional analysis of the Moenkopi Formation, southeastern Utah: Utah Geological and Mineral Survey Bulletin 104, 81 p.

—1996, Permian eolian deposits, sequences, and sequence boundaries, Colorado Plateau, *in* Longman, M.W., and Sonnenfield, M.D., editors, Paleozoic Systems of the Rocky Mountain Region, USA, Rocky Mountains Section: Society for Sedimentary Geology, Denver, p. 405-426.

Blakey, R.C., Basham, E.L., and Cook, M.J., 1993, Early and Middle Triassic paleogeography of the Colorado Plateau and vicinity *in* Morales, Michael, editor, Aspects of Mesozoic geology and paleontology of the Colorado Plateau: Museum of Northern Arizona, Bulletin 59, p. 13-26.

Bowers, W.E., 1975, Geologic map and coal resources of

the Henrieville quadrangle, Garfield and Kane Counties, Utah: U.S. Geological Survey Coal Investigation Map C-74, scale 1:24,000.

—1983, Geologic map and coal sections of the Butler Valley quadrangle, Kane County, Utah: U.S. Geological Survey Coal Investigation Map C-95, scale 1:24,000.

Buranek, A.M., 1945, Notes on the Manganese King property near Kanab, Kane County, Utah: Utah Department of Publicity and Industrial Development, Circular 33.

Butler, B.S., Loughlin, G.F., Heikes, V.C., and others, 1920, Ore deposits of Utah: U.S. Geological Survey Professional Paper 111, 672 p.

Cassity, Michael, and Truman, Kathleen, in preparation, Historical resources overview of Grand Staircase-Escalante National Monument: Grand Staircase-Escalante National Monument, Kanab, Utah.

Davidson, E.S., 1967, Geology of the Circle Cliffs area, Garfield and Kane Counties, Utah: U.S. Geological Survey Bulletin 1229, 140p.

Doelling, H.H., 1968, Southern Utah oddities lure rockhounds: Utah Geological and Mineral Survey Quarterly Review v. 2, no. 3, p. 7.

—1972, Coal in Utah—1970, *in* Doelling, H.H., Central Utah coal fields: Utah Geological and Mineralogical Survey Monograph 3, p. 543-560.

—1975, Geology and mineral resources of Garfield County, Utah: Utah Geological and Mineral survey Bulletin 107, 175 p.

Doelling, H.H., and Davis, F.D., 1989, The geology of Kane County, Utah—geology, mineral resources, geologic hazards: Utah Geological and Mineral Survey Bulletin 124, 192 p.

Doelling, H.H., and Graham, R.L., 1972, Kaiparowits Plateau coal field in Southwestern Utah Coal fields: Utah Geological and Mineral Survey Monograph I, p. 67-249.

Dubiel, R.F., 1994, Triassic deposystems, paleogeography, and paleoclimate of the western interior, *in* Caputo, M.V., Peterson, J.A., and Franczyk, K.J., editors, Mesozoic Systems of the Rocky Mountain Region, USA, Rocky Mountain Section: Society for Sedimentary Geology, Denver, p. 133-168.

Eaton, J.G., Cifelli, R.L., Hutchison, J.H., Kirkland, J.I., and Parrish, J.M., 1999, Cretaceous vertebrate faunas from the Kaiparowits Plateau, south-central Utah, *in* Gillette, D.D., editor, Vertebrate paleontology in Utah: Utah Geological Survey Miscellaneous Publication 99-1, p. 345-354.

Foster, J.R., Titus, A.L., Winterfeld, G.F., Hayden, M.C., and Hamblin, A.H., 1999, Paleontological survey of the Grand Staircase-Escalante National Monument, Garfield and Kane Counties, Utah: Utah Geological Survey unpublished report to the Bureau of Land Management, 40 p.

Gieb, P.R., Huffman, Jim, and Spurr, Kimberly, 1999, An archaeological sample survey of the western Kaiparow-

its Plateau: Navajo Nation Archaeological Department Archaeological Report 98-112, p. 4-11.

Gillette, D.D., and Hayden, M.C., 1997, A preliminary inventory of paleontological resources within the Grand Staircase-Escalante National Monument, Utah: Utah Geological Survey Circular 96, 34 p.

Gloyn, R.W., Park, G.M., and Reeves, R.G., 1997, Titanium-zirconium-bearing fossil placer deposits in Cretaceous Straight Cliffs Formation, Garfield and Kane Counties, Utah, *in* Hill, L.M., 1997, Grand Staircase-Escalante National Monument Science Symposium proceedings: Bureau of Land Management, Utah State Office, Utah, p. 293-303.

Goldstrand, P.M., and Mullett, D.J., 1995, The Paleocene Grand Castle Formation; a new formation on the Markagunt Plateau of southwestern Utah, *in* Maldonado, Florian and Nealey, L.D., editors, Geologic studies in the Basin and Range-Colorado Plateau transition in southeastern Nevada, southwestern Utah, and northwestern Arizona: U.S. Geological Survey Bulletin 2153, p. 59-77.

Gregory, H.E., and Moore, R. C., 1931, The Kaiparowits region, a geographic and geologic reconnaissance of parts of Utah and Arizona: U.S. Geological Survey Professional Paper 164, 161 p.

Hamblin, A.H., 1998, Mesozoic vertebrate footprints in the Grand Staircase-Escalante National Monument, Utah: Journal of Vertebrate Paleontology, v. 18, supplement to no. 3, p. 48A.

Hecker, Suzanne, 1993, Quaternary tectonics in Utah with emphasis on earthquake-hazard characterization: Utah Geological Survey Bulletin 127, 2 pts.

Hettinger, R.D., Roberts, L.N., Biewick, L.R., and Kirschbaum, M.A., 1996, Preliminary investigations of the distribution and resources of coal in the Kaiparowits Plateau, southern Utah: U.S. Geological Survey Open-File Report 95-539, 72 p., 1 plate.

Hintze, L.F., 1988 (reprinted 1993), Geologic history of Utah: Provo, Utah, Brigham Young University Geology Studies Special Publication 7, 204 p.

Jahanbani, F.R., 1997, 1996 annual review and forecast of Utah coal production and distribution: Office of Energy and Resource Planning, Department of Natural Resources, 28 p.

Kirkland, J.L., Lucas, S.G., and Estep, J.W., 1998, Cretaceous dinosaurs of the Colorado Plateau, *in* Lucas, S.G., Kirkland, J.I., and Estep, J.W., editors, Lower and Middle Cretaceous terrestrial ecosystems: New Mexico Museum of Natural History and Science, Bulletin no. 14, p. 79-90.

Lawrence, J.C., 1965, Stratigraphy of the Dakota and Tropic Formations of Cretaceous age in southern Utah, *in* Geology and resources of south-central Utah: Utah Geological Society Guidebook 19, p. 71-91.

Lawson, A.C., 1913, The gold of the Shinarump at Paria: Economic Geology v. 8, p. 434-448.

Lohrengel, C.F., 1969, Palynology of the Kaiparowits Formation, Garfield County, Utah: Brigham Young University Geology Studies, v. 16, pt. 3, p. 61-180.

Lucchitta, Ivo, 1972, Early history of the Colorado River in the Basin and Range Province: Geological Society of America Bulletin v. 83, p. 1933-1948.

McKee, E.D., 1938, The environment and history of the Toroweap and Kaibab Formations of northern Arizona and southern Utah: Washington D.C., Carnegie Institute, Publication 492, 268 p.

McKee, E.D. and McKee, E.H., 1972, Pliocene uplift of the Grand Canyon region: Time of drainage adjustment: Geological Society of America Bulletin v. 83, p. 1923-1932.

Peterson, Fred, 1969a, Cretaceous sedimentation and tectonism in the Kaiparowits region, Utah: U.S. Geological Survey Open-File Report, 259 p.

—1969b, Four new members of the Upper Cretaceous Straight Cliffs Formation in the southeastern Kaiparowits region, Kane County, Utah: U.S. Geological Survey Bulletin 1274-J, 28 p.

Peterson, Fred, and Waldrop, H.A., 1965, Jurassic and Cretaceous stratigraphy of south-central Kaiparowits Plateau, Utah, *in* Geology and resources of south-central Utah: Utah Geological Society Guidebook no. 19, p. 47-69.

Pipiringos, G.N., and O'Sullivan, R.B., 1978, Principal unconformities in Traissic and Jurassic rocks, western interior United States—a preliminary survey: U.S. Geological Survey Professional Paper 1035-A, 29 p.

Spangler, Jerry, and Metcalf, Duncan, in preparation, Archaeological overview of Grand Staircase-Escalante National Monument: Grand Staircase-Escalante National Monument, Kanab, Utah.

Stewart, J.H., Poole, F.G., and Wilson, R.F., 1972, Stratigraphy and origin of the Chinle Formation and related Upper Triassic strata in the Colorado Plateau region: U.S. Geological Survey Professional Paper 690, 336 p.

Thompson, A.E., and Stokes, W.L., 1970, Stratigraphy of the San Rafael Group, southwest and south-central Utah: Utah Geological and Mineral Survey Bulletin 87, 54 p.

University of Utah Seismology Catalog, 1986, Earthquake data, 1979 to February 1986: University of Utah, Department of Geology and Geography.

U.S. Department of Interior, 2000, Grand Staircase-Escalante National Monument approved management plan and record of decision: Bureau of Land Management, Grand Staircase-Escalante National Monument, Cedar City, Utah, February 2000, 111 p.

Utah Geological Survey, 1998, New study suggests oil, gas deposits in Grand Staircase may have been moved by CO_2: Utah Geological Survey, Survey Notes, v. 31, no. 1, p. 8.

Zeller, H.D., and Stephens, E.V., 1973, Geologic map and coal resources of the Seep Flat quadrangle, Garfield and Kane Counties, Utah: U.S. Geological Survey Coal Investigations Series Map C-65, 1:24,000.

Owachomo Bridge, Natural Bridges National Monument
Photo courtesy of the Utah Travel Council

Geology of Utah's Parks and Monuments
2000 Utah Geological Association Publication 28
D.A. Sprinkel, T.C. Chidsey, Jr., and P.B. Anderson, editors

Geology of Natural Bridges National Monument, Utah

Jacqueline E. Huntoon[1], John D. Stanesco[2], Russell F. Dubiel[3] and Jim Dougan[4]

ABSTRACT

Natural Bridges National Monument was established to protect three large natural bridges as well as ancient masonry structures constructed by ancestral Puebloan people. Streams in White Canyon and its tributary canyons are primarily responsible for formation of the bridges. Although the bridges are probably less than 30,000 years old, they occur in Permian Cedar Mesa Sandstone. The Cedar Mesa Sandstone was deposited during the Wolfcampian Epoch of the Permian Period (about 270 million years ago). Deposition of the Cedar Mesa Sandstone and the other formations that comprise the Permian Cutler Group occurred along the western margin of North America in a variety of terrestrial and marine environments. After it was deposited, the Cedar Mesa Sandstone was gradually buried to a depth of 5,000 to 10,000 feet (1,500-3,000 m). Some of the overlying rock formations, including the Triassic Moenkopi and Chinle Formations and the Jurassic Wingate Sandstone, are present in the mesas that surround Natural Bridges National Monument. The overlying rocks began to be eroded from the Natural Bridges area sometime between 74 and 65 million years ago, during the Late Cretaceous to Tertiary Laramide orogeny. Most of the erosion occurred during the last 6 million years, as the Colorado River and its tributaries cut down through the rising Colorado Plateau. Although the ages of the bridges are difficult to determine, they probably began to form during the Pleistocene Epoch of the Quaternary Period (1.64 million-10,000 years before present). At that time the climate in southeastern Utah was considerably wetter than it is today.

INTRODUCTION

Natural Bridges National Monument (NABR) is located in southeastern Utah along the northern margin of the physiographic feature known as Cedar Mesa (figure 1). Natural Bridges can be reached via Utah State Route 275, a 4-mile (6.5-km) entry road that connects to Utah Highway 95 between Blanding and Hite Marina. Entry fees are collected at the Visitor Center where exhibits, a bookstore, and a 10-minute video orient visitors and explain the significance of NABR. A 13-site campground is located a short distance from the Visitor Center.

Two steep-sided canyons, Armstrong Canyon and White Canyon, cut through NABR. Three large natural bridges are located within the two canyons. Visitors to NABR can view the bridges from overlooks along Bridge

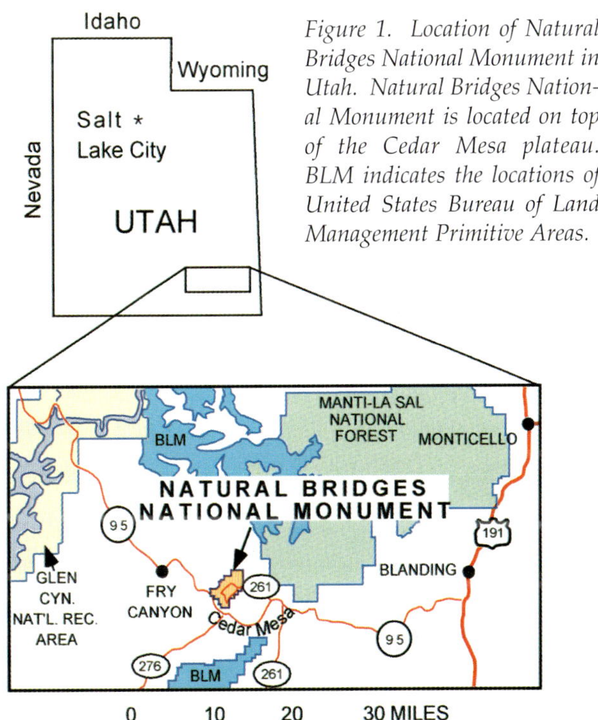

Figure 1. Location of Natural Bridges National Monument in Utah. Natural Bridges National Monument is located on top of the Cedar Mesa plateau. BLM indicates the locations of United States Bureau of Land Management Primitive Areas.

[1]Department of Geological Engineering and Sciences,
  Michigan Technological University, Houghton, MI 49931
[2]Department of Geology, Red Rocks Community College,
  Lakewood, CO 80228
[3]U.S. Geological Survey, Lakewood, CO 80225
[4]Natural Bridges National Monument, Lake Powell, UT 84533

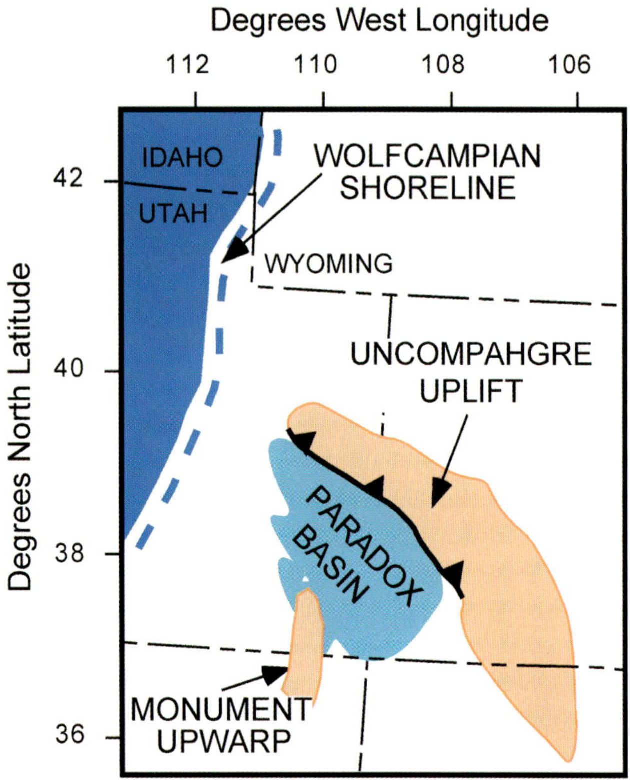

Figure 2. *Early Permian paleotectonic elements of southeastern Utah. The Permian shoreline position fluctuated to the east and west parallel to the line shown on the map.*

Figure 3. *Eolian features. A) Cross-bedding in the Cedar Mesa Sandstone in Natural Bridges National Monument. B) A modern dune located near Hanksville, Utah. Wind blew from the upper left toward the lower right of the photo during formation of this dune.*

View Drive, a paved 9-mile (14.5-km) loop. From the road, hikers can reach each of the bridges by following well-maintained trails that descend into the canyons. The bridges are linked by a marked but otherwise unmaintained 9-mile (14.5-km) loop hiking route.

The three bridges in NABR are among the ten largest in the world. Sipapu is the largest bridge in NABR and the first bridge that visitors see as they drive along Bridge View Drive. It is considered a mature bridge. Symmetrical in shape with a smooth, rounded opening, Sipapu's abutments lie above the level of the present-day streambed. At 220 feet (67 m) high, with a span of 268 feet (82 m), Sipapu is second only to Rainbow Bridge (located on Lake Powell) in size (see the paper by Chidsey and others in this volume for information about the geology of Rainbow Bridge National Monument). Kachina Bridge is located near the confluence of White and Armstrong Canyons. It is a massive, youthful bridge that is still growing in size. Kachina is 210 feet (64 m) high with a span of 204 feet (62 m). The rock making up the span is 93 feet (28 m) thick, and as recently as June, 1992 a major rockfall occurred as an estimated 4,000 tons (3.6 x 10⁶ kg) of sandstone sloughed off the underside of the bridge on its west abutment. The third bridge, Owachomo, is the oldest in NABR and is nearing collapse. It is 106 feet (32 m) high with a span of 180 feet (55 m). Because it is only 9 feet (3 m) thick at the crest of its span, it is very fragile. Located adjacent to Armstrong Canyon, Owachomo lies above and

parallel to the present-day streambed.

Geologic Overview

The three bridges are all developed in Lower Permian Cedar Mesa Sandstone. The Cedar Mesa Sandstone was deposited about 270 million years ago (Ma), at a time when the western shoreline of North America trended approximately north-south (in modern coordinates) and ran through the central part of present-day Utah (figure 2). Most of the rocks in the park were deposited by immense windblown sand dunes that migrated inland from the shoreline. The migrating dunes generated cross-bedding, the most prominent sedimentary structure that can be seen in the rocks in NABR (figure 3). As the dunes were buried by other sediments, they were compacted and cemented into rock. Detailed descriptions of the Cedar Mesa Sandstone and the rock units that occur above and below it are included later in this paper.

A: Sipapu Bridge Evolution

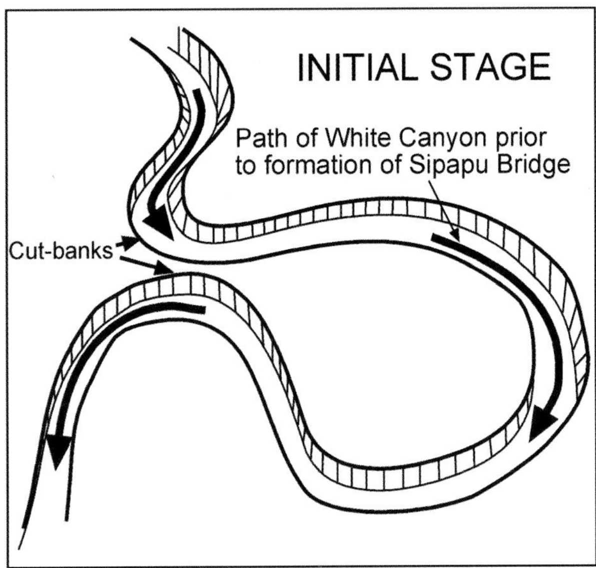

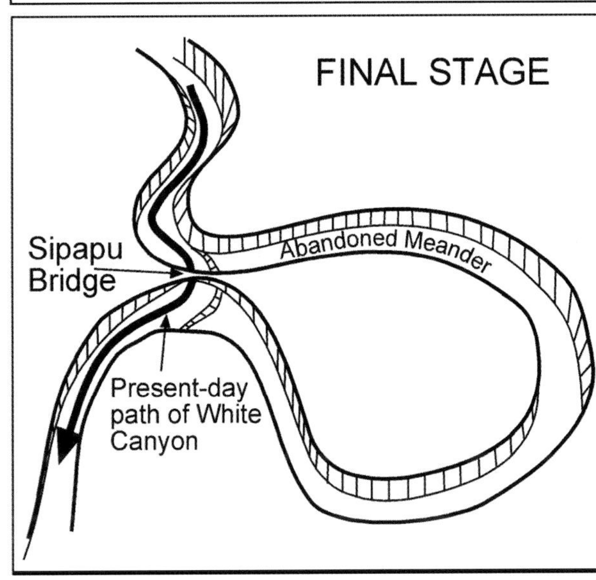

B: Kachina Bridge Evolution

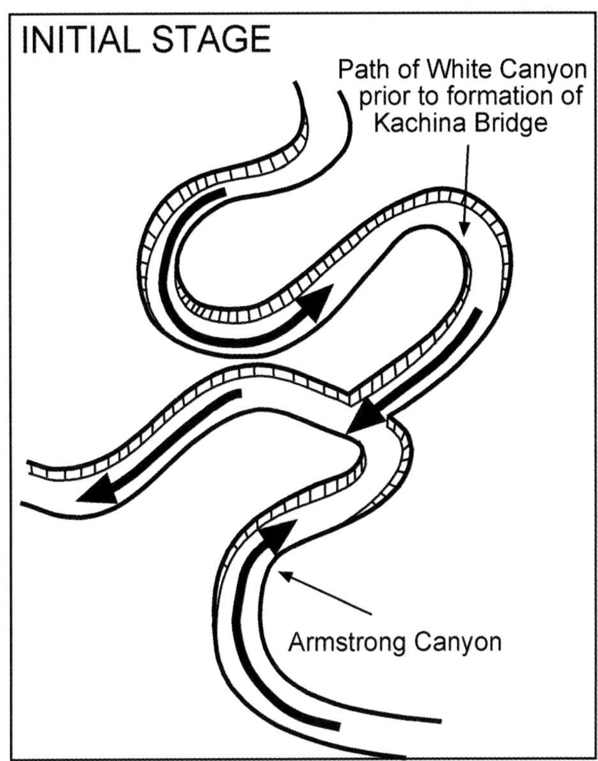

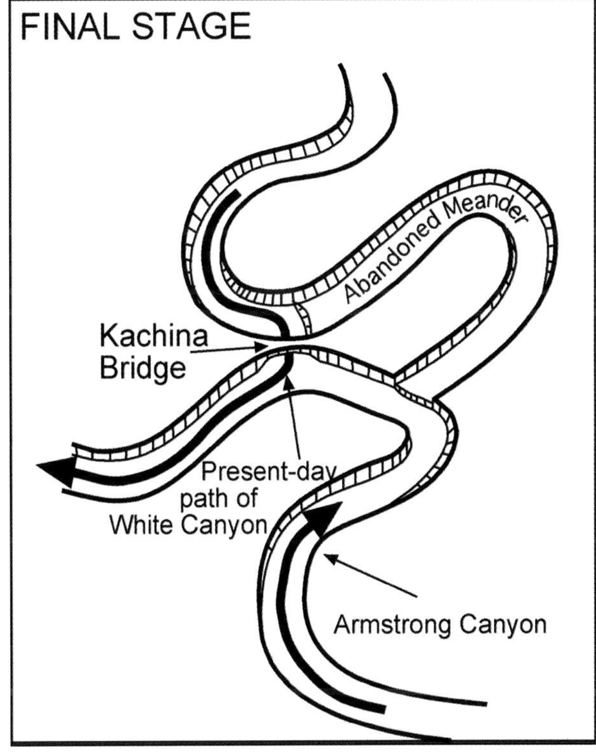

Figure 4. Intrepreted evolution of the three natural bridges. In each part of this figure, the Initial Stage corresponds to time prior to formation of the bridge. The Final Stage corresponds to the present-day configuration of the canyons. A) Sipapu Bridge. B) Kachina Bridge. C) Owachomo Bridge.

Although the bridges are carved out of the approximately 270 Ma Cedar Mesa Sandstone, the bridges themselves are likely less than 30,000 years old. Between the time that the Cedar Mesa Sandstone was deposited and the time that the bridges formed, the Cedar Mesa was buried beneath at least 5,000 feet (1,500 m) of overlying rock and sediment. The lower portion of this package of sedimentary rocks is equivalent to the rock units that are exposed in the cliffs and mesas that surround NABR. Most of the overlying rock was probably removed relatively recently, during the last 6 million years (m.y.). Once

the Cedar Mesa Sandstone was again exposed at the surface of the Earth, water flowing in White Canyon and Armstrong Canyon began to cut down into it. The natural bridges formed as the canyons cut through necks in the Cedar Mesa Sandstone and channel meanders were abandoned.

C: Owachomo Bridge Evolution

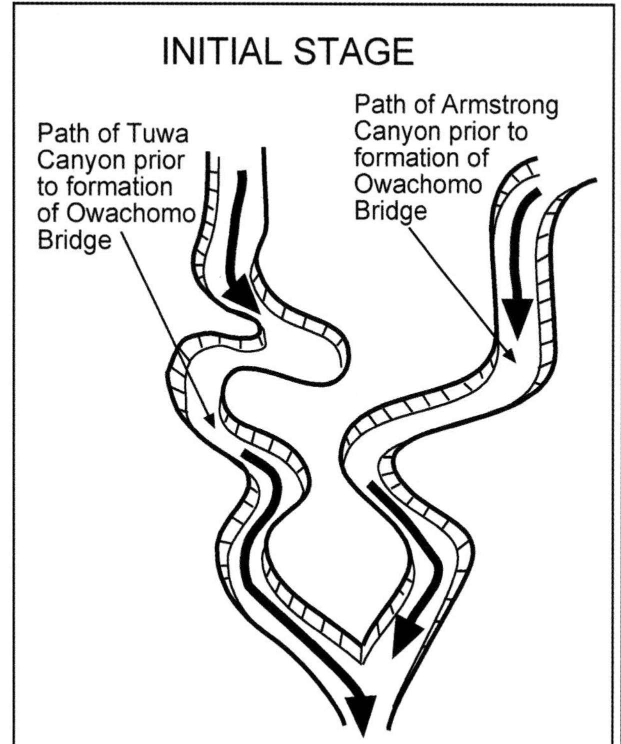

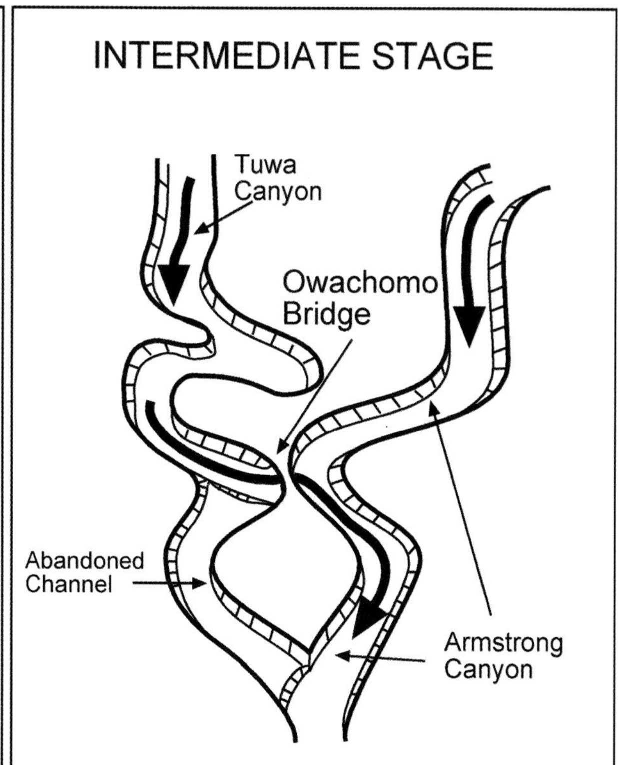

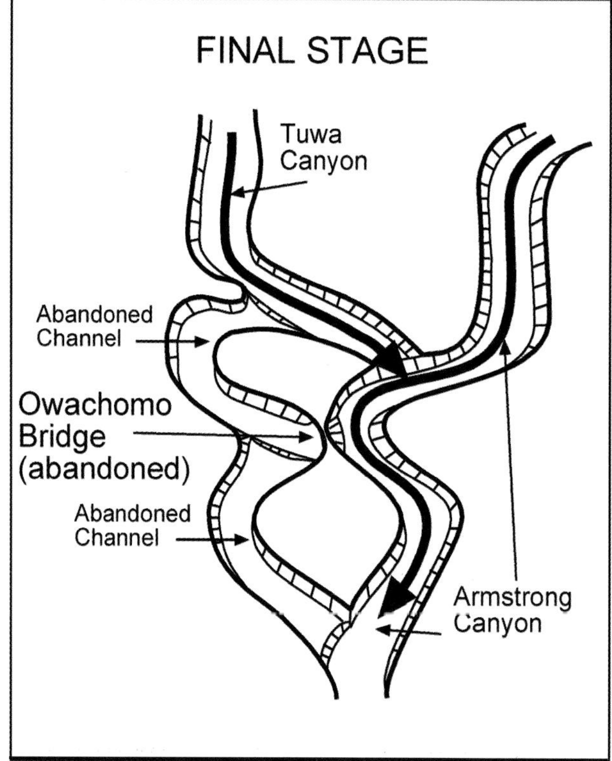

Bridges differ from arches in that they are formed by flowing water. The bridges probably began to form during the last glacial stadial, the Pinedale Glacial, that lasted from about 30,000 to12,000 years before present (ybp). Although the Natural Bridges area was not directly in contact with glacial ice, high levels of precipitation during the glacial stadial may have produced large floods that periodically flowed through Armstrong and White Canyons. Thin canyon walls that blocked and diverted the flow into meanders may have been penetrated during the floods. The bridges are the remnants of the thin canyon walls (figure 4). In addition to flowing water, other processes were

Figure 5. The natural bridges. A) Sipapu Bridge. B) Kachina Bridge as viewed from Armstrong Canyon. Kachina Bridge is partly hidden by vegetation in the photo and its location is highlighted with a white line. C) Owachomo Bridge as viewed from the overlook on the Owachomo Bridge trail. Owachomo Bridge's opening is highlighted with white in the photo so that it can be seen more easily.

also instrumental in formation and expansion of the bridges. Development of the bridges is discussed in detail later in this paper.

History of Natural Bridges National Monument and Its Bridges

In 1883, Cass Hite wandered up White Canyon from the Colorado River searching for gold. He found treasure of a different sort. Three massive stone bridges towered near the head of the White Canyon drainage (figure 5). In the years that followed, cowboys and adventurers found their way to Cedar Mesa to see the unusual spans. In 1904, National Geographic Magazine published a story, "The Colossal Bridges of Utah," that introduced the world to the bridges. A year later a local cowboy named John Scorup led the first scientific expedition to photograph, measure, and study the natural bridges.

United States citizens were extremely interested in the bridges during the first decade of the 20th century, and were equally fascinated with ancient masonry structures found on Cedar Mesa. In 1906 Congress passed the Antiquities Act in an attempt to stem wholesale looting and destruction of the archeological resource. On April 16, 1908, Theodore Roosevelt established Natural Bridges as Utah's first National Monument to protect both the natural bridges and the ruins.

In conducting a survey of the newly created monument the following year, the General Land Office assigned the Hopi names Sipapu, Kachina, and Owachomo to the three bridges that had previously been known as Augusta, Caroline, and Edwin respectively. Sipapu means "the place of emergence," an entryway by which the Hopi believe their ancestors came into this world. Kachina Bridge is named for rock art symbols on the bridge that resemble symbols commonly used on Kachina dolls. Owachomo means, "rock mound," in honor of a feature atop the bridge's east abutment. These Hopi names were chosen because it was at that time widely (and correctly) supposed that the modern-day Hopi (as well as other modern-day Puebloans) are descendents of the people who occupied these remote canyons in ancient times.

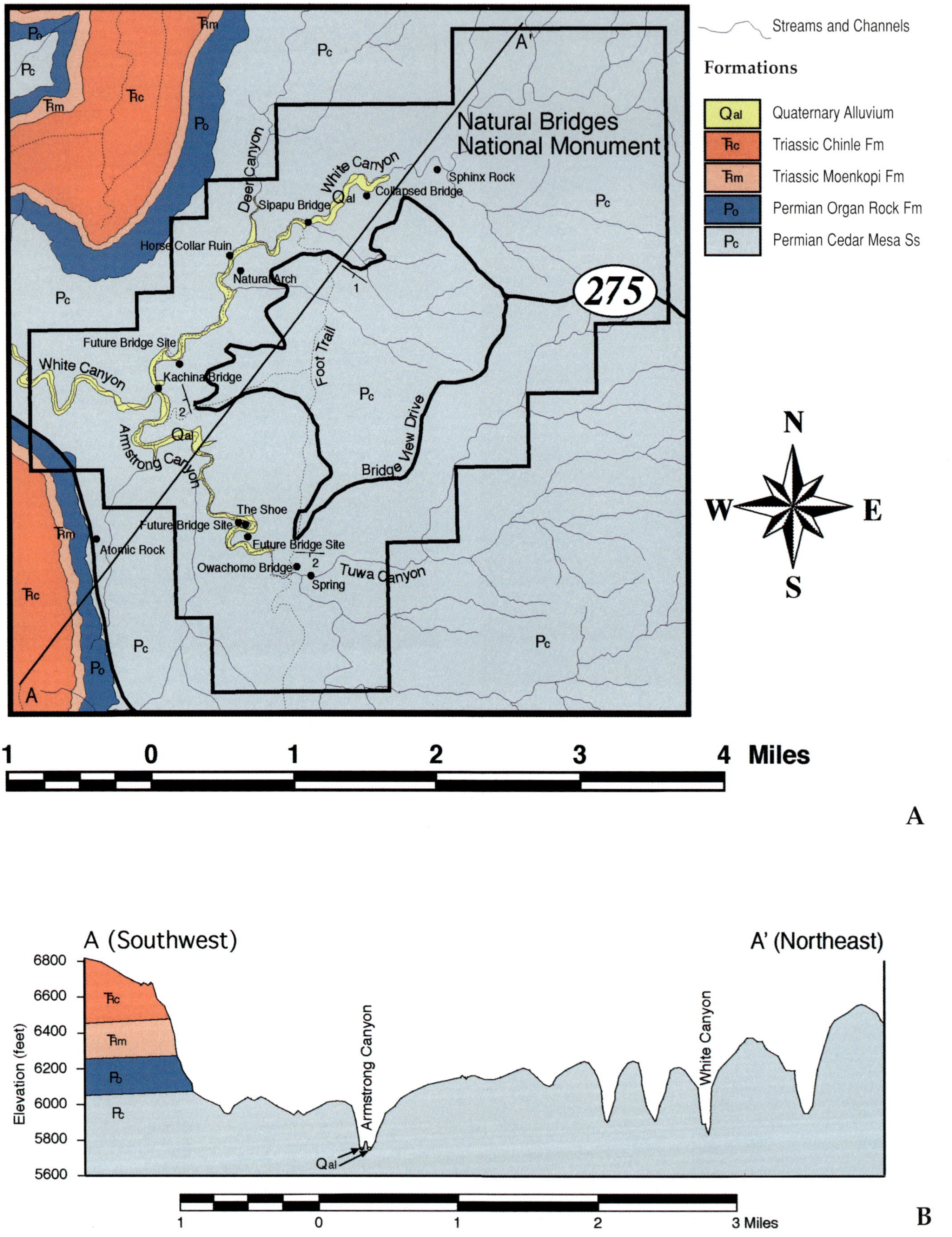

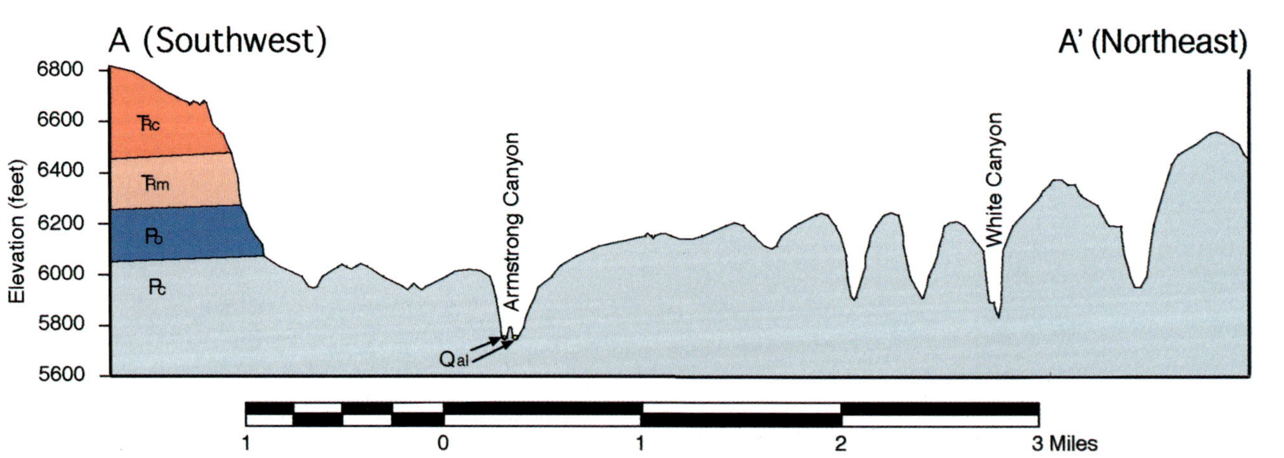

Figure 6. Geologic map (6A) and cross section (6B) for Natural Bridges National Monument.

GEOLOGY OF NATURAL BRIDGES NATIONAL MONUMENT

In this section the paleotectonic setting of the Natural Bridges area during deposition of two bedrock formations exposed in NABR (the Cedar Mesa Sandstone and Organ Rock Formation) is first discussed. After the Cedar Mesa and Organ Rock were deposited, they were buried beneath younger rocks, some of which can be seen in the cliffs surrounding NABR. The sedimentology and stratigraphy of the rock units present in and near Natural Bridges are described in the second part of this section. The final part of this section describes the evolution of the natural bridges.

Permian Paleotectonic Elements of Southeastern Utah

Natural Bridges National Monument encompasses an area underlain almost entirely by the Lower Permian Cedar Mesa Sandstone and Organ Rock Formation (figure 6). Deposition of the Cedar Mesa Sandstone occurred during the Wolfcampian Epoch of the Permian Period (270 to 290 Ma), and the Organ Rock Formation was deposited during the Leonardian Epoch (255 to 270 Ma) (Harland and others, 1989; Blakey, 1996; Stanesco and others, this volume). Three major paleotectonic elements (Uncompahgre uplift, Paradox basin, and Monument upwarp) influenced deposition in southeastern Utah during the Early Permian (figure 2). The Uncompahgre uplift was part of the Ancestral Rocky Mountains. The Ancestral Rockies formed during the Pennsylvanian Period, concurrent with collision of a microcontinent or an island arc and the southern part of North America near Texas and Oklahoma (Ouchita orogeny) (Harry and Mickus, 1998). Stress produced by the collision may have been responsible for development of fault-bounded uplifts and basins across what is now the south-central United States (Kluth and Coney, 1981). The Uncompahgre uplift is bounded by a high-angle reverse fault along its southwestern side (Frahme and Vaughn, 1983). Movement along the Uncompahgre fault resulted in development of a foreland basin, the Paradox basin, adjacent to the uplift. Although the Paradox basin began subsiding during the Pennsylvanian, both the basin and the uplift were still active during the Permian (Huffman and Taylor, 1994).

The third paleotectonic element that influenced deposition in southeastern Utah during the Early Permian is the Monument upwarp. The Monument upwarp is approximately coincident with the southwestern edge of the Paradox basin in southeastern Utah. Isopach maps and correlated sections (for example, Baars, 1962; Blakey, 1996; Condon, 1997) demonstrate that the Monument upwarp influenced deposition during the late Paleozoic and possibly the Early Triassic (Kelley, 1955; Huntoon and others, 1994; Stanesco and others, this volume). During the Permian, the upwarp was a broad, elongate, low-lying topographic high that extended from Monument Valley to approximately the confluence of the Green and Colorado Rivers

(figure 2). Blakey (1996) described the effect of the upwarp on deposition of late Paleozoic eolian rocks (including the Cedar Mesa Sandstone). Stanesco and others (this volume) document the Monument upwarp's influence on deposition of the Organ Rock Formation. The Monument upwarp was also active during the Laramide orogeny (late Mesozoic to early Cenozoic). Evidence of this relatively recent activity can be seen at Comb Ridge, where rocks along the upwarp's eastern margin are bent into a steep monocline. Because rocks on the upwarp are bent upward, late Paleozoic and younger rocks are well exposed in cliff faces near the axis of the upwarp where erosion has penetrated into its core.

During the Permian, boulder conglomerates were deposited in proximal alluvial fan environments adjacent to the Uncompahgre fault in the Paradox basin (Campbell, 1980; Mack and Rasmussen, 1984). Feldspar-rich sandstones and silty sandstones were deposited in the distal portions of the fans. Fluvial systems deposited feldspar-rich silty sandstones throughout the Paradox basin and at times prograded from the Paradox basin toward the paleoshoreline. The Organ Rock Formation consists of rocks that were primarily derived from the Uncompahgre uplift (Stanesco and others, this volume).

The Organ Rock's feldspar-rich composition contrasts with the high quartz content of the Cedar Mesa Sandstone. The Cedar Mesa Sandstone, like other Permian sandstones on the Colorado Plateau, was probably derived from a source area other than the Uncompahgre uplift (Scott, 1965; Irwin, 1976; Campbell and Stanesco, 1985). Paleocurrent data from the Cedar Mesa Sandstone suggest that it was deposited by northwesterly winds. Poole (1962) suggested that the Cedar Mesa, as well as other late Paleozoic sandstones on the Colorado Plateau, were derived from recycling of older eolian sandstones. Based on paleogeographic and paleoclimatic reconstructions (Parrish, 1985), paleocurrent data (Poole, 1962), and composition data (Scott, 1965; Campbell and Stanesco, 1985), the Cedar Mesa is interpreted to have been primarily derived from the shallow-marine shelf environment located to the northwest (in terms of modern latitude and longitude) of NABR (Stanesco and Campbell, 1989). Sediments were made available for transport from the shelf to the Natural Bridges area during times of lowered sea level when the shelf was subaerially exposed (Loope, 1984; Peterson, 1988).

Regional Stratigraphy and Sedimentology

In the Natural Bridges region, the Organ Rock Formation is the top of the Permian System. Triassic and Jurassic rocks that overlie the Organ Rock Formation are exposed along the skyline that is visible from NABR. These rocks include the Lower Triassic Moenkopi Formation, the Upper Triassic Chinle Formation, and the Lower Jurassic Wingate Sandstone. The Organ Rock, along with the underlying Cedar Mesa Sandstone and the informally named lower Cutler beds, are part of the Cutler Group. The lower

Ma	Period	Unit	Member	Lithology	Scale (feet)	Weathering Column and Interpretation
208	JURASSIC	Wingate Sandstone		Dark red to dark orange, cliff-forming, vertically jointed sandstone.	1900–1600	Wind-blown dunes with minor sand-sheet and sabkha deposits.
	TRIASSIC	Chinle Formation	Church Rock; Owl Rock; Petrified Forest; Moss Back; Monitor Butte; Shinarump	Gray, red, pink, orange, and purple mudstone, sandstone, and conglomerate, with local thin limestone. The Shinarump Cgl. Mbr. hosts major uranium deposits along White Canyon.	1500–1100	Stream systems, floodplains, and lakes, with abundant paleosols.
245		Moenkopi Formation	Moody Canyon; Torrey; Sinbad; Black Dragon; Hoskinnini	Red, red-brown, and brown mudstone and sandstone with local conglomerate and gypsum.	1000–800	Coastal plain mudflat with minor marine influence. Stream or tidal channels and deltas are present.
	PERMIAN	Organ Rock Formation		Reddish-brown very fine- to fine-grained sandstone.	700–500	Stream channels with floodplain mudstones. Loess and wind-blown dunes, all with paleosols.
		Cedar Mesa Sandstone		White to gray very fine- to fine-grained sandstone and thin beds of red mudstone to very fine-grained sandstone.	400–100	Wind-blown dunes with mudstones on stream and floodplain surfaces.
290		"Lower Cutler Beds"**		Sandstone, mudstone, and limestone. **Informal unit.		Tidal flats, deltas, wind-blown dunes, shallow-marine shelf.

7A

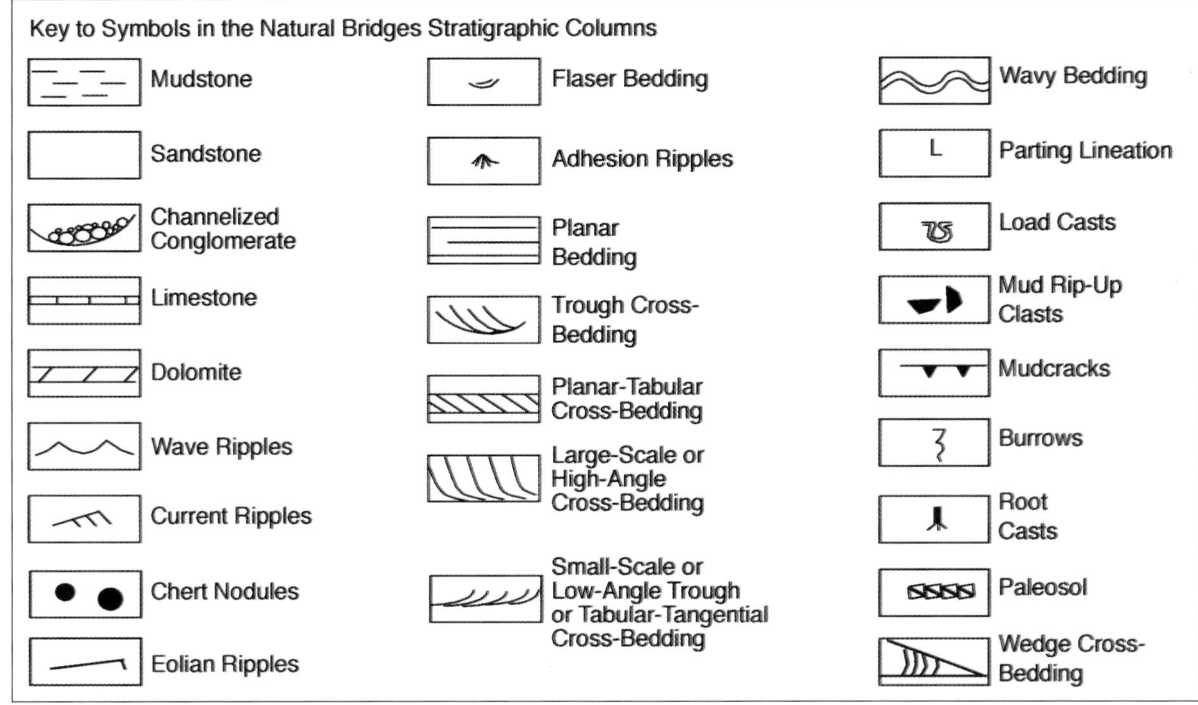

Figure 7. Generalized stratigraphy (7A) of the Paleozoic and Mesozoic rock units exposed on Cedar Mesa. 7B is a key to the symbols used in figures 7A and 9.

Cutler beds are the oldest Permian rocks exposed on Cedar Mesa. Toward the north and northeast, the Cutler Group grades into the coarser Cutler Formation undivided. The Cutler Formation undivided consists of sandstones and conglomerates deposited in fluvial and alluvial fan environments adjacent to the Uncompahgre uplift. The Cutler Group and the Triassic and Jurassic formations that can be seen from Natural Bridges are described in this section (figure 7).

Lower Cutler Beds

The lower Cutler beds are not exposed in Natural Bridges, but they are present elsewhere on Cedar Mesa. The lower Cutler beds consist of interlayered sandstones, mudstones, and limestones. Tidal flats, deltas, coastal sand dunes, fluvial systems, and shallow-marine shelf environments are all represented in the lower Cutler beds (Loope, 1984; Campbell, 1987; Condon, 1997). Lateral shifts in the location of these environments resulted in interbedding of rock types in the lower Cutler beds. Figure 8a depicts the geography of southeastern Utah during deposition of the lower Cutler beds. Feldspar-rich sediment was shed from the Uncompahgre uplift. Some of this sediment was transported by fluvial systems to a shallow sea whose shoreline fluctuated back and forth across the present-day location of Natural Bridges. Sand and dust were blown through the Natural Bridges region when relative sea level was low and the marine shelf to the northwest was exposed (Campbell, 1987). Southeast of Natural Bridges, the upper part of the lower Cutler beds grades into the thickly bedded red siltstones and very fine-grained sandstones of the Halgaito Formation. The Halgaito is interpreted as loess deposits that formed downwind of sand dunes located in the Natural Bridges area (Murphy, 1987).

Cedar Mesa Sandstone

Almost all of the bedrock exposed within the boundaries of NABR is Cedar Mesa Sandstone (figure 6). White Canyon is named for the light colored sandstone. The contact between the Cedar Mesa and the underlying lower Cutler beds cannot be seen within NABR. In exposures located to the east and west of Natural Bridges, the contact is gradational, indicating a gradual change of environments from those represented by the lower Cutler beds. The Cedar Mesa Sandstone's contact with the overlying Organ Rock Formation is well exposed along White Canyon near NABR and is also gradational.

In the Natural Bridges area, the Cedar Mesa consists of three lithofacies (rock assemblages). The dominant facies is a white sandstone. The second facies occurs as thin interbeds of red mudstone that are underlain and overlain by the white sandstone facies. The third facies is a gypsum and limestone facies that is exposed about 20 miles (32 km) to the southeast of Natural Bridges. Only the first two facies are common within NABR (figure 9).

White Sandstone Facies: The white sandstone facies consists of quartz-rich sandstones. Grains are subrounded to well rounded in shape and range from very fine to very coarse in size. Sand-sized marine fossil fragments are rarely present (Stanesco and Campbell, 1989). This facies contains abundant large-scale, high-angle cross-beds (fig-

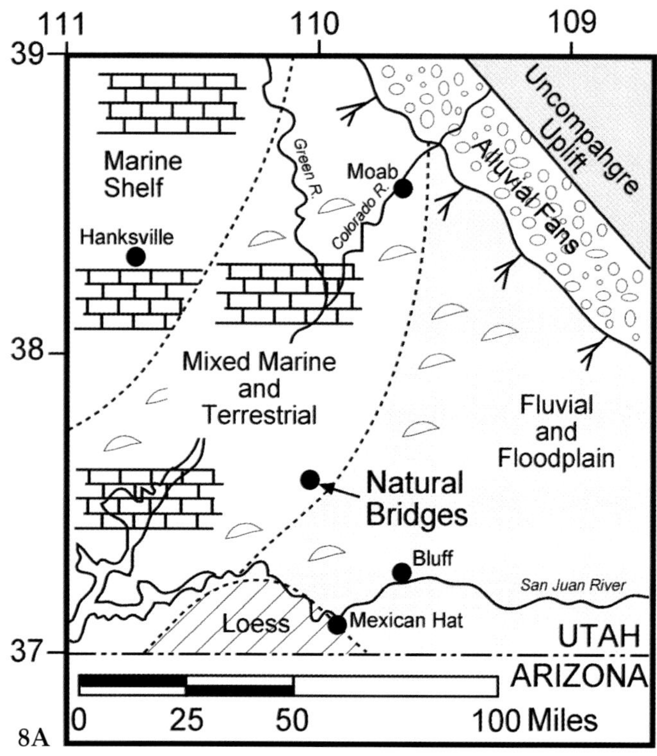

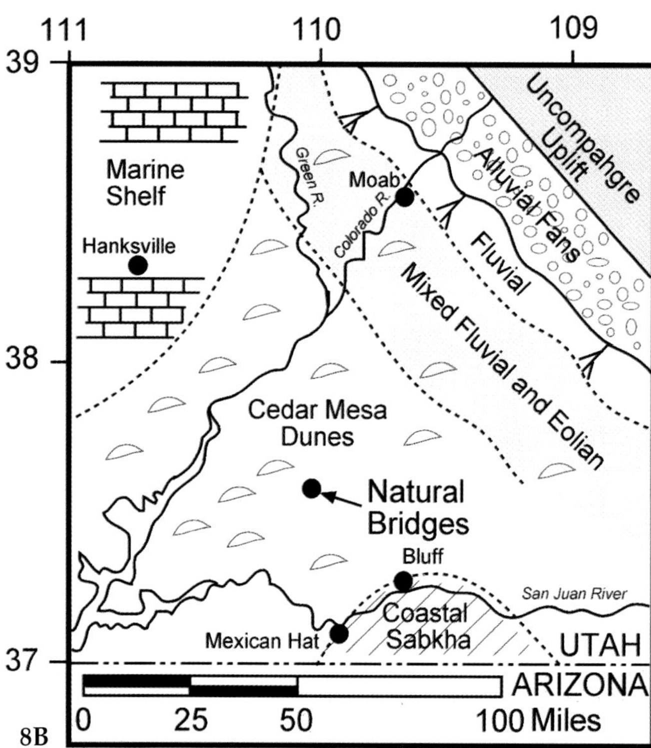

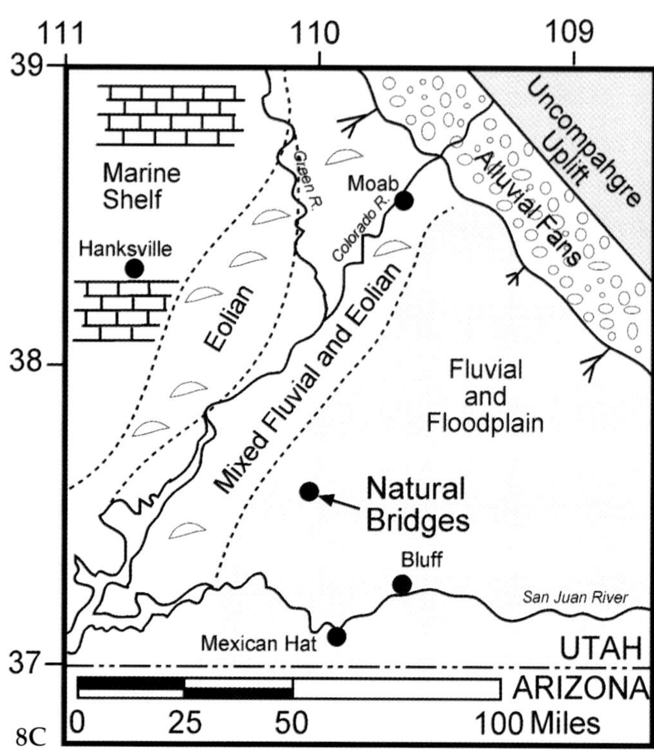

Figure 8. Early Permian depositional environments in southeastern Utah during the: A) Early Wolfcampian (lower Cutler beds) B) Wolfcampian (Cedar Mesa Sandstone), and C) Leonardian (Organ Rock Formation).

dune. Ripple marks at the top of the dune, in the upper-left corner of the photo, were produced as the sand moved over the crest of the dune. These ripple marks have high ripple indices (length to height ratios). They are generally less than 3/8 of an inch (5 mm) high. If there is sufficient sand supply, the ripples produce inversely graded lamination as they migrate downwind. These coarsening upward laminations that result from wind ripple migration are known as translatent strata.

As sand is blown over the crest of the dune it falls out of suspension on the dune's slipface, producing grainfall stratification. Sand accumulates most rapidly near the top of the slipface. Eventually the slipface becomes oversteepened and sand avalanches down the slope producing grainflow stratification. The toes of the avalanche lobes flow onto the dune apron, another site of ripple formation. Note that the crests of the ripples on the dune apron (figure 3b) run parallel to the direction of dune migration. Wind currents that are deflected by the dune and blow around its sides produce these ripples. In figure 10, wedge-shaped grainflow layers in the Cedar Mesa override and interfinger with translatent strata.

All of the features mentioned above can be seen in the white sandstone facies in Natural Bridges. The Geologic Guide to Sipapu Bridge Trail on CD-ROM (UGA Publication 29) contains photographs and descriptions of cross-bedding, ripple marks with high ripple indices, translatent

ure 3a). The cross-bedding is interpreted to be the product of deposition by large, migrating eolian dunes. The white sandstone facies contains many other features that are common in modern eolian dunes.

Figure 3b shows a modern sand dune near Hanksville, Utah. The dune is moving toward the area shown in the lower-right corner of the photo. In active dunes the wind blows sand up the windward slope and over the top of the

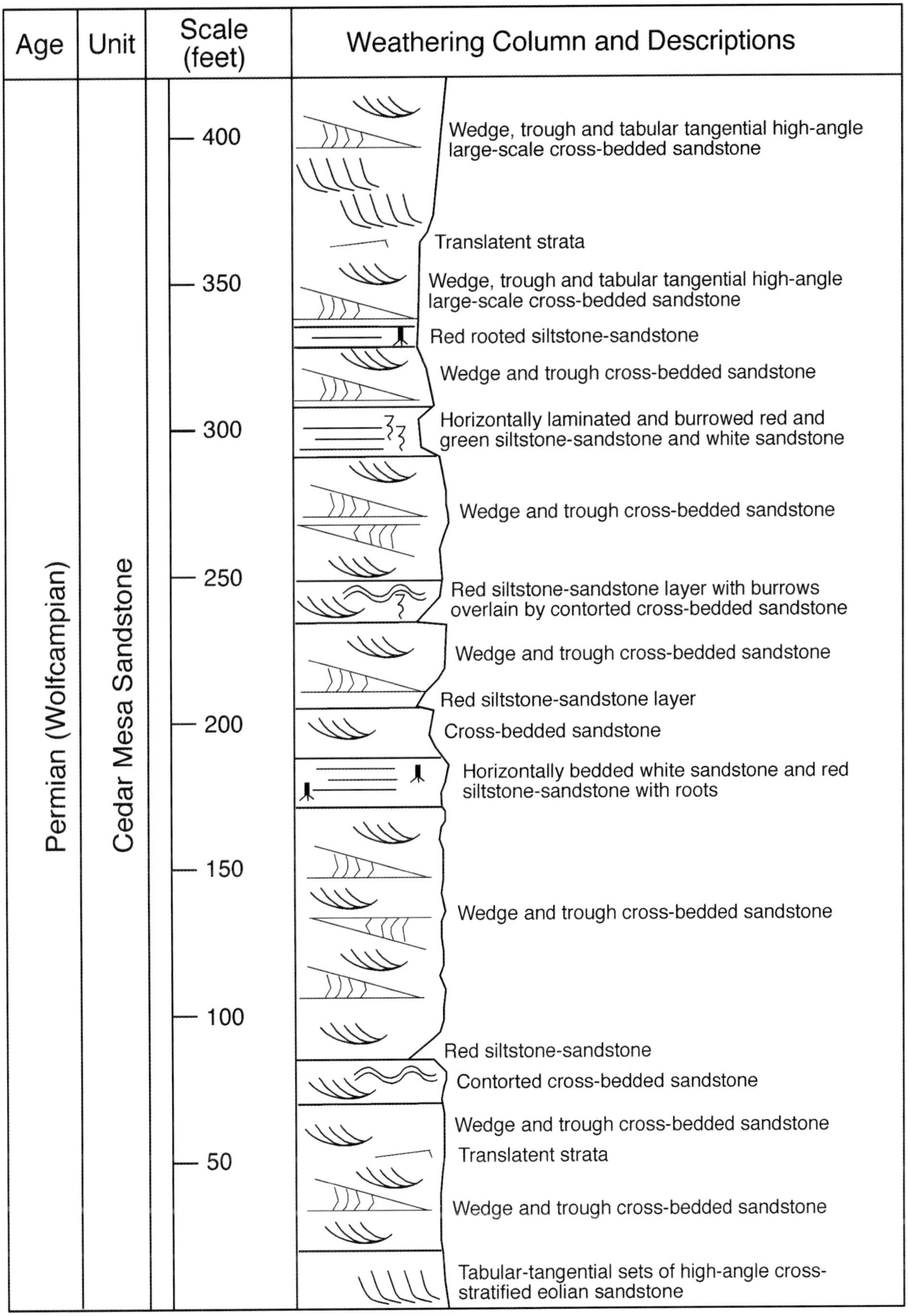

Figure 9. Detailed stratigraphy of the Cedar Mesa Sandstone in Natural Bridges National Monument. Stratigraphic section was measured along the Sipapu Bridge Trail. The top and base of the formation are not present along the trail and are not included in this section.

Figure 10. Sand avalanche layers (grainflow strata) overlying and interfingering with wind-ripple laminae (translatent strata) in the Cedar Mesa Sandstone.

Figure 11. A red mudstone layer underlain and overlain by the white sandstone facies of the Cedar Mesa Sandstone at the Sipapu Bridge overlook along Sipapu Bridge Trail. At this location the white sandstone directly above the mudstone layer is contorted. This suggests the red mudstone was still wet when the white sandstone dune migrated onto it.

Figure 12. Sand-filled mudcrack in the red mudstone facies of the Cedar Mesa Sandstone in Natural Bridges.

strata, grainflow stratification, as well as grainfall stratification.

The white sandstone facies also contains interdune and sand-sheet deposits. Interdunes are low-lying areas between dunes. Sand-sheets are planar areas that lie adjacent to dune fields. These environments are represented in the white sandstone facies by horizontally laminated units that commonly contain translatent strata but lack abundant cross-beds. The red mudstone facies (described below) is also present in the interdune and sand-sheet environments.

Red Mudstone Facies: Horizontally laminated beds of red mudstone 1 to 10 feet (0.3-3 m) thick separate the much thicker sections of white sandstone in the cliffs of Natural Bridges (figure 11). This facies consists of micaceous mudstone and very fine grained sandstone. Discontinuous unfossiliferous limestones are rarely present. The red mudstone layers are generally massive. Some contain mudcracks filled with sand from overlying units (figure 12), root casts, and burrows. At Natural Bridges some of the red mudstone layers extend laterally for miles. These laterally extensive red beds probably formed during floods that inundated numerous interdune areas and formed a continuous surface. Dunes composed of the white sandstone facies eventually migrated across the flood deposit. In Canyonlands National Park, red mudstones within the Cedar Mesa can be traced toward the northeast into fluvial sandstones and conglomerates of the Cutler Formation undivided (Langford and Chan, 1988). Recent flooding of a dunefield in Peru's altiplano is a modern analogue of the flood events that occurred during deposition of the Cedar Mesa Sandstone. In contrast to the laterally continuous red mudstone layers, some red mudstones pinch out into the white sandstone facies. This type of lateral relationship suggests that some of the red mudstones formed adjacent to active eolian dunes. We interpret these discontinuous red mudstone layers as the product of deposition in isolated interdune ponds that formed during floods or because of rising water tables.

Gypsum and Limestone Facies: Approximately 20 miles (32 km) southeast of Natural Bridges the white sandstone and red mudstone facies interfinger with gypsum and algal limestone in a section almost 1,000 feet (300 m) thick. Some of the gypsiferous layers are massive suggesting they formed from evaporation of ponded surface water. Other gypsum layers displace or deform surrounding sandstone and mudstone layers indicating gypsum grew within the clastic sediment. The algal limestone beds are light gray in color. They contain chert nodules up to 1 foot (30 cm) in diameter. The chert is commonly bright red in color. Many of the limestones exhibit fracturing and brecciation that is interpreted to reflect early, subaerial cementation (Ginsburg, 1957). The characteristics of this facies suggest deposition in a sabkha. Sabkhas form in intertidal or supratidal zones along coastlines under highly evaporative conditions. Results of analysis of carbon, oxygen, and sulfur isotopes, as well as the presence of rare marine fossils, indicate the Cedar Mesa sabkha formed along a marine shoreline that opened to the south (Stanesco and Campbell, 1989; Lock and Pelfrey, 1997).

Paleogeography: During deposition of the Cedar Mesa Sandstone, much of southeastern Utah was covered by a large dune field or erg consisting of sand sheets and barchanoid dunes that migrated toward the southeast (figure 8b). The dunes were fed by sand blown inland from a marine shelf located to the northwest. Sand-sized marine fossil fragments increase in abundance toward the northwest in the Cedar Mesa (Stanesco and Campbell, 1989). The dunefield was bordered along its southern margin by a coastal sabkha that opened toward the marine environment on its southern side. Streams originating in the Uncompahgre uplift encroached on the northeastern margin of the erg and occasionally flooded low-lying areas. Natural Bridges National Monument is located near the center of the Cedar Mesa erg. This accounts for the predominance of eolian dune, interdune, and sand sheet deposits in the walls of White Canyon. Elsewhere, near the margins of the dune field, fluvial and sabkha strata are more significant components of the Cedar Mesa Sandstone.

The Cedar Mesa erg and sabkha were deposited in arid climate conditions. Replacement of the Cedar Mesa erg and sabkha by Organ Rock Formation fluvial and floodplain deposits is interpreted to reflect an increase in precipitation, particularly in the Uncompahgre uplift source area.

Organ Rock Formation

The Organ Rock Formation is the youngest formation in the Cutler Group in the vicinity of NABR. To the west, along Lake Powell in Glen Canyon National Recreation Area, the White Rim Sandstone of the Cutler Group overlies the Organ Rock. The White Rim was removed from the Natural Bridges area by erosion that occurred at the end of the Permian Period or the beginning of the Triassic Period. To the southeast of NABR, in the vicinity of Monument Valley, the De Chelly Sandstone of the Cutler Group overlies the Organ Rock. Where the White Rim and De Chelly Sandstones are absent, across the crest of the Monument upwarp, the Organ Rock is unconformably overlain by the Lower Triassic Moenkopi Formation. The Organ Rock is thin along the axis of the Monument upwarp, averaging about 300 feet (100 m) thick near NABR. To the east of the Monument upwarp, near Monument Valley, the Organ Rock is over 700 feet (210 m) thick, and to the west of Natural Bridges near Glen Canyon National Recreation Area the Organ Rock is about 400 feet (130 m) thick.

The Organ Rock is a reddish-brown to light-red, slope-forming unit composed of feldspar-rich very fine- to fine-grained sandstone, siltstone, mudstone, and minor carbonate-pebble conglomerate that was deposited primarily in continental fluvial, floodplain, and eolian environments (figure 8c). Marginal-marine mudflat and tidal channel environments are locally present. The lower part of the Organ Rock was deposited by fluvial systems that flowed to the southwest off the Uncompahgre uplift, and by intrabasinal fluvial systems that flowed to the northwest near Monument Valley. Fine-grained floodplain deposits, many exhibiting root casts, trace fossils, and paleosol (ancient soil) development, are interbedded with the fluvial channel deposits.

To the west of Natural Bridges (near Lake Powell), the lower part of the Organ Rock consists of broad, shallow cut-and-fill deposits. The cut-and-fill deposits may represent distal fluvial and floodplain environments on a low-gradient coastal plain, or marginal-marine mudflat and tidal-channel deposits. To date, no definite marine indicators have been identified. Rain-drop impressions, vertical and horizontal burrows, and adhesion ripples are typically associated with the cut-and-fill deposits. Adhesion ripples form when dry sand blows across a damp surface and adheres to the wet surface in low wrinkled domes that are less than about 1/4 inch (6 mm) high.

Also near Lake Powell, the upper part of the Organ Rock contains abundant large-scale cross-bedded sandstone units. These cross-bedded sandstones are interpreted as eolian dune deposits. On the east side of the crest of the Monument upwarp the upper part of the Organ Rock is composed of sandstone beds containing root casts and adhesion ripples. This succession is interpreted as the product of eolian sand sheet deposition. Loess deposits composed of massive very fine-grained sandstones and siltstones that contain root casts are rare within the Organ Rock, but are present in the upper part of the formation. The sedimentary structures within the Organ Rock indicate deposition in an environment that was occasionally flooded, and generally contained sufficient moisture to sustain plant growth.

Moenkopi Formation

In the immediate vicinity of NABR, the Permian-Triassic unconformity separates the Permian Organ Rock Formation from the overlying Lower to early Middle Triassic Moenkopi Formation (Blakey and others, 1993). The unconformity between the Organ Rock and the Moenkopi is difficult to identify near Natural Bridges because Moenkopi red beds directly overlie Organ Rock red beds. The major difference between the two formations is that the lower part of the Moenkopi contains very coarse to medium-sized, well-rounded quartz grains. These grains were likely derived from erosion of the uppermost parts of the White Rim Sandstone and/or De Chelly Sandstone. The White Rim and De Chelly Sandstones are not present in the Natural Bridges area because Natural Bridges lies close to the crest of the Monument upwarp. During development of the Permian-Triassic unconformity these two units were eroded from the crest of the Monument upwarp near Natural Bridges.

The Moenkopi Formation is mainly composed of reddish-brown sandstone, siltstone, and mudstone. Locally it contains chert-pebble conglomerate. The Moenkopi Formation was deposited in a variety of fluvial channel and floodplain, marginal-marine mudflat and tidal channel, sabkha, and marine environments (Stewart and others, 1972a). The Moenkopi along White Canyon varies from about 300 to 400 feet (100-130 m) in thickness, and forms a red-brown slope between the Organ Rock and Chinle Formations. Large-scale wavy bedding is present in the lower part of the Moenkopi (Hoskinnini Member) near Natural Bridges. The wavy bedding is interpreted to be the result of precipitation and dissolution of evaporites in the Hoskinnini.

Like parts of the Cutler Group below, the Moenkopi was deposited by fluvial and floodplain systems that drained the Uncompahgre uplift and other minor positive areas throughout central Utah. These continental systems connected with marginal-marine mudflat and marine depositional settings to the west and northwest. Gypsum is common in the lower members of the formation, indicating arid conditions at the time of deposition. Upsection, the Moenkopi contains fossilized plants and animals that indicate deposition in a warm tropical setting that may have experienced a monsoonal, wet-dry climate (Stewart and others, 1972a; Dubiel and others, 1991).

Chinle Formation

The Upper Triassic Chinle Formation unconformably overlies the Moenkopi Formation. The Chinle forms a pastel-colored slope composed of entirely continental deposits along the rim of the mesa that lies to the north of NABR. The Chinle varies in thickness from about 300 to 600 feet (100-200 m) near Natural Bridges. The basal member of the Chinle, the Shinarump Conglomerate Member, contains quartz- and chert-pebble conglomerate deposited by fluvial systems that eroded paleovalleys into the underlying Moenkopi Formation. Above the Shinarump Conglomerate Member, Chinle sediments were deposited in fluvial channel, floodplain, marsh, and lake systems. Fluvial trunk-stream systems flowed mainly to the northwest, toward the shoreline located in western Utah. Chinle sediments were derived from both the Uncompahgre uplift and the interior of North America (Stewart and others, 1972b; Dubiel, 1994. The climate during deposition of the Chinle is interpreted to have been monsoonal with pronounced alternation between wet and dry seasons (Dubiel and others, 1991).

Wingate Sandstone

The Lower Jurassic Wingate Sandstone unconformably overlies the Chinle Formation in the area surrounding NABR. The Wingate forms the massive to joint-ed reddish-orange cliff that rims the highest mesas seen from NABR. The Wingate is composed of fine- to medium-grained quartz and feldspathic sandstones. It is characterized by large-scale cross-bedding. The Wingate was deposited by eolian dunes in an arid climate setting. The Wingate Sandstone averages 300 to 400 feet (100-130 m) in thickness along White Canyon.

Development of the Bridges

At one time all of the rocks described above (with the exception of the lower Cutler beds) were present above the Cedar Mesa Sandstone in the vicinity of NABR. Other, younger rocks, that range in age from Jurassic to Cretaceous, were also present. The maximum depth of burial of the Cedar Mesa Sandstone was between 5,000 to 10,000 feet (1,500-3,000 m). Depth of burial estimates are based on the present-day thickness in nearby areas of the formations that once existed above the Cedar Mesa Sandstone (Hintze, 1993). Because the Cedar Mesa was deposited at or near sea level during the Permian, the Natural Bridges region must have subsided from the Permian to the Cretaceous to accommodate deposition of all of the overlying sedimentary rock.

Regional subsidence apparently ended in the Late Cretaceous. The effects of the Laramide orogeny were first expressed during the Maastrichtian (74-65 Ma) (Dickinson and others, 1987). This orogeny probably resulted from shallowing of the angle of subduction along the west coast of North America (Dickinson, 1981). The Natural Bridges area lies near the crest of the Monument upwarp, and rocks on this structure were bent into a broad, approximately north-south trending arch during the Laramide orogeny.

Removal of extensive amounts of rock from above the Cedar Mesa Sandstone did not occur until the entire Colorado Plateau began to rise during the Cenozoic. Uplift of about 6,000 feet (2,000 m) occurred in the eastern part of the plateau during the late Eocene (Gregory and Chase, 1992; Parsons and McCarthy, 1995), approximately 39 to 35 Ma (Harland and others, 1989). As the land surface rose, rivers began to cut down through the rock. When the rivers cut through soft, easily eroded rocks (like the Organ Rock Formation) they established meandering patterns and flowed through relatively wide, gentle valleys. When the rivers cut down into resistant rocks (like the Cedar Mesa Sandstone), the meandering channel paths that were established in a non-resistant overlying layer were superimposed on the resistant rock. The amount of downcutting in the Natural Bridges area was controlled by the elevation of the Colorado River's channel. Until as recently as 6 Ma, the Colorado River had not cut through the Grand Canyon and its channel's elevation was about 0.6 miles (1 km) higher than it is today (Parsons and McCarthy, 1995). During the last 6 m.y. the Colorado River cut through the Grand Canyon (Lucchitta, 1989), lowering local base level for rivers throughout southeastern Utah. The rate of downcutting by the Colorado River was rapid, and the rivers that drained into it cut down into the rocks beneath their beds faster than they cut into the rock on the sides of their channels. The meandering streams that cut into the Cedar Mesa Sandstone became entrenched in the rock (Stokes, 1969).

The natural bridges in NABR began to form after the streams were entrenched in the Cedar Mesa Sandstone. At some locations along the streams' paths thin walls separated the cut-bank side of one meander bend from the cut-bank side of another meander (figure 4). At these locations, the river eroded both sides of the thin walls. Erosion by the river, alone or in concert with other processes (described below), eventually produced a break in the wall. Once the wall was penetrated, the stream flowed through the wall, widening and smoothing the hole. The result was a natural bridge.

At the present time, the climate in southeastern Utah is arid, and streams in the canyons in NABR only rarely carry large volumes of water. It is likely that the natural bridges formed at a time high runoff events were more common than they are today. During the Pleistocene Epoch of the Quaternary Period the climate in Utah was significantly wetter than it is today. The Pinedale Stadial glacial period (30,000-12,000 ybp) is one of the last glacial advances that occurred during the Pleistocene. Although NABR was not directly in contact with ice, most of Utah experienced relatively wet conditions during the Pinedale Stadial. The natural bridges probably began to form at that time.

Although river flows were instrumental in development of the bridges, other processes such as frost wedging (Gregory, 1938), plant root growth, ground-water seeps (Culmer, 1908; Gregory, 1917, 1938), stress-release exfoliation (Gregory, 1938), and wind all weakened the Cedar Mesa before and after the bridges formed. Most visitors to NABR arrive during the summer months, and do not experience the freezing temperatures that affect NABR during winter. Precipitation or ground water that flows into cracks along exposed rock faces may freeze during winter, resulting in an increase in volume that breaks the rock apart. Plant roots pry rock apart along existing joints or fractures in the same way.

Ground-water seeps are common in White and Armstrong Canyons, and ground water preferentially migrates laterally along the top of the relatively fine-grained red layers within the Cedar Mesa Sandstone. Ground water exiting the formation at a seep carries dissolved minerals with it. Through time these seeps substantially weaken the rock and if they occur on a cliff, the cliff face retreats faster around the seep than elsewhere. Overhanging cliffs are therefore common above seeps.

The relatively fine-grained red layers are efficient at retaining the water that enters them due to capillary effects. Plant roots penetrating into the red layers are able to utilize the moisture and survive dry periods. These plant roots change the chemical conditions in the rock and their presence speeds the rate of erosion. In addition, the plant roots mechanically break apart the rock, also leading to accelerated erosion rates.

Because the Cedar Mesa was deeply buried until relatively recently, it is still responding to the change in stress at free surfaces. In the canyons, cliff walls respond to the drop in stress by developing fractures that are nearly parallel to the trend of the canyon. The fractures are widened by frost wedge action or plant root growth until the rock breaks and the canyon is enlarged by a small amount. Finally, wind in the canyons carries abundant quartz grains that sandblast and erode all surfaces they encounter.

Currently there are three large natural bridges in NABR (figures 4 and 5). Sipapu bridge was produced as the stream in White Canyon cut off a meander bend. The abandoned meander can be seen from the Sipapu Bridge Trail (see the Geologic Guide to Sipapu Bridge Trail on CD-ROM, UGA Publication 29). Kachina Bridge formed when the stream in White Canyon broke through a wall just upstream of its original junction with Armstrong Canyon (Barnes, 1987). Owachomo Bridge formed when the stream in a Tuwa Canyon (a tributary to Armstrong Canyon) twice cut through meander bends into Armstrong Canyon (Barnes, 1987). The bridge is now isolated from the main channel, because the second cutting event resulted in abandonment of the part of Tuwa Canyon that passed under the bridge. Several smaller unmarked spans are present in White and Armstrong Canyons. All of the bridges are temporary and will eventually collapse. Remnants of older, collapsed bridges can also be observed within the canyons (figure 6a). New bridges will form in the future. On figure 6a, three sites are indicated where the walls separating upstream and downstream parts of meanders are thin and are currently being eroded. At some time in the future, the walls will be penetrated by the streams in White or Armstrong Canyons, and new bridges will probably be formed as a result.

CONCLUSION

The natural bridges in NABR are the result of Quaternary erosion of Permian bedrock. Hikers in NABR will find their access routes into the canyons controlled by geology. Like the ancestral-Puebloan people who occupied this area over 1,000 years ago, modern visitors will make use of the ledges formed at the contact between the white sandstone facies (below the ledges) and the red mudstone facies (above the ledges) of the Cedar Mesa Sandstone to travel through the region. The exposures of the Cedar Mesa Sandstone and Organ Rock Formation contained within NABR are excellent and indicate that the bedrock in this area was deposited in an arid environment with a climate similar to that experienced by the region today.

ACKNOWLEDGEMENTS

The reviews of this manuscript provided by Paul Anderson, Ron Blakey, Jack Campbell, and Tom Chidsey, Jr.

contributed to its improvement. We thank them for taking the time to read and comment on this paper. We also appreciate the computer-assisted drafting performed by Dave Linari, an undergraduate student at Michigan Technological University. Preparation of this paper was partially supported by the National Science Foundation (Grant Number: DUE-9950213), and by the National Park Service, Geologic Resources Division. We also thank the staff at Natural Bridges for making our time in the field as enjoyable as possible.

REFERENCES

Baars, D.L., 1962, Permian System of Colorado Plateau: American Association of Petroleum Geologists Bulletin, v. 46, p. 149-218.

Barnes, F.A., 1987, Canyon country arches and bridges: Moab, Utah, Canyon Country Publications, 416 p.

Blakey, R.C., 1996, Permian eolian deposits, sequences, and sequence boundaries, Colorado Plateau, *in* Longman, M.W., and Sonnenfeld, M.D., editors, Paleozoic systems of the Rocky Mountain region: Rocky Mountain Section SEPM (Society for Sedimentary Geology), p. 405-426.

Blakey, R.C., Basham, E.L., and Cook, M.J., 1993, Early and Middle Triassic paleogeography, Colorado Plateau and vicinity, *in* Morales, M., editor, Aspects of Mesozoic geology and paleontology of the Colorado Plateau: Flagstaff, Arizona, Museum of Northern Arizona Bulletin 59, p. 13-26.

Campbell, J.A., 1980, Lower Permian depositional systems and Wolfcampian paleogeography, Uncompahgre basin, eastern Utah and southwestern Colorado, *in* Fouch, T.D., and Magathan, E.R., editors, Paleozoic paleogeography of the west-central United States: Rocky Mountain Section SEPM (Society for Sedimentary Geology), p. 327-340.

—1987, Stratigraphy and depositional facies; Elephant Canyon Formation, *in* Campbell, J.A., editor, Geology of Cataract Canyon and vicinity: Four Corners Geological Society 10th Field Conference, p. 91-98.

Campbell, J.A., and Stanesco, J.D., 1985, Textural and compositional variation in a Lower Permian sand sea-- Cedar Mesa Member of the Cutler Formation, southeastern Utah [abs.]: Society of Economic Paleontologists and Mineralogists, Annual Midyear Meeting Abstracts, v. 2., p. 16.

Condon, S.M., 1997, Geology of the Pennsylvanian and Permian Cutler Group and Permian Kaibab Limestone in the Paradox basin, southeastern Utah and southwestern Colorado: U.S. Geological Survey Professional Paper 2000-P, 46 p.

Culmer, H.L.A., 1908, Country of Natural Bridges: The technical world magazine.

Dickinson, W.R., 1981, Plate tectonic evolution of the southern Cordillera: Arizona Geological Society Digest, v. 14, p. 113-135.

Dickinson, W.R., Klute, M.A., Hayes, M.J., Janecke, S.U., Lundin, E.A., McKittrick, M.A., and Olivares, M.D., 1987, Laramide tectonics and paleogeography inferred from sedimentary record in Laramide basins of central Rocky Mountain region [abs.]: Geological Society of America Abstracts with Programs, v. 19, no. 5, p. 271.

Dubiel, R.F., 1994, Triassic deposystems, paleogeography, and paleoclimate of the Western Interior, *in* Caputo, M.V., Peterson, J.A., and Franczyk, K.J., editors, Mesozoic Systems of the Rocky Mountain region, USA: Rocky Mountain Section SEPM (Society for Sedimentary Geology), p. 133-168.

Dubiel, R.F., Parrish, J.T., Parrish, J.M., and Good, S.C., 1991, The Pangean megamonsoon—evidence from the Upper Triassic Chinle Formation: Palaios, v. 6, no. 4, p. 347-370.

Frahme, C.W., and Vaughn, E.B., 1983, Paleozoic geology and seismic stratigraphy of the northern Uncompahgre front, Grand County, Utah, *in* Lowell, J.D., editor, Rocky Mountain foreland basins and uplifts: Rocky Mountain Association of Geologists, p. 201-211.

Ginsburg, R.N., 1957, Early diagenesis and lithification of shallow-water carbonate sediments in south Florida, *in* LeBlanc, R.J., and Breeding, J.G., editors, Regional aspects of carbonate deposition: Society of Economic Paleontologists and Mineralogists Special Publication 5, p. 80-99.

Gregory, H.E., 1917, Geology of the Navajo country; a reconnaissance of parts of Arizona, New Mexico, and Utah: U.S. Geological Survey Professional Paper 93, 161 p.

—1938, The San Juan County, a geographic and geologic reconnaissance of southeastern Utah: U.S. Geological Survey Professional Paper 188, 123 p.

Gregory, K.M., and Chase, C.G., 1992, Tectonic significance of paleobotanically estimated climate and altitude of the late Eocene erosion surface, Colorado: Geology, v. 20, no. 7, p. 581-585.

Harland, W.B., Armstrong, R.L., Cox, A.V., Craig, L.E., Smith, A.G., and Smith D.G., 1989, A geologic time scale 1989: New York, Cambridge University Press, 263 p.

Harry, D.L., and Mickus, K.L., 1998, Gravity constraints on lithospheric flexure and the structure of the late Paleozoic Ouachita orogen in Arkansas and Oklahoma, south-central North America: Tectonics, v. 17, no. 2, p. 187-202.

Hintze, L.F., 1993, Geologic history of Utah: Brigham Young University Geology Studies, Special Publication 7, 202 p.

Huffman, A.C., Jr., and Taylor, D.J., 1994, Pennsylvanian thrust faulting along the northeastern margin of the Paradox basin, Colorado and Utah [abs.]: Geological Society of America Abstracts with Programs, v. 26, no. 6, p. 19.

Huntoon, J.E., Dolson, J., and Henry, B., 1994, Seals and migration pathways in paleogeomorphically trapped petroleum occurrences: Permian White Rim Sandstone, Tar-Sand Triangle area, Utah, *in* Dolson, J.C., Hendricks, M.L., and Wescott, W.A., editors, Unconformity-related hydrocarbons in sedimentary sequences: Rocky Mountain Association of Geologists, p. 99-118.

Irwin, C.D., 1976, Permian and Lower Triassic reservoir rocks of central Utah, *in* Hill, J.G., editor, Geology of the Cordilleran hingeline: Rocky Mountain Association of Geologists Field Conference Guidebook, p. 193-202.

Kelley, V.C., 1955, Tectonics of the Four Corners region: Four Corners Geological Society Guidebook, p. 108-117.

Kluth, C.F., and Coney, P.J., 1981, Plate tectonics of the Ancestral Rocky Mountains: Geology, v. 9, p. 10-15.

Langford, R.P., and Chan, M.A., 1988, Flood surfaces and deflation surfaces within the Cutler Formation and Cedar Mesa Sandstone (Permian), southeastern Utah: Geological Society of America Bulletin, v. 100, p. 1541-1549.

Lock, B.E., and Pelfrey, G.M., 1997, Erg to sabkha transition in the Cedar Mesa Formation (Wolfcampian), Comb Ridge area, San Juan County, southeast Utah [abs.]: Geological Society of America Abstracts with Programs, v. 29, no. 6, p. A480.

Loope, D.B., 1984, Eolian origin of Upper Paleozoic sandstones, southeastern Utah: Journal of Sedimentary Petrology, v. 54, no. 2, p. 563-580.

Lucchitta, I., 1989, History of the Grand Canyon and of the Colorado River in Arizona, *in* Jenney, J.P., and Reynolds, S.J., editors, Geologic evolution of Arizona: Arizona Geological Society Digest, v. 17, p. 701-715.

Mack, G.H., and Rasmussen, K.A., 1984, Alluvial-fan sedimentation of the Cutler Formation (Permo-Pennsylvanian) near Gateway, Colorado: Geological Society of America Bulletin, v. 95, no. 1, p. 109-116.

Murphy, K., 1987, Eolian origin of late Paleozoic red siltstones, Mexican Hat, Utah: Lincoln, Nebraska, University of Nebraska, M.S. thesis, 128 p.

Parrish, J.T., 1985, Latitudinal distribution of land and shelf and absorbed solar radiation during the Phanerozoic: U.S. Geological Survey Open-file Report 85-31, 21 p.

Parsons, T., and McCarthy, J., 1995, The active southwest margin of the Colorado Plateau; uplift of mantle origin: Geological Society of America Bulletin, v. 107, no. 2, p. 139-147.

Peterson, Fred, 1988, Pennsylvanian to Jurassic eolian transportation systems in the western United States, *in* Kocurek, Gary, editor, Late Paleozoic and Mesozoic eolian deposits of the Western Interior of the United States: Sedimentary Geology, v. 56, p. 207-260.

Poole, F.G., 1962, Wind directions in Late Paleozoic to Middle Mesozoic time on the Colorado Plateau; Article 163 Geological Survey Research 1962: U.S. Geological Survey Professional Paper 450-D, p. D147-D151.

Scott, G.L., 1965, Heavy mineral evidence for source of some Permian quartzose sandstones, Colorado Plateau: Journal of Sedimentary Petrology, v. 35, p. 391-400.

Stanesco, J.D., and Campbell, J.A., 1989, Eolian and noneolian facies of the Lower Permian Cedar Mesa Sandstone Member of the Cutler Formation, southeastern Utah: U.S. Geological Survey Bulletin 1808-F, 13 p.

Stewart, J.H., Poole, F.G., and Wilson, R.F., 1972a, Stratigraphy and origin of the Triassic Moenkopi Formation and related Triassic strata in the Colorado Plateau region: U.S. Geological Survey Professional Paper 691, 3195 p.

—1972b, Stratigraphy and origin of the Chinle Formation and related Triassic strata in the Colorado Plateau region with a section on sedimentary petrology by R.A. Cadigan and on conglomerate studies by W. Thordarson, H.F. Albee, and J.H. Stewart: U.S. Geological Suvey Professional Paper 690, 336 p.

Stokes, W.L., 1969, Scenes of the plateau lands and how they came to be: Salt Lake City, Utah, Starstone Publishing Co., (10th printing, 1983), 66 p.

Rainbow over Lake Powell, Glen Canyon National Recreation Area
Photo by Douglas A. Sprinkel

Geology of Utah's Parks and Monuments
2000 Utah Geological Association Publication 28
D.A. Sprinkel, T.C. Chidsey, Jr., and P.B. Anderson, editors

Geology of Rainbow Bridge National Monument, Utah

Thomas C. Chidsey, Jr.[1], Grant C. Willis[1], Douglas A. Sprinkel[1], and Paul B. Anderson[2]

ABSTRACT

Rainbow Bridge, in southern Utah, has a height of 290 feet above its floor and a span of 275 feet, and is one of the largest natural bridges in the world. It was designated a national monument in 1910 by President William Howard Taft. The bridge is composed entirely of Jurassic Navajo Sandstone with each abutment resting on a foundation of Kayenta Formation; these are the only two bedrock formations exposed in the monument. Three structural events helped shape the Rainbow Bridge National Monument area: the Laramide orogeny, the formation of Navajo Mountain, and Tertiary-Quaternary regional uplift of the Colorado Plateau. Rainbow Bridge formed as the result of a favorable combination of entrenchment of the meandering stream, ideally located and oriented joints, running water supplied from Navajo Mountain, and a key lithologic change.

In addition to Rainbow Bridge, the monument offers other fascinating displays of ancient depositional environments and geologic features. The Navajo Sandstone was deposited in a great coastal to inland dune field and is distinguished by spectacular large-scale cross-bedding. The Navajo in the monument also contains deposits representing wadis (desert streams) and oases. The underlying Jurassic Kayenta Formation was deposited in a river-dominated environment and contains dinosaur tracks. A large alcove with a beautiful hanging garden and classic examples of conjugate joint sets can be observed within Rainbow Bridge Canyon.

Rock falls that developed along tension-formed joints and by exfoliation, and other weathering and erosive processes, continue to shape Rainbow Bridge. These natural processes have not caused any major loss in bridge stability for many thousands of years, nor have weathering and erosion accelerated due to Lake Powell flooding the canyon under the bridge. Under existing conditions, Rainbow Bridge will continue to stand for many thousands of years for all to enjoy.

INTRODUCTION

One of the most spectacular geologic sites in Utah, and a crown jewel of the National Park System, is Rainbow Bridge National Monument (figure 1). With a span of 275 feet across Bridge Creek and a height of 290 feet (National Park Service, 1998), Rainbow Bridge is one of the largest natural bridges in the world. To put Rainbow Bridge size into perspective, the bridge is nearly the height of the United States Capitol. A combination of rock strata, geologic structure, regional uplift, and running water created a favorable setting for natural bridge development -- a relatively rare geologic feature. A natural bridge is formed primarily by the erosive process of running water and spans a ravine or valley as opposed to a natural arch which is formed by weathering and rock falls along joints

Figure 1. Rainbow Bridge, Rainbow Bridge National Monument, Utah. View to the southeast with Navajo Mountain just barely visible in the upper left and bridge viewing area in the lower left. Junipers near the base of the bridge are about 15 feet tall.

[1]*Utah Geological Survey, Salt Lake City, UT 84114-6100*
[2]*Salt Lake City, UT 84102*

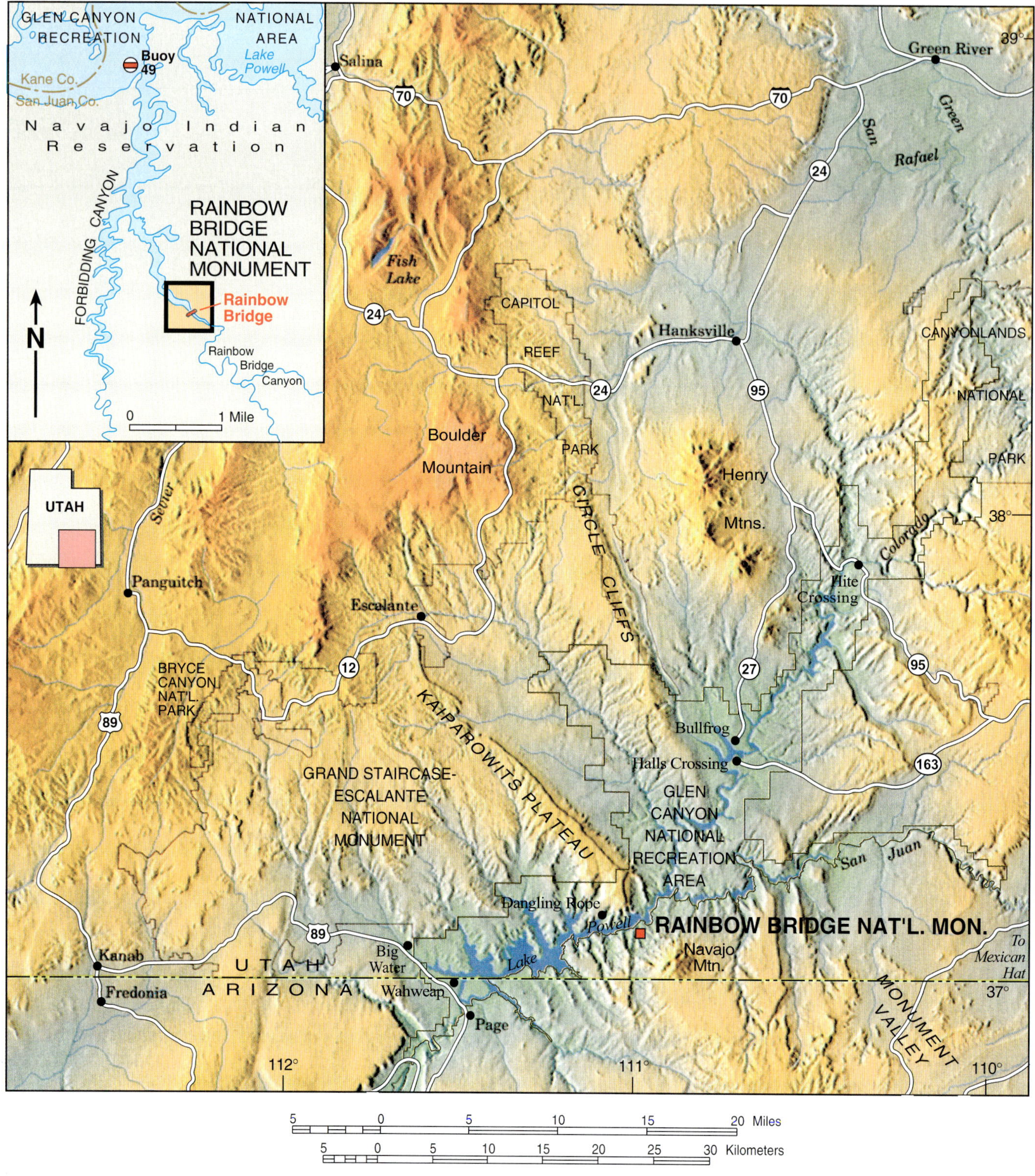

Figure 2. Index map to Rainbow Bridge National Monument showing surrounding towns, highways, and Lake Powell (modified from Hintze, 1997; topographic relief base map modified with permission, courtesy of Chalk Butte, Inc., Boulder, Wyoming).

and fractures, and does not span a ravine or valley.

Rainbow Bridge National Monument is located in the Colorado Plateau physiographic province in southern Utah, about 5 miles north of the Arizona border. The bridge is composed entirely of Navajo Sandstone resting on a base of Kayenta Formation, both units being Early Jurassic in age. It was carved by Bridge Creek, which is fed by springs and the runoff from Navajo Mountain to the southeast. Desert plants such as sagebrush, saltbush, yucca, and Mormon tea are common in the dry sunny parts of the Rainbow Bridge Canyon; sacred datura, oak, juniper, redbud, and buffalo berry grow in the moist, shaded parts of the canyon (National Park Service, 1998).

The monument is surrounded by lands of the Navajo Nation. Glen Canyon National Recreation Area, centered around Lake Powell, is located to the north and the lake has flooded up Rainbow Bridge Canyon under the bridge (figure 2). The monument is about 50 lake miles from Wahweap, Halls Crossing, and Bullfrog Marinas, and 15 lake miles from Dangling Rope Marina (figure 2). Rainbow Bridge Canyon is a branch of Forbidding Canyon, which is entered from the main channel of Lake Powell at buoy 49 (figure 2). The monument can also be reached by rugged trails across the Navajo Nation (permits are required from the Navajo Nation Recreation Department). The entire monument covers a one-half square mile area.

Rainbow Bridge was known for centuries by Native Americans and was probably seen in the 1800s by various cowboys and trappers. It was "discovered" on August 14, 1909, through the combined efforts of University of Utah's Byron Cummings, government surveyor W.B. Douglas, Paiute guides Nasja Begay and Jim Mike, and explorer John Wetherill (National Park Service, 1998). On May 30, 1910, President William Howard Taft designated Rainbow Bridge a national monument and proclaimed this "extraordinary natural bridge, having an arch which is in form and appearance like a rainbow . . . is of great scientific interest as an example of eccentric stream erosion" (National Park Service, 1998). Although Theodore Roosevelt journeyed to the monument in 1913, its remoteness made for few early visitors. Access to the monument improved dramatically with the closing of the gates of Glen Canyon Dam in 1963 and the subsequent flooding of Glen Canyon, including Forbidding and Rainbow Bridge Canyons. A courtesy dock and short trail to a viewing area now allow thousands of visitors each year to enjoy and be inspired by this unique geologic feature.

After his 1913 visit, Roosevelt said, " . . . I noticed that the Navajo rode around outside [the bridge]. His creed bade him to never pass under an arch for the arch is the sign of the rainbow, the sign of the sun's course over the earth, and to the Navajo it is sacred. This great natural bridge, so recently 'discovered' by white men, has for ages been known to the Indians" (Roosevelt, 1916). Rainbow Bridge is still considered sacred by Native American nations and the National Park Service requests voluntary compliance in not approaching or walking under the bridge.

STRATIGRAPHY

Only two bedrock formations–the Kayenta Formation and Navajo Sandstone–crop out in Rainbow Bridge National Monument. Both formations belong to the Glen Canyon Group (figure 3) and were deposited between 187 and 200 million years ago during Early Jurassic time. Older rocks exposed throughout nearby Glen Canyon National Recreation Area are present in the subsurface. The Navajo Sandstone dominates the terrain in the monument

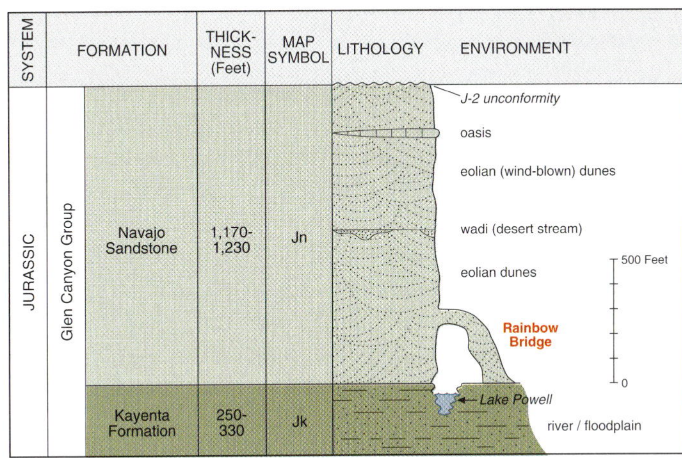

Figure 3. Column showing formations exposed in Rainbow Bridge National Monument, including environments of deposition, thickness, weathering habits, and lithology.

(figure 4). The Kayenta Formation is exposed only along the channel of Bridge Creek, much of which is now inundated by Lake Powell (figure 4). Locally, these bedrock formations are covered by unconsolidated boulders, cobbles, sand, silt, and clay of Quaternary age.

Jurassic

Kayenta Formation

The Kayenta Formation was deposited in a hot, river floodplain (fluvial) environment. It weathers into a series of ledges and low cliffs, and is easily distinguished from the massive cliffs of the overlying Navajo Sandstone. The contact between the two formations is sharp and is best seen near the base of Rainbow Bridge. Unconsolidated alluvial deposits have been cleared away from the bridge viewing area by the National Park Service, providing an excellent exposure for close examination of the Kayenta (figure 4).

The Kayenta Formation is composed of pale-red to dark-orange, moderately hard to hard, fine- to medium-grained sandstone. Two units of the Kayenta Formation are exposed beneath Rainbow Bridge (two others are now well below the lake level and cannot be seen). The upper unit consists of flaggy and lenticular beds 0.5 to 1 foot thick; the total thickness is 4 to 7 feet. The lower unit is blocky to massive with a pre-lake exposed thickness of 40 to 45 feet (Dames & Moore, 1972). It is now partially below the present level of the lake.

Sandstone beds in these units consist of moderately sorted, subrounded to subangular sand grains composed of quartz, minor amounts of feldspar, and traces of mica (Dames & Moore, 1972). Sedimentary structures associated with the fluvial depositional environment include ripple laminations, current ripples, and small-scale trough cross-beds that indicate stream flow was in a west-northwest direction. Silty beds contain clay rip-up clasts and burrows. A tridactyl (three toed), theropod (bipedal) dinosaur track is well displayed at the bridge

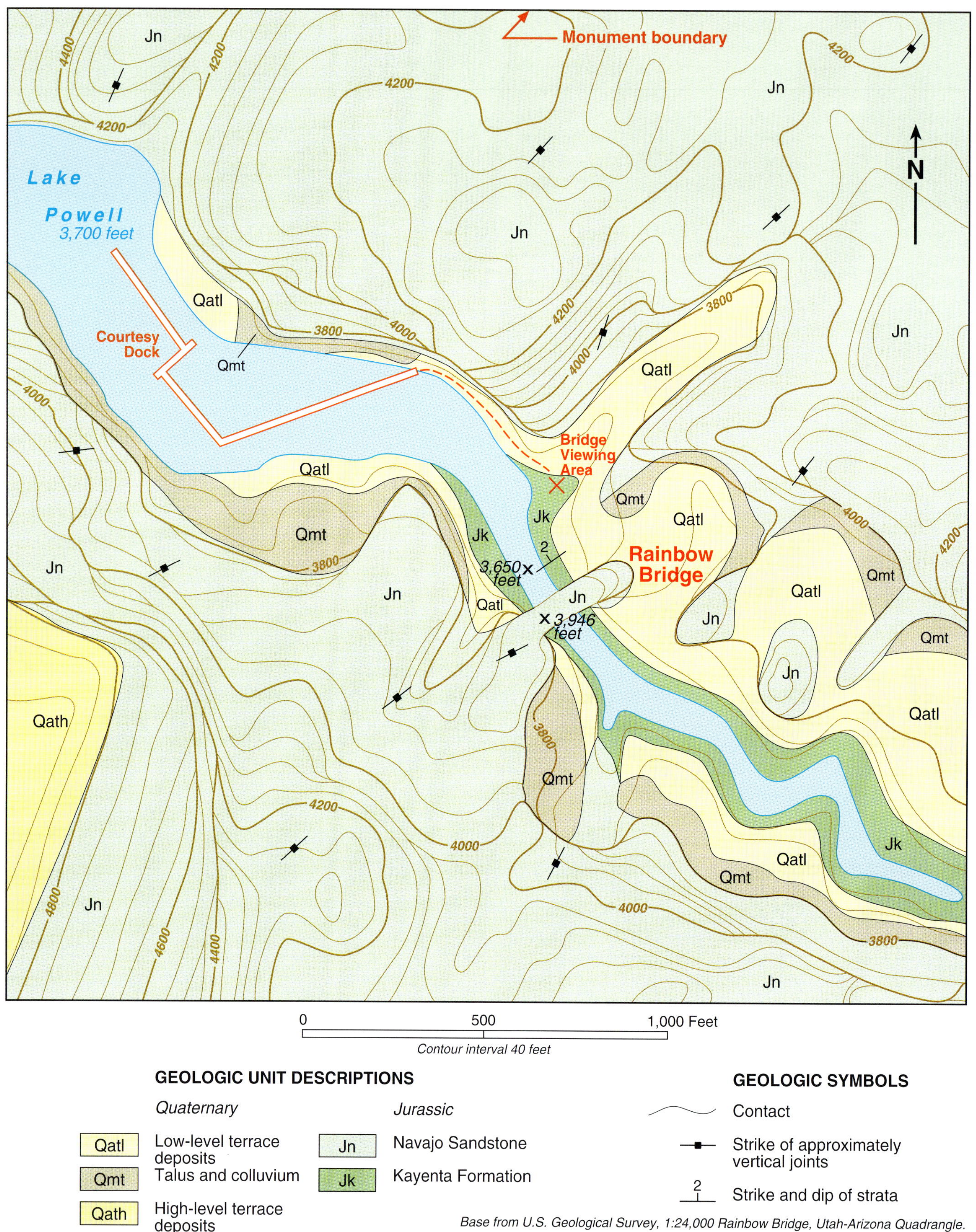

0   500   1,000 Feet

Contour interval 40 feet

GEOLOGIC UNIT DESCRIPTIONS

Quaternary

Qatl — Low-level terrace deposits

Qmt — Talus and colluvium

Qath — High-level terrace deposits

Jurassic

Jn — Navajo Sandstone

Jk — Kayenta Formation

GEOLOGIC SYMBOLS

Contact

Strike of approximately vertical joints

Strike and dip of strata

Base from U.S. Geological Survey, 1:24,000 Rainbow Bridge, Utah-Arizona Quadrangle.

Figure 4. Geologic map of Rainbow Bridge National Monument, San Juan County, Utah (after Hackman, 1956; Dames & Moore, 1972).

Figure 5. Track (wet) from a tridactyl (three-toed), theropod (bipedal) dinosaur in the Kayenta Formation at the bridge viewing area.

viewing area (figure 5).

The Kayenta Formation is 250 to 330 feet thick in the Rainbow Bridge–Glen Canyon area (figure 3; Blakey and others, 1983; Hintze, 1993; Doelling, 1997). Prior to Lake Powell, 70 feet of the formation was exposed in Rainbow Bridge Canyon (Dames & Moore, 1972). About 20 to 30 feet can be seen today depending on the lake level.

Navajo Sandstone

The Navajo Sandstone was deposited in a great coastal to inland dune field (erg) comparable to the present Sahara. In Early Jurassic time, Utah had an arid climate and lay about 15 degrees north of the equator (Hintze, 1993). The Navajo Sandstone is distinguished by spectacular large-scale cross-bedding representing eolian (wind-blown) dunes, which weather into domes above vertical canyon cliffs.

The Navajo Sandstone is very uniform in Rainbow Bridge National Monument and is composed of tan to light-reddish-brown, fine- to medium-grained sandstone. Sand grains are moderately to well-sorted, rounded to subrounded, frosted (an indication of eolian origin) quartz. Calcite is the main cementing agent, with some secondary silica and iron oxide.

The large-scale cross-beds that dominate the Navajo Sandstone are etched out by weathering and are often highlighted by desert varnish (iron oxide staining). Cross-bed types include tabular planar, wedge-planar, and trough, all associated with eolian deposition (Ahlbrandt and Fryberger, 1982). They occur in sets up to 25 feet thick. Dips of cross-beds between set boundaries vary as much as 40 degrees from the nearly horizontal structural attitude of the formation. Dip directions on the cross-bed laminae (dune slipfaces) indicate paleowinds were from the north and northwest. Less common planar beds, composed of generally finer grained material, were deposited in inter-dune areas or playas. These beds and thin horizontal lines,

Figure 6. This spectacular rock fall of Navajo Sandstone in 1983 on the south side of the canyon near the courtesy dock clearly demonstrates the process of exfoliation and the geologic hazard it poses to visitors. It was captured on film by Tom Tyler, a park visitor, who regularly comes to Rainbow Bridge and Lake Powell and donated it to the National Park Service. National Park Service poster photo.

the bedset boundaries, represent upper water-table surfaces (Doelling, this volume).

Leaching of calcite cement by rainwater has caused the outer 1 to 3 inches of the Navajo to become soft and friable (Dames & Moore, 1972). Stress-release exfoliation of this weaker, outer sandstone and frost wedging along joints have led to massive rock falls (figure 6), the main type of erosion presently occurring in the monument. Small holes, often referred to as "stonepecker holes" or tafoni, have been weathered out of the sandstone along cross-beds and bedset boundaries. They are most likely caused by differential erosion in areas where ground water has weakened the cement. Once started, they form voids in which water, protected from evaporation, can accumulate, promoting continued weathering and further growth of the holes.

The Navajo Sandstone is between 1,170 and 1,230 feet thick in the Rainbow Bridge-Glen Canyon area (Blakey and others, 1983; Hintze, 1993; Doelling, 1997). The contact with the overlying Page Sandstone cannot be seen in the monument due to erosion of the entire Middle Jurassic through Cretaceous section. Where present, that contact marks the J-2 regional unconformity dividing the Lower Jurassic from the Middle Jurassic (Pipiringos and O'Sullivan, 1978).

Quaternary

High-Level Terrace Deposits

High-level terrace deposits cap the high, gently sloping mesa above the lake west of Rainbow Bridge (figure 4). They consist of poorly sorted boulders to silt and clay. Boulders are up to several feet in diameter, indicating higher energy deposition. These deposits are reworked older alluvial fan material shed from the flanks of Navajo Mountain, with the Jurassic Navajo, Carmel, and Morrison Formations as the sources of the clasts. The high-level terrace is over 1,200 feet above the pre-lake channel of Bridge Creek and the main Colorado River. Based on average downcutting rates from other parts of the Colorado River basin of about 0.6 feet per thousand years (Willis, 1994), we estimate the terrace gravels are latest Tertiary to middle Pleistocene in age. A group led by T. Hanks (U.S. Geological Survey, written communication, 2000), using somewhat experimental methods, determined that these high-level deposits are less than 780,000 years old, and are probably between 350,000 and 500,000 years old. If these ages are valid, then the deposits are middle Pleistocene in age. This implies that Glen Canyon was cut in just the last 500,000 years, which would be some of the highest cutting rates of any part of the Colorado River system.

Low-Level Terrace Deposits

Low-level terraces deposits, unlike high-level terrace deposits, consist of unconsolidated sand, granules, pebbles, and cobbles intermixed with silt and minor clay deposited by Bridge Creek. These low-level terrace deposits are adjacent to Bridge Creek and are the youngest alluvial sediments exposed in the monument; younger alluvial deposits in the channel bottom are present beneath the lake. These accumulations are generally poorly sorted and were deposited during periods of high runoff. Gravels and boulders, principally sandstone, were derived from Navajo Mountain to the southeast and thus are composed mostly of the Jurassic formations that crop out there. These sandstones are weathered dark brown to almost black, some having the appearance of basalt, and are extremely well indurated (hard) because the normal calcium carbonate cement has been replaced with quartz cement.

These deposits accumulated in active channels and now form small terraces in abandoned meanders along Rainbow Bridge Canyon (figure 4). Most low-level terrace deposits are less than 25 feet thick, range from 50 to 100 feet above the active channels, and are probably late Pleistocene in age. Higher, slightly older deposits may be up to

50 feet thick. An excellent example of an older alluvial terrace deposit abuts Rainbow Bridge and is easily observed from the bridge viewing area.

Talus and Colluvium

Talus and colluvium consist of rock-fall blocks, boulders, smaller angular gravel, sand, and silt that accumulate on the slopes below the Navajo Sandstone cliffs. These deposits are derived entirely from the Navajo and the older terrace gravels in Rainbow Bridge National Monument. Talus is formed when exfoliation and frost wedging cause large slabs of rock to fall from the cliffs and break into small pieces (figure 6). Colluvium is heterogeneous soil and weathered rock fragments deposited by unconcentrated surface runoff (sheet wash) and downslope creep; in this desert environment, colluvium includes a large component of windblown sand. Talus and colluvium deposits are generally 15 feet thick or less. They are Holocene to late Pleistocene in age.

STRUCTURAL AND GEOLOGIC HISTORY

Throughout the early Mesozoic, the Colorado Plateau area that includes Rainbow Bridge National Monument was a broad, low, continental shelf that intermittently accumulated shallow marine to coastal plain sediments. Three structural events helped shape the Rainbow Bridge National Monument area: the Laramide orogeny, the formation of Navajo Mountain, and late Tertiary-Quaternary regional uplift of the Colorado Plateau. Millions of years of erosion have removed much of the rocks uplifted by these events and the remaining rocks are now displayed in an arid environment along the shore of a man-made lake. The final results of these events provide us with a national monument that has spectacular views and fascinating geologic features.

Depositional History

During the Early Jurassic, shallow sinuous rivers meandered across a broad floodplain. Though the climate was fairly dry, dinosaurs tracks in this and other areas indicate that plants and animals flourished. Over time the climate became drier, perhaps aided by rain-shadow effects of ancient mountains to the west, and the environment gradually changed to a coastal dune field. The water table was high and oasis-type settings were common. Desert washes occasionally migrated across the area.

Though not preserved in the monument, nearby Middle and Late Jurassic deposits indicate that the region continued to lie near sea level and received continental and shallow marine deposition. During the Early Cretaceous the area likely underwent slow erosion with limited additional continental deposition. During the Late Cretaceous, based on outcrops on the Kaiparowits Plateau and on top of Navajo Mountain, shallow marine deposition was dominant.

Laramide Orogeny

Large uplifts and basins developed during the mountain-building event known as the Laramide orogeny between latest Cretaceous (Maastrichtian) and Eocene time (about 70 to 38 million years ago [Ma]) (Hintze, 1993). Nearby Laramide features include the Circle Cliffs uplift to the north, the Monument upwarp to the east, and the Kaiparowits structural basin to the west.

Gentle north- to northwest-trending anticlines and synclines, secondary folds of the Kaiparowits basin, extend into the Rainbow Bridge area. The folds developed over deep faults in Precambrian basement rocks. Dips on the flanks of the anticlines are up to 7 degrees, and plunge is to the north (Doelling and Davis, 1989). These folds are tens of miles in length and have been targets for petroleum exploration. The axis of the northwest-trending Rock Creek anticline crosses the mouth of Forbidding Canyon, just north of Rainbow Bridge National Monument (Doelling and Davis, 1989; Doelling, 1997).

Navajo Mountain

Navajo Mountain, southeast of Rainbow Bridge National Monument, is a broad, structural dome that dominates the view up Rainbow Bridge Canyon. It is about 6 miles in diameter and its summit is 10,388 feet above sea level. Jurassic strata on the flanks dip between 4 and 21 degrees; the steepest dips are on the west and northwest flanks (Baker, 1936; Hackman, 1956). The Jurassic Wingate, Kayenta, Navajo, Page(?), Carmel, Entrada, and Morrison Formations crop out on the flanks and in canyons, such as Forbidding and Rainbow Bridge Canyons, which radiate from Navajo Mountain (Baker, 1936; Hackman, 1956). Cretaceous Dakota Sandstone is exposed at the top of the dome.

Navajo Mountain is an example of a laccolith - a dome-shaped structure formed when igneous intrusions were injected along bedding planes and bowed up layers of overlying sedimentary rocks. Navajo Mountain is one of several laccoliths in Utah; these include the Henry Mountains near the northern end of Lake Powell (figure 2). These laccoliths are granodioritic in composition and were intruded about 31.2 to 23.3 Ma during the late Oligocene (Nelson and others, 1992). Unlike the other laccoliths in the Colorado Plateau, very little is known about the intrusive body that underlies Navajo Mountain because it has not been exposed by erosion. Only a small syenite porphry intrusive body is exposed on Navajo Mountain's south-southwest flank (Condie, 1964).

The doming at Navajo Mountain is so localized that it does not affect regional dips beyond 5 miles from the center of the structure (Baker, 1936). Dips in the monument area only deflect 1 to 2 degrees. However, this doming had a major impact on the drainage patterns and possibly the development of joints (rock fractures) in the Rainbow Bridge National Monument area.

Tertiary-Quaternary Regional Uplift and Erosion

The Colorado Plateau began rising in early Cenozoic time, with limited uplift probably continuing through the remaining Cenozoic (Hunt, 1956; Lucchitta, 1979; Graf and others, 1987; Fleming, 1994). This regional uplift changed the landscape from one of deposition to one of massive erosion. Several thousand feet of sedimentary rocks have been removed by the erosive processes of rock falls, running water, and wind. Most of this material has been carried to the sea by the Colorado River system.

As the Colorado Plateau rose, and as the Grand Canyon was cut about 5 million years ago (Lucchitta, 1989), the rejuvenated Colorado River drainage system rapidly cut through the underlying strata and headward erosion increased. The results of this downcutting are the countless canyons and entrenched meanders in Glen Canyon and its tributary canyons, including Rainbow Bridge Canyon. The rate of downcutting along the tributary canyons was controlled by the elevation of the Colorado River channel (Huntoon and others, this volume). Over the last few million years, the effects of rapid downcutting along the Colorado River caused the local base levels of tributary rivers to be lowered, and their channels to cut downward faster than they cut laterally into their sides (Huntoon and others, this volume). Thus, the drainages, such as the one that evolved into Bridge Creek, became entrenched by rapid headward erosion.

Erosion rates were also higher during parts of the Pleistocene than at the present because the area experienced increased precipitation and lower temperatures. The higher volumes of water in Bridge Creek allowed more material to be eroded and carried to the Colorado River.

Jointing

Regionally, Rainbow Bridge National Monument is in an area where the strata dip gently, about 2 to 4 degrees, to the northwest. However, the dominant structural features are the large sets of joints that ultimately played an important role in the formation of Rainbow Bridge.

Sandstones within the Navajo and Kayenta Formations near Rainbow Bridge are brittle and developed joints in response to regional tectonics, local doming at Navajo Mountain, and the erosional unloading of thousands of feet of overlying rock. Joints are closely spaced in many areas, but spacing varies with bedset thickness and lithology. Three types of joints are present in Rainbow Bridge National Monument (Dames & Moore, 1972): (1) inclined northeasterly trending joints, (2) near-vertical northeasterly trending joints, and (3) surficial joints.

The inclined joints consist of two sets, one dipping 70 degrees to the northwest and the other dipping 60 to 70 degrees to the southeast. These form conjugate pairs spectacularly displayed in the Navajo Sandstone above the trail to the bridge viewing area (figure 7). They are spaced

Figure 7. Excellent example of conjugate joint sets (forming X shapes) in the Navajo Sandstone that are probably related to doming at Navajo Mountain. Both sets trend northeasterly and are inclined with dips of 70 degrees; one set dips northwest and the other southeast. View above the trail to the bridge viewing area.

from 5 to hundreds of feet apart, and are as much as several miles in length. The near vertical joints are best developed in the Kayenta Formation and are closely spaced, 2 to 10 feet apart. However, some very prominent examples are present in the Navajo. Both the inclined and near-vertical joints formed in response to regional tensional stresses, including doming at Navajo Mountain. The surficial joints are near-parallel to the Navajo cliff face and formed from expansion of the sandstone after the removal of the overlying strata by rapid erosion (Dames & Moore, 1972). Spalling of large slabs of rock along these joints can result in massive rock falls (figure 6). In cross section, the surficial joints are closely spaced near the cliff face, from inches to a few feet apart, but disappear at depth.

GEOLOGIC UNIQUENESS

Wadis and Oases

In addition to "seas" of wind-blown sand dunes, large deserts such as the Sahara contain many other features, including wadis and oases. A wadi is a stream bed or channel in desert regions that is usually dry. It may be a steep-sided, bouldery ravine that is the site of torrential flooding during rainy seasons. An oasis is a vegetated area in desert regions where springs are present because the water table is close to the surface. There is evidence of both of these features in the Navajo Sandstone within Rainbow Bridge National Monument.

A wadi deposit can be observed from the courtesy dock and is represented by several dark, iron-stained channels present on the south side of the canyon (figure 8A); others are located in other parts of Rainbow Bridge Canyon, and possibly belong to the same ancient wadi system. A large block of a wadi deposit fell to the terrace bench near the bridge viewing area **(visitors are not per-**

Figure 8. Wadi deposits in the Navajo Sandstone. (A) Wadi channel, filled with strongly cemented sand, on the cliff face of the south side of the canyon near the courtesy dock; channel deposit is about 5 feet thick (taken with a telephoto lens). (B) Wadi "pudding stone" consisting of sandstone and dolomitic limestone rip-up clasts in a medium- to coarse-grained sandstone matrix. Note horizontal stratification and small-scale cross-beds at base of photo.

mitted to stray off the bridge viewing area; however, another block similar to the one described below may be examined in the bridge viewing area). The large block was derived from a channel bed about 2.5 to 3 feet thick about 50 feet up the cliff. The base and top are abrupt and slightly irregular. The deposit is a "pudding stone" consisting of tan to reddish-orange, rounded sandstone fragments or clasts, and gray to dark-gray, subangular to subrounded dolomitic limestone clasts (figure 8B). Clasts vary from pea to small boulder size. The matrix is medium- to coarse-grained sandstone cemented with iron-bearing quartz and minor calcite. The fallen block is horizontally stratified and has some small-scale cross-beds. It contains rip-up clasts of lime muds; some imbricated rip-up clasts are inclined in the upstream direction.

An oasis is represented by a light-gray, 5-foot-thick, thin-bedded limestone. It can be observed from the bridge viewing area up the wash and across the canyon, just to the right of Rainbow Bridge. The limestone represents a small freshwater lake (based on geochemical analysis of a similar deposit along the Colorado River near Canyon-

Figure 9. Navajo Sandstone alcove with a hanging garden of vegetation where ground water seeps along an impervious horizontal bed. Note south-southeast-dipping cross-beds that indicate paleowind direction in the Jurassic Navajo sand dune field. View looking north from the north end of the courtesy dock.

lands National Park [Gilland, 1979]). This lake was an oasis for life, one of many oases that existed in the Navajo erg and that can now be seen in the Navajo Sandstone throughout the Glen Canyon National Recreation Area. Fresh ground water at a shallow depth had to persist for prolonged periods of time, perhaps many thousands of years, to allow the lake or pond deposits of these oases to develop (Stokes, 1991). The continuous supply of fresh water provided favorable environments for life and the deposition of carbonate rocks. Limestones in several Navajo outcrops have yielded fossil plants and invertebrates (Stokes, 1991; Santucci, this volume).

Alcoves and Hanging Gardens

A large alcove with a beautiful hanging garden can be seen on the north side of the canyon from the north end of the courtesy dock (figure 9). Alcoves are arch-like recesses in the sandstone. Alcoves form where ground water percolating down through pores in the sandstone encounters a low-permeability bed that is impervious to water flow. Such beds have a higher silt or clay content, and represent interdunal areas or the boundaries between dune bedsets. Because the infiltrating ground water can no longer continue downward, it exits the rock along the impervious bedding plane in the form of seeps and springs. The water dissolves and removes cementing minerals in the sandstone, causing the rock there to weaken relative to the rock elsewhere on the cliff face. The processes of weathering and erosion proceed faster on the weakened rock and eventually form a recess or alcove in the cliff. The increased moisture and shade are ideal for a variety of plants that further aid in the breakdown of the rock. The wet surfaces are often covered with mats of various kinds of algae, ferns such as maidenhair and bracken, grasses, and sedges (Everhart, 1983).

Rainbow Bridge

The spectacular cross-beds, hanging gardens, and limestone oasis are well displayed in Rainbow Bridge National Monument, but they are relatively common in many areas of Utah where the Navajo Sandstone is exposed. Of course, the main reason visitors come to the monument is Rainbow Bridge. Aside from its massive size, the bridge's characteristics and current setting make this rare geologic feature even more unusual.

Physical Characteristics

Rainbow Bridge has a height of 290 feet above its base and a span of 275 feet. It is composed entirely of Navajo Sandstone with each abutment resting on a foundation of Kayenta Formation at an elevation of about 3,725 feet above sea level (figure 4). At the apex, the bridge arch is 42 feet thick and 33 feet across (Dames & Moore, 1972). The west (right) abutment is about 200 feet wide; the east (left) abutment is about 90 feet wide.

Although joints of this orientation are relatively rare in the Navajo, major sets of near vertical joints that strike north 65 degrees east are present on the north and south faces of the bridge (Dames & Moore, 1972). Sets of inclined joints are also present on the top of the bridge, dipping 30 to 50 degrees north along the south side, and dipping 37 to 60 degrees south on the western half of the north side. The weight of the bridge has caused a tensional joint to develop at a right angle to the axis on the underside (Dames & Moore, 1972). Surficial joints are also common.

Bridge Evolution

Rainbow Bridge formed as a result of a favorable combination of regional uplift, structure, running water, and lithology. In the middle to early-late Cenozoic, the ancestral Colorado River and its tributaries flowed through meandering channels in wide valleys where the channels crossed easily eroded rocks, or in the case of Bridge Creek, alluvial fan deposits on the flank of Navajo Mountain (figure 10A). The stream path was partially controlled by joints. After these river channels were established, they became superimposed and entrenched, eroding into the resistant rocks such as the Navajo Sandstone. Small side canyons such as Forbidding and Rainbow Bridge Canyons are probably the evolved result of old superimposed channels, influenced by joints and other heterogeneities in the rocks (figure 10B). Several meanders in the evolving Rainbow Bridge Canyon were separated by very short land distances. At these locations, erosion into the canyon walls occurred at cutbanks on both sides of the rock wall by the meandering or migrating stream, creating narrow necks and setting the stage for bridge formation (figure 10B). Stream flow in Bridge Creek at the level of the lower gravel terraces likely increased during the wetter conditions of the Pleistocene, increasing the rate of erosion.

Development of Rainbow Bridge was assisted by

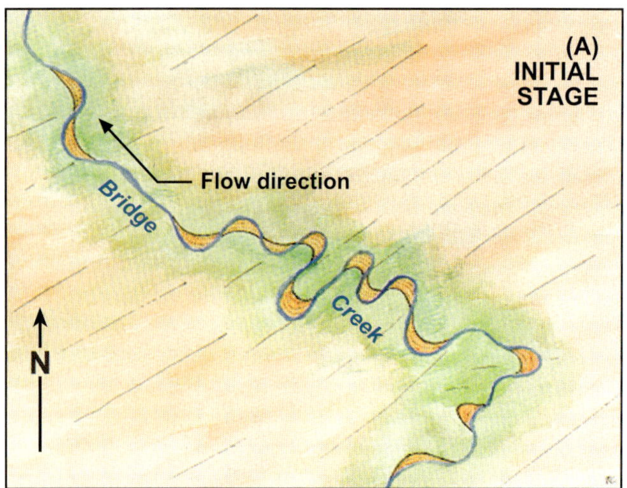

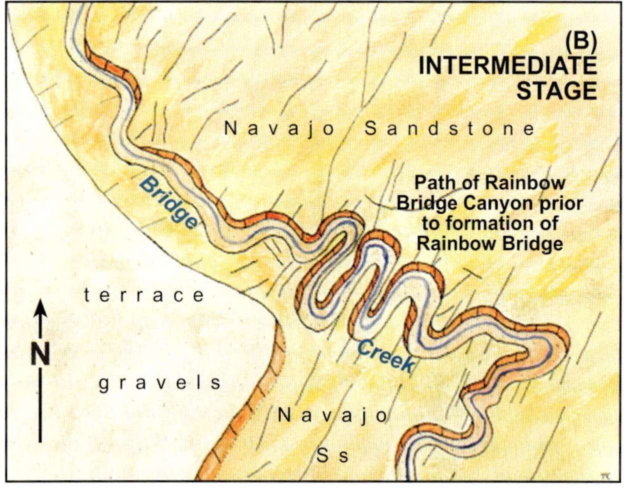

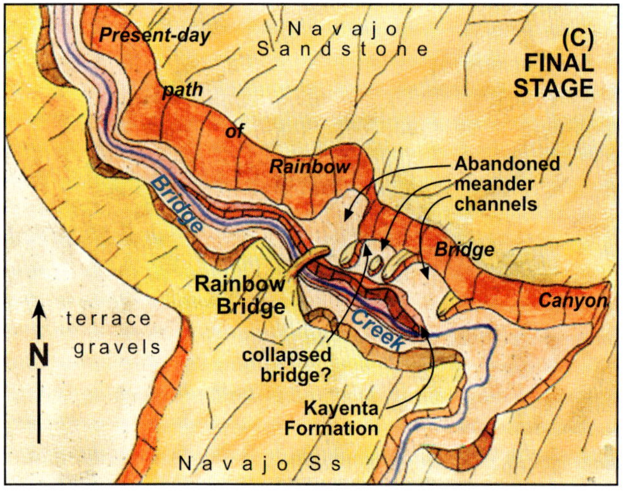

Figure 10. Interpreted stages of Rainbow Bridge evolution. The general course of Bridge Creek and canyon development can be tied to the pair of vertical stereo aerial photographs in figure 11. (A) Initial stage (latest Tertiary to early Pleistocene) - Bridge Creek meanders in a valley eroding soft rocks or alluvial fan deposits. The stream path was partially controlled by joints; green = vegetation, orange = point bars along meandering stream, tan = alluvial fan deposits/soft rocks. (B) Intermediate stage (middle Pleistocene) - Bridge Creek is entrenched and erosion occurs on the cutbanks between narrow meander necks. (C) Final stage (present) - wall of meander neck is penetrated and Rainbow Bridge is formed.

weak partings or bedding layers in the lower Navajo, (such as seen at the hanging gardens), rock falls off of the meander neck along the near-vertical joints (ideally located on the north and south faces), the inclined joints, and exfoliation. Finally, several thousand years ago, the narrow wall beneath the incipient bridge was penetrated and Rainbow Bridge was born (figure 10C). (The window first opened approximately halfway up the current opening.) Other bridges may have existed at other meanders upstream from Rainbow Bridge but have since collapsed. Later, Bridge Creek cut into the much softer Kayenta Formation, quickly increasing the depth of incision (figures 10C and 11). This significantly increased the vertical height of the opening of the bridge. It probably also served to confine Bridge Creek in a narrow, straighter channel, protecting the bridge footings from continued lateral migration of the stream.

The postulated age of the high-level terrace deposits of about 500,000 years discussed previously provides a means of estimating downcutting rates, and thus of indirectly estimating the time of bridge formation. Bridge Creek apparently cut down from the elevation of the terrace deposits at about 4,840 feet to its current level of about 3,655 feet at Rainbow Bridge in about 500,000 years, yielding an incision rate of about 2.4 feet per thousand years. This implies that the creek was flowing at the level of the top of the bridge about 125,000 years ago, and at the level at which the opening was cut about 30,000 years ago. It is important to remember that these figures are based on many suppositions, such as that the downcutting rate was constant, which it probably was not. Thus, the numbers are at best only rough approximations; the actual ages could be less than one-half to more than double these numbers.

Processes Currently Affecting the Bridge

The natural processes affecting Rainbow Bridge today also affect sandstone cliff faces and arches throughout this arid region of Utah. Rock falls that develop along tension-formed joints and by exfoliation are common occurrences over geologic time. These processes are assisted during winter months when freezing moisture forces apart fractures, joints, and the spaces between sand grains in the rock. Chemical weathering and wind abrasion have minor impacts on the bridge.

Dames & Moore (1972), who studied the bridge from an engineering perspective, stated that these natural processes have not caused any major loss in bridge stability for many thousands of years. They also concluded that the bridge is not threatened by its own weight. Finally, the study evaluated the effects of Lake Powell under the bridge and increased levels of sulphur dioxide emitted from the Navajo Power Generating Plant to the southwest in Arizona. The findings concluded that these human-induced changes will not significantly alter the integrity of Rainbow Bridge. They estimated that for the bridge to collapse, over one-half of the foundation rock on each leg

Figure 11. Pair of vertical stereo aerial photographs of Rainbow Bridge National Monument and surrounding area. Hold the photograph approximately 12 inches away with one image in front of each eye. Concentrate on focusing on a scene in the far distance – as if you are looking at the ground from an airplane. If you have one weaker eye, you may not be able to see the image in stereo. Note that the marina has moved since this photo pair was taken in 1991 by the U.S. Department of the Interior.

would have to be removed. Under existing conditions, Rainbow Bridge will continue to stand for many thousands of years to come.

ACKNOWLEDGMENTS

We thank Bruce Heise, Tim Connors, and Joe Gregson of the National Park Service, Geological Resources Division, and Norm Henderson and Dave Gustafson of the Glen Canyon National Recreation Area, National Park Service, for providing enthusiastic support, funding, access, and transportation to Rainbow Bridge National Monument. The Utah Geological Survey (UGS) covered field expenses and provided transportation to the Glen Canyon Recreation Area. Jim Parker (UGS) turned our rough drawings into fine illustrations. We thank David Tabet and Mike Hylland of the UGS for their careful review and constructive criticism of the manuscript.

REFERENCES

Ahlbrandt, T.S., Fryberger, S.G., 1982, Introduction to eolian deposits, *in* Scholle, P.A., and Spearing, Darwin, editors, Sandstone depositional environments: American Association of Petroleum Geologists Memoir 31, p. 11-47.

Baker, A.A., 1936, Geology of the Monument Valley-Navajo Mountain region, San Juan County, Utah: U.S. Geological Survey Bulletin 865, 106 p.

Blakey, R.C., Peterson, Fred, Caputo, M.V., and Voorhees, B.J., 1983, Paleogeography of Middle Jurassic continental shoreline and shallow marine sedimentation, southern Utah, *in* Reynolds, M.W., and Dolly, E.D., editors, Symposium on Mesozoic paleogeography of west-central United States: Denver, Rocky Mountain Section, Society of Economic Paleontologists and Mineralogists, p. 77-100.

Condie, K.C., 1964, Crystallization PO2 of syenite porphyry from Navajo Mountain, southern Utah: Geological Society of America Bulletin, v. 75, no. 4, p. 359-362.

Dames & Moore, 1972, Geological and structural evaluation of Rainbow Bridge, Rainbow Bridge National Monument, Utah: Unpublished consultant's report for the Upper Colorado River Commission, 39 p., 4 appendices.

Doelling, H.H., 1997, Interim geologic map of the Smoky Mountain 30' X 60' quadrangle, Kane and San Juan Counties, Utah and Coconino County, Arizona: Utah Geological Survey Open-File Report 359, 2 plates, scale 1:100,000.

Doelling, H.H., and Davis, F.D., 1989, Geology of Kane County, Utah: Utah Geological and Mineral Survey Bulletin 124, 192 p., 10 plates, scale 1:100,000.

Everhart, R.E., 1983, Glen Canyon-Lake Powell - the story behind the scenery: Las Vegas, KC Publications, Inc., p. 10-11.

Fleming, R.F., 1994, Cretaceous pollen in Pliocene rocks - implications for Pliocene climate in the southwestern United States: Geology, v. 22, p. 787-790.

Gilland, J.K., 1979, Paleoenvironment of a carbonate lens

in the lower Navajo Sandstone near Moab, Utah: Utah Geological and Mineral Survey, Utah Geology, v. 6, no. 1, p. 29-38.

Graf, W.L., Hereford, R., Laity, J., and Young, R.A., 1987, Colorado Plateau, *in* Graf, W.L., editor, Geomorphic systems of North America: Geological Society of America Centennial Special Volume 2, p. 259-302.

Hackman, R.J., 1956, Photogeologic map of the Navajo Mountain-13 quadrangle, Kane and Garfield Counties, Utah and Coconino County, Arizona: U.S. Geological Survey Miscellaneous Geologic Investigations Map I-184, scale 1:24,000.

Hintze, L.F., 1993, Geologic history of Utah: Brigham Young University Geology Studies Special Publication 7, 202 p.

—1997, Geologic highway map of Utah: Brigham Young University Geology Studies Special Publication no. 3., scale 1:1,000,000.

Hunt, C.B., 1956, Cenozoic geology of the Colorado Plateau: U.S. Geological Survey Professional Paper 279, 99 p.

Lucchitta, Ivo, 1979, Late Cenozoic uplift of the southwestern Colorado Plateau and adjacent Colorado River region: Tectonophysics, v. 61, p. 63-95.

—1989, History of the Grand Canyon and of the Colorado River in Arizona, *in* Jenney, J.P., and Reynolds, S.J., Geologic evolution of Arizona: Arizona Geological Society Digest 17, p. 701-715.

National Park Service, 1998, Rainbow Bridge National Monument, Utah - official map and guide: National Park Service, U.S. Department of the Interior, 2 p.

Nelson, S.T., Heizler, M.T., and Davidson, J.P., 1992, New ^{40}Ar/^{39}Ar ages of intrusive rocks from the Henry and La Sal Mountains: Utah Geological Survey Miscellaneous Publication MP 92-2, 24 p.

Pipiringos, G.N., and O'Sullivan, R.B., 1978, Principal unconformities in Triassic and Jurassic rocks, western interior United States - a preliminary survey: U.S. Geological Survey Professional Paper 1035-A, 29 p.

Roosevelt, Theodore, 1916, A book-lover's holiday in the open: New York, Charles Scribners & Sons, 373 p.

Stokes, W.L., 1991, Petrified mini-forests of the Navajo Sandstone, east-central Utah: Utah Geological Survey, Survey Notes, v. 25, no. 1, p. 14-19.

Willis, G.C., 1994, Geologic map of the Harley Dome quadrangle, Grand County, Utah: Utah Geological Survey Map 157, 18 p., scale 1:24,000.

Geology of Utah's Parks and Monuments
2000 Utah Geological Association Publication 28
D.A. Sprinkel, T.C. Chidsey, Jr., and P.B. Anderson, editors

Geology and Hydrogeology of Timpanogos Cave National Monument, Utah

Alan L Mayo[1], David Herron[2], Stephen T. Nelson[1], David Tingey[1], and Mike J. Tranel[3]

ABSTRACT

The Timpanogos Cave system consists of three major caves, Hansen, Middle, and Timpanogos, which have been connected by tunnels. The cave system occurs in the Mississippian Deseret Limestone high on the steep southern wall of American Fork Canyon. Rocks in the American Fork Canyon region record a complex geologic history that includes: (1) deposition of a thick sequence of Late Precambrian and Paleozoic age sedimentary rocks, (2) thrust faulting and folding during the Late Cretaceous Sevier orogeny, (3) extensional faulting that culminated with the uplift of the Wasatch Range beginning about 17 million years ago as part of Basin and Range extension, (4) down-cutting of the deep stream channels accompanying the Wasatch Range uplift, and (5) and Pleistocene glaciation.

Locations and orientations of cave passages are greatly influenced by faulting. Cave morphology suggests that most cave dissolution was deep phreatic (that is, below the water table). Cave sediments indicate that water from the American Fork River moved through the cave system prior to uplift to the present cave location. After the cave was elevated above the bed of the American Fork River and erosion opened the face of the cave system to the atmosphere, widespread deposition of calcite speleothems began in response to the evaporation of infiltrating groundwater recharging in the overlying soil mantle. The rate of groundwater inflow into the cave system is greatest in Hansen Cave, which is located near the cliff face.

INTRODUCTION

While cougar hunting in 1887, Martin Hansen discovered a small cave entrance high on the steep southern slope of American Fork Canyon, east of the town of American Fork, Utah. Although the cave was well decorated, it was not until 1921 that two other large and well-decorated caves were discovered close by (figures 1 and 2, and table 1). Discovery of the new caves brought national attention to the cave system and in 1922 President Warren Harding proclaimed Timpanogos Cave a national monument.

The known cave system consists of the three large caves, Hansen, Middle, and Timpanogos Caves, which have been connected by tunnels for access by cave visitors, and numerous smaller passages (figures 1, 2, and 3). The cave system formed in the Mississippian Deseret Limestone by dissolution along fractures and bedding surfaces.

PREVIOUS INVESTIGATIONS

Bullock (1942, 1954, and 1962) investigated the geolo-

gy and origin of the cave system, described the various speleothems, and outlined the human history and management of the caves. White and VanGundy (1974) re-examined the geology and origin of the cave system, mapped the prominent passages, and investigated the minerals and coloring agents of the cave decorations.

Figure 1. Decorated Coral Garden in Middle Cave where stalactites, draperies, stalactites, and frostwork can be seen. (Kim Despain photo.)

[1]*Department of Geology, Brigham Young University, Provo, UT 84602*
[2]*Mayo and Associates, Lindon, UT 84042*
[3]*U.S. National Park Service, American Fork, UT 84003*

Table 1. Discovery dates and lengths of known caves in the Timpanogos Cave system.

Cave	Length (feet)	Discovered	Discovered By
The Grotto	40	1887	Martin Hansen
Hansen Cave	1,500	1887	Martin Hansen
Timanogos Cave	2,900	1915?	James Cough
		1921	Vearl Manwell
Middle Cave	1,100	1921	Wayne and Heber Hansen
Root Canal Cave	32	1988	David Herron

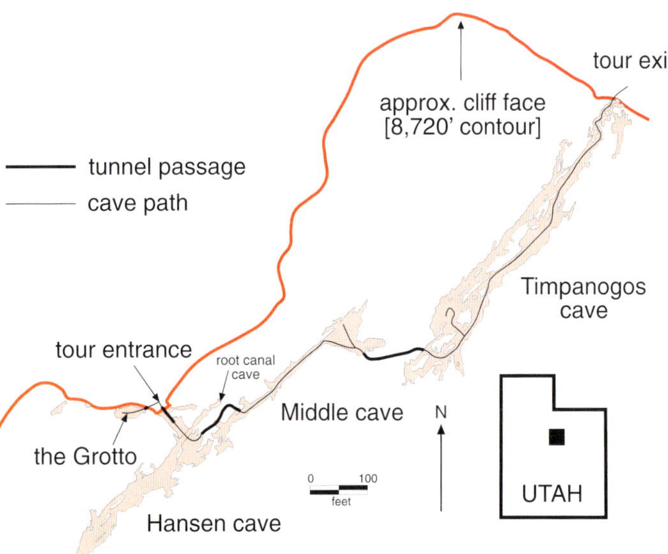

Figure 2. Map of Timpanogos Cave system showing trail system. Tunnels connect the three caves.

Figure 3. Bridge over Middle Cave Lake along the developed trail. A large column is at the head of the bridge. (Timpanogos Cave National Monument photo.)

Perkins (1955) described the structure and stratigraphy of the American Fork Canyon area and Baker and Crittenden (1961) published a geologic map of the Timpanogos Cave Quadrangle. Constenius (1998) and Paulsen and Marshak (1998) re-examined the tectonics of the American Fork Canyon region. Herron (1997) re-examined the origin and history of the cave.

Tranel and others (1991) presented the preliminary results of an investigation of the groundwater systems in the cave.

Several maps of the cave system have been made. The most complete map prepared by Horrocks (1993) is available from Timpanogos Cave National Monument. Horrocks and Tranel (1994) included a smaller version of the map. Other cave maps include those by White and Van-Gundy (1974), Green (1975), and several unpublished maps prepared by the National Park Service.

REGIONAL SETTING

The Timpanogos Cave system is located in the southern portion of the Wasatch Range, a large uplifted, north-south trending fault block. The 8- to 16-mile-wide Wasatch Range extends approximately 125 miles between Brigham City to the north and Nephi to the south. The western margin of the range is a sharp and prominent scarp that rises locally as much as 7,000 feet along the seismically active Wasatch fault. The Wasatch fault separates the Basin and Range geologic province to the west from the Middle Rocky Mountain Province to the east.

Streams have dissected the fault block into a series of large segments separated by deep narrow canyons. These canyons are particularly pronounced on the western side of the range. Most of the canyons, such as American Fork Canyon, originate at the crest of the range. However, a few canyons, such as Provo Canyon located south of American Fork Canyon, cut though the range and carry streams that originate in mountains located farther to the east.

Many of the segments contain north-south-trending, high narrow ridges that have one or more mountain peaks. The skyline of the segment located south of American Fork Canyon is dominated by a 3.5-mile-long, 11,000-foot-high, narrow ridgeline that includes the 11,750-foot Mount Timpanogos. On the western and northern flanks of Mount Timpanogos, a somewhat undulating, 8,000-foot-high upland surface, known as Sagebrush Flat, breaks the steep slope. American Fork River has dissected Sagebrush Flat, cutting the narrow, 2,700-foot-deep, precipitously sided American Fork Canyon. Down cutting of the canyon exposed the Timpanogos Cave system, which occurs approximately halfway up the southern wall of the canyon at an elevation of about 6,700 feet. The segment north of American Fork Canyon is the dominated by the 11,101-foot Box Elder Peak.

GEOLOGIC SETTING

Rocks in the American Fork Canyon region record a complex geologic history that includes:

(1) a thick sequence of Late Precambrian and Paleozoic age rocks that were deposited as gravel, sand, mud, till, and limey ooze;

(2) thrust faulting and folding during the Late Cretaceous Sevier orogeny;

(3) extensional faulting, which initiated along the sole of Charleston thrust fault about 40 million years ago (Constenius, 1998), and culminated with the uplift of the Wasatch Range beginning about 17 million years ago as part of Basin and Range extension;

(4) down cutting of the deep stream channels accompanying the Wasatch Range uplift; and

(5) Pleistocene glaciation.

This history and the timing of cave events are illustrated in figure 4.

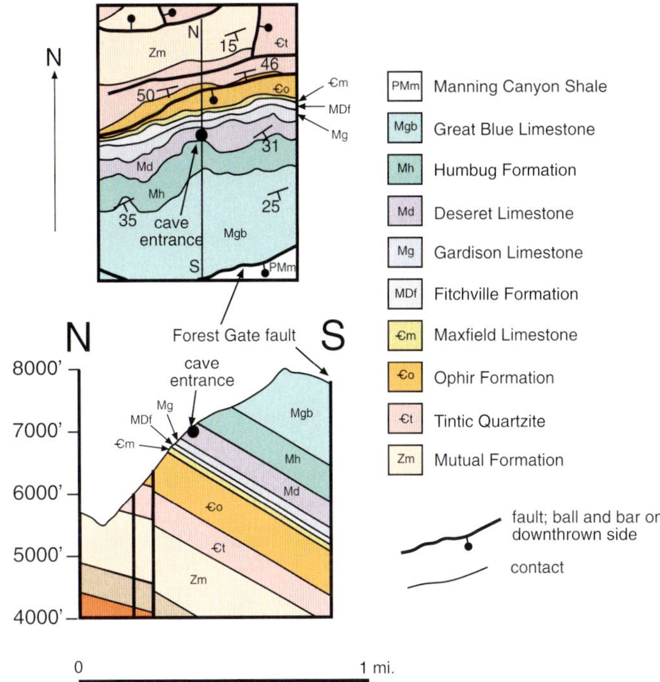

Figure 5. Simplified geologic map and cross section in the vicinity of Timpanogos Cave. The caverns are located in the south dipping beds of the Deseret Limestone (after Baker and Crittenden, 1961).

Precambrian and Paleozoic Deposition

Bedrock exposed in the vicinity of American Fork Canyon represent four major episodes of deposition. Bedrock units are described in table 2 and the formations exposed in the vicinity of the Timpanogos Cave system are illustrated in figure 5, a simplified geologic map and a simplified north-south cross section of the southern wall of American Fork Canyon.

The known geologic history begins in Late Precambrian time with the deposition of layers of sand and mud of the Big Cottonwood Formation that were shed from a highland whose locations is unknown. Following this, an episode of Precambrian glaciation resulted in the deposition of great bodies of glacial till, which are now known as the Mineral Fork Tillite. After the glaciers retreated the region underwent a period of tectonism and extensive erosion. On the erosional surface, Precambrian age red mud, sand, and gravel, shed from a nearby upland, were laid down. In Early Cambrian time the region underwent another period of uplift and erosion. Following this uplift the region subsided and an eastward advancing sea laid down more than 1,000 feet of sand (Tintic Quartzite), a few hundred feet of mud (Ophir Formation), and finally, as the sea deepened, thousands of feet of limy ooze (Maxfield Limestone). Most of the Maxfield Limestone was subsequently removed by erosion.

During Ordovician, Silurian, and Early Devonian time the geologic history of the region is uncertain because no sedimentary rocks, that may have been deposited, remain.

In the late Paleozoic (Mississippian, Pennsylvanian,

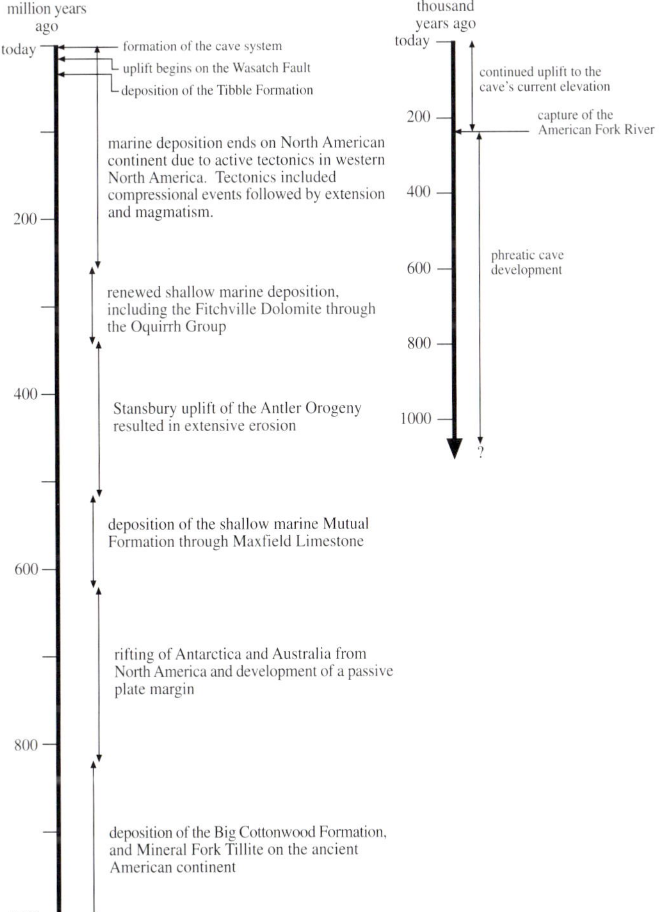

Figure 4. Timing of geologic events related to the history of Timpanogos Cave.

Table 2. Summary of the bedrock units in the vicinity of American Fork Canyon (modified after Baker and Crittenden, 1961; Davis, 1983a, 1983b; and Hintze, 1993).

Age	Name	MYA	Maximum Thickness (feet)	Description
Tert.	Tibble Fork Formation	<30	0-2,500	Fluvial pebble-to boulder-conglomerate, sandy to shaly tuffaceous sediments of fluvial origin with thin interbeds of limestone.
Pennsylvanian	Oquirrh Group	>256	4,000+	Thin to thick-bedded, tan-weathering sandstone and quartzite near the top and medium-to dark-gray limestone(Bridal Vale Falls Limestone) at the bottom. Crops out on the slopes of Mount Timpanogos.
Pennsylvanian	Manning Canyon Shale		1,600	Black shale interbedded with fine-grained and gritty sandstone and gray to black limestone. Exposures are generally poor and it forms a broad bench north and west of Mount Timpanogos.
Mississippian	Great Blue Limestone		2,800	Calcitic thin-bedded, dark-gray to black limestone and shaly limestone. Weathers to light-gray to pinkish tan flake or thin slabs.
Mississippian	Humbug Formation		800+	Alternating dark- to light-gray, fine- to coarse-grained dolomite with tawny weathering, fine- to medium-grained limey sandstone.
Mississippian	Deseret Limestone		500+	Massive, cliff-and-cave forming, dark- to light-gray, fine- to coarse-grained dolomite. Contains the Timpanogos Cave system.
Mississippian	Gardison Limestone	>342	600+	Ten to thirty feet of dark-gray, coarse-grained limestone at the base that is overlain by 80 to 100 feet of thin-bedded, blue-gray limestone with silty partings. The silty partings make the middle unit banded. About 400 feet of dark-gray, massive limestone and dolomite, containing masses of white chert 2 to 4 inches thick form the upper unit.
Mississippian	Fitchville Formation	<517	500+	Basal beds are 2 to 10 feet thick consisting of cross-bedded dolomitic sandstone. Two thick layers of massive- to medium-bedded, dark- to pale-gray dolomite above the base.
Cambrian	Maxfield Limestone		0-300	Thin-to thick-bedded, blue-gray, mottled magnesian limestone and dolomite. Oolitic to pisolitic beds at the base an a conspicuous layer of laminated white dolomite at the top.
Cambrian	Ophir Formation		300	Brown calcareous sandstone (upper), massive gray limestone (middle), and olive-green shale (lower).
Cambrian	Tintic Quartzite	543	1,300	Nearly pure, medium- to coarse-grained, white to pinkish quartzite. Lower beds are generally cross-bedded and pebbley.
Precambrian	Mutual Formation	543 / 620	0 -1,300	Rusty to red-purple quartzite, grit and conglomerate with minor shale. The coarser sandstones are tan, gray or greenish-gray. The finer sandstones are grayish red. The conglomerates contain pebbles and boulders up to 5 feet in diameter.
Precambrian	Mineral Fork Tillite	820 / 860	0 -200	Black massive conglomerate quartzite and sandstone with thin layers of bedded siltstone. The massive tillite contains rounded pebbles, cobbles, and boulders in a sand matrix cemented by glacial flour.
Precambrian	Big Cottonwood Formation		1,300	Rusty- to buff-weathering, massive quartzite and gray to dull-purple shale.

and Permian) the Oquirrh basin formed in response to passive-margin tectonics along the western U.S. Cordillera. In this shallow, slowly subsiding basin, widespread layers of marine carbonate, sand, and mud accumulated. To the west and south more than 30,000 feet of sediments were laid down in center of the basin. The American Fork Canyon area, located on the eastern margin of the basin, contains considerably thinner deposits that are now known as the Fitchville Formation through the Oquirrh Group (table 2). The 500 plus foot thick Deseret Limestone, which now contains the Timpanogos Cave system, was deposited in the Oquirrh basin during the Mississippian. In the Permian, when carbonates of the Park City Formation were forming in the basin, stagnant water was widespread for a time and phosphatic shale was deposited. Permian rocks have subsequently been removed by erosion in the American Fork Canyon area; however, they crop out to the north and east.

Mesozoic and Cenozoic Deformation

In Late Jurassic time the western margin of North America transitioned into a convergent-margin boundary. The convergent boundary, which existed through early Tertiary time, resulted in thin-skinned crustal shorting (that is thrust faulting) of the Sevier orogeny, uplifts of the Laramide orogeny, and localized igneous intrusion (Paulsen and Marshak, 1998). The Sevier orogeny mostly involved Late Precambrian through Mesozoic age sedimentary rocks along the craton margin, whereas, the Laramide orogeny resulted in a series of discontinuous reverse-fault uplifts that involved basement rocks of the craton.

Late Precambrian through late Paleozoic rocks in the American Fork Canyon region are located at the northern end of the Provo salient of the Sevier fold-thrust belt. The Provo salient, which is a single thrust sheet known as the Charleston allochthon, is floored by the Charleston thrust fault. Rocks of the allochthon were transported about 18 to 25 miles eastward over similar but thinner rocks. In American Fork Canyon the bedrock in the allochthon is folded and broken by a complex array of low-angle thrust, high-angle thrust, and high-angle normal faults (Paulsen and Marshak, 1998). The region of intense deformation is bounded by the Deer Creek normal fault in the north and by the Forest Gate normal fault in the south. The complex folds and faults, which are well displayed in the walls of American Fork Canyon, formed during Sevier thrust faulting and during subsequent post-compression extensional relaxation. Constenius (1998) attributes the Tibble Formation to infilling of half-grabens accompanying the post-thrust faulting extension. The Tibble Formation is well exposed on the east dam abutment of Tibble Reservoir, located about 5 miles east of the cave system in the north fork of American Fork River.

Uplift of the Wasatch Range, which is part of the great Basin and Range extension, is the latest tectonic event. Uplift began in the Miocene about 17 million years ago and continues to the present. Uplift along the Wasatch fault has tilted the Wasatch Range eastward and created the great grabens of Utah and Salt Lake Valleys. These grabens have been filled with thousands of feet of sediments derived from the erosion of the uplifted mountain blocks and carried by rivers emerging from the mountains. The rivers, such as American Fork River, have down cut the canyons contemporaneous with the uplift. In American Fork Canyon this down cutting first removed the northern portions of the Timpanogos Cave system. As the canyon cut deeper the cave systems was abandoned progressively higher on the canyon wall.

Timpanogos Cave is about 1,100 feet higher than the elevation of the floor of American Fork Canyon immediately down slope. Knowledge of the uplift rate of the Wasatch Range provides information that constrains the minimum age in the past when the cave was at the elevation of the American Fork River. Prior to this minimum age, the cave would likely have been below the water table as well as being capable of capturing the American Fork River as recorded in stream sediments found within the cave system.

A number of studies have examined uplift rates along the Wasatch fault. Evans and others (1985) and Kowallis and others (1990) determined an uplift rate of 0.030 and 0.027 inches per year (in/yr) on the nearby Little Cottonwood stock which is an Oligocene age intrusion to the north, although this uplift rate may be related to movement along the Salt Lake segment of the Wasatch fault that may not be directly related to the Provo segment. However, Swan and others (1980) and Machette and Lund (1987) found similar values of 0.039 in/yr (3,280 feet per million years) for the Provo and American Fork areas. Using this value, the 1,100 feet of uplift and down cutting of the American Fork River could have been accomplished in probably no less than 335,000 years. What this means is that the minimum age of the cave system is approximately 335,000 years, but may be considerably older as described below.

FORMATION OF THE CAVE SYSTEM

Dissolution Reactions

Formation of cave passages involves the dissolution of carbonate rock, which requires an acidic solution or other source of hydrogen (H^+) ions. In most vadose zones, groundwater recharge is acidic due to the abundance of soil zone carbon dioxide gas (CO_2), which forms during root respiration and by organic matter decay. (The vadose zone is the region above the water table where the soil and bedrock are usually not fully saturated and the where there is a free exchange with atmospheric gases.) Soil zone CO_2 forms carbonic acid (H_2CO_3), which dissociates into H^+ and bicarbonate (HCO_3^-) ions. The H^+ ions are then available to dissolve carbonate minerals. These reactions are show below:

Eq. 1 $CO_{2(g)} + H_2O = H_2CO_3$

Eq. 2 $H_2CO_3 = H^+ + HCO_3^-$

Eq. 3 $2H^+ + CaMg(CO_3)_2 = Ca^{2+} + Mg^{2+} + 2HCO_3^-$
             dolomite

Eq. 4 $H^+ + CaCO_3 = Ca^{2+} + HCO_3^-$
             calcite

Many cave systems, particularly where karst features such as sinkholes occur, are thought to form in the vadose zone and upper portion of the underlying phreatic zone. (The phreatic zone is where all open pores are filled with water. In an unconfined aquifer the upper surface of the phreatic zone is called the water table.)

Almost all deep phreatic groundwater is depleted in soil zone H^+ because dissolution processes in the shallow subsurface generally consume the H^+. Cave passage morphology, described below, suggest a deep phreatic origin for the Timpanogos Cave systems, thus an external source of H+ ions was required. Potential external sources include oxidation of iron-bearing minerals, thermal decarbonization of carbonate rocks accompanying low-temperature metamorphism, decomposition of organic matter, magmatic fluids, mantle fluids, and hydrothermal fluids, and other processes. Mayo and Muller (1997) have described thermal decarbonization reactions and Carothers and Kharaka (1980), Kharaka and others (1986), and Surdam and others (1989) have described decomposition of organic matter.

Identification of specific external H^+ sources is problematic. In deep groundwater systems iron oxidation is unlikely because free oxygen is generally consumed in the shallow subsurface. There is no direct evidence of decarbonization; however, carbonate rocks are abundant and decarbonization has been identified as the probable source of excess CO_2 in the nearby Midway thermal groundwater system (Mayo and Loucks, 1995). Organic-rich sediments are also abundant in the area, but there is no direct evidence that they contributed H^+ ions. Direct contributions of magmatic and mantle fluids are unlikely because the most recent igneous activity predates the uplift of the Wasatch Range. Contributions from hydrothermal fluids from an unknown origin are possible. Metal oxide deposits, described below, suggest the presence of some hydrothermal fluids during part of the cave history. However, many of the other features commonly associated with hydrothermal fluids, such as hydrothermal speleogens and speleothems, bedrock recrystalization along cave passages, and bedrock spar and calcite-filled vugs near cave passages are not present.

Structural Controls

Faults have greatly affected the orientation of cave passages. Damage zones along these faults created a fracture flow system along which fluids could readily migrate. The primary passages of the three large caves developed

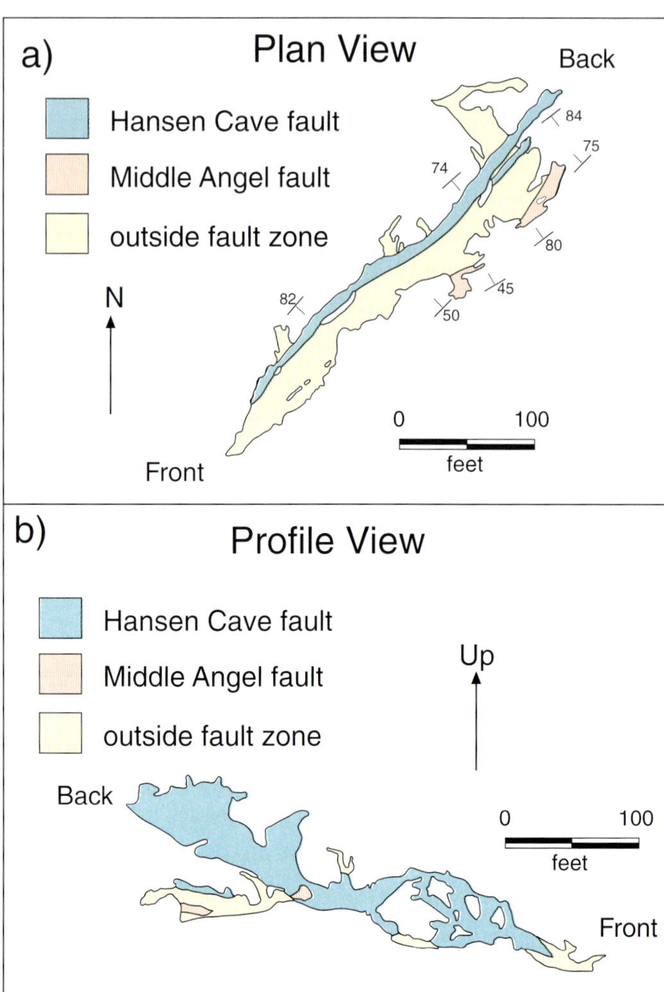

Figure 6. Plan and profile views of Hansen Cave illustrating the influence of faults on cave morphology.

along three different faults, each of which bear the name of their respective cave. Displacement of the Timpanogos Cave fault is at least 130 feet (Bullock, 1962) and the Hansen Cave fault has a similar offset. The Middle Cave fault has about 10 feet of displacement (Herron, 1997). Fault controlled passages are typically narrow and tall features. Fault passages are commonly 10 feet wide or less and have heights as great as 50 to 100 feet. The influence of faults and the aspect ratios of fault-controlled passages (horizontal to vertical) are shown on figure 6, which contains plan and profile views of Hansen Cave.

Although most passages are partially to strongly influenced by bedding, the passages in the Timpanogos Cave system do not follow either the strike or dip of the beds. Instead the passages follow the intersections of bedding surfaces with other features such as minor faults and joints. The geometry of many passages has also been influenced by the collapse of cave roofs and walls.

Cave Morphology

Cave passage morphology often provides valuable insight into the origin of the cave. Vadose origin (above the water table) and phreatic origin (below the water table)

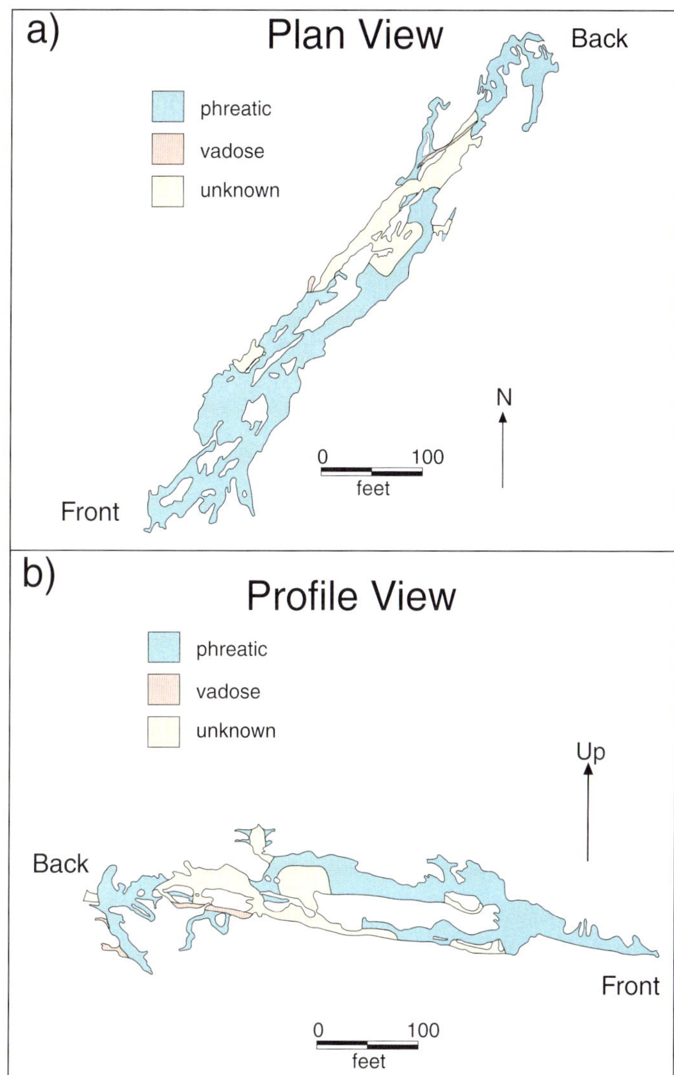

Figure 7. Plan and profile views of Timpanogos Cave showing regions of phreatic and vadose origins.

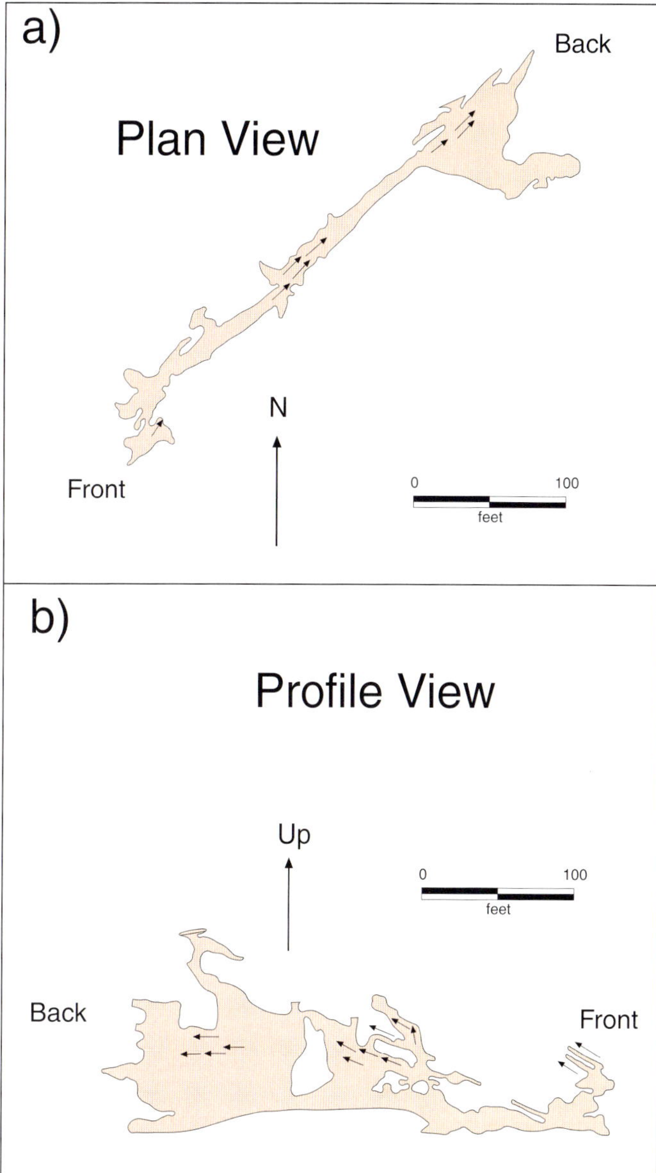

Figure 8. Plan and profile views of Middle Cave showing the direction of groundwater flow as indicated by scallops on cave walls.

caves often have different cave passage morphology (Palmer, 1991). The morphology and spelogens of vadose caves include dome pits and waterfall shafts, stream slots, stream meanders, vertical fluting, and ceiling infeeders. Morphologies which may indicate a vadose origin also include small scallops, which are indicative of fast-moving water, horizontal or gently descending passages, vertical drops alternating with horizontal passages, and passages that cross-cut bedding or other structures to maintain a consistent gradient.

Phreatic cave morphology and speleogens include rounded passage cross sections, steeply angled but not vertical passages, the absence of apparent horizontal controls in passage distribution, and repeated changes in passage gradient in response to structural controls. Morphologies that may indicate a phreatic origin include the absence of vadose morphology, the absence of coarse-grained allogenic sediments (that is they were formed outside of the cave environment), and large scallops indicative of slow water flow. Scallops are smooth shallow con-

cave depressions that sometimes occur on cave walls.

Herron (1997) mapped the distribution of vadose and phreatic passage morphologies and found that majority of the cave system has a predominant phreatic morphology (figure 7). Figure 7 illustrates the occurrence of vadose and phreatic cave wall morphology in Timpanogos Cave. Herron also evaluated the style of vertical relief of the cave passages and found it largely indicates a phreatic origin.

The cave system has a few well-formed scallops, several areas of poorly formed scallops, and large areas without scallops. Scallops are caused by bedrock dissolution accompanying turbulent water flow. The length of the scallops is related to the wavelength associated with turbulent water flow, which is related to water velocity (Curl, 1974).

Herron (1997) mapped scallop locations and implied groundwater flow directions are illustrated in figure 8 (previous page), which includes a plan and profile view of Middle Cave.   Incomplete scallop development suggests that only the last phase of dissolution occurred when groundwater-flow rates were relatively rapid.   The scallops also indicate that groundwater flow during this last dissolution phase was slightly upward in a northeast direction, from Hansen Cave toward Timpanogos Cave. This means that groundwater in the cave system flowed away from the front of the present day Wasatch Range, in a direction opposite to the flow of the nearby American Fork River. This direction of groundwater flow is counterintuitive, and suggests that the most cave development occurred well below the water table. It is possible the cave system predates the ancestral American Fork River, which formed sometime after initiation of the Wasatch Range uplift, about 17 million years ago. It is more likely that cave dissolution occurred at sufficient depth, such that both the location and direction of flow in the American Fork River were relatively unimportant. The upward component of flow means that the cave system has been rotated since dissolution or that groundwater in the cave system was rising.

POST DISSOLUTION SEDIMENTATION

The cave system contains large volumes of cave sediment including dissolution residues, metal-oxide precipitates, stream deposited clastic sediments (laminated silt, sand, well-rounded gravel, and angular gravel), break down debris (collapse debris), and dripstone deposits. Metal-oxide precipitates are discussed below. Dissolution residues are thin and poorly preserved.

Large portions of the cave system are partially or completely filled with deposits of fine-grained silt.   The silts are light tan in color, indicating oxidizing conditions, and are very fine grained. Bedding laminations are typically less than 1/8 of an inch. The silts consists almost entirely of very small quartz grains, with lesser amounts of calcite and dolomite, and traces of magnetite, partially cemented into larger aggregate grains by a thin film of carbonate (Herron, 1997).   Some silt deposits have horizontal bedding, but most are inclined or curved, reflecting an uneven and sloping floor onto which the silt was deposited. The silt deposits were laid down slowly when the cave system was filled with slow moving water.   Faint cross-bedding suggests a southwesterly flow, opposite in direction to the flow that produced scalloping.

Sandy sediments, dominated by well-rounded quartz grains, occur in several places. The mineral assemblage of quartz and the minor concentrations of the minerals calcite, black amphibole, biotite, muscovite, feldspar, and pyrite are similar to modern sands in the American Fork River. The cave sand is dissimilar to sand found in local ephemeral drainages that are tributary to American Fork River and that flow down the walls of American Fork Canyon.

Gravels occur as small and isolated deposits through-out much of the cave system. The gravels range in sized from the sand matrix to 7 inches or more in diameter. The gravels include well-rounded allogenic quartzite, smaller amounts of less-rounded autogenic carbonate rock and rip-up silt, and minor amounts of allogenic chert, mica-shale, red sandstone, and andesite. Allogenic particles originated outside of the cave environment and autogenic material originated from inside the cave. The gravels are similar to modern gravels in the American Fork River, but are dissimilar to gravel in local ephemeral drainages that are tributary to the American Fork River. The ephemeral drainages do not contain appreciable amounts of quartzite clasts.

The metal oxide deposits include black tubes, gossans, and iron oxide sediments. These deposits contain iron, manganese, nickel, zinc, barium, and other trace metals. Although the deposits are small and are not obvious to the casual cave observer, they provide insight into the history of the cave system.   Black tubes are recently discovered curved speleothems that have grown onto cave walls and ceilings from upward flowing fluids. Gossans, which extend several inches into the walls of Hidden Mine Cave, a small subsidiary cavern, formed by replacement of the carbonate bedrock during and before the main phase of cave dissolution.

The thin metal-rich sediments in the cave system were deposited prior to the silt invasion and the black tube speleothems formed after the deposition of the gravels. The fact that the metal oxide deposits formed at different times means that mineralized waters, that were perhaps thermal, were present during the underwater history of the cave.

MODERN HYDROGEOLOGY OF THE CAVE SYSTEM

An appreciable quantity of groundwater flows through the cave system. Groundwater inflows occur as both conduit flow along fault surfaces and diffuse flow along bedding surfaces. Groundwater inflow exhibits both spatial and temporal variations and inflow rates are related to the distance from the cliff face (figure 9). Both Hansen and Middle Cave exhibit considerable conduit flow along fault surfaces, responding rapidly to major precipitation and snowmelt events. Hansen Cave, which is close to the cliff face, has substantially more inflow than Middle Cave. By contrast groundwater flow in Timpanogos Cave, which is the furthest away from the cliff face, is largely bedding plane flow, with maximum drip rates occurring two to six months later than in Hansen Cave. The large inflow rates and the occurrence of conduit flow in Hansen and Middle Caves is attributed to the close proximity of the caves to the cliff face. Near the cliff face, the unbounded bedrock is under tension and appreciable aperture has developed along faults and associated fractures. In places the open fractures extend to the land surface.   Faults and fractures encountered in Timpanogos

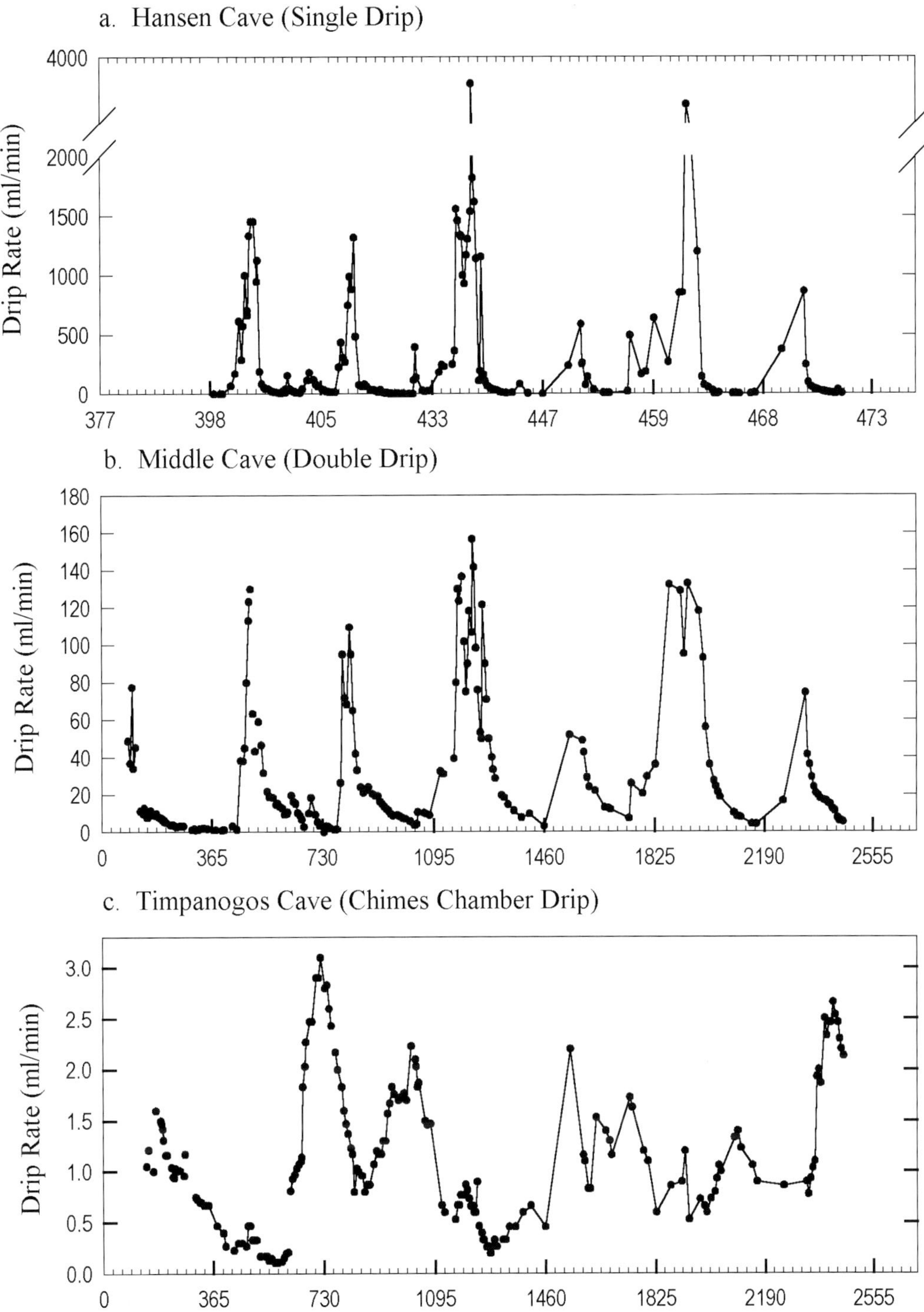

Figure 9. Typical drip rates in Hansen, Middle, and Timpanogos Caves between 1990 and 1997. Day 0 = January 1, 1990.

Cave, which are located farther from the cliff face and deeper below land surface, are not under tension, and thus do not support conduit flow and very small drip rates as illustrated by the Chimes Chamber drip (figure 9).

Water Chemistry

Inflow groundwater exhibits both spatial and temporal variations in solute compositions (Tranel and others, 1991). Inflow waters are of the Ca^{2+}-Mg^{2+}-HCO_3^- type with appreciable amounts of sulfate (SO_4^{2-}; table 3). These com-

positions are consistent with the dissolution of carbonate minerals containing gypsum or anhydrite. Overall solute compositions and total dissolved solids content (TDS) are lowest in Hansen Cave and highest in Timpanogos Cave. The lower TDS concentrations are attributed to lower rock/water ratios. For example, in Timpanogos cave drip rates of many individual roof drips are less than 0.005 gallons per week.

Chemical compositions of roof-drip water (table 3) have relatively high levels of carbonate mineral dissolu-

Table 3. Mean solute composition of roof drip waters in Timpanogos Cave. Modified after Tranel and others, 1991.

	n	TDS meq/l[1]	pH	°C	Ca^{2+}	Mg^{2+}	Na$^+$	K$^+$	HCO$_3^-$	SO$_4^{2-}$	Cl$^-$
Hansen Cave											
Hansen Cave Drip	16	11.6	7.84	7.6	3.75	1.89	0.13	0.01	4.62	1.09	0.107
Middle Cave											
Middle Cave Drip	16	12.32	7.93	7.7	3.16	2.63	0.09	0.03	4.55	1.58	0.148
Timpanogos Cave											
Chimes Chamber Drip	14	14.76	7.92	8.9	4.10	3.05	0.20	0.17	5.87	1.34	0.150
Cavern of Sleep Drip	1		8.30	8.9	1.76	4.21	0.25	0.02	4.22	1.75	0.199

[1] meq/l = milliequivalents per liter. Milliequivalents per liter are used rather than parts per million (ppm) or milligrams per liter (mg/l) because they provide a measure of chemcial reacting equivalents. For example, 1 meq/l of Na$^+$ will combine with 1 meq/l of Cl$^-$ to form the mineral halite. In terms of ppm or mg/l the concentrations would be 23.0 and 35.45 ppm or mg/l, respectively. In most groundwaters ppm and mg/l are approximately equal.

tion products (Equations 3 and 4) indicating the dissolution of limestone and dolomite in the recharge area above the cave system. Total dissolved solids are elevated in all of the caves and the concentrations can be correlated with roof-drip rates. Hansen Cave has the greatest drip rates and the lowest TDS. All of the waters have appreciable SO$_4^{2-}$ contents indicating the dissolution of some gypsum in the carbonate rocks.

Plots of the mineral saturation indices (SI) vs. time show considerable temporal variation (figures 10 and 11). The SI provides an indication if the water is supersaturated, saturated, or under saturated with respect to mineral phases. Saturation is defined as log SI = 0 ± 0.1. Values greater than 1 means that the water can precipitate the mineral and values less than 1 means that the water can dissolve the mineral. Precipitation of cave decorations can only occur when the water is supersaturated. When the water is under saturated the groundwater can dissolve cave decorations.

There is a strong correlation between saturation indices and groundwater inflow rates. For example in Hansen Cave (figure 10) all waters have carbonate minerals SI's greater than one when the drip rate is relatively low. However, when the flow of groundwater into Hansen Cave increases in during spring snowmelt and summer thunderstorms the water will dissolve carbonate minerals. Timpanogos Cave on the other hand, has a very muted response to surface recharge events and thus the water infiltrating into the cave remains carbonate-mineral saturated (figure 11). Thus cave decorations are continually growing.

In the cave environment, mineral saturation is affected by two factors: (1) the solute composition of the inflow

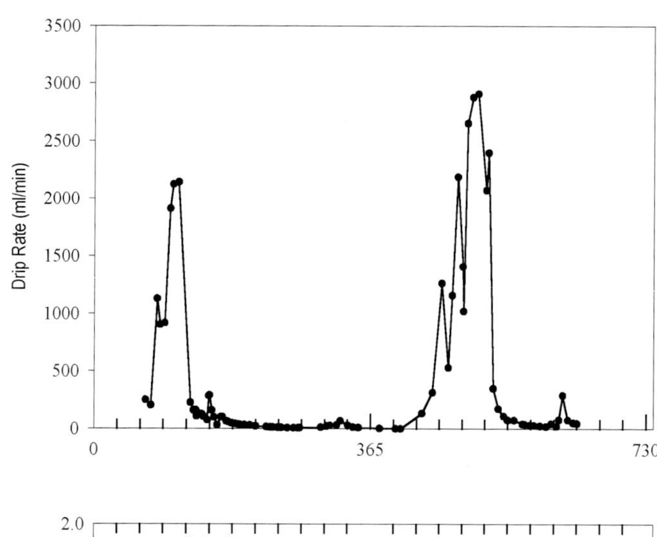

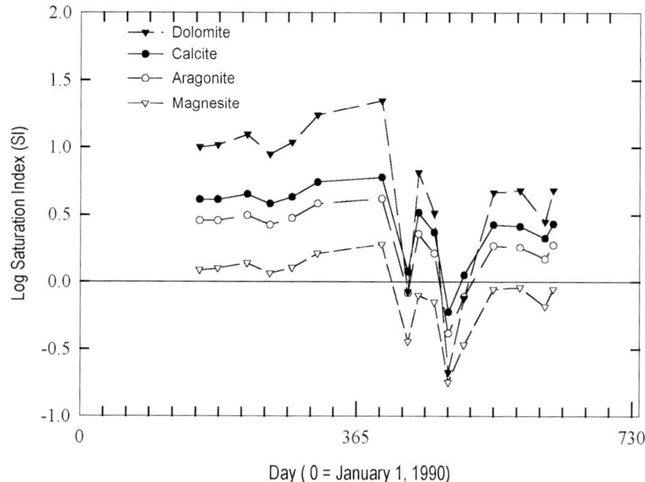

Figure 10. Hansen cave drip rates and corresponding saturation indices for selected carbonate minerals vs. sampling date.

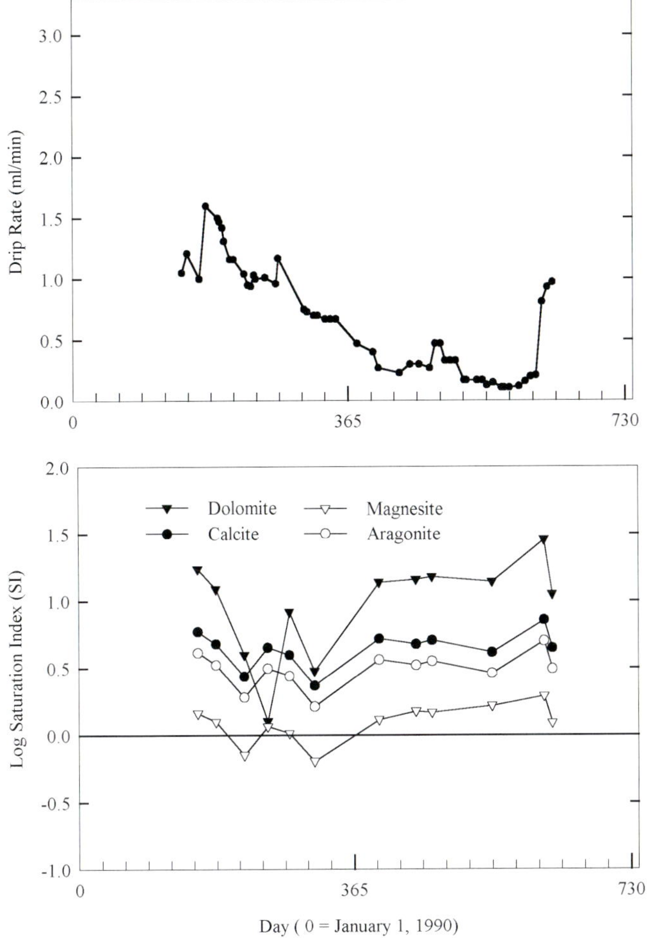

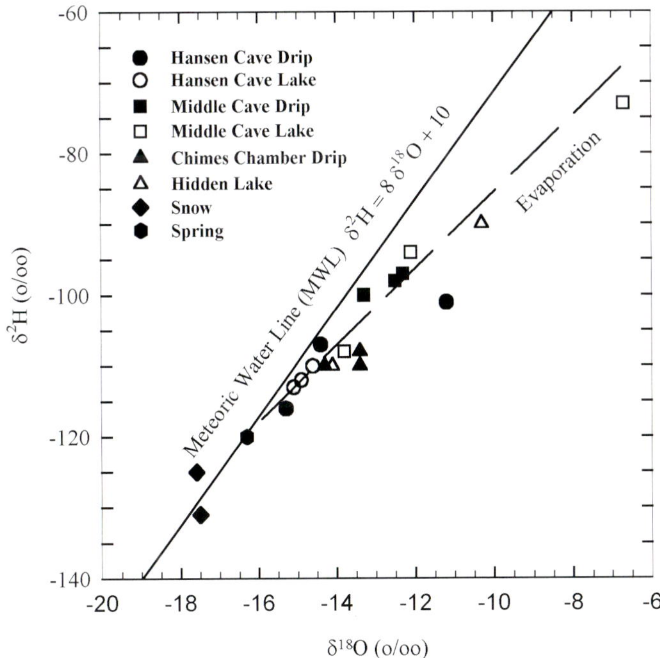

Figure 11. Timpanogos Cave (Chimes Chamber) drip rates and corresponding saturation indices for selected carbonate minerals vs. sampling date.

Figure 13. Actively forming soda straw with helictites in Timpanogos Cave. (Timpanogos Cave National Monument photo.)

Figure 12. Plot of the stable isotopic compositions of cave and recharge waters relative to the meteoric water line. The dashed line is an evaporation trajectory showing the extent of evaporation of caves waters.

groundwater, and (2) the extent of evaporation in the cave. Inflow water solute compositions are controlled by the mineralogy of the overlying soil and bedrock, and by the extent of plant growth in the soil zone. In this case there is abundant plant growth in the groundwater recharge area so that the inflow water is well charged with CO_2 gas and it can readily dissolve the carbonate rocks in the soil and bedrock. The stable isotopic compositions of roof drip and lakes in the cave system show that considerable evaporation occurs in the cave environment (figure 12). The stable isotopic composition of the waters is set at the time of recharge and is not effected by dissolution processes. Snow and spring discharge water outside of the cave system plot along the meteoric water line, where as the composition of cave waters tend to plot along an evaporation trajectory.

Cave Decorations

The Timpanogos Cave system contains considerable quantities of carbonate speleothems including stalactites, stalagmites, draperies, flowstone, helictites, anthodites, aragonite frostwork, moonmilk, and others (figures 3, 13, 14, and 15). Where groundwater inflow rates are relatively stable, precipitation of cave decorations is an active

Figure 14. A cluster of frostwork surrounded by flowstone, popcorn and helictites in Timpanogos Cave. (Timpanogos Cave National Monument photo.)

Figure 15. Calcite crystal growth in a droplet of water on the end of a soda straw in Timpanogos Cave. (Timpanogos Cave National Monument photo.)

Figure 16. Soda straws and helictites in Timpanogos Cave. (Kim Despain photo.)

process. Where rapid and large influxes of groundwater periodically occur, the waters become under saturated and they have the potential to dissolve some cave decorations during some times of the years. At other times the water can precipitate cave decorations.

The speleothems of the Timpanogos Cave system are significant in that they tend to occur in a greater range of colors than in most caves and also because of the greater abundance of typically rare helictites and anthodites (figure 16). The colors, including a very rare deep green and bright yellow are attributed the metal nickel. The nickel is likely the result of the elevated metal content of the cave walls and cave sediments.

SUMMARY OF THE HISTORY OF THE CAVE SYSTEM

The Timpanogos Cave system began approximately 340 million years ago with the deposition of the Deseret Limestone. After deposition, faulting and folding of the bedrock, during the Sevier and Laramide orogonies created faults and associated joints along some of which the cave system may have developed. The Little Cottonwood Stock, a quartz monzonite intrusion, was emplaced near the cave about 30.5 million years ago (Vogel and others, 1997). Thermal fluids from the intrusion were responsible for mineralization in the area, but it is unlikely that the intrusion was responsible for cave dissolution as the cavern system is outside the contact aureole.

About 17 million years ago uplift of the Wasatch Range began along the Wasatch fault zone as part of the Basin and Range extension. Cave system faults may have formed during this time, but is more likely that the uplift created aperture along previously existing faults and associated fractures. Either way, aperture in the fault damage zones was critical to the initiation of the cave system and to determining the location and orientation of the cave system. Openings in the damage zones became preferred pathways for the movement of acidic groundwater in the deep subsurface, thus the faults controlled the orientation of the cave system.

The origin of the acidic, deep phreatic, groundwater is uncertain. Some potential sources include CO_2 gas released by low-temperature metamorphism of carbonate rocks, decay of buried organic sediments, and hydrothermal fluids. Initial dissolution formed small vugs and pockets, then short tubes, and eventually well-connected and open conduits. As groundwater pathways became large and more interconnected, higher flow rates allowed more aggressive dissolution. Although the timing of the dissolution is unknown, the cave system probably spent millions of years slowly developing in the deep phreatic zone.

Regional uplift of the Wasatch Range and down cutting of American Fork Canyon raised the cave system closer to the surface where shallow phreatic conditions prevailed. In the shallow phreatic zone rapid dissolution was possible because large quantities of locally recharged groundwater could pass through the system. The scallops on the cave walls probably developed in the shallow phreatic zone. Fast cave dissolution and high groundwater-flow rates under shallow phreatic conditions probably did not last long, because the scallops in the cave system are not fully developed and uplift along the Wasatch Fault rapidly elevated the cave above the shallow phreatic horizon.

With continued regional uplift and down cutting of the American Fork River, vadose conditions eventually prevailed. Paleomagnetic analysis of cave sediments indicates that some time less than 760,000 years ago the cave system captured all or part of the American Fork River. Whether the river was captured underground, or whether it merely contributed water and sediments to the cave system, is unknown. However, much of the cave system was rapidly buried with surface sediments, supplied by the river. The deposition was rapid because the sediment-laden waters do not appear to have removed significant amounts of bedrock from the cave floors and walls. Capture of the American Fork River did not last long because deep phreatic dissolution created large sediments traps. These traps did not allow effective transport of coarse sediments, leading to rapid burial and blockage of key passages with coarse clastic sediments.

As regional uplift raised the cave system above the level of American Fork River, excavation of previously deposited sediments by small, local stream flows began. Cobbles and silt deposits high on cave walls, in several places, reveals that large volumes of sediments were locally removed. Gravels in the upper passage of Timpanogos Cave suggest that at least 20 feet of sediments were excavated from this location.

With continued uplift of the mountains, the cave system was raised well above the river level and has remained essentially high and dry ever since. Once relatively dry, deposition of carbonate speleothems began from infiltrating shallow groundwater under largely vadose conditions. Widespread deposition of calcite speleothems probably did not occur during the stream invasions because the stream would have dissolved them. However, even after the cave system drained, it is unlikely that many speleothems grew for some time because the cave entrances were plugged with sediments, which limited airflow and associated CO_2 loss for the cave water and air. Because carbonate speleothems grow dominantly by CO_2 loss from carbonate-saturated solutions, accompanied by evaporation, they would not have grown rapidly until a new entrance opened by erosion along the cliff face.

Both Hansen and Middle Caves, which are located close the cliff faces, have direct and very rapid hydraulic communication with surface waters along faults and fractures. Drip-rate responses in Timpanogos Cave, which is located away from the cliff face and is deeply buried, are more muted and appreciably smaller in magnitude that the other caves. The muted drip-rate response indicates diffuse flow along closed fractures and bedding surfaces.

Groundwater flowing into the caves is supersaturated with respect to carbonate minerals, except during very high inflow events. The stable isotopic compositions of cave waters indicate that cave water evaporation is an ongoing process. The combined factors of carbonate mineral supersaturation and evaporation indicates that the cave decorations are currently growing, except during large groundwater inflow events. Such large events only affect small portions of the cave system.

REFERENCES

Baker, A.A., and Crittenden, M.D., Jr., 1961, Geologic map of Timpanogos Cave Quadrangle Utah: U.S. Geological Survey Map GQ-132, scale 1:24,000.

Bullock, K.C., 1942, A study of the geology of the Timpanogos Caves: Provo, Brigham Young University, M.S. thesis, 66 p.

—1954, Geologic notes on the Timpanogos Cave: Technical Note no. 14, Salt Lake Grotto, National Speleological Society, p. 1-6.

—1962, Geology of Timpanogos Cave National Monument: unpublished manuscript, Timpanogos Cave National Monument Archives, 9 p.

Carother, W.W., and Kharaka, Y.K., 1980, Stable carbon isotopes of HCO_3^- in oil-field waters- implications for the origin of CO_2: Geochim. Cosmochim. Acta, v. 44, p. 323-332.

Constenius, K.N., 1998, Extensional tectonics of the Cordilleran foreland fold and thrust belt and the Jurassic-Cretaceous great valley forearc basin: Tuscon, University of Arizona, Ph.D. dissertation, 270 p.

Curl, R.L., 1974, Deducing flow velocity in cave conduits from scallops: National Speleological Society Bulletin, v. 6, p. 1-6.

Davis, F.D., 1983a, Geologic map of the Southern Wasatch Front, Utah: Utah Geological and Mineral Survey, Map 54A, 2 sheets, scale 1:100,000.

—1983b, Geologic map of the Central Wasatch Front, Utah: Utah Geological and Mineral Survey, Map 55A, 2 sheets, scale 1:100,000.

Evans, S.H., Parry, W.T., and Bruhn, R.L., 1985, Thermal,

mechanical and chemical history of the Wasatch fault cataclastic and phyllonite, Traverse Mountains area, Salt Lake City, Utah - age and uplift rates from K/Ar and fission tract measurements: U.S. Geological Survey Open-File Report 86-31, p. 410-415.

Green, D.J., 1975, Results of detailed mapping in Timpanogos Cave National Monument, Utah County, Utah: Technical Note no. 76, Salt Lake Grotto, National Speleological Society, p. 1-2.

Herron, D.C., 1997, Origin and geologic history of the Timpanogos Cave system, Timpanogos Cave National Monument, Utah County, Utah: Provo, Brigham Young University, M.S. thesis, 115 p.

Hintze, L.F., 1993, Geologic history of Utah: Brigham Young University Geologic Studies, Special Publication 7, 202 p.

Horrocks, R.D., 1993, Timpanogos Cave system: Timpanogos Cave National Monument, Archives, unpublished map.

Horrocks, R.D., and Tranel, M.J., 1994, Timpanogos Cave research project 1991-1992: National Speleological Society News, v. 52, no. 1, p. 15-21.

Kharaka, Y.K., Law, L.M., Carothers, W.W., and Goerlitz, D.F., 1986, Role of organic species dissolved in formation waters from sedimentary basin in mineral diagenesis, *in* Gautier, D.L., editor, Roles of organic matter in sedimentary diagenesis: Society of Economic Paleontologist and Mineralogist Special Publication 38, p. 111-122.

Kowallis, B.J., Ferguson, J., and Jorgensen, G., 1990, Uplift along the Salt Lake segment of the Wasatch fault form apatite and zircon fission tract dating in the Little Cottonwood Stock: Nucl. Tracts Radiat. Meas., v. 17, no. 3, p. 325-329.

Machette, M.N., and Lund, W.R., 1987, Late Quaternary history of the American Fork segment of the Wasatch fault zone, Utah [abs]: Geological Society of American Abstracts with programs, v. 19, p. 317.

Mayo, A.L, and Loucks, D.L., 1995, Solute and isotopic geochemistry and ground water flow in the central Wasatch Range, Utah: Journal of Hydrology, v. 172, p. 31-59.

Mayo, A.L., and Muller, A.B., 1997, Low temperature digenetic-metamorphic and magmatic contributions of external CO_2 gas to a shallow ground water system: Journal of Hydrology, v. 194, p. 286-304.

Palmer, A.N., 1991, Origin and morphology of limestone caves: Geological Society of America Bulletin, v. 103, p. 1-21.

Paulsen, T., and Marshak, S., 1998, Charleston transverse zone, Wasatch Mountains, Utah - Structure of the Provo salient's northern margin, Sevier fold-thrust belt: Geological Society of America Bulletin, v. 110, no. 4, p. 512-522.

Perkins, R.F., 1955, Structure and stratigraphy of the lower American Fork Canyon – Mahogany Mountain area, Utah County, Utah: Brigham Young University Research Studies, v. 2, no. 1, 39 p.

Swan, F.H., III, Schwartz, D.P., and Cluff, L.S., 1980, Recurrence of moderate to large magnitude earthquakes produced by surface faulting on the Wasatch fault zone, Utah: Bulletin Seismological Society of America, v. 70, p. 1431-1432.

Surdam, R.C., Crossey, L.J., Hagen, E.S., and Heasler, H.P., 1989, Organic-inorganic interactions and sandstone diagenesis: American Association of Petroleum Geologists Bulletin, v. 73, p. 1-23.

Tranel, M.J., Mayo, A.L., and Jensen, T.J., 1991, Preliminary investigation of the hydrogeology and hydrogeochemistry at Timpanogos Cave National Monument, Utah and its implications for cave management: 1991, National Cave Management Symposium Proceeding, Bowling Green Kentucky, p. 164-178.

Vogel, T.A., Cambray, F.W., Feher, L., and Constenius, K.N., 1997, Petrochemistry and emplacement history of the Wasatch igneous belt, central Wasatch Mountains, Utah [abs]: Geological Society America, Abstracts with Programs, v. 29, no. 6, p. A-282.

White, W.B., and VanGundy, J.J., 1974, Reconnaissance geology of Timpanogos Cave, Wasatch County, Utah: National Speleological Society Bulletin, v. 30, no. 1, p. 5-17.

Geology of Utah's Parks and Monuments
2000 Utah Geological Association Publication 28
D.A. Sprinkel, T.C. Chidsey, Jr., and P.B. Anderson, editors

Geology of Flaming Gorge National Recreational Area, Utah-Wyoming

Douglas A. Sprinkel[1]

ABSTRACT

Flaming Gorge National Recreation Area encompasses 207,363 acres of land and water that stretches from the north flank of the eastern Uinta Mountains of northeast Utah northward into the Green River Basin of southwestern Wyoming. Flaming Gorge was named for the vivid red Triassic rocks that rise above the water by Major John Wesley Powell during his historic boat trip down the Green and Colorado Rivers in 1869.

About 3 billion years of geologic history are showcased within the recreation area, from some of the oldest rocks in Utah to the classic faults and folds of the Laramide orogeny that uplifted the Uinta Mountains about 70 to 40 million years ago. Thirty-three formations that comprise about 72,000 feet of rock are exposed in east-trending bands that dip northward; the oldest rocks are exposed in the southern part of the recreation area and the bands of rock young to the north.

The oldest rocks in Flaming Gorge National Recreation Area are Precambrian (Archean through Middle Proterozoic) in age. These rocks include the 2.7 billion-year-old Owiyukuts Complex and the 2.4-1.7 billion-year-old Red Creek Quartzite. These formations, which are separated by about 2 billion years, represent multiple periods of metamorphism, continental accretion, uplift, and erosion. The 1.1-0.77 billion-year-old Uinta Mountain Group was deposited during a period of rifting. After deposition of the Uinta Mountain Group, a prolonged period—about 450 million years—of interspersed deposition and erosion occurred with erosion prevailing.

Rocks of Mississippian age were laid down on the unconformable (erosion) surface formed on the Uinta Mountain Group. Marine conditions dominated the rest of the Paleozoic with an interruption during Late Pennsylvanian to Early Permian time as the eolian Weber Sandstone was deposited.

Alternating shallow marine and continental formations, punctuated by several unconformities, characterize the early and middle Mesozoic Erathem. Colorful Triassic and Jurassic rocks exhibit shades of red, orange, green, gray, and purple that most everyone readily identifies with the red-rock country of Utah. Well-preserved sedimentary structures and fossils are common in many of these formations; the Jurassic Morrison Formation has been described as the "real" Jurassic Park because it contains a rich collection of dinosaur remains. The balance of the Mesozoic is dominated by yellowish-gray fluvial to shallow marine sandstone and gray marine shale deposited during Early and early Late Cretaceous time. Classic sedimentary structures and fossils are well preserved in this section, most notably the abundant fish scales found in the Mowry Shale. The uppermost Cretaceous rocks record the final withdrawal of seas from the area as the Uinta Mountains begin to rise and take form during the Laramide orogeny. As the Uinta Mountains rose along the Uinta and other faults during latest Cretaceous through early Tertiary time, Paleozoic and Mesozoic rocks were tilted steeply northward, folded into monoclines, and faulted. Thousands of feet of rock were eroded from the growing highlands and deposited as thick coarse-grained sandstone and conglomerate in a developing Green River Basin to the north.

The southern shore of a large lake, Lake Gosiute, lapped onto the north flank of the Uinta Mountains during early Tertiary time. Lake Gosiute covered much of southwestern Wyoming for nearly 20 million years and deposited the Eocene Green River Formation, which is known throughout the world for its well-preserved fossil fish remains. Most of the Wyoming sector of the recreation area consists of Green River Formation.

The landscape and drainage system of the Flaming Gorge area continued to change as the Gilbert Peak erosion surface formed in Oligocene time and was later tilted during Miocene extension of the Uinta Mountains. Relative uplift of the Colorado Plateau concurrent with Basin and Range extension began about 15 to 10 million years ago and rejuvenated the

---

[1]Utah Geological Survey, Salt Lake City, UT 84114-6100

upper Colorado River Basin, which caused active headward erosion of many rivers. Capture of the ancestral Green River by tributaries of the Colorado River system, within the past 5 million years, diverted its flow southward from near Green River, Wyoming, cutting a huge gorge through the Uintas, and ultimately reaching the Gulf of California.

INTRODUCTION

About 3 billion years ago, the area of what is now Flaming Gorge National Recreation Area (NRA) sat on the edge of an ancient continent that was located in the southern hemisphere. The landscape was likely stark and barren of visible life. Since then the landscape at Flaming Gorge has continually changed as a rift valley formed and was later inverted, oceans flooded and retreated several times, and mountains rose only to be eroded away and then reborn. Evidence of this changing landscape, along with the animals that flourished and died there, is preserved in the rocks that form the spectacular scenery of Flaming Gorge. Examples of shallow tropical marine environments, Saharan-type sand dune fields, and coastal environments are all exposed within the recreation area. Flaming Gorge National Recreation Area also contains examples of multiple episodes of deformation, dominated by the classic faults and folds associated with the Laramide orogeny.

Flaming Gorge National Recreation Area contains 207,363 acres of land and water, and is an excellent place to experience and learn about the Earth's geologic history

(figure 1). It includes Flaming Gorge Reservoir and the lands that surround it in northeastern Utah and southwestern Wyoming. The U.S. Congress created Flaming Gorge National Recreation Area on October 1, 1968 and gave administrative responsibilities to Ashley National Forest. However, the dam and related facilities are operated by the U.S. Bureau of Reclamation. The reservoir stretches about 91 miles from the dam to near Green River, Wyoming (figure 2).

The southern part of Flaming Gorge National Recreation Area is on the north flank of the eastern Uinta Mountains. The peaks in this part of the Uintas are generally below 10,000 feet in elevation, which is less than the high peaks of the western part, but are still impressive. Northward near the town of Manila, Utah, the land begins to flatten and the recreation area consists of broad valleys, rolling hills, and hogbacks that take on a badlands appearance typical of southwestern Wyoming.

The recreation area contains a network of paved, graveled, and dirt roads that allows vehicular access to many parts. A network of trails in the mountainous areas provides access to the more remote parts. Finally, Flaming Gorge Reservoir provides excellent access by boat through

Figure 1. Sheep Creek Bay as seen from an overlook along Utah Highway 44. The rocks exposed along the right shore are Permian Park City Formation (dipslopes). The rocks exposed left of the bay are Triassic Dinwoody Formation through the Jurassic Glen Canyon Sandstone. The gray rocks along the shore are Dinwoody, the red slopes consist of the Triassic Moenkopi and Chinle Formations, and the Glen Canyon Sandstone caps the ridge. View to the northeast.

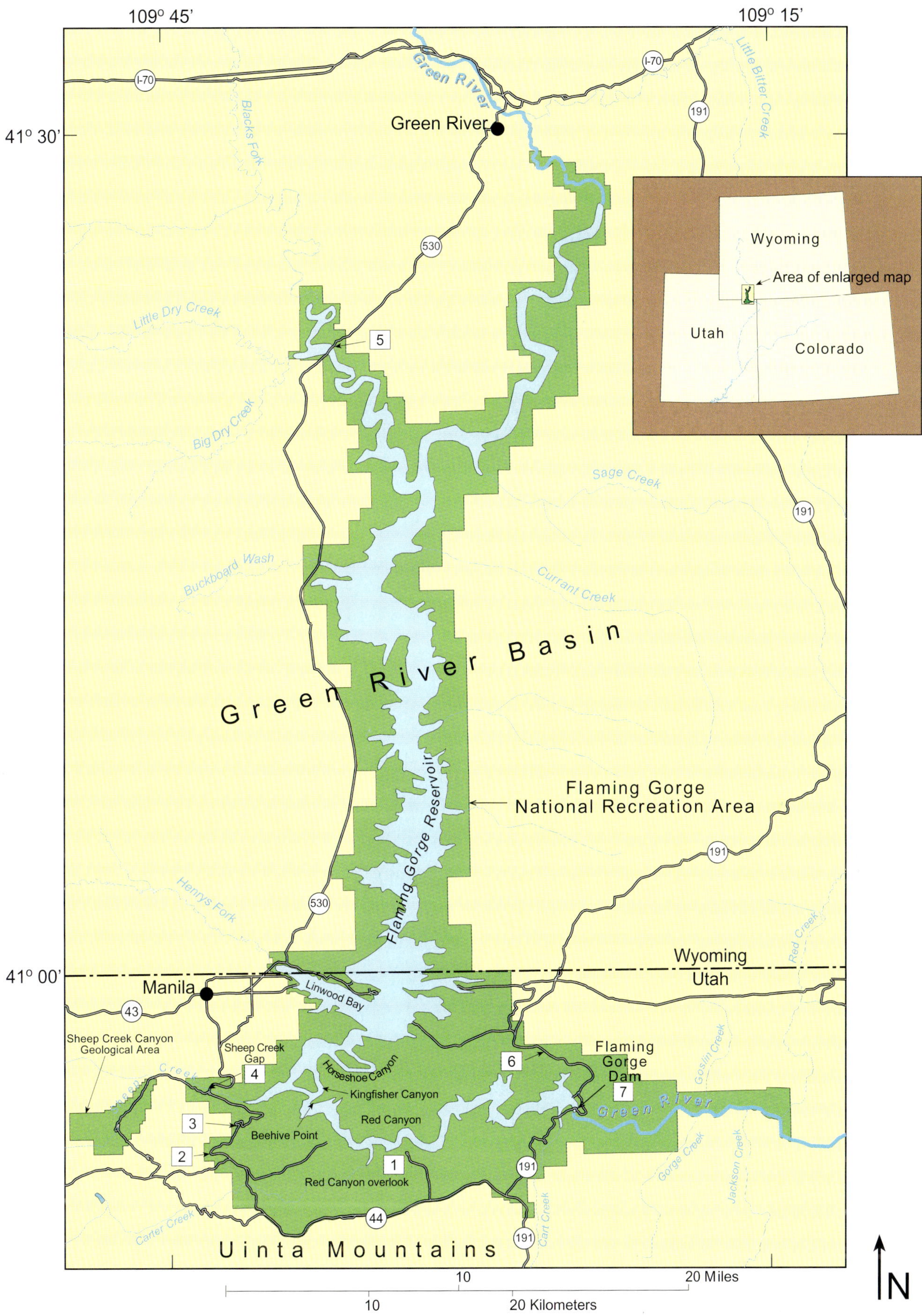

Figure 2. Index map of Flaming Gorge National Recreation Area, northeastern Utah and southwestern Wyoming. Key geographic features and classic geologic sites that are discussed in the article are shown on the map. Classic geologic sites are shown as numbers in boxes.

Figure 3. The entrance to Flaming Gorge. Major John Wesley Powell named the gorge for the brilliant red rocks that rise above the reservoir. The red rocks consist of the Triassic Moenkopi and Chinle Formations. The cliff that caps the ridge is the Glen Canyon Sandstone. Stratigraphically above (to the right) the Glen Canyon Sandstone are the Carmel, Entrada, and Curtis Formations as shown in the inset photograph. The rocks at the entrance to Flaming Gorge are sharply folded northward, presumably by a thrust fault in the subsurface that moved during the Laramide orogeny. Views of photographs are west (inset) and southwest.

the heart of the recreation area. Visitors are encouraged to consult detailed maps and Ashley National Forest personnel for road conditions and travel restrictions.

Several early investigations explored the vast western territories after the Civil War to describe the geology and other natural resources. Three of the four competing geological surveys visited the Flaming Gorge area and eastern Uinta Mountains between 1869 and 1875 (Hansen, 1975). These included the King survey in 1869 and 1871, the Hayden survey in 1870, and the Powell survey in 1869, 1871, 1874, and 1875—although Powell first visited the area in 1868. The geologic work of S.F. Emmons (1877), as part of the King survey, most completely described the geology of the Uinta Mountains; however, it was Powell's work (Powell, 1875, 1876) that most people remember because of his insightful geologic observations and his first-ever exploration of the Green and Colorado Rivers by boat (Hansen, 1975).

On May 24, 1869, Major John Wesley Powell and nine other men pushed off in four boats from the shore of the Green River near Green River, Wyoming, near the north end of the recreation area. Two days later, Powell and the others had floated to the entrance of Flaming Gorge (Powell, 1875).

> *It enters the range by a flaring, brilliant, red gorge that may be seen from the north more than a score of miles away…We name it Flaming Gorge.*
> Major John Wesley Powell, May 26, 1869

The "flaming colors" that impressed Major Powell belong to the Triassic formations that are currently mapped as the Moenkopi and the Chinle and not to the red quartzites of the Middle Proterozoic Uinta Mountain Group (figure 3). Powell (1875) also named many other geographic features, including Kingfisher Canyon, Beehive Point, and Swallow Canyon (Swallow Canyon is a few miles east of the recreation area along the Green River in Browns Park near the Colorado state line). Powell and his companions spent 10 days in what is now Flaming Gorge National Recreation Area exploring the Green River and its side canyons and surrounding peaks, making scientific measurements and describing the geology.

Since the Powell and the other two surveys, many more geological investigations stimulated by scientific curiosity and the search for minerals and petroleum have been conducted in and around the recreation area. A summary of the early geologic work can be found in Hansen (1965). The most comprehensive geologic work in the recreation area was conducted by Wallace Hansen prior to and during the construction of Flaming Gorge Dam.

THE ROCKS

Flaming Gorge National Recreation Area contains 33 exposed formations that regionally adds up to nearly 72,000 feet—almost 14 miles—of rock, representing more than one billion years of geologic history (figure 4). Fourteen known unconformities represent about two billion years of missing rocks.

The rocks within Flaming Gorge National Recreation Area are generally distributed in east-trending bands in which the oldest rocks crop out in the southern part of the recreation area and get younger towards the north (figure 5). However, the youngest rocks are exposed as patches in the mountainous southern and southeastern part of the recreation area. Most of the stratigraphic information is summarized from Hansen (1962, 1965, 1986), Hansen and Bonilla (1956), and Rowley and others (1985).

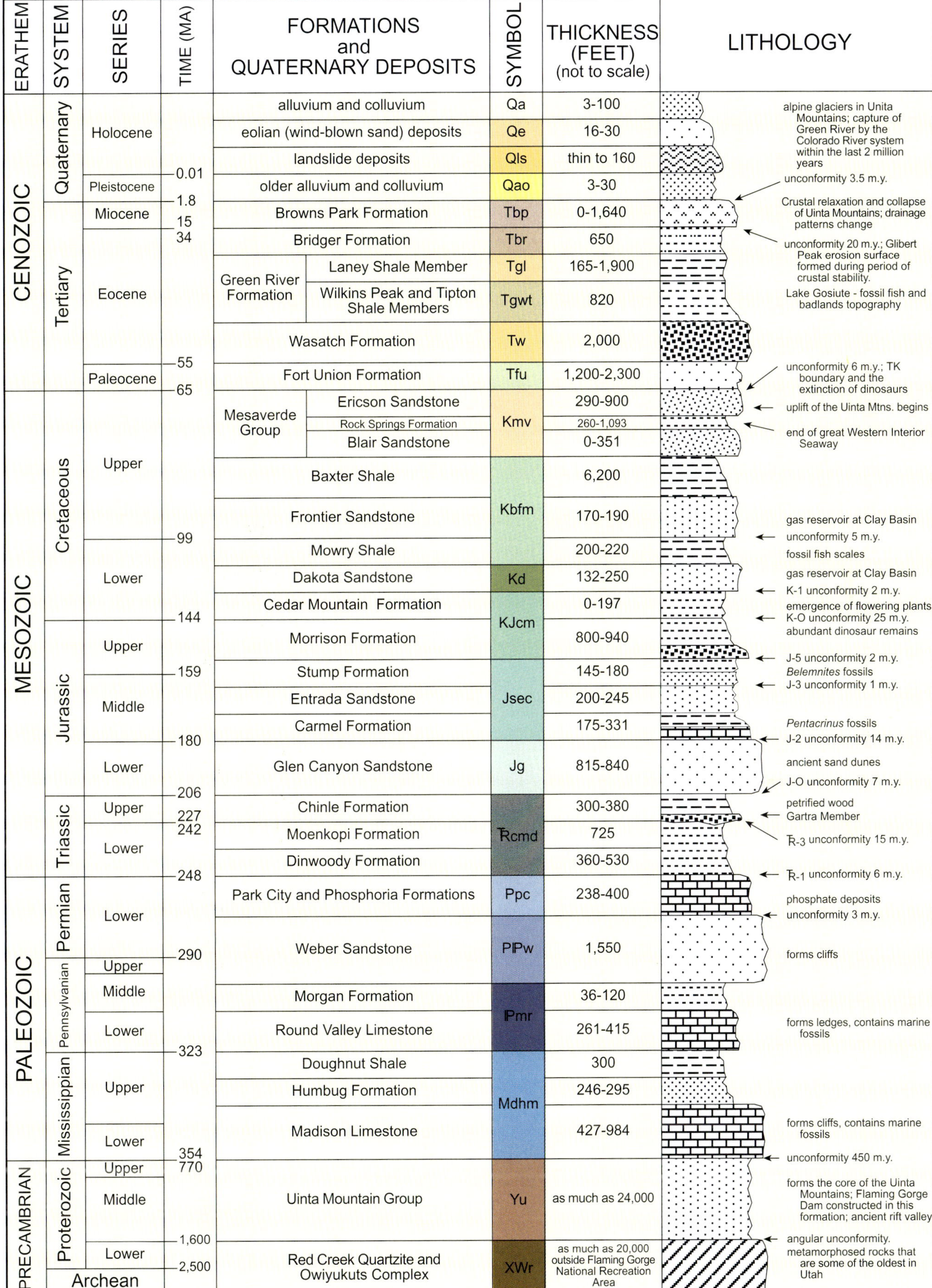

Figure 4. Stratigraphic column of rock formations and Quaternary deposits within Flaming Gorge National Recreation Area.

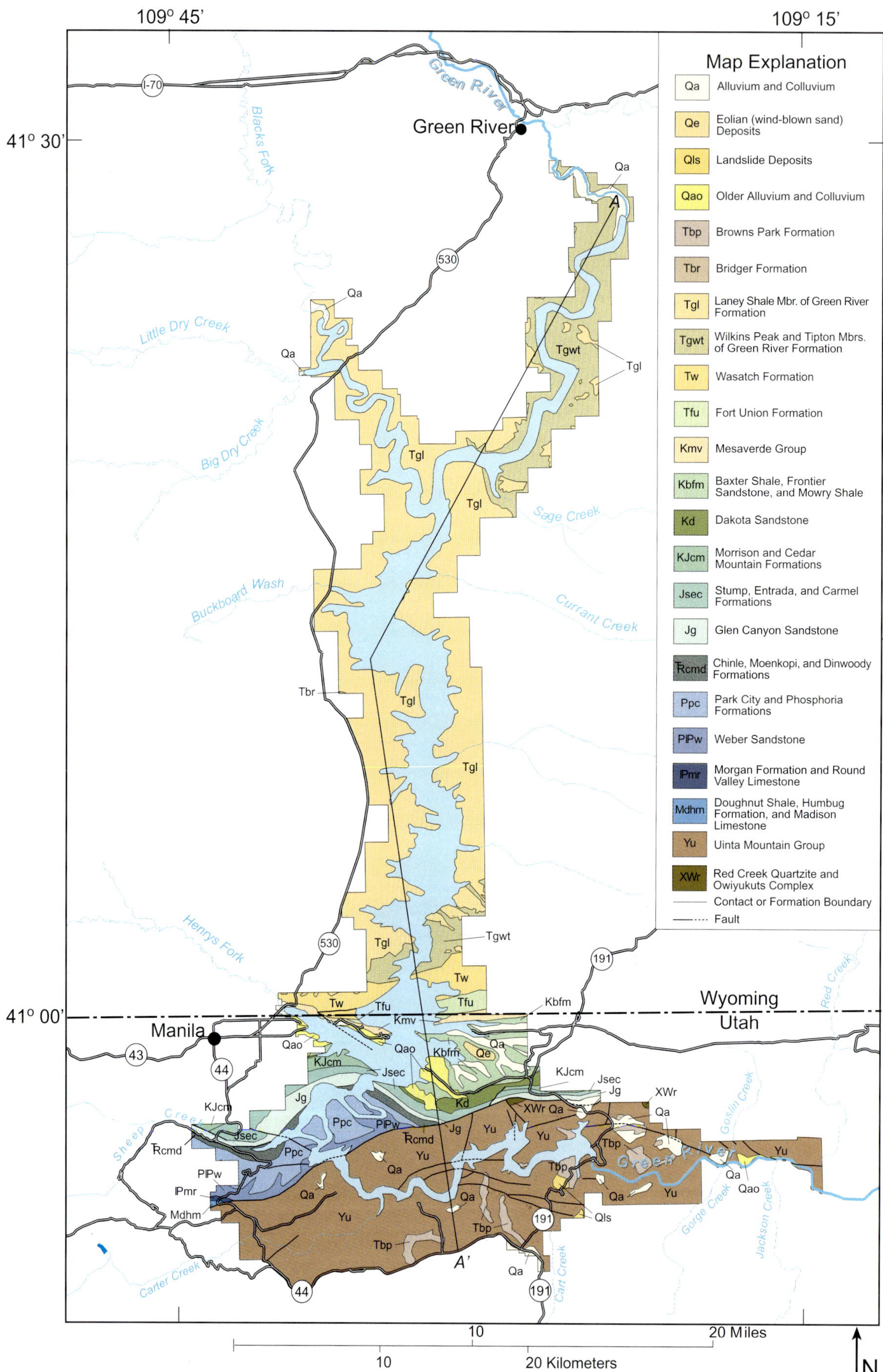

Figure 5. Generalized geologic map of Flaming Gorge National Recreation Area; created and modified from digital Geographic Information System (GIS) files of U.S. Geological Survey (1994) and Hintze and others (2000). Cross section A-A' shown on figure 8.

Archean to Lower Proterozoic Rocks

The oldest rocks in the recreation area, which are also some of the oldest rocks in Utah and possibly in the western United States, are the metamorphic rocks that comprise the Owiyukuts Complex and Red Creek Quartzite. Together these two formations are as much as 20,000 feet thick—although the entire thickness is not exposed in the Flaming Gorge area—and represent about one billion years of geologic history (Hansen, 1965; Sears and others, 1982).

The older unit in the recreation area, the high-grade gneiss of the Archean Owiyukuts Complex, is mostly exposed along the Uinta fault north of the reservoir. Outcrops are generally altered and brecciated and likely represent the upper part of the formation (Sears and others, 1982). The lower part of the Owiyukuts Complex crops out east and northeast of the recreation area in more extensive, yet isolated, structural blocks. Sears and others (1982) reported an age of 2.7 billion years for the Owiyukuts from outcrops in the O-wi-yu-kuts Mountains about 10 miles east of the recreation area, and suggested that the Owiyukuts Complex is part of an Archean-age continent called the Wyoming province. The contact with the overlying Red Creek Quartzite is unconformable; however, that surface later became a zone of ductile shearing before deposition of the Middle Proterozoic Uinta Mountain Group (Sears and others, 1982; Stone, 1993). Rocks of the Owiyukuts Complex were grouped with the Red Creek Quartzite on maps by Hansen (1965) and in this article (figures 5 and 6).

Like the Owiyukuts Complex, the Red Creek Quartzite is exposed in the same small outcrops along the Uinta fault (figure 6). Outcrops of the Red Creek Quartzite are also more extensive east and northeast of the recreation area. The Red Creek is a metamorphic unit that contains three main rock types: fine-grained and vitreous metaquartzite, quartz-muscovite schist, and amphibolite. The basal part of the formation has been altered to mylonite by ductile deformation along a fault zone (Sears and others, 1982). The balance of the formation is dominated by metaquartzite; however, amphibolite may be equally abundant (Hansen, 1965). Other minor rock types include marble and pegmatite. Prior to metamorphism, the Red Creek Quartzite consisted of sandstone, limestone, and other fine-grained sedimentary rocks that were deposited in a shallow marine environment offshore of the Archean continent (Hansen, 1965; Sears and others, 1982). The Red Creek Quartzite is late Archean to Early Proterozoic with a age of 2.4 to 1.7 billion years (Hansen, 1965; Sears and others, 1982).

Middle to Upper Proterozoic Rocks

The youngest of the Precambrian units is the Uinta Mountain Group, which forms the backbone of the Uinta Mountains and is the dominant formation in the southern part of Flaming Gorge National Recreation Area (figure 6).

It consists of mostly dark-red siliceous sandstone with abundant shale and conglomerate, all of which may have been subjected to metamorphism. The rocks of the Uinta Mountain Group form the impressive red cliffs of Red Canyon, along Carter Creek, and at Flaming Gorge Dam. The Uinta Mountain Group lies unconformably on the Red Creek Quartzite (figure 4). In general, the rocks of the Uinta Mountain Group dip less steeply than the rocks of the underlying Red Creek Quartzite (Hansen, 1965).

The Uinta Mountain Group was deposited in a rift valley that developed during Middle Proterozoic time. Great volumes of clastic sedimentary rocks (conglomerate, sandstone, siltstone, and mudstone) were deposited as rifting continued. Eventually more than 24,000 feet of rock was deposited in the rift valley. In the Flaming Gorge area, the Uinta Mountain Group consists of non-marine rocks that were deposited by alluvial and fluvial processes. To the west, however, the rift was submerged by ancient seas and marine rocks were deposited (Wallace, 1972; Sanderson, 1984, 1986). The Uinta Mountain Group is Middle and Late Proterozoic ranging in age from 1,100 to 770 million years (Crittenden and Peterman, 1975; Bressler, 1981).

Mississippian Rocks

The next youngest set of rocks exposed in Flaming Gorge National Recreation Area belongs to the Mississippian System. These rocks are separated from the Precambrian rocks by the Uinta fault (figure 6). However, the Mississippian-age rocks do rest unconformably on the Proterozoic Uinta Mountain Group not too far west of the recreation area near Sheep Creek. This unconformity represents about 550 to 450 million years of missing rock.

Mississippian rocks in the recreation area include the Madison Limestone, Humbug Formation, and Doughnut Shale (figure 4). These formations represent as much as 1,580 feet of rock originally deposited in an ocean about 30 million years ago. The Madison, Humbug, and Doughnut only crop out within the recreation area near the western boundary along the Uinta fault (figure 6). Excellent exposures of the formations and the Uinta fault are in a road cut along Utah Highway 44. There, the rocks are attenuated (structurally thinned) because of faulting; however, a complete section of these formations is exposed in the adjoining Sheep Creek Canyon Geological Area to the west (figure 2) (Hansen, 1965; Sprinkel and others, 2000).

Typically, the Madison Limestone is very thick bedded, gray limestone that forms resistant cliffs. The limestone contains light-gray chert and a few marine fossil beds. Solution cavities are common in the Madison in which ground water can find its way to the surface as springs. The age of the Madison Limestone is Early and Late Mississippian.

Conformably overlying the Madison is the Humbug Formation. It consists of light-gray to red sandstone, light-gray limestone, and red to black shale. The formation is generally soft and forms slopes with some resistant ledges. The Humbug is also a shallow marine unit that was likely

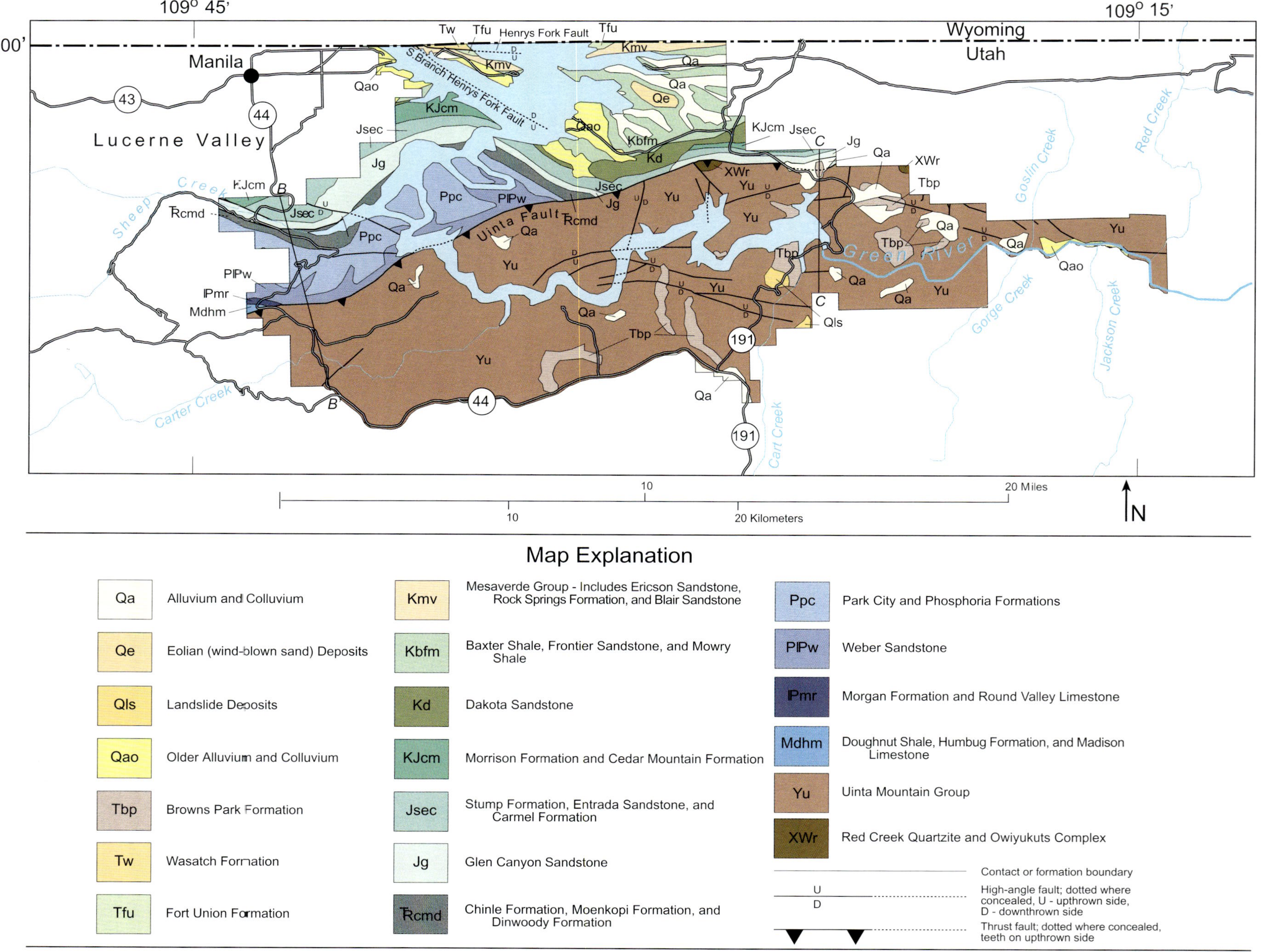

Figure 6. *Generalized geologic map of the Utah sector of the Flaming Gorge National Recreation Area; created and modified from digital Geographic Information System (GIS) files of U.S. Geological Survey (1994) and Hintze and others (2000). Cross sections B-B' and C-C' shown on figure 8.*

deposited in an intertidal zone. Intraformational breccias near the top of and karst in the Humbug indicate that the formation became exposed and was subjected to erosion prior to deposition of overlying units (Hansen, 1965).

The Doughnut Shale marks the top of the Mississippian System in the region. It consists of dark-gray shale with minor sandstone, limestone, and coal. The Doughnut is a soft unit that generally forms slopes. It is also a shallow marine unit; however, the coarse sandstone and thin coal beds indicate that part of the Humbug was deposited in a coastal environment. Diagnostic fossils collected from the Doughnut indicate a Late Mississippian age (Hansen, 1965).

Pennsylvanian Rocks

The rocks that represent the Pennsylvanian System include the Round Valley Limestone, Morgan Formation, and the lower part of the Weber Sandstone (figure 4). The Round Valley and Morgan Formations have a maximum thickness of about 535 feet. The Weber Sandstone spans the Pennsylvanian-Permian boundary and it will be discussed in the next section.

The Round Valley Limestone and Morgan Formation crops out near the western boundary of the recreation area along the Uinta fault (figures 5 and 6). Similar to the Mississippian rocks, these formations are best exposed in a road cut along Utah Highway 44. There, the rocks are likely attenuated (structurally thinned) because of faulting; however, a complete section of these two formations is well exposed in the adjoining Sheep Creek Canyon Geological Area to the west (Hansen, 1965; Sprinkel and others, 2000).

Typically, the Round Valley Limestone is light-gray, thin-bedded to very thick bedded limestone with some interbedded red shale. The limestone beds are resistant and form cliffs and ledges. The limestone beds also contain blue-gray and yellowish-gray chert, but may include pink or red jasperoid chert (Hansen, 1965). Fossil beds are common within the Round Valley and contain a variety of marine fossils such as brachiopods, echinoid spines, bryozoans, and mollusks (Hansen, 1965). The age of the Round Valley is Early and Middle Pennsylvanian.

The overlying Morgan Formation is a varicolored formation that consists of interbedded fine-grained sandstone, siltstone, fossiliferous and cherty limestone, and minor amounts of red shale. The formation is generally thin, less than 120 feet thick, and is often combined with the underlying Round Valley Limestone for mapping purposes. The contact between the Round Valley and the Morgan is placed above the thick limestone beds of the Round Valley and below the first appearance of significant quantities of clastic beds (Hansen, 1965). The age of the Morgan Formation is Middle Pennsylvanian.

Pennsylvanian and Permian Rocks

The Weber Sandstone is one of the most recognized formations in northeastern Utah. It forms the spectacularly steep sandstone cliffs at Split Mountain in Dinosaur National Monument (about 40 miles southeast from Flaming Gorge National Recreation Area) and the shear, massive-weathering, highly cross-bedded sandstone cliffs in the adjoining Sheep Creek Canyon Geological Area to the west. The Weber Sandstone is also a major oil and gas reservoir in the region making it an economically important formation. In Flaming Gorge National Recreation Area, the Weber Sandstone crops out parallel to the Uinta fault from about Utah Highway 44 northeastward across Flaming Gorge Reservoir (figure 6). Along the reservoir, the Weber Sandstone forms the highly cross-bedded cliffs of Beehive Point and the steep walls of Horseshoe Canyon (figures 2 and 6).

The Weber Sandstone is divided into a lower light-gray to yellowish-gray, thick-bedded sandstone with limestone interbeds and an upper light-yellowish-gray massive-weathering and highly cross-bedded sandstone (Hansen, 1965). The horizon that separates the lower and upper parts is subtle. It is placed where the rock type becomes exclusively sandstone and the outcrops change from the slightly darker, more angular ledges of the lower part to the lighter, more rounded ledges of the upper part. In addition, the lower part tends to be a little more resistant to erosion than the upper part because of the interbedded limestone. The Weber Sandstone generally forms steep cliffs. It is 1,550 feet thick.

The Weber Sandstone was deposited mostly in an eolian (wind-blown sand) environment, but the thin marine limestone beds in the lower Weber indicate it is transitional between marine and eolian conditions. The Weber Sandstone is Middle Pennsylvanian to Permian based on marine fossils, mainly corals and brachiopods, preserved in the limestone units in the lower part and foraminifera preserved near the top of the formation (Bissell and Childs, 1958; Bissell, 1964; Hansen, 1965).

Permian Rocks

The Park City and Phosphoria Formations represent the top of the Permian System in the area and are divided into three members: the lower Grandeur Member of the Park City Formation, the middle Meade Peak Phosphatic Tongue of the Phosphoria Formation, and the upper Franson Member of the Park City Formation (Hansen, 1965; Schell, 1969). The Meade Peak is an important economic unit in the area because it contains rich phosphate deposits (Schell and Dyni, 1973) and it is the source of oil produced from Weber Sandstone reservoirs (Maughan, 1984; Sprinkel and others, 1997). In the Flaming Gorge area, the Park City Formation crops out along Utah Highway 44 where the road descends steeply to Sheep Creek and along the southeast shore of Flaming Gorge Reservoir north of the Uinta fault (figure 6). In these areas, the Park City forms impressive flatirons and dip slopes.

Light-gray sandstone with some limestone and dolomite characterize the Grandeur Member. The Meade

Peak is easy to identify because of the dark-gray phosphatic shale beds. The Franson is dominantly a chert limestone and dolomite with interbedded sandstone. The limestone and dolomite beds are hard and protect the underlying softer rocks from erosion (Hansen, 1965).

Shallow marine conditions prevailed during the deposition of the Grandeur and Franson Members, and probably during deposition of the Meade Peak Member as sediments were circulated up from greater depths and deposited on the shelf (Maughan, 1984; Hintze, 1988). The age of the Park City and Phosphoria Formations is Early Permian (Hansen, 1965).

All of the rocks of Late Permian age are missing in the Flaming Gorge area. The contact separating the Park City Formation from the overlying Triassic Dinwoody Formation is the TR-1 unconformity. Pipiringos and O'Sullivan (1978) estimated the unconformity represents as much as 6 million years.

Triassic Rocks

Flaming Gorge's name is derived from the brilliant red Triassic rocks that rise above the reservoir just inside the entrance to the gorge. These Triassic rocks signal a change in the landscape and the animals at the beginning of the Mesozoic time. In Flaming Gorge National Recreation Area, the Triassic rocks form a narrow belt that extends from the western boundary along Sheep Creek northeastward to Flaming Gorge Reservoir, where much of the section is underwater. Near the entrance of Flaming Gorge, the outcrop belt swings southeastward to where the Uinta fault truncates the Triassic section (figure 6). These rocks have been mapped as the Dinwoody, Moenkopi, and Chinle Formations (Hansen, 1965), and those names are used in this article (figure 4). However, the Woodside and Ankareh Formations are correlative to the Moenkopi and Chinle Formations, respectively (Thomas and Krueger, 1946), and it may be appropriate to use the Woodside and Ankareh names for these rocks in Flaming Gorge National Recreation Area.

The Dinwoody Formation consists of light- to greenish-gray siltstone and shale with interbedded fine-grained sandstone, thin limestone, and stringers of gypsum. The Dinwoody is well exposed along Utah Highway 44 near Sheep Creek. Marine fossils are preserved in the Dinwoody; however, they are uncommon in the Flaming Gorge area (Hansen, 1965).

The Moenkopi Formation consists of mostly reddish-brown siltstone, shale, and fine-grained sandstone with local gypsum and limestone beds. It is well exposed along Sheep Creek (although attenuated by faulting) and above the shore of Flaming Gorge Reservoir (figure 6). The Moenkopi Formation signals the end of marine domination in the region, which was so prevalent during the Paleozoic. Although invertebrate fossils are rare in the Moenkopi (Hansen, 1965), phytosaur and amphibian tracks (as well as swim tracks) are preserved in Moenkopi beds south of Flaming Gorge at Red Fleet State Park

(Hamblin and others, 2000).

The Chinle Formation can be divided into two members, the basal Gartra Member and an overlying unnamed member. The Chinle is separated from the underlying Moenkopi by the TR-3 unconformity (Poole and Stewart, 1964; Hansen, 1965; Pipiringos and O'Sullivan, 1978). The Gartra Member consists of fluvial conglomeratic sandstone in which the bottom of the member is irregular, cuts into the underlying Moenkopi Formation, and commonly contains petrified wood fragments. The upper unnamed member consists of varicolored mudstone and siltstone of fluvial and lacustrine (lake) origin (Hansen, 1965). Cross-bedding, ripple marks, and desiccation cracks are sedimentary features commonly preserved in the Chinle Formation. In addition, dinosaur roamed the Chinle landscape. Dinosaur tracks have been reported at several locations in the region, and the remains of a phytosaur was found in Dinosaur National Monument (Hansen, 1965; Hamblin and others, 2000).

The age of the Dinwoody and Moenkopi Formations is Early Triassic. The Chinle is Late Triassic in age (Hansen, 1965). Pipiringos and O'Sullivan (1978) estimated that the TR-3 unconformity separating the Gartra from the underlying formation represents nearly 15 millions years of time.

Jurassic Rocks

Jurassic rocks are among the most scenic in Utah, from the shear red and white sandstone cliffs of the Navajo Sandstone that embrace Zion National Park to the world class dinosaur bone deposits of the Morrison Formation. Even Utah's centennial license plate displays Jurassic rocks in the rendition of Delicate Arch, an arch formed in the Entrada Sandstone and Curtis Formation in Arches National Park. The Jurassic rocks in Flaming Gorge National Recreation Area are no less spectacular.

Five formations comprise the Jurassic System in the Flaming Gorge area preserving about 60 millions years of alternating continental and marine deposits (figure 4). These rocks crop out from the western boundary of the recreation area near Sheep Creek northeastward to Linwood Bay (figures 2 and 6). From there, they swing southeastward forming the entrance gate to Flaming Gorge. The Jurassic outcrop belt continues southeastward to the Uinta fault, where the section is partly truncated (figure 6).

The Glen Canyon Sandstone is the foundation of the Jurassic section in the Flaming Gorge area. It is well exposed along Utah Highway 44 at Sheep Creek, where the road cuts through the massive sandstone hogback forming Sheep Creek Gap. It is a pink to light-brown, massive quartzitic sandstone (Hansen, 1965). Like its counterpart to the south—the Navajo Sandstone—large-scale cross-bedding is its signature characteristic. The Glen Canyon Sandstone is correlative to the Glen Canyon Group and Nugget Sandstone. The Glen Canyon Sandstone rests unconformably on the Triassic Chinle Formation. This surface is the J-0 unconformity, which Pipiringos and O'Sullivan (1978) believed represents at least seven million years. The top of the Glen Canyon Sandstone probably includes beds correlative to the Page Sandstone. Typically, the Page Sandstone is nearly identical to the underlying Glen Canyon Sandstone, but it can be separated from the Glen Canyon by a lag deposit of chert pebbles. The chert pebbles mark the base of the Page and identify the J-2 unconformity, which separates Lower Jurassic and Middle Jurassic rocks (Pipiringos and O'Sullivan, 1978). The road cut at Sheep Creek Gap beautifully displays the chert pebbles of the J-2 unconformity. For mapping purposes in the Flaming Gorge area, the Page Sandstone was included in the Glen Canyon Sandstone (Hansen, 1965).

The Glen Canyon Sandstone is a thick (as much as 840 feet) eolian sandstone deposited in a large dune field that covered parts of six states and was likely similar to the modern Sahara Desert. Ford and Gillman (2000) discuss the details of this extensive dune deposit. Fossils are rarely preserved in the Glen Canyon Sandstone; however, dinosaur tracks have been discovered near the top of the formation around Red Fleet Reservoir to the south (Hamblin and others, 2000), and Stokes (1991) described petrified wood in the correlative Navajo Sandstone. The age of the Glen Canyon Sandstone is Early Jurassic (Imlay, 1980).

The Carmel Formation is a colorful unit sandwiched between the light-colored beds of the underlying Glen Canyon and overlying Entrada Sandstones (figure 4). It includes a mixture of red, green, and gray siltstone, fine-grained sandstone, limestone, and calcareous mudstone (Hansen, 1965; Imlay, 1967). Significant amounts of bedded gypsum may also be present. Gray oolitic limestone and sandy shale are common lithologies of the lower Carmel, which grades upward to mostly red and green mudstone, siltstone, and interbedded gypsum. The lower limestone beds were deposited in an open, shallow marine environment that eventually gave way to more restricted marine conditions (tidal flat) indicated by the deposition of gypsum (Hansen, 1965; Imlay, 1980). The Carmel Formation is mostly a slope-forming unit; however, the limestone beds are resistant to erosion and form ledges. The well-dated age of the Carmel Formation is Middle Jurassic (Imlay, 1980).

The Entrada Sandstone conformably overlies the Carmel Formation (figure 4). In the Flaming Gorge area, it consists of lower massive-weathering light-gray to light-brown and yellow sandstone and an upper reddish-brown siltstone and fine-grained sandstone (Hansen, 1965). Large-scale cross-beds are common within the lower Entrada, owing to its eolian deposition. The upper Entrada is likely marine in origin because of grain size, planar bedding, and oscillation ripple marks (Hansen, 1965; Imlay, 1980). The lower Entrada Sandstone is resistant to erosion, forming massive cliffs typical of the exposures along Utah Highway 44 north of Sheep Creek Gap (Hansen, 1965). Some of the Quaternary eolian deposits may be derived from the upper part of the Entrada Sandstone. The Entrada Sandstone lacks fossils; however, the Middle Jurassic

age is assigned based on the bracketing age of the underlying Carmel Formation and overlying Stump Formation (Hansen, 1965; Imlay, 1980).

The Stump Formation records the last Jurassic sea that invaded Utah. Regionally, it is divided into two members, the lower Curtis Member and the upper Redwater Member (Pipiringos and Imlay, 1979). Near Manila, Utah, the Stump contains a lower gray shale and interbedded thin limestone and an upper gray limestone (Thomas and Krueger, 1946), which is unlike typical descriptions (Pipiringos and Imlay, 1979) of the members. Belemnites are commonly preserved in the sandstone beds of the Stump Formation. The Stump Formation is bounded by the J-3 unconformity at the bottom and the J-5 unconformity at the top. Internally, the J-4 unconformity separates the Middle Jurassic Curtis from the Upper Jurassic Redwater. Locally, at the J-4 unconformity, much of the Curtis Member has been removed by erosion (Pipiringos and O'Sullivan, 1978; Pipiringos and Imlay, 1979).

The Morrison Formation represents the top of the Jurassic System in Utah. It unconformably overlies the Stump Formation and unconformably underlies the Lower Cretaceous Cedar Mountain Formation (figure 4). The Morrison is a soft varicolored unit that contains shades of green, gray, and purple rocks of diverse lithologies. It consists mainly of bentonitic shale, claystone, and siltstone (Hansen, 1965). It is also locally interbedded with lenticular sandstone, grit, and limestone (Hansen, 1965). Most of the Morrison is poorly exposed within the recreation area because of its soft, non-resistant habit. An unusually good exposure of the Morrison is in Finch Draw, which is about a mile northwest of Flaming Gorge and near the west shore of Linwood Bay. Access to the outcrops is easiest by boat.

In 1909, Earl Douglass discovered dinosaur remains within the Morrison Formation about 40 miles south of Flaming Gorge near Jensen, Utah (Gregson and Chure, 2000). Since then dinosaur bones and tracks have been discovered within the Morrison in several locations in eastern Utah (Hintze, 1988; DeCourten, 1998). The Morrison Formation is now synonymous with dinosaurs and has been referred to as the "real" Jurassic Park (Gregson and Chure, 2000). In Flaming Gorge National Recreation Area, Hansen (1965) reported finding dinosaur bone fragments and some petrified wood. The Morrison is an Upper Jurassic non-marine formation deposited in a fluvial-lacustrine environment (Peterson, 1986; Peterson and Turner-Peterson, 1987).

Cretaceous Rocks

Cretaceous rocks within Flaming Gorge National Recreation Area include the Cedar Mountain Formation, Dakota Sandstone, Mowry Shale, Frontier Sandstone, Baxter Shale, and Mesaverde Group (figure 4). They consist mostly of alternating light-colored sandstone and thick gray shale with a basal varicolored mudstone. The basal Cretaceous unit, the Cedar Mountain Formation, is similar to the Morrison in color and lithology. The Cedar Mountain Formation is grouped with the Morrison because the lithologic similarities make selecting a contact to distinguish between the two formations difficult at best. The Cedar Mountain was deposited in a fluvial environment and is Early Cretaceous in age (Hansen, 1965; Rowley and others, 1985). In the recreation area, the Cretaceous sandstone formations (Dakota, Frontier, and Mesaverde) are generally resistant to erosion and form the subdued hills and prominent hogbacks along the north and south margins of Antelope Flat east of the reservoir (Hansen, 1962, 1965). The shale formations (Mowry and Baxter) are less resistant, generally poorly exposed, and form strike valleys.

The Dakota consists of medium- to coarse-grained sandstone separated by carbonaceous shale and coal (Hansen, 1965). The base of the Dakota is conglomeratic and is unconformable with the underlying Cedar Mountain Formation. The Dakota grades from fluvial to coastal marsh deposits and is Early Cretaceous in age (Hansen, 1965).

The Mowry is easy to identify. It is a dark-gray siliceous shale that typically weathers silver gray and contains abundant fossil fish scales. The Mowry is a marine deposit and is Early Cretaceous in age (Hansen, 1965).

The Frontier Sandstone is mostly light-brown to light-gray, fine-grained sandstone with minor coal beds. The formation also contains some petrified wood, invertebrate fossils, and was the preferred rock for petroglyphs made by ancient Native Americans (Hansen, 1965). The Frontier is mostly marine, although coastal marsh conditions existed for a period of time to deposit coal beds and preserve the petrified wood. The Frontier is Late Cretaceous in age (Hansen, 1965; Love and others, 1993).

The Baxter Shale is thick, gray carbonaceous shale with many fine-grained, rippled-marked sandstone beds. The Baxter was deposited in shallow marine conditions and is Late Cretaceous in age (Hansen, 1965; Love and others, 1993). Antelope Flat is underlain by alluvial- and eolian-covered Baxter Shale (Hansen, 1962, 1965).

The Glades, a prominent double hogback north of Antelope Flat and sometimes called the "Devils Racetrack," consists of the Mesaverde Group (Hansen, 1965). The Mesaverde Group is divided into three formations: the lower Blair Formation, the middle Rock Springs Formation, and the upper Ericson Sandstone (figure 4). The southern hogback is the Blair Formation. It consists of fine-grained sandstone with some interbedded marine shale (Hansen, 1965). The northern hogback is the Ericson Sandstone. It consists of coarse-grained sandstone and conglomerate (Hansen, 1965). The intervening strike valley is the less resistant Rock Springs Formation, which consists of fine-grained sandstone with carbonaceous shale and coal (Hansen, 1965). Together, these formations record the last time an ocean occupied the region and the beginning of Laramide-age Uinta Mountain uplift. The age of the Mesaverde Group is latest Cretaceous (Hansen, 1965).

Tertiary Rocks

Tertiary rocks exposed in Flaming Gorge National Recreation Area were deposited in a continental setting that began a little more than 65 million years ago and occurred during Paleocene, Eocene, and Miocene time. Sandstone, siltstone, mudstone, and shale are the principal rock types; however, significant amounts of conglomerate, claystone, and volcanic tuff beds are also preserved in the rock column. Tertiary units include the Fort Union, Wasatch, Green River, Bridger, and Browns Park Formations (figure 4).

The oldest Tertiary formation exposed in the recreation area is the Fort Union Formation. It crops out in an east-trending belt east of Manila, Utah, and north of The Glades near the Utah-Wyoming state line. The Fort Union Formation is light-gray to yellowish-gray sandstone, siltstone, and claystone (Hansen, 1965). The sandstone is lenticular, noncalcareous, and friable. Conglomerate beds are also common. These beds contain pebble fragments derived from Mesozoic formations that were eroded from the rising Uinta Mountains during the early stage of uplift (Hansen, 1965). The Fort Union rests unconformably on the Mesaverde Group in angular discordance. The Fort Union is nonmarine and was deposited under mostly fluvial conditions; however, some fine-grained beds are lacustrine in origin (Hansen, 1965). Fossils are rare in the Fort Union. However, fossil plant remains collected from beds north of The Glades provide a Paleocene age (Hansen, 1965).

The Wasatch Formation is lithologically varied and complex, and grades vertically and laterally into the fine-grained lacustrine Green River Formation (Bradley, 1961; Hansen, 1965). The Wasatch Formation is varicolored, ranging from shades of red to gray. It consists of conglomerate, sandstone, siltstone, and claystone. The conglomerate beds contain pebble- to boulder-size fragments of Paleozoic to Mesozoic rocks (Hansen, 1965). Mesozoic fragments derived from the Glen Canyon, Entrada, Morrison, Dakota, and Mowry Formations are more common in the lower beds. Paleozoic fragments derived from the Mississippian formations, Weber Sandstone, and Park City Formation are more common in the upper beds. In a few locations, rock fragments derived from the Middle Proterozoic Uinta Mountain Group are preserved in the Wasatch Formation (Hansen, 1965). The inverse stratigraphy reflected by the fragments in the Wasatch Formation records denuding of the Mesozoic and then Paleozoic formations off the rising Uinta Mountains. Furthermore, Uinta Mountain Group fragments indicate that the core of the Uinta Mountains was locally exposed to erosion (Hansen, 1965). The Wasatch Formation is mostly fluvial in origin. Fossils are generally uncommon in the Wasatch Formation within the recreation area; however, they have been collected from lacustrine interbeds that provide an Eocene age (Hansen, 1965; Love and others, 1993).

The Green River Formation is a soft, muddy unit that

in part weathers to badlands topography that is characteristic of southwest Wyoming. It consists of several members, many of which are separated by tongues of the Wasatch Formation (Bradley, 1961, 1964; Surdam and Stanley, 1980). Three members of the Green River Formation crop out in Flaming Gorge National Recreation Area (figure 5). These are the lower Tipton Tongue, the middle Wilkins Peak, and the upper Laney Shale Members (Bradley, 1961); however, the Tipton and Wilkins Peak Members are shown as one map unit (figures 4 and 5). The Tipton-Wilkins Peak unit crops out on both shores of Flaming Gorge Reservoir near the Utah-Wyoming state line and along the northeast arm of the reservoir in Wyoming (figure 5). The rest of the Wyoming sector of the recreation area is comprised of the Laney Shale Member (figure 5). All three members consist of shale, organic mudstone and marlstone, tuffaceous sandstone, limestone, and oil shale (Bradley, 1961, 1964; Hansen, 1965; Surdam and Stanley, 1980). Subtle differences in color and mixture of rock types distinguish one member from another. The Green River Formation was deposited in a large lake called Lake Gosiute (Bradley, 1964; Surdam and Stanley, 1980). Fossils are preserved in numerous zones within the Green River Formation. Petrified wood can also be found within the formation. Most fossils preserved in the Green River Formation are invertebrate fresh-water faunas, but extremely well-preserved fish skeletons are its signature fossil. The age of the Green River Formation is Eocene (Bradley, 1964; Hansen, 1965).

The Bridger Formation is a soft, banded formation and, like the Green River Formation, weathers to badlands topography that is typical of southwest Wyoming. It forms the unvegetated buttes and mesas west of Flaming Gorge Reservoir; only a small exposure of the Bridger Formation makes it into the recreation area. It is located along the western boundary of the recreation area south of Buckboard Wash (figure 5). The Bridger Formation is green, gray, and pink tuffaceous mudstone and gray, pink, and brown tuffaceous sandstone. Other rocks include shale, cherty limestone, and white tuff (Bradley, 1961; Hansen, 1965). Deposition of the Bridger Formation is contemporaneous with the lower Laney Shale Member of the Green River along the margins of Lake Gosiute; but as deposition continued, the Bridger eventually filled and covered the Green River Basin (Hansen, 1965). The Bridger Formation is Eocene in age.

A sustained period of erosion followed deposition of the Bridger Formation and broad pediments were cut across the landscape. The most extensive was the Gilbert Peak erosion surface. Remnants of the Gilbert Peak erosion surface are preserved in the recreation area and can be easily seen on Bear Mountain, the Red Caynon overlook, and Dutch John Bench (Hansen, 1986). The Bishop Conglomerate, which is not preserved in the recreation area, probably began to accumulate soon after the surface formed (Hansen, 1986). Radiometric potassium-argon ages of about 29 million years were obtained from biotite

and hornblende crystals, which dates the Bishop Conglomerate and the Gilbert Peak erosion surface as Oligocene (Hansen, 1986).

The Browns Park Formation is well exposed just east of Flaming Gorge National Recreation Area in Browns Park—the area for which the formation was named. In the recreation area, isolated outcrops are preserved near Flaming Gorge Dam, on Dutch John Bench just northeast of the dam, and in areas south of the dam (figure 6). In general, the Browns Park Formation is a heterogeneous mix of rock types, colors, and origins. In the recreation area, it consists of sandstone, conglomerate, and air-fall tuff (Hansen, 1986). These beds are moderately to well cemented; however, some beds within the Browns Park Formation are so poorly cemented that they can be readily crushed by hand (Hansen, 1986). In some areas of the eastern Uinta Mountains, Browns Park deposition probably began soon after the Bishop Conglomerate was deposited with no significant time gap; however, in most places, including the recreation area, millions of years likely passed before the Browns Park was deposited (Hansen, 1986). The variety of rock types is due to the varying environmental settings in which the formation was deposited. Most of the formation is fluvial in origin, but it also contains alluvial-fan, eolian, and lacustrine deposits. Several radiometric ages have been obtained from the ash beds using potassium-argon and fission track methods. These range from about 25 to 10 million years, but the rocks are probably no older than 15 million years based on physiographic constraints (Hansen, 1986). Thus, the Browns Park Formation is Miocene in age.

Quaternary Deposits

Alluvium and colluvium are the most common Quaternary deposits in the recreation area. They consist of silt, sand, gravel, and boulders deposited in and along streams, in alluvial fans, and on slopes. Pleistocene alluvium includes several levels of unconsolidated bench deposits that lie above modern drainages (Hansen, 1965). The benches formed during successive periods of alluvial deposition and stream entrenchment. Holocene alluvium includes all unconsolidated deposits in and along modern drainages. Normally the deposition of Holocene alluvium is uneventful; however, these depositional processes can be destructive and deadly during periods of flooding triggered by rapid snowmelt, sustained rainfall, or locally intense heavy rainfall (cloudbursts).

Eolian deposits consist of unconsolidated sand and silt derived from soft-sandstone-bearing formations and from reworked Quaternary deposits. The most extensive eolian deposit is on Antelope Flat east of Flaming Gorge Reservoir (figure 6). The eolian deposits have likely accumulated in Flaming Gorge National Recreation Area during the past 10,000 years; however, eolian deposits in many areas of Utah can be older. Thus, eolian deposits in the recreation area are shown as Holocene in age, but parts of these deposits may be as old as Pleistocene.

Landslide deposits include slope failures, rock falls, and talus. These deposits can be small, covering a few hundred square feet, to large deposits that cover several square miles. All can be destructive and deadly. Only the larger of these deposits are depicted on the accompanying geologic maps (figures 5 and 6). Clay-bearing formations such as the Morrison, Baxter, and Browns Park, as well as unconsolidated deposits, are susceptible to failure where present on steep slopes. Slope failures are commonly triggered when these susceptible formations become too saturated or they become oversteepened either by natural processes or by human meddling. Most landslide deposits are Holocene in age, but some may be as old as Pleistocene.

STRUCTURE

The rocks in Flaming Gorge National Recreation Area have been bent, broken, and tilted during periods of mountain building and basin formation. Some rocks have been deformed many times since their deposition. The oldest structural features are in the Precambrian section and formed more than a billion years ago, and the youngest structural features formed within the Browns Park Formation in the past two million years. However, the dominant set of structural features exposed in Flaming Gorge National Recreation Area was created by the uplift of the Uinta Mountains during the Laramide orogeny about 70 to 40 million years ago (latest Cretaceous to latest Eocene time).

The oldest structural features in the eastern Uinta Mountains include faults, folds, lineations, and an array of metamorphic features in the Owiyukuts Complex and Red Creek Quartzite. Nearly all of the features lie outside of the recreation area where the Owiyukuts Complex and Red Creek Quartzite outcrops are more extensive. Regional metamorphism caused gneissic banding, foliation, schistosity, and other related features within the Owiyukuts Complex and Red Creek Quartzite (Hansen, 1965; Sears and others, 1982). Part of a Red Creek Quartzite exposure less than five miles northeast of Flaming Gorge Dam (figure 6) may be the only place in the recreation area where schistosity and foliation can be viewed.

The region contains faults and associated folds that deformed only Precambrian rocks. Some of these faults and folds formed prior to deposition of the Uinta Mountain Group and were associated with mountain building that fringed the Wyoming province (Sears and others, 1982). The faults juxtapose rocks of the Owiyukuts Complex against rocks of the Red Creek Quartzite, but do not cut the overlying Uinta Mountain Group (Hansen, 1965; Sears and others, 1982). In addition, reconstruction of the Owiyukuts Complex-Red Creek Quartzite stratigraphic section shows an estimated 13,000 to 23,000 feet of relative uplift of some of the blocks before the Uinta Mountain Group was deposited (Sears and others, 1982). Also associated with this relative uplift, is a mylonite zone that was formed by ductile shearing along a fault zone, called the Cheyenne suture zone, that separates the Owiyukuts Complex from the Red Creek Quartzite (Sears and others, 1982; Stone, 1993).

Other faults, such as the Goslin, Bender, Beaver Creek, and many unnamed faults, juxtapose the Uinta Mountain Group against the older Precambrian rocks (Hansen, 1965). These faults were reported by Hansen (1965) as high- and low-angle overthrusts that clearly predate the Laramide orogeny and may have a Precambrian origin associated with rifting. In addition, Hansen (1965) reported that faults that cut the Browns Park Formation or cut only the Uinta Mountain Group may also have a Precambrian ancestry. The Uinta fault is a Laramide structure; however, it too may have originally formed in Precambrian time as the north-bounding fault of the Middle Proterozoic rift (Bruhn and others, 1986; Stone, 1993).

The Laramide orogeny created the structural features that deformed the bedrock and set the stage for the spectacular landscape seen throughout Flaming Gorge National Recreation Area. The dominant Laramide structures in the Flaming Gorge region are the Uinta arch and related Uinta fault zone. The Uinta arch is a great asymmetrical fold that has an axial length of about 160 miles, an average width of 30 miles, and generally coincides with the Uinta Mountains (Hansen, 1965). The rocks on the north flank dip more steeply than the rocks on the south flank giving the fold its asymmetry (Hansen, 1965). As Hansen (1965) pointed out, the Uinta arch consists of two domes that are aligned east-west and separated by a shallow structural swale. The swale is crossed by U.S. Highway 191-Utah Highway 44 from Vernal to Manila, Utah. The Uinta arch is bounded on the north by the steeply dipping faults of the North Flank-Uinta-Sparks fault zone and on the south by the South Flank-Willow Creek fault zone (Hansen, 1965; Ritzma, 1969; Bruhn and others, 1986; Bryant, 1990; Stone, 1993; Gregson and Chure, 2000).

Flaming Gorge National Recreation Area lies on the north flank of the Uinta arch. Consequently, all of the rocks dip generally northward and increase in north dip as they approach the Uinta fault zone (Hansen, 1965). Local folds, however, have modified dips and alter the regional strike of the beds. The Uinta fault zone cuts through the southern part of the recreation area (figure 6). A great thickness of Middle Proterozoic Uinta Mountain Group was uplifted from the south along the fault and placed on Mississippian and Pennsylvanian rocks near the western boundary of the recreation area along Utah Highway 44 (figures 6 and 7), on Pennsylvanian-Permian Weber Sandstone along the reservoir south of Beehive Point, and on Jurassic Glen Canyon Sandstone along U.S. Highway 191 a few miles north of the dam (figures 6 and 8). Still farther east and outside of the recreation area, the Uinta fault placed Uinta Mountain Group on Eocene Wasatch Formation (Hansen, 1965). Hansen (1965) estimated as much as 34,000 feet of stratigraphic throw along the Uinta fault zone.

Figure 7. Uinta fault zone along Utah Highway 44 placed red Middle Proterozoic Uinta Mountain Group, on the left, up next to gray Mississippian rocks, on the right. The fault zone dips south. The Uinta fault may have originally formed during Middle Proterozoic rifting about 1.5 billion years ago, near the northern margin of the rift valley. Rock relations preserved in the road cut indicate reverse movement that occurred during the Laramide orogeny between 70 and 40 million years ago. Middle to late Miocene collapse of the Uinta Mountains may have produced movement along the Uinta fault in the opposite (normal) sense. View is to the west.

Subsidiary, steeply dipping faults are exposed north of the Uinta fault zone, including an unnamed set of faults along lower Sheep Creek Canyon and the Henrys Fork fault zone (figure 6). Both sets of faults cut younger rock and have much less stratigraphic throw than the Uinta fault. In the lower Sheep Creek Canyon area one fault placed the Triassic Moenkopi Formation over the Jurassic Glen Canyon Sandstone and the other fault placed Lower to Middle Jurassic rocks over Upper Jurassic rocks (Hansen and Bonilla, 1956; Hansen, 1965). The Henrys Fork fault zone consists of two branches (figure 6). The south branch is submerged under Linwood Bay, but just outside of the recreation area it is within the Cretaceous Baxter Shale (Hansen, 1965). The north branch of the Henrys Fork fault is exposed on the peninsula north of Linwood Bay. There, it placed rocks of the Upper Cretaceous Mesaverde Group over the Paleocene Wasatch Formation (Hansen, 1962, 1965).

Uplift of the Uinta Mountains along the Uinta and subsidiary faults created impressive monoclines and drag folds on the hanging wall, and asymmetrical to overturned synclines on the footwall during uplift of the Uinta Mountains. The north flank monocline is well expressed in the Park City Formation along Sheep Creek Canyon (figure 9).

Normal faults that displace and warp the Gilbert Peak erosion surface and Browns Park Formation are the youngest structural features in Flaming Gorge National Recreation Area. Most of the normal faults are concentrated in the southeastern part of the recreation area south of the Uinta fault zone (figure 6). The faults are steeply dipping, generally east-trending, and are mostly downthrown on the south or west side. Fault movement probably began in late Tertiary (Miocene) time—perhaps as early as middle Tertiary (Oligocene), and there is no evidence to suggest that these faults have moved in the Quaternary (Hansen, 1965). However, many of these faults may have a history of movement that predates the middle to late Tertiary movement (Hansen, 1965).

GEOLOGIC HISTORY

About 3 billion years of geologic history unfolds in Flaming Gorge National Recreation Area. The geologic history begins in the mountainous southern part of the recreation area where the oldest rocks are exposed. A traverse from there northward passes through younger and younger rocks, revealing a rich history of shallow oceans teeming with life, ancient river systems, vast sand dune fields, and an extensive lake. The most recent chapter in the recreation area's geologic history requires a return to the southern mountainous part where it all began.

The story begins with the Archean Owiyukuts Complex. The early history of this formation is uncertain, because it has been subjected to multiple periods of deformation and high-grade metamorphism. We do believe, however, that the rocks of the Owiyukuts Complex were deformed and metamorphosed between 2.7 and 2.5 billion years ago (most likely about 2.6 billion years ago) as they became part of the southern margin of the newly assembled Archean-age Wyoming province (Hansen, 1965; Sears and others, 1982).

Marine sediments accumulated offshore from the Archean Wyoming province, and eventually became the Red Creek Quartzite. Deposition of the Red Creek Quartzite was followed by high-grade metamorphism and deformation that began about 2.4 billion years ago and spanned about 700 million years (Hansen, 1965; Sears and others, 1982). Compressional deformation about 1.7 billion years ago thrusted the Red Creek northward against the Owiyukuts Complex (the Wyoming province) by ductile shearing along the Cheyenne suture zone (Sears and others, 1982; Stone, 1993). Subsequent block faulting uplifted the Red Creek Quartzite as much as 23,000 feet. Erosion reduced the Red Creek highlands to rolling hills prior to rifting and deposition of the Uinta Mountain Group (Hansen, 1965).

Collapse of part of the continent along a long linear rift zone approximately 30 miles wide began about 1.5 billion years ago (Hansen, 1965; Sears and others, 1982; Stone, 1993). In the Flaming Gorge area, fluvial sediments of the Middle and upper Proterozoic Uinta Mountain Group accumulated in the rift, and by the time rifting ended about 770 million years ago, more than 24,000 feet of rock was deposited (Hansen, 1965). Uplift followed rifting, which tilted and eroded the Uinta Mountains.

The Flaming Gorge area was at or just above sea level during much of early Paleozoic time. However, there is no record of Cambrian through Devonian rocks, and any sed-

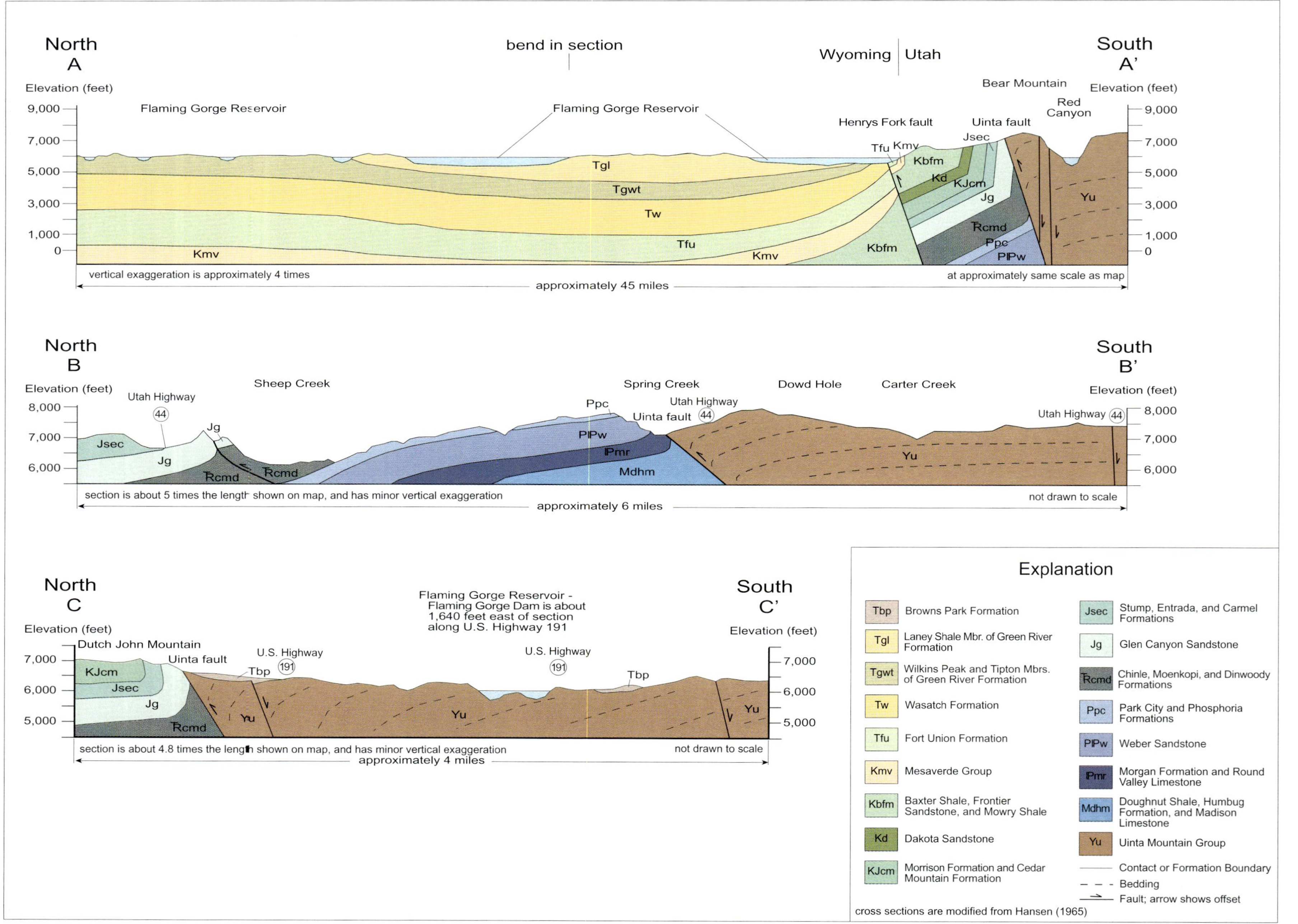

Figure 8. Simplified geologic cross sections showing the major structural features of Flaming Gorge National Recreation Area. Cross section line A-A' is shown on figure 5 and traverses the length of the recreation area. Cross section lines B-B' and C-C' are shown on figure 6. All sections were modified from Hansen (1965). Note that vertical exaggeration makes fault and bedding dips appear to dip steeper than they actually are.

Figure 9. *The north flank monocline is expressed in the rocks of the Permian Franson Member of the Park City Formation that increase dip northward towards lower Sheep Creek Canyon. The monocline formed by movement along the Uinta fault zone during the Laramide orogeny between 70 and 40 million years ago. View is to the west from a spot along Utah Highway 44 below the Sheep Creek Bay overlook.*

iments that were deposited (and lithified) in the Flaming Gorge area during that time were removed by erosion before Mississippian sedimentation began. Mississippian-age seas substantially flooded the region beginning about 354 million years ago. Sea level fluctuated throughout the remaining Paleozoic time and created two shallowing-up sequences. The first sequence includes the Madison-Humbug-Doughnut Formations. The shallow marine environment of the Madison Limestone was ideal for carbonate deposition, and animals such as brachiopods, crinoids, and corals flourished. As the seas became shallower, the Humbug and Doughnut Formations were deposited closer to shore; there was even a time when rocks of the Doughnut were deposited within a coastal marsh environment. The second shallowing-up sequence includes the Round Valley-Morgan-Weber Formations. The seas again became deeper during Round Valley Limestone time in which limestone deposition returned and marine life flourished. As before, sea level dropped, but this time the seas withdrew from the region and eolian conditions prevailed during deposition of the Weber Sandstone. The end of the Paleozoic saw the return of shallow marine conditions.

Sea level significantly dropped worldwide in the latter part of the Permian (Hintze, 1988). Consequently, Upper Permian rocks are not preserved in the Flaming Gorge area, as well as in much of Utah. In addition, an uncon-

formity (TR-1) separates Lower Permian rocks from the overlying Lower Triassic rocks, and represents about 6 millions years of missing time.

The Flaming Gorge region remained at or near sea level during much of the Mesozoic Era, a time of alternating marine and continental deposition. Early Triassic time began with marine deposition of the Dinwoody Formation. That gave way to a mostly nonmarine environment that was dominated by broad fluvial plains of the Moenkopi Formation. Early Triassic time also heralded the appearance of early dinosaurs in the region. A 15-million-year hiatus (TR-3 unconformity) separates the Moenkopi and overlying Chinle Formation (Pipiringos and O'Sullivan, 1978). The basal Chinle Formation—Gartra Member—signaled a return of fluvial deposition. The Gartra consists of coarse fluvial-channel deposits that are deeply incised into the underlying Moenkopi Formation. The formation typically contains petrified wood.

Another hiatus created the J-0 unconformity in which about 7 million years passed between deposition of the fluvial Chinle Formation and the great sand dune desert of the Lower Jurassic Glen Canyon Sandstone (Pipiringos and O'Sullivan, 1978; Imlay, 1980). Conditions similar to the modern Sahara Desert existed for about 25 million years and deposited more than 800 feet of sand before the ocean again flooded the region. The Carmel Formation represents a time of shallow marine to tidal flat deposition.

Clams, crinoids, and oolites are preserved within the lower limestone beds, indicating shallow marine conditions. Gypsum and fine-grained sand, silt, and shale—along with sedimentary features—indicate tidal flat conditions prevailed during much of the later part of Carmel time. The Middle Jurassic Carmel sea continued to retreat and dust blew from the newly exposed seabed and dried tidal flat areas; sand dunes again drifted across the region and deposited the Entrada Sandstone. The end of the Middle Jurassic and beginning of the Late Jurassic marked a time when the sea returned and deposited the Stump Formation. The Stump was deposited in a nearshore to shallow marine environment that teemed with life. Belemnites are commonly preserved in the sandstone beds. A brief hiatus within the Stump interrupted marine deposition for about one million years and created the J-4 unconformity (Pipiringos and O'Sullivan, 1978; Pipiringos and Imlay, 1979). The last Jurassic unconformity, the J-5, formed on a surface that separates the Stump from the overlying Morrison Formation (Pipiringos and O'Sullivan, 1978). Although the time between deposition of the two formations was brief, the depositional environments on either side of the unconformity are contrasting. The Morrison Formation was dominated by fluvial and lacustrine (rivers and lakes) environments (Hansen, 1965). Land animals, including a variety of dinosaurs, populated the Morrison landscape; some geologists and paleontologists refer to the Morrison as the "real" Jurassic Park (Gregson and Chure, 2000). It probably was a great time to be a dinosaur and alive in this region.

Fluvial and lacustrine conditions continued in Early Cretaceous time with the deposition of the Cedar Mountain Formation. The Cedar Mountain is a fluvial and lacustrine unit that contains dinosaur remains and the fossil pollen of the first flowering plants, angiosperms (Kemp, 1968; Tschudy and others, 1984; Kirkland and others, 1999; Sprinkel and others, 1999). Depositional patterns began to change during Dakota Sandstone time. The Dakota records the transition from fluvial deposition to coastal marsh as the great Cretaceous Western Interior Seaway began to flood the region. By the time the Mowry Shale was deposited, the region was fully submerged by the Cretaceous sea and abundant schools of fish probably swam in its waters. A profusion of fish scales is preserved in the Mowry, which attests to the fish population about 100 million years ago. For about 25 million years (Mowry to Mesaverde Formations), the Cretaceous seaway dominated the landscape. By the end of Mesaverde deposition, however, the landscape had changed again. This region that had hovered around sea level since Mississippian time—being submerged for most of the Paleozoic, part of the Jurassic, and most of the Cretaceous—started to rise (Hintze, 1988). The Cretaceous seabed was warped upward in latest Cretaceous time, causing the sea to retreat and the seabed to reach the surface. Uplift would be so complete that the region would never be inundated by the sea again. The mountain building event of the Laramide

orogeny had begun!

The Laramide orogeny was responsible for raising the Uinta Mountains from the sea. Its intermittent, yet persistent, deformation for about 30 million years folded and faulted the rocks (Hansen, 1965). A basin (Green River Basin) formed north of the rising highlands and caught the debris shed off of the Uinta Mountains. This debris lithified forming part of the Late Cretaceous Ericson Sandstone and the Paleocene Fort Union Formation. A regional angular uniformity at the base of the Fort Union Formation records the intermittent nature of movement along the Uinta fault zone that cumulatively displaced 34,000 feet of rock (Hansen, 1965). The coarse- to fine-grained Paleocene Wasatch Formation was also the product of material shed off the Uintas and reworked into the adjacent Green River Basin. By the end of the Paleocene, however, a brackish to saline lake—Lake Gosiute—formed and flooded the Green River Basin, depositing the Green River Formation. Throughout the late Wasatch Formation and early Green River Formation history, a dance of dominance was played out between the two formations. Synorogenic deposits that were typical of the Wasatch Formation were able to push the lake margin northward during periods of uplift and possible climatic change; but periods of tectonic quiescence or basin subsidence, and a possible wetter climate, allowed the Green River Formation to flood southward covering the Wasatch beds (Bradley, 1964; Hansen, 1965). Ultimately the Green River won. A similar dance of dominance played out between the upper Green River Formation and the lower Bridger Formation of middle Eocene age This time the Green River lost and Lake Gosiute eventually dried up about 45 to 44 million years ago (Bradley, 1964; Mauger, 1977).

Crustal stability replaced basin subsidence and uplift of the Uinta Mountains about 30 million years ago (Hansen, 1986). Consequently, an extensive pediment called the Gilbert Peak erosion surface developed across the flanks of the highland leaving only the higher parts of the range above the surface. The Bishop Conglomerate was deposited on the Gilbert Peak erosion surface; however, the Bishop does not crop out in Flaming Gorge National Recreation Area. In addition, a radial drainage system developed on the mountain range that crossed the Gilbert Peak surface and Bishop Conglomerate. In the Flaming Gorge region, the streams likely flowed north into the Green River Basin and to the ancestral Green River, which likely flowed eastward to the North Platte River (Hansen, 1986; Stokes, 1986).

Regional deformation resumed in early Miocene time, but this time the region was subjected to extension instead of compression. Collapse of the eastern Uinta Mountains along the Uinta fault zone tilted the range north and warped and faulted the Gilbert Peak erosion surface (Hansen, 1986). The radial drainage system was also altered by the lowering of the eastern Uinta Mountains. A new east-trending drainage developed along the former crest of the Uinta Mountains and bifurcated the north-flowing streams, causing a reversal of flow of the streams north of the newly formed river (Hansen, 1986). Soon after the initial lowering and tilting of the eastern Uintas, the Browns Park Formation was deposited on the deformed Gilbert Peak erosion surface and filled in the newly created low areas. Initial folding of the Browns Park Formation was likely caused by compaction, but continued downward movement and tilting of the eastern Uinta Mountains enhanced the folds and faulted the Browns Park Formation (Hansen, 1986).

As Basin and Range extension continued in the middle Miocene, relative regional uplift of the Colorado Plateau rejuvenated rivers and streams to the south of the Uintas, and caused vigorous northward headward erosion (Stokes, 1986). Ultimately, the ancestral Green River was captured by the Colorado River system (Hansen, 1986; Stokes, 1986). The exact cause and timing of capture of the Green River is speculative. The discussion below is largely summarized from the concepts presented by Hansen (1986).

Persistent headward erosion from the south by a tributary (the future Green River) of the Colorado River captured parts of the eastern Uinta drainage system (Hansen, 1986). Capture by the Colorado River system of the east-trending drainage that flowed through Flaming Gorge and Red Canyon to Browns Park took place at Lodore Canyon in western Colorado about 35 miles southeast of Flaming Gorge Dam. The cause and timing of capture at Lodore Canyon is speculative. Expanding on the work by Sears (1924), Bradley (1936) suggested that headward erosion by a small vigorous stream captured the stream that flowed eastward through Browns Park at Lodore Canyon and diverted it southward. Hansen (1986), on the other hand, believed that the stream in Browns Park ponded and filled the valley with sediments. Ultimately, this caused water to overtop the valley rim at Lodore Canyon and spill its contents southward, possibly taking advantage of a small pre-existing drainage. Whatever the cause for capture, this drainage was now part of the Colorado River system with a lower base level. Downcutting of Lodore Canyon in late Pliocene time—perhaps less than 5 million years ago—rejuvenated the drainage upstream, which incised the meander loops that form Flaming Gorge, Horseshoe Canyon, and Red Canyon (Hansen, 1986). Continued entrenchment and headward erosion of this invigorated drainage across the Green River Basin, captured streams that had flowed north to the ancestral Green River. Finally, the east-flowing ancestral Green River itself was captured by middle Pleistocene time, perhaps about 1 million years ago, turning its waters southward and completing the link to the Colorado River (Hansen, 1986).

The Pleistocene was a time of glaciation in the high Uinta Mountains; however, there is no evidence that glacial ice ever covered any part of Flaming Gorge National Recreation Area. The balance of the Quaternary sculpted the final touches to the present landscape by continued downcutting of the Green River, landsliding, debris flows, and other active geomorphic processes. The most recent change within the recreation area was the impoundment of the Green River by the Flaming Gorge Dam, which temporarily stopped river entrenchment above the dam.

CLASSIC GEOLOGIC SITES

Flaming Gorge National Recreation Area contains countless sites that display classic geological features; so many that not every site can be discussed within the limits of this article. However, a few sites are briefly discussed in the following sections. Figure 2 shows the approximate location of these sites as boxed numbers. The boxed numbers correspond to the following numbered site names.

1. Red Canyon Overlook

The Red Canyon overlook is north of Utah Highway 44 at the end of the paved road (site 1 on figure 2). The turnoff from Utah Highway 44 is well marked. The overlook offers a great view of Flaming Gorge Reservoir, Red Canyon, and the Gilbert Peak erosion surface across Red Canyon on Bear Mountain. The overlook and surrounding area is constructed on the Gilbert Peak erosion surface, which formed during a period of crustal stability in the late Oligocene, perhaps about 30 million years ago. Subsequently, the Gilbert Peak surface has been warped by the collapse and tilting of the eastern Uintas beginning about 25 million years ago. Less than 5 million years ago, the proto-Green River incised itself through the Gilbert Peak erosion surface and underlying Middle Proterozoic Uinta Mountain Group. Waters of the Green River probably began to flow down Red Canyon about 1 million years ago. The Uinta Mountain Group consists of quartzite and shale at this location. The view of Flaming Gorge Reservoir is spectacular from the Red Canyon overlook (figure 10). From here, the reservoir is about 1,350 feet below the canyon rim.

2. Uinta Fault Zone on Utah Highway 44

The Uinta fault zone is well exposed along Utah Highway 44 not far north of the Sheep Creek Canyon Geological Area loop turnoff (site 2 on figure 2). The fault is easy to see because it placed the red Middle Proterozoic Uinta Mountain Group on the south against the attenuated gray Mississippian limestone and shale beds (figure 7). These rocks were juxtaposed during the Laramide orogeny about 70 to 40 million years ago. The Uinta fault zone may have originally formed about 1.5 billion years ago near the beginning of the Middle Proterozoic as a fault near the northern margin of a rift valley.

3. North Flank Monocline

Utah Highway 44 is built across a monocline on the approach to Sheep Creek Canyon (site 3 on figure 2). The monocline is well expressed in the Franson Member of the Permian Park City Formation, which forms the dip slope

Figure 10. The Red Canyon overlook provides a spectacular view of Flaming Gorge Reservoir along Red Canyon. The Uinta Mountain Group forms the impressive red cliffs that rise about 1,350 feet above the reservoir. The planar surface in the foreground (near the skyline to the right of the reservoir and just below the snow capped mountains to the left of the reservoir) is the Gilbert Peak erosion surface, which form during a period of crustal stability about 30 million years ago. The surface was tilted during lowering of the Uinta Mountains that began in middle to late Miocene time about 25 million years ago. Red Canyon was cut from the Gilbert Peak erosion surface to its present level in less than 5 million years. Downcutting likely accelerated when the ancestral Green River was captured near Green River, Wyoming, about 1 million years ago.

and flatirons (figure 9). A scenic overlook offers a spectacular view of the monocline and the Triassic-Jurassic rocks that rise above Sheep Creek Bay (figure 1). The ridge above the red Moenkopi and Chinle Formations is the Lower Jurassic Glen Canyon Sandstone.

4. Sheep Creek Gap

Just across Sheep Creek, Utah Highway 44 passes through a road cut known as Sheep Creek Gap (site 4 on figure 2). The Gap is cut through the Glen Canyon Sandstone, which dips moderately north. This is one of the best places to view the probable J-2 unconformity near the top of the Glen Canyon, represented by a single line of chert pebbles within the sandstone. Although the sandstone is seemingly identical below and above the chert pebbles, the rocks below the chert pebbles belong to the Lower Jurassic Glen Canyon Sandstone and above the pebbles the rocks may be equivalent to the Middle Jurassic Page Sandstone. However, the Page is mapped with the Glen Canyon Sandstone here because it is thin and hard to separate from the underlying Glen Canyon without the pebbles. The colorful Carmel Formation and the overlying light-brown Entrada Sandstone cliffs can be viewed through the Gap. Fossils, gypsum, and an array of sedimentary features can be discovered by taking a short hike up the Carmel to the Entrada cliffs.

5. Green River Formation

The Green River Formation is one of the best examples of lacustrine deposits within the United States. Its sedi-

mentary features, oil shale beds, and well-preserved fossil fish are exciting to discover and photograph. This site was arbitrarily chosen; several sites need to be examined to fully appreciate this unique formation (site 5 on figure 2).

6. Uinta Fault Zone at U.S. Highway 191

The Uinta fault zone can be viewed along U.S. Highway 191 north of Flaming Gorge Dam (site 6 on figure 2). Here, the Uinta fault separates Middle Proterozoic Uinta Mountain Group on the south from Upper Triassic Chinle Formation and Lower Jurassic Glen Canyon Sandstone. The fault zone is more difficult to see at this location than at site 2, but can generally be picked out where the rocks change from red quartzite to reddish mudstone and light-brown sandstone. The road is cut through the Glen Canyon Sandstone.

7. Flaming Gorge Dam

Flaming Gorge Dam was constructed from 1958 to 1964 on the Green River. The dam is 43 miles from Vernal, Utah, and about 6 miles south of the Utah-Wyoming state line (site 7 on figure 2). It is a medium-thick-arch concrete dam that has a structural height of 502 feet and a crest length of 1,180 feet (U.S. Bureau of Reclamation, 2000) (figure 11). The crest width is 27 feet and the base widens to 131 feet (U.S. Bureau of Reclamation, 2000). The volume of concrete used to construct the dam was 986,600 cubic yards of cement (U.S. Bureau of Reclamation, 2000).

Impoundment of the Green River created Flaming Gorge Reservoir, which stretches 91 miles from the dam to near Green River, Wyoming (Murdock, 1969). The capacity of the reservoir is 3,788,900 acre-feet at a maintained surface elevation of 6,040 feet (U.S. Bureau of Reclamation, 2000). The water is more than 400 feet deep at the dam, about 300 feet deep near the Red Canyon Overlook, and about 180 feet deep in the middle of the reservoir east of Linwood Bay. The primary purpose of the reservoir is to generate electricity, provide irrigation water, and recreation.

Flaming Gorge Dam was constructed in the Uinta Mountain Group (Hansen, 1965). The rocks at the damsite dip about 16 degrees north and consist of red quartzite, sandstone, and thin to thick interbedded shale. Because of the interbedded shale in the abutments, special foundation treatment was performed to stabilize the shale zones (Murdock, 1969). Two fault zones are in the damsite area, but neither cut through the abutments. One of the faults, however, is about 82 feet upstream from the dam (Murdock, 1969).

Geology Along the Reservoir

Viewing the geology along Flaming Gorge Reservoir is one of the best ways to see many more classic geologic features within the recreation area. A boat trip down the reservoir provides nearly the same feel and geologic views as experienced by Major Powell in 1869, less a couple of

Figure 11. Flaming Gorge Dam was built between 1958 and 1964. Flaming Gorge Reservoir stretches 91 miles from the dam to near Green River, Wyoming.

rapids and being 200 to 400 feet higher up the canyon wall. Classic sites along the reservoir include Finch Draw, Flaming Gorge entrance, Horseshoe Canyon, Beehive Point, and Red Canyon. Finch Draw is along the south shore of Linwood Bay. There, the Upper Jurassic Morrison through Upper Cretaceous Frontier Sandstone is unusually well exposed. The entrance to Flaming Gorge is where the Moenkopi and Chinle slopes inspired Major Powell to name the gorge after their brilliant red color. Horseshoe Canyon offers a view of the sheer cliffs of the Weber Sandstone. Beehive Point offers a view of the Uinta fault zone where the Middle Proterozoic Uinta Mountain Group is faulted up against the Pennsylvanian-Permian Weber Sandstone. Finally, Red Canyon displays the red rocks of the Uinta Mountain Group.

ACKNOWLEDGMENTS

I am indebted to Ashley National Forest for all of their logistical and financial support. Without their help, access to the geology along the lake and printing this article in color would not have been possible. A special thanks goes to Louis Wasniewski, Flaming Gorge Ranger District, for taking time out of his busy schedule to captain the boat on Flaming Gorge Reservoir for two days. A special thanks also goes to Darlene Koerner, Ashley National Forest, for loaning me air photos and providing general support while on the forest. I thank Jon King, Mike Hylland, and Grant Willis (Utah Geological Survey) for reviewing the manuscript.

REFERENCES

Bissell, H.J., 1964, Lithology and petrography of the Weber Formation, in Utah and Colorado, *in* Sabatka, E.F., editor, Guidebook to the geology and mineral resources of the Uinta Basin, Utah's hydrocarbon storehouse, 13th Annual Field Conference: Intermountain Association of Petroleum Geologists, p. 67-91.

Bissell, H.J., and Childs, O.E., 1958, The Weber Formation of Utah and Colorado, *in* Curtis, Bruce, and Warner, H.L., editors, Symposium on Pennsylvanian rocks of Colorado and adjacent areas: Rocky Mountain Association of Geologists, p. 26-30.

Bradley, W.H., 1936, Geomorphology of the north flank of the Uinta Mountains: U.S. Geological Survey Professional Paper 185-I, p. 163-199.

—1961, Geologic map of a part of southwestern Wyoming and adjacent states: U.S. Geological Survey Miscellaneous Geologic Investigations Map I-332, scale 1:250,000.

—1964, Geology of the Green River Formation and associated Eocene rocks in southwestern Wyoming and adjacent parts of Colorado and Utah: U.S. Geological Survey Professional Paper 496-B, 86 p.

Bressler, S.L., 1981, Preliminary paleomagnetics and correlation of the Proterozoic Uinta Mountain Group, Utah and Colorado: Earth and Planetary Science Letters, v. 55, no. 1, p. 53-64.

Bruhn, R.L., Dane, P.M., and Isby, J.S., 1986, Tectonics and sedimentology of Uinta Arch, western Uinta Mountains and Uinta Basin, *in* Peterson, J.A., editor, Paleotectonics and sedimentation: American Association of Petroleum Geologists Memoir 41, p. 333-352.

Bryant, Bruce, 1990, Geologic map of the Salt Lake City 30' x 60' quadrangle, north-central Utah, and Uinta County, Wyoming: U.S. Geological Survey Miscellaneous Investigations Series Map I-1944, scale 1:100,000.

Crittenden, M.D., and Peterman, Z.E., 1975, Provisional Rb/Sr age of the Precambrian Uinta Mountain Group, northeastern Utah: Utah Geology, v. 2, p. 75-77.

DeCourten, Frank, 1998, Dinosaurs of Utah: Salt Lake City: University of Utah Press, 300 p.

Emmons, S.F., 1877, Descriptive geology: U.S. Geological Exploration 40th Parallel (King) volume 2, p. 890.

Hansen, W.R., 1962, Geology of the Flaming Gorge quadrangle, Utah-Wyoming: U.S. Geological Survey Geologic Quadrangle Map GQ-75, scale 1:24,000.

—1965, Geology of the Flaming Gorge area Utah-Colorado-Wyoming: U.S. Geological Survey Professional Paper 490, 196 p.

—1975, The Geologic story of the Uinta Mountains: U.S. Geological Survey Bulletin 1291, 144 p.

—1986, Neogene tectonics and geomorphology of the eastern Uinta Mountains in Utah, Colorado, and Wyoming: U.S. Geological Survey Professional Paper 1356, 78 p.

Hansen, W.R., and Bonilla, M.G., 1956, Geology of the Manila quadrangle, Utah-Wyoming: U.S. Geological Survey Miscellaneous Geologic Investigations Map I-156, scale 1:24,000.

Hintze, L.F., 1988 (revised 1993), Geologic history of Utah: Brigham Young University Geology Studies Special Publication 7, 202 p.

Hintze, L.F., Willis, G.C., Laes, D.Y.M, Sprinkel, D.A., and Brown, K.D., 2000, Digital geologic map of Utah: Utah Geological Survey Map 179DM, 17 p., scale 1:500,000.

Imlay, R.W., 1967, Twin Creek Limestone (Jurassic) in the western interior of the United States: U.S. Geological Survey Professional Paper 540, 105 p.

—1980, Jurassic paleobiogeography of the conterminous United States in its continental setting: U.S. Geological Survey Professional Paper 1062, 134 p.

Kemp, E.M., 1968, Probable angiosperm pollen from British Barremian to Albian strata: Palaeontology, v. 11, p. 421-434.

Kirkland, J.I., Cifelli, R.L., Britt, B.B., Burge, D.L., De-Courten, Frank, Eaton, J.G., and Parrish, J.M., 1999, Distribution of vertebrate faunas in the Cedar Mountain Formation, east-central Utah, *in* Gillette, D.D., editor, Vertebrate Paleontology in Utah: Utah Geological Survey Miscellaneous Publication 99-1, p. 201-218.

Love, J.D., Christiansen, A.C., and Ver Ploeg, A.J., 1993, Stratigraphic chart showing Phanerozoic nomenclature for the State of Wyoming: Wyoming Geological Survey Map Series 41.

Mauger, R.L., 1977, K-Ar ages of biotites from tuff in Eocene rocks of the Green River, Washakie, and Uinta basins, Utah, Wyoming, and Colorado: University of Wyoming Contributions to Geology, v. 15, no. 1, p. 17-41.

Maughan, E.K., 1984, Geological setting and some geochemistry of petroleum source rocks in the Permian Phosphoria Formation, *in* Woodward, Jane, Meissner, F.F., and Clayton, J.L., editors, Hydrocarbon source rocks of the greater Rocky Mountain region: Rocky Mountain Association of Geologists, p. 281-294.

Murdock, J.N., 1969, Geology of Flaming Gorge Dam and Reservoir, *in* Lindsay, J.B., editor, Geologic guidebook of the Uinta Mountains-Utah's maverick range: Intermountain Association of Geologists and Utah Geological Society 16th Annual Field Conference, p. 23-31.

Peterson, Fred, 1986, Jurassic paleotectonics in the west-central part of the Colorado Plateau, Utah and Arizona, *in* Peterson, J.A., editor, Paleotectonics and sedimentation in the Rocky Mountain region, United States: American Association of Petroleum Geologists Memoir 41, p. 563-596.

Peterson, Fred, and Turner-Peterson, C.E., 1987, The Morrison Formation of the Colorado Plateau-recent advances in sedimentology, stratigraphy, and paleotectonics: Hunteria, v. 2, no. 1, p. 1-18.

Pipiringos, G.N., and Imlay, R.W., 1979, Lithology and subdivisions of the Jurassic Stump Formation in southeastern Idaho and adjoining areas: U.S. Geological Survey Professional Paper 1035-C, p. C1-C25.

Pipiringos, G.N., and O'Sullivan, R.B., 1978, Principal unconformities in Triassic and Jurassic rocks, western interior United States-a preliminary survey: U.S. Geological Survey Professional Paper 1035-A, 29 p.

Poole, F.G., and Stewart, J.H., 1964, Chinle Formation and Glen Canyon Sandstone in northeastern Utah and northwestern Colorado: U.S. Geological Survey Professional Paper 501-D, p. D30-D39.

Powell, J.W., 1875, Exploration of the Colorado River and its tributaries: Washington D.C.: U.S. Government Printing Office, 218 p.

—1876, Report on the geology of the eastern portion of the Uinta Mountains and a region of country adjacent thereto: U.S. Geological and Geographical Survey of the Territories (Powell), 218 p.

Ritzma, H.R., 1969, Tectonic resume, Uinta Mountains, *in* Lindsay, J.B., editor, Geologic guidebook of the Uinta Mountains-Utah's maverick range: Intermountain Association of Geologists and Utah Geological Society 16th Annual Field Conference, p. 57-63.

Rowley, P.D., Hansen, W.R., Tweto, Ogden, and Carrara, P.E., 1985, Geologic map of the Vernal 1° x 2° quadrangle, Colorado, Utah, and Wyoming: U.S. Geological Survey Miscellaneous Investigations Series Map I-1526, scale 1:250,000.

Sanderson, I.D., 1984, The Mount Watson Formation, an interpreted braided-fluvial deposit in the Uinta Mountain Group (upper Precambrian), Utah: The Mountain Geologist, v. 21, no. 4, p. 157-164.

—1986, The Jesse Ewing Canyon Formation, an interpreted fan deposit in the basal Uinta Mountain Group (Middle Proterozoic), Utah: The Mountain Geologist, v. 23, no. 3, p. 77-89.

Schell, E.M., 1969, Summary of the geology of the Sheep Creek Canyon Geological Area and vicinity, Daggett County, Utah, *in* Lindsay, J.B., editor, Geologic guidebook of the Uinta Mountains-Utah's maverick range: Intermountain Association of Geologists and Utah Geological Society 16th Annual Field Conference, p. 143-152.

Schell, E.M., and Dyni, J.R., 1973, Preliminary geologic strip maps of the Park City and Phosphoria Formations, Vernal phosphate area, Uintah County, Utah: U.S. Geological Survey Open File Report OFR 73-248, scale 1:24,000.

Sears, J.D., 1924, Relation of the Browns Park Formation and the Bishop Conglomerate and their role in the origin of the Green and Yampa Rivers: Geological Society of America, v. 35, p. 279-304.

Sears, J.W., Graf, P.J., and Holden, G.S., 1982, Tectonic evolution of lower Proterozoic rocks, Uinta Mountains, Utah and Colorado: Geological Society of America Bulletin, v. 93, no. 10, p. 990-997.

Sprinkel, D.A., Castaño, J.R., and Roth, G.W., 1997, Emerging plays in central Utah based on regional geochemical, structural, and stratigraphic evaluation [abs.]: American Association of Petroleum Geologists Official Program, v. 6, p. A110.

Sprinkel, D.A., Weiss, M.P., Fleming, R.W., and Waanders, G.L., 1999, Redefining the Lower Cretaceous stratigraphy within the central Utah foreland basin: Utah Geological Survey Special Studies 97, 21 p.

Stokes, W.L., 1986, Geology of Utah: Salt Lake City: Utah Geological Survey and Utah Museum of Natural History Occasional Paper Number 6, 280 p.

—1991, Petrified mini-forest of the Navajo Sandstone, east-central Utah: Utah Geological Survey, Survey Notes, v. 25, no. 1, p. 14-19.

Stone, D.S., 1993, Tectonic evolution of the Uinta Mountains: Palinspastic restoration of a structural cross section along longitude 109°15', Utah: Utah Geological Survey Miscellaneous Publication 93-8, 19 p.

Surdam, R.C., and Stanley, K.O., 1980, The stratigraphic and sedimentologic framework of the Green River Formation, Wyoming, *in* Harrison, A., editor, Stratigraphy of Wyoming: Wyoming Geological Association Guidebook, p. 205-222.

U.S. Bureau of Reclamation, 2000, Flaming Gorge Dam: U.S. Bureau of Reclamation DataWeb, <http://dataweb.usbr.gov/dams/ut10121.htm>.

U.S. Geological Survey, 1994, Bedrock geology of Wyoming: U.S. Geological Survey <http://www.sdvc.uwyo.edu/clearinghouse/>, scale 1:500,000.

Thomas, H.D., and Krueger, M.L., 1946, Late Paleozoic and early Mesozoic stratigraphy of Uinta Mouintains: American Association of Petroleum Geologists, v. 30, no. 8, p. 1255-1293.

Tschudy, R.H., Tschudy, B.D., and Craig, L.C., 1984, Palynological evaluation of Cedar Mountain and Burro Canyon Formations, Colorado Plateau: U.S. Geological Survey Professional Paper 1281, 24 p.

Wallace, C.A., 1972, A basin analysis of the upper Precambrian Uinta Mountain Group, Utah: Santa Barbara, University of California-Santa Barbara, Ph.D. dissertation, 412 p.

Lake Powell, Glen Canyon National Recreation Area
Photo courtesy of the Utah Travel Council

Geology of Utah's Parks and Monuments
2000 Utah Geological Association Publication 28
D.A. Sprinkel, T.C. Chidsey, Jr., and P.B. Anderson, editors

Geology of Glen Canyon National Recreation Area, Utah-Arizona

Paul B. Anderson,[1] Thomas C. Chidsey, Jr.[2], Douglas A. Sprinkel[2], and Grant C. Willis[2]

ABSTRACT

Glen Canyon National Recreation Area contains some of the best examples of the spectacular and unique geology that the Colorado Plateau has to offer. The recreation area is located in southeastern Utah and in a small part of northern Arizona. It includes the shores of Lake Powell—the reservoir behind Glen Canyon Dam—and parts of other main drainages of the Colorado River system like the Dirty Devil and San Juan Rivers. The canyons in the recreation area formed within the past 5 million years by vigorous downcutting of the Colorado and San Juan Rivers and their tributaries to expose more than 8,000 feet of bedrock that spans about 300 million years.

The recreation area is dominated by sparsely vegetated, spectacularly exposed layers of classic Colorado Plateau rocks. The bedrock units range in age from Late Pennsylvanian (300 million years ago) to Late Cretaceous (about 85 million years ago), and record a fascinating history of deposition in shallow seas, tidal flats, sabkhas, vast alluvial plains, and enormous sand dune-covered deserts dotted with oases. Glen Canyon National Recreation Area also contains a surprising variety of unconsolidated surficial deposits that provide clues to the age of the canyons. Active surficial processes continue to shape the recreation area, such as large-scale landslides and rock falls involving the Triassic Chinle Formation and Jurassic Wingate Sandstone.

The recreation area has literally had its "ups and downs." The tectonic history of the area is recorded in the stratigraphy and consists of repeated periods of subsidence and deposition alternating with periods of uplift and erosion. Recent uplift to its present high-desert elevation has caused aggressive downcutting by the Colorado and Green Rivers and their many tributaries, to form a unique combination of beauty, isolation, and geologic history.

INTRODUCTION

So we have a curious ensemble of wonderful features— carved walls, royal arches, glens, alcove gulches, mounds, and monuments. From which of these features should we select a name? We decide to call it Glen Cañon.

Major John Wesley Powell, August 3, 1869

One hundred and three years after Powell wrote these words during his first expedition into the canyons of the Colorado River, Glen Canyon National Recreation Area was established by Congress on October 27, 1972. The recreation area protects lands primarily adjacent to Lake Powell, a reservoir named after the famous explorer and geologist John Wesley Powell (figure 1), and created by the construction of Glen Canyon Dam on the Colorado River.

Glen Canyon National Recreation Area (GCNRA) is located principally in southeastern Utah, with a small portion within northernmost Arizona (figure 2). Most of the western boundary of the recreation area is shared with

Figure 1. Lake Powell in Glen Canyon National Recreation Area. Navajo Mountain in the background; view to the southeast. Photo courtesy of Utah Travel Council.

[1] Salt Lake City, UT 84102
[2] Utah Geological Survey, Salt Lake City, UT 84114-6100

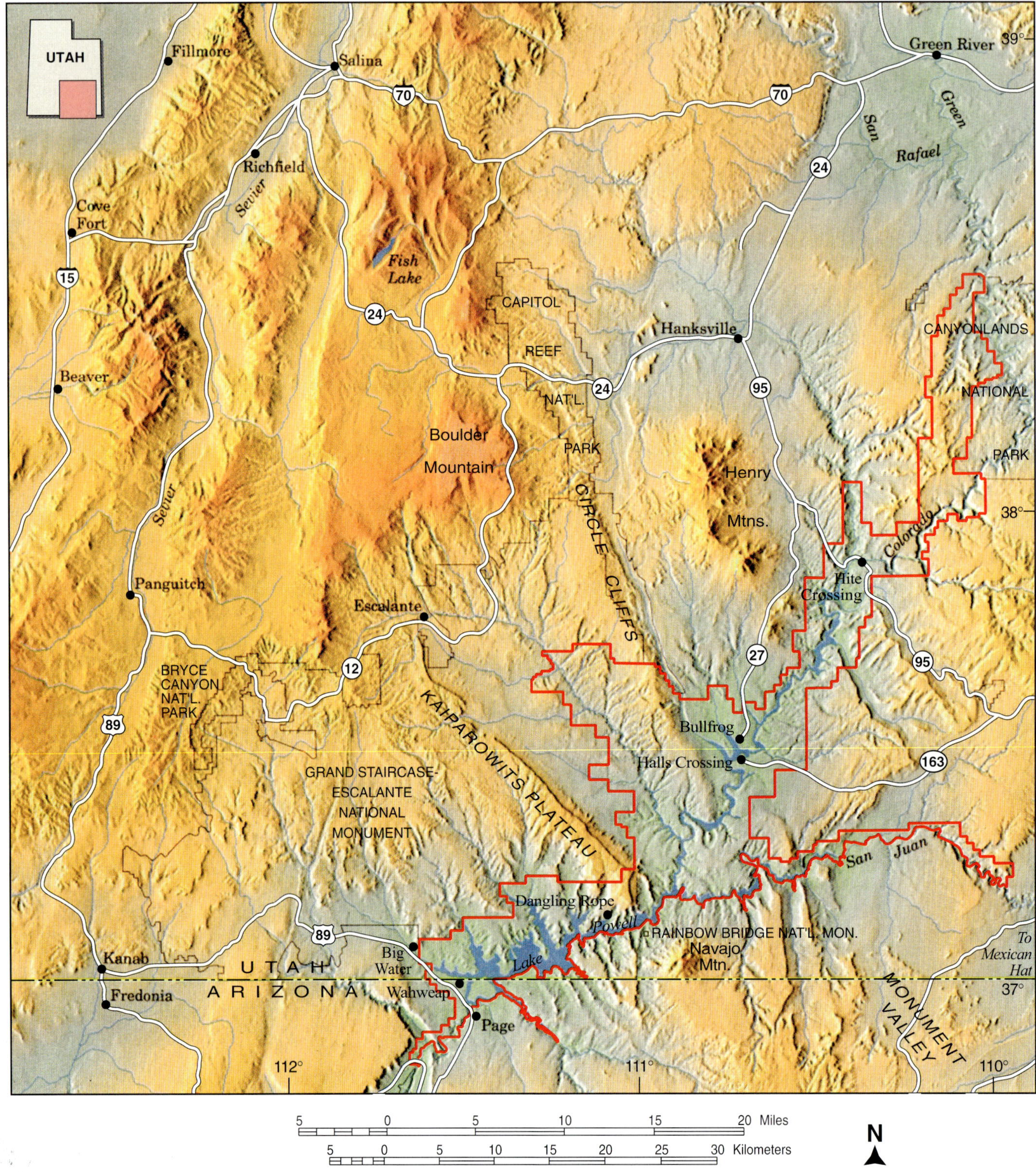

Figure 2. *Index map to Glen Canyon National Recreation Area, Utah and Arizona, showing surrounding towns, highways, and parks (modified from Hintze, 1997; topographic relief base map modified with permission, courtesy of Chalk Butte, Inc., Boulder, Wyoming).*

Grand Staircase-Escalante National Monument, and the northeastern boundary is shared with Canyonlands National Park, both subjects of other papers in this volume. U.S. Highway 89 provides access to the park headquarters, the large Wahweap Marina, and Page, Arizona—the largest town near the recreation area. Road access to boat-ing facilities in Utah is from State Highway 95 to Bullfrog, Hite Crossing, and Halls Crossing Marinas. Dangling Rope Marina is accessible only by boat. Page, Bullfrog, and Hite Crossing all are serviced by small airstrips.

Glen Canyon National Recreation Area is located on the Colorado Plateau, a high-desert physiographic feature

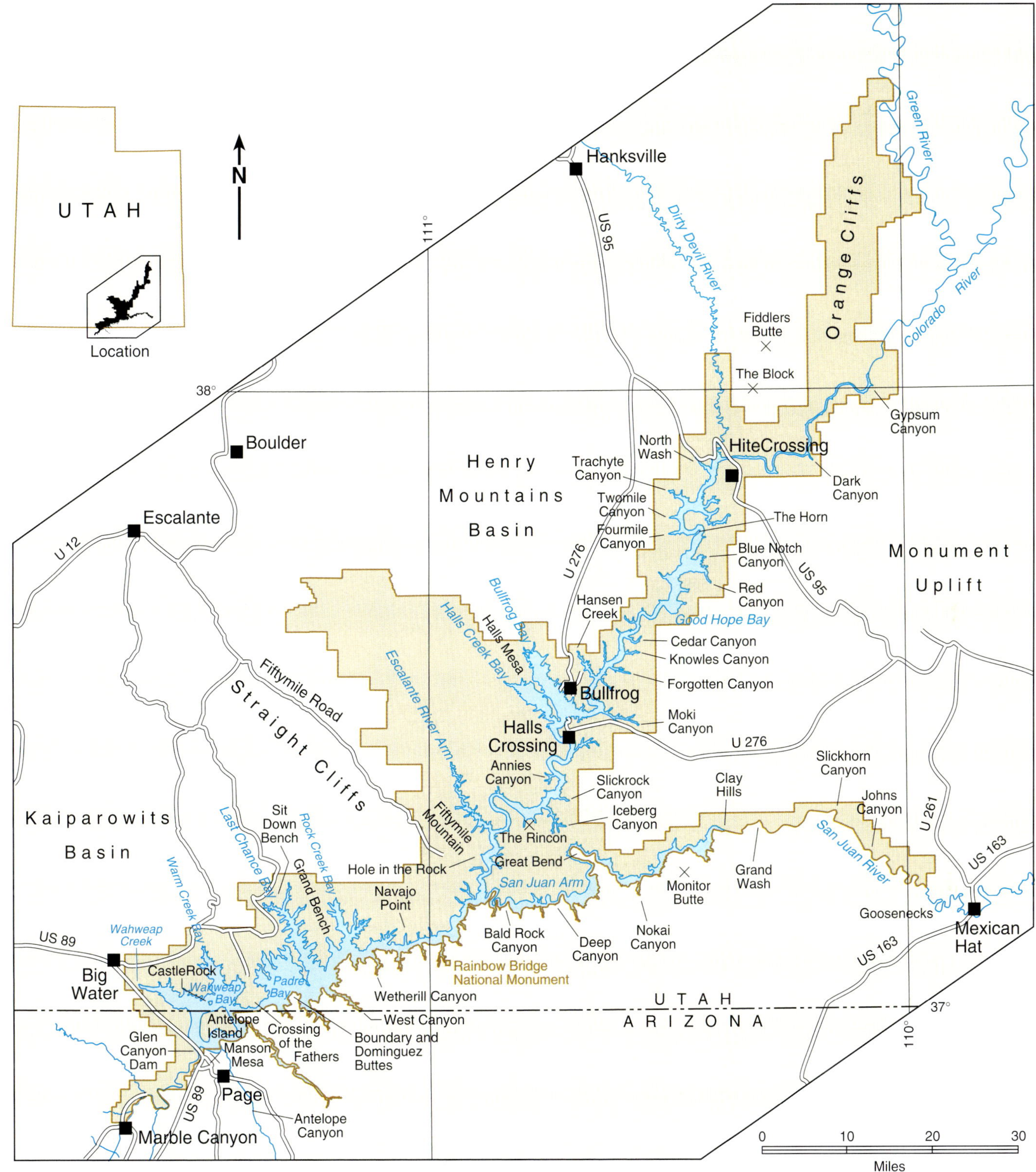

Figure 3. Location map of geologic and lake features within and around Glen Canyon National Recreation Area as referred to in the text.

that spreads across parts of Utah, Colorado, Arizona, and New Mexico. Vegetation is sparse except in riparian areas and a few high mountainous regions. Precipitation ranges from 8 to 12 inches per year over most lower elevation areas. The topography is rugged with broad plateaus and mesas separated by steep, narrow canyons. When full, the elevation of Lake Powell is 3,700 feet above sea level, while elevations in adjacent mountains (Navajo and Henry Mountains) range from 8,000 to 11,000 feet.

Over 8,000 feet of sedimentary rocks are exposed in the recreation area, representing 300 million years of earth history. Deposition of these rocks records marine, marginal marine, coastal plain, alluvial plain, vast desert, and small oasis conditions. Sandstone is the dominant rock type, but a variety of finer grained sedimentary rocks are found throughout the section. Carbonate rocks are found in the older outcrops of the recreation area, and a variety of igneous and metamorphic clasts occur chiefly in Quaternary unconsolidated river gravels. Folds, faults, and jointing provide evidence of an interesting structural history. Erosion of the rocks is primarily by running water and mass wasting. Classic laccoliths (igneous intrusions) are adjacent to Glen Canyon in the Henry Mountains and Navajo Mountain.

Glen Canyon Dam, located near Page, Arizona (figure 3), was authorized by Congress in 1956 to provide water storage in the upper Colorado River Basin, and construction began that same year. Lake Powell stores water from the Colorado River and several major tributaries, such as the Green, Yampa, White, Dolores, Dirty Devil, and San Juan Rivers. The gates of the Glen Canyon Dam were closed on March 13, 1963. However, the lake did not reach full capacity until June 22, 1980, and again in 1983 and 1984. Lake Powell is now the second-largest reservoir in the United States (Lake Mead in Nevada and Arizona is the largest). The lake is 186 miles long and it has more than 1,960 miles of shoreline and 96 major side canyons (figures 2 and 3). The lake's surface area is 266 square miles (U.S. Department of the Interior, 1996; National Park Service, 1999).

When Lake Powell is at its maximum volume of 27 million acre-feet, the water depth at the dam is 560 feet. The average daily legal range of outflow is 5,000 to 20,000 cubic feet per second. The maximum flow in flood times is 322,000 cubic feet per second. Eighty-five percent of the water from Lake Powell goes to agricultural production, and the rest for urban use in California, Arizona, and Nevada. The hot, arid climate causes an average annual evaporation of 2.6 percent of the lake's volume. The rate of siltation in the lake averages 37,000 acre-feet per year, brought in principally from the San Juan and Colorado Rivers (National Park Service, 1994; U.S. Department of the Interior, 1996).

Lake Powell comprises only 13 percent of the total area of GCNRA; the remaining 87 percent is where the geology is found!

STRATIGRAPHY

Rocks exposed in GCNRA were deposited over the past 300 million years and range in age from Late Pennsylvanian to Holocene (figure 4). Using average thicknesses, about 8,500 feet of strata are exposed within the recreation area. These rocks are well exposed and the gently inclined (dipping) beds make them easy to study.

In addition to the bedrock formations in the recreation area, a variety of unconsolidated deposits, made up of material ranging in size from house-size boulders to clay, are found unconformably upon the full range of bedrock strata. Water, wind, mechanical weathering, and gravity are the mechanisms responsible for forming these deposits.

Rock descriptions, thickness, color, and other attributes of the exposed formations in the recreation area are summarized in table 1. A series of generalized geologic maps shows the distribution of rock units in the vicinity of the recreation area (figures 5 through 9).

Pennsylvanian Rocks

Hermosa Group

The Pennsylvanian Hermosa Group comprises the oldest rocks exposed in GCNRA (figure 4 and table 1). The Hermosa Group consists of three formations (in ascending order): the Pinkerton Trail, Paradox, and Honaker Trail. Only the Paradox and Honaker Trail Formations are exposed in the recreation area—the Pinkerton Trail Formation has been penetrated in the subsurface by exploration wells. We have not differentiated these formations of the Hermosa Group on the geologic maps (figures 5, 6, and 8). The Hermosa Group generally thickens from southwest to northeast across the region (Doelling, 1975; Stevenson, this volume).

The Paradox Formation is exposed in a narrow band along the San Juan River in the very southeastern limits of the recreation area (Gianniny and others, 1993), where it forms gray ledgy outcrops and vertical cliffs. The Paradox Formation is also exposed in the northern part of the recreation area in Gypsum Canyon, about 3.5 miles up from the junction with the Colorado River. There, Shoemaker and Stephens' (1975) Paradox Formation includes gray limestone, black shale, and gypsum beds that underlie the gray and tan interbedded limestone and sandstone beds of the Honaker Trail Formation.

The Paradox Formation exposed along the San Juan River was deposited in a shallow marine, carbonate shelf environment, whereas exposures in the northern part of the recreation area were deposited nearer the basin center. The basin center was periodically restricted from the main body of marine waters to the southeast, resulting in thicker evaporite deposits.

The Honaker Trail Formation is exposed along Lake Powell in the northern part of the recreation area, a few miles north of Hite Crossing (figure 6). Honaker Trail exposures continue northward along the Colorado River out of the recreation area into the adjoining Canyonlands National Park, where the lower walls of Cataract Canyon consist of the upper half of this formation (Doelling, 1975). The Honaker Trail Formation is also exposed along the eastern part of the San Juan Arm of the lake (figure 8). In fact, the type section of the Honaker Trail Formation is about 0.5 miles south of the easternmost point in the recreation area in the Goosenecks section of the San Juan River along the Honaker Trail (Wengerd and Matheny, 1958; Stevenson, this volume).

The upper contact of the Honaker Trail Formation with the overlying Rico Formation in the northern part of the recreation area is difficult to identify because both formations have similar lithologies. In general, the contact is

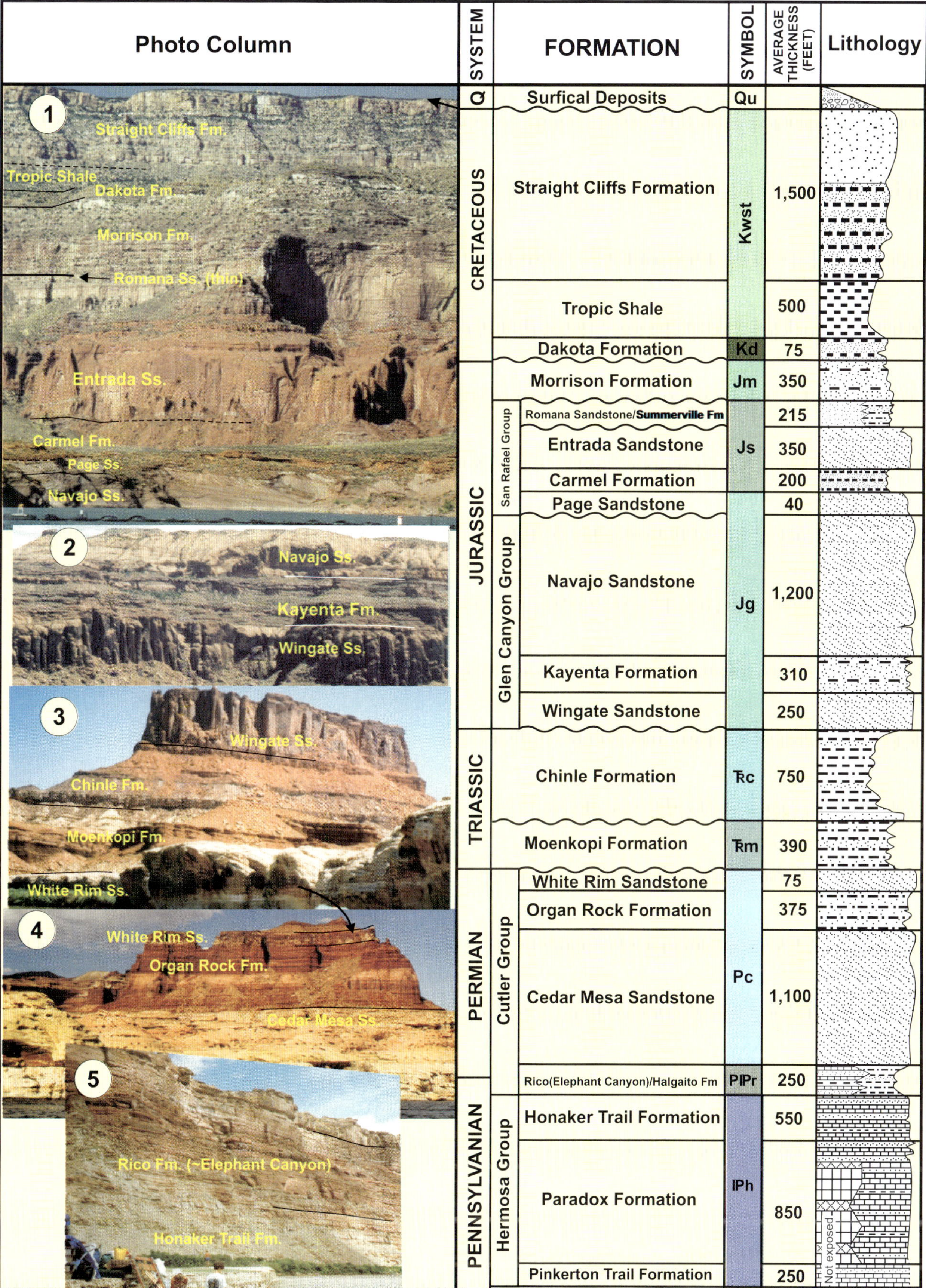

Figure 4. Stratigraphic column of Glen Canyon National Recreation Area and vicinity, including thickness, age, weathering habits, and lithology. Photographs: (1) View north from Dangling Rope Marina. (2) View east near Red Canyon. (3) Stillwater Canyon, Green River. (4) Junction of Dirty Devil and Colorado Rivers, near Hite Crossing. (5) Confluence of the Green and Colorado Rivers, view up Colorado River. Page Sandstone is mapped with the Navajo Sandstone.

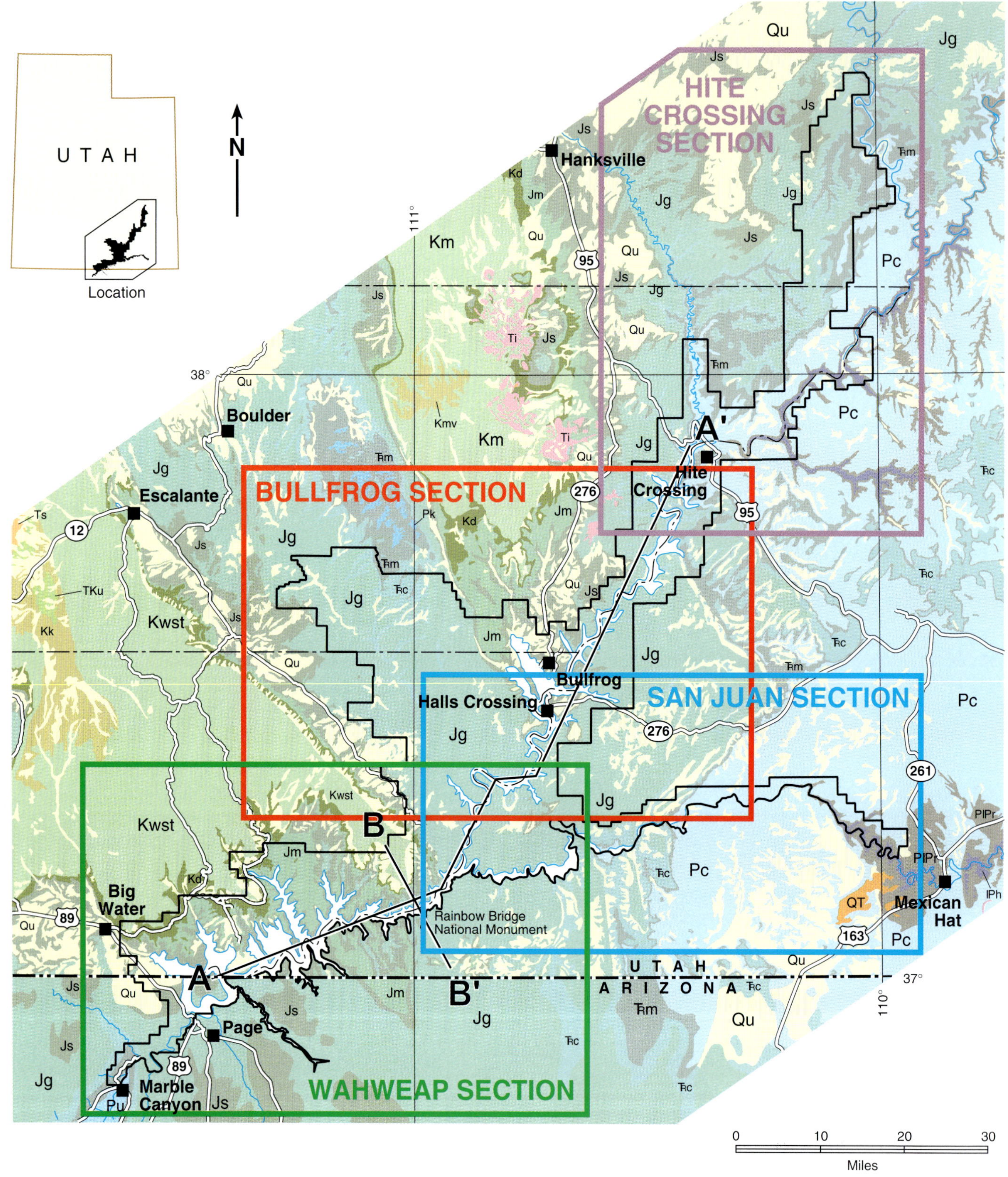

Figure 5. *Geologic map of the entire Glen Canyon National Recreation Area with simplified geologic cross sections (northeast-southwest and northwest-southeast) showing major structural features. Geologic maps of the Hite Crossing, Bullfrog, San Juan, and Wahweap sections are shown in figures 6 through 9, respectively. Geologic map modified after Baars (1973), Doelling (1975), Hintze (1980), Doelling and Davis (1989), and Doelling (1997).*

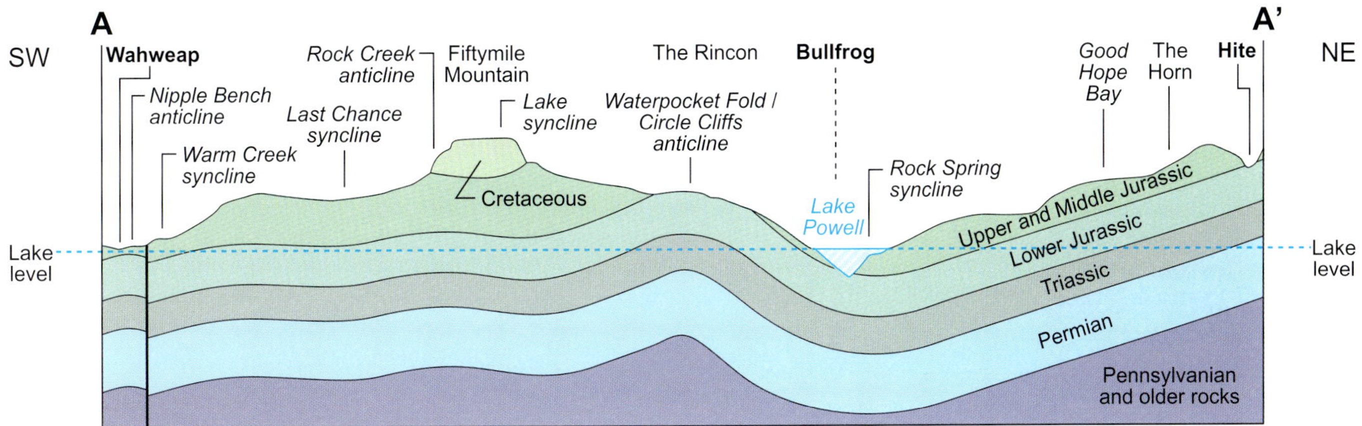

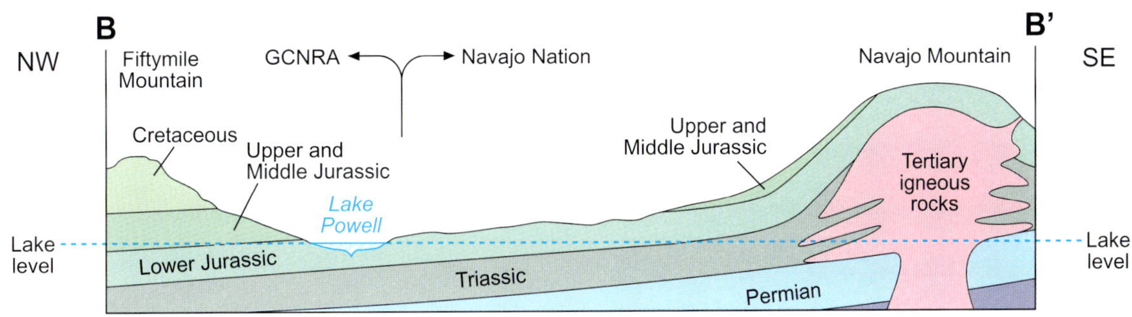

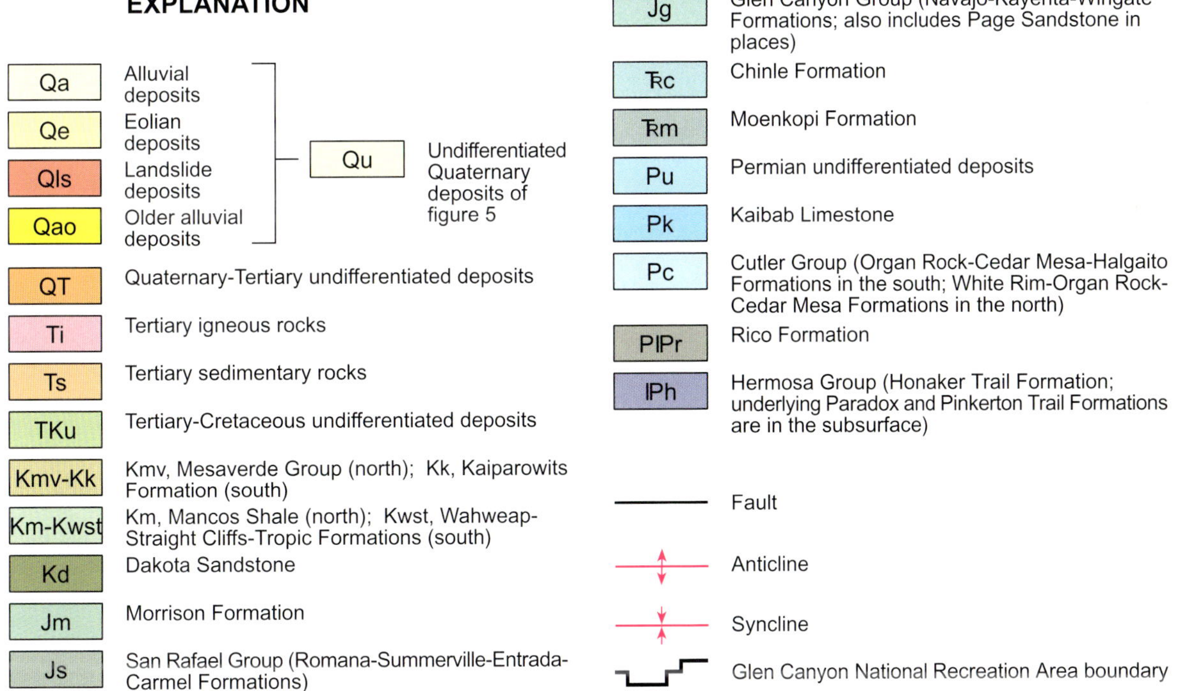

EXPLANATION

Qa	Alluvial deposits
Qe	Eolian deposits
Qls	Landslide deposits
Qao	Older alluvial deposits

Qu — Undifferentiated Quaternary deposits of figure 5

QT	Quaternary-Tertiary undifferentiated deposits
Ti	Tertiary igneous rocks
Ts	Tertiary sedimentary rocks
TKu	Tertiary-Cretaceous undifferentiated deposits
Kmv-Kk	Kmv, Mesaverde Group (north); Kk, Kaiparowits Formation (south)
Km-Kwst	Km, Mancos Shale (north); Kwst, Wahweap-Straight Cliffs-Tropic Formations (south)
Kd	Dakota Sandstone
Jm	Morrison Formation
Js	San Rafael Group (Romana-Summerville-Entrada-Carmel Formations)

Jg	Glen Canyon Group (Navajo-Kayenta-Wingate Formations; also includes Page Sandstone in places)
Ŧc	Chinle Formation
Ŧm	Moenkopi Formation
Pu	Permian undifferentiated deposits
Pk	Kaibab Limestone
Pc	Cutler Group (Organ Rock-Cedar Mesa-Halgaito Formations in the south; White Rim-Organ Rock-Cedar Mesa Formations in the north)
PlPr	Rico Formation
IPh	Hermosa Group (Honaker Trail Formation; underlying Paradox and Pinkerton Trail Formations are in the subsurface)

——	Fault
↕	Anticline
↓	Syncline
⌐_⌐	Glen Canyon National Recreation Area boundary

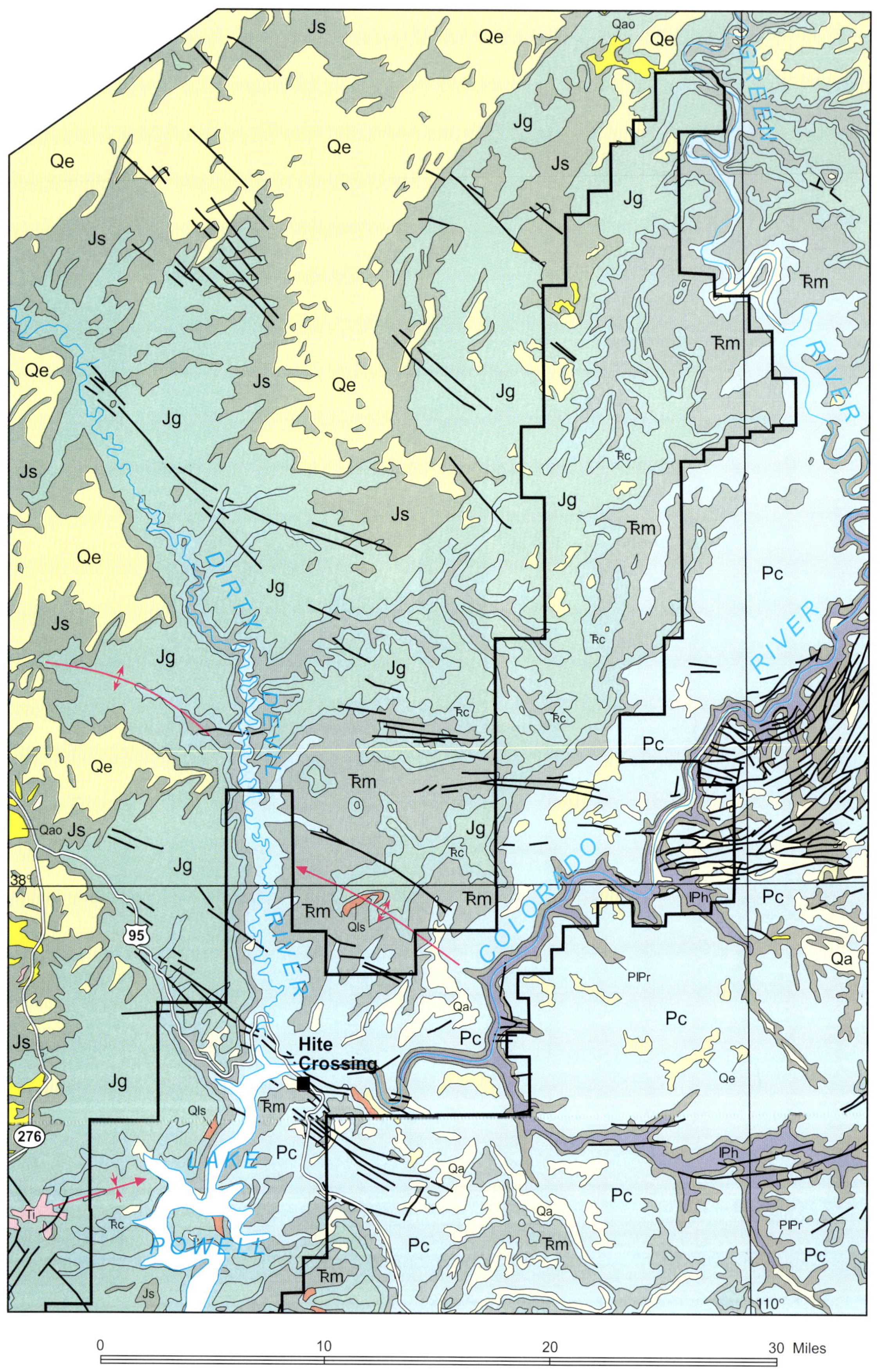

Figure 6. Geologic map of Hite Crossing section of Glen Canyon National Recreation Area. See figure 5 for explanation.

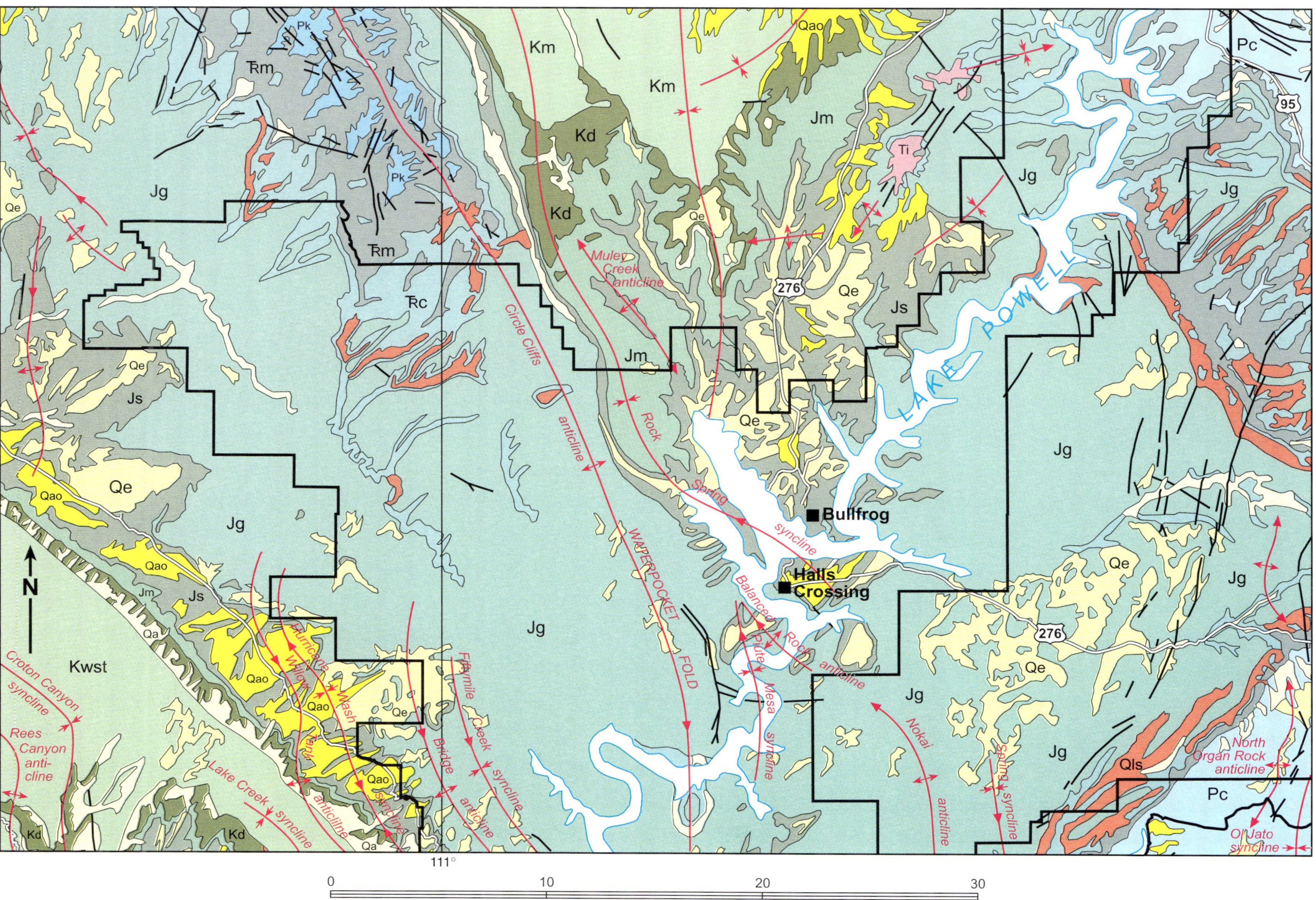

Figure 7. Geologic map of Bullfrog section of Glen Canyon National Recreation Area. See figure 5 for explanation.

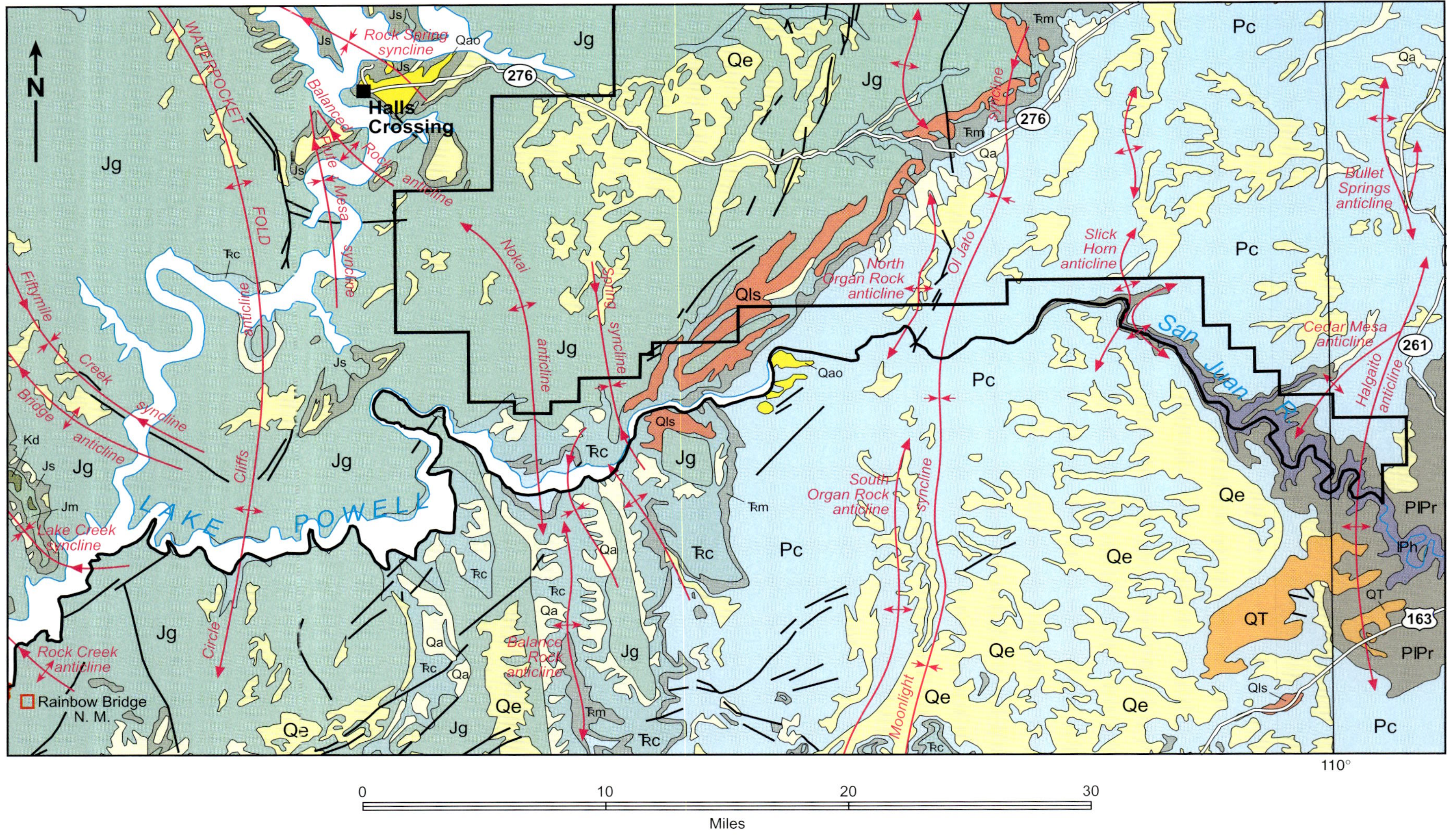

Figure 8. Geologic map of San Juan section of Glen Canyon National Recreation Area. See figure 5 for explanation.

Figure 9. Geologic map of Wahweap section of Glen Canyon National Recreation Area. See figure 5 for explanation.

Table 1. Stratigraphic units in Glen Canyon National Recreation Area, Utah and Arizona.

Unit	Age (m.y.)		Thickness (feet)	Lithology	Color	Depositional Environment / Other Attributes	Cross Reference (this volume)*
Surficial Deposits	Present ~1	TERTIARY-QUATERNARY	0-200+	Highly variable: metamorphic and igneous intrusives, sandstone, limestone, dolomite, quartzite, siltstone and shale	Variable, similar to bedrock to gray in river gravel	Deposited by water, wind, mass wasting and freeze-thaw cycles. Chiefly un-consolidated, except caliche deposits.	
Straight Cliffs and Tropic Shale/Mancos Shale	100	?CRETACEOUS	1,860-2,140	Interbedded sandstone and shale with minor siltstone and coal	Dark-gray sh, tan to brown ss	Thick beach to coastal plain sandstone sequences intertongue with marine shale. Contains large coal reserves. Common fossil ammonites and minor pelecypods in shales.	Ar, CR, GS, Tindall
Dakota Formation — K-0			20-170	Sandy conglomerate, sandstone, shale, and minor coal	Tan to brown ss; gray sh	The unit is divided into a lower sandy conglomerate, middle mudstone with minor coal, and upper sandstone. Fossil oysters common at the top of the unit. Stream and nearshore marine deposits.	Ar, CR, GS
Morrison Formation — J-5	149		0-710	Sandstone, conglomerate, siltstone, and minor mudstone.	Tan ss, maroon to gray-green shale	Probable Salt Wash Member-equivalent beds occur in the south as ledgy outcrops. Minor dinosaur bone fragments and commercial uranium. Mudstones in the upper Brushy Basin Member are mined in other places for clay products. Flood-plain and overbank deposits	Ar, CR, GS
Romana Sandstone/		JURASSIC	0-230	Sandstone, fine- to coarse-grained, minor siltstone and red shale.	Light-tan to gray-green, red at base	Thick bedded cliff-former. Often indistinct contacts. Deposited by streams, some eolian deposits.	GS
Summerville Fm. (north) — J-3			38	Bedded sandstone/siltstone	Red/white	Distinctive banded red and white ss/siltstone	Ar, CR
Entrada Sandstone			120-850	Sandstone, very fine grained, siltstone and minor shale	Reddish-orange to white	Rounded slickrock outcrops in the south with numerous "injection features" and upper cliff-forming banded unit; chiefly eolian deposits.	Ar, CR, GS, Tindall
Carmel Formation			110-250	Sandstone, siltstone, platy limestone, shale and minor gypsum.	Reddish-brown, gray to white	Interbedded red hues and white bands, slope-former, often disturbed bedding, gypsiferous veinlets. Formed in and marginal to a shallow seaway.	Ar, CR, D, GS Tindall
Page Sandstone — J-2			0-300	Sandstone, fine- to medium-grained, rounded quartz, calcareous & iron cement	Tan to light-reddish-brown	Very similar to the underlying Navajo, difficult to find lower contact. Local cherty lag at the basal unconformity. Ancient sand dune deposits.	Ar, D, GS, R, Tindall
Navajo Sandstone	180		1,170-1,230	Sandstone, fine- to medium-grained rounded quartz, calcareous & iron cement	Tan to light-reddish-brown	Large-scale cross-beds, steeply dipping laminae, exposures are typically "slickrock." Forms many alcoves and Rainbow Bridge; contains thin "oasis" limestone beds.	Ar, CR, CY, D, GS, R, Tindall
Kayenta Formation			250-330	Sandstone, fine- to medium-grained, minor siltstone and shale.	Pale-red to dark-orange	Ledgy appearance, flood-plain channel deposits, rare dinosaur tracks.	Ar, CR, CY, D, GS, R, Tindall
Wingate Sandstone — J-0	205		100-400	Sandstone, very fine to fine quartz grains, well sorted, chiefly calcareous cement.	Light-brown to orange-brown	Forms prominent vertical cliff, large-scale cross-beds, "desert varnish" common on weathered faces. Ancient sand dune deposits.	Ar, CR, CY, D, Tindall
-continued next page-				-continued next page-		-continued next page-	

San Rafael Group

Glen Canyon Group

Unit		Age m.y.	Thickness (feet)	Lithology	Color	Depositional Environment Other Attributes	Cross Reference (this volume)*
	Chinle Formation · · · · · · · · · · Shinarump Member	TRIASSIC	460-1,195	Sandstone, mudstone, silt-stone, claystone, limestone, gritstone, and conglomerate.	Red, orange, purple, green, and dark-brown	Changing rock types both laterally and vertically; channel-deposited basal Shinarump Member is discontinuous, thin and erodes into the underlying formation. Upper member deposited in a broad plain with lakes and streams. Some freshwater limestones.	Ar, CR, CY, D, GS, Tindall
	Moenkopi Formation	TRIASSIC	270-500	Siltstone, sandstone, clay-stone, limestone, and con-glomerate; with minor gypsum in veins and blobs.	Reddish-brown, yellow-gray, pale-green, white	Slope-former, flat continuous thin to medium beds; lime-stone beds locally fossiliferous (chiefly pelycepods). Transitional from marginal marine to non-marine.	Ar, CR, CY, D, GS, N, St, Tindall
Cutler Group	White Rim Sandstone	PERMIAN	0-150	Sandstone, very fine to fine-grained, with medium to coarse grains; rounded, pre-dominantly quartz, minor chert	White to yellowish-gray	In the Orange Cliffs the formation is divided into a lower eolian unit and an upper reworked marine unit (Huntoon and Chan, 1987). The lower unit is dominated by large-scale cross-beds with southeasterly dipping foresets.	CY, D, GS, St, Tindall
Cutler Group	Organ Rock Formation	PERMIAN	200-450	Sandstone, fine-grained to silty, minor siltstone and sandy shale. Chiefly quartz with minor muscovite, magnetite, feldspar and chert.	Reddish-brown with minor gray to green mottling.	Even, medium to thick bedded, forms steep slopes to ledgy cliffs. Formed in a marginal to shallow marine environment on the edge of a large dune field.	CR, CY, D, N, St
Cutler Group	Cedar Mesa Sandstone	PERMIAN	700-1,400	Sandstone, fine- to medium-grained, chiefly subangular quartz. Minor coarse-grained sandstone, red siltstone, and limestone.	Yellowish-tan to brown, red to east	Forms massive cliffs and broad slickrock benches with thin unconsolidated dunal deposits. Principally eolian with minor marine and fluvial deposits. Halgaito interfingers to the southeast, is silty, and deposited in distal streams near the sea's edge.	CR, CY, D, G, N, St
Cutler Group	Lower beds/Rico and Halgaito Formations	PERMIAN	0-500	Limestone and sandstone; silty sandstone, fine- to med-ium-grained, calcareous, poorly sorted	Yellowish-tan to brown	Interbedded cabonates, sandstone, and minor shale, forms a ledgy outcrop; exposed only in the northern reach of GCNRA and in the eastern San Juan Arm. Marine to mar-ginal marine environments.	Ar, CR, CY, D, G, N, St
Hermosa Group	Honaker Trail Formation	PENNSYLVANIAN	100-1,3000	Limestone with minor sand-stone; calcareous, poorly sorted	Gray to tan	Red jasperized fossils, forms a vertical cliff; only the upper portion of the formation is exposed in the northern reach of GCNRA and in the eastern San Juan Arm. Chiefly marine carbonates with clastics from distant highlands.	Ar, CY, D, G
Hermosa Group	Paradox Formation	PENNSYLVANIAN	100-1,800	Limestone/dolomite/shale in San Juan Arm; chiefly evap-orites (salt, potash, anhydrite) north and subsurface	Gray	Along San Juan River - platform carbonates and bioherms, abundant marine fossils, important reservoir rocks for oil in Paradox Basin. Northwest area, thick salts.	Ar, CY, G
Hermosa Group	Pinkerton Trail Formation	PENNSYLVANIAN	100-400	Limestone, dolomite with some sandstone and shale	Gray	Subsurface only - possible exposure just outside GCNRA in the Goosenecks area of the San Juan River (Stevenson, this volume).	CY, G

Age boundaries (m.y.): 205, 227, 248, 290

* Abbreviations for surrounding papers: Arches NP (Ar), Capitol Reef NP (CR), Canyonlands NP (CY), Dead Horse Point SP (D), Goosenecks SP (G), Grand Staircase-Escalante NM (GS), Rainbow Bridge NM (R), Stanesco and others (St)

placed above the gray and tan ledgy beds of the Honaker Trail and below yellowish-tan to brown ledgy and slightly less resistant beds of the Rico Formation. In the southeast part of the recreation area, the contact with the overlying Halgaito Formation is much easier to pick. Here, the contact is at the top of the gray and tan interbedded carbonate and clastic rocks of the Honaker Trail, and below the red, moderately resistant beds of the Halgaito Formation.

Permian Rocks

Cutler Group

The mostly Permian Cutler Group crops out in the northern part of the recreation area from about Hite Crossing northward along Lake Powell, the Colorado River, and the lower Dirty Devil River (figure 6). It is also exposed along much of the San Juan Arm of Lake Powell and the San Juan River in the eastern part of the recreation area (figure 8). The Cutler Group includes (in ascending order) the partly Pennslyvanian Rico and Halgaito Formations, and the Permian Cedar Mesa Sandstone, Organ Rock Formation, and White Rim Sandstone. These formations are regionally intertonguing (figure 10) and record the complex depositional environments that existed at a time of upheaval during the uplift of the ancestral Uncompahgre highland (see Baars; Doelling, Chidsey, and Benson; Doelling and others; Stanesco and others; Huntoon and others; all this volume). The nomenclature of the lower Cutler Group formations (Rico-Elephant Canyon-Halgaito) has a complex history, which is confusing even to the most seasoned geologist. The intent of this article is to briefly describe the stratigraphy and relationships of these units.

<u>Rico and Halgaito Formations:</u> The Rico and Halgaito Formations are similar in stratigraphic position but are lithologically different (figure 10). The Rico Formation is a series of mixed carbonate and siliciclastic rocks that lie above the Hermosa Group and below the Cedar Mesa Sandstone (figure 4 and table 1). The Halgaito Formation is composed primarily of silty sandstone that also lies above the Hermosa Group and below the Cedar Mesa Sandstone (Wengred and Matheny, 1958; Doelling, 1975). The name Elephant Canyon Formation was introduced (Baars, 1962) as a partially equivalent unit to the Rico Formation (figure 10).   Biostratigraphic work (Loope and others, 1990; Sanderson and Verville, 1990) established the Permian-Pennsylvanian contact within the Rico and Elephant Canyon Formations. The simplified maps in this paper (figures 6 and 8) are based on Hintze (1980), who showed the Rico Formation as a separate unit from the Cutler Group.

The Rico Formation is found in the northern section of the recreation area between Hite Crossing and Gypsum Canyon in the walls of the canyon along the Colorado River. Narrow side canyons along this stretch of the lake are also excellent places to view these rocks. The Rico Formation forms a series of small ledges and slopes that give

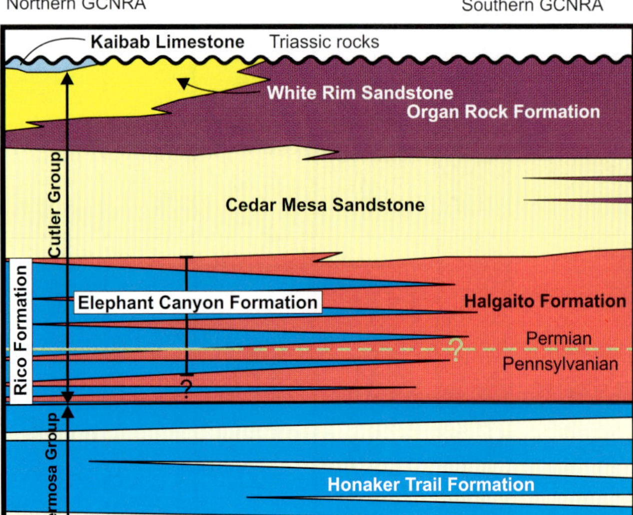

Figure 10. Pennsylvanian and Permian stratigraphic relationships northwest to southeast across Glen Canyon National Recreation Area. Yellow and red colors are dominantly clastic rocks; blue colors are dominantly carbonates.

way to the massive-weathering cliffs of the overlying Cedar Mesa Sandstone.   Abundant marine fossils are found in limestone beds of the Rico Formation.

Rico-equivalent beds—the Honaker Trail Formation (Wengerd and Matheny, 1958) and Halgaito Formation— are also exposed along the San Juan Arm of Lake Powell. Although we concur with the placement of Rico beds into the Honaker Trail Formation by Wengerd and Matheny (1958), our simplified geologic maps (figures 5, 6, and 8) show those beds in the San Juan River drainage area as the Rico Formation.

The Halgaito Formation is the basal formation of the Cutler Group in the San Juan River drainage area (Hintze, 1980). A narrow band of the Halgaito crops out beneath the resistant Cedar Mesa Sandstone, which forms the top of the San Juan River gorge east of Clay Hills. At Johns Canyon, a tributary to the San Juan, the gorge widens and the Halgaito is exposed near the northern boundary of the recreation area. East of the recreation area is the town of Mexican Hat and its famous landform "Mexican Hat," a pedestal within the Halgaito Formation outcrop. The formation forms distinctive reddish, moderately resistant slopes that underlie the tan cliff-forming Cedar Mesa Sandstone.

<u>Cedar Mesa Sandstone:</u> The Cedar Mesa Sandstone makes an impressive "slickrock" unit in the northeastern part of the recreation area and along the upper reaches of the San Juan Arm, east of Clay Hills (figures 6 and 8). The formation is exposed at lake level at Hite Crossing, and both steel arch suspension bridges on State Highway 95 over the Dirty Devil and Colorado arms are anchored in Cedar Mesa Sandstone. Along both sides of the main Colorado River canyon north of Hite, the Cedar Mesa Sandstone forms the top of the inner gorge. In the San Juan

Figure 11. The Organ Rock, White Rim, and Moenkopi Formations (sandstone on skyline); view east just south of Hite Marina.

River area, the formation is exposed for hundreds of square miles both north and south of the river along a broad and gently arching anticline. This extensive outcrop is dissected by numerous small drainages, forming miles of narrow "slickrock" canyons.

The Cedar Mesa Sandstone contains large-scale cross-beds, frosted quartz grains, and other sedimentary features that are typical of eolian deposits (table 1). However, the Cedar Mesa also contains some horizontally bedded sandstone, algal limestone, and gypsum that suggest deposition in a sabkha environment (Huntoon and others, this volume; Stanesco and others, this volume). Thus, the Cedar Mesa Sandstone was deposited in an eolian to coastal environment (Baars, this volume; Huntoon and others, this volume; Stanesco and others, this volume).

Organ Rock Formation: The Organ Rock Formation is a moderately resistant, reddish-brown silty sandstone and shale unit that overlies the white sandstone cliffs of the Cedar Mesa Formation (Blakey, 1980). The Organ Rock crops out in the northern part of the recreation area and along the San Juan Arm at Clay Hills. The formation is relatively easy to identify in the Hite Crossing area because its deep red-colored rocks are sandwiched between the light-colored sandstone beds of the underlying Cedar Mesa and the overlying White Rim Sandstone (table 1). In addition, numerous mesas and buttes that lie on top of the Cedar Mesa Sandstone in the northern part of the recreation area are composed of the Organ Rock Formation.

Regionally, the Organ Rock interfingers with both the underlying Cedar Mesa Sandstone and the overlying White Rim Sandstone (figures 10 and 11) (Stanesco and others, this volume). Laterally, the unit intertongues with and grades into the Cutler Formation of eastern Utah and southwestern Colorado. To the west, the Organ Rock thins and pinches out in the Cedar Mesa Sandstone.

White Rim Sandstone: As the name implies, the White Rim Sandstone is both light colored and typically caps rims or benches above the softer Organ Rock Formation (table 1). Only the northern section of the recreation area has exposures of the White Rim Sandstone (figures 4 and 11). Southeastward, the White Rim thins and pinches out between Hite and White Canyon along the main canyon of the Colorado River. This relation has been covered by the waters of Lake Powell; however, the White Rim pinchout can easily be seen from Dead Horse Point State Park overlook (see Doelling, Chidsey, and Benson, this volume). The top of the White Rim Sandstone is unconformable with the overlying Triassic Moenkopi Formation in the northern part of the recreation area. This bounding surface is named the TR-1 unconformity (Pipiringos and O'-Sullivan, 1978). Along the San Juan Arm of Lake Powell, the White Rim is absent and the TR-1 unconformity separates Permian Organ Rock Formation from the overlying Triassic Moenkopi Formation (Stewart and others, 1972b). However, a small outcrop of DeChelly Sandstone has been identified in the San Juan Arm, at the mouth of Nokai Canyon. The DeChelley lies above the Organ Rock Formation, and is lithologically similar to the White Rim, but is older than the White Rim (Blakey, 1996).

The White Rim Sandstone was likely deposited in an eolian environment (Heylmun, 1958; Stanesco and others, this volume). However, several authors have interpreted all or part of the White Rim as marine in origin, perhaps related by short-duration transgressions of the sea prior to Moenkopi deposition (Baars and Seager, 1970; Orgill, 1971). Huntoon and Chan (1987) indicated that most of the White Rim Sandstone is eolian, but the top the formation is marine and has been locally reworked by marine processes.

Kaibab Limestone: The Kaibab is present in the subsurface on the central-western side of the recreation area, but

Figure 12. Chinle Formation with paleosols (inset is closeup) beneath a channel sandstone; west shore between Twomile and Fourmile Canyons.

no outcrops are found within the park boundaries, and it is not included in table 1.

Triassic Rocks

Moenkopi Formation

The Moenkopi Formation is the oldest Triassic unit in the recreation area. It is exposed north and south of Hite, along the eastern shores of Lake Powell in the San Juan Arm, and in the upper part of the Escalante Canyons in the northwestern part of the recreation area (figures 6, 7, and 8). The Moenkopi Formation contains mostly siltstone, sandstone, and mudstone; however, some limestone beds are exposed in the northern part of the recreation area (table 1). The Moenkopi Formation is regionally divided into several members (Blakey, 1974; Doelling and others, this volume; Morris and others, this volume), but these members are not shown on the simplified geologic maps or discussed individually in this article.

The Moenkopi Formation was deposited during Early Triassic time on a broad continental plain that was periodically flooded by an ocean (Stewart, 1972b; Dubiel, 1994). Classic terrestrial sedimentary features such as mudcracks, petrified wood, and dinosaur tracks are preserved in the Moenkopi. The Moenkopi is separated from the underlying Permian beds by the TR-1 unconformity (Pipiringos and O'Sullivan, 1978).

Chinle Formation

Colorful banded slopes typify the Chinle Formation in

the recreation area (table 1). The Chinle Formation is one of the most fascinating formations in the recreation area because it forms huge landslides and slumps and contains ancient soil horizons (mottled and poorly bedded units called paleosols [figure 12]), gypsum, petrified wood, uranium-bearing logs and carbonaceous debris, and dinosaur tracks and bones. The Chinle is best exposed along Lake Powell in the Good Hope Bay area, the San Juan Arm, and at The Rincon (figures 5 through 8). Regionally, the Chinle consists of several members (Phoenix, 1963; Blakey, 1970; Stewart and others, 1972a; Doelling, 1975; Doelling and Davis, 1989; Dubiel, 1987, 1994). However, the accompanying maps (figures 5 through 8) do not show these members. In addition, we follow the simple terminology of Doelling and Davis (1989), who divided the Chinle into the lower Shinarump Member and an informal upper member.

The basal Shinarump Member is typically resistant, gritty to conglomeratic channel sandstone that forms a tan to brown broken ledge. The Shinarump is discontinuous, but where present, cuts into the underlying Moenkopi Formation. Where the Shinarump Member is not present, the lower part of the Chinle is dominated by volcanic ash-derived bentonitic claystone. In the San Juan Arm, the Shinarump crops out at the mouth of Neskahi and Nokia Washes, and on the north shore in the narrow channel just before Clay Hills. In the main channel of the lake, the best shore exposures of the Shinarump are in the small bay formed at the mouth of Blue Notch Canyon, about 10 miles south of Hite Crossing.

Figure 13. Massive slumps and landslide scarp (at the base of the Wingate cliff) in Chinle Formation. The colluvium on the Chinle slope has moved down about 20 to 30 feet revealing fresh, non-desert varnish-coated Wingate Sandstone. Slumping postdates Lake Powell. Note jointing in Wingate. Photo of east shore of Good Hope Bay.

The informal upper member consists mostly of varicolored (green, gray, purple, brown), bentonitic, non-resistant mudstone and claystone with some locally interbedded, resistant channel sandstone (figure 12). The upper member crops out in similar locations to those mentioned above for the Shinarump. The upper member is typically poorly exposed and littered with rockfall debris from the overlying cliffs of the Glen Canyon Group. Landslides and slumps are common features in this unit because of its high claystone (bentonitic) content, and they present a danger to visitors along the lake shore where this unit forms the beach (figure 13, see also "Classic Geologic Sites" section of this article).

The Chinle Formation was deposited under continental conditions by streams and in lakes (Dubiel, 1994). Abundant volcanic ash rained down on the countryside during Chinle time. The Chinle is bounded by unconformities. The basal TR-3 unconformity separates Upper Triassic Chinle Formation from the Lower Triassic Moenkopi Formation (Pipiringos and O'Sullivan, 1978). The top of the Chinle unconformably underlies the Lower Jurassic Wingate Sandstone, separated by the J-0 unconformity (Pipiringos and O'Sullivan, 1978).

Jurassic

Glen Canyon Group

In ascending order, the Glen Canyon Group consists of the Wingate Sandstone, Kayenta Formation, and Navajo Sandstone (figure 4 and table 1). These three Jurassic formations form a remarkable vertical topographic boundary for many landforms in the central core of the recreation area. The Glen Canyon Group was named for exposures in Glen Canyon (near the present-day Glen Canyon Dam) along the Colorado River (Gregory and Moore, 1931). Al-

though some of the exposures from which the group was named are now submerged, the formations that comprise the group are visible in many other places in the central part of the recreation area.

Resistant, cliff-forming sandstone is the Glen Canyon Group's signature rock type, which dominates the scenery of Lake Powell from just south of Rainbow Bridge to Escalante Canyon and northward to The Horn. Rocks of the Glen Canyon Group also form magnificent and rugged country of the Circle Cliffs, Orange Cliffs, The Block, and Fiddlers Butte (figure 3).

Wingate Sandstone: The Wingate Sandstone is the basal member of the Glen Canyon Group. Although previously thought to be Triassic in age, Pipiringos and O'Sullivan (1978) placed all of the formation above an unconformity (J-0) marking the beginning of the Jurassic rocks. Excellent exposures of the Wingate are along Utah Highway 95 in North Wash, just south of Hog Springs rest area, and northward along the Orange Cliffs to the northern extent of the recreation area. The best lakeshore exposures are from the south side of The Horn to Good Hope Bay, around The Rincon near the Escalante drainage, and a short distance up the San Juan Arm. Wilson (1965) mapped 42 feet of Wingate at the base of the Glen Canyon Group south of the recreation area at Lee's Ferry, Arizona. Doelling and Davis (1989) indicated that the formation intertongues with a westward equivalent, the Moenave Formation, which forms the basal cliffs near the town of Kanab, Utah. From drilling, the formation is about 100 feet thick on the western border of the recreation area and thickens to about 400 feet to the east (Doelling and Davis, 1989).

The Wingate commonly forms vertical cliffs rising up from the slope-forming Chinle Formation below. The pale-yellow-tan to light-orange-brown cliffs are often stained black to dark brown by desert varnish, an iron-magnesium-oxide veneer (table 1).

Kayenta Formation: The contact between the Wingate Sandstone and overlying Kayenta Formation is gradational, representing a depositional change from an eolian (wind-blown) dune environment to a fluvial (stream) environment (Blakey, 1994). The Kayenta weathers into a series of ledges and low cliffs, and is easily distinguished from the massive rounded cliffs of the overlying Navajo Sandstone (figure 14) and the vertical face formed by the Wingate Sandstone (table 1 and figure 4). The Kayenta is found along the shore of Lake Powell at Good Hope Bay and to the south a few miles; from The Rincon to several miles south of the junction of Escalante Canyon along the main channel; and in the San Juan Arm at Bald Rock Canyon, Deep Canyon, and Great Bend.

The Kayenta Formation is 250 to 330 feet thick in GCNRA (Hintze, 1993; Doelling, 1997). A few outcrops contain dinosaur tracks from a large theropod (Santucci, this volume).

Figure 14. *Kayenta Formation at lake level with overlying Navajo and Page Sandstones. Thin Carmel Formation on skyline; view of east shore just north of Cedar Canyon.*

Navajo Sandstone: The Navajo Sandstone is distinguished by spectacular cross-bedding of eolian dunes, and it weathers into domes above vertical canyon cliffs (figures 4 and 14). Navajo Sandstone outcrops cover about 85 percent of the central part of GCNRA (Hintze and Stokes, 1964), and approximately one-third of the surface area of the entire recreation area. North of Bullfrog Bay to Good Hope Bay and south to Rainbow Bridge National Monument, the Navajo Sandstone dominates the shoreline of the lake.

The large-scale cross-beds that dominate the Navajo Sandstone are etched out by weathering and are often highlighted by desert varnish. They occur in sets up to 25 feet thick. Dips of cross-beds between set boundaries vary as much as 40 degrees. Dip directions on the cross-bed laminae (dune slipfaces) indicate paleowinds were from the north and northwest. Less common planar beds, composed of generally finer grained material, were deposited in interdune areas or playas. These beds and thin horizontal lines, the bedset boundaries, represent upper water-table surfaces (Doelling, this volume). Thin lenticular carbonate beds occur in the formation and represent deposition in stable oases. These features are discussed further in the section on "Classical Geologic Sites."

The Navajo Sandstone was deposited in a great coastal to inland dune field (erg) comparable to the present Sahara. In Early Jurassic time, Utah had an arid climate and lay about 15 degrees north of the equator (Hintze, 1993).

San Rafael Group

Middle Jurassic rocks in GCNRA consists of the San Rafael Group. The formations comprising the group were deposited in a continental setting that alternated between eolian, fluvial, and marine conditions. The San Rafael Group consists of the Page Sandstone, Carmel Formation, Entrada Sandstone, Romana Sandstone, and Summerville Formation (figure 4). The San Rafael Group dominates shoreline outcrops at Bullfrog and Halls Crossing Marinas and from Dangling Rope Marina to Wahweap (figure 5).

Page Sandstone: The Page Sandstone is very similar to the underlying Navajo in appearance and environment of deposition (table 1). The contact between the Navajo and the Page marks the J-2 unconformity (figure 15) and represents a period of minor erosion (Pipiringos and O'Sullivan, 1978). Locally, distinct truncation of dunal cross-beds in the Navajo helps define the contact, but in most places the contact is very difficult to identify (figure 16). In places, the contact is marked by a chert-rich lag (Fred "Pete" Peterson, U.S. Geological Survey, verbal communication, 1999).

The Page Sandstone is included with the underlying Glen Canyon Group on the accompanying maps (figures 5 through 9) because it is difficult to distinguish from the underlying Navajo Sandstone. In addition, the Page varies in thickness from about 300 feet near Page, Arizona (the type section) to 15 feet near the Straight Cliffs (Peter-

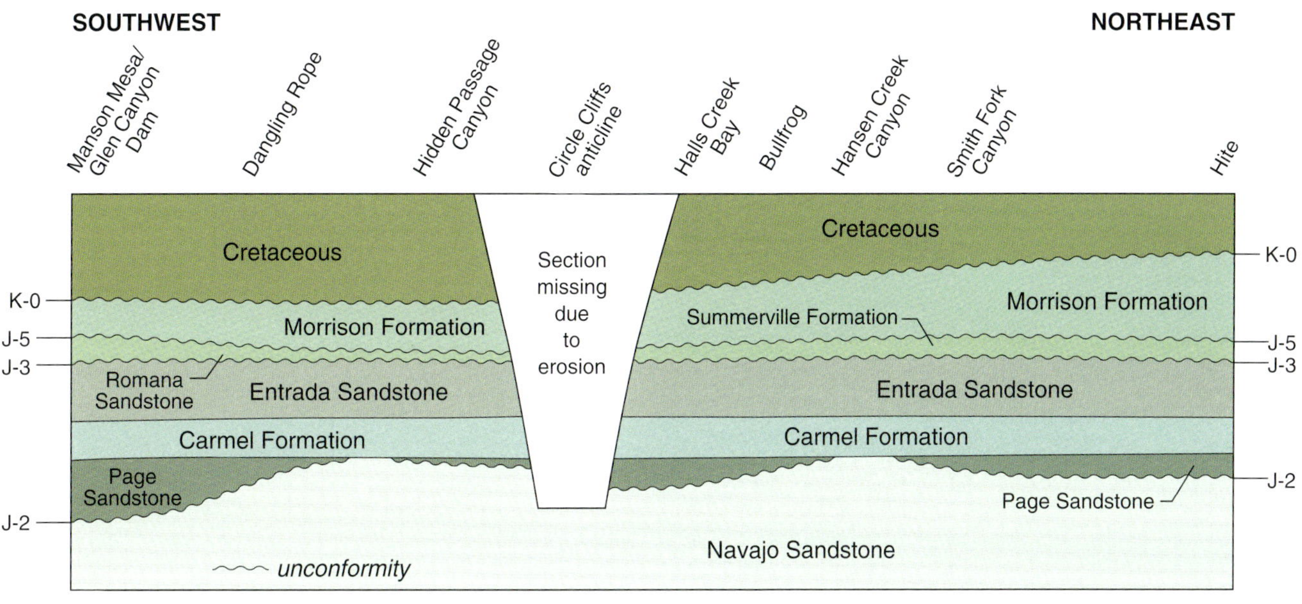

Figure 15. Diagram showing Navajo-Page and Romana-Summerville relationships, and Jurassic unconformities northeast to southwest across Glen Canyon National Recreation Area.

son and Pipiringos, 1979). Locally, the Page is absent and the Carmel Formation rests on the Navajo Sandstone (figure 15).

Carmel Formation: The Carmel Formation is a distinctive, earthy, reddish-brown unit that separates thick sandstone beds of the underlying Navajo/Page and the overlying Entrada Sandstone (table 1). Thickness and character of the Carmel are consistent and show only minor variations along the shores of Lake Powell. Good exposures of the Carmel Formation are along Bullfrog Bay, near Dangling Rope Marina, and in the upper parts of Rock Creek. The Carmel thickens to the northwest from the recreation area into western Kane County, where it is divided into five members (Doelling and Davis, 1989). In outcrops near Bullfrog (figure 16), the upper two members of the formation, the Paria River and Winsor, can be identified

(Doelling and Davis, 1989). However, we have not attempted to divide the Carmel into members in the recreation area because it is relatively thin, it contains no thick limestone beds that help distinguish members of the Carmel to the west, and the outcrops are commonly poorly exposed here.

Contorted bedding is common in the Carmel Formation in the Rock Creek area and along the main channel of Lake Powell just north of Rock Creek. The contorted beds are usually associated with deformed beds of the overlying Entrada Sandstone.

Entrada Sandstone: Reddish-orange to tan and white "slickrock" of the Entrada Sandstone dominates the outcrops in the Bullfrog area, between Bullfrog Marina and Hansen Creek, and south along the western shoreline of Lake Powell surrounding Last Chance, Padre, and Wah-

Figure 16. Middle Jurassic stratigraphy, Navajo Sandstone to basal Entrada Sandstone; view of west shore from main channel north of Moki Canyon (dashed where contact is inferred).

Figure 17. Boundary and Dominguez Buttes with Page Sandstone at lake level and Morrison Formation on the skyline.

weap Bays (table 1). The Entrada Sandstone thickens from southwest to northeast across the recreation area.

The formation is divided into three informal members (Doelling and Davis, 1989): a lower reddish-orange, tan and white cross-bedded member, a middle white and orange-red banded member, and an upper white cliff-forming member. Only the lower two members are preserved in the southern part of the recreation area, but all three are preserved to the north. The lower member is referred to as "slickrim" by Doelling and Davis (1989) because of its distinctive steep, but rounded and barren outcrops (figure 17). The middle member typically is marked by a break in slope to a steeper to vertical cliff, and is colored with white and orange-red banding (figure 17). The contact with the overlying Romana Sandstone is sharp and placed at the base of a thin red bed. Regionally, the contact between the Entrada and overlying Romana is the J-3 unconformity (Pipiringos and O'Sullivan, 1978).

The quartz sandstone of the Entrada contains cross-beds, horizontal beds, and contorted beds. Of these, the most fascinating are the large-scale deformation features that are well exposed along the shores of Lake Powell between Wahweap and Dangling Rope Marinas. A description of these features is presented in the "Classic Geologic Sites" section of this article.

Romana Sandstone/Summerville Formation: The upper part of the San Rafael Group consists of the Romana Sandstone and the Summerville Formation. The Summerville is exposed northeast of the Circle Cliffs uplift (Waterpocket Fold) near Bullfrog Bay, and the Romana is well exposed south of the Circle Cliffs uplift along most of the northwest side of the southern part of the lake (Peterson, 1975). These formations are generally stratigraphically equivalent because both formations are bounded by the J-3 and J-5 unconformities (Pipiringos and O'Sullivan, 1978; Peterson and Pipiringos, 1979) (figure 15); however, the exact

stratigraphic relations between the Summerville and Romana are uncertain because they cannot be traced laterally across the Circle Cliffs uplift (figure 15) since erosion has removed these rocks (as well as the overlying Upper Jurassic rocks).

Unlike the Summerville Formation, the lower and upper contacts of the Romana Sandstone are difficult to pick, in spite of the unconformities present, because the Romana is not lithologically distinctive from the underlying Entrada and overlying Morrison (table 1). The Romana Sandstone consists chiefly of cliff-forming sandstone (figure 17). The lower Romana contact is usually placed at the base of a thin red bed that is thought to be a tongue of the Summerville. The upper contact of the Romana is placed underneath a distinctive overhang of the basal Morrison Formation (Fred "Pete" Peterson, verbal communication, 2000). The Romana Sandstone was named for the exposures at Romana Mesa, which lies between Padre and Warm Creek Bays in the southern part of the recreation area (Peterson and Pipiringos, 1979).

The Summerville Formation is a distinctive unit that consists of alternating medium to thin beds of brown, red, minor purple, and white siltstone and sandstone that are crosscut by white gypsum veinlets. It is generally bracketed by thick, cliff-forming sandstone formations.

Morrison Formation

Resistant, thick sandstone beds of the Morrison Formation cap several benches between the drainages from Wahweap Bay to Dangling Rope Marina in the southwest portion of the recreation area and between West and Wetherill Canyons along the east shore. In these areas, the Morrison ranges from 0 to 710 feet in thickness (table 1). Erosion of the formation associated with the regional K-0 (or sub-Cretaceous) unconformity accounts for its varying thickness. The J-5 unconformity marks the basal contact of the formation (Pipiringos and O'Sullivan, 1978).

In other areas of the Colorado Plateau the Morrison Formation is divided into the Tidwell, Salt Wash, and Brushy Basin Members (Doelling and others, this volume); however, only rocks equivalent to the Salt Wash Member are found here. Ledgy, conglomeratic sandstone and interbedded pale-green to maroon mudstone that are probably equivalent to the Salt Wash Member are exposed in the southern part of the recreation area. To the north in Halls Creek Bay (southwest shore), thick exposures of the Salt Wash Member cap many of the landforms (for example, Halls Mesa). The Morrison Formation is famous for containing dinosaur fossils and yielding uranium ore. In GCNRA, the Morrison has produced uranium, but only dinosaur bone fragments have been found (Doelling and others, this volume).

Cretaceous Rocks

Dakota Formation

A widespread unconformity punctuates the top of the Jurassic (K-0 unconformity; Pipiringos and O'Sullivan, 1978). Coarse, sandy to conglomeratic stream deposits of the Dakota Formation represent the onset of Cretaceous deposition in the recreation area following a long gap in the rock record (table 1). The Dakota Formation crops out in a narrow band between Wahweap and Fiftymile Mountain. Two large outcrops lie on the northwest end of Sit Down Bench and Grand Bench, at the head of and north of Last Chance Bay. Peterson (1969a) divided the Dakota into three informal units: lower, middle, and upper. The conglomeratic lower unit is overlain by mixed sandstone, mudstone, bentonitic claystone, and coal of the middle unit. Coal beds in the middle unit are generally thin and discontinuous. The upper unit is chiefly sandstone with abundant fossils (oysters and clams) from marine to brackish water environments. These units are present in the recreation area, but are too thin to differentiate in mapping. The Dakota Formation often forms a "step" outcrop because the upper member is more resistant and caps and protects the generally slope-forming middle member.

Tropic Shale and Straight Cliffs Formation

Conformably overlying the Dakota Formation is the Tropic Shale, which is overlain by the Straight Cliffs Formation in the Kaiparowits Plateau sector of the recreation area (table 1). The Tropic Shale and overlying Straight Cliffs Formation crop out within the recreation area at the end of Fiftymile Mountain, making up the highest rocks visible on Navajo Point from Dangling Rope Marina (figure 4). The Tropic Shale is dark gray and easily erodes into barren and landslide-riddled outcrops along the Straight Cliffs sector of the Fiftymile Mountain escarpment. Numerous landslides involving the Tropic Shale are large enough to cover the Dakota Sandstone and upper formations of the San Rafael Group. The Straight Cliffs Formation overlies the Tropic Shale and caps Fiftymile Mountain. The Straight Cliffs Formation is a thick sequence of sandstone, shale, siltstone, and coal that is divided into four members (Peterson, 1969b). Thick, minable coal deposits are found across a vast region of the Kaiparowits Plateau northwest of GCNRA, which is now within the neighboring Grand Staircase-Escalante National Monument (see Doelling and others, this volume).

The Mancos Shale, roughly similar in age to the Tropic Shale and Straight Cliffs Formations, is present outside the recreation area in the Henry Mountains basin (figure 5). In the Henry Mountains basin, the Mancos Shale is divided into several members that have been correlated to rocks in the Kaiparowits Plateau (Peterson and Ryder, 1975; Shanley and McCabe, 1995).

Quaternary Deposits

Though GCNRA is best known for the stark beauty of its bare redrock exposures, it also contains a surprising quantity and variety of unconsolidated surficial deposits. These sediments are of five general types: (1) alluvium - sediment deposited in stream and river channels by flowing water and as alluvial fans, (2) eolian - wind-blown sand, silt, and clay, (3) mass-wasting deposits - landslide, slump, and rock-fall debris (talus), (4) colluvium - materials that accumulate on moderate slopes; and (5) residuum - a residual lag of weathered, in-place bedrock. The geologic maps (figures 5 through 9) show only large, more continuous surficial deposits; an equal or greater amount is too widely dispersed to show on these maps. Unconsolidated surficial deposits range in age from possibly Late Tertiary to modern (2 million years ago [Ma] to present).

Alluvium

Alluvial deposits are certainly the most diverse surficial deposits in GCNRA, and probably reveal the most about the recent geologic history of the area. They consist of three general types: alluvium deposited by the large rivers, alluvium deposits by local streams and washes, and alluvial fans deposited at the mouths of washes and canyons.

River alluvium consists primarily of moderately to well-sorted cobble to pebble gravel and minor small to large boulders in a sand and silt matrix. Clasts are well rounded due to the constant grinding as they were transported many tens of miles along the river bottoms. River gravels of the Colorado and San Juan Rivers are particularly interesting because they are composed of a wide variety of rock types, including sedimentary and metamorphic quartzite, intrusive igneous (granitic) rocks, metamorphic gneiss and schist, volcanic rocks, limestone, chert, and well-cemented sandstone (figure 18). Many clasts consist of rock types that could only have been eroded from Precambrian and Paleozoic rocks exposed in central and western Colorado, and transported more than 150 miles from their sources. Locally derived clasts are easily identified because they are composed of the same rocks as the local bedrock, they are generally much less rounded, and in many cases they are poorly lithified rocks that

Figure 18. River gravels consisting of volcanic, quartzite, chert, metamorphic, and other types of clasts; south of Antelope Island.

Figure 19. Navajo Mountain, domed up by igneous intrusions, looms over Glen Canyon National Recreation Area. The Navajo Sandstone is at lake level. It is overlain by the Carmel and Entrada Formations. The Morrison Formation forms the dip slopes off the flanks of the dome. High-level alluvial fans shed off of Navajo Mountain cap outcrops of the Entrada in the middle distance. The high-level fan deposits have been tentatively dated at about 500,000 years old, suggesting that all of the main canyon of Glen Canyon was cut after that time (T. Hanks, U.S. Geological Survey, written communication, 2000).

Figure 20. River-cut terrace near Oak Canyon capped by alluvial cobbles carried in by the Colorado and San Juan Rivers, and by large boulders derived from old, high-level alluvial fans that were shed off nearby Navajo Mountain. Boulders and cobbles accumulate down the slope below the terrace cap as talus that mostly mantles the Navajo Sandstone.

would not have survived bouncing down a river bed for many miles.

Early prospectors quickly recognized that much of the river gravel was derived from central Colorado, the site of many gold deposits. Panning revealed that gold is present in most gravel bars, and many attempts have been made to develop placer gold mines, including several in the recreation area. Unfortunately for the miners, the gold is "flour gold," tiny specks the size of finely sifted flour particles that are extremely difficult to separate from the silt and clay, and few mines proved profitable.

Alluvium is also common along small streams and washes. This material is easy to distinguish from river alluvium because it consists of locally derived clasts, is more angular, and is much more poorly sorted. The deposits consist mostly of boulder- to cobble-size clasts of sandstone, siltstone, and other local rock types. In washes in the western part of the recreation area, the material includes volcanic clasts eroded from the high plateaus to the west.

Alluvial-fan deposits form at the points where drainages decrease in gradient and consist of poorly sorted angular debris up to large boulders deposited mostly by debris flows from violent afternoon thunderstorms in the summer months. They range from small fans at the mouths of small washes to large coalesced fans and fan remnants found around the Henry Mountains, Navajo Mountain, the Kaiparowits Plateau, and high mesas (figure 19). They are graded (slope toward) the major drainages that existed at the time they were deposited and are of corresponding ages.

Alluvial deposits are found in active channels as well as erosional remnants that are up to 1,600 feet above the level of the modern rivers (figures 18, 19, and 20) (Hunt, 1969; Doelling and Davis, 1989). The high-level river terrace deposits reflect the long downcutting history of possibly more than a million years. Many attempts have been made to date the terrace deposits. By dating a deposit of volcanic ash of known age preserved in an alluvial terrace northeast of Moab, Willis (1992) determined that the Colorado River has cut down in that area about 400 feet in the last 640,000 years, an average of 0.6 feet per thousand years. A group led by T. Hanks (U.S. Geological Survey, written communication, 2000), using somewhat experimental methods, determined that high-level alluvial-fan remnants sloping off of Navajo Mountain are less than 780,000 years old, and are probably between 350,000 and 500,000 years old (figure 19). If these ages are valid, then the deposits are middle Pleistocene in age. Today, these deposits are about 1,200 feet above active drainages, suggesting an average downcutting rate of up to 2.4 feet per thousand years. This implies that Glen Canyon was cut in just the last 500,000 years, which would indicate some of the highest downcutting rates of any part of the Colorado River system.

Eolian and Residual Deposits

Eolian deposits blanket surfaces in wind shadows, anchored by vegetation, and in areas not subjected to runoff during violent thunderstorms. The most easily recognized deposits consist of well-sorted, rounded, fine- to medium-grained quartz sand. Most sand is derived from the easily weathered Navajo and Entrada Formations, though the other formations contribute their share as well. Wind-blown silt and clay are also common, especially on the high-level plateaus such as the Kaiparowits Plateau, primarily because less wind-blown sand reaches those higher levels. The wind-blown silt and clay form medium- to dark-reddish-brown deposits that are sometimes called loess, or simply "soil."

Pedogenic carbonate ("caliche") deposits are common on older surfaces. These deposits form "hardpan," a pale gray to white calcium-carbonate layer within the soil profile that ranges from a few inches to several feet thick. Because caliche accumulates a few feet below the ground surface, it is generally only exposed in recent stream or road cuts. Excellent examples are exposed in road cuts near Wahweap and Bullfrog Marinas. The caliche is essentially wind-blown calcium-carbonate dust. It accumulates on the ground surface and is leached into the subsurface by water where it accumulates in the soil profile. Caliche is a valuable indicator of the age of deposits since it takes time to accumulate, and accumulation rates can be calculated for a given area (Birkeland and others, 1991).

Residuum is a lag deposit of weathered bedrock. Since sandstone is the most common rock type in the recreation area, most residuum is sand and appears similar to wind-blown sand piles; some has undoubtedly been reworked by the wind. It accumulates on stable, weathered surfaces, and generally has a thick caliche zone.

Colluvium and Mass-Wasting Deposits

Colluvium consists of a mixture of alluvial, eolian, minor mass-wasting, and residual deposits that accumulate on moderate slopes. Mass-wasting deposits in GCNRA are of five general types: (1) landslides that mostly involve colluvium and talus piles on steep slopes, (2) bedrock slumps and slides, (3) talus and rock-fall debris, (4) slumps and slides induced by waters of Lake Powell, and (5) debris flows. Mass wasting is a concern because it can damage or destroy roads, buildings, and other facilities, and can be deadly.

Colluvium and talus landslides are common and consist of thick piles of extremely poorly sorted, angular rubble that forms hummocky mounds on moderate slopes. Thick piles of colluvium and talus tend to accumulate on the non-resistant, slope-forming units at the base of cliffs and ledges. Under normal conditions, these deposits are stable; however, during periods of increased precipitation, water percolates through the loose rubble, increasing load, and decreasing friction. Continued erosion along gullies and washes also tends to destabilize the rubble. Eventual-

ly, the piles begin to slide downslope.

Bedrock slumps and slides generally form as continued erosion oversteepens slopes and undercuts resistant layers of bedrock. Joints, which are common in the recreation area, aid the process by allowing water to percolate down to the base of the resistant rock where it will perch on the less porous clayey rock layers. The water then weakens cement and moistens clay particles, which decreases friction and increases load. Eventually, the bedrock fails and slumps or slides downslope.

Mass wasting of bedrock in the recreation area involves clay-bearing formations overlain by jointed rock units that typically form steep cliffs. The formations that are most susceptible to mass wasting include the Triassic Chinle Formation, the Jurassic Wingate and Navajo Sandstone, and the Cretaceous Tropic Shale. However, the most abundant and largest mass-wasting deposits involve the Chinle Formation and the overlying Wingate Sandstone. Spectacular landslides, slumps, rock falls, and rock slides involving the Chinle and Wingate are exposed in the San Juan Arm of Lake Powell, and around Good Hope Bay and The Rincon along the main channel of Lake Powell (figures 3, 5, and 13). See the section on "Classic Geologic Sites" for a more complete description of the Chinle and Wingate mass wasting.

Debris flows (commonly called flash floods) are caused by thunderstorms that occur during the summer monsoon season in southern Utah. The cloudbursts create fast-moving water—laden with rock, silt, vegetation, and other debris—that flows down drainages. These debris flows can quickly overwhelm hikers in slot canyons, leaving little time or place to escape. On August 12, 1997, a debris flow swept away 11 hikers in Antelope Canyon, a popular hike near the southeast part of the recreation area (Zoellner, 1997) (figure 3). Only one person survived the ordeal by riding an 11-foot wave of water and debris before pulling himself out to safety. Mud and debris buried the other 10 hikers—only one body was found and recovered. The cloudburst that caused the debris flow originated 15 miles southwest of the canyon. In fact, the skies above the trailhead were sunny at the time. Thus, it is wise to consult National Park Service personnel for weather information before hiking any of the slot canyons in the recreation area.

Rock falls also pose a threat to life in the recreation area. Camping is risky at the base of steep cliffs that are jointed. Rock falls are sudden and often follow rainstorms, but they can come without warning (figure 21). Most rock falls are uneventful; however, people have been killed. In 1999, a biologist was crushed in his tent by a rock fall in the upper reaches of the San Juan Arm.

Most forms of mass wasting have been greatly accelerated along the shorelines of Lake Powell. They are generally the result of three processes working together: (1) the constant water supply soaks deep into the clay-bearing rocks, decreasing stability of clay minerals and increasing load, (2) the water gradually dissolves soluble cements in

Figure 21. Rock fall (cloud of dust) from jointed Wingate; north shore just east of Bald Rock Canyon along the crest of the Circle Cliffs anticline, San Juan River Arm.

some rocks, and (3) wave action greatly increases erosion of less resistant rocks, undercutting and destabilizing overlying cliffs and ledges.

STRUCTURAL AND GEOLOGIC HISTORY

Three structural events helped shape the region in and around GCNRA: the Laramide orogeny, the laccolithic intrusions of the Henry Mountains and Navajo Mountain, and Tertiary-Quaternary relative uplift of the Colorado Plateau. Millions of years of erosion have removed much of the rocks uplifted by these events and the remaining rocks are now displayed in an arid environment along the shore of a man-made lake. Lake Powell provides the access to observe fascinating evidence of these events and spectacular geologic features associated with them.

Depositional History

The oldest rocks exposed in GCNRA are Pennsylvanian in age. During that time, the northern part of the recreation area was part of a subsiding basin that alternated from restricted-marine conditions with limited communication to the ocean to open-marine conditions where the connection with the ocean was unimpeded and waters circulated freely into the embayment (Hermosa Group and Rico Formation and equivalents). Pennsylvanian deposition was thin over platforms separating basins in the region (Doelling and Davis, 1989). Deposits were laid down in shallow marine, beach, lagoonal, and deltaic environments.

The Early Permian was a time when the climate was warm and dry in the region (Stokes, 1986). An extensive coastal dune field covered most of southeastern Utah (Cedar Mesa Sandstone and Organ Rock Formation) with winds from the north-northwest (Kamola and Chan, 1986; Cole and others, 1996; Stanesco and others, this volume). However, shallow marine transgressions occurred period-

ically, resulting in littoral (White Rim Sandstone), mudflat, and beach environments (Doelling and Davis, 1989). The boundary between the Early Permian and the Early Triassic is marked by the major TR-1 unconformity (Pipiringos and O'Sullivan, 1978).

Throughout the early Mesozoic, the Colorado Plateau region that includes the recreation area was a broad, low, continental shelf that intermittently accumulated shallow marine to coastal plain sediments (Moenkopi Formation). Utah was near the equator during the Triassic and the region received more moisture (Scotese, 1999). Tidal flat environments followed by river floodplain and lacustrine settings were prevalent (Chinle Formation).

During the Early Jurassic, the climate was dry and wind-blown dunes dominated the region (Wingate Sandstone). Later, shallow sinuous rivers meandered across a broad floodplain (Kayenta Formation). Though the climate was fairly dry, dinosaur tracks in this and other areas indicate that plants and animals flourished. Over time, the climate became drier, perhaps aided by wind-shadow effects of mountains to the west, and the environment gradually changed back to a coastal dune field (Navajo Sandstone). Middle and Late Jurassic deposits indicate that the region continued to lie near sea level and received continental and shallow marine deposition. Environments included tidal flat, sabkha, beach (Carmel Formation, Entrada Sandstone, and Summerville Formation), braided stream, and floodplain (Romana Sandstone and Morrison Formation).

During the Early Cretaceous, the area likely underwent slow erosion with limited additional continental deposition (no deposits prserved). During the Late Cretaceous, the environment of the region was coastal plain to shallow marine. Deposition was from rivers carrying sediment from the Sevier orogenic belt to the west (lower Dakota Formation). Other environments included lagoonal, beach, and paludal (swamp) (upper Dakota Formation). A major transgression of the sea from the east (Tropic Shale and Tununk Member of the Mancos Shale) was followed by deposition during later regression in shoreface, beach, lagoon, and paludal environments (Straight Cliffs Formation). Peat beds in the swamps and lagoons yielded thick coal deposits.

Laramide Orogeny

Large uplifts and basins developed during the mountain-building event known as the Laramide orogeny between latest Cretaceous time (about 70 Ma) and the Eocene (about 38 Ma) (Hintze, 1993). Laramide features in and adjacent to GCNRA include the Kaiparowits and Henry Mountains structural basins, and the Circle Cliffs (Waterpocket Fold) and Monument uplifts (figures 2 and 3).

Gentle north- to northwest-trending anticlines and synclines, secondary folds of the Kaiparowits basin (figures 5, 7, and 9), extend into the southern part of the recreation area and are easily recognized because the horizontal lake surface serves as a perfect datum. The folds de-

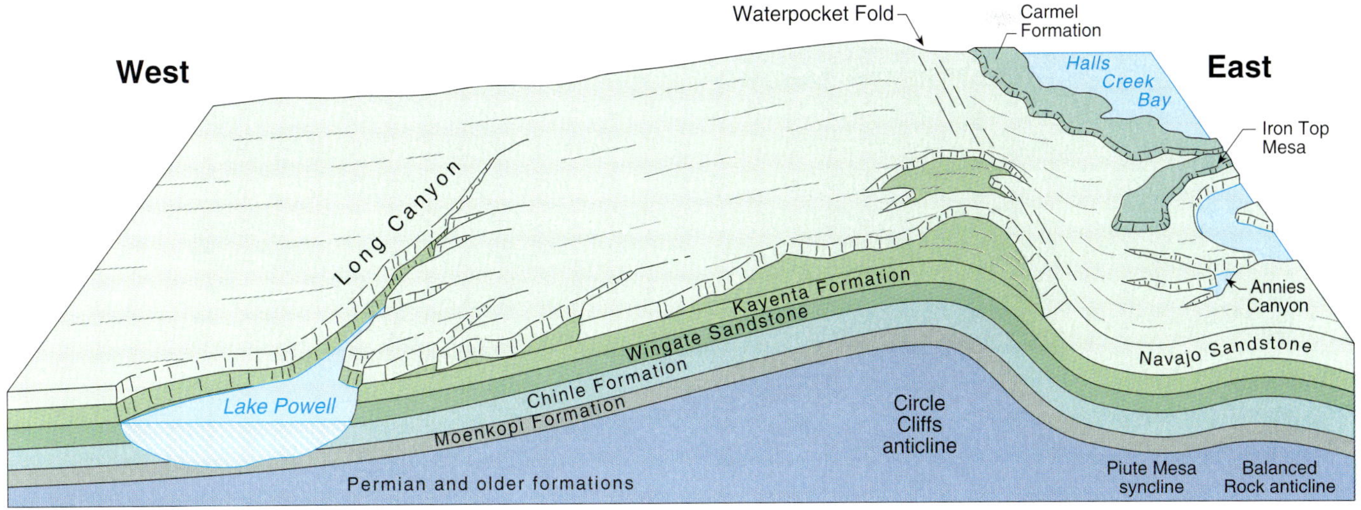

Figure 22. Diagrammatic block diagram across the Circle Cliff anticline, the large doubly plunging structure that trends north-south to northwest-southeast through the center of Glen Canyon National Recreation Area. The steeply dipping Waterpocket Fold defines the east flank and extends northward into Grand Staircase-Escalante National Monument and Capitol Reef National Park.

veloped over deep faults in Precambrian basement rocks. Jurassic strata are the oldest rocks exposed on the crests of anticlines. Dips on the flanks of the structures are up to 7 degrees, and plunge is to the north (Doelling and Davis, 1989). These folds are tens of miles in length and have been targets for petroleum exploration. A few minor normal faults developed parallel to the axes of some of the structures. These faults are typically high angle, down to the west, and have less than 100 feet of displacement. One notable fault is found at Hole-In-The-Rock. The Mormon pioneers took advantage of the weaker fractured rock to complete a "road" in 1880 through the canyon wall that dropped nearly 2,000 feet to the Colorado River below.

The Monument uplift is a large, broad, north-south-trending, asymmetrical monocline that exposes Upper Paleozoic rocks over much of southeastern Utah and northeastern Arizona (figures 3 and 5). The gently dipping western flank is located, in part, in the eastern part of the recreation area. Numerous secondary folds wrinkle the uplift along the eastern San Juan Arm of Lake Powell and the canyon of the San Juan River (figure 8) (Baars, 1973). The flanks of these structures have gentle dips similar to folds in the Kaiparowits basin to the west. They are also tens of miles in length, but are generally oriented in a north-south direction.

The southeastern part of the Henry Mountains basin lies in the north-central part of the recreation area (figure 3). This basin is asymmetric with steep dips on the west limb and gentle dips on the east limb (the west flank of the Monument uplift) (Doelling, 1975; Irwin and others, 1980). The axis of the basin trends north-northwest between the Henry Mountains on the east and the Circle Cliffs uplift to the west (figure 7). In the southern part of the basin just north of the Bullfrog Bay area, the basin axis is divided in two with the Muley Creek anticline (the site of several unsuccessful petroleum exploration wells) in between. Juras-

sic Entrada Sandstone is exposed on the crest of the structure. The two axes merge again to the south into the Rock Spring syncline which roughly parallels Halls Creek Bay (figure 7).

The most prominent structure within GCNRA, in terms of both areal extent and elevation, is the north-northwest to south-southeast-trending Circle Cliffs uplift (figures 5, 7, 8, and 22). The steep east limb of the uplift, referred to as the Waterpocket Fold, has dips of up to 15 degrees (the fold has dips as great as 60 degrees north of the recreation area) (Doelling, 1975; Doelling and Davis, 1989). The gentle west limb has dips of 4 degrees or less and extends southwest to the Escalante Canyon area (Doelling and Davis, 1989). The south-plunging nose of the uplift crosses the lake in The Rincon area. The Navajo Sandstone is exposed along most of the crest of the uplift within the recreation area. Across the main channel of the lake near Iceberg Canyon, the Kayenta Formation forms a major dip slope along the Waterpocket Fold. A belt of faults along the Waterpocket Fold extends from the lake north for 12 miles. These faults are down to the east with small displacements (Doelling and Davis, 1989).

The Henry Mountains and Navajo Mountain Laccoliths

The Henry Mountains are located along the northern end of Lake Powell (figure 2) and consist of five dome-shaped mountains: from north to south they are Mount Ellen (11,522 feet), Mount Pennell (11,371 feet), Mount Hillers (10,723 feet), Mount Holmes (7,930 feet), and Mount Ellsworth (8,235 feet). The southern four mountains are 6 to 8 miles in diameter at the base; Mount Ellen is about 12 miles in diameter. Each mountain consists of a stock (a discordant igneous intrusion) surrounded by laccoliths (Hunt, 1980). The Henry Mountains are the type locality for laccoliths as first described by Gilbert (1877). A

Figure 23. Large, silt-filled mudcracks (inset is closeup) in the shale of the Moenkopi Formation, Red Canyon.

laccolith is a dome-shaped structure formed when igneous intrusions were injected along bedding planes (concordant) and bowed up layers of overlying sedimentary rocks. In the Henry Mountains, these laccoliths are intruded in the Jurassic Morrison Formation and Cretaceous units (Hunt, 1980). The igneous rocks are granodioritic (diorite porphyry) in composition (Doelling, 1975) and were intruded 31.2 to 23.3 Ma during the late Oligocene (Nelson and others, 1992). All of the Henry Mountains except Mount Ellsworth have numerous folds and domes developed from underlying laccoliths and other intrusive bodies superimposed on top (Hunt, 1980). Triassic through Cretaceous strata crop out on the flanks of these mountains. Along the western side of the northern part of Lake Powell, Permian and Triassic formations dip gently west into a subtle syncline which lies east and trends parallel to Mounts Ellsworth and Holmes (Doelling, 1975).

Navajo Mountain is a broad structural dome that dominates the eastern skyline in the southern GCNRA (figures 2 and 19). Unlike the other laccoliths in the Colorado Plateau, very little is known about the intrusive body that underlies Navajo Mountain because it has not been exposed by erosion (figure 5). Only a small syenite porphyry intrusive body crops out on Navajo Mountain's south-southwest flank (Condie, 1964). Navajo Mountain is about 6 miles in diameter and its summit is 10,388 feet above sea level. The Jurassic Morrison, Entrada, Carmel, Page (?), Navajo, Kayenta, and Wingate Formations crop out on the flanks and canyons that radiate from Navajo Mountain (Baker, 1936; Hackman, 1956). Cretaceous Dakota Sandstone is exposed at the top of the dome.

Tertiary-Quaternary Regional Uplift and Erosion

The Colorado Plateau was uplifted along with a much broader area that included the Basin and Range Province to the west and southwest in early Cenozoic time, with limited uplift probably continuing through the remaining Cenozoic (Hunt, 1956; Lucchitta, 1979; Graf and others, 1987; Fleming, 1994). This regional uplift changed the landscape from one of deposition to one of massive erosion. Several thousand feet of sedimentary rocks have been removed by the erosive processes of running water and mass wasting. Most of this material has been carried to the sea by the Colorado River system.

As the Colorado Plateau continued to rise and downcutting of the Grand Canyon accelerated about 5 million years ago (Lucchitta, 1989), the rejuvenated Colorado River drainage system was able to rapidly carve through strata as headward erosion increased. The results of this downcutting are the countless canyons and entrenched meanders in Glen Canyon and its tributary canyons. The rate of downcutting along the tributary canyons was controlled by the elevation of the Colorado River channel (Huntoon and others, this volume). Over the last few million years, the effects of rapid downcutting along the Colorado River caused the local base levels of tributary rivers to be lowered, and their channels to cut downward faster than they cut laterally into their sides (Huntoon and others, this volume). Thus, the drainages like the Escalante River drainage system became entrenched by rapid headward erosion.

Erosion rates were also higher during parts of the Pleistocene than at the present because the area experienced increased precipitation and lower temperatures. The higher volumes of water allowed more material to be eroded and carried to the Colorado River.

Jointing

Prominent structural features of rocks in GCNRA are the large sets of joints observed principally in sandstone formations of the Kayenta, Navajo, and Wingate Formations. These brittle sandstones developed joints in response to regional tectonics, Laramide folds, and the erosional unloading of thousands of feet of overlying rock. Joints are closely spaced in many areas, but spacing varies with bedset thickness and lithology. Three types of joints are present in GCNRA: (1) near-vertical, (2) inclined, and (3) surficial. Slot canyons, rocks falls, and the development of numerous natural arches found in GCNRA are controlled, in part, by the location and orientation of near-vertical and inclined joints. Surficial joints contribute to dome-like shapes above vertical canyon cliffs in the Navajo Sandstone as well as to numerous rock falls.

CLASSIC GEOLOGIC SITES

Moenkopi Mudcracks and Chinle Paleosols

Mudcracks are common sedimentary features in many of the terrestrial rock units that can be found throughout much of the recreation area. However, the Moenkopi Formation exposed in Red Canyon—about half way between Hite and Bullfrog—contains excellent examples of mudcracks in profile. The Moenkopi mudcracks are easy to identify because the v-shaped cracks are developed in the red siltstone and mudstone and were filled with light-gray, fine-grained sandstone (figure 23). The red siltstone and mudstone are generally softer and weather more easily than the sandstone. Thus, the sandstone-filled cracks stand out in relief as light-colored cones.

The Chinle Formation contains classic examples of paleosols (fossil soils). Some of the best developed paleosols within the formation are found at the base of a channel sandstone between Twomile and Fourmile Canyons (figures 3 and 12). The paleosols are soft, varicolored mudstone and siltstone that contain mottled light-colored bedding, which typically are carbonate (caliche) zones. These carbonate zones generally form near the ancient ground surface. Roots zones are also preserved in the paleosols as light-colored, steeply inclined veinlets of carbonate rock.

Massive Chinle and Wingate Slides

Landslides, slumps, and rock falls involving the Chinle Formation and Wingate Sandstone are found in the recreation area wherever these units are exposed, but the mass wasting of these units is most impressive along the shores of Lake Powell at Good Hope Bay, near The Rincon, and along sections of the San Juan Arm (figures 3 and 5).

Figure 24. Major slide/slump in the Wingate Sandstone at the mouth of Ticaboo Canyon.

Nearly everywhere the Chinle Formation is exposed above (or just below) the water line, landslides and slumps have formed. Outcrops of the Chinle in the recreation area commonly have a hummocky topographic expression and often contain fresh landslide and slump scarps (figure 13). The Chinle Formation is susceptible to mass wasting because it contains swelling clays that are derived from altered volcanic beds. These swelling clays have very low strength and are unstable when they become wet. Lake Powell provides a constant source of water for the unstable clay beds. In addition, the lake level annually rises and falls with the spring runoff and planned water release associated with power generation. The cyclic wetting and dewatering of parts of the Chinle aggravates the already unstable condition.

Rock falls and slides can occur at anytime and at any place where jointed, steep, rocky cliffs overlie softer, unstable rocks (figure 21). Rock falls involving the Wingate Sandstone are often particularly large because of a combination of the jointing and the Wingate's stratigraphic position on top of the unstable Chinle Formation (figure 24). The Chinle is commonly mantled with large Wingate Sandstone blocks, a testament to its susceptibility to rock falls.

Navajo Oases

In addition to "seas" of wind-blown sand dunes, large deserts such as the Sahara contain features such as oases. Oases are vegetated areas in desert regions where springs are present because the water table is close to the surface. Excellent examples of oasis deposits in the Navajo Sandstone are exposed in Forgotten, Moki, Annies, Slick Rock, Iceberg, and Escalante Canyons, to name a few, and along the main channel of Lake Powell.

Oasis deposits are typically represented by light-gray, 5- to 10-foot-thick, thin and horizontally bedded limestone that commonly contains oscillation ripples and mudcracks (figure 25A and B). They generally pinch out over very

Figure 25. A - Typical limestone oasis deposit near the top of the Navajo Sandstone; Forgotten Canyon. B - Mudcracks in oasis limestone mud above bed containing ripple marks; Forgotten Canyon. C - Rapid pinch-out of thin limestone bed in the Navajo Sandstone; Moki Canyon. D - Algal laminae within the limestone oasis beds in the Navajo Sandstone; Moki Canyon.

short distances (figure 25C), and can be observed on both sides of the narrower canyons. Limestones in several Navajo outcrops have yielded fossil plants and invertebrates (Stokes, 1991; Santucci, this volume). Some limestone beds also contain possible algal heads (figure 25D) and evidence of salinity (voids from dissolved gypsum crystals now filled with large calcite crystals).

Other limestones represent small freshwater lakes based on geochemical analysis of a similar deposit along the Colorado River near Canyonlands National Park (Gilland, 1979). Fresh ground water at a shallow depth had to persist for prolonged periods of time, perhaps many thousands of years, to allow the lake or pond deposits of these oases to develop (Stokes, 1991). The continuous supply of fresh water provided favorable environments for life and the deposition of carbonate rocks.

Alcoves and Hanging Gardens

Large alcoves with beautiful hanging gardens can be seen in many side canyons, such as Escalante Canyon, and along the main channel of Lake Powell (figure 26). They are best developed in the Navajo Sandstone. Alcoves form where ground water percolating down through pores in the sandstone encounters a low-permeability bed that impedes continued downward water flow. Such beds have a

higher silt or clay content, and represent interdunal areas or the boundaries between dune bedsets. Because the infiltrating ground water's downward flow is restricted, it moves horizontally along a less resistant flow path and exits the rock near these low-permeability bedding planes, forming seeps and springs. The water dissolves and removes cementing minerals in the sandstone, causing the rock to weaken relative to the rock elsewhere on the cliff face. The processes of weathering and erosion proceed faster on the weakened rock and eventually form a recess or alcove in the cliff. The increased moisture and shade are ideal for a variety of plants, which further aid in the breakdown of the rock. The wet surfaces are often covered with mats of various kinds of algae, ferns such as maidenhair and bracken, grasses, and sedges (Everhart, 1983).

Oddities of the Navajo Sandstone

Ironstone deposits and tafoni are just some of the oddities found in the Navajo Sandstone. The ironstone deposits include concretions called "Navajo berries" or "Moki marbles." The ironstone concretions weather out of the Navajo (figure 27A) and consist of a well-cemented limonite shell around a friable (loosely cemented) sandstone core (Doelling, 1968, 1975). Most are nearly spherical and range from pea size up to 4 inches in diameter.

Figure 26. Navajo Sandstone alcove with a hanging garden of vegetation where ground water seeps along an impervious horizontal bed. Note south-southeast-dipping cross-beds high on the cliff face which indicate paleowind direction in the Jurassic Navajo sand dune field. View looking north in Knowles Canyon.

Figure 27. A - Navajo berries/Moki marbles; east shore, Arizona, main channel west of Crossing of the Fathers. B - Navajo Sandstone with iron-stone sheets along bedding planes; west shore east of Bullfrog Marina. C - Spectacular soft-sediment deformation in Navajo beds; south side of Antelope Island, Arizona. D - Numerous holes in the Entrada Sandstone; Dry Rock Creek Canyon.

Figure 28. A - J-2 unconformity at the Navajo/Page contact; type locality of the Jurassic Page Sandstone, Manson Mesa, Arizona. B - shrinkage (desiccation) cracks filled with Page Sandstone at the J-2 unconformity shown on A. C - angular chert granules (closeup) at the J-2 unconformity.

Navajo berries form in the subsurface, probably after the sand is lithified to sandstone. They are composed mostly of quartz sand bound by the dense mineraloid goethite ($FeO.OH$), with some formation of hematite (Fe_2O_3). The process is uncertain, but they form as minute amounts of iron in ground water is precipitated. Ground water moving through the sandstone typically has about 0.1 to 0.2 parts per million dissolved iron. Slight changes in the oxygen content of the water, either by interaction with ground water from different sources, or possibly from hydrocarbons migrating through the rock, can cause the iron to precipitate. The precipitation probably first occurs around a small impurity or void in the rock, and grows as more iron is precipitated, forming concretions. The round shape that attracts attention is an efficient shape and occurs naturally as additional iron is precipitated around the core. In some Navajo berries, the iron migrates outward toward the precipitation front, leaving the core of the concretion weakly cemented, and forming a dense shell around soft sand. The Navajo berries form right within the sandstone; examination under a microscope shows that quartz sand grains are embedded in the ironstone, though in more ad-

vanced stages, the cements tend to push the sand grains aside. Precipitation of iron from ground water may also be responsible for the ironstone sheets often found along Navajo cross-beds (figure 27B) (Doelling and Davis, 1989). These sheets are typically thin, dark brown, and harder than the sandstone. They are common in sandstone beds that were previously contorted into tight, recumbent folds as found on Antelope Island (figure 27C).

Small holes, commonly referred to as "stonepecker holes" or tafoni, have been weathered out of the Navajo Sandstone (also observed in the Cedar Mesa, White Rim, Wingate, Page, and Entrada [figure 27D] Sandstones) along cross-beds and bedset boundaries in many areas. They are most likely caused by differential erosion in areas where ground water has weakened the cement at small variations or imperfections in the rock. Once started, they form voids where water can accumulate protected from evaporation, thus promoting further growth.

J-2 Unconformity

The J-2 regional unconformity divides the Early Jurassic from the Middle Jurassic, representing a gap of 2 million years, and is found at the contact between the Navajo

Figure 29. *Major injection features in the Entrada Sandstone at lake level, Padre Bay, north of Cookie Jar Butte. Note how the beds adjacent to the vertically oriented massive injection feature are undisturbed.*

Figure 30. *Cylindrical injection or deformation features in the Entrada Sandstone. Arrows mark three such features with a rind of bleached sandstone. Diameter of features in the tens of feet. View east, near the mouth of Rock Creek Bay.*

and overlying Page Sandstones (Pipiringos and O'Sullivan, 1978). The J-2 unconformity is best observed at Manson Mesa, Arizona (figure 28A, B, and C), the type locality of the Page Sandstone, where it was first described in detail by Pipiringos and O'Sullivan (1975). At this locality the unconformity is marked by angular chert granules (figure 28C). The sources for the chert are (1) Navajo carbonate lenses (limestone oases) which were removed by erosion, and (2) winnowing of the Navajo sand itself (Fred "Pete" Peterson, U.S. Geological Survey, verbal communication, 1999). The chert is angular due to breakage from large temperature changes in the desert environment. The chert was spread out at the J-2 unconformity as a residual lag, as opposed to being a water-lain deposit. The unconformity is also marked by shrinkage (desiccation) cracks filled with sands from the overlying Page Sandstone (figure 25B), breccia zones, alteration zones up to 30 feet thick,

Figure 31. *Entrada Sandstone and small displacement intraformational faults associated with deformation features. Note faults at both arrows and the lack of displacement in the bed above the upper arrow. Last Chance Bay, north side near entrance.*

bleaching caused by ground water (humic [organic] acids, carbon dioxide gas, or hydrocarbons removed much of the iron from the iron-bearing cements), and carbonate concretions.

Entrada Sandstone Deformation Features

The Entrada Sandstone contains some of the most unique and puzzling features within GCNRA. These features are secondary structures of large to small, irregular, homogeneous masses of sandstone that disrupt and deform normal bedding within the Entrada Sandstone (figures 29 and 30). In addition, small-displacement faults are associated with some of the nearby secondary structures (figure 31). Deformation related to the emplacement of the secondary structures does not affect the uppermost beds of the Entrada or the overlying Romana Sandstone. The secondary structures are fascinating because some of the sandstone masses were clearly injected into the surrounding Entrada host, whereas other sandstone masses have collapsed into openings or possible scoured zones carved into the underlying beds (figure 32). The sandstone masses are generally cylindrical (figure 30) in form, are as much as 240 feet wide, and have an exposed height of as much as 300 feet (Netoff, 1999; M.A. Chan, University of Utah, written communication, 2000). They generally lack bedding and have a sharp boundary with the adjacent host beds. Commonly the adjacent host beds are undeformed and the contact is often marked by a thin white or light-colored bleached zone.

The origin of these secondary structures is enigmatic, and additional study is needed. Some geologists attribute the origin of these features to ground water activity while others ascribe them to soft-sediment deformation, seismically induced deformation by paleoearthquakes, or meteor impact (Gabelman, 1955; Phoenix, 1958; Davidson, 1967; Alvarez and others, 1998; Netoff and Shroba, 1998; Netoff, 1999).

Figure 32. Entrada collapse and infill features near entrance (north shore) of Padre Bay.

The sandstone deformation masses are preserved in many places in the recreation area, but are concentrated along the shores of Padre, Last Chance, and Rock Creek Bays, and along the main channel from Rock Creek Bay to Dangling Rope Marina. The largest ones are along the shores of Padre and Last Chance Bays. These features are also recognized and described elsewhere in Utah, Arizona, New Mexico, and Scotland (Parker, 1933; Allen, 1961; Barrington and Kerr, 1963; Schlee, 1963; Wenrich, 1985; Nocita, 1988; Hunter and others, 1992).

Clusters of giant weathering pits (figure 33) are associated with the secondary structures near Cookie Jar Butte in the Padre Bay area. The most spectacular of these pits are cylindrical shaped with vertical walls. Some are over 100 feet deep and 120 feet wide, possibly among the deepest weathering pits on Earth (Netoff and Shroba, 1997). The injected structures in which the pits developed are composed of very fine grained, highly porous arkosic sandstone weakly cemented with smectite clays and calcite (Netoff and Shroba, 1995). Weathering processes on the sides and floors of the pits include: calcite and gypsum crystal growth in pores, hydration of smectite clays (swelling clays), dissolution of calcite cement, and spalling along surficial joints (Netoff and Shroba, 1995). The weathered sediments have been removed by strong winds (Netoff, 1997). These pits are probably no older than early Pleistocene (Netoff and others, 1994).

The Rincon

The Rincon was once an entrenched meander of the Colorado River and is located on the crest of the Circle Cliffs anticline on the east side of the main channel of Lake Powell (figures 3 and 7). The Chinle Formation is at lake level, followed by jointed Wingate, and Kayenta with some Navajo on top of the butte. The Rincon was one of many meander goosenecks along the Colorado River. Several thousand years ago the river cut off the meander through the Wingate Sandstone, and shortened its length by about 6 miles. The Rincon butte, representing the old

Figure 33. Giant weathering pit in the Entrada Sandstone, one of many clustered near Cookie Jar Butte along Padre Bay.

"peninsula," stands 600 to 750 feet above the now-abandoned channel.

ACKNOWLEDGMENTS

We thank Bruce Heise, Tim Connors, and Joe Gregson of the National Park Service, Geological Resources Division, and Norm Henderson and Dave Gustafson of Glen Canyon National Recreation Area, National Park Service for providing enthusiastic support, funding, access, and transportation to Glen Canyon National Recreation Area. The Utah Geological Survey (UGS) covered most field expenses and provided transportation to the Glen Canyon National Recreation Area. We thank Stephen M. Richard, Arizona Geological Survey, for providing the GIS files used to construct the Arizona section of the geologic map. Jim Parker (UGS) turned many of our rough drawings into fine illustrations. We thank Dave Tabet and Mike Hylland of the UGS for their careful reviews and constructive criticisms of the manuscript and Marjorie Chan for assistance with Entrada deformation features.

REFERENCES

Allen, J.R.L., 1961, Sandstone-plugged pipes in the lower Old Red Sandstone of Shropshire, England: Journal of Sedimentary Petrology, v. 31, p. 325-335.

Alvarez, W., Staley, E., O'Connor, D., and Chan, M.A., 1998, Synsedimentary deformation in the Jurassic of southeastern Utah - a case of impact shaking?: Geology, v. 26, p. 579-582.

Baars, D.L., 1962, Permian system of Colorado Plateau: American Association of Petroleum Geologists Bulletin, v. 46, no. 2, p. 149-218.

—1973, Geology of the canyons of the San Juan River -- a river runner's guide: Four Corners Geological Society, Seventh Field Conference, p. 1-7.

Baars, D.L., and Seager, W.R., 1970, Stratigraphic control of petroleum in White Rim Sandstone (Permian) in and near Canyonlands National Park, Utah: American Association of Petroleum Geologists Bulletin, v. 54, no. 5, p. 709-718.

Baker, A.A., 1936, Geology of the Monument Valley-Navajo Mountain region, San Juan County, Utah: U.S. Geological Survey Bulletin 865, 106 p.

Barrington, J., and Kerr, P.F., 1963, Collapse features and silica plugs near Cameron, Arizona: Geological Society of America Bulletin, v. 74, p. 1237-1258.

Birkeland, P.W., Machette, M.N., and Haller, K.M., 1991, Soils as a tool for applied Quaternary geology: Utah Geological Survey Miscellaneous Publication 91-3, 63 p.

Blakey, R.C., 1970, Geology of the Paria NW quadrangle, Kane County, Utah: Salt Lake City, University of Utah, M.S. thesis, 171 p.

—1974, Stratigraphic and depositional analysis of the Moenkopi Formation, southeastern Utah: Utah Geological and Mineral Survey Bulletin 104, 81 p.

—1980, Pennsylvanian and Early Permian paleogeography, southern Colorado Plateau and vicinity, *in* Fouch, T.D., and Magathan, E.R., editors, Paleozoic paleogeography of west- central United States: Society of Economic Paleontologists and Mineralogists, Rocky Mountain Section, p. 239-257.

—1994, Paleogeographic and tectonic controls on some Lower and Middle Jurassic erg deposits, Colorado Plateau, *in* Caputo, M.V., Peterson, J.A., and Franczyk, K.J., editors, Mesozoic systems of the Rocky Mountain region, USA: Denver, Rocky Mountain Section, Society of Economic Paleontologists and Mineralogists, p. 273-298.

—1996, Permian eolian deposits, sequences, and sequence boundaries, Colorado Plateau, *in* Longman, M.W., and Sonnenfield, M.D., editors, Paleozoic systems of the Rocky Mountain region, USA, Rocky Mountains Section: Society for Sedimentary Geology, p. 405-426.

Cole, R.D., Moore, G.E., Trevena, A.S., Armin, R.A., and Morton, M.P., 1996, Lithofacies definition in Cutler and Honaker Trail Formations, northeastern Paradox basin, *in* Huffman, A.C., Jr., Lund, W.R., and Godwin, L.H., editors, Geology and resources of the Paradox basin: Utah Geological Association Publication 25, p. 161-172.

Condie, K.C., 1964, Crystallization PO_2 of syenite porphyry from Navajo Mountain, southern Utah: Geologic Society of America Bulletin, v. 75, no. 4, p. 359-362.

Davidson, E.S., 1967, Geology of the Circle Cliffs area, Garfield and Kane Counties, Utah: U.S. Geological Survey Bulletin 1229, 140 p.

Doelling, H.H., 1968, Southern Utah oddities lure rock hounds: Utah Geological Survey Quarterly Review, v. 2, no. 3, p. 7.

—1975, Geology and mineral resources of Garfield County, Utah: Utah Geological and Mineral Survey Bulletin 107, 175 p., 1 plate, scale 1:250,000.

—1997, Interim geologic map of the Smoky Mountain 30' X 60' quadrangle, Kane and San Juan Counties, Utah and Coconino County, Arizona: Utah Geological Survey Open-File Report 359, 2 plates, scale 1:100,000.

Doelling, H.H., and Davis, F.D., 1989, Geology of Kane County, Utah: Utah Geological and Mineral Survey Bulletin 124, 192 p., 10 plates, scale 1:100,000.

Dubiel, R.F., 1987, Sedimentology of the Upper Triassic Chinle Formation, southeastern Utah: Boulder, Colorado, University of Colorado, Ph.D. dissertation, 132 p.

—1994, Triassic deposystems, paleogeography, and paleoclimate of the Western Interior, *in* Caputo, M.V., Peterson, J.A., and Franczyk, K.J., editors, Mesozoic systems of the Rocky Mountain region, USA: Rocky Mountain Section-Society for Sedimentary Geology (SEPM) Publication, p. 133-168.

Everhart, R.E., 1983, Glen Canyon-Lake Powell -- the story behind the scenery: Las Vegas, KC Publications, Inc., p. 10-11.

Fleming, R.F., 1994, Cretaceous pollen in Pliocene rocks -- implications for Pliocene climate in the southwestern United States: Geology, v. 22, p. 787-790.

Gabelman, J.W., 1955, Cylindrical structures in Permian (?) siltstone, Eagle County, Colorado: Journal of Geology, v. 63, p. 214-227.

Gianniny, G.L., Kelly, M.A., and Simo, A.T., 1993, Facies mosaics and mixed carbonate/siliciclastic ramp depositional dynamics, Paradox basin, Utah: unpublished field guide, 61 p.

Gilbert, G.K., 1877, Report on the geology of the Henry Mountains: U.S. Geographical and Geological Survey, Rocky Mountain Region (Powell), 160 p.

Gilland, J.K., 1979, Paleoenvironment of a carbonate lens in the lower Navajo Sandstone near Moab, Utah: Utah Geological and Mineral Survey, Utah Geology, v. 6, no. 1, p. 29-38.

Graf, W.L., Hereford R., Laity, J., and Young, R.A., 1987, Colorado Plateau, *in* Graf, W.L., editor, Geomorphic systems of North America: Geological Society of America Centennial Special Volume 2, p. 259-302.

Gregory, H.E, and Moore, R.C., 1931, The Kaiparowits region, a geographic and geologic reconnaissance of parts of Utah and Arizona: U.S. Geological Survey Professional Paper 164, 161 p.

Hackman, R.J., 1956, Photogeologic map of the Navajo Mountain-13 quadrangle, Kane and Garfield Counties, Utah and Coconino County, Arizona: U.S. Geological Survey Miscellaneous Geologic Investigations Map I-184, scale 1:24,000.

Harrison, T.S., 1927, Colorado-Utah salt domes: American Association of Petroleum Geologists Bulletin, v. 11, p. 111-133.

Heylmun, E.B., 1958 Paleozoic stratigraphy and oil possibilities of the Kaiparowits region of Utah: American Association of Petroleum Geologists Bulletin, v. 42, p. 1781-1811.

Hintze, L.F., 1980, Geologic map of Utah: Utah Geological and Mineral Survey, scale 1:500,000.

—1993, Geologic history of Utah: Brigham Young University Studies Special Publication 7, 202 p.

—1997, Geologic highway map of Utah: Brigham Young University Geology Studies Special Publication 3, scale 1:1,000,000.

Hintze, L.F., and Stokes, W.L., 1964, Geologic map of southeastern Utah: University of Utah and Utah Geological and Mineralogical Survey, unnumbered map, scale 1:250,000.

Hunt, C.B., 1956, Cenozoic geology of the Colorado Plateau: U.S. Geological Survey Professional Paper 279, 99 p.

—1969, Geologic history of the Colorado River: U.S. Geological Survey Professional Paper 669-C, p. 59-130.

—1980, Structural and igneous geology of the Henry Mountains, Utah, *in* Picard, M.D., editor, Henry Mountain symposium: Utah Geological Association Publication 8, p. 25-106.

Hunter, R.E., Gelfenbaum, G. and Rubin, D.M., 1992, Clastic pipes of probable solution-collapse origin in Jurassic rocks of the southern San Juan Basin, New Mexico: U.S. Geological Survey Bulletin 1808-L, 19 p.

Huntoon, J.E., and Chan, M.A., 1987, Marine origin of paleotopographic relief on eolian White Rim Sandstone (Permian), Elaterite Basin, Utah: American Association of Petroleum Geologists Bulletin, v. 71, no. 9, p. 1035-1045.

Irwin, C.D., Clark, W.R., and Peabody, W.W., 1980, Petroleum geology of the Henry Mountains basin, *in* Picard, M.D., editor, Henry Mountain symposium: Utah Geological Association Publication 8, p. 353-366.

Kamola, D.L., and Chan, M.A., 1986, Coastal dune facies, Permian Cutler Formation (White Rim Sandstone), Capitol Reef National Park area, southern Utah: Sedimentary Geology, v. 56, p. 341-356.

Loope, D.B., Sanderson, G.A., and Verville, G.J., 1990, Abandonment of the name "Elephant Canyon Formation" in southeastern Utah; physical and temporal implications: The Mountain Geologist, v. 27, no. 4, p. 119-130.

Lucchitta, Ivo, 1979, Late Cenozoic uplift of the southwestern Colorado Plateau and adjacent Colorado River region: Tectonophysics, v. 61, p. 63-95.

—1989, History of the Grand Canyon and of the Colorado River in Arizona, *in* Jenney, J.P., and Reynolds, S.J., Geologic evolution of Arizona: Arizona Geological Society Digest 17, p. 701-715.

McGill, G.E, and Stromquist, A.W., 1975, Origin of graben in the Needles District, Canyonlands National Park, Utah, *in* Fassett, J.E., and Wengred, S.A., editors, Canyonlands country: Four Corners Geological Society Guidebook, Eighth Field Conference, p. 235-243.

National Park Service, 1994, Glen Canyon-where does the water go?: National Park Service, unnumbered brochure, 2 p.

—1999, Glen Canyon-official map and guide: National Park Service, U.S. Department of the Interior, 2 p.

Nelson, S.T., Heizler, M.T., and Davidson, J.P., 1992, New ^{40}Ar/^{39}Ar ages of intrusive rocks from the Henry and La Sal Mountains: Utah Geological Survey Miscellaneous Publication MP-92-2, 24 p.

Netoff, D., 1999, Seismogenically-induced fluidization of Jurassic erg sands in a wet eolian-sabkha environment, south-central Utah [abs.]: Geological Society of America Program with Abstracts, v. 31, no. 7, p. A-160.

Netoff, D.I., and Shroba, R.R., 1995, Physical weathering processes and probable deflation in the development of giant sandstone weathering pits in southeastern Utah [abs.]: Geological Society of America Abstracts with Programs, v. 27, no. 3, p. 76.

—1997, Evidence of deflational removal of sandy sediment from giant weathering pits in southeastern Utah [abs.]: Geological Society of America Abstracts with Programs, v. 29, no. 6, p. 255.

—1998, The nature and origin of clastic pipes in the Jurassic Entrada Sandstone, southeastern Utah [abs.]: Geological Society of America, Rocky Mountain Section Meeting Program with Abstracts, v. 30, no. 6, p. 33.

Netoff, D.I., Cooper, B.J., and Shroba, R.R., 1994, Origin and development of the giant sandstone weathering pits near Cookie Jar Butte, southeastern Utah [abs.]: Geological Society of America Abstracts with Programs, v. 26, no. 6, p. 56.

Nocita, B.W., 1988, Soft-sediment deformation (fluid escape) features in a coarse grained pyroclastic-surge deposit, north-central New Mexico: Sedimentology, v. 35, p. 275-285.

Orgill, J.R., 1971, The Permian-Triassic unconformity and its relationship to the Moenkopi, Kaibab, and White Rim Formations in and near San Rafael Swell, Utah: Brigham Young University Geology Studies, v. 18, pt. 3, p. 131-179.

Parker, B.H., 1933, Clastic plugs and dikes of the Cimarron Valley area of Union County, New Mexico: Journal of Geology, v. 41, no. 1, p. 38-51.

Peterson, Fred, 1969a, Cretaceous sedimentation and tectonism in the Kaiparowits region, Utah: U.S. Geological Survey Open-File Report, 259 p.

—1969b, Four new members of the Upper Cretaceous Straight Cliffs Formation in the southeastern

Kaiparowits region, Kane County, Utah: U.S. Geological Survey Bulletin 1274-J, 28 p.

—1975, Geologic map of the Sooner Bench quadrangle, Kane County, Utah: U.S. Geological Survey Miscellaneous Geologic Investigations Map I-874, 1:24,000.

Peterson, Fred, and Pipiringos, G.N., 1979, Stratigraphic relations of the Navajo Sandstone to Middle Jurassic formations, southern Utah and northern Arizona: U.S. Geological Survey Professional Paper 1035-B, 43 p.

Peterson, Fred, and Ryder, R.T., 1975, Cretaceous rocks in the Henry Mountains region, Utah and their relation to neighboring regions, *in* Fassett, J.E., and Wengred, S.A., editors, Canyonlands country: Four Corners Geological Society Guidebook, Eighth Field Conference, p. 167-189.

Pipiringos, G.N., and O'Sullivan, R.B., 1975, Chert pebble unconformity at the top of the Navajo Sandstone in southeastern Utah, *in* Fassett, J.E., and Wengred, S.A., editors, Canyonlands country: Four Corners Geological Society Guidebook, Eighth Field Conference, p. 149-156.

—1978, Principal unconformities in Triassic and Jurassic rocks, western interior United States--a preliminary survey: U.S. Geological Survey Professional Paper 1035-A, 29 p.

Phoenix, D.A., 1958, Sandstone cylinders as possible guides to paleomovement of ground water: New Mexico Geological Society Ninth Field Conference, p. 194-196.

—1963, Geology of Lees Ferry area, Coconino County, Arizona: U.S. Geological Survey Bulletin 1137, 86 p.

Sanderson, G.A., and Verville, G.J., 1990, Fusulinid zonation of the General Petroleum No. 45-5-G core, Emery County, Utah: The Mountain Geologist, v. 27, no. 4, p. 131-136.

Schlee, J.S., 1963, Sandstone pipes of the Laguna area, New Mexico: Journal of Sedimentary Petrology, v. 33, p. 112-123.

Scottese, C.R., 1999, PALEOMAP animations: 1999 PALEOMAP Project, CD.

Shanley, K.W., and McCabe, P.J., 1995, Sequence stratigraphy of Turonian-Santonian strata, Kaiparowits Plateau, southern Utah, U.S.A. -- implications for regional correlation and foreland basin evolution, *in* Van Wagoner, J.C., and Bertram, G.T., Sequence stratigraphy of foreland basin deposits: American Association of Petroleum Geologists Memoir 64, p. 103-136.

Shoemaker, E.M., and Stephens, H.G., 1975, First photographs of the Canyonlands, *in* Fassett, J.E., and Wengred, S.A., editors, Canyonlands country: Four Corners Geological Society Guidebook, Eighth Field Conference, p. 111-122.

Stewart, J.H., Poole, F.G., and Wilson, R.F., 1972a, Stratigraphy and origin of the Chinle Formation and related Upper Triassic strata in the Colorado Plateau region: U.S. Geological Survey Professional Paper 690, 336 p.

—1972b, Stratigraphy of the Triassic Moenkopi Formation and related strata in the Colorado Plateau region: U.S. Geological Survey Professional Paper 691, 195 p.

Stokes, W.L., 1986, Geology of Utah: Utah Geological and Mineral Survey Miscellaneous Publication MP-S, 317 p.

—1991, Petrified mini-forests of the Navajo Sandstone, east-central Utah: Utah Geological Survey, Survey Notes, v. 25, no. 1, p. 14-19.

U.S. Department of the Interior, 1996, Glen Canyon Dam - - facts & figures: U.S. Department of the Interior, Bureau of Reclamation and National Park Service, 2 p.

Wengerd, S.A., and Matheny, M.L., 1958, Pennsylvanian system of the Four Corners region: American Association of Petroleum Geologists Bulletin, v. 42, no. 9, p. 2048-2106.

Wenrich, K.J., 1985, Mineralization of breccia pipes in northern Arizona: Economic Geology, v. 80, p. 1722-1735.

Willis, G.C., 1992, Lava Creek "B" volcanic ash in pediment mantle deposits, Colorado Plateau, east central Utah -- implications for Colorado River downcutting and pedogenic carbonate accumulation rates [abs.]: Geological Society of America Program with Abstracts, v. 24, no. 6., p. 68.

Wilson, R.F., 1965, Triassic and Jurassic strata of southwestern Utah, *in* Goode, H.D., and Robison, R.A., editors, Geology and resources of south-central Utah - resources for power: Utah Geological Society Guidebook 19, p. 88-90.

Zoellner, Tom, 1997, Heavenly canyon turns into hell: Salt Lake City, Salt Lake Tribune, August 14, 1997.

Antelope Island
Photograph from Utah Geological Survey

Geology of Utah's Parks and Monuments
2000 Utah Geological Association Publication 28
D.A. Sprinkel, T.C. Chidsey, Jr., and P.B. Anderson, editors

Geology of Antelope Island State Park, Utah

Grant C. Willis[1], W. Adolph Yonkee[2], Hellmut H. Doelling[1], and Mark E. Jensen[3]

ABSTRACT

Antelope Island is the largest island in Great Salt Lake and is one of the jewels in the Utah State Park system. The geology is diverse and well exposed, making the island a superb outdoor classroom. It is one of the best places in Utah to observe high-grade metamorphic and intrusive igneous rocks, ancient continental glacial deposits, the effects of Cretaceous thrust faulting on deeply buried rocks, rotated Tertiary mega-boulder conglomerate and volcanic ash beds, Basin and Range fault blocks, Lake Bonneville shorelines, and other geologic features.

Exposed rocks include Archean(?) to Early Proterozoic high-grade metamorphic and intrusive igneous rocks of the Farmington Canyon Complex; Late Proterozoic and Cambrian low-grade metasedimentary rocks of the Mineral Fork Formation, Kelley Canyon Formation, and Tintic Quartzite; Eocene to Oligocene conglomeratic rocks; and Miocene rocks of the Salt Lake Formation. Most of the rock units are separated by major unconformities that represent long periods of time. A few small igneous dikes intrude older rocks, and Quaternary lacustrine, alluvial, colluvial, eolian, and mass-movement deposits mantle much of the island.

The Farmington Canyon rocks have a protracted history, possibly including an older phase of Archean deposition and metamorphism, followed by an Early Proterozoic episode of widespread granitic igneous intrusion, high-grade metamorphism, and intense deformation about 1.7 billion years ago. Late Proterozoic strata record an episode of glaciation and initial rifting of the western margin of North America. The Cambrian Tintic Quartzite reflects deposition in high energy marine and coastal environments, which was followed by Paleozoic slow subsidence with deposition of carbonates in shallow, tropical epicontinental seas. During the Late Jurassic, Cretaceous, and early Tertiary Sevier orogeny (150 to 50 million years ago), island rocks were buried, thrust eastward, retrogressively metamorphosed, and internally deformed. Listric normal faults, formed during early and late Tertiary to Quaternary extension, rotated parts of the island block up to 45 degrees east, producing basins that filled with mostly locally derived deposits.

Between 28,000 and 10,000 years ago, Lake Bonneville covered much of the island, forming shoreline terraces, and depositing gravel, sand, silt, clay, and tufa. Since the retreat of Lake Bonneville, erosion, landsliding, and alluvial-fan deposition have modified the face of the island. Currently, active geologic processes on and near the island can produce earthquakes, landslides, rock falls, debris flows, and lake flooding. Several small prospect pits and mines were dug on the island, and oil and gas discoveries have been made in the Great Salt Lake basin around the island. A petroleum exploration well was started on Antelope Island, but never completed.

358 AN OUTDOOR CLASSROOM

Antelope Island State Park's well-exposed geology provides a unique outdoor classroom for students of all levels (figure 1). Of all the parks and monuments described in this guidebook, Antelope Island alone represents the Basin and Range Province, which covers the western half of Utah (figure 2). Thus, the park portrays many important aspects of Utah geology not seen in any other park (figures 3 and 4). The island is a showcase for metamorphic and igneous rocks of the Farmington Canyon Complex, some of the oldest rocks in the state (figure 5). These rocks display the results of intense metamorphism produced at deep crustal levels during a long Precambrian history of profound mountain building. The Mineral Fork, Kelley Canyon, and Tintic Formations are key markers that provide a record of rifting along the

[1]*Utah Geological Survey, Salt Lake City, UT 84114-6100*
[2]*Department of Geosciences, Weber State University, Ogden, UT 84408-2507*
[3]*Utah Department of Environmental Quality, Division of Drinking Water, Salt Lake City, UT 84114-4830*

Figure 1. View to northwest of Antelope Island, the largest island in Great Salt Lake. Frary Peak is the highest point. Lake Bonneville and Great Salt Lake shoreline terraces are some of the most prominent geomorphic features on the island. Photograph from Utah Geological Survey, taken in 1988.

western margin of North America, and were deposited in a variety of ancient environments from glaciers to tropical seas. Zones of highly altered rocks, complex folds, stretched clasts, and other deformation features are overprinted by low-grade metamorphism and shear deformation produced at middle crustal levels by the Late Jurassic to early Tertiary Sevier orogeny. Outcrops of tilted Tertiary rocks and Basin and Range structures viewed from the island provide key evidence for unraveling the recent structural history. Shorelines and a variety of lake deposits from ancestral Lake Bonneville, one of Utah's geologic icons, are also well exposed on the island.

In addition to the geology, the abundant wildlife — coupled with the sparse vegetation that allows frequent sightings, the sandy beaches, the novelty of Great Salt Lake, and the scenic views add to the outdoor classroom. The island is nearly pristine, a remarkable fact considering the close proximity to the urbanized Wasatch Front.

BACKGROUND

Antelope Island is the largest island in Great Salt Lake. It is approximately 15 miles (24 km) long, up to 5 miles (8 km) across, and about 40 square miles (104 km^2) in area. The highest point, Frary Peak, stands at 6,597 feet (2,011 m) above sea level, about 2,400 feet (732 m) above the lake level (figure 1).

Indians of the early Fremont culture inhabited and hunted on the island approximately 2,000 to 8,000 years ago (Roberts, 1983). More recently, members of the Shoshone and Gosiute tribes lived on and used the island. Captain John C. Fremont, the first official government explorer in Utah, rode his horse to the island in October 1845 and found the son of Chief Wanship and his two wives living there. The Indians called the island "Pa-ri-bi-na," meaning "antelope breeding place," though Fremont actually named the island "in memory of the grateful supply of food (several antelope)..." (Roberts, 1983). The Mormon pioneers reached Salt Lake Valley in 1847; by 1848 they moved cattle to the island, and Fielding Garr constructed a ranch house. This house, which still stands, was continuously occupied from 1849 until 1979 (at that time, the longest continuously inhabited home in Utah), during which time the island was used for grazing cattle and sheep, limited farming, and recreation. Bison were first transported to the island in 1893. In 1967, the State of Utah purchased the northern 2,000 acres and began constructing the north causeway and park facilities, creating Antelope Island State Park. Following a legislative resolution and court condemnation proceedings, Utah purchased the remainder of the island in 1980. In 1983, due to unusually high precipitation, the rising lake cut off access to the island and the park was closed. In 1992, a few years after the lake receded, Davis County rebuilt the causeway at a higher level. The park reopened in 1993. Since that time, Antelope Island has been one of the most popular parks in Utah with annual visitation of over 350,000 people.

Antelope Island has piqued the interest of geologists since the first exploration parties visited Salt Lake Valley. Fremont noted that as he rode to the island, the water just reached the belly of his horse, thus giving scientists the earliest indirect record of the level of Great Salt Lake (Roberts, 1983). He collected a few rocks, which were described by the famous New York geologist, James Hall (Hall, 1845). In 1850, Howard Stansbury explored the Great Salt Lake basin. He too visited Antelope Island and collected samples, which Hall also described (Stansbury, 1852). Later, the Beckwith (1855) and King (1878) surveys reported on the geology of the island. Bywater and Barlow (1909) first mapped the island geology. Larsen (1957) produced a much more detailed map and study. Bryant and Graff (1980) and Bryant (1988b) conducted reconnaissance studies of Farmington Canyon rocks on the island. The Utah Geological Survey supported a comprehensive geologic study of the island between 1987 and 1989 that included a detailed geologic map (Doelling and others, 1990) and topical studies (King and Willis, 2000, and papers therein).

ROCKS OF ANTELOPE ISLAND

Archean(?) to Early Proterozoic Farmington Canyon Complex

Well over half of the exposed rocks on Antelope Island are part of the Farmington Canyon Complex, which includes some of the oldest "basement" rocks in Utah (fig-

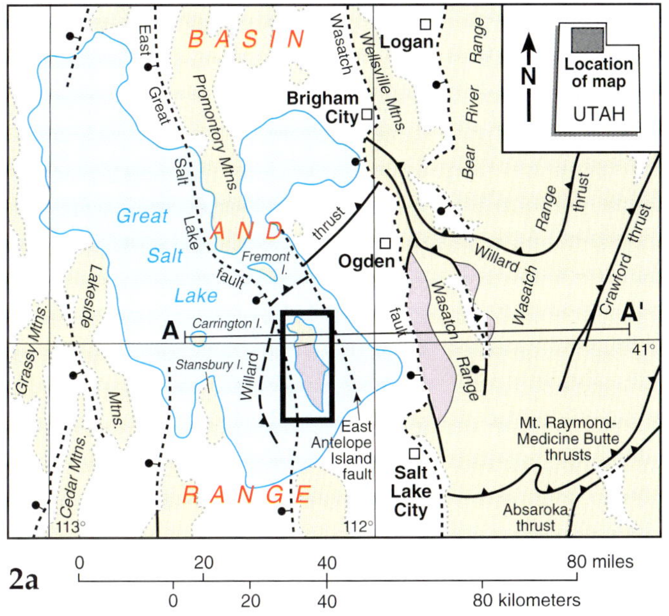

2a

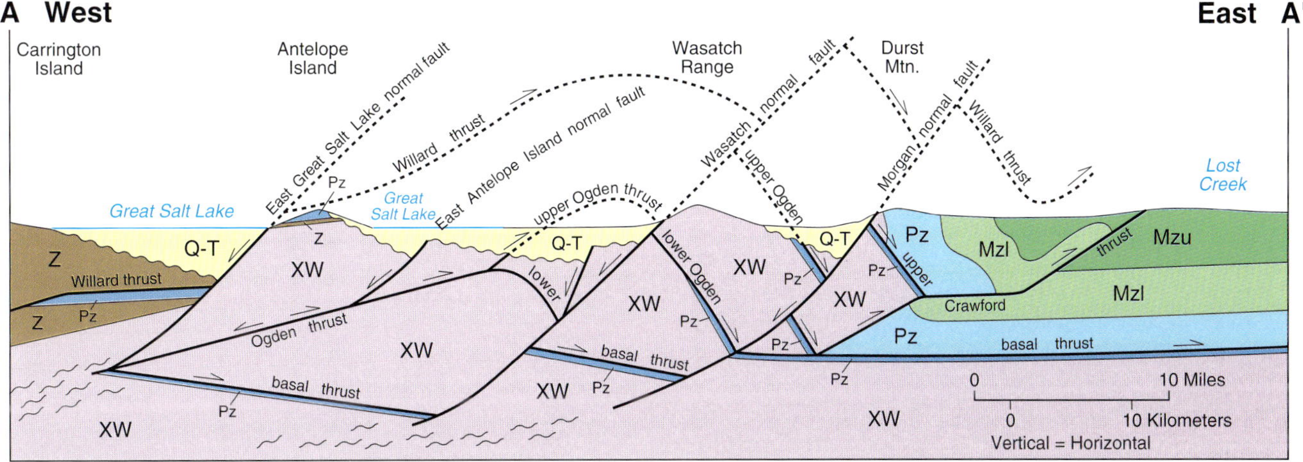

2b

Figure 2. (a) Schematic regional map showing position of Antelope Island relative to major structural and topographic features of northern Utah; Farmington Canyon Complex rocks are shown in purple. (b) Cross section across part of northern Utah showing Antelope Island, position of overlying Willard and underlying Ogden and basal thrust faults, west-facing listric normal faults east and west of the island, and wedges of early and late Tertiary half-graben deposits that thin away from the faults. Rock symbols: XW - Farmington Canyon Complex, Z - Late Proterozoic, Pz - Paleozoic, Mzl - lower Mesozoic, Mzu - upper Mesozoic, Q-T - Quaternary and Tertiary.

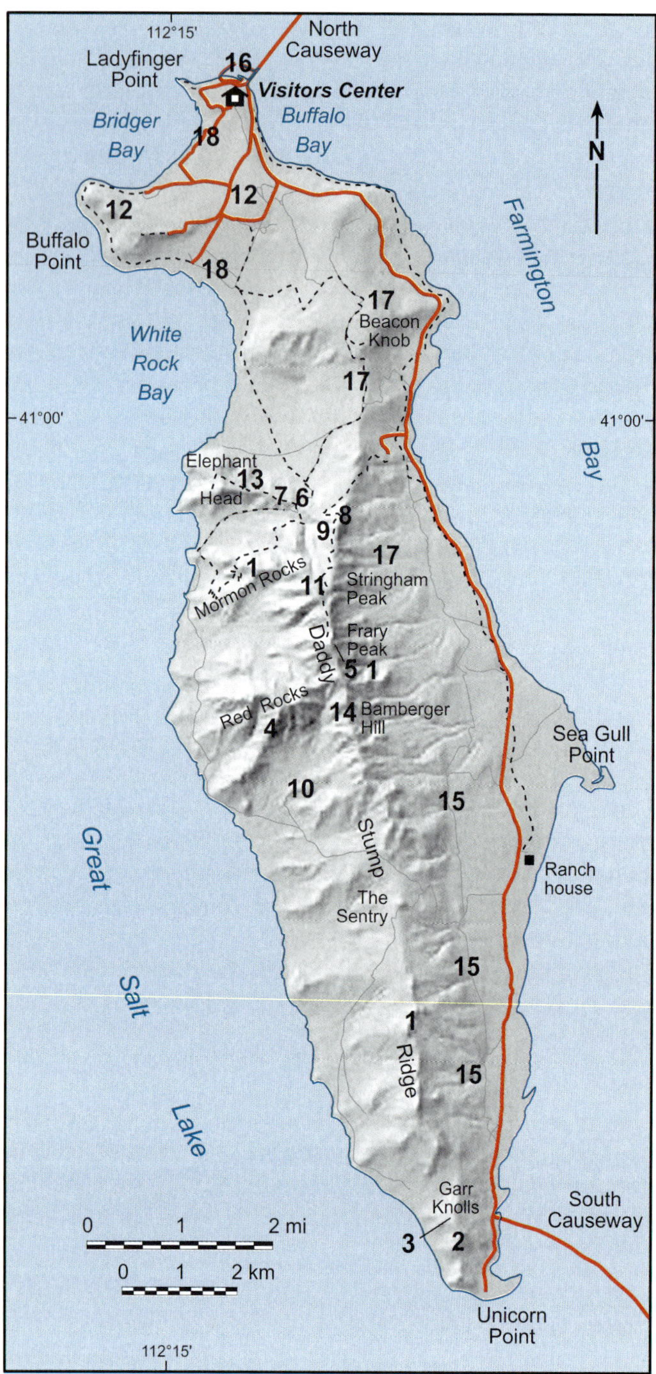

Figure 3. Major roads, trails, and key geologic sites (numbers keyed to locations discussed in text).

ures 5 and 6). Basement rock is old (generally Precambrian) igneous and metamorphic rock that forms the core or foundation of most continents. Because it is generally mantled by younger sedimentary "cover" rock, it is seldom exposed at the surface. Antelope Island is one of just three Farmington Canyon exposures in northern Utah (figure 2), and island outcrops are among the most easily accessed. Like the name suggests, the Farmington Canyon consists of a complex assemblage of rock types that can be overwhelming even to seasoned geologists. However, when considered in parts, they can be more easily under-

stood. On Antelope Island, the Farmington Canyon Complex consists of eight rock types that formed deep within the earth during Precambrian high-grade metamorphic and igneous activity, plus three main rock types related to Cretaceous retrograde metamorphism (Yonkee and others, 2000a). General characteristics of the various rock types are summarized in table 1. Four rock types, including layered gneiss (figure 7), quartz-rich gneiss (figure 8), biotite schist, and metamorphosed ultramafic rocks may have Archean protoliths (the parent rocks before metamorphism) that were possibly deformed during an early phase of high-grade metamorphism about 2.6 billion years ago. Hornblende-plagioclase gneiss (figure 9) has various protoliths, including possible Archean mafic dikes and Early Proterozoic dikes and igneous bodies. Banded gneiss (figure 10) and granite gneiss represent granitic igneous rocks that were intruded into the older rocks. All of these rocks were metamorphosed about 1.7 billion years ago at high temperatures (1,200-1,500°F [650-800°C]) and deep crustal levels (7-12 miles [12-20 km]) with intense deformation and local partial melting of older rocks (Barnett and others, 1993). Near the end of this metamorphism, coarse granite and pegmatite intruded the older rocks (figures 9, 10, and 11). Chloritic gneiss, mylonite, and phyllonite represent younger retrograde metamorphism and deformation of the Late Jurassic to early Tertiary Sevier orogeny (figures 12 and 13).

Late Proterozoic

Late Proterozoic rocks on Antelope Island occur in two formations, the Mineral Fork and the Kelley Canyon. Both formations are exposed as isolated patches in the central part of the island and in a band across the northern third of the island (figure 4). Based on correlation with other areas, the Mineral Fork is probably 770 to 720 million years old (Armstrong, 1982; Devlin and others, 1988), and is separated from the Farmington Canyon Complex by an unconformity representing almost one billion years (figure 5). The age of the Kelley Canyon is roughly constrained between 720 and 600 million years old (Christie-Blick and others, 1988; Christie-Blick and Levy, 1989; Yonkee and others, 2000b). Basaltic dikes and flows occur locally in Late Proterozoic rocks elsewhere in northern Utah (Crittenden and others, 1971; Christie-Blick, 1985), but are not found on Antelope Island. The thickness of Late Proterozoic rocks on Antelope Island ranges from about 70 to 480 feet (20-145 m). During Cretaceous thrust faulting, the Late Proterozoic rocks were metamorphosed to low-grade greenschist facies and were variably deformed.

Mineral Fork Formation

The Mineral Fork Formation consists of dark-brownish-black, matrix-supported diamictite (a very poorly sorted, non-layered mixture of clasts and matrix) (figure 14), with minor interbedded argillite, quartzite, and conglomerate near the top of the unit (Yonkee and others, 2000b). Three distinct kinds of clasts are recognized: (1) subround-

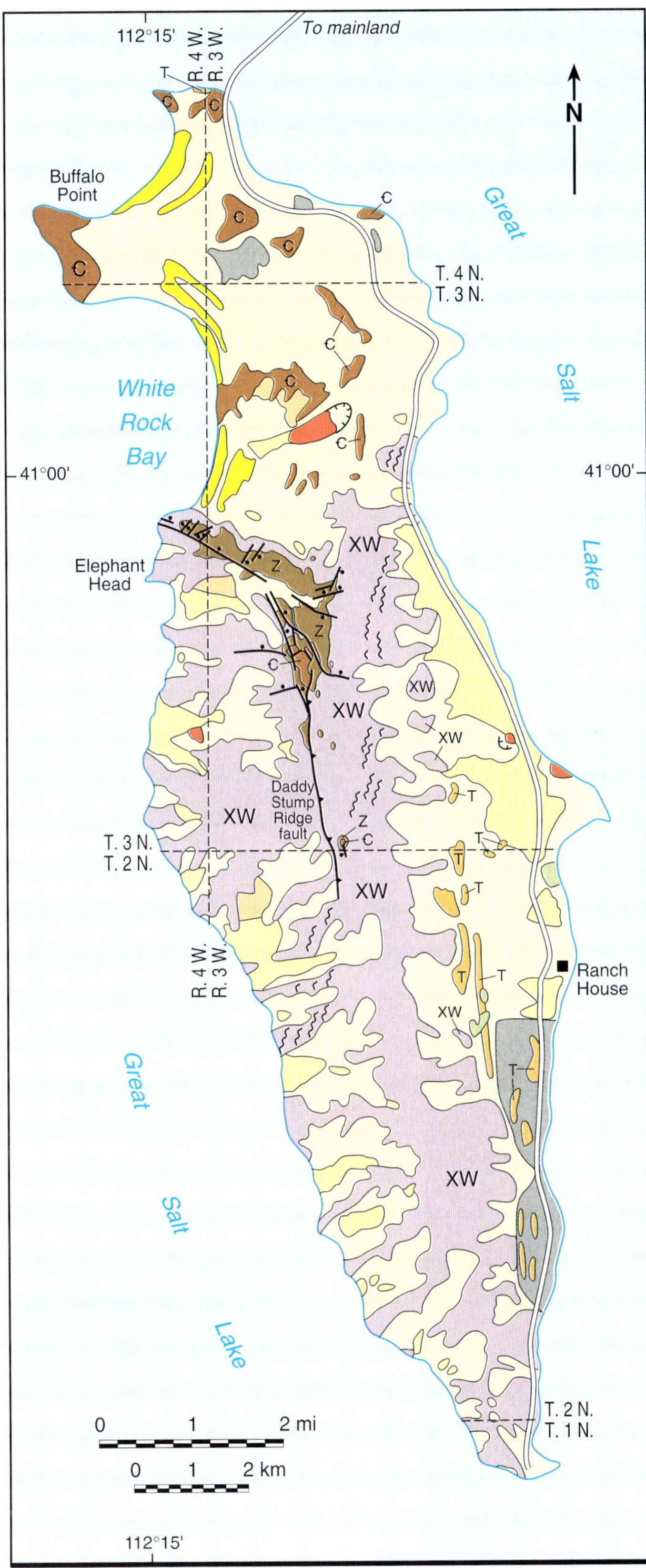

Figure 4. *Simplified geologic map of Antelope Island. Shear zones are common throughout the island, but only the most prominent Antelope Island shear zone is shown.*

ed to subangular clasts of quartz-feldspar gneiss, biotite schist, granite, and amphibolite probably derived from the Farmington Canyon Complex; (2) well-rounded, white to reddish-purple and rare chrome-green quartzite clasts; and (3) subangular white to pale-gray quartzite boulders up to 7 feet (2 m) in length. Micaceous, clay- to sand-sized matrix constitutes 30 to 60 percent of the diamictite. Bedding is generally poorly developed, but rare lenses of fine-grained argillite and conglomerate exhibit subhorizontal bedding. This unit forms dark-colored ledgy exposures, and nonconformably overlies the Farmington Canyon Complex along a sharp contact. In many areas gneissic and granitic clasts are altered (chloritized) and strongly deformed into flattened and stretched bodies with indistinct boundaries, whereas quartzite clasts are much less deformed. Cleavage is typically well developed. Thickness of the unit averages 10 to 20 feet (3-6 m), but varies from 0 to 200 feet (0-60 m), reflecting deposition over an irregular surface and later structural deformation.

Kelley Canyon Formation

The Kelley Canyon Formation on Antelope Island consists of two informal members, a lower dolomite member

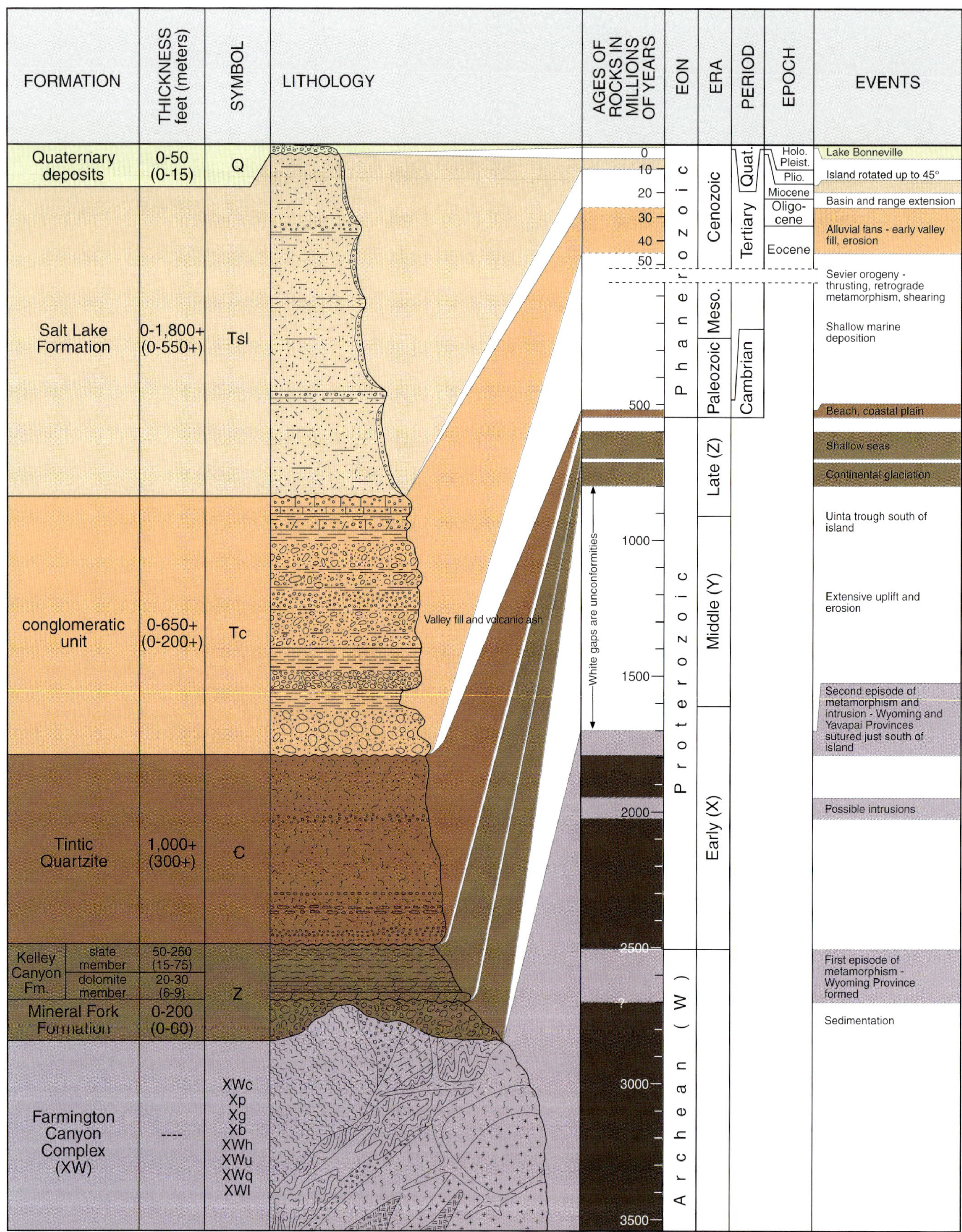

Figure 5. Lithologic column showing relative thicknesses and ages of formations, and timing of major events that affected rocks of Antelope Island.

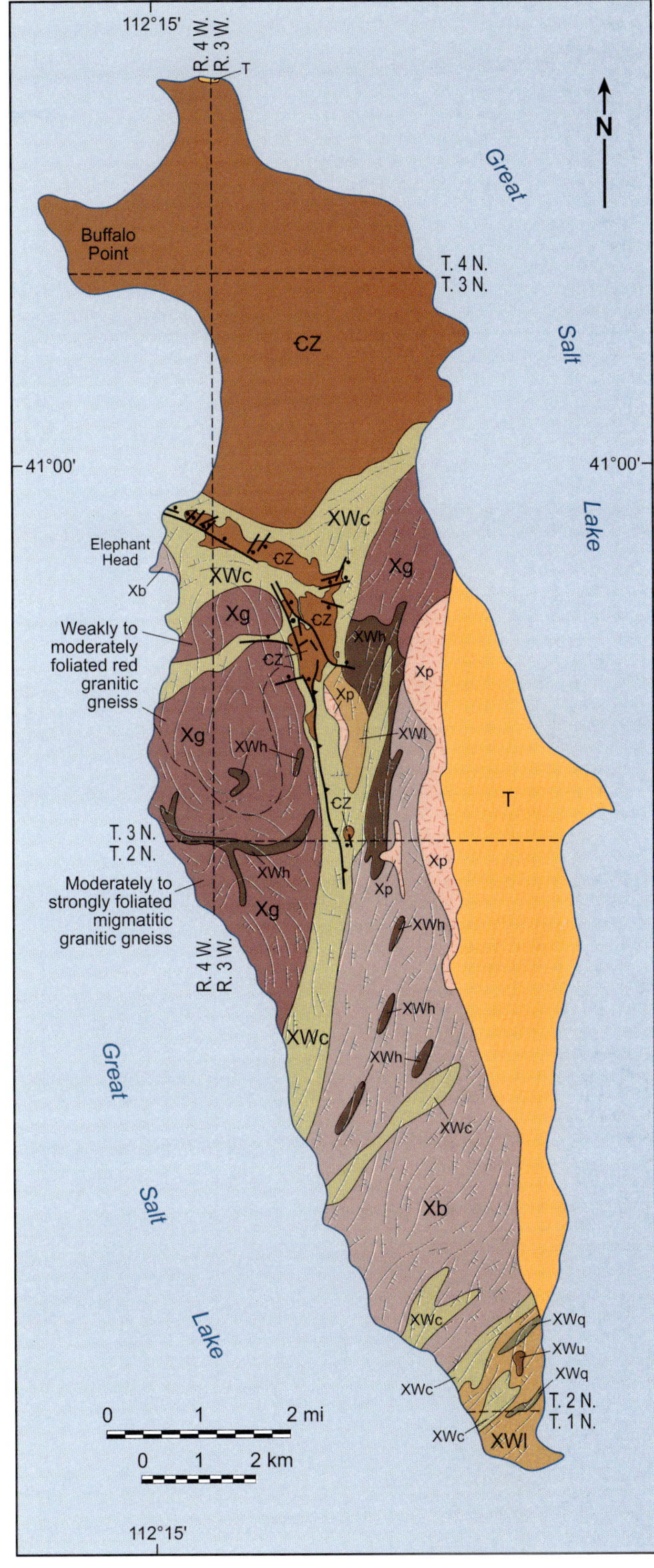

Figure 6. Bedrock geologic map of Antelope Island emphasizing Farmington Canyon Complex map units and dominant metamorphic foliation. Foliation deflects around a major granitic intrusion in the west-central part of the island.

Table 1. Rock types of the Farmington Canyon Complex.

Rock Type	Setting	Outcrop Appearance	Metamorphic Fabrics	General Mineralogy (a)	Interpreted History
Layered gneiss (biotite-bearing, quartz-feldspar gneiss with well-developed compositional layering)	elongate zones in central and southern parts of island; mixed with lenses of biotite schist and quartz-rich gneiss	forms variably resistant slopes with well-developed layering; many layers contain minor amounts of garnet	strong foliation and compositional layering, isoclinal folds with local fold interference patterns, migmatitic with widespread pegmatitic dikes	quartz 20-45%, plagioclase 25-45%, K-feldspar 5-15%, biotite 5-30%, garnet 0-10%, rare sillimanite, cordierite	probably metamorphosed sediments (graywacke and feldspathic sandstone); Archean(?) protoliths with Early Proterozoic high-grade metamorphic overprint that obliterates most Archean fabrics
Biotite schist	lenses up to 20 feet (6 m) wide associated with layered gneiss	forms brown to black, non-resistant, small swales	strong foliation, small-scale tight to isoclinal folds, locally migmatitic, widespread chlorite alteration	biotite 40-55% (b), quartz 0-15%, plagioclase 0-10%, rare garnet, sillimanite	metamorphosed clay-rich sediments; Archean(?) protoliths with Early Proterozoic metamorphism
Quartz-rich gneiss	lenses up to 100 feet (30 m) wide associated with layered gneiss	forms blocky white to greenish-gray, resistant outcrops; cut by widespread fractures	foliation defined by preferred orientation of mica; quartz highly recrystallized	quartz 80-95%, plagioclase 5-10%, biotite 0-5%, muscovite 0-5%	metamorphosed quartz-rich sediments; Archean(?) protoliths with Early Proterozoic metamorphism
Metamorphosed ultramafic rock	pods up to 100 feet (30 m) across; locally rimmed by hornblende-rich gneiss	forms dark green to black outcrops with very abundant mafic minerals	weak to strong foliation; widespread alteration to serpentine and talc	amphibole 15-30% (b), pyroxene 10-15%, olivine 0-10%	may represent parts of ultramafic lava flows, layered mafic complex, or oceanic crust; age uncertain
Hornblende-plagioclase gneiss	variable settings: dikes in layered gneiss; large mafic body in central part of island; amphibolite pods in banded and granitic gneiss	forms gray to black outcrops with abundant mafic minerals	weak to strong foliation and local folding, depending on setting	hornblende 20-60%, plagioclase 25-65%, quartz 0-15%, rare biotite, pyroxene	variable origins: early Archean(?) mafic dikes, parts of mafic lava flows, layered mafic complex, or oceanic crust; some may be later mafic dikes associated with Early Proterozoic granitic intrusions
Banded gneiss (hornblende-bearing, quartz-feldspar gneiss)	dominant rock type in south-central part of island; gradational with granitic gneiss	forms light gray to pink, moderately resistant, distinctly banded outcrops	strong gneissic foliation; small-scale compositional layering, locally migmatitic with abundant concordant to discordant pegmatite dikes	quartz 30-35%, plagioclase 25-40%, K-feldspar 15-30%, hornblende 5-10%, biotite 5-10%	margin of Early Proterozoic granitic intrusion; intruded prior to or synchronous with metamorphism
Granitic gneiss (hornblende-bearing, quartz-feldspar gneiss)	dominant rock type in west-central part of island; gradational with banded gneiss	forms light gray to pink, resistant, massive outcrops; commonly displays distinct jointing	weak to strong gneissic foliation; local compositional layering; concordant to discordant pegmatite dikes; in Red Rocks area, foliation has elliptical pattern	quartz 30-35%, plagioclase 20-30%, K-feldspar 25-40%, hornblende 5-10%, rare pyroxene	core of Early Proterozoic granitic intrusion; intruded prior to or synchronous with metamorphism
Granite and pegmatite	variable settings: small dikes within other units; large pegmatitic bodies on east side of island; red granite bodies on south side; some bodies have distinctive garnet	larger bodies form white to pink, resistant, knobby exposures; in Garr Knolls area, two non- to weakly foliated bodies have sharp boundaries and are associated with brecciated country rock	weakly to non-foliated, except some early phase concordant dikes are well foliated	quartz 25-40%, plagioclase 20-35%, K-feldspar 30-50%, some bodies contain minor garnet, biotite, and/or muscovite	variety of origins: partial melting of layered gneiss, late stage granitic plugs, dikes of various ages
Chloritic gneiss, mylonite (strongly deformed and recrystallized rock), and phyllonite (mylonite with abundant mica)	associated with shear zones; common in broad region in north part of Farmington Canyon outcrops near contact with cover rocks	greenish colored due to retrograde metamorphism; variably fractured and veined outcrops; some outcrops have dark red hematitic and silicic alteration	fractures; micaceous cleavage; quartz ribbons; variably deformed quartz veins	variable depending on parent rock type and degree of alteration; chlorite and muscovite locally abundant	produced by retrograde alteration and plastic to brittle deformation of various rock types during Cretaceous thrusting

(a) retrograde metamorphism and alteration are common on Farmington Canyon Complex rocks; mineral percentages are pre-alteration; alteration minerals include: chlorite, muscovite, epidote, and albite.

(b) mineral percentages do not total 100% because pervasive alteration prevents determination of pre-alteration assemblages.

Figure 7. Layered gneiss near the south end of the island contains biotite-rich to quartz-feldspar-garnet-rich layers and may represent metamorphosed Archean sedimentary rock.

Figure 8. Quartz-rich gneiss forms white, blocky outcrops near the south end of the island and is probably metamorphosed Archean quartz sandstone.

Figure 9. Hornblende-plagioclase gneiss cut by light-colored granitic pegmatite dikes near the south end of the island.

and an upper slate member (Doelling and others, 1990; Yonkee and others, 2000b). The lower member consists of pale-pink to pinkish-gray, crystalline dolomite, with local minor interbedded slate (figure 15). It weathers to form resistant, pale-pinkish-brown to tan ledges that contrast sharply with the darker units above and below, making the member an important marker bed. The dolomite is generally massive, but thin bedding is preserved in some areas. The member is weakly deformed by fractures, thin veins, and open folds in most areas, but tight folds and crenulation cleavage are locally developed near Elephant Head. The lower contact with the Mineral Fork Formation is generally sharp, and the unit has a uniform thickness of 20 to 30 feet (6-9 m), except in strongly deformed areas.

The upper slate member consists primarily of laminar to thin-bedded, purple, greenish-gray, and yellowish-gray slate, with minor fine-grained quartzite and dolomite (figure 16). The unit typically forms smooth, partly covered slopes with purple hues generally dominant in the upper

part, and greenish hues widespread in the lower part. The contact with the underlying dolomite is gradational, with thin dolomite beds interfingering with the lower half of the slate unit. Thin, fine-grained quartzite beds are more widespread in the upper third of the unit. This member is variably deformed with weakly to strongly developed slaty cleavage at low to high angles to bedding, minor folds, and small-scale faults. Recrystallized mica imparts a sparkly sheen on some bedding and cleavage surfaces in more highly deformed areas. This member varies from 50 to 250 feet (15-75 m) thick, probably reflecting erosion of the upper part of the unit prior to deposition of the Tintic Quartzite, and structural deformation.

Cambrian Tintic Quartzite

The Tintic Quartzite consists of tan to pale-gray to greenish-gray, fine- to coarse-grained quartzite, conglomerate, and minor siltstone (Doelling and others, 1990; Yonkee and others, 2000b). Fine- to medium-grained quartzite

Figure 10. Coarse granitic pegmatite dikes intrude migmatitic banded gneiss in the west-central part of the island.

Figure 11. Late-stage pegmatite dikes intrude fractured fragments of hornblende-plagioclase gneiss near Garr Knolls.

Figure 12. Chloritic gneiss of the Farmington Canyon Complex (lower 2/3 of dark outcrop) is overlain by a thin band of Mineral Fork Formation (upper 1/3 of dark outcrop) and pale-gray dolomite of the Kelley Canyon Formation. The right half of the outcrop is cut by a shear zone with near-vertical cleavage that has mostly obscured the depositional contacts. Outcrop is just west of the Frary Peak trail near Stringham Peak.

Figure 13. Quartz veins cut chloritized gneiss of the Farmington Canyon Complex near Garr Knolls.

constitutes about 60 percent of the unit; coarse-grained, pebbly quartzite about 20 percent; and conglomerate about 20 percent. The conglomerate contains moderately well sorted, rounded clasts ranging from 0.4 to 2 inches (1-5 cm) in diameter (figure 17). Some quartzite and conglomerate layers are arkosic, containing significant amounts of feldspar and mica, especially in the lower part of the unit. Bedding is overall medium and most easily recognized where conglomerate beds are present, but is difficult to recognize in more fractured, homogeneous quartzite in the upper part of the unit. The contact with the underlying slate member of the Kelley Canyon Formation is sharp, has minor local relief, and is commonly marked by a basal conglomerate, and thus probably represents an unconformity. The Tintic Quartzite forms ledges and blocky slopes. The unit is variably deformed with locally well developed cleavage, quartz-filled veins, and minor folds. Deformation has elongated and flattened clasts oblique to bedding in many areas (figure 17). The top of the formation is not exposed on the island, so the total thickness can only be estimated at greater than about 1,000 feet (300 m).

Cretaceous(?) Quartz Veins

Quartz veins are widespread in all of the Precambrian and Cambrian rocks on the island, especially near shear and fault zones, but are absent in the overlying Tertiary strata (figure 13). Outcrops consist of white to greenish-white, coarse- to fine-crystalline quartz with trace amounts of muscovite and opaque minerals. Although most veins are less than 10 feet (3 m) thick, some can be traced for over 1,000 feet (300 m) as resistant, protruding ledges. A particularly large body of quartz cuts across rocks on Elephant Head. Most quartz veins and the quartz body apparently formed during Cretaceous thrust faulting, though some of the veins could be older or younger. Sericite in similar veins near the Willard and Ogden thrust faults in the Wasatch Range yielded Early Cretaceous

Figure 14. Large quartzite boulder clast in outcrop of Mineral Fork Formation east of Elephant Head. The Mineral Fork was deposited by continental glaciers. Mottled streaks around the boulder are gneiss and granite boulder clasts that are intensely stretched along cleavage that dips westward from the upper left to lower right. Shear deformation mostly deflected around the resistant quartzite boulders but strongly deformed the weaker rocks.

^{40}Ar/^{39}Ar ages between 110 and 140 million years old (Yonkee and others, 1989).

Tertiary

Stratified Tertiary rocks are exposed in two areas on Antelope Island, on the southeast side, and on the north end (figure 4). In addition, a few small felsic dikes of assumed Eocene to Oligocene age cut Precambrian rocks near the south end of the island. The stratified rocks unconformably overlie Precambrian and Cambrian rocks, though the contact is rarely exposed. This unconformity represents a gap in the rock record of more than 500 million years. Approximately half of the southeast exposures and all of the north exposures were created during excavation for road and causeway fill during the 1970s and 1980s.

Bedding in outcrops on the southeast part of the island strike generally north and dip from 20 to 45 degrees east, averaging 35 degrees (Doelling and others, 1990); dips appear to decrease upsection. The exposures at the north

Figure 15. Dolomite member of Kelley Canyon Formation near Elephant Head with strong crenulation cleavage.

Figure 16. Slate member of Kelley Canyon Formation north of Stringham Peak near the Frary Peak trail. Person is holding an original wooden mallet that was used by early settlers to split slate layers.

end of the island form a narrow outcrop belt along the shoreline. The rocks are strongly fractured, rotated to locally overturned, and cut by numerous minor faults.

Conglomeratic Unit

The conglomeratic unit is only exposed on the southeast part of the island where it is locally at least 650 feet

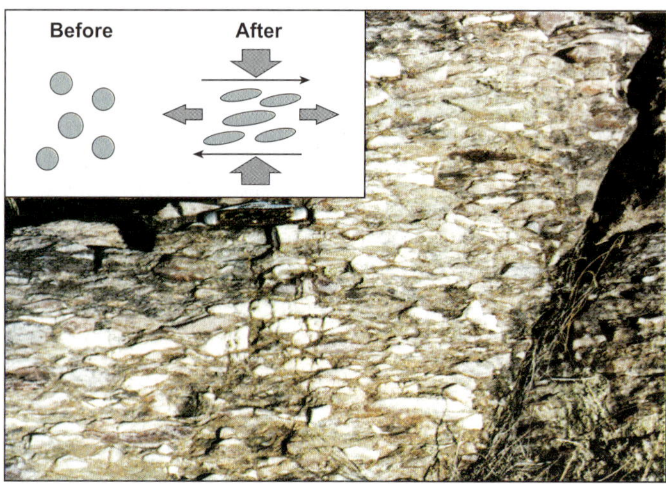

Figure 17. *Conglomerate bed in the Tintic Quartzite. Originally rounded pebble clasts were stretched during Cretaceous deformation (inset). Arrows indicate primary directions of shear, extension, and shortening.*

Figure 18. *These large boulders of Tintic Quartzite were probably originally deposited in debris flows shed off of thrust-generated highlands, forming large clasts in the Tertiary conglomeratic unit. The boulders were later eroded out of the conglomerate beds and redeposited by Lake Bonneville wave action.*

(200 m) thick (Willis and Jensen, 2000). It consists of interbedded conglomerate, breccia, limestone, sandstone, and mudstone. Conglomerate beds are amazingly varied in composition, ranging from well-sorted and well-rounded pebble conglomerate, to poorly sorted boulder conglomerate, to conglomeratic breccia; and with clasts consisting of varying percentages of Paleozoic limestone, dolomite, and quartzite; Precambrian metamorphic and granitic rock; and Tertiary volcanic rock (Willis and Jensen, 2000). The lower part of the unit contains boulders commonly 3 to 5 feet (1-1.5 m) in diameter, but ranging up to 11 feet (3.4 m) (figure 18).

A few small, poorly exposed outcrops of medium- to thin-bedded, grayish-purple, greenish-gray, and reddish-brown, biotite-bearing, bentonitic mudstone with sandy to conglomeratic lenses overlie the lower conglomerate. The upper part of the unit consists of interbedded pebble- to cobble-conglomerate, conglomeratic limestone, and fine-grained limestone.

The conglomeratic unit is not cut by Cretaceous thrust deformation features, but contains deformed clasts, indicating that at least 40,000 feet (13,000 m) of strata were structurally and erosionally removed from what is now Antelope Island in order to expose the sources of the clasts. This denudation probably started during Cretaceous thrusting, but was not completed before early Eocene time (Yonkee, 1992; DeCelles,1994; Willis and Jensen, 2000; Miller and others, in press). The lowermost conglomerate beds contain no volcanic material, suggesting that they predate late Eocene volcanic activity in the region. Three biotite-bearing samples from reworked bentonitic claystone and volcanic clasts in the middle part of the unit yielded late Eocene K-Ar ages of 39 to 48 million years; the lower part of the conglomeratic unit may be Eocene in age, and the rest of the unit is probably late Eocene to Oligocene (Willis and Jensen, 2000).

Salt Lake Formation

The Salt Lake Formation is exposed in the southeast outcrop belt (figure 19) and on the north end of the island (figure 20). In the southeast outcrops, it consists of a thick interval of fine-grained volcanic ash, tuffaceous sandstone, marl, mudstone, and a few thin pebble-conglomerate beds (Doelling and others, 1990; Willis and Jensen, 2000). The volcanic ash beds consist of up to 100 percent angular volcanic glass shards, and weather to very pale gray (figure 19). Pebble conglomerate beds consist of subangular to subrounded quartzite, limestone, and minor metamorphic cobbles up to 3 inches (8 cm) in diameter in a sandy, calcareous matrix. The upper part of the Salt Lake Formation is not exposed so the total thickness cannot be measured, but it is at least 1,800 feet (550 m).

The Salt Lake Formation on the north end of the island consists of very poorly sorted sedimentary breccia and conglomerate interbedded with volcanic ash and pale-reddish-gray mudstone (figure 20). Clasts in the breccia and conglomerate consist of angular quartzite, nonresistant olive-green shale, and silty limestone as large as 3 feet (1 m) in diameter. The immature nature and large size of the clasts indicate that they were transported only a short distance from their source. Most clasts were probably derived from deformed rocks beneath the Willard thrust plate, which was just above rocks of the north end of the island before being eroded.

The Salt Lake Formation has not yielded materials suitable for standard radiometric dating. However, electron microprobe analyses on ten samples from the island were compared with similar analyses of over 2,200 samples of volcanic ash from the western U.S. (Perkins and others, 1995, 1998; Willis and Jensen, 2000). The comparison indicated that the ash beds are 8 to 11 million years old (late Miocene), and were erupted from volcanoes on the central Snake River Plain in Idaho (figure 5).

Figure 19. *Well-stratified, tilted volcanic ash in Salt Lake Formation on the southeastern part of Antelope Island. View is to the north. Inset shows glass shards in volcanic ash as viewed under a microscope. The shards are the remnants of frothy bubbles of molten glassy rock that hardened and then were shattered as they were blasted out of a volcano. Bar in lower right equals 0.004 inches (0.1 mm).*

Intrusive Rocks

A few felsic dikes about 5 feet (1.5 m) wide cut Precambrian metamorphic rock on the southern part of the island. Chemically, they are alkali-rich trachyte (64 percent SiO_2), and are not chloritized or altered by low-grade metamorphism as are their host rocks (Willis and Jensen, 2000). The dikes are probably late Eocene or Oligocene in age based on their proximity to similar-aged trachytic intrusions in the Oquirrh Mountains to the south (Tooker and Roberts, 1971; Moore and McKee, 1983), and the fact that they post-date the Cretaceous metamorphism that affected the host rocks.

Quaternary

Quaternary deposits mantle much of Antelope Island and consist mostly of lacustrine sediments deposited by late Pleistocene Lake Bonneville and Holocene Great Salt Lake (figure 1). Sand, pebble to cobble gravel, and large boulders are present up to about 1,000 feet (305 m) above the present Great Salt Lake shoreline. They are concentrated on beach ridges, wave-built terraces, and wave-cut benches along four prominent and several intermediate shorelines that represent stillstands of the rising and falling Lake Bonneville. Fine-grained deposits are locally exposed in wave-sheltered Lake Bonneville coves, and beneath regressive shoreline deposits. Some deposits con-

Figure 20. *Intensely faulted outcrop of interbedded conglomerate and volcanic ash of the Salt Lake Formation at the north end of Antelope Island.*

tain reworked marl with ostracods. Tufa and calcium-carbonate-cemented sand and gravel (beachrock) locally form a prominent "crust" along the major Lake Bonneville shorelines that is sometimes referred to as the "bathtub ring."

Organic-rich sand, silt, and clay deposits are localized in lagoons behind Holocene beach ridges and spits on the gently sloping east side of the island, and in wet areas surrounding modern springs. Colluvium and talus form a thin mantle on the flanks of ridges above the Bonneville shoreline. Slumps and large landslides are present in coarse-grained lacustrine deposits and in colluvium. Alluvial fans post-date regression of the lake. The alluvium is dominantly sand and gravel debris-flow and flash-flood deposits derived from lacustrine deposits and colluvium. Channelized alluvium is common along ephemeral drainages. Oolites (spherical accretionary grains formed when brine shrimp fecal pellets are coated with calcium carbonate mud as they are rolled back and forth by waves) are abundant on beaches along the west side of the island. Oolitic beach sand is blown into dunes in Bridger and White Rock Bays. Dunes and thin sheets of wind-blown quartz sand extend landward from the oolitic dunes. The quartz sand dunes are older and more subdued than the oolitic dunes, indicating a change in environment, source, and/or lake salinity between times of deposition.

Construction fill and recontoured excavations are present in several areas (figure 4). In some of the excavations, especially in the large pits on the southeast part of the island, reclamation has redistributed overburden, waste piles, and soil.

STRUCTURAL GEOLOGY

Archean(?) to Early Proterozoic High-grade Metamorphic Structures

High-grade metamorphic rocks of the Precambrian Farmington Canyon Complex exhibit extensive structural features, including: foliation, gneissic layering, tight to isoclinal folds, and mineral lineations. Most of these features formed during a main phase of Early Proterozoic deformation and metamorphism about 1.7 billion years ago. Most Farmington Canyon rocks, except late-phase granites and pegmatites, have a strong northeast-striking, steeply dipping foliation that is defined by preferred orientation of mica, hornblende, and quartz grains. Gneissic layering, which formed by transposition of original sedimentary layering, metamorphic differentiation, and intrusion of dikes that were deformed and rotated into parallelism, is developed parallel to foliation in many outcrops. Gneissic layers and dikes are locally contorted into a variety of fold shapes, and mineral lineations tend to parallel the hinges of the folds. This dominant foliation and gneissic layering, as well as most folds, formed during the main phase of Early Proterozoic metamorphism, but locally preserved fold interference patterns and multiple foliations in some fold hinges within layered gneiss may record an earlier period of possible Archean deformation (Yonkee and others, 2000a). Granitic gneiss in the Red Rocks area on the west side of the island has a weak foliation that forms a crude circular pattern, which may reflect intrusion shape. A few small cross-cutting plugs of red granite appear to have contorted and brecciated the surrounding foliated rocks during intrusion.

Mesozoic Thrust-Related Structures

Thrust faulting and deformation associated with the Late Jurassic to early Tertiary Sevier orogeny had widespread effects on basement and cover rocks on Antelope Island. In general, cooler rocks near the earth's surface deform by brittle fracturing, whereas hotter rocks at deeper levels deform plastically; during thrusting, rocks on Antelope Island were at intermediate depths and temperatures, and thus deformed by a combination of processes. Variations in the geometry of structures on the island also define two domains, a southern domain in which structures were produced mostly by shortening above the underlying Ogden thrust system, and a northern domain in which structures were produced by deformation beneath the overlying Willard thrust fault (figure 2) (Yonkee, 1992, 1997).

Thrust-related structures in the Farmington Canyon Complex include fractures, quartz veins, cleavage, and shear zones (bands of concentrated deformation) that cut across older high-grade metamorphic structures. Fractures provided pathways for fluids that altered minerals to chlorite and sericite, forming chloritic gneiss, particularly along edges of shear zones. Veins formed as open fractures filled with quartz and minor mica. Shear zones contain mylonite and phyllonite (highly deformed fine-grained rocks) with strong micaceous cleavage. Quartz within shear zones is highly recrystallized, whereas feldspar is fractured and variably altered to mica. Most shear zones range from inches to tens of feet in width, but one major zone in the central part of the island has a 300-foot-thick (90-m) core bounded by a zone of more diffuse alteration about 1 mile (1.6 km) wide (figure 4). In the southern domain, most shear zones trend north to northeast and form east- and west-dipping sets with reverse slip and steeply dipping cleavage, reflecting shortening of the basement above the Ogden thrust (Yonkee, 1992). In the northern domain, widespread minor shear zones, veins, and moderately northwest-dipping cleavage reflect shearing and shortening of basement rocks near the contact with cover rocks.

Thrust-related features in Late Proterozoic and Cambrian rocks include minor folds, cleavage, quartz and mica veins, and stretched clasts. Bedding dips overall gently to the north to northwest, but is locally rotated into minor folds. Folds in the southern domain trend north and are mostly upright; folds in the northern domain trend northeast and vary from mostly upright in the Tintic Quartzite to inclined in Late Proterozoic strata. Weak to strong cleavage is widely developed, and is defined by flattened clasts, preferred orientation of mica, and mica seams where quartz has been dissolved and removed. Cleavage strikes north and is steeply dipping in the southern domain, whereas it strikes northeast in the northern domain and varies from generally steeply dipping in the Tintic Quartzite to gently dipping and intense in the Mineral Fork Formation. Complex vein sets are widely developed

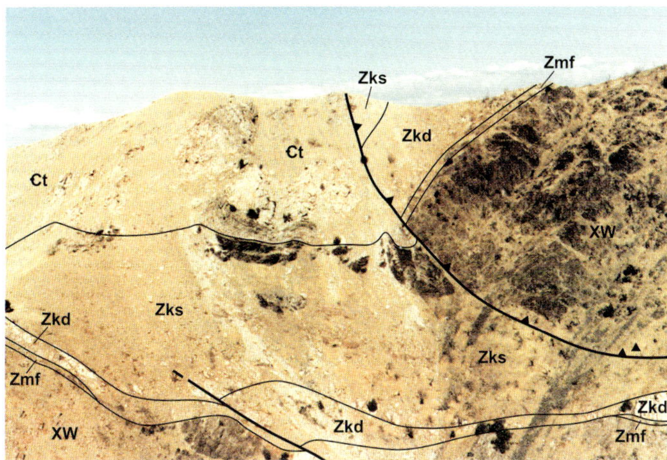

Figure 21. View looking northeast of the Daddy Stump Ridge backthrust fault (barbed line) in which Farmington Canyon rock (XW) has been thrust over younger Mineral Fork Formation (Zmf), Kelley Canyon Formation dolomite(Zkd) and slate (Zks), and Tintic Quartzite (Ct). The normally brittle Tintic Quartzite was deformed into a series of tight folds near the bend in the fault at the center of the photograph.

in the Tintic Quartzite. In many outcrops, clasts in the Mineral Fork Formation, and quartz pebbles in the Tintic Quartzite, are stretched and flattened; their average shape provides a measure of the strain that accompanied deformation (figure 17). Many mica-rich clasts in the Mineral Fork Formation are strongly stretched and flattened to more than six times their original length in outcrops near Elephant Head, reflecting intense shearing and flattening of weaker mica-rich rocks beneath the Willard thrust, although stronger quartzite clasts are less deformed (figure 14). Clasts become less deformed farther southeast, possibly reflecting less footwall deformation as the Willard thrust ramped up to the southeast. Quartz pebbles in the Tintic Quartzite are moderately stretched and flattened 1.5 to 3 times their original length, reflecting less deformation in these stronger rocks.

Interestingly, angular cobbles of highly deformed, Middle Cambrian shale and limestone are preserved in the Salt Lake Formation conglomerate at the north end of the island (figure 20). The matrix around the cobbles is undeformed, indicating that the cobbles were deformed during thrusting, before being eroded out of their bedrock source. The intense deformation indicates that the thrust was located just above this bedrock source, although the thrust and the Middle Cambrian strata have been eroded from the island (Yonkee, 1997; Willis and Jensen, 2000). In comparison, Tertiary conglomerate beds on the southeast part of the island (figure 18) contain clasts of deformed Mississippian limestone, indicating that the Willard thrust ramped up to the southeast across the island rocks prior to erosion.

Several discrete faults displace Late Proterozoic rocks (figure 4) (Doelling and others, 1990). The north-trending, vertical to east-dipping Daddy Stump Ridge fault places Farmington Canyon rocks on the east over folded Late Proterozoic and Cambrian rocks on the west (figure 21).

Offset of Late Proterozoic rocks indicates a minimum apparent displacement of 800 feet (240 m), but actual slip may be greater and appears to increase farther south where the fault becomes a broad shear zone in Farmington Canyon Complex rocks. We interpret the Daddy Stump Ridge fault as a minor, west-directed backthrust related to shortening above the Ogden thrust. The East and West Stringham Peak, Elephant Head, and several other small faults also show evidence of thrust deformation, and were also probably produced by Cretaceous shortening. Most indicate evidence of renewed normal movement during Cenozoic extension. Additional faults probably cut Farmington Canyon and Tintic rocks, but the lack of distinctive markers in these units prevents their recognition.

Cenozoic Extension Structures

Regionally, two phases of extension have affected northern Utah: a first phase during early Cenozoic collapse of the Sevier mountain belt, and a second phase related to late Cenozoic Basin and Range crustal extension (Constenius, 1996). Cenozoic structural features on and near Antelope Island include major normal faults located both east and west of the island beneath Great Salt Lake, tilted Cenozoic deposits, and small-displacement secondary normal faults. In some cases, it is difficult to determine if Cenozoic features are related to the early or late extension; some were active during both episodes.

The island is part of a large structural block bounded on the west by the East Great Salt Lake fault zone and on the east by the East Antelope Island fault zone. Movement on these listric (curved) normal faults during early and late extension was largely responsible for forming the island block and tipping it eastward up to 45 degrees (figure 2).

The East Great Salt Lake fault zone parallels the island approximately 1 mile (1.6 km) west of the west shore (Cook and others, 1980; Viveiros, 1986; Pechman and others, 1987) (figure 2). This fault zone bounds a large half graben that contains up to 14,000 feet (4,300 m) of Cenozoic basin fill (Bortz and others, 1985). Total slip on the fault is probably greater than 20,000 feet (6,000 m). This major fault is still active and capable of generating large earthquakes (Pechman and others, 1987).

The East Antelope Island normal fault, which underlies Great Salt Lake between Antelope Island and the Wasatch normal fault, bounds a large half-graben basin east of the island (Cook and others, 1966; Wilson and others, 1986) (figure 2). This listric fault appears to merge downward into the old, gently west-dipping Ogden thrust fault zone at depth (McNeil and Smith, 1993). The half graben contains up to 8,000 feet (2,500 m) of older basin fill that is tilted eastward, and that is overlain unconformably by younger, less tilted sediments. The older fill appears to be continuous with surface exposures of the conglomerate unit and possibly the lower part of the Salt Lake Formation exposed on the east side of Antelope Island.

Extensional structures are limited and hard to identify

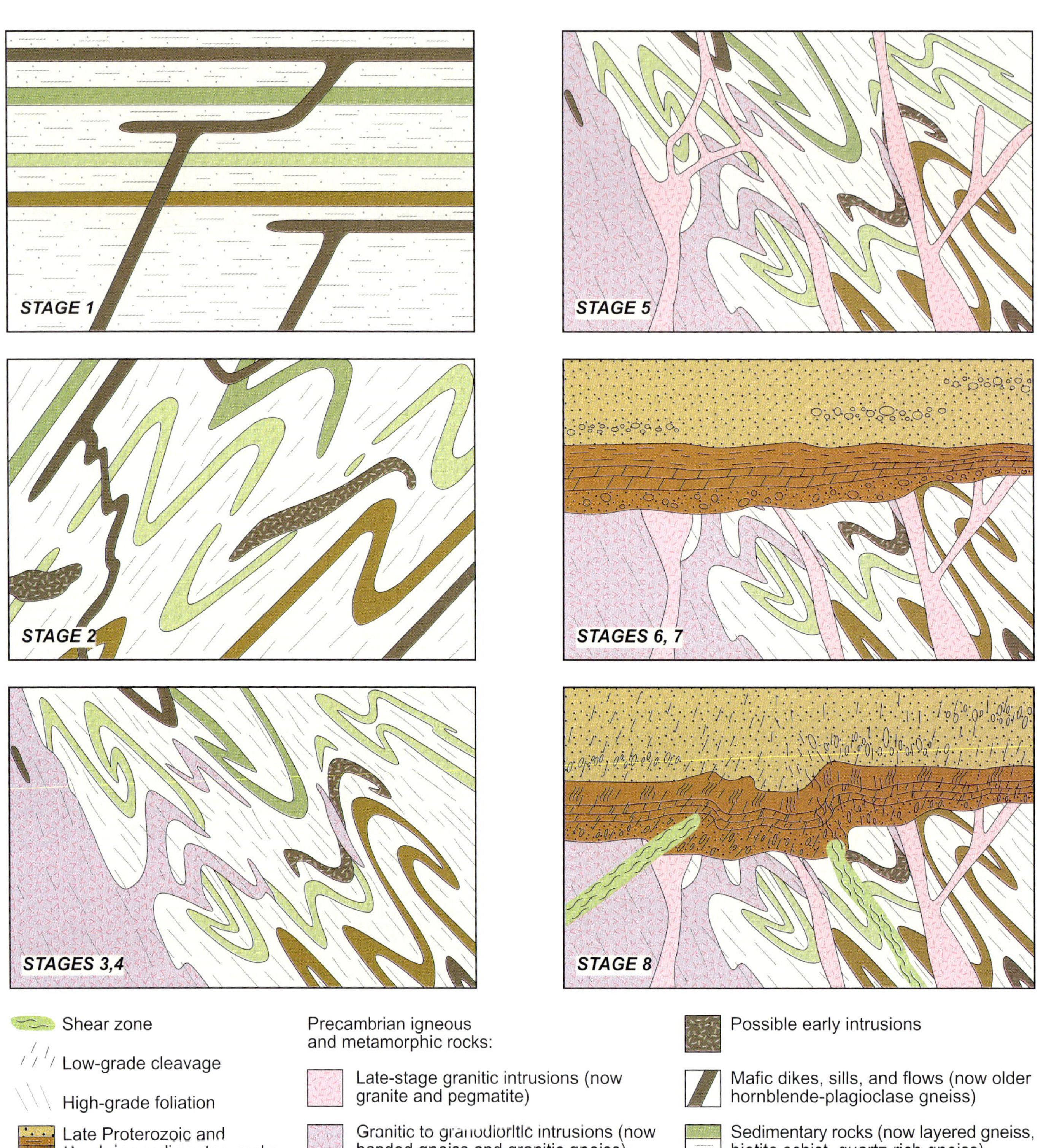

Figure 22. Schematic diagram showing stages in geologic history of Antelope Island: stage 1 - Archean(?) deposition of sedimentary rocks, followed by intrusion of mafic dikes and sills; stage 2 - Late Archean(?) metamorphism with intrusion of igneous bodies; stage 3 - Early Proterozoic intrusion of large granitic plutons, with or shortly followed by stage 4 - main-phase metamorphism during collision of island arc terrains with the Wyoming province about 1.7 billion years ago, which produced most structures and foliation seen in the Farmington Canyon Complex today; stage 5 - Early Proterozoic intrusion of pegmatitic dikes shortly following main-phase metamorphism; stage 6 - Middle to Late Proterozoic uplift with over 6 miles (10 km) of rock removed by erosion; stage 7 - deposition of Late Proterozoic through middle Mesozoic marine and terrestrial strata (most strata not shown); stage 8 - mostly Cretaceous thrust faults load island rock with 40,000 or more feet (13,000 m) of rock and cause pervasive deformation, shearing, and greenschist-facies metamorphism; stage 9 - during Late Cretaceous to Early Tertiary, island rocks tilted westward by movement on lower-level thrust faults; stage 10 - Early Tertiary extensive erosion and structural collapse of thrust belt remove most of Willard thrust sheet and form half-graben basins that begin filling with older basin-fill deposits (Tc); stage 11 - late Tertiary Basin and Range extension and block rotation with deposition of Salt Lake Formation (note "fan" pattern of Tertiary strata), and continued erosion of highlands; stage 12 - Late Pleistocene Lake Bonneville covers most of island; stage 13 - Lake Bonneville recedes, leaving shorelines, a mantle of lacustrine deposits, and its salty remnant - Great Salt Lake.

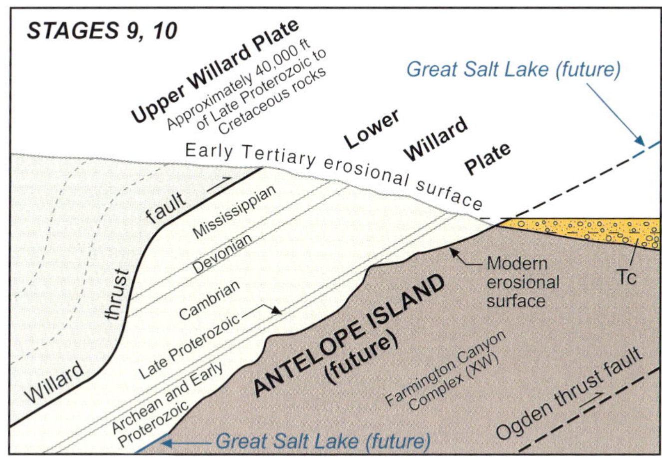

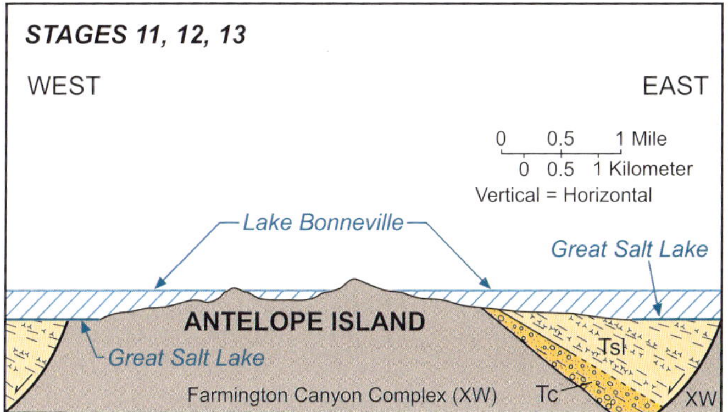

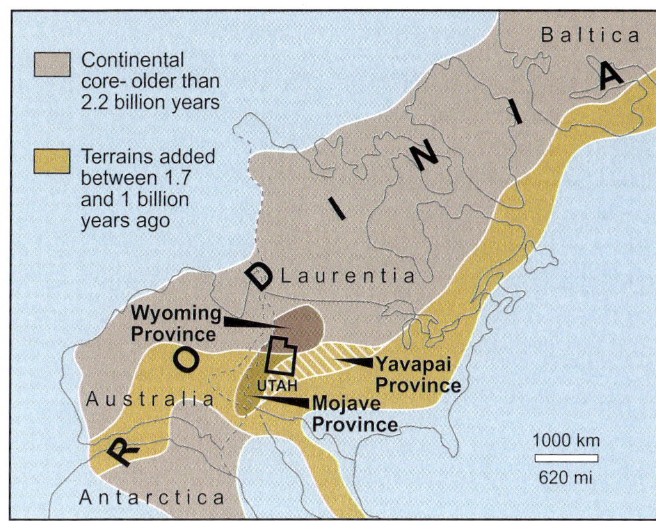

Figure 23. The supercontinent of Rodinia about 1 billion years ago. It consisted of several blocks of terrain assembled over the previous several hundred million years. Antelope Island was near the collision zone between the Wyoming province (part of the Archean core of North America), the Mojave province (a belt of Early Proterozoic and possible Archean crust deformed during the Early Proterozoic), and the Yavapai province (terrain accreted to North America during the Early Proterozoic). The deformation zone along the southern side of the Wyoming province is the Cheyenne belt. For reference, modern boundaries are shown in light gray. Modified from Karlstrom and others, 1999.

on the island. A complex, east-trending, late-extensional phase fault zone on the north tip of the island places highly fractured Tintic Quartzite on the south against tilted, fractured Salt Lake Formation on the north. The East and West Stringham Peak faults and the Elephant Head fault may also have been reactivated during early and/or late Cenozoic extension, and a splay of the East Great Salt Lake fault zone may extend onto the southwest part of the island (Doelling and others, 1990).

GEOLOGIC HISTORY

Rocks on Antelope Island preserve a long, rich geologic history, with multiple stages of mountain building, erosion, and sedimentation (figure 22, stages 1-13).

Archean(?) Deposition and Metamorphism

Though most evidence was obliterated by later metamorphism, limited data suggest that during the Middle or Late Archean, sedimentary strata, including graywacke, feldspar-rich sandstone, quartz-rich sandstone, and clay-rich mudstone, were deposited, possibly on oceanic crust (Hedge and others, 1983; Yonkee and others, 2000a) (figure 22, stage 1). Mafic dikes and flows apparently intruded these layered rocks. These sedimentary and intrusive rocks were apparently metamorphosed and deformed during the Late Archean, about 2.6 billion years ago based on limited Rb-Sr isotopic data from similar rocks in the Wasatch Range (Hedge and others, 1983; Bryant, 1988a;

1988b; Yonkee and others, 2000a) (figure 22, stage 2). Magma may have intruded during this metamorphism. The metamorphosed sedimentary rocks now form layered gneiss, quartz-rich gneiss, and biotite schist outcrops on the central and southern parts of the island; the possible oceanic crust forms pods of metamorphosed ultramafic rock and mafic gneiss; the mafic dikes form outcrops of hornblende-plagioclase gneiss; and the intrusive rock may form some granitic gneiss outcrops (alternatively, all granitic gneiss outcrops may be from Early Proterozoic granitic intrusions). Although data are limited, the Late Archean metamorphism and intrusions apparently correlate with a widespread episode of mountain building associated with collision of small plates of the earth's crust about 2.7 to 2.5 billion years ago. This mountain building occurred as a major part of the Archean continental core of North America called the Wyoming province became consolidated (Bryant, 1988a; Houston and others, 1989). Antelope Island is near the southwestern edge of the Wyoming province (figure 23).

Early Proterozoic Granitic Intrusion and Metamorphism

The southern part of the Wyoming province appears to have been in a passive continental margin setting from about 2.5 to 1.8 billion years ago, with local accumulation of thick sediments and possible local intrusions (Houston and others, 1989), though evidence for such sediments is not preserved on Antelope Island. A profound period of mountain building, igneous activity, and metamorphism then ensued from about 1.8 to 1.6 billion years ago, as a series of island arcs with Early Proterozoic crust and sediments were accreted onto the southern margin of the province (Houston and others, 1989). This was part of an even larger mountain-building event in which several Archean blocks and Early Proterozoic mountain belts were "stitched together" to form the continent of Laurentia (the major part of the ancient North American continent) (Karlstrom and others, 1999) (figure 23). Large granitic plutons, now represented by banded and granitic gneiss such as in the Red Rocks area on Antelope Island, were intruded about 2.0 to 1.8 billion years ago and appear to have incorporated partial melts from older continental crust (Hedge and others, 1983; Bryant, 1988a) (figure 22, stage 3). Metamorphism peaked about 1.7 billion years ago, as island rocks were buried 7 to 12 miles (12-20 km) deep and reached metamorphic temperatures of 1,200 to 1,500°F (650-800°C) (upper amphibolite to granulite facies) (Barnett and others, 1993) (figure 22, stage 4). These temperatures are hotter than normal for rocks buried at these depths, and may indicate extra heating caused by widespread granitic intrusions (Yonkee and others, 2000a). Such intense metamorphism and deformation produced strong foliation and isoclinal folds in layered gneiss and associated rock types, weak to strong foliation and migmatitic (partially melted) textures in banded and granitic gneiss, and obliterated most evidence of previous events.

Such pervasive Early Proterozoic metamorphism is not found in the main part of the Wyoming province, but it is characteristic of the Mojave province, a belt of deformed crustal rock that extends southwest from the Antelope Island area (figure 23). It is also common in island arc terrains of the Yavapai province, which accreted to the southern margin of the Wyoming province along a suture zone called the Cheyenne belt (Chamberlain and Bowring, 1990; Karlstrom and others, 1999). The Cheyenne belt has been largely covered by younger deposits in Utah, but it appears to project westward from Wyoming toward the Antelope Island area, and the pervasive deformation in Antelope Island rocks may reflect close proximity to this suture zone (Bryant, 1988a). Thus, Antelope Island lies near the junction of three main provinces of the ancient continent, and appears to bear elements of each.

Sometime shortly following peak metamorphism, coarse-grained pegmatitic granite, red granite plutons, and late-stage, discordant pegmatite dikes intruded into the older metamorphic rocks of Antelope Island (figure 22, stage 5). These bodies are much less deformed than older rocks, indicating that the rocks had been uplifted above the level of the Precambrian high-grade metamorphism. By about 1.6 billion years ago, Laurentia and other continental pieces were stitched together to form the main part of a supercontinent called Rodinia, with Utah located in a relatively passive setting far inland from the supercontinent margin (Houston and others, 1989; Karlstrom and

others, 1999) (figure 23).

Middle Proterozoic Uplift and Erosion

A profound unconformity representing 900 to 1,000 million years separates highly metamorphosed Farmington Canyon rocks from Late Proterozoic low-grade metasedimentary rocks on Antelope Island, and the history for this time period must be largely inferred from regional relations. Between 1.7 billion and about 750 million years ago, Farmington Canyon Complex rocks underwent relatively slow uplift in which over 6 miles (10 km) of rock were eroded off (Barnett and others, 1993) (figure 22, stage 6). About 1 billion years ago, parts of Rodinia experienced limited extension and local development of rift or extensional basins, including one along part of the weakened Cheyenne belt (Constenius, 1998; Karlstrom and others, 1999). This basin, called the Uinta trough, lay south of Antelope Island and accumulated over 16,000 feet (4,800 m) of sediment of the Big Cottonwood Formation (see Willis and Willis, this volume), part of which may have been eroded from uplifted rocks of the Antelope Island area (Christie-Blick, 1997).

Late Proterozoic Rifting and Sedimentation

At about 800 to 700 million years ago, Rodinia broke apart as the Antarctica-Australia block pulled away from western North America (Unrug, 1997; Karlstrom and others, 1999). The rifting, possibly in multiple pulses, continued until the start of the Paleozoic and led to development of a passive continental margin in central Nevada and weakened crust that extended into Utah (Bennett and DePaolo, 1987); Antelope Island was again near the edge of the continent. This extension set the stage for most of the remaining geologic history of Antelope Island. West of the island, weakened, attenuated crust gradually subsided, accumulating a thick sequence of shallow marine strata. East of the island, a more stable crust formed a shelf that varied from being eroded, to accumulating thin layers of strata. Antelope Island lay near the "hingeline" or transition between the subsiding and more stable crust. Late Proterozoic strata are about 300 feet (90 m) thick on Antelope Island, whereas similar strata are over 10,000 feet (3,000 m) thick in sections of rock deposited west of the island, and are absent in the central Wasatch Range east of the island (figure 22, stage 7).

The Late Proterozoic deposits on the island record an interesting history. Diamictite of the Mineral Fork Formation and correlative rocks in northern Utah were deposited by glaciers that may have extended off the continents into shallow oceans (Christie-Blick, 1983, 1985; Crittenden and others, 1983); the region must have looked much like modern Antarctica. Directly overlying the diamictite is dolomite of the lower Kelley Canyon Formation. The abrupt change represents either an unconformity or a dramatic shift in environment. Similar Late Proterozoic diamictite-dolomite associations in other parts of the world have been interpreted to record a dramatic change from a "snowball" to a "hothouse" earth (Hoffman and Schrag, 2000). According to this theory, global cooling indirectly related to shifting tectonic plate positions led to world-wide glaciation. This glaciation then disrupted the carbon cycle, leading to buildup of carbon dioxide in the atmosphere, eventually triggering an intense greenhouse effect. The rapid global warming melted the ice and caused rapid deposition of a carbonate (now dolomite) layer. Siltstone of the upper Kelley Canyon Formation (now converted to slate) represents deposition of fine-grained sediments in a low-energy environment as the climate stabilized, which was followed by a period of minor erosion during the latest Proterozoic.

Paleozoic to Early Mesozoic Sedimentation

The basic pattern set during the Late Proterozoic continued into the Paleozoic, with a broad subsiding basin to the west, a more stable platform to the east, and Antelope Island at the transition. A final pulse of rifting appears to have occurred at the Proterozoic-Paleozoic boundary, based on an influx of feldspar and quartz cobbles at the base of the Cambrian Tintic Quartzite, Latest Proterozoic basalt flows in correlative rocks elsewhere in northern Utah (Crittenden and others, 1971), and regional subsidence patterns (Christie-Blick and Levy, 1989). On Antelope Island, the Early Cambrian Tintic Quartzite was deposited mostly in energetic near-shore marine environments, with some possible stream deposits near the base of the formation.

Middle Cambrian to Jurassic rocks have been eroded from Antelope Island, but similar-aged rocks are found in surrounding areas (Hintze, 1993), and clasts of early to middle Paleozoic rocks are present in Tertiary conglomerate outcrops on the island. Thus, we know that island rocks were covered by Paleozoic rocks, which were deposited in a shallow, tropical epicontinental sea as Utah lay near the equator (figure 22, stage 7). Some tectonic activity occurred to the west in the later Paleozoic, but it probably had little impact on Antelope Island rocks. During the early Mesozoic, regional patterns were somewhat complex, with periodic deposition of terrestrial sediments in river flood plain, sand dune, and tidal flat settings.

Late Mesozoic Deformation and Low-Grade Metamorphism

During the Late Mesozoic, the North American plate was moving westward and the Farallon plate (floor of an ancestral Pacific Ocean) was being subducted. As subduction proceeded, a fold-thrust belt developed east of a volcanic belt in central California, and deformation advanced eastward over time. By Late Jurassic time the deformation had spread to western Utah and surrounding areas, beginning the Sevier orogeny (Armstrong, 1968). The Early Cretaceous was marked by significant crustal thickening and metamorphism in eastern Nevada and northwestern Utah

(Camelleri and others, 1997). About 140 to 100 million years ago, the Willard thrust fault peeled up a thick sheet of basin rocks from west of the island, and transported it about 30 miles (50 km) eastward over the island rocks on a gently dipping thrust fault system (Yonkee, 1997) (figure 2). Island rock, buried by the 7- to 10-mile-thick (11-16 km) Willard plate, reached temperatures of 550 to 750°F (300-400°C). Rocks of the Willard plate are now eroded from Antelope Island, but they are well exposed on nearby Fremont Island (Yonkee, 1997). The combination of increased temperatures, widespread fluid flow, and differential stress produced widespread deformation, and metamorphosed the rock to a low grade called greenschist facies (figure 22, stage 8).

As thrusting continued during the Cretaceous and into the earliest Tertiary, the lower-level Ogden thrust fault and an even deeper basal thrust fault translated island rocks more than 20 additional miles (30 km) eastward from where they formed (figure 2). Whereas the Willard thrust carried thick sedimentary rocks from west of the hinge line, the Ogden thrust system shaved off a sliver of basement and thin sedimentary rock along the hinge line (Camelleri and others, 1997). These lower-level thrusts produced major uplifts and large-scale folding to form the Wasatch culmination, a huge anticlinal stack of thrust plates, which was a dominant feature in the Sevier belt of northern Utah (Yonkee, 1992). Antelope Island lies on the gently dipping west limb of this anticlinal feature (the steeply dipping eastern limb is exposed in the central Wasatch Range) (figure 22, stage 9). During thrusting, huge mountains probably existed in the area of Antelope Island. Erosion of these mountains provided tremendous amounts of sediment that was shed eastward, accumulating in front, and locally on top, of the growing thrust belt as slip was transferred progressively eastward onto new frontal thrust faults from about 90 to 50 million years ago (DeCelles, 1994; Willis, 1999).

Early Cenozoic Extension, Deposition, and Igneous Activity

As thrusting waned about 50 million years ago, the Sevier mountain belt continued to be rapidly eroded, and was also locally extended as thrust sheets "collapsed" back to the west along listric normal faults (Constenius, 1996) (figure 22, stage 10). Boulder gravels accumulated along mountain fronts, and fine-grained alluvial and lacustrine deposits accumulated away from the mountain fronts in subsiding half-graben basins. From about 40 to 25 million years ago, volcanism also developed across parts of Utah, including a broad belt south of Antelope Island (Tooker and Roberts, 1971; Moore and McKee, 1983). The conglomeratic unit on Antelope Island, with boulders from eroding mountains to the west and volcanic debris from the south, accumulated within a tilted half-graben. During this time, peripheral igneous dikes were also intruded into the Farmington Canyon Complex on the southern part of the island.

Today, Tertiary rocks on the east side of Antelope Island strike northerly and dip 20 to 45 degrees to the east into the East Antelope Island half graben. Exposures are limited, but overall the lower conglomeratic sequence appears to be more steeply tilted than the younger Salt Lake Formation, indicating that tilting occurred over a protracted period of early and late Cenozoic normal faulting. Thus, although the East Antelope Island and East Great Salt Lake faults are generally regarded as late Cenozoic features, it appears that they were active in the early Cenozoic as well.

Late Cenozoic Basin and Range Extension and Deposition

Sometime after 20 million years ago, western Utah and Nevada began to experience crustal-scale extension that produced a series of major north-south-trending normal faults that bounded large uplifted blocks and down-dropped basins, forming the basin and range topography that characterizes the area today (Bryant and others, 1989) (figure 2). Mixtures of clastic, lacustrine, and volcanic deposits filled the basins. The Salt Lake Formation on Antelope Island was deposited in one of these rotated, down-dropped basins between about 11 and 8 million years ago (Willis and Jensen, 2000) (figure 22, stage 11). The formation represents a mix of local clastic debris shed from adjacent mountains, silt and mud deposited in lakes in the basins, and volcanic ash derived from voluminous volcanism in the central Snake River Plain, which was then the site of the hot spot that characterizes Yellowstone National Park today (Miller, 1990; Miller and others, in press; Perkins and others, 1998). The island block has continued to rotate on the listric faults to the present time.

Late Pleistocene (28,000-10,000 years ago) Lake Bonneville

Most of the Quaternary deposits that mantle the island are of Lake Bonneville age and younger, ranging from about 28,000 years ago to the present (figure 24). By this time, the island block had rotated to its current position. Lake Bonneville was the latest of many large late Cenozoic lakes to fill basins in the Basin and Range Province (figure 22, stage 12). At its maximum extent, it covered much of western Utah and the border areas of southeastern Idaho and northeastern Nevada (Currey and others, 1984). The many horizontal terraces and benches visible on hillsides on the island represent old shoreline levels of the lake as it rose and fell (figure 1). The deepest part of Lake Bonneville was near the Newfoundland Mountains, 40 miles (64 km) west of Antelope Island, where the water was more than 1,000 feet (305 m) deep at its maximum (Doelling, 1980). After Lake Bonneville receded, the lake basin rose as the weight of the water was removed (isostatic rebound) (Crittenden, 1963). As a result, today Lake Bonneville shorelines on the island are about 150 feet (45

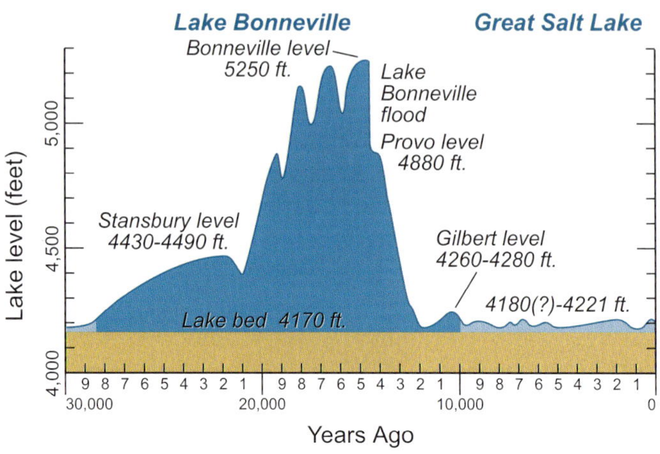

Figure 24. Rise and fall of Lake Bonneville between 28,000 and 10,000 years ago, and Great Salt Lake in the last 10,000 years. The shoreline elevations shown for Antelope Island are about 150 feet (45 m) higher than correlative shorelines near the margin of the ancient lake basin. Modified from Doelling and others, 1990; Oviatt, 1997; and Murchison and Mulvey, 2000.

m) higher than equivalent shorelines at the margins of the basin (Crittenden, 1963; Currey, 1982; Bills and others, in press) (figure 24).

The oldest prominent basinwide shoreline, the Stansbury shoreline, was constructed from 23,000 to 22,000 years ago during a pause in the lake rise (Oviatt, 1997) (figure 24). This shoreline is discontinuous, but locally well developed on Antelope Island at elevations ranging from approximately 4,430 to 4,490 feet (1,351-1,369 m), approximately 300 feet (90 m) above the present level of Great Salt Lake.

After Stansbury time, the lake fluctuated irregularly but gradually rose to its highest level, marked by the Bonneville shoreline, by about 16,000 years ago (Oviatt, 1997) (figure 24). The Bonneville level was controlled by the low point on the basin rim at an elevation of approximately 5,090 feet (1,550 m) in southern Idaho where water spilled northward into the Snake River drainage. The lake oscillated near the threshold elevation, producing several different shorelines within a zone of 45 feet (14 m) (Currey, 1980). The dominant Bonneville shoreline on Antelope Island is at an elevation of about 5,250 feet (1,600 m), about 150 feet (40 m) higher than the same shoreline on mountains near the edge of the Bonneville basin, reflecting isostatic rebound.

About 14,500 years ago (Oviatt, 1997) the low point was breached and the outlet quickly eroded down to the level of a bedrock sill. The ensuing catastrophic flood into the Snake River lowered the surface of Lake Bonneville approximately 360 feet (110 m) within a few months to the Provo level (Jarrett and Malde, 1987). The Provo shoreline is at an elevation of 4,850 to 4,880 feet (1,480-1,490 m) on Antelope Island. As the climate became warmer and drier, Lake Bonneville receded until by 12,000 to 11,000 years ago it was smaller than the modern Great Salt Lake (Currey and others, 1984).

About 11,000 to 10,000 years ago, a wetter climate caused the lake to rise, forming the Gilbert shoreline approximately 80 feet (24 m) above the present level of Great Salt Lake. This represents the last stage of Lake Bonneville. The Gilbert shoreline is displayed on Antelope Island at elevations of approximately 4,260 to 4,280 feet (1,293-1,305 m), especially near Sea Gull Point (Murchison and Mulvey, 2000) (figures 1 and 3).

Holocene (10,000 years ago to present) Great Salt Lake and Post-Bonneville Deposition

Great Salt Lake, the Holocene remnant of Lake Bonneville, has fluctuated between elevations of 4,220 feet and 4,180 feet (1,286-1,275 m) for the last 10,000 years (figure 22, stage 13), including historical highs of 4,212 feet (1,284 m) in 1873 and 1986-87, and a historical low in 1963 of 4,191 feet (1,278 m) (Currey and others, 1984, 1988; Atwood and Mabey, 2000) (figure 24).

Post-Bonneville alluvial fans, composed of debris-flow and debris-flood deposits, bury older lacustrine deposits and locally extend down to modern shorelines. Toes of these fans have undergone wave erosion during rises of Great Salt Lake. Several post-Bonneville landslides have occurred in lacustrine deposits, and numerous small slumps in colluvium occurred during the mid-1980s "wet period." Locally, lake sediments are remobilized as sand dunes.

PAST, PRESENT, AND FUTURE

Exploration and Economic Geology

The early settlers quickly noted the geologic resources of Antelope Island. They apparently attempted to quarry the slate in the Kelley Canyon Formation in large sheets or plates, but it was difficult to maintain size uniformity because the rock plates were too thin and broke easily (figure 16). Some slate may have been broken into small pieces to be used as roofing gravel or to be incorporated into asphalt roofing shingles. However, it appears that little, if any, was shipped from the island (Doelling and others, 1990).

The discovery of gold, silver, and copper in the rich Bingham district in the Oquirrh Mountains directly south of Antelope Island spurred prospectors' interest in the nearby island. They quickly discovered copper and iron stains on quartz veins near the center of the island, enticing them to dig several shallow shafts, inclines, and pits, and one adit that was cut to intersect a large quartz vein at depth. Most prospecting probably took place between 1900 and the end of World War II, with the greatest effort during World War I (Doelling and others, 1990). It is doubtful that more than a few test lots of ore were ever shipped. Today, in the prospect areas, trace amounts of the copper minerals malachite, chrysocolla, azurite, chalcanthite, bornite, and chalcopyrite; and the iron minerals

hematite, magnetite, limonite, jarosite, and pyrite; form small blebs in the quartz veins, and crusts and stains on joint surfaces.

Oil seeps at Rozel Point north of Antelope Island, and other oil and gas discoveries in the Great Basin, triggered sporadic exploration in the Antelope Island area. The Anschutz Corporation obtained a permit in 1981 to drill a 20,000-foot (6,000 m) exploration well on Antelope Island to test a theory that Mesozoic and Paleozoic source and reservoir rocks underlie a thrust fault under the island. They only drilled to a depth of about 133 feet, and then abandoned the well (F.C. Moulton, Anschutz Corporation, retired, verbal communication, 1989). The well pad is now the parking lot for the Frary Peak trailhead (figure 3). Our studies indicate that little or no stratified rocks underlie the island (figure 2), thus the potential for significant oil and gas discoveries appears low (Willis and Jensen, 2000). Better potential lies in fault-bounded basins filled with thick Cenozoic sediments east and west of the island (Bortz and others, 1985).

In 1979 and 1980 about 16 million cubic yards (12 million m³) of fill were excavated from the south part of the island for construction of the Interstate 80 highway and ramps near the Salt Lake International Airport (Davis, 2000) (figure 4). The material was carried by a 13-mile-long (21 km) conveyor belt to a stockpile and loading facility west of Salt Lake City. At that time, the conveyor belt system was the longest ever built in the world. Large amounts of fill and riprap have also been removed for construction of the north and south causeways to the island.

Ground Water

Ground water is undoubtedly the most important geologic resource on Antelope Island, making it possible to maintain the herds of wildlife for which the island is famous. Unlike other islands in Great Salt Lake, Antelope Island has numerous perennial springs that issue from bedrock and surficial deposits, with an estimated combined dry-season discharge of 100 gallons (400 L) per minute (Mayo and Klauk, 2000). Mayo and Klauk showed that the ground water is derived from local precipitation rather than plumbing interconnected with the Wasatch Range. It may seem surprising that an island the size of Antelope Island in a desert setting has that amount of reliable ground water. Several factors contribute: (1) the island is high enough to "catch" winter storms, some of which are augmented by "lake effect" (storms that increase in intensity as they move over the relatively warm lake water); (2) the highly fractured and jointed bedrock and loose surficial cover allow the water to move into subsurface aquifers rather than to run off; and (3) fine-grained, impermeable Tertiary and Quaternary deposits at low elevations on the sides of the island cause the water to discharge on the island as springs (otherwise most of the water would emerge offshore under Great Salt Lake where it would have no value).

Though the ground water is suitable for wildlife,

above-acceptable levels of sodium, chlorine, and sulfate make it unsuitable for human consumption. Most of these dissolved ions are attributed to aerosols (fine mists of salty lake water blown onto the island during storms) (Mayo and Klauk, 2000). The better quality springs are generally above an elevation of 4,400 feet (1,340 m) on the east side of the island.

Active Geology

Certainly some of the interest of Antelope Island lies in the geologic processes that are active today. Fifty miles (80 km) of coastline, proximity to major faults, and steep, rocky slopes combine with local geology to produce lake flooding, wave erosion, landslide, debris flow, rock fall, and earthquake-induced ground shaking risks (Hecker and Case, 2000).

Though fluctuating lake levels are viewed as climatic or meteorological phenomena, it was the geology that created the closed Great Basin and the ultimate size of the watershed. Fluctuations in the level of Great Salt Lake cause flooding and erosion in coastal areas. The 1983-87 rise of the lake to about 4,212 feet (1,284 m) destroyed road access to the island and inundated public beaches (figure 25). However, such dramatic lake-level rises have been relatively infrequent. Efforts in 1987-1988 to control the level of the lake by pumping water to the West Desert have helped to reduce lake flooding and erosion hazards (Atwood and Mabey, 2000; Gwynn, 2000). The north causeway to Antelope Island was reconstructed in 1992 with the road surface at an elevation of 4,208.5 feet (1,282.8 m), and

is engineered to handle a lake level up to about 4,205 feet (1,282 m).

Mass movements on Antelope Island include landslides, debris flows, rock falls, creep, and other gravity-induced rock or soil movement (Hecker and others, 2000). Landslides exist in areas of wave erosion along the modern shore, on and beneath abandoned wave-built lake terraces, and on colluvial slopes above the Bonneville shoreline.

Nearby major fault zones present a significant earthquake hazard (Hecker and others, 2000). The central portion of the Wasatch fault zone, with surface-rupture zones about 15 miles (24 km) east of Antelope Island and potential earthquake epicenters much closer (because the fault dips toward the island), has experienced numerous large earthquakes of magnitudes 7.0 to 7.5 during the Holocene (Schwartz and Coppersmith, 1984). The East Great Salt Lake fault zone has an average rate of movement that is about one-half that of the Wasatch fault zone, but may be capable of generating similarly large earthquakes (Pechmann and others, 1987). The largest earthquakes since 1850 near Antelope Island had magnitudes of 5.5 (in 1910 and 1914 near Salt Lake City and Ogden) and 6.4 (in 1934 about 50 miles [80 km] northwest of Antelope Island) (Arabasz and others, 1980). Strong ground shaking during earthquakes could initiate landslides and rock falls, generate large waves (seiches) in Great Salt Lake, and cause liquefaction in saturated sandy and silty deposits around springs or near the lake shore.

Figure 25. Picnic facilities at Bridger Bay destroyed by wave erosion during the 1985-1987 highstand of Great Salt Lake.

KEY GEOLOGIC SITES AND FEATURES ON ANTELOPE ISLAND

Several of these sites and features are in areas that are generally closed to public access – check with park rangers before visiting them. Numbers refer to locations on figure 3. In some cases, features are visible in several areas. We recommend that you consult the geologic map of the island that shows geologic exposures in more detail (Doelling and others, 1990). Many of these sites and features are pointed out on the road and trail logs.

1. Farmington Canyon Complex. As the name implies, this unit is a complex mixture of at least ten different rock types with varying metamorphic structures, which are exposed across the southern two-thirds of the island (see text discussion, figure 6, and table 1). Comparing and contrasting the various rock types allows parts of Antelope Island's long history to be understood, from periods of intense Precambrian mountain building, to thrusting during the Sevier orogeny. Unfortunately, you have to visit several different parts of the island to see examples of all the different rock types and features. Several key sites are listed separately below. The number "1" on the map (figure 3) is placed on sites at Mormon Rocks, south of The Sentry, and east of Frary Peak, but many other sites also have excellent exposures.

2. Layered gneiss and related rocks on southern end of island. Interlayered biotite-bearing gneiss, quartz-rich gneiss, biotite schist, and metamorphosed ultramafic rock form the oldest and one of the most interesting suites of rock in the Farmington Canyon Complex. These rocks provide one of the few glimpses of old Archean(?) folds and rock types that have not been completely overprinted by younger metamorphism. The best way to view these features is to start near Great Salt Lake shoreline at the south end of island and follow the ridge crest north for about 0.5 mile (0.8 km) (figure 6). Layered gneiss (figure 7), quartz-rich gneiss (figure 8), hornblende-plagioclase gneiss (figure 9), biotite schist, metamorphosed ultramafic rocks, and tight interference folds (figure 7) can be seen along the traverse.

3. Granite intrusions at Garr Knolls. Granite pegmatite has intruded metamorphic gneiss and schist in several areas, brecciating the host rock. The best exposures are in the Garr Knolls area on the southern part of the island, where deformation in and around the edges of granite intrusions is well exposed (figure 11). The host rock is contorted and broken into many large angular fragments.

4. Granite gneiss in the Red Rocks area. Granitic gneiss is spectacularly exposed in the Red Rocks area on the west-central part of the island, and forms the core of a large granitic pluton intruded prior to, or during, main-phase metamorphism. The igneous body was massive enough to deflect the main metamorphic foliation, forming an elliptical foliation pattern in this area (figure 6). Dark-gray hornblende-plagioclase gneiss bodies create striking contrast to the lighter granitic rocks.

5. Frary Peak and trail. Frary Peak, the island's highest point, affords spectacular views of classic Basin and Range features both on and around the island (figure 1). The peak is capped by a small erosional remnant of Kelley Canyon and Mineral Fork Formations, forming a key control point for reconstructing the island geology. The Daddy Stump Ridge backthrust fault is visible in the slope just below the trail northwest of the peak (see site 11). The peak also offers an overview of the Red Rocks intrusive body (site 4). In addition, the trail to the peak passes near several different rock types of the Farmington Canyon Complex, and good outcrops of the Mineral Fork, Kelley Canyon, and Tintic Formations. Watch for tight folds, crenulation and planar cleavage, shear zones, quartz veins, mineral alteration, and stretched clasts in these rocks. To the east, the Wasatch fault can be traced for miles at the base of the Wasatch Range. Several horsts (uplifted and rotated blocks) of the Basin and Range Province are visible south, north, and west of the island (figure 2). Broad, sediment-filled, down-faulted basins are visible on all sides of the island. From this location, it is easy to visualize the island as an uplifted and rotated horst in an extended terrain. Lake Bonneville erosional and depositional shorelines are very well exposed on the island and surrounding ranges.

6. Diamictite of the Mineral Fork Formation. Some of the most outstanding exposures of diamictite (very poorly sorted conglomerate) in Utah can be found on Antelope Island. The Mineral Fork diamictite was deposited by glaciers that covered much of North America about 750 million years ago. The diamictite consists of small cobbles to very large boulders of metamorphic and igneous rock eroded from the Farmington Canyon Complex and deposited in a micaceous matrix. In some areas, mica-rich clasts were stretched almost beyond recognition during Cretaceous thrusting, whereas quartzite boulders were less stretched as the deformation deflected around the boulders through the much weaker matrix. Two impressive outcrops are on Elephant Head (figure 14) and along the Frary Peak trail.

7. Dolomite in the Kelley Canyon Formation. This layer forms a prominent, tannish-gray, easy-to-recognize marker bed that extends across the island near Elephant Head (figure 15). The dolomite commonly displays strong recrystallization and locally has crenulation cleavage produced during Sevier deformation. White Rock, in White Rock Bay (figure 3), is composed of this unit.

8. Slate quarries. Several small excavation pits where slate of the Kelley Canyon Formation was quarried by early pioneers are visible along the Frary Peak trail (figure 16). The slate is quite colorful and locally is of good quality. The rock breaks along cleavage planes that commonly cut across the bedding. In some areas, bedding is tightly folded with pervasive cleavage parallel to the fold planes.

9. *Breccia dikes in slate beds.* Several intriguing dikes of brecciated slate intrude the Kelley Canyon slate and dolomite beds north of Stringham Peak (Doelling and others, 1990). The dikes are up to about 2 feet (0.6 m) wide and can be traced for several tens of feet. They could be soft-sediment deformation features formed soon after deposition of the slate, or later features formed during thrust deformation.

10. *Greenschist-facies metamorphism and shear zones in Precambrian rocks.* Excellent examples of low-grade metamorphism that produced chloritic gneiss, mylonite, and phyllonite, and shear deformation are abundant on the island (figures 12 and 13). Most outcrops show some effects; however, the largest and most impressive example is the Antelope Island shear zone on the west-central part of the island, where the shear zone and associated alteration band is almost 1 mile (1.6 km) wide (figure 4). Medium-size shear zones and regions of minor anastomosing shear zones are north of Garr Knolls, along the Frary Peak trail near Stringham Peak (figure 12), and on Elephant Head (figure 14). The latter two sites allow the opportunity to trace the effects of shearing and alteration from the basement rock into the cover rock where clasts are stretched and sheared. A small shear zone with low-grade metamorphism is accessible by car near the paved east-side road a short distance north of the Frary Peak trailhead turnoff.

11. *Daddy Stump Ridge backthrust fault.* The Daddy Stump Ridge fault is a north-trending, steeply east-dipping backthrust (reverse) fault that lies along the west slope of Daddy Stump Ridge just below the trail between Frary and Stringham Peaks (figure 21). An excellent exposure in which Farmington Canyon rock is thrust over Kelley Canyon slate is about 300 feet (90 m) down the ridge directly west of Frary Peak (see site 5). Near its north end, the Tintic Quartzite is folded into a series of tight folds. Well-exposed rocks of the Farmington Canyon Complex are thrust over younger Late Proterozoic and Cambrian rocks with a minimum displacement of 800 feet (240 m). The tight folds are accessible by dropping down the west slope of the ridge from near the radio facility on the Frary Peak trail about 0.25 miles (0.4 km) north of Frary Peak.

12. *Stretched pebbles in Tintic Quartzite.* Shear deformation, flattening, and stretching produced by thrusting are easily recognized in stretched pebbles in the Tintic Quartzite (figure 17). The deformed pebbles provide clear evidence that the deformation and related retrograde metamorphism post-date, and were not produced during Precambrian deformation. Pebbles are locally stretched to ratios of 3:1 or greater. Best exposures are in the large flat north of the park headquarters and maintenance building, and in some outcrops on Buffalo Point and near White Rock Bay.

13. *Quartz dikes and shear zones on Elephant Head.* Quartz dikes are common in Precambrian and Cambrian rock throughout the island. However, the most impressive examples are large outcrops on Elephant Head. Some outcrops are substantial enough to map separately (Doelling and others, 1990). Similar quartz veins in the Wasatch Range yielded Cretaceous ages, indicating that the quartz was emplaced during Sevier thrust deformation (Yonkee, 1992).

14. *Copper mineralization.* Several large quartz dikes are present near Bamberger Hill in the central part of the island. One dike forms an impressive resistant rib about 15 feet (5 m) high that is strongly stained with the copper minerals chrysocolla and malachite. The mineralization is probably contemporaneous with Tertiary mineralization in areas south of the island. The extent of mineralization is small, but was enough to entice prospectors to dig several pits, adits, and shafts in the area.

15. *Tertiary conglomerate.* Tertiary conglomerate is exposed in several outcrops along the southeast side of the island (figure 4). The conglomerate beds display an amazing variety of clast lithology, size, and sorting (Willis and Jensen, 2000). The number 15 on figure 3 is placed on three of the most interesting exposures, but other outcrops are instructive as well. The northern site exposes megaconglomerate with clasts up to 5 feet (1.5 m) in diameter in outcrops and nearby weathered-out clasts up to 11 feet (3.4 m) in diameter (figure 18). These boulders probably accumulated at the foot of an ancient mountain range in large debris-flow deposits. The center site exposes mixed conglomerate and lacustrine limestone, and the southern site exposes outcrops with mixed metamorphic, quartzite, and volcanic clasts.

16. *Tertiary outcrop near Ladyfinger Point.* This relatively small outcrop, approximately 1,200 feet (370 m) long and 75 feet (23 m) wide, trends east-west along the north shoreline near Ladyfinger Point and was exposed during excavation of a gravel pit (figure 20). The outcrop consists of pale-gray volcanic ash interbedded with brownish-gray breccia and conglomerate. It is cut by numerous east-striking minor faults that may be associated with a larger fault zone north of the island. The outcrops have degraded since they were first exposed, but are still fascinating. When fresh, horizontal striae visible on some faults indicate strike-slip motion. Beds are locally rotated and overturned. Some clasts in this deposit were eroded from highly deformed footwall (lower plate) rocks of the Willard thrust, as well as from the basal part of the upper plate of the Willard thrust, which, prior to erosion, was present above the Tintic Quartzite at this location (Willis and Jensen, 2000).

17. *Lake Bonneville shorelines.* Lake Bonneville covered most of the island between about 28,000 and 10,000 years ago (figures 1 and 24). Shoreline deposits and erosional features are abundant around the island (shown on Doelling and others, 1990). These features vary dramati-

cally depending upon the exposure to waves, composition and resistance of the bedrock, and slope angles. The number 17 on the map refers to a few key localities, but the shoreline features can be viewed almost anywhere. Features include boulder beach deposits, wave-built terrace deposits, shorelines cut into bedrock by wave action, and tufa (a thick crust of limestone deposited by algae in the wave zone along shorelines). Shorelines on Antelope Island are 150 feet (45 m) higher in elevation than equivalent shorelines along the Wasatch Range because the island is closer to the center of the lake basin, which rebounded or rose after the weight of the water was removed.

18. *Great Salt Lake shorelines.* Great Salt Lake has fluctuated between about 4,220 and less than 4,180 feet (1,286-1,275 m) over the past 10,000 years, leaving a number of shorelines around the margin of Antelope Island (Atwood and Mabey, 2000) (figures 1 and 24). The historical highstand shoreline formed in 1986-87 is near the 4,212-foot (1,284 m) elevation, and can be identified by the human-made debris included in the deposits. Other Holocene shorelines are just above and below. Oolites, such as found on sandy beaches on the northwest part of the island, are indicators of high-salinity, high-calcium lake waters (Burke and Gerhard, 2000). They are spherical sand-size grains formed as aragonite (calcium carbonate) was concentrically deposited around the tiny fecal pellets of brine shrimp or sand grains. In some places, the oolites are strongly cemented, forming rock. Some of these newly formed rocks may be only a few years old (Burke and Gerhard, 2000).

19. *Dunes of quartz and oolitic sand.* Oolite and quartz sand dunes are present along the shorelines in Bridger Bay and White Rock Bay (same location as site 18). The oolites formed in Great Salt Lake, washed ashore as beach deposits, and then were blown into dunes. Quartz sand dunes are present inland of the oolite dunes and are related to the Gilbert-level transgression of Lake Bonneville about 10,000 years ago. The quartz indicates that at Gilbert time, offshore sediments were clastic and water was of lower salinity, as opposed to the modern highly saline, calcareous environment.

ACKNOWLEDGMENTS

The Utah Geological Survey supported our original mapping and research in 1987-1988, when road access to the island was cut off by the high-water stand of Great Salt Lake. The Utah Division of Parks and Recreation provided logistical support, including the use of boats and vehicles. We thank Dave Miller, Don Currey, and Michael Perkins for many helpful suggestions and insights into the geology of this great outdoor classroom. Mike Hylland, Julie Willis, Doug Sprinkel, Tom Chidsey, and Elizabeth Balls provided many helpful review comments, and Jim Parker turned our crude drawings into polished illustrations.

REFERENCES

Arabasz, W.J., Smith, R.B., and Richins, W.D., 1980, Earthquake studies along the Wasatch Front, Utah—network monitoring, seismicity, and seismic hazards: Bulletin of the Seismological Society of America, v. 70, p. 1,479-1,499.

Armstrong, R.L., 1968, Sevier orogenic belt in Nevada and Utah: Geological Society of America Bulletin, v. 19, p. 429-458.

—1982, Cordilleran metamorphic core complexes, from Arizona to southern Canada: Annual Reviews Earth and Planetary Sciences, v. 10, p. 129-154.

Atwood, G., and Mabey, D.R., 2000, Shorelines of Antelope Island as evidence of fluctuations in the level of the Great Salt Lake, *in* King, J.K., and Willis, G.C., editors, The geology of Antelope Island, Davis County, Utah: Utah Geological Survey Miscellaneous Publication 00-1, p. 85-97.

Barnett, D., Bowman, J.R., and Smith, H.A., 1993, Petrologic and geochronologic studies in the Farmington Canyon Complex, Wasatch Mountains and Antelope Island, Utah: Utah Geological Survey Contract Report 93-5, 34 p.

Beckwith, E.G., 1855, Report of explorations of a route for the Pacific Railroad near the 41st parallel: U.S. Pacific Railroad Exploration Report 2, Section 2, 41st parallel, p. 1-20.

Bennett, V.C., and DePaolo, D.J., 1987, Proterozoic crustal history of the western United States as determined by neodymium isotopic mapping: Geological Society of America Bulletin, v. 99, p. 674-685.

Bills, B.G., Wambeam, T.J., and Currey, D.R., in press, Geodynamics of Lake Bonneville, *in* Gwynn, J.W., editor, Great Salt Lake: Utah Geological Survey Miscellaneous Publication.

Bortz, L.C., Cook, S.A., and Morrison, O.J., 1985, Great Salt Lake area, Utah, *in* Gries, R.R., and Dyer, R.C., editors, Seismic exploration of the Rocky Mountain region: Rocky Mountain Association of Geologists and Denver Geophysical Society, p. 275-281.

Bryant, B., 1988a, Evolution and early Proterozoic history of the margin of the Archean continent in Utah, *in* Ernst, W.G., editor, Metamorphism and crustal evolution of the western United States: Englewood Cliffs, N.J., Prentice-Hall, p. 431-445.

Bryant, B., 1988b, Geology of the Farmington Canyon Complex, Wasatch Mountains, Utah: U.S. Geological Survey Professional Paper 1476, 54 p.

Bryant, B. and Graff, P., 1980, Metaigneous rocks on Antelope Island [abs.]: Geological Society of America Abstracts with Programs, v. 12, no. 5, p. 269.

Bryant, B., Naeser, C.W., Marvin, R.F., and Mehnert, H.H., 1989, Ages of late Paleogene and Neogene tuffs and the beginning of rapid regional extension, eastern boundary of the Basin and Range Province near Salt Lake City, Utah: U.S. Geological Survey Bulletin 1787-

K, 11 p.

Burke, R.B., and Gerhard, L.C., 2000, Aragonite cementation and related sedimentary structures in Quaternary lacustrine deposits, Great Salt Lake, Utah, *in* King, J.K., and Willis, G.C., editors, The geology of Antelope Island, Davis County, Utah: Utah Geological Survey Miscellaneous Publication 00-1, p. 99-115.

Bywater, G.G. and Barlow, J.A., 1909, Antelope Island, Great Salt Lake: Salt Lake City, University of Utah, B.S. thesis, 21 p.

Camilleri, P., Yonkee, W.A., Coogan, J.C., Decelles, P.G., McGrew, A., and Wells, M., 1997, Hinterland to foreland transect through the Sevier orogen, northeast Nevada to north central Utah - structural style, metamorphism, and kinematic history of a large contractional orogenic wedge, *in* Link, P.K., and Kowallis, B.J., editors, Proterozoic to Recent stratigraphy, tectonics, and volcanology, Utah, Nevada, southern Idaho and central Mexico: Brigham Young University Geology Studies, v. 42, part 1, p. 297-309.

Chamberlain, K.R., and Bowring, S.A., 1990, Proterozoic geochronologic and isotopic boundary in NW Arizona: Journal of Geology, v. 98, p. 399-416.

Christie-Blick, N., 1983, Glacial-marine and subglacial sedimentation, Upper Proterozoic Mineral Fork Formation, Utah, *in* Molnia, B.F., editor, Glacial-marine sedimentation: New York, Plenum Press, p. 703-776.

—1985, Upper Proterozoic glacial-marine and subglacial deposits at Little Mountain, Utah: Brigham Young University Geology Studies, v. 32, pt. 1, p. 9-18.

—1997, Neoproterozoic sedimentation and tectonics in west-central Utah, *in* Link, P.K., and Kowallis, B.J., editors, Proterozoic to Recent stratigraphy, tectonics, and volcanology, Utah, Nevada, southern Idaho and central Mexico: Brigham Young University Geology Studies, v. 42, pt. 1, p. 1-30.

Christie-Blick, N., Grotzinger, J.P., and von der Borch, C.C., 1988, Sequence stratigraphy in Proterozoic successions: Geology, v. 16, p. 100-104.

Christie-Blick, N., and Levy, M., 1989, Stratigraphic and tectonic framework of Upper Proterozoic and Cambrian rocks in the western United States in 28th International Geological Congress, *in* Christie-Blick, N. and Levy, M., editors, Late Proterozoic and Cambrian tectonics, sedimentationm and record of Metazoan radiation in the western United States: American Geophysical Union Field Trip Guidebook T331, p. 7-21.

Constenius, K., 1996, Late Paleogene extensional collapse of the Cordilleran foreland fold and thrust belt: Geological Society of America Bulletin, v. 108, no. 1, p. 20-39.

—1998, Extensional tectonics of the Cordilleran fold-thrust belt and the Jurassic-Cretaceous Great Valley forearc basin: Tucson, University of Arizona, Ph.D. dissertation, 116 p.

Cook, K.L., Berg, J.W., Johnson, W.W., and Novotny, R.T., 1966, Some Cenozoic structural basins in the Great Salt Lake area, Utah, indicated by regional gravity surveys, *in* Stokes, W.L., editor, The Great Salt Lake: Utah Geological Society, Guidebook to the Geology of Utah no. 20, p. 57-76.

Cook, K.L., Gray, E.F., Iverson, R.M., and Strohmeier, M.T., 1980, Bottom gravity meter regional survey of the Great Salt Lake, Utah: Utah Geological and Mineral Survey Bulletin 116, p. 125-143.

Crittenden, M.D., Jr., 1963, New data on the isostatic deformation of Lake Bonneville: U.S. Geological Survey Professional Paper 454-E, 31 p.

Crittenden, M.D., Jr., Christie-Blick, N., and Link, P.K., 1983, Evidence for two pulses of glaciation during the late Proterozoic in northern Utah and southeastern Idaho: Geological Society of America Bulletin, v. 94, p. 437-450.

Crittenden, M.D., Jr., Schaeffer, F.E., Trimble, D.E., and Woodward, L.A., 1971, Nomenclature and correlation of some Upper Precambrian and basal Cambrian sequences in western Utah and southeastern Idaho: Geological Society of America Bulletin, v. 82, p. 581-602.

Currey, D.R., 1980, Coastal geomorphology of Great Salt Lake and vicinity: Utah Geological and Mineral Survey Bulletin 116, p. 69-82.

—1982, Lake Bonneville - selected features of relevance to neotectonic analysis: U.S. Geological Survey Open-File Report 82-1070, 30 p.

Currey, D.R., Atwood, G., and Mabey, D.R., 1984, Major levels of Great Salt Lake and Lake Bonneville: Utah Geological and Mineral Survey Map 73, scale 1:750,000.

Currey, D.R., Berry, M.S., Douglass, G.E., Merola, J.A., Murchison, S.B., Ridd, M.K., Atwood, G., Bills, B.G., and Lambrechts, J.R., 1988, The highest Holocene stage of Great Salt Lake, Utah [abs.]: Geological Society of America Abstracts with Programs, v. 20, no. 6, p. 411.

Davis, F.D., 2000, Construction materials, Antelope Island, *in* King, J.K., and Willis, G.C., editors, The geology of Antelope Island, Davis County, Utah: Utah Geological Survey Miscellaneous Publication 00-1, p. 131-134.

DeCelles, P.G., 1994, Late Cretaceous-Paleocene synorogenic sedimentation and kinematic history of the Sevier thrust belt, northeast Utah and southwest Wyoming: Geological Society of America Bulletin, v. 106, p. 32-56.

Devlin, W.J., Brueckner, H.K., and Bond, G.C., 1988, New isotopic data and a preliminary age for volcanics near the base of the Windemere Supergroup, northeastern Washington, U.S.A.: Canadian Journal of Earth Sciences, v. 25, p. 1,906-1,911.

Doelling, H.H., 1980, Geology and mineral resources of Box Elder County, Utah: Utah Geological and Mineral Survey Bulletin 115, 251 p., scale 1:125,000.

Doelling, H.H., Willis, G.C., Jensen, M.E., Hecker, S., Case, W.F., and Hand, J.S., 1990, Geologic map of Antelope Island, Davis County, Utah: Utah Geological and Mineral Survey Map 127, 27 p., scale 1:24,000.

Gwynn, J.W., 2000, The waters surrounding Antelope Island, Great Salt Lake, Utah, *in* King, J.K., and Willis, G.C., editors, The geology of Antelope Island, Davis County, Utah: Utah Geological Survey Miscellaneous Publication 00-1, p. 117-129.

Hall, J., 1845, Descriptions of organic remains collected by Captain J.C. Fremont in the geographical survey of Oregon and North Carolina, *in* Fremont, J.C., A report of the exploring expedition to Oregon and North Carolina in the years 1843-44: U.S. 28th Congress, Senate Ex. Document 174, p. 304-310.

Hecker, S. and Case, W.E., 2000, Engineering geology for park planning, Antelope Island State Park, Davis County, Utah, *in* King, J.K., and Willis, G.C., editors, The geology of Antelope Island, Davis County, Utah: Utah Geological Survey Miscellaneous Publication 00-1, p. 151-163.

Hedge, C.E., Stacey, J.S., and Bryant, B., 1983, Geochronology of the Farmington Canyon Complex, Wasatch Mountains, Utah, *in* Miller, D.M., Todd, V.R., and Howard, K.A., editors, Tectonic and stratigraphic studies in the eastern Great Basin: Geological Society of America Memoir 157, p. 37-44.

Hintze, L.F., 1993 (revised), Geologic history of Utah: Brigham Young University Geology Studies Special Publication 7, 202 p.

Hoffman, P.F., and Schrag, D.P., 2000, Snowball Earth: Scientific American, January 2000, p. 68-75.

Houston, R.S., Duebendorfer, E.M., Karlstrom, K.E., and Premo, W.R., 1989, A review of the geology and structure of the Cheyenne belt and Proterozoic rocks of southern Wyoming, *in* Grambling, J.A., and Tewksbury, B.J., editors, Proterozoic geology of the southern Rocky Mountains: Boulder, Colorado, Geological Society of America Special Paper 235, p. 1-12.

Jarret, R.D., and Malde, H.E., 1987, Paleodischarge of the late Pleistocene Bonneville flood, Snake River, Idaho, computed from new evidence: Geological Society of America Bulletin, v. 99, p. 127-134.

Karlstrom, K.E., Williams, M.L., McLelland, J., Geissman, J.W., and Ahall, K., 1999, Refining Rodinia - geologic evidence for the Australia-Western U.S. connection in the Proterozoic: Geological Society of America, GSA Today, v. 9, no. 10, p. 1-7.

King, C., and others, 1878, Systematic geology: U. S. Geological Exploration, 40th parallel, v. 1 and 2, 502 p.

King, J.K., and Willis, G.C., editors, 2000, The geology of Antelope Island, Davis County, Utah: Utah Geological Survey Miscellaneous Publication 00-1, 163 p., (compilation of 12 papers).

Larsen, W.N., 1957, Petrology and structure of Antelope Island, Davis County, Utah: Salt Lake City, University of Utah, Ph.D. dissertation, 142 p., scale 1:24,000.

Mayo, A.L., and Klauk, R.H., 2000, Hydrogeology of Antelope Island, Great Salt Lake, Utah, *in* King, J.K., and Willis, G.C., editors, The geology of Antelope Island,

Davis County, Utah: Utah Geological Survey Miscellaneous Publication 00-1, p. 135-150.

McNeil, B.R., and Smith, R.B., 1993, Upper crustal structure of the northern Wasatch front, Utah, from seismic reflection and gravity data: Utah Geological Survey Contract Report 92-7, 62 p.

Miller, D.M., 1990, Mesozoic and Cenozoic tectonic evolution of the northeastern Great Basin, *in* Shaddrick, D.R., Kizis, J.A., Jr., and Hunsaker, E.L., III, editors, Geology and ore deposits of the northeastern Great Basin: Geological Society of Nevada, p. 43-73.

Miller, D.M., Nakata, J.K., Hillhouse, W.C., and Hamachi, B., in press, New K-Ar ages for Cenozoic volcanic rocks in the northeastern Great Basin and implications for Cenozoic tectonics: U.S. Geological Survey Bulletin 1988.

Moore, W.J., and McKee, E.H., 1983, Phanerozoic magmatism and mineralization in the Tooele 1- by 2-degree quadrangle, Utah, *in* Miller, D.M., Todd, V.R., and Howard, K.A., editors, Tectonic and stratigraphic studies in the eastern Great Basin: Geological Society of America Memoir 157, p. 183-190.

Murchison, S.B., and Mulvey, W.E., 2000, Late Pleistocene and Holocene shoreline stratigraphy on Antelope Island, *in* King, J.K., and Willis, G.C., editors, The geology of Antelope Island, Davis County, Utah: Utah Geological Survey Miscellaneous Publication 00-1, p. 77-83.

Oviatt, C.G., 1997, Lake Bonneville fluctuations and global climate change: Geology, v. 25, no. 2, p. 155-158.

Pechmann, J.C., Nash, W.P., Viveiros, J.J., and Smith, R.B., 1987, Slip rate and earthquake potential of the East Great Salt Lake fault, Utah [abs.]: EOS, Transactions of the American Geophysical Union, v. 68, no. 44, p. 1,369.

Perkins, M.E., Brown, F.H., Nash, W.P., and Fleck, R.J., 1995, Fallout tuffs of Trapper Creek, Idaho—A record of Miocene explosive volcanism in the Snake River plain volcanic province: Geological Society of America Bulletin, v. 107, no. 12, p. 1,484-1,506.

Perkins, M.E., Brown, F.H., Nash, W.P., McIntosh, W., and Williams, S.K., 1998, Sequence, age and source of silicic fallout tuffs in middle to late Miocene basins of the northern Basin and Range Province: Geological Society of America Bulletin, v. 110, no. 3, p. 344-360.

Roberts, A.D., 1983, History of Antelope Island in the Great Salt Lake, Utah: Salt Lake City, Utah, Wallace N. Cooper 2 & Associates, 114 p.

Schwartz, D.P., and Coppersmith, K.J., 1984, Fault behavior and characteristic earthquakes - examples from the Wasatch and San Andreas fault zones: Journal of Geophysical Research, v. 89, no. B7, p. 5,681-5,698.

Stansbury, H., 1852 (reprinted 1988), Exploration and survey of the valley of the Great Salt Lake, including a reconnaissance of a new route through the Rocky Mountains (reprinted with the title "Exploration of the valley of the Great Salt Lake": (reprinted by) Washington,

D.C., Smithsonian Institution Press, 421 p.

Tooker, E.W., and Roberts, R.J., 1971, Geologic map of the Garfield quadrangle, Salt Lake and Tooele Counties, Utah: U.S. Geological Survey Geologic Quadrangle Map GQ-922, scale 1:24,000.

Unrug, R., 1997, Rodinia to Gondwana - the geodynamic map of Gondwana supercontinent assembly: Geological Society of America, GSA Today, v. 7, no. 1, p. 1-6.

Viveiros, J.J., 1986, Cenozoic tectonics of the Great Salt Lake from seismic reflection data: Salt Lake City, University of Utah, M.S. thesis, 81 p.

Willis, G.C., 1999, The Utah thrust system–an overview, *in* Spangler, L.D. and Allen, C.J., editors, Geology of northern Utah and vicinity: Utah Geological Association Publication 27, p. 1-9.

Willis, G.C., and Jensen, M.E., 2000, Tertiary rocks of Antelope Island, Utah, *in* King, J.K., and Willis, G.C., editors, The geology of Antelope Island, Davis County, Utah: Utah Geological Survey Miscellaneous Publication 00-1, p. 49-70.

Wilson, E.A., Saugy, L., and Zimmermann, M.A., 1986, Cenozoic tectonics and sedimentation of the eastern Great Salt Lake area, Utah: Bulletin de Societe Geologique Francaise, v. 2, no. 5, p. 777-782.

Yonkee, W.A., 1992, Basement-cover relations, Sevier orogenic belt, northern Utah: Geological Society of America Bulletin, v. 104, p. 280-302.

—1997, Kinematics and mechanics of the Willard thrust sheet, central part of the Sevier orogenic wedge, north-central Utah, *in* Link, P.K., and Kowallis, B.J., editors, Proterozoic to Recent stratigraphy, tectonics, and volcanology, Utah, Nevada, southern Idaho and central Mexico: Brigham Young University Geology Studies, v. 42, pt. 1, p. 341-354.

Yonkee, W.A., Parry, W.T., Bruhn, R.L., and Cashman, P.H., 1989, Thermal models of thrust faulting - constraints from fluid-inclusion observations, Willard thrust sheet, Idaho-Utah-Wyoming thrust belt: Geological Society of America Bulletin, v. 101, p. 304-313.

Yonkee, W.A., Willis, G.C., and Doelling, H.H., 2000a, Petrology of Precambrian rocks of the Farmington Canyon Complex, Antelope Island, Utah, *in* King, J.K., and Willis, G.C., editors, The geology of Antelope Island, Davis County, Utah: Utah Geological Survey Miscellaneous Publication 00-1, p. 5-36.

—2000b, Proterozoic and Cambrian sedimentary and low-grade metasedimentary rocks on Antelope Island, Utah, *in* King, J.K., and Willis, G.C., editors, The geology of Antelope Island, Davis County, Utah: Utah Geological Survey Miscellaneous Publication 00-1, p. 37-47.

Geology of Utah's Parks and Monuments
2000 Utah Geological Association Publication 28
D.A. Sprinkel, T.C. Chidsey, Jr., and P.B. Anderson, editors

Geology of Coral Pink Sand Dunes State Park, Kane County, Utah

Richard L. Ford[1] and Shari L. Gillman[1]

ABSTRACT

Coral Pink Sand Dunes State Park, located in southwestern Kane County, Utah, contains a variety of geologic features including one of the largest areas of freely migrating dunes in the Colorado Plateau. The semiarid climate, strong prevailing southerly winds, sparse vegetation, and abundant supply of sand-sized sediment make this area susceptible to aeolian processes.

Picturesque exposures of Jurassic rocks are present within the park. The stratigraphic sequence ranges from the Lower Jurassic Moenave Formation to the Middle Jurassic Carmel Formation. The most widespread bedrock unit exposed within the park is the Navajo Sandstone (Lower Jurassic). The Navajo Sandstone is also widely exposed across the Moccasin Terrace southwest of the park and is the most likely source for the sand that comprises the dune field. The coral-pink color of the dune sand is the result of iron-oxide stains on the surface of the sand grains.

Coral Pink Sand Dunes lies within the structural transition zone between the Great Basin section of the Basin and Range province to the west, and the core of the Colorado Plateau to the east. The north-south-trending Sevier fault cuts through the length of the park. The fault trace is marked by a west-facing bedrock escarpment that divides the park into two topographic units (a forested plateau to the east and a relatively low-lying valley floor to the west) and acts as a major control over the accumulation of sand within the dune field.

Important events recorded in the geologic features of the park include the Jurassic depositional history of the Glen Canyon Group, the Cretaceous to Cenozoic structural history of the Colorado Plateau, and the Quaternary history of the active dunes. Although the chronology and evolution of the dune field is poorly known, the park provides easy access to textbook examples of a wide variety of dunes.

Migrating dunes, whose morphology is primarily a function of wind characteristics, include transverse ridges, barchanoid ridges, and a solitary star dune. Dunes influenced or impeded by topographic obstacles or vegetation include climbing dunes, echo dunes, parabolic dunes, vegetated linear dunes, and nebkhas.

We divide the dune field into major geomorphic units based on the dominant dune type. A largely stabilized (vegetated) sand sheet and partially stabilized, poorly organized dunes are present at the southern (upwind) end of the dune field. The active core of the dune field contains transverse ridges and barchanoid ridges. Barchanoid ridges at the northern (downwind) end of the active core grade into climbing dunes that ramp up the bedrock escarpment associated with the Sevier fault. The climbing dunes in turn grade into large parabolic dunes that dominate the downwind end of the dune field.

The succession of dunes present at Coral Pink Sand Dunes reflects a complex interplay between topographic controls, sediment availability, and vegetation.

INTRODUCTION

Geographic Setting

Sand dunes occur in two distinct habitats; along the coasts of seas and rivers, on the one hand, and on the barren waterless floors of deserts, on the other....Here [in deserts] instead of finding chaos and disorder, the observer never fails to be amazed at a simplicity of form, an exactitude of repetition and geometric order unknown in nature on a scale larger than that of crystalline structure.

— Ralph A. Bagnold, 1942

[1]*Department of Geosciences, Weber State University, Ogden, UT 84408*

The many geologic wonders of southern Utah include a picturesque area of active dunes in southwestern Kane County, located about 27 miles (43 km) northwest of Kanab near the Utah-Arizona border (figure 1). This is one of the largest areas (approximately 5.4 square miles or 14 km^2) of freely migrating dunes within the Colorado Plateau Province. This dune field has become known as the Coral Pink Sand Dunes. The term "coral" in this case refers to the deep orange pink color of the sand and has nothing to do with the marine reef-building organisms of the same name. Using a soil-color chart, geologists or soil scientists would formally describe the sand as reddish yellow (5YR 6/8); it is probably a good thing that a geologist did not name these dunes. A wide variety of aeolian (an adjective referring to wind activity, derived from the name of the Greek god of the wind, Aeolus; also commonly spelled as eolian) features and landforms are present within the Coral Pink Sand Dunes, making this an excellent field laboratory in which to learn about the role of wind in shaping the surface of the Earth.

The northern half of the dune field is federal land administered by the Bureau of Land Management (BLM). The southern half of the dune field and adjacent land (3,730 acres or 15 km^2) comprises Coral Pink Sand Dunes State Park (CPSDSP), the subject of this paper. The Yellowjacket Canyon 7.5-minute topographic quadrangle covers the park area.

Upon its establishment in 1963, the park was visited primarily by off-highway vehicle (OHV) enthusiasts. Over the years visitation has greatly increased and today the majority of park visitors arrive without OHVs to enjoy the scenic beauty of this distinctive landscape. Park facilities include a 22-unit campground, modern restrooms with hot showers, a boardwalk overlook, and a one-half-mile nature trail. In addition, CPSDSP serves as an excellent base for exploring other areas of geologic interest in southern Utah, including Zion and Bryce Canyon National Parks, Cedar Breaks and Grand Staircase-Escalante National Monuments, and Kodachrome Basin State Park.

Access to the park is provided by either Sand Dune Road, a paved road that runs south from U.S. Highway 89 through Yellowjacket Canyon, or Hancock Road, a paved road that runs southwest from U.S. Highway 89 (figure 1). Together, Sand Dune Road and Hancock Road comprise the state-designated Ponderosa/Coral Pink Sand Dunes Scenic Backway.

Topography

Topographically, the park can be divided into two distinct units. The eastern half is a forested upland, part of the Moquith Mountains, bounded by a west-facing escarpment. This escarpment forms the eastern redrock backdrop to the dunes, visible from the dune field and campground to the west (figure 2). This escarpment is fault-controlled (see Structure section) and increases in height from north to south, reaching a maximum of approximately 700 feet (213 m) near the southern end of the park. Although given the name "mountains," the Moquiths are actually a deeply incised plateau that is tilted toward the northeast. The highest elevation within the park, 6,977 feet (2,126 m), lies on this plateau. The fault-controlled escarpment exposes the same rock units that form

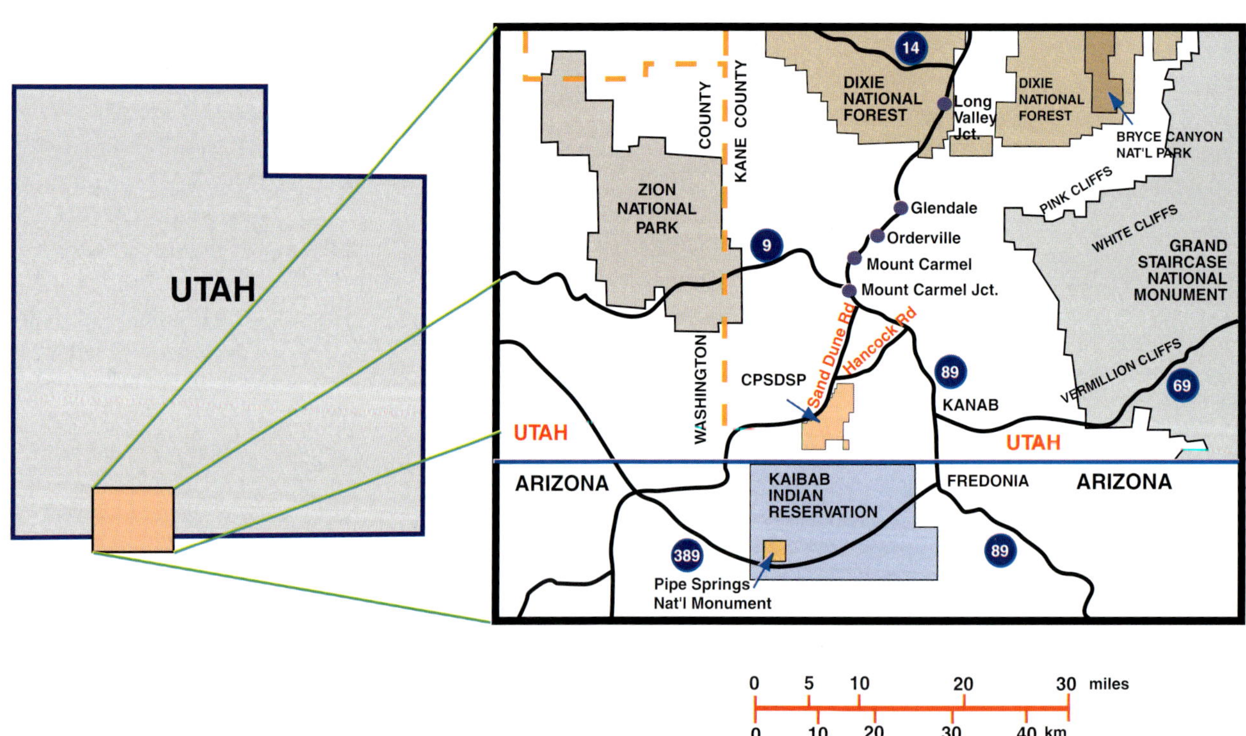

Figure 1. Location of Coral Pink Sand Dunes State Park (CPSDSP) in Kane County, Utah.

Figure 2. View to the east from the boardwalk overview of the bedrock escarpment that forms the eastern boundary of the dune field. The escarpment was created by movement along the Sevier fault (see Structure section) and forms the western boundary of the forested Moquith Mountains in the background. A solitary star dune (see Classic Geological Sites section) is visible in the middle gound.

the Vermillion Cliffs of the Grand Staircase, which lie generally east and south of the park. For a complete description of the rock units and features that comprise the Grand Staircase of southwestern Utah, see Doelling and others in this volume.

The western half of the park is relatively low terrain lying between the Moquith Mountains and the mesa just northwest of the park. Though unnamed on modern topographic maps, this mesa was called Esplin Point by Gregory (1950) in his early regional study, a name we will use in this paper. Esplin Point lies at the eastern end of a line of cliffs and mesas that extends from Elephant Butte to the park, which collectively form the western expression of the White Cliffs of the Grand Staircase. Esplin Point has a maximum elevation of approximately 6,850 feet (2,090 m). Most of the dune field within the park boundaries lies on this lowland at the base of the scarp bounding the Moquith Mountains. Near the northern end of the park the dunes climb the escarpment and continue to the northeast, forming that part of the dune field on land administered by the BLM.

The park area is drained by a number of ephemeral streams whose channels extend from the upland areas, on either side of the dune field, to the margin of the dune field itself. Channels are largely absent within the dunefield, owing to the high infiltration rates within the dune sand. However, the steep ephemeral channels that drain the eastern escarpment act as tributaries to Sand Canyon Wash, lying at the base of the escarpment and along the eastern margin of the dune field. Sand Canyon Wash flows southward to Kanab Creek and hence to the Colorado River. The lowest elevation within the park, approximately 5,620 feet (1,710 m), is in the channel of Sand Canyon Wash where it crosses the park's southern boundary. Thus, the total topographic relief within the park is approximately 1,357 feet (416 m). The drainage divide between Sand Canyon Wash and Yellowjacket Canyon to the north is located near the intersection of Hancock and Sand Dune roads, approximately 0.9 miles (1.4 km) north of the park. North of this divide, Sand Dune Road descends Yellowjacket Canyon, a north-flowing tributary of the East Fork of the Virgin River.

Climate and Vegetation

Aeolian processes are important in areas with strong prevailing winds, sparse vegetation, and an abundant supply of sand-sized sediment. This is why most of the world's major dune fields are found in association with arid or semiarid climates. The Coral Pink Sand Dunes are no exception, being located within the extensive semiarid climatic zone of Utah known as steppe (Köppen climatic classification: BS). In Utah, the steppe climate is transitional between the true arid/desert climates of the Great Basin and the moister climates of the state's mountainous regions (Murphy, 1981). The mean annual temperature in Kanab, Utah, is 54.4° F (12.4° C); the mean annual precipitation is 13.3 inches (33.8 cm) (Utah Climate Center, as reported in Pope and Brough, 1996). The distribution of precipitation in this area, as evidenced by the data from Kanab, is distinctly bimodal with winter-summer precipitation peaks and spring-autumn drought. The closest weather station to the park with long-term wind data is Las Vegas, Nevada, located approximately 140 miles (225 km) to the southwest. The mean annual surface wind at this location blows from the southwest at 9.3 mph (15.0 kph). It is interesting to note that in Las Vegas, the two months of May and June have the greatest average wind speed, which coincides with the two driest months of the year in the Kanab area. If this relationship is extrapolated to the Coral Pink Sand Dunes, one would hypothesize that aeolian activity would generally peak during this time.

Outside of the distinctive habitats of the dune field itself (see Castle, 1954), the dominant vegetation of the western half of the park is typical of pinyon-juniper woodlands (*Pinus edulis, Juniperus* spp.) and sagebrush scrub (*Artemisia* spp.) of the Colorado Plateau -- with one notable and scenic exception. Impressive stands of ponderosa pine (*Pinus ponderosa*) are present within the more stabilized areas of the dune field. Ponderosa pines also dominate the forested upland of the eastern side of the park.

Previous Investigations

Geologic aspects of Coral Pink Sand Dunes have been previously reported in more broad-based investigations, most notably Gregory (1950), Doelling and others (1989), Anderson and Christenson (1989), and Davis (1999). Castle (1954) investigated the soil conditions and vegetation communities within the dune field. We are greatly indebted to these researchers, as much of this paper is a synthesis of their work. However, this is the first work to focus specifically on the geology of Coral Pink Sand Dunes. Our major contribution to the geologic knowledge of this area lies in the complete characterization of the dune field, including its subdivision into distinct geomorphic units that reflect the relationship between surface forms and dominant surface processes. In addition to our literature review, we conducted an analysis of color aerial photography (scale 1:4,000), augmented by reconnaissance-level field research during the spring and fall of 1999.

STRATIGRAPHY AND GEOMORPHOLOGY

Figure 3 is a generalized geologic map of the park area and figure 4 is a diagrammatic cross section through the park. The general geology of the park can be characterized as an area of cliff-and-bench topography, developed on Mesozoic sedimentary rocks, with a Quaternary dune field at the surface. The oldest Mesozoic unit exposed at CPSDSP is the Moenave Formation (Lower Jurassic). If one were to drill below the dune field, the Chinle (Upper Triassic) and Moenkopi (Lower Triassic) Formations would be successively encountered below the Moenave Formation (figure 4). The youngest bedrock unit exposed within the park boundary is the lowest member of the Carmel Formation (Middle Jurassic); the Co-op Creek Limestone Member of Doelling and others (1989). The various unconsolidated aeolian deposits and active dunes, for which the park is named, are the youngest of all the geologic units in the area.

Mesozoic Stratigraphy

The picturesque Moenave/Wingate, Kayenta, and Navajo Formations make up the Glen Canyon Group. These units have historically been regarded to be Triassic and Jurassic in age; however subsequent stratigraphic work has shown that the Glen Canyon Group is entirely Early Jurassic in age (Pipiringos and O'Sullivan, 1978; Imlay, 1980; and Doelling and others; 1989). The general stratigraphy and depositional environments of the various Jurassic-age bedrock formations exposed in the park area are discussed below. A generalized stratigraphic column is presented in figure 5.

Moenave Formation (Jmo)

In western Kane County, the Moenave Formation (Lower Jurassic) overlies the basal unconformity (J-0) separating rocks of the Triassic and Jurassic systems (figure 5). Although most workers (for example Doelling and others, 1989) typically divide the Moenave Formation into three members (in ascending order, the Dinosaur Canyon, Whitmore Point, and Springdale Sandstone Members), these are generally unmappable at common map scales because of their steep outcrop topography (Doelling and others, 1989). In the park, the Springdale Sandstone Member is exposed in fault slices along the base of the Moquith Mountains (figure 3). The unit, 160 to 185 feet (49-56 m) thick, consists of very fine grained, pale-reddish-brown sandstone with subordinate amounts of cliff-forming conglomerate (Doelling and others, 1989).

The presence of paleo-channels with low-angle crossbeds in the Springdale Sandstone Member and freshwater-fish fossils in the Whitmore Point Member suggest a terrestrial depositional environment for the Moenave Formation. Specific environments probably included lakes, mudflats, and fluvial channels as part of a broad floodplain (Doelling and others, 1989).

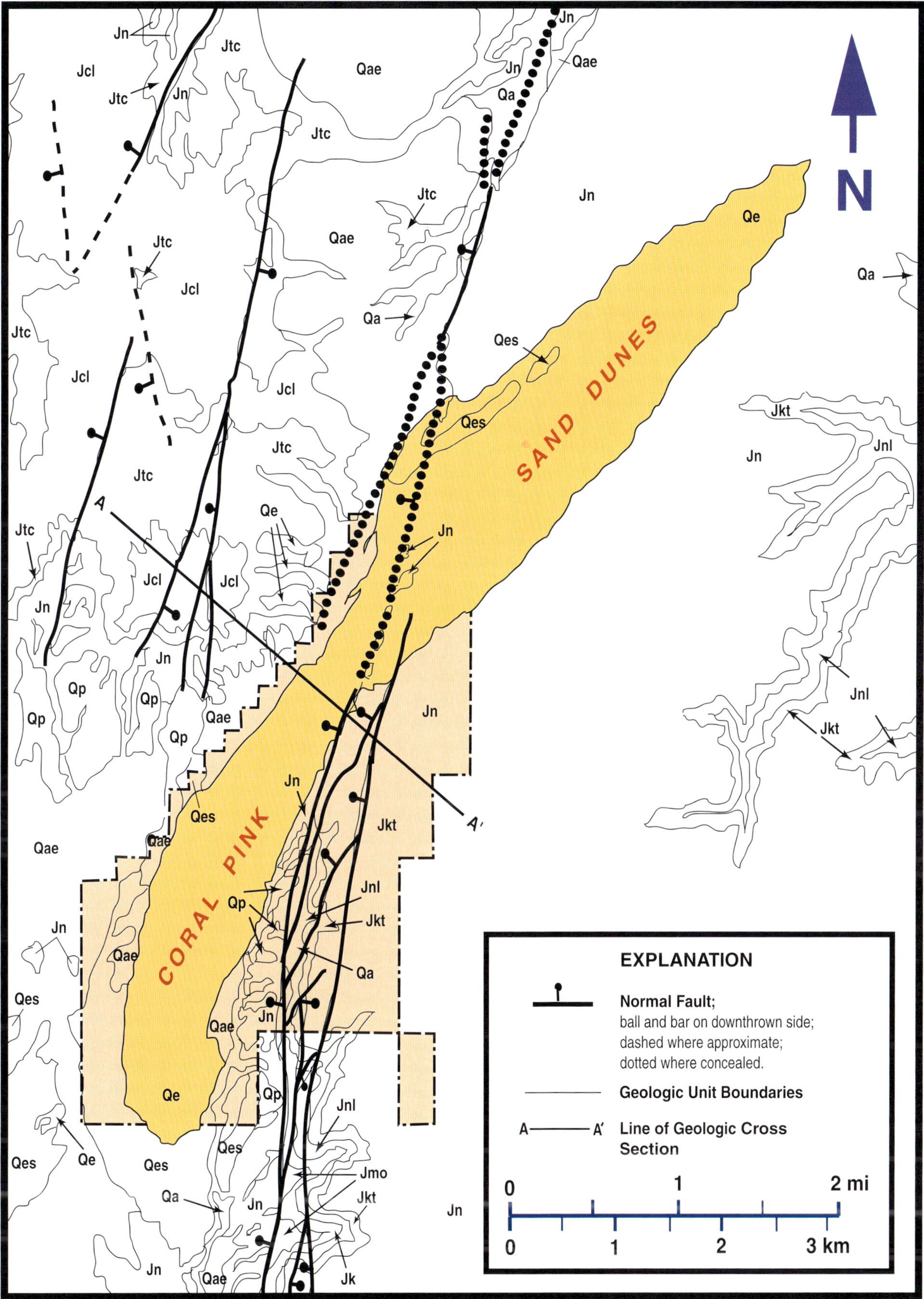

Figure 3. Geologic map of the Coral Pink Sand Dunes area in Kane County, Utah (after Sargent and Philpott, 1987). The map legend is included with the cross section shown in figure 4 and identifies the geologic units and symbols used. Note the trace of the Sevier fault running north-south the length of the park.

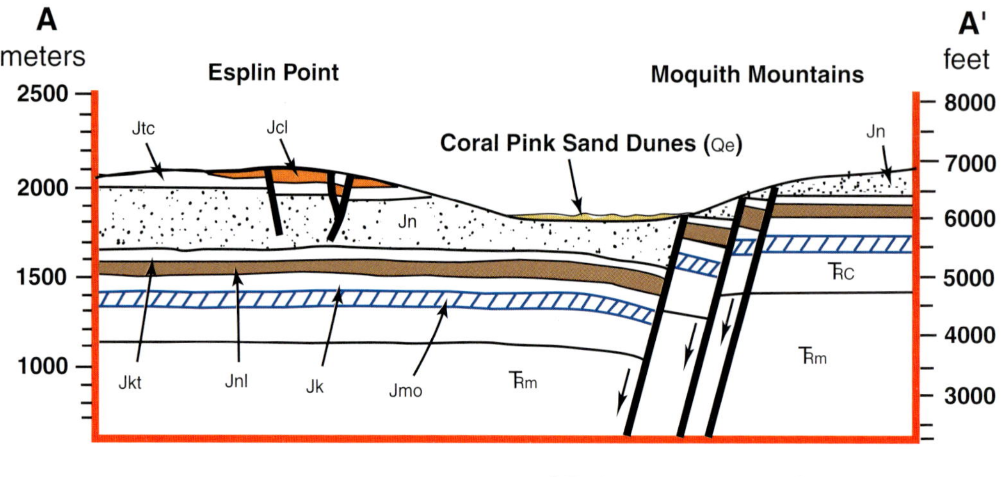

MAP AND CROSS SECTION EXPLANATION

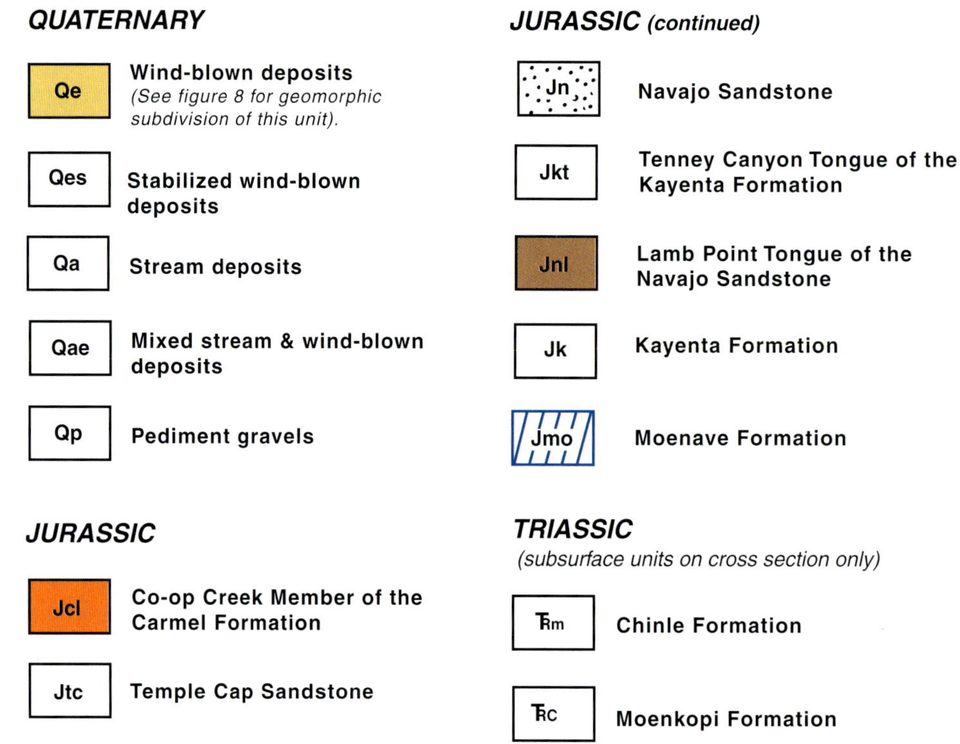

Figure 4. Cross section along line A-A' shown in figure 3. Note the offset in the geologic units created by movement along the Sevier fault zone.

Kayenta Formation (Jk)

The Kayenta Formation (Lower Jurassic) conformably overlies the Moenave Formation (figure 5). Like the underlying Moenave Formation, the Kayenta Formation is exposed within the park in the Sevier fault zone along the base of the escarpment that forms the western edge of the Moquith Mountains (figure 3). Here the Kayenta Formation consists primarily of deep red siltstones and claystones. Smaller amounts of lenticular, medium-grained, trough-cross-bedded sandstone are also present. In Kane County, the thickness of the Kayenta Formation varies from 190 to 340 feet (58-104 m) (Doelling and others, 1989).

Although the Kayenta Formation is mostly fluvial in origin (formed by shifting braided streams), some aeolian sandstone and lacustrine limestone beds, deposited in interfluve areas, are locally present (Doelling and others, 1989). These streams originated in highlands to the east, probably the Ucompahgre uplift (Barnes, 1993).

A thin, though mappable, tongue of sandstone, known as the Tenney Canyon Tongue, extends eastward from the main body of the Kayenta Formation into the lower portion of the overlying Navajo Sandstone (figure 5). The

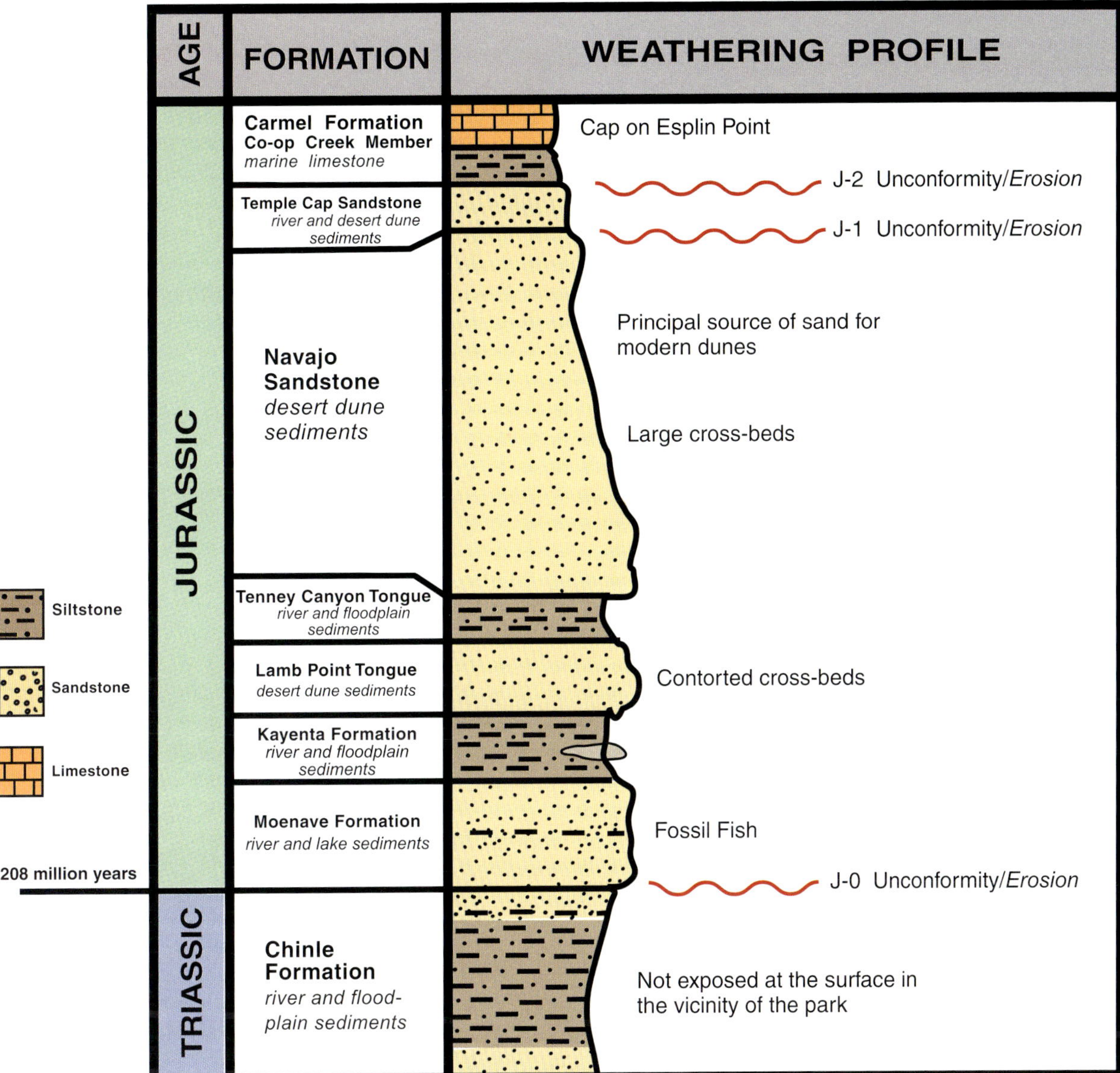

Figure 5. Stratigraphic column of the Mesozoic bedrock units present within Coral Pink Sand Dunes State Park (modified from Doelling and others, 1989).

portion of the Navajo Sandstone lying between the main body of the Kayenta Formation and the Tenney Canyon Tongue is called the Lamb Point Tongue of the Navajo Sandstone (Doelling and others, 1989). These two bedrock units are also exposed within the park along the trace of the Sevier fault (figure 3).

Lamb Point Tongue of the Navajo Sandstone (Jnl)

The Lamb Point Tongue (Lower Jurassic) is named for a location on the Vermilion Cliffs south of the park. The unit consists of white, tan, or gray fine-grained sandstone with thick sets of aeolian crossbeds, locally greater than 25 feet (7.6 m). The lower and upper contacts with the Kayenta Formation are sharp. This tongue is 90 to 410 feet (27-125 m) thick and pinches out to the west of the park. The Lamb Point Tongue contains distinctive contorted cross-beds in the upper 10 to 15 feet (3-4.6 m) of the unit. These contorted beds have been interpreted to be the re-

sult of slumping on the steep downwind side of dunes or possibly the result of earthquake-induced liquefaction (Doelling and others, 1989). Like the main body of the Navajo Sandstone, the Lamb Point Tongue represents widespread aeolian deposition in Early Jurassic time.

Tenney Canyon Tongue of the Kayenta Formation (Jkt)

The Tenney Canyon Tongue (Lower Jurassic) of the Kayenta Formation is pale-reddish brown in color and comprised of siltstone, mudstone, and very fine thin-bedded to laminated sandstone, representing floodplain and channel deposition. It is 90 to 170 feet (27-52 m) thick and typically displays low-angle cross-bedding. This unit has sharp contacts with both the underlying Lamb Point Tongue and the overlying main body of the Navajo Sandstone (Doelling and others, 1989). The tongue thins from west to east and pinches out east of Kanab, Utah.

Figure 6. View to the northwest of Esplin Point, part of the White Cliffs. Navajo Sandstone (Jn), Temple Cap Sandstone (Jtc), and the Co-op Creek Limestone Member of the Carmel Formation (Jcl) are exposed in the cliff face. Foreground area is covered by mixed aeolian and alluvial sediments (Qae).

Navajo Sandstone (Jn)

The Navajo Sandstone (Lower Jurassic) stands out as the premier formation of the remarkable scenery of the Colorado Plateau. The Navajo Sandstone and its related equivalent formations (Nugget Sandstone of northern Utah and southwestern Wyoming, and the Aztec Sandstone of southern Nevada) form the largest aeolian deposit in North America (Peterson and Turner-Peterson, 1989). In the vicinity of CPSDSP, the Navajo Sandstone is a thick unit, 1,800 to 2,300 feet (549-701 m), of well-sorted, fine-grained quartz sandstones of varying colors and degrees of cementation. In addition to the cross-bedded sandstone, the Navajo contains a few lenticular beds of dense limestone or dolostone. These carbonate rocks are thought to have accunmulated in interdune lakes or playas. Being more resistant than the sandstones, the limestones and dolostones commonly form benches or shelves (Doelling and others, 1989).

The Navajo Sandstone is world-renowned for its elaborate array of high-angle cross-beds and stark erosional forms, including cliffs, domes, and monuments. The light colors of the Navajo have been described variously as white, tan, buff, salmon, pink, vermillion, brown, red, yellow, cream, orange and gray. The sandstone is weakly cemented by calcite or dolomite and varying amounts of iron oxides. Hematite cement, in addition to the more abundant calcite and dolomite, produces the reddish colors, limonite the yellows, and ferrous-iron minerals the browns and occasional greens (Doelling and others, 1989).

The Navajo Sandstone is the most extensive bedrock unit within the park (figure 3). The lower and upper parts of the formation are more strongly cemented than the middle third and thus are cliff-forming units. The lower cliff-forming unit is typically reddish in color and, along with the underlying Kayenta Formation, form the Vermillion Cliffs of southwestern Utah. The upper cliff-forming

sandstones typically lack the reddish hues characteristic of lower section and thus form the White Cliffs of the Grand Staircase. The lower reddish cliff-forming portion of the Navajo is exposed in the bedrock escarpment east of the active dunefield, whereas the upper white cliff-forming portion of the Navajo is exposed in the face of Esplin Point (figure 6), the prominent mesa located due north of the park's campground. In active gullies and washes along the margin of the Coral Pink Sand Dunes, the Navajo Sandstone—presumably the middle to upper third of the formation—directly underlies the modern dunes.

Deposition of the Navajo Sandstone occurred in a large coastal to inland desert, possibly similar to the modern Sahara. Orientation of the cross-bedding, essentially the lithified slip faces of the Jurassic dunes, indicates that the Jurassic winds blew primarily from the north and northwest (Stokes, 1986). The mineralogy of the Navajo Sandstone, 90 to 98 percent clear quartz with minor amounts of feldspar, magnetite, tourmaline, staurolite, zircon, garnet, and mica, suggests that the source area of the sand was dominated by metamorphic rocks (Doelling and others, 1989).

Geologists use the Arabic term "erg" to refer to large ($\geq$ 48 square miles or 125 km^2) desert areas dominated by wind-deposited sand and complex dune forms (smaller areas of dunes, such as the Coral Pink Sand Dunes, are defined as "dune fields" [Pye and Tsoar, 1990]). Although most geologists today accept the erg origin of the Navajo Sandstone, some have pointed to the lack of iron (as is typical of beach sands), the presence of small amounts of glauconite (a mineral characteristic of shallow marine environments), and the presence of contorted bedding to suggest deposition under water, most likely a shallow sea (Stokes, 1986). Those who favored the marine origin (for example Stanley and others, 1971) see the Navajo as large offshore sandbars cross-bedded by ocean currents. This controversy has been essentially put to rest by the work of Hunter (1976, 1977), who established the criteria for distinguishing aeolian and water-laid cross stratification. The discovery of small occurrences of petrified trees within the sandstone, presumably spring-fed desert oases, and the discovery of vertebrate, including dinosaurs, and invertebrate tracks preserved within the interdune limestones added further evidence of terrestrial deposition (Barnes, 1993).

Temple Cap Sandstone (Jtc)

A major unconformity (J-1) marks the top of the Navajo Sandstone (figure 5). Above it is the Temple Cap Sandstone of Middle Jurassic age, named for the East and West Temple features of Zion National Park. This formation contains, at its base, a prominent reddish, slope-forming siltstone and sandy siltstone, that is 40 to 50 feet (12-15 m) thick (Sinawava Member). This member is overlain by up to 150 feet (46 m) of light-gray to tan, cross-bedded, cliff-forming sandstone (White Throne Member) (Doelling and others, 1989). The sandstones and siltstones of the lower

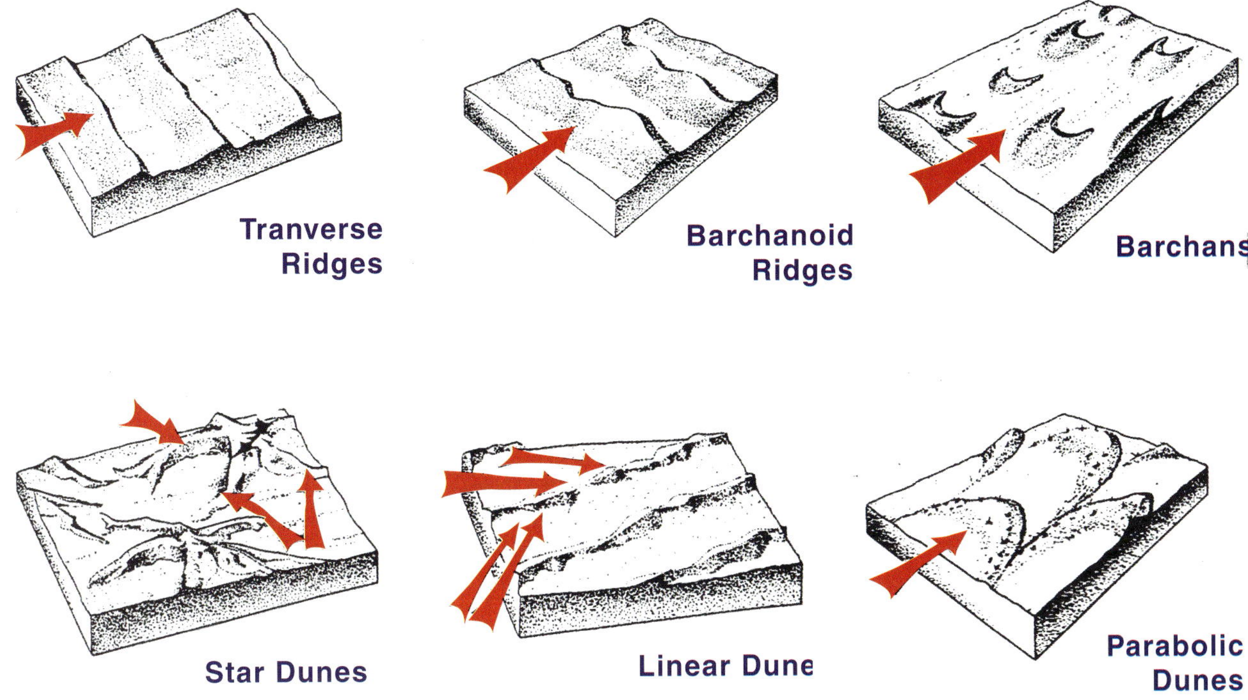

Figure 7. Morphology of the major types of dunes. Arrows indicate the formative prevailing wind direction (modified from McKee, 1979).

Sinawava Member are fluvial in origin; the crossbedded sandstones of the White Throne Member represent aeolian deposition. However, the two members are difficult to separate owing to the extensive interfingering between the two (Doelling and others, 1989).

The Temple Cap Sandstone is exposed in the central portion of the face of Esplin Point north of the campground (figure 6). This outcrop belt extends to the western edge of the park (figure 3).

Co-op Creek Limestone Member of the Carmel Formation (Jcl)

The Carmel Formation (Middle Jurassic), named for Mt. Carmel, Utah, is a lithologically complex unit of limestones and sandstones that is subdivided into numerous members (Hintze, 1988; Doelling and others, 1989). The lowermost Co-op Creek Limestone Member caps Esplin Point (figure 6). Co-op Creek beds also occur just west of the road near the northern boundary of the park. The Co-op Creek Member consists of a basal siltstone, 10 to 20 feet (3-6 m) thick, overlain by more than 200 feet (61+ m) of thin- to medium-bedded light-gray limestone and shaly limestone (Doelling and others, 1989).

The Co-op Creek Limestone Member of the Carmel Formation unconformably overlies the Temple Cap Sandstone along the J-2 unconformity surface (figure 5). The Carmel Formation in turn is locally truncated by the unconformity at the base of the Cretaceous System. Most importantly, the Carmel Formation marks the end of terrestrial deposition and the return of shallow marine conditions to this part of Utah during Middle Jurassic time. Subsequent geologic events uplifted the sediments of the

Carmel Formation from below sea level and raised them to their present elevation of over 6,600 feet (2,011 m) in the vicinity of the park.

Quaternary Stratigraphy and Geomorphology of the Dune Field

Although the local Jurassic bedrock units are impressive, the foremost geologic features of this park are the various unconsolidated aeolian deposits and landforms that make up the dune field. Whereas the Jurassic formations provide information about ancient depositional environments, the modern dunes are the result of recent and on-going geological processes during the Quaternary Period (approximately the last 2 million years of Earth's history).

For a dune to form, a small patch of sand must first accumulate where the wind speed has been reduced, generally by an increase in surface roughness. Once formed the patch of sand grows by trapping bouncing (saltating) grains which are unable to rebound upon impact as easily as those that impact harder non-sandy surfaces (an example of a positive feedback). As a result of the separation and deceleration of the airflow on the lee (downwind) side of the growing sand body, sand accumulates more rapidly than it is removed by aeolian erosion; thus the dune increases in size (Summerfield, 1991). A mature dune is thus shaped by the airflow over it and in turn modifies the airflow. As a result, many dunes attain a characteristic equilibrium profile of three components: (1) facing upwind is a gently inclined (typically 10-15 degrees) backslope, (2) facing downwind is a steep slipface, standing at the angle of

Table 1. *Classification of dune types present at Coral Pink Sand Dunes State Park (modified from Summerfield, 1991). See figure 7 for diagrams of the major dune types.*

DUNE TYPE	MORPHOLOGY	WIND REGIME / MODE OF DEVELOPMENT
A. FREE DUNES		
Transverse ridge	asymmetric ridge, straight crest	unidirectional winds
Barchanoid ridge	asymmetric ridge, sinuous crest	unidirectional winds
Star dune	central peak with 3 or more arms	multidirectional winds
B. IMPEDED DUNES		
Blowout	elliptical depression	localized deflation
Parabolic dune	u-shaped in plan, arms point upwind	locally deflated sand partially anchored by vegetation
Nebkha	elliptical mound	accumulation around a clump of vegetation
Climbing dune	sandy ramp on the windward side of large topographic obstruction	accumulation in zone of disrupted airflow
Echo dune	asymmetric ridge parallel to and separated from the windward side of a large topographic obstruction	accumulation in zone of disrupted airflow
Vegetated linear dune	symmetric ridge parallel to prevailing wind	remnant arm of an eroded parabolic dune

repose for sand (generally 30-34 degrees), and (3) separating the two slopes, a dune crest (Ritter and others, 1995). This asymmetric equilibrium profile can be seen in a variety of dune types with differing plan forms (figure 7).

Wind direction and velocity, sand supply, and the presence of topographic obstacles or stabilizing vegetation are the most important factors influencing dune morphology or type. Considering these factors, it is useful to classify the various dune types as either free dunes, whose morphology is primarily a function of wind direction and sediment supply, or impeded dunes whose form is greatly influenced by the effects of vegetation, topographic obstacles, or highly localized sediment sources (Summerfield, 1991). Many of the classic dune types are present within Coral Pink Sand Dunes State Park (table 1).

Sargent and Philpott (1987) divide the dune field into two units: (1) a larger core of active sand dunes and (2) a smaller area of inactive aeolian sand along the southern margin of the dune field. Doelling and others (1989) map the dune field as a single unit. Neither report identifies the various types of dunes present in the area. Based on field observations and an analysis of aerial photography, we subdivide the active core of the dune field into five (5) map units that reflect the dominant dune type present (figure 8). In addition, we retain the stabilized-sand unit (Qes) of Sargent and Philpott (1987). These units are described below in order of their occurrence, starting at the south end of the dune field.

Stabilized Aeolian Sand Sheet (Qes)

In the southwestern corner of the park, and extending beyond the park boundaries, is an area of aeolian sand largely stabilized by sagebrush scrub (figure 8). Although slipfaces are not preserved on the dune forms, this unit does retain some original depositional relief in the form of rolling hills of sand. The western and southern boundary of this unit is gradational with the mixed aeolian and alluvial sediments of the valley floor (Qae), which support a pinyon-juniper woodland. The interior boundary with the partially stabilized transverse dunes (Qeps) is sharper, being marked by a distinct change from sagebrush scrub to a more sparsely vegetated area. This low-relief accumulation of aeolian sand is best termed a sand sheet. Sand sheets develop under conditions unfavorable to dune formation, including a high water table, periodic surface flooding, and a vegetative cover (Lancaster, 1995). Each of these conditions, which act to limit the amount of sand available for dune formation, may be significant in this area, especially the cover of vegetation.

Partially Stabilized Dunes (Qeps)

Located at the southern (upwind) end of the dune field and interior of the stabilized sand sheet is an area of partially stabilized dunes (figure 8). Dune morphology within this map unit is poorly developed and somewhat chaotic, but includes small transverse and parabolic-like forms (discussed in detail in following sections). Many of

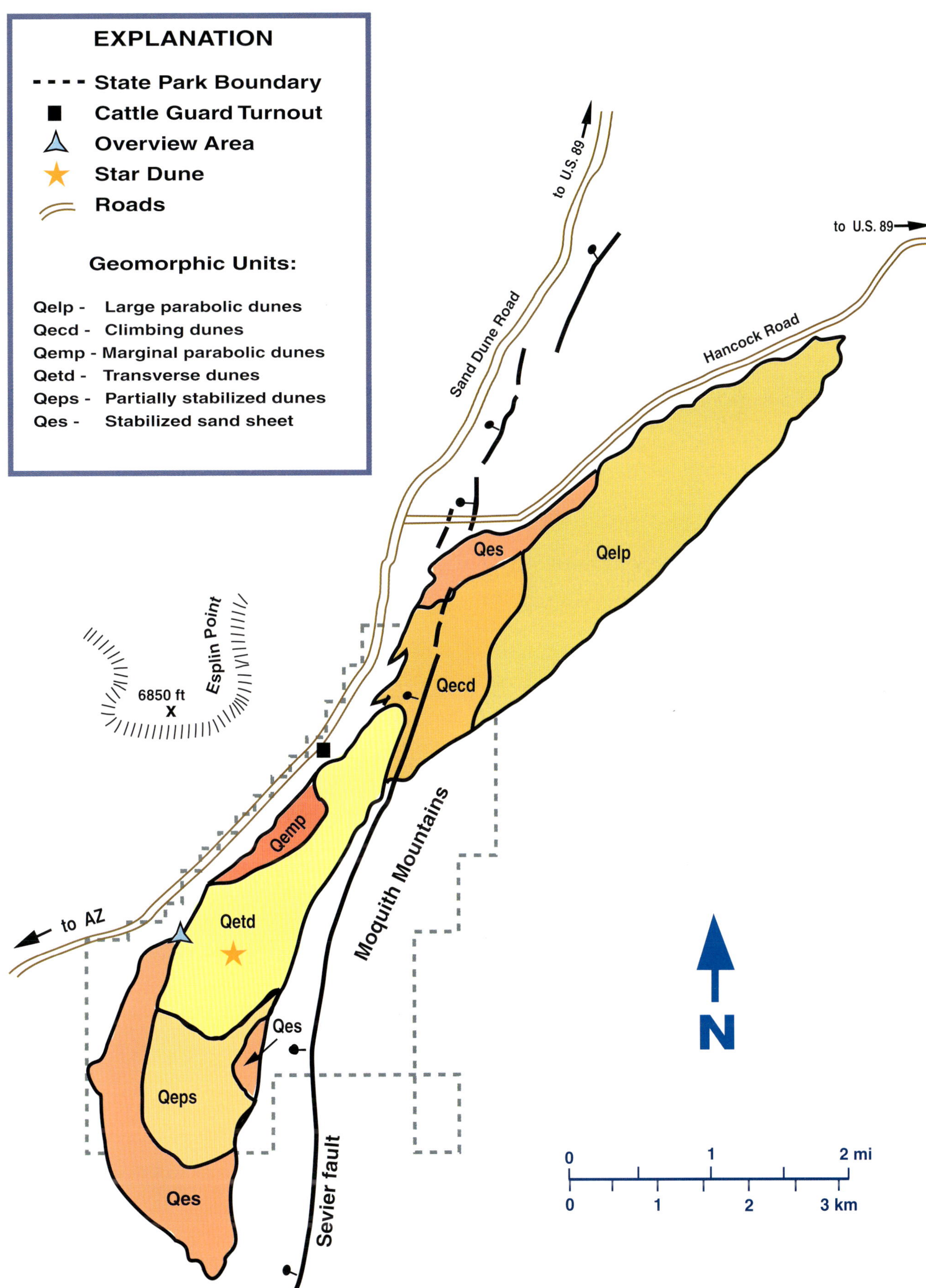

Figure 8. Geomorphic map of the Coral Pink Sand Dunes. Trace of the Sevier fault from Sargent and Philpott (1987). See text for detailed decriptions of the Quaternary-age map units.

Figure 9. View to the south of ponderosa pines (Pinus ponderosa) growing among partially stabilized dunes (Qeps) at the southern end of the dune field.

the low rolling dunes in this area lack obvious slipfaces. Geomorphically, this map unit is transitional, in terms of dune activity and relief and vegetative cover, between the stabilized sand sheet (Qes) to the south and the core of active dunes (Qetd) to the north.

The most distinctive characteristic of this geomorphic unit is the presence of scattered ponderosa pines (*Pinus ponderosa*) amongst the dunes (figure 9). Ponderosa-pine forests are best developed on the Colorado Plateau on mesa tops and mountain slopes at elevations between 6,900 and 8,200 feet (2,100-2,500 m) (Betancourt, 1990). Their presence at this relatively low elevation, approximately 5,680 to 5,800 feet (1,731-1,768 m), on a basin floor otherwise dominated by a pinyon-juniper woodland, is curious. Ponderosa pines can tolerate a variety of soil conditions, but trees on thin, dry soils are usually dwarfed (Harlow and Harrar, 1968). These trees are not dwarfed and thus indicate a moisture regime more typical of cooler habitats at higher elevations. We speculate that the southward slope of the dune field, combined with the high hydraulic conductivity of dune sand, produces a localized southward flow of shallow groundwater. The water table and ground surface may converge as one moves south to a point that is within the rooting depth of ponderosa pines. Four-year-old trees may have taproots 4 to 5 feet (1.2-1.5 m) long (Harlow and Harrar, 1968).

Active Core of Transverse Dunes (Qetd)

The most sparsely vegetated and active portion of the dune field is characterized by large, well developed transverse dunes. These are the signature dunes of the park, and this area is the most popular with the OHV recreationists. This portion of the dune field lies on the valley floor immediately below the west-facing escarpment of the Moquith Mountains (figure 8).

Transverse dunes, generally associated with unidirectional winds, are asymmetric ridges of sand with a single slipface orientation. The ridge crests are oriented perpendicular or transverse to the prevailing winds (Summer-

field, 1991). The crest of the transverse dunes at CPSDSP have a prominent northwest-southeast orientation, indicating a prevailing southwesterly wind, and rise 30 to 50 feet (9-15 m) above their adjacent interdune swales.

Two of the three major types of transverse dunes are present in the Coral Pink Sand Dunes (isolated barchans are not present here). In the southern portion of the map unit, the dunes have relatively straight crests and are thus classified as transverse ridges (figure 7). The crest-to-crest spacing of the ridges is typically 600 to 700 feet (183-213 m). Simple transverse ridges are relatively rare. Apparently, minor surface irregularities commonly create corkscrew-like vortices in the airflow over a transverse ridge. These vortices distort the ridge into a sinuous form called a barchanoid ridge (Summerfield, 1991). The transverse ridges at CPSDSP grade downwind (to the north) into classic barchanoid ridges (figure 10), with an increase in the dune spacing (up to 1,000 feet or 305 m). These barchanoid ridges display the characteristic alternating linguoid (protruding) and barchanoid (recessed) elements (figure 7). Owing to the complex airflow over these sinuous ridges, the barchanoid element of one ridge is commonly aligned with a linguoid element in the adjacent ridge, creating a complex crestal network referred to as aklé or fishscale patterns (Pye and Tsoar, 1990). A weak aklé pattern is present at the northernmost end of this map unit, where the barchanoid ridges impinge upon the bedrock escarpment to the east.

The convergence between the barchanoid ridges and the bedrock escarpment has also produced several echo dunes (figure 11). Echo and climbing dunes (discussed below) are examples of topographically controlled dunes, dunes that owe their existence and morphology to interactions between sand-transporting winds and topographic obstacles (Lancaster, 1995). Echo dunes commonly form in front of cliffs (slope > 50 degrees). A vortex forms immediately upwind of the cliff that acts to "sweep out" a corridor between the cliff and the slipface of the dune (Cooke and others, 1993). The result is the slipface of the dune tends to parallel, or echo, the shape of the cliff face. Echo dunes are best developed where the prevailing wind is near perpendicular to the trend of the cliff or escarpment. Since the sand-transporting winds within the park strike the bedrock escarpment obliquely, only the eastern end of some of the barchanoid ridges display echo morphology.

Small Marginal Parabolic Dunes (Qemp)

Along the western margin of the dune field, approximately a quarter mile south of the "cattle guard" area (see Classic Geological Sites section) is an area dominated by small parabolic dunes (figure 8). Parabolic dunes are U- or V-shaped in plan with two trailing arms which point upwind (figure 7). Typically, there is a large mound of sand with a steep slipface at the downwind end of the dune. The outside slopes of the trailing arms are almost always vegetated (Pye and Tsoar, 1990). Parabolic dunes are common in sand accumulations stabilized by vegetation. Lo-

Figure 10. View to the east of barchanoid ridges within the active core of transverse dunes (Qetd). Note the steep slipface and sinuous crest of the dune.

calized disturbance of the vegetative cover and subsequent aeolian erosion can give rise to circular or elliptical depressions called blowouts. The eroded sand is then deposited downwind, near the edge of the disturbed area, as a parabolic dune (Summerfield, 1991).

The orientation of the parabolic dunes in this portion of the dune field suggest they are controlled by the same wind regime responsible for the large area of transverse dunes. However, these are much smaller features, generally less than 12 feet (3.7 m) in height.

Climbing Dunes (Qecd)

Wind encountering the windward face of a topographic obstacle, such as a hill or scarp, with a slope of 30 to 50 degrees will be decelerated such that a dune is deposited upwind of the obstacle. In this situation, unlike an echo dune, the fixed eddy or vortex is small or absent. Thus, the dune can bank up against the scarp as a sandy ramp, creating a so-called climbing dune. When the ramp attains an equilibrium profile sand can then be carried up and over it (Cooke and others, 1993). This is the process that has taken place at the north end of the park where the active transverse dunes obliquely converge with the fault-line scarp of the Sevier fault (figures 8 and 12). The scarp

is buried by a ramp of climbing dunes that has a slope of 5 to 12 degrees. The original slope of the bedrock scarp is estimated to have been 45 to 50 degrees, based on the profile of small outcrops of Navajo Sandstone poking through the sand ramp. The area of climbing dunes is more heavily vegetated than the active core of transverse dunes. The dune morphology is a mixture of poorly developed transverse and parabolic forms.

Large Parabolic Dunes (Qelp)

Where the climbing dunes reach the top of the escarpment they grade into a large geomorphic unit dominated by parabolic dunes (figure 8). This geomorphic unit, essentially the northern half of the dune field, lies beyond the park on land administered by the BLM. Slipface orientation in this part of the dune field indicates a more westerly prevailing wind (S. 50° W.) compared to the area of transverse dunes (S. 40° W.), probably owing to deflection as the regional wind is funneled through the gap between the eastern escarpment and Esplin Point.

These parabolic dunes are much larger than those along the margin of the dune field further south. The complex pattern of coalesced and nested dunes in this area, typical of most occurrences of vegetated parabolic dunes,

Figure 11. View to the east of a barchanoid ridge (modern dune sand) impinging on an outcrop of Navajo Sandstone (Jurassic dune sand). Local airflow has modified the barchanoid ridge into an echo dune. Young field assistant in the lower left corner is approximately 4.6 feet (1.5 m) tall.

Figure 12. View to the northeast of climbing dunes (Qecd) at the north end of the park which bury the bedrock escarpment created by the Sevier fault.

is suggestive of alternating periods of dune migration and stabilization (Cooke and others, 1993). Here the rows of coalesced dunes have an average crest-to-crest spacing of approximately 1,300 feet (396 m). Large circular to elliptical blowouts are present upwind of many of the dunes. A characteristic feature of this part of the dune field is the presence of small groves of ponderosa pines in the interdune swales. Unlike the ponderosa pines present at the extreme southern end of the dune field, these occur at more typical elevations of 6,100 to 6,500 feet (1,859 to 1,981 m).

Most of the eastern and western boundaries of this geomorphic unit are marked by what is best termed a vegetated linear dune. The western feature is quite evident as one travels on Hancock Road. Linear dunes are oriented roughly parallel to the prevailing wind (figure 7). There are many subtypes and their origin is generally poorly understood (Cooke and others, 1993). However, these features are clearly the remnant arms of vegetated parabolic dunes, the noses and other arms having been blown away.

Fluvial Deposits (Qa, Qp, Qae)

Besides the aeolian deposits and landforms, a variety of unconsolidated water-laid deposits occur in the park area (figures 3 and 4). The sand and gravel associated with active stream courses are mapped as alluvium (Qa). The largest accumulation of alluvium within the park coincides with the channel of Sand Wash, located along the eastern margin of the dune field. The most widespread group of unconsolidated deposits in the park area is best classified as mixed aeolian and alluvial deposits (Qae) (figure 3). These deposits form when accumulations of windblown sand are later reworked by sheetwash or channel flooding during torrential rains (Doelling and others, 1989). These mixed deposits cover much of the area im-

mediately west of the dune field, including the park campground. Unconsolidated gravel deposits lying on bedrock at elevations significantly above the active channels are pediment or terrace deposits (Qp). These remnant deposits indicate that the valley floor once stood at a higher elevation and has since been lowered by erosion. In the park area, pediment gravels are located along both the base of the fault-controlled escarpment to the east and the base of Esplin Point to the west (figure 3). The pediment gravels (Qp) are the oldest of the Quaternary deposits in the area, probably deposited during the Pleistocene Epoch (approximately 2 million to 10,000 years ago). Some may be as old as Tertiary age (Doelling and others, 1989). All of the other Quaternary units, both aeolian and fluvial, were most likely deposited during the Holocene Epoch, or the last 10,000 years.

Succession of Dune Forms at Coral Pink Sand Dunes

The succession of dune types within this dune field can be generalized as a downwind sequence (south to north) of stabilized and partially stabilized sand sheets and dunes, transverse ridges, barchanoid ridges, climbing dunes, and parabolic dunes. This is a complex sequence that reflects the interplay between topography, sediment supply, vegetation, and possibly age. The progression of forms at Coral Pink Sand Dunes is best understood by considering it to be two subsequences with different primary controls.

The southern half of the sequence represents adjustments in form and process to a topographically controlled increase in sand accumulation with increasing distance from the source area. This subsequence culminates in the deposition of the climbing dunes against the fault-line scarp of the Sevier fault. Other dune fields of the western United States with similar sequences and a pronounced topographic control on dune successions include the Lynndyl Dunes of Utah and Great Sand Dunes National Monument, Colorado (Sack, 1987).

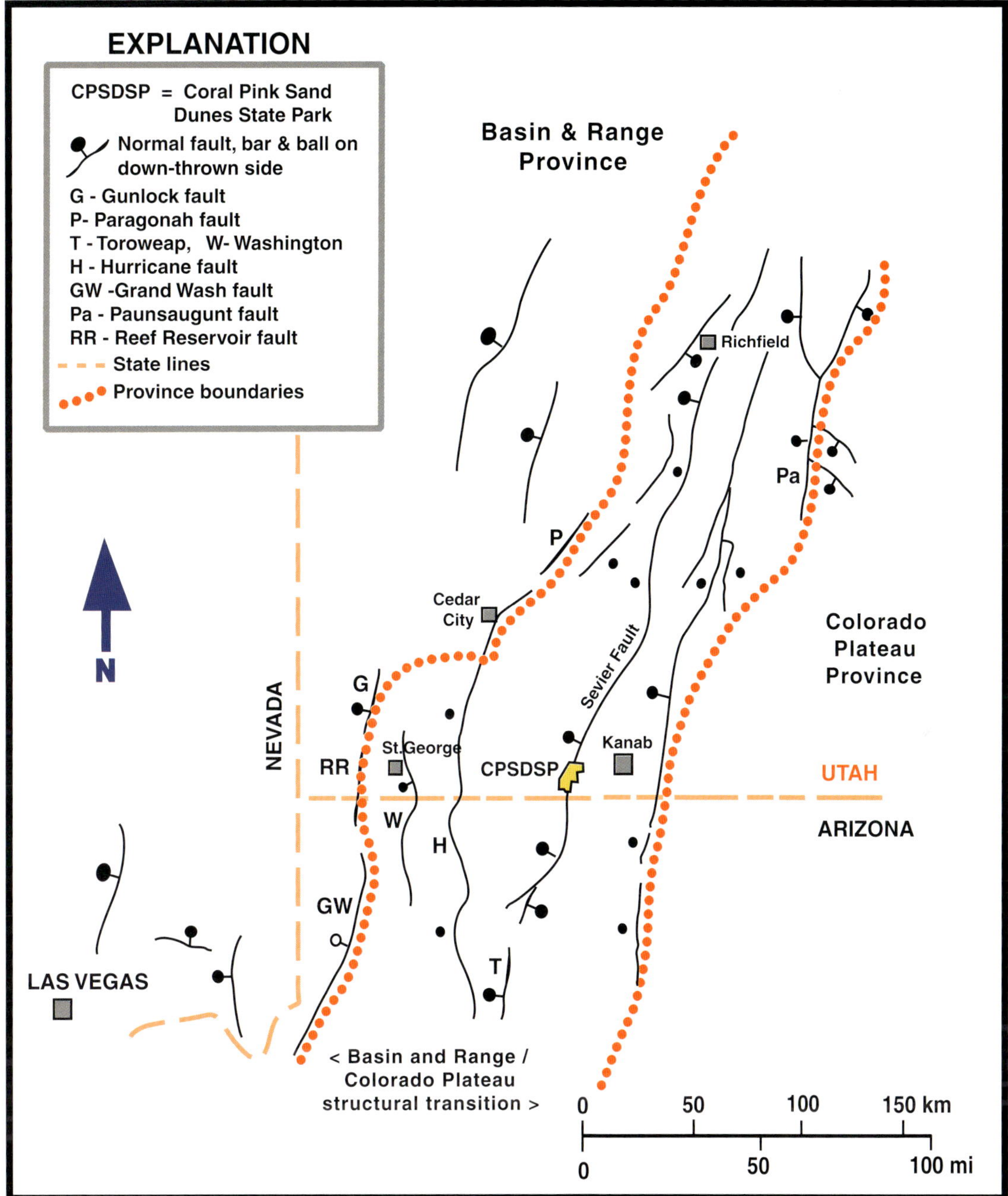

Figure 13. Basin and Range/Colorado Plateau structural transition zone in southwest Utah (modified from Anderson and Christenson, 1989). Note the location of Coral Pink Sand Dunes State Park along the trace of the Sevier fault.

The northern subsequence, climbing dunes to parabolic dunes, reflects a decrease in sand accumulation downwind of the source area, owing to a progressive decrease in the sediment supply and an accompanying increase in vegetation. Similar controls affect the sequence of dunes at the Killpecker Dunes of Wyoming and White Sands National Monument, New Mexico (Sack, 1987).

STRUCTURAL GEOLOGY

Regional Setting

Coral Pink Sand Dunes State Park (CPSDSP) lies within the zone of structural transition between two major geologic or geomorphic provinces of western North America; the Great Basin section of the Basin and Range Province, and the Colorado Plateau province (figure 13). These two provinces are distinguished from one another based on differences in their depositional history and style of structural deformation and related differences in their topography. West of Cedar City and the Hurricane Cliffs (figure 13) lies the Great Basin, an area characterized by north-south-trending fault-block mountain ranges separated by broad intervening basins with internal drainage and filled with Tertiary to Quaternary alluvium and lake deposits. The boundary between the transition zone and the Great Basin coincides with the trend of the Paragonah,

Gunlock, and Grand Wash faults (figure 13). The boundary between the transition zone and the more stable Colorado Plateau interior to the east is not as sharply demarcated, but generally coincides with the Paunsaugunt fault (Anderson and Christenson, 1989).

The transition zone, designated the High Plateaus section (of the Colorado Plateau) by some workers (for example Davis, 1999), lies between the core areas of the Basin and Range and Colorado Plateau and thus displays characteristics of both major provinces. In simplest terms, the transition zone is that part of the Colorado Plateau that was affected by Basin and Range extensional faulting, more characteristic of the style of deformation further to the west. Basin and Range extension was initiated during Miocene time (approximately 15 million years ago) and is still active today (Davis, 1999). This deformation created east-west-tilted structural blocks bounded by widely spaced, north-south-trending, high-angle normal faults; namely the Hurricane, Sevier, and Paunsaugunt faults (Anderson and Christenson, 1989; Davis, 1999). Coral Pink Sand Dunes State Park lies astride the Sevier fault (figures 3 and 13), the central of the three major Basin-and-Range faults of southern Utah.

Sevier Fault

The Sevier fault in Utah is the northern portion of a 300-mile-long (500 km) fault zone that includes the Toroweap and Aubray faults in Arizona (Anderson and Christenson, 1989; Davis, 1999). The fault extends from the Grand Canyon to central Utah, where it loses its discrete character within Miocene volcanic rocks. The north-south trace of the Sevier fault cuts CPSDSP into two roughly equal halves (figure 3).

In the vicinity of the park, the Sevier fault strikes approximately N. 30° E. and dips about 75° W. It is not a single fault plane but rather a complex zone of braided fault segments (figures 3 and 4). As a normal fault, the Sevier fault was created by extensional stresses that produced relative motion along the fault zone such that rocks lying above the fault plane and west of the fault's surface trace moved down relative to the up-thrown block of rocks beneath the dipping fault zone and east of the surface trace (figure 4). Strata within the western down-thrown block dip very gently (< 5°) to the north, as evidenced by the exposures in the face of Esplin Point. The blocks between the fault braids, within the up-thrown eastern block, are locally tilted up to 60° (Doelling and others, 1989). Further east, away from the fault zone, the strata again display a very gentle north to northeast dip.

Total normal displacement along the Sevier fault zone increases from south to north, ranging from approximately 1,560 feet (475 m) at the Utah-Arizona border to 4,920 feet (1,500 m) in southern Sevier County. The stratigraphic displacement within the park is obvious because beds of the upper portion of the Navajo Sandstone (Jurassic), exposed on the western down-thrown side of the fault, are abutted against rocks of the up-thrown block ranging from

Moenave Formation (Upper Triassic) to lower portions of the Navajo Sandstone (figures 3 and 4). Anderson and Christenson (1989) estimated the total displacement in the vicinity of CPSDSP at 1,560 feet (475 m). This fault offset has produced the prominent west-facing bedrock escarpment, a fault-line scarp, east of the campground and main area of active dunes (figure 2).

Movement along the Sevier fault probably began 15 to 12 million years ago, corresponding to the beginning of Basin and Range deformation in this area (Davis, 1999). Assessing the recent history of movement along this fault has proven to be difficult. Throughout most of its length in southern Utah, the Sevier fault cuts through Mesozoic-age bedrock. This limits the opportunity to document the recent history of movement, which is typically accomplished through the study of fault scarps and stratigraphic offset within unconsolidated surficial deposits (Quaternary age). However, studies of the Sevier fault north and south of the park area suggest movements resulting in surface faulting during the late Tertiary to Pleistocene (approximately 4 to 0.56 million years ago) (Anderson and Christenson, 1989). Two geomorphic aspects of the fault in the general vicinity of the park provide indirect support for Pleistocene deformation (Anderson and Christenson, 1989). First, the west-facing bedrock scarp displays a distinctive profile, with a moderately sloping rounded upper part and steeper cliff-forming lower part. In several places within the park these two slope elements are separated by a small bench or step in the scarp profile. Anderson and Christenson (1989) suggest that recent movement, rather than differential erosion, is responsible for these profile characteristics. The second feature suggestive of recent movement along the fault is the presence of a small but distinctive closed basin at Clay Flat, approximately 1 mile (1.6 km) north of the park. This area of deposition (depocenter) is located at a major left step in the trace of the Sevier fault. The local stress field has apparently created a small pull-apart basin which interrupts the northward transport of sediment by ephemeral streams in Yellow Jacket and Sethys Canyons. In order to maintain such a local depocenter, active fault movement and related subsidence during the late Quaternary is probably required (Anderson and Christenson, 1989).

Coral Pink Sand Dunes State Park lies within the southern end of the Intermountain Seismic Belt (ISB), the north-south-trending zone of seismicity extending from northwestern Montana to the Las Vegas, Nevada, area. The Wasatch fault of northern Utah is the most infamous feature within this zone of active earthquake activity. Earthquakes in the southern portion of the ISB are generally small to moderate in size, typically less than Richter magnitude (M_L) 4.0, and in many cases are not associated with the mapped Quaternary faults of the area (Anderson and Christenson, 1989). The largest historic earthquake in the vicinity of CPSDSP was the magnitude 6.3 (M_L) Pine Valley earthquake in 1902, located 21 miles (33 km) north of St. George. Estimated magnitude-5.7 and 5.5+ (M_L)

earthquakes occurred east of the park near Kanab in 1887 and 1959, respectively. Compared to the Hurricane fault 40 miles (64 km) to the west, which generated the 1992 St. George earthquake (M_w = 5.8), the Sevier fault has had a much lower level of seismicity during historic time. Only two historic (1900-1985) earthquakes have been recorded along the main trace of the Sevier fault in Utah (Davis, 1999), neither of them within the park. Anderson and Christenson (1989) raise the possibility that the Sevier fault may be locally deforming by continuous aseismic fault creep, as opposed to large ground-rupturing earthquakes. Either way, the low-level earthquake activity, coupled with the geomorphic character of the fault-line scarp noted above, suggest that the Sevier fault is still active today.

Deformation-Band Shear Zones

The Navajo Sandstone of southwestern Utah displays a variety of outcrop-scale structures that resemble veins or dikes weathering out in positive relief from their host sandstone. These features, called deformation bands, have been recently studied and analyzed in careful detail by Davis (1999). Deformation bands are the result of porosity reduction, grain crushing, grain fracturing, and grain flow that occur during the deformation of porous granular materials. Davis recognizes two varieties of deformation bands, cataclastic and noncataclastic, both of which are present in the Navajo Sandstone within the vicinity of CPSDSP. Cataclastic deformation bands are closely associated with the regional faults and folds of the area, including the Sevier fault. Slip within these features is indicated by slickensides, and a distinctive ladder structure is common. The most distinctive manifestation of cataclastic deformation bands are the formation of "fault fins," triangular blades of sandstone up to 26 feet (8 m) tall (see cover photograph of Davis, 1999). Fault fins are produced by differential weathering and erosion; the reduced porosity within the deformation bands increases their resistance. Tilted deformation bands then serve to protect underlying sandstone from erosion (Davis, 1999).

The second or noncataclastic type of deformation band is present in almost every outcrop of the uppermost 33 to 50 feet (10-15 m) of the Navajo Sandstone (Davis, 1999). The noncataclastic deformation bands are vein-like structures that weather in positive relief but show minimal evidence of grain-scale fracturing and no slickensides. Davis (1999) concludes that noncataclastic deformation bands formed in Jurassic time by the loading of undercompacted dune sand of the Navajo Sandstone by sediments that now make up the Carmel Formation. Aided by groundwater infiltration, the Navajo sands failed by vertical compaction. The deformation bands mark the zones where this volume reduction took place. The uppermost part of the Navajo Sandstone outcrops near the northwest corner of the park. Large blocks of sandstone, apparently quarried from that area, have been placed at camp sites and along the loop road. "These blocks are museum pieces of . . . noncataclastic deformation bands" (Davis,

Figure 14. *Noncataclastic deformation bands in a boulder of Navajo Sandstone along the campground loop, Coral Pink Sand Dunes State Park.*

1999, p. 66) (figure 14).

GEOLOGIC HISTORY

A complete geologic history of the area around Coral Pink Sand Dunes State Park (CPSDSP) is beyond the scope of this paper. Interested readers should consult Peterson and Turner-Peterson's (1989) overview of the Colorado Plateau, as well as other papers in this volume. We will focus on those geologic events that have specifically left their mark on the landscape of the park. The most important events are the Jurassic deposition of the Glen Canyon Group (Moenave, Kayenta, and Navajo Formations), the Cretaceous to Cenozoic structural deformation of the Colorado Plateau, and the Quaternary formation and evolution of the active dunes. This selective history is primarily abstracted from the work of Baars (1983), Stokes (1986), Harris and Tuttle (1990), Patton and others (1991), Barnes (1993), Morris and Stueben (1994), Elias (1997), and Davis (1999).

Jurassic Environmental Change

For much of the Paleozoic Era (570 to 245 million years ago), Utah was situated on the western edge of the North American continent and dominated by shallow-marine deposition. During Middle Triassic time (240 to 230 million years ago) western Utah was cut off from the ocean to the west by an highland barrier, termed the Mesocordilleran High (Stokes, 1986), that was located in what is now eastern Nevada. To the east, in what is now western Colorado, was another highland area called the Uncompahgre uplift, that was the eroded remnant of the Ancestral Rockies. Thus, the subsequent Jurassic formations of the Glen Canyon Group were deposited in a sedimentary basin that formed between these two highlands, dominated by terrestrial depositional environments. The Mesocordilleran High blocked moisture-ladden air masses and served to enhance arid conditions in Utah by creating a rainshadow. The Mesocordilleran High was also a source area for rivers flowing eastward and carrying sediment into the basin.

Fluvial and lacustrine deposition during the Early Jurassic resulted in the sandstones, siltstones, and freshwater limestones of the Moenave Formation. During this time (approximately 203 to 196 million years ago) the North American continent was drifting northward through equatorial latitudes. The lithologies and sedimentary structures preserved within the Moenave suggest a landscape of low-gradient stream channels with broad floodplains containing lakes and mudflats. Fossil remains of large freshwater fish, similar to sturgeon, have been found in the Whitmore Point and Springdale Sandstone Members.

As North America drifted north away from the equator, the climate in what is now southern Utah became cooler with wet summers and dry winters (Barnes, 1993). Streams deposited silt and sand in channels and on floodplains; dinosaurs left their footprints in the damp sediments that would become the Kayenta Formation (196 to 191 million years ago).

Continued northward drift brought a large portion of North America under the influence of subtropical high pressure, resulting in increasing aridity and the establishment of a huge Jurassic sand sea or erg. One estimate indicates that the erg may have covered 256 million square miles (6.63 x 105 km^2) (Marzolf, 1988). However, the intertonguing of the Kayenta and Navajo formations represented by the Lamb Point and Tenney Canyon indicates an initial period of time during which fluvial and aeolian systems vied for dominance in southern Utah. A Jurassic desert, represented by the Lamb Point Tongue, appears to have advanced from the east, burying and replacing the fluvial channels and floodplains of the Kayenta Formation. The margins of the sandy desert temporarily receded back to the east, replaced by fluvial environments of the Tenney Canyon Tongue. The desert once again advanced and overwhelmed the fluvial landscape. Aeolian deposition, represented by the main body of the Navajo Sandstone, then dominated this area for approximately 20 million years (191 to 171 million years ago).

Paleogeographic reconstructions suggest that the erg was situated near the western edge of the continent between approximately 18° and 25° north latitude, under the influence of onshore north-northwesterly winds associated with the eastern edge of a subtropical high (Marzolf, 1988; Peterson, 1988). A shallow marine shelf, estuary, or large lake bordered the lowland desert on the west. Peterson (1988) suggests that the source area for the sand was an uplifted area in central Montana. Rivers carried sediment westward to the coast from this upland, longshore currents moved the sediment southward, and then waves and northwesterly winds delivered the sediment to Utah. Marzolf (1988) suggests a different source for the sand. He suggests that rivers draining northwestward from upland areas in Arizona delivered sediment to the head of the marine embayment to the west, where the silt and clay was winnowed and the sand was returned inland by the onshore winds.

Navajo Sandstone deposition ended, possibly the result of climate change, in the vicintiy of CPSDSP when streams, loaded with red mud, flooded the dunes and partially truncated them. These sediments became the Sinawava Member of the Temple Cap Sandstone (Middle Jurassic). Aeolian deposition quickly resumed producing the White Thrown Member of the Temple Cap Sandstone.

For wind-blown sediments to be preserved as aeolian sandstones, they must be deposited in an actively subsiding basin. In the case of a coastal erg, if deposition does not keep pace with subsidence, the sea will transgress or flood the lowland. This is what occurred along the western edge of the Navajo erg during Middle Jurassic time, resulting in a major unconformity (J-2) (figure 6). A shallow seaway extended into southwestern Utah from the north. Wave action planed off the tops of the dunes and calcareous silt buried them. This is the depositional environment represented by the limestones of the Co-op Creek Member of the Carmel Formation (Middle Jurassic).

Upper Jurassic through Lower Cretaceous beds are not present in the vicinity of the park and were probably removed by a long period of uplift and erosion associated with the Laramide orogeny. The nearest outcrops of Cretaceous rocks are poor exposures of Tropic Shale and Dakota Sandstone, both Upper Cretaceous, located near Mt. Carmel. Thus, the modern aeolian sediments of the park lie directly on Lower Jurassic formations, most notably the Navajo Sandstone. The boundary between the two aeolian units, one lithified and one still moving, represents a hiatus or gap in the stratigraphic record of approximately 190 million years.

Cretaceous to Cenozoic Tectonics

Towards the end of Mesozoic time, and continuing into the Cenozoic, western North America was subjected to a mountain-building episode known as the Laramide orogeny (approximately 90 to 50 million years ago). This orogeny was the result of compressional stresses generated by plate-tectonic convergence between the North American plate and the oceanic Farallon plate to the west. Subduction of the Farallon plate, and related folding and thrust faulting, gave rise to the Rocky Mountains. The Colorado Plateau was also greatly affected by this deformational event. Compression of the Colorado Plateau region was accomodated by basement-cored reverse faulting and associated folding which produced the Kaibab uplift, the San Rafael Swell, and the numerous broad anticlines and synclines of the Kaiparowits Plateau, among other major structures. Since the beginning of the Laramide orogeny the nearly circular Colorado Plateau has acted as a coherent structural block and has been uplifted more than 6,600 feet (2,012 m) (Morris and Stubben, 1994).

One hypothesis (Beghoul and Barazangi, 1989) suggests that the Farallon plate may have been key to this uplift, becoming attached during subduction to the bottom of the North American plate in the vicinity of the Colorado

Plateau. During mid-Cenozoic time the Farallon plate separated from the North American plate and sank into the mantle. As the Farallon plate remnant sank, hot material from the asthenosphere rose to fill the void. This material thermally expanded as it rose and some of it intruded the lower continental crust, thereby increasing its thickness and temperature. Thus the Colorado Plateau is seen to have been uplifted by isostatic compensation resulting from a combination of heating and increased crustal thickness.

The intrusion of molten material mentioned above caused a second phase of deformation during early part of the Miocene Epoch (approximately 25 to 19 million years ago). This period of magmatism is not directly evident in the geology of CPSDSP but it resulted in the nearby Marysvale volcanic field and the laccoliths of the Henry Mountains (see Davis, 1999).

A third deformational event that did have a pronouced effect of the geology of the park was the Basin and Range extension. This episode of normal faulting and crustal extension began approximately 15 million years ago, in mid-Miocene time, and is still active today (Davis, 1999). There is no consensus among geoscientists as to the plate-tectonic explanation for this extension. Some (for example Stewart, 1971) suggest that a slowing of convergence between the Farallon and North American plates coupled with a rollback of the subducting Farallon plate essentially created back-arc spreading within the continental crust. Others (for example Dickinson, 1979) have suggested that the North American plate completely overrode the mid-ocean ridge along the western boundary of the Farallon plate, thus creating a window in the subducting slab through which heat and magma from the asthenosphere could rise to lift and thin the overlying continental crust. Either way, the beginning of this extensional deformation was coincident with the cessation of subduction along the California coast and the initiation of the transform boundary between the North American and Pacific plates marked by the San Andreas fault.

Whatever its cause, this extensional deformation created the distinctive topography of the Basin and Range Province, including the Great Basin section in Nevada and western Utah, as well as the three major high-angle normal faults located within the southwestern margin of the Colorado Plateau -- namely the Hurricane, Sevier, and Paunsaugunt faults (figure 13). The Sevier fault has had a major influence on the geologic history of the Coral Pink Sand Dunes State Park because the present topography is dominated by a fault-line scarp resulting from periodic movement along this fault. Without this fault scarp, the varied Mesozoic strata would not be exposed within the park. In addition, this scarp is in part responsible for the concentration and accumulation of wind-blown sand at this location.

The uplift of the Colorado Plateau caused a major change in the nature of the dominant geologic processes. Whereas the the Mesozoic Era was dominated by deposi-

tion, the subsequent Cenozoic geologic history of the Colorado Plateau has been dominated by erosion, producing the world-renowned canyonlands and cliff-and-bench topography. This erosion is very evident in the landscape of CPSDSP, exposing the picturesque formations of the Glen Canyon Group. However, localized aoelian deposition during the Quaternary Period has created the features for which the park is named.

Late Quaternary History of the Colorado Plateau

The Quaternary Period is characterized by major climatic changes that had significant impacts on ecosystems and geologic processes. Unfortunately, the late Cenozoic erosional history of the Colorado Plateau, including the Quaternary, has left little in the way of a stratigraphic record. However, a general paleoecological history of the Colorado Plateau has been pieced together (see summaries by Betancourt, 1990, and Elias, 1997).

The Quaternary Period is subdivided into the Pleistocene and Holocene Epochs, with the boundary between the two occurring approximately 10,000 years ago. The Pleistocene is noted for its alternating glacial and inter-glacial conditions. The Holocene is essentially the most recent and on-going inter-glacial time period that began when the last ice age (the Wisconsin glaciation) ended. Late Pleistocene full-glacial (22,000 to 18,000 years ago) conditions on the Colorado Plateau probably inhibited major aeolian transport and deposition. Paleobotanical evidence suggests that late Wisconsin winters were wetter and summers were cooler and drier than present (Betancourt, 1990). Drier summers probably reflect a decrease in the availability of subtropical moisture via the southwest monsoon, whereas wetter winters were caused by a southern shift in the polar jet and an increased occurrence of Pacific storms and associated frontal precipitation over the Plateau. The result was coniferous woodlands, including limber pine, juniper, Colorado blue spruce, Douglas-fir, and sagebrush, were present in areas that now support pinyon-juniper woodlands. The area of the Coral Pink Sand Dunes may have supported a coniferous woodland during the late Pleistocene. Notably, ponderosa pine was apparently absent from the Colorado Plateau during this time, due to a lack of summer moisture and/or a reduction of thunderstorm activity and lightning strikes; ponderosa pine distribution is in part linked to fire (Betancourt, 1990).

The Pleistocene-Holocene transition on the Colorado Plateau is generally marked by gradual changes in vegetation which indicate warming and a progressive decrease in effective moisture. Macrobotanical remains from the Escalante River basin indicate decreased abundances of mesophytic plants and an upslope retreat of Douglas fir and spruce (Withers and Mead, 1993). However, the early to mid-Holocene (10,000 to 6,000 years ago) on the Colorado Plateau saw a significant increase in summer precipitation (and thunderstorm activity?) (Betancourt, 1990). Ponderosa pine expanded during this period beyond even its present distribution. Even during the latter part of this period, commonly associated with hot-dry conditions in other parts of the southwest (the altithermal), the Colorado Plateau appears to have been wetter than today. The most likely explanation is more abundant subtropical moisture from an intensified Bermuda High and southwest monsoon (Betancourt, 1990).

Pollen evidence from Posy Lake on the Aquarius Plateau, north of the park, indicates that the period of enhanced summer precipitation persisted until 5,500 years before present (B.P.) (Shafer, 1989). Lake levels were lowest at this site from about 5,000 to 3,500 years B.P., indicating greater aridity than today (the altithermal?). Summer precipitation reintensified after 3,500 years B.P.

The presence of inactive dune forms, stabilized by vegetation, as well as the active dune field suggests at least two major periods of aeolian activity at Coral Pink Sand Dunes State Park during the Holocene. Could the mid-Holocene dry period documented by Shafer (1989) have resulted in vegetation changes, a decrease in soil moisture, and the initiation of aeolian activity in the park area? Or are the Coral Pink Sand Dunes even younger, the result of one of several periods of regional aeolian reactivation and mobilization suggested for the southwestern United States during the last 1,000 years? Stokes (1994) noted a correlation between two phases of aeolian reactivation (790 to 620 and 520 to 430 years ago) and extended periods of drought based on tree-ring data. These questions cannot be answered at this time. As far as we know no radiocarbon dates have ever been obtained from the Coral Pink Sand Dunes and thus no correlation can be made with the paleoclimatic events mentioned above.

GEOLOGIC UNIQUENESS OF THE PARK

Naturalist Freeman Tilden (1970) concluded that sand dunes are nature's nudes. Indeed, there is something very pleasing, even sensual, about the curves and bare contours of active dunes. Dunes bring to mind romantic adventures in Old World deserts, as well as frontier tales from the American west. It is no wonder then that the Coral Pinks Sand Dunes have been used as locations for several Hollywood films: *Arabian Nights* (1942) -- "corny escapist stuff" with an enslaved Sheherazade and a retired Sinbad the Sailor; *Mackenna's Gold* (1969) -- "overblown adventure saga about search for lost canyon of gold," and *One Little Indian* (1973) -- "AWOL cavalry corporal escaping through the desert with young Indian boy and a camel" (Maltin, 1997). Geologic history, OHV recreation, film making, and wildlife habitat (to be discussed below) -- all make this is an interesting, important, and valuable landscape.

Source of the Sand

Although the commercial use of the Coral Pink Sand Dunes dates to 1942, the earliest scientific treatment of the dune field is Herbert Gregory's (1950) description of the dunes in his general survey of the geology and geography of the Zion National Park area:

Likewise the disintegrated products from the bare sandstones of South Mountain are carried eastward across Moccasin Terrace to form the dunes along the cliffs at Sand Canyon and the great sand flats at the head of Three Lakes Canyon. With local accretions en route these deposits are redistributed over Wygaret Terrace and eastward to the base of the Kaiparowits plateau. During sandstorms great quantities of the finest dust rise high into the air and move eastward to distant places or after darkening the skies with whirling clouds return to the place from which they came. . . . Another large area of dunes extends from the head of Cottonwood and Water Canyons northwestward across Sand and Yellow Jacket Valleys to the base of the Block Mesas near Esplin Point. For a distance of about 8 miles northwest of Riggs Spring dunes as much as 200 feet high are nearly stationary; they support growths of piñon and juniper and in wet seasons hold lakes and give rise to springs. At the head of Sand Canyon they are in motion and in their migration are burying and uncovering trees and converting the original escarpment of the Sevier fault into a slope (Gregory, 1950, p. 188).

Botanist Elias Castle (1954) may have been the first to use the term "coral pink" to describe the color of the dunes. His report, probably the first to focus specifically on the dunes in the park area, summarizes the soil conditions and their influence on the various vegetation communities within the dune field.

Kane County has many aeolian deposits though most are quite small. In addition to the Coral Pink Sand Dunes, the Sand Hills, which extend across U.S. 89 between the Sevier fault and Kanab Creek, are large enough to be portrayed on regional geologic maps (Sargent and Philpott, 1987; Doelling and others, 1989). Of the many Jurassic sandstone units exposed in the vicinity, the Navajo, Page, and Entrada Sandstones are thought to be especially productive in supplying sand for dunes. Doelling and others (1989) suggest that the friable and poorly cemented middle portion of the Navajo Sandstone provided the bulk of the reddish sand for the Coral Pink Sand Dunes. The reddish color is the result of iron-oxide staining on the surface of the quartz sand grains.

Although Gregory (1950) indicates a western source (South Mountain) for the sand, the prominent southwest-northeast orientation of the dune field and prevailing southwesterly winds suggests to us a source to the southwest. The middle pink portion of the Navajo Sandstone is exposed extensively across the Moccasin Terrace, southwest of the park. In addition, extensive surficial deposits, primarily deposits of fine-grained sand deposited by mixed alluvial and aeolian processes (Qae), cover the Moccasin Terrace (Doelling and others, 1989). These unconsolidated deposits are a likely source for the sand that comprises the Coral Pink Sand Dunes.

This suggested source indicates a very interesting path through the rock cycle for these sand grains -- ancient aeolian sandstones weathering to produce modern aeolian sediments. Recall that some geologists (for example Peterson, 1988) suggest that metamorphic rocks exposed in central Montana were weathered and eroded to produce sediment that was transported westward by rivers to a marine embayment during Jurassic time. This sediment was transported southward by ocean currents, progressively winnowed by wave and tidal action, and eventually transported back to land by onshore winds. These sand grains were then deposited in large dunes of a lowland erg. The dunes were buried by younger sediments and eventually lithified to sandstone, what we now call the Navajo Sandstone. These aeolian sandstones remained buried for perhaps 125 million years or more. Uplift of the Colorado Plateau during the Tertiary Period set the stage for the recent and on going weathering and erosion, releasing the sand grains from the ancient rocks. Once again, perhaps 190 million years later, the sand grains are eroded and again transported by wind. The modern wind regime has concentrated many of these sand grains in the Coral Pink Sand Dunes and continues to slowly transport them to the northeast, to encroach on and bury Jurassic Navajo Sandstone outcrops (figure 11).

Formation of the Dune Field

An obvious question is why have these modern aeolian sediments been concentrated here? Although no local wind data are available, a park brochure (Utah State Parks and Recreation, no date) and interpretive signage describe the existence of several regional winds that converge in the vicinity of the park. A break in the Vermillion Cliffs south of the park, due to offset on the Sevier fault, likely allows winds to accelerate through the gap between the Moquith and Moccasin Mountains and to entrain loose sediment on the Moccasin Terrace. As the gap widens in the vicinity of the park and the winds impinge upon the bedrock scarp of the Sevier fault, velocity may decrease to allow deposition. Named for an Italian physicist, the acceleration of air or liquid as it is forced through a narrow constriction is called the Venturi effect. The southern portion of the dune field has a distinct north-south orientation, possibly reflecting the influence of this southerly wind.

About two miles (3.2 km) north of the southern end of the dune field, in the generally vicinity of the park campground, the orientation of the dune field changes to southwest-northeast. This may reflect the influence of prevailing southwesterly winds blowing up from Rosy Canyon, another low in the Vermillion Cliffs to the southwest. These southwesterly winds may be funneled between the Moccasin Mountains to the south and the Block Mesas, including Esplin Point, to the north. The fault-related scarp

on the eastern edge of the dune field may act to slow these winds as well, thus initiating deposition at the base of the scarp. The sand deposited at the base of the scarp is the obvious source for the dunes that climb the fault scarp and extend approximately four miles (6.4 km) northeast onto BLM land. This secondary sand movement may be facilitated by an acceleration of the wind as it flows through the narrow, one-mile (1.6 km) gap between Esplin Point and the scarp of the Sevier fault. Thus, the Coral Pink Sand Dunes appear to owe their existence to an abundant supply of fine-grained sand from the Navajo Sandstone and other units, strong prevailing southerly and southwesterly winds, and the decelerating influence of the Sevier fault-line scarp. Specific data about the local wind regime are needed to confirm the highly speculative hypothesis presented above.

LOCATION AND DESCRIPTION OF CLASSIC GEOLOGICAL SITES WITHIN THE PARK

Overview Area and Nature Trail

A parking lot and overview area (figure 8) is located on the east side of the campground road between the ranger station and the campground. Most non-OHV visitors to the park utilize the boardwalk here to access the dune field. The overview is built atop what is best termed a vegetated linear dune (Tsoar and Moller, 1986) that marks the eastern boundary of this portion of the dune field. Unlike the vegetated linear dunes along the margins of the dune field to the north, the origin of this feature is not obvious. The best interpretation we can provide for this example is that it is the result of complex airflow along the boundary between the dunefield and the vegetated valley floor.

From this vantage point one can look to the south and see the gap between the Moquith Mountains (east, left) and Moccasin Mountain (west, right) through which southerly winds may be accelerated by the Venturi effect. One can also look to the southwest across much of the Moccasin Terrace, the probable source area for much of the sand in the dunes. To the north-northeast is the narrow gap between Esplin Point and the west-facing escarpment of the Sevier fault, which may facilitate acceleration of the wind and the transport of sand over the escarpment to form the large parabolic dunes at the northern end of the dune field (Qelp). Directly east of the overview are the active core of the dune field (Qetd) and the prominent bedrock escarpment of the Sevier fault (figure 2).

Nebkhas

A short nature trail begins beyond the boardwalk overview and traverses into the dune field. Interpretive signs along the trail focus on the relationships between vegetation and certain dune forms. Here one can see excellent examples of nebkhas (also called shrub-coppice

Figure 15. View to the west of a nebkha (shrub-coppice dune), anchored by Wyethia scabra (known commonly as mule ears), within the active core of transverse dunes (Qetd). Young field assistant is approximately 4.6 feet (1.5 m) tall.

dunes), mounds or hummocks of sand trapped by clumps of vegetation (figure 15). Although present in each geomorphic unit of the dune field, nebkhas are particulary abundant here along the soutwestern margin of the active core of transverse dunes (Qetd).

On flat surfaces wind velocities may decrease as much as 50 percent on the downwind side of a bush or shrub (Francis, 1994). Both the decrease in velocity and the physical obstruction of the stems or branches cause deposition of wind-blown particles within the plant, including sand, silt, organic debris, and nutrients attached to dust nuclei. Such accumulations of material locally increases the soil fertility. A nebkha will develop where the plants grow fast enough to remain on top of the accumulating mound. Nebkhas may eventually reach 3 to 15 feet (1-3 m) in height and 6 to 30 feet (2-5 m) in diameter. Typically they are oval or elliptical in plan form. The nebkhas in the Coral Pink Sand Dunes are generally less than 6 feet (2 m) in height. Here, several different plant species at are adapted to the stress of progressive burial by wind-blown sand, but *Wyethia scabra* (mule ears) is by far the most common. *Wyethia scabra* nebkhas are particularly abundant along the margins of the dune field. In some areas the relief of the nebkha has been increased by deflation or aeolian erosion of the ground adjacent to the nebkha, locally exposing the matted and twisted stems and roots of the mound-forming plant for a considerable depth below the top of the dune (Castle, 1954).

Star Dune

The large dune directly east of the boardwalk overview is an excellent example of a star dune (figures 2 and 8). Star dunes commonly have a high central peak and three or four curving arms, with multiple slipfaces, that extend radially. Star dunes form where winds from more than two directions have contributed to dune growth. They tend to grow vertically, rather than migrating horizontally, and contain a greater volume of sand than any other dune type (Lancaster, 1995). McKee (1982) noted that most of the star dunes of the Namib Desert, southwestern Africa, developed from linear dunes, although some are associated with transverse dunes, as is the case in the Coral Pink Sand Dunes.

The exact nature of the wind regime responsible for the single star dune within the park is not known. If it was the result of a seasonal change in wind direction, as is the case for many star dunes, then one might suspect that more than one transverse dune would be modified into this form. We speculate that this dune is located at the convergence of the several local winds previously discussed.

Star dunes typically achieve heights of 45 to 450 feet (14-137 m), though some modern star dunes in the Namib Desert are reported to rise as much as 900 feet (274 m) above their interdune base (McKee, 1982). The large star dune at CPSDSP rises approximately 100 feet (30 m) above its base and has three sinuous arms and several smaller secondary arms.

Barchan (Current Crescent)

Also visible from the boardwalk overview is a large barchan-like dune, approximately 0.2 miles (0.3 km) south-southwest of the star dune. Barchans are characterized by a distinctive crescentic shape in plan view, a steep concave slipface, and "horns" extending downwind from the central mass of the dune (figure 8). Barchans are the stable dune type in areas where the directional variability of the wind is less than 15°. Isolated barchans generally occur in areas with a limited sand supply; as the sand supply increases barchans coalesce to form barchanoid ridges (Lancaster, 1995).

Lancaster (1995) noted that one of the settings in which barchans typically form are sand transport corridors that link source areas with depositional zones. Interestingly, the isolated barchan at Coral Pink Sand Dunes is located in a transitional area between the partially stabilized transverse dunes (Qesp) to the south and the active core of transverse dunes (Qetd) to the north. However, it is puzzling that this dune type so indicative of a unidirectional wind regime is in such close proximity to a star dune, indicative of multidirectional winds. A mitigating factor may be the fact that the isolated barchan at CPSDSP is not a freely migrating dune, but instead has formed largely upwind of a small knob of Navajo Sandstone, which can be observed in the dune's slipface. We believe this dune is not a true barchan, but instead is best termed a current crescent. Current crescents are horseshoe-shaped dunes that accumulate where winds are deflected around and over topographic obstacles such as boulders, escarpments, or hills (Pye and Tsoar, 1990). Sand is deposited both in front of the obstacle and on either side in two tapering wings that resemble the horns of a true barchan.

Tiger Beetle Conservation Area ("Cattle Guard Turnout")

Approximately 1.6 miles (2.6 km) north of the ranger station, on the east side of the road, is a turnout and small parking area locally referred to as the "cattle guard" area (figure 8). This site provides easy access to the active core of transverse dunes (Qetd) and the area of small marginal parabolic dunes (Qemp). From this area one can also see the barchanoid ridges (figure 10) impinge upon the bedrock escarpment, transforming into echo dunes and climbing dunes. This is also an excellent location to observe the ecological differences between the largely unvegetated dune ridges and the vegetated interdune swales. Some of the interdune swales are incised, exposing their shallow stratigraphy. This stratigraphy, which includes mudcracks and darker, organic-rich (?) layers, indicates cycles of water ponding and desiccation and periods of weak soil development within these interdune areas.

This general location is also the habitat of the Coral Pink Sand Dunes (CPSD) tiger beetle (*Cicindela limbata albissima*). The biology and ecology of the CPSD tiger beetle has been largely revealed through the research of entomologists Barry Knisley (Randolph-Macon College, Ashland, Virginia) and James Hill. The following account is summarized from their work, primarily Knisley and Hill (in press).

Tiger beetles are predatory insects which prefer open, sparsely vegetated habitats, such as dune fields. Among the many Cicindela species that inhabit dune fields of the western United States are several endemic species or subspecies, including the CPSD tiger beetle. This subspecies of the Cicindela limbata group is only known from the Coral Pink Sand Dunes. Surprisingly, the CPSD tiger beetle appears to regularly inhabit only a small portion (approximately 200 acres or 81 ha) of the total dune field, making its geographical range one of the smallest of any organism known to science.

In 1994 the Southern Utah Wilderness Alliance petitioned the U.S. Fish and Wildlife Service (USFWS) to list the CPSD tiger beetle as an endangered species. Currently, the CPSD tiger beetle is recognized as a candidate for listing as an endangered or threatened species. In 1998 a conservation agreement was signed by the USFWS, BLM, Utah Department of Natural Resources, and Kane County that established a 200-acre (81 ha) conservation area within CPSD State Park. Off-highway vehicles are not permitted in the western portion of the conservation area where most of the tiger beetles are found. The eastern portion of the conservation area serves as a travel corridor between the southern and northern portions of the dune field. An additional 370 acre (121 ha) conservation area has been established on BLM-administered land at the extreme northern end of the dune field where a small number of dispersing tiger beetles have been observed.

Although the range of the CPSD Tiger beetle is quite small, as is its total population, there is no evidence of a progressive decline in CPSD tiger beetles during the time that Knisley and Hill (in press) have monitored their population (1992-present). They believe that the implementation of the conservation plan in 1998, which protects the beetles' primary habitat, will promote the long-term existence of this species within the Coral Pink Sand Dunes.

A puzzling question, for which there is presently no definitive answer, is why is the distribution of the CPSD tiger beetle so restricted within the overall dune field? Knisley and Hill (in press) point out that there is significant variation in the geomorphology, vegetation, prey insects, and OHV activity throughout the dune field. They note that the percent vegetation cover in the interdune swales of the primary habitat/conservation area is significantly greater than in the swales of other areas of the dune field. Probably related, the numbers and types of prey species are also significantly greater in the conservation area compared to other areas of the dune field. Are these differences related to purely natural factors, such as the geomorphic transition from more active, less vegetated barchanoid dunes in the southern portion of the dune field to the less active, more vegetated climbing and parabolic dunes to the north? Or are the habitat differences related to OHV activity? Knisley and Hill (in press) suggest that high OHV use contributes to the highly dynamic nature of the southern portion of the dune field, decreasing the cover of vegetation in interdune swales. These questions point out the distinctly interdisciplinary (biology and geology in this case) nature of many of the resource and land-use issues or concerns now faced by human societies.

Final Comments

This paper has attempted to summarize our current understanding of the particular geomorphic system known as the Coral Pink Sand Dunes. We know of no other dune field in Utah, with the possible exception of the Lynndyl Dunes (BLM Little Sahara Recreation Area) (Sack, 1987), that contains the diversity of aeolian landforms present here. Hopefully we have shown that much can be learned at Coral Pink Sand Dunes State Park, both informally and individually by observant visitor-naturalists and formally and cooperatively by professional scientists. Coral Pink Sand Dunes will continue to provide a natural laboratory in which to observe and discern the complex interactions among atmospheric, geomorphic, and ecological processes. The lead author plans to continue research here in the hopes of developing a chronology of dune formation and evolution during the Holocene. Of course one doesn't have to be a scientist to appreciate the importance and beauty of this landscape.

To stand in the midst of a sea of great dunes is to have the sensation of being utterly alone, and vulnerable, in a world of scorching elements and soul-shaking beauty.

— Jan DeBlieu, 1999

ACKNOWLEDGMENTS

We would like to thank Margie Chan (University of Utah), Greg Schlenker (Kleinfelder), and Sarah George (Utah Museum of Natural History) for their careful and thoughtful review of our manuscript. In addition, the comments and suggestions of editors Doug Sprinkel and Paul Anderson greatly improved the final paper. Barry Knisley (Randolph-Macon College) generously shared his knowledge of tiger beetle ecology and dune environments and materials related to the park. Stephanie Rodgers donated her time and expertise in preparing some of the figures. Thanks are also due to the staff of the Utah State Film Commission for researching the use of the park area as a film location. Stuart Ford provided assistance and comic relief during several of the field sessions. Lastly, we thank the park staff, especially Rob Quist (Park Manager) and Carl Davis (retired), for facilitating our field work and, more importantly, for their professional management of this important site. Their job is not easy as the constituencies who use and value this park are diverse. We all owe them our gratitude.

REFERENCES

Anderson, R.E., and Christenson, G.E., 1989, Quaternary faults, folds, and selected volcanic features in the Cedar City 1°x 2° quadrangle, Utah: Utah Geological and Mineral Survey Miscellaneous Publication 89-6, 29 p.

Baars, D.L., 1983, The Colorado Plateau - a geologic history: Albuquerque, University of New Mexico Press, 279 p.

Bagnold, R.A., 1942, The physics of blown sand and desert dunes: New York, William Morrow & Company, 265 p.

Barnes, F.A., 1993, Geology of the Moab area: Moab, Canyon Country Publications, 264 p.

Beghoul, N., and Barazangi, 1989, Mapping high Pn velocity beneath the Colorado Plateau constrains uplift models: Journal of Geophysical Research, v. 94, p. 7083-7104.

Betancourt, J.L., 1990, Late Quaternary biogeography of the Colorado Plateau, *in* Betancourt, J.L., Van Devender, T.R., and Martin, P.S., editors, Packrat middens - the last 40,000 years of biotic change: Tucson, The University of Arizona Press, p. 259-292.

Castle, E.S., 1954, The succession of vegetation on a southern Utah sand dune: Provo, Brigham Young University, M.S. thesis, 98 p.

Cooke, R., Warren, A., and Goudie, A., 1993, Desert geomorphology: London, UCL Press, 526 p.

Davis, G.H., 1999, Structural geology of the Colorado Plateau region of southern Utah with special emphasis on deformation bands: Geological Society of America Special Paper 342, 157 p.

DeBlieu, J., 1999, Wind: how the flow of air has shaped life, myth, and the land: Boston, Mariner Books, 294 p.

Dickinson, W.R., 1979, Cenozoic plate tectonic setting of the cordilleran region in the United States, *in* Armentrout, J.M., Cole, M.R., and Terbest, H., editors, Cenozoic paleogeography of the western United States: Society of Economic Mineralogists and Paleontologists, Pacific Coast Paleogeography Symposium 3, p. 1-13.

Doelling, H.H., Davis F.D., and Brandt, C.J., 1989, The geology of Kane County, Utah: Utah Geological and Mineral Survey Bulletin 124, 192 p.

Elias, S.A., 1997, The ice-age history of southwestern national parks: Washington, D.C., Smithsonian Institution Press, 200 p.

Francis, C.F., 1994, Plants on desert hillslopes, *in* Abrahams, A.D., and Parsons, A.J., editors, Geomorphology of desert environments: London, Chapman and Hall, p. 243-254.

Gregory, H.E., 1950, Geology and geography of the Zion Park region Utah and Arizona: U.S. Geological Survey Professional Paper 220, 200 p.

Harlow, W.M., and Harrar, E.S., 1968, Textbook of dendrology - covering the important forest trees of the United States and Canada (5th edition): New York, McGraw-Hill Book Company, 512 p.

Harris, A.G., and Tuttle, E., 1990, Geology of national parks (4th edition): Dubuque, Kendall/Hunt Publishing, 652 p.

Hintze, L.F., 1988, Geologic History of Utah: Brigham Young University Geology Studies, Special Publication 7, 202 p.

Hunter, R.E., 1976, Comparison of eolian and subaqueous sand-flow cross strata [abs.]: American Association of Petroleum Geologists Bulletin, v. 60, p. 683-684.

—1977, Basic types of stratification in small eolian dunes: Sedimentology, v. 24, p. 361-387.

Imlay, R.W., 1980, Jurassic paleogeography of the conterminous United States in its continental setting: U.S. Geological Survey Professional Paper 1062, 134 p.

Knisley, C.B., and Hill, J.M., in press, Biology and conservation of the Coral Pink Sand Dunes tiger beetle, *Cicindela limbata albissima*: Western North American Naturalist, v. 60.

Lancaster, N., 1995, Geomorphology of desert dunes: London, Routledge, 290 p.

Maltin, L., editor, 1997, Movie and video guide (1998 edition): New York, Signet Reference, 1620 p.

Marzolf, J.E., 1988, Controls on late Paleozoic and early Mesozoic eolian deposition of the western United States: Sedimentary Geology, v. 56, p. 167-191.

McKee, E.D., 1979, Introduction to a study of global sand seas, in McKee, E.D., editor, A study of global sand seas: U.S. Geological Survey Professional Paper 1052, p. 1-19.

—1982, Sedimentary structures in dunes of the Namib Desert, South West Africa: Geological Society of America Special Paper 188, 64 p.

Morris, T.H., and Stubben, M.A., 1994, Geologic contrasts of the Great Basin and Colorado Plateau, *in* Harper,

K.T., St. Clair, L.L., Thorne, K.H., and Hess, W.M., editors, Natural history of the Colorado Plateau and Great Basin: Niwot, University of Colorado Press, p. 98-25.

Murphy, D.R., 1981, Climatic zones, *in* Atlas of Utah: Provo, Brigham Young University Press, p. 55.

Patton, P.C., Biggar, N., Condit, C.D., Gilliam, M.L., Love, D.W., Machette, M.N., Mayer, L, Morrison, R.B., and Rosholt, J.N., 1991, Quaternary geology of the Colorado Plateau, *in* Morrison, R.B., editor, Quaternary nonglacial geology - Coterminous U.S.: Boulder, Colorado, Geological Society of America, The Geology of North America, v. K-2, p. 373-406.

Peterson, Fred, 1988, Pennsylvanian to Jurassic eolian transportation systems in the western United States: Sedimentary Geology, v. 56, p. 207-260.

Peterson, Fred, and Turner-Peterson, C.E., 1989, Geology of the Colorado Plateau, *in* Hanshaw, P.M., editor, Sedimentation ands basin analysis in siliciclastic rock sequences, Volume 1, Field trips for the 28th International Geological Congress: Washington, D.C., American Geophysical Union, 65 p.

Pipiringos, G.N., and O'Sullivan, R.B., 1978, Principle unconformities in Triassic and Jurassic rocks, western interior United States - a preliminary survey: U.S. Geological Survey Professional Paper 1035-A, 29 p.

Pope, D., and Brough, C., 1996, Utah's weather and climate: Salt Lake City, Publishers Press, 245 p.

Pye, K., and Tsoar, H., 1990, Aeolian sand and sand dunes: London, Unwin Hyman, 396 p.

Ritter, D.F., Kochel, R.C., and Miller, J.R., 1995, Process geomorphology (3rd edition): Boston, WCB/McGraw-Hill, 546 p.

Sack, D., 1987, Geomorphology of the Lynndyl Dunes, west-central Utah, *in* Kopp, R.S., and Cohenour, R.E., editors, Cenozoic geology of western Utah - sites for precious metal and hydrocarbon accumulations: Utah Geological Association Publication 16, p. 291-299.

Sargent, K.A., and Philpott, B.C., 1987, Geologic map of the Kanab quadrangle, Kane County, Utah, and Coconino County, Arizona: U.S. Geological Survey Geologic Quadrangle Map GQ-1603, scale 1:62,500.

Shafer, D.S., 1989, Holocene climatic patterns inferred from pollen and macrofossil records of Holocene lakes of the northern Colorado Plateau, Utah and Arizona [abs.]: Geological Society of America Abstracts with Programs, v. 21, no. 5, p. 142.

Stanley, K.O., Jordan, W.M., and Dott, R.H., 1971, New hypothesis of Early Jurassic paleogeography and sediment dispersal for western United States: American Association of Petroleum Geologists Bulletin, v. 55, p. 10-19.

Stewart, J.H., 1971, Basin and Range structure - a system of horsts and grabens produced by deep seated extension: Geological Society of America Bulletin, v. 82, p. 1019-1050.

Stokes, S., 1994, Latest Holocene mobilisation (sic) events in the southwestern United States [abs.]: Geological Society of America Abstracts with Programs, v. 26, no. 7, p. A-89.

Stokes, W.L., 1986, Geology of Utah: Utah Museum of Natural History Occasional Paper 6, 309 p.

Summerfield, M.A., 1991, Global geomorphology: New York, Longman Scientific & Technical, 537 p.

Tilden, F., 1970, The national parks (revised and enlarged edition): New York, Alfred A. Knoff, 608 p.

Tsoar, H., and Moller, J.T., 1986, The role of vegetation in the formation of linear dunes, *in* Nickling, W.G., editor, Aeolian geomorphology (Proceedings of the 17th Annual Binghamton Geomorphology Symposium): Boston, Allen & Unwin, p. 75-95.

Utah State Parks and Recreation, no date, Coral Pink Sand Dunes State Park - geology of the park and surrounding area: Utah State Parks and Recreation brochure, 4 p.

Withers, K., and Mead, J.L., 1993, Late Quaternary vegetation and climate in the Escalante River basin on the central Colorado Plateau: Great Basin Naturalist, v. 53, p. 145-161.

Legends of Dead Horse Point

Bonnie J. Benson[1]

Dead Horse Point is truly a paradise for anyone who likes rocks and spectacular scenery. An abundance of both is present at the park as nearly 300 million years of the Earth's geologic history is revealed in the staggering panorama visible from The Point. Time and geologic forces have worked together to create a vista of canyon scenery rivaled with few equals. The geologic formations visible from Dead Horse Point each tell a story about the events that shaped them into the extraordinary forms we marvel at today. But what about the horses that gave the park its name? What happened to them and how do they fit into the fascinating saga of rock, wind, and water? The rocks were molded by the forces of nature and the resultant landscape played its role in the legend that enshrouds the place called Dead Horse Point.

Old timers around the area have told many legends about the origin of the name Dead Horse Point. Some stories are more believable than others, and a few are just downright fun, but the fact remains that no one seems to know how this particular promontory of sandstone acquired its grim epithet. One of the most widely believed stories (and the official park legend recounted by the rangers) about how Dead Horse Point got its name goes something like this:

Around the turn of the 19th century, bands of wild mustangs roamed the high windswept mesa top. Cowboys liked these hot-blooded horses because they were fast, smart, and free for the taking -- if they could be caught. The challenge was how to catch these clever, fleet-footed equines who did not want to be captured. Dead Horse Point provided just the right trap. To get on Dead Horse Point you have to negotiate a narrow track of land bounded on both sides by vertical sandstone cliffs that drop several hundred feet straight down. This feature of the park, referred to as The Neck, is about 30 yards wide and is the only connection between the mesa and the rock peninsula known as The Point.

One way the cowboys found to catch the wild horses was to herd them across The Neck and out onto The Point. They would then build a barrier of juniper branches across the neck, turning The Point into a natural corral. Look for the reconstructed fence on each side of the road as you drive out to Dead Horse Point. Since The Point is surrounded on all sides by sheer cliffs, there was no escape for the horses from this 40-acre enclosure. Here the cowboys could round up the horses, choose the ones they wanted, and let the culls or broomtails go free. Legend tells that one time the cowboys forgot to take down the fence when they left. A band of horses left corralled on The Point died a long, slow death of thirst within sight of the Colorado River far below.

Another twist on this particular legend says that the thirst-crazed horses trapped on The Point could see and smell the Colorado River below, and plunged to their deaths at the bottom of the sheer red-brown cliffs as they tried to get down to the water.

There is yet another legend associated with the dramatic Wingate Sandstone cliffs below The Point. The story tells of a diminutive cowboy called Shorty who had a pinto pony whom he called Paint. One day Shorty and Paint were riding on the mesa top looking for stray cows and enjoying the view. Since Shorty had been out late the night before, he decided it was time for a little siesta. It was a warm day, so he kicked off his boots, and took off his chaps, and settled down under a juniper tree with his hat down over his eyes, leaving Paint to graze. Well, being such a hot day, Paint got pretty thirsty and began looking around for some water. He wandered over to the cliff rim and spotted the Colorado River. Now although Paint was quite a fine horse, he had one minor problem: Paint was very near-sighted. Paint really needed spectacles, but Shorty couldn't afford to take him to the eye doctor. So Paint, seeing all that cool water down there, decided he would just mosey on over and get himself a nice long drink. Poor near-sighted Paint didn't realize that the water was 2,000 feet below him, and much to his surprise and astonishment, his first step sent him plummeting straight down into thin air!

At Dead Horse Point, there are some very strong thermals, or updrafts, created by the warming of the air around the cliffs in the sunshine on hot days. The ravens like to catch these thermals and use them to perform acrobatic stunts for fun. Well, as it happened, when Shorty had removed his chaps for his nap, he had tied them onto the horn of Paint's saddle for safe keeping. Amazingly, just as Paint was about to smash into smithereens on the rocks below, those chaps caught a hot-air thermal, started spinning around like a helicopter blade, and carried Paint right back up that cliff! It is a little hard to believe, but as you know Paint was a small pony and those thermals can be very strong. The only problem is that those darned thermals have an annoying habit of petering out at the rim of the cliff. Wouldn't you know it, just when he got up to the rim, poor Paint lost his thermal and went plummeting back down. As you may have guessed, Shorty was considerably upset about losing his favorite pony and the place known as Dead Horse Point.

While you admire the view and contemplate the rock strata from Dead Horse Point, you may notice a layer of light-colored rock near the Colorado River. This is called the White Rim Sandstone and it involves another, lesser known legend. Look closely, just to the left of the Gooseneck of the Colorado River. Can you see the shape of a horse in the white rock below? You don't have to have a very wild imagination to see: the legs, tail, back, withers, mane, ears, nose, and even an eye, looking right at you! Do you suppose that some giant, prehistoric horse could have stumbled off the big cliff thousands of years ago and left his impression in stone?

[1]*Utah Division of Parks and Recreation, Moab, Utah 84532*

Geology of Utah's Parks and Monuments
2000 Utah Geological Association Publication 28
D.A. Sprinkel, T.C. Chidsey, Jr., and P.B. Anderson, editors

Geology of Dead Horse Point State Park, Grand and San Juan Counties, Utah

Hellmut H. Doelling[1], Thomas C. Chidsey, Jr.[1], and Bonnie J. Benson[2]

ABSTRACT

Dead Horse Point State Park is in the heart of the Canyonlands region of Utah between Canyonlands and Arches National Parks. The view is spectacular, sublime, awe-inspiring, and majestic, and would be hard to surpass anywhere. The mood of the vista changes by season and time of day. One of nature's engineers, in this instance the Colorado River, has carved this arresting and striking panorama of colorful strata of Pennsylvanian to Jurassic age. Past structural events have locally folded and fractured these rocks in a manner that favored the deposition or accumulation of economic natural resource deposits. The signs of human activity to extract these deposits are apparent as one approaches the park or looks from the canyon edge.

Since the preeminent attraction of the park is its viewpoint, most of the unique sites associated with the park are not within its boundaries. Nevertheless, the visitor may hike about and see some typical characteristics of the Colorado Plateau region, such as sandstone, potholes, arches, microbiotic soil, and examples of plateau life. The myths and history associated with this state park add to the interesting geologic history that is inscribed in the rocks.

INTRODUCTION

Dead Horse Point State Park was created on December 18, 1959. It comprises about 5,300 acres of land, most on a mesa top. The elevation at Dead Horse Point (figure 1), near the observation shelter, is 5,933 feet. The Colorado River, at an elevation of about 3,950 feet, flows about 2,000 feet below Dead Horse Point. The park offers 10 miles of hiking and self-guided nature trails, interpretive exhibits, a junior ranger program, and ranger talks in the evenings. The observation shelter at The Point was erected in 1961, and the wheel-chair accessible Visitor Center was constructed in 1965. Stone walls along the edge of Dead Horse Point were emplaced in 1963, for the safety of park visitors.

Dead Horse Point State Park lies in the Bench and Canyonlands region of east-central Utah, between Arches and Canyonlands National Parks (figure 2). The nearest town is Moab, the Grand County seat, which lies about 35 miles east of the park by road. Moab is located about 240 miles southeast of Salt Lake City.

A layer of rock that is very important at Dead Horse Point State Park is the one we stand on: the Jurassic Kayen-

ta Formation. The Kayenta is the youngest geologic formation in the park; all younger layers above have been eroded away over the millennia. The Kayenta forms the resistant caprock that protects the softer cliffs in the Jurassic Wingate Sandstone from erosion, helping to keep them vertical. From The Neck, try to spot the obscure vertical arch in the Wingate Sandstone cliff to the west (figure 3). A thin sliver of light is visible through it for only a few hours each day at certain times of the year. Without the

Figure 1. View of the Gooseneck of the Colorado River from Dead Horse Point. Utah Division of Parks and Recreation photo.

[1]*Utah Geological Survey, Salt Lake City, UT 84114-6100*
[2]*Utah Division of Parks and Recreation, Moab, UT 84532*

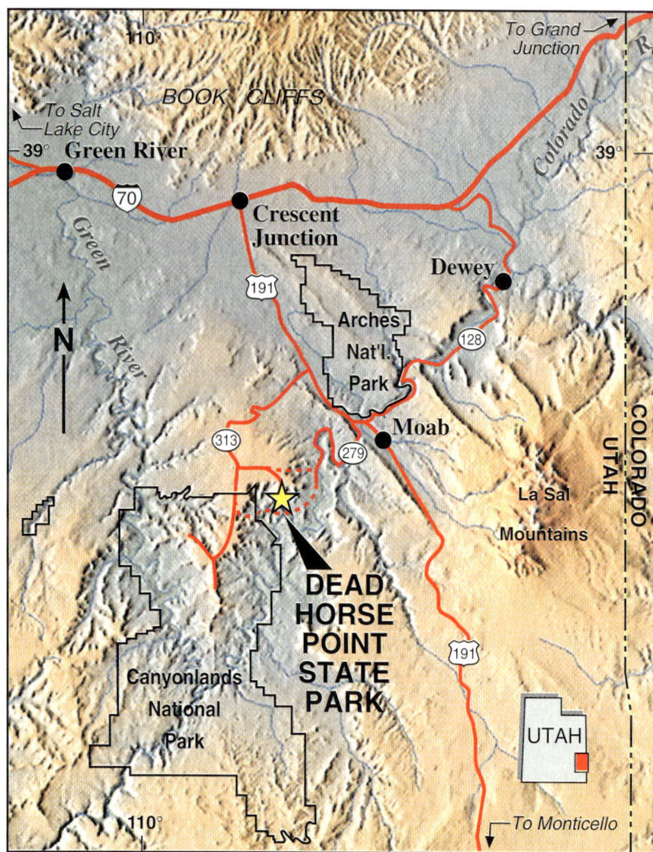

Figure 2. Index map to Dead Horse Point State Park showing surrounding towns, highways, and parks (modified from Hintze, 1997; topographic relief base map modified with permission, courtesy of Chalk Butte, Inc., Boulder, Wyoming).

Figure 3. Jug-handle arch at Dead Horse Point. A thin sliver of light is visible through it for only a few hours each day at certain times of the year. Note the vertical nature of the Wingate Sandstone cliff capped by the more ledgy Kayenta Formation.

Figure 4. Dinosaur footprint in the Kayenta Formation at Dead Horse Point State Park. U.S. quarter for scale.

Kayenta, The Neck would erode through and The Point would collapse into the river. The Kayenta Formation is also interesting because it contains dinosaur tracks (figure 4).

Another interesting thing to look for in the Kayenta while hiking at Dead Horse Point are the depressions called potholes (figure 5). These often water-filled potholes, also called waterpockets, tanks, or tinajas in some regions, are natural catchment basins for rainwater and snowmelt. They are created when water seeps into the sandstone and dissolves the calcium carbonate cement that holds the grains of sand together. A shallow depression is formed where more rainwater and snowmelt can collect, continuing to erode and enlarge the pool. Most potholes are only a few inches deep, but some become very deep and will hold water for months at a time or even year-round in wet years. Sometimes, given enough time and the right conditions, a pothole will erode through a cliff overhang and form a pothole arch. Potholes contain the only water on the mesa top, but are not particularly reliable sources, especially during long dry periods.

Potholes create fascinating miniature ecosystems. They are home to creatures that have developed extraordinary adaptations for survival in extreme conditions. They are sensitive to very minute changes, even when they are

Figure 5. Potholes in the Kayenta Formation, Dead Horse Point State Park.

dry, so be careful not to disturb them. There are some very deep potholes in the Kayenta Formation. However, these deeper potholes are not out on The Point. They are located a few miles back to the north along the rim of the east fork of Shafer Canyon. Some of these pools are so deep and very sheer-sided that occasionally animals who try to drink water from them have the sad misfortune of getting down in and not being able to get back out again. Indeed, another legend about how the park got its name claims that some poor thirsty horse fell into a nearby pothole and drowned! (see Legends of Dead Horse Point State Park on page 390)

Maybe you have a favorite legend or just want to make up one of your own. Or perhaps you have a favorite rock with a story to tell. Whether you are partial to views, rocks, or you just like a good old-fashioned horse story, at Dead Horse Point the legend is in the landscape.

STRATIGRAPHY AND DEPOSITIONAL HISTORY

Consolidated sedimentary rocks seen in the vistas from Dead Horse Point include strata of Late Pennsylvanian to Early Jurassic age. These strata have a cumulative thickness of 2,700 to 3,600 feet depending on which direction you look (figure 6). The panoramic views from The Point encompass much more area than is contained in the legal limits of the park. Within this area changes in the strata's color, percentage of rock types, thickness, composition, or weathering habit allow geologists to interpret the geologic processes, environments, and history that formed this area of magnificent sights.

Pennsylvanian Rocks

Pennsylvanian rocks were deposited in a subsiding basin beneath a restricted sea or embayment of an ocean that extended to the west of the park. To the northeast of this embayment, a land mass, known as the Uncompahgre Highland, emerged and rose. The boundary between the embayment and mountainous uplift was a sharp north-west-trending fault that lay to the northeast of Dead Horse Point. Rivers and streams carried the erosional debris from the mountains to the embayment where it was deposited. The uplift did not occur at a uniform rate. When the mountains rose rapidly, more erosional debris and sediment was dumped into the embayment and moved farther to the southwest. When the uplift slowed, only marine precipitates, such as gypsum, limestone, and salt were deposited in the embayment. In Middle Pennsylvanian time, when the Paradox Formation was laid down, the embayment became cut off from open-ocean circulation and thick salt was deposited. In Late Pennsylvanian time, when the Honaker Trail Formation was laid down, ocean waters freely circulated into the subsiding embayment, which continued to receive erosional debris shed from the Uncompahgre Highland.

Paradox Formation

Although not exposed in the area observed from Dead Horse Point, the Paradox Formation has played an important role here. It was deposited some 315 to 310 million years ago as a marine deposit consisting of layered salts, anhydrite, shale, siltstone, limestone, and dolomite. These rocks were laid down within the subsiding basin in cycles that alternated from restricted-marine conditions with limited communication to the ocean to open-marine conditions where the connection with the ocean was unimpeded and waters circulated freely into the embayment. More often than not, physical barriers were established that cut off circulation with the ocean. The area had a hot, dry climate with high rates of evaporation. As the water evaporated, the dissolved chemical matter (salts which all ocean waters carry) was precipitated out in the bottom of the bay. Most of this salt is halite (NaCl) or common table salt. However, at times the magnesium and potassium content of the seawater increased to the point where sylvite (KCl) and carnallite ($KC1 \cdot MgCl_2 \cdot 6H_2O$) were also deposited. A typical cycle began when connection with the open ocean was reestablished, and limestone and dark shales were deposited; ensuing evaporation led to deposition of dolomite, gypsum, and finally salt. Geologists have defined as many as 29 such depositional cycles in the Paradox Formation.

The Paradox Formation is probably 3,000 to 5,500 feet thick beneath the area one can see from Dead Horse Point. Of this amount, 75 percent consists of soluble salts. A single salt bed may be as much as 300 feet thick. Salt beds are much more ductile and less dense than the rocks that contain them, and buoyant forces often cause them to exchange places with the overlying heavier beds of rock. As a result of forces active deep in the Earth's crust, the salt locally moved to lines of weaknesses such as faults. The salt was literally squeezed into these weak zones by the weight of the rock deposited on top of it. Moab Valley, east of Dead Horse Point, is aligned along one of these weak zones. Moab Valley is underlain by a wall of salt that is more than 10,000 feet thick and more than a mile wide. In

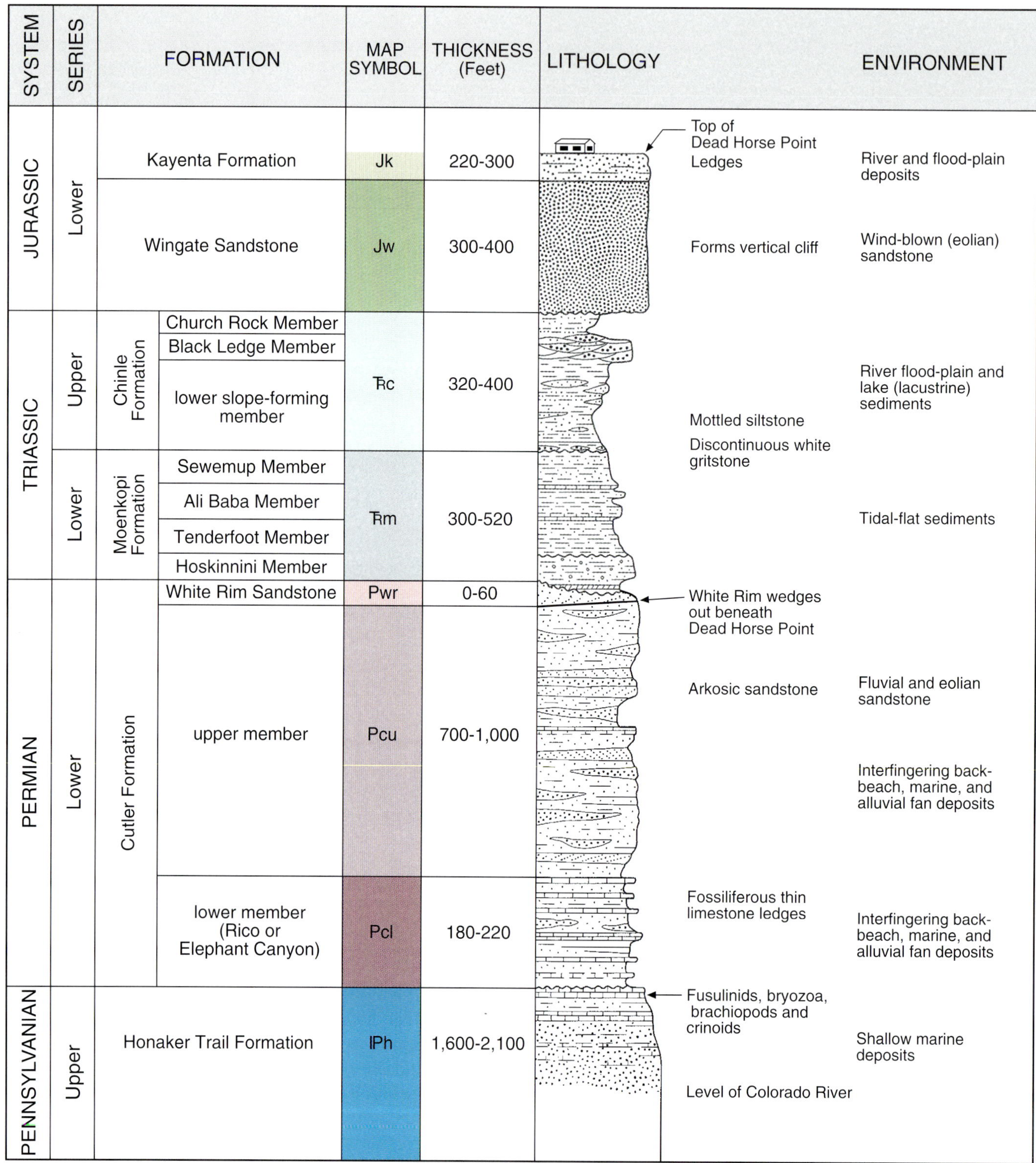

Figure 6. Lithologic column showing formations and members exposed below Dead Horse Point, including environments of deposition, thickness, age, weathering habits, and lithology. See also figure 8.

the Dead Horse Point area, the salt locally formed bulges, pushing up and raising overlying strata, while in intervening areas the salt was squeezed and thinned. The process involved salt recrystallization. Pressure on salt crystals causes them to dissolve and to recrystallize in areas of lower pressure. This is something like in a tube of toothpaste. If you keep the cap on and push in the middle, the ends will bulge. If you remove the cap the paste (salt) will move out of the tube as it did in the Moab Valley area.

Two of these bulges can readily be seen from Dead Horse Point. These bulges are called anticlines (when elongate) or domes (when circular) by geologists. The most obvious is the Cane Creek anticline, seen looking northeast of Dead Horse Point. Rock strata can be seen

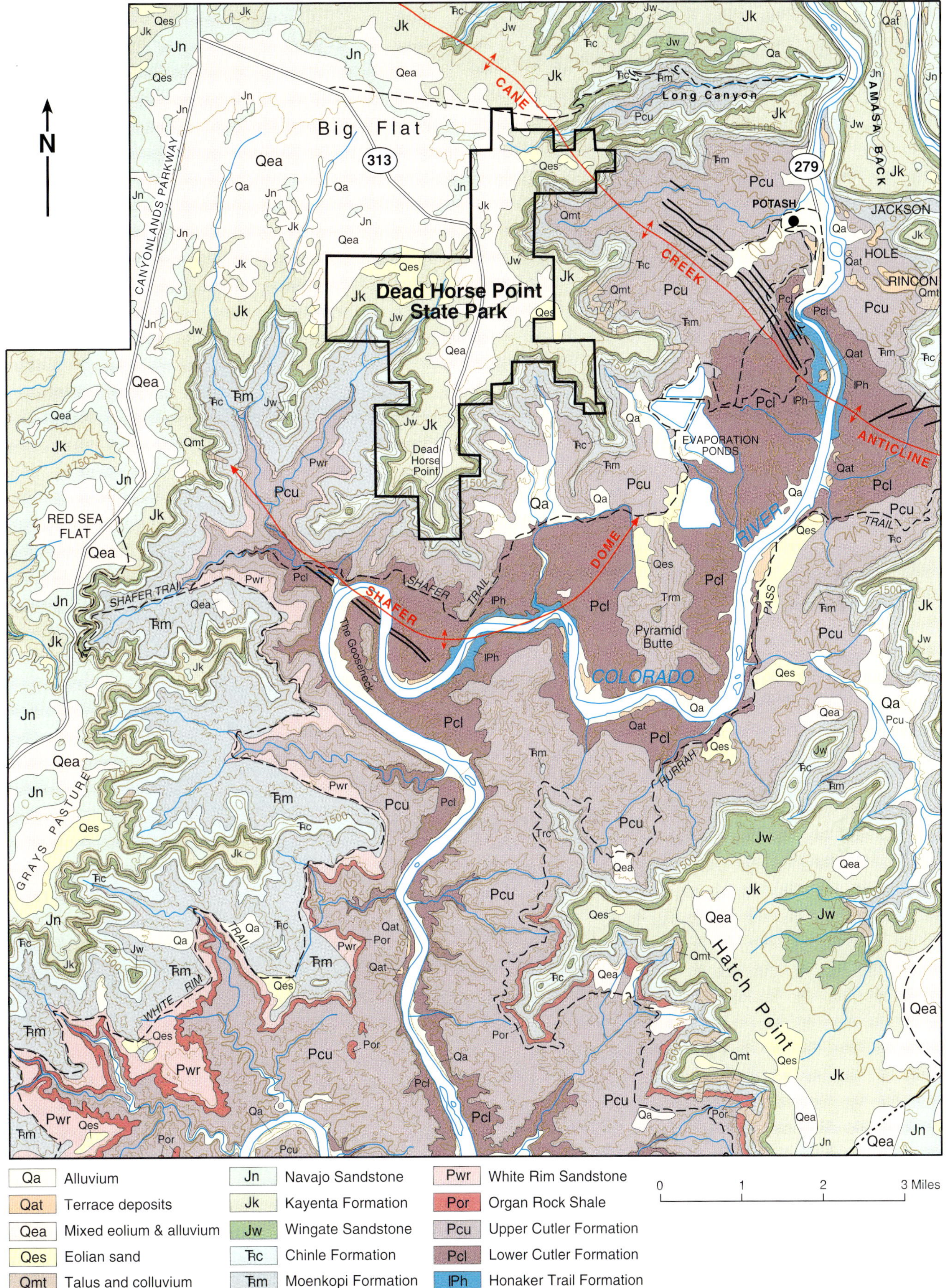

Qa — Alluvium
Qat — Terrace deposits
Qea — Mixed eolium & alluvium
Qes — Eolian sand
Qmt — Talus and colluvium
Jn — Navajo Sandstone
Jk — Kayenta Formation
Jw — Wingate Sandstone
Ŧrc — Chinle Formation
Ŧrm — Moenkopi Formation
Pwr — White Rim Sandstone
Por — Organ Rock Shale
Pcu — Upper Cutler Formation
Pcl — Lower Cutler Formation
IPh — Honaker Trail Formation

0   1   2   3 Miles

Figure 7. Geologic map of the Dead Horse Point area, Grand and San Juan Counties, Utah (modified from Hinrichs and others, 1967; Huntoon and others, 1982; Doelling, 1993).

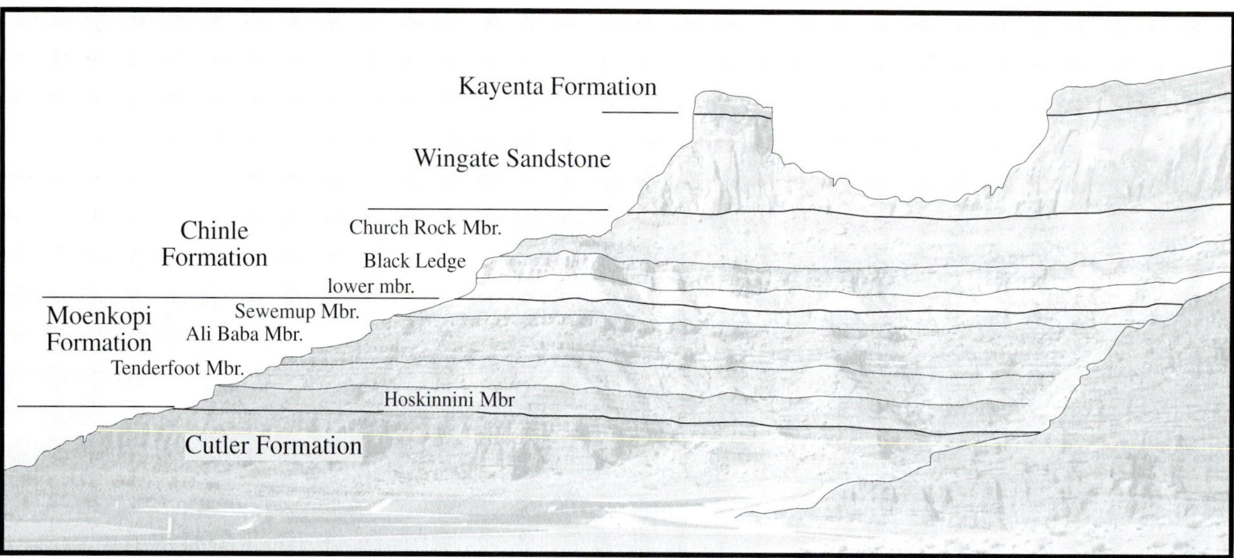

Figure 8. Profile of rocks exposed in the Dead Horse Point area, showing contacts of most formations given on figure 6. Solar evaporation ponds associated with potash production are in the lower left corner.

bending up and over the buried salt bulge. The Shafer dome or anticline can be seen near the Gooseneck of the Colorado River and immediately below Dead Horse Point. Additional discussion of the Cane Creek and Shafer anticlines is given in the section on structural geology.

Honaker Trail Formation

Like the Paradox Formation, most of the Honaker Trail Formation is found in the subsurface. However, the uppermost strata of the formation are exposed on the tops of the anticlines and domes, as a part of the structures (bulges) that elevate the older rocks (figure 7). The outcrops expose interbedded sandstone, limestone, and siltstone, the same lithologies found in subsurface drill-hole samples. The sandstone is mostly yellow gray to gray, very fine to fine grained, well to moderately sorted, micaceous, and calcareous. Some beds are cross-bedded. Bedding is thick to massive (figure 6). Limestone interbeds are gray to very light gray, variably argillaceous (clayey), and are 1 to 10 feet thick. Some of the limestone beds are fossiliferous, containing a marine fauna of crinoid debris, brachiopods, bryozoans, gastropods, foraminifera, and rare trilobites. The siltstone is micaceous, green to yellow-gray, is locally bioturbated (contains worm burrows), and is cross-stratified.

The Honaker Trail Formation was deposited in the same embayment as the Paradox Formation. However, the circulation of seawater with the open ocean was no longer impeded. Deposition was in very shallow water and the deposits were laid down in shallow marine, beach, lagoonal, and deltaic depositional environments. Some of the rocks contain terrestrial plant remains (Melton, 1972). Identified marine fusulinids indicate a latest Pennsylvanian age (Virgilian) for the Honaker Trail Formation below Dead Horse Point (Doelling and others, 1994). The formation was deposited between 305 and 295 million years ago.

Figure 9. Panorama from the The Gooseneck of the Colorado River on the left (south) and the Shafer Trail in the center; Permian Cutler Formation at river level to Jurassic Navajo Sandstone on the skyline in the distance in Canyonlands National Park (left of center). Dead Horse Point is in the transition area between the areas where Cutler facies change. The point where the White Rim Sandstone pinches out is visible below Dead Horse Point (right of center). In this area, beds below the White Rim Sandstone are more like the northeast facies than the other four formations of the Cutler Group. Thus, these arkosic beds are considered Cutler Formation. View south-southwest to west from Dead Horse Point Overlook.

From subsurface data we learn that the total Honaker Trail Formation is 1,600 to 2,100 feet thick. The contact between the Pennsylvanian Honaker Trail Formation and the overlying Permian rocks is a paraconformity--rocks above and below the contact show little or no erosional relief, with beds of both formations parallel to one another but separated by a 10 million year time gap.

Permian Rocks

During the Permian, the Uncompahgre Highland to the northeast continued to rise, and erosion eventually exposed granitic and mafic (iron-manganese-rich) rocks that were very old (Proterozoic, 570 to 2,000 million years old). The clastic erosional debris shed to the southwest into the Dead Horse Point area was deposited as a series of alluvial fans at the foot of the mountain range; the embayment was filled and the ocean shorelines retreated farther to the southwest. The iron content of the source rocks imparted a red coloration to the rocks deposited in this area. Granites, made up of quartz, feldspar, mica, and small percentages of dark iron-bearing minerals, were eroded and provided source material for sandstones rich in feldspar, or arkoses. The Permian rocks below Dead Horse Point were deposited between 285 to 270 million years ago.

Permian rocks in the Dead Horse Point area are part of the Cutler Formation/Group. Northeast of Dead Horse Point, these rocks are part of a thick sequence of conglomeratic, arkosic alluvial-fan sediments deposited in front of the Uncompahgre Highland and are given formation status (figures 6 and 8). These strata grade southwest into fluvial, coastal dune, and tidal flat deposits that are exposed in Canyonlands National Park southwest of Dead Horse Point, and are divided into five units (see Baars, Geology of Canyonlands National Park, this volume). In that area, the Cutler is elevated to group status and the five units are considered formations. The upper formation is the White Rim Sandstone. Dead Horse Point is in the transition between these areas. The point where the White Rim Sandstone pinches out is visible below Dead Horse Point (figure 9). In this area, beds below the White Rim Sandstone are more like the northeast facies than the other four formations of the Cutler Group. Thus, these arkosic beds are still considered Cutler Formation. They are divided into informal upper and lower members. In other geologic publications, the lower member has been given the names Rico (McKnight, 1940) or Elephant Canyon Formation (Huntoon and others, 1982). However, the validity of these names is still debated and they are not used here.

The upper and lower members of the Cutler Formation are similar and consist of interbedded arkosic sandstone, subarkosic sandstone, sandstone, conglomerate, micaceous siltstone, and limestone. Many of the arkosic and subarkosic sandstone beds display trough cross-bedding, and cut-and-fill structures indicating deposition by rivers and streams (fluvial deposition). Conglomeratic lenses locally contain pieces of granite as much as 6 inches in diameter. Quartzose sandstones are mostly fine grained, well sorted, and micaceous. Many were deposited by the wind (eolian deposited). The eolian rocks are mostly orange and red-orange, whereas the fluvially deposited arkoses, subarkoses, and conglomerates are dark red to purple. The gray limestones are marine deposits laid down during short intervals when the sea was able to push shorelines northeastward. These beds are more prevalent in the lower member of the Cutler Formation and form the basis for dividing the lower from the upper member. The number of limestone beds decreases northeastward. These are locally fossiliferous, containing brachiopods, bryozoans, gastropods, crinoid debris, and rare cephalopods and trilobites.

The White Rim Sandstone is only present southwest of Dead Horse Point and forms a white rim around the Island-in-the-Sky in Canyonlands National Park. The White Rim is a fine- to medium-grained quartzose sandstone exhibiting both planar and cross-stratified beds. The White Rim formed as a near-shore, beach, and back-beach deposit.

The upper contact of the Permian strata with the overlying Triassic beds is sharp, marked by local scouring and channeling and is unconformable. In most cases the plane of unconformity appears flat. The unconformity is regional and indicates a period of non-deposition lasting at least 30 to 35 million years. The lower member of the Cutler Formation is 220 to 350 feet thick. The upper member of the Cutler Formation is 600 to 800 feet thick in the Dead Horse Point area. The White Rim Sandstone is 0 to 250 feet thick, thinning to the northeast.

Triassic Rocks

The Triassic Period is represented by the Moenkopi and Chinle Formations. During Moenkopi time, the open sea or ocean retreated farther to the southwest and deposition in the area was from sluggish streams migrating over broad tidal flats that were at or near sea level. The Uncompahgre Highlands to the northeast were now much lower and the sediments derived from them contain much mica. During Chinle time, deposition was dominated by fluvial environments and the influence of the sea was gone. Toward the end of Chinle time, the highlands of the Uncompahgre were completely leveled, and the terrain there began to subside and receive sediments. Moenkopi deposits were laid down approximately 244 million years ago (Ma) and again between 242 and 238 Ma. Chinle deposits were laid down about 220 to 215 Ma. Events occurring between Moenkopi and Chinle time are not recorded by rocks. Sediments may have been deposited during these 18 million years and then eroded.

Moenkopi Formation

The Moenkopi Formation is divided into four members in the Dead Horse Point area (figures 6 and 8), which in ascending order are: Hoskinnini, Tenderfoot, Ali Baba, and Sewemup (Sew-em-up). All four members total about 300 to 520 feet thick at Dead Horse Point. Thicknesses of the four members vary independently.

The Hoskinnini Member consists mostly of a chocolate-brown, fine-grained, poorly sorted, micaceous to sub-arkosic sandstone. It is poorly bedded, and displays irregular to wavy laminae. Locally, it has a thin bed of gypsum near the base (especially in Long Canyon). It forms a steep slope in its lower part and a cliff in its upper part. The Hoskinnini Member is generally 60 to 110 feet thick in the Dead Horse Point area. Its upper contact with the Tenderfoot Member is generally sharp and is considered an

unconformity leaving as much as 2 million years with no record.

The Tenderfoot Member forms a 100- to 160-foot-thick slope of light chocolate-brown, thin-bedded siltstone with widely spaced, 1- to 3-foot-thick sandstone ledges. Ripple cross-stratification is particularly widespread.

The Ali Baba Member forms a 100- to 160-foot-thick series of chocolate-brown ledges and slopes. It consists of thin- to medium-bedded siltstone with numerous sandstone beds. The sandstone beds are 1 to 10 feet thick and display low-angle cross-stratification. The Ali Baba Member locally contains a thin, yellow-gray limestone and calcareous siltstone at its base, which may correlate with the Sinbad Member of the Moenkopi Formation in the San Rafael Swell and Circle Cliffs areas of Utah.

The Sewemup Member is a 60- to 120-foot-thick slope-forming unit consisting of homogeneous, gray-red to pale-red-brown siltstone, with widely spaced, thin (less than 3 feet thick) sandstone ledges. The siltstone displays horizontal and ripple cross-lamination, and is criss-crossed by thin gypsum veinlets. The contact with the overlying Chinle Formation is sharp and unconformable, but commonly poorly exposed. It is placed at the base of a distinctive white to mottled gritstone, or between the gray-red or gray-green mudstone and siltstone of the lower part of the Chinle and the orange-red siltstones of the upper part of the Moenkopi.

Chinle Formation

The Chinle Formation is divided into three members in the cliffs below Dead Horse Point: a lower slope-forming member, the Black Ledge, and an upper Church Rock Member (figures 6 and 8). The formation consists of complex interbedding and lensing arrangements of sandstone, pebble conglomerate, siltstone, mudstone, and rare limestone. The red-brown, tan, and gray-red sandstones are very fine to coarse grained, moderately to well sorted, quartzose, and slightly micaceous. Primary sedimentary structures include low-angle cross-stratification, horizontal stratification, asymmetric ripples, and channeling, all of which point to deposition in fluvial and lacustrine environments (stream channel, floodplain, and lake environments). Soft-sediment deformation, including disharmonic folds and low-angle detachments, is common, especially below thick sandstone ledges. Pebble and intraformational conglomerates occur as lenses and in scour channels concentrated in the lower parts of sandstone beds. Quartzose and micaceous siltstone is interbedded with the sandstones and conglomerates, and displays low-angle cross-stratification and ripple lamination. Mudstone is gray-red to gray-green, bentonitic, and poorly exposed. A few gray-red nodular limestone beds are locally present.

White to variegated gritstone locally marks the base of the Chinle Formation. The grit is poorly sorted, and contains rounded to angular, coarse to pebble-sized grains of quartz. Where variegated, the gritstone may have existed as a paleosol (ancient soil). Mudstones and siltstones dominate in the lower slope-forming member. Sandstones and conglomerate channels, when found in the lower slope-forming member, are locally mineralized with uranium, vanadium, and copper minerals. Finely divided carbonaceous plant debris is abundant in these channels. The lighter overall color of this lower member is caused by the reduced iron in this part of the formation. This reduction of iron commonly extends as much as 3 feet into the underlying Moenkopi Formation. The lower slope-forming member is 70 to 90 feet thick, and the upper contact is abrupt.

The Black Ledge is dominated by red-brown sandstone and black, desert varnish-stained conglomerate. The sandstones commonly contain scattered logs and branches of petrified wood. Lowermost lenses of sandstone are locally mineralized with uranium and copper minerals. The Black Ledge is about 90 to 110 feet thick. The upper contact is gradational into the Church Rock Member.

The Church Rock Member is mostly a red-brown sandstone and siltstone, but sandstone ledges are more common in the lower part. The bedding in much of this unit is indistinct, and the rock breaks into equidimensional fragments. Blocky, red-brown, fine-grained, well-sorted, thick-bedded sandstone, that mimics the overlying Wingate Sandstone, is common in the upper 10 to 30 feet of the member. The Wingate Sandstone, however, rarely contains distinct bedding-plane partings as found in the Church Rock Member. These upper sandstones have informally been referred to as the Hite beds. The Church Rock Member is 160 to 200 feet thick.

The contact of the Church Rock Member with the overlying Wingate Sandstone is sharp and accordant (disconformable) in most areas, commonly being placed below the massive cliff of well-sorted sandstone typical of the Wingate. No regional channeling or angular unconformity is apparent. Nevertheless, most investigators believe an erosional hiatus is present between the two formations that may account for 15 million years of geologic history.

Jurassic Rocks

With the exception of the modern (Quaternary) unconsolidated sediments, Jurassic strata form the top of the geologic column at Dead Horse Point. These strata include the Wingate Sandstone, Kayenta Formation, and Navajo Sandstone, and were deposited between 205 and 187 Ma. The Wingate and Navajo were deposited in a sand-dune desert, the Kayenta in a flood-plain environment. A few sandstone beds in the upper Kayenta were also deposited by the wind.

Wingate Sandstone

The Wingate Sandstone is a prominent cliff former below the promenade at Dead Horse Point, and below the Island-in-the Sky bench to the southwest (figures 6 and 8). The Wingate forms red-brown, nearly vertical cliffs streaked and stained with desert varnish. The Chinle and

Moenkopi slopes below the cliff are generally littered with large blocks of the Wingate Sandstone (figure 8). Partings or bedding planes are rare in the Wingate which is commonly described as one massive unit. The Wingate consists mostly of light-orange-brown, moderate-orange-pink, or pale-red-brown, fine-grained, well-sorted, cross-bedded sandstone. The rock is usually well cemented and well indurated; weathered exposures are nearly smooth. The Wingate is a wind-blown sand deposit as indicated by the high-angle cross-beds.

The formation is 300 to 400 feet thick in the Dead Horse Point area. The contact of the Wingate with the overlying Kayenta Formation is generally sharp and conformable, but difficult to identify. Generally, the line is placed at the horizon where the smooth cliff is replaced by thick cliffy ledges.

Kayenta Formation

The Kayenta Formation caps most of the upper benches at Dead Horse Point and is the unit on which one stands (figures 1, 6, 7, and 8). The Kayenta consists mostly of stream-deposited sandstone lenses, with lesser amounts of eolian sandstone, intraformational conglomerate, siltstone, and shale. The unit is primarily red, but individual lenses and beds vary considerably in color; some are purple, lavender, tan, orange, or white. In outcrop, the Kayenta is ledgy and step-like. Sandstone in the Kayenta exhibits both high-angle and low-angle cross-bedding. Some lenses display channeling, current ripple marks, and rare slump features. The grain size is more variable than in the Wingate and Navajo, ranging mostly from fine to medium. Siltstone, shale, and intraformational conglomerate appear as partings or are interlayered with the sandstone. These softer constituents are rare in the lower half of the formation and become common in the upper part.

The Kayenta Formation is 220 to 300 feet thick in the Dead Horse Point area. It forms the bench tops and is rarely completely exposed. The upper contact is mostly sharp, but intertonguing between the Kayenta and the overlying Navajo Sandstone is common. Remnants of the Navajo Sandstone rest on the benches, and at least at Dead Horse Point, are far from the cliff edge.

Navajo Sandstone

Navajo Sandstone is mostly seen as cliffy to rounded bare-rock exposures. The lower parts are cliffy and the tops are commonly rounded. The Navajo is a classic example of an eolian (wind-deposited) unit.

The Navajo is a mostly orange to light-gray, mostly fine grained, generally well-sorted, massive sandstone. Locally, thin, hard, lenticular gray limestone (lacustrine) is also found in the unit, and is interpreted to have developed in oases, playas, or interdune lakes (Stokes, 1991). Partings, where present, occur at the contacts of cross-bed sets, which are as much as 20 feet thick. High-angle, cross-bed laminae lie as much as 30 degrees from the true attitude of the unit. Navajo cross-beds etch out in relief in contrast to the smooth-weathering habit of the Wingate Sandstone. The top of this formation is not exposed in the Dead Horse Point area.

Quaternary Deposits

Quaternary deposits are the most recent sediments deposited in the Dead Horse Point area (figure 7). They are the products of weathering and erosion, and are in the process of being transported by the Colorado River and its tributaries to the sea. Gravity and wind work the rock outcrops, break them up, and move the debris short distances from their original locations. Torrential rains, which occur sporadically each summer, pick up these accumulated materials and transport them to the river.

Essentially these unconsolidated rock materials are temporary deposits. As older materials move riverward and down the river, additional erosional debris is manufactured. The Colorado Plateau, the larger area in which the Canyonlands and Dead Horse Point are found, has been rising for the last 15 million years while the Colorado River and its tributaries continue to cut deeper and deeper into the bedrock. What you see from Dead Horse Point may change little in your lifetime, but has changed dramatically in geologic time.

Modern Alluvium

Alluvium is stream-deposited unconsolidated sand and gravel intermixed with silt and minor clay. This is the material found beneath the water in the Colorado River channel and on the floodplain of the river. Generally, the coarser materials are found nearest the river, and the finer materials on the floodplain. During the spring runoff, when the mountain snows melt, or when torrential summer storms strike, the river water may escape its channel and sand, silt, and clay may be deposited on its floodplain. During these floods, the river may abandon its channel, form a new one, destroy part of its old floodplain, and gain access to fresh bedrock on one side of the canyon or the other. The important tributaries and washes act in the same manner.

Because the drainage basin of the Colorado River is very large, much of the gravel it carries has come from distant places upstream. The cobbles and pebbles include Tertiary volcanic rocks (from the La Sal Mountains), Precambrian high-grade metamorphic rocks (banded gneiss from the Uncompahgre uplift that straddles the Colorado-Utah line), and Paleozoic and Mesozoic sandstone and limestone from the local area. Tributaries and washes generally contain only the gravels and sands derived from the bedrock of the immediate area.

The Colorado River is classed as a superposed stream. It crosses structures formed long before it began to flow. The Colorado River probably came into existence synchronously with the uplift of the plateau. As it flowed across softer, younger formations it meandered back and forth. However, as the downcutting proceeded into hard, resistant cliff-formers, it entrenched its meandering course.

Terrace Gravel Deposits

Terrace gravel deposits have the same composition as that of modern alluvium. They represent old channel deposits now stranded above the current level of the drainages (figure 7). The proof that many of these gravels were deposited by the ancestral Colorado River is found in the igneous and quartzitic cobbles they contain, which were derived from rocks exposed many miles upstream.

Prominent terraces are found 30 to 40 feet, 70 to 100 feet, at 200 feet, 240 to 260 feet, 320 to 340 feet, and at 450 feet above the present river level. The highest are the oldest remaining channel deposits of the river. Willis (1994) obtained an age of 620,000 years for a volcanic ash found in a terrace a little over 300 feet above current river levels; this gives us some idea of how quickly the downcutting has taken place.

Many of these terraces are nicely displayed in the Jackson Hole rincon, opposite Potash to the east of Dead Horse Point. The river meandered through this rincon before it was able to straighten out its course.

Mixed Eolian and Alluvial Deposits

The Colorado River had more difficulty cutting through the hard, cliff-forming formations, such as the Wingate Sandstone and lower part of the Kayenta Formation. The softer units above were stripped off, leaving relatively flat benches, such as on Dead Horse Point itself. Drainages developed on these benches are generally weak when compared with the Colorado River and its more important tributaries below. These drainages are mainly washes that are dry most of the time. Mixed eolian and alluvial deposits cover large areas of the benches. Eolian sand and silt fills hollows on these table-lands, which become significantly modified by sheetwash and shallow-channel flow.

These deposits consist mostly of well-sorted, very fine to medium-grained sand and silt that have been reworked and mixed with gravel from surrounding bedrock areas by fluvial processes. The uppermost surfaces of these deposits are dominated by wind-blown sand and silt.

Eolian Sand and Sand Dune Areas

Eolian, or wind-blown, sand deposits are found locally on the benches and in protected areas beneath the benches. The wind-blown material occurs in sheets or undulatory dunes, and consist of light red-orange to light red-brown, fine- to medium-grained, quartz-rich sand. Much of this sand is stabilized by vegetation, and active transport is limited. On the benches, these deposits commonly grade into the mixed eolian and alluvial deposits. The sand is locally derived, and some may have been winnowed out of the mixed eolian and alluvial deposits.

Talus and Colluvium

Talus and colluvium commonly mantle the steep slopes beneath vertical cliffs. This material includes rock-

Figure 10. Panorama of the Cane Creek anticline (middle ground), solar evaporation ponds, with jointed Navajo outcrops of the Behind the Rocks area in front of the La Sal Mountains in the distance. The Jurassic Kayenta Formation forms the rim of the overlook followed down section by Wingate, Chinle, Moenkopi, and Cutler at the base. View east from between Dead Horse Point Overlook and The Neck. Monolith at left is the same as on figure 8.

fall blocks, and muddy sand, silt, and clay derived from the weathering of the slope-forming rock. Now generally removed from the action of running water, the higher cliffs recede as the softer slope-forming rocks beneath them weather and are slowly removed by creep and sheetwash to develop a recess. Fractures then open in the hard rock above, and large slabs of the cliff eventually crash down onto the slope below and break up into smaller pieces called talus. Colluvium is the weathered surface material of softer rocks that has moved by gravity creep and sheetwash.

STRUCTURAL AND GEOLOGIC HISTORY

Regional Setting

Dead Horse Point State Park is located in a region known as the Paradox fold and fault belt of the Paradox basin. This structural belt extends southeast from here into Colorado and is characterized by a series of northwest-trending anticlines and faults that developed in response to movement caused by crustal forces or by shallow deposits of Pennsylvanian salt.

The most obvious structural feature observed from Dead Horse Point State Park is the spectacular Cane Creek anticline that fills the panoramic view to the east (figure 10). The events that caused this and other structural features to form in the region began over a billion years ago during the Precambrian (Proterozoic) and continues to the present.

The Paradox basin of southeastern Utah and southwestern Colorado, like the fold and fault belt within it, is an elongate, northwest-southeast-trending evaporitic basin that predominantly developed during Pennsylvanian (Desmoinesian) time about 330 to 310 Ma. However, the stage was set for development of many of its structural features in the Proterozoic when movement began on high-angle basement faults and fractures 1,700 to 1,600 Ma (Stevenson and Baars, 1987).

During the Pennsylvanian, a pattern of basin and fault-bounded uplifts developed in the area of what is now Utah to Oklahoma, possibly the result of the collision of South America, Africa, and southeastern North America (Kluth and Coney, 1981; Kluth, 1986), or the result of a smaller scale collision of a microcontinent with south-central North America (Harry and Mickus, 1998). One result of this tectonic event was the uplift of the Ancestral Rockies in the western United States. The Uncompahgre Highland of eastern Utah and western Colorado formed the westernmost range of the Ancestral Rockies during this ancient mountain-building period. The Uncompahgre Highland (uplift) is bounded along its southwestern flank by a large basement-involved, high-angle reverse fault. This fault has been identified from geophysical seismic surveys and exploration drilling. As the mountains rose, movement along this fault caused an accompanying depression, a foreland basin, to form to the southwest -- the Paradox basin (see Huntoon and others, this volume). Rapid basin subsidence, particularly during the Pennsylvanian and into the Permian, accommodated deposition of large volumes of deeper basin evaporitic and marine sediments which intertongued with basin-margin non-marine arkosic material shed from the mountain area to the northeast (Hintze, 1993).

Later, the Uncompahgre Highland was eroded down during the Triassic and Jurassic. The area was uplifted again during the Late Cretaceous and early Tertiary Laramide orogeny to form the Uncompahgre uplift observed today (Stokes, 1986; Hintze, 1993). Also, periodic movement of the deep basement-involved faults underlying the Paradox basin continued during both the Laramide and earlier Cretaceous Sevier (to the west) orogenies (Shoemaker and others, 1958; Cater, 1970; Case and Joesting, 1973; Friedman and others, 1994).

Figure 11. *Panorama of the north-dipping Permian Cutler Formation of the Shafer anticline (center and left in bottom of the photo), Pyramid Butte (left), and the Colorado River; Abajo Mountains in the distance (right). The light band in the distant cliffs is in the lower part of the Chinle with the vertical cliffs of the Wingate above. View to southeast from between Dead Horse Point Overlook and The Neck.*

Salt Movement

Salt, which was deposited as part of the Paradox Formation, has a low specific gravity, behaves plastically, and moves when under high confining pressure from the weight of the overlying column of rocks or sediments. This movement (often piercing the strata above [diapiric movement]) progresses along zones of weakness or areas of low confining pressure, forming large folds such as the Cane Creek and Shafer anticlines (figures 7, 10, and 11). The weak zones likely developed above and along the northwest-trending basement faults in the region which experienced continued movement (Shoemaker and others, 1958). Salt-cored anticline development has been active intermittently from the Pennsylvanian to the present day (Shoemaker and others, 1958; Cater, 1970; Case and Joesting, 1973; Baars and Doelling, 1987; Doelling, 1988; Oviatt, 1988).

During the Permian-Triassic, rapid diapiric salt movement caused the crests of some of these features to influence surface topography and depositional patterns. Sediments were deposited as thin layers (or not deposited at all) over the crests of structures, and as thick layers in adjacent low areas. Where the rocks were upturned by the movement of the salt, localized angular unconformities are displayed, particularly in the Chinle Formation. During the Jurassic and Early Cretaceous, the salt-cored anticlines were dormant and became buried by 3,000 to 6,000 feet of sediments (Stokes, 1987; Doelling, 1988).

Jurassic and Cretaceous Sedimentation

As described in the stratigraphy section (and as shown on figure 6), the region continued to lie near sea level and received continental deposition through Early Jurassic time. Because no bedrock units younger than the Early Jurassic Navajo Sandstone are present near the park, no record exists of the geologic events that happened in the interval from 187 to 1.5 Ma. The area likely received continental deposition during remainder of the Jurassic and the Early Cretaceous and shallow-marine deposition dur-

ing the Late Cretaceous.

Late Cretaceous-Early Tertiary Folding, Faulting, and Intrusions

Large uplifts and basins developed in the Colorado Plateau during the Laramide orogeny between the latest Cretaceous (Maastrichtian, about 70 Ma) and the Eocene (about 38 Ma). The northern end of the Laramide Monument upwarp can be viewed to the south from Dead Horse Point (figures 1 and 11). Other nearby Laramide features include the San Rafael Swell to the west, the Circle Cliffs uplift to the southwest, the Uinta Basin to the north, and the rejuvenated Uncompahgre uplift to the northeast.

The regional dip of strata in the area is 2 to 4 degrees northward. The gentle northwest-trending anticlinal and synclinal folds in the Dead Horse Point area disrupt this regional slope. The axes of the Cane Creek and Shafer anticlines (figure 7) are aligned directly over local bulges of Paradox salt. The overlying rocks were fractured and locally extended by minor faults just off the crest of the anticlines (figure 7) (Morgan and others, 1991). Other anticlines in the Paradox fold and fault belt that are aligned with salt walls have major normal faults such as the Moab fault to the northeast. The Moab fault has over 2,400 feet of displacement (Doelling and others, 1994). The timing of these events is unclear, except that they occurred between 80 and 15 Ma.

The La Sal Mountains (figure 10), on the horizon to the east above the Cane Creek anticline, are a classic example of a laccolith (for discussion of laccoliths, see Geology of Goblin Valley State Park by Milligan, this volume). The La Sal Mountains are a complex of granitic (diorite porphyry) rocks intruded into a salt wall about 25.1 to 27.9 Ma during the Oligocene (Nelson and others, 1992). These peaks are more than 12,000 feet above sea level and were glaciated during the Pleistocene ice ages (Hintze, 1993). In the distance to the southeast, another laccolithic intrusion, the Abajo Mountains, can be seen. This intrusion is dated between 23 and 29 Ma (Hintze, 1993).

Jointing and Fractures

The sandstones in and around Dead Horse Point are brittle, and when folded or bent produce joints and fractures. Fracture patterns and joint sets are related to regional tectonics and salt movement. Large-scale, northeast-trending fractures are found along the Cane Creek anticline (Morgan, 1992). Jointing is prevalent in the Cutler, Wingate, and Kayenta Formations. A dominant set of joints strikes northwest to north-northwest (Doelling and others, 1994). Joints are closely spaced in many areas, but vary with lithology and bed thickness. Another joint set and fracture zone strikes northeast and represents the northeast-trending Roberts rift. This fracture zone may represent high fluid pressure created by fault movement beneath the salt (Doelling and others, 1994) or wrench faulting of competent rocks below the Paradox Formation moving independently of the competent strata above the salt (Hite, 1975). The age of the Roberts rift is unknown (Hite, 1975).

Late Tertiary-Quaternary Regional Uplift and Erosion

The Colorado Plateau began rising in late Cenozoic time during the Miocene (Hunt, 1956; Lucchitta, 1979; Fleming, 1994). This regional uplift changed the landscape from one of deposition to one of massive erosion. Several thousand feet of sedimentary rocks have been removed by the erosive processes of mass wasting, wind, and running water. Most of this material has been carried to the sea by the Colorado River system.

As the Colorado Plateau rose, the Colorado River and its tributaries were rejuvenated, and rapidly cut through the underlying strata. The results of this action are the countless canyons and entrenched meanders visible from Dead Horse Point. Downcutting by the ancestral Colorado River allowed fresh water to reach Paradox salt along fractures, joints, and faults. Major salt dissolution by the downward infiltration of fresh water, and the resulting subsequent structural collapse, has caused many valleys north of the park to widen and develop secondary anticlines (for further discussion, see Geology of Arches National Park by Doelling, this volume).

ECONOMIC GEOLOGY

A unique aspect of Dead Horse Point State Park is that it is surrounded by activity associated with the extraction of three principal minerals -- potash, petroleum, and uranium (figure 12). All three have seen periods of boom and bust during the 20th century. They have been, and remain, an important part of the local economy, as well as the subject of debate in how the lands around the park should be managed.

Potash

The most common question asked at Dead Horse

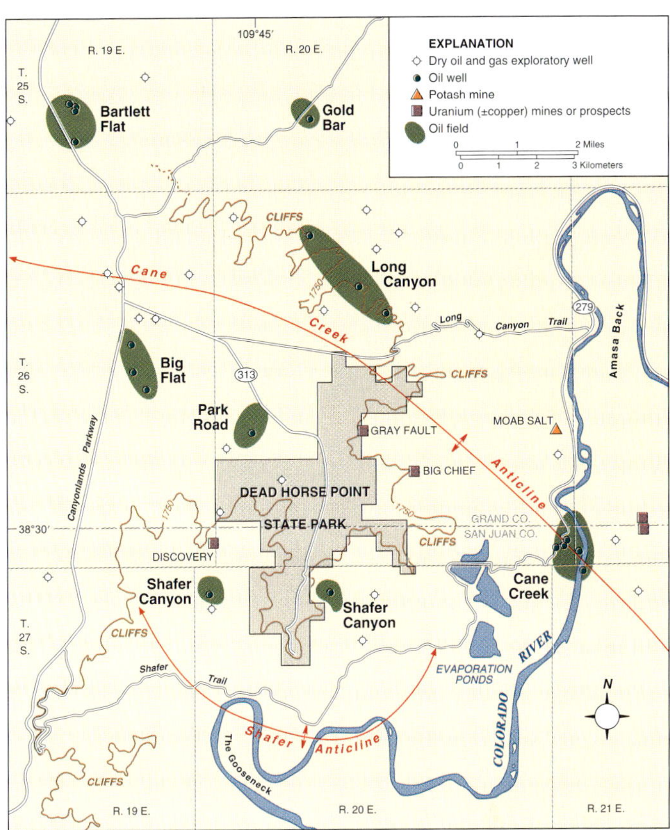

Figure 12. Location of potash, petroleum, and uranium deposits and exploration activities in the Dead Horse Point area, Grand and San Juan Counties.

Point State Park is "what are those big blue things off to the east?" The "big blue things" are solar evaporation ponds (figures 8 and 10) which are designed to extract potash (used for fertilizer, chemicals, pharmaceuticals, and other products) from brines pumped from wells penetrating the Paradox Formation. Seventeen of the 29 depositional cycles in the Paradox Formation contain halite (common table salt) and potash salts (Doelling and others, 1994). The most common of the potash minerals are carnallite and sylvite (Ritzma, 1969). The sylvite is less abundant, but it is the primary commercial mineral composed of 52.4 percent potassium and 47.6 percent chlorine.

In 1964, Texas Gulf Sulfur Inc. (now Moab Salt LLC) began underground room-and-pillar mining of potash from the Paradox Formation cycle number 5 along the Cane Creek anticline at depths between 2,500 and 3,000 feet. Underground mining operations were difficult due to pockets of natural gas, high temperatures, and contorted beds (Phillips, 1975). Before mine operations began, 18 miners were killed in a gas explosion while constructing lateral shafts (Huntoon, 1986). In 1970, the operations were converted to solution mining. Colorado River water is now pumped into the old mine workings dissolving the potash and salt (figure 13). The resulting brine is pumped out and piped to the solar evaporation ponds where the minerals are eventually harvested.

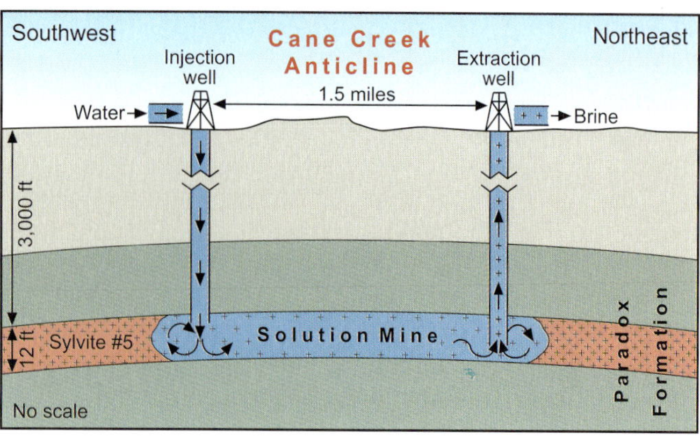

Figure 13. Schematic cross section showing solution mining process on the Cane Creek anticline where salt and potash in the sylvite number 5 depositional cycle of the Paradox Formation are dissolved by injecting river water. The resulting brine is withdrawn by an extraction well and pumped to the solar evaporation ponds where the minerals are eventually harvested.

Figure 14. The Midwest Exploration and Utah Southern No. 1 Shafer wildcat well, section 31, T. 26 S., R. 21 E., Salt Lake Base Line and Meridian, Grand County, drilled in 1924; view down river to the southwest. Used by permission, Utah State Historical Society, all rights reserved.

Potash production is roughly 60,000 tons annually (Eric York, Moab Salt LLC, verbal communication, 2000). For the past ten years, about 200,000 tons of halite have been produced annually as a by-product.

Petroleum

Since the early 1920s, the immediate area around and within Dead Horse Point State Park has been the site of oil and gas exploration drilling (figure 12). There are seven oil fields, three currently active, near the park. Oil and gas have been produced from the Cane Creek shale zone of the Paradox Formation, and the Mississippian Leadville Limestone. The Cane Creek shale zone consists of thinly interbedded, black, organic-rich marine shale, dolomitic siltstone, dolomite, and anhydrite (Smith, 1978a; Morgan, 1992; Grove and others, 1993). Petroleum is trapped in fractured reservoirs, usually on the crest of anticlinal closures. These traps are identified by a combination of geophysical seismic surveys, and subsurface and surface geology. There are no oil and gas pipelines in the area. The oil is trucked to refineries in Salt Lake City and the gas produced along with the oil is flared on site (occasionally seen at night) because it cannot be transported.

The Cane Creek anticline was the most obvious structural drilling target and has been tested sporadically in the Cane Creek oil field near the Colorado River eight times since 1924 (figure 14). However, only 1,887 barrels of oil (BO) and 25 million cubic feet of gas (MMCFG) have been produced, primarily from the Cane Creek shale, in the Cane Creek field (Stowe, 1972). In 1960, lands on the crest of the Cane Creek anticline were withdrawn from oil and gas leasing to prevent interference with potash mining (Smith, 1978e). The oil field area has been abandoned since then to the production of movies and television commercials (for more details, see road logs on CD-ROM [UGA Publication 29] and Cane Creek anticline discussion).

The first commercial production (now abandoned) came with the discovery of Big Flat field just northwest of the park (figure 12). Over 92,000 BO and 50 MMCFG were produced from vertically fractured crystalline limestone and dolomite in an anticlinal closure of the Leadville Limestone (Smith, 1978b; Utah Division of Oil, Gas and Mining, 2000). "Shows" of oil from the Paradox shale zones in Big Flat field lead explorationists to three oil discoveries in 1962: Shafer Canyon, Long Canyon, and Bartlett Flat fields (Smith, 1978a, 1978c, 1978d). Of these fields, Shafer Canyon is the closest to Dead Horse State Park (figure 12). It consisted of two wells: one in the canyon just east of the visitor center and the other in the East Fork of Shafer Canyon just west of the Shafer Canyon overlook. Unlike the other fields in the area, Shafer Canyon produced oil from a generally northwest-trending syncline that separates the Cane Creek and Shafer anticlines. The wells were abandoned in 1967, having produced only about 68,000 BO and 64 MMCFG from the Cane Creek shale zone (Stowe, 1972; Smith, 1978c).

Long Canyon field (figure 12) was the only commercial success of the 1962 discoveries, having encountered a highly fractured, 70-foot-thick Cane Creek interval along the northeast flank of the Cane Creek anticline. The discovery well, and main producer, initially flowed 660 BO per day, and the field has now produced over 1,064,000 BO and 1,119 MMCFG (Smith, 1978d; Utah Division of Oil, Gas and Mining, 2000).

Bartlett Flat field to the northwest (figure 12) produced 37,975 BO from the Cane Creek shale zone on a narrow, faulted, northwest-trending anticline identified by geophysical seismic data (Smith, 1978a). However, the field was abandoned in 1964 when the well casing collapsed due to salt flow (Smith, 1978a).

The late 1980s and 1990s saw dramatic improvements

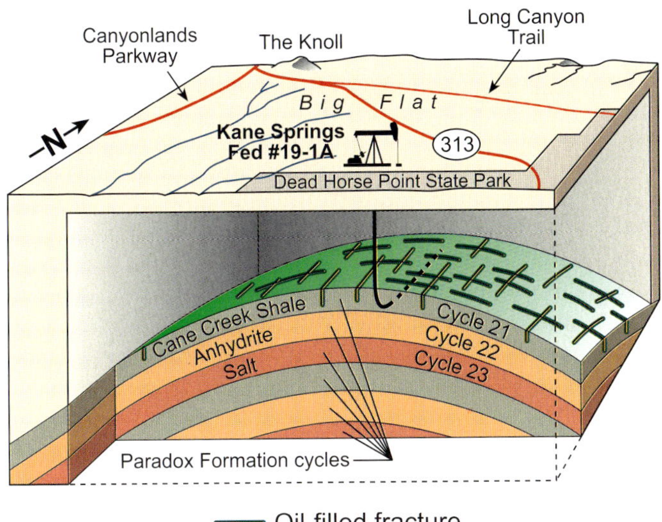

Figure 15. Schematic block diagram showing a horizontal well encountering oil-filled vertical fractures in the Cane Creek shale along a north-northeast-plunging structural nose, Park Road oil field.

in the ability to successfully complete wells in fractured reservoirs by the use of horizontal drilling technology. This technology allows the well bore to be deviated from a vertical to a horizontal position. The direction and depth of the well bore can be carefully controlled, both in relatively thin beds and over distances of several thousand feet. This technology greatly increases the chance of encountering oil-filled fractures over conventional vertical wells (figure 15). Besides being a fractured reservoir, the Cane Creek shale zone also has the following characteristics favorable for horizontal drilling: (1) it contains organic-rich, petroleum-generating source rocks with total organic carbon as high as 15 percent (Hite and others, 1984); (2) it has proven production of high-gravity oil; (3) it is overpressured; (4) it has wide regional extent (cycle 21 of the Paradox Formation); and (5) it has little associated water (Morgan, 1992). In addition, one horizontal well may drain an area that would have required several vertical wells. This made horizontal drilling particularly attractive in the environmentally sensitive Dead Horse Point area.

In 1991, Columbia Gas Development Corporation began drilling a series of horizontal wells in the area north of the park. They returned production to Bartlett Flat field and added a new discovery, Park Road field. Park Road field is about half a mile north of Dead Horse Point State Park between Highway 313 and the park boundary (figures 12 and 16). The Kane Springs No. 19-1A discovery well was drilled 2,011 feet horizontally in the Cane Creek shale in a north-northeast direction (away from the park) to encounter fractures on an anticlinal nose (figures 15 and 16). The well initially tested 1,158 BO per day and is expected to ultimately recover between 475,000 and 1 million barrels (Grove and others, 1993). It has produced over 247,000 BO and 228 MMCFG as of January 1, 2000 (Utah Division Oil, Gas and Mining, 2000).

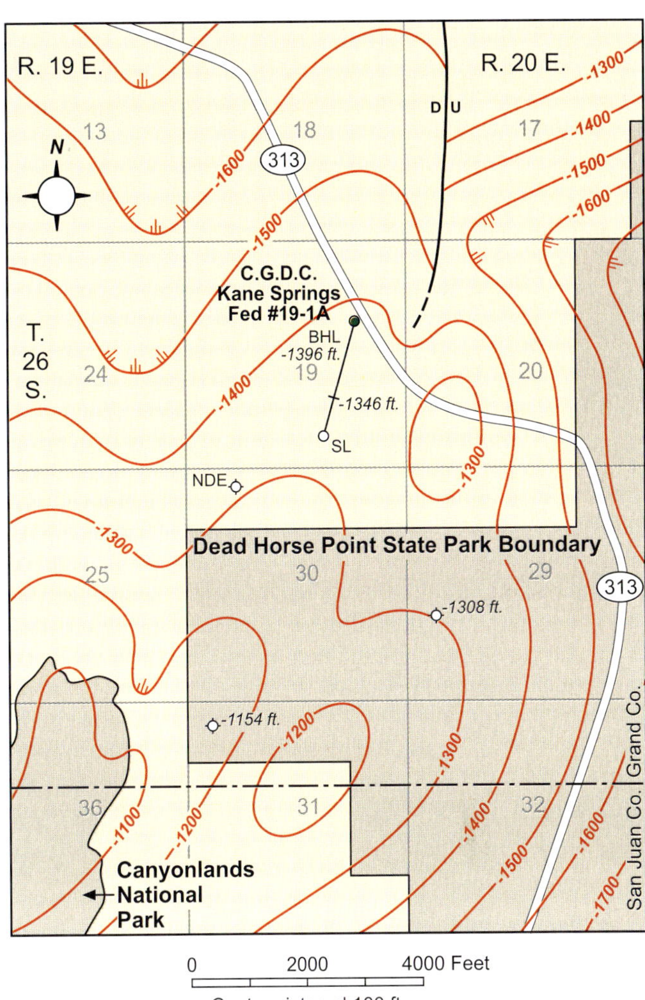

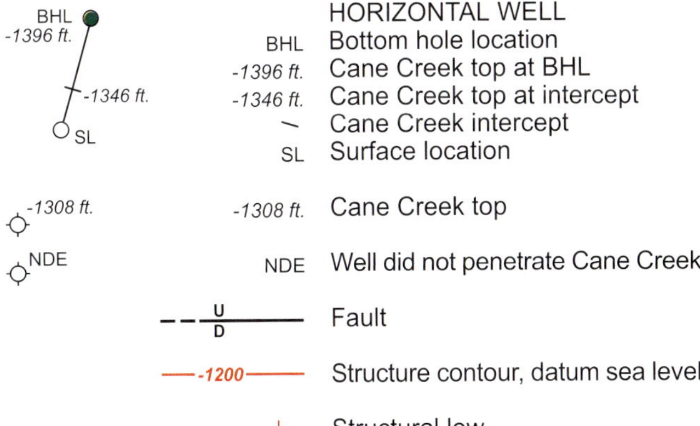

Figure 16. Cane Creek shale structure map, Park Road oil field, Grand County. Surface location, direction, and length of horizontal well shown (after Grove and others, 1993).

Uranium

The results of uranium exploration in Dead Horse Point State Park, and in the surrounding area, is less noticeable than potash and petroleum. However, during the uranium boom of the 1950s, uranium exploration was a major activity throughout southeastern Utah, especially around Moab where there was a large processing mill. Dead Horse Point lies within the Inter-river uranium area. Uranium deposits were found in three small mines near the park (figure 12); the Big Chief, Gray Fault, and Discovery mines. All three mines are abandoned.

All uranium production around Dead Horse Point State Park was from the Chinle Formation (Chenoweth, 1996). The uranium-bearing minerals were found in the bases of carbonaceous sandstone and conglomerate lenses deposited in channels scoured into the top of the Moenkopi Formation (Doelling and others, 1994; Chenoweth, 1996). The principal ore mineral produced was uraninite (a mixture of uranium oxides). Secondary minerals included uranium-bearing schrockingerite, autunite, and possibly carnotite; and copper-bearing chalcocite, malachite, chalcopyrite, and azurite (Utah Geological and Mineral Survey, 1974). These minerals coat fractures, bedding planes, and ore-body contacts (Doelling and others, 1994). Alteration by mineralization is indicated where the reddish-purple sandstone has been bleached to greenish-gray (Chenoweth, 1996).

The three mines around the park consisted of small adits (from less than 100 feet to as long as 800 feet in length) and several "dog holes." Mineralized zones were between 2 and 8 feet thick. Total production from the three mines was only 1,830 pounds of U_3O_8 (Utah Geological and Mineral Survey, 1974; Doelling and others, 1994).

GEOLOGIC UNIQUENESS AND CLASSIC GEOLOGIC SITES

The most unique thing about Dead Horse Point State Park is its panoramic view (figures 1, 9, 10, and 11). Although there are some points of interest on The Point itself, most would agree that the exciting thing is the vantage point looking over the Canyonlands area of Utah. There are several classic geological sites that can be seen from this vantage point, and along the roads that lead to the park; none are in the park itself (figure 17). The Point is the place that puts it all together. Nevertheless, if at all possible, the visitor should take advantage of following the road logs found on CD-ROM (UGA Publication 29). Dead Horse Point should be visited before and after enjoying the sites along these roads.

Cane Creek Anticline

The axis of the northwest-trending Cane Creek anticline cuts across the northeasternmost part of Dead Horse Point State Park (figure 17). It is the largest structural feature in the area (figure 10). Beds dip gently, 5 to 8 degrees in both directions away from the crest. The oldest rocks exposed by the Colorado River canyon on the anticline belong to the Pennsylvanian Honaker Trail Formation. A series of minor, high-angle extension faults parallel the axis of the anticline along the northeast limb (figure 7). The Cane Creek anticline developed from a likely combination of salt bulging and renewed movement on deep, older

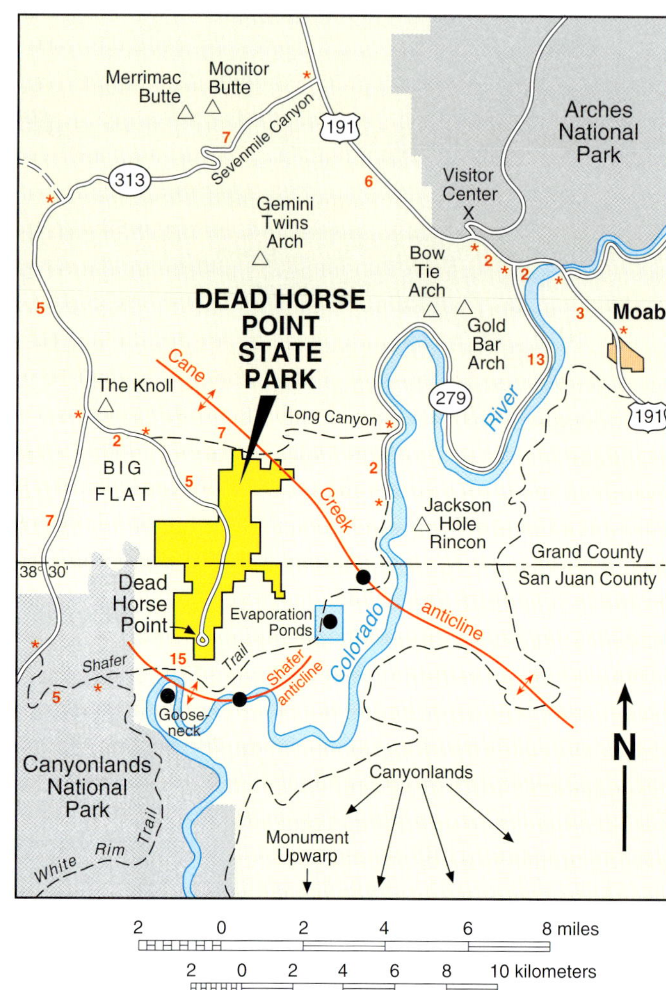

Figure 17. Road map for Dead Horse Point State Park and vicinity. Classic geologic sites discussed in the text are shown with black dots. Red numbers indicate miles between starred junctions. Solid lines are paved roads, dashed lines are dirt roads. See also figure 14 for road detail nearer the park.

structures.

Drilling for oil on the Cane Creek anticline began in 1924 using a cable-tool rig (figure 14). This rig was floated 20 miles down the Colorado River, a practice which continued into the 1950s (Smith, 1978e). The No. 1 Shafer wildcat well (section 31, T. 26 S., R. 21 E., Salt Lake Base Line and Meridian) blew out and caught fire after reaching a depth of 2,028 feet in the Paradox salt (Smith, 1978e). Seven more wells were drilled between 1928 and 1958. "Shows" of hydrocarbons were encountered in the Cane Creek shale zone of the Paradox Formation and the Mississippian Leadville Limestone. All that remains of these activities are several iron stand pipes (dry hole markers).

Gooseneck of the Colorado River

This magnificent entrenched meander of the Colorado River is easily seen just below Dead Horse Point to the southwest (figure 1). At the narrowest neck of the peninsula, the distance across bedrock between the river is less than a quarter mile. Here, it is entrenched into about 400 feet of the lower Cutler Formation. The river level is about 2,000 feet below the elevation of the pavilion at the Dead Horse Point overlook. For a distance of about 4 river miles along the Gooseneck, the river proceeds less than 0.25 land miles! The river is capable of cutting through the 400-foot wall of lower Cutler rocks, and has cut through similar "necks" in other areas, but it will probably take thousands of years to do so!

When the Colorado Plateau rose in the late Cenozoic, the ancestral Colorado River and its tributaries flowed through meandering channels in wide valleys on easily eroded rocks such as the now-removed Cretaceous Mancos Shale. Once these river channels were established, they later became superimposed and entrenched into buried structures, such as the Cane Creek and Shafer anticlines, and into resistant rocks such as the Wingate and Navajo Sandstones. The deeply entrenched Gooseneck of the Colorado (figures 1, 7, 12, and 17) is a classic example of this geomorphologic process.

Shafer Anticline

The Shafer anticline (sometimes referred to as Shafer dome) can be seen just south of Dead Horse Point (figures 11, 12, and 17). The axis curves essentially around The Point, trending northwest on the west, east-west to the south, and northeast to the east of Dead Horse Point (figure 7). Although less obvious than the Cane Creek anticline, the Shafer anticline is a major structural feature. Beds dip 5 to 10 degrees from the crest, where rocks as old as the Pennsylvanian Honaker Trail Formation are exposed along the Colorado River on the eastern axis of the structure. A series of minor, high-angle extension faults generally parallels the northwest-trending axis along the southwest limb (figure 7). Like the Cane Creek anticline, the Shafer anticline most likely developed from salt bulging in the Paradox Formation, and movement on deep, older faults. The structure was drilled in a few localities, but no petroleum was found.

Solar Evaporation Ponds

The brine pumped from the solution mine (described earlier) to the large solar evaporation ponds observed from the park is saturated with respect to salt (NaCl) and close to saturation with respect to sylvite (KCl). Halite is a contaminant and is partially removed in a carefully controlled evaporative process. Brine, upon evaporating to a suitable concentration, is successively drained into a new pond, each time leaving some of the halite behind. The process is repeated several times before the final liquid becomes suitably concentrated in potassium salts. The slurry is then pumped to a processing facility where the potash is separated from the remaining salt by flotation (Eric York, Moab Salt LLC, verbal communication, 2000). The potash is then bagged and sold.

The potash solar evaporation ponds so prominently displayed in the Shafer Basin east of Dead Horse Point ac-

tually consist of 23 ponds in four areas. The ponds cover a total of 400 acres and are 2 to 3 feet deep. The beautiful blue color of the water is the result of a dye which is introduced to enhance evaporation. If the product cannot be harvested within two years the operation becomes uneconomical. The operators do not like wet years and cloudy skies.

ACKNOWLEDGMENTS

We thank the staff at Canyonlands National Park and Dead Horse Point State Park for providing access to park lands, and Mary Tullius of the Utah Division of Parks and Recreation, who enthusiastically endorsed this paper and guidebook. The Utah Geological Survey (UGS) covered field expenses and provided field vehicles. We thank Jim Parker, UGS, who drafted several figures from rough drawings. Finally, we thank David Tabet, Grant Willis, and Mike Hylland of the UGS for their careful review and constructive criticism of the manuscript.

REFERENCES

Baars, D.L., and Doelling, H.H., 1987, Moab salt-intruded anticline, east-central Utah: Geological Society of America Centennial Field Guide-Rocky Mountain Section, p. 275-280.

Case, J.E., and Joesting, H.R., 1973, Regional geophysical investigations in the central Colorado Plateau: U.S. Geological Survey Professional Paper 736, 31 p.

Cater, F.W., 1970, Geology of the salt anticline region in south-western Colorado: U.S. Geological Survey Professional Paper 637, 80 p.

Chenoweth, W.L., 1996, The Uranium industry in the Paradox basin, *in* Huffman, A.C., Jr., Lund, W.R., and Godwin, L.H., editors, Geology and resources of the Paradox basin: Utah Geological Association Publication 25, p. 95-108.

Doelling, H.H., 1988, Geology of the Salt Valley anticline and Arches National Park, Grand County, Utah, *in* Salt deformation in the Paradox region: Utah Geological and Mineral Survey Bulletin 122, p. 1-60.

—1993, Interim geologic map of the Moab 30' x 60' quadrangle, Grand County, Utah: Utah Geological Survey Open-File Report 287, 16 p., 1 pl., scale 1:100,000.

Doelling, H.H., Yonkee, W.A., and Hand, J.S., 1994, Geologic map of the Gold Bar Canyon quadrangle, Grand County, Utah: Utah Geological Survey Map 155, 26 p., scale 1:24,000.

Fleming, R.F., 1994, Cretaceous pollen in Pliocene rocks - implications for Pliocene climate in the southwestern United States: Geology, v. 22, p. 787-790.

Friedman, J.D., Case, J.E., and Simpson, S.L., 1994, Tectonic trends of the northern part of the Paradox basin, southeastern Utah and southwestern Colorado, as derived from Landsat multispectral scanner imaging and geophysical and geological mapping: U.S. Geological

Survey Bulletin 2000-C, 30 p.

Grove, K.W., Horgan, C.C., Flores, F.E., and Bayne, R.C., 1993, Bartlett Flat Big Flat (Kane Springs unit), *in* Hill, B.G., and Bereskin, S.R., editors, Oil and gas fields of Utah: Utah Geological Association Publication 22, non-paginated.

Harry, D.L., and Mickus, K.L., 1998, Gravity constraints on lithopheric flexure and the structure of the Late Paleozoic Ouachita orogen in Arkansas and Oklahoma south-central North America: Tectonics, v. 17, no. 2, p. 187-202.

Hinrichs, E.N., Krummel, W.J., Jr., Connor, J.J., and Moore, H.J., II, 1967, Geologic map of the southeast quarter of the Hatch Point (Shafer Basin) quadrangle, San Juan County, Utah: U.S. Geological Survey Miscellaneous Geologic Investigations Map I-513, scale 1:24,000.

Hintze, L.F., 1993, Geologic history of Utah: Brigham Young University Studies Special Publication 7, 202 p.

—1997, Geologic highway map of Utah: Brigham Young University Geology Studies Special Publication No. 3., scale 1:1,000,000.

Hite, R.J., 1975, An unusual northeast-trending fracture zone and its relations to basement wrench faulting in northern Paradox basin, Utah and Colorado, *in* Fassett, J.E., editor, Canyonlands country: Four Corners Geological Society Guidebook, 8th Annual Field Conference, p. 217- 223.

Hite, R.J., Anders, D.E., and Ging, T.G., 1984, Organic-rich source rocks of Pennsylvanian age in the Paradox basin of Utah and Colorado, *in* Woodward, J., Meissner, F.F., and Clayton, J.L., editors, Hydrocarbon source rocks of the Greater Rocky Mountain region: Rocky Mountain Association of Geologists Guidebook, p. 225-274.

Hunt, C.B., 1956, Cenozoic geology of the Colorado Plateau: U.S. Geological Survey Professional Paper 279, 99 p.

Huntoon, P.W., 1986, Incredible tale of Texasgulf well 7 and fracture permeability, Paradox basin, Utah: Ground Water, v. 24, no. 5, p. 643-653.

Huntoon, P.W., Billingsley, G.H., Jr., and Breed, W.J., 1982, Geologic map of Canyonlands National Park and vicinity, Utah: Moab, Utah, Canyonlands Natural History Association, scale 1:62,500.

Kluth, C.F., 1986, Plate tectonics of the Ancestral Rocky Mountains: American Association of Petroleum Geologists Memoir 41, p. 353-369.

Kluth, C.F., and Coney, P.J., 1981, Plate tectonics of the Ancestral Rocky Mountains: Geology, v. 9, p. 10-15.

Lucchitta, Ivo, 1979, Late Cenozoic uplift of the southwestern Colorado Plateau and adjacent Colorado River region: Tectonophysics, v. 61, p. 63-95.

McKnight, E.T., 1940, Geology of area between Green and Colorado Rivers, Grand and San Juan Counties, Utah: U.S. Geological Survey Bulletin 908, 147 p.

Melton, R.A., 1972, Paleoecology and paleoenvironments of the upper Honaker Trail Formation near Moab, Utah: Provo, Utah, Brigham Young University Geology Studies, v. 19, part 2, p. 45-88.

Morgan, C.D., 1992, Horizontal drilling potential of the Cane Creek shale, Paradox Formation, Utah, *in* Schmoker, J.W., Coalson, E.B., and Brown, C.A., editors, Geologic studies relevant to horizontal drilling -- examples from western North America: Rocky Mountain Association of Geologists Guidebook, p. 257-265.

Morgan, C.D., Yonkee, W.A., Tripp, B.T., 1991, Geological considerations for oil and gas drilling on state potash leases at Cane Creek anticline, Grand and San Juan Counties, Utah: Utah Geological Survey Circular 84, 24 p.

Nelson, S.T., Heizler, M.T., and Davidson, J.P., 1992, New $^{40}Ar/^{39}Ar$ ages of intrusive rocks from the Henry and La Sal Mountains: Utah Geological Survey Miscellaneous Publication MP-92-2, 24 p.

Oviatt, C.G., 1988, Evidence for Quaternary deformation in the Salt Valley anticline, southeastern Utah, *in* Salt deformation in the Paradox region: Utah Geological and Mineral Survey Bulletin 122, p. 61-76.

Phillips, Margie, 1975, Cane Creek mine solution mining project, Moab potash operations, Texasgulf Inc., *in* Fassett, J.E., editor, Canyonlands country: Four Corners Geological Society, 8th Annual Field Conference, p. 261.

Ritzma, H.R., 1969, Potash in the San Juan Project area, Utah and Colorado, *in* Mineral resources, San Juan County, Utah, and adjacent areas: Utah Geological and Mineral Survey Special Studies 24, p. 17-33.

Shoemaker, E.M., Case, J.E., and Elston, D.P., 1958, Salt anticlines of the Paradox basin: Intermountain Association of Petroleum Geologists 9th Annual Field Conference, p. 39-59.

Smith, K.T., 1978a, Bartlett Flat, *in* Fassett, J.E., editor, Oil and gas fields of the Four Corners area: Four Corners Geological Society, v. 2, p. 1061-1063.

—1978b, Big Flat, *in* Fassett, J.E., editor, Oil and gas fields of the Four Corners area: Four Corners Geological Society, v. 2, p. 596-598.

—1978c, Shafer Canyon, *in* Fassett, J.E., editor, Oil and gas fields of the Four Corners area: Four Corners Geological Society, v. 2, p. 700-702.

—1978d, Long Canyon, *in* Fassett, J.E., editor, Oil and gas fields of the Four Corners area: Four Corners Geological Society, v. 2, p 676-678.

—1978e, Cane Creek, *in* Fassett, J.E., editor, Oil and gas fields of the Four Corners area: Four Corners Geological Society, v. 2, p. 624-626.

Stevenson, G.M., and Baars, D.L., 1987, The Paradox -- a pull-apart basin of Pennsylvanian age, *in* Campbell, J.A., editor, Geology of Cataract Canyon and vicinity: Four Corners Geological Society, 10th Field Conference, p. 31-55.

Stokes, W.L., 1986, Geology of Utah: Utah Geological and Mineral Survey Miscellaneous Publication MP-S, 317 p.

—1987, Geology of Utah: Utah Geologic and Mineral Survey, Occasional Paper 6, 280 p.

—1991, Petrified mini-forests of the Navajo Sandstone, east-central Utah: Utah Geological Survey, Survey Notes, v. 25, no. 1, p. 14-19.

Stowe, Carlton, 1972, Oil and gas production in Utah to 1970: Utah Geological and Mineral Survey Bulletin 94, 179 p.

Utah Division of Oil, Gas and Mining, 2000, December 1999 oil and gas production report: Salt Lake City, Utah Division of Oil, Gas and Mining, non-paginated.

Utah Geological and Mineral Survey, 1974, Uranium-vanadium occurrences of Utah: unpublished report for the U.S. Bureau of Mines, non-paginated.

Willis, G.C., 1994, Geologic map of the Harley Dome quadrangle, Grand County, Utah: Utah Geological Survey Map 157, 18 p., scale 1:24,000.

Coral Pink Sand Dunes State Park
Photo courtesy of the Utah Travel Council

Geology of Utah's Parks and Monuments
2000 Utah Geological Association Publication 28
D.A. Sprinkel, T.C. Chidsey, Jr., and P.B. Anderson, editors

Geology of Escalante State Park, Utah

Susan K. Morgan[1], *Bradford W. Lindsay*[1], *and Anthony P. Williams*[1]

ABSTRACT

Escalante State Park contains exposures of three stratigraphic formations spanning the late Middle Jurassic to Early Cretaceous within its boundaries. In ascending order they are the late Middle Jurassic Escalante Member of the Entrada Sandstone, the Late Jurassic Morrison Formation, and, in the northeast corner of the park, the Early to Late Cretaceous Dakota Formation. The Morrison Formation consists of three members, the lower Tidwell Member, the middle Salt Wash Member, and the upper Brushy Basin Member. In the southwestern corner of the park the sedimentary rocks are overlain by a Quaternary gravel cover composed of Tertiary-age basalt and rhyolite that was fluvially transported and deposited from adjacent plateaus. Most sedimentary beds in the park are nearly horizontal. However, strata in the southern and eastern margins of the park experienced compression that created open anticlinal and synclinal folds. Petrified wood, most likely from conifers, occurs in the upper brown conglomeratic bed of the Brushy Basin Member of the Morrison. The wood is agatized and highly colorful and occurs as centimeter-size fragments to nearly entire logs 10 feet long.

INTRODUCTION

Escalante State Park is located 0.6 miles west of the town of Escalante in southeastern Utah (figure 1) and is nestled amidst the stark yet hauntingly beautiful geologic wonderland of the Colorado Plateau. This is an area with a rich geologic history that unfolds layer by geologic layer, easily seen and often laced with fossils from life of the past. Escalante State Park's uniqueness in this vast area of geologic fascination is the abundance of often large and colorful specimens of agatized petrified wood. A short hike along a well-maintained trail displays everything from small chips of petrified wood to large, nearly whole tree trunks. In addition to the spectacular display of wood, pockets of dinosaur bone litter remote areas, testifying to the presence of the mighty beasts that roamed the area millions of years ago. The geologic story of the park unfolds like pages of a book as each layer reveals startling and dramatic changes of environments that, through time, led to the landscape of rocks and fossils we see and enjoy today.

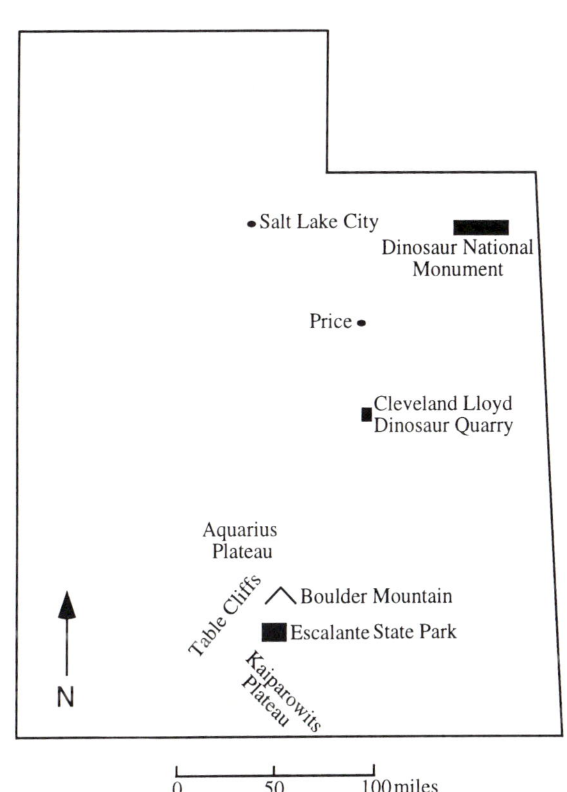

Figure 1. *Location map of Escalante State Park (modified from Stephens, 1973).*

[1] *Geology Department, Utah State University, Logan, Utah 84322-4505*

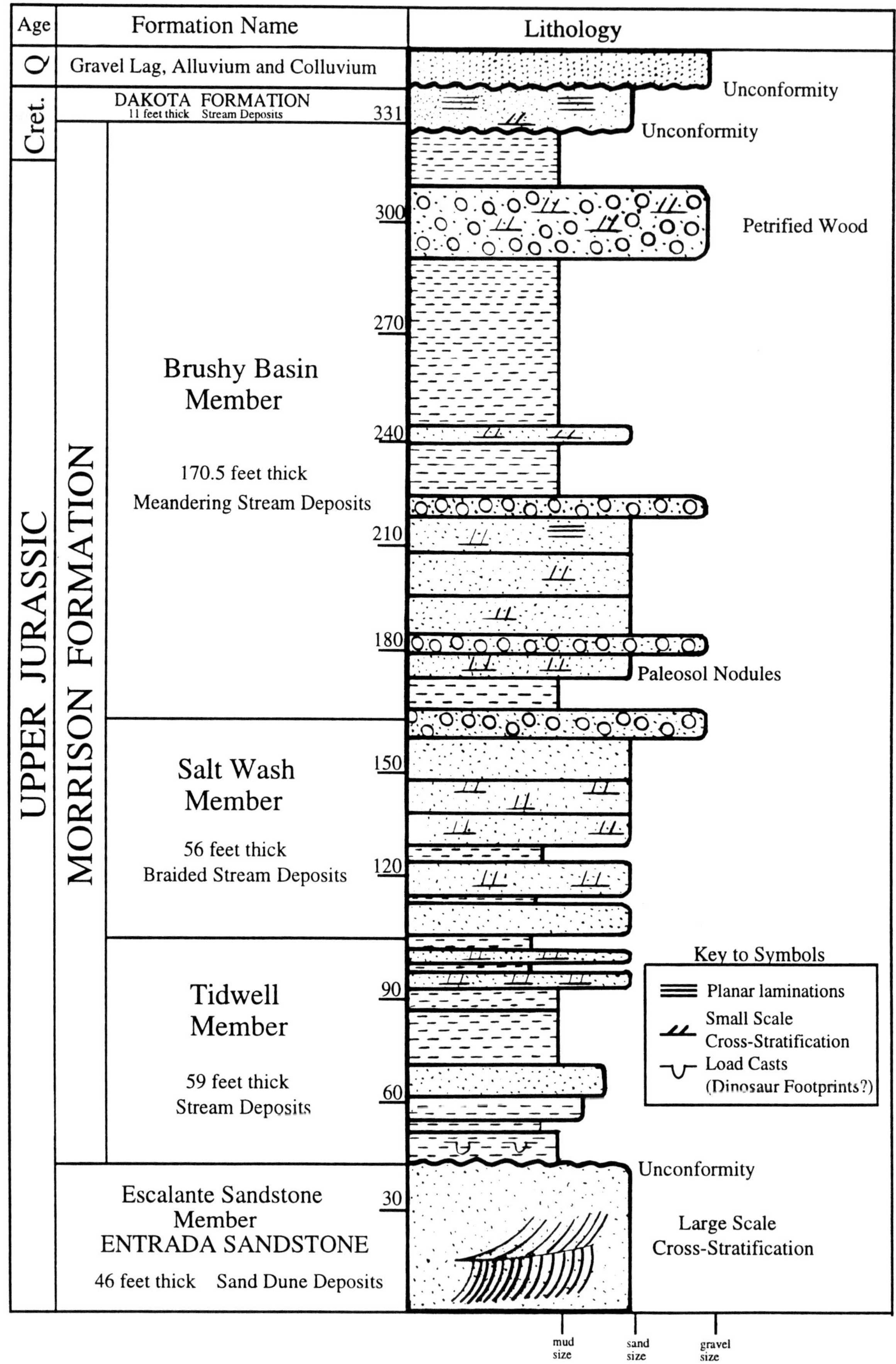

Figure 2. Stratigraphic section of rocks exposed in Escalante State Park. Thickness along column in feet.

STRATIGRAPHY AND HISTORY OF DEPOSITION

Escalante State Park contains exposures of three stratigraphic formations spanning the late Middle Jurassic to Early Cretaceous within its boundaries and was originally mapped by Peterson (1971) and Stephens (1973) (figure 2). The oldest unit in the park, exposed at the base of the cliffs, is the late Middle Jurassic Escalante Member of the Entrada Sandstone. The Late Jurassic Morrison Formation unconformably overlies the Entrada and consists of three members, the lower Tidwell Member, the middle Salt Wash Member, and the upper Brushy Basin Member. In the northeast corner of the park, the Early to Late Cretaceous Dakota Formation unconformably overlies the Morrison Formation. In the southwestern corner of the park the sedimentary rocks are overlain by a Quaternary gravel cover composed of Tertiary-age basalt and rhyolite transported and deposited by streams from adjacent plateaus. Quaternary alluvium blankets Baily Wash whereas colluvium covers slopes adjacent to the park's cliffs. Most sedimentary beds in the park are nearly horizontal; however, strata on the southern and eastern margins of the park experienced compression that created open anticlinal and synclinal folds.

Entrada Sandstone

The late Middle Jurassic age Entrada Sandstone (153 million years old) was named by Gilluy and Reeside (1928) for strata exposed at Entrada Point in the northeastern San Rafael Swell. At the type locality it consists of mostly reddish-brown earthy siltstone and minor interbedded clean sandstone in an undivided sequence more than 295 feet thick (Craig and Shawe, 1975). The Entrada is well exposed at Pine Creek, about 3 miles north of Escalante State Park, where it can be subdivided into distinct members. The upper Escalante Sandstone Member is described as consisting of light-gray, largely cross-stratified, cliff-forming sandstone (Doelling, 1975; Peterson, 1988a; Doelling and others, 1989).

Only part of the upper Escalante Sandstone Member of the Entrada Sandstone is exposed in the park; the lower contact is not exposed (figure 3). Outcrops of the Escalante Sandstone Member are in the campground, northward along the dirt road that parallels Wide Hollow Reservoir, and at the base of the cliffs rimming the southern boundary of the park (figure 4). The Escalante Sandstone Member is up to 46 feet thick near Wide Hollow Reservoir and is a moderately cemented, massive, white to light-gray eolian (wind blown dune) sandstone dominated by large-scale cross-stratification.

Prior to deposition of the Escalante Sandstone, this region of Utah was at the southern boundary of an extensive Middle Jurassic seaway, the Sundance Sea (Hintze, 1988; Peterson, 1994). During this time, Utah was at a latitude of 30-35° N. and had a warm and dry paleoclimate (Robinson and McCabe, 1998). As the Sundance seaway regressed

Figure 3. *Exposure of lower, white Escalante Member of the Entrada Sandstone, red Tidwell Member and buff cliff-forming Salt Wash Member, capped by slopes of the Brushy Basin Member of the Morrison Formation. Photograph taken northwest from the campground.*

northward in late Middle Jurassic, strong south winds reworked shoreline deposits, spreading coastal sand dunes across southeastern Utah creating the Escalante erg (sandy desert) (Peterson, 1994).

Morrison Formation

The Late Jurassic Morrison Formation (146-138 million years old) was named and described by Cross (1894) and redefined at its type locality near the town of Morrison, Colorado, by Emmons and others (1896). The Morrison is famous for its collection of dinosaur bones and occasional petrified wood. The Morrison extensively covers the Colorado Plateau and is divided in up to seven members in eastern Colorado and locations in Utah (Peterson and Turner-Peterson, 1989). Three of those members crop out in Escalante State Park: the lower Tidwell Member, the middle Salt Wash Member, and the upper Brushy Basin Member (figure 4).

Tidwell Member

Thin-bedded red mudstone and thin- to medium-bedded white sandstone beds overlie the Escalante Sandstone Member of the Entrada. These beds have previously been mapped as the Summerville Formation. This unit is now recognized as the Tidwell Member of Morrison Formation (Peterson, 1988a ; O'Sullivan, 1992; Baars, 1995). The Summerville is restricted to thin-bedded mudstone, sandstone, and siltstone beds truncated by the J-5 unconformity, whereas the Tidwell Member, which displays similar lithologies, lies above the unconformity (Peterson 1988b). Six regional unconformities occur in Jurassic age rocks in Utah and are labeled J-0 through J-5. The J-5 unconformity marks the base of the Morrison Formation (Anderson and Lucas, 1998; Hintze, 1988).

The Tidwell Member is well exposed in the park. Near the campground, it forms cliffs that increase in height south and east, framing the southern boundary of the park (figure 3). In addition, Baily Wash is eroded into the Tid-

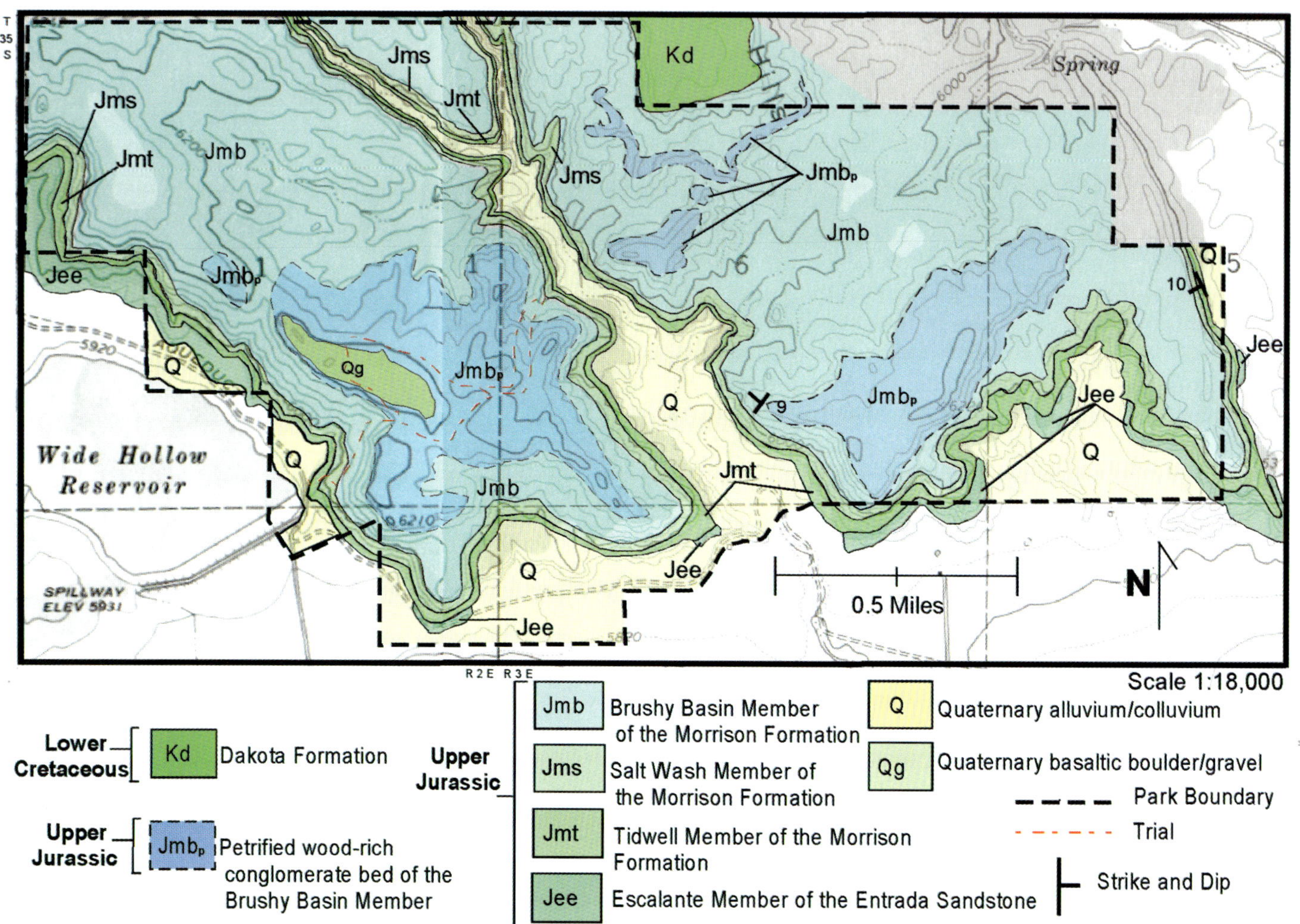

Figure 4. Geologic map of Escalante State Park.

well Member. A stroll up the mostly dry stream bed provides ample opportunity to investigate the sediment and rock layers exposed in the walls of the wash.

The Tidwell Member is 59 feet thick north and east of Wide Hollow Reservoir. It contains 2- to 30-inch-thick beds of well-cemented, mostly red and some white sandstone interbedded with 2- to 55-inch-thick beds of red mudstone and siltstone and green siltstone. Most of the mudstone and siltstone layers are thinly laminated; some display wavy bedding planes. Load casts occur in the mudstone and siltstone layers near the bottom of the member. Often, what appear to be load casts in the Morrison Formation are actually casts of dinosaur footprints (Bilbey, verbal communication, 2000). With limited exposures, the authors were unable to determine the true nature of these features.

Toward the top of the member, two 28-inch-thick sandstone beds contain low-angle cross-stratification and pinch out laterally. The lower sandstone bed pinches out within 12.5 feet and the upper bed extends to 42 feet. The top of the Tidwell Member was placed at the contact of the last 55-inch-thick mudstone bed and the first medium-bedded sandstone of the Salt Wash Member. Although the Tidwell Member can contain gypsum and bedded chert in some locations (Peterson, 1988b, Bilbey, written communication, 2000) no gypsum or chert were found in exposures in the Escalante State Park region.

The Tidwell Member represents fluvial (river) deposition sourced from nearby highlands. The Sevier highlands westward in Nevada and the Mogollon highlands in southwestern Arizona (Young, 1987; Peterson, 1988a; Peterson, 1988b) were created by compression as a result of Late Jurassic subduction off the west coast of North America. Sediment-choked streams drained the uplifted regions, transporting and depositing material to the newly created foreland basin in central and eastern Utah (Robinson and McCabe, 1988). Mudstone and siltstone were deposited on broad floodplains studded with occasional lakes and ponds whereas sporadic channel-point bar deposits were preserved as sandstone interbeds. Continued uplift of the highlands resulted in eastward progradation of coarsening channel deposits across floodplain and lacustrine mud recorded by the thicker cross-stratified sandstone beds near the top of the Tidwell (Peterson, 1988b).

Salt Wash Member

The Salt Wash Member was named by Lupton (1914) and is present throughout the Colorado Plateau. The

Figure 5. The base of the white sandstone cliff marks the contact with the underlying upper mudstone of the Brushy Basin Member and the overlying Dakota Formation. The Dakota consists of three units; the lower white sandstone is overlain by carbonaceous slope-forming mud and capped by an orange-yellow cliff-forming sandstone.

Figure 6. Petrified conifer 10 feet long embedded in the upper brown conglomerate of the Brushy Basin Member (staff is 4 feet long).

member is described as consisting of cliff-forming lenticular, cross-bedded, channel-fill sandstone and conglomeratic sandstone interbedded with reddish-brown to grayish and purple laminated mudstone (Doelling, 1975; O'Sullivan, 1992; Petersen and Roylance, 1982; Peterson, 1988a). The Salt Wash Member is well exposed in the park, forming cliffs that cap the Tidwell Member (figure 3). The base of the Salt Wash contains 2-to 8-feet-thick, white cross-stratified sandstone beds divided by red and white mudstone and green siltstone layers less than 1.6 feet thick. The mudstone layers pinch out within 10 to 13 feet and contain load casts (possible dinosaur footprint casts?) from the overlying sandstone. Above the mudstone are intensely cross-stratified sandstone and conglomeratic sandstone beds capped by a white cross-stratified conglomerate with a basal scour surface.

Sandstone and conglomerate beds of the Salt Wash Member represent fluvial (river) channel deposits, whereas mudstone and siltstone beds are probably overbank deposits (Robinson and McCabe, 1998). Continued uplift of the Sevier highlands to the west in Utah, Nevada, and California and the Mogollon highlands to the south in Arizona provided coarsening clastic sediments eroded from exposed Paleozoic and Mesozoic rocks (Robinson and McCabe, 1998). The sediment was transported into the depositional basin northeastward and eastward by a braided river complex with few overbank deposits (Peterson, 1988a; Robinson and McCabe, 1998).

Brushy Basin Member

The Brushy Basin Member forms the top of the Morrison Formation in most of the Colorado Plateau (Craig and Shawe, 1975; Petersen, 1988a). It is characteristically composed of dominantly variegated, slope-forming, bentonitic mudstone with interbeds of cross-stratified dark brown conglomerate and buff to white cross-stratified sandstone (Peterson, 1988a; Peterson, 1988b; Johnson, 1988). The Brushy Basin was thought to be latest Jurassic age; how-

ever, an age date from zircon crystals in the upper mudstone indicates the uppermost part of the unit is Early Cretaceous (Peterson, 1988a). The Brushy Basin Member covers broad expanses of Escalante State Park, capping the sandstone cliffs (figure 5). The unit is 170.5 feet thick in the park and was measured and described east of Baily Wash. The basal contact of the Brushy Basin is placed at the first 10-foot-thick red mudstone on top of the Salt Wash sandstone and sandy conglomerate cliffs. An overview of Baily Wash reveals that the red mudstone pinches out laterally to cross-stratified sandstone and conglomerate; therefore, the lithologies involved in the basal contact will vary but can still be placed at the top of the Salt Wash sandstone cliff (Craig and Shawe, 1975).

The lower 59 feet of the Brushy Basin contain 7- to 1-foot-thick, cross-stratified white sandstone with distinctive orange and red clasts and a 6-foot-thick interval of cross-stratified, clast-supported conglomerate with brown and red clasts. The sandstone and conglomerate beds all display basal scour surfaces and pinch out laterally. The middle 65.5 feet are composed of slope-forming red, white, gray, yellow, purple, and green bentonitic mudstone interrupted by a lone 3-foot-thick, cross-stratified white sandstone interval. A cliff-forming 24.5 foot interval of 1.6- to 12-foot-thick cross-stratified dark brown conglomerate occurs above the variegated mudstone. A basal scour surface separates the conglomerate from the underlying mudstone. A significant amount of multicolored agatized petrified wood occurs in the conglomerate ranging from small 1- to 2-inch clasts to 10- to 11.5-foot-long tree trunks (figure 6). Clast composition is used to distinguish Morrison conglomerate from the overlying Cretaceous Cedar Mountain conglomerate (Peterson and others,

1980; Johnson, 1988). The cliff-forming conglomerate is characteristic of other Morrison conglomerates in that the clasts are predominantly colorful orange, green, and rusty red chert pebbles and are cemented with silica. The Cedar Mountain clasts are predominantly white, gray, and brown chert with gray quartzite and limestone, and minor red chert and have a calcite cement (Peterson and others, 1980; Peterson 1988a).

A white to light-green-gray mudstone forms a gentle slope above the conglomerate and contains minor amounts of silicified (not agatized) dull brown to tan 2 to 10 inch pieces of petrified wood. Mudstones of the upper Brushy Basin are often white to light gray. The light color has been attributed to bleaching as a result of weathering on the overlying unconformity that separates the Brushy Basin from the younger Cretaceous Dakota Formation (Young, 1987). It is possible that this upper mudstone unit may be the Cretaceous age Cedar Mountain Formation that crops out in Capitol Reef National Park to the north and the Henry Mountains to the east. However, Hintze (1988), Stephens, (1973) and Peterson (1971) do not recognize the Cedar Mountain Formation in the region of Escalante State Park. An analysis of petrified wood from the formation would determine whether, in fact, it is part of the Brushy Basin Member or the Cedar Mountain Formation (Medlyn, verbal communication, 2000).

The Brushy Basin Member represents changing environments as the braided streams of the Salt Wash were gradually replaced by migrating fluvial channel sandstone and conglomerate and increasing floodplain and lacustrine mudstone (Johnson, 1988; Peterson, 1988a). Johnson (1988) believes the fluvial systems changed from bedload to mixed and suspended-load channels when large amounts of volcanic ash covered the rivers' headwaters in the western and southern highlands. The tephra, or volcanic ash, was reworked and redeposited as floodplain mudstone. Smectite, a clay mineral that is a major component of the Brushy Basin mudstone, forms from altered volcanic ash. In the latest Jurassic to earliest Cretaceous, active subduction tectonics to the west and southwest of Utah (Nevadan orogeny) resulted in violent volcanic eruptions, the source for air-fall tephra (Stokes, 1980; Peterson, 1988b). Lacustrine marlstone and thin limestone beds also occur in the Brushy Basin Member, however, none are present in the park. The upper conglomerate layer in the Brushy Basin is rich with agatized petrified wood. Most of the wood is from conifers (D.A. Medlyn, verbal communication, 2000) and is evidence that large trees grew on the floodplain (Stokes, 1994).

An enigma of the Brushy Basin, described by Peterson (1988a), is the occurrence of high-energy fluvial conglomerate and sandstone within a thick succession of low-energy mudstone. Johnson (1988) suggests that changing magmatic activity to the west influenced the fluvial systems. Periods of high activity with large amounts of tephra produced suspended-load streams and overbank deposits whereas low activity allowed bed-load channels to develop.

Dakota Formation

The name Dakota Formation was applied by Meek and Hayden (1862) to Early Cretaceous deposits near Dakota, Nebraska. In most localities in southern Utah, the Dakota contains three lithologic units: a lower, often conglomeratic sandstone, a middle carbonaceous shale and coal, and an upper sandstone (Brown, 1973; Young, 1973; Peterson and Ryder, 1975; Doelling and others, 1989). In south-central to southwestern Utah, the Dakota Formation crops out mostly west and south of Escalante State Park in the Table Cliff and Kaparowits Plateaus (Brown, 1973). However, in the very northeastern corner of the park, a sliver of the base of the Dakota lies within the park boundary (figure 5). Because the Dakota straddles the park boundary, all of the unit will be described; however, only the lowermost section was measured and described in detail.

The contact of the Dakota with the underlying Brushy Basin Member of the Morrison Formation is covered by sand and mud; however, it is considered to be the K-0 regional unconformity (Peterson and Ryder, 1975; Doelling and others, 1989). The lowermost Dakota is 11 feet thick and forms cliffs. It is a poorly to moderately-cemented buff to white sandstone that is cross-stratified to planar-laminated. Dark-gray to black carbonaceous, laminated mudstone overlies the basal sandstone and in turn is overlain by a cap rock of thick, orange-yellow cliff-forming sandstone. The sandstone is rich with 1- to 3-inch-long *Ostera* fossil oyster shells. In addition, the Dakota can also contain the oysters *Exogyra* and *Gryphaea* (Doelling and others, 1989).

The influx of sediment during Morrison time slowly waned, and, as the Sevier orogenic belt gradually uplifted the area to the west, erosion and subsequent transport of material to the northwest ensued, creating an unconformable surface (Young, 1973; Cole, 1987). Renewed tectonic activity in the west once again uplifted western Utah, eastern Nevada and southern Idaho to create the Sevier highlands (Young, 1973). Subsiding land created a foreland basin east of the highlands that became the site of the Interior Cretaceous Seaway. The lower Dakota sandstone formed as streams eroded sediment from the young highlands, often depositing it as blanket sandstones, as they flowed toward the seaway (Young, 1973).

The middle carbonaceous shale accumulated as sea level rose, creating estuarine to marine lagoonal deposits. The upper orange-yellow sandstone records littoral to offshore marine deposition (Young, 1973; Doelling and others, 1989). Rocks of the Dakota sequence record the first incursion of the Cretaceous Sea from the east (Doelling and others, 1989; Peterson and others, 1980).

Quaternary Basaltic Boulder and Gravel Lag

Igneous activity in the later Tertiary produced a 370- to 500-foot-thick cap of basalt and rhyolite on the Aquarius Plateau and Boulder Mountain to the north (Smith and others, 1963). During the late Pleistocene, glaciers covered these high regions, depositing till in moraines and minor amounts of outwash (Flint and Denny, 1958). Glacier melt-water streams and debris flows transported the dark-red and black boulders, cobbles, and gravel to their present resting place on top of the small plateau transected by the park's main hiking trail (figure 4) (Smith and others, 1963).

The Quaternary lag deposit is composed of dark-red rhyolite and black basaltic igneous rocks that range in size from boulders, up to 1.6 to 3 feet in length, to smaller cobbles and gravel. The boulder and gravel lag has been mapped as a pediment surface by Stephens (1973). Pediments are broad plains of low relief developed by stream erosion that truncates bedrock at the base of a plateau escarpment. Due to poor exposures on the plateau, a truncated bedrock surface was not directly observed. The undersides of the igneous-rock-derived boulders and gravel displayed up to 0.5 inch thick coats of white caliche, a characteristic attributed to pediment gravels (Smith and others, 1963). However, without exposures revealing the relationship of the boulder-and-gravel cap with the underlying rock, the cap is referred to as a lag deposit and not pediment.

Quaternary Alluvium/Colluvium

Quaternary alluvium blankets the intermittent stream bed of Baily Wash whereas colluvium extends from the base of the park's cliffs outward into broad valleys. Alluvium is unconsolidated sand, gravel, silt and clay that is transported and deposited by streams in recent geologic time (Bates and Jackson, 1987). Colluvium refers to any unconsolidated material that collects at the base of hillsides, cliffs and slopes (Bates and Jackson, 1987). Weathering of the sandstone and mudstone cliffs in the park provided sediment that was transported by rainwash and wind and collected downslope as a colluvium blanket.

INTERESTING FEATURES

Several interesting geologic phenomena occur in the park and are worth noting. They include petrified wood, dinosaur bones, and a calcrete horizon of a paleosol (fossil soil). Please remember petrified wood and dinosaur bones are protected by law; collecting is not permitted. Enjoy looking at and taking photographs of the petrified wood and bones, but leave them in their place.

Petrified Wood

A unique attribute of Escalante State Park is the abundance of colorful agatized petrified wood. Most of the wood occurs in the uppermost dark-brown conglomerate of the Brushy Basin Member of the Morrison Formation. Large logs up to 10 feet long and as much as 3 feet in diameter are encased in the conglomerate (figure 6). Many of the petrified wood pieces have weathered out of the overlying conglomerate and have rolled downslope to rest on the Brushy Basin variegated mudstones. Small pieces of dull brown to tan silicified petrified wood occur above

Figure 7. Scattered of fragments of bone, most likely dinosaur, on the variegated mudstone of the Brushy Basin Member (hacky-sack for scale).

the brown conglomerate, in the upper gray mudstone of the Brushy Basin.

Petrification occurs through a process of replacement. As wood tissue begins to decay in the presence of water containing dissolved ions, the organic material is replaced by minerals. When this occurs slowly the microscopic structure of the wood is duplicated. However, when replacement is rapid the original wood structure is destroyed (Fenton and Fenton, 1989). The wood is replaced by a variety of silica called agate. The colors seen in the park's petrified wood are a result of very small amounts of elements or specific minerals contained within the agate. Common elements and the colors they produce are: copper, cobalt and chromium produce shades of green and blue; manganese tinges the rock pink; carbon and manganese cause black; and iron produces various shades of red, brown, yellow, and green.

None of the agatized wood in the park is preserved well enough to identify (D.A. Medlyn, verbal communication, 1999); however, it is thought that most are conifers that lived adjacent to the fluvial systems. Four genera of conifers, *Protopicieoxylon, Tasaceoxylon, Mesembrioxylon,* and *Araucaioxylon,* have been identified from the Morrison Formation in the Henry Mountains to the east (Medlyn and Tidwell, 1975). For additional information on the flora and fauna of the Morrison Formation see Chure and others (1998).

Dinosaur Bones

The Morrison Formation is well known for its dinosaur fauna (Chure, 1987; Baars, 1995; Chure and others, 1998). Significant quarries are developed within the Salt Wash and Brushy Basin members in the Colorado Plateau and include the Cleveland Lloyd Dinosaur Quarry, Utah, and the Douglass Quarry at Dinosaur National Monument, Utah and Colorado (Bilbey, 1998). Fragments of dinosaur bone, some of which are displayed at the park office, have been found in remote sites in Escalante State Park (figure 7). Dinosaur bones are vertebrate fossils, and, as all vertebrate fossils, are protected by law. Collecting even the smallest fragment of bone is not allowed. If you

Figure 8.　Concretions in a sandstone bed of Brushy Basin Wash Member exposed on the Sleeping Rainbows Trail just above the Baily Wash overlook.

are lucky enough to find pieces of bone, enjoy them but leave them as you find them.

Paleosol

Another interesting geologic feature in the park occurs along the Petrified Forest and Sleeping Rainbows Trails. Once past sign post number 1 on the Petrified Forest Trail, the trail moves over the lower Brushy Basin Member of the Morrison Formation. Several sandstone outcrops that contain many small, 0.5 to 1 inch diameter spherical nodules occur in the lower Brushy Basin. These nodules also occur along the Sleeping Rainbows Trail. The trail descends through the Brushy Basin Member of the Morrison Formation to an overlook of Baily Wash where it begins back uphill. Sandstone of the lower Brushy Basin Member is exposed along the uphill trail in 1.5- to 3.5-foot-thick beds. The calcite-cemented sandstone is composed of numerous spherical nodules from 0.33 to 1 inch in diameter (figure 8).

The nodules mark a calcrete zone in soil horizon C of a paleosol, an ancient soil horizon that formed on the sandstone. Calcretes develop either as a precipitate from groundwater supersaturated with calcium carbonate or from rain leaching calcium carbonate dust into the soil that was carried there by the wind (Machette, 1985; Retallack, 1997). Once exposed, the calcrete weathered into spherical, calcite-cemented sandstone nodules.

SUMMARY

Escalante State Park is an ideal location to see abundant specimens of very colorful agatized petrified wood. Most of the wood samples are poorly preserved specimens of Mesozoic conifers, and occur in the upper conglomerate of the Brushy Basin Member of the Morrison Formation. In addition, weathering of the Morrison reveals occasional fragments of dinosaur bones that litter the hillsides. The fossils and the rocks tell a story of changing environments through the late Middle Jurassic to Early Cretaceous time. Eolian sand dunes of the Escalante Member of the Entrada Sandstone gave way to Morrison Formation fluvial sandstone, conglomerate, and mudstone, whereas the Dakota Formation records the advance of the encroaching Early Cretaceous seaway.

ACKNOWLEDGMENTS

Thanks to geology student Alayna Hoffman for joining us in the field. In addition, Gayle Pollock took a day from his busy schedule to meet us in Escalante State Park and discuss the Mesozoic and Cretaceous rocks exposed in the area. Dan Richards, park ranger of Escalante State Park, was helpful in providing information and maps and for accommodating us in the campground. We also would like to thank the reviewers Sue Ann Bilbey, Peter T. Kolesar, and Gayle Pollock for their helpful comments and insights. In addition, Sue Ann provided some hard-to-find references.

REFERENCES

Anderson, O.J., and Lucas, S.G., 1998, Redefinition of Morrison Formation (Upper Jurassic) and related San Rafael group strata, southwestern U.S.: Modern Geology, v. 22, p. 39-69.

Baars, D.L., 1995, Navajo Country: Albuquerque, University of New Mexico Press, 138 p.

Bates, R. L., and Jackson, J. S., editors, 1987, Glossary of Geology: Alexandria, Virginia, American Geological Institute, 788 p.

Bilbey, S.A., 1998, Cleveland-Lloyd dinosaur quarry - age, stratigraphy and depositional environments: Modern Geology, v. 22, p. 87-120.

Brown, H.H., 1973, The Dakota Formation in the plateau area, southwest Utah, *in* Fassett, J.E., editor, Cretaceous and Tertiary rocks of the southern Colorado Plateau: Four Corners Geological Society Memoir, p. 52-56.

Chure, D.J., 1987, Dinosaur National Monument—a window on the past, *in* Avertt, W.R., editor, Paleontology and geology of the Dinosaur triangle: Museum of Western Colorado Guidebook, p. 5-20.

Chure, D.J., Carpenter, K., Litwin, R., Hasiotis, S., Evanoff, E., 1998, The fauna and flora of the Morrison Formation: Modern Geology, v. 23, p. 507-537.

Cole, R.D., 1987, Cretaceous rocks in the Dinosaur Triangle, *in* Avertt, W.R., editor, Paleontology and geology of the Dinosaur triangle: Museum of Western Colorado Guidebook, p. 5-20.

Craig, L.C. and Shawe, D.R., 1975, Jurassic rocks of east-central Utah, *in* Fassett, J.E., editor, Canyonlands country: Four Corners Geological Society, Eighth Field Conference, p. 157-165.

Cross, Whitman, 1894, Pikes Peak folio: Unites States Geological Survey Atlas.

Doelling, H.H., 1975, Geology and mineral resources of Garfield County, Utah: Utah Geological and Mineral Survey Bulletin 107, 175 p.

Doelling, H.H., Davis, F.D., and Brandt, C.J., 1989, The geology of Kane County, Utah: Utah Geological and Mineral Survey Bulletin 124, 192 p.

Emmons, S.F., Cross, C.W., and Eldridge, G.H., 1896, Geology of the denver basin in Colorado: U.S. Geological Survey Monograph 27.

Fenton, C.L., and Fenton, M.A., 1989, The fossil book: New York, Doubleday, 740 p.

Flint, R.F., and Denny, C.S., 1958, Quaternary geology of Boulder Mountain, Aquarius Plateau, Utah: U.S. Geological Survey Bulletin 1061-D, 164 p.

Gilluly, James, and Reeside, J.B., Jr., 1928, Sedimentary rocks of the San Rafael Swell and some adjacent areas in eastern Utah: U.S. Geological Survey Professional Paper 150-D, p. 61-110.

Hintze, L.F., 1988, Geologic history of Utah: Brigham Young University Geology Studies Special Publication 7, 202 p.

Johnson, J.A., 1988, The sedimentology, paleohydrology, and paleogeography of the Brushy Basin Member, Morrison Formation in the Henry Basin, Wayne and Garfield Counties, Utah: Berkeley, University of California, Ph.D. dissertation, 112 p.

Lupton, C. T., 1914, Oil and gas near Green River, Grand County, Utah: United States Geological Survey Bulletin, 541, p. 115-133.

Machette, M. N., 1985, Calcic soils of the southwestern United States, *in* Weide, D.L., editor, Soils and Quaternary geology of the southwestern United States: Geological Society of America, Special Paper 203, p. 1-21.

Meek, F.B., and Hayden, F.V., 1862, Description of new Lower Silurian (Primordial), Jurassic, Cretaceous, and Tertiary fossils collected in Nebraska Territory...with some remarks on the rocks from which they were obtained: Proceedings Academy National Science, Philadelphia, vol. 12, p. 419-20.

Medlyn, D.A., and Tidwell, W.D., 1975, Conifer wood from the Upper Jurassic of Utah Part I—Xwnoxylon morrisonesc sp. nov.: American Journal of Botany, v. 62, 2, p. 203-208.

O'Sullivan, R.B., 1992, The Jurassic Wanakah and Morrison Formation in the Telluride-Ouray-western Black Canyon area of southern Colorado: U.S. Geological Survey Bulletin 1927, 24 p.

Peterson, Fred, 1988a, Stratigraphy and nomenclature of Middle and Upper Jurassic rocks, western Colorado Plateau, Utah and Arizona: U.S. Geological Survey Bulletin 1633-B, p.17-56.

Peterson, Fred, 1988b, A synthesis of the Jurassic system in the southern Rocky Mountain region, *in* Sloss, L.L., editor, Sedimentary cover—North American craton, U.S.: Geological Society of America Geology of North America, v. D-2, p. 65-76.

— 1994, Sand dunes, sabkhas, streams, and shallow seas—Jurassic paleogeography in the southern part of the western interior basin, *in* Caputo, M.V., Peterson, Fred, and Franczyk, K.J., editors, Mesozoic systems of the Rocky Mountain region, USA: Denver Rocky Mountain Section of Society of Economic Paleontologists and Mineralogists, p. 233-298.

Peterson, Fred, and Ryder, R.T., 1975, Cretaceous rocks in the Henry Mountains region, Utah and their relation to neighboring regions, *in* Fassett, J.E., editor, Canyonlands country: Four Corners Geological Society Guidebook, Eighth Field Conference, p. 167-1?.

Peterson, Fred, Ryder, R.T., and Law, B.E., 1980, Stratigraphy, sedimentology, regional relationships of the Cretaceous system in the Henry Mountains region, Utah, *in* Picard, M.D., editor, Henry Mountains symposium: Utah Geological Association Publication 8, p. 151-170.

Peterson, Fred, and Turner-Peterson, Christine, 1989, Geology of the Colorado Plateau: American Geophysical Union, Guidebook T 130, 65 p.

Petersen, L.M., and Roylance, M.M., 1982, Stratigraphy and depositional environments of the Upper Jurassic Morrison Formation near Capitol Reef National Park, Utah: Brigham Young University Geology Studies, v. 29, p. 1-12.

Peterson, P.R., 1971, Geology of the Escalante-Boulder area Garfield, County, Utah: Utah Geological and Mineralogical Survey, Map 31, scale 1:63,360.

Retallack, G.J., 1997, A color guide to paleosols: New York, John Wiley & Sons, 175 p.

Robinson, J.W., and McCabe, P.J., 1998, Evolution of a braided river system—the Salt Wash Member of the Morrison Formation (Jurassic) in southern Utah, *in* Shanley, K.W., and McCabe, P.J., editors, Relative role of eustasy, climate, and tectonism in continental rocks: Society of Economic Paleontologists and Mineralogists Special Publication 59, p. 93-107.

Smith, J.R., Jr., Huff, L.C., Hinrichs, E.N., and Luedke, R.G., 1963, Geology of the Capitol Reef area, Wayne and Garfield Counties, Utah: U.S. Geological Survey Professional Paper 363, 101 p.

Stephens, E.V., 1973, Geologic map and coal resources of the Wide Hollow Reservoir quadrangle, Garfield County, Utah: U.S. Geological Survey, Coal Investigations Map C-55, scale 1:24,000.

Stokes, W.L., 1944, Morrison and related deposits in and adjacent to the Colorado Plateau: Geological Society of American Bulletin 55, p. 951-992.

—1980, Stratigraphic interpretations of Triassic and Jurassic beds, Henry Mountains area, *in* Picard, M.D., editor, Henry Mountains symposium: Utah Geological Association Publication 8, p. 113-122.

Young, R.G., 1973, Depositional environments of basal Cretaceous rocks of the Colorado Plateau, *in* Fassett, J.E., editor, Cretaceous and Tertiary rocks of the southern Colorado Plateau: Four Corners Geological Society Memoir, p. 10-27.

—1987, Triassic and Jurassic rocks in the dinosaur triangle, *in* Avertt, W.R., editor, Paleontology and Geology of the Dinosaur Triangle: Denver, Museum of Western Colorado Guidebook, p. 5-20.

Geology of Utah's Parks and Monuments
2000 Utah Geological Association Publication 28
D.A. Sprinkel, T.C. Chidsey, Jr., and P.B. Anderson, editors

Geology of Goblin Valley State Park, Utah

Mark R. Milligan[1]

ABSTRACT

Goblin Valley State Park exhibits the sub-horizontal sedimentary red beds that typify the Colorado Plateau. Within the park this sub-horizontal strata includes the Jurassic Entrada, Curtis, Summerville, and Morrison Formations. Quaternary deposits and soils, many with microbiotic and mechanical crusts, complete the geologic succession at Goblin Valley.

Found exclusively within the Entrada Sandstone, a multitude of bizarrely shaped hoodoos are the park's preeminent attraction. Within the Entrada Sandstone, fracture patterns form angular blocks in fine-grained sandstone beds. Spheroidal weathering removes the angular sides and corners from these blocks creating rounded goblins. The fine-grained sandstone beds are interbedded with siltstones and shales that weather and erode more rapidly, giving goblins an elongated and stacked appearance. Additionally, variation in the amount and type of cementation may act as a secondary control on the unusual shapes of individual goblins.

INTRODUCTION AND GEOLOGIC SETTING

One of Utah's most remote and isolated state parks, Goblin Valley lies 14 road miles (23 km) west of State Highway 24 between Hanksville and Green River (figure 1). This isolated desert setting adds to the mystique of the bizarre stone sculptures that are the park's main attraction.

As with the other southeastern Utah parks included in this publication, Goblin Valley State Park lies within the Colorado Plateau physiographic province (figure 2). Across the Colorado Plateau, buttes, mesas, and deep narrow canyons expose layer upon layer of nearly undeformed, flat-lying sedimentary rock (figure 3). Goblin Valley State Park and its goblin- bearing beds follow this rule of "layer-cake" geology (figure 4). However, two notable exceptions to the rule can be seen from the park: the San Rafael Swell directly to the northwest and the Henry Mountains to the south.

San Rafael Swell

Lying about one mile (1.6 km) northwest of the park entrance is a large anticline, the San Rafael Swell. Although originally horizontal, the rock layers that make up this structure have been compressed into a convex-upward fold, with the older rocks exposed in the center (figure 5). This anticline is roughly 75 miles (120 km) long (extending northeast-southwest) and 30 miles (48 km) wide (Stokes, 1986). The limbs or sides of this anticline are not symmetric. As seen from Goblin Valley State Park, the

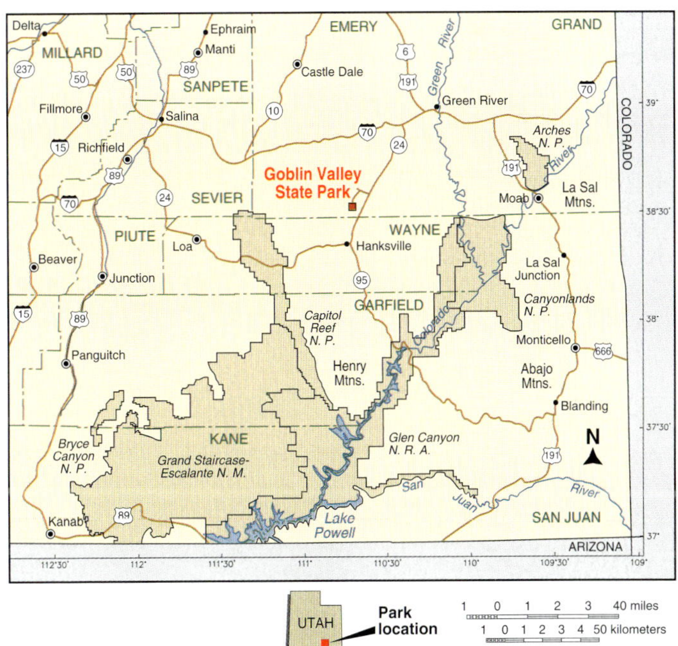

Figure 1. Location of Goblin Valley State Park, Utah.

[1]*Utah Geological Survey, Salt Lake City, UT 84114-6100*

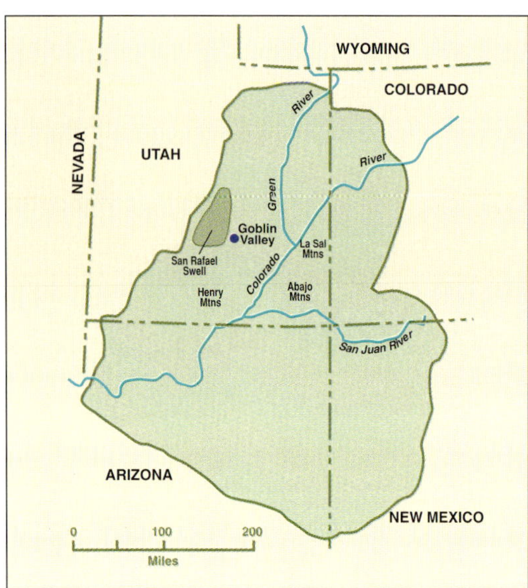

Figure 2. *Goblin Valley State Park lies within the Colorado Plateau physiographic province (shown in green).*

Figure 3. *Wild Horse Butte near the park's entrance, viewed from the west. Typical of the Colorado Plateau, steep cliffs expose nearly flat-lying beds of sedimentary rock.*

Figure 4. *True to the regional pattern of flat-lying beds, the goblins develop in laterally continuous, horizontal, fine-grained sandstone beds interbedded with and underlain by siltstone and shale beds. Notice the goblins forming in this cliff face of such rock layers. The apparently isolated goblins in the foreground were once part of the same, once-continuous horizontal beds exposed at the base of the cliff face.*

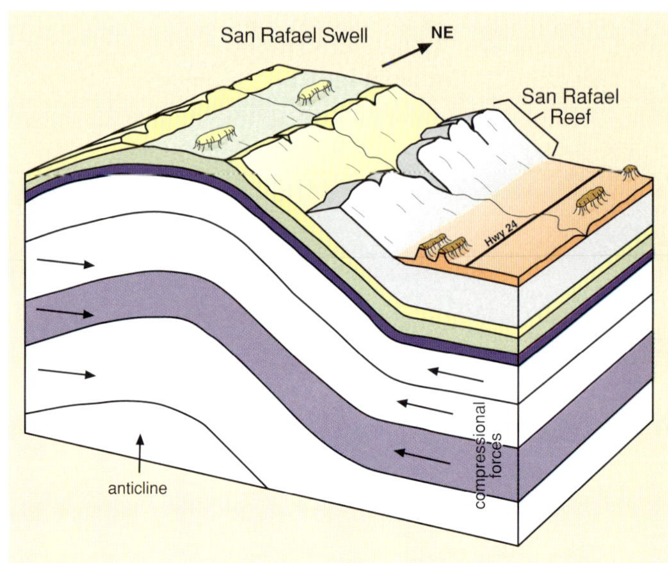

Figure 5. *Diagrammatic illustration of the structure of the San Rafael Swell. Because they have been partially removed by erosion, the uppermost rock layers are no longer continuous over the anticline.*

Figure 6. *As seen from Goblin Valley State Park, the San Rafael Swell forms a ridge against the skyline. An exception to the flat-lying beds found across the Colorado Plateau, the slope seen from this view is due to the steep incline of the beds.*

eastern limb, called the San Rafael Reef, is steeply inclined to nearly vertical, in contrast with the more gently inclined western limb (figures 5 and 6). Alternating hard and soft rock layers dissected at nearly right angles by washes account for some of the San Rafael Swell's spectacular scenery. In ascending stratigraphic order, the Moenkopi, Chinle, Wingate, Navajo, and Carmel Formations constitute the Swell in the immediate vicinity of Goblin Valley State Park. The beds of these formations are laterally continuous toward the park, but dip deeply beneath the surface.

The San Rafael Swell has a complex history. It was probably originally upwarped approximately 60 to 65 million years ago during the Laramide orogeny (Stokes, 1986), a regional-scale mountain-building event that also formed Waterpocket Fold in Capitol Reef National Park to the southwest and the Uinta Mountains in northeastern Utah. Laramide mountain building presumably resulted from events that happened far to the west when two plates, the

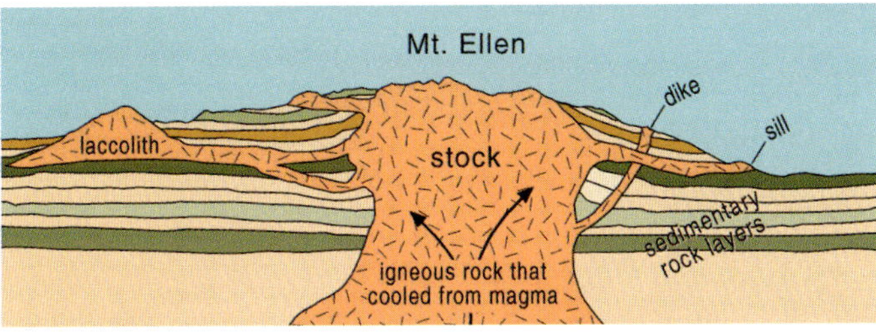

Figure 7. Mount Ellen, at the northern end of the Henry Mountains, is a prominent feature seen from Goblin Valley State Park. As shown in the illustration, Mount Ellen is composed of igneous rock bodies that include a stock with dikes, sills, and laccoliths.

North American plate and the precursor to the Pacific plate, collided in the area that is now coastal California (Coney, 1978, 1981). This head-on collision created compressional forces far inland causing the crust to buckle and create features like the San Rafael Swell.

Following the Laramide orogeny, the crest of the original San Rafael anticline was removed by erosion and may have been partially buried (Stokes, 1986). It was not until the last 10 million years when the entire Colorado Plateau was uplifted and the modern Colorado River drainage system developed, that erosion re-exhumed the pre-existing structure of the San Rafael Swell.

Henry Mountains

Another prominent skyline feature is the Henry Mountains, which lie to the south (figure 7). In contrast to the layers of sedimentary rocks that compose most of the Colorado Plateau, intrusive igneous rocks constitute the heart of the Henry Mountains. These intrusive igneous rocks formed approximately 23 to 29 million years ago,

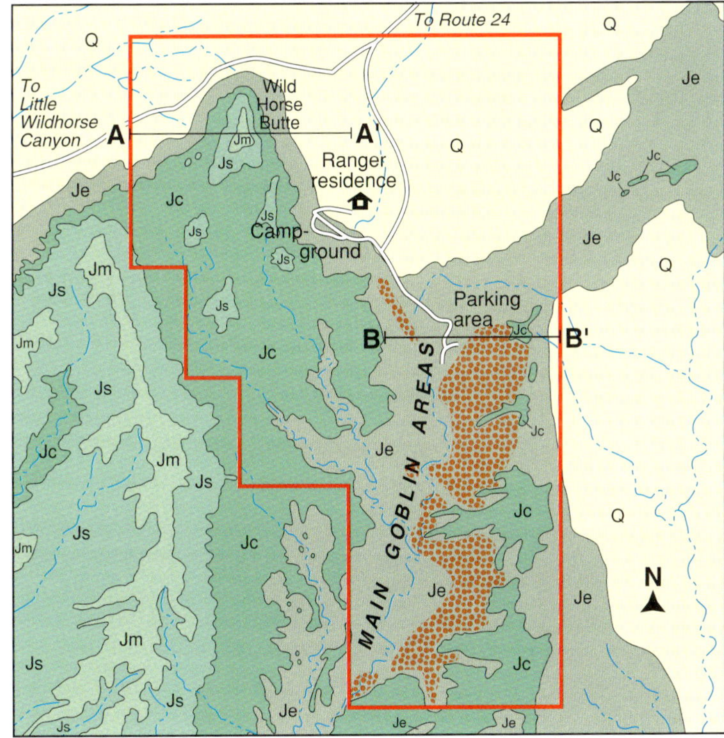

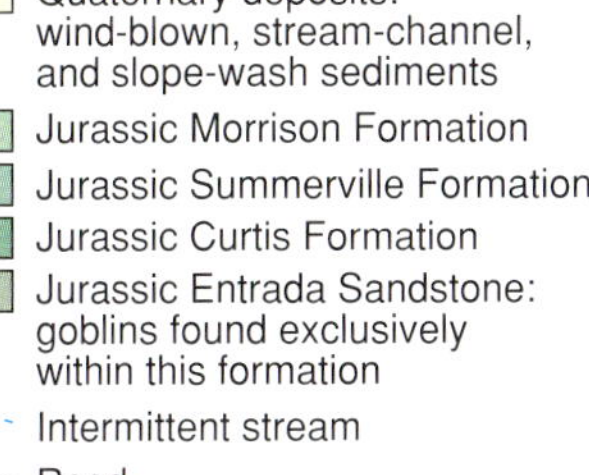

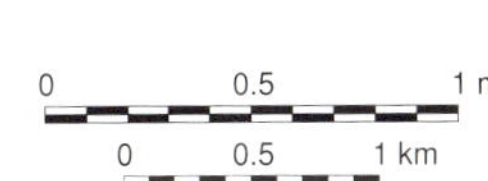

Geology modified from Orkild, 1953

Figure 8. Geologic map and cross section of Goblin Valley State Park. Geology modified from Orkild (1953).

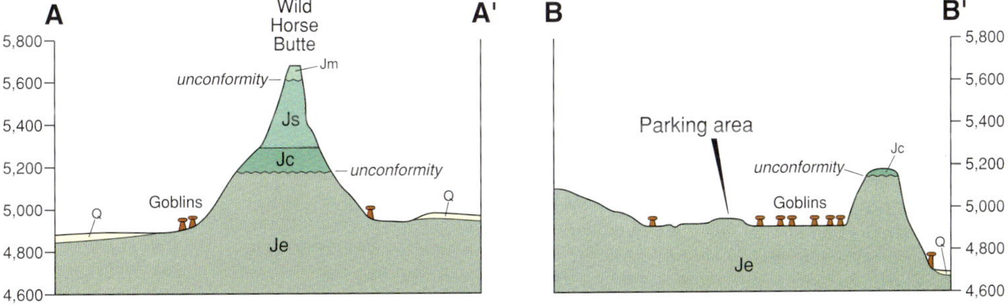

DIAGRAMMATIC CROSS-SECTIONS
2.5x vertical exaggeration

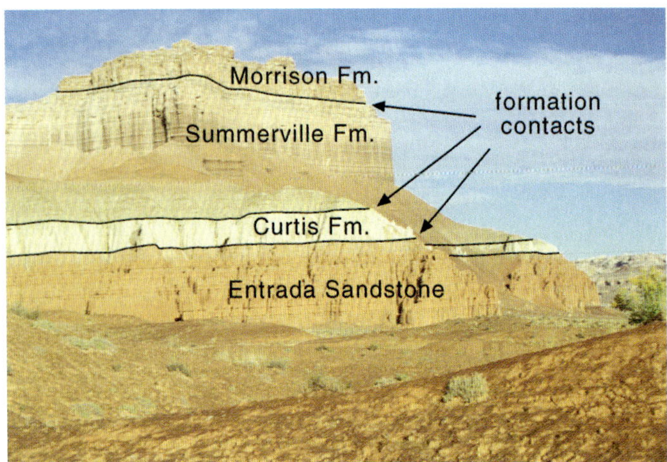

Figure 9. Wild Horse Butte exposes all four rock formations found within Goblin Valley State Park. View from south-southeast.

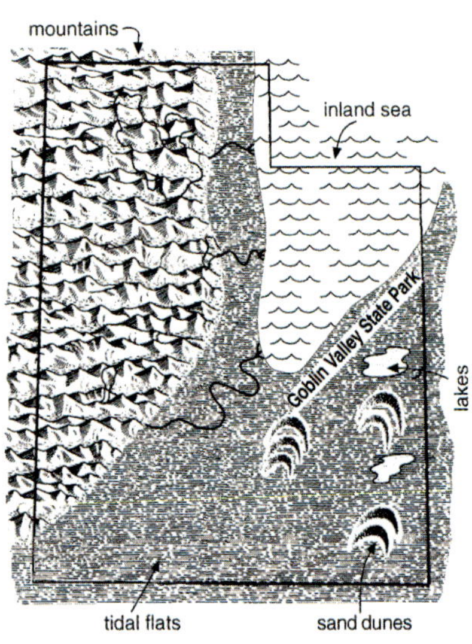

Figure 10. A diagrammatic representation of how Utah may have looked approximately 170 million years ago (Middle Jurassic) during deposition of the goblin-forming Entrada Sandstone (modified from Stokes, 1986).

when magma that was injected between and across the sedimenatry rock layers cooled before reaching the surface (Hintze, 1988). Since the intrusive igneous rocks are more resistant to weathering than the sedimentary host rocks, they stand out in prominent relief as erosion lowers the surrounding landscape. On a clear day, two more igneous intrusions may be visible on the horizon: the La Sal Mountains to the east and Abajo Mountains to the southeast.

STRATIGRAPHY AND GEOLOGIC HISTORY

Four formations are exposed in Goblin Valley State Park. From oldest to youngest, they are: the Entrada Sandstone, Curtis Formation, Summerville Formation, and Morrison Formation; the latter three are part of the San Rafael Group (figures 8 and 9). The sedimentary layers comprising these formations were deposited approximately 145 to 170 million years ago, during the Middle to Late Jurassic (Orkild, 1953; Williams and Hackman, 1971). During this time, North America and Eurasia were pulling apart from South America and Africa as part of the

Figure 11. Found only within the reddish-brown Entrada Sandstone, goblins are composed of fine-grained sandstone interbedded with and underlain by shale and siltstone. Though now an erosional island, the beds that form this goblin were once laterally continuous. Below the goblin, bedding is masked by colluvium.

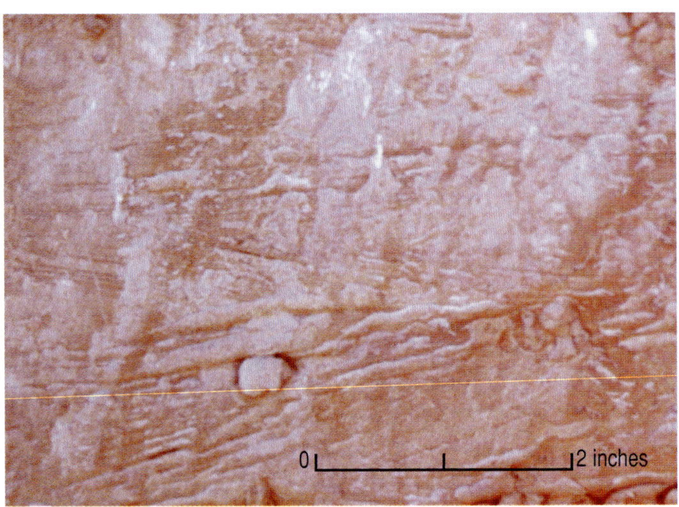

Figure 12. Careful observation of some of the Entrada's sandstone beds reveals herringbone cross-bedding. The thin banding slants in opposite directions, left near the bottom, then right, then left caused by the alternating direction of the incoming flood tide and outgoing ebb tide.

breakup of the supercontinent Pangea (Irving, 1983). The area that we now call Utah was closer to the equator. Much of eastern Utah was a dry Sahara-like desert (Stokes, 1986), but shallow seas intermittently transgressed across the area that is now Goblin Valley State Park. Northwestern Utah consisted of granitic highlands (Stokes, 1986). The silts, sands, and clays that comprise the rocks now exposed in Goblin Valley State Park were formed primarily from erosional debris shed from these highlands and redeposited in seas, on shorelines, in river channels, and on playas (figure 10).

Goblin-Forming Entrada Sandstone

Approximately 425 vertical feet (130 m) of shale, siltstone, and fine-grained sandstone comprise the Entrada Sandstone at Goblin Valley State Park (figure 11). Similar to many rocks across the Colorado Plateau, the Entrada's reddish hue comes mainly from hematite (iron oxide).

Figure 13. This cut and fill structure is the remnant of a tidal channel in the Entrada Sandstone, produced when water flowing toward the open sea cut a channel that later filled with mud and silt. In this picture water would have been flowing either towards or away from the camera.

Figure 14. Just north of the park's main parking area, this road cut exposes an eolian dune in Entrada Sandstone. Lines formed by slight variations in grain size define individual beds of sand. These beds slope downward to the right. The single direction and relatively large scale of this cross-bedding (vs. the cross-bedding in figure 12) along with the grain-size and sorting suggests that this rock layer may have once been a sand dune.

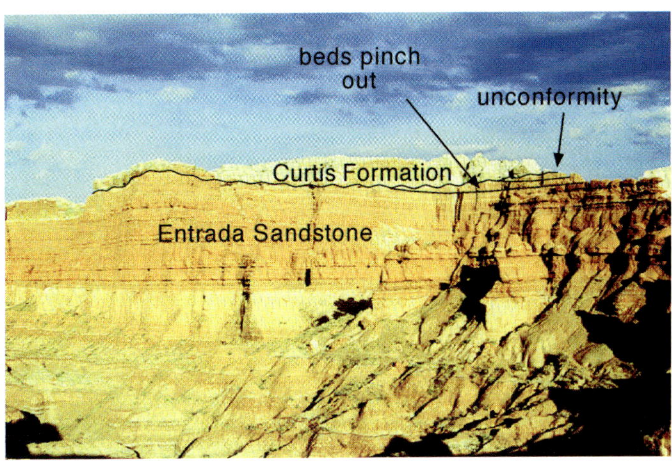

Figure 15. As seen in this cliff face at the eastern edge of the park, an angular unconformity separates the Entrada Sandstone from the overlying Curtis Formation. Note how the uppermost Entrada beds are truncated below the unconformity.

Figure 16. A block of the Curtis Formation displays a surface of ripple marks frozen in time. Note how some ripple crests fork. The oscillating action of waves created these bifurcating or branching ripple marks on the beach of the ancient Curtis Sea. The block is approximately 3 feet (1 m) long.

Named after Entrada Point in the northern part of the San Rafael Swell (Gilluly and Reeside, 1928), it is the same formation that erodes to arches, fins, and spires in Arches National Park and hoodoos in Cathedral Valley of Capitol Reef National Park. The Entrada in Cathedral Valley is similar to that of Goblin Valley State Park, and consists of interbedded shale, siltstone, and sandstone deposited on tidal flats (Billingsley and others, 1987). In Arches, however, sandstone, originally deposited as sand dunes, dominates the Entrada (Doelling, 1985). Hence this formation changes laterally, much the same way modern landscapes change while driving across southern Utah.

The rhythmically interbedded nature of the siltstone and shale beds (tidal bedding), herringbone cross-bedding (figure 12), plane parallel lamination, and cut and fill structures (figure 13) attest to tidal-flat deposition. Although this area was predominantly a wide tidal flat between the sea to the north and continental highlands to the west, coastal sand dunes also existed on parts of the tidal area (figure 14).

Curtis Formation

The Curtis Formation overlies the Entrada, forming the greenish-gray cap rock on the buttes east of the goblins (figure 15). An angular unconformity marks the Entrada - Curtis contact. This is the J-3 unconformity described in detail by Pipiringos and O'Sullivan (1978). Within the park the Curtis is approximately 85 feet (26 m) thick. The Curtis Formation takes its name from Curtis Point in the northern part of the San Rafael Swell (Gilluly and Reeside, 1928). Fossils in locations outside the park suggest the sandstones and siltstones comprising the Curtis are Late Jurassic in age and marine in origin (Brenner, 1983). The greenish color comes from minor amounts of glauconite, a

Figure 17. Surrounding Wild Horse Butte near the park entrance, cliffs of the Summerville Formation expose chocolate- to bone-colored shale beds interlayered with thin, whitish gypsum beds.

Figure 18. Veinlets of gypsum form a lace-like pattern in cliffs of the Summerville Formation around Wild Horse Butte. Rock hammer for scale.

clay mineral that contains iron and forms in modern ocean sediments (Stokes and Cohenour, 1956). Within the park, bifurcating ripple marks and planar cross-bedding argue for deposition on the beach of the ancient Curtis sea (figure 16). The pieces of orange agate and other varieties of quartz found throughout the park generally erode from an approximately 3-inch-thick (8 cm) bed near the conformable contact with the overlying Summerville Formation.

Summerville Formation

In Late Jurassic time the deeper waters of the Curtis Sea retreated northward, and again the area took on the attributes of a seaside tidal flat (Brenner, 1983). The sediments preserved in these tidal flats are called the Summerville Formation. This formation gets its name from Summerville Point in the northern part of the San Rafael Swell (Gilluly and Reeside, 1928). Locally, the Summerville can be seen overlying the Curtis Formation on the highest buttes at the north end of the park. Wild Horse Butte displays approximately 340 vertical feet (104 m) of Summerville. This formation consists of distinctive, thin beds of chocolate- to bone-colored shale and siltstone with minor sandstone (figure 17). Thin beds and veinlets of white gypsum found within the shale suggest a dry climate where ponded tidal water readily evaporated (figure 18).

Morrison Formation

Following deposition of the Summerville, this area again experienced slight uplift and erosion. Hence the disconformity between the Summerville and Morrison Formations (the J-5 unconformity of Pipiringos and O'Sullivan [1978]). When deposition resumed, the seas had not returned and exclusively continental conditions existed across the Colorado Plateau (Hintze, 1988). Flood plains or playas left behind varicolored mudstones, and streams crossed the area depositing sandstones and conglomerates in the channels (Hallam, 1982; Peterson and Turner-Peterson, 1987). These deposits compose the Morrison Formation, which takes its name from exposures near the town of Morrison in Jefferson County, Colorado (Eldridge, 1896; Waldschmidt and LeRoy, 1944). Within the park the formation is only found on the top of Wild Horse Butte where it is approximately 150 feet (46 m) thick but generally inaccessible. The Morrison Formation is famous for the fossil dinosaur bones found within it. No dinosaur bone discoveries have been reported on Wild Horse Butte, but bones have been found just west of the park in this formation.

The Morrison is the uppermost formation in the park. Overlying formations have long since been removed by erosion in the park; however, some of these formations can be found outside the park and as many as eleven formations totaling thousands of feet overlie the Morrison elsewhere.

Quaternary Deposits

Quaternary deposits in Goblin Valley State Park include: (1) talus consisting of blocks, boulders, and smaller angular rock fragments at the bases of cliffs and steep slopes, (2) colluvium, (3) alluvium (figure 19), and (4) eolian (wind) dunes. Quaternary deposits such as these are fundamental in identifying areas containing geologic hazards. For example, large talus blocks at the foot of a cliff

Figure 19. Erosion actively disassembles goblins and redeposits their sediments in modern intermittent stream channels. Such modern environments are important analogs for deciphering the conditions under which ancient formations were deposited. Notice the subtle differences between these modern stream bed ripples and the ancient beach ripples shown in figure 16.

are a reminder of the danger of rock falls. Many of the Entrada slopes are covered with colluvium that exhibits a "popcorn" texture called gilgai (figure 20) (Costa and Baker, 1981). Gilgai is indicative of unstable, expansive soils that expand when wet and shrink while drying. Without proper building techniques, this instability can heave and crack foundations, road surfaces, sidewalks, and buried utilities and cause failure of wastewater disposal systems. Alluvium in normally dry stream channels may serve as a warning of the potential for flooding. Sand dunes and other wind-blown deposits can be unstable. Even dunes stabilized by vegetation can be disturbed and reactivated, leading to migration over roads and other structures.

Microbiotic and Mechanical Crusts

Microbiotic and mechanical crusts often cap Quaternary soils (figure 20). These crusts stabilize soil and affect infiltration of rainwater, seed germination, and plant growth.

Mechanical crusts develop on the clay-rich soils derived from the Entrada Sandstone. These crusts are formed by a thin upper coating of clay particles oriented parallel to the surface (Cooke and Warren, 1973).

Figure 20. Soil covering this slope is self-derived from the Entrada Sandstone. The popcorn-like texture (gilgai) indicates expansive soil that shrinks and expands with drying and wetting cycles. Mechanical and microbiotic crusts form a thin but hard veneer on the top of this expansive soil. The darker areas on the left are due to the presence of microbiotic crusts.

Figure 21. A web of filaments secreted by microscopic cyanobacteria and green algae create this microbiotic crust. Such crusts are found throughout the park.

Figure 22. In a microbiotic crust, a web of organic filaments binds soil particles together, forming an interlocking network of grains. The filaments are composed of sticky sheath material secreted around the cells of cyanobacteria and green algae. Magnification 90x. Photo courtesy Jayne Belnap, U.S. Geological Survey, Biological Resources Division.

Figure 23. *An area of goblins near the park's southern boundary (view to the north) illustrates the roughly north-south-trending set of near-vertical joints in the Entrada.*

Figure 24. *Looking east from the main parking area, the light-colored Curtis Formation caps the reddish-brown Entrada Sandstone.   Notice the apparent east-west-trending set of near-vertical joints in the goblin-forming sandstone beds of the Entrada.*

In contrast, microbiotic crusts are produced by living organisms and their by-products that bind together soil particles at or very near the surface (figures 21 and 22). Many names (cryptogamic, cryptobiotic, microphytic, biological) have been applied to a variety of these organic crusts that are found throughout the world's deserts and semiarid grasslands, shrublands, and woodlands. The existence and type of microbiotic crust depends upon variables such as soil texture, conductivity, pH (acidity), and moisture (Johnston, 1988). The general appearance of microbiotic crust varies widely, depending upon the relative abundance of different crust-forming organisms. Across the Colorado Plateau, cyanobacteria are the most abundant crust-forming organisms (Jayne Belnap, U.S. Geological Survey, Biological Resources Division, verbal communication, April 30, 1998).

Cyanobacteria are a group of microscopic organisms that harvest the sun's energy through photosynthesis. The cyanobacteria are not alone, as they are commonly found with green algae (another group of photosynthetic organisms). Mosses and lichen can also grow on crusts already stabilized by cyanobacteria and green algae. In Goblin Valley State Park, well-developed crusts with abundant mosses and lichen are present, but cyanobacteria-dominated crusts (without mosses and lichen) are most common.

Both microbiotic and mechanical crusts help stabilize soil. By stabilizing soil, they may also help stabilize the goblins. With microbiotic crust, filamentous sheaths hold soil particles in place and directly improve resistance to wind and water erosion. Microbiotic crust may also increase infiltration of rainwater, help retain soil moisture, and encourage seed germination and growth of native plants. Similar to microbiotic crust, mechanical crust greatly enhances resistance to wind erosion. However, mechanical crust is not nearly as resistant to erosion by water. Mechanical crust may also form an impermeable layer that decreases rainwater infiltration, further increasing runoff and downstream erosion.

Foot traffic impacts both microbiotic and mechanical crusts. A single footprint can break mechanical crust and the filaments that create microbiotic crusts. Repeated foot traffic can completely remove this protective layer. Once damaged, the erosive powers of wind are unleashed and soil particles easily blow away. The loss of microbiotic crusts increases the erosive power of water as well. Fortunately, damage done to crusts is reversible, though it can take a long time.

The recovery time for mechanical vs. microbiotic crust varies greatly. Mechanical crusts begin substantial recovery with the first intense rainstorm. Microbiotic crusts take much longer to recover. Cyanobacteria and green algae secrete soil-binding sheaths only when wet, and therefore need repeated wet periods to reconstruct their crust-forming network of filaments. Microbiotic crusts can begin to substantially recover in as little as one to five years, or may take more than 50 years, depending upon crust type, soil type, climate, and extent of initial disturbance (Johnston, 1988). These estimates are generalizations taken from other areas of the Colorado Plateau; no detailed studies have yet been undertaken in Goblin Valley State Park. Visitor impacts on soil and goblin stability is in need of further study.

STRUCTURAL GEOLOGY

Although the impressive geologic structure of the San Rafael Swell anticline looms just north of the park, rock layers within Goblin Valley State Park have maintained a nearly horizontal orientation. The park lies near the edge of an area that exhibits a regional system of east southeast-west northwest-trending faults that cut across the San Rafael Swell (Baker, 1946; Fossen and Hesthammer, 1997). Detailed studies conducted about a mile (~2 km) north of the park and any goblin-bearing outcrops, reveal multiple sets of microfaults that divide the Entrada Sandstone into yard-scale rhombohedral blocks (Aydin, 1978; Aydin and

Figure 25. This cliff face shows progressive goblin development within the Entrada Sandstone. In the cliff face in the left half of the photo, continuous sandstone beds display fresh, unweathered vertical fracture or joint patterns. These vertical joints form zones of weakness that are more susceptible to attack by weathering. In the right half of the photo, cliff retreat and erosion along the joints leave rounded goblins standing out in relief.

Figure 26. Softer shale and siltstone beds weather more readily than the harder sandstone beds. Alternating sandstone, shale, and siltstone beds cause this goblin to have a flattened and elongated shape, and a stacked appearance. A thin veneer of soil (colluvium) covers the base of the goblin.

Johnson, 1978, 1983; Aydin and Reches, 1982). These micro faults exhibit mechanical fracturing of the grains (Fossen and Hesthammer, 1997, 1998). This cataclastic deformation reduces grain size, which results in decreased porosity (pore space) and permeability (ability to transmit fluid) within the fracture. Within Goblin Valley State Park structures are limited to presumably similar, small-scale fractures that exhibit little (less than an inch) to no discernible offset. As discussed in the following section, these fractures or joints play a role in goblin formation.

GEOLOGIC UNIQUENESS

WEATHERING AND EROSION - SCULPTORS OF THE GOBLINS

The park's bedrock geology and its 170 million plus years of geologic history have merely set the stage for the master sculptors in the park - weathering and erosion. Erosion excavated and exposed the Entrada Sandstone, as well as carved the individual goblins from within it.

Joint sets within the Entrada's fine-grained sandstone beds play an important role in goblin development by creating initial zones of weakness (figures 23 and 24). Unweathered joints intersect to form sharp edges and corners (figure 25). These edges and corners are more susceptible to weathering because they have a greater surface-area-to-volume ratio than the faces. As a result, they weather more quickly, producing rounded goblins through a process called spheroidal weathering. Spheroidal weathering helps shape the goblins, but it is only part of the larger erosion process that forms and exhumes the goblins.

The interbedded and underlying shale and siltstone beds are less resistant to weathering and erosion than the sandstone beds that form the goblin bodies. Combined

Figure 27. Minerals precipitated in the tiny spaces between individual sand grains provide a degree of hardness to the sandstone beds. Variations in the amount and type of cement may also contribute to the unusual shapes of specific goblins. Perhaps the neck on this "turtle" can be attributed to varying degrees or types of cementation?

Figure 28. Goblins appear and disappear. This toppled goblin will eventually weather to oblivion, while erosion continues to excavate new goblins.

with spheroidal weathering of the sandstone beds, these softer shale and siltstone beds give the goblins their often elongated shapes, flat bottoms, stacked appearance, and the pedestals upon which they are displayed (figure 26).

Additionally, variation in the amount and type of cementation (between grains in sedimentary rocks) may act as a secondary control on the unusual shapes of individual goblins (figure 27). However, a detailed study of cementation has not been done at the park.

Old goblins eventually topple and weather to oblivion as erosion unearths new goblins (figure 28). Thus, on a geologic time scale, the park is being renewed and regenerated. However, the rate of goblin excavation and creation vs. goblin destruction is not known.

ACKNOWLEDGMENTS

This paper is an outgrowth of The Geology of Goblin Valley State Park, a booklet published by the Utah Geological Survey in 1999. The Utah Division of Parks & Recreation provided funding for field expenses. Field research for the original booklet was done while I served on the Goblin Valley State Park Resource Management Planning Team. During the planning process other team members contributed to the success of the booklet.

Jayne Belnap, U.S. Geological Survey, Biological Resources Division, introduced me to the soils of the Colorado Plateau. Utah Geological Survey geologists Sandy Eldredge, Mike Hylland, and Christine Wilkerson provided helpful reviews.

REFERENCES

Aydin, Atilla, 1978, Small faults formed as deformation bands in sandstone: Pure and Applied Geophysics, v. 16, p. 913-930.

Aydin, Atilla, and Johnson, A.M., 1978, Development of faults as zones of deformation bands and as slip surfaces in sandstones: Pure and Applied Geophysics, v. 16, p. 931-942.

—1983, Analysis of faulting in porous sandstones: Journal of Structural Geology, v. 5, no. 1, p. 19-31.

Aydin, Atilla, and Reches, Ze'ev, 1982, Number and orientation of fault sets in the field and in experiments: Geology, v. 10, p. 107-112.

Baker, A.A., 1946, Geology of the Green River Desert - Cataract Canyon region, Emery, Wayne and Garfield Counties, Utah: U.S. Geological Survey Bulletin 951, 122 p.

Billingsley, G.H., Jr., Huntoon, P.W., and Breed, W.J., 1987, Geologic map of Capitol Reef National Park and vicinity, Utah: Utah Geological and Mineral Survey Map 87, scale 1:62,500.

Brenner, R.L., 1983, Late Jurassic tectonic setting and paleogeography of Western Interior, North America, *in* Reynolds, M.W., and Dolly, E.D., editors, Symposium on Mesozoic paleogeography of west-central U.S.: Rocky Mountain Section of Society of Economic Paleontologists and Mineralogists, Denver, Colorado, p. 119-132.

Coney, P.J., 1978, Mesozoic-Cenozoic Cordilleran plate tectonis, *in* Smith, R.B., and Eaton, G.P., editors, Cenozoic tectonics and regional geophysics of the western Cordillera: Geological Society of America Memoir 152, p. 33-50.

—1981, Accretionary tectonics in western North America, *in* Dickinson, W.R., and Payne, W.D., editors, Relations of tectonic to ore deposits in the southern Cordillera: Arizona Geological Society Digest, v. 15, p. 23-37.

Cooke, R.U., and Warren, Andrew, 1973, Geomorphology in deserts: Berkeley and Los Angeles, University of California Press, 374 p.

Costa, J.E., and Baker, V.R., 1981, Surficial geology - building with the earth: New York, John Wiley & Sons, 498 p.

Doelling, H.H., 1985, Geology of Arches National Park: Utah Geological and Mineral Survey Map 74, scale 1:50,000, 15 p.

Eldridge, G.H., 1896, Mesozoic geology, *in* Emmons, S.F., Cross,W., and Eldridge, G.H., editors, Geology of the Denver Basin in Colorado: U.S. Geological Survey Monograph 27, p. 51-151.

Fossen, Haakon, and Hesthanner, Jonny, 1997, Geometric analysis and scaling relations of deformation bands in porous sandstone: Journal of Structural Geology, v. 19, no. 12, p. 1479-1493.

—1998, Deformation bands and their significance in porous sandstone reservoirs: First Break, European Association of Geoscientists & Engineers, v. 16, no. 1, p. 21-25.

Gilluly, James, and Reeside, J.B., Jr., 1928, Sedimentary rocks of the San Rafael Swell and some adjacent areas in eastern Utah: U.S. Geological Survey Professional Paper 150 D, p. 61-110.

Hallam, Anthony, 1982, The Jurassic climate, *in* Climate in Earth history, studies in geophysics: National Academy Press, Washington, D.C., p. 159-163.

Hintze, L.F., 1988, Geologic history of Utah: Brigham Young University Geology Studies Special Publication 7, 202 p.

Irving, E., 1983, Fragmentation and assembly of the continents, mid-Carboniferous to present: Geophysical Surveys, v. 5, p. 299-333.

Johnston, Roxanna, 1988, Introduction to microbiotic crusts: U.S. Department of Agriculture, 13 p.

Orkild, P.P., 1953, Photogeologic map of the Stinking Spring Creek-15, Emery County, Utah: U.S. Geological Survey Open-File Report 53-209, scale 1:24,000.

Pipiringos, B.N., and O'Sullivan, R.B., 1978, Principal unconformities in Triassic and Jurassic rocks, Western Interior United States - a preliminary survey: U.S. Geological Survey Professional Paper 1035-A, 29 p.

Peterson, Fred, and Turner-Peterson, C.E., 1987, The Morrison Formation of the Colorado Plateau–recent advances in sedimentology, stratigraphy, and paleotectonics: Hunteria, v. 2, no. 1, p. 1-18.

Stokes, W.L., 1986, Geology of Utah: Utah Geological and Mineral Survey Miscellaneous Publication S, 317 p.

Stokes, W.L., and Cohenour, R.E., 1956, Geologic atlas of Utah: Utah Geological and Mineral Survey Bulletin 52,

92 p.

Williams, P.L., and Hackman, R.J., 1971, Geology, structure, and uranium deposits of the Salina quadrangle, Utah: U.S. Geological Survey Miscellaneous Geologic Investigations Map I-591, scale 1:250,000.

Waldschmidt, W.A., and LeRoy, L.W., 1944, Reconsideration of the Morrison Formation in the type area, Jefferson County, Colorado: Geological Society of America Bulletin, v. 55, p. 1097-1114.

Goosenecks State Park
Photo courtesy of the Utah Travel Council

Geology of Utah's Parks and Monuments
2000 Utah Geological Association Publication 28
D.A. Sprinkel, T.C. Chidsey, Jr., and P.B. Anderson, editors

Geology of Goosenecks State Park, San Juan County, Utah

Gene M. Stevenson[1]

ABSTRACT

The goosenecks of the San Juan River consists of a series of deeply entrenched meanders that are spectacularly preserved in deep limestone canyons formed by the persistent down-cutting action of the river as it dissects the Monument upwarp. Although access to river level is impossible from Goosenecks State Park due to impenetrable vertical cliffs, one can access the inner canyon from the Honaker Trail, located a short distance west of the park. Whether gazing into the canyon below, or looking at the incredible colorful vistas of the region, Goosenecks State Park is an exceptional place to visit.

INTRODUCTION

Goosenecks State Park is located near the center of the Colorado Plateau physiographic province where rocks of late Paleozoic age are magnificently exposed along the course of the San Juan River (figure 1). The central Colorado Plateau has been steadily uplifted in an arid to semi-arid climate throughout the Quaternary resulting in erosional features that have been intensely developed, as characterized by the rugged topography and classic desert landforms as seen from the Goosenecks State Park and vicinity. Here, the Monument upwarp dominates the physiography of the "San Juan Country" and is superbly sculpted by the combined processes of uplift and erosion. The Monument upwarp is one of several large-scale, "bean-shaped" folds that characterize the Colorado Plateau (figure 2). They were formed by tangential compressional forces that were episodically repeated throughout the Phanerozoic, and most magnificently accentuated by Laramide and younger tectonism. These uplifts differ significantly from the middle to late Tertiary laccolithic domes and volcanic mountains that also typify the plateau country. The Monument upwarp is one of the larger uplifts on the Colorado Plateau, extending approximately 110 miles from north to south, and 50 miles from east to west (figure 2). It is asymmetrical with a sharply defined east face, represented by the Comb Ridge monocline (figure 3), and a gradual west dip into the Henry Mountains

Figure 1. Oblique aerial view of "the goosenecks" of the San Juan River. The dead-end road leading to the overlook at Goosenecks State Park can be seen on left (north) side of photo. (Photo courtesy of Don Baars).

basin. The crest of the Monument upwarp has been deeply incised by the San Juan River, exposing strata of early Pennsylvanian age in the bottom of the canyons (figure 4). Mild wrinkling of the crest of the uplift is well exhibited by the subparallel orientation of en echelon folds that are visible from Goosenecks State Park (figure 5).

Goosenecks State Park is actually no bigger than many roadside rest areas. The park is located 4 miles west of Mexican Hat, Utah and accessed from U.S. Highway 163

[1] Bluff, Utah 84512

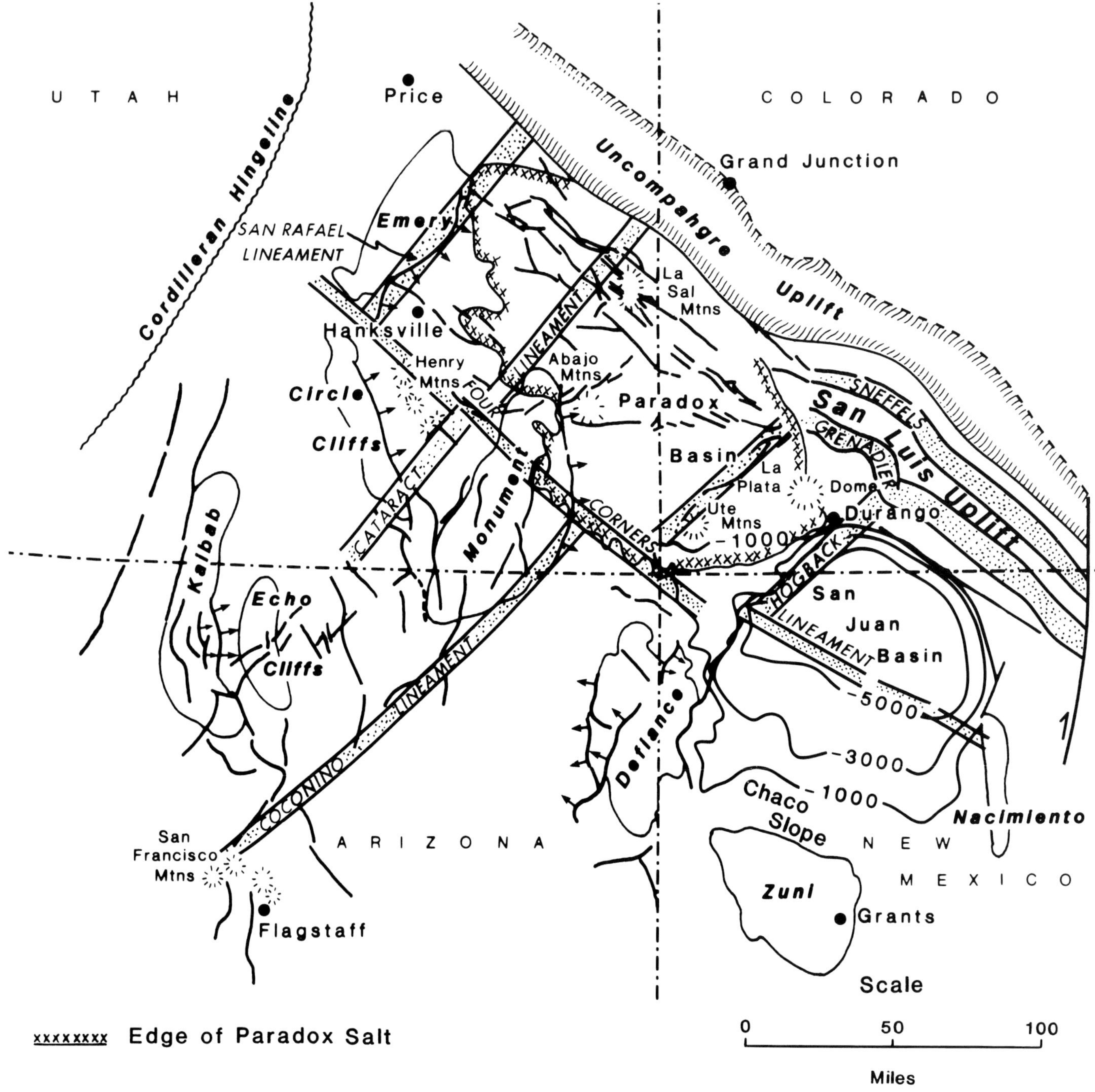

Figure 2. *Location map showing major paleostructural features of the central Colorado Plateau (greater Four corners region). Major lineaments are shown in stippled patterns and major uplifts are shaded. The Paradox basin outline is defined by the distal limit of Paradox salt. Structural contours in the San Juan basin are on a Middle Pennsylvanian marker horizon (from Stevenson and Baars, 1986).*

and State Highways 261 and 316 (figure 3). Although the park is small, the view is immense and simply spectacular (figure 1). Over 1,100 feet below, one can see the San Juan River lazily meandering through the incised canyons while the sandstone monoliths of Monument Valley loom to the south. The tightly folded Raplee anticline is exposed to the east, and the prominent Cedar Mesa escarpment to the north. The Red House Cliffs near Clay Hills and Lake Powell merge below the skyline with Navajo Mountain in the distance to the west (figure 5).

Headwaters of the San Juan River are in the 14,000 foot high peaks of the San Juan Mountains, near Wolf Creek Pass, in southwestern Colorado. The alpine stream flows from there southwestward   into Navajo reservoir and northern New Mexico, then westward past the Four Corners through the Blanding subbasin, and across the Monument upwarp in southeastern Utah (figure 2). The San Juan River maintains a relatively high gradient and carries a large suspended and bottom load of sediments eroded from the exposed arid uplands of the Four Corners region.

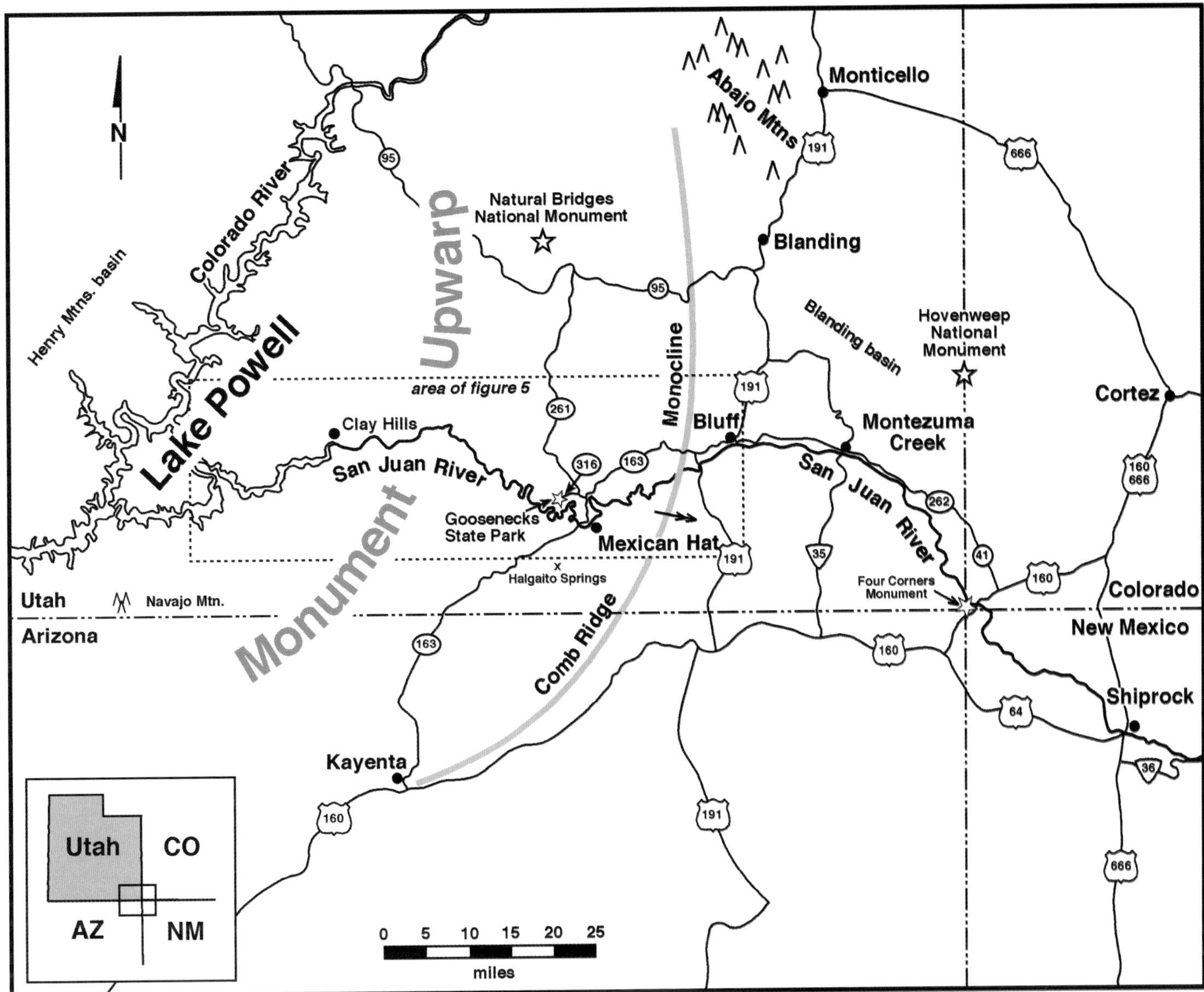

Figure 3. Map showing location of Goosenecks State Park, westerly course of the San Juan River from northwest New Mexico to Lake Powell. All paved highways in the area are shown. Note the dashed inset that shows the area mapped in figures 5 and 7.

Prior to the construction of the Navajo and Glen Canyon dams in the early 1960s, the San Juan River was a major tributary to the Colorado River. Today, that confluence is a drowned arm of Lake Powell (figure 3). And yet, the mean suspended-sediment load still arrives at an average rate of over 25 million tons *per year*, only to settle out as the prograding delta system of Powell reservoir. No data has been compiled for bottom-load sediment transport.

The course of the San Juan River in southeastern Utah generally approximates the southern shallow marine shelf of the Paradox basin, where it has carved majestic canyons through a thick succession of dominantly marine sedimentary rocks of Pennsylvanian age (figure 6). The superimposed canyons were cut across the huge Monument upwarp in late Tertiary to Holocene times, exposing a natural cross section of cyclic marine strata for a distance of nearly 60 river miles (figure 4), including ooid shoals, phylloid algal and chaetetid bioherms, and numerous subtle vari-

eties of bioclastic shelf carbonates in unexcelled magnificence (figure 7). The deepest and oldest rocks exposed are evaporites and carbonates of the Paradox Formation (Middle Pennsylvanian) along the southwestern shelf of the Paradox evaporite basin. The upper canyon walls are composed of mixed carbonate and siliciclastic cycles of the Late Pennsylvanian Honaker Trail Formation (figure 4).

Red beds of Permian, Triassic, and Jurassic age express the eroded margins of the Monument Upwarp along either flank of the structure. These rock units dip sharply into the Blanding basin toward the east along the flanking Comb Ridge monocline, and dip gently westward into the Henry Mountains basin and the course of the Colorado River, now inundated by Lake Powell (figure 6). Consequently, these younger strata are not seen in the deeper canyons that have been cut across the axis of the Monument upwarp (figures 5 and 6).

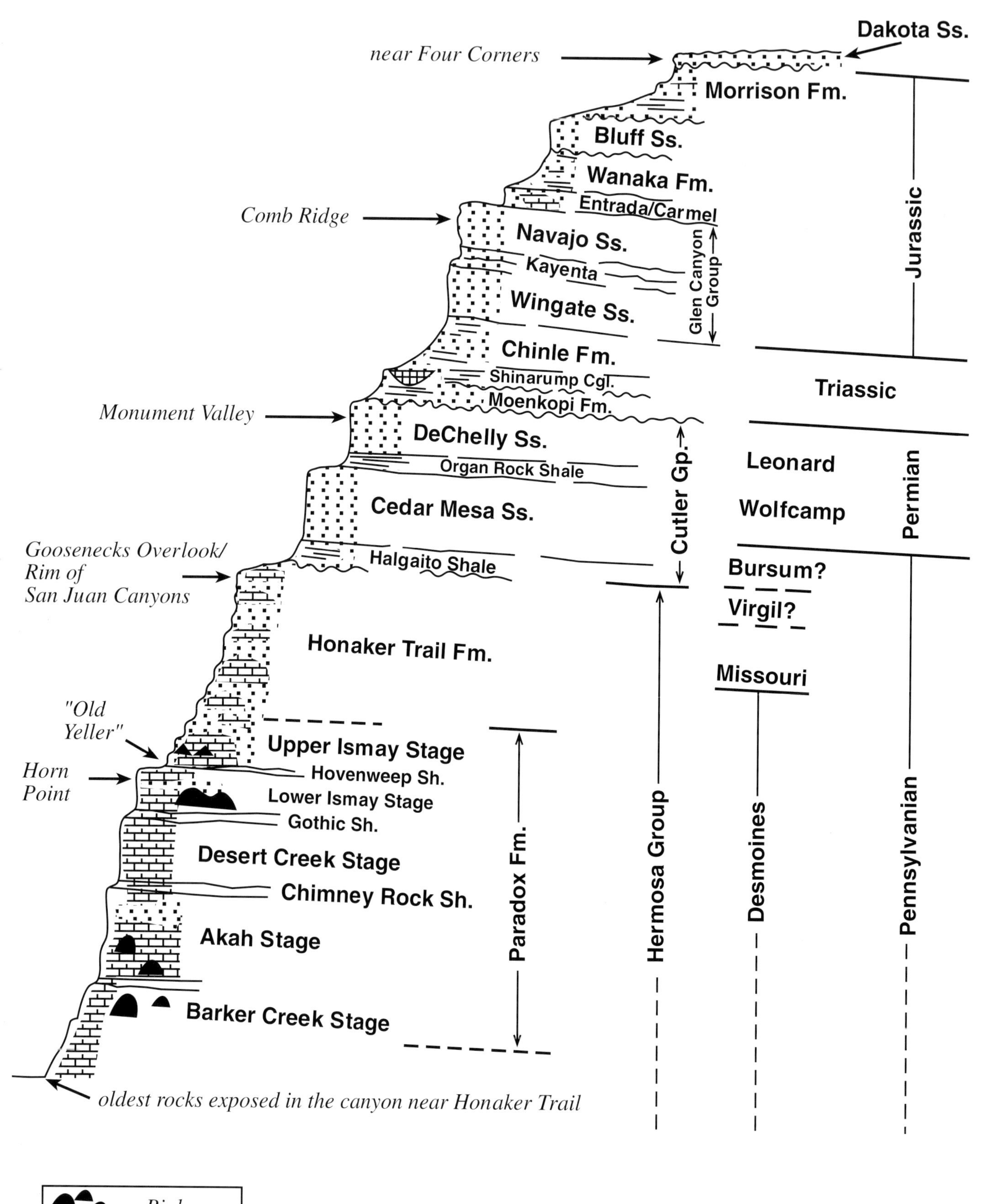

Figure 4. *Generalized stratigraphic column showing rock units exposed along the San Juan River corridor from near the Colorado/Utah border to Honaker Trail west of Goosenecks State Park. Prominent geographic locations and stratigraphic horizons are labeled to left. Refer to figures 3, 5, and 7 for general course of river and geographic locations.*

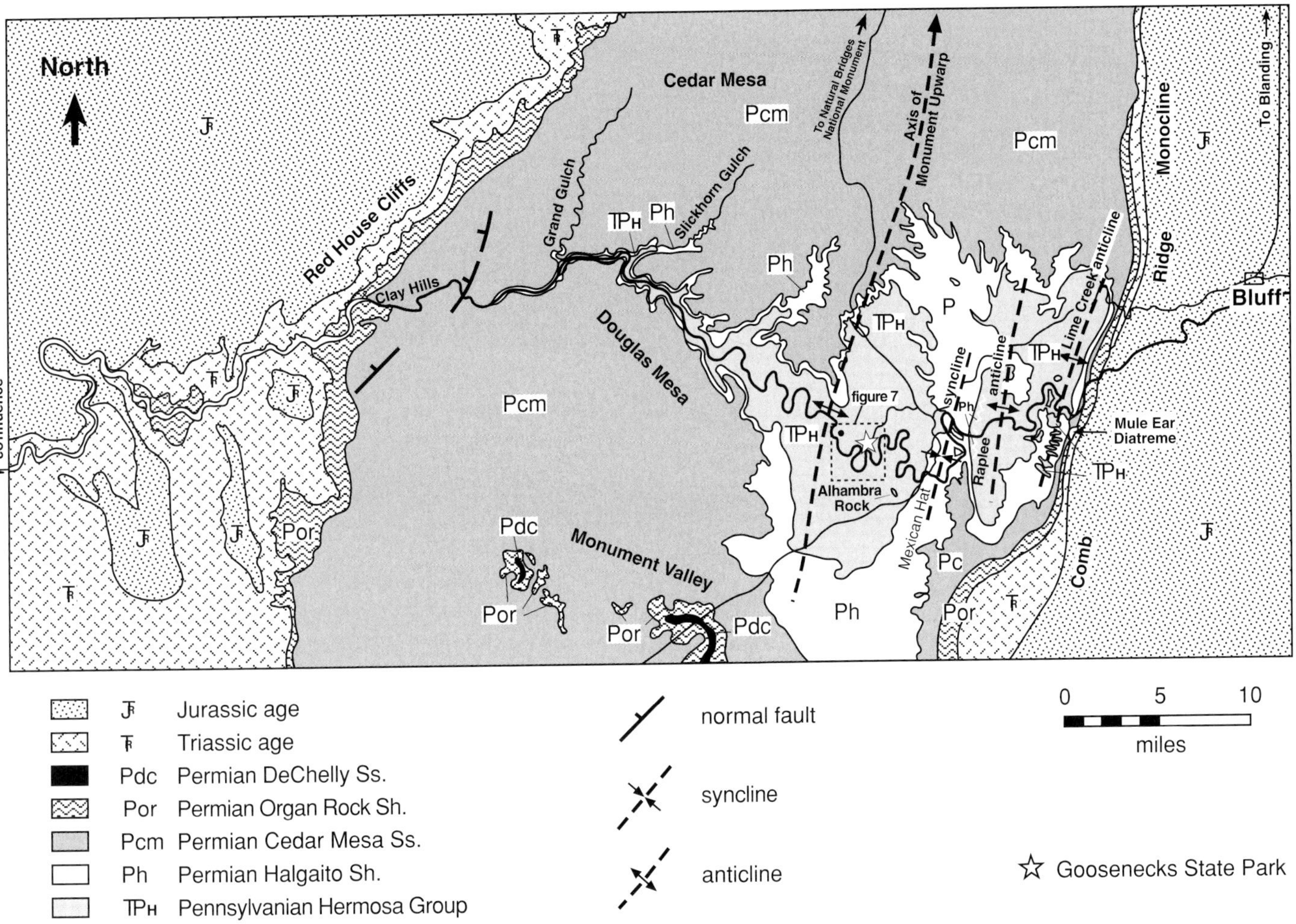

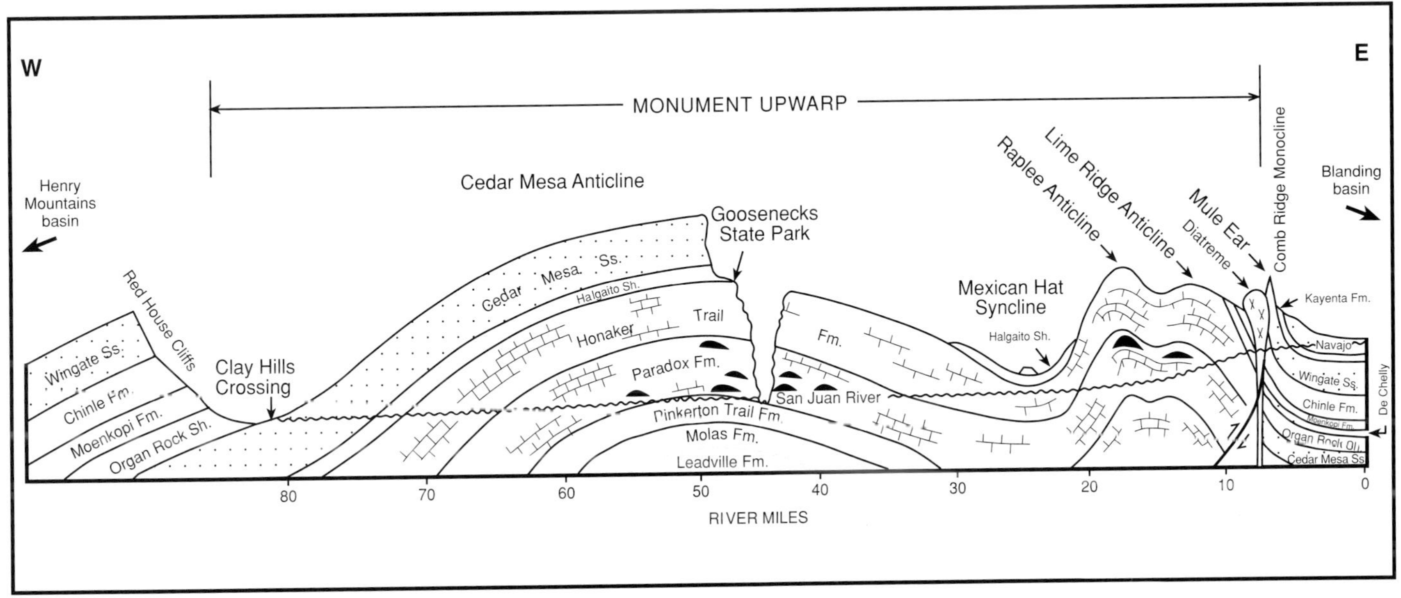

Jurassic age — Jr
Triassic age — Tr
Pdc — Permian DeChelly Ss.
Por — Permian Organ Rock Sh.
Pcm — Permian Cedar Mesa Ss.
Ph — Permian Halgaito Sh.
TPн — Pennsylvanian Hermosa Group

normal fault
syncline
anticline
☆ Goosenecks State Park

Figure 5. Generalized geologic map of Monument upwarp where incised by the San Juan River. Note location of Goosenecks State Park and other areas discussed in text. See figures 2 and 3 for regional location, and figure 6 for schematic cross section from Bluff to Clay Hills Crossing (modified from Haynes, and others, 1972; Hackman and Wyant, 1973).

Figure 6. Schematic west-to-east cross-section across Monument upwarp following general course of the San Juan River. Refer to figures 3, 5, and 7 for course of river and geologic details (modified from Baars and Stevenson, 1986).

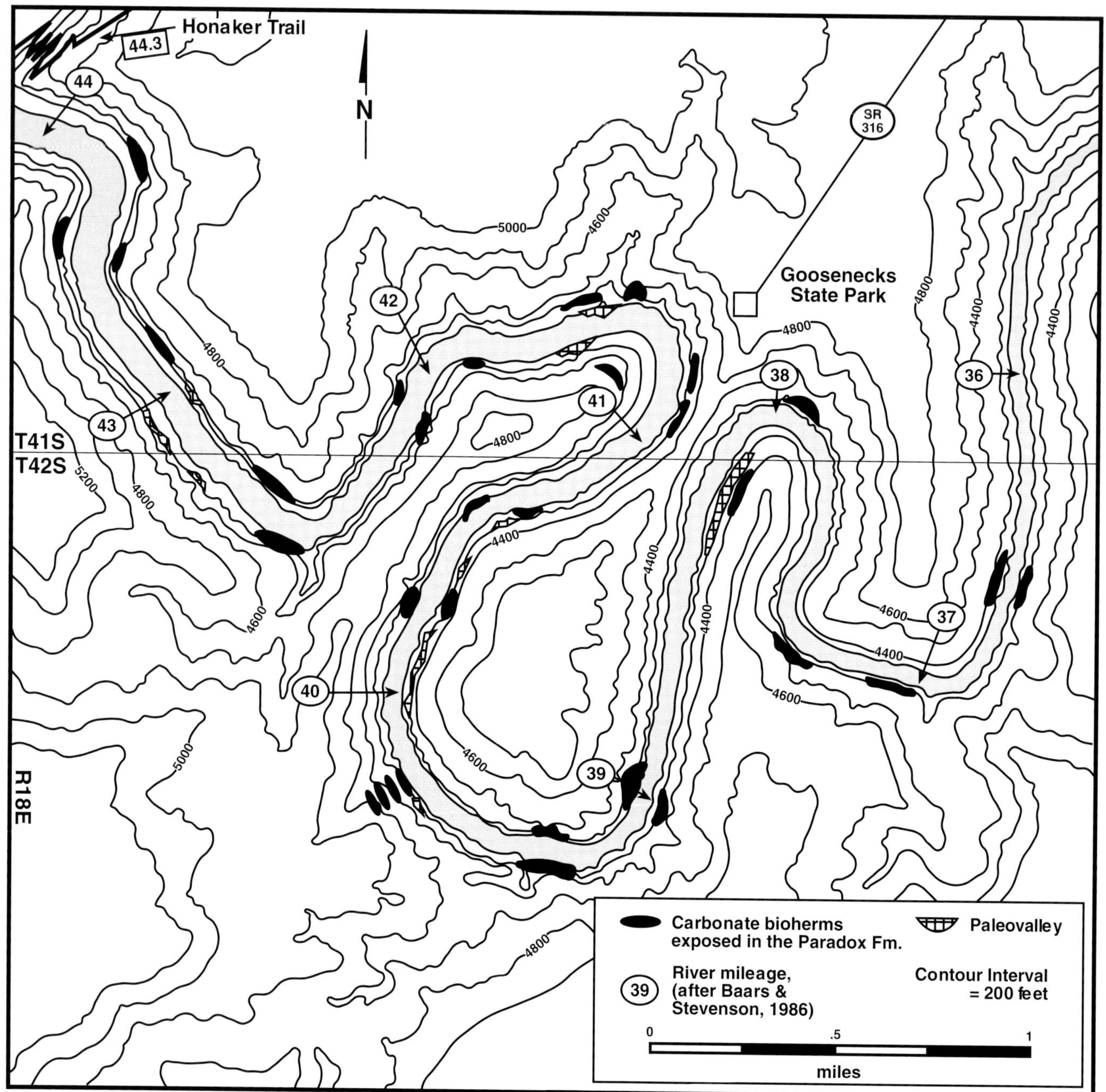

Figure 7. *Map showing location of major bioherms scattered throughout the Paradox Formation along the main "gooseneck" meanders of the San Juan River. Note location of Honaker Trail at river mile (RM) 44.3. Oblique aerial view of figure 1 is from the left side of map. Bioherm locations from Wengerd (1955) and Gianniny and others (1993).*

STRATIGRAPHY

Pre-Pennsylvanian

Most of our knowledge of the pre-Pennsylvanian history of the Colorado Plateau is based on geologic data derived from thousands of subsurface exploratory wells drilled over the past hundred years across the Four Corners region, and tied to excellent outcrop exposures in the San Juan Mountains of southwestern Colorado and the Grand Canyon of northern Arizona. The pre-Pennsylvan-

ian depositional setting across the Colorado Plateau is one of relatively stable and widespread deposition of shallow water, marine carbonates and siliciclastics. These sedimentary rocks were associated with regional encroachment of the early Paleozoic seas across the gently sloping platform shelves of the region (Ohlen and McIntyre, 1965; Baars and Stevenson, 1982). In late Mississippian time, the shelf underwent regional uplift that resulted in emergence and the development of a well-developed, reworked, soil horizon. By early Pennsylvanian time (Atokan), extensional faulting and rapid subsidence initiated, resulting in

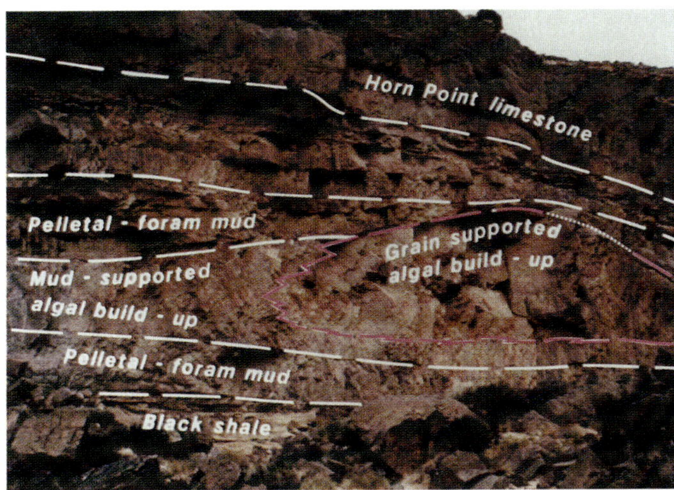

Figure 8. Algal mounds exposed in the Lower Ismay stage of the Paradox Formation in the upper San Juan Canyon east of Mexican Hat, Utah near RM 17.0. The phylloid-algal mound is approximately 25 feet (8 m) thick and typical of productive analogs from the Blanding basin (from Baars and Stevenson, 1982, p.144).

Figure 9. Raplee anticline as seen from river level near Mexican Hat (RM 24).

the development of the asymmetric Paradox basin (Wengerd and Matheny, 1958; Baars, 1966; Baars and See, 1968; Baars and Stevenson, 1981; Stevenson and Baars, 1986).

Pennsylvanian

Early Pennsylvanian

Early Pennsylvanian stratigraphy consists of the basal Molas Formation, a red paleosol that disconformably overlies the Mississippian Leadville Formation, or older rock units, and is gradational with the overlying Hermosa Group (figure 6). The Pinkerton Trail Formation is a relatively thin succession of marine carbonates and fine-grained, dark gray to black siliciclastics which gradationally overlies the Molas Formation and gradationally underlies the Paradox Formation. This unit was assigned a late Atokan to Early Desmoinesian age based on fusulinid biostratigraphy (Wengerd and Strickland, 1954; Baars and others, 1967). The Pinkerton Trail Formation, along with the Paradox and Honaker Trail Formations comprise the Hermosa Group (figure 4) (Cross and others, 1899; Baker, 1933; Wengerd and Matheny, 1958).

Middle Pennsylvanian

The Paradox basin is an elongate, northwest - southeast trending, evaporitic basin that extends from the northwestern part of New Mexico across southwestern Colorado into east-central Utah (figure 2). The basin covers an area of approximately 17,000 square miles (27,200 km²) (Stevenson and Baars, 1986; 1988). The Paradox is an extensional basin that sagged into existence during the Ancestral Rockies orogeny, the North American counterpart to the Hercynian orogeny of Eurasia. Although the basin

was most actively subsiding and accumulating sediments during the Late Pennsylvanian and Permian Periods, the basin's structural framework developed by late Precambrian time (Baars and Stevenson, 1981; Stevenson and Baars, 1986). Recurrent tectonic movement throughout the Paleozoic resulted in vertical movements along basement fractures (Baars and Stevenson, 1982). In the basin center, shale, gypsum, salt, and potash were deposited whereas along the northern Uncompahgre uplift, thick siliciclastic arkosic wedges accumulated. Deposition on the Paradox shelf farther to the south and west was characterized primarily by cyclical deposition of carbonates with subordinate shales and siliciclastics.

The Paradox Formation is a thick cyclic sequence of basin-filling evaporites and time-equivalent carbonates and siliciclastics deposited on the southwestern shelf. Historically, anywhere from 29 to 40 major cycles of evaporite/carbonate deposition have been recognized in the Paradox Formation (Peterson and Hite, 1969; Goldhammer and others, 1991), and are wonderously exposed in the canyons of the San Juan River (figure 9). On the shelf, the cycles are grouped into five major intervals, or stages, which in ascending order are the Barker Creek, Akah, Desert Creek, Lower Ismay, and Upper Ismay (Baars, and others, 1967; Baars and Stevenson, 1982). The names are derived from areas in the region where oil was first recovered from their respective zones. Of these, the Desert Creek, Lower Ismay, and Upper Ismay cycles have proven to be the most productive.

Late Pennsylvanian

The Honaker Trail Formation is the uppermost unit of the Hermosa Group (figure 4) and consists of cyclically alternating marine carbonates and siliciclastics that grade vertically into more massive arkosic sandstones and siltstones derived from the emergent Ancestral Rockies to the east. This vertical and eastward thickening of arkosic clastics indicates the gradual withdrawal of the Paleozoic sea from the uplifting Paradox shelf. The type section for the formation is located less than two miles west of the Goosenecks overlook at Honaker Trail, and was upgraded to formation status by Wengerd and Matheny (1958).

Permian

The rise of the Uncompahgre uplift in Middle Pennsylvanian through Early Permian time provided the bulk of the huge volume of arkosic sediments deposited across the Colorado Plateau. The Uncompahgre was a major mountain range that extended from east of Santa Fe, New Mexico northwesterly past Price, Utah, and thus forms the easternmost fault-bounded uplift of the Colorado Plateau (figure 2). The coarse arkoses (known as the Cutler Group) are stacked in aggradational and westward-verging progradational sequences ranging from proximal fan delta conglomerates, to bajadas, to low coastal floodplain and wind-blown deposits. Due to a combination of emergence of the Uncompahgre uplift and subsidence of the Paradox basin, and verified by seismic and deep drilling, the Cutler section is at least 18,000 feet thick along the Uncompahgre front and varies dramatically in thickness across the Paradox salt anticlines, the "Paradox fold and fault belt," before it grades south and westerly into fine-grained redbeds of the Abo, Organ Rock and Halgaito shales (Baars, 1962). These fine-grained siltstones and mudstones extend across much of the Colorado Plateau (with different formation names, of course), as far as the Grand Canyon and south of Flagstaff along the Mogollon Rim. Farther to the southwest and immediately to the northwest, these redbeds interfinger with marine carbonates and siliciclastics from different provenances. In those regions where distinctive facies are prominent, several formations are readily discernable. This interfingering of facies is most impressively exhibited across the backbone of the Monument upwarp, from Monument Valley to Canyonlands National Park, and we get a glimpse at Raplee anticline near Goosenecks State Park (figure 5).

Lower Permian/Upper Pennsylvanian Dilemma

The Halgaito Shale consists of red, very fine-grained siltstone and shale deposited in arid coastal floodplains. Current and swash ripples, fern imprints, flaser bedding, and load casts are some of the sedimentary structures frequently found in this unit. The Halgaito is well developed in the area, as the type locality is southwest of Mexican Hat in Halgaito Springs (figure 3) (Baker and Reeside, 1929). Frequent carbonate tidal channels exhibiting algal-coated lithoclasts, and scattered thin, carbonate lenses further attest to the low-lying tidal flat coastal setting.

The Halgaito facies extends over most of the central and southern Colorado Plateau, and has been historically referred to as early Permian in age (Baars, 1962; 1979). The Halgaito was considered the basal redbed unit of the Permian due to lithostratigraphic correlation to Wolfcampian

strata to the northeast and west, which was based on an assumed Missourian/Wolfcampian disconformity found in the Raplee anticline immediately east of Goosenecks. These ages have been recently challenged and modified (Ross and Ross, 1994; 1998; D.L. Baars, verbal communication, 1999) such that the Halgaito Shale now represents deposition during latest Pennsylvanian time (Virgil-Bursum) and therefore, the Raplee disconformity represents a probable (?) Missourian/Virgillian boundary. Furthermore, since the Halgaito grades vertically northward into the Elephant Canyon Formation in Cataract Canyon, at least the lower two-thirds of the Elephant Canyon should be raised to a Virgillian age. The top third of the Elephant Canyon Formation is still regarded as early Permian (Wolcampian) based on fusulinid biostratigraphy (D.L. Baars, verbal communication, 1999). Obviously, additional detailed studies are needed in this area to further delineate these important time-stratigraphic boundaries.

At Goosenecks overlook, the massive limestone rimrock defines the lithostratigraphic boundary between the overlying Halgaito redbeds and the underlying Honaker Trail Formation (figures 4 and 5). Closer examination reveals that several layers of red siliciclastics are interbedded with the underlying carbonates, and that thin, discontinuous limestone beds extend upward into the Halgaito siltstones. This alternating pattern of gray ledge-forming limestone with softer, slope-forming redbeds is beautifully exposed on the west dipping flank of the nearby Raplee anticline, forming a prominent "zig-zag" pattern (figure 9).

Early Permian

The prominent white, cliff-forming unit that overlies the Halgaito Shale in the Monument Valley-Goosenecks area is the Cedar Mesa Sandstone (figures 4 and 5). The type section is that which can be seen from the Goosenecks overlook, named by Baker and Reeside (1929) and raised to formation status by Wengerd and Matheny (1958). The Cedar Mesa is best described as a coastal complex of eolian, fluvial, and marine-reworked siliciclastics. North of Goosenecks, the upper Halgaito and lower Cedar Mesa grade into Elephant Canyon carbonates (Baars, 1962; 1979). The Cedar Mesa Sandstone reaches thicknesses of over 1,400 feet west of the Colorado River and can be traced in the subsurface from the San Rafael Swell to the north, into the Esplanade Sandstone through Grand Canyon and into the Mogollon rim country to the south, and to the Queantoweap Sandstone to the west (Baars, 1962; 1979; Blakey, 1979). Along the eastern margin of the Monument upwarp, the distinctively white, cross-bedded sandstones interfinger rather abruptly with the Cutler redbeds in the Needles district of Canyonlands National Park, and change facies to tidal flat mudstones and gypsum beds between the towns of Mexican Hat and Bluff. This facies change occurs within a few thousand feet and can be "walked out" from near the Highway 163 roadcut in Comb Wash to the San Juan River. The extent of this facies change from the Needles district to Comb Wash suggests that the Monument upwarp was mildly positive during Cedar Mesa deposition. The lagoonal gypsiferous facies continues in the subsurface to near the Four Corners and southward of the Defiance uplift (Baars, 1979).

Late Permian

The redbeds that overlie the Cedar Mesa Sandstone in the Monument Valley-Goosenecks area comprise the Organ Rock Shale (figures 4 and 5). The unit was named by Baker and Reeside (1929) for a prominent monolith in the western portion of Monument Valley. The Organ Rock consists of red, fine-grained siltstone and shales that contains semi-arid vertebrate and plant remains of lower Leonardian age (Baars, 1979). This widespread redbed unit can be traced regionally, and is equivalent to the Hermit Shale in Grand Canyon. From the Goosenecks overlook, the Organ Rock can be seen to overlie the south-dipping Cedar Mesa Sandstone, and forms the base of the monoliths in Monument Valley (figure 4).

The massive sandstone that forms the spectacular buttes and spires in Monument Valley is the DeChelly Sandstone (figure 4). The unit was named by Gregory (1917) for exposures in Canyon de Chelly, Arizona. The formation is considered to be eolian in origin, and is stratigraphically equivalent to the Meseta Blanca Sandstone Member of the Yeso Formation in New Mexico (Baars and Stevenson, 1977), and the Schnebly Hill Formation for exposures near Sedona, Arizona (Blakey, 1979). The DeChelly has been erroneously correlated to the Cedar Mesa, Coconino, and White Rim Sandstones. None of these rock units are time eqivalent to the DeChelly. More importantly, the DeChelly and equivalents are reddish colored sandstones, with individual quartz grains coated with hematite and cemented by iron minerals. Conversely, the other sands are generally white in color and cemented by silica (Baars, 1979).

Tertiary

Alhambra Rock is a prominent elongated spire that is visible immediately south of the overlook. It is an intrusive basaltic dike, or minette, of Middle Tertiary age, and is considered to be part of the "Navajo volcanic field," an informal name given to the region due to the high occurrence of diatremes and related basaltic dike swarms (Kelley, 1955). All are Oligocene to early Miocene in age (30-25 my).

SIGNIFICANCE OF PENNSYLVANIAN OUT-CROPS IN SAN JUAN RIVER CANYONS

The Pennsylvanian Period was a time of extensive glaciation in the southern hemisphere (Crowell, 1978), and is well documented by cyclical sedimentation in numerous sedimentary basins around the world. These characteristic cyclicity patterns have been shown to be related to short term glacio-eustatic pulses (Milankovitch bands) that dominated the sedimentary record throughout much of North America during this period (for example, Wanless and Shepard, 1936; Wanless, 1972; Heckel, 1980, 1986; Goldhammer and others, 1991; Grammer and others, 1996). In the canyons carved across the Monument upwarp, this cyclicity is recorded in a mixed system of carbonates and siliciclastics deposited on the Paradox shelf (figure 9). In turn, these facies can be related to time-equivalent basin-centered evaporites, and to oil and gas producing intervals in the upper Paradox Formation (Wengerd and Matheny, 1958; Choquette and Traut, 1963; Pray and Wray, 1963; Peterson and Hite, 1969; Hite, 1970; Hite and Buckner, 1981; Baars and Stevenson, 1982; Grammer and others, 1996).

The huge expanse (up to 60 river miles) of laterally continuous outcrops through these canyon walls provides an extraordinary opportunity to study the detailed stratigraphy of Pennsylvanian strata on the exposed Paradox shelf. This expansive outcrop has been most useful for petroleum geologists to better correlate their observations from the canyon walls to the subsurface of the Blanding basin regarding the distribution and three-dimensional architecture of both hydrocarbon-bearing phyloid algal and chaetetid/foram biohermal reservoirs (figure 8). Furthermore, the timing of mound growth and porosity development to high-frequency sea level changes seen on the exposed shelf help petroleum geologists further understand their associated hydrocarbon-producing facies in the subsurface. This lateral variability in reservoir and associated facies occurs within very short distances (10s to 100s of feet), as well as on a scale of miles, and is a function of paleotectonics, paleotopography, facies types, periods of subaerial exposure, and the amplitude and frequency of relative sea level change (Baars and Stevenson, 1982; Grammer, and others, 1996).

STRUCTURE

The San Juan River has carved a natural cross section through the Monument upwarp, a huge anticlinal flexure in the Earth's crust (figure 6). The north-trending structure extends a distance of some 110 miles from the confluence of the Green and Colorado Rivers in Canyonlands National Park to near Kayenta, Arizona (figures 2 and 3). The axis of the upwarp passes through Monument Valley, the Goosenecks, and Cedar Mesa (figure 5). The eastern margin of the east-facing asymmetrical fold is expressed by the distinctly apparent Comb Ridge monocline, where the sharp flexure drapes Mesozoic and Paleozoic rocks over a deep-seated, high-angle reverse, basement fault into the Blanding basin with vertical structural displacement of nearly 5,000 feet (figures 5 and 6). The west flank of the large fold is much more gentle, as the long gradual homoclinal dip of the Paleozoic and Mesozoic rocks subside beneath Lake Powell into the Henry Mountains basin. Thus, its width of approximately 50 miles is defined by the erosional edges of the Jurassic Glen Canyon Group where these rocks crop out and define the basin margins (figure 6).

Numerous smaller en echelon folds occur as secondary wrinkles across the surface of the much larger upwarp. One of the more spectacular of these smaller tight folds, known as the Raplee anticline, can be seen to the east of the Goosenecks overlook (figures 5 and 9). Here, red beds of the Permian Halgaito Shale drape onto the steep west-facing arm of the Raplee anticline forming a prominent zig-zag erosional pattern. As the course of the river departs from the upper canyon, it enters the Mexican Hat syncline which separates the Raplee anticline to the east from the Halgaito anticline on the west (figures 5 and 6). Downstream, or west, from the town of Mexican Hat, the river enters a second deep gorge as it cuts through the structural backbone of the Monument upwarp. Here the Monument upwarp appears to be a single, broad structurally high plateau, although it is actually composed of several smaller anticlines superimposed onto the larger structure (figures 5 and 6). In a distance of some 60 river miles from Mexican Hat to Paiute Farms Wash (located west of Clay Hills) on Lake Powell the river bisects six anticlines with modest amplitudes. Other than the broad crestal Cedar Mesa anticline, the remaining five individual structures are nearly imperceptible from river level.

GEOMORPHOLOGY

Perhaps the most striking geologic attribute of the area is that of a strongly meandering river deeply incised across one of the Colorado Plateau's uplifts. For a distance of some 12 river miles (RM), from RM 30 to RM 42, the river only proceeds 5 land miles; a portion from RM 35.5 to 44.3 is shown in figure 7. How does a river flow across an uplift? Shouldn't it go around? In 1869, Major John Wesley Powell was mystified as to how the Green River in northeastern Utah could behave similarly where crossing the Split Mountain anticline in Dinosaur National Monument, rather than flowing around. His erroneous conclusion was that the river must be much older than the structures, having preceded the uplift, thereby making the huge monoclinal structures on the Colorado Plateau very young. We now know differently.

Erosional fluvial, eolian, and mass movement processes operating in an overall arid to semi-arid climate for the region became significant with uplift during the mid-Tertiary orogeny (Oligocene-early Miocene) of the Colorado Plateau. These processes have been the major driving forces in shaping the region and the evolution of the landscape, triggering landscape rejuvenation, and the subsequent removal of several thousand feet of sedimentary rocks (Hunt, 1956; Bird, 1979). Hunt (1969) and Larson, and others (1975) surmise that the ancestral Colorado River system probably developed on a surface underlain by Tertiary age rock several thousand feet above the present-day plateau surface. These estimates have been confirmed by independent research in basin history modeling

(Hite, and others, 1984; Nuccio and Condon, 1996). In general, the river course(s) formed in Tertiary lake and river deposits and were subsequently superimposed onto the underlying bedrock and buried structures across the province. Overall, the rates of canyon incision on the Colorado Plateau are considered comparable to the rate of plateau uplift, or approximately 0.8 feet (0.2 m) per thousand years for the Colorado River system (Woodward-Clyde Consultants, 1982).

HISTORY

In 1879 E. L. Goodridge made the first known traverse of the San Juan and Animas Rivers from near Durango, Colorado past the confluence with the Colorado River to Lee's Ferry, Arizona prospecting for gold. In April 1880 the town of Bluff was settled by the beleagured Mormon "hole-in-the-rock" pioneers. These two closely spaced events had a significant impact on the early history of anglo emigration into the San Juan canyon country.

During his traverse, Goodridge noted extremely small quantities of very fine-grained placer gold at several places along the river and further reported the discouraging associated costs (Gregory, 1938, p. 108). Nevertheless, word from Goodridge and Cass Hite that the Bluff settlers were panning gold from the banks of the San Juan River exploded into full rumors of rich gold deposits in the canyons of the San Juan River and Glen Canyon, leading to the "gold excitement" of 1892-93. Miser (1924) wrote that prospecting for gold in the San Juan River canyons began in 1892, when tales of fabulously rich deposits caused 1,200 men to stampede to the canyon. After spending a few months there they went away empty-handed, but prospecting continued at a few places as late as 1912. Miser (1924) also described the gold as "extremely fine in grain, being known as flour gold, and occurs mostly in placer deposits along river channel and in terrace gravels."

Most of the hopeful prospectors arrived by land to the canyon rims where they followed game trails and lowered themselves and their supplies over the cliffs. A long stretch of the San Juan River through the "goosenecks" was prospected, with Honaker Trail being built in 1893 to reach the canyon bottom near the future site of Goosenecks State Park (figures 5 and 7). In 1892, Henry Honaker obtained a permit from the San Juan County courthouse to build a horse trail in which to supply the prospectors and to haul out the gold. The trail was completed in June 1894, and the first horse to attempt the descent fell to its death near Horn Point. However, by January 1893, the gold boom was already a bust, as reported by the *Salt Lake Tribune*. According to Miser (1924, p. 21-22), the largest amount of gold was obtained from the Nephi claim located about 4 miles below Honaker Trail, where $3,000 worth was panned in 30 days. Unprofitable gold operations continued in the region until 1912, and Honaker Trail was never used as it was originally designed (Baars, 1979; Baars and Stevenson, 1986). Today, it is hiked by mostly river runners and geol-

Figure 10. Hikers view from Honaker Trail showing Paradox and Honaker Trail Formations. The hikers are standing near the top of the Barker Creek Stage. View looking southeast. Refer to the stratigraphic column in figure 4.

Figure 11. View of hikers on Honaker Trail looking west. The hikers are standing in the Chimney Rock Shale which separates the underlying Akah Stage from the overlying Desert Creek Stage. Refer to the stratigraphic column in figure 4.

ogists (figures 10 and 11).

A number of years passed by following the gold excitement, but E.L. Goodridge remembered seeing "little streams of oil coming from loose boulders on the bottom of the canyon" above the mouth of Slickhorn Gulch in 1879, and located an oil claim in 1882 near some oil seeps from rock ledges beneath the present-day bridge at Mexican Hat (Gregory, 1938). Following years of discouraging efforts to find funding, Goodridge discovered oil on March 4, 1908, at a drilling depth of 225 feet below the surface, where the well was reported as a "gusher" and started the Mexican Hat oil boom. The success of this wildcat well (the Crossing No. 1) led to a flurry of drilling in 1908 and 1909 (Lauth, 1983). A road was built from Bluff to Mexican Hat so that drilling equipment and supplies could be hauled to the "San Juan Oil Field."

By the summer of 1910 considerable capital had been enlisted to exploit the field. One standard rig was in operation, and others were reported to have been ordered. There were 10 portable deep-well rigs in the area and several more on the way to it. During midsummer active development was somewhat retarded on account of

the heat, but in the later part of August preparations were made to renew operations with greater vigor than before. Reports received from reliable sources during the winter of 1910-11 indicate that the expection of activity has been fully realized. On February 1, 1911, according to a report by A. L. Raplee, there were 27 drilling rigs in the field and equipment for more on the way. Two oil wells were brought in during the winter, and there was considerable improvement at old wells. A small town had been established near Mexican Hat, and the roads and general facilities much improved.

Woodruff, 1912, p. 98-99

Scores of additional wells have now been drilled in the immediate region on the north side of the river, since those glory days, with a rather meager total reported cumulative recovery of only 257,287 barrels of oil as of January 1, 1999 (Utah Division of Oil, Gas and Mining Monthly Production Report, December, 1998). The Mexican Hat oil field was a bust.

Following the oil discovery in 1908 at Mexican Hat, Goodridge constructed a primitive road overland along the north rim of the San Juan River past the Honaker trail-

Figure 12. View looking west at the top of the trail head of Honaker Trail.

head and across John's Canyon to the mouth of Slickhorn Gulch where other oil seeps had been earlier discovered.

Three unsuccessful wells were drilled near the mouth of Slickhorn Gulch between 1908 and 1952, in which there was some oil recovered, but in unsustainable and uneconomic amounts.

By the early 1950s, oil exploration in the Four Corners region was just about at a standstill when major discoveries were made approximately 35 miles east of Mexican Hat at Desert Creek (1954) and Aneth (1956). Subsequent drilling of thousands of wells over the past hundred years in the Paradox basin has led to significant oil and gas production of nearly 500 million barrels of oil and nearly a trillion cubic feet of gas. Most of this oil and gas is recovered from porous carbonates in the Paradox Formation, which are well exposed in the canyons of the San Juan River, thereby causing innumerable petroleum geologists to visit these outcrops either by river boats, or on foot.

LOCATION AND DESCRIPTION OF HONAKER TRAIL

Honaker Trail is located 1.6 miles northwest of the Goosenecks overlook, and is accessible by the John's Canyon dirt road that intersects State Road 316 (figures 3 and 7). The length of the trail is approximately 2 miles (one way), and the route should be treated as a wilderness access (that is, self-supported by foot, and plenty of drinking water). The view from the trailhead is magnificent, exposing over 1,300 feet of Pennsylvanian age rocks from the canyon rim to the San Juan River below (figure 12). The trail descends in a stair-step fashion through the approximate crest of the Cedar Mesa anticline thereby exposing the oldest layers in the Barker Creek cycle (figures 4 and 10). Recent workers (Gianniny, and others, 1993) have even conjectured a Pinkerton Trail formational contact.

The upper section of the trail stair-steps through limestone and sandstone ledges and red shale slopes that

Figure 13. View looking west approximately half way down the Honaker Trail.

grade downward into gray-green slopes (figure 13). From Horn Point, and continuing through the Paradox section to river level, the trail makes sharp descents through manmade corridors, then contours along cycle-bounding black shale benches to the next descent. The time and effort involved in constructing this trail in such a remote place, and based on a rumor of possible wealth is astounding. Important fusulinid biozones, phyloid algal and chaetetid bioherms, skeletal and ooid carbonates, siliciclastics, and numerous disconformities are well exposed along the trail.

Today, the trail is hiked mostly by river runners or backcountry hikers who are interested, for the most part, in the scenery (figures 10, 11, 12 and 13). But among them are a few geologists who have taken the time to record the interval by measured section. Regardless, hikers are very much exposed to vertical drops of 600 feet or more in a number of places, so acrophobics beware!

The first geologist to publish his findings was Sherman Wengerd (1951), and the first complete measured section from rim to river in 1963. Pray and Wray (1963) provided the first detailed measured section of the upper Paradox strata (Lower Ismay - upper Desert Creek cycles).

Field geology conducted in the 1950s commonly relied on painted numbers for referenced descriptions and are still preserved along the trail. Unfortunately, the formation and stage boundaries are incorrect, but the numbers are still useful for refining correlations. Since oil was discovered in the mid 1950s at Aneth, any number of oil company geologists have come and measured and sampled various parts of the section exposed, with most emphasis on the reservoir facies in phylloid-algal mounds, and the non-phylloid, chaetetetid-foram mounds. Other workers who have measured partial to complete sections at Honaker Trail include: Goldhammer, and others, 1990; Weber and others, 1994; and, Grammer, and others, 1996.

SUMMARY

Much of our geologic knowledge of the San Juan country is due to the economic importance of the natural resources these rocks contain, but beyond that, the Goosenecks State Park is just simply a wonderful place to visit and see the grandeur of this spectacular landscape carved across the backbone of the Monument upwarp. The area provides something for everyone; from the novice geologist in awe of the scenery, to the hardcore, who wants to trek the Honaker Trail and view the details of the geologic history of the region laid open to all visitors.

ACKNOWLEDGMENTS

Thanks to Theresa Breznau of *Living Earth Studios, Inc.* for computer designed illustrations and her patience for all my revisions, and to Don Baars for his aerial photos. Thanks also to Tom Chidsey and Paul Anderson for reviewing the manuscript.

REFERENCES

Baars, D.L., 1962, Permian system of the Colorado Plateau: American Association of Petroleum Geologists Bulletin, v. 46, p. 149-218.

—1966, Pre-Pennsylvanian Paleotectonics - key to basin evolution and petroleum occurrences in Paradox basin: American Association of Petroleum Geologists Bulletin, v. 50, p. 2082-2111.

—1979, The Permian System, *in* Baars, D.L., editor, Permianland: Four Corners Geological Society Guidebook, p. 1-6.

Baars, D.L., Parker, J.W., and Chronic, J., 1967, Revised stratigraphic nomenclature of Pennsylvanian system, Paradox basin: American Association of Petroleum Geologists Bulletin, v. 51, p. 393-403.

Baars, D.L., and See, P.D., 1968, Pre-Pennsylvanian stratigraphy and paleotectonics of the San Juan Mountains, southwestern Colorado: Geological Society of America Bulletin, v. 79, p. 333-350.

Baars, D.L., and Stevenson, G. M., 1977, Permian rocks of the San Juan Basin, *in* Fassett, J.E., and James, H.L., editors, Permianland: Four Corners Geological Society Guidebook, p. 133-138.

—1981, Tectonic evolution of the Paradox basin, Utah and Colorado, *in* Wiegand, D.L., editor, Geology of the Paradox basin: Rocky Mountain Association of Geologists Guidebook, p. 23-31.

—1982, Subtle stratigraphic traps in Paleozoic rocks of Paradox basin, *in* Halbouty, M.T., editor, Deliberate search for the subtle trap: American Association of Petroleum Geologists Memoir 32, p. 131-158.

—1986, San Juan Canyons - a river runner's guide and natural history of San Juan River canyons: Grand Junction, Canon Publishers, Ltd, 64 p.

Baker, A.A., 1933, Geology and oil possibilities of the Moab district, Grand and San Juan Counties, Utah: U.S. Geological Survey Bulletin 841, 95 p.

Baker, A.A., and Reeside, J.B., 1929, Correlation of the Permian of southern Utah, northern Arizona, northwestern New Mexico and southwestern Colorado: American Association of Petroleum Geologists Bulletin, v. 13, p. 1413-1448.

Blakey, R.C., 1979, Lower Permian stratigraphy of the southern Colorado Plateau, *in* Baars, D.L., editor, Permianland: Four Corners Geological Society Guidebook, p. 115-130.

Bird, P., 1979, Continental delamination and the Colorado Plateau: Journal of Geophysical Research, v. 84, p. 7561.

Choquette, P.W., and Traut, J.D., 1963, Pennsylvanian carbonate reservoirs, Ismay field, Utah and Colorado, *in* Bass, R.O., editor, Shelf carbonates of the Paradox basin: Four Corners Geological Society Guidebook, p. 157-184.

Cross, W., Spencer, A.C., and Purington, C.W., 1899, La Plata Colorado: U.S. Geological Survey Geology Atlas, Folio 60.

Crowell, J.C., 1978, Gondwana glaciation, cyclothems, continental positioning, and climate change: American Journal of Science, v. 278, p. 1345-1372.

Gianniny, G.L., Kelly, M.A., and Simo, J.A.T., 1993, Facies mosaics and mixed carbonate/siliciclastic ramp depositional dynamics, Paradox basin, Utah: unpublished field guide, 61 p.

Gianniny, G.L., and Simo, J.A.T., 1996, Implications of unfilled accomodation space for sequence stratigraphy on mixed carbonate-siliciclastic platforms: an example from the lower Desmoinesian (Middle Pennsylvanian), southwestern Paradox basin, Utah, *in* Longman, M.W., and Sonnenfeld, M.D., editors, Paleozoic systems of the Rocky Mountain region: Rocky Mountain Section - SEPM (Society for Sedimentary Geology), p. 213- 234.

Goldhammer, R.K., Dunn, P.A., and Hardie, L.A., 1990, Depositional cycles, composited sea-level changes, cycle stacking patterns, and the hierarchy of stratigraphic forcing - examples from Alpine Triassic platform carbonates: Geological Society of America Bulletin, v. 102, p. 535-562.

Goldhammer, R.K., Oswald, E.J., and Dunn, P.A., 1991, The hierarchy of stratigraphic forcing - an example from Middle Pennsylvanian shelf carbonates of the Paradox basin, *in* Franseen, E.K., Watney, W.L., Kendall, C.G., and Ross, W., editors, Sedimentary modeling - computer simulations and methods for improved parameter definition: Kansas Geological Survey Bulletin 233, p. 361-413.

Grammer, G.M., Eberli, G.P., Van Buchem, F.S.P., Stevenson, G.M., and Homewood, P., 1996, Application of high-resolution sequence stratigraphy to evaluate lateral variability in outcrop and subsurface - Desert Creek and Ismay intervals, Paradox basin, *in* Longman, M.W., and Sonnenfeld, M.D., editors, Paleozoic systems of the Rocky Mountain region: Rocky Mountain Section, SEPM (Society of Sedimentary Geology), p. 235-266.

Gregory, H.E., 1917, Geology of the Navajo country, a reconnaissance of parts of Arizona, New Mexico, and Utah: U.S. Geological Survey Professional Paper 93, 161 p.

—1938, The San Juan country, a geographic and geologic reconnaissance of southeastern Utah, with contributions by M. R. Thorpe and H. D. Miser: U.S. Geological Survey Professional Paper 188, 123 p.

Hackman, R.J., and Wyant, D.G., 1973, Geology, structure, and uranium deposits of the Escalante quadrangle, Utah and Arizona: U.S. Geological Survey Miscellaneous Geologic Investigations Map I-744, scale 1:250,000, 2 sheets.

Haynes, D.D., Vogel, J.D., and Wyant, D.G., 1972, Geology, structure, and uranium deposits of the Cortez quadrangle, Colorado and Utah: U.S. Geological Survey Miscellaneous Geologic Investigations Map I-629, scale 1:250,000, 2 sheets.

Heckel, P.H., 1980, Paleogeography of eustatic model for deposition of Midcontinent Upper Pennsylvanian cyclothems, *in* Fouch, T.D. and Magathan, E.R., editors, Paleozoic paleogeography of the west-central United States: Rocky Mountain Section, SEPM (Society of Sedimentary Geology), Symposium 1, p. 197-215.

—1986, Sea-level curve for Pennsylvanian eustatic marine transgressive-regressive depositional cycles along Mid-continent outcrop belt, North America: Geology, v. 14, p. 330-334.

Hite, R.J., 1970, Shelf carbonate sedimentation controlled by salinity in the Paradox basin, southeast Utah, *in* Ron, J.L. and Dellwig, L.F., editors, Third symposium on salt: Northern Ohio Geologic Society, v. 1, p. 48-66.

Hite, R.J. and Buckner, D.H., 1981, Stratigraphic correlation, facies concepts, and cyclicity in Pennsylvanian rocks of the Paradox basin, *in* Wiegand, D.L., editor, Geology of the Paradox basin: Rocky Mountain Association of Geologists Guidebook, p. 147-159.

Hite, R.J., Anders, D.E., and Ging, T.G., 1984, Organic-rich source rocks of Pennsylvanian age in the Paradox basin of Utah and Colorado, *in* Woodward, J., Meiss-ner, F.F., and Clayton, J.L., editors, Hydrocarbon source rocks of the greater Rocky Mountains region: Rocky Mountain Association of Geologists Guidebook, p. 255-274.

Hunt, C.B., 1956, Cenozoic geology of the Colorado Plateau: U.S. Geological Survey Professional Paper 279, 99 p.

—1969, Geologic history of the Colorado River, the Colorado River region and John Wesley Powell: U.S. Geological Survey Professional Paper 669-C, p. 59-130.

Kelley, V.C., 1955, Regional tectonics of the Colorado Plateau and relationship to the origin and distribution of uranium: University of New Mexico Publications in Geology, no. 5, 120 p.

Larson, E.E., Ozima, M., and Bradley, W.C., 1975, Late Cenozoic basin volcanism in northwestern Colorado and its implications concerning tectonism and the origin of the Colorado River system: Geological Society of America Memoir 144, p. 155-178.

Lauth, R.E., 1983, Mexican Hat oil field, *in* Fassett, J.E., editor, Oil and gas fields of the Four Corners area, Volume III: Four Corners Geological Society, p. 682-687.

Miser, H.D., 1924, The San Juan Canyon, southeastern Utah: U.S. Geological Survey Water Supply Paper 538, p. 1-80.

Nuccio, V.F., and Condon, S.M., 1996, Burial and thermal history of the Paradox basin, Utah and Colorado, and petroleum potential of the Middle Pennsylvanian Paradox Formation, *in* Huffman, A.C. Jr., Lund, W.R., and Godwin, L.H., editors, Geology and resources of the Paradox basin: Utah Geological Association Publication 25, p. 57-76.

Ohlen, H.R., and McIntyre, L.B., 1965, Stratigraphy and tectonic features of Paradox basin, Four Corners area: American Association of Petroleum Geologists Bulletin, v. 49, p. 2020- 2040.

Peterson, J.A., and Hite, R.J., 1969, Pennsylvanian evaporite-carbonate cycles and their relation to petroleum occurrence, southern Rocky Mountains: American Association of Petroleum Geologists Bulletin, v. 53, p. 884-908.

Pray, L.C., and Wray, J.L., 1963, Porous algal facies (Pennsylvanian) Honaker Trail, San Juan Canyon, Utah, *in* Bass, R.O., editor, Shelf carbonates of the Paradox basin: Four Corners Geological Society Guidebook, p. 204-234.

Ross, C.A., and Ross, J.R.P., 1998, Bursumian Stage, Uppermost Carboniferous of Midcontinent and Southwestern North America: Carboniferous Newsletter, v. 16, p. 40-42.

—1994, The need for a Bursumian Stage, Uppermost Carboniferous, North America: Permophyles, v. 24, p.3-6.

Stevenson, G.M., and Baars, D.L., 1977, Pre-Carboniferous paleotectonics of the San Juan Basin, *in* Fassett, J.E., and James, H.L., editors, San Juan Basin III: New Mexico Geological Society Guidebook, p. 99-110.

—1986, The Paradox: a pull-apart basin of Pennsylvanian

age, *in* Peterson, J.A., editor, Paleotectonics and sedimentation in the Rocky Mountain region: American Association of Petroleum Geologists Memoir 41, p. 513-539.

—1988, Overview - carbonate reservoirs of the Paradox basin: Rocky Mountain Association of Geologists, Carbonate Symposium, p. 149-162.

Wanless, H.R., 1972, Eustatic shifts in sea level during the deposition of Late Paleozoic sediments in the central United States, *in* Elam, J.G., and Chuber, S., editors, Cyclic sedimentation in the Permian Basin: Second Edition, West Texas Geological Society Publication 72-60, p. 41-54.

Wanless, H.R., and Shepard, F.P., 1936, Sea level and climatic changes related to late Paleozoic cycles: Geological Society of America Bulletin, v. 47, p. 1177-1206.

Weber, L.J., Sarg, J.F., Wright, F.M., and Huffman, A.C., 1994, High resolution sequence stratigraphy: reservoir description and geologic setting of the giant Aneth oil field, SE Utah - a field guide to exposures along the San Juan River canyon: American Association of Petroleum Geologists/Rocky Mountain Association of Geologists Field Trip Guidebook, 45 p.

Wengerd, S.A., 1951, Reef limestones of Hermosa Formation, San Juan Canyon, Utah: American Association of Petroleum Geologists Bulletin, v. 35, p. 1038-1051.

—1955, Biohermal trends in Pennsylvanian strata of San Juan Canyon, Utah, *in* Geology of parts of the Paradox, Black Mesa, and San Juan basins: Four Corners Geological Society Guidebook, p.70-77.

—1963, Stratigraphic section at Honaker Trail, San Juan Canyon, San Juan County, Utah, *in* Bass, R.O., editor, Shelf carbonates of the Paradox basin: Four Corners Geological Society Guidebook, p. 235-243.

Wengerd, S.A., and Matheny, M.L., 1958, Pennsylvanian system of Four Corners region: American Association of Petroleum Geologists Bulletin, v. 42, p. 2048-2106.

Wengerd, S.A., and Strickland, J.W., 1954, Pennsylvanian stratigraphy of the Paradox salt basin, Four Corners region, Colorado and Utah: American Association of Petroleum Geologists Bulletin, v. 38, p. 2157-2199.

Woodruff, E.G., 1912, Geology of the San Juan oil field, Utah: U.S. Geological Survey Bulletin 471, p. 76-104.

Woodward-Clyde Consultants, 1982, Geologic characterization report for the Paradox basin study region, Utah study areas: Office of Nuclear Waste Isolation (ONWI-290), v. I-V.

Kodachrome Basin State Park
Photo courtesy of Utah Division of Parks and Recreation

Geology of Utah's Parks and Monuments
2000 Utah Geological Association Publication 28
D.A. Sprinkel, T.C. Chidsey, Jr., and P.B. Anderson, editors

Geology of Kodachrome Basin State Park, Kane County, Utah

James L. Baer[1] and Robert H. Steed[2]

ABSTRACT

Kodachrome Basin State Park has an area of approximately three and a quarter square miles. The geology of the park is flat to gently dipping, mostly Jurassic age sedimentary rocks. The most intriguing feature of the park's geology is the presence of tens of sedimentary pipes. These pipes penetrate rocks representing the Carmel Formation and Entrada Sandstone. In many places the pipes stand alone, while some are still totally or partially encased in the Jurassic age rock.

These pipes are suspected to be the result of rising sand slurries that scoured their way into the overlying rock by following a variety of lower resistant pathways. Pipes range widely in size, ranging in diameter from less than one foot to over 38 feet.

The pipes are thought to be intruded into the overlying sedimentary rocks as the result of over-pressured pods of sabkha water-charged sediments. The duration of the event is not known but is postulated to have occurred during the deposition of the Henrieville sandstone.

INTRODUCTION

The geology of the Kodachrome Basin State Park (KBSP) is characterized in two features (figure 1). One, is the rocks display typical Colorado Plateau style geology, with Jurassic and Cretaceous age, horizontal to gently dipping, sedimentary rocks. These rocks make up a series of mesas, buttes, and spires. This style of geology is relatively straight forward as the rock units are well exposed and structurally uncomplicated. The major structural features of the region are long, widely spaced, nearly north-south trending normal faults and occasional monoclines. The KBSP is approximately three and a quarter square miles of typical Colorado Plateau style geology with the majority of the rocks being Middle to Upper Jurassic sedimentary units that have been disturbed by only minor faulting (figure 2). Two, is the presence of sedimentary sand pipes that penetrate the Jurassic age country rock. These "pipes" are concentrated in KBSP with numbers exceeding 54 within the park area (Hannum, 1980) and 67 of these curious features were mapped in and around the park by Hornbacher (1984). Many of these "pipes" stand in stark contrast with their surroundings (figures 3a, 3b). The gray to buff

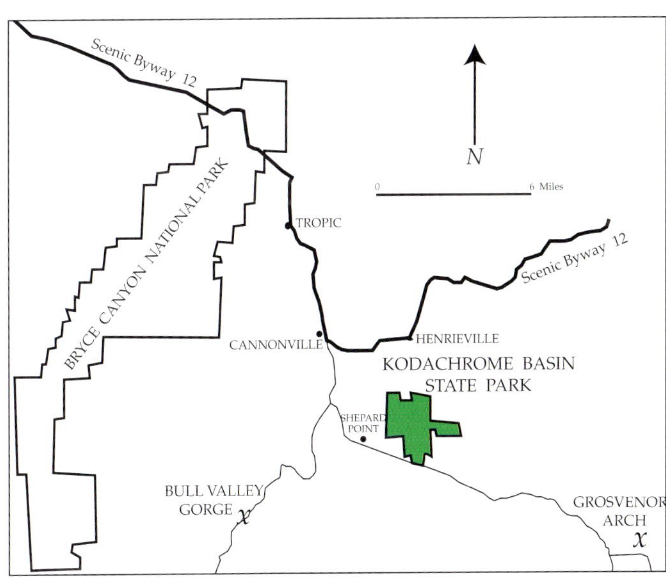

Figure 1. Index map of Kodachrome Basin State Park.

spires are "sore thumbs" when compared to the adjacent red strata of the Entrada units. Some of the "pipes" stand as monoliths and appear as if they are man-made columns from some ancient civilization. A closer examination of these "pipes" reveals an intertwining network of injected sedimentary bodies. It is the enigma of these "pipes" that intrigues the geologist in KBSP.

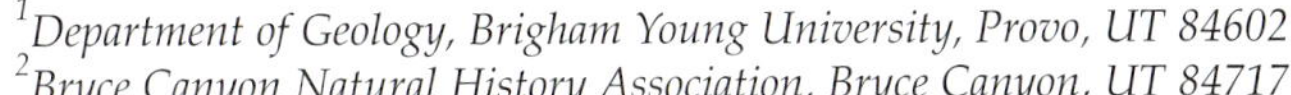

[1]*Department of Geology, Brigham Young University, Provo, UT 84602*
[2]*Bryce Canyon Natural History Association, Bryce Canyon, UT 84717*

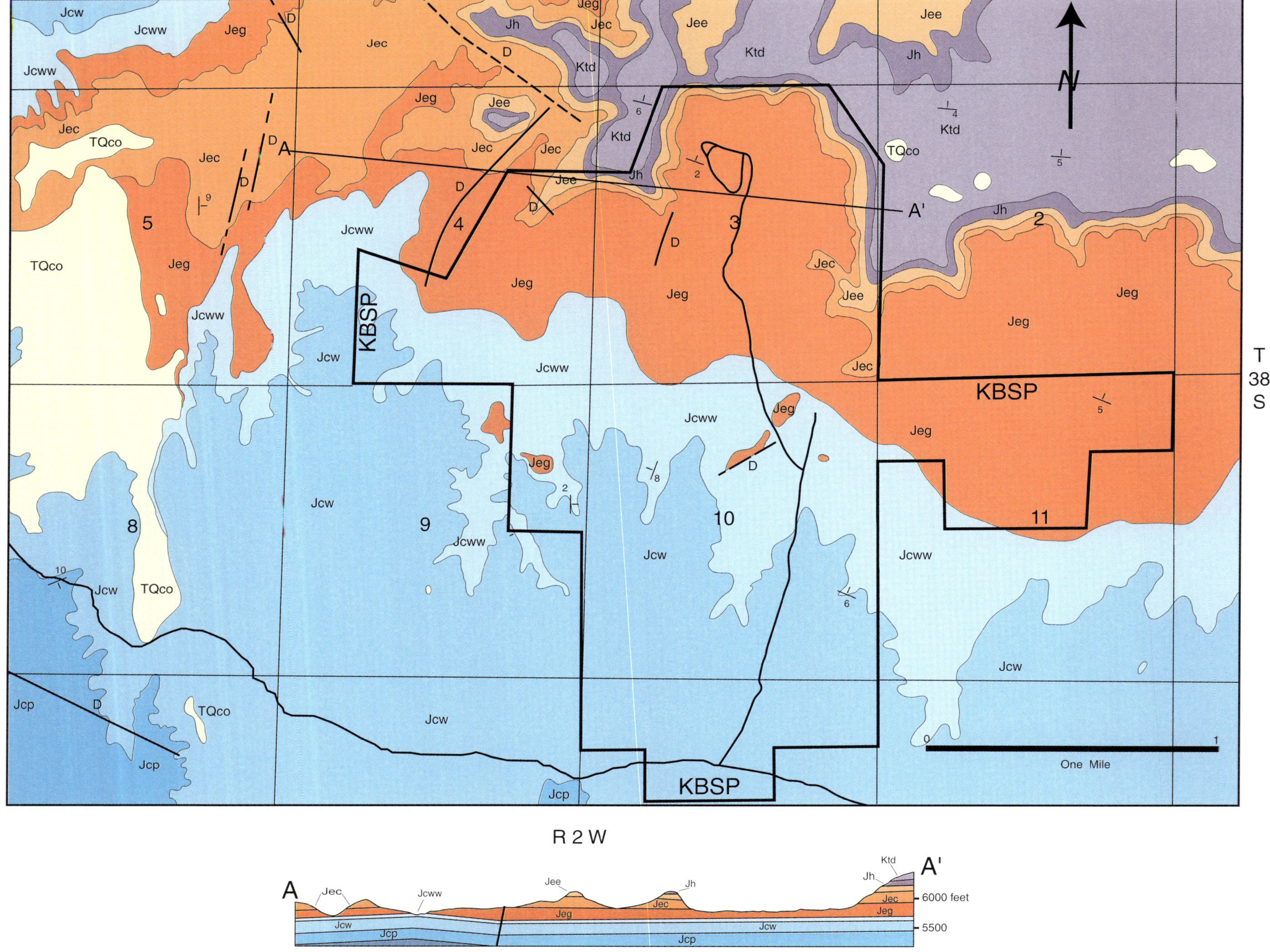

Figure 2. Geologic map and cross section of bed rock units of Kodachrome Basin State Park. Cross section is 1.5 times vertical exaggeration. Rock units are found on figure 4.

Figure 3a. The Kodachrome Basin State Park is characterized by the occurrence of a large number of sedimentary pipes. Here two pipes can be easily viewed on the cliff face.

Figure 3b. Some of the pipes stand out prominently as erosional remnants.

STRATIGRAPHY

Bedrock units exposed in KBSP are Jurassic to Quaternary in age (figure 4). The prominent unitswithin the park proper are the Winsor and Wiggler Wash Members of the Carmel Formation, the Gunsight Butte, Cannonville and Escalante Members of the Entrada Formation, the Henrieville sandstone, the Dakota Formation-Tropic Shale (undivided), and an unnamed resistant conglomerate that is Plio-Pleistocene age (Hornbacher,1984). Additional sedimentary units that are exposed along the roadways to Bull Valley Gorge and to Grosvenor Arch include the Jurassic Navajo Sandstone, Judd Hollow Tongue of the Carmel Formation, the Page Sandstone, and the Paria River Member of the Carmel Formation. While these four named units do not appear in the park proper, they are briefly described so as to aid the park visitor with rocks seen as they travel to the park. Each of these units general lithologies will be described. Short discussions of the sedimentary environments are included. Unconsolidated sedimentary deposits will not be described or discussed.

Jurassic Rocks

Navajo Sandstone (Jn)

The Navajo Sandstone is one of the most prominent and widely recognized rock formations in the southern part of Utah. Anyone who has viewed the Great White Throne or Checkerboard Mesa of Zion Park can easily see the important role it plays in the landscape. The Navajo Sandstone is a gray to orange, highly cross-bedded, fine-to medium-grained sandstone. This magnificent rock unit also forms extensive cliff faces throughout southwest Utah. The Navajo Sandstone was deposited in a Sahara-like desert with an abundance of large, sweeping sand dunes. Bowers (1975) reports thicknesses of 1,550-1,700

feet (472-518 m). The only place where the Navajo Sandstone is exposed in the subject area is at Bull Valley Gorge. Here the formation forms a vertical walled narrow canyon. The cross-bedding is prominent and an examination of the sand grains with a hand lens, reveals frosted grain surfaces, another indicator of wind blown deposition.

Carmel Formation (Jc)

Few formations are as varied as the Carmel Formation, which has several lithologies including limestone, gypsum, sandstone, mudstone, siltstone, and shale. The contact with the underlying Navajo Sandstone is sharp. The Carmel Formation is subdivided into three members, the Paria River Member, the Winsor Member, and the Wiggler Wash member. The Judd Hollow Tongue and the Thousand Pockets Tongue of the Page Sandstone intertongue with the Carmel Formation (figure 4). The total thickness for the Carrmel Formation is 650 feet (198 m).

The upper three members of the Carmel Formation makeup most of the rocks in KBSP. The older units can be seen west and south of the park.

Judd Hollow Tongue (Jcj)

This unit is approximately 75 feet (23 m) thick. It is a thin bedded unit with red, sandy shale, gray-brown, calcareous sandstone, medium gray, calcareous shale, and gray calcareous sandstone making up the bulk of the unit. Outcrops of the Judd Hollow weather to a moderate slope and the unit is distinctive as it is the generally reddish-gray beds above the gray sandstones of the Navajo Sandstone ledge former. The Judd Hollow Tongue is the result of sedimentation on a wide tidal flat. Some of the layers have prominent ripple marks and mudcracks. This unit is found well exposed near Bull Valley Gorge and south of the park.

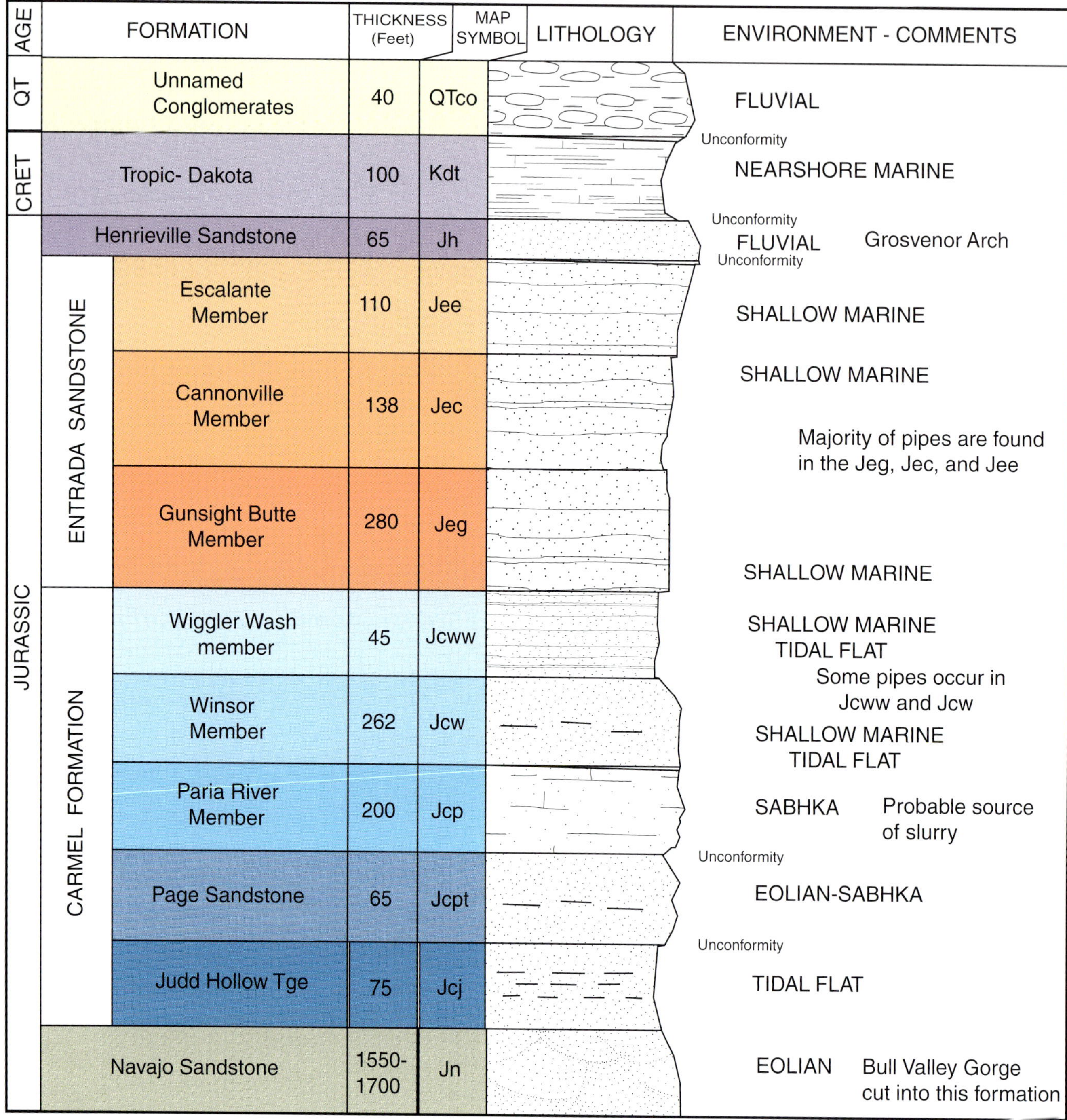

Figure 4. Stratigraphic column of Kodachrome Basin State Park, not to scale.

Page Sandstone (Thousand Pockets Tongue) (Jpt)

The gray cross-bedded sandstones of the Page Sandstone makes the return of subaerial sedimentation as the conditions that promoted desert dune development returned. This unit is quite similar to the Navajo Sandstone but differs as the cross-beds are less striking and of lower amplitude. The unit forms a moderate slope and is 65 feet (20 m) thick. The Page Sandstone can be seen easily on the road to Bull Valley Gorge. The lower contact of the Page Sandstone is an unconformity.

Paria River Member (Jcp)

Thompson and Stokes (1970) assigned 200 feet (61 m) of light gray gypsum, limestone, and red to white sandstones and siltstones that are well exposed along the Paria River near KBSP to the Paria River Member. While this unit is not exposed within the park proper its position in the rock column and lithologies are thought to play an important part in the genesis of the "sedimentary pipes." The Paria River Member is thin-bedded and forms a low to moderate slope. The presence of gypsum is important to note. Gypsum has been found in 3 to 7 foot (1-2 m) thick

Figure 5.   Exposures of Winsor Member of the Carmel Formation (Jurassic) in roadcut just west of Shepard's Point. Note pipe just to left of man. This pipe has a bulky texture with fragments of country rock and some cobbles. Pipe cuts through prominent mud crack bearing unit. This unit is seen in closer view in figure 6.

Figure 7. Exposure of Winsor Member of the Carmel Formation makes up the cliff face of Shepard's Point. Note that at least three pipes transect the Winsor beds and terminate at the contact of the unnamed Plio-Pleistocene conglomerate unit.

Figure 6.   Closer view of mud crack. Sand, perhaps windblown over a shallow tidal flat, fill in two sets of mud cracks.

Figure 8. Sandstone dike-like structure in the Wiggler Wash member fine-grained sandstones.

beds as well as thinner beds scattered throughout the member but concentrated near the middle of the member. This lithology is indicative of a sabhka environment. This member can be seen along the road to Bull Valley Gorge and south of the road from Shepard Point and KBSP. In general the outcrops are a series of low, knobby hills.

Winsor Member (Jcw)

The oldest rocks found in KBSP are assigned to the Winsor Member. The road cut just southwest of Shepard Point reveals the characteristic lithology of the Winsor Member. Here cliffs of thickly-bedded to massive, reddish-brown to chocolate brown sandstone layers are fully exposed. Above these rocks are thin- to medium-bedded red-brown sandstone and shale layers that form cliffs in some areas but knobby rounded hills in other areas. While the red to brown colors dominate the section, there are a number of light colored, thin- to medium-bedded sandstone layers that are obscured by the red-brown weathering material that drapes over them. In the lower part of the member are a series of thin- to thick-bedded white, to light gray, often highly cross-bedded sandstone. The Winsor

Member is interpreted to have been deposited in a clastic dominated tidal flat. Some of the sandstones are representative of channels that formed on the tidal flat. Mudcracks are well developed and some can be seen in the road cut just southwest of Shepard Point (figures 5, 6, and 7). Thompson and Stokes (1970) reported 262 feet (80 m) of the unit.

Wiggler Wash member (Jcww)

The lithologies of the Wiggler Wash member and the Winsor Member are similar with color being foremost. But the Wiggler Wash Member differs in that it has a variety of gypsum occurrences within it , the presence of green shale beds, and the near absence of thick- bedded sandstones. In some places there is a thin limestone layer at the top of the unit. A fairly prominent gypsum layers also found near the middle of the unit. There is a sufficient amount of gypsum in the unit to cause disruption of adjacent layers. The gypsum is found in beds, small dikes and veins and displays colors of white, (alabaster quality), reddish-brown to orange and some light to malachite green. There are some "sedimentary pipes" that penetrate the Wiggler Wash and terminate in this unit (figure 8). The Wiggler Wash member often weathers to a moderate irregular slope. It is a thin unit reaching a maximum thickness of 45 feet (14 m). The sedimentary environment for the Wiggler Wash member is also tidal flat with a few channels and a more restricted waterway. The gypsum deposits are indicative of deposition in sabkhas.

Entrada Sandstone (Je)

The Entrada Sandstone, along with the Carmel Formation and the Navajo Sandstone, are among the most regionally extensive formations in southern Utah. The Entrada Sandstone is found in nearly all the major national parks in that region and makes up a large portion of the rocks in the KBSP. It is also the formation that contains the majority of the "sedimentary pipes" in the park. Depositional environments for the Entrada Sandstone is also tidal flat dominated with local sabkhas, sand dunes, and some channel deposits. Unlike the underlying Carmel Formation, the Entrada is more clastic, with some sandstone units making resistant ridges for several miles. In KBSP, the Entrada is divided into three members: in ascending order, the Gunsight Butte Member—mostly red siltstones; in contrast to these redbeds are the alternating bands of red and white siltstones and fine-grained sandstones that make up the Cannonville Member; and the Escalante Member, which displays gray to gray-green mudstones. Total thickness of the Entrada Sandstone is 530 feet (162 m)

Gunsight Butte Member (Jeg): The basal units of the Gunsight Butte Member are massive red-brown silty, sandstone beds. The edges of these massive blocks are often rounded by weathering. Most of the unit is red to red-brown sandstone that displays cross-beds. Near the top of this member there are some blue to lavender to purple shales that form a mild but colorful slope. A thin, fine-grained white sandstone makes up the top of this member. This member is also a tidal flat deposit. Thompson and Stokes (1970) reported a thickness of 280 feet (85 m) for this member.

Cannonville Member (Jec): A distinct character of the Cannonville Member is the alternating red and white sandstone layers, commonly referred to as "banding." The lower half of this member is a series gray shales with interbeds of brown to purple tuffs (volcanic ash) and thin quartz sandstone layers. Buff to tan fine-grained massive, with numerous yellow limonite nodules, sandstone beds mark the upper portion of this member. These light colored layers are easily seen and serve as means to identify the Cannonville Member (figure 9). Hornbacher (1984) measured 138 feet (42 m) of this member.

Escalante Member (Jee): Buff to tan colored, fine-grained, massive, sandstones make up of this member. Less apparent are the gray shales and the red tuffs that are layered in between the sandstones. Some gypsum layers are also present, The sandstones have many limonite concretions

Figure 9. View looking west over Cannonville, Utah. Red beds are the Gunsight Butte Member of the Entrada Sandstone, these are overlain by the reddish-brown to buff siltstones and fine- grained sandstones of the Cannonville Member, which in turn are overlain by the light tan sandstones of the Escalante Member. The Henrieville Sandstone and portions of the Dakota Formation make up the near and far skyline.

and are conspicuously planar bedded. Again a tidal to slightly sub-aerial sedimentary environment prevails. An added factor is the presence of the volcanic tuff units. These ashfalls introduce more silica and provide for the lavender to red colors. A thickness of 110 feet (34 m) was measured by Hornbacher (1984).

Thompson and Stokes (1970) described a subtle but significant unconformity that occurs at the top of the Escalante Member. Jurassic units such as the Curtis and the Summerville found near KBSP were removed by this erosional event. The Henrieville Sandstone was deposited upon this surface and got many of its sediments from the reworking and erosion of older sandstone units.

Henrieville Sandstone (Jh)

The Henrieville Sandstone is bounded by unconformities (Thompson and Stokes, 1970) This unit is not widespread and is considered by some to be the equivalent of the Salt Wash Member of the Morrison Formation (Thompson and Stokes, 1970). The Henrieville Sandstone marks a change in the sedimentary depositional environment. Tidal flat, sabkha, and some fluvial conditions prevailed in the older rocks, with the upper portion including a series of volcanic ash deposits. Henrieville Sandstone deposition becomes one of a more active shoreline with coarser clastic units being deposited by shoreline activities and some by fluvial processes. Initial deposition of the Henrieville Sandstone included fine clastics with mud and silt being deposited. These beds are now gray, yellow-green shales and siltstones that are heavily limonite stained. White to buff, fine-grained, quartz-rich, cross-bedded sandstones with occasional conglomerate layers make up the upper 80 percent of the unit. The cross-beds are a blend of wave and fluvial caused features. Streaks of limonite stain give the sandstone an "almost petroglyph" appearence (figure10). Hornbacher (1984) reported a thick-

Figure 10. Typical exposure of the fluvial sandstones that make up the Henrieville Sandstone. The Henrieville Sandstone is bracketed by unconformities. Cretaceous rocks of the Dakota Sandstone and the Tropic Shale can be seen capping the mesa.

Figure 11. Grosvenor Arch is sculptured in the Henrieville Sandstone.

ness of the Henrieville Sandstone at 65 feet (20 m).

After the Henrieville was indurated, it was subjected to tectonic forces, causing the unit to be fractured and uplifted, thereby exposing the rock to the surface weathering agents. This combination of rock character, weathering, and position on a cliff corner allowed for the formation of the spectacular Grosvenor Arch (figure 11). A trip to see the arch is worthwhile provided the road conditions are favorable.

Above the Henrieville Sandstone is another unconformity. This sub-Cretaceous unconformity is much more widely recognized than the previously noted unconformity. This unconformity marks the stripping away of several hundreds of feet of Jurassic rocks when much of the region was uplifted epeirogenically. The subsequent sinking of the region allowed a basal conglomerate of fluvial origin to be deposited upon the stripped surface. These conglomerates mark the contact between the Jurassic and Cretaceous rocks throughout the region.

Figure 12. An unnamed Plio-Pleistocene conglomerate caps the Winsor Member with its intruded sandstone pipes at Shepard's Point.

Cretaceous Rocks

Dakota Formation-Tropic Shale (Kdt)

A small portion of KBSP has rocks assigned to these Cretaceous units. Because the sandstones of the Dakota and the shales of the Tropic interfinger in this area the formations are not divided. Also these rocks are not easily seen within the park but are seen along the roads leading into the park. The reader is referred to that log for information on these units.

In general, the Dakota Formation has a basal conglomerate and tan to gray sandstones with interbeds of dark-gray to black shales and some thin, coal seams. The Tropic Shale is mostly dark-gray to black shale with thin tuffs and some gypsum-filled veins. These units mark the beginning of marginal marine sedimentation and have a modern analog in parts of the Gulf Coast of the United States.

While the Cretaceous Dakota-Tropic Shale is present in the high skyline, the low hills within KBSP are capped in several places by a thin conglomerate unit. Hornbacher (1984) described this unit as being deposited upon a local erosional surface. This unconformity is one of limited areal extent and appears to represent an irregular erosional surface created by the ancestral Paria River (Gregory, 1951). The age of this surface and the age of the rocks that are deposited upon it play an important role in timing the emplacement of the "sedimentary pipes."

Tertiary-Quaternary Rocks

Pliocene-Pleistocene Conglomerates (QTc)

At Shepard Point an unnamed conglomerate caps the mesa (figure 12). It is also obvious that several of the "sedimentary pipes" terminate at the lower contact of this unit. The conglomerate is relatively thin, ranging from 5 to 6 feet (1-1.5 m) to 12 to 15 feet (3-5 m) thick. Chert and limestone cobbles dominate the unit, with some red-brown sand channel fills found throughout the unit. In most

Figure 13. Local slumping associated with sedimentary pipe intrusions create a minor syncline as seen at Shepard's Point in the Winsor Member.

places the unit is not well cemented and therefore makes well rounded knobs. The cobbles are in cut- and fill-channels with the largest clasts approximately 2 feet (0.5 m). This conglomerate was deposited in a fluvial environment.

STRUCTURE

Geologic structure of the Colorado Plateau is one that is caused by differential uplift of basement blocks. This uplift causes the development of long, linear normal faults, like the Paunsaugunt fault, and long, linear monoclines such as the Waterpocket Fold ,that makes the eastern edge of Capitol Reef National Park. Between these main features are flat to moderate dipping rocks that makeup most of the structures of the region. In addition at least two sets of high-angle fractures often control the direction of drainage and erosional patterns.

Structure within KBSP is rather simple. The rocks dip gently to the northeast and are broken by a few minor normal faults. All faults trend northeast and have less than 100 feet (30 m) of displacement. Bowers (1975) mapped a gentle northeast plunging syncline in the eastern half of KBSP. The fracture system is not well developed but two sets of fractures are present. One strikes north 10 to 20 degrees east, and the other, less well developed, strikes north 70 to 80 degrees west. A few local structures seen near some of the pipes are a consequence of "sedimentary pipe" emplacement (figure 13).

GEOLOGIC HISTORY

The rock sequence of KBSP and surrounding area is so well exposed that the geologic history can be well documented. Geologists look at modern analogs to explain the perceived ancient counterparts. However there are not always modern regimes that fit well, for example extensive epicontinental seas interpreted for the Cretaceous units are not present today. Another aspect to any geologic history is the scale of time that it represents. The rock record in the region of the park represents approximately 200 million years. An overriding concept with the geologic history is the plate tectonic model. The Earth's outer lithosphere is broken into large slabs referred to as "plates". What is referred to now as Utah is a part of the North American plate. These plates move about through time and change position in respect to such geographic features as the north pole and the equator. A portion of the North American plate is the lithosphere called the Colorado Plateau. This segment has a generally thicker crust then areas on all sides. As the plate moves the Colorado Plateau portion moves up and down through the last 200 million years. It is these up and down movements (epeirogenic movements) that control the sedimentaion and geologic structure development of KBSP.

The oldest rock in the area is the Jurassic Navajo Sandstone, seen near Bull Valley Gorge. These rocks represent a time when a broad, sweeping dunes dominated the scene. These sand dunes developed when the area was much further south and east than the present. It was also near sea level. The desert conditions gradually gave way to shallow marine environment as fine clastics, evaporites, and limestones that make up the members of the Carmel Formation and the Entrada Sandstone were deposited. This shallow basin experienced periodic uplifts and subsequent subsidence as the thick crustal blocks of the Colorado Plateau reacted to plate motion while the plate moved slowly north and west. These uplifts with the attendant erosion made surfaces that were eventually buried by younger sedimentation, thus creating unconformities. These unconformities became the telltale evidence of this style of tectonic behavior. These Jurassic rocks make up about 60 million of the 200 million history.

Near the end of the Jurassic the area began to feel the effects of the a converging plates to the west. An ancient mountain range developed on what is now Nevada and western Utah. As this range grew subaerial erosion created the surface that would eventually represent the unconformity that makes the division between the Jurassic and the Cretaceous rocks. It was in a gradually subsiding foredeep basin that the clastics washed from the western mountains were deposited. This sea differs from the previous Jurassic sea in that it is a sea caused by the converging plates, was deeper, and was strongly clastic dominated. Subtropic conditions prevailed and the lush vegetation that grew along the shorelines will eventually become the extensive coal deposits found in the region. These rocks, represented in part by the Dakota Formation and Tropic Shale in this area, reached thicknesses in excess of 7,000 feet (2,135 m) of alternating units of sandstone and shale. The top of these rocks is marked with a major unconformity. Approximately 80 million years is represented by these rocks. As the area is rising the plate is also heading further north and west.

From Tertiary times on the area began a slow rise as the North American plate reacted to the subduction of the

Figure 15. Sandstone pipes can be seen on the cliff face and seem to wind their way through the Winsor Member rocks.

Figure 14. Portion of pipe seen in roadcut near Shepard's Point. The surrounding rock is Winsor Member sandstones and siltstones. Pipe has several internal features such as conglomerate, displaced siltstone blocks, flow structures, and slump features.

Pacific plate. While the whole of the western United States was uplifted some portions were lifted higher and at differing rates than others, such is the case for the Colorado Plateau. During this uplift phase, marking the past 65 million years, the sedimentation was all continental with stream and inland lake deposition dominating. Within KBSP there are few Tertiary rocks, the exception being the unnamed conglomerate that caps a few of the local mesas. During these times the majority of the movement on the large faults occurred and several of the areas had active volcanoes.

GEOLOGICAL FEATURES

The features that stand out both figuratively and literally are the "sedimentary pipes" (figures 14 and 15). The shape, the geometry, the petrology, the distribution, and the method of emplacement are the intriguing aspects of these intrusive bodies. These rock bodies have been the subject of study in some detail by Hannum (1980) and Hornbacher (1984). Hannum (1980) in her study mapped 54 of the sedimentary pipes, while Hornbacher (1984) mapped 67 of these sedimentary intrusive bodies in and near KBSP. These curious sedimentary features occur in areas that are readily accessible as well as areas that are almost inaccessible. We will not enumerate these features as did Hannum and Hornbacher but we will draw on their observations as well as our own to discuss these interesting sedimentary features.

These features have been classified by Hannum (1980) as sandstone pipes, conglomerate pipes, thick dikes, and thin dikes dependent upon the lithology and orientation of the intrusive body. Hornbacher (1984) makes little distinction of these intrusive bodies other than to refer to them an pipes and dikes. In our discussion we will follow Hornbacher by referring to the dikes and pipes as connected intrusives.

Basically, these sedimentary intrusives can be considered as a collection of small dikes some of which are connected to prominent sedimentary pipes. These structures are the result of an intricate invasion of a thick slurry originating from stratigraphic units below those that hold these structures now. Hannum (1980) and Hornbacher (1984) describe individual structures. Rather than repeat their observations we chose to deal with the intrusives and the intrusion collectively.

A general description of these pipes and dikes is not an easy task as there is a great variety in shape, size, and lithology. But a view based upon a model of emplacement reduces the differences and allows for a better understanding of the variation.

A description of the intrusive bodies can be divided into the small to moderate size dikes and sills that serve as feeder and connective bodies for the larger and more prominent sedimentary pipes, and the pipes themselves. Dikes and sills differ from pipes because dikes and sills tend to be slab like while the pipes are vertical and are mostly equate in diameter. Dikes range in size from a few inches to 3 to 4 feet (1 m). Most of the dikes penetrate rocks at near normal to the bedding, making the dikes vertical in the near horizontal strata. A few of the dikes intersect the bedding planes at angles ranging from 20 to 70 degrees. Some dikes are near circular while others take on the

Figure 16. Sandstone dike and sill follow previously existing channel deposits of the Wiggler Wash member. Sandstone intrusives appear to wrap around these features and branch out to make prominent pipes farther east.

Figure 18. Pebble units that can be found in some of the sedimentary pipes. Pebbles may have been carried up from the Paria River Member.

Figure 17. Angular pieces of siltstone found inside a prominent pipe found in the roadcut by Shepard's Point. Many of the pipes have rock fragments in them.

Figure 19. Lone pipe stands amid rocks of the Wiggler Wash member. It is thought that many of the pipes are more resistant to erosion because they have a calcareous cemented matrix.

shape of a linear fin-like structure. Some dike and sill structures are governed by the pre-existing sedimentary fabrics (figures 8 and 16). Where dikes and pipes can be seen at length, for instance 20 feet or more (6-7m), many of them display a sinuous nature as if they follow the path of least resistance as they were emplaced. The majority of the dikes are gray to tan with a few reddish brown. The dikes are mostly sand but contain small fragments of country rocks and pockets of pebbles (figures 17 and 18). There appears to be no preferred orientation to the dikes except to note that they are found more abundantly near faults and fractures. There is little or no indication that the emplacement of the dikes caused the bedding of the host rock to be disturbed. Most of the dikes stand out, probably because of their calcium carbonate cement that makes them more weather resistant.

Although they are less numerous it is the sedimentary pipes that are so prominent and give KBSP its distinction.

Figures 19 and 20 illustrate the single sentinel-like appearance that some of these pipes take on. It is thought that these prominent circular structures came about because the intrusive slurry rose at the intersection of two fractures. While the ones shown in the figures are large the largest of these pipes is 172 feet (52 m) high and the largest diameter is 50 feet (15 m). While some of these pipes are nearly circular some are ovate and others are roughly rectangular. The shape of these pipes may be controlled by previously existing sedimentary properties and the amount of slurry available.

The internal features of the pipes are varied. Some pipes have a rather consistent fine sandstone interior while others have a mixture of pebbles, cobbles, blocks (mostly near by country rock), brown shale clasts, and some carbonized wood fragments. Some of the larger clasts appear as if they are floating in the fine grained matrix. Some pipes, however, have a bedded appearance with blocks of conglomerate transecting the breadth of the pipe. The larger pipes have a pseudo-bedding blocky look.

Figure 20. This lone sentinel is slighty over 45 feet (14 m) high and has a rind of calcareous sandstone that girds the monolith.

Figure 22. Bleached or reduced country rock is evidence of the reducing nature of the rising slurry. Probably as the result of organic matter carried in the slurry.

Figure 21. A girdle of fine sandstone surrounds this pipe. It is thought that this sandstone girdle is the result of dewatering of the pipe and the sandstone rind is much like mudcake in a well.

Figure 23. Pipe with bedrock contact which is bleached. Notice also the flow structures that occur just inside the fine sandstone rind.

While not found in all the pipes, many exhibit a concentric banding with a fine sand rind that surrounds the pipe (figure 21). This fine sand band appears to be much like the mudcake found in oil well bores. These types of pipes often display a reduction zone or bleached area next to the pipe (figure 22). Some of the pipes show flow structures (figure 23). A few of the pipes have a remarkable display of flute and groove structure on there exterior (figure 24).

Even though the pipes are prominent and some of the smaller dikes are readily visible the relationship of the dikes to the pipes is obscure. It is suspected that the dikes are secondary and may originate from the pipes (Hannum, 1980). Or they could possibly be feeder structures through which the sand slurry was transported to the pipes. Hornbacher (1984) suggested that the small dikes are neither of the aforementioned but rather are just small intrusive structures that these structures may or may not connect to the main pipes (figure 16). We prefer Hornbacher's hypothesis.

Figure 24 . Some of the solitary pipes show a strong flute and groove structure indicative of a fairly mobile slurry.

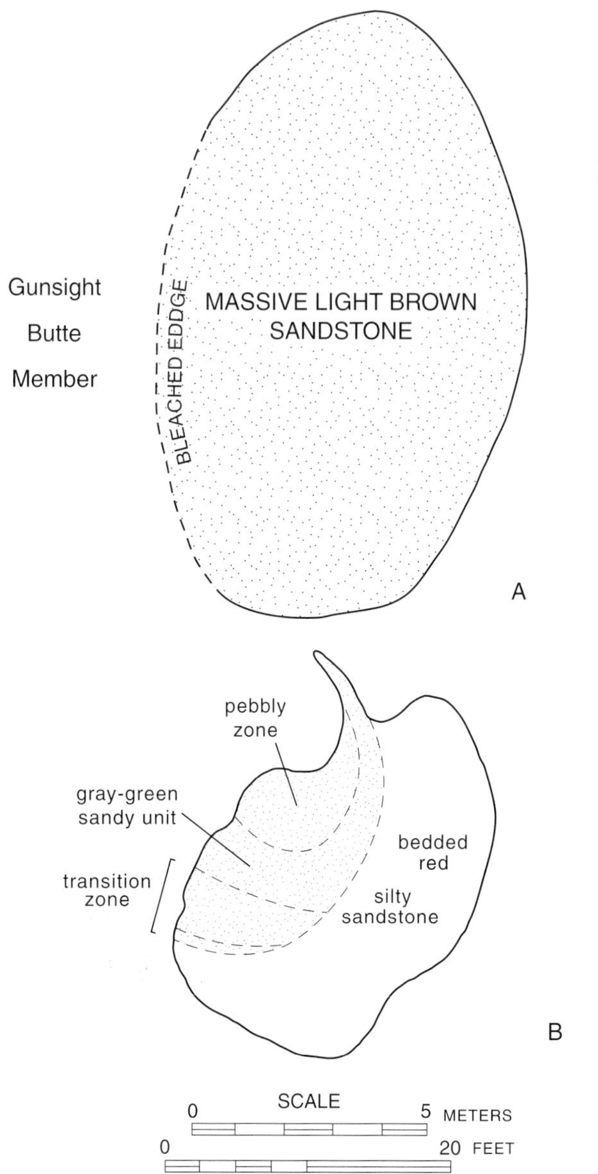

Figure 25. Outlines of two pipe types. A- Pipe A is over 35 feet (10 m) long in its longest dimension and is mostly made of sandstone. B- A partially eroded pipe with a variety of lithologies. It is suspected that the material is from rafted bedrock. (Modified from Hannum, 1980).

While these intrusive sand structures present a widely diverse picture, consensus as to the means of their emplacement is also diverse (figure 25). Any suggestion for mode of emplacement needs to account for the lack of apparent disturbance of host rock, apparent volume for volume replacement or rearrangement, tie the intrusive material to a mobile lithology that exists below the host rock, and have the mechanics of the intrusion placed in a feasible time of occurrence.

Hannum(1980) suggested that the pipes and dikes are the product of a cold water springs that carried the fine sand from below and made the pipes particularly the smaller ones. She also suggests that an earthquake could have liquified already water bearing units and the resulting injection would cause these structures to come about. The cold water spring suggestion may serve to explain the smaller pipes but the presence of cobbles and gravel within the pipe is difficult to explain through a cold water spring mechanism. Hornbacher (1984) discussed several mechanisms that range from some type of rapid loading of sediments that would cause entrapped water bearing sediments to eventually expel these water- rich sediments into the overlying host rocks in a diapiric style structure to having an earthquake trigger intrusion of water-rich sediments in a liquefaction style of mechanism. Hornbacher (1984) favored the earthquake triggered mechanism because the intrusives are closely related to the two small fault traces that lie just north of Shepard's Point. Further he stated that the intrusives are not brecciated or rotated in the lower portion of a monocline and, according to his preferred mechanism, the water saturated environment required for the intrusion event was available near an ancestral Paria River (Hornbacher, 1984).

Any suggestion for mechanism must consider the timing of the intrusion. Hannum (1980) made no attempt to date the intrusives other than to note that the majority of the pipes cut or are encased in the Gunsight Butte Member of the Entrada Sandstone. She further stated that she did not observe these sandstone intrusives in rocks younger than the Gunsight Butte Member and only a few were observed in the Wiggler Wash member of the Carmel Formation. Hannum's observation that limited exposure of the pipe hosting units, differential erosion, and restrictive access precludes an accurate assessment of the pipe distribution. Hannum (1980) stated that the base of any one pipe is not exposed but she also suggests that the material making up the intrusives came from the lower part of the Winsor member and the Paria River member of the Carmel Formation. Hornbacher (1984) made many of the same observations as Hannum but he offers a more detailed suggestion as to the timing of the intrusives. Hornbacher (1984) stated that one of the pipes penetrates the Escalante Member of the Entrada Sandstone there by dating the intrusion later than that member. He further states that one pipe he found had a convoluted, massive, tan-brown conglomerate at its top. By comparing pebble counts and sieve analysis of this conglomerate with conglomerates that he collected from two units of the Plio-Pleistocene conglomerate he concluded that the intrusions occurred after the deposition of the lower conglomerate unit, the channel conglomerate, but before the deposition of the upper conglomerate unit, the sheet conglomerate. This allows the area to be saturated with water from the river or rivers that transported the cobbles and finer clasts that make up the Plio-Pleistocene conglomerate. While these sediments were saturated a movement on the Paunsaugunt Fault generated an earthquake with sufficient energy to mobilize saturated sediments from the underlying units namely the Paria River and Winsor Members as well as contributions from the Thousand Pockets Tongue of the Page Sandstone and the Judd Hollow Tongue of the Carmel Formation (Hornbacher,1984).

While there is some merit to the mechanism as proposed by Hornbacher (1984) we think that it is much more complicated than the data indicate. Our proposed mechanism is much simpler and meets a critical factor that Hornbacher's model ignores, namely the time interval from deposition of the Jurassic units in question and the Plio-Pleistocene intrusion event. If one approximates the age of the Carmel Formation at 155 to 160 million years and the Plio-Pleistocene conglomerates deposited 1 to 2 million years ago then the units from which the pipe making material came were largely dormant for 150 million years or more. Another concern is the need to saturate the Jurassic rocks at this late time in order to make them mechanically more susceptible to earthquake initiated intrusion. It may be that the timing of the intrusion as proposed by Hornbacher is driven more by the earthquake part of the mechanism than any other factor. In our model the Plio- Pleistocene conglomerates are not considered to be important as time constraints.

Figure 26 illustrates our general concept of the geometries of the intrusive pipes and dikes. Figure 27 shows a schematic of the timing and mechanism for these intrusions. We agree that the source material for the pipes and dikes come from the units suspected by Hannum (1980) and Hornbacher(1984). We interpret these source units as being deposited in a sabkha dominated environment. As a result these units were composed of fine sands, with occasional pebble deposition, but the dominate sediments

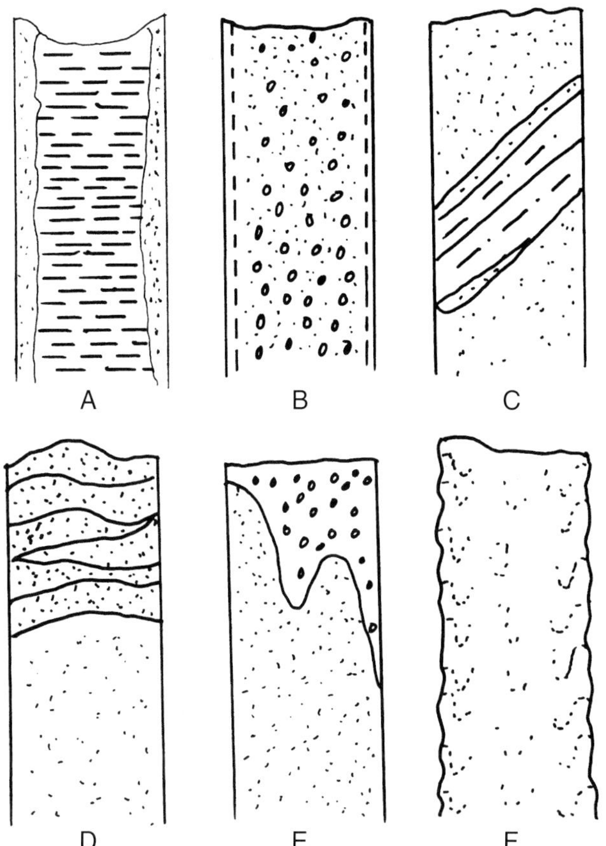

Figure 26. Diagrams of some pipe interiors. A- Pipe with clay-siltstone interior and sandstone exterior. B- Pipe with suspended pebbles in the interior and a sandstone exterior with a reduction or bleached contact with the country rock. A pipe similar to this can be seen in figures 21 and 22. C- Pipe with bedded country rock inclusion. Commonly these inclusions can be determined to originate from nearby country rock. D- Pipe with pseudo-bedded appearance. These "beds" appear to be the result or either multiple extrusions or partial collapse of the pipe when it was newly formed. E- Pipe with conglomerate core. These conglomerates can be from underlying rock or the result or interaction with cobble bearing strata that lie above the pipe. F- Pipe with strong cast and flute surface. These pipes are often composed of fine sand.

were evaporites, mostly gypsum, with some limestones that formed in and around laterally constrained basins. It is common that these shallow basins that lie just above the normal tide line to also have stromatolites as well as some salt tolerant reeds and rushes. There are sabkha facies found in the Judd Hollow and Thousand Pockets Tongues as well as most of the Paria River and part of the Winsor Members. We think these sabkha facies allow for formation waters to be trapped by seals, perhaps gypsum beds, and as the sediments deposited over these sealed pods they become more and more pressured and eventually become over-pressured. The sediments that makeup the greater part of the Carmel Formation and the Entrada Sandstone are deposited in shallow marine environments. And as these sediments pile up they pressurize the sabkha facies below.

Hornbacher (1984) reported a total penetration of one of his pipes, from the Paria River Member of the Carmel

                    Geology of Kodachrome Basin State Park, Utah

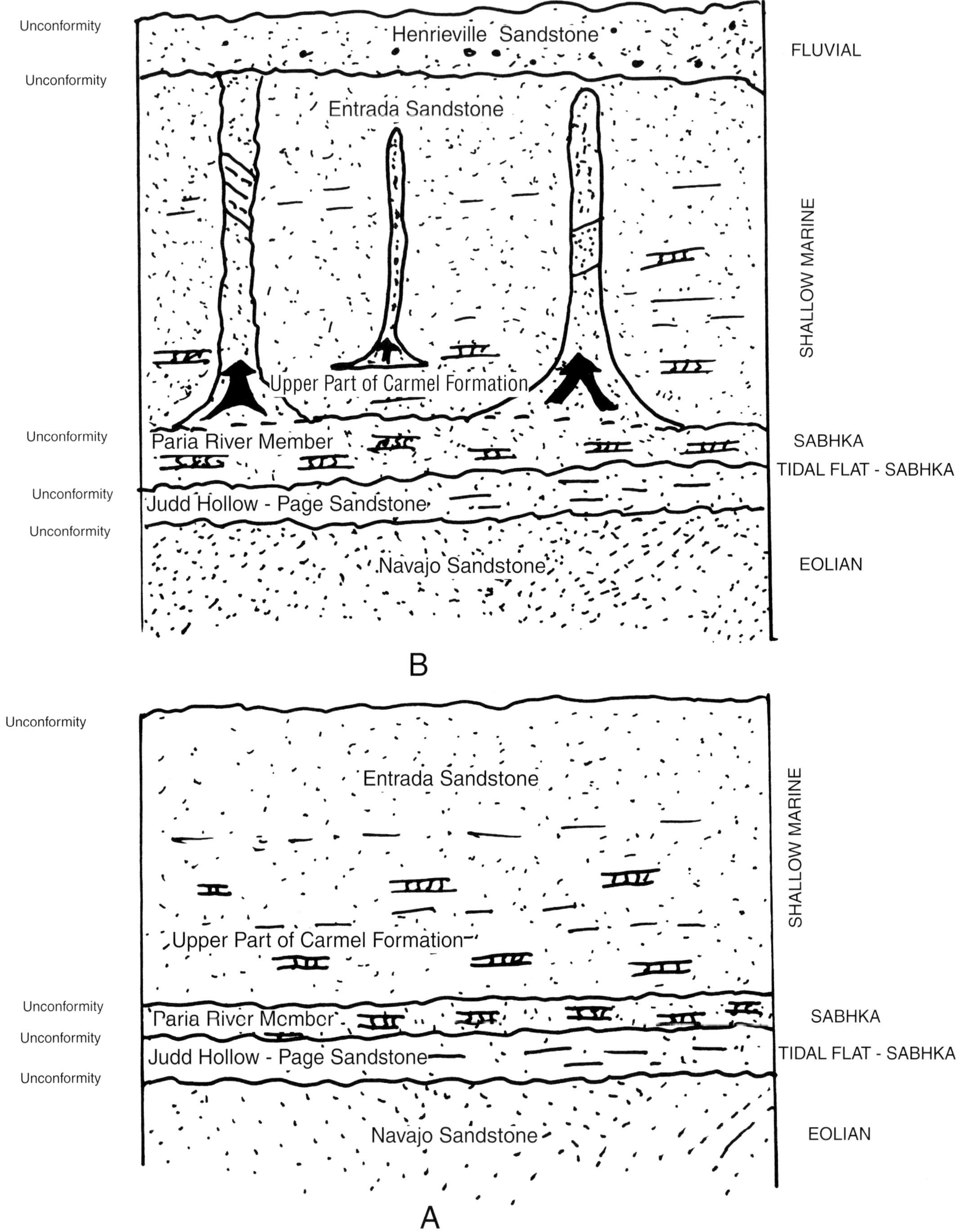

Figure 27. Diagrammatic scheme of sedimentary pipes intrusion. A- Setting before intrusion of slurry. Slurry comes from over-pressured pods of sabhka pods of the Paria River Member. B- Slurry is thought to scour its way into the overlying rock during or slightly after deposition of the Henrieville Sandstone.

Formation to the Escalante Member of the Entrada Sandstone, as a total of 395 feet (120 m). He also states that the youngest formation penetrated by a sand intrusion is the Escalante Member. The Henrieville Sandstone directly overlies the Escalante Member with an unconformity separating these two sedimentary bodies. The fact that the youngest demonstrable unit penetrated by the sand intrusives is the Escalante Member and there is no evidence that younger units such as the Henrieville Sandstone and the Cretaceous rocks having been affected by the intrusives leads us to suggest that the intrusions of the sandstone bodies was much earlier than the Plio-Pleistocene age as postulated by Hornbacher. We think the intrusions are post Escalante Member and penecontemporaneous with the deposition of the Henrieville Sandstone when the Jurassic host rocks were in their early diagenetic stage. This allows for the host rocks to be partially indurated, soft enough to be scoured by the rising sedimentary slurry yet not so hard as to be disrupted and heavily brecciated by that activity.

Further, the sabkha environment allows for the intruding slurry to range in composition and volume. This may account for the variety of lithologies found in the structures and why they are of different sizes. It is highly likely that the sabhka pods could also be initiated at different times as the loading caused by the deposition of the Henrieville Sandstone sediments progressed. Each of the pods would release their water saturated, over-pressured slurry as the circumstances dictated. The rising slurry would follow a path of least resistence and develop a variety of structures as situations would permit. The two small faults found north of Shepard's Point was a prominent weakness and many of the sand intusions formed near them. Intersection of fractures were loci for many of the bigger circular pipes (figure 25). In some cases previously existing sedimentary structures, such as amalgamated channels, cause the slurry to work its way round and about. Other features, such as reduction of iron (bleaching) along the contacts of some of the intrusions, presence of large pieces of the country rock found in the pipes, pseudo-layering that is selective in some pipes, volume problems, and the presence of "mudcake" layers on some pipes can all be accommodated in the sabkha pod originated, load triggered, forceful injection of a sand slurry (figures 21 and 22). The slurry, in some places, contained sufficient amounts of organic matter to reduce the iron compounds in the host rocks as the slurry injected and often times scoured its way. Hannum (1980) reported the finding of pieces of carbonized wood in some dikes. This fossil wood, along with other organic matter, from the sabhka sediments produced the reducing slurry. The presence of large blocks found in some of the pipes can be explained by the scouring and buoyancy associated with the rising slurry. As the slurry worked its way upward it would scour out sections of the country rock and in some instances raft them along as the pipe developed. Where these rafted blocks settled back into the scoured structure

the blocks can take on a pseudo- layered effect. Such a feature would be like pipe three of Hannum (1980). Hornbacher (1984) addressed the room problem, in essence how do the structures accommodate the introduction of the sand slurry and the volume of rock that occupied the space before the intrusion. Because there is little or no evidence of forced entry that disrupted and brecciated the country rock how was the introduced slurry compensated for ? This lends credence to the structures to be the result of scouring action. As the slurry rose and scoured away some of the country rock the resulting volume was filled with either the slurry sand or portions of the country rock that were now rafted in the rising slurry. It is suspected that some of these intrusions reached the surface and vented material as sand boils, thereby leaving the volume excavated occupied by the slurry and remnants of the country rock. In regard to the concentric layer, "mudcake", found in some pipes, it is postulated that this was the result of the dewatering of the slurry subsequent to the intrusion. Water escaped slowly into the confining country rock with the resulting of the finer sand being carried and deposited at this interface (figure 21).

In addition there are flow structures found in the pipes (figure 23). Some of these flow structures infer a two directional flow regime. After the scouring intrusion phase the energy driving this phase would ultimately reduce to zero. Then the slurry would dewater and consolidate over time. This suggests that some pipes may have had voids develop at their tops, however none have yet been found.

In summary the Kodachrome Basin State Park is characterized by two main geological features. First, is the colorful sculptured landscape consisting of mostly Jurassic marine sedimentary rocks and second is the concentration of intriguing sedimentary intrusions, pipes and dikes. Either one of these features can justify the state park designation on their own. Together they make the park a must see.

REFERENCES

Bowers, W.E., 1975, Geologic map and coal resources of the Henrieville Quadrangle, Garfield and Kane Counties, Utah: U.S. Geological Survey Coal Investigations Map C-74

Hannum, Cheryl, 1980, Sandstone and conglomerate-breccia pipes and dikes of the Kodachrome Basin area, Kane County, Utah: Brigham Young University Geology Studies, v. 27, p. 31-50

Gregory, H.E., 1951, Geology and geography of the Paunsaugunt region, Utah: U.S. Geological Professional Paper 226, 116 p.

Hornbacher, Dwight, 1984, Geology and structure of Kodachrome Basin State Reserve and vicinity, Kane and Garfield Counties, Utah: Loma Linda, Loma Linda University, M.S. thesis, 179 p.

Thompson, A.E., and Stokes, W.L., 1970, Stratigraphy of the San Rafael Group, southwest and south central Utah: Utah Geological and Mineralogical Survey Bulletin 87, 53 p.

Bryce Canyon National Park
Photo courtesy of the Utah Travel Council

Geology of Utah's Parks and Monuments
2000 Utah Geological Association Publication 28
D.A. Sprinkel, T.C. Chidsey, Jr., and P.B. Anderson, editors

Geology of Quail Creek State Park, Utah

Robert F. Biek[1]

ABSTRACT

Quail Creek State Park and Quail Creek Reservoir lie cradled in the eroded core of the Virgin anticline, one of the most remarkable geologic features in southwestern Utah. The park is best known as a wonderful place for fishing, boating, and swimming, and it is operated jointly as an off-line reservoir for storage of Virgin River water and as a recreational facility. Although Quail Creek State Park is small, it offers truly exceptional views of Triassic strata that form this part of the anticline. At the park, the Shnabkaib Member and upper red member of the Moenkopi Formation form the eroded core of the anticline, and the overlying Shinarump Conglomerate Member of the Chinle Formation forms surrounding cliffs and a resistant carapace. These strata are offset by minor thrust and normal faults associated with formation of the Virgin anticline. The park is also host to a variety of Quaternary deposits, including reworked debris-flow deposits that contain igneous clasts from the distant Pine Valley Mountains. Quail Creek State Park is the site of a major engineering catastrophe that occurred on January 1, 1989, when the Quail Creek south dike suddenly failed. Approximately 25,000 acre-feet (30,492,000 m^3) of water - more than half the capacity of Quail Creek Reservoir - flowed through a breach in the dike over a 12-hour period. The effects of this flooding can still be seen below the dam.

INTRODUCTION

The first thing most visitors to Quail Creek State Park notice, apart from the improbably blue and refreshing waters of the reservoir itself, are the brightly colored, layered rocks of the surrounding cliffs (figure 1). In fact, Quail Creek State Park lies astride one of the most remarkable geologic features in southwestern Utah. The park is cradled in the eroded core of the Virgin anticline, a Late Cretaceous or early Tertiary compressional feature formed during the Sevier orogeny. The flanks of the fold provide spectacular exposures of parts of the late Early Triassic Moenkopi Formation and overlying Late Triassic Chinle Formation, and Quaternary boulder deposits at the northwest end of the reservoir provide a glimpse into the rock types of the distant Pine Valley Mountains. Quail Creek State Park is also the site of a major engineering catastrophe that occurred on January 1, 1989, when the Quail Creek south dike suddenly failed.

While this paper focuses on the geology of Quail Creek State Park, the park is surrounded by a landscape of

Figure 1. *View northeast across the reservoir at Quail Creek State Park.*

[1]*Utah Geological Survey, Salt Lake City, UT 84114-6100*

465

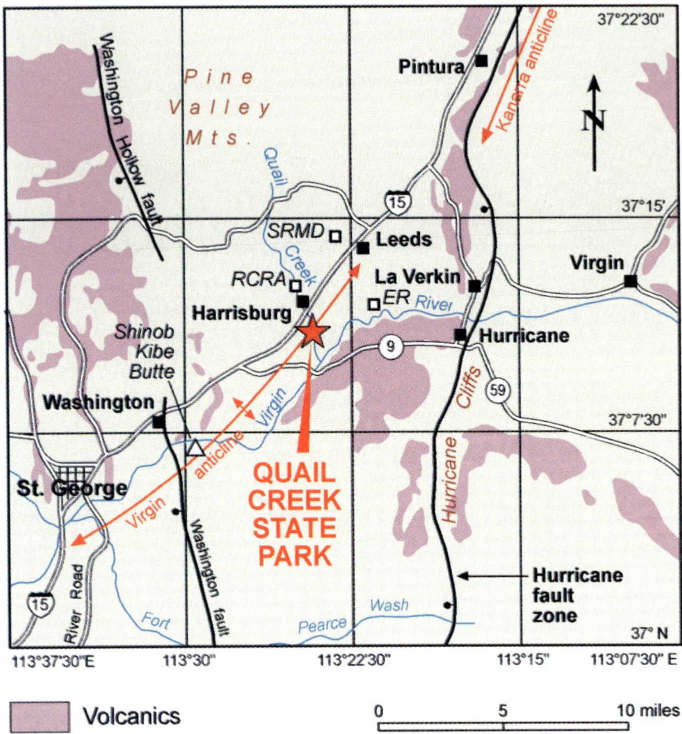

Figure 2. *Location of Quail Creek State Park (QCSP). Red Cliffs Recreation Area (RCRA), Silver Reef Mining District (SRMD), and East Reef (ER) are also shown.*

Figure 3. *The old Harrisburg town site, an early Mormon settlement established in 1861, immediately west of Quail Creek State Park. The Pine Valley Mountains, an early Miocene laccolith, are in the distance.*

enormous geological and human interest (figure 2). Long before Mormon pioneers settled this region, an Anasazi farming community occupied the area intermittently from about A.D. 600 to A.D. 1050 (Eardley and Schaack, 1991). The remains of stone- and clay-lined rooms used for storage of corn and other crops can be seen at the Red Cliffs Recreation Area, just west of Quail Creek State Park. After the Anasazi, Southern Paiute Indians lived in this area for hundreds of years before the first European explorers arrived in the 1700s. The junction of Quail Creek and the Virgin River was an important crossroads for these Native Americans. In 1859, Mormon pioneers spent their first winter in this immediate area at a site called Harrisville, near the confluence of Quail Creek and the Virgin River. In 1861, they moved about 2 miles (3 km) upstream on Quail Creek and established Harrisburg, where remains of early dwellings can still be seen (figure 3). Due to insufficient water and arable land, most Harrisburg settlers moved about 3 miles (5 km) north to establish Leeds in 1867.

In 1866, while traveling through the Harrisburg area, an itinerant prospector discovered high-grade silver ore in sandstone (Proctor and Shirts, 1991). The mineral occurrence - ore-grade silver chloride (cerargyrite or horn silver) in sandstone, unaccompanied by obvious alteration or substantial base-metal ores - was so unusual that he doubted his own findings and moved on to the silver boom town of White Pine, Nevada. Still, the Harrisburg

area attracted him, and he returned and eventually established the first claim in 1871 in what was to become the Silver Reef mining district. The Silver Reef mining district consists of four "reefs" located along the northeast-plunging nose of the Virgin anticline, immediately north of Quail Creek State Park: White, Buckeye, and Butte Reefs are located on the anticline's northwestern flank, while East Reef is located on the anticline's northeastern flank (Proctor, 1953; Proctor and Brimhall, 1986; Biek, 1997, 1998). The ore horizons are contained within the Springdale Sandstone Member of the Jurassic Moenave Formation, which is repeated by thrust faults on the anticline's northwest flank to form the three "reefs." In *Silver, Sinners, and Saints: A History of Old Silver Reef, Utah*, published in 1991, Paul Proctor and Morris Shirts provide a fascinating account of the discovery, disbelief, re-discovery, and development of this unusual mineral occurrence. The mining district, located immediately northwest and east of Quail Creek State Park, produced about 8 million ounces (226,800,000 gm) of silver prior to 1910, and sporadically produced silver, copper, gold, and uranium through the 1960s.

Although Quail Creek State Park is located in the middle of a truly exceptional geologic setting - the view east from the park boundary is but one example (figure 4) - the park may be best known for its fishing and boating. Trout, bass, crappie, bullhead catfish, and bluegill attract anglers from throughout the west, and its warm waters make for a swimmer's paradise. Quail Creek Reservoir is operated as on off-line reservoir by the Washington County Water Conservancy District for storage of Virgin River water. At its maximum pool elevation of 2,985 feet (910 m), the lake covers 640 acres (one square mile, 256 hectares) and stores 40,325 acre-feet (49,746,000 m3) of water. Most of the water is diverted from the Virgin River east of Hurricane and is piped to the reservoir in order to avoid the salty water discharge at Pah Tempe Hot Springs between Hur-

Figure 4. The view east up the Virgin River, across the east limb of the Virgin anticline, to Hurricane-area cinder cones, with Hurricane Mesa and Zion National Park in the distance. The photo was taken from the eastern Quail Creek State Park boundary in the NW1/4 section 25, T. 41 S., R. 14 W.

ricane and LaVerkin. The annual yield of the reservoir is about 20,000 acre-feet (26,136,000 m^3), an important part of the St. George basin water supply (Horrocks-Carollo Engineers, 1993).

STRATIGRAPHY

Only four members of two Triassic bedrock formations - the Shnabkaib Member and upper red member of the Moenkopi Formation, and the Shinarump and Petrified Forest Members of the Chinle Formation - crop out in Quail Creek State Park, but Permian-age strata are exposed to the south along the axis of the anticline, and progressively younger strata are exposed on the flanks of the anticline (figures 5 and 6). These enclosing formations are described in Biek and others (this volume).

Moenkopi Formation

The Moenkopi Formation (late Early Triassic) in southwestern Utah consists of three transgressive members (the Timpoweap, Virgin Limestone, and Shnabkaib Members) each overlain by a regressive, informally named red-bed member (the lower, middle, and upper red members, respectively); the Rock Canyon Conglomerate Member, whose channel-form conglomerates and regolithic breccias record erosion associated with the Permian-Triassic unconformity, locally forms the base of the Moenkopi Formation (Reeside and Bassler, 1921; Stewart and others, 1972; Nielson, 1991; and Dubiel, 1994). The Moenkopi Formation records a complicated series of ma-

Figure 5.

Rocks present in Quail Creek State Park and surrounding area. Only those intervals highlighted in color are present in the park; enclosing rock units are found in nearby areas.

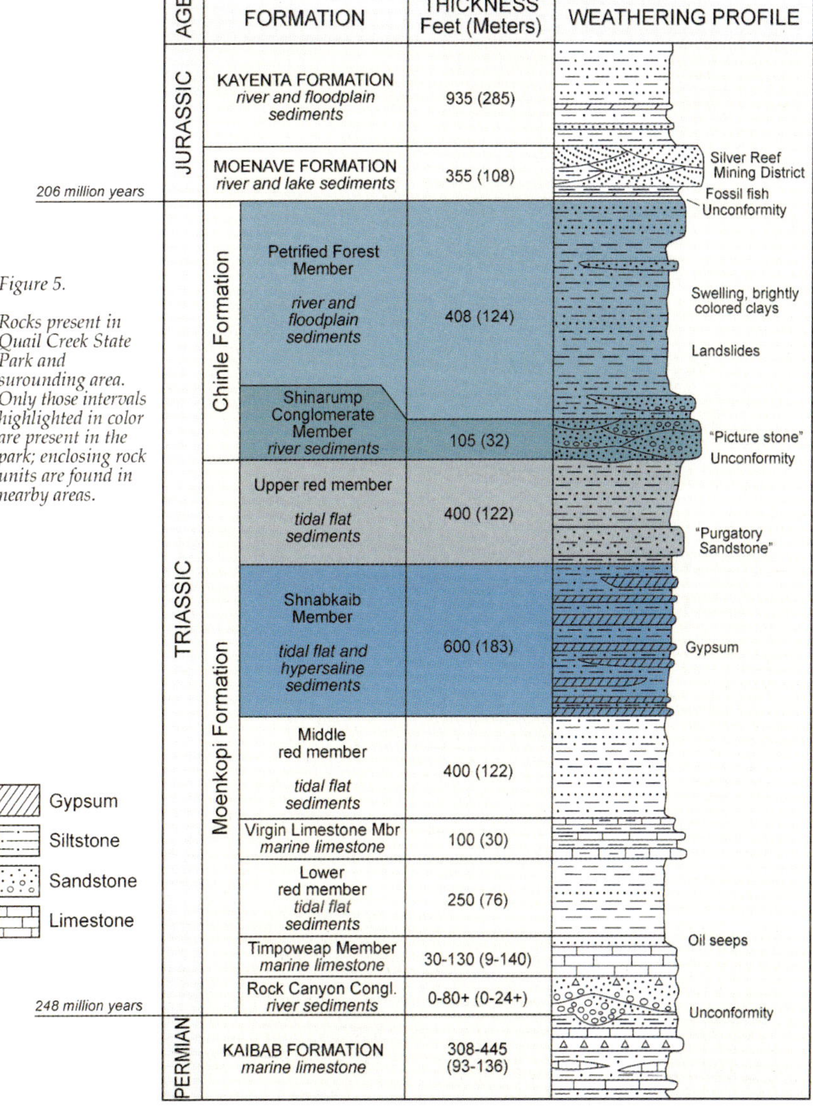

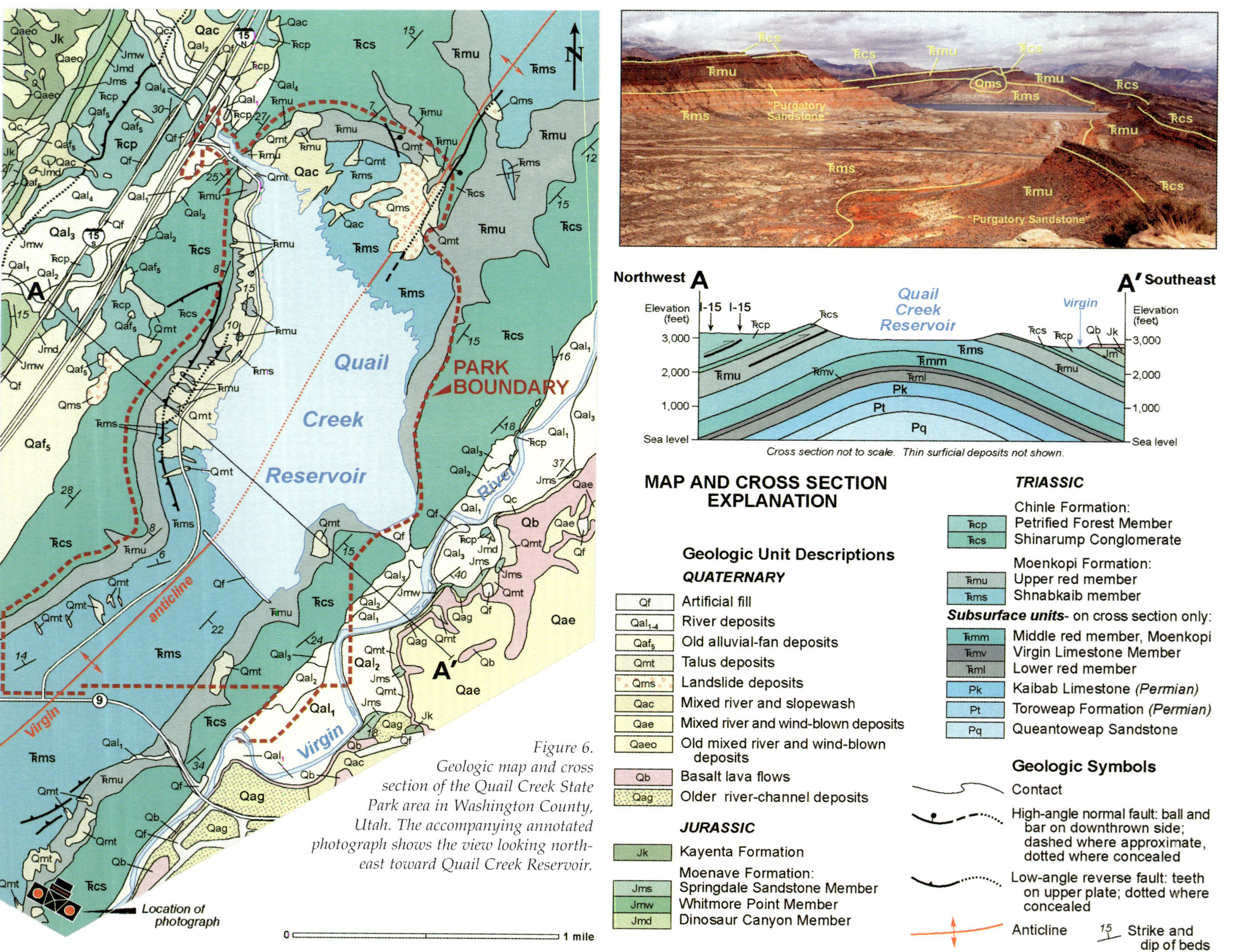

Figure 6. *Geologic map and cross section of the Quail Creek State Park area in Washington County, Utah. The accompanying annotated photograph shows the view looking northeast toward Quail Creek Reservoir.*

rine transgressions and regressions across a very gently sloping continental shelf, where sea level changes of a few feet translated into shoreline changes of many miles (Dubiel, 1994). The transgressive members generally thicken, and the red-bed members thin, from east to west across southwestern Utah. As a whole, the Moenkopi Formation thickens westward from about 1,500 feet (457 m) thick at Hurricane Mesa, northeast of Hurricane, to about 2,150 feet (655 m) thick in the St. George area (Higgins and Willis, 1995; Biek, 1998).

Shnabkaib Member: The Shnabkaib Member is well exposed in the core of the Virgin anticline where it forms a striking red- and white-banded sequence of interbedded, pale-red to moderate-reddish-brown, slope-forming mudstone and siltstone, and white to greenish-gray, ledge- or ridge-forming gypsum (figure 7). Where protected by resistant Shinarump strata, the Shnabkaib Member forms steep, ledgy slopes; elsewhere, and more commonly, it weathers to low, rounded, strike ridges that are upheld by relatively resistant gypsum beds. The type section of the Shnabkaib Member is a few miles to the southwest at Shinob Kibe butte. It was originally named the Shnabkaib shale member by Reeside and Bassler (1921), who stated that the name *Shnabkaib* is probably a corruption of an old Indian name meaning *Coyote Mountain*. Gregory (1950), however, indicated that the name *Shnabkaib* may be a misspelling of the Piute *Shinob* (Great Spirit) and Kaib (mountain), loosely translated as *Mountain of the Lord*.

The mudstones and siltstones of the Shnabkaib Member are commonly gypsiferous in laminated to thin beds, rarely with ripple cross-stratification. Gypsum is present in laterally continuous, massive beds; finely laminated, commonly silty or muddy beds; nodular horizons; and as secondary cavity fillings and cross-cutting veins. The gypsum beds vary from less than one inch (< 1 cm) to about 9 feet (3 m) thick, and weather to a soft, powdery soil, commonly covered with delicate microbiotic crust. The Shnabkaib Member also contains thin, laminated, light-gray dolostone beds that, being more resistant than enclosing rocks, weather out, causing dolostone debris to accumulate at the surface.

The upper contact of the Shnabkaib Member is gradational and corresponds to the top of the highest, thick gypsum bed, above which are found laminated to thin-bedded, moderate-reddish-brown mudstone and siltstone beds of the upper red member. The contact is marked by a prominent color change from generally lighter colored Shnabkaib strata below, which are dominated by white, greenish-gray, and pale-red hues, to darker colored, moderate reddish brown upper red beds above. The Shnabkaib Member is about 600 feet (183 m) thick at Quail Creek State Park (Biek, 1997).

Upper red member: The upper red member is well exposed below cliffs of Shinarump Conglomerate in the core of the Virgin anticline. The upper red member consists of a generally upward-coarsening sequence of interbedded,

Figure 7. View north of brightly colored hillside of Shnabkaib, upper red, and Shinarump strata just north of Highway 9, immediately south of Quail Creek State Park. These are the bedrock units seen surrounding Quail Creek Reservoir. Note the "bacon-striped" appearance of the Shnabkaib Member; the yellowish-brown sandstone, locally known as the "Purgatory Sandstone," near the base of the upper red member; and the cliff-forming Shinarump Conglomerate. Note also the veneer of talus that locally conceals bedrock.

mostly thin- to medium-bedded, uniformly colored, moderate-reddish-orange to moderate-reddish-brown siltstone, mudstone, and very fine- to fine-grained sandstone. A massive yellowish sandstone, described below, is present near the base of the member (figure 7). Planar, low-angle, and ripple cross-stratification, and well-preserved ripple marks, are common. With the exception of the yellowish sandstone, the lower part of the member generally forms ledgy slopes. The upper part of the member forms ledges and low cliffs.

A prominent, normally cliff-forming, pale-yellowish-orange to grayish-orange, fine-grained sandstone with Liesegang banding is found about 50 feet (15 m) above the base of the member along the central portion of the Virgin anticline; this yellowish sandstone is informally known as the "Purgatory Sandstone." It is medium to very thick bedded with both planar and low-angle cross-stratification, and includes minor, similarly colored, thin- to medium-bedded siltstone and very fine-grained sandstone interbeds. The "Purgatory Sandstone" is 108 feet (33 m) thick southeast of Quail Creek Reservoir, in the NE1/4 section 35, T. 41 S., R. 14 W., and the entire upper red member is about 400 feet (122 m) thick at Quail Creek State Park (Biek, 1997).

Chinle Formation

The Chinle Formation of southwestern Utah consists of the Shinarump Conglomerate and Petrified Forest Members. The Shinarump Conglomerate forms a prominent carapace along the central portion of the Virgin anticline, whereas the overlying Petrified Forest Member is both poorly and exceptionally well exposed in adjacent strike valleys. The Chinle Formation is Late Triassic in

Figure 8. View west of a small channel (in Highway 9 road cut just above the car) at the contact of the upper red member of the Moenkopi Formation and the overlying Shinarump Conglomerate Member of the Chinle Formation.

Figure 9. View north of the east flank of the Virgin anticline, with Quail Creek State Park at the left side of the photo. Note how the resistant Shinarump Conglomerate forms a protective carapace over the more easily eroded Moenkopi Formation. From this angle, the anticline looks like a great whale protruding from the Virgin River lowlands.

age, based principally on vertebrate and plant remains, and was deposited in a variety of fluvial and lacustrine environments (Stewart and others, 1972; Dubiel, 1994). Dubiel (1994) assigned Chinle strata to the early Carnian to late Norian (Late Triassic) with an unconformity of several million years separating the two members. In southwestern Utah, the TR-3 regional unconformity (Pipiringos and O'Sullivan, 1978) - the third major unconformity of the Triassic Period in southwestern Utah - separates Early Triassic (Moenkopi Formation) and Late Triassic (Chinle Formation) rocks and marks a change from mostly shallow-marine to continental sedimentation. In the Quail Creek State Park area, the TR-3 unconformity is a disconformity with minor channeling at the base of the Shinarump Conglomerate Member; a small channel is exposed in the Highway 9 road cut just south of the park (figure 8).

Shinarump Conglomerate Member: Because of its resistance to erosion, the Shinarump Conglomerate Member forms a prominent carapace along the central portion of the Virgin anticline (figure 9). It is well exposed in cliffs along the interior of the anticline surrounding Quail Creek State Park. The Shinarump Conglomerate is a laterally and vertically variable sequence of cliff-forming, fine- to very coarse-grained sandstone, pebbly sandstone, and minor pebbly conglomerate It is commonly thick to very thick bedded with both planar and low-angle cross-stratification, although thin, platy beds with ripple cross-stratification are locally present. The sandstone beds are predominantly pale- to dark-yellowish orange, but pale-red, grayish-red, very pale-orange, and pale-yellowish-brown hues are common. Small, subrounded pebbles are primarily quartz, quartzite, and chert.

Along the Virgin anticline, joints in the Shinarump Conglomerate trend subparallel to the strike and dip of bedding. Well-developed slickensides, with a wide variety of orientations, are common throughout the Shinarump Conglomerate Member and suggest minor move-

ment along and between bedding planes. Shinarump strata are also nearly everywhere heavily stained by iron-manganese oxides, commonly in the form of Liesegang banding. This banding invariably follows joints, so that large blocks become concentrically zoned in a variety of interesting patterns. Where these color bands are in fine- to medium-grained sandstones, they are much sought after as "picture stone" or "landscape stone" (figure 10). Coarser sandstones and pebbly sandstones locally contain poorly preserved petrified wood, commonly replaced in part by iron-manganese oxides; small logs several feet in length are common though not abundant. Plant fragments, re-

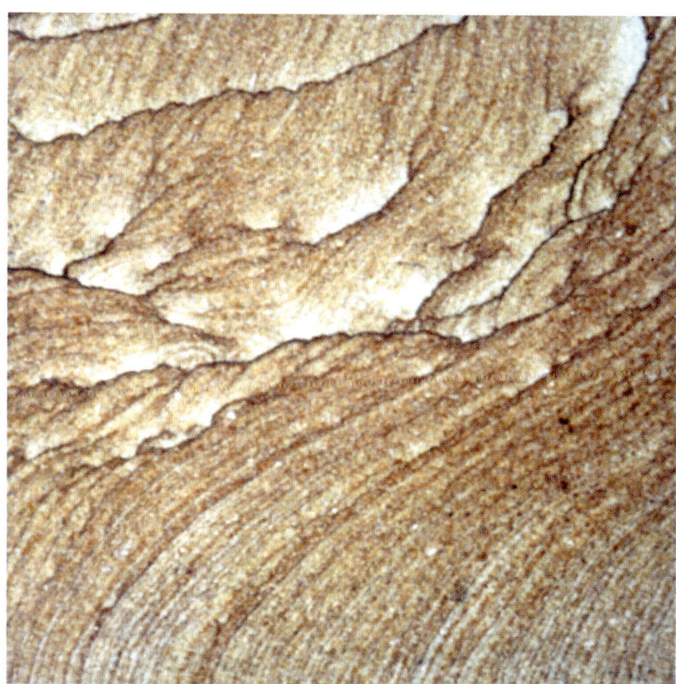

Figure 10. Picture stone from the Shinarump Conglomerate Member of the Chinle Formation, the same unit that forms the high cliffs around Quail Creek Reservoir. The banding is due to naturally occurring iron-manganese oxides. This coaster is about 4 inches (10 cm) square.

placed by iron-manganese oxides, are also common.

The Shinarump Conglomerate varies from about 5 to 200 feet (1.5-61 m) thick in the St. George basin, and it is about 105 feet (32 m) thick at Quail Creek State Park. Such wide variations in thickness are likely due to deposition over paleotopography on the underlying TR-3 unconformity, deposition in braided-stream channels, and difficulty in placing the locally gradational upper contact.

In a gross sense, the contact between the Shinarump Conglomerate and Petrified Forest Members corresponds to a prominent lithologic and color change, from yellowish-brown sandstone and pebbly sandstone of the Shinarump Conglomerate below to the bright, varicolored swelling claystones of the Petrified Forest Member above. However, Shinarump-like sandstone beds in the lower Petrified Forest Member suggest that the contact is gradational and intertonguing (Biek, 1997).

Petrified Forest Member: Only a small part of the lower Petrified Forest Member crops out at Quail Creek State Park, and there only in the northwest corner of the park, west of where Quail Creek passes through the water gap formed by the resistant, west-dipping Shinarump Conglomerate. However, some of the best and most complete exposures of Petrified Forest strata in southwestern Utah are found at East Reef, immediately northeast of the park on the northeast flank of the Virgin anticline (Stewart and others, 1972; Biek, 1998).

The Petrified Forest Member consists of varicolored mudstone, claystone, siltstone, lesser sandstone and pebbly sandstone, and minor chert and nodular limestone - a wider lithologic variation than might be expected given the prominent varicolored swelling mudstones that typify the member. Mudstones and claystones of the Petrified Forest Member are typically various shades of purple, although grayish-red, dark-reddish-brown, light-greenish-gray, brownish-gray, olive-gray, and similar hues are common. Bentonitic clays that swell conspicuously when wet are common and give weathered surfaces a "popcorn" appearance. These swelling clays are responsible for numerous foundation problems and landslides in the greater St. George area.

The upper contact of the Petrified Forest Member, known as the J-0 unconformity, represents a gap of about 10 million years during the Late Triassic and Early Jurassic (Pipiringos and O'Sullivan, 1978), but it is not exposed at Quail Creek State Park. Stewart and others (1972) measured 408 feet (124 m) of Petrified Forest strata at East Reef.

Quaternary Deposits

Quaternary deposits within Quail Creek State Park include alluvial, mixed alluvial and colluvial, mass-movement, and artificial deposits. The northwest corner of the park includes a small part of the Cottonwood Creek and Quail Creek drainages, where alluvial and terrace gravels are incised into older alluvial-fan deposits shed off the Pine Valley Mountains. The terrace deposits consist of

Figure 11. Granite-like boulders of quartz monzonite porphyry at the north end of Quail Creek Reservoir. These boulders were eroded from the Pine Valley Mountains and transported nearly 10 miles (16 km) by ancient floods and debris flows to their present location. Limestone clasts with distinctive star-shaped fossils are also common in these deposits at the north end of the reservoir. The fossils are a type of crinoid, or sea lily, known as Pentacrinus and come from Jurassic rocks that crop out on the flanks of the Pine Valley Mountains.

moderately to well-sorted sand, silt, clay, and pebble to boulder gravel that form isolated, level to gently sloping surfaces above modern drainages. Most clasts in these terrace deposits are reworked from the older alluvial-fan deposits, and include clasts from the Miocene Pine Valley intrusive complex, the Middle Jurassic Carmel Formation, and the Late Cretaceous Iron Springs Formation. The terrace deposits exposed within the park are probably late Pleistocene in age and correspond to deposits near the Virgin River that are 30 to 90 feet (9- 27 m) above modern base level (Biek, 1997).

Mixed alluvial and colluvial deposits at the north end of the reservoir are characterized by large igneous boulders derived from the Pine Valley intrusive complex (figure 11). The boulders form a protective lag along the reservoir's northwest shoreline, where the fine-grained sediments have been winnowed away by wave action. These deposits also contain Carmel and Iron Springs clasts and are doubtless reworked from older alluvial-fan and terrace deposits present west of the park.

The western shore and nearby slopes of Quail Creek Reservoir are mantled by talus. The talus consists of poorly to moderately sorted, angular, clay- to boulder-size, locally derived sediment deposited principally by rock fall. Large blocks of Shinarump and upper red strata characterize talus in this area. The talus grades downslope into colluvium.

A large, deeply dissected landslide at the north end of Quail Creek Reservoir involves Shnabkaib and upper red strata, and is partly covered by large blocks derived from the Shinarump Conglomerate (figure 12). The landslide is deeply eroded and thus of probable late Pleistocene age,

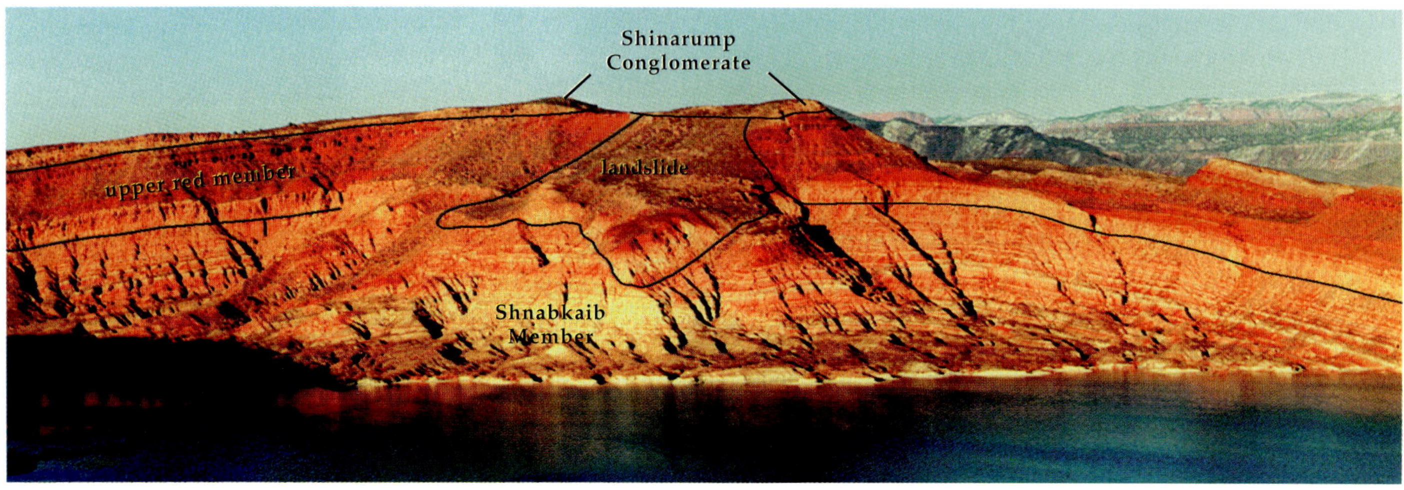

Figure 12. Old, deeply eroded landslide just north of Quail Creek Reservoir. The base of the landslide is in Shnabkaib strata, which are comparatively weak and unstable. Undisturbed Shnabkaib and upper red members of the Moenkopi Formation, and the Shinarump Conglomerate Member of the Chinle Formation, are also visible.

and is characterized by chaotically oriented blocks above the basal slip surface, which is in comparatively weak and unstable, gypsiferous Shnabkaib strata.

STRUCTURE

Regional Setting

The St. George basin, including Quail Creek State Park, lies in the transition zone between the Colorado Plateau and Basin and Range physiographic provinces. Strata in the basin are characteristic of the generally flat-lying rocks of the Colorado Plateau physiographic province, but they were folded into the Virgin anticline and subsidiary folds during the Sevier orogeny, cut by three principal late Tertiary-Quaternary fault zones, and partially covered by Quaternary basaltic flows and cinder cones. In southwestern Utah, the transition zone includes several major down-to-the-west normal fault zones that step down from the Colorado Plateau to the Basin and

Range. Quail Creek State Park is on an intermediate structural block bounded on the west by the Gunlock-Grand Wash faults and on the east by the Hurricane fault zone (figure 13). As discussed by Schramm (1994), the Gunlock-Grand Wash and Hurricane faults probably form a displacement transfer zone, in which decreasing slip on one fault is compensated for by increasing slip on another. Such a transfer zone accounts for the relatively wide span of the transition zone in southwestern Utah.

Virgin Anticline

The Colorado Plateau-Basin and Range transition zone also roughly coincides with the leading edge of the Sevier orogenic belt, and it is this middle Cretaceous to early Tertiary compressional event that gives the basin its most prominent structural feature - the Virgin anticline (figure 14). The Virgin anticline is a 30-mile (48-km) long, northeast-trending, generally symmetrical fold that is co-linear with the Kanarra anticline to the north. At Quail Creek State Park, as along most of the fold's length, the Virgin anticline has flank dips of 25 to 35 degrees. About 2 miles (3 km) northeast of the park, the nose of the anticline plunges about 10 to 15 degrees to the northeast. The anticline has three similar structural domes along its length. From south to north these are Bloomington dome, Washington Dome, and Harrisburg Dome, each of which is cored by the Harrisburg Member of the Kaibab Formation (late Early Permian). A number of comparatively shallow, west-dipping thrust faults repeat Triassic and Jurassic strata on the northwest flank of the anticline, near Leeds (Proctor, 1953; Proctor and Brimhall, 1986; Biek, 1997, 1998). The nose of the anticline is complicated by numerous normal faults and subsidiary folds, which doubtless formed during the Sevier orogeny to accommodate tight folding on the nose of the Virgin anticline (Biek, 1998). A basal detachment is postulated in underlying Cambrian and Precambrian strata (Davis, 1999).

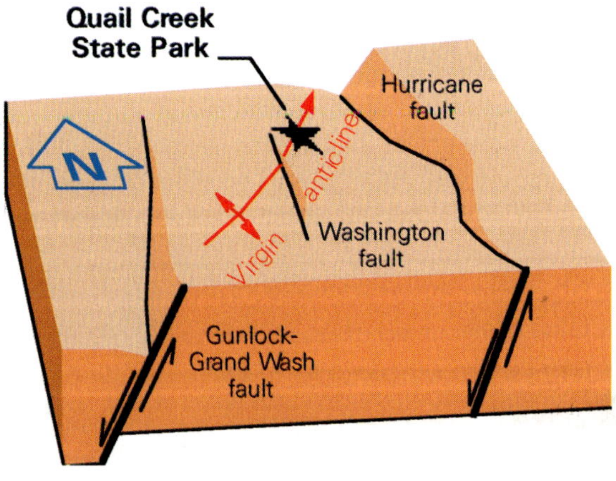

Figure 13. Schematic block diagram showing the relationship between the Gunlock-Grand Wash and Hurricane faults.

Figure 14. Aerial view of the Virgin anticline, looking northeast to Quail Creek Reservoir. The Virgin River bisects the anticline, with Washington Dome on the south and Harrisburg Dome on the north. Photo by Janice Higgins, Utah Geological Survey.

Faults

Quail Creek State Park lies in the middle of a large structural block (figure 13), so it is not surprising that few large faults are found in this area. However, both normal faults and thrust faults of small displacement are present at Quail Creek State Park (Biek, 1997). Two small, west-dipping thrust faults associated with formation of the Virgin anticline displace Shnabkaib, upper red, and Shinarump strata along the west side of Quail Creek Reservoir. These thrust faults are best observed where they duplicate the yellowish-brown "Purgatory Sandstone" at the base of the upper red member of the Moenkopi Formation (figure 15). Kink folds and a small back thrust associated with these thrust faults are exposed in Shnabkaib strata in a small, steep wash in the SW1/4 section 26, T. 41 S., R 14 W., about 400 feet (121 m) north of the south section line and

about 2,200 feet (670 m) east of the west section line. A small down-to-the-east normal fault at the north end of Quail Creek Reservoir, at the crest and parallel to the axis of the Virgin anticline, likely formed to accommodate local tensional forces during folding of the Virgin anticline.

GEOLOGIC HISTORY

With only parts of two Triassic bedrock formations exposed in Quail Creek State Park, the geologic history revealed by these strata is just a glimpse into the larger history of the rocks of southwestern Utah. Additional portions of this fascinating geologic history are described in papers on Snow Canyon State Park (Higgins, this volume) and Zion National Park (Biek and others, this volume).

Perhaps the best way to visualize the geologic history recorded in the rocks of Quail Creek State Park is to expand our view to one of global proportions. During the Triassic, the area we now call Utah lay near the equator, straddling the western shore of the supercontinent Pangea. The Sonoma orogeny affected the western margin of Pangea during this time, creating a back-bulge basin in what is now southwestern Utah (Lawton, 1994). A back-bulge basin is a broad, shallow basin formed in response to loading of the Earth's crust and is the distal part of a typical thrust system (see, for example, Willis, 1999). The Moenkopi Formation was deposited in this back-bulge basin setting in a variety of shallow-marine and coastal-plain environments (Morales, 1987; Blakey, 1989; Dubiel, 1994).

In southwestern Utah, the interbedded evaporites and red beds of the Shnabkaib Member of the Moenkopi Formation were deposited in a variety of supratidal, intertidal, and subtidal environments on a broad, coastal shelf of very low relief (Lambert, 1984). The intricate interbedding of evaporites and red beds suggests complex water

Figure 15. View north of a small, west-dipping thrust fault that places the "Purgatory Sandstone" on top of itself. The inset shows a small kink fold associated with this west-dipping thrust fault.

Figure 16. *Aerial view to the north of the Virgin anticline and Quail Creek Reservoir. The snow-covered Pine Valley Mountains are to the west and the Kolob Canyons section of Zion National Park is to the east. Photo by Janice Higgins, Utah Geological Survey.*

Figure 17. *Quail Creek south dike, shortly after its catastrophic failure on January 1, 1989. Note how floodwaters scoured the bedrock clean of loose, overlying sediments just below the dike. Photo courtesy of Ben Everitt, Utah Division of Water Resources.*

table fluctuations, probably associated with minor sea level fluctuations (Dubiel, 1994). Stewart and others (1972) noted that the amount of gypsum and carbonate in the Shnabkaib Member decreases to the north and east away from the Quail Creek State Park area, and that red beds increase. These facies changes reflect deposition on a gentle, westward-sloping basin margin. Red beds of the upper red member were probably deposited in arid tidal-flat and coastal-plain environments.

In southwestern Utah, the TR-3 regional unconformity, which separates Early Triassic Moenkopi Formation and Late Triassic Chinle Formation rocks, marks a change from mostly shallow-marine to continental sedimentation. Rocks of Middle Triassic age are largely lacking in Utah, but extensive Middle Triassic marine strata are exposed farther west in Nevada (Dubiel, 1994). Chinle strata were also deposited in a back-bulge basin setting (Lawton, 1994). Shinarump strata were deposited principally in braided-stream channels that flowed generally to the north and northwest; Petrified Forest fluvial systems mimicked this paleoflow, but with a much greater abundance of high-sinuosity stream deposits and floodplain mudstones (Dubiel, 1994). Dubiel (1994) also noted that parts of the Petrified Forest Member were deposited in lacustrine environments, and that mottled, variegated mudstones with calcareous nodules probably represent paleosols. Abundant bentonitic mudstones in the Petrified Forest Member are probably reworked volcanic ash from a magmatic arc along the continental margin to the west (Dubiel, 1994). Petrified wood is common in channel deposits of the Chinle Formation, where it is found in a horizontal position, the result of driftwood being swept downstream during floods.

These Triassic and enclosing units were folded into the Virgin anticline during the Sevier orogeny, but the timing of deformation is poorly constrained, in part due to a lack of proximal synorogenic deposits. The folding probably occurred in the Late Cretaceous or early Tertiary, during the latter part of the orogeny (Willis, 1999).

CLASSIC GEOLOGIC FEATURES

Virgin Anticline

Quail Creek State Park owes its existence to the Virgin anticline, which, with two small dams, forms a natural catchment for off-line storage of Virgin River water (figure 16). The 30-mile (48-km) long, northeast-trending Virgin anticline is a generally symmetrical fold with flank dips of 25 to 35 degrees. Small thrust and normal faults associated with formation of the anticline are present in the park. Because the anticline is so clearly expressed, and only sparsely covered by vegetation and Quaternary deposits, it is a mecca for geology field camp teachers and students.

Catastrophic Failure of the Quail Creek South Dike

At 12:30 a.m. on January 1, 1989, the Quail Creek south dike failed catastrophically, unleashing a torrent of water and causing millions of dollars of damage. Fortunately, the downstream area was evacuated in time to avoid fatalities. Approximately 25,000 acre-feet (30,492,000 m^3) of water - more than half the reservoir's capacity - flowed through a breach in the dike over a 12-hour period (figure 17).

The original Quail Creek south dike was a 78-foot (24-m) high, 2,000-foot (610-m) long earthen dam constructed in 1984. The dam was poorly designed and seepage under the dam occurred immediately after filling the reservoir. Seepage and sinkhole development increased in succeeding years despite efforts to seal the leaks (O'Neill and Gourley, 1991; Gourley, 1992). Seepage water probably passed under the dike, or at the dike-foundation contact, and began to erode the dike materials and in-situ soils. Ultimately, seepage and erosion of the dike and foundation materials continued and accelerated until caving occurred on a developing opening in the dike. Frantic last-minute efforts to stem the seepage were unsuccessful and the dike finally breached. Evidence of the flood caused by the catastrophic failure of the Quail Creek south dike is still visible downstream from the new dam, where the Shanbkaib Member was scoured clean of overlying loose bedrock and sediment.

The dike's failure was principally due to poor foundation design and construction coupled with inadequate oversight by engineering geologists (O'Neill and Gourley, 1991; Gourley, 1992). Factors that contributed to the failure of the dike included the assumption of a low-permeability foundation, inadequate preparation of the foundation, and placement of unprotected, erodible embankment material on the dam's foundation. The dike was built mostly on the Shnabkaib Member of the Moenkopi Formation, except for the southeast abutment which lies on the "Purgatory Sandstone" of the upper red member. Both of these units contain abundant joints, and the Shnabkaib Member contains abundant gypsum, which readily dissolves in water. Joints allowed water to infiltrate rapidly, creating dissolution channels up to 70 feet (21 m) deep below the dike.

The new dike, called the Quail Creek south dam, was completed in 1990 as a roller-compacted concrete gravity dam (Payton, 1992). The dimensions of the dam are basically the same as the old dike, except that it now includes a new impermeable cutoff trench up to 75 feet (23 m) deep, which is designed to prevent water from seeping under the dam (figure 18).

Gypsum

Gypsum is a common evaporite mineral and a major component of the Shnabkaib Member of the Moenkopi Formation. Gypsum is soft and can be easily scratched with one's fingernail, and it is easily cleaved or parted in one direction. At Quail Creek State Park, gypsum is found in a variety of forms: as thick, white, massive beds; laminated, commonly silty or muddy beds; nodular horizons; and as large, transparent crystals called selenite and satin spar that form in small vugs and cross-cutting veins. Gypsum weathers to a soft, powdery soil, commonly covered by a delicate microbiotic crust. It is an important industrial mineral and is used to make plaster and gypsum board, as a filler in the paper and textile industries, to loosen clay-rich soils, and in the production of sulfuric acid. Dissolution of gypsum may lead to local foundation problems, and it was an important factor in the failure of the Quail Creek south dike (Gourley, 1992). Gypsum is also a structurally weak material that has a low bearing strength, unsuitable for typical foundations (Mulvey, 1992). Sulfuric acid and sulfate derived from gypsum dissolution can react with certain types of cement, weakening foundations.

Figure 18. Cutoff trench being excavated at the bottom of the new Quail Creek south dam in January 1990. Photo by Bill Lund, Utah Geological Survey.

"Picture Stone"

The "picture stone" of southwestern Utah is sandstone naturally stained by iron-manganese oxides. The staining can produce intricate patterns of twisted, swirling light and dark bands and even images reminiscent of landscapes, thus giving rise to its other common name, "landscape stone" (figure 10). The sandstone comes from the Shinarump Conglomerate Member of the Chinle Formation, the same rock unit that forms the high cliffs around Quail Creek State Park. Look closely at the Shinarump Conglomerate and you can see that the banding parallels joints in the rock, so that large blocks become concentrically zoned in a variety of interesting patterns. The staining is caused by mineralized groundwater that moves through the rock, locally precipitating iron-manganese oxides.

ACKNOWLEDGMENTS

Many geologists have helped unravel the geologic story recorded in the rocks of Quail Creek State Park and southwestern Utah, and the story told here would be much abbreviated were it not for their curiosity and scholarship. Several of their reports are listed below, while a more complete list of references accompanies the geologic maps and reports of the Harrisburg Junction and Hurricane quadrangles (Biek, 1997, 1998), which straddle Quail Creek State Park.

Geologic mapping of the Harrisburg Junction and Hurricane 7.5' quadrangles was jointly funded by the Utah Geological Survey (UGS) and the U.S. Geological Survey under cooperative STATEMAP agreements. Grant Willis and Janice Higgins, both with the UGS, and numerous participants who attended the field reviews of this new mapping, offered valuable advice in the field. Grant Willis, Sandy Eldridge, and Mike Hylland of the UGS, and Gary Pascoe, Superintendent of Quail Creek State Park, provided insightful reviews of *The Geology of Quail Creek State Park* (Biek, 1999), the educational booklet from which this paper was in part derived. The UGS graciously allowed me time to put together this report and road log. Thanks also to Bill Lund (UGS) and Ben Everitt (Utah Division of Water Resources) who provided photos of the Quail Creek dike collapse and reconstruction, to Bill Case (UGS) for providing the picture-stone coaster shown in figure 10, and to Janice Higgins for aerial photographs of the Virgin anticline. Jim Parker (UGS) turned my crude drawings into superb illustrations. Grant Willis and Mike Hylland (UGS) reviewed this manuscript.

REFERENCES

Biek, R.F., 1997, Interim geologic map of the Harrisburg Junction quadrangle, Washington County, Utah: Utah Geological Survey Open-File Report 353, 124 p., scale 1:24,000.

—1998, Interim geologic map of the Hurricane quadrangle, Washington County, Utah: Utah Geological Survey Open-File Report 361, 154 p., scale 1:24,000.

—1999, The Geology of Quail Creek State Park: Utah Geological Survey Public Information Series 63, 21 p.

Blakey, R.C., 1989, Triassic and Jurassic geology of the southern Colorado Plateau, *in* Jenny, J.P., and Reynolds, S.J., editors, Geologic evolution of Arizona: Arizona Geological Society Digest 17, p. 369-396.

Davis, G.H., 1999, Structural geology of the Colorado Plateau region of southwestern Utah, with special emphasis on deformation bands: Geological Society of America Special Paper 342, 168 p.

Dubiel, R.F., 1994, Triassic deposystems, paleogeography, and paleoclimate of the Western Interior, *in* Caputo, M.V., Peterson, J.A., and Franczyk, K.J., editors, Mesozoic systems of the Rocky Mountain region, USA: Rocky Mountain Section of Society of Economic Paleontologists and Mineralogists, p. 133-168.

Eardley, A.J., and Schaack, J.W., 1991, Zion - The story behind the scenery: Las Vegas, Nevada, KC Publications, 46 p.

Gourley, Chad, 1992, Geological aspects of the Quail Creek dike failure, *in* Harty, K.M., editor, Engineering and environmental geology of southwestern Utah: Utah Geological Association Publication 21, p. 17-38.

Gregory, H.G., 1950, Geology and geography of the Zion Park region, Utah and Arizona: U.S. Geological Survey Professional Paper 220, 200 p.

Higgins, J.M., and Willis, G.C., 1995, Interim geologic map of the St. George quadrangle, Washington County, Utah: Utah Geological Survey Open-File Report 323, 114 p., scale 1:24,000.

Horrocks-Carollo Engineers, 1993, Culinary water resources study: Unpublished consultant's report for St. George City Water and Power Department, June 1993, 128 p.

Lambert, R.E., 1984, Shnabkaib Member of the Moenkopi Formation -- Depositional environment and stratigraphy near Virgin, Washington County, Utah: Brigham Young University Geology Studies, v. 31, pt. 1, p. 47-65.

Lawton, T.F., 1994, Triassic deposystems, paleogeography, and paleoclimate of the Western Interior, *in* Caputo, M.V., Peterson, J.A., and Franczyk, K.J., editors, Mesozoic systems of the Rocky Mountain region, USA: Rocky Mountain Section of Society of Economic Paleontologists and Mineralogists, p. 1-25.

Morales, Michael, 1987, Terrestrial fauna and flora from the Triassic Moenkopi Formation of the southwestern United States, *in* Morales, Michael, and Elliott, D.K., editors, Triassic continental deposits of the American Southwest: Journal of the Arizona-Nevada Academy of Science, v. 22, p. 1-19.

Mulvey, W.E., 1992, Engineering geologic problems caused by soil and rock in southwestern Utah, *in* Harty, K.M., editor, Engineering and environmental geology of southwestern Utah: Utah Geological Association Publication 21, p. 139-144.

Nielson, R.L., 1991, Petrology, sedimentology and stratigraphic implications of the Rock Canyon Conglomerate, southwestern Utah: Utah Geological Survey Miscellaneous Publication 91-7, 65 p.

O'Neill, A.L., and Gourley, Chad, 1991, Geologic perspectives and cause of the Quail Creek dike failure: Bulletin of the Association of Engineering Geologists, v. 28, no. 2, p. 127-145.

Payton, C.C., 1992, Geotechnical investigation and foundation design for the reconstruction of Quail Creek dike, *in* Harty, K.M., editor, Engineering and environmental geology of southwestern Utah: Utah Geological Association Publication 21, p. 39-51.

Pipiringos, G.N., and O'Sullivan, R.B., 1978, Principal unconformities in Triassic and Jurassic rocks, western Interior United States - a preliminary survey: U.S. Geological Survey Professional Paper 1035-A, 29 p.

Proctor, P.D., 1953, Geology of the Silver Reef (Harrisburg) mining district, Washington County, Utah: Utah Geological and Mineral Survey Bulletin 44, 169 p.

Proctor, P.D., and Brimhall, W.H., 1986, Silver Reef mining district, revisited, Washington County, Utah, *in* Griffen, D.T., and Phillips, W.R., editors, Thrusting and extensional structures and mineralization in the Beaver Dam Mountains, southwestern Utah: Utah Geological Association Publication 15, p. 159-177.

Proctor, P.D., and Shirts, M.A., 1991, Silver, sinners and saints - a history of old Silver Reef, Utah: Provo, Utah, Paulmar, Inc., 224 p.

Reeside, J.B., Jr., and Bassler, Harvey, 1921, Stratigraphic sections in southwestern Utah and northwestern Arizona: U.S. Geological Survey Professional Paper 129-D, p. 53-77.

Schramm, M.E., 1994, Structural analysis of the Hurricane fault in the transition zone between the Basin and Range Province and the Colorado Plateau, Washington County, Utah: Las Vegas, University of Nevada, M.S. thesis, 90 p., scale 1:12,000.

Stewart, J.H., Poole, F.G., and Wilson, R.F., 1972, Stratigraphy and origin of the Triassic Moenkopi Formation and related strata in the Colorado Plateau region, with a section on sedimentary petrology by R.A. Cadigan: U.S. Geological Survey Professional Paper 691, 195 p., scale 1:2,500,000.

Willis, G.C., 1999, The Utah thrust system - an overview, *in* Spangler, L.E., and Allen, C.J., editors, Geology of northern Utah and vicinity: Utah Geological Association Publication 27, p. 1-9.

Snow Canyon State Park
Photo courtesy of Utah Division of Parks and Recreation

Geology of Utah's Parks and Monuments
2000 Utah Geological Association Publication 28
D.A. Sprinkel, T.C. Chidsey, Jr., and P.B. Anderson, editors

Geology of Snow Canyon State Park, Southwestern Utah

Janice M. Higgins[1]

ABSTRACT

Snow Canyon is carved into the Navajo Sandstone with the upper member of the underlying Kayenta Formation exposed at the mouth of the canyon. Weathering accentuates cross-beds in the sandstone that formed during the Jurassic Period as sand dunes of a low-latitude desert migrated in response to a prevailing wind generally from the north. During this time period, this part of North America was only about 15 degrees north of the equator. The color of the Navajo Sandstone changes from red at the mouth of Snow Canyon to white at the head of the canyon; the change is well exposed in the canyon where the colors interfinger. The rock has been fractured by two sets of joints: one set of relatively closely-spaced fractures that trend northeast, and another set of more widely spaced fractures that trend just west of north. Erosion along this second set forms the major canyons in the area.

In the bottom of Snow Canyon, rounded "turtle back" monoliths of sandstone protrude above lobes of lava that flowed around them only 10 to 20 thousand years ago. Originating from vents at the base of two cinder cones next to State Route 18, the Santa Clara flow cascaded into Snow Canyon and filled the V-shaped, stream-cut canyon with basalt. Downcutting along the edge of the flow has begun the topographic inversion process.

Three levels of basaltic lava flows document the eruptive and erosional history of Snow Canyon. The oldest, the Lava Ridge flow, came from cinder cones one mile (1.6 km) east of Snow Canyon State Park and now caps a ridge east of Snow Canyon behind the Winchester Hills subdivision (Willis and Higgins, 1995). A small portion of this 1.41 ± 0.01 million year old (Ma) flow cascaded down a small channel and into an ancestral Snow Canyon near the present location of State Route 18. The Lava Ridge flow effectively displaced the drainage and was buried by the Snow Canyon Overlook flow 1.16 ± 0.03 Ma. The Snow Canyon Overlook flow displaced the drainage to the west, which subsequently created the modern Snow Canyon. The Santa Clara flow partially filled this canyon only 10 to 20 thousand years ago. Downcutting and widening of West Canyon is once again causing the location of Snow Canyon to shift to the west.

INTRODUCTION

Snow Canyon State Park is located in the southwest corner of Utah in Washington County, northwest of St. George (figure 1). The canyon is approximately 5 miles (8 km) long, with elevations in the park ranging from 3,000 feet (915 m) at the mouth of the canyon to 5,024 feet (1,532 m) at the top of a sandstone peak northwest of the canyon. Because of southwest Utah's mild winter climate, the park, including the campground, is open all year. There are more than 20 miles (32 km) of hiking and biking trails, and more than 5 miles (8 km) of equestrian trails.

The park is physiographically located in the transition zone between the Colorado Plateau to the east and the Basin and Range Province to the west, which also roughly coincides with the leading edge of the Sevier orogenic belt. The rocks of Snow Canyon have been uplifted and tilted northeastward as part of the west limb of the poorly defined St. George syncline (Higgins and Willis, 1995). This movement caused the brittle, massively bedded, Jurassic Navajo Sandstone to fracture in two intersecting sets of parallel cracks, called joints. These joint sets, along with the very uniform nature of the cross-bedded Navajo Sandstone, control the weathering pattern of the rock to form the intricate landscape of the canyon (figure 2). The jagged and irregular, dark surface of Quaternary basaltic flows creates a stark contrast with the rounded shapes of the red and white sandstone. Three episodes of volcanic activity document the continued uplift and subsequent downcutting of the area.

[1]*Utah Geological Survey, Salt Lake City, UT 84114-6100*

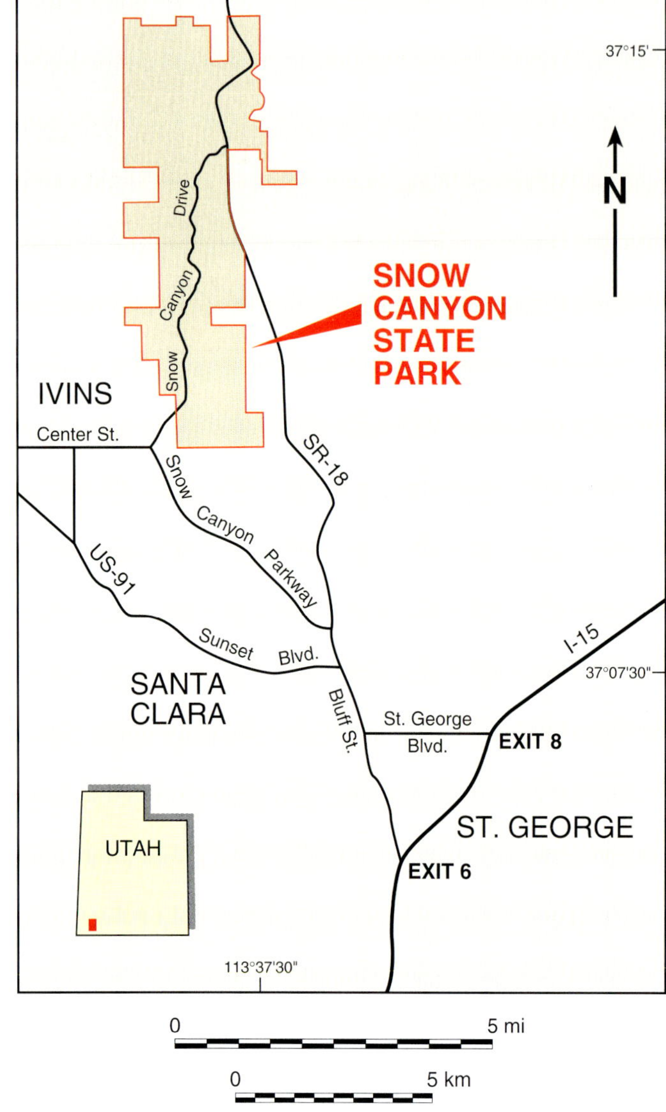

Figure 1. *Location of Snow Canyon State Park.*

Figure 2. *Oblique aerial view looking north from the mouth of Snow Canyon. Padre Canyon, to the west, is along the left edge of the photo. State Route 18 is near the right edge. Weathering pattern is controlled by joints in the Navajo Sandstone.*

STRATIGRAPHY

Sedimentary rocks within Snow Canyon State Park include the upper member of the Kayenta Formation and the overlying Navajo Sandstone, both Early Jurassic in age. These two units comprise nearly all of the rock in the park, but their contact is gradational and difficult to correlate across the region. The Quaternary section of Snow Canyon State Park includes three lava flows—Lava Ridge flow, Snow Canyon Overlook flow, and Santa Clara flow—as well as a variety of unconsolidated deposits (figure 3).

Jurassic

Kayenta Formation

Only the upper member of the Kayenta Formation (Jku) is exposed within the park. It is 800 feet (244 m) thick (Willis and Higgins, 1996). It forms the horizontally bedded, lower slope of the mountains at the mouth of the canyon beneath the massive Navajo Sandstone. The Kayenta Formation is Early Jurassic in age (Imlay, 1980) and was deposited in fluvial, distal fluvial/playa, sabkha and minor lacustrine environments (Sansom, 1992). This formation contains nearly all of the known dinosaur footprints found in the St. George area; however, none are known within Snow Canyon State Park.

The gradational contact between the Kayenta Formation and the Navajo Sandstone has previously been placed at the top of the highest playa sand, thereby including transitional strata in the Kayenta Formation (Bugden, 1992; Hintze and Hammond, 1994). This included a significant section of eolian sand in the Kayenta Formation and placed the contact high on the cliff, since the transition zone in this region is up to several hundred feet thick (Tuesink, 1989; Sansom, 1992). However, placing the contact at the base of the transition beds makes it easier to map and coordinates this area with mapping in the region to the east, including Zion National Park (Doelling and others, Utah Geological Survey, unpublished mapping). Also, this placement of the contact can be easily correlated on well logs and seismic lines. The contact, placed at the top of the highest mudstone interval, corresponds to a slight color change with darker reddish brown, thinner bedded, horizontal strata of the Kayenta Formation below and lighter, moderate-reddish-orange, planar to massively cross-bedded and vertically jointed Navajo Sandstone above (figure 4) (Willis and Higgins, 1996).

Navajo Sandstone

The Navajo Sandstone and correlative sandstones are famous as one of the world's largest coastal and inland paleodune fields, which covered much of what is now Utah and portions of adjacent states in the Early Jurassic (Blakey and others, 1988). Except for the basal transition beds, the 2,500-foot-thick (760 m) Navajo Sandstone consists of massively cross-bedded, fine- to medium-grained, well-rounded and frosted quartz grains that are poorly to moderately

ERA	PERIOD	FORMATION	MAP SYMBOL	THICKNESS feet (meters)	WEATHERING PROFILE	
CENOZOIC	QUATERNARY	Surficial deposits	Q	0-50 (0-15)		Dunes (Qed), eolian sand (Qes), stream and colluvial/eolian deposits (Qac, Qae), talus (Qmt) Est. 10,000-20,000 yr.
		Santa Clara flow/cone	Qbs/Qbsc	0-60 (0-18)		1.16±0.03 Ma
		Snow Canyon overlook flow	Qbso	0-30 (0-9)		1.41±0.01 Ma
		Lava Ridge flow	Qbl	0-40 (0-12)		
MESOZOIC	JURASSIC	Navajo Sandstone	Jn	2,500 (760)		Eolian coastal and inland paleodune field High-angle cross-beds TRANSITION BEDS Wind-blown sand deposited on sabkha surface
		Upper member of the Kayenta Formation	Jku	800 (244)		River and floodplain sediments

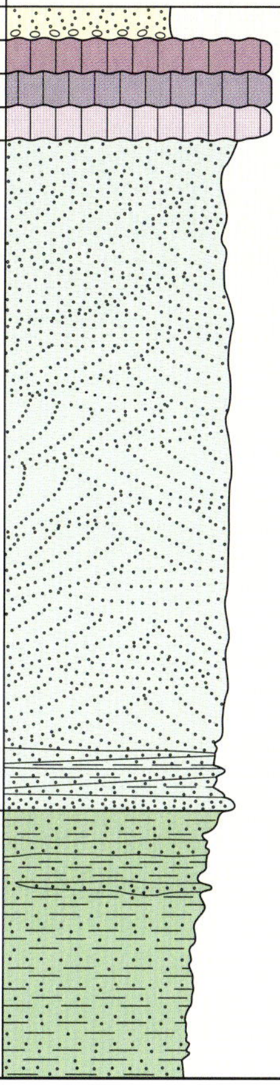

Figure 3. Stratigraphic column of units in Snow Canyon State Park.

well cemented (Willis and Higgins, 1996). This highly jointed sandstone weathers to form the bold, rounded cliffs for which southern Utah is famous. The basal transition beds consist of thick cross-bedded eolian intervals, interbedded with thin, planar-bedded sandstone, muddy sandstone, and minor mudstones with crinkle bedding, tepee structures and mineral casts formed by the growth of minerals such as gypsum and halite. These transition beds represent wind-blown sand deposited on a sabkha surface (Sansom, 1992). The planar bedding formed by eolian sand blowing across the sabkha and adhering to the wet surface.

The Navajo Sandstone is very uniform in composition having greater than 90 percent quartz sand, although geochemical analyses of representative samples indicate great variability in the minerals that cement the sand grains together. Cement of "typical" moderate-reddish-orange sandstone includes 5 percent each of sodium and aluminum and 2 percent iron of the total volume of the rock. By contrast, the "white" Navajo Sandstone has 3 percent aluminum, 1 percent sodium and only 0.5 percent iron (Willis and Higgins, 1996). Also common in the Navajo Sandstone throughout the park are some horizons where secondary enrichment of cementing minerals results in a

Figure 4. Contact between the Jurassic Kayenta Formation (Jk), and the Navajo Sandstone (Jn), at the mouth of Snow Canyon. Note the Santa Clara flow in the foreground. View looking east.

very dark-brownish-black sandstone (ironstone) with total rock volume comprising 20 percent iron, 2 percent aluminum, and manganese concentration as high as 5 percent (Willis and Higgins, 1996). These iron-manganese-rich horizons are more resistant to weathering and erosion and thus commonly cap stacks of rock called "hoodoos." The iron and manganese oxides commonly form concentric

Figure 5. *"Moki marbles," ironstone concretions that develop as iron and manganese oxides form concentric rings around a central point, weather out of the Navajo Sandstone. The concretions average 0.75 inches (2 cm) in diameter.*

Figure 6. *The surface of the Navajo Sandstone is commonly stained by surface runoff and by the formation of desert varnish. Photo looking east at the west cliff face of Island in the Sky.*

Figure 7. *Across the canyon from the Lava Flow Overlook, in the west wall of Snow Canyon, is the interfingering pattern of red and white Navajo Sandstone.*

rings to create ironstone concretions, nicknamed "Moki marbles," that are more resistant to erosion than the surrounding rock (figure 5).

The Navajo Sandstone is the major aquifer in the area (Willis and Higgins, 1996; Hurlow, 1998). St. George City operates several water wells in the northwest part of the park in West Canyon. These wells, drilled to depths of 500 to 850 feet (150-258 m), produce between 200 and 700 gallons per minute (656-2,646 liters/minute) (Horrocks-Carollo Engineers, 1993). Ground water also seeps to the surface, creating springlines along some horizons in the Navajo Sandstone. Water gradually but effectively dissolves the cementing minerals from between the sand grains. The sand grains are then easily removed by water or wind. This sapping process commonly leads to the formation of blind or incipient arches.

The weathered surface of the Navajo Sandstone is commonly discolored (figure 6). Deposits of desert varnish on the cliff face have a slightly different origin than streaks originating from the top of the cliff. Both are deposited as a surface stain as water carrying dissolved minerals evaporates, but desert varnish originates as water percolates through the rock while the streaks from the top of the cliff are created by surface runoff. The minerals dissolved in the water are deposited as a laminated coating or "patina" on the surface of the rock. The formation of desert varnish is aided by an organic process as the wind deposits clay particles and microorganisms (bacteria) on the sandstone. The microorganisms then extract manganese and iron oxides from the rock and clay particles to form a layer of varnish (Warneke, 1993). This process takes a very long time to form a thin layer. Native Americans would peck through this varnish layer to expose the lighter colored sandstone to make petroglyphs. Older petroglyphs are darker in color because the desert varnish has started to reform.

On the west wall in the middle of Snow Canyon, the interfingering pattern of red and white Navajo Sandstone

is truly spectacular (figure 7). South of this point, the sandstone is nearly all red, whereas to the north, it is nearly all white. Unlike the red wall of the Grand Canyon or the Altar of Sacrifice at Zion National Park where the red color of the rock is simply a surface stain, the red cementing minerals of the Navajo Sandstone here color the entire rock. The discoloration or "whitening" of the rock occurs after lithification. The subsequent loss of color is caused by fluid interaction that either dissolves the cementing minerals out from between the sand grains, leaving the sandstone very friable, or reduces the cementing minerals (chiefly iron) through chemical reactions that change the oxidation state. In other areas, such as Zion National Park, the cementing minerals have been dissolved from the upper portion of the Navajo Sandstone, leaving the sandstone quite "white." However, there the color change does not interfinger. Perhaps fluid associated with the intrusion of the Pine Valley laccolith, emplaced 20.9 ± 0.6 million years ago to the northeast (McKee and others, 1995), was at least partially responsible for the interfingering color change of the Navajo Sandstone in this area. The sandstone is white from the interfingering area all the way to

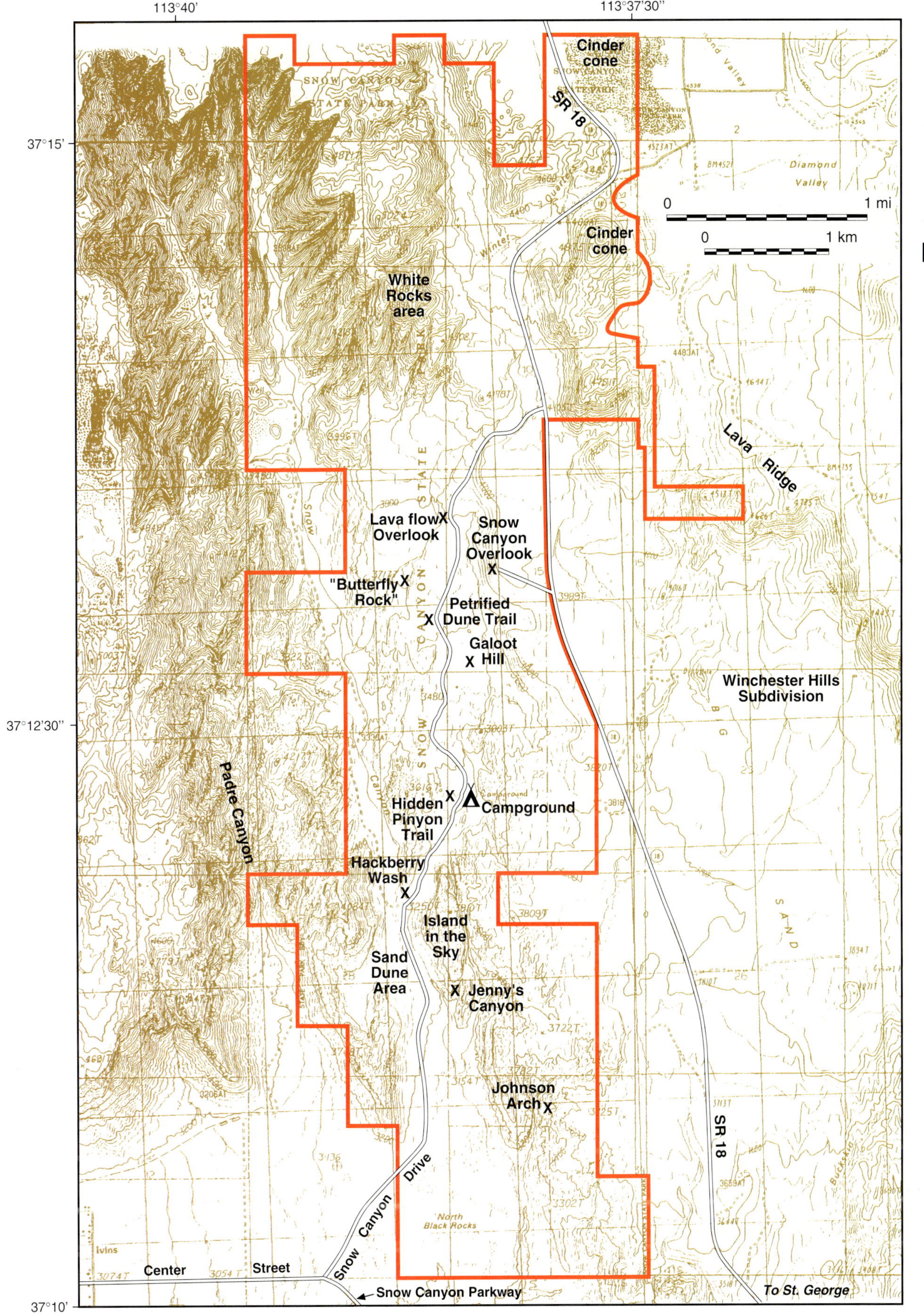

Figure 8. Location map of place names in Snow Canyon State Park.

Figure 9. *Differential weathering accentuates cross-bedding and small vertical cracks in the Navajo Sandstone to give it a "checkerboard" or "elephant skin" look. Photo looking east at the west side of Galoot Hill. Note the Snow Canyon Overlook flow capping the east rim of Snow Canyon in the background.*

the base of the Pine Valley Mountains, formed by the intrusion, including the White Rocks area (figure 8) near the head of Snow Canyon.

The surface of the sandstone is more deeply weathered farther up the canyon than it is near the mouth of the canyon where the walls are nearly vertical. This differential weathering accentuates the cross-bedding (figure 9). Some isolated monoliths of Navajo Sandstone, nicknamed "turtle backs," weather to resemble stacks of pancakes. Each of these cross-beds was once the front or face of a migrating sand dune, before it was buried by the next layer. Small vertical cracks in the rock give it a "checkerboard" or "elephant skin" look. These shallow cracks are not joints, but are expansion cracks that form as load is removed and as temperature changes.

Quaternary

Quaternary units within Snow Canyon State Park include three lava flows - Lava Ridge flow, Snow Canyon Overlook flow, and Santa Clara flow - which document the uplift and downcutting history of this area and unconsolidated eolian, talus, and alluvial/colluvial deposits (figures 10 and 11). The mapping of these deposits, as shown on figure 10, is simplified, for the most part, from maps by Willis and Higgins (1995,1996).

Basaltic Flows and Cinder Cones

The three basaltic lava flows within Snow Canyon State Park form steps down to the west with decreasing age (figure 11). Throughout the region, downcutting of the streams along the sides of the resistant basalt flows creates "inverted" valleys (Hamblin, 1970,1987). The oldest inverted valleys are now at the highest elevations above present drainages. Just east of Snow Canyon State Park, the Lava Ridge flow caps the ridge at approximately 4,600 feet (1,403 m) elevation. A portion of this flow cascaded

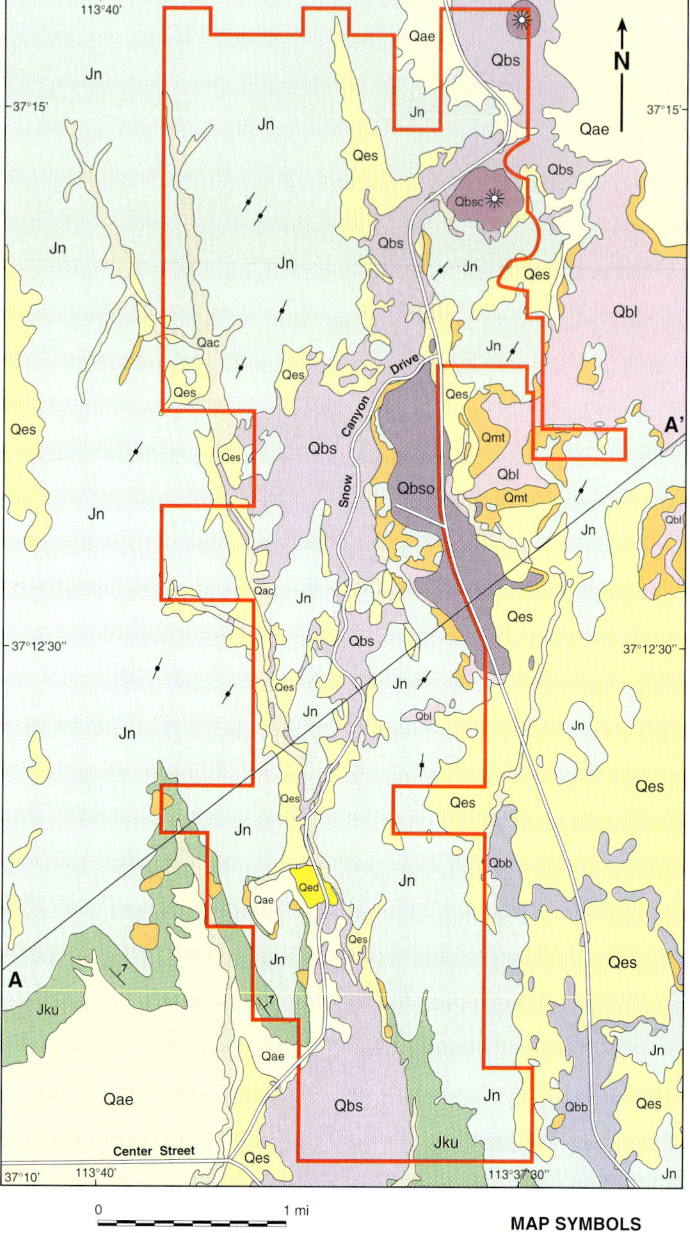

Figure 10. *Geologic map of the Snow Canyon State Park area (modified from Willis and Higgins, 1995; 1996). Description of map units and cross section A-A' shown on figure 11.*

down to partially fill a lower valley and was subsequently covered by the Snow Canyon Overlook flow. Just west of Lava Ridge (figure 8) and south of the Snow Canyon Overlook, the Snow Canyon Overlook flow caps the overlook rim at approximately 3,800 feet (1,159 m) elevation. To the southwest and in line with these two points, the Santa Clara flow fills the bottom of Snow Canyon near the active drainage level at 3,400 feet (1,037 m) elevation. The cinder cones of only this youngest flow are within park boundaries.

Lava Ridge flow (Qbl):   The Lava Ridge flow erupted

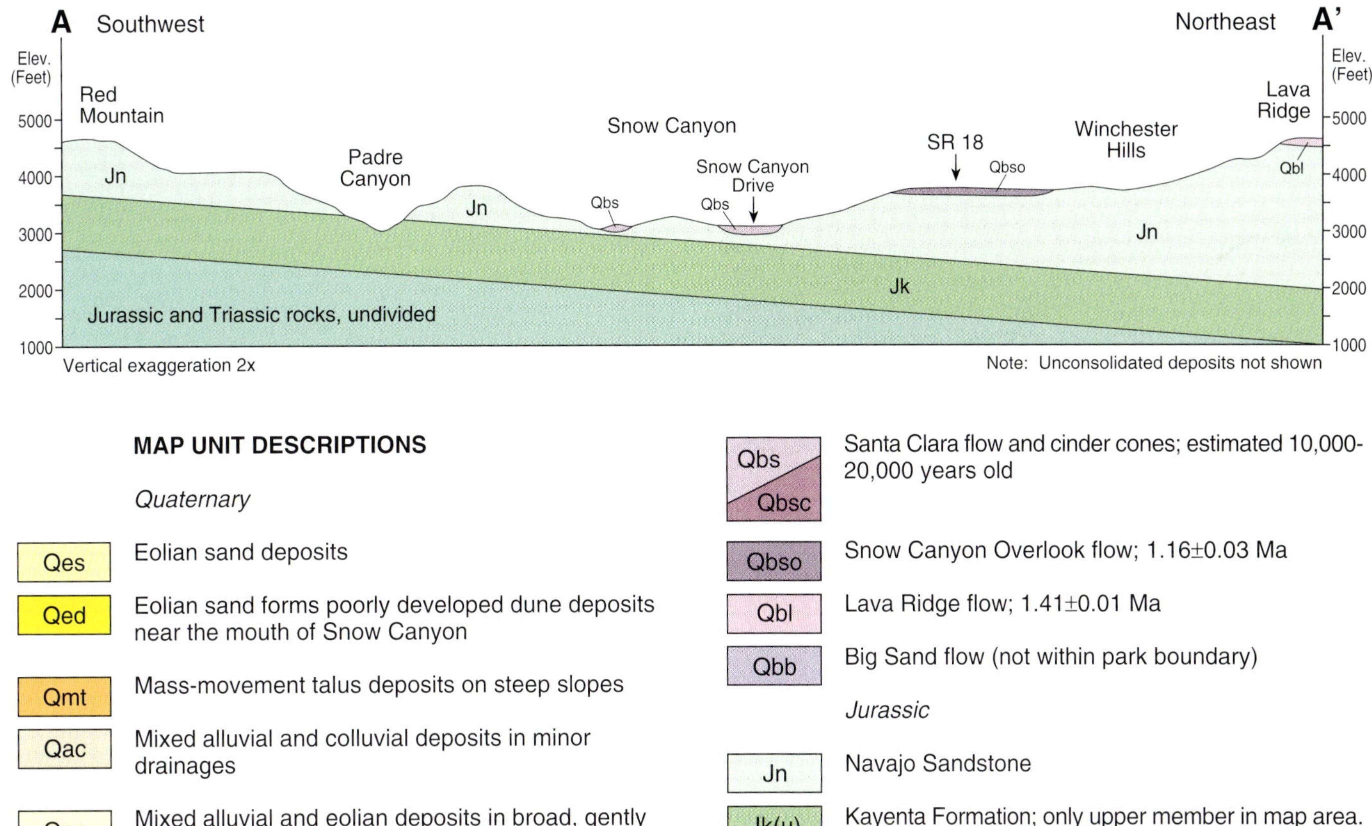

MAP UNIT DESCRIPTIONS

Quaternary

Qes — Eolian sand deposits

Qed — Eolian sand forms poorly developed dune deposits near the mouth of Snow Canyon

Qmt — Mass-movement talus deposits on steep slopes

Qac — Mixed alluvial and colluvial deposits in minor drainages

Qae — Mixed alluvial and eolian deposits in broad, gently sloping areas

Qbs / Qbsc — Santa Clara flow and cinder cones; estimated 10,000-20,000 years old

Qbso — Snow Canyon Overlook flow; 1.16±0.03 Ma

Qbl — Lava Ridge flow; 1.41±0.01 Ma

Qbb — Big Sand flow (not within park boundary)

Jurassic

Jn — Navajo Sandstone

Jk(u) — Kayenta Formation; only upper member in map area. Entire formation shown on cross section.

Figure 11. Map units and symbols for the geologic map of Snow Canyon State Park. Unconsolidated map units are not shown on the generalized cross section A-A'.

from a group of heavily weathered cinder cones on Lava Ridge, about one mile (1.6 km) east of the park. The Lava Ridge flow is a moderate- to dark-gray to dark-brownish-gray, quartz-bearing rock classified as basaltic trachyandesite, according to the total alkali-silica (TAS) classification of Le Bas and others (1986). Euhedral plagioclase phenocrysts are prominent, and quartz, pyroxene, and olivine phenocrysts are common. The Middleton lobe of this flow to the south and east of the park yielded an ^{40}Ar/^{39}Ar age of 1.41 ± 0.01 Ma, making it the oldest volcanic unit in the park (Willis and Higgins, 1995). The Lava Ridge flow caps the ridge to the east of Snow Canyon and is also visible half way up Snow Canyon in the east canyon wall. There, the Lava Ridge flow fills the bottom of an old channel in the Navajo Sandstone, after cascading over 600 feet (180 m) in 0.25 miles (0.4 km) to reach the channel. It is capped by the Snow Canyon Overlook flow (Willis and Higgins, 1995). The two flows may be separated by stream gravels, although exposures are poor. The Lava Ridge flow is about 250,000 years older than the overlying Snow Canyon Overlook flow. This is the only place in the park where a younger flow is at a higher elevation than an older flow. Usually, so much downcutting occurs between flows that the younger flow lies at a lower level than the older flow.

Snow Canyon Overlook flow (Qbso): The Snow Canyon Overlook flow is classified as a trachybasalt on the TAS di-

agram of Le Bas and others (1986) and labeled hawaiite by Best and Brimhall (1974). It is dense, strongly jointed, and weathers very dark brown with abundant, small olivine phenocrysts that weather out in relief, forming a "sandpaper" texture (Willis and Higgins, 1996). Vesicles in this basalt are elongated in the direction of flow. The Snow Canyon Overlook flow yielded an ^{40}Ar/^{39}Ar age of 1.16 ± 0.03 Ma and probably originated along the flank of the Pine Valley Mountains 5 to 10 miles (8-16 km) northeast of the park. The two small, basalt-capped hills (too small to map separately on figure 10) northwest of the State Route 18/Snow Canyon Drive intersection mark the northernmost extent of this isolated remnant. South of that point, it caps the sandstone bench that forms the east rim of the canyon. This flow, burying a portion of the Lava Ridge flow, apparently followed the course of an ancestral Snow Canyon and now forms a classic example of inverted topography (figure 12). The ancestral Snow Canyon drainage subsequently shifted west of the resistant basalt flow and cut the modern Snow Canyon in the softer sandstone, similar to the downcutting that has started along the edge of the Santa Clara flow at Hackberry Wash (figure 8).

Along the edge of Snow Canyon Overlook, fractures in the Snow Canyon Overlook flow are caused by the widening of the columnar joints as the softer sandstone is eroded from beneath the basalt. Eventually, the basalt breaks off to become talus on the sandstone slope below.

Figure 12. *The younger Santa Clara flow fills the bottom of Snow Canyon, while the older Snow Canyon Overlook flow caps the ridge on the east side of the canyon. This is an excellent example of inverted topography.*

Figure 13. *Originating from vents at the base of two well-preserved cinder cones next to SR 18, the Santa Clara flow cascaded into Snow Canyon and partially filled the V-shaped, stream-cut canyon with basalt. View shows only the southernmost cone and is from east of the park, looking west. The Beaver Dam Mountains are in the background.*

A significant stage VI caliche layer (pedogenic carbonate soil) has developed on the surface of the basalt (Machette, 1985; Willis and Higgins, 1996).

Santa Clara flow and cinder cones (Qbs, Qbsc): The youngest lava flow within Snow Canyon State Park, and the entire region, is the Santa Clara flow. It is geochemically classified as hawaiite by Best and Brimhall (1974). Using the classification of Le Bas and others (1986), it plots as a subalkaline basalt. It has a distinctly higher iron content than other flows in the area (Willis and Higgins, 1996). The rock is dark-brownish-black, dense, and aphanitic, with abundant small olivine crystals.

The Santa Clara flow has not been radiometrically dated. The flow is too young to obtain a reliable ^{40}Ar/^{39}Ar age, and attempts to find charcoal beneath the flow for carbon-14 dating have been fruitless. Hamblin (1963, 1987, and unpublished mapping) classified the flow as a stage IV (in a modern drainage but shows little evidence of erosion or alteration) and estimated it as slightly more than 1,000 years old. However, in 1985, hikers discovered human skeletal remains along with an atlatl partially buried by 2.5 inches (6 cm) of sand inside a lava tube cave. Features of the atlatl indicate that it was probably manufactured during late Archaic to Basketmaker II times, some 1,500 to 2,500 years ago (Madsen, 1992). A similar atlatl from nearby Antelope Cave, just south of the Utah and Arizona border, dates to 1,850 ± 60 years before present (Janetski, 1984). The flow must be sufficiently older than these dates to allow enough weathering time for the roof of the lava tube to collapse, permitting access to the cave.

Additionally, a drainage nick point with an approximately 40 foot (12 m) vertical drop has been created by headward erosion of the intermittent drainage returning to a former base level along the edge of the flow near the mouth of the canyon. There are no cuts across the flow that would help determine whether the wash has been cut lower than the thickest part of the flow. Also, the irides-

Figure 14. *View south from the Snow Canyon Overlook toward the mouth of Snow Canyon, showing rounded "turtle back" monoliths of sandstone protruding above lobes of the Santa Clara lava flow that flowed around them only 10 to 20 thousand years ago.*

cent sheen typical of young basalt flows has been mostly weathered away, and pedogenic carbonate, which typically takes a few thousand years for noticeable amounts to accumulate (Machette, 1985; Birkeland and others, 1991), coats joints in road cuts along State Route 18 to the north. For these reasons, the flow is probably between 10,000 and 20,000 years old (Willis and Higgins, 1996).

Vents at the base of two cinder cones east of State Route 18 at the head of Snow Canyon are the sources of the Santa Clara flow (figure 13). Although the cones themselves are extinct and local volcanism is considered dormant since there have been no eruptions during historical time, the extensional tectonic setting that caused these eruptions along joint systems in the Navajo Sandstone is still present (Condit and others, 1988; Sanchez, 1995; Smith and others, 1999). The symmetry of the cones is preserved because cinder cones typically form near the final phase of

Figure 15. Aerial photograph shows the excellent alignment of the lava tube cave collapse features, which delineate the lava tube within the Santa Clara flow. Note Snow Canyon Drive along the right (east) edge of the photo.

Figure 16. One of the largest lava tube cave collapse structures in the park is 100 feet by 150 feet (30 X 45 m). The tube-shaped cave is accessible because gravity has caused part of the roof of the lava tube to collapse. The cave entrance is about 15 feet by 25 feet (5 X 8 m).

Figure 17. Poorly formed sand dunes at the mouth of a small side canyon near the mouth of Snow Canyon.

the eruptive cycle. Cinder cones that do form early in the cycle are usually torn apart by the undermining flow. In the small side canyon just south of the southernmost cone, a dike associated with the Santa Clara flow protrudes out of the Navajo Sandstone. Additional dikes are present near the ridge crest.

To the west of State Route 18 at the head of Snow Canyon, the Santa Clara flow is nearly at the same level as the Snow Canyon Overlook flow. The Santa Clara flow then cascaded into Snow Canyon, partially filling the stream-eroded, V-shaped canyon with basalt and flattening out the canyon floor (figure 14). Only the tallest ridges, nicknamed "turtle backs," were left uncovered as isolated sandstone monoliths. Just how deep the canyon was, or how thick the flow is, is a matter of speculation because the base of the flow is not exposed; however, drainage level was still controlled by, and must be graded to, the Santa Clara River. Most of the flow has a rough aa surface, but there are some pahoehoe areas and pressure ridges near where the lava cascaded into West Canyon.

A well-developed lava tube in the Santa Clara flow is one of the most popular hiking destinations in the park. Lava tubes form as the surface of the flow cools and hardens, thus insulating the underlying molten lava. As the lava drains from the tube, a cave forms. Weathering eventually leads to a gravity collapse of the roof, which allows access to the tube-shaped cave. Aerial photographs show the excellent alignment of these collapse features, which delineates the lava tube (figure 15). Some of the largest lava tube cave collapse structures in the park measure approximately 100 feet by 150 feet (30 X 45 m), while the cave entrance measures about 15 feet by 25 feet (5 X 8 m) (figure 16). Inside the cave, some interesting collapse and flow structures within the flow are seen by flashlight.

Eolian Deposits

Eolian sand (Qes, Qed): Well- to very well sorted, fine- to very fine grained, well- rounded, mostly quartz sand has accumulated in thin sheets and irregular hummocky mounds on gently sloping areas in Snow Canyon and in depressions and protected areas on the Navajo Sandstone. Most of the sand has weathered from the Navajo Sandstone. The deposits are 0 to 20 feet (0-6 m) thick. Near the mouth of Snow Canyon the sand is locally more extensive. There, in the mouth of a small side canyon, the sand is up to 50 feet (15 m) thick and forms poorly developed dunes (figure 17) (Willis and Higgins, 1996).

Mass-movement Deposits

Talus deposits (Qmt): Talus deposits are very poorly sorted, angular boulders with minor fine-grained interstitial materials that have accumulated on and at the base of steep slopes. Most talus deposits at the mouth of Snow Canyon consist of individual blocks of Navajo Sandstone that tumble down slopes as the supporting softer red beds of the Kayenta Formation erode. Similarly, farther up the canyon, blocks of basalt accumulate on the Navajo Sandstone. Thickness of talus deposits varies from 0 to 20 feet (0-6 m).

Mixed-environment Deposits

Mixed alluvial and eolian deposits (Qae): These deposits consist of moderately to well-sorted sand, clay, silt, cobbles, and boulders. They are present primarily over broad, gently sloping areas where eolian materials were reworked by ephemeral streams and mixed with alluvial sediments. The deposits are 0 to 30 feet (0-9 m) thick.

Mixed alluvial and colluvial deposits (Qac): Poorly to moderately sorted clay- to boulder-sized sediment is present in the larger drainages throughout the area. The alluvial deposits were transported along washes during heavy

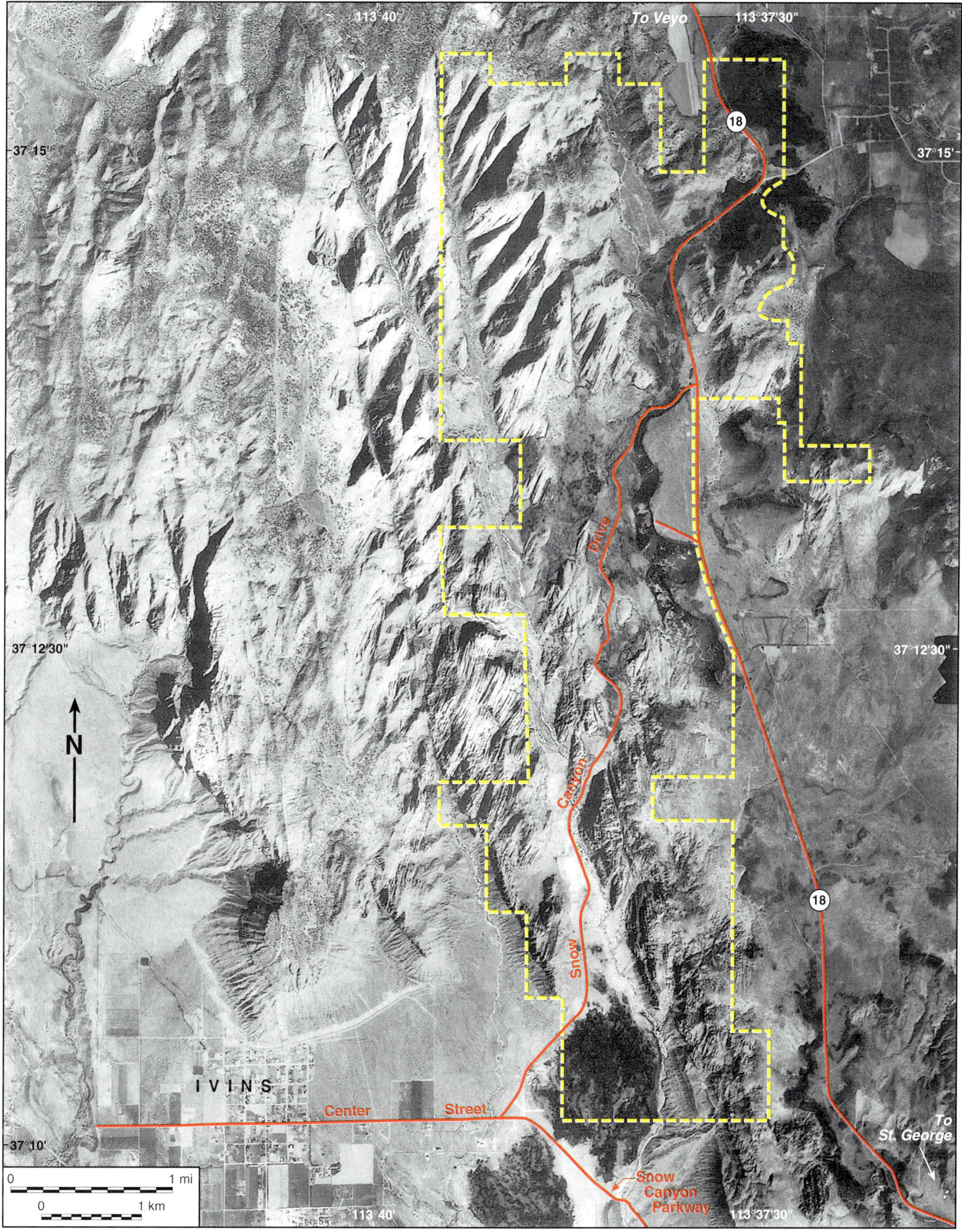

Figure 18. Aerial photograph of Snow Canyon State Park. The most prominent structural features are the numerous joints and fractures that cross the massive Navajo Sandstone. The sandstone is fractured into two intersecting sets of joints that control the weathering of the canyon. Padre Canyon is left (west) of the larger Snow Canyon. Note the two cinder cones near the top of the photo. Park boundary is outlined.

rainstorms by ephemeral streams and debris flows; colluvial material was derived from side slopes along the washes. They vary in thickness from 0 to 10 feet (0-3 m).

STRUCTURAL GEOLOGY

Regional Setting

Snow Canyon State Park is in the transition zone between the Colorado Plateau to the east and the Basin and Range Province to the west (Hamblin, 1970; Hintze, 1986). This transition zone also roughly coincides with the leading edge of the Sevier orogenic belt, and it is this Late Cretaceous to early Tertiary compressional event that formed the St. George syncline (Higgins and Willis, 1995). Additionally, the area is in the active southern segment of the Intermountain seismic belt, which in southwestern Utah also coincides with the Basin and Range-Colorado Plateau transition zone, and which is characterized by high-angle normal faults (Arabasz and Julander, 1986). In the area that includes Snow Canyon State Park, the transition zone consists of a series of down-to-the-west normal faults that "step down" from the Colorado Plateau into the Basin and Range. The fault block that includes the park is bounded on the east by the Hurricane fault and on the west by the Grand Wash-Reef Reservoir-Gunlock fault system. The Hurricane fault, located 18 miles (29 km) east of the park, has a total stratigraphic separation of 6,000 to 7,000 feet (1,830-2,135 m) near the latitude of Snow Canyon State Park (Biek, 1998); the amount of separation increases northward (Pearthree and others, 1998). The Grand Wash-Reef Reservoir-Gunlock fault system is about 6 miles (9.6 km) west of the park and has about 1,500 to 3,000 feet (457-915 m) of down-to-the-west displacement (Hintze, 1986; Hammond, 1988). Rocks west of that fault system are intensely deformed, whereas rocks to the east, including those of Snow Canyon State Park, are only slightly deformed.

Local Structures

St. George Syncline

A minor thrust detachment of the Late Cretaceous Sevier orogenic thrust belt is postulated in Cambrian strata about 4,000 feet (1,200 m) beneath the surface (Willis and Higgins, 1996; Davis, 1999). Movement along this thrust fractured and deformed overlying rock to form the St. George syncline. The rocks of Snow Canyon have been uplifted and tilted northeastward as part of the west limb of this northward plunging syncline. The axis of the St. George syncline trends through the city of St. George. The rocks dip uniformly 7 degrees northeast, towards the axis of the syncline (figures 4 and 10).

Joints and Fractures

The most prominent structural features in Snow Canyon State Park are the numerous joints and fractures

Figure 19. The prominent peak in the White Rocks area directly north of Lava Flow Overlook appears creased by a deeply weathered vertical gash. This crack is one of several, widely spaced, heavily eroded joints that trend just west of north. Erosion along these lineaments forms Snow Canyon, West Canyon, Padre Canyon to the west, and almost detaches Island in the Sky to the south.

that cross the massive Navajo Sandstone. The sandstone is fractured into two intersecting sets of parallel cracks, called joints (figure 18). Formed as the brittle rock is stressed by tectonic events or undergoes stress reduction because of erosional unloading, these cracks increase the surface area of the rock, thereby increasing the weathering rate of the rock. Many of the features of the park are formed by weathering along joints. Fluted hillsides form as weathering proceeds at a faster rate along northeast trending joints than it does between the joints. Differential weathering also locally exposes joint surfaces coated with desert varnish.

The prominent peak in the White Rocks area at the north end of the park appears creased by a deeply weathered vertical gash (figure 19). This crack is one of several widely spaced, heavily eroded joints that trend just west of north. Erosion along these lineaments forms Snow Canyon, West Canyon, Padre Canyon (houses Tuacahn Amphitheater west of the park), and almost detaches Island in the Sky to the south (figure 2). Some of these lineaments are several miles in length and have brecciated zones 5 to 30 feet (1.5-9 m) wide (Willis and Higgins, 1996). Brecciation and siliceous and calcareous recementation is generally intense along these fractures. Any significant offset is difficult to recognize on these fractures, largely because the Navajo Sandstone has few stratigraphic markers, but strata may be offset along some of these joints. Hurlow (1998) considered the West Canyon area as a separate structural compartment for a regional ground-water study because of assumed movement on these lineaments.

Another prominent set of joints in the Navajo Sandstone trends northeast (figure 20). These joints don't show evidence of micro-faulting as there is no brecciation and minor or no silicification along the joints. They are not evenly spaced, as seen to the east of SR 18, just north of the intersection with Snow Canyon Drive.

Figure 20. Oblique aerial view looking northward at northeast-trending joints in the Navajo Sandstone just east of the southern end of Snow Canyon State Park. The paved road in the picture is State Route 18.

GEOLOGIC HISTORY

During the Early Jurassic Period, the sand and silt that was to become the Kayenta Formation was deposited in fluvial, distal fluvial/playa, sabkha, and minor lacustrine environments (Sansom, 1992). The area then began to be inundated by desert sand that would become the Navajo Sandstone. The gradational nature of the contact between these two formations indicates that this transition from sabkha- and stream-deposited beds to wind-deposited sand did not occur overnight. The environment vacillated between a slowly encroaching desert and an extensive system of braided and meandering streams (Blakey and others, 1988; Bugden, 1992). Along these streams dinosaurs pressed footprints into the sand that are preserved in the rock. Rivers eventually ceased flowing as water became scarce and windy desert conditions prevailed, perhaps because this area was only about 15 degrees north of the equator at that time in a climate belt of an arid, west coast, low-latitude desert (Peterson, 1988).

The Sahara-like desert blasted and enveloped an extensive area of North America between 190 and 180 million years ago during the late Early Jurassic (Peterson and Pipiringos, 1979). Paleowinds that blew mostly from the north created dunes that would become the Navajo Sandstone (Sansom, 1992). The source of the sand is unknown. Peterson (1988) suggested that it is likely recycled from Paleozoic and Triassic sandstone to the north in Montana, and perhaps as far away as Alberta, Canada, with minor additions from the east margin of the marine embayment to the west. However, Marzolf (1988) proposed that the ultimate source of sand was the marine embayment as sand was blown back onshore to form dunes after it had been transported northwest by Kayenta streams and reworked along the shore.

Following the deposition of the Navajo Sandstone, this area experienced a period of erosion. Subsequent deposition created younger rocks that formed in later Jurassic and early Cretaceous time. These rock layers have now been removed from on top of the Navajo Sandstone within the area of the park by a more recent period of erosion.

Compressional deformation occurred during the Late Cretaceous to early Tertiary Sevier orogeny. A minor detachment of the thrust belt is postulated in Cambrian strata about 4,000 feet (1,200 m) beneath the surface (Willis and Higgins, 1996; Davis, 1999). The upper plate of this thrust includes the Navajo Sandstone and Kayenta Formation of Snow Canyon State Park, which have been transported from west to east. Movement along this thrust fractured and deformed overlying rock. The compression formed the broad, northward-plunging St. George syncline, creating the 7 degree northeast dip of the rocks of Snow Canyon.

During late Tertiary and Quaternary time, tectonic stress changed from compression to tension. This resulted in normal faulting and thinning of the crust due to extension. Magma, already closer to the surface because of crustal thinning, was able to erupt along joint systems (Condit and others, 1989; Sanchez, 1995; Smith and others, 1999).

Three distinct basaltic lava flows document the Quaternary eruptive and erosional history of Snow Canyon. The oldest, the Lava Ridge flow, now caps a ridge east of Snow Canyon, behind the Winchester Hills subdivision (figure 8) (Willis and Higgins, 1995). A small portion of this 1.41 ± 0.01 Ma Lava Ridge flow cascaded down a small channel into an ancestral Snow Canyon near the present location of State Route 18. The Lava Ridge flow effectively displaced the drainage and was buried by the Snow Canyon Overlook flow 1.16 ± 0.03 Ma. Sand Bench, just east of State Route 18 and between these two flows, is an unusually old surface because it has been isolated and protected by this stream shift. The Snow Canyon Overlook flow displaced the drainage to the west, which subsequently created the modern Snow Canyon. The Santa Clara flow filled the bottom of this canyon only 10 to 20 thousand years ago. Downcutting and widening of West Canyon because of erosion by intermittent streams of the softer Navajo Sandstone instead of the more resistant basalt is once again causing the location of Snow Canyon to shift westward.

Weathering of the rock produces unconsolidated deposits, such as the sand dunes, and creates the varied landscape of Snow Canyon State Park. Many of the features of the park are formed by weathering along joints. Johnson Arch, a natural arch in the Navajo Sandstone 200 feet (60 m) in length, formed in a narrow fin of sandstone as joints were enlarged by weathering. Undercutting of the sandstone along a spring line occurs as cementing minerals are removed from between the sand grains. This sapping leads to spalling which creates an incipient arch in the rock. With continuing weathering and erosion along joints and spring lines, the arch that has formed will eventually collapse.

CLASSIC GEOLOGIC ATTRIBUTES/SITES

Snow Canyon State Park includes several geologic features that are unique and easily seen within park boundaries (figure 8).

- A slot canyon is easily accessed by hiking the Jenny's Canyon Trail. This 0.5 mile (0.8 km) round trip walk leads to a narrow slot canyon in the Navajo Sandstone along the southeast edge of Island in the Sky.

- Sand dunes are a favorite stop with locals as well as visitors. The largest dune area is located near the mouth of the canyon, west of Snow Canyon Drive.

- Desert varnish is common on the Navajo Sandstone, and is particularly well developed on the north side of Island in the Sky.

- Johnson Arch, a natural arch in the Navajo Sandstone, is accessed from a trailhead near the south fee station. Currently, the trail is only open November 15th through March 1st due to the presence of nesting peregrine falcons and other sensitive species. When open, hiking is allowed only on the designated trail because of the delicate riparian area created by springs in the side canyon near the arch. Hiking to the top of the arch is prohibited, but the view from the base of the arch justifies the 1.5 mile (2.4 km) round trip hike.

- Cross-bedding in the Navajo Sandstone is accentuated by weathering in the upper half of the canyon. Both Galoot Hill and the Petrified Dunes Trail provide easy access to get a close look.

- Interfingering color change in the Navajo Sandstone is best seen from a distance from the Lava Flow Overlook or from the Snow Canyon Overlook. To reach the area, a hike from the Lava Flow Overlook or on the Petrified Dunes Trail then across the Santa Clara flow is necessary.

- Excellent examples of secondary enrichment of cementing minerals in the Navajo Sandstone, which create areas of the sandstone that are more resistant to erosion and form "hoodoos," are found along the Hidden Pinyon Trail and the Petrified Dunes Trail to the lava tube caves at "butterfly rock." "Moki marbles" are especially well developed at Galoot Hill and along the Petrified Dunes Trail.

- Joints in the Navajo Sandstone are present throughout the park. The Snow Canyon Overlook provides a good perspective to get a sense of intersecting joint relationships.

- Cinder cones that are only 10 to 20 thousand years old are located in the northeast corner of the park just east of State Route 18.

- The youngest lava flow in the region, the Santa Clara flow, erupted from vents at the base of the cinder cones in the northeast corner of Snow Canyon State Park. From there, the flow cascaded into and flowed the entire length of Snow Canyon, and beyond. The Santa Clara flow is easily accessed at the cinder cones, from the Lava Flow Overlook, from the Petrified Dunes Trail to the lava tube caves, and the trail to Johnson Arch.

- Lava tube collapse structures and caves in the Santa Clara flow are reached with a 1 to 1.5 mile (1.6-2.4 km) hike from either the Petrified Dunes Trail or the Lava Flow Overlook.

- Inverted topography is best viewed from Snow Canyon Overlook where the Lava Ridge flow (1.41 ± 0.01 Ma) caps the ridge to the east of Snow Canyon behind Winchester Hills subdivision, the Snow Canyon Overlook flow (1.16 ± 0.03 Ma) caps the east rim of Snow Canyon, and the Santa Clara flow (estimated 10 to 20 thousand years old) fills the bottom of the canyon. A more in-depth study of the inversion process should include stops at Hackberry Wash, where the drainage was diverted to the edge of the Santa Clara flow and is downcutting through the softer Navajo Sandstone, and at the erosional nick point of the Santa Clara flow along the Johnson Arch Trail.

ACKNOWLEDGMENTS

Kendall Farnsworth, Assistant Superintendent of Snow Canyon State Park, provided much information on trail availability and length and was very helpful in preparing this report. His patience in answering numerous questions during a time when the park was undergoing major transitions is greatly appreciated. Wes Johnson, Utah State Parks Division, furnished information on current park boundaries. Kelly Bringhurst, Dixie College, reviewed preliminary manuscripts and made several valuable suggestions, as did Bob Biek and Grant Willis of the Utah Geological Survey. The oblique aerial photographs were obtained with the assistance of Harold D. Mitchell, who graciously took me flying.

REFERENCES

Arabasz, W.J., and Julander, D.R., 1986, Geometry of seismically active faults and crustal deformation within the Basin and Range - Colorado Plateau transition in Utah: Utah Geological and Mineral Survey Miscellaneous Publication 89-6, 29 p.

Best, M.G., and Brimhall, W.H., 1974, Late Cenozoic alkalic basaltic magmas in the western Colorado Plateaus and the Basin and Range transition zone, U.S.A., and their bearing on mantle dynamics: Geological Society of America Bulletin, v. 85, no. 11, p. 1,677-1,690.

Biek, R. F., 1998, Interim geologic map of the Hurricane quadrangle, Washington County, Utah: Utah Geological Survey Open-File Report 361, 154 p., scale 1:24,000.

Birkeland, P.W., Machette, M.N., and Haller, K.M., 1991, Soils as a tool for applied Quaternary geology: Utah Geological and Mineral Survey, Miscellaneous Publication 91-3, 63 p.

Blakey, R.C., Peterson, Fred, Kocurek, Gary, 1988, Late Paleozoic and Mesozoic eolian deposits of western interior of the United States: Sedimentary Geology, v. 56, p. 3-125.

Bugden, Miriam, 1992, The Geology of Snow Canyon State Park, Washington County, Utah: Utah Geological Survey Public Information Series 13, 16 p.

Condit, C.D., Crumpler, L.F., Aubele, J.C., and Elston, W.E., 1989, Patterns of volcanism along the southern margins of the Colorado Plateau-Springerville field: Journal of Geophysical Research, v. 94, p. 7,975-7,986.

Davis, G.H., 1999, Structural geology of Colorado Plateau region of southern Utah with special emphasis on deformation bands: Geological Society of America Special Paper 342, 168 p.

Hamblin, W.K., 1963, Late Cenozoic basalts of the St. George basin, Utah, *in* Heylmun, E.B., editor, Guidebook to the geology of southwestern Utah: Intermountain Association of Petroleum Geologists Twelfth Annual Field Conference, p. 84-89.

—1970, Structure of the western Grand Canyon region, *in* Hamblin, W.K., and Best, M.G., editors, The western Grand Canyon district: Utah Geology Society Guidebook to the Geology of Utah, no. 23, p. 3-20.

—1987, Late Cenozoic volcanism in the St. George basin, Utah: Geological Society of America Centennial Field Guide--Rocky Mountain Section, p. 291-294.

Hammond, B.J., 1988, Analysis of the Grand Wash-Reef Reservoir-Gunlock fault zone, Washington County, Utah, and Mohave County, Arizona: Provo, Brigham Young University, M.S. thesis, 57 p.

Higgins, J.M., and Willis,G.C., 1995, Interim geologic map of the St. George quadrangle, Washington County, Utah: Utah Geological Survey Open-File Report 323, 90 p., scale 1:24,000.

Hintze, L.F., 1986, Stratigraphy and structure of the Beaver Dam Mountains, southwestern Utah, *in* Griffen, D.T., and Phillips, W.R., editors, Thrusting and extensional structures and mineralization in the Beaver Dam Mountains, southwestern Utah: Utah Geological Association Publication 15, p. 1-36.

Hintze, L.F., and Hammond, B.J., 1994, Geologic map of the Shivwits quadrangle, Washington County, Utah: Utah Geological Survey Map 153, 21 p., scale 1:24,000.

Horrocks-Carollo Engineers, 1993, Culinary water resources study: St. George City Water and Power Department, June 1993, 128 p.

Hurlow, H.A., 1998, The geology of the central Virgin River basin, southwestern Utah, and its relation to ground-water conditions: Utah Geological Survey, Water Resources Bulletin 26, 53 p., 6 plates.

Imlay, R.W., 1980, Jurassic paleogeography of the conterminous United States in its continental setting: U.S. Geological Survey Professional Paper 1062, 134 p.

Janetski, J.C., 1984, An archaeological and geological assessment of Antelope Cave (NA5507), Mohave County, Northwestern Arizona: Addendum to Brigham Young University Department of Anthropology Technical Series No. 83-73; Provo, Brigham Young University, M.S. thesis, 93 p.

Le Bas, M.J., Le Maitre, R.W., Streckeisen, A., and Zanettin, B., 1986, A chemical classification of volcanic rocks based on the total alkali-silica diagram: Journal of Petrology, v. 27, p. 745-750.

Machette, M.N., 1985, Calcic soils of the southwestern United States: Geological Society of America Special Paper 203, p. 1-21.

Madsen, D.B., 1992, An atlatl from Snow Canyon State Park, *in* Utah Archaeology 1992: Utah Statewide Archaeological Society, v. 5, no. 1, p. 133-136.

Marzolf, J.E., 1988, Controls on late Paleozoic and early Mesozoic on eolian deposition of the western United States, *in* Kocurek, Gary, editor, Late Paleozoic and Mesozoic eolian deposits of the western interior of the United States: Sedimentary Geology, v. 56, p. 167-191.

McKee, E.H., Blank, H.R., and Rowley, P.D., 1995, Potassium-Argon ages of Tertiary igneous rocks in the eastern Bull Valley Mountains and Pine Valley Mountains, southwestern Utah, *in* Maldonado, Florian and Nealey, L.D., editors, Geologic studies in the Basin and Range-Colorado Plateau transition in southeastern Nevada, southwestern Utah, and northwestern Arizona: U.S. Geological Survey Bulletin 2153, p. 241-252.

Pearthree, P.A., Lund, W.R., Steiner, H.D., and Everett, B.L., 1998, Paleoseismologic investigation of the Hurricane fault in southwestern Utah and northwestern Arizona - A final project report: National Earthquake Hazards Reduction Program, External Research Program, Element One, 131 p.

Peterson, Fred, 1988, Pennsylvanian to Jurassic eolian transportation systems in the western United States: Sedimentary Geology, v. 56, p. 207-260.

Peterson, Fred and Pipiringos, G.N., 1979, Stratigraphic relations of the Navajo Sandstone to Middle Jurassic formations, southern Utah and northern Arizona: U.S. Geological Survey Professional Paper 1035-B, 43 p.

Sanchez, Alexander, 1995, Mafic volcanism in the Colorado Plateau/Basin and Range transition zone, Hurricane, Utah: Las Vegas, University of Nevada, M.S. thesis, 92 p.

Sansom, P.J., 1992, Sedimentology of the Navajo Sandstone, southern Utah, USA: Oxford, England, Department of Earth Sciences at Wolfson College, Ph.D. dissertation, 291 p.

Smith, E.I., Sanchez, Alexander, Walker, J.D., and Wang, Kefa, 1999, Geochemistry of mafic magmas in the Hurricane volcanic field, Utah- Implications for small- and large-scale chemical variability of the lithospheric mantle: Journal of Geology, v. 107, p. 433-448.

Tuesink, M.F., 1989, Depositional analysis of an eolian-fluvial environment - the intertonguing of the Kayenta Formation and Navajo Sandstone (Jurassic) in southwestern Utah: Flagstaff, Northern Arizona University, M.S. thesis, 189 p.

Warneke, Al, 1993, An introduction to the geology of Zion National Park: Zion Natural History Association, 23 p.

Willis, G.C., and Higgins, J.M., 1995, Interim geologic map of the Washington quadrangle, Washington County, Utah: Utah Geological Survey Open-File Report 324, 113 p., scale 1:24,000.

—1996, Interim geologic map of the Santa Clara quadrangle, Washington County, Utah: Utah Geological Survey Open-File Report 339, 87 p., scale 1:24,000.

Geology of Utah's Parks and Monuments
2000 Utah Geological Association Publication 28
D.A. Sprinkel, T.C. Chidsey, Jr., and P.B. Anderson, editors

Geology of Wasatch Mountain State Park, Utah

Julie B. Willis[1] and Grant C. Willis[2]

ABSTRACT

Wasatch Mountain State Park, located on the east side of the Wasatch Range and the west side of Heber Valley, is near the junction of several major geologic structures. The oldest of these, the east-west-trending Cheyenne belt, is a suture formed about 1.7 billion years ago during the collision between two protocontinents that now form much of North America. This zone of structural weakness trends under Wasatch Mountain State Park. The park is located just east of another major structure, the north-south-trending Utah hinge line, which marks the eastern extent of crustal attenuation that developed when North America rifted from the supercontinent Rodinia in the late Proterozoic.

During the late Proterozoic to early Mesozoic, the hinge line was the boundary between a subsiding marine basin to the west and the continental shelf to the east. The park was part of the continental shelf just east of the hinge line, with shallow marine and near-shore deposition, or erosion. During the late Mesozoic and early Tertiary, the east-directed Charleston-Nebo thrust fault juxtaposed thick-facies strata from the west side of the hinge line onto thin-facies strata of similar age in southern Wasatch Mountain State Park. The Deer Creek detachment fault, a low-angle extensional fault, developed when the thrust-faulted terrain "relaxed" and moved back to the west. In the middle Tertiary, several igneous stocks, which are exposed in northern Wasatch Mountain State Park, were intruded along the Cheyenne belt. Since the Late Tertiary, movement on the Wasatch fault, which is the easternmost major fault of the Basin and Range Province, has elevated the park, and smaller subsidiary faults have formed Heber Valley. Erosion, alpine glaciation, and landslides have shaped the elevated terrain in the last few million years. Hot springs, formed by ground water circulating deep underground along the extensional fault system, have deposited thick mounds of tufa and travertine along the eastern edge of the park in Heber Valley. In historical times, mining and recreation, directly and indirectly related to the geology, influenced the establishment of Wasatch Mountain State Park.

Figure 1. *Wasatch Mountain State Park is known for its alpine scenery. The brush covered slope is Mississippian and Permian sedimentary rock. The treeless peaks are Sunset Peak (left) and Pioneer Peak (right). The tops of these peaks are cut by the Grizzly (Alta) thrust zone, which juxtaposes Cambrian and lower Mississippian strata over middle Mississippian rocks (Baker and others, 1966). Photo courtesy Alan Day Photography, Heber City, Utah.*

[1]*Heber City, UT 84032*
[2]*Utah Geological Survey, Salt Lake City, UT 84114-6100*

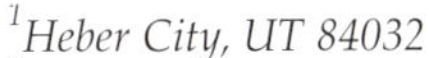

495

INTRODUCTION

Wasatch Mountain State Park (WMSP), located on the east side of the Wasatch Range with park headquarters in Heber Valley, is best known for its beautiful alpine scenery, attractive golf course, campground, and cross country ski trails (figures 1 and 2). The park is one of the most visited state parks in Utah; however, most visitors don't realize how large it is or the significance of its geologic history (Willis and Willis, 1994).

The park sits at the junction of several geologic boundaries (figure 3). Perhaps the most significant of these are the east-west-trending Cheyenne belt, a suture between two parts of the continental core of North America, and the north-south-trending Utah hinge line, a long-lasting boundary between the stable continental shelf to the east and a subsiding marine basin to the west. Both boundaries exerted major tectonic influences on deposition and structure in and near the park since the Precambrian (see Structure and Geologic History). The latest geologic boundary to affect WMSP is the Wasatch fault, which elevated and tilted the Wasatch Range, the fault block on which the park sits.

ROCKS OF THE PARK

Middle Proterozoic to Oligocene sedimentary rocks (total thickness about 17,000 feet [5,200 m]) and Oligocene intrusive and extrusive igneous rocks are exposed in WMSP (figures 4 and 5). Paleozoic rocks are primarily marine-deposited limestone, dolomite, shale, and quartzite (Hintze, 1993). Earliest Mesozoic rocks are also marine deposits, but by the Late Triassic most deposition was on land, reflecting changing tectonics in the western United States (Blakey and others, 1993). Igneous rocks exposed in WMSP and vicinity are part of the Oligocene Wasatch igneous belt (John, 1989; Vogel and others, 1997). Hydrothermal fluids that attended emplacement of the stocks resulted in the economic vein and replacement ore deposits of the Park City and Snake Creek Canyon mining districts (Presnell, 1997; John, 1997a). A middle Tertiary conglomerate records extensional collapse of the Cretaceous Charleston-Nebo thrust sheet (Constenius, 1996). Surficial deposits record glacial, hot spring, alluvial, and mass movement events of the last million years.

Most stratified rocks exposed in WMSP can be grouped into two packages: "upper plate" and "lower plate." Upper plate rocks were deposited 20 to 30 miles (30-50 km) west of their current position and were transported into the area on the Charleston-Nebo thrust fault during the Sevier orogeny (Levy and Christie-Blick, 1989) (figure 3). Lower plate rocks have not been transported significantly and were deposited at or near their current position.

Prior to thrusting, upper and lower plate rocks were on opposite sides of the Utah hinge line; rocks deposited west of the hinge line are as much as ten times thicker

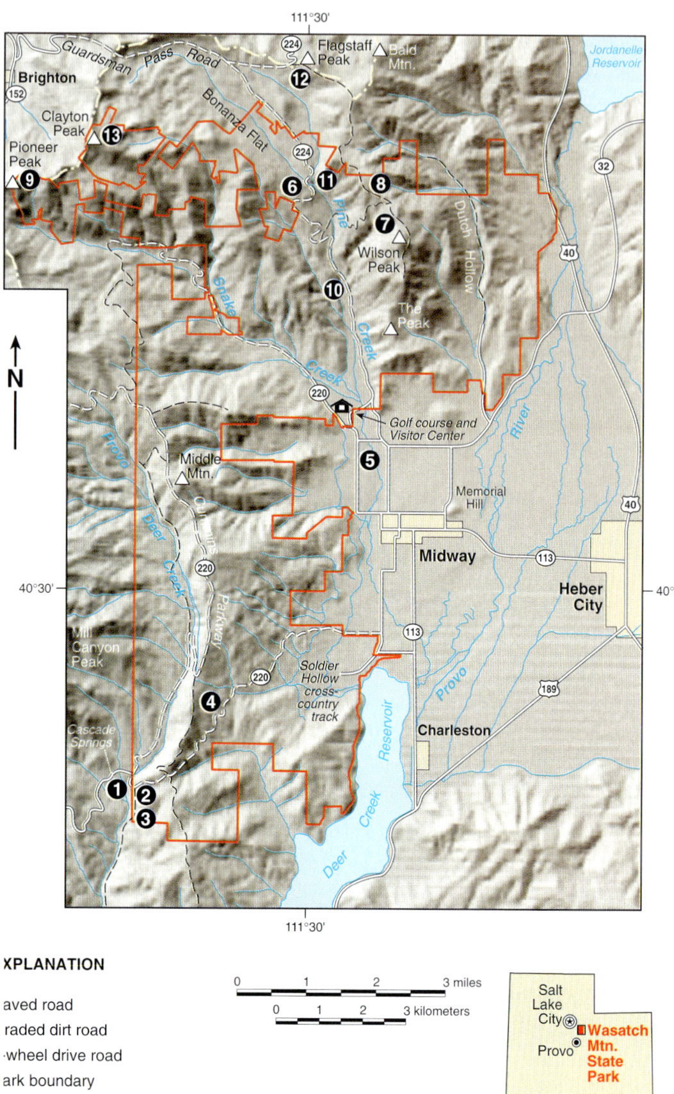

Figure 2. Index map of Wasatch Mountain State Park. Numbers indicate classic geologic sites: (1) Cascade Springs, (2) Charleston-Nebo thrust fault, (3) Deer Creek detachment fault, (4) Bedding plane landslides, (5) Midway thermal system, (6) Glacial till with megaboulders, (7) Wilson Peak, (8) Mineral Fork Formation, (9) Pioneer Peak and upper Snake Creek Canyon, (10) Pine Creek stock, (11) Valeo stock, (12) Flagstaff stock, (13) Clayton Peak and Clayton Peak stock. Road log routes are: Road Log 1–Visitor Center to Cascade Springs and the Cummins Parkway via State Route 220; Road Log 2–Visitor Center up Pine Creek Canyon to Bonanza Flat and the Guardsman Pass Road via State Route 224; Road Log 3–Guardsman Pass Road to Wilson Peak; Road Log 4–Visitor Center up Snake Creek Canyon to the Cummins Parkway via State Route 220.

(thick facies) than correlative deposits east of the hinge line (thin facies). In some cases, correlative strata on the upper and lower plates in WMSP are lithologically similar and bear the same formation name; in other cases, the strata are distinct and different names are applied (Baker, 1964; Baker and others, 1966; Bromfield and others, 1970; Bryant, 1990, 1992).   Thicknesses and stratigraphic rela-

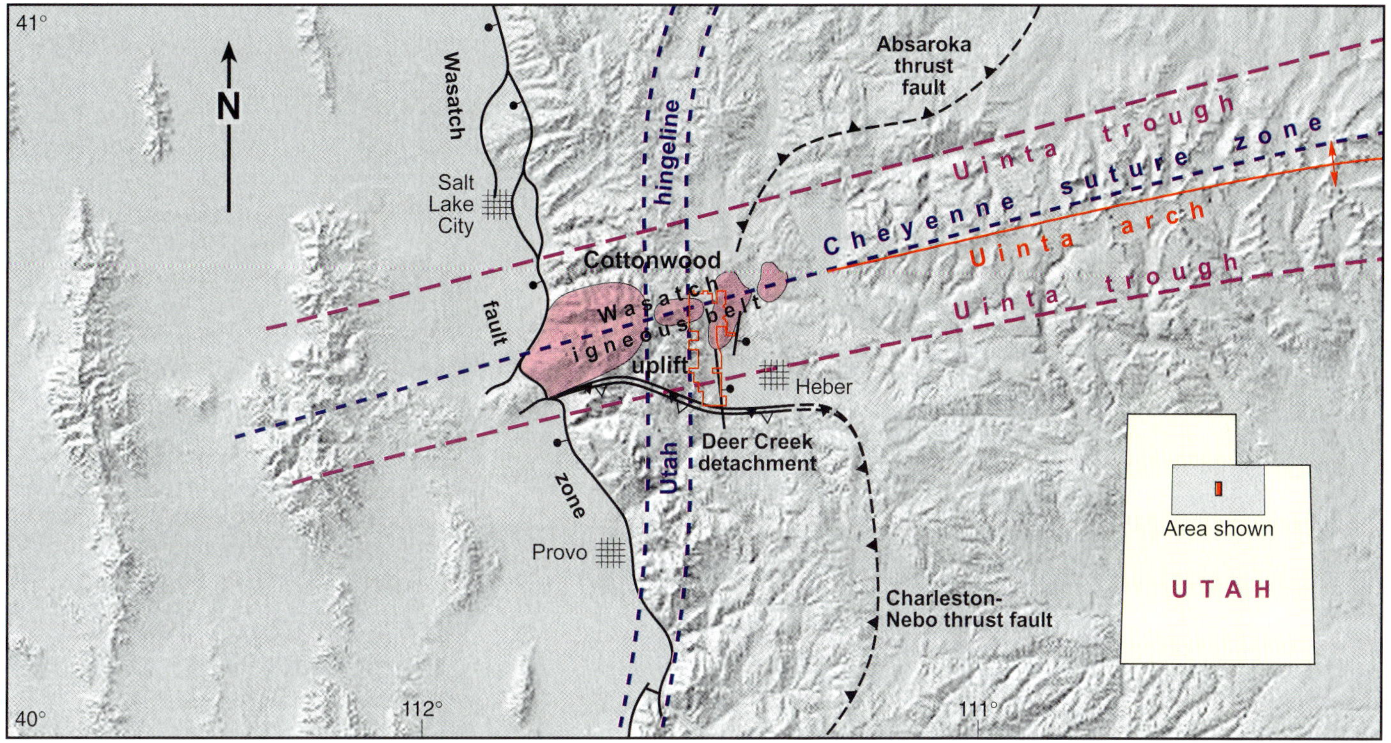

Figure 3. Regional structure map of the central Wasatch Range (after Bryant, 1992; John, 1997a; Vogel, 1997; Constenius, 1998). The oldest structures are the east-west-trending early Proterozoic Cheyenne belt and the north-south-trending Proterozoic-Mesozoic Utah hinge line. Wasatch Mountain State Park lies near the junction of these structures, which exerted a strong influence on more recent geologic events.

tionships of sedimentary rocks are given on figure 5.

Proterozoic

Big Cottonwood Formation (upper plate)

The 1,000- to 850-million-year-old Big Cottonwood Formation is the oldest formation exposed in WMSP (figures 4 and 5) (Link and others, 1993). It is white and purple quartzite and quartzitic conglomerate with minor beds of sandstone and olive-green micaceous shale. In southern WMSP, the Big Cottonwood crops out discontinuously along the trace of the Charleston-Nebo thrust fault where it forms the most common basal unit of the upper plate. Exposures are exceptionally poor because the rock was shattered and contorted during thrusting. One relatively intact outcrop is found near the railroad tracks on the west shore of Deer Creek Reservoir. Mapped exposures of the Big Cottonwood Formation may include some overlying Tintic Quartzite and structurally intermixed beds of younger formations (Baker, 1964).

The Big Cottonwood Formation is not exposed in northern WMSP but it is probably present in the subsurface. West of the park, the formation contains the oldest known tidal rhythmites (layered rock in which deposition of each thin layer was controlled by rising and falling ocean tides), and east of the park it correlates with, and may be equivalent to, the 25,000-foot-thick (7,600 m) Uinta Mountain Group (Link, and others, 1993; Chan and others, 1994).

Mineral Fork Formation (lower plate)

The Mineral Fork Formation is a rusty to olive, drab-weathering, gritty sandstone interbedded with dark-gray quartzite and conglomerate (figure 6). It contains abundant angular to rounded dropstones (large boulders to cobbles "floating" in a fine-grained matrix). The conglomerate beds contain well-rounded cobbles and boulders of predominately white and pink quartzite with less numerous clasts of schist, granitic rock, and limestone. The Mineral Fork is exposed adjacent to the northwest intrusive contact of the Pine Creek stock in northern WMSP. Exposures are poor and outcrops are rare; a dark-greenish-gray soil is commonly the only sign of the formation. A good outcrop is located north of Wilson Peak (figure 2) (see Road Log 3).

Lower to Middle Cambrian

Tintic Quartzite (upper and lower plates)

The Lower to Middle Cambrian Tintic Quartzite consists mainly of white to light-tan, medium- to coarse-grained, strongly cemented sedimentary quartzite with a few pink, dark-red, and lavender quartzite bands. It contains lenses of gritstone and quartz pebble conglomerate with pebbles up to 2 inches (5 cm) in diameter. Tintic Quartzite of the lower plate is locally well exposed around the edges of the Pine Creek and Valeo intrusions in northern WMSP. Considering their proximity, the intrusions

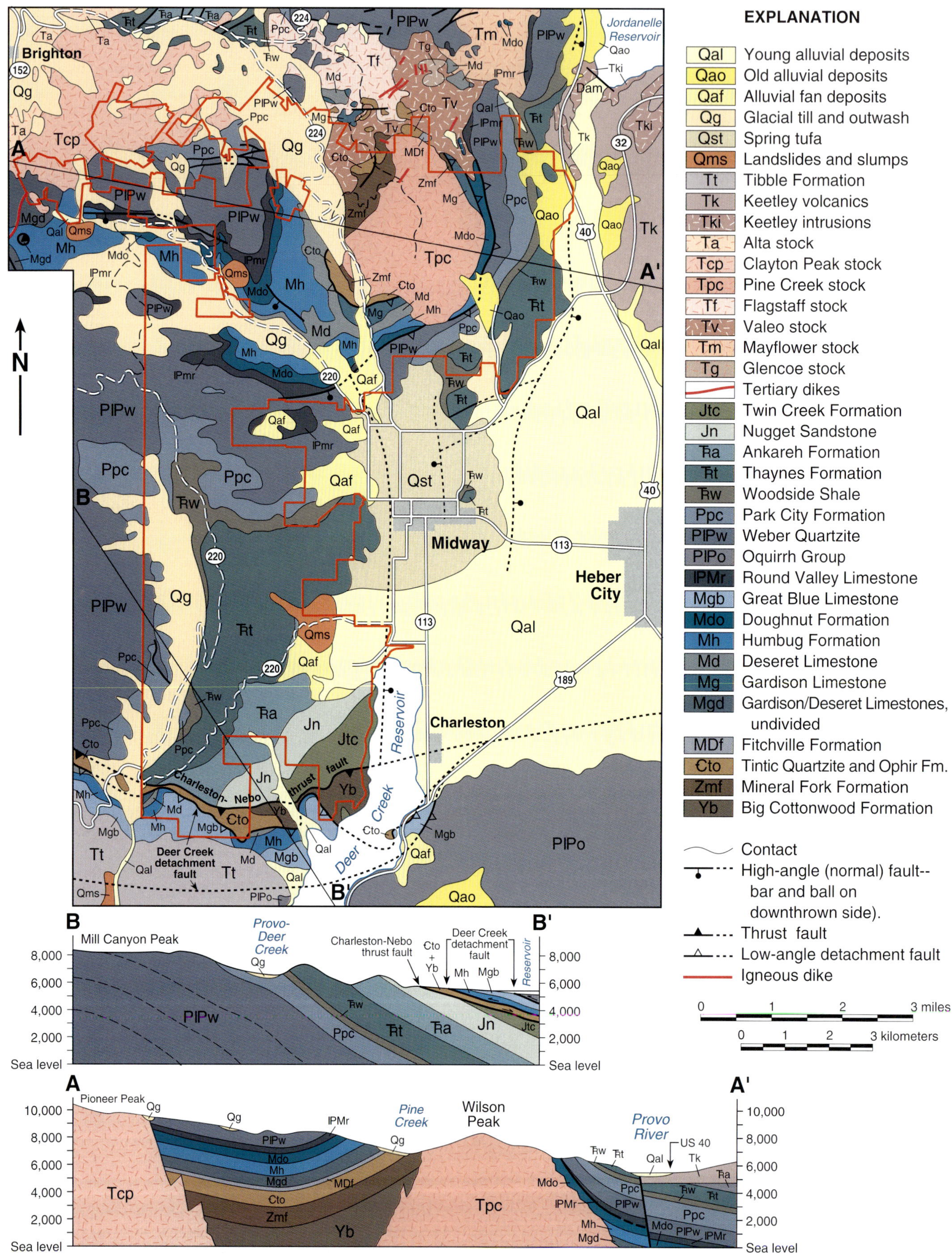

Figure 4. Geologic map of Wasatch Mountain State Park (heavy red line) and vicinity with cross sections (mapping compiled from Baker, 1964; Baker and others, 1966; Bromfield and others, 1970; Baker, 1976; Bryant, 1990; Bryant and others, 1992).

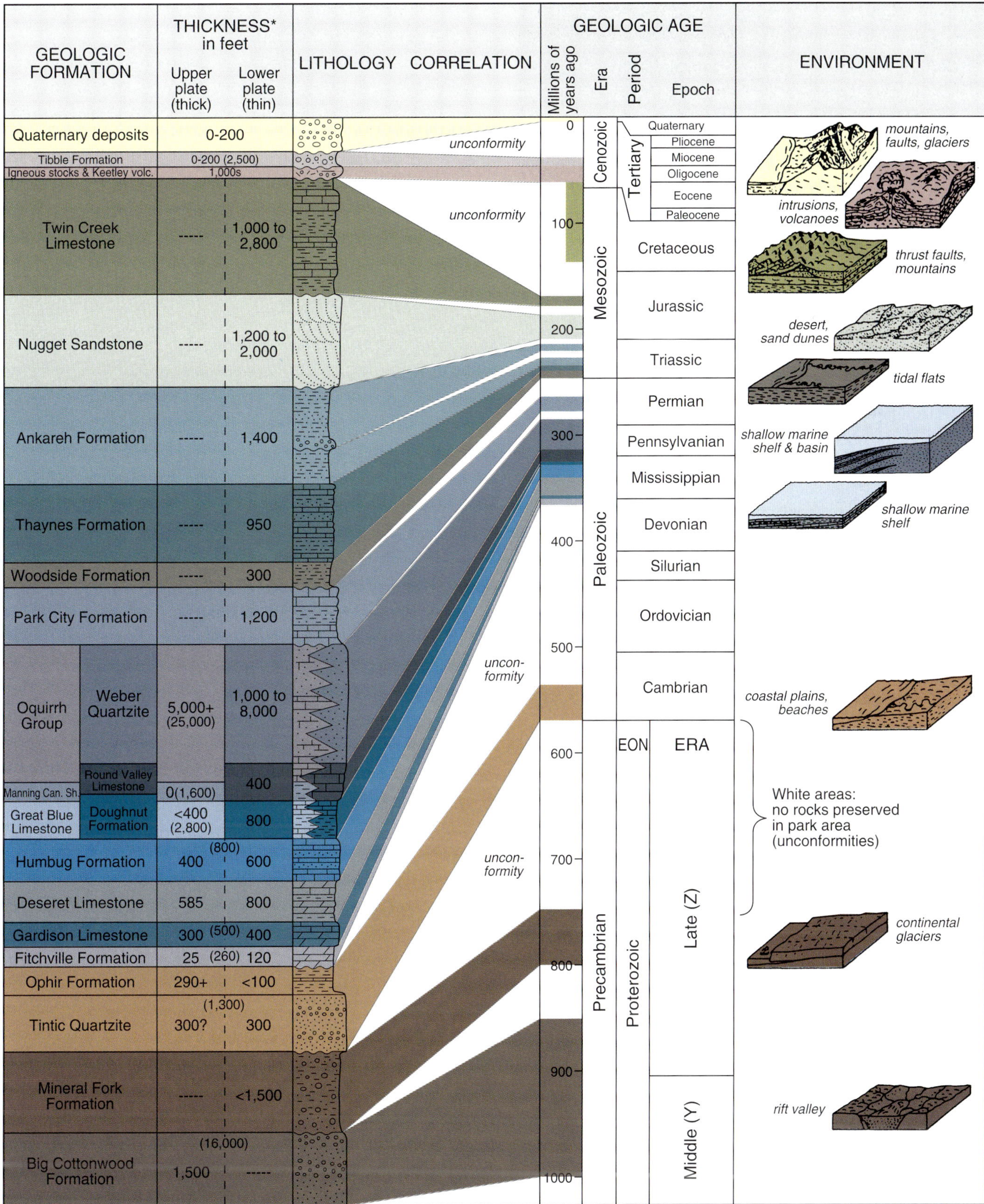

Figure 5. Stratigraphic column and correlation diagram showing time relationships and thicknesses of rocks found in Wasatch Mountain State Park. Major geologic events are also illustrated. Gaps in the time line (no color) represent times when rock either was never deposited, or was eroded away before deposition of overlying rock (after Willis and Willis, 1994).

Figure 6. The Late Proterozoic Mineral Fork Formation, which consists of debris dropped by melting glacial ice in a shallow ocean, is exposed in this slope. The slope is protected by a resistant conglomerate bed (the source of the boulder in the foreground).

generally had minor impact on the Tintic. Outcrops are mostly undeformed with only a few minor faults marked by slickensides and limited brecciation. Tintic Quartzite of the upper plate is exposed in southern WMSP where movement on the Charleston-Nebo thrust and the Deer Creek detachment faults intensely shattered and sheared it. The faulting cut out some of the stratigraphic sequence and distorted the rock, making it difficult to distinguish from the Big Cottonwood Formation; so, in some areas, Baker (1964) mapped these two units as undifferentiated.

Ophir Formation (upper and lower plates)

Ophir Formation of the lower plate consists of drab-olive to dark-green, micaceous, sandy shale with a few thin beds of micaceous quartzite. It is present in the Pine Creek Canyon area where it is faulted against Mississippi-an limestones. Ophir Formation of the upper plate consists of two units of olive-green micaceous shale and sandstone separated by a middle unit of gray limestone mottled brownish yellow on bedding planes (Baker, 1964). The rock is generally nonresistant and is rarely exposed. It is present in southern WMSP, near Cascade Springs, where it crops out discontinuously between the Charleston-Nebo thrust fault and the Deer Creek detachment.

Upper Devonian - Mississippian

Fitchville Formation (upper and lower plates)

The Upper Devonian - Lower Mississippian Fitchville Formation is light- to dark-gray, thin- to thick-bedded dolomite. It is exposed in small slivers in only two locales in WMSP: on the north edge of the Pine Creek intrusion (lower plate) and near Cascade Springs (upper plate). The upper plate section is brecciated by thrusting and contains numerous calcite-filled vugs.

Gardison Limestone (upper and lower plates)

The Lower Mississippian Gardison Limestone is medium- to dark-bluish-gray, thin- to thick-bedded, fossil-iferous limestone with interbedded tan to gray dolomite. In some areas it has black clastic dolomite at the base (Crittenden, 1959). The upper part of the Gardison is typically thin bedded with an abundant hash of broken Lower Mississippian brachiopods, gastropods, bryozoans, and corals; it is the most fossiliferous unit in WMSP.

Gardison Limestone of the lower plate is exposed along the northeast edge of the Pine Creek intrusion and in Pine Creek Canyon, where it is faulted against the Cambrian Tintic Quartzite. Along the edge of the intrusion, some of the formation is intensely brecciated and slightly metamorphosed (Road Log 3). In southern WMSP, the basal beds of the Gardison Limestone are faulted out and only the upper few hundred feet of the section is present on the upper plate (Baker, 1964).

Deseret Limestone (upper and lower plates)

The Middle Mississippian Deseret Limestone is light- to dark-gray, fine- to coarse-grained limestone and dolomite that contain abundant lenses and thin beds of chert. The limestone and dolomite weather dull brownish gray and the chert weathers black to brown. Deseret Limestone of the upper plate is exposed discontinuously above the Charleston-Nebo thrust fault near Cascade Springs. Deseret Limestone of the lower plate is exposed in Snake Creek and Pine Creek Canyons.

Humbug Formation (upper and lower plate)

The Middle to Upper Mississippian Humbug Formation consists of thin- to thick-bedded, light- to dark gray-, cherty limestone interbedded with tan- to buff-colored, limy or quartzitic sandstone. The interbedded buff sandstone and gray limestone gives outcrops of the Humbug a distinctive color and it is readily recognized even at a distance (Baker, 1964) (figure 7). The Humbug Formation of the lower plate is poorly exposed in Pine Creek and Snake Creek Canyons where it is typically covered with vegetation (see Road Log 4). The Humbug of the upper plate is poorly exposed in southern WMSP (Baker, 1964).

Great Blue Limestone (upper plate)

The Upper Mississippian Great Blue Limestone is dark-gray to black, thin-bedded limestone with some black limy shale beds and intermittent thin beds of fine-grained, dark-gray quartzitic sandstone. It is thick-facies rock carried on the upper plate of the Charleston-Nebo thrust fault into southern WMSP where only the lower few hundred feet of the formation is exposed.

Doughnut Formation (lower plate)

The Upper Mississippian Doughnut Formation is the thin-facies equivalent of the Great Blue Limestone (figure 5). The basal part of the Doughnut is black or greenish-

Figure 7. The Humbug Formation in a road cut in Snake Creek Canyon. The Humbug forms blocky outcrops of interbedded limestone and sandstone. This cyclical marine deposition may be related to global sea-level fluctuations.

black shale with some rusty weathering beds of gray limy sandstone; the upper part consists of dark- to medium-gray, thin-bedded limestone similar to the Great Blue Limestone. The Doughnut Formation is present in Snake Creek and Pine Creek Canyons, though vegetation and colluvium cover most of the beds. It is also found along the eastern edge of the Pine Creek intrusion contact zone where it is brecciated and slightly metamorphosed.

Upper Mississippian and Pennsylvanian

Round Valley Limestone (lower plate)

The Upper Mississippian to Lower Pennsylvanian Round Valley Limestone is pale-gray weathering, gray to dark-gray limestone with sparse orange, white, and black chert, interbedded with thin beds of shaly sandstone and fine-grained quartzite. Pale-reddish-orange silicified fossils are characteristic. It is locally exposed in Snake Creek Canyon, but is otherwise mostly covered by vegetation and colluvium.

Manning Canyon Shale (upper plate)

The Manning Canyon Shale is a "greasy" dark-gray to black organic shale that is responsible for the landslides that deform Highway 189 in Provo Canyon a few miles southwest of the park (Baker, 1964; Biek and others, 2000). It is not exposed in the park, but is probably present under the thin cover of the Tibble Formation (south WMSP) and is included on figure 5.

Pennsylvanian and Permian

Weber Quartzite (lower plate)

The Weber Quartzite consists mainly of pale-yellowish-gray to buff, cross-bedded quartzite and calcareous sandstone with a few cherty limestone beds. It is one of the most resistant units in the park, and forms many of the ridges. It is the primary host rock for vein deposits in the Park City mining district (John, 1997a). The lower part of the Weber is Middle Pennsylvanian and the upper part is probably Lower Permian; although lithologically similar, the two parts are likely separated by an unconformity (Bissell, 1962).

Oquirrh Group (upper plate)

The Oquirrh Group is a cyclic accumulation of sandstone and sandy limestone deposited in a rapidly subsiding basin. It is mostly equivalent to the Weber Quartzite of the lower plate (Baker, 1964). Although the Oquirrh is the dominant formation south of WMSP (Biek and others, 2000) and is included on figure 4, it is not exposed within park boundaries.

Permian

Park City Formation (lower plate)

The Lower Permian Park City Formation is gray to pinkish-gray cherty and fossiliferous limestone generally exposed as a ledgy slope. The limestone is separated into upper and lower members by a tongue of the Meade Peak Phosphatic Shale Member of the Phosphoria Formation (not mapped separately; Baker and others, 1966), which represents unusual deposition in a deep-water oxygen- and sediment-starved basin (Sheldon and others, 1967). The Park City Formation has a high organic content and is a petroleum source rock in other parts of the state (Maughan, 1979; Sprinkel, 1991). In this area the formation is the primary ore host rock for replacement deposits in the Park City mining district, and it may contain mineable quantities of phosphate (John, 1997a). Good outcrops are found along the Cummins Parkway near the western edge of the park.

Triassic

Woodside Formation (lower plate)

The Lower Triassic Woodside Formation consists of thin layers of interbedded brownish-red to purplish-red siltstone, shale, and fine-grained sandstone (figure 8). It forms poorly exposed slopes and strike valleys, and it is characterized by numerous ripple marks and a lack of fossils. Good outcrops of the Woodside are found along roads east and north of Cascade Springs.

Thaynes Formation (lower plate)

The Lower Triassic Thaynes Formation consists of interbedded limestone, sandstone, and shale (figure 8). The limestone is medium gray, weathers brown, and varies from thin bedded to massive with some sandy or cherty beds; the limy sandstone beds are light gray to buff; the shale beds are reddish brown or greenish gray, and some contain ripple marks. The Thaynes interfingers with the underlying Woodside Formation and represents the trans-

Figure 8. This classic example of a normal fault moved pale-brown limestone of the Thaynes Formation (right) down relative to reddish siltstone of the Woodside Formation (left). Limestone caught in the fault zone forms the white gouge zone. This roadcut is near Provo Deer Creek about 2 miles (3 km) north of Cascade Springs.

Figure 9. This boudinage (structurally deformed "ball" of rock) in the Twin Creek Limestone, near Deer Creek Reservoir, was shattered and shaped by movement on the closely overlying Charleston-Nebo thrust fault. In some areas near the reservoir, the Twin Creek forms the glide plane for the thrust.

gression of a shallow sea onto the tidal flats of the Woodside. The Thaynes Formation is well exposed east of Cascade Springs where it is involved in a large landslide complex (see Road Log 1).

Ankareh Formation (lower plate)

The Middle and Upper Triassic Ankareh Formation is divided into three members. The upper and lower members consist of repeated thin beds of reddish-brown to purplish-red sandy shale and sandstone, some with ripple marks; the lower unit has a few beds of massive sandstone. The middle member is a massive bed of coarse, sugary to quartzitic, light-colored conglomeratic sandstone about 35 feet (11 m) thick. An unconformity separates the middle and lower units. The Ankareh Formation is locally well-exposed north and east of Cascade Springs where it is involved in a large landslide complex along with the underlying Thaynes Formation.

Jurassic

Nugget Sandstone (lower plate)

The Lower Jurassic Nugget Sandstone consists of homogeneous, fine- to medium-grained, pale-grayish-orange, planar and cross-bedded sandstone deposited in a remarkably uniform sheet (Stokes, 1959). A few small dinosaur tracks have been found in the Nugget in quarries east of Heber. The Nugget is well exposed in southern WMSP near Soldier Hollow and in cuts for the Heber Valley Historic Railroad.

Twin Creek Limestone (lower plate)

The Middle Jurassic Twin Creek Limestone consists predominantly of gray, locally fossiliferous limestone with some interbedded grayish-green shale and thin-bedded siltstone. It typically weathers to a mass of small chips

and splinters. In some areas in and near WMSP, the Twin Creek forms the glide surface for the Charleston-Nebo thrust fault, which has deformed the formation and cut out the upper part (figure 9). It is exposed in southern WMSP in the Soldier Hollow area and near the railroad tracks on the west side of Deer Creek Reservoir.

Tertiary

Tertiary rocks exposed in WMSP include igneous rocks of the Wasatch igneous belt and the mostly non-volcanic Tibble Formation (Constenius, 1996; John and others, 1997; Presnell, 1997; Vogel and others, 1997).

Igneous Rocks

Four stocks (igneous intrusions generally up to a few miles across) and a few small dikes of the Wasatch igneous belt are locally well exposed in northern WMSP (Road Logs 2 and 3). Three other stocks (Alta, Mayflower, and Glencoe) and the Keetley Volcanics are located just outside park boundaries and are shown on figure 4. The stocks are mostly high-potassium, calc-alkaline granodiorites (granite-like rocks with less silica than in granite) that were likely derived from partial melting of the lower crust (Vogel and others, 1997; Presnell, 1997). Variations in chemical composition indicate each stock cooled from a separate magma and not from differentiation of a single magma body. The Keetley Volcanics are the extrusive equivalent of these stocks.

Most rocks of the Wasatch igneous belt were emplaced between 36.6 and 33.5 million years ago, although some age differences between individual stocks are not conclusively resolved (Vogel and others, 1997) (table 1). The portion of the stocks now exposed in the park cooled at depths of about 2 miles (3 km) below the surface (John, 1989).

Figure 10. Hand samples of the igneous stocks found in WMSP are characterized by variations in matrix and in phenocryst (crystal) assemblage: plagioclase (white rectangles), hornblende (dull black needles), biotite (generally shiny black flakes), quartz (glassy gray beads). (A) Pine Creek stock: abundant large plagioclase and less abundant biotite and hornblende phenocrysts imbedded in a fine-grained light-gray groundmass. The dark area (lower left) is an inclusion of country rock. (B) Flagstaff stock: abundant large plagioclase phenocrysts imbedded in a dark-green to black, fine-grained matrix. (C) Valeo stock (light-colored rock): unusually crystal-rich with abundant phenocrysts of plagioclase and lesser amounts of quartz, biotite, and hornblende imbedded in a fine-grained, medium- to dark-gray matix; dark-colored rock is a dike that cuts the Valeo. (D) Clayton Peak stock: light- to dark-gray, medium- to fine-grained, equigranular with small phenocrysts of plagioclase and scarcely visible phenocrysts of hornblende and biotite.

Table 1. Ages of igneous rocks in WMSP area (from Vogel and others, 1997; and Kurt Constenius, written communication, 2000).

Igneous Body	Probable age of emplacement (millions of years)
Clayton Peak stock	35.5 ± 1.5
Pine Creek stock	35.1 - 35.6
Flagstaff stock	33.5 - 36.6
Valeo stock	34.6 ± 1.6
Mayflower stock	33.5 - 36.6
Glencoe stock	33.5 - 36.6
Alta stock	35.0 ± 2.0
Keetley Volcanics	33.5 - 36.6

Pine Creek Stock: The Pine Creek stock is fine- to medium-grained granodiorite porphyry (61 - 63 weight percent SiO_2; John, 1997b). Visible phenocrysts include plagioclase crystals up to 0.5 inch (1 cm) long, less abundant 0.1-to-0.2 inch (0.25-0.5 cm) biotite crystals that appear as tiny "books" or as "pencils," and hornblende (figure 10a). The groundmass is fine-grained quartz and feldspar.

Flagstaff Stock: The Flagstaff stock is coarse-grained granodiorite porphyry (60 - 65 weight percent SiO_2) that contains 20 to 30 percent phenocrysts (John, 1997b) (figure 10b). In hand sample, the most distinctive characteristic of the Flagstaff is abundant large, white plagioclase phenocrysts, 0.1 to 0.5 inch (0.2-1.3 cm) in length, imbedded in a dark-green to black, fine-grained matrix (Baker and others, 1966). Less abundant phenocrysts include hornblende, biotite, and rare quartz. The Flagstaff is commonly altered and locally contains abundant epidote, chlorite, and sericite.

Valeo Stock: The Valeo stock is medium- to coarse-grained granodiorite porphyry (62-67 weight percent SiO_2)

(John, 1997b) that is unusually crystal-rich (30 - 50 volume percent phenocrysts), which makes it easy to identify in hand sample (figure 10c). Identifiable phenocrysts include coarse-grained white plagioclase 0.2 to 0.4 inch (0.5-1 cm) in length, prominent rounded quartz "eyes" 0.04 to 0.12 inch (0.1-0.3 cm) in diameter, biotite, and hornblende in a fine-grained groundmass (Bromfield and others, 1970). Weathered surfaces of the rock have a "vuggy" appearance because the plagioclase crystals readily weather out.

Clayton Peak Stock: The Clayton Peak stock mostly lies west of WMSP, but it is locally exposed in the park and is the source of much of the glacial debris in Pine Creek and Snake Creek Canyons. It is the oldest, most compositionally zoned, and internally varied stock in the Wasatch igneous belt (Presnell, 1997). It is fine- to medium-grained, equigranular to porphyritic, mafic (iron and manganese rich) granodiorite to monzodiorite (49 - 61 weight percent SiO_2) (John, 1997b) (figure 10d). In the park, most samples are dark gray with scarcely visible hornblende and biotite.

Intrusive Dikes: A few small dikes cut the rocks in northern WMSP (figure 4). The dikes vary in composition from lamprophyre on the mafic end to monzodiorite and granodiorite on the silicic end (Baker and others, 1966). The dikes are generally dark greenish gray to greenish black, and fine grained with hornblende and plagioclase phenocrysts. They range from a few feet to 10 feet (1-3 m) wide, and can be traced for a few tens to a few hundred feet. The dikes are typically covered by colluvium and generally weather similar to stocks they cut, so they are not very noticeable. They can be located by watching for darker colored float in areas where they are mapped.

Keetley Volcanics (and intrusions): The Keetley volcanics are not found in WMSP, but are exposed just a few feet outside the east park boundary, and they undoubtedly covered at least parts of the park at one time (figure 4). They form the easternmost extent of the Wasatch igneous belt. Though generally referred to as "volcanics," the Keetley includes several small stocks and dikes of rhyodacite porphyry, in addition to volcanic breccia and interlayered welded tuff of andesitic to rhyodacitic composition (Leveinen, 1994; Fehr, 1997).

Tibble Formation

The Tibble Formation forms a poorly exposed mantle over the low hills in southern WMSP. It is primarily cobble to boulder conglomerate with subrounded to subangular quartzite, andesite, and sandstone clasts. It is moderately to poorly cemented, and thus, is easily weathered. In the park, it is typically exposed as a cobble and small boulder lag in a sandy soil.

The Tibble Formation records the development of half-grabens that formed during middle Tertiary extension (Constenius, 1998). Datable volcanic clasts and ash, and progressive levels of deformation within the deposits, provide good constraints on timing of the extension: (1) the

Figure 11. A shallow wash cut into bedrock of the Woodside Formation near Provo-Deer Creek is filled with thick colluvium. White caliche has accumulated in spaces around the rubble and in fractures in the bedrock.

lower part of the Tibble contains no volcanic clasts and is older than 36.6 million years; (2) a volcanic ash in the next interval is 36.4 ± 0.2 million years old; (3) the upper part contains clasts of Keetley volcanics that are 33 to 36 million years old; (4) the Tibble is overlain with angular unconformity by another conglomerate (not present in the park) with volcanic clasts about 28 million years old (Constenius, 1998). These younger rocks are tilted about half as much as the Tibble Formation, indicating that most early extension ended about 28 million years ago.

Quaternary Surficial Deposits

Alluvium

Alluvium is present in the larger canyons and washes and in Heber Valley. It consists of moderately to well-sorted mud to boulder material deposited by streams and washes. It ranges from silt, sand, and well-sorted gravel in parts of Heber Valley, to moderately sorted cobble and boulder alluvium in the upper canyons.

Two distinct ages of alluvium are present in the park. Young alluvium (Holocene) consists of post-glacial deposits in active channels or stranded at low levels (generally less than 30 feet [9 m]) above the active streams. Older alluvium, found in the Jordanelle-Dutch Hollow area, caps dissected benches and terraces about 150 feet (45 m) above active streams and the valley floor. It is distinguished, where exposed in fresh cuts, by a thick soil profile that includes a well-developed caliche zone (stage IV to stage V of Birkeland and others, 1991). The advanced stage of the caliche, which appears as white or pale-gray chalky limestone, suggests an early to middle Pleistocene age for the older alluvium.

Colluvium

Colluvium is ubiquitous throughout WMSP, and if mapped, would obscure most other map relationships. Therefore, it is not shown on figure 4, and is shown only to

Figure 12. This large tufa mound is 55 feet (16 m) high and is part of an extensive accumulation of calcareous spring deposits in the Midway area. This mound once overflowed with hot, calcium-enriched spring water. Now the spring feeds a large, warm-water-filled cavern under the mound.

Figure 13. Several glacial features can be seen in this view of the upper part of Pine Creek Canyon: a glacial pond (historically enhanced) near the center of the photo, the sharp drop off to the left of the pond marks a terminal moraine (temporary front edge of the glacier), the hummocky terrain is deposits of glacial debris, and the sharp peaks in the background were shaped by glaciers plucking rocks from their slopes.

a limited extent on detailed geologic maps of the area (Baker, 1964; 1976; Baker and others, 1966; Bromfield and others, 1970). The colluvium is a generally thin mantle of weathered bedrock, slope wash, windblown silt and loess, small landslides, and slope creep deposits (figure 11). It is most extensive on north-facing slopes where increased moisture accelerates weathering.

Hot Spring Tufa Deposits

Western Heber Valley, near WMSP headquarters, contains the largest concentration of hot spring tufa deposits in the state. The deposits consist primarily of calcareous tufa in platforms or in hollow mounds and cones (craters) (figure 12). The tufa is pale-grayish-yellow, soft, porous rock that is extremely vuggy, giving it the appearance of a coarse sponge. The spring deposits are locally at least 200 feet (60 m) thick and cover about 4.5 square miles (11 km^2) (Bromfield and others, 1970; Kohler, 1979; Mayo and Loucks, 1995). Because the tufa is abundant, many older homes and buildings in Midway are constructed from tufa "bricks." The extensive deposits suggest that the hot springs have been active for hundreds of thousands to millions of years.

Glacial Deposits

Glacial deposits and erosional features are common in the upper parts of WMSP (figure 13). The deposits consist mostly of till in moraines, and of alluvial outwash on, between, and downstream of the moraines. The moraines consist of an extremely poorly sorted mixture of angular rubble to rock flour. Boulders in the rubble are up to 50 feet (15 m) across, and were carried down the canyons from outcrops 2 to 3 miles (3-5 km) away (figure 14). The main moraines are in the Bonanza Flat/Pine Creek Canyon area and in Snake Creek Canyon. The outwash consists of moderately sorted mud, silt, sand, and poorly

Figure 14. This megaboulder of Clayton Peak stock was transported by a glacier about 2 miles (3.5 km) down Pine Creek Canyon from its source near Clayton Peak.

to moderately rounded cobbles and small boulders.

Most glacial deposits in the park are indistinct. A large glacial deposit shown on figure 4 in Provo Deer Creek is mostly outwash with some moraine material; and many deposits mapped as alluvium and alluvial fans are composed partially of glacial outwash. It is difficult to tell how far glaciers advanced down the canyons, but they probably extended to near the upper end of the golf course in Snake Creek Canyon and to near the lowermost outcrop of the Pine Creek stock in Pine Creek Canyon. The glacial deposits were emplaced primarily 30,000 to 12,000 years ago during the latest glacial epic (called Pinedale Glaciation in this area) (Madole, 1986). Previous glacial epics probably also affected the park, but deposits tied to these events were obscured or reworked by the latest glaciation, and have not been recognized.

Figure 15. These beds of the Ankareh Formation exposed along State Route 220 east of Cascade Springs were deformed and tilted during landslide movement. The Ankareh and the underlying Thaynes Formations form a large landslide complex on the eastern side of the ridge east of Provo Deer Creek.

Mass-Movement Deposits

Mass-movements are common in WMSP. They are of two general types: (1) landslides, slumps, and slope creep that involve surficial deposits (mostly colluvium); and (2) landslides and slumps that involve bedrock. Only the larger and more continuous mass movements are shown on the geologic map (figure 4). Mass-movement features are recognized by hummocky surfaces, non-sorted rubble with chaotic angular blocks, and open or partially healed fractures and scarps. The timing of last movement for most slumps and landslides in the park probably ranges from the last glacial episode to recent times. Some landslides are active today (Klauk and Mulvey, 1987).

One interesting mass-movement is in southern WMSP on the eastern side of the ridge east of Provo Deer Creek. In that area, the Thaynes and Ankareh Formations are tilted 20 to 35 degrees east to southeast, and they consist of competent beds of sandstone and limestone interbedded with incompetent beds of mudstone and shale—an ideal situation for bedding-plane sliding. The bedrock has slid in many areas, forming surficial folds, duplicated beds, tilted and displaced beds, and brecciation (figure 15). The extent of the slide complex is not known and it is not shown on the geologic map (figure 4) but the deformation is well exposed in road cuts and outcrops along State Route 220 between Midway and Cascade Springs (Road Log 1).

GEOLOGIC HISTORY AND STRUCTURE

Earth's rocks record over 4 billion years of geologic changes. Rocks found in Wasatch Mountain State Park (WMSP) span almost one billion of those years, and reveal an intriguing geologic story of environmental variation and structural deformation. The park lies near the junc-

tion of several major geologic structures, and jointed, shattered, and brecciated rocks chronicle the park's tumultuous past and the forces exerted along major faults and intrusions.

Late Archean to Middle Proterozoic – Building the North American Continent

Although the oldest rocks exposed in WMSP are only about a billion years old, the geologic history of the park goes back about 2.6 billion years to the Late Archean. At that time, North America was much smaller than it is now, and most of the western United States, including the southern two thirds of Utah, did not exist. The northern third of Utah was part of the Wyoming province, a segment of the ancient continental core of North America. The Wyoming province consists of at least 2.6 billion-year-old metamorphic rock, and its sedimentary protolith (parent rock) may be more than 3 billion years old (Bryant, 1988). The park area was near the western and southern edges of the Wyoming province (and thus on the edge of North America).

About 1.7 billion years ago, rocks of the Proterozoic (2.2 to 1.7 billion year old) Mojave and Yavapai provinces collided with and were sutured to the Wyoming province (figure 16). The collisions formed the Cheyenne belt, a zone of weakly welded crust that underlies the park and stretches eastward into Wyoming and westward into Nevada (Condie, 1987; Houston and others, 1989; Presnell, 1997). The Cheyenne belt consists of intensely sheared rock that is altered to weaker rocks and minerals, and is cut by large-scale thrust and strike-slip faults. Because of its structural weakness, later tectonic stresses applied to western North America concentrated deformation along the Cheyenne belt, influencing the development of several major geologic features seen in the park: the Uinta trough (an intracontinental Proterozoic rift), the Charleston-Nebo thrust fault, the Deer Creek detachment fault, the Uinta Mountain uplift, the Cottonwood arch, the Wasatch igneous belt, and the Park City mining district (figure 3).

After the collisions between the oceanic Mojave/Yavapai provinces and the cratonic Wyoming province, North America was much bigger than before and included all of Utah. Later collisions further increased the size of North America and by 1 billion years ago it was the central part of the supercontinent Rodinia, which included Australia and Antarctica as its western part (Dalziel and others, 1997; Unrug, 1997; Karlstrom and others, 1999) (figure 16).

Late Proterozoic – Rifting and Glaciation

The oldest rock exposed in WMSP was deposited 1,000 to 850 million years ago as intracontinental extension within Rodinia opened an east-west-trending rift (aulocogen or fault-bounded valley) along the pre-existing weakness of the Cheyenne belt (Karlstrom and others, 1999).

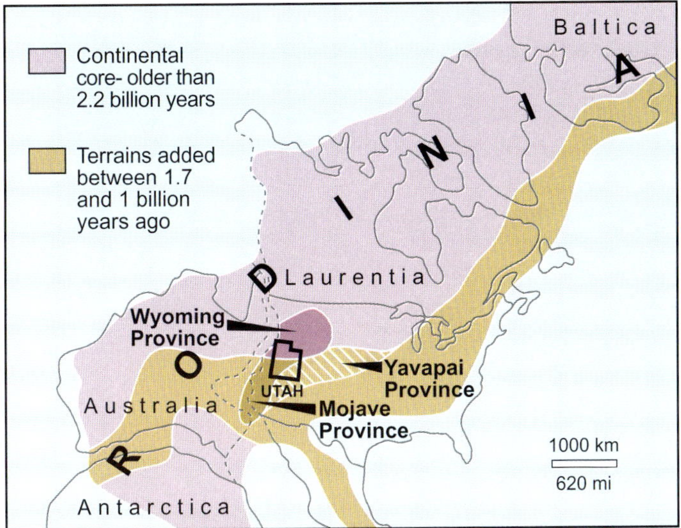

Figure 16. The supercontinent Rodinia formed between 1.7 and 1 billion years ago. It included Laurentia (North America), Australia, Antarctica, Greenland, and Baltica (northern Europe). Wasatch Mountain State Park straddles a 1.7-billion-year-old suture zone (the Cheyenne belt) that formed when the Yavapai and Mojave Provinces were accreted to the Archean Wyoming Province. Breakup of Rodinia occurred in the Late Proterozoic when Australia and Antarctica rifted away from Laurentia. The north-south rift (dashed lines) cut through present-day central Nevada and created a broad zone of attenuated and weakened crust that reached into central Utah. The eastern edge of the attenuated crust is marked by the Utah hinge line. Modified from Karlstrom and others, 1999.

The rift, called the Uinta trough, extended from west of what is now Salt Lake City, through WMSP, to the eastern end of the Uinta Mountains. As the rift deepened and widened, it filled with thousands of feet of coarse to fine debris deposited in marginal marine to terrestrial environments (the Big Cottonwood Formation and the equivalent Uinta Mountain Group). The rift was aborted before it split the continents apart.

Between 800 and 750 million years ago, North America, still part of Rodinia, underwent two or more episodes of glaciation (Christie-Blick, 1983; Crittenden and others, 1983). The Mineral Fork Formation records at least one of these glacial periods (figures 5 and 6). It was deposited as ice from continental glaciers melted in a shallow ocean, dropping loads of poorly sorted sediment.

About 725 million years ago, Rodinia began to break apart as a north-south-trending rift opened through present-day central Nevada, and Australia and Antarctica tore away from North America (Unrug, 1997; Karlstrom and others, 1999). The effects of the rifting were felt in a broad zone of attenuated (thinned) crust that reached as far inland as central Utah. The boundary between the unstable attenuated crust and the stable continent is called the Utah hinge line. West of the hinge line, the attenuated crust formed a broad subsiding marine basin that affected depositional patterns from the time of its formation into the early Mesozoic. East of the hinge line was the stable continental shelf. The area that is now WMSP was just east of

the hinge line on the shelf (figure 3).

No rocks of the latest Precambrian are present in the park; they were probably stripped off by erosion near the end of the Proterozoic. It is likely that during this time, WMSP was part of a low-relief continental shelf and North America was moving slowly toward the equator.

Paleozoic – Shallow Seas and Subsiding Basins

The Paleozoic marks a time when plant and animal life began to thrive and diversify, evolving from simple marine organisms to complex plants and animals. Fossils and rocks indicate that during this time, the park area lay near the equator, and was at or below sea level.

During much of the Paleozoic, Utah was tectonically quiet. To the west, somewhere near present-day western California, tectonic activity was concentrated along a subduction zone (Scotese, 2000). East of this subduction zone, in present-day Nevada and western Utah, the broad subsiding basin, which formed during the late Proterozoic breakup of Rodinia, accumulated tremendous thicknesses of shallow marine limestones, dolomites and shales (thick facies).

Just east of the hinge line, on the stable continental shelf, Paleozoic sedimentary deposits in the WMSP area are comparatively thin (thin facies) and record many different environments and events. Lower and Middle Cambrian thin-facies sediments were deposited in beach and coastal plain to shallow marine settings (Tintic Quartzite and Ophir Formation) (figure 5). Upper Cambrian to Middle Devonian deposits are not present in the park; they were eroded during the Devonian, indicating a period of regional uplift. Above the Devonian unconformity, Upper Devonian and Lower Mississippian shallow marine strata record incursions of the sea onto the continental shelf, including the most widespread shallow marine incursion in Utah (Gardison Limestone) (Sandberg and others, 1982; Hintze, 1993). Upper Mississippian interbedded sandstones and limestones (Humbug Formation) record cyclic marine sedimentation that may have been related to sea-level fluctuations caused by glaciation in high-latitude areas of the world (Veevers and Powell, 1987) (figure 7).

During the Pennsylvanian and Permian, a unique, fault-bounded ocean basin formed in the Oquirrh Mountains area west of Salt Lake City (Bissell, 1962; Welsh and Bissell, 1979). This basin deepened rapidly and collected over 25,000 feet (7,600 m) of sediments shed from ancient mountains to the southeast and west (the Ancestral Rockies and the Antler orogenic belt). The park was near the edge of this basin, and the well-sorted quartz sands of the Weber Quartzite were deposited on a shelf and slope that bordered the basin, as evidenced by a dramatic thickening of the Weber across the width of the park (Koelmel, 1986). The Paleozoic ended with another incursion of the sea onto the stable continent as recorded by the Park City Formation.

Mesozoic – Deserts and Mountains

Early Mesozoic – Time for a Change

Early in the Triassic, deposition in Utah was still affected by the Utah hinge line. Western Utah continued its long history as a subsiding shallow marine basin, and eastern Utah continued as part of the flat continental shelf. In the park, the Woodside, Thaynes, and lower Ankareh Formations were deposited on tidal flats and in warm, shallow seas on the continental shelf (Blakey and Gubitosa, 1993). Lithologic changes within the formations (from limestone to sandstone or shale) record subtle fluctuations in sea level and variations in the influx of sediments from the east.

By the Late Triassic, however, a major change occurred. North America began to move westward, colliding with the dense, oceanic Farallon plate, which plunged beneath the lighter continent. The results were immediate and dramatic. The collision faulted and deformed the western continental margin, forming a chain of large mountains and volcanoes in Arizona and California. In Utah, environments changed from marine to mostly terrestrial, and Upper Triassic rocks (middle and upper Ankareh Formation) deposited in river and lake environments contain much more volcanic ash than older deposits – a distant influence of the volcanoes.

During the Late Triassic and Early Jurassic, North America gradually moved northward into the hot, dry trade winds belt. In addition, the newly formed western mountains blocked most coastal precipitation. Consequently, the climate changed from tropical to desert conditions, and by the Early Jurassic, a huge, sandy desert spread across Utah and surrounding states, depositing the Nugget and Navajo (in southern Utah) Sandstones (Kocurek and Dott, 1983).

Late Mesozoic – Sevier Mountain Building and Thrust Faults

One of the most dramatic events in Utah's geologic history was an episode of intense mountain building during the latest Jurassic to early Tertiary (figure 5). As subduction of the Farallon plate continued, the zone of structural deformation migrated eastward into Utah. In the deformation zone, which reached from Mexico to Alaska, immense sheets of rock were folded, buckled, and thrust several miles eastward over younger rock (Royse and others, 1975; Coogan, 1992).

In the Utah area, this great mountain-building event is known as the Sevier orogeny (from the Greek "oro" [mountain] and "gen" [building]); it is named after the Sevier River region in central Utah. The Sevier orogeny holds economic interest because oil and gas are trapped in many folds that formed near the front of the thrust sheets about 40 miles (60 km) northeast of the park. Effects of Sevier deformation were felt in Utah as early as the Middle Jurassic with the development of a broad back-bulge basin

(a very shallow basin commonly formed far to the front of thrust faulting) (DeCelles, 1984; Willis, 1999). The Twin Creek Limestone was deposited in a shallow sea that occupied this basin, which extended from arctic Canada to northern Arizona (Imlay, 1980; Kocurek and Dott, 1983).

During the Cretaceous, compression associated with the Sevier thrust belt migrated eastward into Utah. As it did so, the back-bulge basin also migrated eastward, to be replaced by a forebulge high (a broad area of slow erosion to minor deposition) and then by a foredeep marine basin (a much deeper basin directly in front of the thrust belt) (Willis, 1999). Upper Jurassic and Cretaceous strata in eastern Utah were deposited in the foredeep marine basin and in a variety of terrestrial settings around the basin. (Rock of this age has been eroded from the park, but it is preserved in nearby areas.) During the Cretaceous, the land lifted enough that the seas receded eastward toward the low relief interior of the continent and debris shed from the Sevier orogenic belt accumulated in thick conglomeratic wedges; this was the last time the park would be "ocean-front" property.

Starting in the middle Cretaceous (about 100 million years ago) and continuing until the Late Eocene (about 40 million years ago), the Charleston-Nebo thrust fault transported rock eastward, eventually reaching southern WMSP (Constenius, 1998) (figure 17). The fault transported a slice of rock about 50,000 feet (15,000 m) thick approximately 25 miles (40 km) eastward, stacking older strata on top of younger strata (Levy and Christie-Blick, 1989). In the park, only the lower few hundred feet of this immense thrust sheet is preserved. However, to the west and south, Mt. Timpanogos and Mt. Nebo preserve huge sections of the upper plate. This fault is named the Charleston-Nebo thrust fault because remnants of its upper plate are found from Charleston (near WMSP) to Mt. Nebo 50 miles (80 km) to the south.

West of WMSP, the Charleston-Nebo thrust rides primarily on thick middle and upper Paleozoic beds of the lower plate. But as thrusting encountered thinner rock east of the Utah hinge line, the thrust plane tended to ramp upward. Thus in the park, we see Middle Proterozoic Big Cottonwood Formation and Cambrian Tintic Quartzite (upper plate) ramping up and over Mesozoic lower plate strata (figure 4 cross section B-B' and figure 17). In the park, the thrust fault itself is poorly exposed because rocks near the fault (both upper and lower plate) are intensely shattered, and therefore weather easily and are covered by colluvium.

Though evidence is unclear, a second, lower-level thrust fault may have displaced lower plate rocks in the park a comparatively short distance 85 to 60 million years ago (DeCelles, 1994; Coogan, 1992). This thrust fault may be a southern extension of the Absaroka thrust system, which extends into Utah from southwestern Wyoming (J.C. Coogan, verbal communication, 1999). The extension of the fault into WMSP is uncertain because exposures are poor and fault relationships are covered by Tertiary ig-

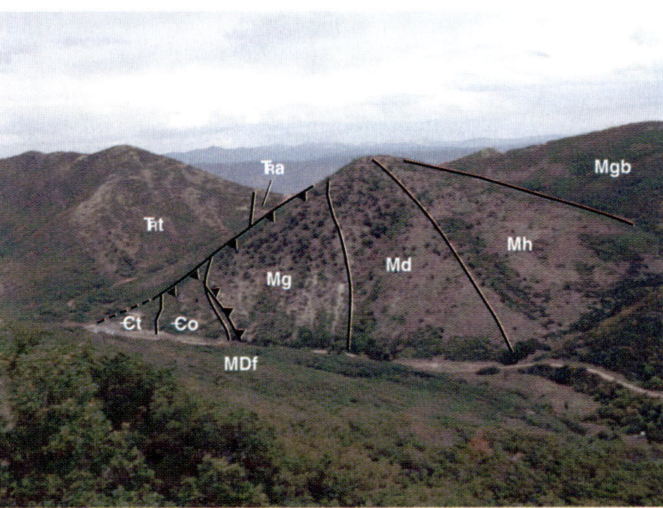

Figure 17. The Charleston-Nebo thrust fault (long barbed line) and the Deer Creek detachment fault (short barbed line) cut through this slope east of Cascade Springs. Formations that were transported eastward on the upper plate of the thrust fault: Big Cottonwood Formation (Yb), Tintic Quartzite (Ct), Ophir Shale (Co), Fitchville Formation (MDf), Gardison Limestone (Mg); Deseret Limestone (Md), Humbug Formation (Mh), and the Great Blue Limestone (Mgb). Formations that are on the lower plate of the thrust: Thaynes (Rt) and Ankareh (Ra) Formations.

neous rocks and valley fill. Folds in lower plate strata provide indirect evidence for the thrusting. Such folds form a broad northwest-trending syncline (structural saddle) near Middle Mountain, a northwest-trending anticline and a north-trending syncline north of Snake Creek Canyon, and smaller secondary folds throughout the park (Baker, 1964; Baker and others, 1966). These folds may also be related to later deformation.

Cenozoic – Mountains, Intrusions, and Glaciers

Early Tertiary – Laramide Mountain Building

Near the start of the Cenozoic era (65 million years ago), compressional deformation extended eastward from the park and the subduction angle of the Farallon plate lessened. As a result, the style of thrust faulting gradually changed (Coogan, 1992; Willis, 1999). Rocks west of the Utah hinge line lent themselves to "thin-skinned thrusting" in which plates "peeled off" and slid up and over adjacent rock. Rocks of the stable continent east of the hinge line were not conducive to this type of deformation. Instead crystalline basement and overlying stratified rock responded to compression as a single unit, producing basement-cored uplifts bounded by high-angle reverse faults. This different style of deformation is called the Laramide orogeny (after the Laramie Mountains in Wyoming). Generally, these uplifts took advantage of preexisting weaknesses in the basement rock. Most Laramide structures in the Utah-Colorado-Wyoming area trend roughly north-south because compressional stresses were directed mostly east-west (examples in Utah include the San Rafael

Swell, Waterpocket Fold, and Monument upwarp). The Uinta Mountains uplift and the related Cottonwood arch are Laramide-type structures that trend east-west because they pushed up along the weak Cheyenne belt. The park sits on the tilted southeastern flank of the Cottonwood arch uplift, and rocks in the park generally dip east to southeast, with some local overprinting by smaller folds (Bryant, 1992). The arch is separated from the Uinta Mountains uplift by a syncline just east of the park.

Middle Tertiary – Extension and Intrusions

Early Extension – the Deer Creek detachment: In the park, the Sevier and Laramide orogenies ended about 40 million years ago as compression waned and east-northeast extension began (Constenius, 1998). The reasons for the switch from compression to extension are not fully understood, but they are attributed to complex tectonics as the North American plate overrode the trailing end of the shallow subducting Farallon plate (Severinghaus and Atwater, 1990; Rowley, 1998). The extension allowed thrust-faulted terrain, which stood as topographic highs, to structurally "relax" and slide back to the west along low-angle normal faults (Vogel and others, 1997). These faults mostly parallel bedding planes and placed younger rock over older rock, cutting out some intervening strata (the opposite of thrust faults).

The largest low-angle normal fault in the park is the Deer Creek detachment. Movement on the detachment occurred 40 to 20 million years ago as the upper plate of the Charleston-Nebo thrust slid 3 to 4.5 miles (5-7 km) back to the west (Constenius, 1998). The detachment fault forms two main splays in southern WMSP, and roughly parallels the plane of the original thrust (figure 4 cross section B-B' and figure 17). One splay places Mississippian strata on Cambrian strata, and one places Pennsylvanian strata on Mississippian strata (Baker, 1964). Rocks caught between these splays and the nearby Charleston-Nebo thrust are shattered and highly deformed.

As the Charleston-Nebo thrust plate slid back to the west, fault-bounded grabens, half-grabens, and other extensional depressions formed on its upper surface. Some of the grabens collected synorogenic sediment eroded from nearby sources. As the grabens continued to develop, older sediments were tilted and deformed, then overlain by younger sediment. Thus, the sediments collected in the grabens contain a record of fault activity and are critical to unraveling the structural history of the area. The Tibble Formation, near the southern boundary of the park, is one of these synorogenic deposits (Constenius, 1998). Datable volcanic clasts and ash within the Tibble Formation indicate the early extension began before 36.6 million years ago and was mostly over by 28 million years ago.

Intrusions and ore deposits – the Wasatch igneous belt: During Sevier and Laramide compression, the crust thickened significantly along the Cheyenne belt and isostatically sagged downward into the upper mantle. A hot, thick

Figure 18.   View across Snake Creek and Pine Creek Canyons northeast to Wilson Peak. The peak is composed of the Pine Creek stock of the Wasatch igneous belt. The hill in the middle distance is mostly Mississippian Deseret and Humbug Formations domed up by the intrusion.

crustal welt developed in the lower crust as a kind of "shadow" of the uplifted Uinta Mountains and Cottonwood arch (Cook and others, 1989; Constenius, 1998). Later, as compressional forces were released and the Charleston-Nebo thrust plate slid back to the west, the reduced crustal load allowed isostatic rebound and decompression melting of the thickened lower crust. Magma, derived from the partially melted lower crust, moved upward, forming intrusive stocks and dikes, and volcanoes – the Eocene to Oligocene Wasatch igneous belt (Presnell, 1997; Vogel and others, 1997) (figures 3 and 10). Most of the magma in the Wasatch igneous belt cooled and solidified before it reached the surface, forming a line of granite-like stocks that stretch from the Wasatch front through northern WMSP (figure 18). Some of the magma found avenues to the surface, forming volcanoes that vented great volumes of hot ash and lava in eruptions that were much larger than the 1980 Mount St. Helens eruption. Volcanic deposits from these eruptions probably once overlay all the intrusions in the park, but have since eroded away. The Keetley Volcanics, which collected in a structural saddle between the Cottonwood arch and the Uinta Mountains uplift, are the only preserved volcanic deposits of the Wasatch igneous belt near the park. They are the likely extrusive equivalent of the stocks in WMSP and of other chemically similar stocks in the area (Vogel and others, 1997).

Several structures in the sedimentary strata surrounding the stocks record the effects of the intruding magma. Paleozoic carbonates around the edges of the stocks are typically highly brecciated, silicified, and slightly metamorphosed, with fractures healed by secondary quartz. East of Pine Creek Canyon, strata are folded into a broad dome centered around the Pine Creek stock. Small normal faults (both low-angle and high-angle) and small sub-

sidiary folds are found near all the stocks (figure 4). The low-angle normal faults are likely related to the forced doming and resultant gravity sliding of strata as the magma moved upward. The high-angle normal faults probably formed in steps simultaneous with intrusion to make room for the rising magma (Vogel and others, 1997).

The intrusions of the Wasatch igneous belt played an important part in the park's recent history as they are responsible for silver, lead, zinc, copper, and gold mineralization in the Park City and Snake Creek Canyon mining districts. Most of the ore occurs in northeast-trending zones in which ore-bearing fluids associated with the intrusions replaced Paleozoic carbonates fractured during earlier structural deformation (Presnell, 1997).

Late Tertiary to Quaternary – Extension and Uplift, Glaciers and Hot Springs

<u>Uplift and late extension – the Wasatch Range and Heber Valley:</u> About 17 million years ago (Miocene), the North American plate overrode the subducting East Pacific Rise (a spreading center and transform fault zone) and the western U.S. began to pull away from the rest of the continent, accelerating and changing the direction of earlier extension (Hamilton and Myers, 1966; Bryant and others, 1989; Severinghaus and Atwater, 1990). As a result, Utah was now stretching and continuing to rise. West of the hinge line, where the underlying rocks are hot and weak, the region stretched and fractured, forming a series of parallel mountains and valleys that are bounded by high-angle normal faults – the Basin and Range Province. Eastern Nevada and western Utah are dominated by many such mountain ranges and basins that formed during late Cenozoic extension (which continues today). East of the hinge line, where the rock is cooler and stronger, early and late Cenozoic regional uplift created the Middle Rocky Mountains and Colorado Plateau physiographic provinces. The park lies on the east flank of the east-tilted Wasatch Range at the boundary between the Basin and Range and the Middle Rocky Mountains Provinces. The Wasatch fault, which bounds the west side of the Wasatch Range and is about 15 miles (24 km) west of the park, is one of the most active faults in the mountain west (Machette and others, 1992). Uplift on the fault has helped shape the park's rugged mountains and canyons.

To estimate offset on the Wasatch fault, Naeser and others (1983) and John (1989) used the early Tertiary igneous stocks in and near WMSP. Microscopic inclusions in the stocks indicate that rocks now exposed at the tops of the mountains cooled at depths that systematically vary from about 36,000 feet (11,000 m) on the west side of the Wasatch Range near Salt Lake City to 3,200 feet (1000 m) on the east side. This means that since the intrusions cooled, rocks exposed in the west part of the range have been elevated almost 7 miles (11 km), and the upper parts of the stocks and overlying sedimentary rock have been eroded away. Constenius (1998) showed that not all

36,000 feet (11,000 m) of uplift was due to movement on the Wasatch fault as surmised by earlier workers. He attributed some of the uplift to localized isostatic rebound of the Cottonwood arch. Also some of the uplift is due to regional uplift of the entire intermountain west.

Heber Valley likely formed in the last 10 million years as late Tertiary to Quaternary extension stepped east of the Wasatch fault. The valley is a half-graben or "trap-door" basin flanked by potentially active down-to-the-east faults on the west side and down-to-the-north faults on the south side (Hecker, 1993) (figure 4). The valley is filled with up to 790 feet (240 m) of sediment (Peterson, 1970; Biek and others, 2000).

The precise locations of the faults that bound Heber Valley are not well constrained, but are inferred on geologic maps of the area (Bromfield and others, 1970; Baker, 1976; Bryant, 1992) (figure 4). One down-to-the-east fault probably parallels the east side of the park between Deer Creek Reservoir and the Visitor Center. Another down-to-the-east fault may roughly parallel the Provo River on the northeast side of the park. These faults are up to 10 miles (16 km) long. Amount of displacement along the faults is unknown but is estimated at between several hundred and a few thousand feet, and is probably greatest near the southwest corner of Heber Valley. The faults developed sometime in the last several million years, with little evidence to indicate more precisely when movement on them first occurred or when they were most active. No faulted surficial deposits or even subdued fault scarps have been identified in Heber Valley – evidence that the latest ground rupture along the faults occurred at least several thousand years ago, and that recurrence intervals are on the order of tens of thousands of years (Hecker, 1993). Even though little is known about these faults, they are potentially active and could produce damaging earthquakes.

Hot Springs: Faults along the west side of Heber Valley are the conduits along which hot water of the Midway thermal system moves. This extensive system of hot springs has probably been active for over a million years, depositing thick layers and mounds of calcareous tufa. Mayo and Loucks (1995) indicated that thermal water in the active springs has average discharge temperatures of 90 to 115°F (31.2-45.5°C). They proposed a model for the hot springs in which precipitation in the Wasatch Range circulates down through open fractures in calcareous rocks to a depth of 1.2 to 1.5 miles (2-2.5 km). At this depth, rocks are hot due to the earth's geothermal gradient. (The temperature in the subsurface increases naturally with depth; in the Wasatch Range area it increases at a rate of about 95°F per mile [35°C/km] [Blackwell and Steele, 1992], which is why deep mines are so hot.) Most ground water in the Heber Valley area remains within 600 feet (200 m) of the ground surface where it stays cool (about 55°F [12°C]) (Blackwell and Steele, 1992). Beneath Midway the deeply circulating hot water intersects a fault system, and rapidly rises along fault-related fractures. Near the sur-

face, the hot water mixes with upper-surface ground water and cools slightly before it discharges from the springs. Mayo and Loucks (1995) also pointed out that the water is most likely not heated by circulation near a shallow, warm igneous body, as postulated by Kohler (1979).

Water discharged from the Midway thermal system is saturated in calcium (contains an average of 34.2 milliequivalents per liter Ca^{2+}) (Mayo and Loucks, 1995). The calcium was dissolved out of calcareous sedimentary rock as the ground water circulated downward. As the calcium-saturated hot water returns to the surface, tufa is deposited through a complex process that involves the release of CO_2 (carbon dioxide) spurred by the growth of algae and other plants (the plants extract CO_2 from the water, which decreases the solubility of the calcium in the water and causes it to precipitate).

Glaciation: Glaciers invaded the Rocky Mountains several times during the recent geologic past. The last two glacial episodes ended about 130,000 and 12,000 years ago (Pierce and others, 1976; Madole, 1986). The glaciers in WMSP were relatively small, and their features are poorly defined when compared with nearby areas, such as the Uinta Mountains or Big and Little Cottonwood Canyons. The glaciers were small for two reasons: first, the park, on average, is at a lower elevation than these other areas; and second, Bonanza Flat, the primary area of glacial accumulation, faces southeast, a direction that receives direct sun. Some glacial features seen in the high mountains in and near the park are U-shaped valleys, polished rock, and angular, poorly sorted sediments deposited in moraines, glacial outwash and rock glaciers (figures 13 and 14) (Road Logs 2 and 3).

Historical Time – Mining and Recreation: In 1869, about 20 years after the arrival of the first settlers in Utah, soldiers discovered quartz veins rich in silver and gold near WMSP (Boutwell, 1912; Bugden, 1991). Within weeks of the discovery, prospectors swarmed over the region studying every rock exposure for a hint of "color" – rust-brown, red, green, or blue stain was taken as a sign of mineralization and an enticement to dig. Most productive mining in the area was done 1 to 3 miles (1.5-5 km) north of WMSP (the Park City mining district) and in Snake Creek Canyon. However, unproductive prospect pits (piles of freshly broken rock that mark where prospectors dug) are located throughout the park, and the park's irregular northern boundary is due to the shape and location of early mining claims (figure 2). The first shipment of silver-lead ore from the district was in 1871 from the Flagstaff mine near the north end of the park; the last shipments of ore were in 1982. Total ore values exceeded $38 billion (1989 value) (Bromfield, 1989). Mining ceased in 1982 for economic and environmental reasons. Today, the value of WMSP lies in its scenic beauty, its wide variety of recreational opportunities, and its role as a critical watershed.

GEOLOGIC UNIQUENESS AND CLASSIC GEOLOGIC SITES

Wasatch Mountain State Park (WMSP) is unique for its location at the junction of several major geologic features including the Cheyenne belt, Utah hinge line, Oquirrh basin, Sevier thrust belt, Cottonwood arch, Wasatch igneous belt, Park City mineral belt, and the east boundary of the Basin and Range Province (figure 3). Because of this setting, the park has experienced some of the longest and most convoluted history of any site of similar size in Utah.

The sites listed below briefly describe some of the classic geologic features in WMSP (numbers refer to numbers shown on figure 2).

1. Cascade Springs

Cascade Springs is a natural cold water spring with an approximate discharge rate of 6,700 gallons (2.5 m^3) per minute (Mundorff, 1971) (figure 19). The spring water originates as precipitation in the mountains to the west and flows downward through fractured Paleozoic rock until it hits an impermeable rock layer and is deflected toward the lowest exit point (somewhat like water spilling over the lowest point of a pond). The water surfaces in bouldery glacial till and outwash that overlie bedrock. The water precipitates calcium as travertine (a hard, dense, often banded form of calcium carbonate), forming picturesque terraced pools (figure 19). The Forest Service has developed the spring area into an attractive nature area, and a small parking fee is required. (See also Quaternary Surficial Deposits and Late Tertiary to Quaternary sections, and Road Log 1.)

2. Charleston-Nebo Thrust Fault

The Charleston-Nebo thrust fault developed during the Sevier orogeny when tectonic forces slowly pushed slabs of rock thousands of feet thick, about 25 miles (40 km) eastward. One of the few accessible places to see the thrust zone is on the east side of the Cascade Springs parking lot (figure 17). The fault itself is not exposed, but highly brecciated and sheared rock of the lower and upper plates is visible. Though the exposures are not impressive, the geologic significance of the site makes this location worth visiting. A less accessible view of the thrust zone is found along the Heber Valley Historic Railroad route near Deer Creek Reservoir (figure 9). (See also Late Mesozoic section and Road Log 1.)

3. Deer Creek Detachment Fault.

The Deer Creek detachment fault is a low-angle normal fault that formed during mid-Tertiary (Eocene) extension. It developed as Sevier orogenic compression subsided and the thickened Charleston-Nebo thrust plate "relaxed" and slid to the east. The detachment fault roughly parallels the Charleston-Nebo thrust fault. Perhaps the best place to see the fault relationships is near Cascade

Figure 19. *Cascade Springs is a natural spring with numerous waterfalls and lush vegetation that draw thousands of visitors each year. Terraces are calcareous travertine formed by the deposition of calcium carbonate from the water.*

Springs (figure 17). The fault itself is not exposed due to weathering of the highly fractured rocks, but rocks involved in the faulting and the fault relationships can be seen. (See also Geologic History and Structure —Middle Tertiary section and Road Log 1.)

4. Landslide on Cascade Springs Road

Much of the road from Midway to Cascade Springs (State Route 220) is built on ancient landslides and slumps. These slides developed in rocks of the Thaynes and Ankareh Formations. The slides detach along weak bedding planes in shale and siltstone. Overlying limestone and sandstone beds are rumpled into small thrusts and folds. Many of these features are well exposed along the road (figure 15). (See also Quaternary Surficial Deposits and Road Log 1.)

5. Midway Thermal System and Travertine Deposits

Much of the area around Midway and WMSP Visitors Center is underlain by thick calcareous tufa deposited by hot springs of the Midway thermal system. Common surface features include tufa mounds (locally called "craters") centered by open pipes or caverns, a few active hot springs, and laterally extensive, thick beds of tufa. The most impressive tufa mound is the 55-foot-high (16 m) mound at the Homestead Resort (figure 12). The upper part of the tufa mound is dry; however, local lore indicates that in the mid-1800s, before many water wells were drilled in the area, water overflowed the rim of this and many smaller craters in the area. (See also Quaternary Surficial Deposits and Road Logs 1 and 2).

Visitors to WMSP often mistake an unusual rounded hill (Memorial Hill) southeast of Homestead Resort for a large tufa mound. This hill is actually Triassic Woodside and Thaynes Formations uplifted as a small fault block within the larger Heber Valley half-graben (Bryant, 1990).

6. Glacial Till with Megaboulders in Pine Creek Canyon

About half way up Pine Creek Canyon, the road switchbacks up a thick glacial moraine. Several interesting glacial features are exposed near the top of the moraine including huge glacial erratics (boulders 10 to 50 feet [3 to 15 m] in diameter carried by glacial ice far from their sources), moraines (mounds formed along the margins of glaciers), and glacial ponds dammed by debris dropped by the receding glaciers (figures 13 and 14). During the last ice age, about 30,000 to 12,000 years ago, Bonanza Flat was a glacial accumulation area. Glaciers moved out of this area and down adjacent canyons, including Pine Creek Canyon. (See also Quaternary Surficial Deposits and Road Log 2.)

7. Wilson Peak

Wilson Peak, at 8,708 feet (2,655 m), is a prominent point in WMSP. It is near the center of the Pine Creek stock and crowns a ridge near the center of the park (figure 18). The top of the peak affords a spectacular regional view of the surrounding mountains and valleys. Many geologic features in the park are visible from this vantage point, including glacial features in Snake and Pine Creek Canyons and on Clayton Peak, the Heber Valley half-graben, the Midway thermal system, the trace of the Charleston-Nebo thrust and Deer Creek detachment faults, regional dip of the strata in the area, and the resistant core of several igneous stocks with domed rock around their flanks.

8. Outcrop of Mineral Fork Formation

The Mineral Fork Formation is a Late Proterozoic glacial deposit that is generally poorly exposed in WMSP. However, an excellent outcrop is found in the park north of Wilson Peak (figure 6). At this location it is possible to see the composition and size of the clasts and the crude bedding of the matrix. (See also Road Log 3.)

9. Pioneer Peak and Upper Snake Creek Canyon Area

Pioneer Peak is the white peak visible west of the Visitor Center. It caps the backbone ridge between Big Cottonwood Canyon (Brighton area) and Snake Creek Canyon (figure 2). The tops of Pioneer Peak and nearby Sunset Peak are cut by the Grizzly or Alta thrust zone, which juxtaposes Cambrian and Lower Mississippian strata over Middle Mississippian rocks (Baker and others, 1966). Many glacial features can be seen from Pioneer Peak. The peak can be reached from the head of Snake Creek Canyon (no trails), or from hiking trails south of Brighton.

Rocks in the upper Snake Creek Canyon and Pioneer Peak area are strongly marbleized and locally mineralized due to proximity to the Alta and Clayton Peak stocks.

Abandoned mines and evidence of contact metamorphism and mineralization can be seen in upper Snake Creek Canyon where mines were in production from 1900 to 1953. Ore taken from the mines consisted of 3 per cent copper, 0.75 ounce per ton silver, and 0.35 ounce per ton gold (Utah Geological Survey, unpublished data, 2000). The now inaccessible Steamboat Tunnel mine extended 4,000 feet (1.2 km) from Snake Creek Canyon through the mountain to producing mines near Brighton. The tunnel was meant to provide access to the backside of the ore deposits but it did not encounter the mineralization and was not productive. Other tunnels were dug to drain water from the mines.

10. Pine Creek Stock and Rock Quarry

The Pine Creek stock is well exposed in an old quarry just west of the Pine Creek Canyon road. Rock from the quarry was removed in large blocks and used in buildings in Heber Valley. Rock surfaces are fresh and it is easy to see phenocrysts (crystals) and xenoliths (inclusions of "host" rock in the intrusion) (figure 10a). (See also Rock Units–Tertiary, Geologic History and Structure–Middle Tertiary, and Road Log 2.)

11. Valeo Stock

The Valeo stock forms a jagged ledge and steep slope covered by a large talus pile of angular fallen boulders about 600 feet (200 m) east of the Pine Creek Canyon road. The talus slope is a prime example of ice wedging in igneous rock. (See also Rock Units–Tertiary, Geologic History and Structure–Middle Tertiary, and Road Log 2.)

12. Flagstaff Stock

The most accessible outcrops of the Flagstaff stock are located just north of the park near Flagstaff Mountain, a short distance east of the Guardsman Pass-Park City Road. The stock is commonly altered. The first mineral discoveries in the Park City mining district were near this site, and the earliest shipment of ore in the district came from the nearby Flagstaff mine. (See also Rock Units–Tertiary, Geologic History and Structure–Middle Tertiary, and Road Log 3.)

13. Clayton Peak and Clayton Peak Stock

Clayton Peak, visible west of the Visitor Center, is on the same ridge line as Pioneer Peak, and forms the triple-divide between the Big Cottonwood, Snake Creek, and Pine Creek drainages. It consists entirely of well-exposed Clayton Peak stock. The Clayton Peak stock is the oldest and most varied stock of the Wasatch igneous belt. The most easily accessed outcrops of the stock are near Guardsman Pass about 1 mile (1.6 km) north of Clayton Peak. The top of the peak, easily accessed by hiking south along the ridge line from Guardsman Pass, provides a spectacular view. The peak was a primary accumulation zone for glaciers during Pinedale glaciation and has the best examples of glacial erosional features (cirques, horns, aretes, u-shaped canyons, glacial-formed lakes, etc.) near the park. Several small rock glaciers (masses of poorly sorted, angular boulders and rock cemented near the base by ice that moves slowly downslope) are preserved in the talus of the upper canyons of the peak (Baker and others, 1966).

ACKNOWLEDGMENTS

This paper is built upon a less technical guide to the geology of Wasatch Mountain State Park (Willis and Willis, 1994) produced through a Mineral Lease grant to the lead author from the Utah Geological Survey. We thank Bob Biek, Kurt Constenius, Jim Coogan, Lehi Hintze, Mike Hylland, Mike Lowe, and Adolph Yonkee for many insightful discussions on the geology of the area. Paul Anderson, Bob Biek, Tom Chidsey, and Mike Hylland provided helpful technical reviews, and Dave Stobart of WMSP provided helpful suggestions for this paper and for our previously published booklet on the park. A special thanks to Tyler, Emily, and Jacob for their good-natured field assistance, willingness to provide scale in the photographs, and patience.

REFERENCES

Baker, A.A., 1964, Geologic map and sections of the Aspen Grove quadrangle, Utah: U.S. Geological Survey Map GQ-239, scale 1:24,000.

—1976, Geologic map of the west half of the Strawberry Valley quadrangle, Utah: U.S. Geological Survey Map GQ-931, scale 1:62,500.

Baker, A.A., Calkins, F.C., Crittenden, M.D., Jr., and Bromfield, C.S., 1966, Geologic map of the Brighton quadrangle, Utah: U.S. Geological Survey Map GQ-534, scale 1:24,000.

Biek, R.F., Hylland, M.D., Welsh, J.E., and Lowe, M., 2000, Interim geologic map of the Center Creek 7.5 minute quadrangle, Wasatch County, Utah: Utah Geological Survey Open-File Report, scale 1:24,000.

Birkeland, P.W., Machette, M.N., and Haller, K.M., 1991, Soils as a tool for applied Quaternary geology: Utah Geological and Mineral Survey Miscellaneous Publication 91 3, 63 p.

Bissell, H.J., 1962, Pennsylvanian-Permian Oquirrh Basin of Utah: Brigham Young University Geology Studies, v. 9, pt. 1, p. 26-49.

Blackwell, D.D., and Steele, J.L., editors, 1992, Decade of North American Geology geothermal map of North America: Geological Society of America, Boulder, Colorado, 1:5,000,000, 4 sheets.

Blakey, R.C., and Gubitosa, R., 1983, Late Triassic paleogeography and depositional history of the Chinle Formation, southern Utah and northern Arizona, *in* Reynolds, M.S., and Dolly, E.D., editors, Symposium on Mesozoic paleogeography of west-central United States: Denver, Colorado, Rocky Mountain Section of Society of Economic Paleontologists and Mineralogists, p. 57-76.

Blakey, R.C., Basham, E.L., and Cook, M.J., 1993, Early and Middle Triassic paleogeography of the Colorado Plateau and vicinity, *in* Morales, M. editor, Aspects of Mesozoic geology and paleontology of the Colorado Plateau: Museum of Northern Arizona Bulletin 59, p. 13-26.

Boutwell, J.M., 1912, Geology and ore deposits of the Park City district, Utah: U.S. Geological Survey Professional Paper 77, 231 p.

Bromfield, C.S., Baker, A.A., and Crittenden, M.D., Jr., 1970, Geologic map of the Heber quadrangle, Utah: U.S. Geological Survey Map GQ-864, scale 1:24,000.

Bromfield, C.S., 1989, Gold deposits in the Park City mining district, Utah, *in* Shawe, D.R. and Ashley, R.P., editors, Gold-bearing polymetallic veins and replacement deposits-part 1: U.S. Geological Survey Bulletin 1857-C, p. 14-26.

Bryant, B., 1988, Evolution and Early Proterozoic history of the margin of the Archean continent in Utah, *in* Ernst, W.C., editor, Metamorphism and crustal evolution of the western United States, Ruby Colloquium VII: Prentice-Hall, New York, p. 432-445.

—1990, Geologic map of the Salt Lake City 30'x60' quadrangle, north-central Utah and Uinta County, Wyoming: U.S. Geological Survey Map I-1944, 1:100,000.

—1992, Geologic and structure maps of the Salt Lake City 1° x 2° quadrangle, Utah and Wyoming: U.S. Geological Survey Miscellaneous Investigations Series Map I-1997, scale 1:125,000, 3 sheets.

Bryant, B., Naeser, C.W., Marvin, R.F, and Mehnert H.H., 1989, Ages of late Paleogene and Neogene tuff and the beginning of rapid regional extension, eastern boundary of the Basin and Range Province near Salt Lake City, Utah: U.S. Geological Survey Bulletin, 1787-J, 22 p.

Bugden, M., 1991, Geology and scenery of the central Wasatch Range: Utah Geological and Mineral Survey, Public Information Series, no. 9, 17 p.

Chan, M.A., Kvale, E.P., Archer, A.W., and Sonett, C.P., 1994, Oldest direct evidence of lunar-solar tidal forcing encoded in sedimentary rhythmites, Proterozoic Big Cottonwood Formation, central Utah: Geology, v. 22, p. 791-794.

Christie-Blick, N., 1983, Glacial-marine and subglacial sedimentation, Upper Proterozoic Mineral Fork Formation, Utah, *in* Molnia, B.F., editor, Glacial-marine sedimentation: New York, Plenum Press, p. 703-776.

Condie, K.C., 1987, Early Proterozoic arc terranes and continental accretion in the southwestern U.S. [abs]: Geological Society of America Abstracts with Programs, v. 19, p. 625.

Constenius, K.N., 1996, Late Paleogene extensional collapse of the Cordilleran foreland fold and thrust belt:

Geological Society of America Bulletin, v. 108, no. 1, p. 20-39.

—1998, Extensional tectonics of the Cordilleran fold-thrust belt and the Jurassic-Cretaceous Great Valley forearc basin: Tucson, University of Arizona, Ph.D. dissertation, 116 p.

Coogan, J.C., 1992, Thrust systems and displacement transfer in the Wyoming-Idaho-Utah thrust belt: Laramie, University of Wyoming, Ph.D. dissertation, 239 p.

Cook, K.L., Bankey, V., Mabey, D.R., and DePangher, M., 1989, Complete bouguer gravity anomaly map of Utah: Utah Geological and Mineral Survey Map 122, scale 1:500,000.

Crittenden, M.D., Jr., 1959, Mississippian stratigraphy of the central Wasatch and western Uinta Mountains, Utah: Intermountain Association of Petroleum Geologists Guidebook 10, p. 63-74.

Crittenden, M.D. Jr., Christie-Blick, N., and Link, P.K., 1983, Evidence for two pulses of glaciation during the late Proterozoic in northern Utah and southeastern Idaho: Geological Society of America Bulletin, v. 94, no. 4, p. 437-450.

Dalziel, I.W.D., 1997, Neoproterozoic-Paleozoic geography and tectonics–review, hypothesis, environmental speculation: Geological Society of America Bulletin, v. 109, no. 1, p. 16-42.

DeCelles, P.G., 1994, Late Cretaceous-Paleocene synorogenic sedimentation and kinematic history of the Sevier thrust belt, northeast Utah and southwest Wyoming: Geological Society of America Bulletin, v. 106, no. 1, p. 32-56.

Fehr, L., 1997, Petrogenesis of the Keetley Volcanics in Summit and Wasatch counties, north-central Utah: East Lansing, Michigan State University, M.S. thesis, 95 p.

Hamilton, W., and Meyers, W.B., 1966, Cenozoic tectonics of the western United States: Reviews of Geophysics, v. 4, p. 509-549.

Hecker, Suzanne, 1993, Quaternary tectonics of Utah with emphasis on earthquake-hazard characterization: Utah Geological Survey Bulletin 127, 157 p., scale 1:500,000.

Hintze, L.F., 1993, Geologic history of Utah: Brigham Young University Geology Studies Special Publication 7, 202 p.

Houston, R.S., Duebendorfer, E.M., Karlstrom, K.E., and Premo, W.R., 1989, A review of the geology and structure of the Cheyenne belt and Proterozoic rocks of southern Wyoming, *in* Grambling, J.A., and Tewksbury, B.J., editors, Proterozoic geology of the southern Rocky Mountains: Boulder, Colorado, Geological Society of America Special Paper 235, p. 1-12.

Imlay, R.W., 1980, Jurassic paleobiography of the conterminous United States: U.S. Geological Survey Professional Paper 1062, 134 p.

John, D.A., 1989, Geologic setting, depths of emplacement, and regional distribution of fluid inclusions in intrusions of the central Wasatch Mountains, Utah: Economic Geology, v. 84, p. 386-409.

—1997a, Geologic setting and characteristics of mineral deposits in the Central Wasatch Mountains, Utah, *in* John, D.A., and Ballantyne, G.H., editors, Geology and ore deposits of the Oquirrh and Wasatch Mountains: Society of Economic Geologists Guidebook, no. 29, p. 11-33.

—1997b, Day one road log, Mid-Tertiary igneous rocks and mineral deposits in the Central Wasatch Mountains, Utah, *in* John, D.A., and Ballantyne, G.H., editors, Geology and ore deposits of the Oquirrh and Wasatch Mountains: Society of Economic Geologists Guidebook no. 29, p. 59-67.

John, D.A., Turrin, B.D., and Miller, R.J., 1997, New K/Ar and ^{40}Ar/^{39}Ar ages of plutonism, hydrothermal alteration and mineralization in the central Wasatch Mountains, *in* John, D.A., and Ballantyne, G.H., editors, Geology and ore deposits of the Oquirrh and Wasatch Mountains: Society of Economic Geologists Guidebook, no. 29, p. 47-57.

Karlstrom, K.E., Halran, S.S., Williams, M.L., McLelland, James, Geissman, J.W., and Ahall, K.I., 1999, Refining Rodinia - geologic evidence for the Australia-western U.S. connection in the Proterozoic: Geological Society of America, GSA Today, v. 9, no. 10, p. 1-7.

Klauk, R.H. and Mulvey, W., 1987, Study of landslides west of the K & J subdivision in Snake Creek Canyon, Wasatch County, Utah: Utah Geological and Mineral Survey Report of Investigations, no. 214, 27 p.

Kocurek, G., and Dott, R.H., Jr., 1983, Jurassic paleogeography and paleoclimate of the central and southern Rocky Mountains region, *in* Reynolds, M.W. and Dolly, E.D., editors, Symposium on Mesozoic paleogeography of west-central U.S.: Rocky Mountain section of Society of Economic Paleontologists and Mineralogists, p. 101-116.

Koelmel, M.H., 1986, Post-Mississippian paleotectonic, stratigraphic, and diagenetic history of the Weber Sandstone in the Rangely field area, Colorado: American Association of Petroleum Geologists Memoir 41, p. 371-396.

Kohler, J.F., 1979, Geology, characteristics, and resource potential of the low-temperature geothermal system near Midway, Wasatch County, Utah: Utah Geological and Mineral Survey Report of Investigation, no. 142, 45 p.

Leveinen, J.E., 1994, Petrology of the Keetley Volcanics in Summit and Wasatch Counties, north-central Utah: Minneapolis, University of Minnesota, M.S. thesis, 175 p.

Levy, M., and Christie-Blick, N., 1989, Pre-Mesozoic palinspastic reconstruction of the eastern Great Basin (western United States): Science, v. 245, p. 1,454-1,462.

Link, P.K., and 12 others, 1993, Middle and Late Proterozoic stratified rocks of the western U.S. Cordillera,

Colorado Plateau, and Basin and Range Province, *in* Reed, J.C., Jr., and others editors, Precambrian–Conterminous U.S.: Geological Society of America, Geology of North America, The Decade of North American Geology (DNAG) Series, v. C2, p. 463-596.

Machette, M.N., Personius, S.F., Nelson, A.R., 1992, Paleoseismology of the Wasatch fault zone–a summary of recent investigations, interpretations, and conclusions, *in* Gori, P.L., and Hayes, W.W., editors, Assessment of regional earthquake hazards and risk along the Wasatch frount, Utah: U.S. Geological Survey Professional Papaer 1500A, p. A1-A71.

Madole, R.F., 1986, Lake Devlin and Pinedale glacial history, Front Range, Colorado: Quaternary Research, v. 25, p. 43-54.

Maughan, E.K., 1979, Petroleum source rock evaluation of the Permian Park City Group in northeastern Great Basin, Utah, Nevada, and Idaho, *in* Newman, G.W,. and Goode, H.D., editors, Basin and Range and Great Basin Field Conference: Denver, Rocky Mountain Association of Geologists and Utah Geological Association, p. 523-530.

Mayo, A.L., and Loucks, M.D., 1995, Solute and isotopic geochemistry and ground water of the central Wasatch Range, Utah: Journal of Hydrology, v. 172, p. 3-59.

Mundorf, J.C., 1971, Nonthermal springs of Utah: Utah Geological and Mineralogical Survey Water Resources Bulletin 16, 70 p.

Naeser, C.W., Bryant, B., Crittenden, M.D., Jr., and Sorensen, M.L., 1983, Fission-track ages of apatite in the Wasatch Mountains, Utah -- an uplift study: Geological Society of America Memoir 157, p. 29-36.

Peterson, D.L., 1970, A gravity and aeromagnetic survey of Heber and Rhodes Valleys: Utah Department of Natural Resources Technical Publication 27, p. 54-60.

Pierce, K.L., Obradovich, J.D., and Friedman, I., 1976, Obsidian hydration dating and correlation of Bull Lake and Pinedale glaciations near West Yellowstone, Montana: Geological Society of America Bulletin, v. 87, no. 5, p. 703-710.

Presnell, R.D., 1997, Structural controls on the plutonism and metallogeny in the Wasatch and Oquirrh Mountains, Utah, *in* John, D.A., and Ballantyne, G.H., editors, Geology and ore deposits of the Oquirrh and Wasatch Mountains: Society of Economic Geologists Guidebook no. 29, p. 1-9.

Rowley, P.D., 1998, Cenozoic transverse zones and igneous belts in the Great Basin, western United States - their tectonic and economic implications, *in* Faulds, J.E., and Stewart, J.H., editors, Accommodation zones and transfer zones-the regional segmentation of the Basin and Range Province: Boulder, Colorado, Geological Society of America Special Paper 323, p. 195-228.

Royse, F., Jr., Warner, M.A., and Reese, D.L., 1975, Thrust belt structural geometry and related stratigraphic problems, Wyoming, Idaho, northern Utah *in* Bolyard, D.W., editor, Symposium in deep drilling frontiers in the central Rocky Mountains: Rocky Mountain Association of Geologists Symposium, p. 41-54.

Sandberg, C.A., Gutschick, R.C., Johnson, J.G., Poole, F.G., and Sando, W.J., 1982, Middle Devonian to Late Mississippian geologic history of the Overthrust Belt region, western U.S.: Rocky Mountain Association of Geologists, Geologic Studies of the Cordilleran Thrust Belt, v. 2, p. 691-719.

Scotese, C.R., 2000, Paleomap project: www.scotese.com

Severinghaus, J., and Atwater, T., 1990, Cenozoic geometry and thermal state of the subducting slabs beneath western North America, *in* Wernicke, B.P., editor, Basin and Range extensional tectonics near the latitude of Las Vegas, Nevada: Geological Society of America Memoir 176, p. 1-22.

Sheldon, R.P., Cressman, E.R., Cheney, T.M., and McKelvey, V.E., 1967, Permian–middle Rocky Mountains and northeastern Great Basin: U.S. Geological Survey Professional Paper 515, p. 157-174.

Sprinkel, D.A., 1991, Stratigraphic and time-stratigraphic cross sections of Phanerozoic rocks, western Uinta Mountains through the San Pitch Mountains--Wasatch Plateau to western San Rafael Swell, Utah (Summit, Wasatch, Utah, Juab, Sanpete, and Emery Counties): Utah Geological Survey Open-File Report 214, 39 p.

Stokes, W.L., 1959, Jurassic rocks of the Wasatch Range and vicinity *in* Williams, N.C., editor, Guidebook to the sedimentation of the Wasatch and Uinta Mountains transition area: Intermountain Association of Petroleum Geologists Guidebook 10, p. 109-114.

Unrug, R., 1997, Rodinia to Gondwana -- the geodynamic map of Gondwana supercontinent assembly: Geological Society of America, GSA Today, v. 7, no. 1, p. 1-6.

Veevers, J.J., and Powell, C.M., 1987, Late Paleozoic glacial episodes in Gondwanaland reflected in transgressive-regressive depositional sequences in Euramerica: Geological Society of America Bulletin, v. 98, no. 4, p. 475-487.

Vogel, T.A., Cambray, W.F., Feher, L., and Constenius, K.N., 1997, Petrochemistry and emplacement history of the Wasatch igneous belt, *in* John, D.A., and Ballantyne, G.H., editors, Geology and ore deposits of the Oquirrh and Wasatch Mountains: Society of Economic Geologists Guidebook No. 29, p. 35-46

Welsh, J.E., and Bissell, H.J., 1979, The Mississippian and Pennsylvanian (Carboniferous) Systems in the United States: U.S. Geological Survey Professional Paper 1110-Y, 35 p.

Willis, G.C., 1999, The Utah thrust system–an overview, *in* Spangler, L.D. and Allen, C.J., editors, Geology of Northern Utah and Vicinity: Utah Geological Association Publication 27, p. 1-9.

Willis, J.B., and Willis, G.C., 1994, A geologic tour through Wasatch Mountain State Park: Utah Geological Survey, Miscellaneous Publication 93-6, 66 p.

Geology of Utah's Parks and Monuments
2000 Utah Geological Association Publication 28
D.A. Sprinkel, T.C. Chidsey, Jr., and P.B. Anderson, editors

Geology of Sheep Creek Canyon Geological Area, Northeastern Utah

Douglas A. Sprinkel[1], Brien Park[2], and Michael Stevens[3]

ABSTRACT

Sheep Creek Canyon Geological Area is located in northeastern Utah on the north flank of the eastern Uinta Mountains. More than 1 billion years of geologic history are showcased within the geological area, from some of the older rocks in Utah to the classic faults and folds of the Laramide orogeny that uplifted the Uinta Mountains about 70 to 40 million years ago. Nine formations that comprise about 8,000 feet of rock are exposed in northwest-trending bands that dip northeastward; the oldest rocks are exposed in the southern part of the geological area and the bands of rock young to the north.

The oldest rocks in Sheep Creek Canyon comprise the Middle and Upper Proterozoic Uinta Mountain Group. These rocks are 1.1 to 0.8 billion year old and were deposited during a period of rifting. After deposition of the Uinta Mountain Group, a prolonged period—about 450 million years—of interspersed deposition and erosion occurred, with erosion prevailing. Any rocks deposited during this time were later eroded. Rocks of Mississippian age were laid down on the unconformable (erosion) surface formed on the Uinta Mountain Group. Marine conditions dominated the rest of the Paleozoic, with an interruption during Late Pennsylvanian to Early Permian time as the eolian Weber Sandstone was deposited. The youngest rocks in the geological area belong to the Triassic Dinwoody Formation.

The Uinta Mountains rose along the Uinta fault zone during latest Cretaceous through early Tertiary time. Precambrian, Paleozoic, and Mesozoic rocks were tilted steeply northward, folded into monoclines, and faulted. Thousands of feet of rock was eroded from the growing highlands, eventually exposing the Precambrian core of the Uinta Mountains.

The landscape and drainage system of the eastern Uinta Mountains, which includes Sheep Creek Canyon, continued to change as the Gilbert Peak erosion surface formed in Oligocene time and was later tilted during Miocene extension of the Uinta Mountains. Renewed uplift of the Colorado Plateau during Basin and Range extension that began about 15 to 10 million years ago rejuvenated the upper Colorado River Basin and caused active headward erosion of many rivers.

INTRODUCTION

More than 1 billion years ago, the area of what is now Sheep Creek Canyon Geological Area sat near the northern margin of a great rift valley that stretched westward for nearly 160 miles. The landscape was likely stark and barren of visible life. Since then the landscape at Sheep Creek Canyon has continually changed as a rift valley was inverted, oceans flooded and retreated several times, and mountains rose only to be eroded away and then reborn. Evidence of this changing landscape, along with the animals that flourished and died there, is preserved in the rocks that form the spectacular scenery of Sheep Creek

Canyon. Examples of shallow tropical marine environments, vast sand dune fields, and coastal environments are all exposed within the geological area (figure 1). Sheep Creek Canyon Geological Area showcases examples of deformation dominated by the classic faults and folds associated with the Laramide orogeny.

The U.S. Forest Service designated nearly 3,600 acres of land as the Sheep Creek Canyon Geological Area on May 13, 1962, to preserve the spectacular geology of the canyon for future generations. This remarkable area is located along part of the Sheep Creek drainage west of Flaming Gorge National Recreation Area (figure 2). Sheep Creek Canyon is an excellent place to learn about the Earth's geologic history.

Sheep Creek Canyon Geological Area is on the north flank of the eastern Uinta Mountains. The peaks in this part of the Uintas are generally below 10,000 feet in eleva-

[1]*Utah Geological Survey, Salt Lake City, UT 84114-6100*
[2]*Department of Geology, Utah State University, Logan, UT 84322-4505*
[3]*Department of Geology and Geophysics, University of Utah,*
Salt Lake City, UT 84112-1183

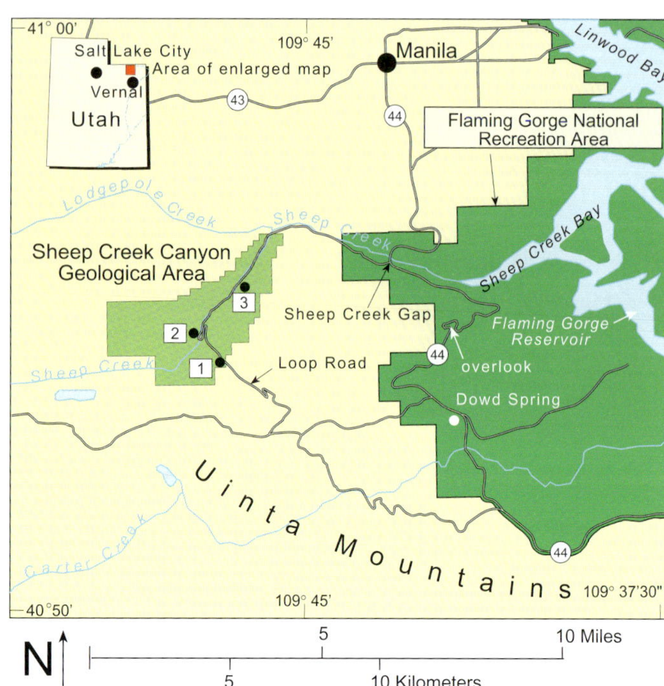

Figure 2. Index map of Sheep Creek Canyon Geological Area, north-eastern Utah, showing key geographic features and classic geologic sites discussed in the text. Classic geologic sites are shown as numbers in boxes.

Figure 1. Tower Rock in the northeast part of Sheep Creek Canyon Geological Area is composed of the upper Weber Sandstone. The upper part of the Weber is interpreted as being deposited in an eolian environment because it consists of quartz-rich, well-sorted sand grains, and contains large-scale cross-bedding. View to the northeast.

tion, which is less than the high peaks of the western part, but are still impressive. The elevation rises to about 9,000 feet along a ridge in the southwestern part of the geological area and drops to 6,400 feet in the northeast part of the geological area where Sheep Creek enters the broader, alluviated valley of the lower Sheep Creek Canyon. The geological area contains one road that is part of a loop that connects with Utah Highway 44 near Dowd Spring on the south and at Sheep Creek Gap on the north.

Several early investigations explored the vast western territories after the Civil War to describe the geology and other natural resources. Three of the competing "Great Four" surveys studied the eastern Uinta Mountains between 1869 and 1875 (Hansen, 1975). These included the King survey in 1869 and 1871, the Hayden survey in 1870, and the Powell survey in 1869, 1871, 1874, and 1875—although Powell first visited the area in 1868. The geologic work of S.F. Emmons (1877), as part of the King survey, most completely described the geology of the Uinta Mountains; however, it was Powell's work (Powell, 1875, 1876)

that most people remember because of his insightful geologic observations and his first-ever exploration of the Green and Colorado Rivers by boat (Hansen, 1975).

Since the Powell, King, and Hayden surveys, many more geological investigations stimulated by scientific curiosity and the search for minerals and petroleum have been conducted in and around the geological area. A summary of the early geologic work can be found in Hansen (1965). The only geologic report that specifically described the geology of the Sheep Creek Canyon Geological Area was by Schell (1969).

THE ROCKS

Sheep Creek Canyon Geological Area contains nine exposed formations that total nearly 8,000 feet of rock, representing more than 1 billion years of geologic history (figure 3). Bedrock formations are separated by three known unconformities separate, which the unconformities represent about 450 millions years of time between rock units. The rocks generally strike northwest and dip northeast such that the oldest rocks crop out in the southern part of the geological area and get younger towards the north (figure 4). Most of the stratigraphic information presented below is summarized from Schell (1969) and Hansen (1965).

Middle to Upper Proterozoic Rocks

The oldest rocks in the geological area make up the Uinta Mountain Group, which forms the backbone of the Uinta Mountains and is the dominant formation in the

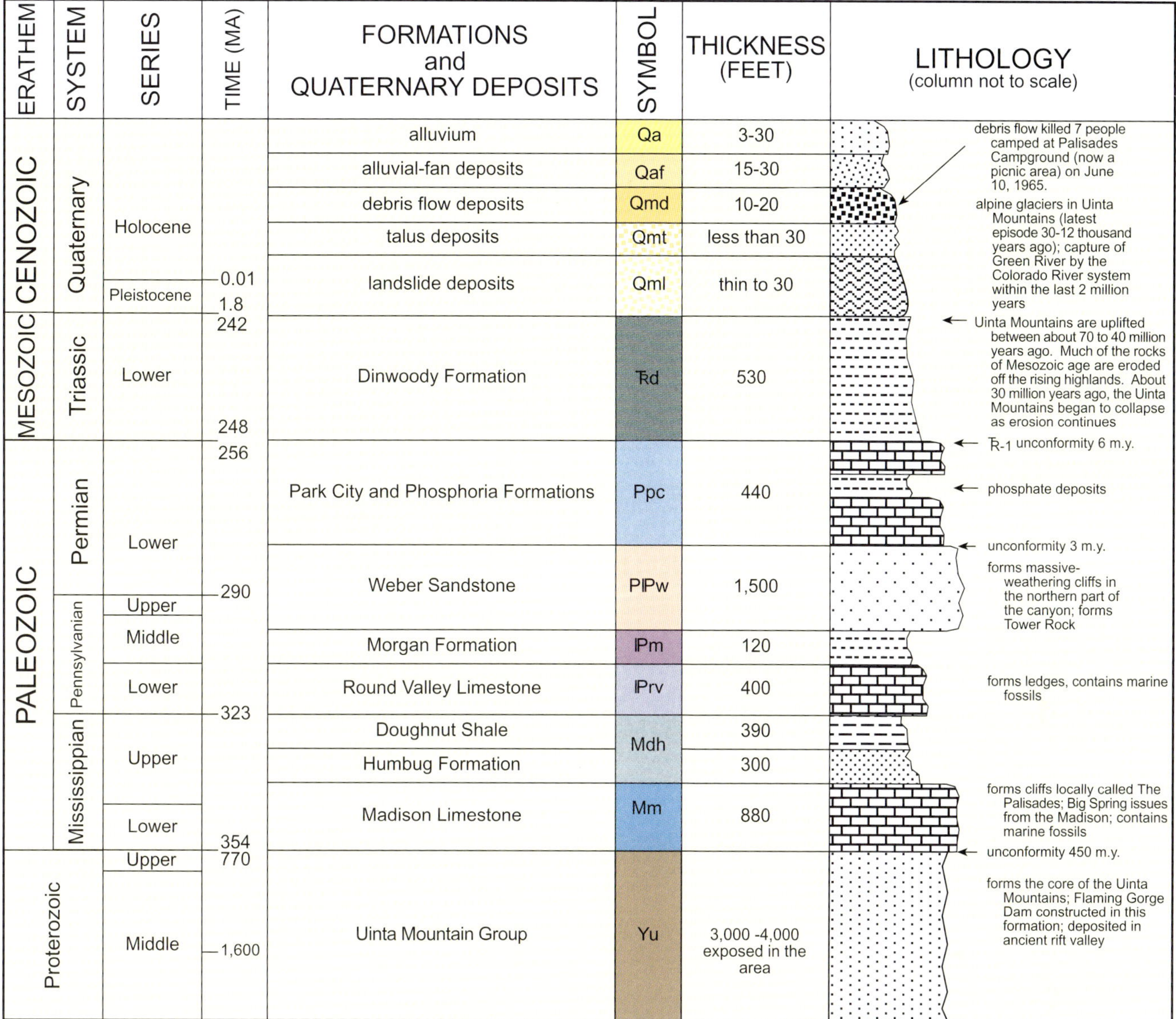

Figure 3. Stratigraphic column of rock formations and Quaternary deposits within Sheep Creek Canyon Geological Area (modified from Hansen, 1965; Schell, 1969). Vertical scale based on geologic time; thus, thicknesses are not shown to scale.

eastern Uinta Mountains. It consists of mostly dark-red siliceous sandstone with abundant shale and conglomerate, all of which may have been subjected to low-grade metamorphism. The rocks of the Uinta Mountain Group are well exposed along Sheep Creek, and form the impressive red cliffs of Red Canyon, Carter Creek, and at Flaming Gorge Dam—all less than 20 miles to the east in the adjacent Flaming Gorge area (figure 2). The Uinta Mountain Group lies unconformably on the Red Creek Quartzite in the Flaming Gorge area. The base of the Uinta Mountain Group and the underlying Red Creek Quartzite is not exposed in Sheep Creek Canyon Geological Area, but is presumed to be in the subsurface.

The Uinta Mountain Group was deposited in a rift valley that slowly opened during Middle Proterozoic time, gradually filling with more than 24,000 feet of clastic sedimentary rocks (conglomerate, sandstone, siltstone, and mudstone). In the Sheep Creek Canyon area, the Uinta

Mountain Group consists of non-marine rocks that were deposited by alluvial and fluvial processes. To the west, however, the rift was submerged by ancient seas and marine rocks were deposited (Wallace, 1972; Sanderson, 1984, 1986; Chan and others, 1994). The Uinta Mountain Group is Middle and Late Proterozoic, ranging in age between about 1,100 and 770 million years (Crittenden and Peterman, 1975; Bressler, 1981).

Mississippian Rocks

The next youngest set of rocks exposed in the geological area belongs to the Mississippian System. In some areas, these rocks are separated from the Precambrian rocks by the Uinta fault (figure 5). In the western part of the geological area, however, the Mississippian-age rocks rest unconformably on the Proterozoic Uinta Mountain Group. This unconformity represents about 550 to 450 million years worth of missing rock.

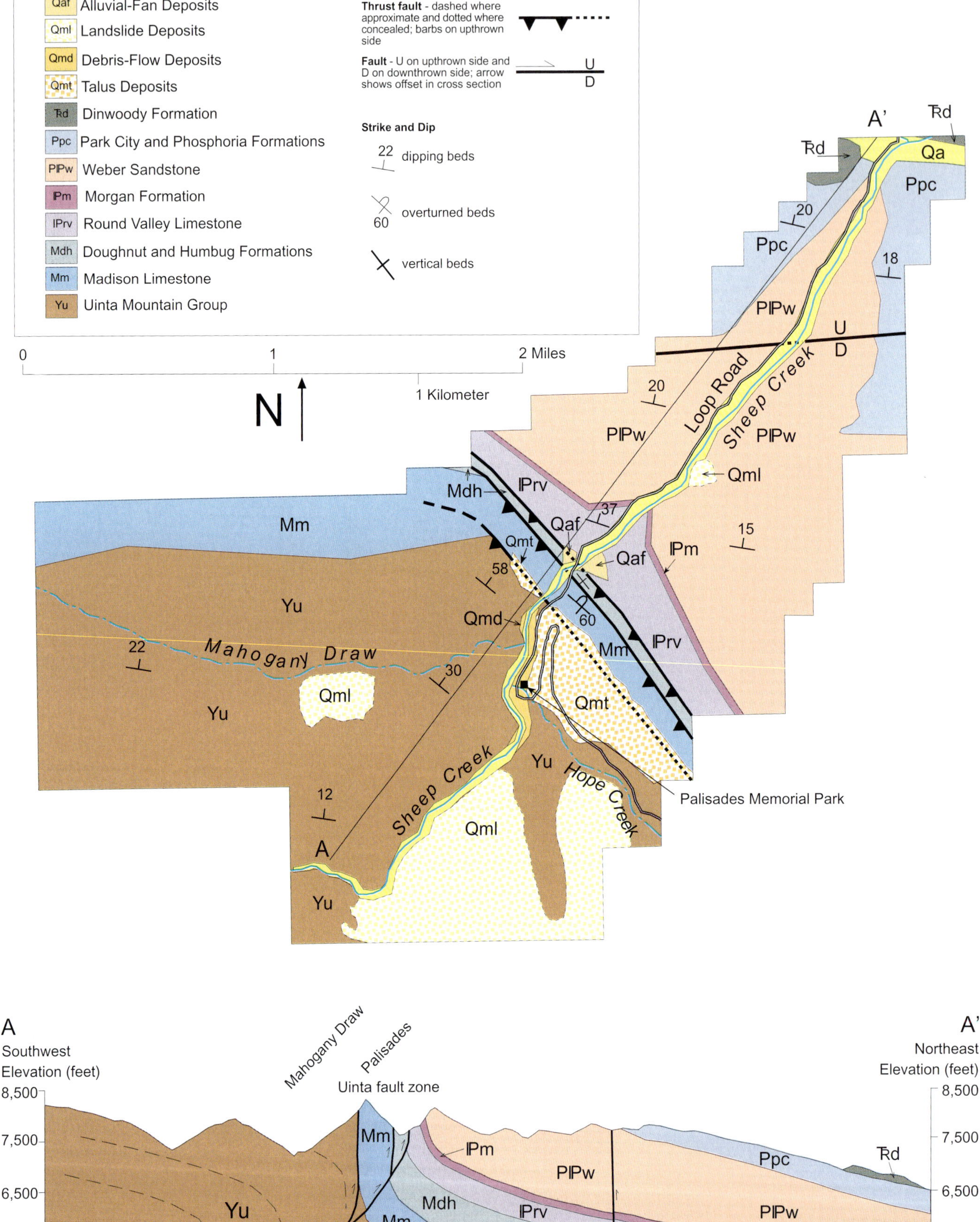

Figure 4. Generalized geologic map and schematic cross section of Sheep Creek Canyon Geological Area; modified from Hintze and others (2000).

Figure 5. Panoramic view of part of Sheep Creek Canyon Geological Area. The southwest branch of the Uinta fault zone (white dashed line) placed deep red rocks of the Uinta Mountain Group (Yu) up next to the gray rocks of the Mississippian Madison Limestone (Mm) during the Laramide orogeny about 70 to 40 million years ago. The Pennsylvanian-Permian Weber Sandstone forms the ridge on the right side of the photograph. The Madison Limestone cliff is locally called The Palisades. View north.

Mississippian rocks in the Sheep Creek Canyon area include the Madison Limestone, Humbug Formation, and Doughnut Shale (figure 3). These formations represent as much as 1,570 feet of sediment deposited in an ocean about 300 million years ago. Typically, the Madison Limestone is very thick bedded, gray limestone that forms resistant cliffs. It forms the steep cliff locally called The Palisades for which nearby Palisades Memorial Park is named (figure 5). The limestone contains light-gray chert and a few marine fossil beds. Solution cavities are common, through which ground water finds its way to the surface as springs, such as Big Spring. The age of the Madison Limestone is Early to Late Mississippian.

Conformably overlying the Madison is the Humbug Formation. It consists of light-gray to red sandstone, light-gray limestone, and red to black shale. The formation is generally soft and forms slopes with some resistant ledges. The Humbug crops out on the northeast side of The Palisades, but is faulted within the Uinta fault zone (Schell, 1969). The Humbug is also a shallow marine unit that was likely deposited in an intertidal zone. Intraformational breccias near the top, and paleokarst features in the Hum-

bug indicate that the formation became exposed and was subjected to erosion prior to deposition of overlying units (Hansen, 1965).

The Doughnut Shale marks the top of the Mississippian System in the region. It consists of dark-gray shale with minor sandstone, limestone, and coal, and is a soft unit that generally forms slopes. It is poorly exposed in the geological area because it is covered by surficial deposits and is broken by faults in the Uinta fault zone (Schell, 1969). The Doughnut Shale is also a shallow marine unit; however, the coarse sandstone and thin coal beds indicate that part of the Doughnut was deposited in a coastal environment. Diagnostic fossils indicate a Late Mississippian age (Hansen, 1965).

Pennsylvanian Rocks

The rocks that represent the Pennsylvanian System include the Round Valley Limestone, Morgan Formation, and the lower part of the Weber Sandstone (figure 3). The Round Valley and Morgan Formations together have a maximum thickness of about 520 feet. The Weber Sandstone spans the Pennsylvanian-Permian boundary and is

Figure 6. View north along the loop road of the Pennsylvanian Round Valley Limestone and Morgan Formation (lPrv-lPm) along the northeastern branch of the Uinta fault zone near the center of the photograph. The Pennsylvanian-Permian Weber Sandstone (PlPw) forms the cliffs in the upper right of the photograph and the Mississippian Madison Limestone (Mm) form the cliffs in the left of the photograph. The northeastern branch of the Uinta fault zone is structurally complicated. In general, the several faults placed vertical to steeply northeast-dipping beds of the Mississippian Humbug and Doughnut Formations (Mdh) over moderately dipping Pennsylvanian Round Valley Limestone and Morgan Formations.

discussed in the next section.

The Round Valley and Morgan Formations crop out in the slopes northeast of the Uinta fault zone (figures 4 and 6). Typically, the Round Valley Limestone is light-gray, thin-bedded to very thick bedded limestone with some interbedded red shale. The limestone beds are resistant and form cliffs and ledges. The limestone beds also contain blue-gray and yellowish-gray, and locally pink or red jasperoid chert (Hansen, 1965; Schell, 1969). Fossil beds are common within the Round Valley and contain a variety of marine fossils such as brachiopods, echinoid spines, bryzoans, and mollusks (Hansen, 1965). The age of the Round Valley is Early and Middle Pennsylvanian.

The overlying Morgan Formation is varicolored and consists of interbedded fine-grained sandstone, siltstone, fossiliferous and cherty limestone, and minor amounts of red shale. The formation is generally thin, about 120 feet thick, and is often combined with the underlying Round Valley Limestone for mapping purposes. The contact between the Round Valley and the Morgan is placed above the thick limestone beds of the Round Valley and below the first appearance of significant quantities of clastic beds (Hansen, 1965; Schell, 1969). The age of the Morgan Formation is Middle Pennsylvanian.

Pennsylvanian and Permian Rocks

The Weber Sandstone is probably one of the most recognized formations in northeastern Utah. It forms the spectacular sandstone cliffs at Split Mountain in Dinosaur National Monument (about 50 miles southeast from the Sheep Creek Canyon area) and the shear, massive-weath-

ering, highly cross-bedded sandstone cliffs in Sheep Creek Canyon Geological Area (figure 1). The Weber Sandstone is also a major oil and gas reservoir in the region, making it an economically important formation. In the geological area, the Weber Sandstone crops out along the loop road and on both sides of the canyon. The Weber Sandstone forms Tower Rock in the geological area (figure 1).

The Weber Sandstone consists of a lower light-gray to yellowish-gray, thick-bedded sandstone with limestone interbeds and an upper light-yellowish-gray, massive-weathering, highly cross-bedded sandstone (Hansen, 1965; Schell, 1969). The contact that separates the lower and upper parts is subtle. It is placed where the rock type becomes exclusively sandstone and the outcrops change from the slightly darker, more angular ledges of the lower part to the lighter, more rounded ledges of the upper part. In addition, the lower part tends to be a little more resistant to erosion than the upper part because of the interbedded limestone. The Weber Sandstone is 1,500 feet thick in the geological area (Schell, 1969).

The Weber Sandstone was deposited mostly in an eolian (wind-blown sand) environment, but the thin marine limestone beds in the lower Weber indicate it is transitional between marine and eolian conditions. The Weber Sandstone is Middle Pennsylvanian to Early Permian based on marine fossils, mainly corals and brachiopods, preserved in the limestone units in the lower part and foraminifera preserved near the top of the formation (Bissell and Childs, 1958; Bissell, 1964; Hansen, 1965).

Permian Rocks

The Park City and Phosphoria Formations represent the top of the Permian System in the area and are divided into three members: the Grandeur Member of the Park City Formation, the intervening Meade Peak Member of the Phosphoria Formation, and the Franson Member of the Park City Formation (Hansen, 1965; Schell, 1969). The Meade Peak is an important economic unit in the area because it contains rich phosphate deposits (Schell and Dyni, 1973) and is the source of oil produced from Weber Sandstone reservoirs (Maughan, 1984; Sprinkel and others, 1997). The three units crop out high above the road in the northeastern part of the geological area and dip northeastward toward the loop road (figure 7). They intersect the loop road in the extreme northeastern part of the geological area. Eastward along strike and outside of the geological area, the Park City Formation forms impressive flatirons along the north flank monocline. The monocline is best viewed at the Sheep Creek Bay overlook along Utah Highway 44 (figure 2).

Light-gray sandstone with some limestone and dolomite characterize the Grandeur Member. The Meade Peak is easy to identify because of the dark-gray phosphatic shale beds. The Franson is dominantly a cherty limestone and dolomite with interbedded sandstone. The limestone and dolomite beds are hard and protect the underlying softer rocks from erosion (Hansen, 1965).

Figure 7. Outcrops of the Permian Park City and Phosphoria Formations in the northeastern part of the geological area. The upper thick cliff is the Franson Member of the Park City and the underlying slope that includes the thick carbonate ledge is the Meade Peak Member of the Phosphoria Formation. Phosphatic shale crops out right above the fence. The top of the Grandeur Member of the Park City is right above the loop road at the extreme left side of the photograph. View south.

Shallow marine conditions prevailed during the deposition of the Grandeur and Franson Members, and probably during deposition of the Meade Peak (Maughan, 1984; Hintze, 1988). The age of the Park City and Phosphoria Formations is Early Permian (Hansen, 1965).

No rocks of Late Permian age are present in the region. The contact separating the Park City Formation from the overlying Triassic Dinwoody Formation is the TR-1 unconformity. Pipiringos and O'Sullivan (1978) estimated the unconformity represents as much as 6 million years.

Triassic Rocks

The Triassic Dinwoody Formation is the youngest rock unit in Sheep Creek Canyon Geological Area and crops out in the extreme northeastern part (figures 3 and 4). It is also well exposed along Utah Highway 44 near Sheep Creek (figure 2). The Dinwoody Formation consists of light- to greenish-gray siltstone and shale with interbedded fine-grained sandstone, thin limestone, and stringers of gypsum. In other areas, marine fossils are preserved in the Dinwoody; however, they are uncommon in the area (Hansen, 1965; Schell, 1969). The age of the Dinwoody is Early Triassic (Hansen, 1965).

Rocks North of Geological Area

The stratigraphic succession of Triassic, Jurassic, Cretaceous, and Tertiary rocks continues and is well exposed north of Sheep Creek Canyon Geological Area. The strike valley that the Sheep Creek Canyon loop road enters just north of the geological area boundary—and in which Sheep Creek flows to Flaming Gorge Reservoir—is cut into the Triassic Moenkopi and Chinle Formations. The ridge that rises northward from the Triassic strike valley is the

Glen Canyon Sandstone. These rocks are exposed in the nearby Flaming Gorge National Recreation Area and are described in Sprinkel (this volume).

Quaternary Deposits

Sheep Creek Canyon Geological Area contains a variety of Quaternary deposits, including alluvium, alluvial fans, talus, landslides, and debris flows. Of these, landslides and debris flows pose the greatest risk to visitors and property.

Alluvium consists of unconsolidated silt, sand, gravel, and boulders deposited in and along Sheep Creek and its tributary drainages. However, the geologic map only depicts larger deposits along Sheep Creek (figure 4). Most alluvium deposited in the geological area is probably Holocene in age.

Alluvial fans consist of unconsolidated, poorly sorted, boulder- to silt-size fragments deposited at the mouths of most steep, straight side canyons. The geologic map only depicts a couple of the largest alluvial-fan deposits (figure 4). Most of the alluvial fans are Holocene in age.

Talus consists of unconsolidated angular blocks of rock that accumulate at the base of steep cliffs. A large talus deposit is at the base of the steep Mississippian Madison cliffs, which form The Palisades (Schell, 1969) (figure 5). The loop road crosses part of this deposit. Other talus deposits are in the geological area but are too small to show on the geologic map. The age of most of the talus deposits is Holocene.

Landslide deposits include large slope failures involving the Uinta Mountain Group south of Sheep and Hope Creeks, and south of Mahogany Draw (Schell, 1969). These landslides are on north-facing slopes where the Uinta Mountain Group beds dip 12 to 30 degrees north to northeast. Blocks of the Uinta Mountain Group failed and slid along weak shaley beds within the formation. Undercutting of the slope by Sheep and Hope Creeks aggravated an already unstable condition. Schell (1969) reported that a large landslide south of Sheep and Hope Creeks had numerous scarps. Some of the scarps are old and overgrown with vegetation, but some scarps formed in June 1965 during an unusually wet period. These deposits rarely pose a risk to human life, but can damage or destroy structures that are built on or near them. The landslide deposits are Holocene in age, but could be as old as Pleistocene.

Debris-flow deposits consist of unconsolidated, poorly sorted boulders, gravel, sand, silt, and mud that was transported along Sheep Creek in the southern part of the geological area. During debris-flow events, the mobilized deposits are destructive to property and can be deadly. In June 1965, a debris flow ripped through the Palisade campground—now Palisades Memorial Park—destroying the campground and killing seven people. A more complete description of this debris flow is in the "Unique Geologic Features" section of this article.

STRUCTURE

The rocks in Sheep Creek Canyon Geological Area have been bent, broken, and tilted during periods of mountain building and basin formation. Some rocks have been deformed many times since their deposition. The oldest structural features in the region are faults that formed more than a billion years ago along the northern part of a rift valley in which the Uinta Mountain Group was deposited. However, their Precambrian ancestry is unclear because of later movement along these faults during the Laramide orogeny and late Cenozoic regional extension. A more complete description of the Precambrian structures is in Hansen (1965) and Sprinkel (this volume). The youngest structural features formed during late Cenozoic regional extension in the past 15 million years. However, the dominant structural features exposed in the geological area were created by the uplift of the Uinta Mountains during the Laramide orogeny about 70 to 40 million years ago (latest Cretaceous to latest Eocene time). These structures set the stage for the spectacular landscape seen in Sheep Creek Canyon Geological Area.

The dominant Laramide structures in the region are the Uinta arch and related Uinta fault zone. The Uinta arch is a great asymmetrical fold that has an axial length of about 160 miles, an average width of 30 miles, and generally coincides with the Uinta Mountains (Hansen, 1965). The rocks on the north flank dip more steeply than the rocks on the south flank, giving the fold its asymmetry (Hansen, 1965). As Hansen (1965) pointed out, the Uinta arch consists of two domes that are aligned east-west and separated by a shallow structural saddle. The saddle is crossed by U.S. Highway 191-Utah Highway 44 from Vernal to Manila, Utah. The Uinta arch is bounded on the north by the thrust faults of the North Flank-Uinta-Sparks fault zone and on the south by the South Flank-Willow Creek fault zone (Hansen, 1965; Ritzma, 1969; Bruhn and others, 1986; Bryant, 1990; Stone, 1993; Gregson and Chure, this volume; Sprinkel, this volume).

Sheep Creek Canyon Geological Area lies on the north flank of the Uinta arch. Consequently, all of the rocks dip generally northeastward and increase in north dip as they approach the Uinta fault zone (Hansen, 1965). Local folds, however, have modified dips and alter the regional strike of the beds. The Uinta fault zone cuts through the central part of the geological area and consists of at least two branches (Schell, 1969) (figure 4). The southwestern branch thrusts a great thickness of Middle Proterozoic Uinta Mountain Group over the Mississippian Madison Limestone (figures 4 and 5). Along the fault, the beds of the Uinta Mountain Group increase their northeastern dip as they approach the fault and locally become overturned (figure 8). The Madison beds are steeply dipping to vertical (figure 8). The northeastern branch of the Uinta fault zone is far more complicated than the geologic map and cross section depict (Schell, 1969) (figure 4). In general, the fault placed steeply dipping to vertical beds of the Missis-

Figure 8. Southwestern branch of the Uinta fault zone along the loop road less than a mile northeast of Palisades Memorial Park. The red middle and upper Proterozoic Uinta Mountain Group (Yu) is thrusted over gray Mississippian rocks (Mm). The thrust fault (long-dash line) is mostly covered by talus (Qmt) and alluvial-fan deposits (Qaf) in this photograph, but dips south where exposed. Beds of the Uinta Mountain Group steepen northward and are overturned along the fault. Beds of the Madison Limestone (Mm) are vertical to overturned. The short-dash line depicts bedding attitudes. The Uinta fault may have originally formed during Middle Proterozoic rifting beginning about 1.5 billion years ago, along the northern margin of the rift valley. Rock relations preserved in the road cut indicate reverse movement that occurred during the Laramide orogeny between 70 and 40 million years ago. Middle to late Miocene collapse of the Uinta Mountains may have produced movement along the Uinta fault in the opposite (normal) sense. View is to the northwest.

sippian Humbug and Doughnut Formations over moderately northeast-dipping beds of the Pennsylvanian Round Valley Limestone (figures 4 and 6).

Schell (1969) estimated about 1,000 feet of stratigraphic throw along the Uinta fault zone in the geological area. Stratigraphic throw decreases generally westward along the fault zone to where the fault eventually dies out. However, the Uinta fault zone increases in stratigraphic throw generally eastward. Hansen (1965) estimated as much as 34,000 feet of stratigraphic throw along the Uinta fault zone in Flaming Gorge National Recreation Area.

Movement on the Uinta and subsidiary faults created impressive monoclines, drag folds, and asymmetrical to overturned synclines. The north flank monocline is well expressed in the Park City Formation along lower Sheep Creek Canyon outside of the geological area.

A small high-angle normal (extensional) fault is the youngest structural feature in Sheep Creek Canyon Geological Area. The fault is east trending and displaced beds of the Weber Sandstone and Park City Formations 15 to 20 feet to the south (Schell, 1969) (figure 4). This fault is similar in structural style to other normal faults outside of the geological area, which are also steeply dipping, generally east trending, and mostly downthrown on the south side (Hansen, 1965). Movement on these extensional faults probably began in late Tertiary (Miocene) time—perhaps as early as middle Tertiary (Oligocene) (Hansen, 1965).

There is no evidence to suggest that these faults have moved in the Quaternary, but it is possible that they remain potentially active.

GEOLOGIC HISTORY

More than 1 billion years of geologic history unfolds in Sheep Creek Canyon Geological Area. A south-to-north traverse along the loop road through the geological area passes through rocks that reveal a rich history of shallow oceans teeming with life and coastal sand dune fields that have been uplifted by faults and folded. The most recent chapter in the area's geologic history includes the ongoing erosion of bedrock formations and the deposition of surficial materials.

The geologic history of Sheep Creek Canyon begins about 1.5 billion years ago with the collapse of part of the Precambrian continent along a long, linear rift zone approximately 30 miles wide (Hansen, 1965; Sears and others, 1982; Stone, 1993; Willis and Willis, 2000). In the eastern Uinta Mountains, fluvial sediments of the middle and upper Proterozoic Uinta Mountain Group accumulated in the rift, and by the time rifting ended about 770 million years ago, more than 24,000 feet of rock was deposited (Hansen, 1965). Late Precambrian to early Paleozoic uplift followed rifting, which tilted and eroded part of the Uinta Mountain Group rocks.

The Sheep Creek Canyon area was at or just above sea level during much of early Paleozoic time. However, there is no record of Cambrian through Devonian rocks, and any sediment that was deposited (and lithified) in the geological area during that time was removed by erosion before Mississippian sedimentation began. Mississippian seas substantially flooded the region beginning about 350 million years ago. Sea level fluctuated throughout the remaining Paleozoic time and created two shallowing-up sequences. The first sequence includes the Madison-Humbug-Doughnut Formations. The shallow marine environment of the Madison Limestone was ideal for carbonate deposition, and animals such as brachiopods, crinoids, and corals flourished. As the seas became shallower, the Humbug and Doughnut Formations were deposited closer to shore; there was even a time when rocks of the Doughnut were deposited within a coastal marsh environment. The second shallowing-up sequence includes the Round Valley-Morgan-Weber Formations. The seas again became deeper during Round Valley time when limestone deposition returned and marine life flourished. As before, sea level dropped beginning with the near-shore deposition of the Morgan Formation, but this time the seas eventually completely withdrew from the region and eolian conditions prevailed during deposition of the upper Weber Sandstone. The late Early Permian saw the return of shallow marine deposition of the Park City and Phosphoria Formations. Sea level significantly dropped worldwide in the latter part of the Permian (Hintze, 1988). Consequently, Upper Permian rocks are not preserved in the Sheep Creek Canyon area, nor in much of Utah. In addition, an unconformity (TR-1) separates Lower Permian rocks from the overlying Lower Triassic rocks, and represents about 6 millions years of missing time.

The Sheep Creek Canyon area remained at or near sea level during much of the Mesozoic Era, a time of alternating marine and continental deposition. Early Triassic time began with marine deposition of the Dinwoody Formation. Although the rocks that lie above the Dinwoody were eroded from area, they are regionally preserved to the north and south and indicate that marine and terrestrial deposition continued intermittently until latest Cretaceous time.

By latest Cretaceous time, the landscape began to change dramatically. This region that had hovered around sea level since late Precambrian time—being submerged for most of the latter part of Paleozoic and parts of Mesozoic time—started to rise (Hintze, 1988). The seabed was warped upward in latest Cretaceous time, causing the sea to retreat and the seabed to reach the surface. The regional mountain building event of the Laramide orogeny had begun! Uplift would be so extensive that the region would never be inundated by the sea again. The Laramide orogeny was responsible for raising the Uinta Mountains, as well as other ranges in the Rocky Mountain region, from the sea (Stone, 1969; Gries, 1983). Its intermittent, yet persistent, deformation for about 30 million years folded and thrust faulted the rocks in Sheep Creek Canyon Geological Area (Hansen, 1965).

Crustal stability replaced uplift of the Uinta Mountains about 30 million years ago (Hansen, 1986). Consequently, an extensive pediment called the Gilbert Peak erosion surface beveled across the flanks of the highland, leaving only the higher parts of the range above the surface. The Gilbert Peak erosion surface is not preserved in Sheep Creek Canyon Geological Area, but it is worthy of mention because it is an important part of the geologic history of the eastern Uinta Mountains. A more complete description of the Gilbert Peak erosion surface is provided by Hansen (1986) and summarized by Sprinkel (this volume).

Regional deformation resumed in early Miocene time, but this time the region was subjected to extension instead of compression. Collapse of the eastern Uinta Mountains by down-to-the-south movement along the Uinta fault zone tilted the rocks north and warped and faulted the Gilbert Peak erosion surface (Hansen, 1986).

As extension continued in the middle Miocene in areas to the west, relative regional uplift of the Colorado Plateau rejuvenated rivers and streams to the south of the Uintas, and caused vigorous northward headward erosion (Stokes, 1986). Ultimately, the ancestral Green River was captured by the Colorado River system (Hansen, 1986; Stokes, 1986). The exact cause and timing of capture of the Green River is speculative (Sprinkel, this volume), but this event probably led to accelerated downcutting of Sheep Creek, creating the spectacular scenery that led to the special designation of this site.

Figure 9. Debris-flow deposit at the Palisades Memorial Park. The debris flow ripped through the Palisade campground on June 10, 1965, destroying the campground and killing seven campers. A high-flowing Sheep Creek, which was swollen by steady rains and a late snowmelt, may have undercut a landslide that was already unstable because of the wet conditions; landslide material that slumped into Sheep Creek likely triggered the debris flow. View is southwest.

Parts of the Pleistocene were times of glaciation in the high Uinta Mountains; however, there is no evidence that glacial ice ever covered any part of Sheep Creek Canyon Geological Area. Erosion during the remainder of the Quaternary sculpted the final touches of the present landscape by continued downcutting of the Green River and its tributaries, landsliding, debris flows, and other active geomorphic processes.

CLASSIC GEOLOGIC SITES

Sheep Creek Canyon Geological Area contains numerous sites that display classic geological features, so many that not every site can be discussed within the limits of this article. However, a few sites are briefly discussed in the following sections. Figure 2 shows the approximate location of these sites as boxed numbers. The boxed numbers correspond to the following numbered site names.

1. Sheep Creek Canyon Overlook

The Sheep Creek Canyon overlook is at the southern entrance to the geological area. A turnout provides a grand view to the west of the Sheep Creek drainage that exposes the Precambrian Uinta Mountain Group, Mississippian Madison Limestone that forms The Palisades escarpment, and the Uinta fault zone (figure 5). The deep red rocks consist of the Uinta Mountain Group, and the gray cliff that forms the Palisedes escarpment is the Madison Limestone. The Uinta fault cuts the two formations and is evident where the rocks are steeply tilted north to overturned to the south. The debris-flow deposit that destroyed the Palisade campground and killed seven people can be seen in the bottom of the canyon.

Figure 10. Debris-flow levee west of the Palisades Memorial Park. Twisted water pipes and other metal from the destroyed campground can still be found in the debris-flow deposit. View is south.

2. Debris Flow at Palisades Memorial Park

The night of June 10, 1965, was stormy with steady rains. The ground was likely already saturated from the melting of a greater-than-normal snow pack, which was still perched in the mountains surrounding the campground due to a late and cool spring, and the wet conditions were aggravated by the heavy rains—a recipe for disaster! Seven people camped at Palisade campground (now Palisades Memorial Park) along Sheep Creek were in their trailer for the night when a devastating debris flow—commonly known as a flash flood—ripped through the campground. The debris flow destroyed the campground and swept the seven campers away to their death. The debris flow continued down Sheep Creek and destroyed five miles of road, three bridges, and four developed campsites. Damage from the debris flow is still evident west of the picnic area near Sheep Creek where twisted water pipes and other metal from the campground are lodged in the debris-flow deposit.

The debris flow originated about one mile upstream where east-flowing Sheep Creek makes a turn to the northeast. At that turn, Sheep Creek cuts into a large landslide (figure 4). Schell (1969) reported that the landslide was moving in June 1965 because of abnormally high runoff. It is likely that Sheep Creek, swollen from steady rains and heavy snowmelt, undercut part of the landslide. That may have caused the landslide and residual (soil and colluvium) material to slump into Sheep Creek and move rapidly downstream, scouring more debris (mud, silt, sand, gravel, boulders, and vegetation) from the unstable eastern bank along the way. By the time the debris flow reached the campground, which probably was only a few minutes, it contained a large volume of material; the force of the flow overturned the car and destroyed the trailer belonging to the doomed campers. We estimated that the debris-flow deposit at the south end of the campground was at least 5 feet thick and covered much of the flood plain (figure 9). Debris-flow levees are still preserved east of the picnic area (figure 10).

Not known at that time by the campers, the old campsite was located on historical debris-flow and alluvial deposits. The death of the seven campers from the new debris flow prompted U.S. Forest Service officials to designate the site as the Palisades Memorial Park and restrict it to day use only; thus, reducing the risk of deaths from future debris flows.

3. Tower Rock

Weathering of the upper, highly cross-bedded part of a Weber Sandstone outcrop gives the appearance of a tower built along the road. The Weber Sandstone at Tower Rock is a fine- to medium-grained sandstone that was deposited in an eolian environment about 285 million years ago during Early Permian time.

ACKNOWLEDGMENTS

Ashley National Forest provided financial support that permitted this article to be printed in color. Special thanks to Darlene Koerner, Ashley National Forest, for loaning us the aerial photos of the Sheep Creek Canyon area and providing general support while on the forest. We thank Jon King, Mike Hylland, and Grant Willis (Utah Geological Survey) for reviewing the manuscript.

REFERENCES

Bissell, H.J., 1964, Lithology and petrography of the Weber Formation, in Utah and Colorado, *in* Sabatka, E.F., editor, Guidebook to the geology and mineral resources of the Uinta Basin, Utah's hydrocarbon storehouse: Intermountain Association of Petroleum Geologists 13th Annual Field Conference, p. 67-91.

Bissell, H.J., and Childs, O.E., 1958, The Weber Formation of Utah and Colorado, *in* Curtis, B., and Warner, H.L., editors, Symposium on Pennsylvanian rocks of Colorado and adjacent areas: Rocky Mountain Association of Geologists, p. 26-30.

Bressler, S.L., 1981, Preliminary paleomagnetics and correlation of the Proterozoic Uinta Mountain Group, Utah and Colorado: Earth and Planetary Science Letters, v. 55, no. 1, p. 53-64.

Bruhn, R.L., Dane, P.M., and Isby, J.S., 1986, Tectonics and sedimentology of Uinta Arch, western Uinta Mountains and Uinta Basin, *in* Peterson, J.A., editor, Paleotectonics and sedimentation: American Association of Petroleum Geologists Memoir 41, p. 333-352.

Bryant, B., 1990, Geologic map of the Salt Lake City 30' x 60' quadrangle, north-central Utah, and Uinta County, Wyoming: U.S. Geological Survey Miscellaneous Investigations Series Map I-1944, scale 1:100,000.

Chan, M.A., Kvale, E.P., Archer, A.W., and Sonett, C.P., 1994, Oldest direct evidence of lunar-solar tidal forcing encoded in sedimentary rhythmites, Proterozoic Big Cottonwood Formation, central Utah: Geology, v. 22, no. 9, p. 791-794.

Crittenden, M.D., and Peterman, Z.E., 1975, Provisional Rb/Sr age of the Precambrian Uinta Mountain Group, northeastern Utah: Utah Geology, v. 2, p. 75-77.

Emmons, S.F., 1877, Descriptive geology: U.S. Geological Exploration 40th Parallel (King) volume 2, p. 890.

Gries, R., 1983, North-south compression of Rocky Mountain foreland structures, *in* Lowell, J.D., and Gries, R., editors, Rocky Mountain basins and uplifts: Rocky Mountain Association of Geologists Symposium, p. 9-32.

Hansen, W.R., 1965, Geology of the Flaming Gorge area Utah-Colorado-Wyoming: U.S. Geological Survey Professional Paper 490, 196 p.

—1975, The geologic story of the Uinta Mountains: U.S. Geological Survey Bulletin 1291, 144 p.

—1986, Neogene tectonics and geomorphology of the eastern Uinta Mountains in Utah, Colorado, and Wyoming: U.S. Geological Survey Professional Paper 1356, 78 p.

Hintze, L.F., 1988, (revised 1993), Geologic history of Utah: Brigham Young University Geology Studies Special Publication 7, 202 p.

Hintze, L.F., Willis, G.C., Laes, D.Y.M., Sprinkel, D.A., and Brown, K.D., 2000, Digital geologic map of Utah: Utah Geological Survey Map 179DM, 17 p., scale 1:500,000.

Maughan, E.K., 1984, Geological setting and some geochemistry of petroleum source rocks in the Permian Phosphoria Formation, *in* Woodward, J., Meissner, F.F., and Clayton, J.L., editors, Hydrocarbon source rocks of the greater Rocky Mountain region: Rocky Mountain Association of Geologists, p. 281-294.

Pipiringos, G.N., and O'Sullivan, R.B., 1978, Principal unconformities in Triassic and Jurassic rocks, Western Interior United States-a preliminary survey: U.S. Geological Survey Professional Paper 1035-A, 29 p.

Powell, J.W., 1875, Exploration of the Colorado River and its tributaries: Washington, D.C.: U.S. Government Printing Office, 218 p.

—1876, Report on the geology of the eastern portion of the Uinta Mountains and a region of country adjacent thereto: U.S. Geological and Geographical Survey of the Territories (Powell), 218 p.

Ritzma, H.R., 1969, Tectonic resume, Uinta Mountains, *in* Lindsay, J.B., editor, Geologic guidebook of the Uinta Mountains-Utah's maverick range: Intermountain Association of Geologists and Utah Geological Society 16th Annual Field Conference, p. 57-63.

Sanderson, I.D., 1984, The Mount Watson Formation, an interpreted braided-fluvial deposit in the Uinta Mountain Group (upper Precambrian), Utah: The Mountain Geologist, v. 21, no. 4, p. 157-164.

—1986, The Jesse Ewing Canyon Formation, an interpreted fan deposit in the basal Uinta Mountain Group (Middle Proterozoic), Utah: The Mountain Geologist, v. 23, no. 3, p. 77-89.

Schell, E.M., 1969, Summary of the geology of the Sheep Creek Canyon Geological Area and vicinity, Daggett County, Utah, *in* Lindsay, J.B., editor, Geologic guidebook of the Uinta Mountains-Utah's maverick range: Intermountain Association of Geologists and Utah Geological Society 16th Annual Field Conference, p. 143-152.

Schell, E.M., and Dyni, J.R., 1973, Preliminary geologic strip maps of the Park City and Phosphoria Formations, Vernal phosphate area, Uintah County, Utah: U.S. Geological Survey Open File Report OFR 73-248, scale 1:24,000.

Sears, J.W., Graf, P.J., and Holden, G.S., 1982, Tectonic evolution of lower Proterozoic rocks, Uinta Mountains, Utah and Colorado: Geological Society of America Bulletin, v. 93, no. 10, p. 990-997.

Sprinkel, D.A., Castaño, J.R., and Roth, G.W., 1997, Emerging plays in central Utah based on regional geochemical, structural, and stratigraphic evaluation [abs.]: American Association of Petroleum Geologists Official Program, v. 6, p. A110.

Stokes, W.L., 1986, Geology of Utah: Utah Geological Survey and Utah Museum of Natural History Occasional Paper Number 6, 280 p.

Stone, D.S., 1969, Wrench faulting and Rocky Mountain tectonics: The Mountain Geologist, v. 6, p. 67-79.

—1993, Tectonic evolution of the Uinta Mountains—Palinspastic restoration of a structural cross section along longitude 109°15', Utah: Utah Geological Survey Miscellaneous Publication 93-8, 19 p.

Wallace, C.A., 1972, A basin analysis of the upper Precambrian Uinta Mountain Group, Utah: Santa Barbara, University of California-Santa Barbara, Ph.D. dissertation, 412 p.

Geology of Utah's Parks and Monuments
2000 Utah Geological Association Publication 28
D.A. Sprinkel, T.C. Chidsey, Jr., and P.B. Anderson, editors

Geology of Monument Valley Navajo Tribal Park, Utah-Arizona

William L. Chenoweth[1]

ABSTRACT

Monument Valley Navajo Tribal Park is located on the Monument uplift in southeastern Utah and northeastern Arizona. The park was created in 1958 by the Navajo Tribal Council, to protect the scenery and archeology, and to develop tourism in the area. It includes the most scenic mesas, buttes, and pinnacles in the entire Monument Valley area. These features rise some 800 feet above the high desert floor, and are composed of the cross bedded, reddish-brown sandstone of the DeChelly Sandstone of Permian age. The base of the mesas and buttes as well as the floor of the central part of the park is the Permian Organ Rock Shale. Some of the buttes are capped with rocks of the Triassic Moenkopi Formation and the tops of many of the mesas are formed by the resistant rocks of the Shinarump Conglomerate Member of the Triassic Chinle Formation. Prior to the area becoming a park, two uranium-vanadium ore bodies were found in paleochannels (ancient river channels) in the base of the Shinarump Conglomerate Member. A 17 mile, unimproved valley drive passes by and around the most spectacular features in the park. The park has been the site of many Hollywood movies beginning with Stagecoach in 1938.

INTRODUCTION

Monument Valley is a vaguely defined area of isolated mesas, buttes and pinnacles in southeastern Utah and northeastern Arizona, within the Navajo Nation. In general, it is the area south of the Eagle Mesa and Saddleback Butte (figure 1). Comb Ridge, 10 miles to the east of the park, is considered to be the eastern and southeastern border of the valley. Hoskinnini and Tyende Mesa, 13 miles west of the park, is the western border. The tribal park contains the most scenic part of the area.

On July 11, 1958, Resolution CF-31-57 of the Advisory Committee of the Navajo Tribal Council created the park, the first in the Navajo Nation. A total of 29,817 acres was withdrawn for the protection of the scenery and archeo-

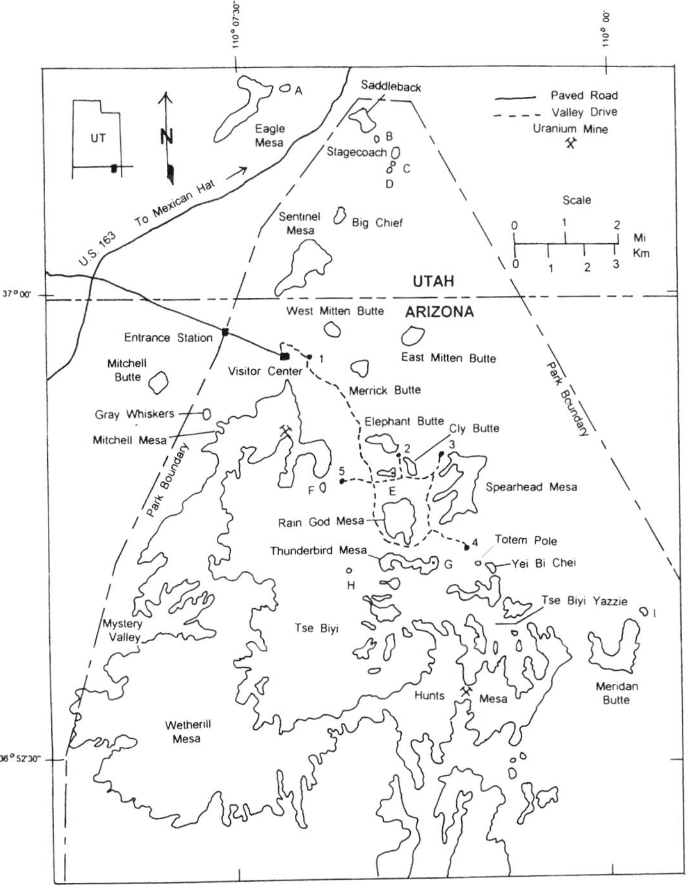

Figure 1. Generalized map of Monument Valley Navajo Tribal Park showing prominent features, points of interest. Stops in road log (1) Mitten Buttes; (2) North Window; (3) Artist Point; (4) Sand Springs; (5) John Ford's Point. Smaller features (A) Setting Hen; (B) King On His Throne; (C) Bear and Rabbit; (D) Castle Rock; (E) Thumb on Camel Butte; (F) Three Sisters; (G) Big Chair; (H) The Hub; (I) Rooster Rock. Map from Navajo Recreational Resources Department.

[1]Grand Junction, CO 81506-3911

529

Figure 2. Geologic map of the northern part of Monument Valley Navajo Tribal Park. Geologic symbols: Pcha-Halgaito Shale; Pccm-Cedar Mesa Sandstone; Pcor-Organ Rock Shale, Pcdc-DeChelly Sandstone; Trmh-Hoskinnini Member of Moenkopi Formation; Trm-upper members of Moenkopi Formation; Trcs-Shinarump Conglomerate Member of Chinle Formation; Trcm-Monitor Butte Member of Chinle Formation; Qd-dune sand; Ti-intrusive igneous rocks. The alignment of U.S. Highway 163 has been changed since this map was published. Also, Saddleback Butte is called Brighams Tomb on this map. From Cooley and others (1969).

logical sites and to develop tourism. The park is roughly triangular shaped with the north corner being at Saddleback Butte, the southeast corner being 4.5 miles southeast of Rooster Rock and the south corner 8 miles south of Wetherill Mesa (figure 1). It has been proposed (Recreational Resources Department and National Park Service, 1983) that the area between the west boundary and U.S. Highway 163 be added and most of the area south of Wetherill and Hunts Mesas be dropped from the park.

This proposal has yet to be implemented. The entrance to the park is 19 miles south of the bridge over the San Juan River at Mexican Hat, Utah. A paved road, from U.S. 163, leads to the Visitor Center, picnic area, campground, and restaurant.

The park contained the most spectacular reddish-brown colored mesas, buttes and pinnacles in the entire Monument Valley area. Many of these features rise 800 feet above the high desert floor. The Navajo name for

Monument Valley is *Tse' Bii' Ndzisgaii* - meaning "treeless areas (cleared) among the rocks."

STRATIGRAPHY

Rocks exposed within the Park include the Halgaito Shale, Cedar Mesa Sandstone, Organ Rock Shale and the DeChelly Sandstone of the Permian Cutler Group, the Moenkopi and Chinle Formations of Triassic age (figure 2). Quaternary sand, some in the form of dunes, covers most of the rock units on the floor of the park.

The Halgaito Shale is the oldest formation exposed in the park. The uppermost beds of the formation are exposed in the northeast corner of the park (figure 2). It consists of reddish-brown shaley siltstone and fine-grained sandstone that were deposited in an ancient coastal plain and intertidal environment. The type locality of the formation is Halgaito Spring, 6 miles northeast of the park.

Above the Halgaito is the Cedar Mesa Sandstone. The formation is exposed in the park in the area east of Spearhead Mesa, East Mitten Butte, and Saddleback Butte (figure 2). The Cedar Mesa, in the park, is comprised of a series of orangish-brown to pink, very fine-grained sandstone silty sandstone, siltstone and limey siltstone, deposited on an ancient coastal plain. It is approximately 300 feet thick in the park. The type locality is Cedar Mesa, 25 miles north of the park.

The Organ Rock Shale overlies the Cedar Mesa and forms the floor of a greater portion of the valley and the lower slopes of many of the buttes and mesas (figure 3). It is comprised of a sequence of reddish-brown mudstone and sandstone, ranging from 600 to 700 feet in thickness. The formation was deposited when this part of Utah and Arizona was a coastal lowland. The Organ Rock correlates with the Hermit Shale in the Grand Canyon. Plant remains found in the Hermit indicate a early Leonardian age, 268 Ma (Blakey and Baars, 1987). The type locality of the Organ Rock Shale is Organ Rock, a butte some 15 miles northwest of the park.

Above the Organ Rock Shale, is the DeChelly Sandstone. This is the unit that forms the massive cliffs of the mesas, buttes and pinnacles. It is a fine-grained, quartzose, cross-bedded sandstone which is reddish-brown colored due to hematite (iron) coatings on the sand grains. This eolian unit is 400 feet thick in the park.

Overlying the DeChelly Sandstone, with a slight unconformity, is the Moenkopi Formation of Early Triassic age. This formation caps many of the buttes and mesas. Where it is overlain by the Shinarump Conglomerate Member of the Chinle Formation, the Moenkopi forms a thin slope. The formation consists of reddish-brown sandstone, mudstone, and siltstone that were deposited on an ancient coastal plain. Within the park the formation is approximately 200 feet thick.

In the Monument Valley area the basal 40 feet of the Moenkopi Formation has been named the Hoskinnini Member. The type locality is Hoskinnini Mesa, 13 miles

Figure 3. Merrick Butte, Arizona. Stratigraphy as follows: (Trcs) Shinarump Conglomerate Member of Chinle Formation, (Trm) Moenkopi Formation, (Pdc) DeChelly Sandstone, (Por) Organ Rock Shale. Steven Semken photo.

west of the park. It consists of dark red, even-bedded, fine-grained sandstone and siltstone. The upper part of the Moenkopi contains rocks of the Torrey and Moody Canyon Members (Blakey and Baars, 1987). These members have not been mapped separately in the area of the park.

The Shinarump Conglomerate is the basal member of the Chinle Formation. The member is very resistant and caps many of the large mesas within the park as well as several of the buttes. This unit unconformably overlies the Moenkopi Formation. Paleovalleys, or ancient channels, filled with Shinarump sediments that have been scoured into the Moenkopi. The Shinarump is a tan colored, cross-bedded, mixture of conglomerate and sandstone deposited in a fluvial environment. It is approximately 50 feet thick, but can be as much as 120 feet thick as in the channel on Mitchell Mesa. The channels in the base of the Shinarump are the location of ore deposits of uranium-vanadium minerals in the Monument Valley area.

Overlying the Shinarump Conglomerate Member is the Monitor Butte Member of the Chinle Formation. In the area of the park shown on figure 2, the basal beds of this member are present on the tops of some of the mesas south of Wetherill Mesa. These beds are composed of cross-bedded conglomerate sandstone interbedded with dark-gray claystone. In the Monument Valley area, the Monitor Butte beds commonly intertongue with the underlying Shinarump Conglomerate (Witkind and Thaden, 1963).

Sand derived mainly from the weathering of the DeChelly Sandstone covers much of the floor of the park. Locally dunes have formed, especially in the southern part of the park. South of Wetherill Mesa is a small lamprophyric dike (figure 2). Outside the park on the southwest is Agathla Peak, a 1,400 foot high volcanic neck of nearly black lamprophyric rock. Agathla, also known as El Capitan, is a prominent landmark in Monument Valley. Neither the dike or Agathla have been dated, but Late

Oligocene to Early Miocene ages have been obtained from similar igneous rocks south of the park (Steven Semken, written communication, 2000).

STRUCTURAL GEOLOGY

Monument Valley is located on the Monument uplift, a large feature that extends from Kayenta, Arizona some 80 miles northward into Canyonlands National Park. Within the Monument Valley area there are numerous north, and northeast-trending synclines and anticlines. The dominant structural feature in the park is the north trending Mitten Butte syncline, also known as the Tse Biyi syncline (Witkind and Thaden, 1963). The syncline can be recognized for approximately 7 miles, with the axis extending from east of East Mitten Butte passing through the area of Artist Point and to the west of Big Chair on Thunderbird Mesa (figure 2). Dips on the western limb are approximately 4 degrees and on the eastern limb are less than 1 degree. The syncline forms a basin-like feature in the park north of Hunts Mesa and east of Wetherill Mesa, known as Tse Biyi, meaning "between the rocks" (figure 1).

The Agathla anticline is southeast of Wetherill Mesa (figure 2). This southwesterly-plunging feature has been mapped for a distance of 16 miles. The dips are steeper on the northwest, where dips a great as 14 degrees have been measured (Witkind and Thaden, 1963). Dips on the southeast flank average 4 degrees.

The Monument uplift began to form in the Late Cretaceous. Erosion in the last 10 million years has created the land forms in Monument Valley.

The geology of the Park, has been mapped by Cooley and others (1969) at a scale of 1:125,000. The Arizona portion of the park is included in a 1:62,500 scale map by Witkind and Thaden (1963).

MINERAL RESOURCES

During the uranium boom of the early 1950s, prospectors scoured the outcrops of the Shinarump Conglomerate in Monument Valley searching for signs of uranium - vanadium minerals. Within the area, that later became the park, two areas of ore grade mineralization were discovered (figure 1).

During 1953, five tons of ore averaging 0.24 percent U_3O_8 and 1.30 percent V_2O_5 were shipped from a rim cut in a Shinarump channel exposed on the north side of Hunts Mesa (Scarborough, 1981). The mine was located on Sam Charlies' Navajo Tribal Mining Permit.

A second mineralized channel was found on the south side of Mitchell Mesa at the head of a large re-entrant, approximately 1 mile northwest of the Three Sisters, one of the famous pinnacles in the park (figure 1). The ground was held by Harry A. Binale's Navajo Tribal Mining Permit issued in May 1952. Due to the remote location of the mineralization it would be several years before it was

Figure 4. West Mitten, East Mitten, and Merrick Buttes, Arizona. View from Mitten Buttes overlook. Steven Semken photo.

mined. A mine road was built up the talus slope in the re-entrant and a few hundred tons of ore were shipped in 1962. The next operator shipped additional tonnage in 1965, but was killed on October 26, 1965, when he fell from the mesa in an ore hauler. An additional tonnage was shipped in 1966. Total production from the Mitchell Mesa mine was 1,764 tons of ore averaging 0.14 percent U_3O_8 and 1.71 percent V_2O_5 (Scarborough, 1981). The operator in 1965 built an airstrip on the top of Mitchell Mesa so he could fly in and out of the isolated location. The remains of the airstrip are still visible in 2000.

FEATURES OF THE PARK

The park contains the most scenic features of the entire Monument Valley area. The clustering of mesas, buttes, and valleys has created a three-fold division in the valley (Baars and others, 1973). The fore-valley includes the isolated mesas and buttes west of Wetherill and Mitchell Mesas and includes Mitchell Butte and Gray Whiskers. The outer valley is the area north of Observation Ridge, when the Visitor Center is located, and includes the Mitten and Merrick Buttes (figure 4), Sentinel Mesa, Big Chief and the northern buttes - Saddleback, Stagecoach, King On His Throne, Bear and Rabbit and Castle Rock (figure 5).

The inner valley includes the area east of Mitchell and Wetherill Mesas and north of Hunts Mesa. To many, this is the "true" Monument Valley. To appreciate the full beauty of the park the valley loop drive should be taken. From the Visitor Center, this 17 miles unimproved, sometimes rough, road takes one through the inner valley. The road passes by the spectacular mesas, buttes, and pinnacles such as the Three Sisters, The Thumb on Camel Butte, Big Chair, Totem Pole and The Yei-Bi-Chei (figure 1). There are four side trips off the main road to the North Window, Artist Point, Sand Springs and John Ford's Point (figure 1). Wetherill and Hunt Mesas are named for two early traders in Monument Valley. Gray Whiskers and Cly

Figure 5. Storm over North Buttes, Utah. Left to right, Saddleback, King On His Throne, Stagecoach, Bear and Rabbit, Castle Rock, and Big Chief. View from U.S. Highway 163. Chenoweth photo.

Buttes are named after Navajo Medicinemen. Mitchell and Merrick Buttes are named for two prospectors, who, according to legend, were killed near these buttes in 1880, while searching for Chief Hoskininni's silver mine. The mine has never been found and is one of the "lost mines" of the southwest.

In order to protect the archeological sites in the park and to insure the privacy of the Navajo families living in the area, tours outside the valley loop drive are by guides only. Information on guided tours is available at the Visitor Center as well as the current conditions of the valley drive. Tours can be arranged at the Visitor Center to areas outside the valley drive, such as to the arches and Anazazi sites in the southern part of the inner valley, that is Tse Biyi and Tse Biyi Yazzie (figure 1). The latter is Navajo for "small area between the rocks." Arches and ancient ruins in Mystery Valley, northwest of Wetherill Mesa (figure 1), is another destination of tours. The caves containing the cliff dwellings and the arches are formed in the lower part of the DeChelly Sandstone.

Hollywood brought the beauty of Monument Valley to the big screen. The Mitten Buttes have been the backdrop for many major productions starting with John Ford's Stagecoach in 1938. Other major productions include My Darling Clementine (1946), Fort Apache (1947), She Wore A Yellow Ribbon (1948), The Searchers (1956), Cheyenne Autumn (1963), How The West Was Won (1972), The Trials of Billy Jack (1973), The Legend Of The Lone Ranger (1986), and Back To The Future III (1988). Many television shows and commercials were also filmed in Monument Valley.

The U.S. Postal Service has recognized the beauty of Monument Valley. In 1996, the service issued a five-cent stamp, for non-profit organizations, featuring the Mitten Buttes.

ACKNOWLEDGMENT

Craig S. Goodknight and Russel Edge, kindly reviewed an earlier version of this paper.

Information on the history of the park was supplied by Herb T. Yazhe of the Navajo Nation's Parks and Recreation Department.

REFERENCES

Baars, D.L., Ash, S.R., and James, H.L., 1973, Second day road log of Monument Valley Navajo Tribal Park, *in* James, H.L., editor, Guidebook of Monument Valley and vicinity, Arizona and Utah: New Mexico Geological Society Guidebook 24, p. 37-45.

Blakey, R.C., and Baars, D.L., 1987, Monument Valley, Arizona and Utah, *in* Beus, S.S., editor, Centennial Field Guide, v. 2: Rocky Mountain Section Geological Society of America, p. 361-364.

Cooley, M.E., Harshbarger, J.W., Akers, J.P., and Hardt, W.F., 1969, Regional hydrogeology of the Navajo and Hopi Indian Reservations, Arizona, New Mexico and Utah: U.S. Geological Survey Professional Paper 521-A, plate 1, sheets 3 and 5.

Recreational Resources Department, no date, Monument Valley Navajo Tribal Park: Navajo Tribe and Beautyway Publications, 10 p.

Recreational Resources Department and National Park Service, 1983, Monument Valley Tribal Park master plan: Monument Valley Navajo Tribal Park, 53 p.

Scarborough, R.B., 1981, Radioactive occurrences and uranium production in Arizona: Arizona Bureau of Geology and Mineral Technology Open-File Report 81-1, 297 p.

Witkind, I.J., and Thaden, R.E., 1963, Geology and uranium-vanadium deposits of the Monument Valley area Apache and Navajo Counties, Arizona: U.S. Geological Survey Bulletin 1103, 171 p.

Lake Powell, Glen Canyon National Recreation Area
Photo courtesy of the Utah Travel Council

A Survey of the Paleontological Resources from the National Parks and Monuments in Utah

Vincent L. Santucci[1]

ABSTRACT

The National Park Service (NPS) administers thirteen park units within the state of Utah. Most of these parks and monuments have been established and are recognized for their significant geologic features. Fossiliferous rocks of Paleozoic, Mesozoic, and Cenozoic age have been identified in all of the National Park System units in Utah. In 1998, the first comprehensive inventory of paleontological resources in the national parks and monuments of Utah was initiated. A wide diversity of fossilized plants, invertebrates, vertebrates, and trace fossils has been documented. Paleontological resources identified from within the parks and monuments have been assessed relative to their scientific significance, potential threats, and management as non-renewable resources. Considerable focus has been directed towards the *in situ* management of the abundant fossil vertebrate tracks identified throughout the Mesozoic formations within at least seven National Park Service areas in Utah. The baseline paleontological resource data obtained during this survey will assist park staff with improved management of their paleontological resources and protection of fossils within their park.

HISTORY OF PALEONTOLOGY IN UTAH NATIONAL PARKS

During five expeditions into Utah led by Captain John C. Fremont between 1842 and 1854 (Rolle, 1991), rock, mineral and fossil specimens were collected and sent to geologist and paleontologist James Hall in New York. Hall contributed descriptions of the Utah fossils as an appendix in Fremont's 1845 report (Fremont, 1845). This work represents the first scientific publication to document Utah's geologic resources (Willis, 1996).

Captain Howard Stansbury explored Utah in 1850, searching for a railroad route across the Wasatch Mountains. During this survey, Stansbury collected fossils that he sent to James Hall for identification. Hall described these fossils in Stansbury's published report (Stansbury, 1852).

In 1859, the remains of the first dinosaur from Utah Territory were discovered by John S. Newberry, a member of Captain John N. Macomb's survey party. This partial skeleton was later studied and described by paleontologist Edward D. Cope who named the specimen *Dystrophaeus viaemalae* (Cope, 1877; Gillette, 1996). The fossil is a Late Jurassic sauropod dinosaur collected in the Morrison Formation.

Figure 1. John Wesley Powell, circa 1870 (National Park Service photo collection).

After the American Civil War, there was renewed interest in westward expansion. Congress funded four great surveys of the western territories during the late 1860s and

[1] *National Park Service, Kemmerer, WY 83101*

Figure 2.   Map showing the locations of the National Park System units in Utah (copyright National Geographic Maps, Trails Illustrated).

1870s (Bartlett, 1962).   Three scientific civilian surveys were organized under Ferdinand V. Hayden, Clarence E. King, and John Wesley Powell (figure 1). One military survey was formed and led by Lieutenant George M. Wheeler. All four of these surveys spent some time mapping and documenting geologic resources in Utah. Paleontologist F.B. Meeks participated in both the Hayden and King surveys and authored reports on fossils collected in Utah.

Yale paleontologist O.C. Marsh conducted field work in the Utah Territory during 1870. Marsh crossed the Uinta Mountains and traveled into the Uinta Basin where his field party discovered Eocene mammals, turtles, the rare Cretaceous crinoid *Uintacrinus*, and the second dinosaur specimen from Utah (Marsh, 1871). Marsh's dinosaur was the first theropod dinosaur known from Utah and was found near the current west boundary of Dinosaur National Monument (Bilbey and Hall, 1999).

A dinosaur bonebed (Carnegie Quarry) was discovered in northeastern Utah in 1909 by Carnegie Museum paleontologist Earl Douglass. Many significant dinosaur skeletons have been collected from the Upper Jurassic Morrison Formation in the Carnegie Quarry. One of the most complete sauropod skeletons ever found (*Apatosaurus louisae*) and a nearly complete specimen of *Allosaurus fragilis* were collected from the quarry (Holland, 1916a). In 1915, the site was established as Dinosaur National Monument through presidential procla-

mation. Carnegie Museum continued field excavations at the quarry between 1915 and 1922.

Over the past 150 years, Utah has been the focus of considerable interest by paleontologists. The 1939 Smithsonian Paleontological Expedition, the 1951 American Museum of Natural History field party led by Dr. Edwin Colbert, and other similar endeavors uncovered a great diversity of ancient plants and animals from Utah's national parks and monuments. During the 1990s, the Morrison Formation Extinct Ecosystem Project was a multi-disciplinary approach to understanding the geology and paleontology of the Upper Jurassic Morrison Formation. Many of the Utah national parks and monuments were assessed during this project. Although the Mesozoic strata and fossils have received the most attention in Utah, recent work in the Late Paleozoic and Early Cenozoic has led to some important paleontological discoveries. Fossil-rich deposits within the national parks and monuments of Utah yield specimens that contribute towards a better understanding of the history of life.

FOSSILIFEROUS UNITS IN THE UTAH NATIONAL PARK AREAS

Most of the National Park Service areas in Utah lie within the Colorado Plateau Province (figure 2). The plateau parks are dominated by a thick sequence of sedimentary rocks. The landscape is composed of colorful, eroded geologic features, punctuated by sparse vegetation in this semi-arid region. The Colorado, Green, and other rivers dissect the plateau rocks, forming canyons and mesas exposing the colorful layers of sedimentary strata that lend so much to the beauty of Utah. The scenic landforms that have formed naturally in Utah have gained the attention of the public and scientific community. Many of these outstanding geologic features of Utah are preserved within the National Park System.

The stratigraphic units vary between the eastern and western parts of the state and facies changes frequently reflect transgressive and regressive marine events. Between the Paleozoic and the Early Triassic, a sea on the western portion of Utah repeatedly advanced to the east. During the Cretaceous, a broad seaway that stretched northward from the Gulf of Mexico across the Great Plains and up to the Arctic Ocean, expanded and contracted intermittently, flooding eastern Utah from time to time. Tertiary and Quaternary fluvial and lacustrine deposits represent more recent geologic events. Stokes (1986), Hintze (1988), and the contributions included within this volume provide comprehensive overviews on the geologic history of Utah and the National Park Service areas within the state.

ARCHES NATIONAL PARK

Arches National Park was originally established as a national monument by presidential proclamation on April 12, 1929. The monument was redesignated as a national park on November 12, 1971, to preserve the extraordinary products of erosion including arches, windows, pinnacles, pedestals, and other landforms. For more detailed information on the geology and a stratigraphic section of Arches National Park see Doelling (this volume), Lohman (1975), and Doelling (1985).

The oldest fossils known from the Arches National Park area occur in the Middle Pennsylvanian Paradox Formation. The Paradox is a marine unit composed largely of limestone that contains the remains of algae, corals, bryozoans, brachiopods, crinoids, and other marine fossils. During the Late Pennsylvanian, cyclic sediments of the Honaker Trail Formation were deposited and are exposed on the western boundary of the park. Melton (1972) reports the following fossils from the Honaker Trail Formation in the Moab area: fusilinids, corals, bryozoans, brachiopods, gastropods, bivalves, crinoids, echinoids, and a variety of marine trace fossils (figure 3). In addition, Tidwell and others (1972) reported on a *Calamites*-like stem that was collected from the Honaker Trail Formation.

Fragmentary vertebrate remains occur in the Moenkopi and Chinle Formations in the Moab area. Just west of Arches National Park vertebrate bone, phytosaur teeth, and one theropod track have been reported from within the Upper Triassic Chinle Formation (S. Duffy, verbal communication, 1999).

Dinosaur tracks have been reported from in and

Figure 3. Marine invertebrates from the Pennsylvanian Honaker Trail Formation at Arches National Park.

around Arches National Park since the 1940's. Paleontologist Roland Bird is reported to have visited some track sites in the Arches area. Two theropod tracks have been identified in the Lower Jurassic Kayenta Formation in the "Petrified Dunes" area of the Arches National Park (S. Duffy, verbal communication, 1999). Tiny theropod tracks and a single quadrupedal trackway are reported from the Entrada Sandstone on the perimeter of the park (Fran Barnes, written communication, 1999). A dinosaur megatracksite, consisting of thousands of theropod tracks, weaves in and out of Arches National Park boundary. The track producing layer was originally identified as the Moab Tongue of the Entrada Sandstone (Lockley, 1990, 1991; Duffy, 1993), but more recent interpretation places the tracks into the basal sandstone bed of the Summerville Formation (Fred Peterson, written communication, 2000). Additional dinosaur track localities occur in the Morrison and Cedar Mountain Formations just outside of Arches National Park (Engelmann and Hasiotis, 1999). Several iguanodontid tracks in the collections at the College of Eastern Utah have been collected from the Cedar Mountain Formation just north of Arches National Park.

The Upper Jurassic Morrison Formation is well exposed in and around Arches National Park. Petrified wood and a partial sauropod skeleton are reported from the Morrison within the park. Large petrified logs occur just west of the park at the contact between the base of the Morrison and the underlying Summerville. The Yellow Cat Flat area northeast of the park was administered as part of Arches National Park until 1971. The Lower Cretaceous Cedar Mountain Formation is capped by the Dakota Sandstone in the Yellow Cat Flat area. The area includes the Robert Gaston Quarry from which the first specimen of *Utahraptor* and the armored nodosaur *Gastonia* were collected along with other vertebrate remains referred to as the "Yellow Cat Fauna." Bodily (1969) reported on the most complete specimen of the nodosaur *Sauropelta* from the Poison Strip Sandstone of the Cedar Mountain Formation. This specimen was found just west of Arches Na-

Figure 4.   A mammoth mandible collected from a rockshelter in Arches National Park.

tional Park in the Dalton Wells Quarry. Other specimens referred to as *Sauropelta* have been found along the north and west sides of the park (Carpenter and others, 1999). A variety of vertebrate tracks, including the first theropod tracks and possible pterosaur feeding traces, have been identified in the Cedar Mountain Formation from within and near Arches National Park (Lockley and others, 1999; J. Kirkland, verbal communication). Specimens of the cycadeoidales *Monanthesia* have been collected from the Cedar Mountain Formation near Arches National Park (Furniss and Tidwell, 1972).

The youngest Mesozoic unit in Arches National Park is the Upper Cretaceous Mancos Shale, which is exposed in the southern portion of Salt Valley. A few marine invertebrate fossils, including bivalves, occur in the Mancos Shale in the park. Plesiosaur and mosasaur remains have been discovered in the Mancos Shale about 35 miles outside of Arches National Park.

During the 1950's, Arches Chief Ranger Lloyd Pierson discovered the remains of a Columbian mammoth in the park. A partial mandible was collected from the site and was determined to be from a juvenile (figure 4). The specimen, nicknamed "Woody", may represent one of the youngest juvenile mammoths from the Colorado Plateau. The remains of a bighorn sheep (*Ovis canadensis*) and a bison (*Bison bison*) were found in rock shelters within Arches National Park (Mead and others, 1991). Packrat middens are common in the dry rock shelters and contain needles from Douglas fir (*Pseudotsuga menziesii*) and Limber Pine (*Pinus flexilis*). Radiocarbon dating of organic remains from the middens have yielded dates between 12,400 to 20,000 years B.P.

BRYCE CANYON NATIONAL PARK

Bryce Canyon National Park was originally established as a national monument on June 8, 1923. The area was designated and renamed Utah National Park on June

7, 1924. Finally, on February 25, 1928, the park was renamed Bryce Canyon National Park. Bryce Canyon National Park lies along the eastern margin of the Paunsaugunt Plateau in south-central Utah. The pink and white spires and cliffs have developed along an eroding fault escarpment within the early Tertiary Claron Formation. Underlying Upper Cretaceous rocks have produced a variety of paleontological resources from within and near Bryce Canyon National Park. For more information on the geology and a stratigraphic section of Bryce Canyon National Park, see Davis and Pollock, (this volume), Gregory (1951), and Bowers (1990).

The Dakota Formation is the oldest exposed unit within Bryce Canyon National Park. A large collection of vertebrate fossils, including the remains of fish, sharks, rays, lizards, crocodiles, turtles, dinosaurs, and early marsupial mammals, occur in the fluvial facies of the Dakota Formation near the park (Jeff Eaton, written communication, 1999). The last North American fossil lungfish is known from the Dakota just east of the park, which documents the last gasp of a largely Jurassic freshwater fish fauna that dies out at the end of the Cenomanian (Kirkland, 1987). Locally, *in situ* stumps, large fragments of silicified and coalified wood, and palynomorphs (spores and pollen) have been found at the top of the Dakota Formation (May and Traverse, 1973). The remains of the bivalve (oyster) *Exogyra* sp. commonly occur at the top of the Dakota Formation (Gayle Pollock, written communication, 1999).

The Tropic Shale and its equivalents are some of the most fossiliferous Upper Cretaceous (Upper Cenomanian to Middle Turonian) marine units in North America. The Tropic contains an abundance of marine invertebrates and the remains of a few marine vertebrates. The lower portion of the Tropic Shale contains the Late Cenomanian index fossil *Sciponoceras gracile* ("*Scip*" Zone) and the upper portion contains the middle Turonian index fossil *Collignoniceras woollgari* (Peterson and Waldrop, 1965). A small collection of invertebrate fossils has been recovered from within the park (Cobban and others, 1996). Gayle Pollock has collected fossil pearls from the Tropic Shale outside of the park near Tropic, Utah (W. Cobban, written communication, 2000). A few localized concentrations of fossil shark and ray teeth have been recovered from the upper portions of the Tropic Shale at nearby localities outside of the park.

The Straight Cliffs and Wahweap Formations contain significant terrestrial vertebrates (theropods and hadrosaurs). Eaton (1993, 1999) suggested that the fauna from the stratigraphically highest Cretaceous rocks of the plateau shows affinities to the Kaiparowits Formation (Judithian Land-Mammal Age). Eaton and his colleagues are continuing their research on the Wahweap and possible Kaiparowits sediments in an effort to refine the biostratigraphy of the uppermost Cretaceous from the Paunsaugunt Plateau. The vertebrate fauna from Bryce Canyon includes fish, dinosaurs, crocodiles, lizards, turtles, and mammals, including a partial upper molar from a marsupial (Eaton, 1994, 1995, 1999; Eaton, and others, 1993; Eaton, and others, 1998; Eaton and Morrow, 1990; Munk, 1998). Chris Shierup of Northern Illinois University surveyed the Wahweap? Formation in the western part of the Paunsaugunt Plateau, including one locality in the park, during 1999. Shierup recovered vertebrae, ribs, shoulder bones, and one theropod tooth that are currently under study.

The Claron Formation (Late Paleocene to Early Eocene) is composed of limestone, mudstone, sandstone, and conglomerate beds that form the scenic landforms of Bryce Canyon National Park. The strata were deposited in lacustrine fluvial and overbank floodplain environments, but have been altered considerably by massive calcretization of many of the beds. A few invertebrate fossils and palynomorphs have been documented from this formation (Eaton, and others, 1999b). A large number of invertebrate trace fossils were recently reported from the Claron Formation (Bown and others, 1997). The ichnofossils include hymenoptera nests, beetle burrows, and scorpion trails.

The Boat Mesa Conglomerate, inferred to be Oligocene in age, overlies the Claron Formation. Permian invertebrates are preserved within chert pebbles from this conglomerate, indicating that Permian age rocks were at least a partial source of the clasts. A single mammoth tooth (*Mammuthus*) is cataloged in the park collections and was allegedly collected from Pleistocene alluvium within Bryce Canyon National Park (Gayle Pollock, written communication, 1999).

CANYONLANDS NATIONAL PARK

Canyonlands National Park was established on September 12, 1964. The park consists of scenic geologic features including spires, mesas, and canyons formed by the downcutting of the Colorado and Green Rivers into the heart of the Colorado Plateau. For more information on the geology and a stratigraphic section of Canyonlands National Park, see Baars (this volume), Lohman (1974), and Huntoon and others (1982).

The Honaker Trail Formation is a very fossiliferous Pennsylvanian limestone exposed in Canyonlands National Park. This unit contains rugose corals, bryozoans, brachiopods, gastropods, a few trilobites, and crinoids.

A fossil-rich locality within the Permian Cedar Mesa Sandstone is reported from the Indian Creek drainage just east of Canyonlands National Park (Stanesco and Campbell, 1989; Sumida and others, 1999). Cranial and vertebral remains of the pelycosaur reptile *Sphenacodon* and fragments identified as the temnospondyl amphibian *Eryops* were collected from within a petrified log jam. The logs at this locality have been identified as conifers and reach nearly a meter in diameter. This site was completely destroyed by vandalism in 1995 (Sumida and others, 1999). There may also be some tracks in the Permian Cedar Mesa Sandstone in the park that are accessible by river (A. Hunt, verbal communication, 1998).

A few poorly preserved steinkerns and gastropod impressions were reported from the Lower Triassic Sinbad Limestone Member of the Moenkopi Formation in Canyonlands National Park (Lucas, 1995). These specimens were first reported by McKnight (1940) and are dominated by the following taxa: the brachiopod *Lingula* sp., *Monotis thaynesiana*, unidentified viviparoid gastropods, and the ammonite *Meekoceras* sp.

The Upper Triassic Chinle Formation is well exposed in Canyonlands National Park and contains diverse faunal, floral, and ichnofossil assemblages. Vertebrate body fossils reported from the park include the remains of semionotid and turseodid fish, metoposaurs, phytosaurs, and the aetosaur *Stagonolepis* (Hasiotis, 1993; Lucas and others, 1997; Heckert and others, 1999;). Fresh water gastropods, bivalves, conchostrachans, and the earliest known crayfish also occur within this unit. An abundance of fossil plants occur in the Owl Rock Member of the Chinle including: *Neocalamites* sp. and *Pagiophyllum* sp.

Burrows produced by lungfish, crayfish, worms, and insects are common in the Chinle Formation in Canyonlands National Park (Hasiotis and Mitchell, 1989; Hasiotis, 1993, 1995). Hasiotis (1993) also reported a horseshoe crab resting trace from the park. A single well-preserved impression of a tridactyl dinosaur footprint (*Grallator* sp.) was found in the Rock Point Member of the Chinle Formation near Upheaval Dome (Hunt and others, 1993b; Lucas and others, 1995). Another Chinle tracksite contains impressions of a tetrapod with a four-toed manus and a five-toed pes. These tracks have blunt toes, lack claw impressions, and have been identified as *Brachychirotherium* sp. There are also two types of large five-toed tracks. One set is associated with an aetosaur-like reptile and the other is attributed to a dicynodont reptile (Santucci and others, 1998).

Fossil vertebrate tracks are also known from the upper part of the Kayenta Formation just below the overlying Navajo Sandstone in Canyonlands National Park (Lockley and Hunt, 1993; Santucci and others, 1998).

CAPITOL REEF NATIONAL PARK

Capitol Reef was established as a national monument on August 2, 1937. The site was redesignated as a national park on December 18, 1971. The park preserves narrow, high-walled gorges cut through the 100-mile-long Water Pocket Fold. For more information on the geology and a stratigraphic section of Capitol Reef National Park, see Morris and others (this volume), Gregory and Anderson (1939), Smith and others (1963), Davidson (1967), Billingsley and others (1987), and Collier (1987).

John C. Fremont traveled through the northern portion of the Capitol Reef area in 1853, during his fifth and final expedition through Utah prior to the Civil War. Fremont's party may have been the first Europeans to enter the area. G.K. Gilbert was probably the first geologist to visit the area which is now within Capitol Reef National

Park. Fossil vertebrate tracks in the park received considerable attention by researchers after their discovery in 1945. A paleontological survey was conducted in 1994 along the GarKane Power Company's Right of Way through Capitol Reef National Park (Burres, 1994).

The Permian White Rim Sandstone (Cutler Group) which crops out locally within the park, is interpreted as a shoreface and coastal dune deposit in Capitol Reef National Park (Kamola and Chan, 1988). The marine trace fossils *Thalassinoides* and *Chondrites* are abundant in some parts of the cross-stratified sandstone facies. The Kaibab Limestone is a fossiliferous marine carbonate unit that interfingers with the White Rim Sandstone. The Kaibab Limestone contains fragmentary marine invertebrates including bryozoans, brachiopods, gastropods, bivalves, and crinoids.

The Triassic Sinbad Limestone Member of the Moenkopi Formation contains brachiopods, gastropods, bivalves, and ammonites. *Lingula* sp. is the only invertebrate fossil to be found outside of the Sinbad Limestone in the Moenkopi (Smith and others, 1963). Fossil vertebrate tracks were first reported from the Moenkopi in the Capitol Reef area by Charles Kelly in 1945. Paleontologist Charles Camp and Zion National Park naturalist Myrl Walker independently visited Capitol Reef in 1950 to survey for additional Moenkopi tracks after learning about Kelly's discovery. Peabody (1948, 1956) and Lammers (1964) published on the fossil vertebrate tracks, including *Chirotherium, Rotodactylus, Palaeophycus*, and *Diplidnites* from the Torrey Member of the Moenkopi Formation within Capitol Reef National Park. McAllister and Kirby (1998) reported on a variety of subaqueous reptile traces including: kick-off scours, z-traces, and buoyancy-size-mitigated, variably preserved traces.

In 1921, R.C. Moore, who was working with H.E. Gregory, collected some leaf impressions from the Upper Triassic Shinarump Formation in the Circle Cliffs area that is now within Capitol Reef National Park (Ash, 1975). These fossil plants were described by Berry (1927) and named *Zamites powelli*. Fossil plants were also collected in the Capitol Reef area by Roland Brown of the U.S. Geological Survey. Brown identified the fossil plants as *Palissya* sp., *Sphenozamites* sp., and an undetermined cycad leaf. The best preserved and most abundant stems of the fossil horsetail *Equisetites* occur in the Shinarump Member in the northern part of the park. *Phlebopteris, Cyneopteris, Cladophlebis, Pagiophyllum,* and *Araucarioxylon* are also known from this locality (Ash, 1975; 1993a). Leaves of a palmlike plant called *Sanmiguelia* cf. *S. lewisi* were reported from the Owl Rock Member of the Chinle Formation at Capitol Reef National Park (Ash, 1982). Petrified wood (figure 5), leaf impressions, bivalves, vertebrate bones, coprolites and trace fossils, including a few tridactyl tracks, have also been found within the Chinle at the park.

Large algal mounds are reported from interdunal playa deposits within the Jurassic Navajo Sandstone in

Figure 5. *Petrified wood from the Upper Triassic Chinle Formation at Capitol Reef National Park.*

Capitol Reef National Park (Len Eisenberg, verbal communication, 1999). The algal mounds occur within carbonate lenses that have been tentatively interpreted as "Oasis deposits."

The Middle Jurassic Carmel Formation in central and southern Utah, including several localities in Capitol Reef National Park, contains a small but notable marine assemblage including *Ostrea* sp., *Trigonia* sp., *Camptonectes* sp. and the star-shaped columnals of the crinoid *Pentacrinus asteriscus* (Imlay, 1964; Sohl, 1965). Jurassic dinosaur bones and petrified logs occur in the upper portion of the Salt Wash Member of the Morrison Formation in and near Capitol Reef National Park. Turtle and dinosaur remains are reported from the Lower Cretaceous Cedar Mountain Formation just north of the park (J. Kirkland, verbal communication, 1999).

The Cretaceous Dakota Sandstone is locally fossiliferous at Capitol Reef and contains a dense oyster shell reef composed of *Pycnodonte* sp. and *Exogyra (Costagyra) olisiponensis*   Marine fossils, including bivalves, gastropods, ammonites, and shark's teeth, have been recovered from the Tununk Shale Member and the Blue Gate Member of the Mancos Shale in and around Capitol Reef National Park (W. Cobban, written communication, 2000).

The Flagstaff Limestone is a fossiliferous unit of Late Paleocene or Early Eocene age in the park. Charophytes, ostracods, bivalves, and gastropods indicate a freshwater origin for the carbonate unit (Smith and others, 1963).

Over two dozen packrat middens from Capitol Reef National Park have been studied in order to assess local vegetational changes from the Pleistocene to the Recent (Cole, 1992; Cole and Henderson, 1993). The oldest midden is dated to somewhat older than 39,000 years B.P. The remains of a Pleistocene mammoth were found on Boulder Mountain, west of Capitol Reef National Park.

CEDAR BREAKS NATIONAL MONUMENT

Cedar Breaks National Monument was established through Presidential proclamation on August 22, 1933. The monument preserves a huge and colorful natural amphitheater eroded from a 2,000-foot-thick escarpment in upper Cretaceous and early Tertiary rocks. For more information on the geology and a stratigraphic section of Cedar Breaks National Monument see Hatfield and others (this volume).

The only reports of paleontological resources from within or near Cedar Breaks National Monument include some marine invertebrates from the Jurassic Carmel Formation just west of the monument (Imlay, 1964) and freshwater gastropods from the early Tertiary Claron Formation. Eaton (written communication, 1999; Eaton, and others, 1999a) reports on vertebrate fossils, including fish, turtles, and dinosaurs, from within the Straight Cliffs Formation in Cedar Canyon just west of the monument.

David Madsen (Utah Geological Survey, verbal communication, 1999) is examining Quaternary pond deposits from two localities that are adjacent to Cedar Breaks National Monument. The remains of insects, plant macrofossils, and palynomorphs (spores and pollen) have been recovered. Radiocarbon dates from these deposits range from 17,000 B.P. to the Recent.

DINOSAUR NATIONAL MONUMENT

Dinosaur National Monument was established by presidential proclamation on October 4, 1915. The site was originally established to protect the famous dinosaur quarry discovered in the Upper Jurassic Morrison Formation by Carnegie Museum paleontologist Earl Douglass. The monument was enlarged in 1938 to include the spectacular canyons cut by the Green and Yampa Rivers. For more information on the geology and a stratigraphic section of Dinosaur National Monument, see Gregson and Chure, (this volume), Untermann and Untermann (1954, 1969), Hansen and others (1983), and Hansen (1996).

The oldest sedimentary unit known from Dinosaur National Monument is the Precambrian Uinta Mountain Group. Hansen (1996) reported on fossilized algal globules *Chuaria* sp. from the Uinta Mountain Group near Manila, Utah, about 70 miles north of the monument.

The Upper Cambrian Lodore Formation consists of variegated, glauconitic shales, and sandstones that contain marine invertebrates and trace fossils. Brachiopods, gastropods, and trilobites have been identified from the Lodore Formation in Dinosaur National Monument (Herr, 1979; Herr and others, 1982; Hansen, 1996).

Corals, brachiopods, gastropods, and echinoderms are preserved, but rare, in the Lower Mississippian Madison Limestone (Hansen and others, 1983). Upper Mississippian brachiopods, fish, and coal beds are present in the Doughnut Formation (Hansen and others, 1983). The Lower Pennsylvanian Round Valley Limestone contains bryozoans, brachiopods, mollusks, and echinoderms (Hansen and others, 1983). Sponge spicules, corals, brachiopods, echinoid spines, crinoids, foraminifera, and conodonts are common in the marine facies of the Middle Pennsylvanian Morgan Formation (Driese, 1982).

The Permian Park City Formation (equivalent to the Phosphoria Formation farther north) consists of limestone, sandstone, and some chert layers. Marine invertebrates including brachiopods, bivalves, cephalopods, gastropods, and other invertebrates have been found in this unit (Hansen and others, 1983).

Peabody (1948) studied some unusual reptile tracks in the Lower Triassic Moenkopi Formation in the vicinity of Dinosaur National Monument. These include some swimming traces now in the collections of the Utah Field House Museum of Natural History in Vernal, Utah. *Scoyenia* traces have been reported from the Moenkopi at Dinosaur National Monument (Lockley and others, 1990).

In the 1960's an important vertebrate tracksite was discovered just northeast of Dinosaur National Monument. Today over two dozen tracksites have been identified within the monument. Numerous tracksites have been discovered in the Upper Triassic Popo Agie and Chinle Formations. Fossil tracks are diverse and include those identified from dinosaurs, mammal-like reptiles, phytosaurs, aetosaurs, lepidosaurs, ?trilophosaurs, and tanystropheids (Lockley and others, 1990, 1992a, 1992b, 1992c; Hunt and others, 1993a). Among these is a swimming trackway of *Gwyneddichnium* that shows webbing between the toes. In addition, there are examples of both walking and swimming types of these tracks. Horseshoe crab-like tracks are documented from the Chinle Formation at Dinosaur National Monument. There is also some petrified wood in the Chinle Formation in the monument.

Tridactyl theropod tracks and a rich *Otozoum* tracksite are known from the Lower Jurassic Glen Canyon Sandstone, which is equivalent to the Navajo Sandstone farther south and the Nugget Sandstone farther west and north (Lockley and others, 1992a; Santucci and others, 1998). The Middle Jurassic Carmel Formation is a shallow marine deposit that locally contains gypsiferous beds. Bivalves, gastropods, echinoderms, and a few rare tridactyl vertebrate tracks have been reported from the Carmel Formation in nearby areas adjacent to Dinosaur National Monument.

Chure (1993) reported on three plesiosaur specimens that may have been collected from the Redwater Member of the Stump Formation (Middle to Upper Jurassic) near the western boundary of Dinosaur National Monument. Belemnites, ammonites, gastropods, and bivalves occur in the Middle Jurassic Curtis Member of the Stump Formation in the Dinosaur National Monument area.

The Upper Jurassic Morrison Formation is widely recognized as one of the most prolific dinosaur-bearing units in the world. In addition to the dinosaurs, the Morrison Formation has produced important collections of Jurassic mammals and other vertebrates (Chure and Engelmann,

Figure 6. Paleontologist Earl Douglass during the excavation of a Diplodocus skeleton in the Douglass Quarry at Dinosaur National Monument, circa 1923 (National Park Service photo collection).

1989).   The Morrison Formation at Dinosaur National Monument contains four members including, from oldest to youngest, the Windy Hill, Tidwell, Salt Wash, and Brushy Basin Members (Turner and Peterson, 1999).

Utah's first theropod dinosaur (also recognized as the second dinosaur discovered in Utah) was found in 1870 near what is today Dinosaur National Monument (Marsh, 1871; Bilbey and Hall, 1999). Earl Douglass made his famous discovery of the dinosaur bonebed in 1909. Under Douglass' direction the Carnegie Museum worked the site until 1922. During 1923, the U.S. National Museum collected a specimen of *Diplodocus*, which was mounted for display in that museum (figure 6). In 1924, the University of Utah collected a skeleton of *Androdemus* (now *Allosaurus*) from the quarry. Holland (1912, 1915, 1916b, and 1924) and Gilmore (1924, 1925a, 1925b, 1926, 1932, 1936a, and 1936b) published extensively on the dinosaur discoveries from Dinosaur National Monument.

Theodore White was hired as the monument's first paleontologist in 1953. White focused his attention on the preparation of the *in situ* bone-bearing layer and talking with the public about the world of dinosaurs. He hired and trained two maintenance men, Tobe Wilkins and Jim Adams, to relief the bones on the Carnegie Quarry cliff face. White published both scientific and popular articles about the fossils at Dinosaur National Monument (White, 1958, 1964, 1967). White liked to call himself the "Chief Ramrod of the Hammers and Chisels" until his retirement in 1973 (Ann Elder, written communication, 1999). Russ King, Dan Chure, Ann Elder, and Scott Madsen have recently worked as staff paleontologists at Dinosaur National Monument (Chure, 1987, 1992; Chure and McIntosh, 1990). Elder (1999) provides an historical overview of the Carnegie Quarry at Dinosaur National Monument..

Between 1989 and 1992, George Engelmann conducted a comprehensive paleontological survey of the Morrison Formation at Dinosaur National Monument (Engelmann, 1992). More than 270 fossil sites were recorded during the survey. Most of the sites were dinosaur bone localities, but sites containing plant remains, invertebrates, and small vertebrates were also reported.

A number of new dinosaurs have been collected in recent years from Dinosaur National Monument. In 1990, the first large carnivorous theropod dinosaur was collected from the Salt Wash Member of the Morrison Formation (Chure and Madsen, 1993; Chure and others, 1993). Chure (1994) reported on the oldest troodontid dinosaur which was recovered from the monument. A partial skeleton of a hatchling dinosaur, identified as *Camptosaurus*, was discovered at the monument in 1991 (Chure and others, 1992). This is the only hatchling of *Camptosaurus* sp. known from the fossil record.

Chure and others (1989) reported on non-mammalian vertebrates collected from the Brushy Basin Member of the Morrison in Dinosaur National Monument. Evans and Chure (1999) reported on lizards from the Morrison Formation that were collected in the monument. The remains of the turtle *Glyptops* sp. and the crocodile *Hoplosuchus kayi* (Gilmore, 1926) and *Goniopholis* sp. have been collected from the monument. Several tiny frog skeletons and many isolated frog bones have been collected from a Brushy Basin microvertebrate locality in the park. Some of the frog remains have recently been described and represent a new pipoid anuran named *Rhadinosteus* (Henrici, 1992, 1993, 1998).

Engelmann and others (1989) reported on microvertebrates, including mammals, that have been collected from quarries in Dinosaur National Monument. The quarries are in the Brushy Basin Member of the Morrison and have yielded hundreds of isolated teeth and a few partial jaws. The skull of a new multituberculate *Glirodon grandis* was also found at the monument (Engelmann and Callison, 1999). Other mammals identified include a triconodont, a symmetrodont, at least two species of dryolestids, and a paurodontid.

Yen and Reeside (1950) described freshwater mollusks from the Morrison Formation. Sohn and Peck (1963) identified the ostracod *Theriosynoecum wyomingense* as a guide fossil for the Salt Wash Member of the Morrison Formation.

Ash (1993b, 1994) reported on an unusual leaf *Czechanowskia* sp. from the Brushy Basin Member of the Morrison Formation in the monument. This plant is considered by some as an indicator of humid paleoclimates. The discovery of this plant in deposits of an alkaline-saline lake farther south brings this interpretation into question (Turner and Fishman, 1991). A ginkgo leaf locality occurs in the middle of the Brushy Basin Member of the Morrison Formation. Tidwell (1990) reported on a plant locality in Orchid Draw in the western part of Dinosaur National Monument. A palynological (fossil pollen) assessment of the Morrison Formation, including several sites within the monument, was conducted by Litwin and others (1998).

Recent evidence shows that dermestid beetle larvae (Coleoptera: Dermestidae) borings are preserved in dinosaur bones collected from the Carnegie Quarry (Hastiotis, and others, 1999). These trace fossils suggest subaerial exposure of the dinosaur carcasses prior to burial and represent the earliest evidence of dermestids in the paleontological record.

Recent work in the Lower Cretaceous Cedar Mountain Formation has produced some spectacular fossil specimens. One site in particular, a river-deposited bonebed, has yielded a nearly complete articulated sauropod skull, elements of a second disarticulated sauropod skull, numerous sauropod post-cranial elements, and a few isolated theropod bones. Though only a preliminary analysis of these fossils has been completed, the cranial material appears to be some of the most complete Cretaceous sauropod specimens found in North America (Ann Elder, written communication, 1999).

The Dakota Formation of Late Early or Early Late Cretaceous age consists of shoreface and terrestrial strata deposited along the western margin of the western interior seaway. Petrified wood and fragmentary invertebrate remains have been found in this formation. Fish scales and bones are locally abundant in the Mowry Shale of Late Cretaceous age. Bivalves, ammonites, and shark teeth are also known from the Mowry Shale in the Dinosaur National Monument area. The Upper Cretaceous Frontier Formation contains bivalves, gastropods, ammonites, petrified wood, and some thin coal beds. The Mancos Shale is not well exposed in the monument, but locally this unit is very fossiliferous and preserves a high diversity of marine invertebrates. Ammonites are reported from the Mancos at Ashley Creek and Brush Creek near the monument (Kennedy and Cobban, 1991).

Sharpe (1991) reported on the Quaternary and Holocene flora in Dinosaur National Monument collected to assess vegetation changes.

GLEN CANYON NATIONAL RECREATION AREA

Initially administered under a cooperative agreement with the Bureau of Reclamation that was signed on April 18, 1958, Glen Canyon National Recreation Area was established as a unit of the National Park Service on October 27, 1972. The recreation area includes the 186-mile-long Lake Powell, which was formed by one of the world's highest concrete dams. For more information on the geology and a stratigraphic section of Glen Canyon National Recreation Area see Anderson and others (this volume).

John Wesley Powell led expeditions down the Colorado River, passing through Glen Canyon in 1869 and 1871. Powell and his survey team traveled the Colorado River by boat and collected a few paleontological specimens. The Geographic and Geologic Survey of the Col-

orado Plateau was established soon thereafter and was under the direction of Powell until 1879, when all of the geographical and geological surveys of the western United States were abolished and their work was incorporated into the newly formed United States Geological Survey. Construction of the Glen Canyon Dam was initiated in 1957 and completed in 1963. Lake Powell was finally filled approximately 17 years after completion of the dam. A systematic paleontological survey was never conducted along the Colorado River in Glen Canyon prior to construction of the dam. Fossils along the lake shoreline experience periods of submergence and periods of emergence due to fluctuations in the lake's water levels. A popular publication by Crampton (1994) provides photos of the natural and cultural resources within the Glen Canyon area prior to the flooding by Lake Powell.

A species of the rare temnospondyl amphibian *Platyhystrix* was collected from the Upper Pennsylvanian Halgaito Shale at a site called the Cedar Point Locality (Sumida and others, 1999). A nearly complete dorsal "sail" from this animal was recovered from the Cedar Point Locality that overlooks the San Juan River Canyon where it winds through the upper part of Glen Canyon National Recreation Area. The fossil was recovered from a conglomeratic stream channel (Vaughn, 1962; Berman and others, 1981). In a locality east of the Cedar Point Locality, just north of Mexican Hat, Utah, Vaughn (1962) documented so many specimens of this amphibian that he designated the site the "*Platyhystrix* Pocket."

Three Permian vertebrate tracksites are known from the Cedar Mesa Sandstone within Glen Canyon National Recreation Area. One of the tracksites documented evidence of a predator attacking a prey, however, only photographs and replicas of this trackway are available for study since the original site is now under the waters of Lake Powell. This tracksite was named the "Dirty Devil Tracksite" and has been interpreted as a "Permian Murder Scene" because *Anomalopus* sp. tracks converge on the smaller *Stenichus* sp. trackway (Lockley and Madsen, 1993). The two other Permian track localities are named "Steer Gulch" and "Grand Gulch" tracksites.

Three types of subaqueous traces, including both vertebrate and invertebrate swim traces, were found at two tracksites in the Middle Triassic Moenkopi Formation within Glen Canyon National Recreation Area (Schultz and others, 1995). The vertebrate traces are preserved as parallel scrape marks, thought to have been formed when a buoyant animal's manus touched the substrate during a swimming stroke. The invertebrate traces are small, crescent-shaped swim traces attributed to limulids. There are also Triassic Moenkopi tracks discovered near Hite on the shores of Lake Powell.

Vertebrate tracks occur in the Upper Triassic Chinle Formation along the northern shores of Lake Powell (Lockley and others, 1992d). These tracks are identified as *Atreipus milfordensis*, which represent the first discovery of these tracks in the western United States. Hunt (A.P.

Figure 7. *Eubrontes dinosaur tracks from the Jurassic Kayenta Formation at Glen Canyon National Recreation Area.*

Figure 8. *Painting of a Cretaceous plesiosaur by artist Rich Penny (copyright 1998).*

Hunt, verbal communication, 1998) reported that fossil vertebrate bones, including a fish, were recovered from the Rock Point Member of the Chinle Formation in the recreation area. Gregory and Moore (1931) also reported on some Chinle vertebrate remains from the Lee's Ferry area. Vertebrate bones are also reported from the Chinle in The Rincon area (Tom Chidsey, written communication, 2000). Petrified wood from the Chinle Formation has been reported from a number of localities within Glen Canyon National Recreation Area including The Rincon, Blue Notch Canyon, and from Neskahi Wash.

At least three tracksites occur in the Wingate Sandstone (basal formation of the Glen Canyon Group) at Glen Canyon National Recreation Area. The three sites are at Lee's Ferry (Riggs, 1904), North Wash, and The Rincon. All the Wingate specimens represent the ichnogenus *Grallator*.

Tracks are known from the upper part of the Kayenta Formation just below the Navajo Sandstone. Large theropod tracks (*Eubrontes* sp.) were removed from the Kayenta in Explorer Canyon and are on display at the Page Visitor Center (figure 7). The Explorer Canyon tracksite was featured in a 1967 National Geographic Magazine (Edwards, 1967). *Eubrontes* sp. represents the first large theropod track type in the fossil record.

There are at least ten tracksites known from the Navajo Sandstone in Glen Canyon National Recreation Area (Lockley and others, 1998). All of these sites are on the west end of the recreation area. A number of theropod dinosaur tracks from the lower portion of the Navajo were discovered and then destroyed during the construction of Glen Canyon Dam (Stokes, 1978). One tracksite from the upper portion of the Navajo has been under water for over a decade. An *Otozoum* sp. "giant animal" tracksite, consisting of at least 28 criss-crossing trackways, has been documented from the Navajo Sandstone (Lockley and oth-

ers, 1998). There are very small theropod tracks in association with the *Otozoum* sp. tracks. Another impressive tracksite occurs in the Navajo on an overhang, about 150 feet above lake level at Tapestry Wall north of Bullfrog. This tracksite contains at least 14 large theropod (*Eubrontes* sp.) tracks on the underside of a long overhanging exposure. A partial reptile skeleton was discovered from a laminated pond limestone in the Navajo Sandstone in Navajo Nation portion of Glen Canyon National Recreation Area (P. Buchheim, verbal communication, 1999).

There are several sauropod footprints with preserved skin impressions found near Lake Powell. These tracks occur near the contact between the Summerville Formation and the Morrison Formation. This site is near Bullfrog, on the north side of Lake Powell. There is also a site just outside of the boundaries of Glen Canyon National Recreation Area that contains possible pterosaur tracks (Lockley and others, 1998). At one Morrison locality in the recreation area, termite nests are preserved by preferential cementation. Therefore, the fossilized nests appeared as cylindrical concretions about 20 cm in diameter that stand 30 to 40 cm above the sandstone surface (Hasiotis and Demko, 1996; Engelmann, 1999).

The bivalve *Exogyra* occurs in the Cretaceous Dakota Sandstone in Glen Canyon National Recreation Area. At least three plesiosaur localities have been reported in the Upper Cretaceous Tropic Shale from within the Glen Canyon area (Gillette and others, 1999). The skeletal material assessed from these sites indicates all of the specimens are associated with adult plesiosaurs (figure 8). Teeth from the extinct skate *Ptychodus* sp., a few unidentified shark teeth, and a variety of marine invertebrates have also been recovered from the Tropic Shale in the national recreation area.

In 1982, a survey team in Glen Canyon National Recreation Area entered a large, dry sandstone cave known as Bechan Cave. The survey team found an organic layer of Pleistocene age preserved in the cave that consists of more than 300 m^3 of plant debris, herbivore dung, and dried animal remains. Radiocarbon dates from the cave deposits range from 11,670 to 12,900 years B.P. (Davis and others, 1984, 1985; Mead and Agenbroad, 1992). Analysis of the dung identified the source of the fecal material came from the megaherbivores *Mammuthus* sp., *Euceratherium collinum, Nothrotheriops shastensis, Bison* sp., and cf. *Oreamnos harringtoni*. Coprolites of rabbits, rodents, and possibly mountain sheep or deer (*Ovis canadensis* or *Odocoileus* sp.) were also recovered from the dung deposits. Preliminary analysis of the hair samples indicated the sources to be from mammoths and two types of ground sloths. A *Euceratherium* lower molar and metapodial were also recovered from Bechan Cave. Microfaunal remains from the cave included: *Scaphiopus intermontanus, S.* cf. *S. bombifrons, Pituophis melanoleucus, Crotalus* cf. *C. viridis*, a grouse-sized bird, *Brachylagus idahoensis, Marmota flaviventris, Spermophilus* sp., *Thomomys* sp., *Lagurus curtatus, Microtus* sp., and *Neotoma cinerea* (Mead and Agenbroad, 1992; Mead and others, 1993b). Pollen analysis of the dung blanket indicated that, away from the riparian area, the predominant plant community may have been sagebrush steppe rather than blackbrush (*Coleogyne* sp.), which is the dominant shrub today (Mead, and others, 1984). In an effort to locate additional Pleistocene remains, a helicopter survey was conducted in 1983 at Glen Canyon, however, no new significant paleontological resources were discovered.

GOLDEN SPIKE NATIONAL HISTORIC SITE

Golden Spike National Historic Site was established on April 2, 1957, in north-central Utah, to commemorate the completion of the first transcontinental railroad in the United States. The site is located at the point where the Central Pacific and Union Pacific Railroads met in 1869.

Late Paleozoic miogeoclinal rocks are exposed in uplifted areas in and around Golden Spike National Historic Site. The Pennsylvanian–Permian Oquirrh Formation is exposed in the nearby Promontory Mountains. The basal limestone member consists of coarse bioclastic beds that contain fusulinids, horn corals, bryozoans, brachiopods, gastropods, and crinoids that have been reported to be Early to Middle Pennsylvanian in age (Miller and others, 1991).

A fossilized mandible from an extinct marmot, *Paenemarmota* cf. *P. sawrockensis*, was collected from an early Pliocene colluvium locality near Golden Spike (Nelson and Miller, 1990).

Fine-grained lacustrine deposits associated with the Late Pleistocene Lake Bonneville Alloformation contain pockets of ostracods, bivalves, and gastropods (Don Currey, verbal communication, 1999).

GRAND STAIRCASE-ESCALANTE NATIONAL MONUMENT

The Grand Staircase-Escalante National Monument was established in south-central Utah on September 18, 1996. Paleontological resources are specifically addressed by President Clinton in the proclamation establishing the monument. Grand Staircase-Escalante National Monument is administered by the Bureau of Land Management. Therefore the monument is not included in this paleontological resource inventory of National Park Service areas in Utah. A preliminary inventory of paleontological resources within the Grand Staircase-Escalante National Monument has been conducted by Gillette and Hayden (1997).

HOVENWEEP NATIONAL MONUMENT

Hovenweep National Monument in southeastern Utah was established on March 2, 1923, to preserve a concentration of Pre-Columbian cliff dwellings, pueblos, and towers. Sedimentary rocks exposed in the monument include the Upper Jurassic Morrison Formation, the Lower Cretaceous Burro Canyon Formation, and the Upper Cretaceous Dakota Sandstone. The only report of paleontological resources from the monument is an unidentified bone found by a Utah Geological Survey geologist (Martha Hayden, written communication, 1999). Although there are not many reports of fossils from within the monument, judging from their known presence nearby, invertebrate fossils most likely are present in Hovenweep National Monument.

NATURAL BRIDGES NATIONAL MONUMENT

Natural Bridges National Monument in southeastern Utah, was established on April 16, 1908 to preserve three spectacular natural bridges. The monument was the first National Park Service unit established in Utah. The natural bridges are formed in the Permian Cedar Mesa Sandstone, which is the oldest geologic unit exposed in the monument. Stratigraphically, the rocks near the monument range from Permian to Jurassic in age. Although a paleontological survey has not been undertaken at the monument, a few isolated fossils have been reported. For more information on the geology and a stratigraphic section of Natural Bridges National Monument see Huntoon and others (this volume).

The Permian Cutler Formation in southeastern Utah was originally divided into five members (Baker and Reeside, 1929). More recent work by Condon (1997) recognized the Cutler as a Group in southeastern Utah and identified the following subdivisions in and near Natural Bridges: lower Cutler beds, Halgaito Formation, Cedar Mesa Sandstone, and Organ Rock Formation. The Cedar Mesa Sandstone is primarily a light-colored, cross-bedded sandstone unit that locally contains pink arkosic sandstone and mudstone beds as well as scarce grey-green limestone lenses. The unit has been interpreted as largely eolian in origin because of the abundant cross-bedded sandstone. However minute fragments of marine invertebrate fossils locally occur within the sandstone. Baars (1975) suggested that the fossils indicate a marine origin of the beds whereas Stanesco and Campbell (1989) concluded that the marine fossils were transported into the eolian sands by wind. Duffy (1998) reported on *in situ* fossilized plant roots or rhizoliths preserved in the Cedar Mesa Sandstone at Natural Bridges National Monument. Poorly preserved horizontal and vertical burrows are also preserved in the fine-grained, green-gray, interdunal sandstone beds (Jackie Huntoon, written communication, 1999).

The Upper Triassic Chinle Formation is exposed near the monument and some isolated petrified wood specimens have been reported from this formation (S. Duffy, verbal communication, 1999). Dubiel (1983, 1987) reported ostracods, conchostracans, unionid bivalves, and various trace fossils from the Chinle Formation nearby in White Canyon.

A large, flat-floored dry rock shelter in the Cedar Mesa Sandstone contains a wealth of indurated late Pleistocene (Rancholabrean) packrat middens and a 100-cm stratigraphic profile that contains skeletal and plant remains. Dung pellets from the shelter were radiocarbon dated and range in age between 39,000 to 9660 years B.P. (Mead and Agenbroad, 1992; Mead and others, 1993b). Two metapodials, identified as those belonging to the extinct mountain goat *Oreamnos harringtoni*, were recovered from the shelter and represent the oldest dated remains of this mountain goat. Plant microfossils indicate that Engelmann spruce (*Picea engelmannii*), limber pine (*Pinus flexilis*), and Douglas fir (*Pseudotsuga menziesii*) grew nearby during the late Pleistocene, whereas a riparian willow (*Salix* sp.) and cottonwood (*Populus* sp.) is now present in the bottom of the canyon and a pinyon-juniper (*Pinus edulis-Juniperus osteosperma*) community now predominates higher up on the canyon walls and in the benchlands above the canyon (Mead and others, 1987).

RAINBOW BRIDGE NATIONAL MONUMENT

Rainbow Bridge in south-central Utah was proclaimed a national monument on May 30, 1910, to preserve the world's largest natural bridge. The bridge is 309 ft (94 m) above the floor of Bridge Canyon and spans 278 ft (85 m) (Hansen, 1959). The bridge is carved in the Lower Jurassic Navajo Sandstone which forms vertical cliffs in the area. The floor of Rainbow Bridge consists of the Lower Jurassic Kayenta Formation. The Kayenta is a reddish-orange fluvial sandstone unit. For more information on the geology and a stratigraphic section of Rainbow Bridge National Monument see Chidsey and others (this volume).

Hall (1934) was the first to report dinosaur tracks near Rainbow Bridge. The tracks were discovered during the University of California's Rainbow Bridge Expedition of 1933. These poorly preserved tracks are named *Eubrontes* sp. and are in the Kayenta Formation.

TIMPANOGOS CAVE NATIONAL MONUMENT

Timpanogos Cave was proclaimed a national monument on October 14, 1922. However, it was administered by the U.S. Forest Service until it was transferred to the jurisdiction of the National Park Service on August 10, 1933. The monument was established to protect a colorful limestone cavern and associated karst features on the north side of Mount Timpanogos near the American Fork River in north-central Utah. For more information on the geology and a stratigraphic section of Timpanogos Cave National Monument see Mayo and others (this volume), Baker and Crittenden (1961), and White and Van Gundy (1974).

The oldest fossils in the monument are trace fossils found within the Precambrian Mutual Formation. Invertebrate fossils are preserved in the Cambrian Maxfield Limestone, Ophir Shale, and the Devonian/Mississippian Fitchville Formation. Walcott reported Early and Middle Cambrian trilobites (*Olenellus*) from the Ophir Shale. Worm burrows and brachiopods also occur within the Ophir (Baker and Crittenden, 1961). The limestone caves in the national monument are developed in the Mississippian Deseret Formation. A variety of fossilized marine invertebrates, including syringoporoid corals and brachiopods, have been found in the formation.

Packrat middens have been found at several localities within the national monument including the Timpanogos Cave System and Hidden Cave Mine. In 1939, Tom Walker found mammal bones in a rockshelter known as the Grotto, which was known to be the den for a mountain lion until 1880. Bones were collected from packrat nests found in the Organ Pipe Room of Hansen Cave. During 1998, George (1999) initiated an assessment of packrat middens from three cave areas within Timpanogos Cave National Monument. Eleven species of mammals were collected and identified from the middens. A partial bison skeleton was found in the gravels at the mouth of Swinging Bridge Canyon in the monument (Rod Horrocks, written communication, 1999).

ZION NATIONAL PARK

The area that is now Zion National Park was originally proclaimed Mukuntuweap National Monument on July 31, 1909. The area was renamed Zion National Monument on March 18, 1918. The site was redesignated as Zion National Park on November 19, 1919. For more information on the geology and a stratigraphic section of Zion National Park see Biek and others (this volume), Gregory (1939,

1945, 1950), and Hamilton (1978, 1984).

Several important expeditions by Europeans came into or near Zion Canyon during the 18th and 19th centuries. The earliest description of the area is in the diaries of the Dominguez-Escalante Expedition of 1776. The federal government initiated scientific surveys into southwestern Utah during 1853, some of which passed into and near Zion Canyon. Some of the more notable surveys were led by George Wheeler and John Wesley Powell. These two surveys mapped and interpreted the geographic and geologic features in a region that covered more than 50,000 square miles.

The Wheeler Survey, also referred to as the U.S. Geographic Surveys West of the One Hundredth Meridian, was a series of military and scientific expeditions undertaken by the U.S. Army. The survey was led by Captain George M. Wheeler. Although field surveys were conducted in 1869 and 1871, Wheeler did not receive funding to organize a regional scientific survey until 1872. The Wheeler Survey continued field work until 1879. Geologists G.K. Gilbert and Edwin E. Howell joined the Wheeler Survey and were involved in geologic field work in Zion Canyon and the surrounding area during 1872. The results of the survey, including descriptions of the geology and paleontology, were published in a series of volumes by the U.S. government.

The following quote is found within the Wheeler Geological Report (1886) in reference to southwestern Utah. "Clambering along the cliff, and while securing a large haul of fossils, the crisp edge of coal crops was noticed, and prospecting which a 12-foot vein of dense bituminous coal, having both above and below a bed of shale 15 to 18 inches thick, was found, with petrified wood strewn in many directions. Fossils were found in sandstones..."

John Wesley Powell followed the Virgin River Valley northward into Zion Canyon during 1871 (Powell, 1875). Powell did not focus much attention on the geology until he employed Howell in 1874 and Gilbert and Dutton in 1875. William Henry Holmes produced several outstanding line drawings of the area that are well known for their geological and topographical accuracy as well as their artistic beauty.

The rocks exposed in and around Zion National Park range from Permian through Cretaceous in age. During this interval, the Zion area was repeatedly covered by marine transgressions from seaways that lay largely to the west, north, or east. The oldest unit exposed in Zion National Park is the Lower Permian Toroweap Formation. The Kaibab Limestone of Late Early Permian age is a marine limestone unit, overlying the Toroweap, exposed in two small areas in the northwest corner of the park along the escarpment produced by the Hurricane fault. Brachiopods, bryozoans, corals, crinoids, and sea urchins have been recovered in the Zion area (McKee, 1952) although fossil preservation generally is poor.

The Moenkopi Formation (Early to Middle Triassic) represents both shallow marine and nearshore terrestrial environments in and near the Zion region. Fossilized marine bivalves, snails, and ammonites (*Meekoceras* sp.) are known from the formation. A few pieces of fossil wood and bone have been found in this unit. The Virgin Limestone Member contains fossilized asteroid starfish and abundant internal molds of mollusks. This unit is well exposed in the northwest and southwest corners of the park. The terrestrial component of the Moenkopi Formation increases upsection, reflecting gradual transgressions and regressions of the early Triassic sea.

The Chinle Formation (Late Triassic) includes petrified wood that was originally transported by streams from the east and southeast. The logs are found in the basal Shinarump Conglomerate Member and has been identified as *Araucarioxylon* sp. and *Woodworthia* sp. Fossilized bones from the labyrinthodont *Metoposaurus* sp. have been collected from freshwater mudstone beds near Cougar Mountain.

The Lower Jurassic Moenave Formation includes, from oldest to youngest, the Dinosaur Canyon, Whitmore Point, and Springdale Sandstone Members. The Dinosaur Canyon Member consists of red mudstone, siltstone, and some sandstone deposited in mudflat, fluvial, and overbank environments. The Whitemore Point Member is a gray mudstone and shale unit deposited primarily in lacustrine environments. Palynomorphs recovered from this member are especially important as they provided the most reliable dating of this formation. The Springdale Sandstone Member is composed largely of red sandstone deposited by high energy streams that originated in a highland source region in the ancestral Rockies of western Colorado. Pond and stream deposits from the Moenave Formation contain the remains of the fish *Semionotus kanabensis* (Hesse, 1935; Day, 1967). Fossil vertebrate tracks have been found in both the Whitmore Point and Springdale Members of the Moenave (Smith and Santucci, 1999).

The Lower Jurassic Kayenta Formation in the Zion region consists primarily of siltstone and sandstone deposited in sabkhas downwind (south) of extensive eolian dune deposits that are included in the Navajo Sandstone. This unit contains several thin limestone beds that preserve fossil trails of aquatic snails or worms. The first vertebrate tracks reported from Zion National Park were tridactyl dinosaur prints in the Kayenta (Stokes and Bruhn, 1960). Additional vertebrate tracksites were discovered in the Kayenta during a paleontological survey in Zion during 1998 and 1999 (Santucci and others, 1998; Smith and Santucci, 1999).

Although the Navajo Sandstone is one of the most easily recognized units in the southwest, the unit appears to be largely devoid of body fossils in Zion National Park, although a few tridactyl dinosaur footprints have been found along the trail to Observation Point (Fred Peterson, written communication, 2000). The large-scale cross-bedding that is so pronounced in the park reflects stratification produced in windblown sand deposits. In an unpub-

Figure 9. Large artiodactyl track from Zion National Park.

Figure 10. Heron-like bird track from Zion National Park.

lished report found in the Zion National Park files, John Bradbury claims that during 1962 poorly preserved fossil wood was found within a shale lens of the Navajo Formation.

The Middle Jurassic Carmel Formation includes several light tan to gray limestone beds that contain marine fossils, including crinoids, pectens, oysters, and other bivalves (Gregory and Williams, 1947). The crinoids are identified as *Isocrinus* sp. An oolitic limestone bed containing algal balls, bivalves, and gastropods is present along Wildcat Canyon Trail.

A small exposure of the Cretaceous Dakota Sandstone is exposed in the northwest corner of the park on top of Horse Ranch Mountain. The formation contains a basal conglomerate overlain by a series of sandstone and mudstone beds, some of which contain freshwater bivalves and plant impressions. A few undescribed vertebrate fossils are reported from the Dakota just east of Zion National Park (Eaton, written communication, 1999; Kirkland, written communication, 1999).

The remains of a plesiosaur were excavated from the Upper Cretaceous Tropic Shale near the eastern boundary of Zion National Park (Gillette and others, 1999).

A large artiodactyl track (figure 9) and a bird track (figure 10) resembling those of herons were collected from Quaternary lacustrine deposits in the Coalpits Wash area (Santucci and others, 1998). The remains of a bison (*Bison antiquus*) were collected in the park many years ago (Wayne Hamilton, verbal communication, 1998). Hevly (1979) analyzed pollen and spore samples taken from Quaternary lacustrine sediments in Zion National Park.

PALEONTOLOGICAL RESOURCE MANAGEMENT AND PROTECTION

The paleontological resources in the national parks and monuments of Utah provide valuable information about ancient plants and animals. The National Park Ser-

vice manages fossils along with other natural and cultural resources for the benefit of the public. Fossils are recognized as non-renewable resources that possess both scientific and educational values. All fossils are protected under federal law and their collection is prohibited except under the terms of a research permit.

Paleontological resources are placed on exhibit in many of the national parks and monuments in Utah. The Quarry Visitor Center at Dinosaur National Monument provides visitors with the opportunity to view the world famous dinosaur bone-bearing rock wall as an *in situ* exhibit. Glen Canyon National Recreation Area has a sandstone slab of dinosaur tracks on display outside of the Visitor Center and mammoth dung and bones are on exhibit within the Visitor Center.

Comprehensive paleontological resource inventories are underway in a number of National Parks Service units in Utah. These surveys are designed to identify the scope, significance, and distribution of the paleontological resources and to assess any natural or human-related threats to the paleontological resources. Fossils reported from areas adjacent to the parks and monuments are also considered in order to assess the potential for stratigraphically equivalent resources within park boundaries. This baseline data will better enable park staff to plan strategies that increase the management, protection, research, and interpretation of park fossils.

Ongoing and future paleontological research in the various National Park Service units within the state of Utah will not only enlarge our knowledge of the fossil record but, more importantly, will expand our understanding of the ancient environments in which the fossils lived.

ACKNOWLEDGEMENTS

I thank the many National Park Service employees who provided their time and expertise during my inventory of paleontological resources in the various National

Park Service units of Utah, including: J. Webster, K. Yeston, and S. Duffy from Arches National Park; G. Pollock from Bryce Canyon National Park; B. Rodgers from Canyonlands National Park; T. Clark, L. Kreutzer, R. Mack, A. Mathis, T. Nordling, D. Worthington, and J. Chrobak-Cox from Capitol Reef National Park; D. Sharrow and S. Robinson from Cedar Breaks National Monument; D. Chure, A. Elder, and S. Madsen from Dinosaur National Monument; J. Ritenour, N. Henderson, and J. Spence from Glen Canyon National Recreation Area; R. Horrocks from Timpanogos Cave National Monument; and, J. Bradybaugh, D. Cohen, D. Falvey, L. Naylor, and D. Rachliss from Zion National Park. Special thanks to paleontology interns C. George, A. Painter, R. Scott, J. Smith, A. Stanton, R. Taylor, and K. Thompson for their volunteer efforts in the Utah parks and monuments.

I extend an additional thanks to U.S. Geological Survey geologists R. Dubiel, F. Peterson, C. Turner, G. Billingsley, W. Cobban, W. Hansen, and D. Miller; Utah Geological Survey geologists G. Willis, D. Sprinkel, T. Chidsey, Jr., D. Madsen, M. Hayden, and Utah State Paleontologist J. Kirkland; J. Mead (Northern Arizona University); B. Britt (Eccles Dinosaur Park); D. Burge (College of Eastern Utah, Prehistoric Museum); J. Eaton (Weber State University); D. Currey (University of Utah); G. Engelmann (University of Nebraska at Omaha); A. Heckert (University of New Mexico); S. Sumida (California State University); P. Anderson (independent consultant); S. Ash (retired paleobotanist); and, F. Barnes (independent writer/publisher), for suggestions and technical review.

Finally, I would like to acknowledge my appreciation to J. Gregson, T. Connors, B. Heise, B. Higgins, D. Shaver, and D. McGinnis of the National Park Service, for providing the opportunity to include paleontology as part of the Geologic Assessments of the Utah National Parks and Monuments.

REFERENCES

Ash, Sidney, 1975, The Chinle (Upper Triassic) flora of southeastern Utah: Four Corners Geological Society Guidebook, 8th Field Conference, Canyonlands, p. 143-147.

—1982, Occurrence of the controversial plant fossil *Sanmiguelia* cf. *S. lewisi* Brown in the Upper Triassic of Utah: Journal of Paleontology, v. 56, no. 3, p. 751-754.

—1993a, Plant megafossils of the Upper Triassic Chinle Formation, Capitol Reef National Park, Utah, *in* Santucci, V.L., editor, National Park Service research abstract volume: National Park Service Technical Report, NPS/NRPO/NRTR-93/11, p. 32.

—1993b, Plant megafossils of the Upper Jurassic Morrison Formation, Dinosaur National Monument, Utah, *in* Santucci, V.L., editor, National Park Service paleontological research abstract volume: National Park Service Technical Report, NPS/NRPEFO/NRTR-93/11, p. 44.

—1994, First occurrence of *Czekanowskia* (Gymnospermae, Czekanowskiales) in the United States: Review of Palaeobotany and Palynology, v. 81, p. 129-140.

Baars, D.L., 1975, The Permian System of Canyonlands country, *in* Canyonlands Country: Four Corners Geological Society Guidebook, 8th Field Conference.

Baker, A.A., and Crittenden, M.D., 1961, Geologic map of the Timpanogos Cave Quadrangle, Utah: U.S. Geologic Survey Quadrangle Map GQ-132, scale 1:24,000.

Baker, A.A., and Reeside, J.B., 1929, Correlation of the Permian of southern Utah, northern Arizona, northwest New Mexico, and southwestern Colorado: American Association of Petroleum Geologists Bulletin, v. 13, p. 1413-1448.

Bartlett, R.A., 1962, Great Surveys of the American West: Norman, University of Oklahoma Press, 408 p.

Berman, D.S., Reisz, R.R., and Fracasso, M.A., 1981, Skull of the Lower Permian dissorophid amphibian (*Platyhystrix rugosus*): Annals of the Carnegie Museum, v. 50, p. 391-416.

Berry, E.W., 1927, Cycads in the Shinarump Conglomerate of southern Utah: Washington Academy of Science Journal, v. 17, p. 303-307.

Biek, R.F., Willis, G.C., Hylland, M.D., and Doelling, H.H., (this volume), Geology of Zion National Park, *in* Sprinkel, D.A., Anderson, P.B., and Chidsey, T.C., Jr., editors, Geology of Utah's parks and monuments: Utah Geological Association Publication 28.

Bilbey, S.A., and Hall, J.E., 1999, Marsh and "*Megalosaurus*" – Utah's first theropod dinosaur, *in* Gillette, D.D., editor, Vertebrate paleontology in Utah: Utah Geological Survey Miscellaneous Publication 99-1, p. 67-69.

Billingsley, G.H., Huntoon, P.W., and Breed, W.J., 1987, Geologic map of Capitol Reef National Park and vicinity, Emery, Garfield, Millard and Wayne Counties, Utah: Utah Geological and Mineral Survey Map M-87, scale 1:24,000.

Bodily, N.M., 1969, An armored dinosaur from the Lower Cretaceous of Utah: Brigham Young University Geology Studies, v. 16, p. 35-60.

Bowers, W.E., 1990, Geologic Map of Bryce Canyon National Park and vicinity, southwestern Utah: U.S. Geological Survey Miscellaneous Investigation Series Map I-2108, scale 1:24,000.

Bown, T.M., Hasiotis, S.T., Genise, J.F., Maldonado, F., and Brouwers, E.M., 1997, Trace fossils of Hymenoptera and other insects, and paleoenvironments of the Claron Formation (Paleocene and Eocene), southwestern Utah: U.S. Geological Survey Bulletin 2153-C, p. 43-58.

Burres, C.L., 1994, Paleontological Survey Report: Capitol Reef National Park GarKane Power Right-of-Way, Capitol Reef Park Archives, 33 p.

Carpenter, K., Kirkland, J.I., Burge, D., and Bird, J., 1999, Ankylosaurs (Dinosauria: Ornithischia) of the Cedar Mountain Formation, Utah, and their stratigraphic distribution, *in* Gillette, D.D., editor, Vertebrate paleontology in Utah: Utah Geological Survey Miscellaneous Publication 99-1, p. 243-251.

Chure, D.J., 1987, Dinosaur National Monument - a window on the past, *in* Averett, W.R., editor, Geology and paleontology of the Dinosaur Triangle: Grand Junction, Museum of Western Colorado, p. 75-77.

—-1992, Leaping lizards, frolicking frogs, swimming salamanders, and minute mammals - the non-dinosaurs of Dinosaur National Monument: Park Science, v. 12, no. 3, p. 7.

—-1993, The first record of ichthyosaurs from Utah: Brigham Young University Geology Studies, v. 39, p. 65-69.

—-1994, *Koparion douglassi*, a new dinosaur from the Morrison Formation (Upper Jurassic) of Dinosaur National Monument - the oldest troodontid (Theropoda: Maniraptora): Brigham Young University Geology Studies, v. 40, p. 11-15.

Chure, D.J., and Engelmann, G.F., 1989, The fauna of the Morrison Formation in Dinosaur National Monument, *in* Flynn, J.J., editor, Mesozoic and Cenozoic vertebrate paleontology - classic localities, contemporary approaches: Washington, D.C., 28th International Geological Congress Field Trip Guidebook T322, American Geophysical Union, p. 8-14.

Chure, D.J., and Madsen, J.H., 1993, A new carnosaurian dinosaur from the Salt Wash Member of the Morrison Formation of Dinosaur National Monument, *in* Santucci, V.L., editor, National Park Service Paleontological Research Abstract Volume: National Park Service Technical Report, NPS/NRPEFO/NRTR-93/11, p. 47.

Chure, D.J., and McIntosh, J.S., 1990, Stranger in a strange land - a brief history of the paleontological operations at Dinosaur National Monument: Earth Sciences History, v. 9, no. 1, p. 34-40.

Chure, D.J., Engelmann, G.F., and Madsen, S.K., 1989, Non-mammalian microvertebrates from the Morrison Formation (Upper Jurassic, Kimmeridgian) of Dinosaur National Monument, Utah-Colorado, USA: Journal of Vertebrate Paleontology, v. 9 (supplement to no. 3), p. 16A-17A.

Chure, D.J., Madsen, J.H., and Britt, B.B., 1993, New data on theropod dinosaurs from the Late Jurassic Morrison Formation. Journal of Vertebrate Paleontology Abstracts with Program 13 (supplement to no. 3).

Chure, D.J., Turner, C.E., and Peterson, Fred, 1992, An embryo of the ornithopod dinosaur *Camptosaurus* from the Morrison Formation (Upper Jurassic) of Dinosaur National Monument: Journal of Vertebrate Paleontology 12 (supplement to no. 3): p. 23A-24A.

Cobban, W.A., Pollock, G.L. and Dyman, T.S., 1996, Correlation of marine and nonmarine facies of lower Upper Cretaceous rocks in southwestern Utah with the Cenomanian-Turonian boundary reference section near Pueblo, Colorado [abs.]: Geological Society of America Abstracts with Programs, v. 28, no. 7, p. 185.

Cole, K.L., 1992, A Survey of the fossil packrat middens and reconstruction of the pregrazing vegetation of Capitol Reef National Park: Final Report to Capitol Reef National Park, October 9, 1992.

Cole, K.L., and Henderson, N.R., 1993, The presettlement vegetation of Capitol Reef National Park reconstructed with fossil packrat middens, *in* Santucci, V.L., editor, National Park Service Research Abstract Volume: National Park Service Technical Report, NPS/NRPO/NRTR-93/11, p. 33.

Collier, M., 1987, The geology of Capitol Reef National Park: Capitol Reef Natural History Association, 48 p.

Condon, S.M., 1997, Geology of the Pennsylvanian and Permian Cutler Group and Permian Kaibab Limestone in the Paradox basin, southeastern Utah and southwestern Colorado: U.S. Geological Survey Bulletin 2000-P, P1-P46.

Cope, E.D., 1877, On a dinosaurian from the Trias of Utah: Proceedings of the American Philosophical Society, v. 16, p. 579-584.

Crampton, C.G., 1994, Ghosts of Glen Canyon - history beneath Lake Powell: Salt Lake City, Tower Productions, 135 p.

Davidson, E.S., 1967, Geology of the Circle Cliffs area, Garfield and Kane Counties, Utah: U.S. Geological Survey Bulletin 1229.

Davis, O.K., Agenbroad, L.D., Martin, P.S., and Mead, J.I., 1984, The Pleistocene dung blanket of Bechan Cave, Utah: Carnegie Museum of Natural History Special Publication No. 8, p. 267-282.

Davis, O.K., Mead, J.I., Martin, P.S., and Agenbroad, L.D., 1985, Riparian plants were a major component of the diet of mammoths in southern Utah: Current Research Pleistocene, v. 2, p. 81-82.

Day, B.S., 1967, Stratigraphy of the Upper Triassic(?) Moenave Formation of southwestern Utah: Salt Lake City, University of Utah, M.S. thesis, 58 p.

Doelling, H.H., 1985, Geologic map of Arches National Park and vicinity, Grand County, Utah: Utah Geological and Mineral Survey Map M-74, scale 1:50,000.

Driese, S.G., 1982, Sedimentology, conodont distribution, and carbonate diagenesis of the Upper Morgan Formation (Middle Pennsylvanian), northern Utah and Colorado: Madison, University of Wisconsin, Ph.D. dissertation, 280 p.

Dubiel, R.F., 1983, Sedimentology of the lower part of the Upper Triassic Chinle Formation and its relationship to uranium deposits, White Canyon area, southeastern Utah. U.S. Geological Survey Open- File Report 83-459, 48 p.

—-1987, Sedimentology and new fossil occurrences of the Upper Triassic Chinle Formation, southeastern Utah: Four Corners Geological Society Guidebook, 10th Field Conference, Cataract Canyon. p. 99-107.

Duffy, Shawn, 1993, Synopsis of the dinosaur megatrack site in Arches National Park, *in* Santucci, V.L., editor, National Park Service paleontological research abstract volume: National Park Service Natural Resources Technical Report, NPS/NRPO/NRTR-93/11, p. 4.

—1998, Permian root traces from Natural Bridges National Monument, *in* Santucci, V.L., and McClelland , L., editors, National Park Service paleontological research volume 3: National Park Service Technical Report, NPS/NRGRD/GRDTR-98/01, p. 107-108.

Eaton, J.G., 1993, Mammalian paleontology and correlation of the uppermost Cretaceous rocks of the Paunsaugunt Plateau, *in* Morales, M., editor, Aspects of Mesozoic geology and paleontology of the Colorado Plateau: Museum of Northern Arizona Bulletin 59, p. 163-180.

—1994, Vertebrate paleontology of Cretaceous rocks in Bryce Canyon National Park, Utah [abs.]: Geological Society of America, Rocky Mountain Section, Abstracts with Programs, v. 26, p. 12.

—1995, Cenomanian and Turonian (early Late Cretaceous) multituberculate mammals from southwestern Utah: Journal of Vertebrate Paleontology, v. 15, no. 4, p. 761-784.

—1999, Vertebrate paleontology of the Paunsaugunt Plateau, Upper Cretaceous, southwestern Utah, *in* Gillette, D.D., editor, Vertebrate paleontology in Utah: Utah Geological Survey Miscellaneous Publication 99-1, p. 335-338.

Eaton, J.G., Diem, S., Archibald, J.D., Schierup, C., and Munk, H., 1999a, Vertebrate paleontology of the Upper Cretaceous rocks of the Markagunt Plateau, southwestern Utah, *in* Gillette, D.D., editor, Vertebrate paleontology in Utah: Utah Geological Survey Miscellaneous Publication 99-1, p. 323-334.

Eaton, J.G., Goldstrand, P.M., and Morrow, J., 1993, Composition and stratigraphic interpretation of Cretaceous strata of the Paunsaugunt Plateau, Utah, *in* Morales, M., editor, Aspects of Mesozoic geology and paleontology of the Colorado Plateau: Museum of Northern Arizona Bulletin 59, p. 153-162.

Eaton, J.G., Hutchison, J.H., Holroyd, P.A., Korth, W.W., and Goldstrand, P.M., 1999b, Vertebrates of the Turtle basin local fauna, Middle Eocene, Sevier Plateau, south-central Utah, *in* Gillette, D.D., editor, Vertebrate paleontology in Utah: Utah Geological Survey Miscellaneous Publication 99-1, p. 463-468.

Eaton, J.G., and Morrow, J., 1990, Preliminary report on the paleontology of Cretaceous rocks and stratigraphic implications, Paunsaugunt Plateau, southwestern Utah: Symposium on Southwestern Geology and Paleontology, Museum of Northern Arizona, p. 6.

Eaton, J.G., Munk, H., and Hardman, M.A., 1998, A new vertebrate fossil locality within the Wahweap Formation (Upper Cretaceous) of Bryce Canyon National Park and its bearing on the presence of the Kaiparowits Formation on the Paunsaugunt Plateau, *in* Santucci, V.L., and McClelland, L., editors, National Park Service paleontological research volume 3: National Park Service Technical Report, NPS/NRGRD/GRDTR-98/01, p. 36-40.

Edwards, W.M., 1967, Lake Powell - waterway to desert wonders: National Geographic Magazine, v. 132, p. 44-75.

Elder, A.S., 1999, The history of Dinosaur National Monument's Douglass Quarry - the Park Service years, *in* Gillette, D.D., editor, Vertebrate paleontology in Utah: Utah Geological Survey Miscellaneous Publication 99-1, p. 71-76.

Engelmann, G.F., 1992, Paleontological survey of the Jurassic Morrison Formation in Dinosaur National Monument: Park Science, v. 12, no. 3, p. 8-9.

—1999, Stratigraphic and geographic distribution of fossils in the upper part of the Upper Jurassic Morrison Formation of the Rocky Mountain region, *in* Gillette, D.D., editor, Vertebrate paleontology in Utah: Utah Geological Survey Miscellaneous Publication 99-1, p. 115-120.

Englemann, G.F., and Callison, G., 1999, *Glirodon grandis*, a new multituberculate mammal from the Upper Jurassic Morrison Formation, *in* Gillette, D.D., editor, Vertebrate paleontology in Utah: Utah Geological Survey Miscellaneous Publication 99-1, p. 161-177.

Englemann, G.F., Chure, D.J., and Madsen, S.K., 1989, A mammalian fauna from the Jurassic Morrison Formation of Dinosaur National Monument [abs.]: Journal of Vertebrate Paleontology Abstracts with Programs, v. 9 (supplement to no. 3), p. 19A.

Englemann, G.F., and Hasiotis, S.T., 1999, Deep dinosaur tracks in the Morrison Formation - sole marks that are really sole marks, *in* Gillette, D.D., editor, Vertebrate paleontology in Utah: Utah Geological Survey Miscellaneous Publication 99-1, p. 179-183.

Evans, S.E., and Chure, D.J., 1999, Upper Jurassic lizards from the Morrison Formation of Dinosaur National Monument, Utah, *in* Gillette, D.D., editor, Vertebrate paleontology in Utah: Utah Geological Survey Miscellaneous Publication 99-1, p. 151-159.

Fremont, J.C., 1845, The report of the exploring expedition to the Rocky Mountains in the year 1842, and to Oregon and north California in the years 1843-1844: Washington D.C., Gales and Seaton, 693 p.

Furniss, B.L., and Tidwell, W.D., 1972, Cycadeoidales from the Cedar Mountain Formation near Moab, Utah: Geological Society of America Abstract 4, p. 377.

George, Christian, 1999, A systematic study and taphonomic analysis of the mammals remains from the packrat middens of Timpanogos Cave National Monument, Utah, *in* Santucci, V.L., and McClelland , L., editors, National Park Service paleontological research volume 4: National Park Service Geologic Resource Technical Report, NPS/NRGRD/GRDTR-99/03, p. 109-117.

Gillette, D.D., 1996, Origin and early evolution of the sauropod dinosaurs of North America – the type locality and stratigraphic position of *Dystrophaeus viae-*

malae Cope 1877, *in* Huffman, A., Lund, W.R., and Godwin, L.H., editor, Geology and resources of the Paradox basin: Utah Geological Association Guidebook 25, p. 313-324.

Gillette, D.D., and Hayden, M.C., 1997, A preliminary inventory of paleontological resources within the Grand Staircase-Escalante National Monument, Utah: Utah Geological Survey Circular 96, 34 p.

Gillette, D.D., Hayden, M.C., and Titus, A.L., 1999, Occurrence and biostratigraphic framework of a plesiosaur from the Upper Cretaceous Tropic Shale of southwestern Utah, *in* Gillette, D.D., editor, Vertebrate paleontology in Utah: Utah Geological Survey Miscellaneous Publication 99-1, p. 275-294.

Gilmore, C.W., 1924, Expedition to the Dinosaur National Monument: Smithsonian Miscellaneous Collection, v. LXXVI, p. 12-16.

—-1925a, A nearly complete, articulated skeleton of *Camarasaurus*, a saurischian dinosaur from the Dinosaur National Monument: Memoirs of the Carnegie Museum, v. 10, p. 347-384.

—-1925b, Osteology of ornithopodous dinosaurs from the Dinosaur National Monument, Utah, part I - on a skeleton of *Camptosaurus medius* Marsh, part II - on a skeleton of *Dryosaurus altus* Marsh, part III - on a skeleton of *Laosaurus gracilis* Marsh: Memoirs of the Carnegie Museum, v. 10, p. 385-409.

—-1926, A new aetosaurian reptile from the Morrison Formation of Utah: Annals of the Carnegie Museum, v. 15, no. 2, p. 326-342.

—-1932, On a newly mounted skeleton of *Diplodocus* in the United States National Museum: Proceedings of the United States National Museum, Article 18, 21 p.

—-1936a, Osteology of *Apatosaurus* with special reference to specimens in the Carnegie Museum: Memoirs of the Carnegie Museum, v. 11, p. 175-300.

—-1936b, The great dinosaurs of the Carnegie Museum: Section of Vertebrate Paleontology, Pamphlet no. 2, 14 p.

Gregory, H.E., 1951, The geology and geography of the Paunsaugunt region, Utah: U.S. Geologic Survey Professional Paper 226, 116 p., 1 plate.

Gregory, H.E., and Anderson, J.C., 1939, Geographic and geologic sketch of the Capitol Reef region, Utah: Bulletin of the Geological Society of America, v. 50, p. 1827-1850.

Gregory, H.E., and Moore, R.C., 1931, Kaiparowits region, a geographic and geologic reconnaissance of parts of Utah and Arizona: U.S. Geological Survey Professional Paper 164, 161 p.

Gregory, H.H., 1939, Geologic sketch of Zion National Park: Zion-Bryce Museum Bulletin No. 3, 28 p.

—-1945, Scientific explorations in southern Utah: American Journal of Science, v. 243, p. 527-549.

—-1950, Geology and geography of the Zion Park region, Utah and Arizona: U.S. Geological Survey Professional Paper 220, 200 p.

Gregory, H.H., and Williams, N.C., 1947, Zion National Monument, Utah: Geological Society of America Bulletin, v. 58, p. 211-244.

Gregson, J.D., and Chure, D.J., (this volume), Geology of Dinosaur National Monument, Utah-Colorado, *in* Sprinkel, D.A., Anderson, P.B., and Chidsey, T.C., Jr., editors, Geology of Utah's parks and monuments: Utah Geological Association Publication 28.

Hall, A.F., 1934, General report on the Rainbow Bridge – Monument Valley expedition of 1933: Berkeley, University of California Press, 32 p.

Hamilton, W.L., 1978, Geological map of Zion National Park, Utah: Zion Natural History Association.

—-1984, The Sculpturing of Zion - guide to the geology of Zion National Park: Salt Lake City, Zion Natural History Association, Paragon Press, Inc., Utah, 132 p.

Hansen, W.R., 1959, A geologic examination of Rainbow Bridge National Monument to review proposed measures to protect the monument from impairment by Glen Canyon reservoir: U.S. Geological Survey, Administrative Report, 19 p.

—-1996, Dinosaur's restless rivers and craggy canyon walls: Vernal, Dinosaur Nature Association, 103 p.

Hansen, W.R., Rowley, P.D., and Carrera, P.E., 1983, Geologic map of Dinosaur National Monument and vicinity, Utah and Colorado: U.S. Geological Survey Miscellaneous Investigations Map I-1407, scale 1:50,000.

Hasiotis, S.T., 1993, Paleontologic, sedimentologic, and paleoecologic examination of the Canyonlands National Park vicinity, Utah, *in* Santucci, V.L., editor, National Park Service research abstract volume: National Park Service Technical Report, NPS/NRPO/NRTR-93/11, p. 28.

—-1995, Crayfish fossils and burrows from the Upper Triassic Chinle Formation, Canyonlands National Park, Utah, *in* Santucci, V.L., and McClelland, L., editors, National Park Service research volume 2: National Park Service Technical Report, NPS/NRPO/NRTR-95/16, p. 49-53.

Hasiotis, S.T., and Demko, T.M., 1996, Terrestrial and freshwater trace fossils, Upper Jurassic Morrison Formation, Colorado Plateau, *in* Morales, M., editor, The continental Jurassic: Museum of Northern Arizona Bulletin 60, p. 355-370.

Hasiotis, S.T., Fiorillo, A.R., and Hanna, R.R., 1999, Preliminary report on borings in Jurassic dinosaur bones - evidence for invertebrate-vertebrate interactions, *in* Gillette, D.D., editor, Vertebrate paleontology in Utah: Utah Geological Survey Miscellaneous Publication 99-1, p. 193-200.

Hasiotis, S.T., and Mitchell, C.E., 1989, Lungfish burrows in the Upper Triassic Chinle and Dolores Formations, Colorado Plateau - new evidence suggests origin by burrowing decapod crustaceans: Journal of Sedimentary Petrology, v. 59, no. 5, p. 871-875.

Heckert, A.B., Lucas, S.G., and Harris, J.D., 1999, An aetosaur (Reptilia:Archosauria) from the Upper Triassic

Chinle Group, Canyonlands National Park, Utah, *in* Santucci, V.L., and McClelland, L., editors, National Park Service paleontological research volume 4: National Park Service Geologic Resources Division Technical Report, NPS/NRGRD/GRDTR-99/03, p. 23-26.

Henrici, A., 1992, Fossil frogs - Dinosaur National Monument: Park Science, v. 12, no. 3, p. 11.

—1993, The first articulated frogs from the Upper Jurassic of North America, *in* Santucci, V.L., editor, National Park Service paleontological research abstract volume: National Park Service Technical Report, NPS/NRPE-FO/NRTR-93/11, p. 53.

—1998, A new pipoid anuran from the Late Jurassic Morrison Formation at Dinosaur National Monument: Journal of Vertebrate Paleontology, v. 18, no. 2, p. 321-332.

Herr, R.G., 1979, Sedimentary petrology and stratigraphy of the Lodore Formation (Upper Cambrian), northeast Utah and northwest Colorado: Salt Lake City, University of Utah, M.S. thesis, 129 p.

Herr, R.G., Picard, M.D., and Evans, S.H., 1982, Age and depth of burial, Cambrian Lodore Formation, northeastern Utah and northwestern Colorado: Contributions to Geology, University of Wyoming, v. 21, no. 2, p. 115-121.

Hesse, C.J., 1935, *Semionotus* cf. *gigas*, from the Triassic of Zion National Park, Utah: American Journal of Science, v. 29, p. 526-531.

Hevly, R.H., 1979, Pollen studies of ancient lake sediments in Zion National Park, Utah, *in* Linn, R.M., editor, Proceedings of the first conference on scientific research in the national parks, volume 2: Department of Interior, National Park Service Transactions and Proceedings, Series 5.

Hintze, L.F., 1988, Geologic History of Utah: Brigham Young University Geology Studies Special Publication 7, 202 p.

Holland, J.W., 1912, Note on the discovery of two nearly complete sauropod skeletons in Utah: Annals of the Carnegie Museum, v. 8, p. 2-3.

—1915, A new species of *Apatosaurus*: Annals of the Carnegie Museum, v. 10, p. 143-145.

—1916a, Paleontology: Annual Report of the Carnegie Museum for 1915, p. 38-42.

—1916b, Skeletons of *Diplodocus* and *Apatosaurus* in the Carnegie Museum of Natural History: Geological Society of America Bulletin, v. 38, p. 153.

—1924, The skull of *Diplodocus*: Memoirs of the Carnegie Museum, v. 9, p. 379-403.

Hunt, A.P., Lockley, M.G., Conrad, K.L., Paquette, M., and Chure, D.J., 1993a, Late Triassic vertebrates from the Dinosaur National Monument area (Utah, USA) with an example of the utility of coprolites for correlation: New Mexico Museum Natural History Science Bulletin, v. 3, p. 197-198.

Hunt, A.P., Lockley, M.G., and Lucas, S.G., 1993b, New Late Triassic dinosaur tracksite discoveries from Col-

orado National Monument and Canyonlands National Park, *in* Santucci, V.L., editor, National Park Service research abstract volume: National Park Service Technical Report, NPS/NRPO/NRTR-93/11, p. 38.

Huntoon, P.W., Billingsley, G.H., and Breed, W.J., 1982, Geologic map of Canyonlands National Park and vicinity, Utah: Moab, Canyonlands Natural History Association, scale 1:62,500.

Imlay, R.W., 1964, Marine Jurassic pelecypods, central and southern Utah: U.S. Geological Survey Professional Paper 483-C, p. C1-C42.

Kamola, D.L., and Chan, M.A., 1988, Coastal dune facies, Permian Cutler Formation (White Rim Sandstone), Capitol Reef National Park area, southern Utah: Sedimentary Geology, v. 56, p. 341-356.

Kennedy, W.J., and Cobban, W.A., 1991, Coniacian ammonite faunas from the United States western interior: The Paleontological Association of London, Special Papers in Palaeontology, No. 45, 96 p.

Kirkland, J.I., 1987, Upper Jurassic and Cretaceous lungfish tooth plates from the Western Interior, the last dipnoan faunas of North America: Hunteria, v. 2, no. 2, 16 p.

Lammers, G.E., 1964, Reptile tracks and the paleoenvironment of the Triassic Moenkopi of Capitol Reef National Monument, Utah: Museum of Northern Arizona Bulletin, Major Brady Memorial Volume, v. 40, p. 49-55.

Litwin, R., Turner, C.E., and Peterson, F.E., 1998, Palynological assessment of the Morrison Formation: Dinosaur National Monument (Utah and Colorado) and the Western Interior, *in* Carpenter, K.E., Chure D.J., and Kirkland, J.I., editors, The Morrison symposium - an interdisciplinary approach: Modern Geology, v. 22, nos. 1-4, p. 297-320.

Lockley, M.G., 1990, Tracking the rise of dinosaurs in eastern Utah: Canyon Legacy, v. 2, p. 2-8.

—1991, The Moab megatracksite - a preliminary description and discussion of millions of Middle Jurassic tracks in eastern Utah, *in* Guidebook for dinosaur quarries and tracksites tour, western Colorado and eastern Utah: Grand Junction Geological Society, Grand Junction, p. 59-65.

Lockley, M.G., Conrad, K., and Paquette, M., 1992a, New vertebrate track assemblages from the Late Triassic of the Dinosaur National Monument area, eastern Utah and western Colorado [abs.]: Geological Society of America, Abstracts with Programs, v. 24, no. 6, p. 24.

—1992b, New discoveries of fossil footprints at Dinosaur National Monument: Park Science, v. 12, no. 3, p. 4-5.

Lockley, M.G., Conrad, K., Paquette, M., and Hamblin, A., 1992c, Late Triassic vertebrate tracks in the Dinosaur National Monument area, *in* Wilson, J.R., editor, Field guide to geologic excursions in Utah and adjacent areas of Nevada, Idaho, and Wyoming: Geological Society of America, Rocky Mountain Region Section, Utah Geological Survey Miscellaneous Publication 92,

p. 383-391.

Lockley, M.G., Flemming, R.F., and Conrad, K., 1990, First semiannual report - distribution and significance of Mesozoic vertebrate trace fossils in Dinosaur National Monument: Report to the National Park Service, Contract Number PX1200-0-C809, 15 p.

Lockley, M.G., and Hunt, A.P., 1993, Fossil footprints - a previously overlooked paleontological resource in Utah's national parks, *in* Santucci, V.L., editor, National Park Service research abstract volume: National Park Service Technical Report, NPS/NRPO/NRTR-93/11, p. 29.

Lockley, M.G., Hunt, A.P., Conrad, K., and Robinson, J., 1992d, Tracking dinosaurs and other extinct animals at Lake Powell: Park Science, v. 12, p. 16-17.

Lockley, M.G., Hunt, A.P., Meyer, C., Rainforth, E.C., and Schultz, R.J., 1998, A survey of fossil footprint sites at Glen Canyon National Recreation Area (western USA) - a case study in documentation of trace fossil resources: Ichnos, v. 5, p. 177-211.

Lockley, M.G., Kirkland, J.I., DeCourten, F.L., Britt, B.B., and Hasiotis, S.T., 1999, Dinosaur tracks from the Cedar Mountain Formation of eastern Utah - a preliminary report, *in* Gillette, D.D., editor, Vertebrate paleontology in Utah: Utah Geological Survey Miscellaneous Publication 99-1, p. 253-257.

Lockley, M.G., and Madsen, J., 1993, Permian vertebrate trackways from the Cedar Mesa Sandstone of eastern Utah - evidence of predator-prey interactions: Ichnos, v. 2, p. 147-153.

Lohman, S.W., 1974, The geologic story of Canyonlands National Park: U.S. Geological Survey Bulletin 1327, 126 p.

—-1975, The geologic story of Arches National Park: U.S. Geological Survey Bulletin 1393, 113 p.

Lucas, S.G., 1995, The Triassic Sinbad Formation and correlation of the Moenkopi Group, Canyonlands National Park, Utah, *in* Santucci, V.L., and McClelland, L., editors, National Park Service research volume 2: National Park Service Technical Report, NPS/NRPO/NRTR-95/16, p. 54-57.

Lucas, S.G., Heckert, A.B., Estep, J.W., and Anderson, O.J., 1997, Stratigraphy of the Upper Triassic Chinle Group, Four Corners Region: New Mexico Geological Society Guidebook, 48th Field Conference, p. 81-107.

Lucas, S.G., Hunt, A.P., and Lockley, M.G., 1995, Dinosaur footprints from the Upper Triassic Rock Point Formation of the Chinle Group, Canyonlands National Park, *in* Santucci, V.L., and McClelland, L., editors, National Park Service paleontological research volume 2: National Park Service Natural Resources Technical Report, NPS/NRPO/NRTR-95/16, p. 58-59.

Marsh, O.C., 1871, On the geology of the eastern Uintah Mountains: American Journal of Science and Arts, Third Series, v. 1, p. 191-198.

May, F.E., and Traverse, A., 1973, Palynology of the Dakota Sandstone (Middle Cretaceous) near Bryce Canyon National Park, southern Utah: Geoscience and Man, v. 7, p. 57-64.

McAllister, J., and Kirby, J., 1998, An occurrence of reptile subaqueous traces in the Moenkopi Formation (Triassic) of Capitol Reef National Park, south central Utah, *in* Santucci, V.L., and McClelland, L., editors, National Park Service paleontological research volume 3: National Park Service Technical, Report NPS/NRGRD/GRDTR-98/01, p. 45-49.

McKee, E.D., 1952, Uppermost Paleozoic strata of northwestern Arizona and southwestern Utah: Utah Geological and Mineral Survey Guidebook, Geology of Utah, no. 7, p. 52-55.

McKnight, E.T., 1940, Geology of the area between Green and Colorado Rivers, Grand and San Juan Counties, Utah: U.S. Geological Survey Bulletin 908, 147 p.

Mead, J.I., and Agenbroad, L.D., 1992, Isotope dating of Pleistocene dung deposits from the Colorado Plateau, Arizona and Utah: Radiocarbon, v. 34, no. 1, p. 1-19.

Mead, J.I., Agenbroad, L.D., Martin, P.S. and Davis, O.K., 1984, The mammoth and sloth dung from Bechan Cave in southern Utah: Current Research Pleistocene, v. 1, p. 79-80.

Mead, J.I., Agenbroad, L.D., Middleton, L., and Phillips, A.M., 1987, Extinct Mountain Goat (*Oreamnos harringtoni*) in southeastern Utah: Quaternary Research, v. 27, p. 323-331.

—-1993a, Extinct Mountain Goat (*Oreamnos harringtoni*) in southeastern Utah, *in* Santucci, V.L., editor, National Park Service research abstract volume: National Park Service Technical Report, NPS/NRPO/NRTR-93/11, p. 86.

Mead, J.I., Agenbroad, L.D., and Stuart, A.J., 1993b, Late Pleistocene vertebrates from Bechan Cave, Colorado Plateau, Utah, *in* Santucci, V.L., editor, National Park Service research abstract volume: National Park Service Technical Report, NPS/NRPO/NRTR-93/11, p. 69.

Mead, J.L., Sharp, S.E., and Agenbroad, L.D., 1991, Holocene Bison from Arches National Park, southeastern Utah: Great Basin Naturalist, v. 51, no. 4, p. 336-342.

Melton, R.A., 1972, Paleoecology and paleoenvironments of the upper Honaker Trail Formation near Moab, Utah: Brigham Young University Geology Studies, v. 19, no. 2, p. 45-88.

Miller, D.M., Crittenden, M.D., and Jordan, T.E., 1991, Geology map of the Lampo Junction Quadrangle, Box Elder County, Utah: Utah Geological Survey Map 136, scale 1:24,000.

Munk, H., 1998, Preliminary report on Late Cretaceous herptiles within or near Bryce Canyon National Park, Utah, *in* Santucci, V.L. and McClelland, L., editors, National Park Service paleontological research volume 3: National Park Service Technical Report, NPS/NRGRD/GRDTR-98/01, p. 41-44.

Nelson, M.E., and Miller, D.M., 1990, A Tertiary record of

the giant marmot *Paenemarmota sawrockensis* in northern Utah: Contributions to Geology, University of Wyoming, v. 28, p. 31-37.

Peabody, F.E., 1948, Reptile and amphibian trackways from the Lower Triassic Moenkopi Formation of Arizona and Utah: California University, Department of Geologic Sciences Bulletin, v. 27, p. 295-468.

—1956, Ichnites from the Triassic Moenkopi Formation of Arizona and Utah: Journal of Paleontology, v. 30, no. 3, p. 731-740.

Peterson, Fred, and Waldrop, H.A., 1965, Jurassic and Cretaceous stratigraphy of south-central Utah – resources for power: Utah Geological Society Guidebook, Geology of Utah, no. 19, p. 47-69.

Powell, J.W., 1875, Exploration of the Colorado River of the West and its tributaries explored in 1869, 1870, 1871, and 1872 under the direction of the Secretary of the Smithsonian Institution: Washington, D.C., Government Printing Office.

Riggs, E.S., 1904, Dinosaur footprints from Arizona: American Journal of Science, v. 57, p. 423-424.

Rolle, A., 1991, John Charles Fremont, character as destiny: Norman, University of Oklahoma Press, 351 p.

Santucci, V.L., Hunt, A.P., and Lockley, M.G., 1998, Fossil vertebrate tracks in National Park Service areas: Dakoterra, v. 5, p. 107-114.

Schultz, R.J., Lockley, M.G., and Hunt, A.P., 1995, New tracksites from the Moenkopi Formation (Lower-Middle Triassic), Glen Canyon National Recreation Area, Utah, *in* Santucci, V.L., and McClelland, L., editors, National Park Service paleontological research volume 2: National Park Service Natural Resources Technical Report, NPS/NRPO/NRTR-95/16, p. 60-63.

Sharpe, S.E., 1991, Late-Pleistocene and Holocene vegetation change in Arches National Park, Grand County, Utah and Dinosaur National Monument, Moffat County, Colorado: Flagstaff, Northern Arizona University, Quaternary Studies, M.S. thesis, 96 p.

Smith, J., and Santucci, V.L., 1999, An inventory of vertebrate ichnofossils from Zion National Park, Utah [abs.]: Journal of Vertebrate Paleontology Abstracts, v. 19, no. 3, p. 77A.

Smith, J.F., Huff, L.C., Hinrichs, E.N., and Luedke, R.G., 1963, Geology of the Capitol Reef area, Wayne and Garfield Counties, Utah: U.S. Geological Survey Professional Paper 363, 102 p.

Sohl, I.G., and Peck, R.E., 1963, *Theriosynoecum wyomingense*, a possible guide ostracode to the Salt Wash Member of the Morrison Formation: U.S. Geological Survey Bulletin 1161-A, p. A1-A10.

Sohl, N.F., 1965, Marine Jurassic gastropods, central and southern Utah: U.S. Geological Survey Professional Paper 503-D, p. D1-D29.

Stanesco, J.D., and Campbell, J.A., 1989, Eolian and noneolian facies of the Lower Permian Cedar Mesa Sandstone Member of the Cutler Formation, southeastern Utah: U.S. Geological Survey Bulletin 1808, p. F1-F13.

Stansbury, H., 1852, Exploration and survey of the valley of the Great Salt Lake, including a reconnaissance of a new route through the Rocky Mountains: Washington D.C., Smithsonian Institution Press, 421 p.

Stokes, W.L., 1978, Animal tracks in the Navajo-Nugget Sandstone: Contribution to Geology, University of Wyoming, v. 16, no. 2, p. 103-107.

—1986, Geology of Utah: Utah Museum of Natural History Occasional Paper 6, 280 p.

Stokes, W.L., and Bruhn, A.F., 1960, Dinosaur tracks from Zion National Park and vicinity: Proceedings Utah Academy Sciences, Arts, and Letters, v. 37, p. 75-76.

Sumida, S.S., Wallister, J.B., and Lombard, R.E., 1999, Late Paleozoic Amphibian-Grade tetrapods of Utah, *in* Gillette, D.D., editor, Vertebrate paleontology in Utah: Utah Geological Survey Miscellaneous Publication 99-1, p. 21-30.

Tidwell,W.D., 1990, Preliminary report on the megafossil flora of the Upper Jurassic Morrison Formation: Hunteria, v. 2, no. 8, p. 1-11.

Tidwell,W.D., Thayn, G., and Terrell, F.M., 1972, New Upper Pennsylvanian fossil plant locality from the Honaker Trail Formation near Moab, Utah [abs.]: Geological Society America, Abstracts with Programs, v. 4, p. 417.

Turner, C.E., and Fishman, N.S., 1991, Jurassic Lake T'oo'dichi – a large alkaline, saline lake, Morrison Formation, eastern Colorado Plateau: Geological Society of America Bulletin, v. 103, p. 538-558.

Turner, C.E., and Peterson, Fred, 1999, Biostratigraphy of dinosaurs in the Upper Jurassic Morrison Formation of the western interior, U.S.A., *in* Gillette, D.D., editor, Vertebrate paleontology in Utah: Utah Geological Survey Miscellaneous Publication 99-1, p. 77-114.

Untermann, G.E., and Untermann, B.R., 1954, Geology of Dinosaur National Monument and vicinity, Utah-Colorado: Utah Geological and Mineralogical Survey Bulletin, v. 42, 227 p.

—1969, A popular guide to the geology of Dinosaur National Monument: Vernal, Dinosaur Nature Association, 126 p.

Vaughn, P.P., 1962, Vertebrates from the Halgaito Tongue of the Cutler Formation, Permian of San Juan County, Utah: Journal of Paleontology, v. 36, p. 529-539.

Wheeler, G.M., 1886, Geographic report, U.S. Geographic Survey West of the 100th Meridian: Government Printing Office.

White, T.E., 1958, The braincase of *Camarasaurus*: Journal of Paleontology, v. 32, no. 3, p. 477-494.

—1964, The Dinosaur Quarry, *in* Sabatka, E.F., editor, Guidebook to the geology and mineral resources of the Uinta Basin: Intermountain Association of Petroleum Geologists, Eigth Annual Field Conference, p. 21-28.

—1967, Dinosaurs at Home: New York, Vantage Press, 232 p.

White, W.B., and Van Gundy, J.J., 1974, Reconnaissance geology of Timpanogos Cave, Wasatch County, Utah: National Speleological Society Bulletin, v. 36, no. 1, p. 5-17.

Willis, G.C., 1996, The history of mapping in Utah prior to statehood: Utah Geological Survey, Survey Notes, v. 29, no. 1, p. 1-7.

Yen, T.G., and Reeside, J.B., 1950, Molluscan fauna of the Morrison Formation: U.S. Geological Survey Professional Paper 233-B, p. 19-51.

Geology of Utah's Parks and Monuments
2000 Utah Geological Association Publication 28
D.A. Sprinkel, T.C. Chidsey, Jr., and P.B. Anderson, editors

Ancient Animal Footprints and Traces in the Grand Staircase-Escalante National Monument, South-Central Utah

Alden H. Hamblin[1] and John R. Foster[2]

ABSTRACT

The Grand Staircase-Escalante National Monument contains exposures of geologic formations ranging from Permian to Cretaceous in age. Several sites with fossil footprints were known prior to monument designation in 1996. There are now 56 known footprint sites occurring in eleven and possibly as many as thirteen of the twenty formations found in the monument. Early and Late Triassic footprints sites in the Moenkopi and Chinle Formations are well represented, as are Early Jurassic footprints in the Moenave, Kayenta, and Navajo Formations. One site is known in the Early Jurassic Wingate Sandstone. New discoveries from the Middle Jurassic include several sites in the upper Entrada Sandstone and a possible small theropod print in the Page Sandstone. Late Cretaceous natural footprint casts have been found associated with coalbeds in the John Henry Member of the Straight Cliffs Formation. Footprint casts have also been found in the Wahweap and Kaiparowits Formations. One possible footprint cast has been found in the Dakota Formation. The footprint localities vary from small sites, with only one or two prints or casts, to large sites with hundreds of footprints. The footprints represent both bipedal and quadrupedal locomotion of animals ranging from very small dinosaurs (*Grallator* and other unnamed footprints), small lizard-like reptiles (*?Gwyneddichnium and Rhynchosauroides*), cat-sized mammal-like reptiles (*Brasilichnium*) and Komodo dragon-sized reptiles, to fairly large carnivorous (*Eubrontes*) and herbivorous dinosaurs. Numerous traces of horseshoe crabs were also found in the Moenkopi Formation within the monument. Most Late Cretaceous footprints represent ornithopod dinosaurs with one possible theropod footprint.

INTRODUCTION

The Grand Staircase-Escalante National Monument (GS-ENM) in southern Utah (figure 1) contains extensive sedimentary rocks of Mesozoic age, most of which are of terrestrial origin with a potential for prehistoric animal footprints. Dinosaur and other reptile footprints had been discovered at several locations prior to designation of the monument in 1996 (Peabody, 1956; Stokes and Bruhn, 1960; Stokes, 1978). Investigations following establishment of the monument have resulted in identifications of more than 50 new footprint localities (appendix). These range in age from Early Triassic to Late Cretaceous. Fossil

Figure 1. Location map. Grand Staircase-Escalante National Monument is divided into three geographic regions: Grand Staircase, Kaiparowits Plateau, and Escalante Canyons.

[1]*Fremont Indian State Park and Museum, Sevier, UT 84766*
[2]*Department of Geology and Geophysics, University of Wyoming, Laramie, WY 82071-3006*

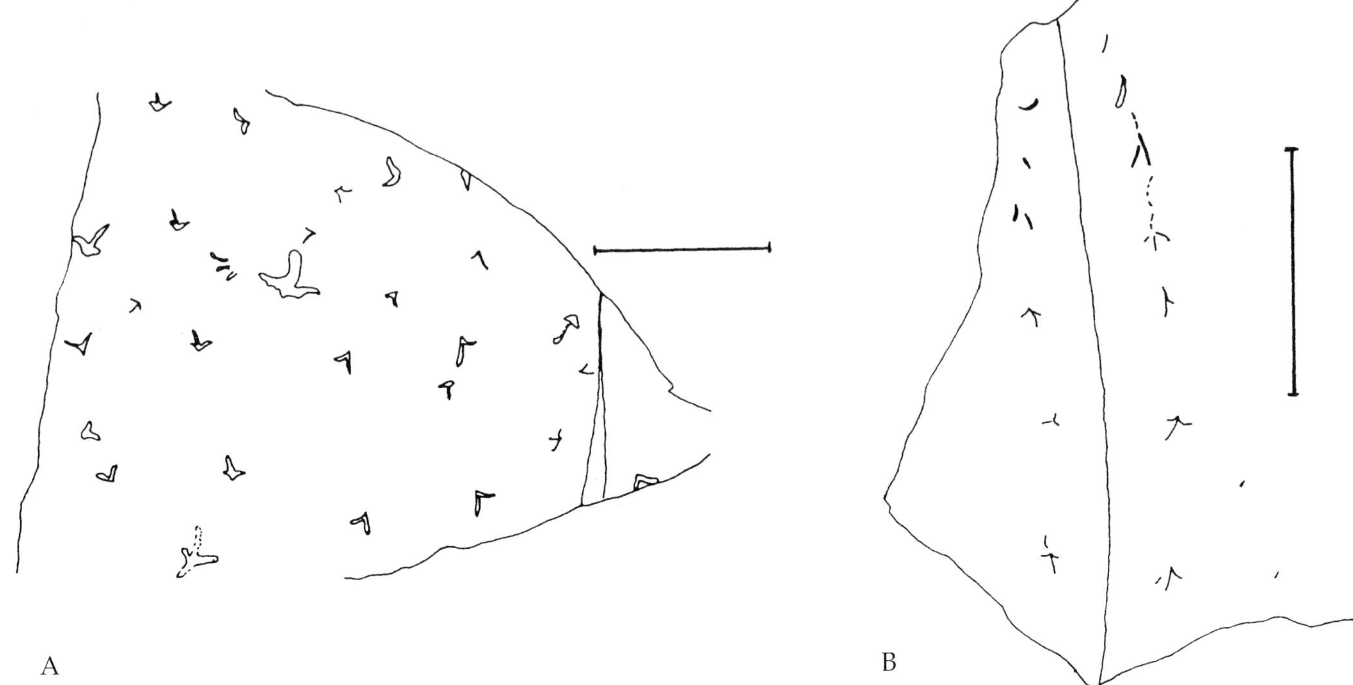

Figure 2. A) Sketch of a slab from the lower Moenkopi Formation of the Circle Cliffs uplift, containing trackways of two limulids (horseshoe crab) and a total of approximately 25 prints. B) Another slab from the same locality containing the trackway of one individual limulid, with telson drag impression. The animal was traveling from bottom to top in this figure. Both scale bars are 10 cm.

animal footprints provide an indication of the fauna present during these times and are particularly valuable in formations that are sparse or lacking in skeletal material. Not all known footprint sites in the monument are discussed here, but examples are given for the formations having sites. While invertebrate trace fossils are fairly common in various formations in the monument, only the more important invertebrate sites will be discussed in this paper. This paper will not address detailed stratigraphy or other aspects of paleontology in the monument. For that information the reader is referred to Doelling and others, this volume.

MOENKOPI FORMATION

The Moenkopi Formation is Early Triassic in age and is exposed in the southern part of the Grand Staircase and in the center of the Circle Cliffs uplift.

Several sites in the Moenkopi Formation in the Circle Cliffs uplift area of GS-ENM contain animal trace fossils, including those of limulids (horseshoe crabs), small reptiles (ichnogenus *Akropus?*), and some scrape marks made by unidentified vertebrates, possibly in shallow water. Footprints assigned to *Akropus* have also been found in the Moenkopi near Paria in the Vermilion Cliffs area, and vertebrate "swim" or scrape marks have been reported from east of GS-ENM in Capitol Reef National Park (Peabody, 1956). One site in the lower Moenkopi Formation of the Circle Cliffs contains hundreds of limulid (horseshoe crab) tracks, and numerous limulid trackways, in a thin unit of thin-bedded, platy siltstone (figure 2). Most of these tracks

are probably undertracks made by the limulid pusher organs (as is common among post-Paleozoic limulid trackways [Goldring and Seilacher, 1971]), though pincer tracks and telson (spike-like posterior end of horseshoe crab) drags are also present in some specimens. The tracks indicate an abundance of horseshoe crab activity on the tidal flats of the seaway in this part of southern Utah during the Early Triassic.

CHINLE FORMATION

The Chinle Formation is Late Triassic in age and is exposed mainly along the Vermilion Cliffs and around the Circle Cliffs uplift.

Trace fossils known from the Chinle Formation within GS-ENM include *Pseudotetrasauropus, Grallator, Apatopus, Rhynchosauroides,* and *Gwyneddichnium?* (figure 3). These reptilian footprints are known from two sites in the Circle Cliffs area. *Pseudotetrasauropus* is believed to represent the footprints of small prosauropod dinosaurs (Ellenberger, 1972: Lockley and others, 1992), and *Grallator* footprints were likely made by small theropod dinosaurs such as *Coelophysis.* The footprints of *Apatopus,* which are pentadactyl in both the manus and pes, and which may include tail drag impressions, probably represent phytosaurs (Baird, 1957; Foster and others, in press). *Rhynchosauroides* and *Gwyneddichnium* are print types representing small, lizard-sized reptiles. Both localities containing these vertebrate print types occur in the Owl Rock Member of the Chinle Formation.

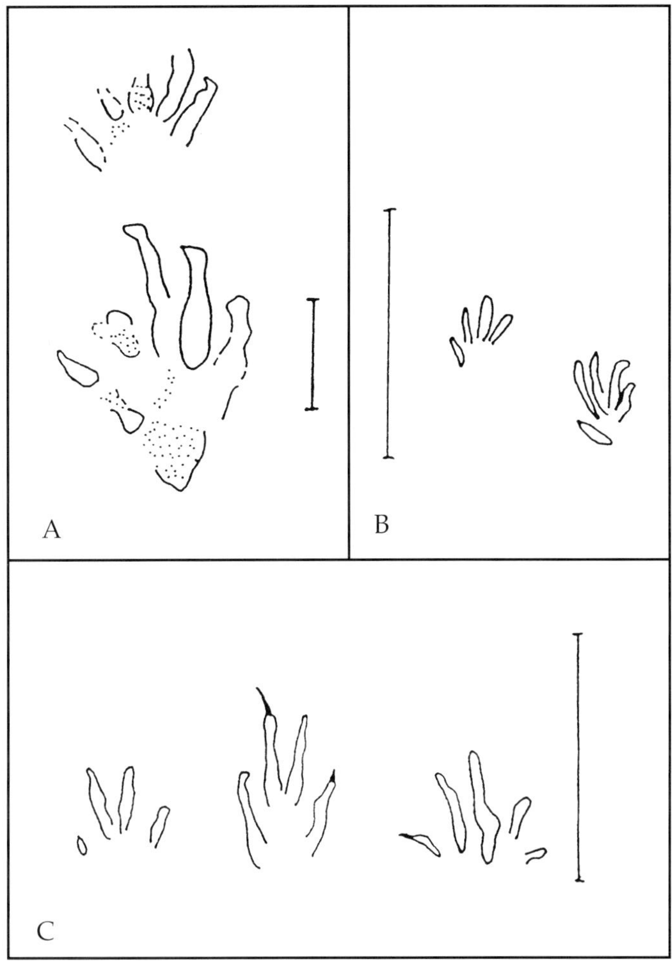

Figure 3. A) Left manus and pes of a trackway assigned to Apatopus *(probably a phytosaur). Scale bar is 10 cm. B) Two individual footprints assigned to* Rhynchosauroides. *Scale bar is 5 cm. C) Three footprints assigned to Gwyneddichnium? Scale bar is 5 cm. All from a site in the upper Owl Rock Member of the Chinle Formation in the northeastern Circle Cliffs. Based on Foster and others (in press).*

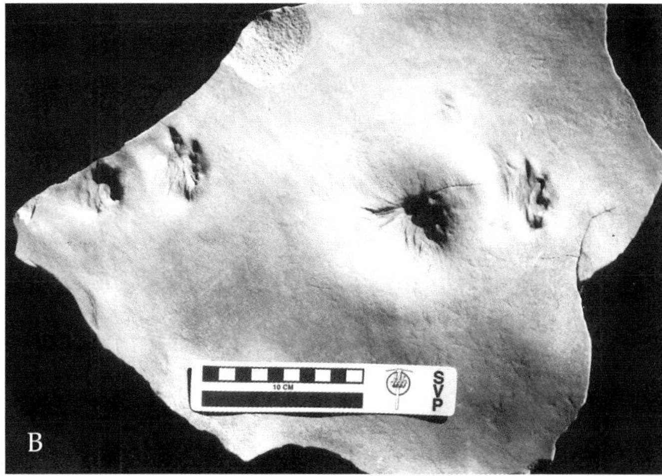

Figure 4. A) Natural cast of small theropod dinosaur footprint, assigned to Grallator, *from the lower Moenave Formation, Vermilion Cliffs. Note claw and pad impressions. Scale bar is 10 cm. B) Two left manus-pes sets of a small crocodylomorph trackway assigned to* Batrachopus, *from the lower Moenave Formation, Vermilion Cliffs. Scale bar is 10 cm.*

MOENAVE FORMATION

The Moenave Formation is Early Jurassic in age and occurs within the monument mainly in the western areas, along the Vermilion Cliffs. To the east it grades laterally into the Wingate Sandstone, which overlies the Chinle Formation around the Circle Cliffs.

The Moenave Formation contains footprints identified as *Grallator, Batrachopus,* and *Anomoepus?* within GS-ENM. Grallator represents the footprints of a small theropod dinosaur and *Anomoepus* may be the tracks of small, bipedal ornithischian dinosaurs. The ichnogenus *Batrachopus* probably represents a crocodylomorph (Olsen and Padian, 1986), possibly *Protosuchus*. However, *Batrachopus* footprints might be confused with synapsid footprints in some cases (Schultz-Pittman and others, 1996). Most of the sites in the Moenave Formation within GS-ENM occur along the Vermilion Cliffs. Here, at a particular stratigraphic level low in the formation, sandstone layers interbedded with thin mudstone layers has yielded numerous foot-

prints as both impressions and natural casts. One site in particular (Park Wash I) has produced a very well preserved *Grallator* footprint cast (figure 4-A) and an impression of two manus-pes sets of *Batrachopus* (figure 4-B). *Grallator* casts have also been found higher up in the Moenave formation in the Springdale Sandstone Member. As few vertebrate fossils are known from the Moenave Formation in GS-ENM, these reptilian footprints furnish most of our current knowledge of the fauna for this area.

WINGATE SANDSTONE

The Wingate Sandstone is best exposed in the northeast part of the GS-ENM, where it forms the massive cliffs that make up the Circle Cliffs.

The Long Canyon site is the only site found so far in the Wingate within GS-ENM. Twelve *Grallator*-type footprints occur on the top side of a 3 m x 3 m sandstone block that is displaced slightly from its original position at the

Figure 5. Sketch of Grallator *footprints on large block of Wingate Sandstone in Long Canyon (Circle Cliffs area) with 5 step trackway and 7 other footprints. Scale bar is 20 cm.*

base of the Wingate Sandstone cliffs. Five of these footprints form a trackway (figure 5). The prints measure 13 cm long and 10.5 cm wide, and the distance of the step from right foot heel to left foot heel is 65 cm. These are the only known Wingate fossils in the monument (Hamblin, 1998; Foster and others, 1999).

KAYENTA FORMATION

The Kayenta Formation is exposed in the Vermilion Cliffs of the Grand Staircase and in the Escalante Canyons and Circle Cliffs areas of the monument. The Kayenta is Early Jurassic in age.

Vertebrate footprints are the most common fossils found in the Kayenta. Nine Kayenta sites are known in the monument. These include several types of dinosaur prints (*Eubrontes, Grallator, Kayentapus and ?Anomoepus*), footprints of mammal-like reptiles (*Brasilichium*) and possible lizard footprints. It has been suggested that the maker of the *Eubrontes* footprints was the dinosaur *Dilophosaurus* and that the *Grallator* footprints were made by the dinosaur *Syntarsus* (DeCourten, 1998). The bones of both

Figure 6. Flag Point tracksite with 3 Eubrontes *footprints and other scattered imprints. The footprint in the foreground measures 46 cm long and 41 cm wide. View is to the south.*

these dinosaurs have been found else-where in the Kayenta Formation.

Several footprint sites have been found northeast of Flag Point. The largest site has over 100 footprints, mostly *Eubrontes*, but with a few *Grallator* (figure 6). Another site near Flag Point has over 50 footprints, most of which are of *Grallator* type plus a *Kayentapus* footprint. One Kayenta site in the Escalante Canyons area exhibits *Brasilichnium*-type tracks which are probably made by small, cat-size mammal-like reptiles (figure 7-A). Another site, in the Grand Staircase area of the monument, has *Grallator* and *Eubrontes* footprints.

NAVAJO SANDSTONE

The Navajo Sandstone is Early Jurassic in age; it forms the White Cliffs of the Grand Staircase and is also exposed throughout much of the Escalante Canyons area.

There are four known footprint sites in the Navajo Sandstone in the monument. All four sites appear to be tracks of animals walking up dune faces. Some of the prints exhibit small mounds at the rear of the foot where the sand bunched up on the down-hill side. The Stokes site (Stokes, 1978), along Highway 12, has a 9-print trackway of a small bipedal, 3-toed dinosaur walking up the dune face; it has a stride of 38 cm and each imprint measures roughly 9 cm long. Several feet to the right of this is

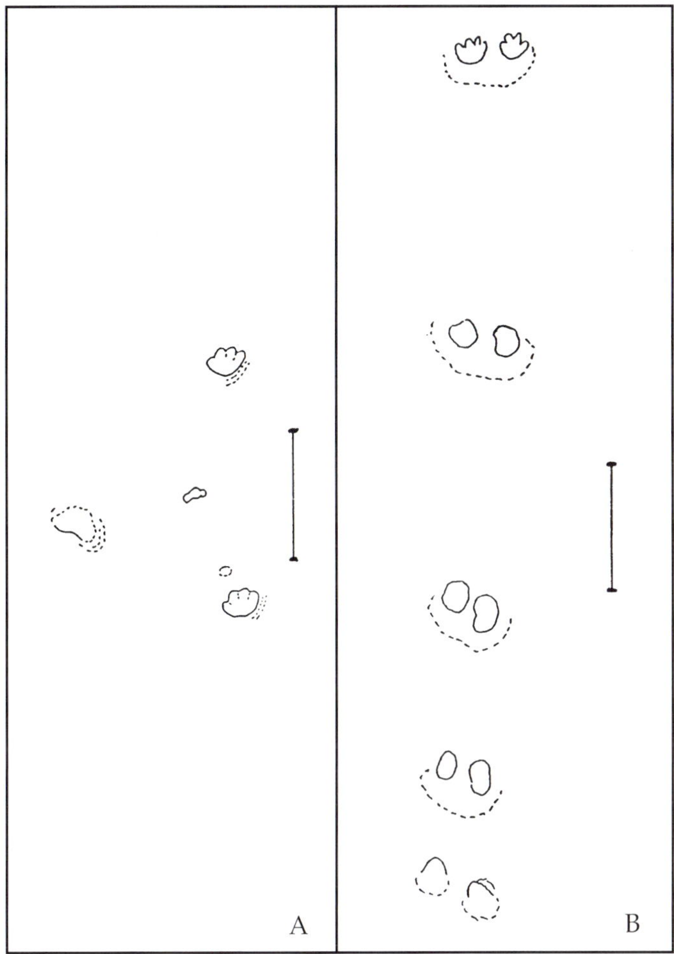

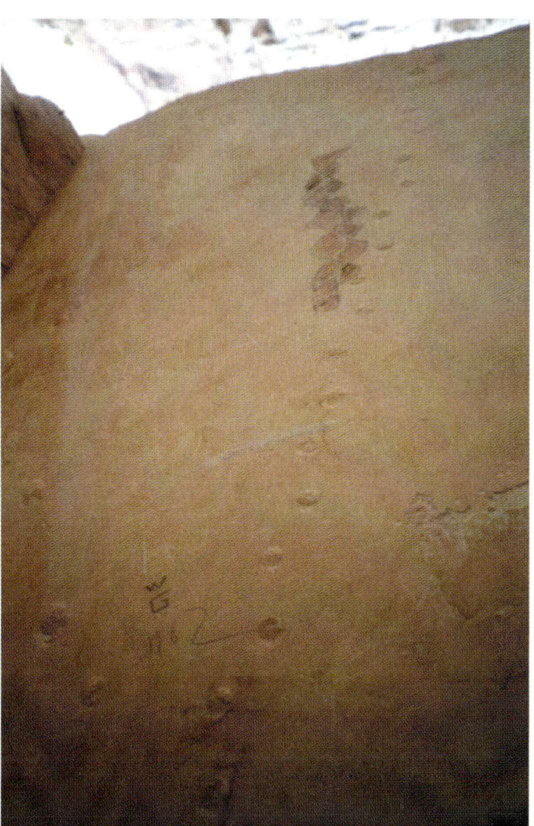

Figure 8. Brasilichnium *footprints on underside of an overhang in the Navajo Sandstone in Escalante Canyon. Footprints of right trackway measure 2.5 cm across and are spaced 13 cm apart.*

Figure 7. Sketches. A) Brasilichnium *footprints in Kayenta Formation in Park Wash area. Scale bar is 10 cm. B) Five sets of paired footprints of hopping mammal or mammal-like reptile in the Navajo Sandstone. Footprints are like* Brasilichnium. *Scale bar is 10 cm.*

another trackway composed of 27 small round to oval imprints referable to the ichnogenus *Brasilichnium*. (*Brasilichnium* footprints resemble modern mammal prints and are thought to have been made by a mammal-like reptile (?therapsid)). Other smaller vertebrate footprints are also known from this site and invertebrate trails have been found several hundred yards northwest of this site.

The Escalante Canyon site is in a small overhang, along with a small prehistoric pictograph. It has 42 footprints in three tracksways made by three different animals. Footprints in two trackways vary slightly in size, forming 2.5 cm and 4 cm circular patterns with indentations showing sand rims or crescents behind the feet as the animals moved up a dune. They also have different gaits. The smaller footprints form a trackway of 28 prints evenly space about 7.5 cm apart (right side of figure 8). The other trackway has sets of two prints, spaced 13 cm apart; these sets are in turn, spaced about 26 cm apart (left side of figure 8). These two trackways start on top of one another at the back of the overhang and after two feet they diverge. The third trackway with three circular imprints, several

times larger than those of the first two trackways, occurs at the back of the overhang. These all appear to be referable to *Brasilichnium*.

The third site has several dune faces with small footprints of *Brasilichnium* type. One particular track is made up of 5 sets of parallel or nearly parallel footprints moving up a dune face. These appear to be in a hopping stride, which increases in length up the dune from 8 cm to 13 cm to 21 cm and 23 cm. The top set of prints are most distinct and measure about 2 x 2 cm, with 4 toes of about equal length (figure 7-B). This is possibly the first example of footprints of hopping vertebrates from the Navajo Sandstone. Similar footprints have been reported from late Triassic to Jurassic rocks in South America by Leonardi (1994), being attributed to a small hopping dinosaur; these were later interpreted as footprints of small hopping mammals or mammal-like reptiles by Rainforth and Lockley (1996). The last pair of prints illustrated in figure 7-B appear to have the morphology of typical *Brasilichnium* footprints.

PAGE SANDSTONE

The Page Sandstone is Middle Jurassic in age and is exposed only in the southern part of the monument, where it lies above the Navajo Sandstone and interfingers with the Carmel Formation. The paleoenvironment represent-

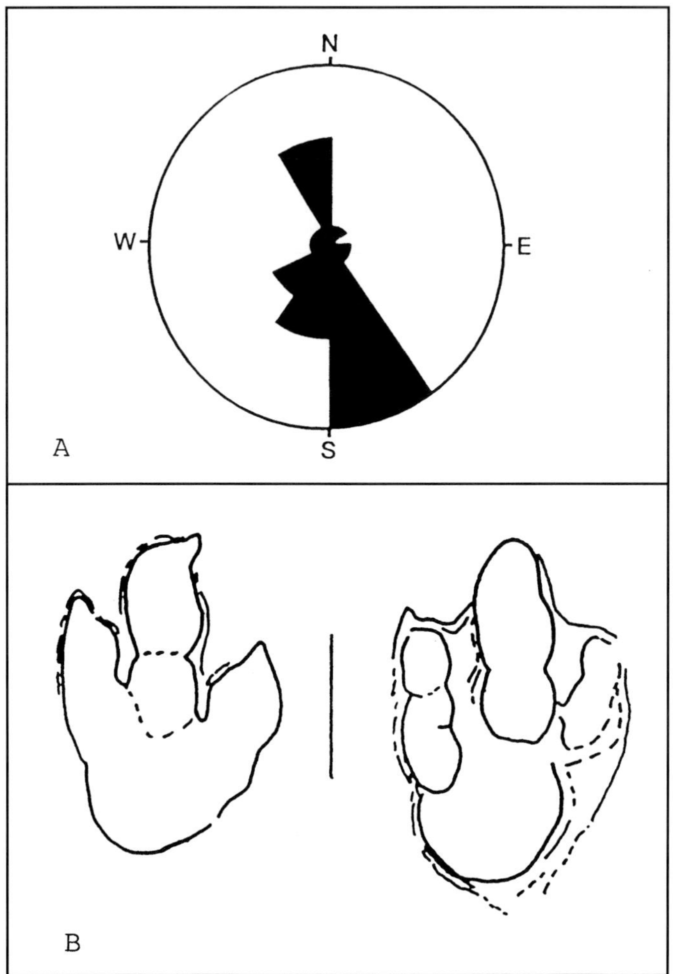

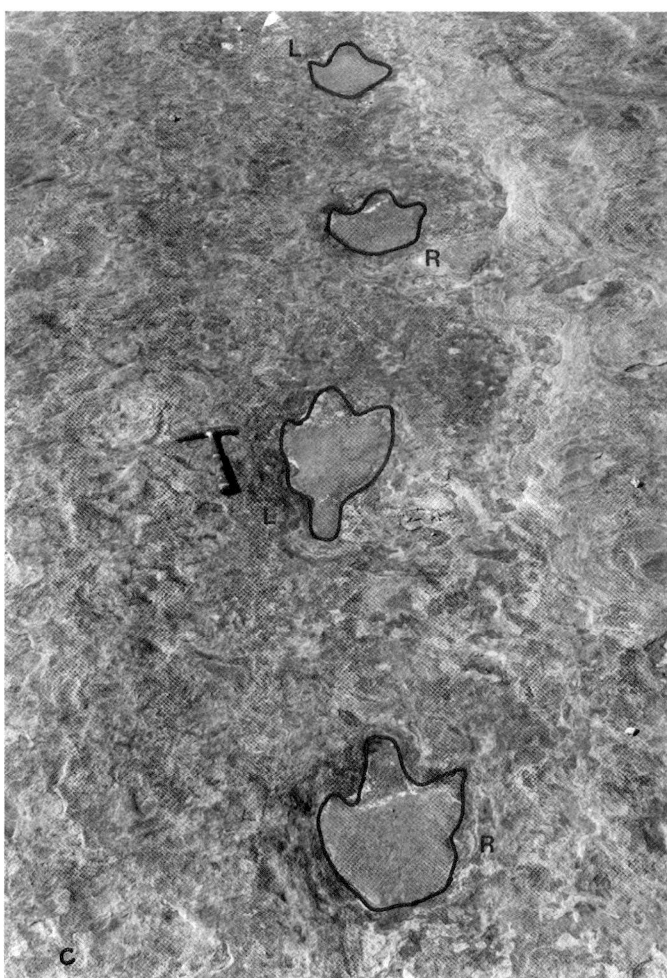

Figure 9. A) Rose diagram of theropod track orientations from the upper Entrada Sandstone near Twentymile Wash along the Straight Cliffs. N=35. B) Outlines of two of the better-preserved theropod dinosaur footprints from the upper Entrada Sandstone, both left feet. Scale bar is 20 cm. Based on Foster and others (in press). C) One of the theropod tracksways from the upper Entrada Sandstone near Twentymile Wash, with left and right steps labeled and footprints outlined for clarity. Note metatarsal impression on second footprint. Rock hammer for scale.

ed by the Page Sandstone may be similar to the eolian dunes of the underlying Navajo Sandstone, but no fossil material has been reported previously from the Page. One site near West Clark Bench, at the southern end of the monument, contains what may be a small (~5 cm) tridactyl dinosaur footprint, and this, along with the lithologic similarities of the Page to the Navajo, suggests that further footprints may be found in the Page Sandstone.

CARMEL FORMATION

The Carmel Formation is Middle Jurassic in age; it is exposed along the Straight Cliffs south of Escalante and in the Grand Staircase, south of the town of Tropic. Fossils from the Carmel Formation are relatively rare within the monument and invertebrate trace fossils are more common than body fossils. The paucity of fossil material within the monument, compared to some areas further west, may be a result of high salinity in this part of the seaway during deposition of the Carmel (Fred Peterson, personal communication, 1998). Invertebrate traces found in the Carmel Formation include grazing trails and burrows, and some larger traces that are similar to the ichnogenus Planolites.

ENTRADA SANDSTONE

The Entrada Sandstone is Middle Jurassic in age; it is exposed along the Straight Cliffs and east of Cannonville. Few fossils are known from the Entrada Sandstone anywhere, but near Moab, Utah, abundant large theropod footprints have been found (Lockley and Hunt, 1995).

Prior to 1998, no fossils were known from the Entrada Sandstone within GS-ENM, but several footprint localities have now been identified near the top of the formation along the Straight Cliffs. These sites reveal nearly 300 footprints of perhaps 50 individual theropod dinosaurs and a trackway with footprints and tail drag of a sauropod dinosaur, which is the lowest stratigraphic evidence of a sauropod in the United States (Foster and others, in press).

Figure 10. Possible natural sandstone cast manus-pes set of a small sauropod dinosaur from the Morrison Formation. For scale, walking stick is approximately one meter.

The theropod trackways show a north-south bimodal orientation, with most of the trackways trending approximately south (figure 9-A). The footprints are in several levels within the top sixteen meters of the upper member of the Entrada Sandstone and are in horizontally bedded sandstones, up to two meters thick, that lie between thick units of cross-bedded sandstone. Cross-bed sets within the sandstones are up to approximately 4-5 m thick and probably represent eolian deposition. The horizontally bedded units containing the footprints may represent wet interdune areas perhaps near a tidal flat, as some of the Entrada may have been deposited by reworking of eolian dunes in shallow marine and beach environments (Doelling and Davis, 1989).

The theropod dinosaur footprints in the Entrada Sandstone at Twentymile Wash are mostly large, about 25-50 cm, with most prints approximately 45 cm long (figure 9B). These foot lengths suggest hip heights for the animals in the range of 2 m. The trackways range from short sets of two or three footprints up to 30-print trackways about 30 m long. Calculations on one trackway with an estimated modal stride length (figure 9-C) indicated a walking speed of 5.3 km/hr. There are also numerous isolated footprints in some layers. Most of the footprints have been identified as *?Megalosauripus* by Foster and others (in press), though some smaller, less well preserved prints about 15-20 cm long may belong to *?Therangopodus*. These same types of theropod footprints have also been found at many sites near to the top of the Entrada Sandstone around Moab, Utah, but the occurrence of a sauropod trackway is unusual in that sauropods have not previously been found anywhere in the Entrada.

MORRISON FORMATION

The Morrison Formation is Late Jurassic in age and is exposed along the Straight Cliffs, east of the Kaiparowits Plateau, and in the southeastern part of the monument, north of Lake Powell. The formation is not present in the western part of the monument, as it was removed by erosion prior to deposition of Cretaceous rocks. Despite the abundance and diversity of fossil collections from the Morrison Formation elsewhere, vertebrate material is rather rare in the Morrison of GS-ENM.

The Morrison Formation contains a number of trace fossil types at many localities, and a few traces are known also from GS-ENM. One site along the Straight Cliffs contains possible traces of a termite nest (Hasiotis and Demko, 1998) in sandstone of the Salt Wash Member. A nearby site consists of a possible natural sandstone cast manus-pes set of a small sauropod dinosaur (figure 10). A site in the Salt Wash Member near the southern boundary of the monument, north of Lake Powell, includes several possible sauropod pes natural casts. The structures found in GS-ENM are not as well preserved as tracks from some other Morrison sites, but their overall shape suggests they probably are tracks of sauropods.

DAKOTA FORMATION

The age of the Dakota Formation has been considered early Late Cretaceous in age (Davidson, 1967), but there is evidence that the lower member is late Early Cretaceous (Doelling and Davis, 1989). The Dakota Formation is exposed north of Cannonville and Henrieville, along the Cockscomb, across the south end of GS-ENM below the Kaiparowits Plateau, and along the base of the Fiftymile Mountain.

The Dakota Formation has not been explored to any extent for tracks within GS-ENM, although dinosaur footprints are quite plentiful in the Dakota Formation in other areas (Lockley and Hunt, 1995). To date, only one possible 3-toed small dinosaur footprint has been found in the monument. This measures 9.5 x 9.5 cm and is possibly that of a very small ornithopod dinosaur. It was found on the bottom of a sandstone block, along with impressions of several leaves and other plant debris (figure 11-A). Further exploration for footprints has a potential for finding new sites in the Dakota Formation.

STRAIGHT CLIFFS FORMATION

The Straight Cliffs Formation is exposed around the edges of the Kaiparowits Plateau, particularly along the Straight Cliffs for which it was named. It is Late Cretaceous in age.

The John Henry Member is the only member of the 4 members so far to produce dinosaur footprints, six sites being known as of this writing. Although the Smoky Hollow Member has a high potential for footprints, it has not been explored to any extent yet. Several sites in the John Henry Member have been found associated with coalbeds just above the Calico bed. Footprints in coalbeds are fairly common in other areas of the Colorado Plateau (Lockley and Hunt, 1995). Footprint have also been found in mud-

Figure 11. Sketches of Cretaceous footprints. A) Outline of possible small ornithopod footprint in the Dakota Formation in the Henrieville area. Scale bar is 5 cm. B) Outlines of footprint casts from John Henry Member of the Straight Cliffs Formation. Drawing made with bottom side up. B-d) has long slender toes compared to others and may be theropod. Others are probably ornithopod footprints. Scale bar is 20 cm. C) Outlines and drawings of casts from Wahweap Formation, thought to be ornithopod footprints. Drawings made with bottom side up. C-b) is on the bottom of a large sandstone block. The others are loose casts. C-f) appears to be multiple footprints. C-h) is the only 4 toed footprint found, possible ceratopsian. Scale bar is 20 cm. D) Two ornithopod casts from the Kaiparowits Formation. Drawing made with bottom side up. D-a) appears to have a heel skid. D-b) is figured with sides of footprint showing striations on sides of cast where the foot went into the mud. Scale bar is 20 cm.

stone-sandstone layers. Most occur as 3-toed casts of ornithopod dinosaurs (figure 11-B-a,b,c). One possible exception is a footprint with narrow toes, which could be that of a theropod dinosaur (figure 11-B-d).

WAHWEAP FORMATION

The Wahweap Formation is Late Cretaceous in age. It is found on the Kaiparowits Plateau from the north central part of the monument, running south to the center of the plateau and hooking to the west in a "j" shaped exposure.

Only recently have fossil footprints been recorded in the Wahweap Formation. Five sites were found in the lower unit in several brief days of exploration, attesting to a high potential for footprints in this formation. Four of these sites occur in interbedded sandstone and mudstone along roads, where the footprints are either eroding out of road cuts or have been graded up by road equipment and deposited with other rocks and debris along the side of the road. They are comprised of 3-toed casts of ornithopods and vary in size from 31 x 31cm to 63 x 57 cm (width x length) (figure11-C). One large cast is 63 cm wide and 82 cm long may represent several footprints (figure11-C-f). A 4-toed footprint cast at one site appears to be that of a quadruped, possibly a ceratopsian (figure 11-C-h).

KAIPAROWITS FORMATION

The Kaiparowits Formation is the youngest Cretaceous formations in the monument. It occurs mainly east of the Cockscomb and in the northwest part of the Kaiparowits Plateau.

The Kaiparowits Formation has not been properly explored for footprints, but several sites have recently been found. One site consists of one 3-toed footprint cast 41 cm wide and 50 cm long which preserves striations on the sides of the center toe where the foot went into the mud (figure 11-D-b). The other site has one large 3-toed footprint cast on the bottom of a large rock. It has a long heel skid and measures 44 cm wide and 78 cm long (figure 11-D-a). These footprints also appear to have been made by ornithopod dinosaurs.

CONCLUSIONS

The identification of 56 sites with fossil footprints in eleven, possibly thirteen, formations of the Grand Staircase-Escalante National Monument is a great illustration of the potential for ichnological research in the monument. These footprint site discoveries give a better indication of the paleofauna present in the monument through the Mesozoic than would be apparent relying solely on body fossils, adding another important dimension to the study of paleontology in this new national monument.

ACKNOWLEDGMENTS

We express appreciation to the Grand Staircase-Escalante National Monument (BLM) who funded the Utah Geological Survey Inventory Study from which much of this information was obtained and to the State of Utah, Utah Division of Parks and Recreation who funded the Paleontologist position (Alden Hamblin) for the Monument Management Plan process when this research was preformed. We thank David Gillette and Mike Lowe for help facilitating field work during the UGS survey and Josh A. Smith for assistance in the field. Appreciation is also given to Martin Lockley and William Sarjeant for their reviews of the manuscript.

REFERENCES

Baird, Donald, 1957, Triassic reptile footprint faunules from Milford New Jersey: Museum of Comparative Zoology Bulletin, v. 117, no. 5, p. 449-520.

Davidson, E.S., 1967, Geology of the Circle Cliffs area, Garfield and Kane Counties, Utah: U.S. Geological Survey Bulletin 1229, 140 p.

DeCourten, F.L., 1998, Dinosaurs of Utah: Universtiy of Utah Press, Salt Lake City, 300 p.

Doelling, H.H., and Davis, F.D., 1989, The geology of Kane County, Utah: Utah Geological and Mineral Survey Bulletin 124, 192 p.

Ellenberger, Paul, 1972, Contribution á la classification des pistes de vertébrés du Trias; les types du Stormberg d'Afrique du Sud (I); Palaeovertebrata, Mémoire Extraordinaire, Montpellier, France, v. 1972, p. 1-117.

Foster, J.R., Hamblin, A.H., and Lockley, M.G., in press, The oldest evidence of a sauropod dinosaur in the western United States and other important vertebrate trackways from the Grand Staircase-Escalante National Monument, Utah: Ichnos, in press.

Foster, J.R., Titus, A.L., Winterfeld, G.F., Hayden, M.C., and Hamblin, A.H., 1999, Paleontology Survey of the Grand Staircase-Escalante National Monument, Garfield and Kane Counties, Utah: A report prepared for the Bureau of Land Managment by the Utah Geological Survey.

Goldring, Roland, and Seilacher, Adolf, 1971, Limulid undertracks and their sedimentological implications: Neues Jahrbuch für Geologie und Paläontologie Abhandlungen, v. 137, no. 3, p. 422-442.

Hamblin, A.H., 1998, Mesozoic vertebrate footprints in the Grand Staircase-Escalante National Monument, Utah: Journal of Vertebrate Paleontology, v. 18, Supplement to no. 3, p. 48A.

Hasiotis, S.T., and Demko, T.M., 1998, Ichnofossils from Garden Park Paleontological Area, Colorado - implications for paleoecological and paleoclimatic reconstructions of the Upper Jurassic: Modern Geology, v. 22, p. 461-479.

Leonardi, Guiseppe, 1994, Annotated atlas of South American tetrapod footprints (Devonian to Holocene): Companhia de Pesquisa de Recursos Minerais, Brasilia, 248 p.

Lockley, M.G., and Hunt, A.P., 1995, Dinosaur tracks and other fossil footprints of the western United States: New York, Columbia University Press, 338 p.

Lockley, M.G., Conrad, Kelly, Paquette, Marc, and Hamblin, A, 1992, Late Triassic vertebrate tracks in the Dinosaur National Monument area: Utah Geological Survey Miscellaneous Publications 92-3, p. 383-391.

Olsen, P.E., and Padian, Kevin, 1986, Earliest records of *Batrachopus* from the southwestern United States, and a revision of some Early Mesozoic crocodylomorph ichnogener, *in* Padian, Kevin, editor, The beginning of the age of dinosaurs: New York, Cambridge University Press, p. 259-273.

Peabody, F.E., 1956, Ichnites from the Triassic Moenkopi Formation of Arizona and Utah: Journal of Paleontology, v. 30, p. 731-740.

Rainforth, E.C., and Lockley, M.G., 1996, Tracks of diminutive dinosaurs and hopping mammals from the Jurassic of North and South America, *in* Morales, Michael, editor, The continental Jurassic: Museum of Northern Arizona Bulletin 60, p. 265-269.

Schultz-Pittman, R.J., Lockley, M.G., and Gaston, Robert, 1996, First reports of synapsid tracks from the Wingate and Moenave Formations, Colorado Plateau Region, *in* Morales, M., editor, The continental Jurassic: Museum of Northern Arizona Bulletin 60, p. 271-273.

Stokes, W.L., 1978, Animal tracks in the Navajo-Nugget Sandstone: Contributions to Geology, University of Wyoming, v. 16, no. 2, p. 103-107.

Stokes, W.L., and Bruhn, A.F., 1960, Dinosaur tracks from Zion National Monument and vicinity, Utah: Utah Academy of Science, Arts, and Letters Proceedings, v. 37, p. 75-76.

APPENDIX, GRAND STAIRCASE-ESCALANTE NATIONAL MONUMENT FOOTPRINT SITES.

	SITE #	FORMATION	DESCRIPTION OF SITES / FOOTPRINTS	SITE NAME / INFORMATION
1	Ga325	Moenkopi	Possible swim marks	The Flats
2	Ga326	Moenkopi	3-toed footprint mold	Lamp Stand
3	Ga464	Moenkopi	Limulid tracks (horseshoe crab)	Canyon View
4	Ga466	Moenkopi	Vertebrate footprints	White Canyon
5	Ga467	Moenkopi	*?Akropus*, small manus/pes, tetradactyl pes, tetra or tridactyl manus footprints	Stud Horse East
6	Ga468	Moenkopi	Possible vertebrate track: swim mark, scrape mark	Northeast Horse Canyon
7	Ga610	Moenkopi	Swim? marks	Moody Creek II
8	Ga612	Moenkopi	Swim? marks and other tracks	Silver Falls Creek
9	Ka004/ Ka667	Moenkopi	Lacertoid footprints resembling *Akopus*	Old Paria Road I /Camp's 1951 site (Peabody, 1956)
10	Ka615	Moenkopi	3 sets of 3-toed marks, also arthropod? tracks	Old Paria Road II
11	Ka689	Moenkopi	Swim marks	Paria South
12	Ga324	Chinle	Vertebrate footprints; *Apatopus, Rhynchosauroides* and *?Gwyneddichnium*	Brinkerhof Spring (Foster, et.al., in press)
13	Ga475	Chinle	Small theropod footprint: *Pseudotetrasauropus,* invert tracks	Long Canyon Pass
14	Ka300/ Ka509	Moenave	Footprint cast of 3-toed dinosaur, *Grallator*	Watson Cabin III
15	Ka299/ Ka510	Moenave	Footprints, *? Grallator*	Watson Cabin II
16	Ka562	Moenave	2 *Grallator* footprints, invert traces, 2 reptile manus/pes sets	Park Wash I
17	Ka563	Moenave	4 *Grallator* footprints, possible tetradactyl footprints	Fin Little Overlook
18	Ka564	Moenave	dinosaur footprints *?Anomoepus*; invertebrate traces	Fin Little II
19	Ka565	Moenave	Small theropod footprints (*?Grallator*)	Park Wash III
20	Ka566	Moenave	Theropod footprints	Paria Movie Set IV
21	Ka690	Moenave	Small 3-toed footprint casts (*?Grallator*)	Park Wash IV
22	Ga323	Wingate	Dinosaur footprints, *Grallator*	Long Canyon
23	Ga322/ Ga477	Kayenta	3-toed dinosaur footprints (*Grallator?, Eubrontes?*), mammal-like reptile footprints *Brasilichnium*	Kiva Koffee House
24	Ga478	Kayenta	Theropod footprints, medium size, 2-4 step tracks	Calf Creek Trail
25	Ka002	Kayenta	3-toed dinosaur footprints, *Eubrontes?* and *Grallator?*	Flag Point Track Site (Stokes & Bruhn, 1960)
26	Ka298	Kayenta	Dinosaur footprints?	Watson Cabin I
27	Ka567	Kayenta	50+ *Grallator* footprints, 1 *Kayentapus* & 1 theropod footprint	Flag Point III
28	Ka568	Kayenta	*Eubrontes* (2), *?Anomoepus* dinosaur footprints	Flag Point II

Appendix continued.

29	Ka569	Kayenta	2 small theropod footprints	Lower Long Canyon
30	Ka570	Kayenta	4 large & 3 small theropod footprints (*Eubrontes, ?Anomoepus*); lacertoid? track	West Swag
31	Ka621	Kayenta	Dinosaur footprints, possibly *Eubrontes*	Flag Point IV
32	Ka571	Navajo	non-dinosaurian vertebrate footprints, *Brasilichnium*	Park Wash II
33	Ga001/ Ga479	Navajo	Vertebrate footprints, *Grallator?, Brasilichnium,* invertebrate trails	Stokes Site (Stokes, 1978)
34	Ga319	Navajo	Vertebrate footrpints, *Brasilichium*	Escalante Canyon
35	Ga609	Navajo	Vertebrate footprints, *Brasilichium*, footprints of small hopping animal	Big Spencer Flat
36	Ka579	Page Sandstone	Possible small theropods footprints	Power Lines
37	Ga480	Entrada	Theropod footprints, 25+	20 Mile Wash West
38	Ga481	Entrada	Track site with 250+ footprints, 3-toed and quadruped tracks, cf. *Brontopodus, ?Megalosauripus, ?Therangospodus*	Twentymile Wash Track Site (Foster, et al., in press)
39	Ga482	Entrada	Theropod footprints	Right Hand Bowl
40	Ga483	Entrada	5 Theropod footprints	Cattle Tank Tracks
41	Ga608	Morrison	2 sauropod(?) footprint casts or other quadruped	Right Hand Collet Canyon
42	Ka580	Morrison	3 probable sauropod footprints, worm borrows	Croton Bench
43	Ga523	Dakota	Possible 3-toed dinosaur footprint cast	South Middle Bench
44	Ka293	Straight Cliffs	3-toed dinosaur footprint	Roger Canyon
45	Ka301/ Ka518/Ka605	Straight Cliffs, John Henry Member	3- toed dinosaur footprint casts, and possible 4-toed footprint cast	The Scorpion
46	Ka682	Straight Cliffs, John Henry Member	3-toed dinosaur footprint casts, mostly ornithopod?, but one possible theropod	Tibbet Canyon I
47	Ka684	Straight Cliffs, John Henry Member	3-toed dinosaur footprint casts above 6" coal bed	Tibbet Canyon II
48	Ka686	Straight Cliffs, John Henry Member	3-toed dinosaur footprints on coal bed	Smokey Hollow Coal
49	Ka691	Straight Cliffs, John Henry Member	2 3-toed ornithopod? dinosaur footprint casts	Lower Trail Canyon
50	Ka687	Wahweap	Several dinosaur footprint casts, 3-toed and one possible 4-toed	Nipple Butte
51	Ka688	Wahweap	1 3-toed ornithopod? dinosaur footprint cast	Tibbet Bench
52	Ga624	Wahweap	3 3-toed dinosaur footprint casts, one also has the mold on opposite side	Star Seep I
53	Ga625	Wahweap	1 large rock with 3-toed dinosaur footprint cast, possibly more than one print	Star Seep II
54	Ga626	Wahweap	2 3-toed dinosaur footprint casts	Star Seep III
55	Ga621	Kaiparowits	1 3-toed ornithopod? Footprint cast, 1 toe broken off, striations on center toe	Shurtz Bush Creek I
56	Ga622	Kaiparowits	1 large 3-toed ornithopod? dinosaur footprint cast with long heel drag, one other possible cast.	Shurtz Bush Creek II

Geology of Utah's Parks and Monuments
2000 Utah Geological Association Publication 28
D.A. Sprinkel, T.C. Chidsey, Jr., and P.B. Anderson, editors

Prehistoric Animal Tracks at Red Fleet State Park, Northeastern Utah

Alden H. Hamblin[1], Sue Ann Bilbey[2], and James Evan Hall[3]

ABSTRACT

Red Fleet State Park sits on the southern flank of the Uinta Mountains in northeastern Utah. Rock strata in and around Red Fleet Reservoir dip steeply to the south resulting in surface exposure of eleven Mesozoic formations. These formations range in age from Early Triassic to Late Cretaceous. Five formations are known to contain fossil footprints in the Red Fleet area. Tracks in the Moenkopi, Chinle and Carmel Formations near Brush Creek were recorded in the 1940s and 1950s, long before the reservoir was constructed. In 1987, several years after the reservoir filled, a major track site with more than 350 tracks was found on an eroded shoreline formed by the fluctuating lake levels that impacted the Glen Canyon Sandstone (Navajo/Nugget Sandstone). The following year, tracks were also discovered on the lake shoreline in the Carmel Formation. Subsequent investigations have lead to the discovery of tracks in the Chinle Formation, both on the shoreline and hills northeast of the reservoir, as well as dinosaur tracks associated with thin coal beds in the Frontier Formation near Red Fleet Dam. Other fluvial and littoral formations in this area have excellent potential for vertebrate ichnofossils, as these units have similar fossils elsewhere in the intermountain west.

INTRODUCTION

Red Fleet State Park is located 19 kilometers (12 miles) northeast of Vernal, Utah (figures 1 and 2). It is situated on the southeastern flank of the Uinta Mountain arch with exposed sedimentary strata that dip steeply to the south (Kinney, 1955; Rowley, and others, 1985). Mapping expeditions beginning in the 1870s, under the auspices of the United States Territorial Survey (later Geological Survey) of Ferdinand Hayden (1872), Clarence King (1877), and John Wesley Powell (1876), established landmark studies for all subsequent geological work in the Uintas. The geology of the Uinta Basin and Uinta Mountains is remarkably complex, and a comprehensive review of their geology is beyond the scope of this synthesis. This presentation, however, is a brief overview of the Mesozoic geologic history of the Uintas near Red Fleet State Park.

In geological terms, the Uinta Mountains and Uinta

Figure 1. *Location of Red Fleet State Park in northeastern Utah with park boundaries indicated relative to the area of the reservoir.*

---

[1]*Fremont Indian State Park, Sevier, UT 84766*
[2]*Utah Field House of Natural History, Vernal, UT 84078*
[3]*Uinta Paleontological Associates, Inc., Vernal, UT 84078*

Figure 2. Photograph of Red Fleet State Park from the hills west of the dam looking northwest.

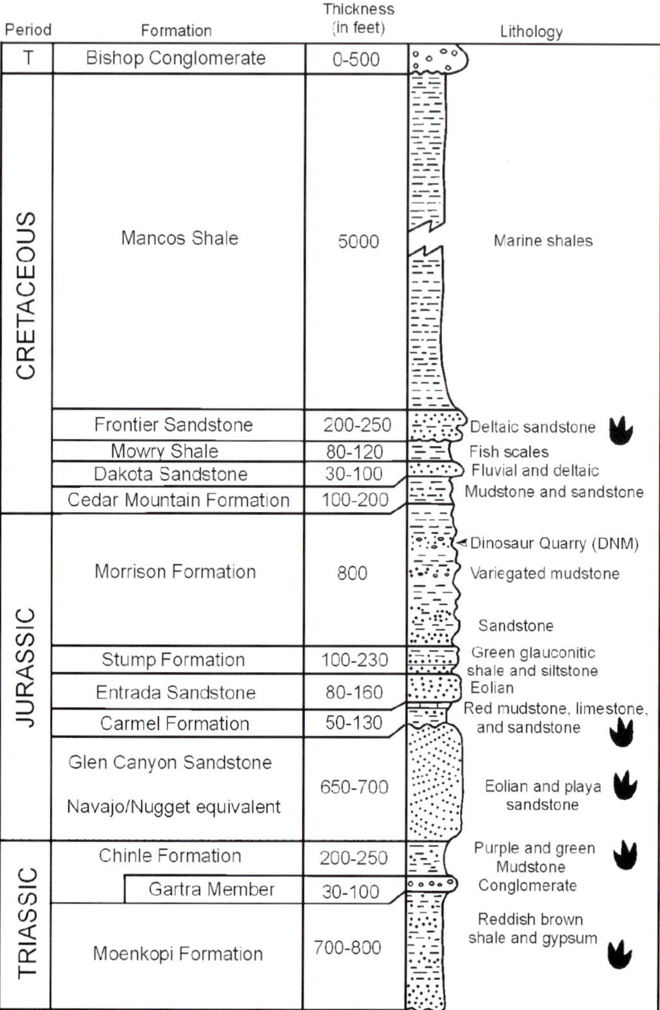

Period	Formation	Thickness (in feet)	Lithology
T	Bishop Conglomerate	0-500	
CRETACEOUS	Mancos Shale	5000	Marine shales
CRETACEOUS	Frontier Sandstone	200-250	Deltaic sandstone
CRETACEOUS	Mowry Shale	80-120	Fish scales
CRETACEOUS	Dakota Sandstone	30-100	Fluvial and deltaic
CRETACEOUS	Cedar Mountain Formation	100-200	Mudstone and sandstone
JURASSIC	Morrison Formation	800	Dinosaur Quarry (DNM) / Variegated mudstone / Sandstone
JURASSIC	Stump Formation	100-230	Green glauconitic shale and siltstone
JURASSIC	Entrada Sandstone	80-160	Eolian
JURASSIC	Carmel Formation	50-130	Red mudstone, limestone, and sandstone
JURASSIC	Glen Canyon Sandstone / Navajo/Nugget equivalent	650-700	Eolian and playa sandstone
TRIASSIC	Chinle Formation	200-250	Purple and green Mudstone
TRIASSIC	Gartra Member	30-100	Conglomerate
TRIASSIC	Moenkopi Formation	700-800	Reddish brown shale and gypsum

Figure 3. Stratigraphic column of Red Fleet Area (adapted from Hintze, 1988). Track prints indicate units that preserve vertebrate track sites. Position of the Dinosaur National Monument quarry is indicated as well.

Basin formed relatively recently during the Tertiary (Crowley, 1955; Untermann and Untermann, 1964; Hansen, 1986). Geological formations exposed in the Red Fleet State Park region represent more than 150 million years of earth history, primarily strata from the Mesozoic Era. The most recent geological events are the erosional processes of the Quaternary that have formed the spectacular canyons of Brush Creek and its drainage where the reservoir is now located The absolute ages of the geological time periods as used here are defined in Hintze (1988). In the following discussion "mya" denotes million years ago.

In a linear distance of approximately 4 kilometers (2.5 miles) trending southeast from the second access road as one travels north on US Highway 191 to the dam, twelve Mesozoic formations are exposed in the Red Fleet Reservoir area (Kinney, 1955; Rowley and others, 1985)(figure 3). Fossil animal tracks described as "swim" tracks were first reported in the Moenkopi Formation in an area just northwest of the present-day reservoir by Peabody (1948; 1956). Shortly thereafter, G.E. and B.R. Untermann (1949) reported track sites in the Chinle and Carmel Formations from nearby rock exposures north and east of Vernal. Red Fleet Dam was constructed and the reservoir filled in 1980. Dinosaur tracks were discovered in the Glen Canyon Sandstone (Navajo/Nugget Sandstone) along the shoreline in 1987. In 1988, dinosaur tracks were found in the Carmel Formation, also along the shoreline. Additional exploration in succeeding years has led to the discovery of tracks in the Chinle Formation along the shoreline and in the hills northeast of the reservoir, and of tracks in the Frontier Formation near the dam site (Hamblin, 1992). Several additional track sites have been discovered recently during a U. S. Bureau of Reclamation paleontological resource survey (Vincent Santucci, verbal communication, 1999; Utah Field House collections).

TRIASSIC PERIOD - 245 mya to 208 mya

Dinwoody and Moenkopi Formations - Early Triassic

The Early Triassic Dinwoody and Moenkopi Formations introduce the first rock units of the Mesozoic Era in northeastern Utah. As part of a regressional sequence, the thin light gray, nearshore marine shales and siltstones of the Dinwoody Formation quickly gave way to red mudflats of the Moenkopi Formation. The Moenkopi Formation is identifiable by the brick-red, micaeous shale and mudstone interbedded with thin layers of gypsum. In western Utah and Idaho, the upper Dinwoody and Thaynes formations are the marine equivalents of the Moenkopi (Hintze, 1988).

Thin red mudstone units of the Moenkopi Formation preserve tracks identified as phytosaurs and amphibians that lived in the area (Peabody, 1948, 1956). Peabody (1956) reported that ". . . extensive surfaces bearing

Figure 4. "Swim" track casts from Moenkopi Formation northeast of Red Fleet State Park. Scale is in 10 cm blocks.

Figure 5a and 5b. Recently discovered footprint casts of Brachy-cheirotherium with tail drag marks from the Chinle Formation at Red Fleet State Park. Scale is in centimeters.

"swim" tracks are fairly common, subaerial tracks are rare. One trackway of a small tetrapod (? reptile) showing an undulate tail mark was found in the lower beds exposed approximately 2 miles up an eastern tributary of Brush Creek north of Vernal. The trackway was preserved as a cast on the under surface of a stratum of massive mudstone and could not be collected readily." Figure 1 of Plate 79 in Peabody (1956) shows the upside-down layer with "swim" track casts. Similar "swim" track casts have been found by the authors northeast of the reservoir in an area assumed to be close to Peabody's site (figure 4). Specimens of these tracks are displayed at the Utah Field House of Natural History State Park Museum in Vernal.

Chinle Formation - Late Triassic

At the close of Moenkopi time, the sea retreated and coarse-grained fluvial sediments were being shed from the Uncompagre Uplift (southeast of the present Uinta Basin)(Dubiel, 1992). Evidence of this transition is preserved as an angular unconformity between these units, although some of the unconformity may be the result of erosional trenching by the encroaching streams of the Gartra Member of the Chinle Formation (Poole and Stewart, 1964a and b; Dubiel, 1992). As in the basal conglomerate members of the Chinle Formation elsewhere, petrified wood is preserved in the conglomeratic fluvial channel deposits of the Gartra Member in the Red Fleet area (Kinney, 1955; Untermann and Untermann, 1964).

The Late Triassic Chinle Formation in the Uinta Basin is the result of tectonic processes that were taking place near the end of the Triassic: the uplift of the Ancestral Rockies to the east, the Uncompagre Uplift to the southeast, as well as island arch volcanic activity to the west (Poole and Stewart, 1964a and b; Dubiel, 1992). Fluvial systems from Colorado carried abundant clastic debris into northeastern Utah, where deltaic and lacustrine conditions predominated. In addition, volcanic ash, later devitrified to smectitic claystone, was carried into the area by west winds. Dark green and purple variegated lacustrine claystone beds dominate the lower portion of the formation north of Vernal, but thin fluvial sandstones with associated overbank deposits are more abundant in the upper portions. The upper variegated Chinle mudstones are intermittently covered with a thin sheet, sandstone units and eventually by the Glen Canyon Group (sometimes known locally as the Navajo or Nugget Sandstone), an eolian sandstone unit that was deposited in Early Jurassic time (Peterson, 1988).

Untermann and Untermann (1964, 1969) reported finding tracks in the Chinle Formation along the south flank of the Uinta Mountains in the Red Mountain area just west of Red Fleet State Park. The senior author discovered two track sites in the Chinle Formation, one along the shoreline of the lake and the other in the hills northeast of the reservoir. These were reported as "Red Fleet West" site and "Red Fleet North" site in Lockley and others, (1992). "Red Fleet North" consists of several footprints that belong to the ichnogenus Agialopus, a small three-toed dinosaur. These tracks are similar to a track type known as Grallator. Footprints at the "Red Fleet West" site are from a quadruped, possibly an aetosaur. These tracks belong to the ichnogenus, Brachycheirotherium. Similar track sites have been found near Dinosaur National Monument and are described by Lockley and others (1992).

Recently during a paleontological resource survey for the U.S. Bureau of Reclamation another track site was discovered in the Chinle Formation along the southern shoreline in the northern end of the reservoir (Vincent Santucci, verbal communication, 1999) (figures 5a and 5b). These tracks are similar to Brachycheirotherium–a four-toed quadruped with associated tail drag marks (up to 22 cm long). However, the footprints are smaller (3.5 cm) than the trackway reported from Cub Creek near Dinosaur National Monument (Lockley and others, 1992). The Red Fleet tracks are cast impressions and occur in a tan fine-grained sandstone that overlay variegated green to reddish-gray siltstone and mudstone as recognized from a few adhering layers.

JURASSIC PERIOD - 208 mya to 144 mya

Glen Canyon Sandstone - Early Jurassic

In the Late Triassic - Early Jurassic, continental plate movements pushed the North American continent over a portion of the East Pacific Rise. A subduction zone with its corresponding island arc and continental uplift was developing in western Nevada and California (Stokes 1986). Erg (wind-blown sand) deposits of the Glen Canyon Sandstone (Wingate, Kayenta, and Navajo Formations as well as the Nugget Sandstones elsewhere) suggest the presence of continental desert conditions over much of the Rocky Mountain province during the Early Jurassic (Lawton, 1994).

The senior author discovered an extensive track site in the Glen Canyon (Navajo/Nugget) Sandstone along the shore of Red Fleet Reservoir in 1987 (Hamblin, 1992). The tracks were found at a popular swimming and diving area of the lake, but had gone unnoticed until their discovery seven years after the lake had filled. Details of this site were reported by Hamblin and Bilbey (1999). More than 350 footprints are recorded in nine different layers of the horizontally-bedded calcareous sandstone (figures 6a and 6b). Two track types were recognized, Grallator and Eubrontes, representing two sizes of bipedal, tridactyl dinosaur track-makers in a series of red to yellow, bioturbated, oasis or playa deposits. There are two hypotheses explaining these track ways: 1) Both track types were made by one species of dinosaur, but represent different age groups; or 2) These are the tracks of two different species of theropod dinosaurs (Hamblin and Bilbey, 1999). Gralla-

Figure 6a and 6b. Grallator and Eubrontes footprints from Glen Canyon (Navajo/Nugget) Sandstone from Red Fleet State Park. Scale is 10 centimeters.

tor and Eubrontes tracks are fairly common in Early Jurassic rocks in other areas, particularly the Connecticut Valley of Massachusetts, USA, where they were first studied and identified. The general interpretation of these tracks elsewhere is that they represent two species of dinosaurs (Lockley, 1991).

Another small site was found by Evan Hall in the Glen Canyon Sandstone on the north side of the Brush Creek channel of the lake. The site is approximately 15 meters (50 feet) above the water line and stratigraphically lower than the Hamblin track site. Splayed quadrupedal footprints cross a parallel-laminated bed within the larger cross-bedded sandstone units of the Glen Canyon Sandstone. They are possibly underprints, round with no toe marks and are about 1.5 cm long. These are probably of the track type Brasilichnium which are similar to modern mammal tracks and are thought to be tracks of a mammal-like reptile (?therapsid). These have been reported elsewhere in the Navajo Sandstone (Lockley and Hunt, 1995; Hamblin, 1998; Hamblin and Foster, in this publication).

Some faint tridactyl footprints about 50 cm in length were also observed at this site. These tracks, found on parallel-laminated beds, suggest an occasional rise in the ground water table in the great erg desert of the Glen Canyon Sandstone. Similar tracks have been found in the Nugget Sandstone near Heber, Utah (Albers, 1975).

Carmel Formation - Middle Jurassic

In the Middle Jurassic, marine incursions into the Western Interior of the United States emerged from the north as the Sundance Sea developed and expanded (Hinman, 1957; Freeman, 1976; Imlay, 1980; Peterson, 1988). The Carmel and Stump Formations are the result of two Jurassic transgressions of the Sundance Seaway (Pipiringos and Imlay, 1979; Imlay, 1980). Deposited between these units are the regressional eolian sandstone beds of the Entrada Formation.

The Carmel Formation is composed of mudflat and shoreline deposits of red claystone, light-greenish-gray, clayey limestone, light-gray sandstone, and gypsum that correlate with the marine Twin Creek Formation in central Utah (Hinman, 1957; Rigby, 1964; Imlay, 1980). A year after discovery of the Glen Canyon track site, Utah State Park Ranger Paul Dixon discovered small dinosaur footprints in a sandstone unit in the Carmel Formation along the western shore of the lake. Subsequent investigation revealed two distinctive layers of sandstone with tracks. The lower layer contains elongate tridactyl footprints measuring 7 cm long and 4 cm wide and the upper layer has nearly symmetrical tridacty prints measuring 6.2 cm long and 6.0 cm wide (Lockley and others, 1998) (figure 7). The dissimilarity in footprint sizes in the lower horizon may suggest the occurrence of two distinct ichnospecies or it may be an artifact of preservation differences for the same species. The better detail of footprints from the upper layer led Lockley and others (1998) to attribute these tracks to Carmelopus, a new Middle Jurassic ichnogenus. These tracks were described from the Red Fleet State Park and Dinosaur National Monument areas. Although this is a significant discovery, Untermann and Untermann (1949) reported occurrences of similar tridactyl dinosaur tracks in the Carmel Formation near Dinosaur National Monument. Examples of these tracks were collected by the Untermanns and are on display in the Utah Field House.

During a Utah State University research project, Emil Stockton discovered a single footprint near the entrance road of the state park. Although this is a solitary footprint, its morphological detail is identical to those found on the shoreline and it occurs in a similar fine-grained, light-gray sandstone. Apparently dinosaurs were feeding along a sandy beach and left their tracks in the sand. These are the only evidence of Middle Jurassic dinosaurs known from this area. No fossil bone has been found in this unit, only tracks and an abundance of marine invertebrate shells (Sohl, 1965).

Figure 7. Carmelopus footprints from the Carmel Formation from Red Fleet State Park. The scale interval is 30 to 40 centimeters.

Entrada Sandstone and Stump Formation - Middle Jurassic

During a brief intermediary regression of the Sundance Sea, winds reworked shoreline sands and deposited the eolian, cross-bedded sandstone of the Entrada Sandstone (Otto and Picard, 1976). Fossils of any type are rare in the Entrada near Vernal, but the inferred depositional environment of the sandstone suggests potential for preservation of ichnofossils similar to those found in this stratigraphic unit near Moab (Lockley and Hunt, 1995). Next, the Stump Formation includes three distinctive marine units: the lower Curtis Member, the Redwater Shale, and the Windy Hill Member (a regressive limestone and sandstone unit sometimes grouped with the Upper Jurassic Morrison Formation but more appropriately placed in the lithostratigraphic grouping of the marine Stump Formation) (Peterson, 1988; Bilbey, 1998). The Curtis Member is composed of near-shore, flaggy-bedded sandstone deposits. The Redwater Member is a transgressive, greenish to dark-gray marine shale. The Windy Hill Member is a regressional unit with nearshore limestone and beach sandstone deposits (Hoggan, 1970). Although no tracks have been found in the Stump Formation, fossil remains of marine reptiles–Icthyosaurs and Pliosaurs–have been discovered near Red Fleet (Bilbey and others, 1990).

Morrison Formation - Late Jurassic

Overall regional uplift of the craton to the west and southwest (the Nevadan and the beginning Sevier orogenies) caused the final northward withdrawal of the Sundance Sea. Continental deposition (fluvial, lacustrine, and paleosol) dominated a large alluvial plain extending from southwestern Utah and northern Arizona to Montana and eastward to Kansas (Stokes, 1944; Craig and others, 1955; Dawson, 1970; Dodson and others, 1980; Imlay, 1980; Brenner, 1983).

This continental sequence began with the deposition

of the Morrison Formation, world renown for its dinosaur fauna (Gilmore, 1924; 1936; Madsen and Miller, 1979; Dodson and others, 1980; Turner and Peterson, 1999; Engelmann, 1999), and continued with the Cedar Mountain and Dakota Formations. Regional uplift to the west and southwest exhumed late Paleozoic and early Mesozoic sedimentary rock that was carried eastward into the depositional basin. Volcanic ash from the emerging island arc and scattered plutons in western Utah and eastern Nevada provided much of the volcanic detritus incorporated in these formations (Cadigan, 1967; Craig and others, 1955; Armstrong and Suppe, 1973; Bilbey, 1992, 1998). Silica released during the devitrification of the ash cemented many of the sandstone units, formed intraformational silcrete horizons, and petrified many of the dinosaur bones (Cadigan, 1967; Bilbey and others, 1974; Bilbey, 1992; 1998). Bones of other, much smaller animals such as mammals, salamanders, turtles, and crocodiles, (Chure and others, 1998) as well as petrified wood (Tidwell, 1990a and b) and small fresh water invertebrates (Yen, 1952; Evanoff and others, 1998) have also been found. Non-dinosaurian animals are quite rare and are preserved primarily in crevasse splay, pond, or overbank deposits. There are a variety of fossil vertebrates and plants known from Morrison Formation in the Red Fleet area. Although no dinosaur tracks have been found in the Morrison Formation near Red Fleet, the abundance of vertebrate fossils suggests that there is potential for the discovery of tracks.

CRETACEOUS PERIOD - 141 mya to 66.4 mya

Cedar Mountain Formation - Early Cretaceous

The Sevier orogeny, which caused uplift and overthrusting throughout central Utah, north to south, as well as eastern Nevada, southwestern Wyoming and western Montana, began in earnest in the Early Cretaceous (Allmendinger and Jordan, 1981; Heller and Paola, 1989). Great detrital sheets of conglomerate record that activity in the western Colorado Plateau and eastern Basin and Range provinces. In northeastern Utah, eastward-thinning conglomerate lenses appear as early as Morrison time, but are more prevalent in the Lower Cretaceous Cedar Mountain Formation (Young, 1960, 1987; Kirkwood, 1976; Bilbey, 1992). Dinosaurs, other terrestrial vertebrates, and freshwater invertebrates are also found in the Cedar Mountain Formation near Vernal, but are locally less abundant than in the Morrison Formation (Stokes, 1944; 1952; Galton and Jensen, 1979; Kirkland and others, 1993; several papers in Lucas and others, 1998; Kirkland and others, 1999). Plant material found in the Cedar Mountain Formation suggests one of the earliest occurrences of angiosperms in North America (Tidwell, 1983). Dinosaur tracks are not common in the Cedar Mountain Formation, but occasionally they are found in crevasse splay deposits particularly in the San Rafael Swell area (Lockley and others, 1999).

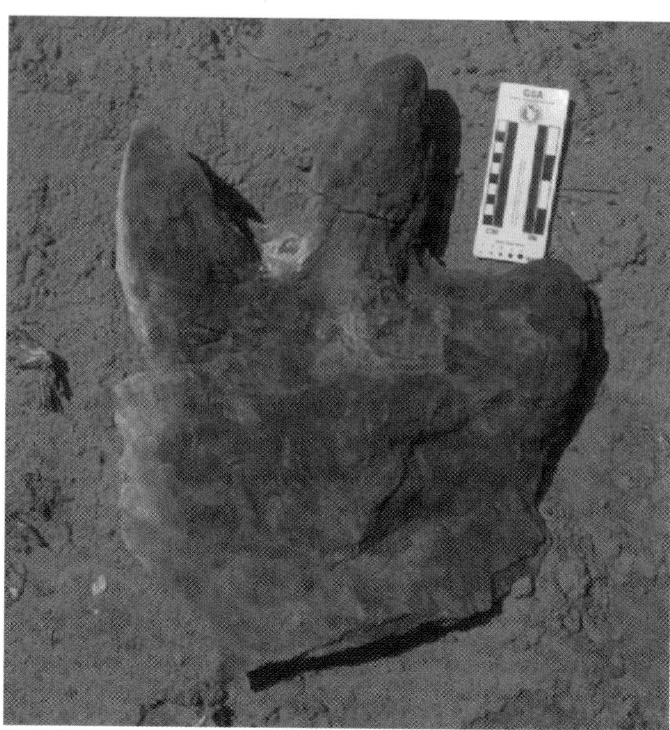

Figure 8. Dinosaur footprint cast from Frontier Formation near the south end of Red Fleet State Park. Scale is in 10 centimeters or 4 inches.

Dakota Sandstone and Mowry Formation - Early Cretaceous

Counteracting the uplift west of the Colorado Plateau region was midcontinental subsidence to the east and the major transgressions of epicontinental seas (Young, 1960, 1987). In the Early Cretaceous a sea encroached from the north depositing first the littoral sands of the Dakota Sandstone and later the marine Mowry Formation.

Interfingering littoral (beach) and fluvial deposits of the Dakota Sandstone (light brown to yellow sandstone with minor coal and gray claystone) are the first evidence of the Cretaceous epicontinental sea incursions. Although no vertebrate trace fossils have been found in this unit in the Red Fleet area, marine invertebrate ichnofossils, like Callianasa burrows, are common. However, dinosaur tracks are known from the Dakota Formation elsewhere, for example, the Alameda Tracksite near Morrison, Colorado (Lockley and Hunt, 1995), so there is potential for finding tracks in the Vernal area.

Overlying the Dakota is the Mowry Formation, a thin-bedded marine shale with minor bentonite beds. The bentonitic clay is indicative of continued volcanic activity primarily to the west and northwest (Stokes, 1986). Silver-gray weathering shale with numerous fish bones, teeth, and scales (Enchodus, Xenyllion, icthyodectiform fishes, and sharks), less common marine reptiles (pliosaur and sea crocodile), and cephalopods, particularly Neogastropolites, help identify this formation (Cockerell, 1915, Stewart and others, 1993).

Frontier Formation - Late Cretaceous

The Frontier Formation, near Vernal, is a fairly thin sequence (90 meters) of interbedded facies of fluvial and beach sandstone, coal, and barrier bar sandstone. These were formed near the eastern extent of a large river delta which prograded from the Sevier Highland into the Cretaceous Mancos epicontinental seaway (Untermann and Untermann, 1964; Armstrong, 1968; Maione, 1971). Farther west along the trend of the Uinta Mountains, the Frontier Formation thickens to more than 3,000 meters of deltaic and marine sandstone units, with interfingering fluvial sandstones, coal, and overbank deposits (Hale, 1959; Ryer, 1977; Molenaar and Wilson, 1990).

Footprints of large bipedal tridactyl dinosaurs, probably ornithopods, have been found associated with thin coal beds in the Frontier Formation near the Red Fleet dam site (figure 8). Another site near the southwest shore of the lake has a possible four-toed footprint. These tracks are significant because few dinosaurs are known from the Turonian Stage of the Cretaceous Period in North America.

Mancos Shale - Late Cretaceous

In northeastern Utah, the Mancos Shale makes up the majority of the Cretaceous rocks, reaching a thickness of more than 1,700 meters (Untermann and Untermann, 1964). It is a dark-gray to light-brownish-gray, marine shale with relatively few fossils. A few types of benthic mollusks, a variety of pelagic ammonites, and a few marine reptiles are occasionally found. The paucity of bottom dwelling invertebrates is due primarily to the inhospitable character of the clay sea bottom (Fouch and others, 1983). The Mancos Shale is the youngest Mesozoic unit exposed at Red Fleet Reservoir. Interfingering with the Mancos and eventually overlying it are fluvial and deltaic deposits of the Mesaverde Group. Although not present at Red Fleet, these beds are found on the southern edge of Ashley Valley, just south of Vernal. These continental units also contain dinosaur tracks that are particularly abundant in the ceilings of coal mines in central Utah and northwestern Colorado.

TERTIARY AND QUATERNARY PERIODS - 66.4 MYA to the Present

After Tertiary folding, faulting, and uplift of the Uinta Mountains associated with the Laramide orogeny, a period of peneplanation occurred. The resulting erosion formed the Bishop Conglomerate, a moderately consolidated unit of conglomerate with sandstone and minor volcanic ash beds, that unconformably overlies small amounts of the Mesozoic and much of Paleozoic and Precambrian rocks in the eastern Uinta Mountains (Hansen, 1986). This unit was deposited primarily in streams flowing from the higher Uinta Mountains, as evidenced by the abundance of Uinta Mountain Group metaquartzite clasts.

Biotite from the ash beds has been dated as far back as the Oligocene (Hansen, 1986). The Bishop Conglomerate is intermittently exposed in the Red Fleet area, capping exposed Mesozoic bedrock.

Quaternary uplift has caused entrenchment of existing streams that flow south from the Uinta Mountains, forming steep canyons like Brush Creek, Ashley Creek, and Dry Fork Canyons. The recent artificial dams on some of these streams form local reservoirs–Red Fleet and Steinaker State Parks.

SUMMARY

Red Fleet State Park is an excellent location area where fossil footprints of animals spanning much of the Mesozoic Era can be examined in a distance of four kilometers (2.5 miles). Footprints ranging in age from Early Triassic to Late Cretaceous are found near the reservoir at eight sites in five different formations. The Glen Canyon Sandstone locality is a large site where tracks can be examined in the field. Seven smaller sites provide important study and exhibit material. Other formations such as the Entrada Sandstone, Morrison Formation, Cedar Mountain Formation and Dakota Sandstone contain fossil tracks in other geographic areas and have potential for fossil footprints around Red Fleet State Park.

ACKNOWLEDGMENTS

We express appreciation to the following people who have helped in the work that resulted in this paper: Peter Laraba, Shauna Witbeck, and Ilene Hamblin participated in the field work. Curtis Sinclear, Vincent Santucci, and Susan Morgan read and reviewed the manuscript and provided suggestions for corrections and improvements. Appreciation is also given to the Utah Division of Parks and Recreation who operates Red Fleet State Park for time and assistance on the research and preparation of the manuscript.

REFERENCES

Albers, Cheryl, 1975, Paleoenvironment of the Upper Triassic-Lower Jurassic(?) Nugget(?) Sandstone near Heber, Utah: Salt Lake City, University of Utah, M.S. thesis, 94 p.

Allmendinger, R.W. and Jordan, T.E., 1981, Mesozoic evolution, hinterland of the Sevier orogenic belt: Geology, v. 9, p. 308-313.

Armstrong, R.L., 1968, Sevier orogenic belt in Nevada and Utah: Geological Society of America Bulletin, v. 79, p. 429-458.

Armstrong, R.L., and Suppe, John, 1973, Potassium-argon geochemistry of Mesozoic igneous rocks in Nevada, Utah, and southern California: Geological Society of America Bulletin, v. 84, p. 1375-1392.

Bilbey, S.A., 1992, A study of the Upper Jurassic - Lower Cretaceous rocks at the Cleveland-Lloyd Dinosaur

Quarry with a comparison to the Dinosaur National Monument Quarry, Utah: Salt Lake City, University of Utah, Ph. D. dissertation, 295 p.

—1998, Cleveland-Lloyd Dinosaur Quarry–age, stratigraphy, and depositional environments: Modern Geology, v. 22, p. 87-120.

Bilbey, S.A., Hall, J.E., and Welles, S.P., 1990, Pliosaurian plesiosaur found in Redwater Member of the Stump Formation (Jurassic–Oxfordian) of northeastern Utah [abs.]: Society of Vertebrate Paleontology Meeting, Oct. 1990.

Bilbey, S.A., Kerns, R.L., Jr., and Bowman, J.T., 1974, Petrology of the Morrison Formation, Dinosaur Quarry Quadrangle, Utah: Utah Geological and Mineral Survey Special Studies 48, 15 p.

Brenner, R.L., 1983, Late Jurassic tectonic setting and paleogeography of Western Interior, North America, *in* Reynolds, M.W., and Dolly, E. D. editors, Mesozoic paleogeography of west-central United States: Denver, Rocky Mountain Section Society of Economic Paleontologists and Mineralogists, p. 119-132.

Cadigan, R.A., 1967, Petrology of the Morrison Formation in the Colorado Plateau region: U.S. Geological Survey Professional Paper 556, 113 p.

Chure, D.J., Carpenter, Kenneth, Litwin, Ron, Hasiotis S.T., and Evanoff, Emmett,1998, The fauna and flora of the Morrison Formation: Modern Geology, v. 23, part 2, p. 507-537.

Cockerell, T.D.A., 1915, Some American Cretaceous fish scales, with notes on the classification and distribution of Cretaceous fishes: U.S. Geological Survey Bulletin 603, p. 34-57.

Craig, L.C., Holmes, C.N., Cadigan, R.A., Freeman, V.L., Mullens, T.E., and Weir, G.W., 1955, Stratigraphy of the Morrison and related formations, Colorado Plateau region–a preliminary report: U.S. Geological Survey Bulletin 1009-E, 168 p.

Crowley, A.J., 1955, A structural history of northwestern Colorado and parts of northeastern Utah: Intermountain Association of Petroleum Geologists and Rocky Mountain Association Geologists, Guidebook to the Geology of Northwest Colorado, p. 53-55.

Dawson, J.C., 1970, The sedimentology and stratigraphy of the Morrison Formation (Upper Jurassic) in northwestern Colorado and northeastern Utah: Madison, University of Wisconsin, Ph.D. dissertation, 125 p.

Dodson, Peter, Behrensmeyer, A.K., Bakker, R.T., and McIntosh, J.S., 1980, Taphonomy and paleoecology of the dinosaur beds of the Jurassic Morrison Formation: Paleobiology, v. 6, no. 2, p. 208-232.

Dubiel, R.F., 1992, Sedimentology and depositional history of the Upper Triassic Chinle Formation in the Uinta, Piceance, and Eagle basins, northwestern Colorado and northeastern Utah: U.S. Geological Survey Bulletin 1787-W, 25 p.

Elder, W.P., and Kirkland, J.I., 1993, Cretaceous biogeography of the Colorado Plateau and adjacent areas, *in* Morales, Michael, editor, Aspects of Mesozoic geology and paleontology of the Colorado Plateau: Museum of Northern Arizona Bulletin 59, p. 129-152.

Englemann, G.F., 1999, Stratigraphic and geographic distribution of fossils in the upper part of the Upper Jurassic Morrison Formation of the Rocky Mountain region, *in* Gillette, D.D., editor, Vertebrate paleontology in Utah: Utah Geological Survey Miscellaneous Studies 99-1, p. 115-120.

Evanoff, Emmett, Good, S.C., and Hanley, J. H., 1998, An overview of the freshwater mollusks from the Morrison Formation (Upper Jurassic, Western Interior, USA): Modern Geology, v. 22, no. 1-4, p. 324-451.

Fouch, T.D., Lawton, T.F., Nichols, D.J., Cashion, W.B., and Cobban, W.A., 1983, Patterns and timing of synorgenic sedimentation in Upper Cretaceous rocks of central and northeast Utah, *in* Reynolds, M.W. and Dolly, E.D., editors, Mesozoic paleogeography of west-central United States: Denver, Rocky Mountain Section of Society of Economic Paleontologists and Mineralogists, p. 305-336.

Freeman, W.E., 1976, Regional stratigraphy and depositional environments of the Glen Canyon Group and Carmel Formation (San Rafael Group), *in* Hill, J.G., editor, Symposium on geology of the Cordilleran hingeline: Rocky Mountain Association of Geologists, p. 247-260.

Galton, P.M., and Jensen, J.A. , 1979, Remains of ornithopod dinosaurs from the Lower Cretaceous of North America: Brigham Young University Geology Studies, v. 25, part 1, p. 1-10.

Gilmore, C.W., 1924, The Dinosaur National Monument and its fossils: Washington Academy of Science Journal, v. 19, no. 15., p. 381.

Hale, L.A., 1959, Intertonguing Upper Cretaceous sediments of northeastern Utah-northwestern Colorado, *in* Haun, J.D. and Weimer, R.J., editors, Symposium on Cretaceous rocks of Colorado and adjacent areas: Rocky Mountain Association Geologists, p. 55-66.

Hamblin, A.H., 1992, Tracking Dinosaurs through 100 million years at Red Fleet State Park, twelve miles north of Vernal, Utah [abs.]: Geological Society of America, Abstracts with Programs, Rocky Mountain Section, v. 24, no. 6, p. 16.

—1998, Mesozoic vertebrate footprints in the Grand Staircase-Escalante National Monument, Utah: Journal of Vertebrate Paleontology, v. 18, Supplement to no. 3 p. 48A.

Hamblin, A.H. and Bilbey, S.A., 1999, A dinosaur track site in the Navajo-Nugget Sandstone, Red Fleet Reservoir, Uintah County, Utah, *in* Gillette, D.D., editor, Vertebrate paleontology in Utah: Utah Geological Survey Miscellaneous Publication 99-1, p. 51-57.

Hansen, W.R., 1986, Neogene tectonics and geomorphology of the eastern Uinta Mountains in Utah, Colorado and Wyoming: U.S. Geological Survey Professional Paper 1356, 78 p.

Hayden, F.V., 1872, Preliminary report of the United States Geological Survey of Wyoming and portions of the contiguous territories, Washington, D.C., Government Printing Office, p. 41-70.

Heller, P.L., and Paola, C., 1989, The paradox of Lower Cretaceous gravels and the initiation of thrusting in the Sevier orogenic belt, United States Western Interior: Geological Society of America Bulletin, v. 101, p. 864-975.

Hinman, E.E., 1957, Jurassic Carmel - Twin Creek facies of northern Utah: The Compass of Sigma Gamma Epsilon, v. 34, no. 2, p. 102- 119.

Hintze, L.F., 1988, Geologic history of Utah: Brigham Young University Geology Studies, Special Publication 7, 202 p.

Hoggan, R.D., 1970, Paleontology and paleoecology of the Curtis Formation in the Uinta Mountains area, Daggett County, Utah: Brigham Young University Geology Studies, v. 17, part 2, p. 31-65.

Imlay, R.W., 1980, Jurassic paleobiogeography of the conterminous United States in its continental setting: U. S. Geological Survey Professional Paper 1062, 134 p.

Kinney, D.M., 1955, Geology of the Uinta River-Brush Creek area, Duchesne and Uintah Counties, Utah: U.S. Geological Survey Bulletin 1007, 185 p.

King, Clarence, 1877, Report of the geological exploration of the Fortieth Parallel, descriptive geology by Arnold Hague and Emmons S. F.: Professional Paper of the Engineering Department United States Army, no. 18, p. 191-309.

Kirkland, J.I., Cifelli, R.L., Britt, B.H., Burge, D.L., DeCorten, F.L., Eaton, J.G., and Parrish, J.M., 1999, Distribution of vertebrate faunas in the Cedar Mountain Formation, east-central Utah, *in* Gillette, D.D., editor, Vertebrate paleontology in Utah: Utah Geological Survey Miscellaneous Publication 99-1, p. 201-217.

Kirkwood, S.G., 1976, Stratigraphy and petroleum potential of the Cedar Mountain and Dakota Formations, northwestern Colorado: Golden, Colorado School of Mines, M.S. thesis, 193 p.

Lawton, T.F., 1994, Tectonic setting of Mesozoic sedimentary basins, Rocky Mountain region, U.S., *in* Caputo, M.V., Peterson J.A., and Franczyk , K.J., editors, Mesozoic systems of the Rocky Mountain region USA: Rocky Mountain Section Society for Sedimentary Geology, p. 1-26.

Lockley, M.G., 1991, Tracking dinosaurs: Cambridge, Cambridge University Press, 238 p.

Lockley, M.G., Conrad, Kelly, Paquette, Marc, and Farlow, J. O., 1992, Distribution and significance of Mesozoic vertebrate trace fossils in Dinosaur National Monument, *in* Plumb, G.E. and Harlow, H.J., editors, National Park Service Research Center 16th Annual Report, p. 74-85.

Lockley, M.G., and Hunt, A.P., 1995, Dinosaur tracks and other fossil footprints of the western United States: New York, Columbia University Press, 338 p.

Lockley, M.G., Hunt, A.P., Paquette, Marc, Bilbey, S.A., and Hamblin, A.H., 1998, Dinosaur tracks from the Carmel Formation, northeastern Utah–Implications for Middle Jurassic paleoecology: Ichnos, v. 5, p. 255-267.

Lockley, M.G., Kirkland J.I., DeCorten, F.L., Britt, B.B., and Hasiotis, S.T.,1999, Dinosaur tracks from the Cedar Mountain Formation of eastern Utah–A preliminary report, *in* Gillette, D.D., editor, Vertebrate paleontology in Utah: Utah Geological Survey Miscellaneous Publication 99-1, p. 253-258.

Lucas, S.G., Kirkland, J.I., and Estep, J.W., 1998, Lower and Middle Cretaceous terrestrial ecosystems: New Mexico Museum of Natural History and Science Bulletin 14, 330 p.

Madsen, J.H., Jr., and Miller, W.E., 1979, The fossil vertebrates of Utah, an annotated bibliography: Brigham Young University Geology Studies, v. 26, part 4, 147 p.

Maione, S.J., 1971, Stratigraphy of the Frontier Sandstone Member of the Mancos Shale (Upper Cretaceous) on the south flank of the eastern Uinta Mountains, Utah and Colorado: Earth Science Bulletin, v. 4, p. 27-58.

McCormick, C.D., and Picard, M.D., 1969, Stratigraphy of the Gartra Formation (Triassic), Uinta Mountain area, Utah and Colorado: Intermountain Association of Geologists 16th Annual Conference Guidebook - Uinta Mountains, p. 169-180.

Molenaar, C.M., and Wilson, B.W., 1990, The Frontier Formation and associated rocks of northeastern Utah and northwestern Colorado: U.S. Geological Survey Bulletin 1787-M, p. M1-M21.

Otto, E.P., and Picard, M.D., 1976, Petrology of Entrada Sandstone (Jurassic), northeastern Utah, *in* Hill, J.G., editor, Symposium on geology of the Cordilleran hingeline: Rocky Mountain Association of Geologists, p. 231-246.

Peabody, F.E.,1948, Reptile and amphibian track ways from the Lower Triassic Moenkopi Formation of Arizona and Utah: Berkeley, University of California Publication, Department of Geological Science., v. 27, p. 295-468.

—1956, Ichnites from the Triassic Moenkopi Formation of Arizona and Utah: Journal of Paleontology, v. 30, no. 3., p. 731-740.

Peterson, Fred, 1988, Stratigraphy and nomenclature of Middle and Upper Jurassic rocks, western Colorado Plateau, Utah and Arizona: U.S. Geological Survey Bulletin 1633-B, p. 17-56.

Pipiringos, G.N., and Imlay, R.W., 1979, Lithology and subdivisions of the Jurassic Stump Formation in southeastern Idaho and adjoining areas: United States Geological Survey Professional Paper 1035-C, p. C1-C25.

Poole, F.G., and Stewart, J.H., 1964a, Chinle Formation and Glen Canyon Sandstone in northeastern Utah and northwestern Colorado, *in* Sabatka, E.F., editor, Guidebook to the geology and mineral resources of the Uinta Basin–Utah's hydrocarbon storehouse: Intermountain Association of Petroleum Geologists Guidebook on

Uinta Basin, 13th Annual Field Conference, p. 93-104.

—1964b, Chinle Formation and Glen Canyon Sandstone in northeastern Utah and northwestern Colorado: U. S. Geological Survey Professional Paper 501-D, p. D30-D39.

Powell, J.W., 1876, Report on the Geology of the eastern portion of the Uinta Mountains and a region of country adjacent thereto: United States Geological and Geographic Survey of the Territories (Rocky Mountain region), Washington D.C., Government Printing Office, 218 p.

Rigby, J.K., 1964, Some observations of the stratigraphy and paleoecology of the Carmel and Twin Creek Formations in the Uinta Mountains, *in* Sabatka, E.F., editor, Guidebook to the geology and mineral resources of the Uinta Basin–Utah's hydrocarbon storehouse: Intermountain Association of Petroleum Geologists Guidebook on Uinta Basin, 13th Annual Field Conference, p. 109-114.

Rowley, P.D., Hansen, W.R., Tweto, Ogden. and Carrara, P. E., 1985, Geologic Map of the Vernal 1° x 2° Quadrangle, Colorado, Utah, and Wyoming: U.S. Geological Survey Map I-1526, scale 1:250,000.

Ryer, T.A., 1977, Patterns of Cretaceous shallow-marine sedimentation, Coalville and Rockport areas, Utah: Geological Society of America Bulletin, v. 88, p. 177-188.

Sohl, N.F., 1965, Marine Jurassic Gastropods, central and southern Utah: U.S. Geological Survey Professional Paper 503-D, 34 p.

Stewart, J.D., Bilbey, S.A., Chure, D.J., and Madsen, S.K. 1994, Vertebrate fauna of the Mowry Shale (Cenomanian) in northeastern Utah [abs.]: Society of Vertebrate Paleontology 1993 Meeting, v. 14, Supplement to Number 3, p 47A.

Stokes, W.L., 1944, Morrison Formation and related deposits in and adjacent to the Colorado Plateau: Geological Society of America Bulletin v. 55, no. 8, p. 951-992.

—1952, Lower Cretaceous in Colorado Plateau: American Association of Petroleum Geologists Bulletin, v. 36, no. 9, p. 1766-1776.

—1986, Geology of Utah: Utah Museum of Natural History and Utah Geological and Mineral Survey, Occasional Paper 6, 280 p.

Tidwell, W.D., 1983, Paleoecology of a small Lower Cretaceous swamp near Ferron, Utah [abs.]: Geological Society of America, Rocky Mountain/Cordilleran Regional Meeting, v. 15, p. 286.

—1990a, Preliminary report on the megafossil flora of the Upper Jurassic Morrison Formation: Hunteria, v. 2, no. 8, 12 p.

—1990b, A new Osmundaceous species (Osmundacaulis lemonii n. sp.) from the Upper Jurassic Morrison Formation, Utah: Hunteria, v. 2, no. 7, 11 p.

Turner, C.E. and Peterson, Fred, 1999, Biostratigraphy of dinosaurs in the Upper Jurassic Morrison Formation of the Western Interior, USA, *in* Gillette, D.D., editor, Vertebrate paleontology in Utah: Utah Geological Survey Miscellaneous Studies 99-1, p. 77-114.

Untermann, G.E., and Untermann, B.R., 1949, Geology of Green and Yampa River Canyons and vicinity, Dinosaur National Monument, Utah and Colorado: American Association of Petroleum Geologists Bulletin, v. 33, no. 5, p. 683-694.

—1964 (revised 1968), Geology of Uintah County: Utah Geological and Mineral Survey Bulletin 72, 112 p.

—1969, Geology of the Uinta Mountain area, Utah-Colorado, *in* Lindsay, S.B., editor, Geologic guidebook of the Uinta Mountains–Utah's Maverick Range: Intermountain Association of Geologists and Utah Geological Society, p. 79-86.

Yen, Teng-Chien, 1952, Molluscan fauna of the Morrison Formation: U. S. Geological Survey Professional Paper 233-B, p. 21-51.

Young, R.G., 1960, Dakota Group of the Colorado Plateau: American Association Petroleum Geologists Bulletin v. 44, no. 2, p. 156-194.

—1987, Triassic and Jurassic rocks in the Dinosaur Triangle, *in* Averett, W.R., editor, Paleontology and geology of the Dinosaur Triangle guidebook: Grand Junction, Museum of Western Colorado, p. 5-21.

Geology of Utah's Parks and Monuments
2000 Utah Geological Association Publication 28
D.A. Sprinkel, T.C. Chidsey, Jr., and P.B. Anderson, editors

Inventory of Dominantly Marine and Brackish-Water Fossils from Late Cretaceous Rocks in and near Grand Staircase-Escalante National Monument, Utah

William A. Cobban[1], Thaddeus S. Dyman[1], Gayle L. Pollock[2], Kenneth I. Takahashi[1], Larry E. Davis[3] and Dennis B. Riggin[1]

ABSTRACT

A digital inventory of predominantly marine and brackish-water invertebrate fossils from Late Cretaceous rocks has been compiled for the newly designated Grand Staircase--Escalante National Monument based on U.S. Geological Survey collections obtained during the past three decades. The inventory contains 168 collections and descriptions of invertebrate fossils from more than 100 localities from the upper part of the Dakota Formation, Tropic Shale, Straight Cliffs Formation, and equivalent units which include rocks of late Cenomanian through late Santonian age. Some of the identified fauna were not previously reported from southwestern Utah.

For many fossil localities in the monument, the inventory provides data on the presence of ammonites and bivalves that are used to correlate marine Cretaceous rocks in southwestern Utah with equivalent rocks in other regions. The inventory also contains (1) information on the geologic age, lithologic characteristics, and depositional environments of rock units; (2) a map of fossil localities within the monument indicated; (3) a chronostratigraphic chart showing the positions of collections within the standard Cretaceous ammonite biozones; (5) six measured sections illustrating the range of lithologies from which the fauna were derived; and (6) photographs of selected ammonites and inoceramids and views of the measured sections from which they were collected.

The oldest marine Cretaceous rocks in the Grand Staircase-Escalante National Monument occur in the early late Cenomanian *Dunveganoceras albertense* biozone of the Dakota Formation in the western part of the monument at Cottonwood Wash. Marine sandstones in the Straight Cliffs Formation represent the overall regressive phase of the seaway and contain biozones ranging from late middle Turonian through the Santonian.

The inventory was compiled using EXCEL 97 and includes fossil name and type, U.S. Geological Survey identification number, collection location information, stratigraphic position of collection, biozone, and general remarks. The inventory can be sorted and modified using standard EXCEL queries.

INTRODUCTION

During the period 1963-1999, 168 collections of Cretaceous invertebrate fossils were made from more than 100 localities in the area now included in the Grand Staircase-Escalante National Monument (figure 1). The collections represent the following stages of the Cretaceous Period (65-142 million years ago): Cenomanian (upper part), Turonian (lower and middle parts), Coniacian (middle and upper parts), and Santonian (middle and upper parts). Pre Cenomanian and post Cretaceous rocks are absent from the monument. Most collections were made by members of the U.S. Geological Survey (USGS). The collectors and years of collection are as follows: H.A. Waldrop (1963-1965), H.D. Zeller (1964-1966), B.E. Law (1966), G.H. Horn

[1]*U.S. Geological Survey, Denver, CO 80225*
[2]*Bryce Canyon National History Association, Bryce Canyon, UT 84717*
[3]*St. Johns University, Department of Biology, Collegeville, MN 56321*

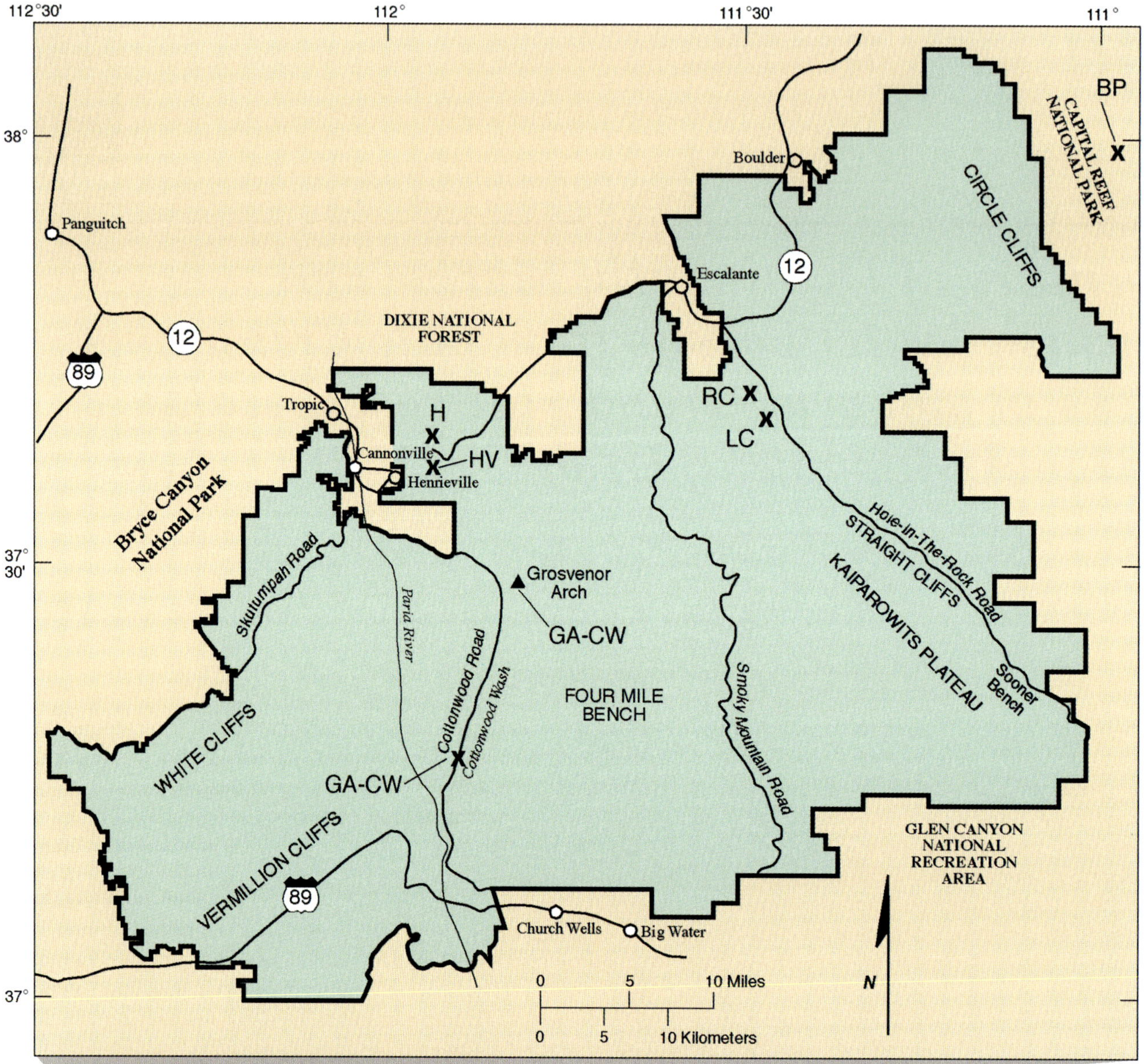

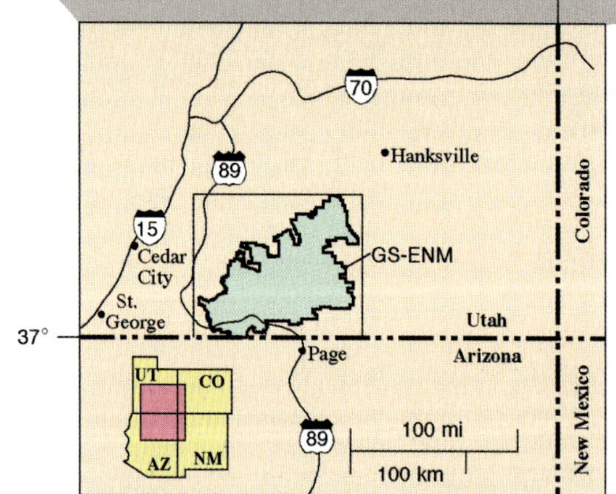

Figure 1. Index map of Grand Staircase-Escalante National Monument illustrating major geographic features, highways, and towns. Measured section localities as follows: GA-CW, Grosvenor Arch-Cottonwood Wash; H, Henrieville; HV, Henrieville Valley; RC, Right-Hand Collet Canyon; LC, Left-Hand Collet Canyon; BP, Bitter Spring Creek-The Post.

(1966), E.V. Stephens (1966, 1967), F. Peterson (1965-1975), W.E. Bowers (1966-1970), F.B. Zelt (1982-1984), G.L. Pollock (1989-1999), T.S. Dyman (1994-1999), C.A. Derewetzky (1997), W.A. Cobban (1966-1999), and I. Walaszczyk (1999). Fossils were identified primarily by W.A. Cobban and G.L. Pollock. The inventory does not include collections of non-USGS personnel, particularly the collections of those researchers published earlier in the last century. In many cases, exact geographic locations of older collections could not be documented by us, and many uncertainties exist due to fossil name changes through the years. For information on other marine Cretaceous collections as well as collections for other rock units in the monument refer to Gillette and Hayden (1997).

The inventory is included on CD-ROM (UGA Publication 29) as an EXCEL data file with supporting files of information. This written report contains: (1) information on the geologic age and lithologic characteristics of the chief rock units from which the fossils were collected; (2) a map of the monument indicating fossil localities; (3) a chronostratigraphic chart showing the positions of collections within the standard Cretaceous ammonite biozones. Other supporting information on CD-ROM includes: (1) graphic displays of six measured sections and accompanying photographs illustrating the range of lithologies from which the fauna were derived; and (2) photographs of selected ammonites and other fossils and views of the measured sections from which many of them were collected.

The purpose of the digital inventory is to present fossil descriptions and supporting information for marine invertebrate collections from the monument as a digital resource for students, teachers, researchers, and the general public. Applications include studies of the energy, mineral, and environmental resources of the monument. Fossil information compiled from the inventory has been incorporated into educational outreach activities in school districts in the form of lectures, field trips, and teacher training programs. Graduate school theses and other academic research projects have incorporated these data. The fossil collections are stored at the USGS in Denver, CO 80225. The authors wish to acknowledge Robert Hettinger and Katherine Varnes, U.S. Geological Survey, Denver, CO for their critical reviews of the manuscript.

CRETACEOUS EPEIRIC SEA

Marine Cretaceous rocks of the monument were deposited along the western margin of a large sea within the continent of North America known as the Cretaceous epeiric sea (figure 2). Sediments were deposited by this sea in a large basin called the Western Interior basin, which is one of the largest and most economically viable sedimentary basins in the world. Energy and mineral resources including coal, uranium, petroleum, natural gas, bentonite, and building stone have been produced in the Western Interior basin for many years. The prairies, mountains, and valleys that today occupy this geographic region offer some of the most scenic and environmentally valuable lands of the American west. Figure 2B illustrates the asymmetric basin profile in which sedimentary rocks range in thickness from more than 20,000 feet in the west in the thrust belt of western Montana, Wyoming, and Utah to less than 1,000 feet in eastern North and South Dakota, and in Nebraska and Kansas. The tectonically active western margin was dominated by coarse clastic sediments deposited in generally nonmarine environments, while the tectonically quiet eastern margin and central shelf were dominated by marine shales and carbonates. The two cross sections of figure 2 illustrate the change in basin configuration through time. During the Early Cretaceous, the basin resembled a wedge thinning to the east (figure 2B), whereas during the Late Cretaceous, this wedge was broken into a series of smaller "Laramide" tectonic basins formed by continental-scale plate-tectonic events along the western margin of North America and by local uplifts and igneous intrusions (figure 2C).

MEASURED SECTIONS

Six measured sections are included on the CD-ROM (UGA Publication29) in graphic form. They represent much of the range in lithologic variation within and near the monument. They are located near: Grosvenor Arch-Cottonwood Wash, Henrieville, Henrieville Valley, Left Hand Collet Canyon, Right Hand Collet Canyon, and The Post-Bitter Creek, and each measured section is named for its locality (figure 1). Each graphical measured section includes the dominant lithologies, significant fossils, comments regarding characteristics of the strata, references to key collection numbers from the digital inventory, and reference numbers which can be used to identify photographs representing parts or all of each measured section. Lithologies have been simplified to accommodate the scale of presentation.

FOSSIL PHOTOGRAPHS

Photographs of 26 of the more than 200 species identified at Grand Staircase-Escalante National Monument are also included in the digital inventory on the CD-ROM (UGA Publication 29). These fossils are either among the most abundant in the monument or represent rarer but important guide fossils. Photographs were taken of line drawings and original photographs from published reports dealing with each species. Photograph captions identify the chief characteristics of each species and list the published source from which the photograph or drawing was taken.

Species include the following:

Inoceramus pictus Sowerby
Mytiloides mytiloides (Mantell)
Euomphaloceras septemseriatum (Cragin)
Sciponoceras gracile (Shumard)
Neocardioceras juddii (Barrois and de Guerne)
Baculites codyensis Reeside
Pycnodonte newberryi (Stanton)
Exogyra (Costagyra) olisiponensis Sharpe
Inoceramus mesabiensis Bergquist
Metoicoceras geslinianum (d'Orbigny)
Collignoniceras woollgari regulare (Haas)
Prionocyclus hyatti (Stanton)
Flemingostrea prudentia (White)
Inoceramus howelli White
Clioscaphites vermiformis (Meek and Hayden)
Volviceramus involutus (Sowerby)
Inoceramus (Magadiceramus?) stantoni Sokolow
Protexanites bourgeoisianus (d'Orbigny)
Gyrodes depressa Meek
Perissoptera prolabiata (White)
Cymbophora utahensis Meek

STRATIGRAPHY AND AGE

Figure 3 is a generalized correlation chart illustrating the stratigraphic position of Cretaceous rocks in the mon-

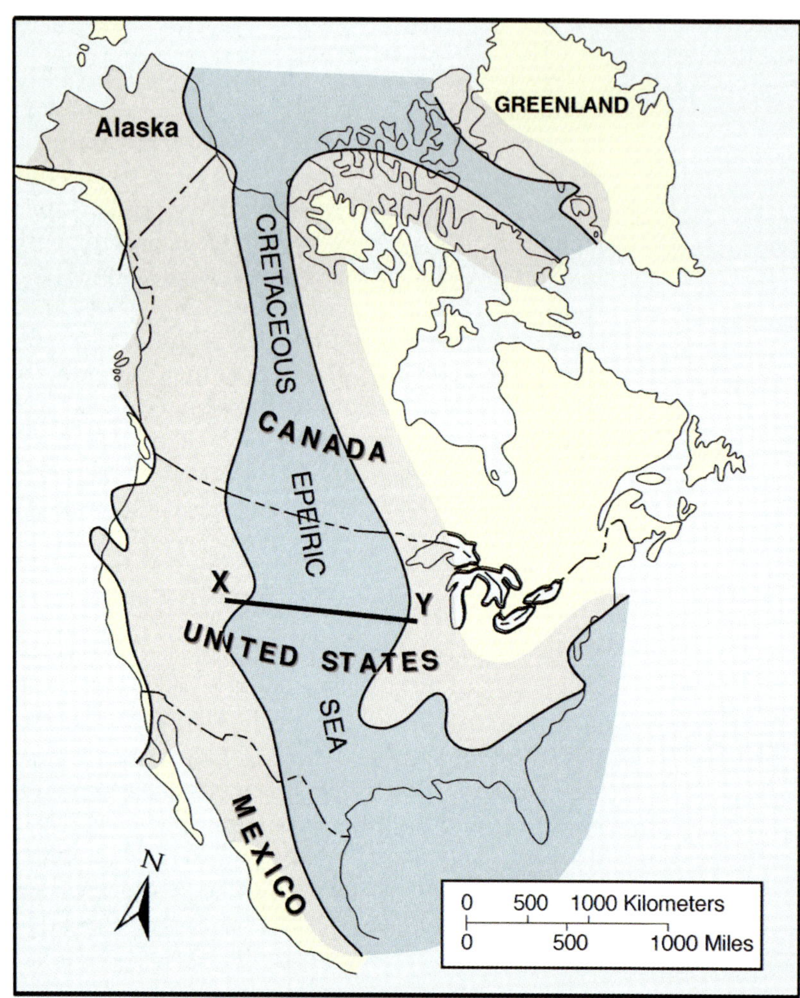

Figure 2. Generalized map and cross sections of Cretaceous eperic sea. (A) Map showing maximum extent of epicontinental seaway during Campanian time (unshaded portion, modified from Gill and Cobban, 1973). Line of cross section X-Y for (B) and (C) shown. Generalized cross sections X-Y shown for late Campanian time (B) and late Maastrichtian time (C). (B) From late Aptian to late Campanian (approximately 115 to 73 million years ago), the Western Interior was a foreland basin bounded on the west by a thrust-faulted tectonically-active area and on the east by a stable craton. Depositionally thick areas occurred along the western margin of the basin and were associated with major western source areas. (C) During the early phase of the Laramide orogeny, crustal blocks were uplifted and the foreland basin was fragmented into smaller synorogenic basins. Abbreviations on cross sections as follows: M, Maastrictian; Ca, Campanian; C-S, Coniacian-Santonian; Ap-T, Aptian-Turonian. Cross sections B and C taken from Dyman and others (1995).

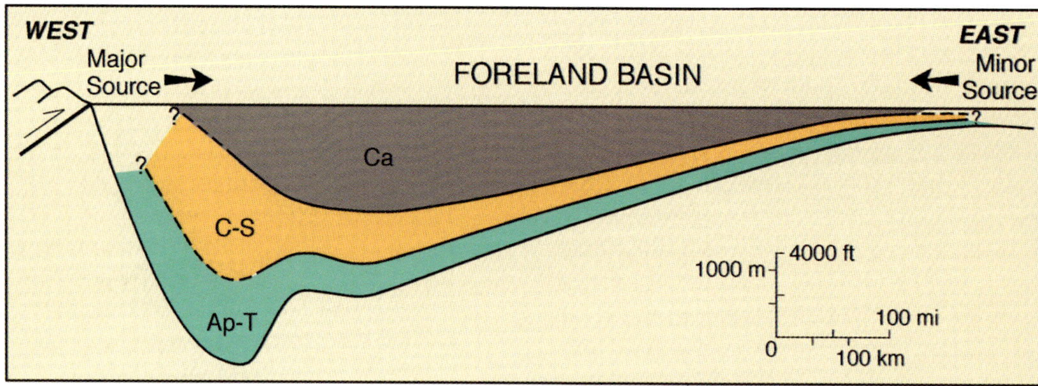

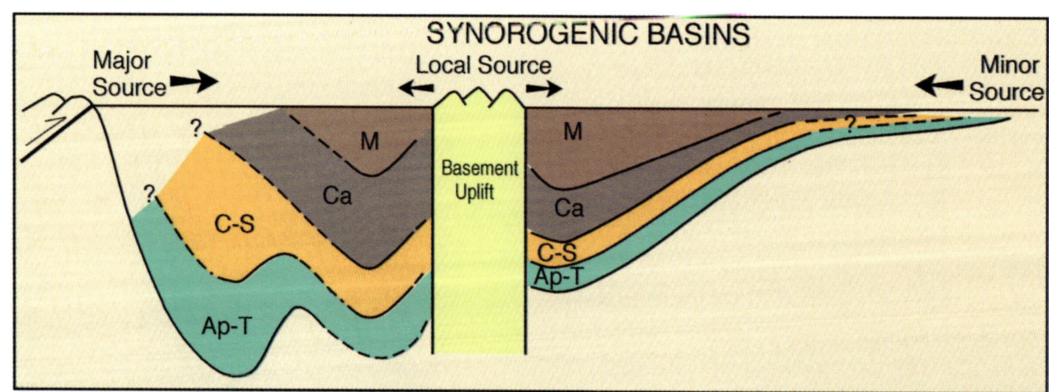

ument, immediately east of the monument in Capitol Reef National Park, and in areas to the west in southwestern Utah. Within the monument, marine rock units include most of the Dakota Formation, Tropic Shale, and Straight Cliffs Formation. At Capitol Reef National Park, marine rocks include most of the Dakota Formation and the overlying Mancos Shale. Figure 4 is a biostratigraphic chart showing Upper Cretaceous stages, formations and members in the Monument, informal stratigraphic units, Western Interior ammonite zones, and localities of biostratigraphically significant fossil collections. These two figures will be helpful in using the digital inventory and reading the following discussion.

The following discussion is divided into two parts: (1) the stratigraphy within and near the monument, and (2) the stratigraphy within and near Capitol Reef National Park.

Grand Staircase-Escalante National Monument

Dakota Formation

In the monument, the oldest marine rocks are found in the upper part of the Dakota Formation (figures 3 and 4). Near the town of Tropic, and southeastward at Grosvenor Arch and Cottonwood Wash (figure 1), the Dakota averages about 300 feet thick and is composed of sandstone, conglomerate, mudstone, siltstone, and coal. The Dakota thins in the eastern part of the monument, where it averages less than 150 feet thick in the Sooner Bench area (figure 1). The base of the formation is identified by a coarse pebble and cobble conglomerate that persists throughout most of the region. Clasts are composed of quartzite, dark-gray chert, and various lithic fragments including sandstone, conglomerate, and mudstone. The basal conglomerate overlies a widespread regional unconformity above Jurassic rocks. Where the conglomerate is absent, the basal Dakota is composed of carbonaceous mudstone, coal, and sandstone. Several distinctive coal zones are present in the middle and upper parts of the Dakota. Sandstones are generally fine to medium grained and lithic rich. At Cottonwood Wash (figure 1), the Dakota was deposited in coastal, floodplain, and shallow marine depositional environments. The Dakota-Tropic Shale contact near the town of Tropic is sharp and marks an abrupt change in lithology from predominantly sandstone to shale.

The oldest marine fossils occur in the uppermost beds of the Dakota which are clearly of late Cenomanian age at the monument (figures 3 and 4). Ammonites are scarce, but the presence of *Metoicoceras mosbyense* and *M. defordi* suggest assignment to some one of the zones of *Vascoceras diartianum, Dunveganoceras conditum,* or *D. albertense.* At most localities, the top of the Dakota contains an extensive fauna of bivalves characterized by the oyster *Exogyra (Costagyra) olisiponensis* Sharpe and *Flemingostrea prudentia* (White). At one locality (figure 4; collection 31), *Metoico-*

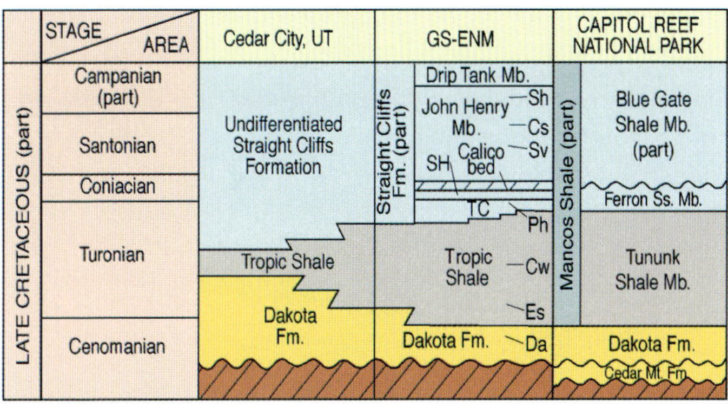

Figure 3. Generalized stratigraphic correlation chart illustrating marine Cretaceous rock units of late Cenomanian through early Campanian in age in the Grand Staircase-Escalante National Monument (GS-ENM), Cedar City area, and equivalent rocks in Capitol Reef National Park. Hatchured areas indicate unconformities. Abbreviations show the stratigraphic location of marine Cretaceous ammonite biozones, associated inoceramids, and stratigraphic units as follows: Cw, Collignoniceras woollgari; Da, Dunveganoceras albertense; Es, Euomphaloceras septemseriatum; Ph, Prionocyclus hyatti; Sv, Scaphites ventricosus; Cs, Clioscaphites vermiformis; Sh, Scaphites hippocrepis; SH, Smoky Hollow Member of Straight Cliffs Formation; TC, Tibbet Canyon Member of Straight Cliffs Formation.

ceras mosbyense was found with *E. olisiponensis,* which suggests that the *E. olisiponensis* assemblage lies at the top of the range of *M. mosbyense.* Inasmuch as the highest *M. mosbyense* occurs in the zone of *Vascoceras diartianum,* the highest beds of the Dakota are assigned to this zone. The occasional presence of *M. mosbyense* lower in the upper part of the Dakota suggests assignment to some one of the *Dunveganoceras* zones, such as *D. conditum* or *D. albertense.*

Tropic Shale

The Tropic Shale in the monument averages about 700 to 900 feet thick and is composed of medium to dark-gray fissile shale with occasional thin siltstone and sandstone lenses. The lower part of the formation is generally calcareous and contains several distinctive concretionary zones. The lowermost concretionary zone, which forms a distinct horizon about 15 to 20 feet above the base of the formation, contains the ammonite *Sciponoceras gracile* and associated fauna of the middle late Cenomanian *Euomphaloceras septemseriatum* biozone (figure 4; collections 7, 94, and 95). The *E. septemseriatum* zone is especially fossiliferous and accounts for 21 of the collections in the inventory. A second horizon about 150 feet above the base of the formation contains fauna of the *Vascoceras birchbyi* biozone of early Turonian age (for example, see collection 30). About 700 feet above the base of the formation, at a distinct color change from calcareous to noncalcareous shale, is the approximate first appearance of the ammonite *Prionocyclus hyatti* of late middle Turonian age (figure 4; collections 15 and 60) which is also found in the overlying Tibbet Canyon Member of the Straight Cliffs Formation. A

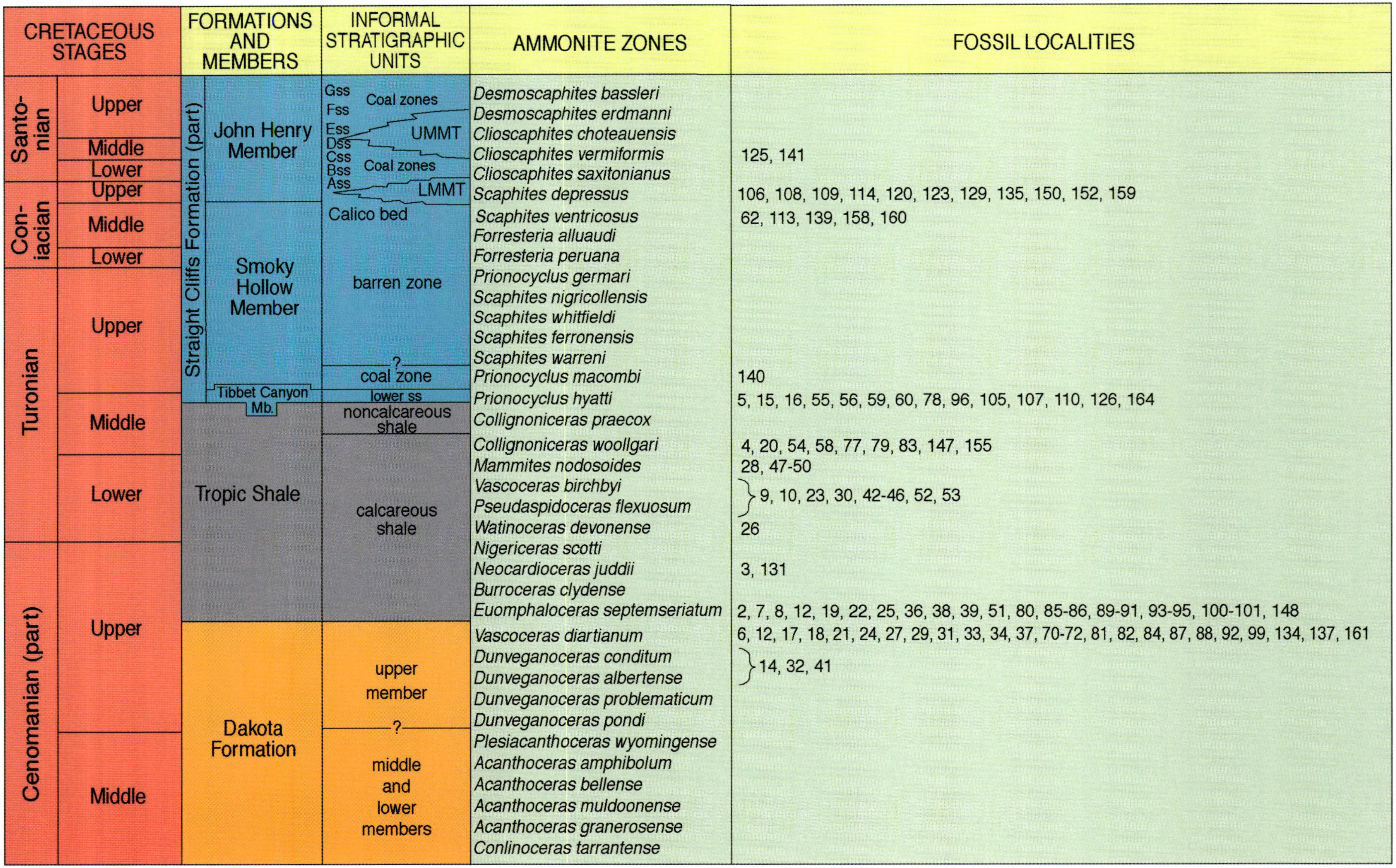

Cretaceous Stages		Formations and Members	Informal Stratigraphic Units	Ammonite Zones	Fossil Localities
Santonian	Upper	Straight Cliffs Formation (part) — John Henry Member	Gss / Fss — Coal zones	Desmoscaphites bassleri	
Santonian	Upper			Desmoscaphites erdmanni	
Santonian	Middle		Ess / Dss — UMMT	Clioscaphites choteauensis	
Santonian	Middle			Clioscaphites vermiformis	125, 141
Santonian	Lower		Css / Bss — Coal zones	Clioscaphites saxitonianus	
Coniacian	Upper		Ass — LMMT	Scaphites depressus	106, 108, 109, 114, 120, 123, 129, 135, 150, 152, 159
Coniacian	Middle	Smoky Hollow Member	Calico bed	Scaphites ventricosus	62, 113, 139, 158, 160
Coniacian	Middle			Forresteria alluaudi	
Coniacian	Lower			Forresteria peruana	
Turonian	Upper		barren zone	Prionocyclus germari	
Turonian	Upper			Scaphites nigricollensis	
Turonian	Upper			Scaphites whitfieldi	
Turonian	Upper			Scaphites ferronensis	
Turonian	Upper			Scaphites warreni	
Turonian	Upper		? coal zone	Prionocyclus macombi	140
Turonian	Upper	Tibbet Canyon Mb.	lower ss	Prionocyclus hyatti	5, 15, 16, 55, 56, 59, 60, 78, 96, 105, 107, 110, 126, 164
Turonian	Middle	Tropic Shale	noncalcareous shale	Collignoniceras praecox	
Turonian	Middle		calcareous shale	Collignoniceras woollgari	4, 20, 54, 58, 77, 79, 83, 147, 155
Turonian	Middle			Mammites nodosoides	28, 47-50
Turonian	Lower			Vascoceras birchbyi	} 9, 10, 23, 30, 42-46, 52, 53
Turonian	Lower			Pseudaspidoceras flexuosum	
Turonian	Lower			Watinoceras devonense	26
Turonian	Lower			Nigericeras scotti	
Turonian	Lower			Neocardioceras juddii	3, 131
Turonian	Lower			Burroceras clydense	
Turonian	Lower			Euomphaloceras septemseriatum	2, 7, 8, 12, 19, 22, 25, 36, 38, 39, 51, 80, 85-86, 89-91, 93-95, 100-101, 148
Cenomanian (part)	Upper	Dakota Formation	upper member	Vascoceras diartianum	6, 12, 17, 18, 21, 24, 27, 29, 31, 33, 34, 37, 70-72, 81, 82, 84, 87, 88, 92, 99, 134, 137, 161
Cenomanian (part)	Upper			Dunveganoceras conditum	} 14, 32, 41
Cenomanian (part)	Upper			Dunveganoceras albertense	
Cenomanian (part)	Upper			Dunveganoceras problematicum	
Cenomanian (part)	Upper		?	Dunveganoceras pondi	
Cenomanian (part)	Middle		middle and lower members	Plesiacanthoceras wyomingense	
Cenomanian (part)	Middle			Acanthoceras amphibolum	
Cenomanian (part)	Middle			Acanthoceras bellense	
Cenomanian (part)	Middle			Acanthoceras muldoonense	
Cenomanian (part)	Middle			Acanthoceras granerosense	
Cenomanian (part)	Middle			Conlinoceras tarrantense	

Figure 4. Biostratigraphic chart showing Upper Cretaceous stages, formations and members in the Grand Staircase--Escalante National Monument, informal stratigraphic units, Western Interior ammonite zones (modified from Cobban, in Obradovich, 1993), and localities of fossil collections. Upper part of informal stratigraphic units modified from Peterson (1969). LMMT and UMMT are lower and upper mudstone tongues. Localities of fossil collections are described in text and shown in figure 4. Each number corresponds to the appropriate collection in the inventory. Refer to inventory for generic names of ammonites identified on chart.

similar sharp color change occurs as far east as west-central Kansas where it marks the contact of the underlying Fairport and Blue Hill Members of the Carlile Shale.

The upper part of the Tropic Shale in the monument is gradational with the overlying Tibbet Canyon Member of the Straight Cliffs Formation. Sandstones increase in abundance upward in the upper part of the Tropic until sandstone is the dominant lithology. The Tropic--Straight Cliffs contact is usually placed where sandstones become more abundant than shale (Peterson, 1969).

Bentonite beds (altered ash beds) are abundant throughout the Tropic. Four widely distributed beds of bentonite, lettered A to D, in the Bridge Creek Member of the Greenhorn Limestone at Pueblo, Colorado, by Elder and Kirkland (1985), were traced across the Western Interior basin from Pueblo to Black Mesa in northeastern Arizona by Elder (1985). Bentonite A, lying in the upper Cenomanian biozone of *Euomphaloceras septemseriatum,* has been dated at 93.49 ± 0.89 million years (Ma) ago by Obradovich (1993). Bentonite B, which lies higher in the upper Cenomanian biozone of *Neocardioceras juddii,* was dated by Obradovich at 93.59 ± 0.58 Ma. Bentonite C, which may lie in the lower Turonian biozone of *Pseudaspidoceras flexuosum,* was dated at 93.25 ± 0.55 Ma by Obradovich. Bentonite D, in the lower Turonian biozone of *Vascoceras birchbyi,* was dated at 93.40 ± 0.63 Ma by Obradovich. These beds of bentonite have recently been treated by Elder (1991) from Black Mesa to Wahweep Wash in the northern part of the monument. Refer to Obradovich's paper for a detailed list of all dated bentonites within the middle Cretaceous of the Western Interior basin. Refer also to Zelt (1985) for an alternative zonation for these bentonites and for bentonites higher in the stratigraphic section.

Straight Cliffs Formation

The Straight Cliffs Formation represents the final regressive phase of the Tropic sea. Lithologic descriptions by Hettinger (1995) of core show the clastic-rich formation is lithologically diverse. It contains four named members designated by Peterson (1969). They include: the Tibbet Canyon, Smoky Hollow, John Henry, and Drip Tank Members (figures 3 and 4). Only the Tibbet Canyon and John Henry Members are known to contain marine invertebrate fauna.

Tibbet Canyon Member: The Tibbet Canyon, the lowest member of the Straight Cliffs Formation, is composed of gray-brown, fine- to medium-grained sandstone and interbedded mudstone and shale. Peterson (1969) identified the base of the Tibbet Canyon in the southeastern Kaiparowits Plateau, where sandstone becomes the dominant lithology above the Tropic Shale. The Tibbet Canyon Member is entirely marine and contains the upper middle Turonian guide fossil *Prionocyclus hyatti.*   The member ranges in thickness from about 70 to 200 feet in the monument.

Smoky Hollow Member: The Smoky Hollow Member of Straight Cliffs Formation is more lithologically and depositionally heterogeneous than the underlying Tibbet Canyon Member and is composed of interbedded sandstone, mudstone, carbonaceous mudstone, and coal. The base of the member is identified by the presence of a coal and carbonaceous mudstone zone that varies in thickness from 0 to 47 feet (Peterson, 1969). The top of the member is composed of a unit of quartz- and chert-rich sandstone and chert-pebble conglomerate referred to as the Calico bed (Peterson, 1969) (figures 3 and 4) or the Calico sandstone or sequence (Hettinger, 1995). The Calico bed varies in thickness from 0 to about 50 feet and is in sharp contact with the overlying John Henry Member. This sharp contact was interpreted to represent a regional unconformity by Peterson (1969). The unconformity was reinterpreted to be located at the base of the Calico bed by Shanley and McCabe (1991), and the sharp contact at the base of the John Henry was reinterpreted to represent a transgressive surface of erosion by Shanley and others (1992).

A late Turonian age is likely for most of the member (Peterson, 1969). Hettinger (1995, p. A 6) noted the occurrence of an inoceramid bivalve identified as *Cremnoceramus deformis* (Meek) (Hettinger, 1995) 12 feet below the top of the Smoky Hollow Member at a locality southwest of Escalante and barely outside the monument. The inoceramid is probably *Volviceramus involutus* (Sowerby). Middle Coniacian inoceramids have been found at two localities in the monument (figure 4; collections 62, 113). Both are presumably from the John Henry Member.

John Henry Member: The John Henry Member varies in thickness from about 600 feet to more than 1,000 feet in the monument and is composed of interbedded sandstone, mudstone, carbonaceous mudstone, and coal. The upper contact of the John Henry Member is placed at the base of the lowest cliff-forming sandstone of the overlying Drip Tank Member. The John Henry-Drip Tank contact was interpreted to be conformable by Peterson (1969) and it was interpreted to be unconformable by Shanley and McCabe (1991).

In the southwestern third of the monument, the John Henry Member seems to be entirely nonmarine but in the central part of the monument, thick marine sandstones intertongue with coal-bearing units, and farther east, two marine mudstone units intertongue with the sandstones. Peterson (1969) referred to the mudstone units as a "lower marine mudstone tongue" and an "upper marine mudstone tongue" (figure 4). The lower tongue usually has pebbles at the base and rests on an unconformable surface developed on the Calico bed of the Smoky Hollow Member. Ammonites and inoceramids date the lower tongue as late Coniacian. The upper tongue is not well dated, but it has yielded a single fragment of an ammonite assigned to *Clioscaphites vermiformis* (Meek and Hayden) of middle Santonian age. Four major sandstone units separate the two mudstone tongues designated by Peterson (1969): A (lowest) to G (highest). The ammonite *Baculites codyensis* Reeside was collected by Peterson at the boundary of the B and C sandstones (collection 102). It is a late Coniacian to middle Santonian species. The bivalve *Endocostea baltica* (Boehm) was collected by Peterson from the upper part of the upper mudstone tongue (collections 116, 125) as well as from the overlying G sandstone (collection 117). This inoceramid has a range of late Santonian to early Campanian. Peterson also collected the late Santonian--early Campanian inoceramid *Sphenoceramus patootensiformis* (Seitz) from near the top of the G sandstone (figure 4; collection 132). Another significant find by Peterson is a good collection of the inoceramids *Endocostea flexuosa* (Haenlein) and *E. flexibaltica* (Seitz) 350 feet below the top of the Straight Cliffs Formation just outside the monument and about 10 miles northwest of Escalante. According to Seitz (1967) *E. flexuosa* came from rocks assigned to the lower Campanian in Germany, and *E. flexibaltica* has a range of late Santonian--early Campanian in Germany. Troeger (1989, figure 5) shows *E. flexibaltica* as having a very narrow range straddling the late Santonian to early Campanian boundary. Until diagnostic ammonites are discovered in the uppermost part of the Straight Cliffs, that part of the formation is herein regarded as of latest Santonian age, as also suggested by Eaton (1991, p. 52).

Drip Tank Member: The Drip Tank is the uppermost member of the Straight Cliffs Formation and ranges from about 140 feet in thickness in the southern part of the monument to more than 500 feet in the northern part. It is composed of cliff-forming, fine- to medium-grained gray-brown sandstone with well-developed cross stratification. It is entirely nonmarine.

Capitol Reef National Park

Middle Cretaceous rocks at Capitol Reef National Park immediately to the east of the monument include the Dakota Formation and overlying Mancos Shale. The Mancos Shale is subdivided into five members in ascending order: Tununk Shale, Ferron Sandstone, Blue Gate Shale, Emery Sandstone, and Masuk Members. Only the Tununk Shale, Ferron Sandstone, and Blue Gate Shale Members are equivalent to rocks at the monument and are discussed in this section.

Dakota Formation

In Capitol Reef National Park, the oldest marine Cretaceous rocks are located in the upper part of the Dakota Formation (figures 3 and 4). Near The Post and along Bitter Spring Creek in the southern part of the Park (figure 1), the Dakota averages less than 150 feet thick and is composed of sandstone, conglomerate, mudstone, siltstone, and coal. The lower part of the Dakota is entirely nonmarine and contains thin coal seams and carbonaceous mudstone. The base of the formation is identified by a coarse pebble and cobble conglomerate that persists throughout most of the region. Clasts are composed of quartzite, dark-

gray chert, and various lithic fragments including sandstone, silicified limestone, and mudstone. The basal conglomerate unconformably overlies the older Cretaceous Cedar Mountain Formation (Peterson and others (1980). The Dakota-Mancos Shale contact near The Post and along Bitter Spring Creek is sharp and marks an abrupt change in lithology from predominantly sandstone in the upper Dakota to shale in the Tununk Member of the Mancos Shale.

The oldest marine fossils occur in the uppermost beds of the Dakota at Capitol Reef National Park (figures 3 and 4). Ammonites were absent from the upper Dakota, but the presence of the oysters *Exogyra (Costagyra) olisiponensis* Sharpe and *Flemingostrea prudentia* (White) supports a late Cenomanian age.

Mancos Shale

Tununk Shale Member: The Tununk Shale Member is the lowest member of the Mancos Shale at Capitol Reef National Park and is composed of medium- to dark-gray bentonitic shale and minor siltstone, mudstone, bentonite, and fine-grained sandstone. It averages about 600 feet thick in the Henry Mountains region east of Capitol Reef National Park and forms low, broad valleys and lowland areas; it is generally poorly preserved (Peterson and others, 1980). The Tununk is about 550 feet thick at the Bitter Spring Creek-The Post measured section.

The contact of the Tununk with the underlying Dakota Formation is poorly exposed but appears sharp in the area of the Bitter Spring Creek-The Post measured section, although Peterson and others (1980) defined the contact as gradational in the Henry Mountains area.

The early middle Turonian guide fossil *Collignoniceras woollgari* has been identified from the middle part of the Tununk Member (figure 3; see collection 155) indicating that the Tununk is corrrelative with the middle part of the Tropic Shale to the west at the monument. *P. hyatti* has been found throughout the region in the Tununk Shale (Peterson and others, 1980; Gardner, 1995).

Ferron Sandstone Member: The Ferron Sandstone Member of the Mancos Shale forms resistant ridges of sandstone between broad lowland areas comprised of less resistant shales in the underlying Tununk and overlying Blue Gate Members. The Ferron also contains abundant mudstone, shale, and coal, and is subdivided into a predominantly marine lower unit and a predominantly nonmarine upper unit (Peterson and others, 1980). The lower unit forms a coarsening-upward sequence capped by a medium- to coarse-grained cross-bedded sandstone. The base of the lower unit is difficult to define because of the interfingering nature of sandstone and shale in the lower part of the lower unit. The unit averages about 150 feet thick in the southern part of Capitol Reef National Park (Peteson and others, 1980), although we measured it to be about 100 feet thick. Some of the difference in thickness may be due to difficulties in interpreting the lower boundary of the lower unit. The upper unit is more heterogeneous lithologically than the lower unit and contains interbedded mudstone, shale, sandstone, and coal. Sandstones form discontinuous channels and are locally conglomeratic. The upper contact of the upper unit and the overlying Blue Gate Shale is sharp and represents a transgressive surface of erosion associated with a sea level rise. The upper unit is about 100 feet thick at the Post-Bitter Spring Creek measured section.

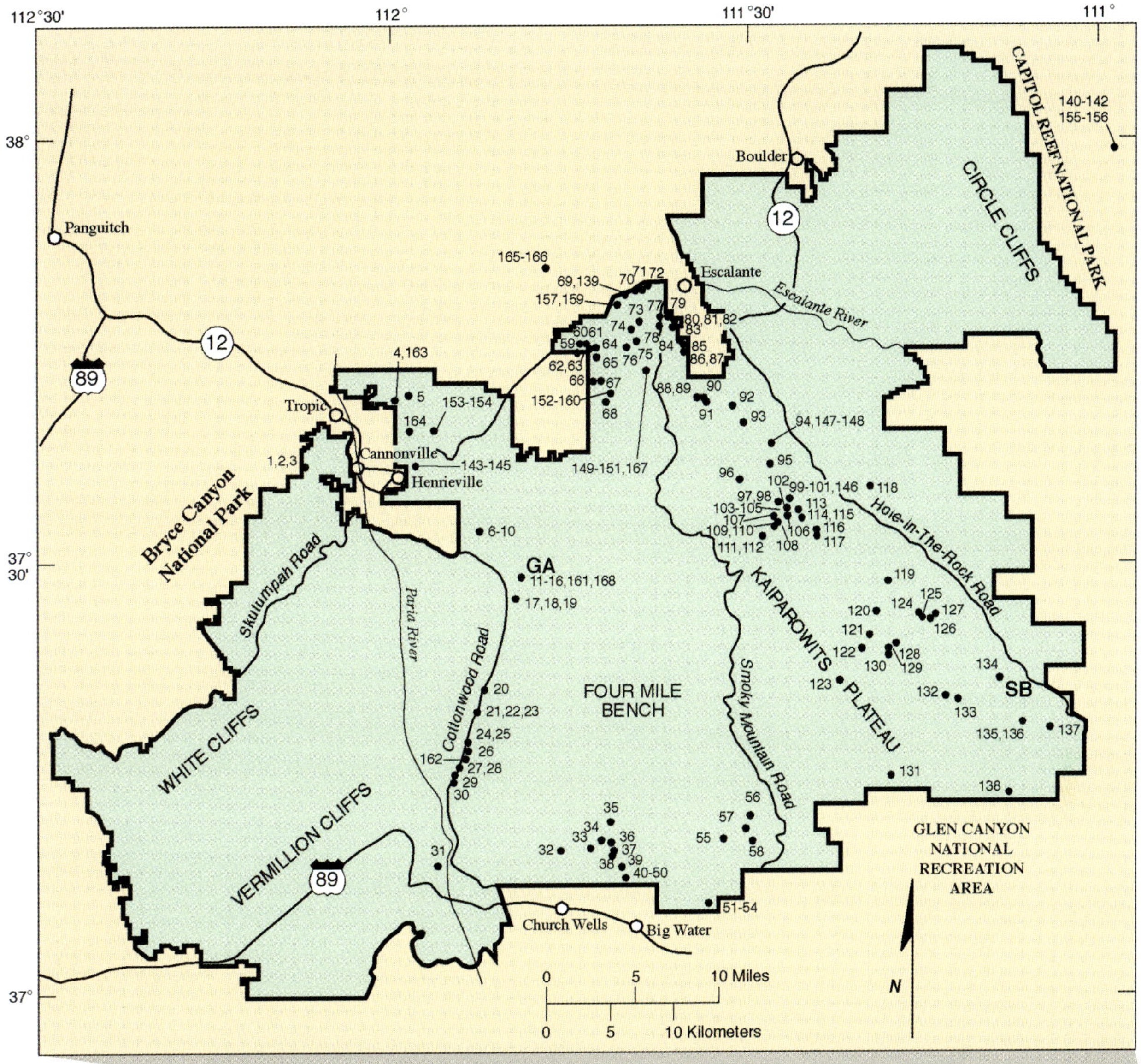

The only marine invertebrate fossil identified by us from the Ferron at The Post-Bitter Spring Creek measured section, *Nicaisolopha bellaplicata*, is a clam which was recognized previously from the middle Turonian zone of *Prionocyclus hyatti* and upper Turonian zone of *Prionocyclus macombi* in New Mexico (see collection 140). Peterson and others (1980) collected *Inoceramus howelli* White from the lower part of the lower unit of the Ferron in the area. The lower part of the Ferron is equivalent to the Tibbet Canyon Member of the Straight Cliffs Formation at the monument (figure 3).

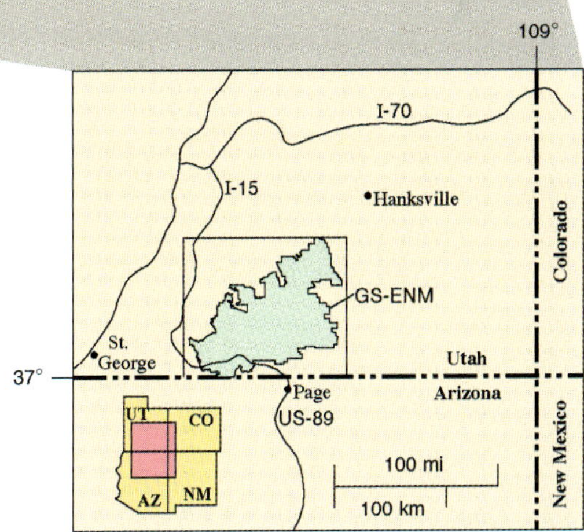

Figure 5. Map of Grand Staircase-Escalante National Monument illustrating major geographic features and the locations of invertebrate marine and brackish-water fossil collections presented in the inventory. Numbers correspond to numbered collections in the inventory. GA, Grosvenor Arch; SB, Sooner Bench.

Blue Gate Shale Member: The Blue Gate Shale Member of the Mancos Shale consists of medium- to dark-gray bentonitic shale and minor bentonite and siltstone. The Blue Gate is very similar to the Tununk Shale Member but is much thicker (Peterson and others, 1980). For this study we measured only the lower part (about 450 feet). The member averages about 1,300 feet thick in the region.

The only fossil assemblage identified (but only noted) from the Blue Gate at the Bitter Spring Creek measured section contains the middle Santonian ammonite *Clioscaphites vermiformis* (Meek and Hayden) (see collection 141).

FOSSIL INVENTORY

Refer also to figures 4 and 5 when using the inventory. Figure 4 illustrates the biozones represented in the monument; collections are identified by number on the chart from this inventory that can be traced to a specific biozone. Figure 4 includes only the ages that span the time included in the marine Cretaceous of the monument. Some collection numbers are not identified on figure 4 because the fossils contained in them are not biozone diagnostic. These collections are left blank in the inventory under biozone. Furthermore, many of the fossils listed in the inventory are not ammonites or are ammonites that are not identified on figure 4. For example, collection 16 includes fossils that are part of the *Prionocyclus hyatti* biozone even if the fossil representing the name of the zone (*P. hyatti*) is not present. The collected fossils are restricted to the named biozone.

Figure 5 is a location map of the monument that illustrates locations of the 168 collections. Each collection is identified by its township, range, and section location, USGS quadrangle map, and county name. Additional locality comments follow the location in the inventory. Stratigraphic location information may vary in precision because of differences in descriptive information provided by collectors. The collection identifiers listed in the inventory (labeled "ID") are USGS Mesozoic locality numbers where D represents Denver, CO. These collections are stored at the Denver Federal Center.

REFERENCES

Dyman, T.S., Porter, K.W., Tysdal, R.G., Cobban, W.A., Fox, J.E., Hammond, R.H., Nichols, D.J., Perry, W.J., Jr., Rice, D.D., Setterholm. D.R., Shurr, G.W., Haley, J.C., Anderson, S.B., and Campen, E.B., 1995, West-east stratigraphic transect of Cretaceous rocks- southwestern Montana to southwestern Minnesota: U.S. Geological Survey Miscellaneous Investigations Map 2474-A.

Eaton, J.G., 1991, Biostratigraphic framework for the Upper Cretaceous rocks of the Kaiparowits Plateau, southern Utah, *in* Nations, J.D., and Eaton, J.G., editors, Stratigraphy, depositional environments, and sedimentary tectonics of the western margin, Cretaceous Western Interior seaway: Geological Society of America Special Paper 260, p. 47-60.

Elder, W.P., 1985, Biotic patterns across the Cenomanian-Turonian extinction boundary near Pueblo, Colorado, *in* Pratt, L.M., Kauffman, E.G., and Zelt, F.B., editors, Fine-grained deposits and biofacies of the Cretaceous Western Interior seaway; evidence of cyclic sedimentary processes: Society of Economic Paleontologists and Mineralogists Fieldtrip Guidebook 4, 1985 Midyear Meeting, Golden, Colorado, p. 157-169.

—1991, Molluscan paleoecology and sedimentation patterns of the Cenomanian-Turonian extinction interval in the southern Colorado Plateau region, *in* Nations, J.D., and Eaton, J.G., editors, Stratigraphy, depositional environments, and sedimentary tectonics of the western margin, Cretaceous Western Interior seaway: Geological Society of America Special Paper 260, p. 113-137.

Elder, W.P., and Kirkland, J.I., 1985, Stratigraphy and depositional environments of the Bridge Creek Limestone Member of the Greenhorn Limestone at Rock Canyon anticline near Pueblo, Colorado, *in* Pratt, L.M., Kauffman, E.G. and Zelt, F.B., editors, Fine-grained deposits and biofacies of the Cretaceous Western Interior seaway--evidence of cyclic processes: Society of Economic Paleontologists and Mineralogists Midyear Meeting, Guidebook No. 4, p. 122-134.

Gardner, M.H., 1995, The stratigraphic hierarchy and tectonic history of the mid-Cretaceous foreland basin of central Utah, *in* Dorobeck, S.L., and Ross, G.M., editors, Stratigraphic evolution of foreland basins: Society for Sedimentary Geology Special Publication No. 52, p. 283-303.

Gill, J.R., and Cobban, W.A., 1973, Stratigraphy and geologic history of the Montana Group and equivalent rocks, Montana, Wyoming, and North and South Dakota: U.S. Geological Survey Professional Paper 776, 37 p.

Gillette, D.D., and Hayden, M.C., 1997, A preliminary inventory of paleontological resources within the Grand Staircase--Escalante National Monument, Utah: Utah Geological Survey Circular 96, 33 p.

Hettinger, R.D., 1995, Sedimentological descriptions and depositional interpretations, in sequence stratigraphic context, of two 300-meter cores from the Upper Cretaceous Straight Cliffs Formation, Kaiparowits Plateau, Kane County, Utah: U.S. Geological Survey Bulletin 2115-A, 32 p.

Obradovich, J.D., 1993, A Cretaceous time scale, *in* Caldwell, W.G.E., and Kauffman, E.G., editors, Evolution of the Western Interior basin: Geological Association of Canada Special Paper 39, p. 379-396.

Peterson, Fred, 1969, Four members of the Straight Cliffs Formation in the southeastern Kaiparowits region, Kane County, Utah: U.S. Geological Survey Bulletin 1274-J, 28 p.

Peterson, Fred, and Kirk, A.R., 1977, Correlation of the Cretaceous rocks in the San Juan, Black Mesa, Kaiparowits and Henry basins, southern Colorado Plateau, *in* Fassett, J.E., editor, San Juan Basin III, northwestern New Mexico: New Mexico Geological Society Guidebook, 28th Field Conference, p. 167-189.

Peterson, Fred, Ryder, R.T., and Law, B.E., 1980, Stratigraphy, sedimentology, and regional relationships of the Cretaceous system in the Henry Mountains, Utah: *in* Henry Mountains Symposium: Utah Geological Association Publication 8, p. 151-170.

Seitz, Otto, 1965, Die Inoceramen des Santon und Unter-Campan von Nordwestdeutschland; II, Teil; Biometrie, Dimorphismus and Stratigraphie der Untergattung *Sphenoceramus* J. Boehm: Geologisches Jahrbuch Beihefte, no. 69, 194 p., 26 plates.

Shanley, K.W., and McCabe, P.J., 1991, Predicting facies architecture through sequence stratigraphy—an example from the Kaiparowits Plateau, Utah: Geology, v. 19, p. 742-745.

Shanley, K.W., and McCabe, P.J., and Hettinger, R.D., 1992, Tidal influence in Cretaceous fluvial strata from Utah—a key to sequence stratigraphic interpretation: Sedimentology, v. 39, p. 905-930.

Troeger, K.-A., 1987, Problems of Upper Cretaceous inoceramid biostratigraphy and paleogeography in Europe and western Asia, *in* Wiedmann, J., editor, Cretaceous of the western Tethys: Proceedings of the Third International Cretaceous Symposium, Tubingen, p. 911-930.

Zelt, F.B., 1985, Natural gamma-ray spectrometry, lithofacies, and depositional environments of selected Upper Cretaceous marine mudrocks, western United States, including Tropic Shale and Tununk Member of Mancos Shale: Princeton, New Jersey, Princeton University, Ph.D. dissertation, 161 p.

Monument Valley
Photo courtesy of the Utah Travel Council

Depositional Environments and Paleotectonics of the Organ Rock Formation of the Permian Cutler Group, Southeastern Utah

John D. Stanesco[1], Russell F. Dubiel[2], and Jacqueline E. Huntoon[3]

ABSTRACT

The Lower Permian Organ Rock Formation of the Cutler Group is exposed in outcrops across southeastern Utah from Monument Valley to Canyonlands National Park. The Organ Rock Formation conformably overlies the Cedar Mesa Sandstone of the Cutler Group throughout the region. The Organ Rock is overlain conformably to erosionally by the De Chelly Sandstone at Monument Valley and by the White Rim Sandstone at Canyonlands. Along the Monument upwarp the Organ Rock is truncated by an erosion surface that is overlain by the Triassic Moenkopi Formation. The Organ Rock Formation grades laterally to the east into undivided Cutler Formation and to the west into marine and eolian deposits of the Cedar Mesa and White Rim Sandstones.

In the vicinity of Monument Valley the Organ Rock consists primarily of pale-red, very fine grained sandstones, siltstones, and limestone-nodule conglomerates deposited in fluvial channels and on floodplains associated with north to northwest-flowing, meandering streams. Numerous rhizolith-bearing horizons indicate extended periods of soil development on the floodplains. Near the top of the unit, very-fine-grained sandstones and siltstones interpreted as loessites grade upward into eolian deposits of the overlying De Chelly Sandstone.

To the northeast, in exposures of the Organ Rock near Canyonlands National Park, eolian dune and sand-sheet deposits are interbedded with arkosic, medium-grained sandstone to conglomeratic fluvial channel deposits. The coarser grain size reflects the proximity of the Uncompahgre Highland source area. Paleocurrents in fluvial rocks in this area indicate west to northwest-directed flow.

West of the Colorado River, near the Maze Overlook in Canyonlands National Park, the Organ Rock interval consists almost exclusively of eolian dune and sand sheet deposits. The size and orientation of cross-strata suggest that the dunes were primarily transverse or barchanoid ridges that migrated toward what is presently the southeast. Several rhizolith-bearing paleosol horizons attest to extended periods of landscape stability in the dune field. The quantity and thickness of eolian deposits in the Organ Rock decrease southeastward toward the axis of the Monument upwarp.

Isopachs and depositional trends in the Organ Rock suggest that, during the Permian, the axis of the Monument upwarp trended northeast-southwest and was located to the west of its present position. Fluvial channels in the Organ Rock were diverted northwestward around the northern edge of the upwarp whereas eolian deposits onlapped the structure from the west. The entire Organ Rock interval was thinned across the axis of the Monument upwarp due in part to truncation by the Permian-Triassic unconformity.

INTRODUCTION

The Permian Organ Rock Formation forms some of the most spectacular scenery that the canyon country of southeastern Utah has to offer. It has a supporting role as the lower slope-forming unit in the mesas and spires of Monument Valley (figures 1 and 2) and forms monoliths of its own near Hite crossing at the northern end of Lake Powell and in the Land of Standing Rocks west of the Colorado River (figures 1 and 3). It is also part of the dramatic scenery near Natural Bridges National Monument and at Canyonlands National Park where its red color stands in stark contrast to the white sandstones that lie above and below (figures 1 and 4).

[1]*Red Rocks Community College, Lakewood, CO 80228*
[2]*U.S. Geological Survey, Denver, CO 80225*
[3]*Michigan Technological University, Houghton, MI 49931*

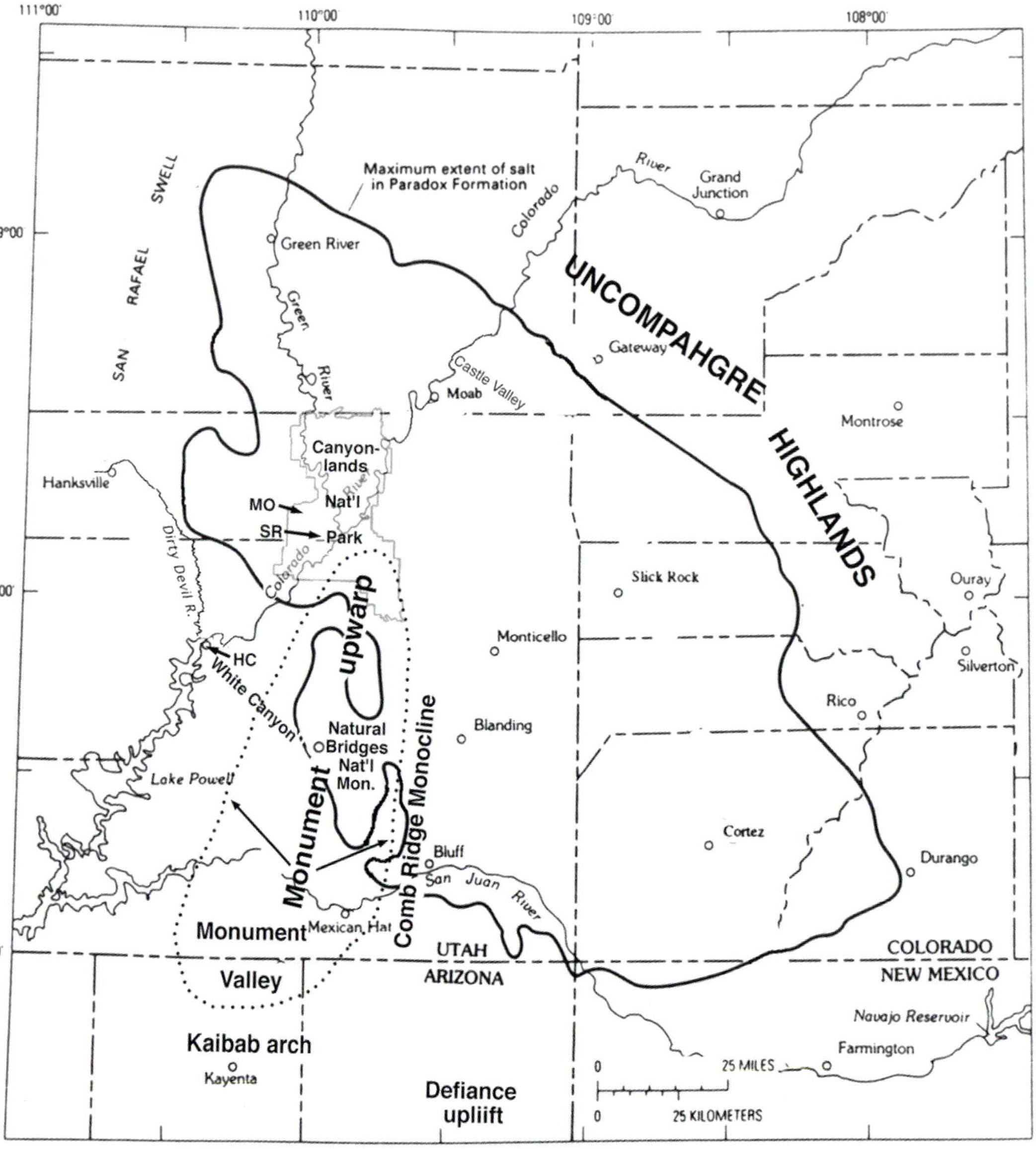

Figure 1. Map showing geographic features in southeastern Utah, southwestern Colorado, northeastern Arizona and northwestern New Mexico. Other locations mentioned in the text are: MO, Maze Overlook; SR, Land of Standing Rocks; HC, Hite Crossing. Outline of Paradox Basin corresponds to maximum extent of salt in the Pennsylvanian-age Paradox Formation.

Figure 2. The Mittens in Monument Valley along the Utah-Arizona border. Fluvial and flood plain deposits in the Organ Rock Formation (Po) form a slope beneath eolian strata of the De Chelly Sandstone (Pd).

Figure 3. Monoliths of the Organ Rock Formation rise above a light-colored bench of eolian Cedar Mesa Sandstone, Land of Standing Rocks in Canyonlands National Park (SR, figure 1). Elaterite Butte in the background consists of Mesozoic sedimentary rocks. View is to the northwest.

Figure 4. Red-colored strata of the Organ Rock Formation (Po) contrast with light-colored layers of the underlying Cedar Mesa Sandstone (Pc) and the overlying White Rim Sandstone (Pw) near the Maze Overlook (MO, figure 1) in Canyonlands National Park. The Organ Rock is of predominantly eolian origin at this location.

Figure 5. Map showing the location of stratigraphic sections in the Lower Permian Organ Rock Formation and equivalent strata that form the basis of this report. Lines A-B and A-C correspond to the cross sections of Permian strata shown in figures 6a and 6b. Stratigraphic sections are labeled as follows: MP, Monument Pass; OR, Organ Rock; CH, Clay Hills Crossing; CR, Comb Ridge; 78, Milepost 78 on U. S. Highway 95; FR, Fry Canyon; 64, Milepost 64; HJ, Happy Jack Mine; 56, Milepost 56; 50, Milepost 50; FC, Farley Canyon; IH, Indian Head Pass; HM, Hite Marina; NW, North Wash; AM, Andy Miller Flat; SM, Sewing Machine Butte; RP, Red Point; CS, Cove Spring; GS, Golden Stairs, MO Maze Overlook; SC Salt Creek, IC, Indian Creek; LC, Lockhart Canyon; ST, Shafer Trail. Solid dark line encloses the outcrop area of the Organ Rock Formation. Dotted line indicates the recognized extent of the Organ Rock Formation in the subsurface. Modified from Condon (1997).

The Organ Rock Formation extends from Monument Valley near the Utah-Arizona border to the northern part of Canyonlands National Park in a broad band defined by Comb Ridge monocline on the east and the Dirty Devil River on the west (figures 1 and 5). The Organ Rock is recognized in the subsurface as far west as the San Rafael Swell in central Utah (Condon, 1997).

Despite its striking character and wide geographic extent, the Organ Rock Formation has received little scientific attention compared to other Permian strata in southeastern Utah. Baker and Reeside (1929) named the unit the Organ Rock Tongue and placed it within the Cutler Formation. The stratigraphy of the unit was discussed in descriptive reports by Gregory (1938), Sears (1956), Mullens (1960), Witkind and Thaden (1963), Lewis and Campbell (1965), and O'Sullivan (1965). Baars (1962) mapped the unit in the subsurface, and presented a summary of the Organ Rock's distribution and general depositional environments (Baars, 1975, 1985, 1987). Condon (1997), in a paper on the Pennsylvanian and Permian Cutler Group of the Paradox basin, constructed isopach maps and described the general geology of the Organ Rock, referencing preliminary studies by the authors of this report (Stanesco and Dubiel, 1992; Dubiel and others, 1996a). Mamay and Breed (1970) and Vaughn (1973) identified terrestrial plant

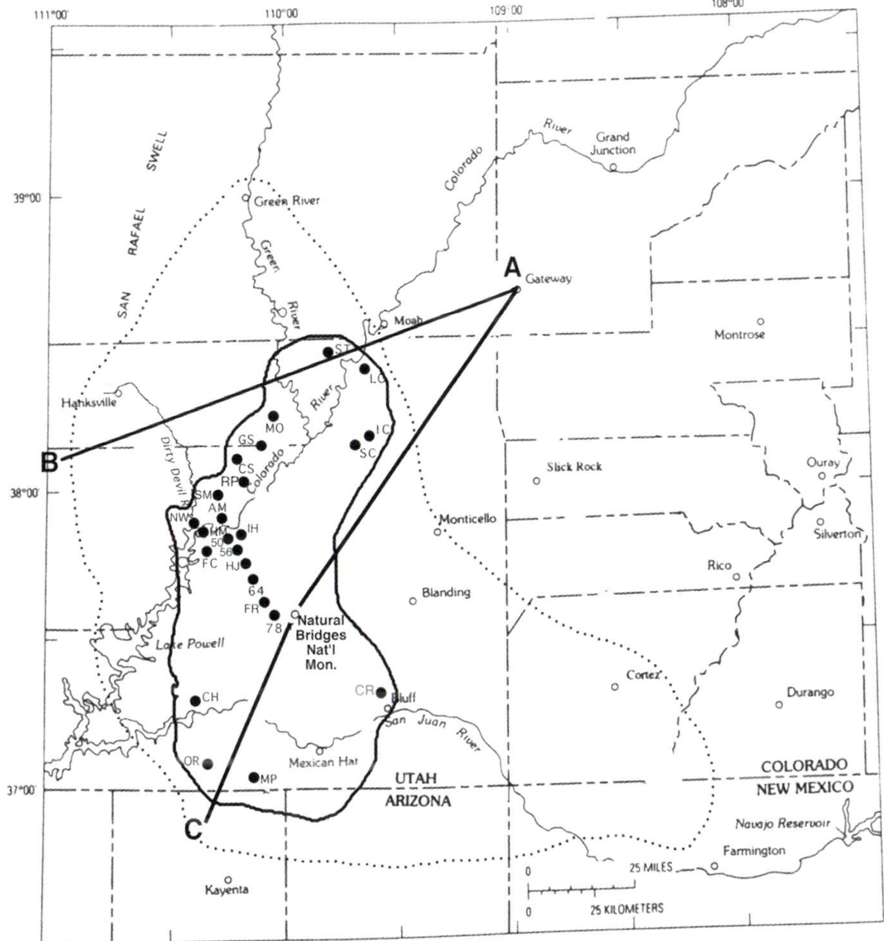

and vertebrate fossils from the Organ Rock.

This paper describes the lithology, sedimentary structures, and inferred depositional environments of the Organ Rock Formation. It also discusses the influence of Permian tectonic features on the stratigraphy and deposition of the unit and on the development of regional unconformities. Twenty-four stratigraphic sections measured in the Organ Rock and equivalent strata form the basis for the interpretations presented in this paper (figure 5).

PALEOGEOGRAPHIC AND PALEOTECTONIC SETTING

Most outcrops of the Organ Rock Formation occur within the Paradox basin, an oval-shaped structural depression that formed during the Pennsylvanian Period and continued to be an active site of deposition during the Permian. The outline of the Paradox basin in figure 1 corresponds to the edge of salt deposits in the Pennsylvanian Paradox Formation (Condon, 1997). Throughout the late Paleozoic, the Paradox basin was bordered on its northeastern margin by the Uncompahgre Highlands (figure 1), the westernmost range of the Ancestral Rocky Mountains. Precambrian granites and metamorphic rocks were exposed in the core of the uplift.

In addition to the Uncompahgre Highlands, elevated areas were present to the south and west of the Paradox basin during the Permian (figure 1). The Defiance uplift and the Kaibab arch were less significant uplifts located to the south of the basin in northern Arizona and New Mexico (Blakey, 1996; Condon, 1997). The Monument upwarp was a broad, low-amplitude feature located near the southwestern edge of the basin (Blakey, 1980; Baars and Stevenson, 1981; Condon, 1997). The structure was active throughout much of the late Paleozoic and was reactivated during the Late Cretaceous Laramide orogeny. The Laramide-age Monument upwarp extends from Monument Valley to the confluence of the Green and Colorado Rivers in Canyonlands National Park (figure 1).

During the Early to Middle Pennsylvanian Period, cyclic deposits of marine shale and evaporites were concentrated in deeper parts of the Paradox basin, while carbonates interfingered in shallow water settings with clastic debris eroded from the Uncompahgre Highlands (Hite and Buckner, 1981). As the basin filled during the late Pennsylvanian, terrestrial fluvial and eolian strata interfingered with marine deposits. Mixed marine and terrestrial deposition continued into the Permian Period.

During the Permian, southeastern Utah and the Paradox basin were situated about 10-15° north of the paleoequator (Scotese and McKerrow, 1990). The Permian shoreline on the western edge of the continent trended approximately north-south across what is now central Utah (Stokes, 1988). Organ Rock strata were deposited on a seaward-sloping coastal plain between the ancestral Uncompahgre Highlands to the east and the marine shoreline to the west (Baars, 1962, 1975; Condon, 1997). However, it should be noted that during the Permian, the basin was rotated as much as 45° clockwise from its present orientation.

STRATIGRAPHY AND DEPOSITIONAL SETTING

The Organ Rock Formation is a member of the Cutler Group, a sequence of sedimentary rocks deposited in southwestern Colorado and southeastern Utah during the Early Permian. The stratigraphy and general thicknesses of units in the Cutler Group are shown in figures 6a and 6b. Along the eastern margin of the Paradox basin the Cutler consists almost exclusively of arkosic (feldspar-rich) conglomerates and sandstones that were shed westward from the ancestral Uncompahgre Highlands. These rocks are referred to as the Cutler Formation, undivided. Westward into the basin, the red arkosic rocks interfinger on a large scale with white quartzose sandstones and gray carbonates. Where the interbedding occurs, the Cutler is elevated to group status and is subdivided into six units. These six units are, in ascending order, the informal lower Cutler beds, the Halgaito Formation, the Cedar Mesa Sandstone, the Organ Rock Formation, the De Chelly Sandstone, and the White Rim Sandstone.

Lower Cutler Beds

The lower Cutler beds are the basal unit of the Permian Cutler Group (Loope and others, 1990; Condon, 1997) (figure 6a, b). The unit consists of interlayered red sandstones and mudstones and gray limestones that were deposited in both marine and terrestrial environments. These environments include shallow-marine shelves, coastal sand dunes, rivers, and fluvial floodplains (Baars, 1985, 1987; Campbell, 1980, 1987). South of Natural Bridges, the upper part of the lower Cutler beds grades into the thick-bedded red siltstones and very fine-grained sandstones of the Halgaito Formation (figure 6b). These rocks have been interpreted as loess deposits, that is, accumulations of wind-blown dust (Murphy, 1987). They may have formed as finer grained eolian deposits downwind of sand dunes preserved in the lower Cutler beds and Cedar Mesa Sandstone.

Cedar Mesa Sandstone

The Cedar Mesa Sandstone (figure 6a, b) is a dominantly white to yellow, cross-bedded quartz arenite that contains interbeds of red mudstone and discontinuous lenses of unfossiliferous gray limestone. Evaporites and algal-laminated limestones are locally present near Comb Ridge southeast of Natural Bridges National Monument (figure 1). Abundant sand-avalanche layers and inversely-graded wind-ripple laminae in the sandstone indicate a primarily eolian origin for the Cedar Mesa (Loope, 1984; Stanesco and Campbell, 1989). Along the eastern boundary of Canyonlands National Park, eolian beds in the Cedar Mesa interfinger with red mudstones, sandstones, and conglomerates that can be traced toward the Uncom-

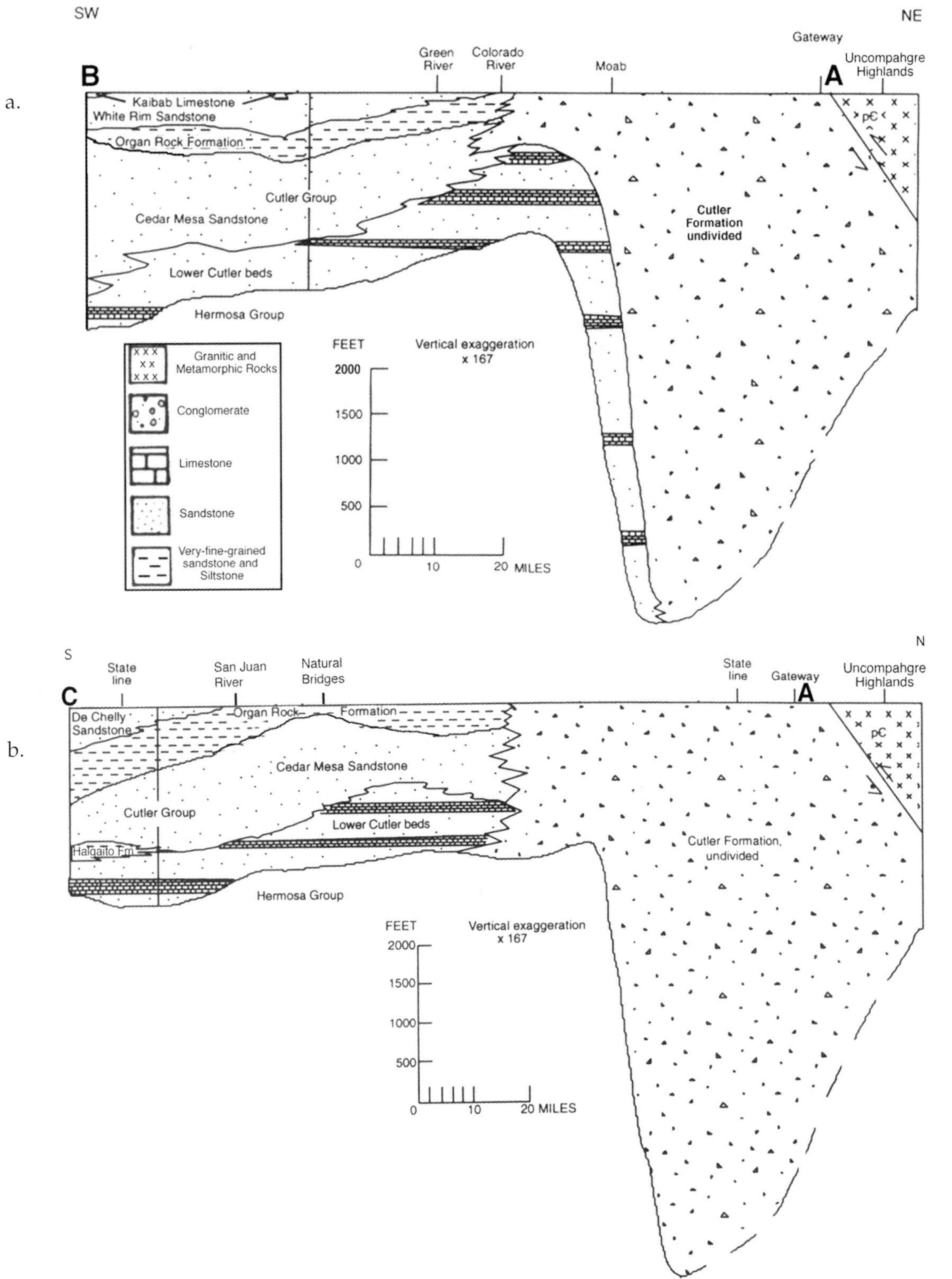

Figure 6 Cross sections showing stratigraphic relationships of Permian strata discussed in this report. Cross section (a) corresponds to line A-B in figure 5. Cross section (b) corresponds to line A-C. Modified from Condon (1997).

pahgre Highlands. These red beds are interpreted as the depositional product of floods that periodically inundated the dune field (Langford and Chan, 1988). The evaporites and algal limestones along Comb Ridge are interpreted to represent a coastal sabkha succession (Stanesco and Campbell, 1989; Lock and Pelfrey, 1997).

Although the contact between the Cedar Mesa Sandstone and the overlying Organ Rock Formation is locally sharp and erosional, the contact is considered to be conformable. On a regional scale the contact is marked by the interbedding of Cedar Mesa and Organ Rock strata, indicating a gradual and fluctuating change of environments from those characteristic of the Cedar Mesa to those of the Organ Rock.

Organ Rock Formation

The Organ Rock Formation (figure 6a, b) is exposed along the canyons of the Colorado, Green, and San Juan Rivers and their tributaries between Monument Valley and Canyonlands National Park (figure 1, figure 5). In the subsurface, the eastern edge of the Organ Rock trends southeastward from Green River, Utah into the San Juan Basin in New Mexico (Condon, 1997). To the east of this trend the Organ Rock merges with the Cutler Formation, undivided (figure 6a). The Organ Rock is also recognized in the subsurface to the northwest in the San Rafael Swell where it pinches out into the Cedar Mesa and White Rim Sandstones (Baars, 1979; Condon, 1997). It may correlate with the Hermit Shale in the Grand Canyon (Blakey, 1996).

The Organ Rock was originally named the Organ Rock tongue of the Cutler Formation (Baker and Reeside, 1929), but Wengerd and Matheny (1958) raised the Cutler to Group status, a terminology subsequently followed by Baars (1962) and many others. In those latter papers, the unit was referred to as the Organ Rock Shale; however it contains little if any shale, being composed primarily of very fine to fine grained sandstone and siltstone, with lesser amounts of mudstone, arkosic sandstone and conglomerate, and carbonate-pebble conglomerate. The unit was referred to as the Organ Rock Formation by Blakey (1980), a terminology also employed by Dubiel and others (1996a, 1996b). Detailed descriptions and interpretations of the Organ Rock Formation form the primary focus of this paper and will be discussed later.

The Organ Rock conformably overlies the Cedar Mesa Sandstone and locally interfingers with it on a regional scale (Condon, 1997). In the Monument Valley area, the Organ Rock appears to be similarly gradational with the overlying De Chelly Sandstone. To the north, near Canyonlands National Park, the Organ Rock Formation is overlain by the White Rim Sandstone. The contact between the two formations ranges from gradational to sharp. Wherever the Permian formations above the Organ Rock were removed by erosion during the Late Permian or Early Triassic, the Organ Rock is unconformably overlain by the Lower Triassic Moenkopi Formation.

De Chelly Sandstone

In the Monument Valley region, the Organ Rock Formation is overlain by the De Chelly Sandstone (figure 6b), a white to yellow quartz arenite of eolian origin (Baars, 1985, 1987, Stanesco, 1991a). The De Chelly is dominated by large-scale, high-angle cross-stratification that dips to the south. Sand-avalanche layers and inversely graded wind-ripple strata are common. The absence of interbedded fluvial or marginal marine strata within the De Chelly

at Monument Valley suggests deposition near the center of an erg. The De Chelly dune field extended southward into New Mexico and Arizona where it prograded into sabkha facies of the Yeso and Schnebly Hill Formations respectively (Stanesco, 1991b; Blakey and others, 1988; Blakey, 1996). Blakey (1996) recognizes an unconformity between the Organ Rock Formation and the De Chelly Sandstone. In the Monument Valley region however, the vertical transition from the Organ Rock to the De Chelly is marked by interbedding of strata characteristic of the two formations. This suggests a conformable relationship between the Organ Rock and the De Chelly in southern Utah.

White Rim Sandstone

In the Canyonlands region, the Organ Rock Formation is overlain by the White Rim Sandstone (figure 6a). Like the De Chelly, the White Rim Sandstone contains stratification types and sedimentary structures indicative of wind deposition and is considered primarily eolian in origin (Huntoon and Chan, 1987). A thin marine veneer at the top of the formation contains wave ripples, small-scale, low-angle cross-beds, granule-size chert clasts, and megapolygons that resulted from displacive salt crystal growth during final deposition of the formation (Huntoon and Chan, 1987).

To the west of the confluence between the Green and Colorado Rivers, the contact between the Organ Rock and the White Rim appears to be sharp, and possibly erosional.

Permian-Triassic Unconformity

The upper portions of both the De Chelly Sandstone and the White Rim Sandstone are truncated by the Permian-Triassic unconformity. The De Chelly thins to the northwest of Monument Valley because of erosion along the unconformity and is completely absent in outcrops along the San Juan River (figure 6b). Similarly, erosion of the White Rim beneath the Permian-Triassic unconformity increases toward the southeast, so that the formation is generally absent south and east of the Colorado River. An isolated outcrop of the White Rim is present in Castle Valley, ten miles northeast of Moab, Utah (Condon, 1997) where it was likely preserved due to subsidence along a salt syncline below the level of erosion along the Permian-Triassic unconformity.

Despite their similar lithology, sedimentary structures, depositional environment, and stratigraphic position below the Permian-Triassic unconformity, the De Chelly and White Rim Sandstones are not correlative (Blakey, 1996). Physical correlation with other eolianites to the south in Arizona and New Mexico indicates that the De Chelly is part of an older erg system than the White Rim (Blakey, 1996).

Moenkopi Formation

Both the De Chelly Sandstone and the White Rim

Sandstone are unconformably overlain by the Lower Triassic Moenkopi Formation in eastern Utah. Where the De Chelly and White Rim Sandstones are completely removed beneath the Permian-Triassic unconformity, the Moenkopi directly overlies the Organ Rock Formation. The basal part of the Moenkopi Formation exhibits a pronounced facies change from west to east between Hite Crossing at Lake Powell and Natural Bridges National Monument (figure 1), (Huntoon and others, 1994). To the west, the Black Dragon Member of the Moenkopi is a fluvial chert-pebble conglomerate. This facies interfingers to the east with sabkha deposits of the Hoskinnini Member of the Moenkopi. (Huntoon and others, 1994; Dubiel and others, 1996a, 1996b).

SEDIMENTOLOGY OF THE ORGAN ROCK FORMATION

The Organ Rock Formation consists of reddish-brown to light-red sandstone, siltstone, carbonate-pebble conglomerate, and minor mudstone. Several distinct depositional facies associations can be recognized in the Organ Rock based on variations in grain size, bedding characteristics, and sedimentary structures.

Floodplain and Channel Facies

In most of the sections measured for this study, the lower half of the Organ Rock Formation is a reddish-brown, generally slope-forming unit composed of two texturally distinct lithofacies (figure 7): a fine-grained facies and a coarse-grained to conglomeratic facies.

The dominant lithologies in the fine-grained facies are silty sandstone, sandy siltstone, and minor mudstone. All exist as thin to thick beds that extend laterally for several hundred yards to over a mile. Many of these beds either change facies into or interfinger with the coarse-grained to conglomeratic facies. Internally the fine-grained beds contain lavender alteration haloes which are tubular, vertically elongated areas of altered iron oxides that branch and bifurcate downward. The haloes are roughly circular in cross section, and are about 1 to 1 1/2 inches in maximum diameter. The beds also locally contain carbonate nodules that range in size from 1/16 of an inch to as much as 1 inch in diameter. The nodules occur as isolated knobs randomly distributed within the beds, as accumulations of coalesced nodules, and as vertically stacked nodules adjacent to the lavender alteration haloes. Fine-grained beds locally contain small horizontal and vertical burrows. Many of the fine-grained beds appear structureless and lack obvious physical sedimentary structures.

The coarse-grained to conglomeratic facies is composed of fine to coarse, subrounded to well-rounded siliciclastic and carbonate sand and carbonate nodules that range in size from 1/8 inch to 1 1/2 inches. Beds within this facies overlie and fill scour surfaces and are broadly lenticular. The beds interfinger laterally with the fine-grained facies described above. Beds range from one foot

Figure 7. Permian and Triassic strata at Monument Pass section (MP, figure 5). The foreground consists of the Permian Cedar Mesa Sandstone (Pc). Prominent ledges composed of the fluvial channel and floodplain facies of the Organ Rock Formation (Po 1) are overlain by slope-forming channel, floodplain and rare loessite deposits (Po 2). Paleosols are common throughout Po 2. Ledges that underlie the massive cliff consist of floodplain, loessite and sand sheet deposits. They mark the gradational transition (Po 3) between the Organ Rock Formation and the overlying De Chelly Sandstone (Pd). The contact between the De Chelly and the overlying Moenkopi Formation (TR) is the Permian-Triassic unconformity. View is to the south.

Figure 8. Massive, conglomeratic fluvial channel in the Organ Rock thins to the left into levee and floodplain sediments. The De Chelly Sandstone, the light-colored unit in the middle of the cliff in the background, is thinned by erosion along the Permian-Triassic unconformity. Organ Rock section (OR, figure 5). View is to the west.

to as much as 20 feet in thickness and are as much as several hundred yards wide. Internally they are characterized by lateral accretion stratification. Small- to medium-scale cross-bedding within the lateral accretion strata is oriented perpendicular to the lateral accretion bedding.

These associated fine-grained and coarse-grained to conglomeratic lithofacies are interpreted to represent associated floodplain and fluvial-channel deposits, respectively (figure 8). The fine-grained sediment was deposited on the floodplains during flood events in the adjacent fluvial

Figure 9. A rhizolith, or root trace fossil, extends down into a bed of sediments deposited in a flood plain environment at Monument Pass (MP, figure 5). Scale is 10 cm (4 in) long.

Figure 10. Floodplain facies at Clay Hills Crossing (CH, figure 5). Color alterations and nodular textures are due to paleosol development on the floodplain strata. Calcareous nodules eroded from paleosols are found as clasts in Organ Rock fluvial channels.

channels. The fluvial channels are interpreted to represent deposition in meandering streams based on the lateral accretion stratification and fine grain size of the adjacent floodplain deposits. Tracing of channel orientations on successive mesas throughout the Monument Valley area indicates a north to northwest paleoflow direction for these streams. The carbonate nodules found along the thalweg of the fluvial channels were sourced from the adjacent floodplain deposits when meandering streams cut their banks into adjacent units. The floodplain deposits are locally structureless due to bioturbation by both plant roots and invertebrate organisms. The lavendar alteration haloes are interpreted as rhizoliths (plant root trace fossils) (figure 9) based on their downward bifurcating morphology and their similarity to rhizoliths in other red-bed units on the Colorado Plateau and elsewhere (Dubiel and others, 1991; Dubiel and Smoot, 1994). The carbonate nodules in the floodplain deposits formed as a result of pedogenic processes in paleosols that developed during episodes of exposure (figure 10). Their penecontemporaneous formation within paleosols is evidenced by the occurrence of re-

worked nodules as clasts in the adjacent channel deposits, indicating that they were already formed when the fluvial systems scoured into the floodplains. The distribution in fine-grained floodplain strata of pedogenic carbonate nodules ranging from isolated to coalesced nodules is typical of tropical paleosols that developed under an arid climate (Dubiel and Smoot, 1994). However, the presence of abundant rhizoliths, the fine-grained floodplain deposits, and the meandering stream channels suggests that at least periodically there was abundant water in the depositional system. Although the channel and floodplain facies are most common at or near the base of the Organ Rock, particularly where the formation is thickest between Monument Pass (MP, figure 5) and the San Juan River, they are also present at stratigraphically higher levels throughout the study area.

In the western part of White Canyon (figure 1), there are several exposures near the base of the Organ Rock composed of broadly lenticular beds overlying scour surfaces. The beds are composed of thin to very thin layers of dark-red sandstone and reddish-brown mudstone. The layers exhibit numerous mud drapes, sand-filled desiccation cracks and abundant small-diameter horizontal and vertical burrows, but there are no occurrences of rhizoliths or other pedogenic features within these strata. These beds possibly formed in low-energy channels on the distal coastal plain, as evidenced from their sedimentary structures and their palegeographic position. Katpah (1995) suggested that these fluvial channels were tidally influenced. A similar interpretation was made by Baars (1962, 1975,1979).

In the northeast part of the study area, near the eastern boundary of Canyonlands National Park (figure 1), floodplain and fluvial channel deposits differ from those described above. Floodplain deposits occur as thick, tabular beds consisting of fine- to medium-grained sandstone and micaceous mudstone. They commonly contain very thin layers of medium- to coarse-grained sand that we interpret as lag deposits caused by eolian reworking of the sediment. The floodplain deposits are a less-significant component of the stratigraphic sections in this region than they are in sections farther to the south, and they are interbedded with eolian sand sheet and dune deposits (described below).

Fluvial channel deposits in the northeast part of the study area are reddish-brown to purple arkosic sandstones and conglomerates. They contain numerous pebble- to cobble-size granitic and metamorphic clasts and occur in stacked channels with few intervening fine-grained floodplain deposits. Mudstone and sandstone rip-up clasts are common, but carbonate clasts are rare. Fluvial channels scour into underlying floodplain, sand sheet, and channel deposits to depths of up to 7 feet. The channels lack the lateral accretion stratification that characterizes the channels in the Monument Valley region. The coarse grain size, as well as the paucity of lateral accretion stratification and associated floodplain deposits, indicates that the fluvial systems in the northeast part of the study area were bedload dominant and probably braided streams. Paleocurrent indicators suggest that the streams in the northeast part of the study area flowed to the west-northwest.

In contrast to the west-northwesterly paleoflow directions of the Organ Rock streams in the northeast part of the study area, streams near Monument Valley flowed more toward the north. This suggests that there were two regional fluvial systems that may have drained distinct source areas during deposition of the Organ Rock Formation.

The fluvial channel facies is most common in the eastern-most sections of the study area. At Salt Creek (SC, figure 5) near Canyonlands National Park, fluvial channel strata comprise 56 percent of the section. At Monument Pass (MP, figure 5) fluvial channel strata comprise 15 percent of a section that is 700 feet thick. Fluvial channel strata become less abundant toward the west. They comprise only 2 percent of a thin section at milepost 64 (64, figure 5) and are absent from the Organ Rock section at Maze Overlook (MO, figure 5).

Figure 11. Light–colored eolian strata within floodplain facies in the Organ Rock Formation near Farley Canyon (FC, figure 5).

Fluvial flood plain beds comprise 75 percent of the section at Monument Pass but only 20 percent of the section at Salt Creek. They comprise 62 percent of the section at milepost 64 in White Canyon (figure 1) but only 20 percent of the section to the northwest at Maze Overlook.

Eolian Dune and Sand Sheet Facies

The second distinct lithofacies in the Organ Rock is characterized by its light- to pale-red and orange coloration that contrasts with the reddish-brown fluvial and floodplain deposits (figure 11). This facies is most common in the westernmost exposures of the Organ Rock and consists of very fine to medium-grained, cross-bedded to horizontally stratified, thin- to thick-bedded sandstone. Both the cross-bedded and horizontally stratified sandstone beds typically consist of repetitive, very-thin, evenly spaced laminations, both horizontal and sloping, that commonly exhibit inverse grading. Cross-bedded units in this lithofacies also contain internally massive laminations 0.25 to 2 inches thick that thin and taper out near the base of the cross-beds.

Both of these small-scale types of stratification are common in eolian dunes. The inversely graded layers are wind-ripple laminae, (figure 12), formed by the migration of wind-generated ripples (Hunter, 1977). They occur most commonly along the crests of eolian dunes and along the gently sloping aprons in front of dune slip faces. The tapered layers within the cross-beds are interpreted to be sand avalanche layers deposited on the slip faces of dunes (figure 13). Sand avalanches are caused by the flow of sand down the over-steepened slip face of the dune. In cross-sectional view, the avalanches commonly pinch out where the slope of the slip face decreases near the base of the dune. Thus, the avalanche deposits are commonly interlayered with the wind-ripple laminations on the dune apron.

Cross-beds in the dune facies range in thickness from 1 to 15 feet. Dune foresets dip uniformly toward the present-day southeast, indicating dune movement driven by

Figure 12. Wind-ripple laminae in eolian strata of the Organ Rock at Farley Canyon (FC, figure 5). Each pinstripe lamination forms by the migration of a wind-generated ripple.

Figure 13. Cross-bedded eolian dune deposit overlies red-colored fluvial floodplain facies at Farley Canyon (FC, figure 5). Sloping sand avalanche layers taper out near the base of the dune. Note sand-filled mud cracks extending downward from the dune into the fluvial deposits.

Figure 14. Root casts at the top of the conspicuous eolian bed (figure 11) near Farley Canyon (FC, figure 5).

Figure 15. Adhesion ripples in inferred loessites near the top of the Organ Rock at Monument Valley. Adhesion structures form when wind-blown silt or sand sticks to wet sediment. Pen is 5 1/2 inches long.

winds blowing from the northwest. The uniform direction of cross-bed dips suggests that the dunes were transverse or barchanoid in shape.

Orange, thin- to medium-bedded strata dominated by horizontally stratified, coarsening-upward wind-ripple laminae that lack sand avalanche layers and cross-beds are associated with the dune deposits. These strata are interpreted as sand sheet deposits that formed on sandy plains lying within and adjacent to the dune fields.

The lower contacts of the eolian dune and sand sheet layers are sharp and commonly marked by sand-filled desiccation cracks that extend down into underlying fluvial and floodplain strata (figure 13). Mud chips, presumably derived from the upturned edges of mudcracks in the underlying units, also occur along these contacts. Stratification near the tops of the beds in the eolian facies commonly becomes indistinct. The uppermost surfaces of these beds often contain rhizolith alteration haloes and root casts (figure 14) consisting of calcite and limonite. These plant trace fossils indicate episodes of stabilization

in the dune field during which dunes ceased migrating and incipient paleosols developed (Loope, 1985). The abundance of root traces replaced by calcite- and limonite within the eolian beds, in contrast to lavender alteration root haloes in the floodplain deposits, may be the result of higher porosity and groundwater flow rates in the eolian strata.

Eolian dune and sand sheet deposits comprise 80 percent of the section at Maze Overlook (MO, figure 5). They thin eastward, comprising only 8 percent of the section at Monument Pass (MP, figure 5).

Loessite Facies

Light-orange to pinkish-red, very fine-grained sandstone to siltstone beds that appear structureless and that exhibit a conchoidal fracture are common in the southernmost sections of the Organ Rock Formation. Locally the beds contain faint horizontal to wavy laminations characterized by very thin mud-laminae partings. On fortuitous exposures, many of the mud laminations exhibit a dimpled texture interpreted here to be adhesion ripples (figure 15). These structures are formed when wind-blown fine-grained sand or silt adheres to wet sediment. The adhesion ripples occur in beds immediately above and below eolian dune and sand sheet deposits within the Organ Rock and are particularly abundant in the beds at the top of the Organ Rock that appear to be transitional with the overlying eolian dune deposits of the De Chelly Sandstone (figure 7). Because the beds lack any other stratification and are uniformly composed of very fine-grained sandstone to siltstone, they are interpreted as loessites (see Murphy, 1987). The loessites within the Organ Rock locally exhibit lavender alteration haloes and dispersed carbonate-nodules similar to those described for the floodplain facies that are also interpreted to be rhizoliths and paleosol carbonate deposits, respectively.

GEOGRAPHIC DISTRIBUTION OF FACIES IN THE ORGAN ROCK FORMATION

Facies in the Organ Rock Formation are not uniformly distributed throughout the study area (figure 16). Floodplain and fluvial channel deposits are more common in the eastern measured sections (figure 5), whereas eolian dune and sand sheet strata dominate the northwest sections. There is also geographic variability within the floodplain and fluvial channel facies itself. Fluvial deposits in the northeast part of the study area are composed of arkosic sandstones and conglomerates. They contain numerous granitic and metamorphic clasts and occur in stacked channels with few intervening fine-grained floodplain deposits. They probably formed in bed-load dominant braided channels that were proximal to the Uncompahgre Highlands source area and that flowed west to northwest away from the mountain front.

Farther south, near Monument Valley, the fluvial channels contain abundant limestone pebbles derived from reworked paleosol carbonates and calcareous rhizoliths within Organ Rock floodplain deposits. Granitic and metamorphic clasts are absent. The composition of the fluvial deposits in Monument Valley suggests a local, intrabasinal source area for the clasts rather than the granite and metamorphic rock-cored Uncompahgre Highland. Thick floodplain deposits as well as abundant lateral accretion deposits interpreted to represent point bars indicate that Organ Rock streams in the Monument Valley area were meandering streams. Paleocurrent indicators suggest north to northwest stream flow. The carbonate-nodule intrabasinal clasts indicate that these streams transported and reworked sediment derived in part from pre-existing beds in the Organ Rock itself.

In the western part of the study area along White Canyon (figure 1), fluvial conglomerates are rare. Channel deposits occur as broad, shallow, mud-filled scours that

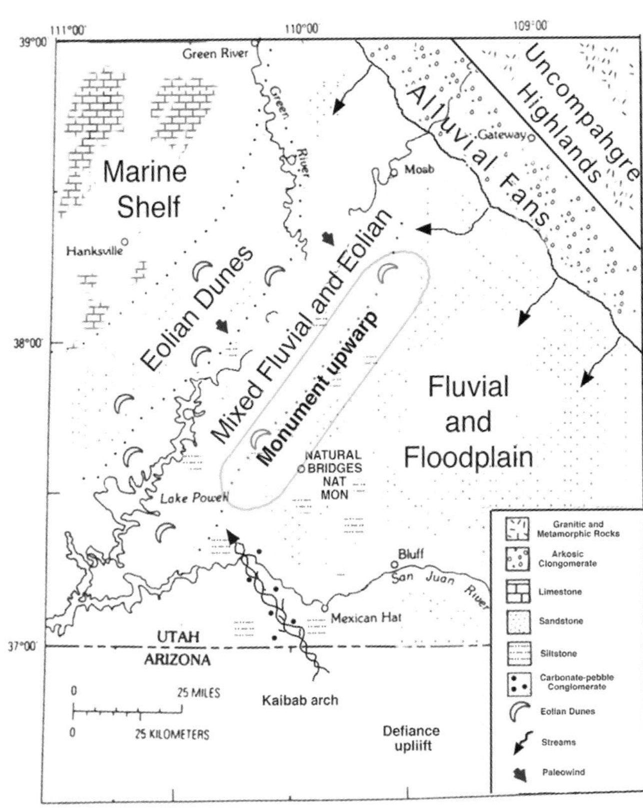

Figure 16. Lower Permian paleogeography of southeastern Utah during deposition of the Organ Rock Formation. Fluvial and floodplain sediments derived from the Uncompahgre Highlands and from areas to the south of the Paradox Basin dominate the eastern part of the study area. Eolian dunes prograde southeastward from a dunefield located to the northwest of the study area and pinch-out on the western flank of the Permian-age Monument upwarp.

exhibit numerous mud drapes, mud cracks, and small trace fossils. These fine-grained, low-energy deposits are interpreted as fluvial channels that flowed westward across a low-relief coastal plain toward a north-south trending marine shoreline.

There is also variation in the geographic distribution of eolian facies in the Organ Rock. Dune and sand sheet deposits comprise 80 percent of the section at the Maze Overlook (MO, figure 5) in the northwestern part of the study area. The dominance of eolian strata in this area probably indicates a continuation of erg deposition from the underlying Cedar Mesa Sandstone. The percentage of eolianites in the Organ Rock decreases southeastward from the area of the Maze Overlook toward White Canyon. A prominent eolian bed, and other minor eolian beds, (figure 11) thin and pinch out in the vicinity of the Happy Jack Mine (HJ, figure 5). In contrast, dune and sand-sheet deposits farther to the southeast near Monument Pass (MP, figure 5) are confined to the top of the Organ Rock where it grades into the overlying De Chelly Sandstone. In the northeast part of the study area, discontinuous eolian strata interfinger with braided stream deposits sourced from the Uncompahgre Highland.

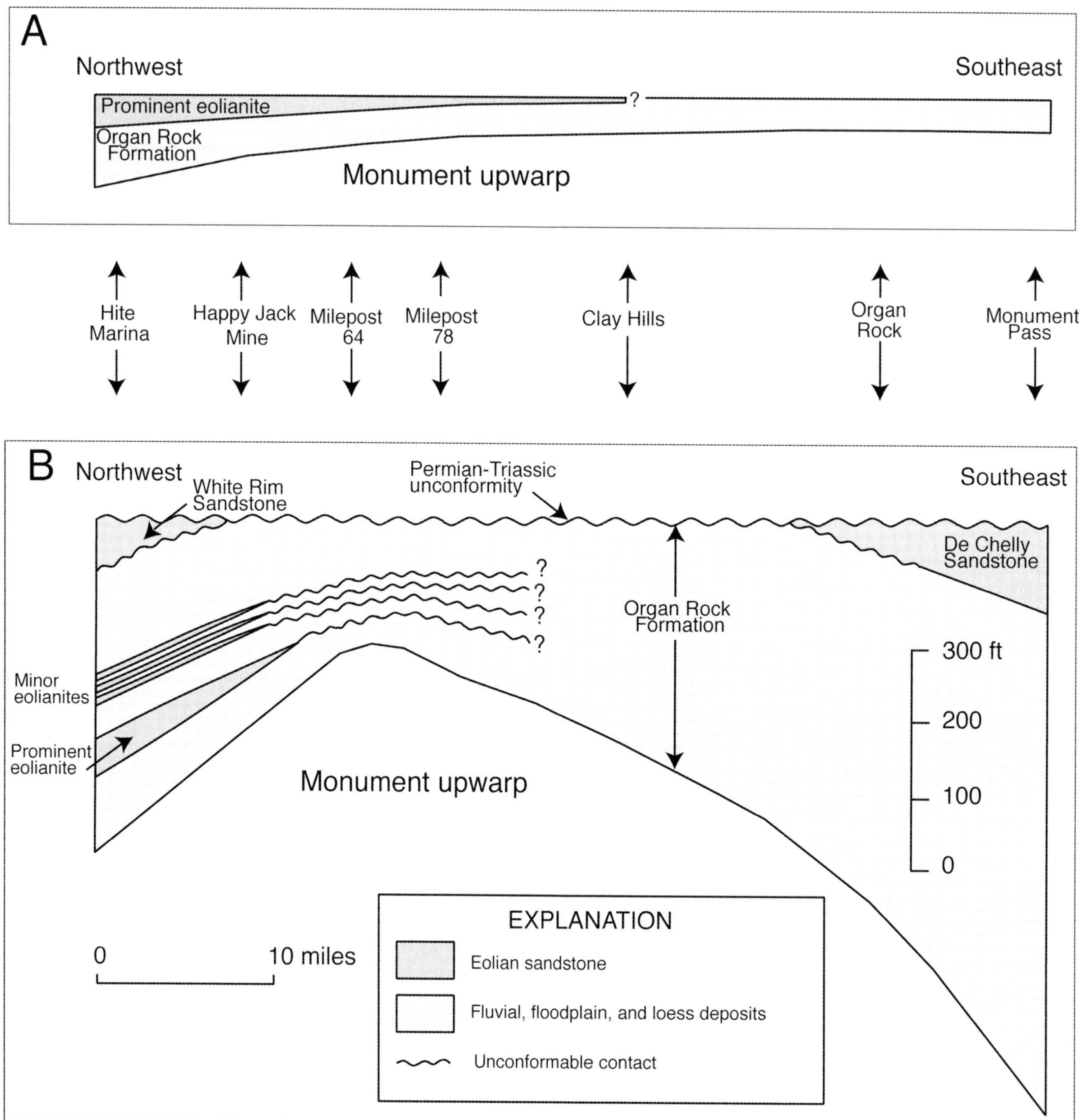

Figure 17. Diagrammatic representation of the Monument upwarp's influence on deposition of the Organ Rock Formation. Measured sections were projected to a line drawn between Hite Marina and Monument Pass (figure 5).

(a) During deposition of the lower part of the Organ Rock (beneath the prominent eolianite shown in figure 11) the Monument upwarp existed as a slightly positive feature. The prominent eolianite pinches out on the northwest side of the Permian-age Monument upwarp, indicating that the upwarp was elevated relative to the surrounding area.

(b) During deposition of the upper part of the Organ Rock Formation the Monument upwarp continued to be a positive feature. During generation of the Permian-Triassic unconformity, the White Rim and De Chelly Sandstones were removed from the central part of the upwarp. Vertical exaggeration in the diagram causes surfaces to tilt more steeply than the 2 to 3° dip measured in the field.

PALEOTECTONIC INFLUENCE ON DEPOSITION OF THE ORGAN ROCK FORMATION

The Uncompahgre Highlands were the primary source of Organ Rock Formation sediment in the northeast part of the study area (Baars, 1962; Rascoe and Baars, 1972; Langford and Chan, 1988). The textural and mineralogic composition of the formation, along with its overall coarsening toward the Uncompahgre Highlands, support this interpretation. There was, however, an additional contribution of clastic sediment from the southeast through the area near Monument Valley (figure 16). These streams may have been sourced in the Kaibab arch or Defiance uplift to the south of the Paradox basin (figure 1) or they may reflect a northward bend in a fluvial system draining the southern end of the Uncompahgre Highlands. These streams reworked pre-existing Organ Rock deposits as evidenced by the abundance of intraformational carbonate nodules in the fluvial channels.

The Monument upwarp also exerted influence on depositional facies distribution within the Organ Rock, and on the development of the unconformity at the top of the Permian system (figure 17). Eolian units within the Organ Rock thin from northwest to southeast along the western side of the Monument upwarp. This thinning is interpreted to indicate that the Monument upwarp was a positive feature at the time of deposition of the eolian rocks. This does not necessarily mean that the upwarp was an area of topographically high relief. At times it merely may have been subsiding at a slower rate than the surrounding basin.

Further evidence that the Monument upwarp was positive during the deposition of the Organ Rock is present within the floodplain and fluvial channel facies. The relatively coarse-grained, arkosic stream deposits on the east side of Canyonlands National Park were deposited by streams flowing west-northwest (figure 16). These streams would be expected to have flowed to the southwest (directly away from the Uncompahgre Highlands) if the Monument upwarp had not influenced their orientation.

Correlated measured sections indicate that the entire Organ Rock Formation thins across an area located northwest of the axis of the present (Laramide) Monument upwarp. Isopach maps based on subsurface data show a similar decrease in thickness of the Organ Rock in this area (Condon, 1997). These two lines of evidence indicate that the structure was oriented more to the northeast-southwest during the Permian as compared to its present north-south orientation. (figure 1, figure 16). In this study we assume that the basal contact of a prominent and extensive eolian unit (figure 11) within the Organ Rock Formation on the west side of the Monument upwarp represented an approximately horizontal surface at the time of deposition. Wherever possible, measured sections were hung on the base of that eolian layer for correlation purposes. Sections correlated in this way clearly demonstrate that the lower portion of the Organ Rock (below the eolian layer) thinned across the Permian-age Monument upwarp (figure 17). The eolian layer onlaps and/or pinches out onto the west side of the Monument upwarp, further supporting the interpretation that the upwarp was a positive feature relative to adjacent areas at the time of deposition of the Organ Rock Formation. Other less laterally extensive eolian units within the Organ Rock on the west side of the uplift also thin and pinch out across the stucture's axis. These layers can be traced laterally into internal diastems or unconformities within the Organ Rock Formation.

Based on the same correlated sections, it is also clear that the upper portion of the Organ Rock, above the distinct eolian layer, thins over the Monument upwarp. The thinning in the upper part of the Organ Rock is interpreted here as evidence that the upwarp continued to be a positive feature and that truncation occurred along the surface now identified as the Permian-Triassic unconformity. Erosion was more intense across the Monument upwarp during generation of the unconformity because the upwarp was elevated relative to the surrounding area.

Following deposition of the Organ Rock, differential erosion at the Permian-Triassic Systems boundary along the crest of the Monument upwarp produced an obvious unconformity, juxtaposing the Organ Rock and overlying Triassic rocks (Huntoon and others, 1994) where the White Rim and De Chelly Sandstones are no longer present.

CONCLUSIONS

Data presented in this paper indicate that the Organ Rock Formation was deposited in a mixed fluvial and eolian system (figure 16). In the southeast part of the study area, meandering streams sourced to the south of the Paradox basin eroded penecontemporaneous floodplain deposits, incorporating pedogenic carbonate nodules into their channels. The floodplains were laterally extensive and characterized by arid climate paleosols. Along the northeast part of the study area, the Organ Rock streams flowed west and northwest from the nearby Uncompahgre Highlands. This part of the fluvial system was dominated by coarse-grained braided streams with fewer floodplain deposits compared to the streams in the Monument Valley area. Winds reworked the floodplain sediments. Near the area of Lake Powell, the Organ Rock streams flowed in broad, shallow, mud-filled channels on a distal, low-relief coastal plain adjacent to marine environments that lay farther west.

Eolian dune and sand sheet deposits dominate the northwestern sections in the Organ Rock outcrop belt. The dunes were transverse or barchanoid ridges that migrated to the southeast. Eolian strata in this area interfinger with fluvial and floodplain deposits in the northeast sections but are rare southeast of the Monument upwarp, except near the contact between the Organ Rock and the overlying De Chelly Sandstone. Rooted horizons and incipient paleosols at the top of some eolian beds indicate periods of stability within the dune field. Loess deposits containing adhesion ripples mark the stratigraphic transitions between many fluvial and eolian dune strata in the Organ Rock.

The Monument upwarp influenced deposition of the Organ Rock Formation. The Permian-age Monument upwarp was located farther to the northwest and elongated more to the northeast than the Laramide-age structure that is prominent today. Eolian strata thin toward and pinch out on the northwestern side of the Monument upwarp, and the course of streams along its northeastern flank was influenced by its position and orientation. The Monument upwarp remained a positive area throughout the Permian, and Permian strata were deeply incised during the development of the Permian/Triassic unconformity.

ACKNOWLEDGEMENTS

The authors thank Debra Mickelson for her able assistance in the field and Steven Condon and Gerilyn Soreghan for their helpful reviews of the manuscript.

REFERENCES

Baars, D.L., 1962, Permian system of the Colorado Plateau: American Association of Petroleum Geologists Bulletin, v. 46, no. 2, p. 149-218.

—1975, The Permian system of Canyonlands country, *in* Fassett, J.E., and Wengerd, S.A., editors, Canyonlands Country: Four Corners Geological Society, Eighth Field Conference Guidebook, p. 123-127.

—1979, The Permian system, *in* Baars, D.L., editor, Permianland: Four Corners Geological Society, Ninth Field Conference Guidebook, p. 1-6.

—1985, Paleozoic rocks of Canyonlands country, *in* Molenaar, C.M., and Baars, D.L., editors, Field and river trip guide to Canyonlands country, Utah: Rocky Mountain Section – SEPM (Society for Economic Paleontologists and Mineralogists) Guidebook for Field Trip No. 7., 1985 SEPM Midyear Meeting Field Guides, p. 7-5 and 7-22.

—1987, Paleozoic rocks of Canyonlands country, *in* Campbell, J.A., editor, Geology of Cataract Canyon and vicinity: Four Corners Geological Society, Tenth Field Conference Guidebook, p. 11-16.

Baars, D.L., and Stevenson, G.M., 1981 Tectonic Evolution of the Paradox basin, Utah and Colorado, *in* Wiegand, D.L., editor, Geology of the Paradox basin, Field Conference Guidebook 1981, p. 23-31.

Baker, A.A., and Reeside, J.B., Jr., 1929, Correlation of the Permian of southern Utah, northern Arizona, northwestern New Mexico, and southwestern Colorado: American Association of Petroleum Geologists Bulletin, v. 13, no. 11, p. 1413-1448.

Blakey, R.C., 1980, Pennsylvanian and Early Permian paleogeography, southern Colorado Plateau and vicinity, *in* Fouch, T.D., and Magathan, E.R., editors, Paleozoic paleogeography of west-central United States: Society of Economic Paleontologists and Mineralogists, Rocky Mountain Section, p. 239-257.

—1996, Permian eolian deposits, sequences, and sequence boundaries, Colorado Plateau, *in* Longman, M.W., and Sonnenfeld, M.D., editors, Paleozoic Systems of the Rocky Mountain Region: Denver Rocky Mountain Section-SEPM (Society of Sedimentary Geology), p. 405-426.

Blakey, R.C., Peterson, F., and Kocurek, G., 1988, Late Paleozoic and Mesozoic eolian deposits of the Western Interior of the United States: Sedimentary Geology, v. 56, p. 3-125.

Campbell, J.A., 1980, Lower Permian depositional systems and Wolfcampian paleogeography, Uncompahgre basin, eastern Utah and southwestern Colorado, *in* Fouch, T.D., and Magathan, E.R., editors, Paleozoic paleogeography of the West-Central United States: Society of Economic Paleontologists and Mineralogists, Rocky Mountain Section, p. 327-340.

—1987, Stratigraphy and depositional facies; Elephant Canyon Formation, *in* Campbell, J.A., editor, Geology of Cataract Canyon and vicinity: Four Corners Geological Society Field Conference, 10th, p. 91-98.

Condon, S.M., 1997, Geology of the Pennsylvanian and Permian Cutler Group and Permian Kaibab Limestone in the Paradox basin, southeastern Utah and southwestern Colorado: U.S. Geological Survey Bulletin 2000-P, 46 p.

Dubiel, R.F., Huntoon, J.E., Condon, S.M., and Stanesco, J.D., 1996a, Permian deposystems, paleogeography, and paleoclimate of the Paradox basin and vicinity, *in* Longman, M.W., and Sonnenfeld, M.D., editors, Paleozoic systems of the Rocky Mountain region: Denver, Rocky Mountain Section-SEPM (Society of Sedimentary Geology), p. 427-444.

Dubiel, R.F., Huntoon, J.E., Stanesco, J.D., Condon, S.M., and Mickelson, D., 1996b, Permian-Triassic depositional systems, paleogeography, paleoclimate, and hydrocarbon resources in Canyonlands, Utah, *in* Thompson, R.A., Hudson, M.R., and Pillmore, C.L., editors, Geologic excursions to the Rocky Mountains and beyond - field trip guidebook for the 1996 annual meeting of the Geological Society of America, October 28-31, 1996: Colorado Geological Survey Special Publication 44/CD-ROM, 24 p.

Dubiel, R.F., Parrish, J.T., Parrish, J.M., and Good, S.C., 1991, The Pangean megamonsoon--evidence from the Upper Triassic Chinle Formation: Palaios, v. 6, no. 4, p. 347-370.

Dubiel, R.F., and Smoot, J.P., 1994, Criteria for interpreting paleoclimate from red beds - a tool for Pangean reconstructions, *in* Beauchamp, B., Embry, A.F., and Glass, D., editors, Pangea - global environments and resources: Canadian Society of Petroleum Geologists Memoir 17, p. 295-310.

Gregory, H.E., 1938, The San Juan country: U.S. Geological Survey Professional Paper 188, 123 p.

Hite, R.J., and Buckner, D.H., 1981, Stratigraphic correlations, facies concepts and cyclicity in Pennsylvanian rocks of the Paradox basin *in* Weigand, D.L., editor, Geology of the Paradox basin: Rocky Mountain Association of Geologists, p. 147-159.

Hunter, R.E., 1977, Basic types of stratification in small eolian dunes: Sedimentology, v. 24, p. 361-387.

Huntoon, J. E., and Chan, M. A., 1987, Marine origin of paleotopographic relief on eolian White Rim Sandstone (Permian), Elaterite basin, Utah: American Association of Petroleum Geologists Bulletin, v. 71, no. 9, p. 1035-1045.

Huntoon, J.E., Dubiel, R.F., and Stanesco, J.D, 1994, Tectonic influence on development of the Permian-Triassic unconformity and basal Triassic strata, Paradox basin, southeastern Utah, *in* Caputo, M.V., Peterson, J.A., and Franczyk, K.J., editors, Mesozoic systems of the Rocky Mountain region, USA: Denver, Rocky Mountain Section Society of Economic Paleontologists and Mineralogists (Society for Sedimentary Geology), p. 109-131.

Katpah, S.S., 1995, Fluvial architecture in the Cutler Group, Paradox basin, southeastern Utah [abs.]: Geological Society of America, Abstracts with Programs, v. 27, no. 6, p. A-381.

Langford, R.P., and Chan, M.A., 1988, Flood surfaces and deflation surfaces within the Cutler Formation and Cedar Mesa Sandstone (Permian), southeastern Utah: Geological Society of America Bulletin, v. 100, p. 1541-1549.

Lewis, R.Q., Sr., and Campbell, R.H., 1965, Geology and uranium deposits of Elk Ridge and vicinity, San Juan County, Utah: U.S. Geological Survey Professional Paper 474-B, 65 p.

Lock, B.E., and Pelfrey, G.M., 1997, Erg to sabkha Transition in the Cedar Mesa Formation (Wolfcampian), Comb Ridge area, San Juan County, Southeast Utah [abs.]: Geological Society of America, Abstracts with Programs, v. 29, no. 6, p. A-480.

Loope, D.B., 1984, Eolian origin of upper Paleozoic sandstones, southeastern Utah: Journal of Sedimentary Petrology, v. 54, no. 2, p. 563-580.

—1985, Episodic deposition and preservation of eolian sands; a late Paleozoic example from southeastern Utah: Geology, v. 13, p. 73-76

Loope, D.B., Sanderson, G.A., and Verville, G.J., 1990, Abandonment of the name Elephant Canyon Formation in southeastern Utah–Physical and temporal implications: Mountain Geologist, v. 27, no. 4, p. 119-130.

Mamay, S.H., and Breed, W.J., 1970, Early Permian plants from the Cutler Formation in Monument Valley, Utah: U.S. Geological Survey Professional Paper 700-B, p. 109-117.

Mullens, T.E., 1960, Geology of the Clay Hills area, San Juan County, Utah: U.S. Geological Survey Bulletin 1087-H, p. 259-336.

Murphy, Kathleen, 1987, Eolian origin of upper Paleozoic red siltstones at Mexican Hat and Dark Canyon, southeastern Utah: Lincoln, University of Nebraska, M.S. thesis, 127 p.

O'Sullivan, R.B., 1965, Geology of the Cedar Mesa-Boundary Butte area, San Juan County, Utah: U.S. Geological Survey Bulletin 1186, 128 p.

Rascoe, Bailey, Jr., and Baars, D.L., 1972, Permian system, *in* Mallory, W.W., editor, Geologic atlas of the Rocky Mountain region: Denver, Rocky Mountain Association of Geologists, p. 143-165

Sears, J.D., 1956, Geology of Comb Ridge and vicinity north of San Juan River, San Juan County, Utah: U.S. Geological Survey Bulletin 1021-E, p. 167-207.

Scotese, C.R., and McKerrow, W.S., 1990, Revised world maps and introduction, *in* McKerrow, W.S., and Scotese, C.R., editors, Paleozoic paleogeography and biogeography: Geological Society Memoir 12, p. 1-21.

Stanesco, J.D., 1991a, Sedimentology and cyclicity in the Lower Permian De Chelly Sandstone on the Defiance Plateau; eastern Arizona: Mountain Geologist, v. 28, no. 4, p. 1-11.

—1991b, Sedimentology and depositional environments of the Lower Permian Yeso Formation in northwestern New Mexico: U.S. Geological Survey Bulletin 1808-M, 12 p.

Stanesco, J.D., and Campbell, J.A., 1989, Eolian and non-eolian facies of the Lower Permian Cedar Mesa Sandstone Member of the Cutler Formation, southeastern Utah: U.S. Geological Survey Bulletin 1808-F, 13 p.

Stanesco, J.D., and Dubiel, R.F., 1992, Fluvial and eolian facies of the Organ Rock Shale Member of the Cutler Formation, southeastern Utah [abs.]: Geological Society of America, Abstracts with Programs, v. 24, no. 6, p. 64.

Stokes, W.L., 1988, Geology of Utah: Salt Lake City, Utah Museum of Natural History Occasional Paper Number 6, 280 p.

Vaughn, P.P., 1973, Vertebrates from the Cutler Group of Monument Valley and vicinity, *in* James, H.L., editor., Guidebook of Monument Valley and vicinity, Arizona and Utah: New Mexico Geological Society Field Conference, 24th, p. 99-105.

Wengerd, S.A., and Matheny, M.L., 1958, Pennsylvanian System of Four Corners region: American Association of Petroleum Geologists Bulletin, v. 42, no. 9, p. 2048–2106.

Witkind, I.J., and Thaden, R.E., 1963, Geology and uranium-vanadium deposits of the Monument Valley area, Apache and Navajo Counties, Arizona: U.S. Geological Survey Bulletin 1103, 171 p.

Great White Throne, Zion National Park
Photo courtesy of the Utah Travel Council

Geology of Utah's Parks and Monuments
2000 Utah Geological Association Publication 28
D.A. Sprinkel, T.C. Chidsey, Jr., and P.B. Anderson, editors

Cyclic Eolian Stratification on the Jurassic Navajo Sandstone, Zion National Park: Periodicities and Implications for Paleoclimate

Marjorie A. Chan[1] and Allen W. Archer[2]

ABSTRACT

Zion National Park and related areas of southern Utah contain exposures of the largest ancient wind-blown (eolian) dune system known in North America, preserved in the Jurassic Navajo Sandstone. Despite the common lack of absolute age constraints, ancient desert sand seas (ergs) and their erg margins can record valuable paleoclimatic proxies in the sedimentary record. The central erg portion of the Jurassic Navajo Sandstone of southwestern Utah contains nested cycles of eolian grainfall and wind-ripple laminae. These rhythmic alternations preserve random "snapshots" in time ranging from annual cycles to decadal climatic variations, influenced by periodic and quasi-periodic oscillators. Based on the established interpretation of annual cycles, nearly 300 of these high-frequency seasonal/annual cycles in the Navajo Sandstone of Zion National Park were measured in a continuous-thickness series of transverse dune foresets. Harmonic analysis reveals prominent periodicities of approximately 30 and 60 years and several other decadal periodicities. These long bedform cycles are interpreted as climatic oscillations/fluctuations of flow related to decadal periodicities that may be driven by solar variability and/or seasonal precipitation (moisture changes). This study demonstrates the utility of spectral analysis as a quantitative tool for interpreting periodic paleoclimatic oscillators in eolian environments.

INTRODUCTION

Ergs and erg margins are sensitive indicators of climatic changes and preserve potential paleoclimatic proxies within the sedimentologic and stratigraphic record. Large, shifting and migrating dunes deposit foresets at the front of the migrating dune. This foreset structure is called cross-bedding. The purpose of this study is to document the utility of harmonic and image analysis to evaluate periodicities within rhythmic and cyclic eolian cross-bedding of the Jurassic Navajo Sandstone of Zion National Park, southwestern Utah.

Rhythmic and cyclic eolian stratification is recognized as repeated variations within the structure and/or texture of cross-beds within a dune set. Cyclic cross-bedding in the Navajo Sandstone was originally recognized by Stokes (1964). Further study by Hunter and Rubin (1983) concluded that the prominent repetitions represent annual cycles based on regularity and cycle thickness (too thick to be daily cycles) as well as on comparisons to modern rates of dune movement. However, initial analyses presented here indicate the presence of additional bedform cycles (herein interpreted as climatic oscillations/fluctuations of flow) related to longer periodicities (for example, semiannual/seasonal to decadal-scale cycles). Drivers for these longer oscillations may be solar variability and/or seasonal changes.

Although daily cycles and winter-summer (annual) stratification changes are recognized in modern dunes of the Oregon coast and Padres Island, Texas (for example, Hunter and Richmond, 1988; Kocurek, 1996), there are currently no documented modern cyclicities with decadal-periodicities. Despite the fact that modern dune mechanics

[1]*Department of Geology and Geophysics, University of Utah, Salt Lake City, UT 84112-1183*

[2]*Department of Geology, Kansas State University, Manhattan, KS 66506*

are well understood, it is generally either too difficult or too expensive to create the types of trenches that would be necessary to study long records of modern deposition. Thus, exposures of ancient eolian dunes can provide data that has not been studied in the modern record. Although decadal cycles may be present in modern dunes, eolian workers indicate that they haven't really looked for such cycles (N. Lancaster, verbal communication, 1997; G. Kocurek, verbal communication, 1998). "Reverse uniformitarianism, " the concept of the ancient as the key to the present or future, may prove fruitful for understanding the modern record.

Recognition of these cycles may be useful in paleoclimate modeling and examining parameters (such as paleogeography) that could have accentuated climate shifts. Cycles encoded in the Jurassic eolian rocks may show prominent periodicities of Mesozoic paleoclimates that can later be used to identify more subtle climatic signals in modern or Holocene analogs. Furthermore, identification of the magnitude and frequency of these well-preserved ancient cycles also help refine tools (image- and harmonic-analysis methodologies) to use in interpreting proxy paleoclimate signals.

GEOLOGIC SETTING AND STRATIGRAPHY

The Jurassic Navajo Sandstone and its related equivalents form the largest erg deposit in North America (Peterson and Turner-Peterson, 1989). This spectacular erg deposit is generally flat lying and well exposed in the Colorado Plateau. The Navajo Sandstone is the uppermost formation of the Glen Canyon Group (figure 1) that has been regionally traced over the Colorado Plateau (Pipiringos and O'Sullivan, 1978; Peterson and Pipringos, 1979). The Navajo Sandstone is underlain by the Kayenta Formation of the Glen Canyon Group, and overlain unconformably (J-1 surface) by the San Rafael Group. Previous work on this erg (for example, Blakey and others 1988; Peterson 1988; Verlander 1995; Blakey and others 1996; Kocurek 1999) provides the framework for the detailed examination of cyclic cross-beds presented here. Jurassic paleogeography and paleoclimatology is summarized in Kocurek and Dott (1983), Blakey and others (1988), Chandler and others (1992), Blakey (1994), Parrish and Peterson (1988), and Peterson (1994). In this study, a locality was chosen along State Highway 9, 2.4 kilometers west of the east gate in Zion National Park (figure 1) which provides a thick series of cyclic cross-beds for evaluation.

CYCLIC CROSS-BEDDING

Expression of Cyclic Eolian Stratification

Cyclic cross-beds are distinguished by alternations of eolian stratification types and fine internal structures originally delineated and defined by Hunter (1977, 1985).

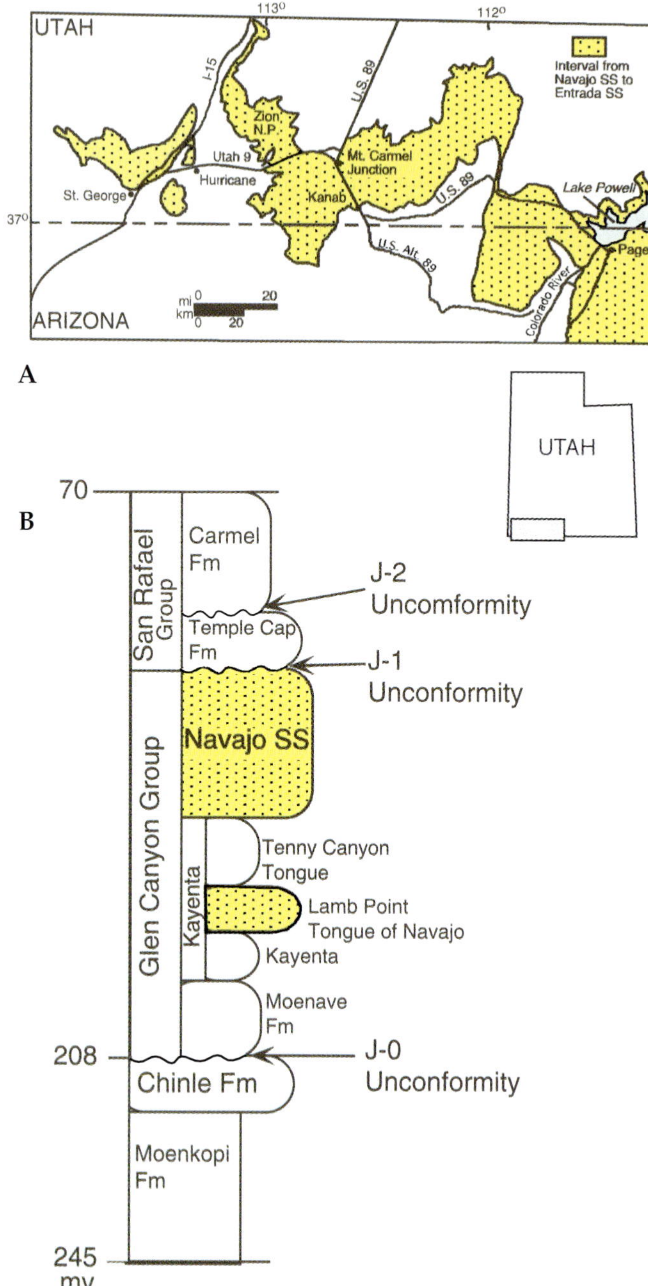

Figure 1. (A) Study area (modified from Rubin and Hunter, 1987) and (B) stratigraphic relationships of Jurassic Navajo Sandstone of the Zion National Park and Kanab areas. J-0 through J-2 indicate major unconformities of Pipiringos and O'Sullivan (1978). Stipple pattern indicates Navajo exposures containing cyclic cross-bedding. Measured locality is along State Highway 9, 2.4 kilometers west of the east gate in Zion National Park.

These lee-face stratification types and structures include: climbing-wind-ripple laminae, grainfall lamination, and grainflow/sandflow or avalanche tongues. In the lee face of dunes, wind ripples occur where tractional processes dominate. Both grainfall (from salting grains passively falling out of suspension) and grainflow (from grains that exceed the angle of repose and avalanche down the slipface) occur where gravitational processes dominate.

The arrangement of internal stratification types within the eolian foresets typically corresponds to how transverse, oblique, or longitudinal the airflow is, with respect to the incident angle of prevailing wind. The shifts in the incident angle appear to be seasonal wind patterns that are most commonly recognized by the variations of the internal stratification.

(1) Grainflow and grainfall strata. Grainflow deposits show a tapering wedge and occur from avalanching produced from the primary, transverse flow patterns of large dunes (for example, summer pattern). Large, modern dune crests typically build up and avalanche about six to ten times/year (G. Kocurek, verbal communication, 1996). Grainfall strata are indistinctly laminated and can also be deposited from primary, transverse flow patterns. These strata (either grainflow, grainfall, or both together) indicate the dominance of gravity-driven processes.

(2) Wind-ripple strata. Traction deposits may represent seasonal (for example, winter) patterns with an oblique incident angle of wind transport. Internally, the wind-ripple laminae are inversely graded (Hunter, 1977; Kocurek,1996). The bottom dune set is reworked to give a wind ripple plinth or apron at the base. This can be a seasonal shift in the wind direction, or could be the secondary (dune-modified) flow, where along-slope wind partly reworks bedforms and modifies the bottom set, producing the fluctuating asymmetry.

The differing stratification types in eolian deposits can be commonly "coded" with respect to color variations as well as weathering/cementation differences. The wind-ripple strata may additionally be better cemented having retained its pervasive initial cements (resulting in positive outcrop relief) in contrast to the more permeable grainflow deposits which were more commonly flushed with diagenetic waters (resulting in negative outcrop relief) (Chandler and others, 1989). These variations in cementation result in good delineation of the cyclic cross-beds in weathered outcrops. The grainflow deposits can be interspersed with grainfall deposits, and are likely to represent the long-term regional wind pattern established by summer winds. Stratification types can also be affected by position on the dune; grainfall is common when the lee face is close to the angle of repose and grainflows might start mid dune and extend to the toe of the dune. Secondary flow on the lee face (particularly developed towards the base) is likely to result in along-slope (or along-strike), traction transport (Kocurek, 1996), perhaps dominant during winter. Counts and analyses of individual events (grainfall vs. wind-ripple strata) within the annual cycles and examination of the primary (transverse) vs. secondary (oblique) wind patterns can provide information about frequency of chang-

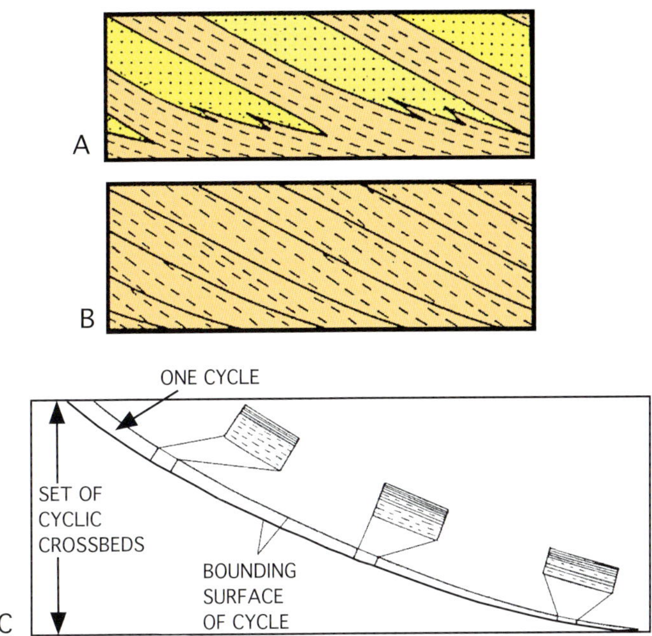

Figure 2. Cyclic cross-bedding from Hunter and Rubin (1983). (A) Concordant cyclic cross-beds (CCC), alternating stratification or grain sizes with parallel bounding surfaces. (B) Compound cross-beds (with foresets separated by erosional surfaces). (C) Amplification of concordant cyclic cross-beds (CCC, figure 2A) and alternating, internal eolian stratification types for the study locality. Dashed lines in bottom portion of inset boxes represent grainfall laminae; solid lines in top portion of inset boxes represent wind-ripple laminae.

ing energy flux on the scale of years and decades.

The interpretations and relations to potential paleoclimate proxies in this study are based on the assumption that the cyclic grainfall and wind-ripple alternations are annual cycles. This yearly interpretation is based, in part, on the scale of the cycles, which are too thick to be related to diurnal wind-flow and directional changes. The annual cyclicity can be attributed to seasonal wind patterns and moisture changes that can produce various internal fine structures (figures 2 and 3). We feel this is a reasonable hypothesis from previous work of Hunter and Rubin (1983) in their examination of Navajo Sandstone cross-bedding, including a portion of this same study area. The concordant nature of the cyclic cross-beds argues for fluctuating flow, dictated by climate changes that could in turn affect migration speed and asymmetry, dune position, and/or shifting wind patterns.

Hunter and Rubin (1983) define two end members of cyclic cross-bedding: "concordant cyclic cross-bedding" (CCC) where lamination within cycles are parallel to the bounding surfaces of the cycle, or "compound cross-bedding" where the cross-beds composing a set are separated by surfaces of erosion and are internally cross-bedded (figure 2). The origins of the cyclic cross-bedding may be due to either superimposed bedforms or fluctuating-flow conditions, although there is not a one-to-one correlation be-

Figure 3.   Measured annual cycles in the Jurassic Navajo Sandstone eolian stratification (figure 4A) in Zion National Park (1.5 miles or 2.4 kilometers west of east entrance station, Highway 9).
(A) View (looking east) of cyclic cross-bedding in canyon walls west of Checkboard Mesa. Specific area of study (B) is shown in the lower left of this photo.
(B) Cross sectional view of migrating dune set (bracketed). Some decadal cyclicity is indicated by packages of the thinner annual wind-ripple (AWR) dominated cycles towards the toes, alternating with thicker annual grainfall and grainflow (AGF) cycles. Surface of exhumed top is shown in (C).
(C) Exhumed top of the same migrating dune form in (B) showing repetitive annual cycles. Wind-ripple portions of the annual cycle marked at the tips of the arrow heads (center part of picture), alternate with thicker grainfall portions.
(D) Close view of annual cycles on exhumed top. Scale card = 16.5 centimeters tall, with cyclic packages ~ 10-15 centimeters thick (also shown by arrow length at left). Arrow indicates direction of dune migration.

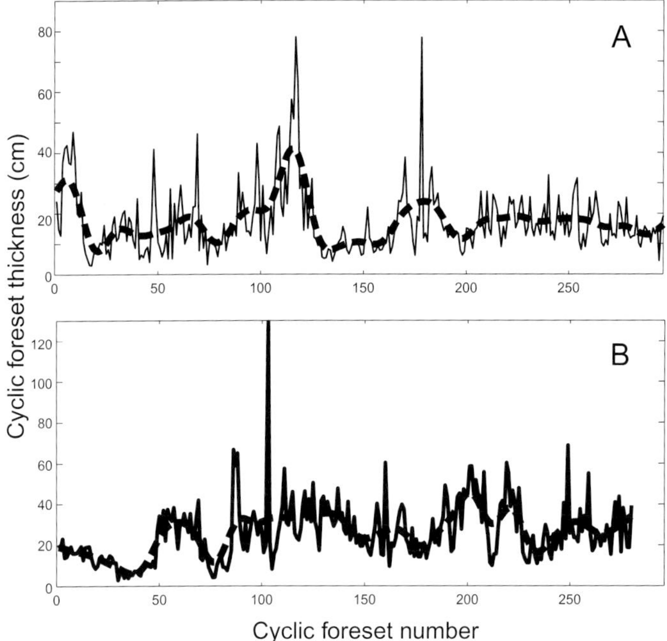

Figure 4. *(A) Annual foreset-thickness data from outcrop measurements of exhumed top on concordant cycle cross-beds in the Navajo Sandstone. (B) Foreset thickness from a similar data set near locality of figure 3, obtained from digitizing graphic dune advance data of Hunter and Rubin (1983, p. 439).*

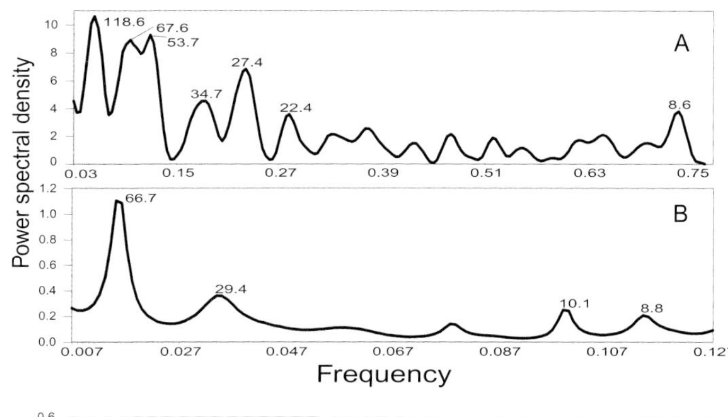

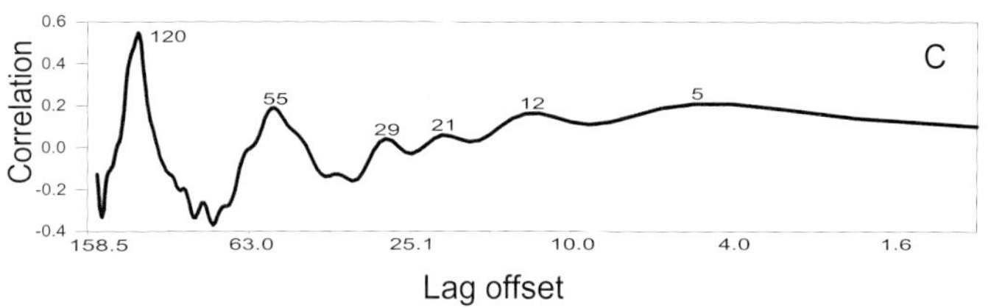

Figure 5. *Comparative analyses of foreset-thickness data from both Navajo outcrop data sets as depicted in figure 4. Time-series analyses from both outcrops have been combined (stacked) in order to accentuate similarities of encoded periodicities.*
(A) FFT (fast Fourier transform) power spectral density (PSD) exhibiting periodicities of 118.6, 67.6, 53.7, and 27.4 foresets.
(B) MEM (maximum entropy method) spectrum exhibiting well-developed periodicities of 66.7 and 29.4 foresets.
(C) Cross-correlation of foreset-thickness from data sets of figure 4. The strongest correlations, which occur at 120, 55, and 29 foresets are generally similar to both the FFT and MEM spectra.

tween the type of cyclic cross-bedding and the origin. Although both types of cyclic cross-bedding occur in the Navajo Sandstone, we focus on the best example of concordant cyclic cross-bedding formed by fluctuating flow (figure 2C). This type yields the best potential for climatic information because cyclicity is likely to be allocyclic (controlled by change in the total energy or material input to the system). In other words, there does not seem to be a change in dune shape, thus the differences in stratification are likely a function of climate parameters such as available sediment, and/or wind variations. In contrast, cyclic cross-bedding developed from superimposed bedforms (for example, Rubin, 1987) can be autocyclic (independent of energy or material input to the system) and thus may not yield useful proxy climate information.

Data Collection

For this analysis we measured continuous series of cyclic cross-beds within the Navajo Sandstone where an exhumed dune top and a side transverse section contain well-developed concordant cyclic cross-beds (CCC). Field relationships of stratification types, bounding surfaces, and interpreted airflow dynamics (see summary in Kocurek, 1996) are used in conjunction with the data gathered by image analysis of outcrops. This locality on the eastern boundary of Zion National Park (figures 1 and 3) was initially described by Hunter and Rubin (1983), and is conducive to study with the preferential weathering that distinguish grainfall and wind-ripple zones. The cycles here are parallel, relatively thin, concordant cyclic cross-

beds in a long series. We could physically walk across the top of an exhumed set which showed no major reactivations nor shifts in the bedform geometry. From the strike of the cross-beds and bounding surfaces, we could determine that the cyclicity of the bedding was produced by cyclic fluctuating flows (cross-beds and bounding surfaces with the same strike), and not the result of superimposed bedforms where the cross-beds and bounding surfaces may have different strikes (Rubin 1987). Additionally, the long series showed that the cyclic eolian stratification appears to occur on a variety of scales; the annual cycles and then longer cyclicities composed of the annual cycles. These conditions enabled measurement of the thicknesses of the CCC.

The strike and dip of the foreset (295°, 24 to 26° south) indicates a south-southwesterly paleoflow of 200 to 210°. A continuous series consisting of 297 CCC (figure 3B) was measured and did not exhibit significant reactivations. The exhumed top allowed us to see our position along the straight 65-meter strike length of the dune foreset (with no visible major lateral migration of the dune). The geometry suggests this measured example is a transverse dune. Following the interpretation that each CCC represents the yearly migration of a dune, the series represents a large, relatively straight-crested dune that marched forward for some 297 annual seasonal (summer-winter) cycles (figures 4 and 5A). Thus, this series of measurements provides paleoclimatic proxy for a window of nearly 300 years during the early Mesozoic (late Triassic to early Jurassic).

Another set of similar data was obtained from Hunter and Rubin (1983). This second data set consists of a series of 281 sequential cyclic foresets (figure 4B), also measured in Zion National Park, but from a longitudinal section of a different dune set. This foreset-thickness series was reconstructed from the original data by digitizing the graphic depiction presented by Hunter and Rubin (1983, p. 439). Comparative harmonic analyses of these two sets of data (figure 4) are presented below and the extracted periodicities are compared to known, climatically significant oscillators.

Periodicities Within Cyclic Foresets

Several techniques were used to test for the presence of periods within the Navajo foreset-thickness series. The fast Fourier transform (FFT) algorithm of Horne and Baliunas (1986) was applied to both data sets. The resulting spectra for both data sets were subsequently averaged. This "stacking," a standard geophysical technique, serves to reduce the more random components while accentuating any similar periodicities occurring in both data sets. The resultant spectrum (figure 5A) has a well-developed periodicity of 118.6 foresets as well as broad spectral peak suggesting a period ranging from about 68 to 54 foresets/cycle. Another significant period occurs at 27.4 foresets/cycle.

Maximum-entropy method (MEM) of spectral estimation was also applied to both data sets; this was based upon algorithms of Press and others (1988). The MEM approach presents a more averaged, less finely split spectrum. Similar to the FFT techniques described above, results for each set of data were "stacked" in order to produce a composite spectral estimate (figure 5B). This spectrum has peaks at 66.7 and 29.4 foresets/cycle. Both the MEM and FFT spectra indicate well-developed periodicities in the 50 to 60 and 30 foreset/cycle. The similarity of periodicities extracted using these disparate techniques and using data measured by different workers strongly suggests that some type of allogenic oscillator was operative during dune deposition. More data sets, however, are needed to verify the statistical significance of these periodicities.

As an additional test, the two data sets were cross-correlated using the algorithm described by Davis (1973). This technique (figure 5C) corroborates the long-term period of about 120 foresets/cycle also documented within the FFT spectrum. A somewhat weaker correlation occurs at a lag offset of 55 foresets; this apparently correlates to the 50-60 foreset cycles that are evident in both the FFT and MEM spectra. Higher frequency periods are not strongly expressed, but there is a weak correlation at an offset of 29 and this probably corresponds to the 27-30 foresets cycles evident in the FFT and MEM spectra.

DISCUSSION

How can we be certain that cycles are allogenic and therefore climatically controlled? The continuous series of concordant cyclic cross-beds without any major lateral shifting of the dune suggests an allogenic origin. In a tectonically stable, non-marine regime of the Jurassic Navajo system, the overriding allogenic control on deposition would be climate. Although dunes are inherently complex, even if there were a systematic autogenic change in the migration of the dune every 30 or 60 years, it would likely be climatically induced (changing wind patterns to affect dune migration). If the cyclicity were a simple mechanical function of the way dunes form, perhaps building/migrating up to a point and then starting over, the cyclicity should be much more prevalent in dunes of all ages and detectable particularly in the modern record. The lack of the cyclicity in most dune deposits (either modern or ancient) seems to argue that well-preserved cyclicity must be caused by factors other than just bedform migration. The presence of strong cyclicity suggests climatic control, perhaps preserved only where there is strong seasonality and an abundant sand supply to record the climatic variability such as the Navajo erg. However, additional data sets are required before statistically significant conclusions can be made regarding the utility of such paleoclimatic proxies.

In comparing the decadal periodicities of cyclic cross-beds to known established decadal-scale climatic oscillators, there are a number of periodicities related to solar activity. The best documented sunspot cycles are at 11 years and 22 years (double sunspot, termed the Hale Cycle). These cycles (for example, Eddy, 1980) are supported by oxygen isotope ratios ($\delta18$) from tree rings (Libby, 1983) and in several long-term fluvial hydrographs (Currie, 1994). There are no well-defined Navajo foreset periods in the range of the simple 10- to 11-year sunspot cycle, although there are weak, 8, 10, and 12-foreset periods. These weakly developed periodicities may relate to cycles of sunspot activity, which over the past several hundred years has been manifested as a quasi-periodic oscillator with a considerable range of variance.

In general, decadal-scale cycles are expressed within regional or local settings, but do not commonly seem to be hemispheric or global in scale (Mörner, 1984). Thus, such cycles are considerably different in geographic range than Milankovitch-scale orbital parameters. However, these decadal-scale cycles would contain important climatic information relevant to General Circulation Model (GCM)-scale modeling. Examples of decadal-scale climate change include droughts in the Sahel with a periodicity of approximately 30 years (Charney, 1975; Charney and others, 1977). Other modern studies of Kenya (Phillipson, 1975) suggest 5, 10, 40, and 50 year drought cycles, with the 50-year drought cycle being the most extreme. If these types of climate droughts occurred in the Jurassic, the response might be reflected in the cyclic eolian stratification by thicker grainfall and/or grainflow strata, and corresponding change in wind-ripple laminae thicknesses.

Although decadal-scale solar variability (Siscoe, 1980) and other longer-term periods have been discussed in the literature, they are controversial and typically rely upon the relatively subjective, historical records of sunspot or auroral activity. Many of the various solar periods are actually quasi-cyclic trends and might be developed only within parts of the longer-term records.

The various techniques of periodicity analyses all yielded cycles in the range of approximately 30 foresets/cycle, with values of 27.4, 29.4, and 29 for the FFT, MEM, and cross-correlation analyses, respectively. Thus, this appears to be one of the most consistently developed periodicities within the foreset series. The relationship of an approximately 30-year period to seasonal (for example, drought or precipitation) cycles might be significant in the understanding of fine-scale Jurassic climatic cyclicity.

A series of periodicities ranging from about 55 up through 67 were extracted in the FFT, MEM, and cross-correlational analyses. Although additional data is required in order to test the significance of these preliminary results, the analyses strongly suggest that periods of this magnitude were operative during the deposition of the Navajo dunes. Analysis of a long, evaporitic varve series from the Upper Jurassic Todilto Formation of New Mexico indicated a number of periods, including a 60-year cycle developed within parts of the sequence (Anderson and Kirkland, 1960). The development of these similar periodicities in a greatly different type of depositional system strongly suggests a well-developed, pervasive periodic oscillator that was affecting early Mesozoic climate in the Western Interior of the U.S.

PALEOCLIMATE IMPLICATIONS

In determining time constraints for interpreting paleoclimate, it is recognized that absolute ages are difficult to obtain from the non-marine rocks described herein. Although there is a lack of chronometric time control for individual bounding sets, there is good control of annual cycles. The rock record still provides random "snapshots" in time to tell us about decadal climatic variations. In principle, sequence stratigraphy and boundaries tied to eustasy could give additional time control, although the Jurassic Page Sandstone is one of the few erg units with that level of detailed stratigraphic analysis (for example, Blakey and others, 1996). The use of harmonic analyses can allow us to test different time periodicities to see conceptually whether or not the longer scales are coincident with observed stratification, and expected scales from interpretations and comparisons of modern eolian annual cycles.

During the deposition of the Early Jurassic eolian sandstones, the paleolatitude of the Navajo study example was close to 20° N, within the northeast trade winds belt (Parrish and Petersen, 1988; Chandler and others, 1992; Peterson, 1994) (figure 6). Resultant wind predictions and measured paleocurrent patterns show a shift from the Triassic to more northerly winds. This appears to correspond to predicted subtropical circulation as well as monsoonal circulation, most pronounced in eastern portions of Pangea (Parrish and Peterson, 1988; Kutzbach and Gallimore, 1989; Parrish, 1993). General circulation models (GCM) simulate warm surface-air temperatures and extreme continental aridity in the low and middle latitudes of western Pangea, as well as deep, low-pressure cells in summer alternating seasonally with winter high-pressure cells (Chandler and others, 1992). Initial results from this study suggest that this locality experienced decadal contrasts of wetter and drier periods during the Early Jurassic, possibly influenced by the one large ocean at this time, Panthalassa. This paleogeography could have had strong seasonal effects on precipitation, thus reflected in cyclic changes in eolian stratification. Outcrops of the Navajo set (figure 3B) show periodicities within groups of annual cycles (in other words, a group of thicker grainfall-dominated annual cycles, followed by a group of thinner wind-ripple-dominated annual cycles). These relationships suggest corroboration of seasonality interpretations for the Jurassic. Similarly, other workers (for example, Bell, 1986; Richmond and Morris, 1998) suggest potential Upper Jurassic Morrison Formation flood and drought cycles that affected shallow lakes and vertebrate populations in the Western Interior.

There are noted Jurassic trends of summer winds which were largely due south, and winter winds largely due west (from northeast winds). Dune crests are typically east-west with superimposed bedforms coming from approximately the northeast quadrant. More detailed paleoclimatic reconstructions for the Jurassic forthcoming by other workers may eventually allow distinction of monsoonal circulation (cyclicity) vs. subtropical flow patterns. Conversely, if future studies can elucidate more of the relationships between climate and dune cyclicity, the proxy information could be an important component for evaluating wind direction (for different seasons) and perhaps even relative wind strength/velocity. This in turn could serve as input for GCM models (for specific time periods, over certain areal extents).

Why does cyclic cross-bedding occur within the Navajo Sandstone? We have seen localized cyclic cross-bedding in a number of Permian through Jurassic erg deposits on the Colorado Plateau. However, cyclic cross-bedding appears to be most prominent within the Navajo Sandstone. This could be the result of several factors.

(1) The Navajo Sandstone may have had all the right conditions for a highly efficient system with a constant sand supply, large dune forms, extreme aridity, consistent wind patterns, perhaps the right continental configuration, and correspondingly the effect of a large ocean.

(2) With the conditions previously stated in (1) above,

the Navajo Sandstone may have thus been sensitive to climate oscillators.

(3) Given the nature of the Navajo erg, there was good preservation potential to capture these snapshots of time.

POTENTIAL FOR FUTURE WORK

This study focussed primarily on one Jurassic Navajo example that is well exposed and contains a long record. Future work can take a number of different approaches to refine the interpretations of cyclic stratification, including a comparison of the exhumed dune top counts (figure 3C) of this Zion locality with an independent evaluation of the 2-D side view cross sectional cross-bedding at the same locality (figure 3B). In the field, it is generally rare to find an exhumed top, thus if the side two-dimensional (2-D) cross-sectional data (that was cross checked with the exhumed top data) could be reliably correlated, then it might be possible to analyze and interpret counts where only 2-D cross-

sectional data is available. Following this comparison, it would also prove useful if mathematical relationships and projections can be determined for relatively short 2-D sections where the number of annual cycles may be only half or less as long as the Zion example of this paper.

More data sets of different types, sizes, and forms of cyclic cross-bedding could help distinguish new and/or recurring periodicities, using both modern and ancient examples. A variety of 2-D cross sections of eolian cross-bedding exist within more exposures of the Navajo Sandstone (figure 7) and the Permian DeChelly Sandstone (figure 8). Some of these would require more detailed examination in order to determine the bedform geometry and whether these are annual cycles also, or a larger, longer periodicity. A comparison of different-aged periodicities (for example, Permian vs. Jurassic) might be able to distinguish paleoclimate proxies, and perhaps ultimate controls of dune sizes and wind transport capacity, sand supply, and sediment availability.

Continued studies of air flow, as well as dune and bedform mechanics (for example, Werner and Kocurek, 1997, 1999) may also help further elucidate on the importance of

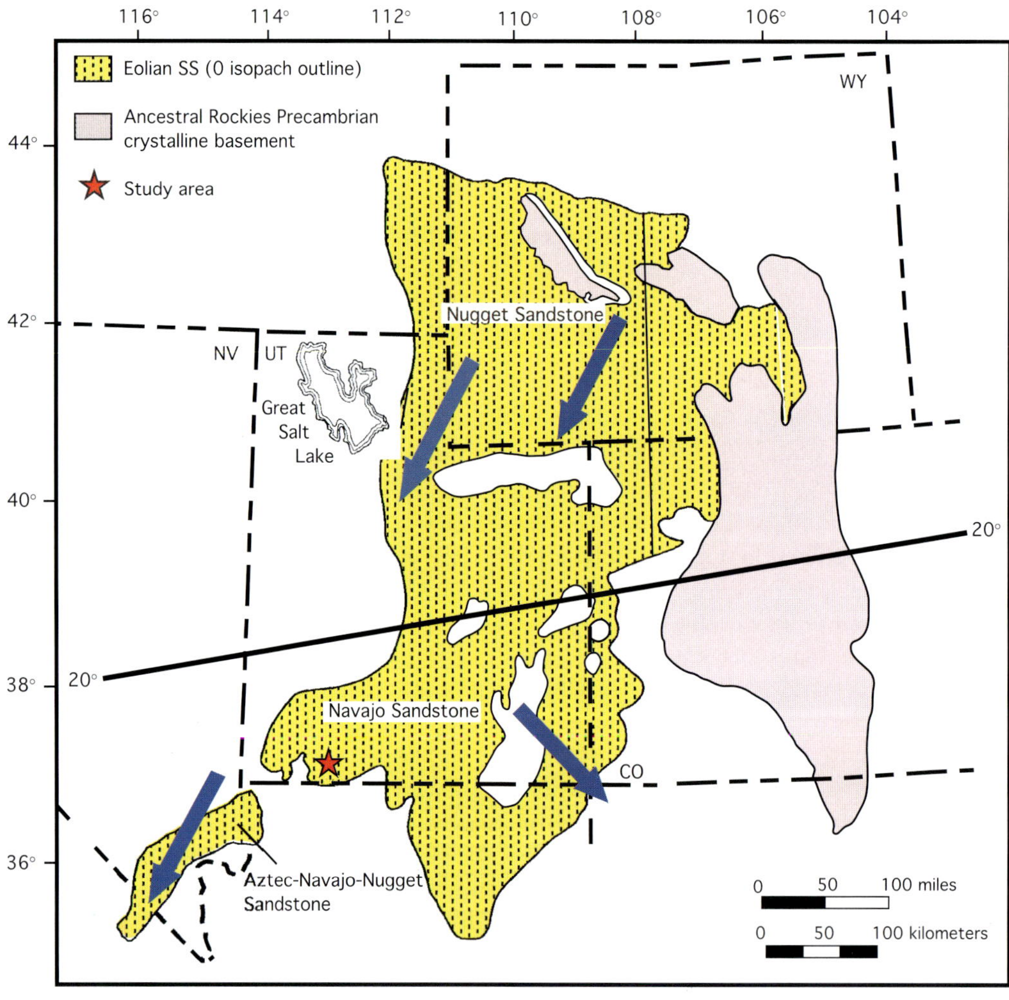

Figure 6.   Paleolatitude and predicted wind patterns (large arrows) from Early Jurassic eolian sandstones, after Peterson (1988) and Parrish and Peterson (1988).

Figure 7.   *Spectacular sections of thick cyclic cross-bedding in the Jurassic Navajo Sandstone of the Coyote Buttes area, Paria Wilderness, Utah-Arizona border, east of Kanab, Utah. All cross-bedding is dipping towards the southwest. The thickest parts of the cycles represent the grainflow and grainfall portions, separated by the thinner, better-cemented basal plinths of wind-ripple laminae. (A) In the dead-center portion of this Navajo Sandstone panel, an indivdual cross-bed set is approximately 4 meters thick. (B) The central cyclic set of this photo panel is estimated at 10 meters thick. Location in GPS coordinates: 36° 59' 42 N, 112° 0' 22 W.*

Figure 8.   *Cyclic cross-bedding in the Permian DeChelly Sandstone near Oljeto, Utah (far southeast corner of Utah). Thick alternating grainflow deposits are separated from thin, better-cemented wind-ripple laminae (wind-ripple laminae shown at arrows). Foresets ~ 2 meters high. The stacked sets at the right show truncations and reactivations, that warrant further study to interpret flow dynamics.*

autocyclic vs. allocyclic effects on cyclic cross-bedding. As more is known about the bedform mechanics, these may help explain the variability in size, and thicknesses of cyclic cross-bedding.

Collaborative work with paleoclimate modelers who can perform detailed comparisons of GCM wind and rainfall results will help refine the relationships of eolian cyclicity with different geologic ages and predicted climate regimes. This type of data can have strong predictive capabilities in both ancient and modern dune settings. As the earth sciences are looking towards the integrative field of global climate change, extraction of numerical values from the ancient stratigraphic record will be important in interpreting Quaternary paleoclimates and in evaluating predictive climatic models.

SUMMARY

Eolian dune seas are particularly sensitive indicators of climatic change and provide good proxy sedimentologic and stratigraphic evidence of paleoclimate. This study focuses on a section of Jurassic Navajo Sandstone in the eastern portion of Zion National Park where there is excellent three-dimensional exposure of cyclic cross-bedding in the dune deposits. Image- and harmonic-analysis are useful methodologies to distinguish and numerically evaluate cyclicity within eolian cross-stratification. These methods show distinction of individual small-scale and stacked larger scale periodicities (particularly those at 30 and 60 years in this example) reflecting annual to seasonal to decadal and longer oscillators that are interpreted to be signals of solar variability and/or seasonality. It is rare to be able to find much control on time in non-marine deposits, however these rhythmic "snapshots" in time can provide important paleoclimate information to help us unlock secrets of the past, and may also provide new keys to search for in the modern record.

ACKNOWLEDGMENTS

We gratefully acknowledge insightful conversations with Ralph E. Hunter, and the helpful reviews of Rick Ford and Thomas Morris. Mark Chandler and an anonymous reviewer provided input on earlier drafts of this manuscript. Portions of this manuscript are used by permission of Gordon and Breach Publishers, which retains the copyright on the earlier paper of Chan and Archer (1999).

REFERENCES

Anderson, R.Y., and Kirkland, D.W., 1960, Origin, varves, and cycles of Jurassic Todilto Formation, New Mexico: American Association of Petroleum Geologists Bulletin, v. 44, p. 37-52.

Bell, T.E., 1986, Deposition and diagenesis of the Brushy Basin Member and upper part of the Westwater Canyon Member of the Morrison Formation, San Juan Basin, New Mexico, *in* Turner-Peterson, C.E., Santos E.S., and Fishman, N.S., editors, A basin analysis case study; the Morrison Formation, Grants uranium region, New Mexico: American Association of Petroleum Geologists Studies in Geology 22, p. 77-91.

Blakey, R.C., 1994, Paleogeographic and tectonic controls on some Lower and Middle Jurassic erg deposits, *in* Caputo, M.V., Peterson, J. A., and Franczyk, K.J., editors, Mesozoic systems of the Rocky Mountain region, USA, Colorado Plateau: Denver, Colorado, Rocky Mountain Society for Sedimentary Geology, p. 273-298.

Blakey, R.C., Peterson, F., and Kocurek, G., 1988, Synthesis of late Paleozoic and Mesozoic eolian deposits of the western interior of the United States: Sedimentary Geology, v. 56, p. 3-125.

Blakey, R.C., Havholm, K.G., and Jones, L.S., 1996, Stratigraphic analysis of eolian interactions with marine and fluvial deposits, Middle Jurassic Page Sandstone and Carmel Formation, Colorado Plateau, U.S.A.: Journal of Sedimentary Research, v. 66, p. 324-342.

Chan, M.A., and Archer, A.W., 1999, Spectral analysis of eolian foreset periodicities -- implications for Jurassic decadal-scale paleoclimatic oscillators: Palaeoclimates, v. 3, no. 4, p. 239-255.

Chandler M., Kocurek G., Goggin D.J., and Lake, L.W., 1989, Effects of stratigraphic heterogeneity on permeability in eolian sandstone sequence, Page Sandstone, northern Arizona: American Association of Petroleum Geologists Bulletin, v. 7, p. 658-668.

Chandler, M., Rind, D., and Ruedy, R., 1992, Pangaean climate during the Early Jurassic- GCM simulations and the sedimentary record of paleoclimate: Geological Society of America Bulletin, v. 104, p. 543-559.

Charney, J.G., 1975, Dynamics of deserts and drought in the Sahel: Quarterly Journal of the Royal Meteorlogical Society, v. 101, p. 193-202.

Charney, J.G., Quirk, W.J., Chow, S.H., and Kornfield, J., 1977, A comparative study of the effects of albedo change on drought in semi-arid regions: Journal of Atmospheric Science, v. 34, p. 1366-1385.

Currie, R.G., 1994, Variance contribution of luni-solar and solar cycle signals in the St. Lawrence and Nile River records: International Journal of Climatology , v. 14, p. 843-852.

Davis, J.C., 1973, Statistics and data analysis in geology: New York, John Wiley, p. 245-246.

Eddy, J.A., 1980, The historical record of solar activity, *in* Pepin, R.O., Eddy, J.A., and Merrill, R.B., editors, The ancient sun -- fossil record in the Earth, moon, and meteorites: New York, Permagon Press, p. 119-134.

Horne, J.H., and Baliunas, S.L., 1986, A prescription for period analysis of unevenly sampled time series: Astrophysical Journal, v. 302, p. 757-763.

Hunter, R.E., 1977, Terminology of cross-stratified sedimentary layers and climbing-ripple structures: Journal of Sedimentary Petrology, v. 47, p. 697-706.

Hunter, R.E., 1985, Subaqueous sand-flow cross-strata:

Journal of Sedimentary Petrology, v. 55, p. 886-894.

Hunter, R.E., and Richmond, B.M., 1988, Daily cycles in coastal dunes: Sedimentary Geology, v. 55, p. 43-67.

Hunter, R.E., and Rubin, D.M., 1983, Interpreting cyclic cross bedding, with an example from the Navajo Sandstone, *in* Brookfield, M.E., and Ahlbrandt, T.S., editors, Eolian sediments and processes: International Association of Sedimentologists Developments in Sedimentology, v. 38, New York, Elsevier, p. 429-454.

Kocurek, G., 1996, Desert aeolian systems, Chapter 5, *in* Reading, H.G., editor, Sedimentary environments-processes, facies and stratigraphy (3rd edition): Oxford, England, Blackwell Science, p. 125-153.

—1999, The aeolian rock record, yes, Virginia, it exists, but it really is rather special to create one, *in* Goudie, A.S., Livingstone, I., and Stokes, S., editors, Aeolian environments, sediments and landforms: New York, John Wiley & Sons, Ltd., p. 239-259.

Kocurek, G., and Dott, R.H., Jr., 1983, Jurassic paleogeography and paleoclimate of the central and southern Rocky Mountain region, *in* Reynolds, M.W., and Dolly, E.D., editors, Mesozoic paleogeography of the west-central U.S: Denver, Colorado, Society of Economic Paleontologists and Mineralogists Rocky Mountain Section, Rocky Mountain Paleogeography Symposium, p. 101-116.

Kutzbach, J.E., and Gallimore, R.G., 1989, Pangean climates- megamonsoons of the megacontinent: Journal of Geophysical Research, v. 94, p. 3341-3357.

Libby, L.M., 1983, Past climates- tree thermometers, commodities, and people: Austin, Texas, University of Texas Press, 143 p.

Mörner, N.A., 1984, Climatic changes on a yearly to millennial basis, an introduction, *in* Mörner, N.A., and Karlén, W., editors, Climatic changes on a yearly to millennial basis: Dordrecht, Holland, D. Reidel, p. 1-13.

Parrish, J.T., 1993, Climate of the supercontinent Pangea: Journal of Geology, v. 101, p. 215-233.

Parrish, J.T., and Peterson, F., 1988, Wind directions predicted from global circulation models and wind directions determined from eolian sandstones of the western United States -- a comparison: Sedimentary Geology, v. 56, p. 261-282.

Peterson, F., 1988, Pennsylvanian to Jurassic eolian transportation systems in the western United States: Sedimentary Geology, v. 56, p. 207-260.

—1994, Sand dunes, sabkhas, streams, and shallow seas -- Jurassic paleogeography in the southern part of the Western Interior basin, *in* Caputo, M.V., Peterson, J. A., and Franczyk, K.J., editors, Mesozoic systems of the Rocky Mountain region, USA, Colorado Plateau: Denver, Colorado, Rocky Mountain Society for Sedimentary Geology, p. 233- 272.

Peterson, F., and Pipiringos, G., 1979, Stratigraphic relations of the Navajo Sandstone to Middle Jurassic formations, southern Utah and northern Arizona: U.S.

Geological Survey Professional Paper 1035-B, 43 p.

Peterson, F., and Turner-Peterson, C., 1989, Geology of the Colorado Plateau, 28th International Geological Congress Field Trip Guidebook T130: American Geophysical Union, 65 p.

Peterson, J.A., 1972, Jurassic system, *in* Mallory, W.W., editor, Geologic atlas of the Rocky Mountain region: U.S.A.: Rocky Mountain Association of Geologists, p. 177-189.

Pipiringos, G.N., and O'Sullivan, R.G., 1978, Principle unconformities in Triassic and Jurassic rocks, Western Interior U.S. -- a preliminary report: U.S. Geological Survey Professional Paper 1035-A, 29 p.

Phillipson, J., 1975, Rainfall, primary production and "carry capacity" of Tsavo National Park, Kenya: East African Wildlife Journal, v. 13, p. 171-201.

Press, W.H., Flannery, B.P., Teukolsky, S.A., and Vetterling, W.T., 1988, Numerical recipes in C, the art of scientific computing: New York, Cambridge University Press, 735 p.

Richmond, D.R., and Morris, T.H., 1998, Stratigraphy and cataclysmic deposition of the Dry Mesa Dinosaur Quarry, Mesa County, Colorado: Modern Geology, v. 22, p. 121-143.

Rubin, D.M., 1987, Cross-bedding, bedforms, and paleocurrents: Society of Economic Paleontologists and Mineralogists Concepts in Sedimentology and Paleontology, v. 1, 187 p.

Rubin, D.M., and Hunter, R.E., 1987, Field guide to sedimentary structures in the Navajo and Entrada Sandstones in southern Utah and northern Arizona, *in* Davis, G.H., and Vanden Dolder, E.M., editors, Geologic diversity of Arizona and its margins -- excursions to choice areas: Geological Society of America 100th Annual Meeting Phoenix Arizona guidebook, Arizona Bureau of Geology and Mineral Technology Geological Survey Branch Special Paper 5, p. 126-139.

Siscoe, G.L., 1980, Evidence in the auroral record for secular solar variability: Reviews of Geophysics and Space Physics, v. 18, p. 647-658.

Stokes, W.L., 1964, Eolian varving in the Colorado Plateau: Journal Sedimentary Petrology, v. 34, p. 429-432.

Werner, B.T., and Kocurek, G., 1997, Bedform dynamics-does the tail wag the dog?: Geology, v. 25, p. 771-774.

—1999, Bedform spacing from defect dynamics: Geology, v. 27, p. 727-730.

Verlander, J.E., 1995, Basin-scale stratigraphy of the Navajo Sandstone -- southern Utah, USA: University of Oxford, Ph.D. dissertation, 159 p.

Mesa Arch, Canyonlands National Park
Photo courtesy of Utah Travel Council

Geology of Utah's Parks and Monuments
2000 Utah Geological Association Publication 28
D.A. Sprinkel, T.C. Chidsey, Jr., and P.B. Anderson, editors

Upheaval Dome, Canyonlands, Utah: Strain Indicators that Reveal an Impact Origin

Peter W. Huntoon[1]

ABSTRACT

Upheaval Dome in the northern part of Canyonlands National Park is the best exposed impact crater on the earth. The 5.5 km (3.4 mi) diameter crater is deeply eroded. Assuming that the impact was responsible for the soft-sediment deformation observed in the Carmel Formation, it dates from Jurassic time so only a small thickness of affected stratigraphy is eroded. Consequently its original size was little bigger than the outer limits of the present deformed zone.

Structures produced during the three stages of cratering are preserved. The conclusion of the contact and compression stage and earliest part of the crater excavation stage are represented by pseudo-shattercones and clastic dikes. Mechanical thickening of the stratigraphic section by conjugate thrust faults and ductile crowding structures adjacent to the opening transient crater remain from the crater excavation stage. A record of the gravity-driven modification stage is preserved as: (1) listric normal faults that carried material back into the transient crater, (2) outwardly plunging anticlines which reveal shortening of the circumferences of the ring-shaped hanging wall blocks as they contracted toward the center, (3) a ring syncline produced by mechanical thinning associated with the listric normal faulting, and (4) a prominent central peak caused by rebound. Destruction of the transient crater by collapse and rebound of the central peak left a small ring structure that is classified as a complex crater.

PURPOSE

The purpose of this article is to describe the structural geology of the Upheaval impact crater. Impact cratering progresses through three stages: (1) contact and compression, (2) excavation, and (3) modification. Care is taken to identify the different types of structures observed in the crater and to relate them to the stage during which they formed. Unraveling how and when particular structures formed is accomplished by deducing the causative stresses from the observed strains and observing the cross-cutting relationships between the various structures.

UPHEAVAL DOME

Upheaval Dome is a small complex impact crater, meaning that it is a multiple ring crater (figure 1). It is the finest exposed complex crater on the earth, a distinction attributed to the fact that the crater is deeply eroded. As

shown on figure 2, it occupies an elevated position in the Island in the Sky district of northern Canyonlands National Park between the deeply entrenched Green and Colorado rivers. The desert setting carries the quality of exposure to the sublime.

The deformed zone which defines the Upheaval impact structure is about 5.5 km (3.4 mi) in diameter. A prominent central peak dominates the structure and is ringed by a syncline. The rocks exposed in the crater range from the Permian Organ Rock Shale in the eroded core to the Jurassic Navajo Sandstone preserved in the ring syncline (figure 3). West-draining Upheaval Canyon heads in the crater, and provides an impressive radial profile through its west side that is 360 m (1,200 ft) in height. The upstream tributaries to Upheaval Canyon have etched into the flanks of the central peak parallel to the crater rings and provide wonderful profiles that expose the ring syncline and other features in the ring structures. One small gulch, eroded through the core of the central peak, exposes the Organ Rock Shale directly under the hypocenter. The south-facing wall of Holeman basin along the Green River Canyon beautifully exposes the outermost ring fault,

[1]*Boulder City, NV 89006*

Figure 1. *Upheaval Dome, Canyonlands National Park, Utah, viewed toward the northwest. The light-colored, rounded rocks beyond the outermost ring are the Navajo Sandstone which is preserved in the ring syncline. The width across the center of the photograph is 2.6 km (1.6 mi).*

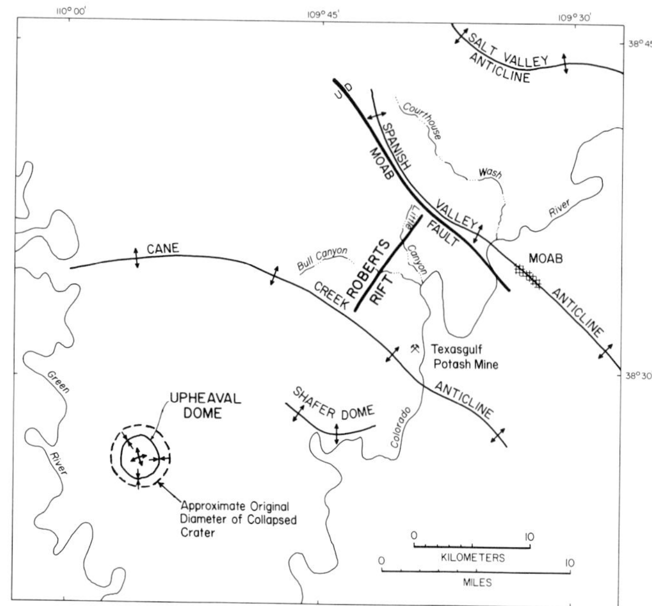

Figure 2. *Location of Upheaval Dome between the Green and Colorado rivers, Canyonlands area, Utah. Upheaval Canyon trends westward from the center of the dome to the Green River. Trail Canyon trends northwestward along the northeast side of the dome. Holeman basin opens to the south toward the Green River along the south side of the dome.*

yielding one of the most definitive structural outcrops present. Trail Canyon along the northeastern margin also profiles the outer ring but not with such clarity.

Upheaval Dome is readily accessible by paved road by taking Utah State Highway 313 south to the Island in the Sky district of Canyonlands National Park and following the signs to the crater rim. Hiking trails provide excellent access to overlooks and to the crater interior.

ORIGIN

The origin of Upheaval Dome has been the subject of speculation in a long, highly-conflicting series of academic and popular articles. Only the most substantive or exotic are cited below. The field seems to have narrowed lately to salt diapirism (doming caused by flowage of buried salt) and impact; but this is not simply a debate about different processes, rather it reflects deeper philosophical divisions.

The diapirists favor mechanisms that are rooted in process gradualism, a manifestation of Darwinian evolution that was merged into the geologic paradigm during the 19th century as uniformitarianism. This was our forbearers means of rejecting the capriciousness of creationism which was prevalent at the time, and which embraced catastrophic events. A consequence is that there is a reticence on the part of many classically trained geoscientists to acknowledge that impactors from space are of supreme but periodic importance as geologic agents (French, 1990). Impactors are often viewed uncomfortably because they seem to be reviving the heretical notions of catastrophic processes which appear ad hoc much like the biblical flood (Hartmann and Miller, 1991, p. 49-50). Unfortunately the pejorative label "ad hoc" is commonly misused in place of "stochastic" when actual catastrophic geologic processes

are discounted by uniformitarianists.

There is a rich literature favoring variations on a salt diapir origin for Upheaval Dome (McKnight, 1940; Fiero, 1958; Mattox, 1968). The latest and most substantive of these appears in Jackson and others (1998). The salt theories pivot on the presence of approximately 500 m (1,600 ft) of Pennsylvanian Paradox salts under the site prior to the impact (Woodward-Clyde Consultants, 1983, figure 5-12). There is, however, no salt in the exposed core of Upheaval Dome or any mineralogical evidence that any salt passed upward through the feature.

As part of a multiple hypothesis screening exercise, McKnight (1940, p. 127) raised the alternate possibility that the dome could be caused by intrusion of an igneous plug which remains buried. Using elements of both salt flowage and igneous intrusion, Joesting and Plouff (1958) proposed a model whereby igneous rocks were fortuitously intruded into the core of an existing salt dome. This conveniently explained a gravity high detected by them over the dome without having to consider the radical alternative of a central peak in an impact structure.

Kopf (1982) proposed an entirely different concept by which the dome was caused by an hydraulic ram mechanism involving overpressured fluids driven and localized by unspecified tectonic forces.

Significantly, Upheaval Dome won a place on Bucher's (1936) cryptovolcanic explosion crater list. The idea here was that the crater was caused by a gaseous explosion of probable volcanic origin but without subsequent intrusion or eruption of igneous rock. Boon and Albritton (1936)

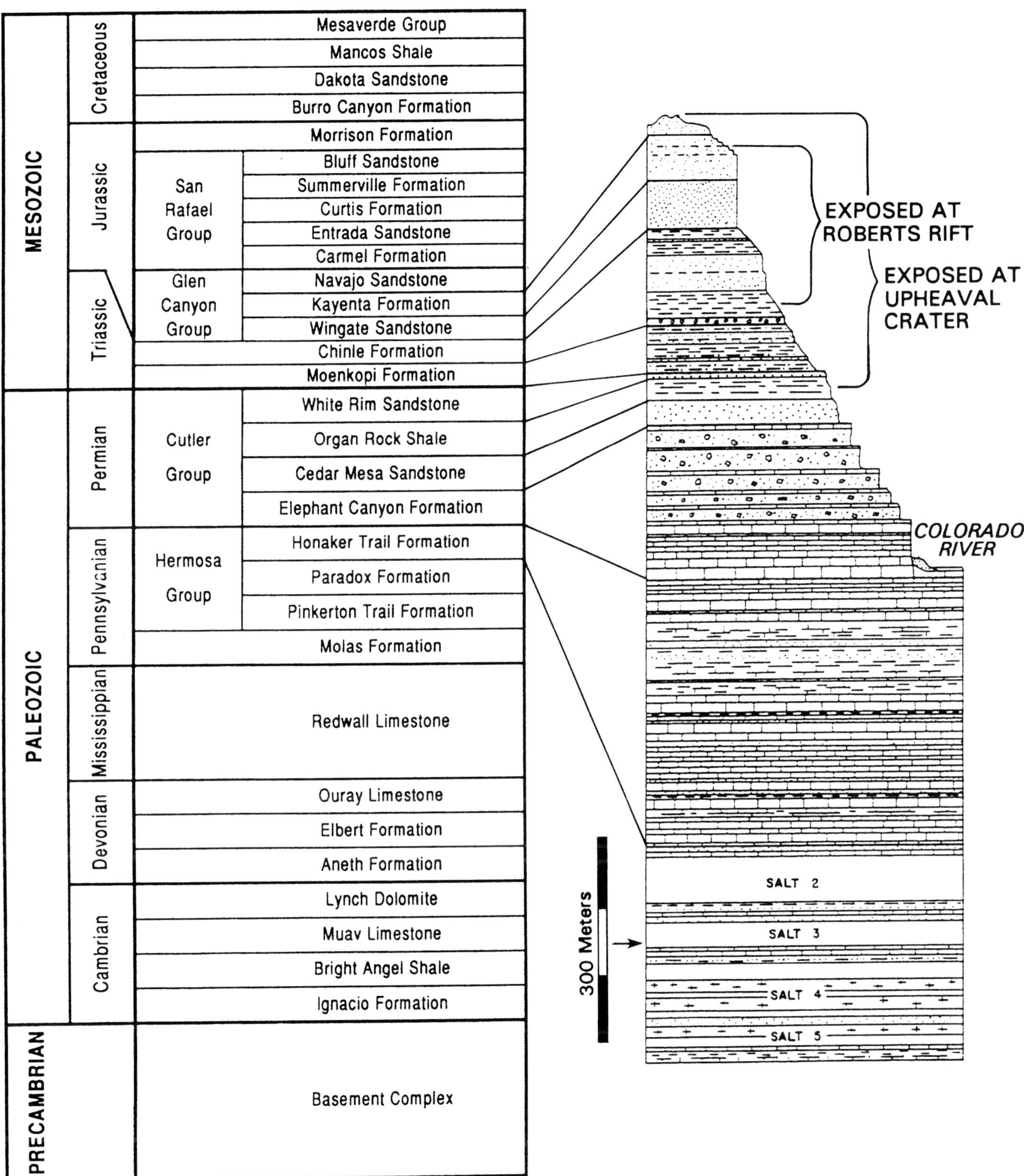

Figure 3. *Stratigraphy in the vicinity of Upheaval Dome and Roberts rift, Canyonlands area, Utah. It is now thought that the land surface at the time of impact was near the top of the Carmel Formation. Only the upper part of the Paradox Formation is shown in the right column. Bar scale goes with the right column; left column is not to scale.*

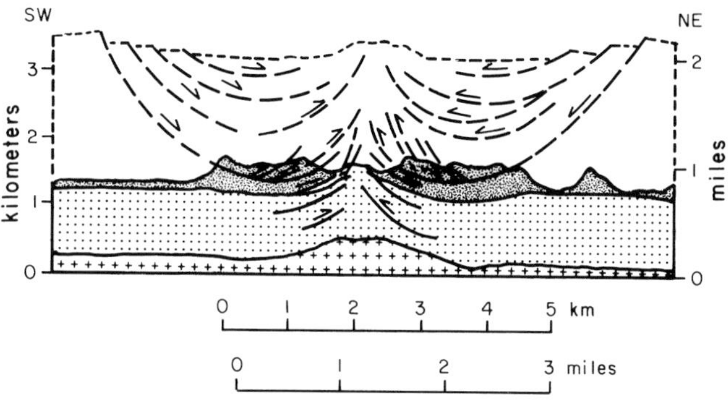

Figure 4. Historic structural cross-sectional sketch through Upheaval Dome, Canyonlands, Utah, redrawn from Shoemaker and Herkenhoff (1984). At the time this cross-section was made, it was assumed that the impact was a Cretaceous-Tertiary event so 2 km (1.2 mi) of eroded Mesozoic strata was inferred to cover the site. It now appears that the impact occurred during Jurassic time when only the thin Carmel Formation mantled the site. To actually fit observations, the structures shown must be scaled down by a factor of 0.6 and dropped down so that the top of the inferred structural profile coincides with the land surface.

had the prescience to argue that many of Bucher's crypto-volcanic structures were in fact impact structures. Bucher's list subsequently proved to be a reliable catalog of impact sites.

Shoemaker and Herkenhoff (1984) revealed that Upheaval Dome is a deeply-eroded impact structure. Their cross section, redrawn here as figure 4, shows the essential character of the crater. A definitive treatment of the impact followed in Kriens and others (1999). Huntoon and Shoemaker (1995) used the energy from the Upheaval impact to explain hydraulic fracturing and clastic dike emplacement found both within the crater and at the curious Roberts rift located 22 to 32 km (14 to 20 mi) along a northeast radii. Similarly, Alvarez and others (1998) used the seismic energy from the impact to explain soft-sediment deformation within the Jurassic Carmel Formation in the vicinity, thus tentatively proposing a timing for the impact.

IMPACT CRATERING

A bullet hitting a wall serves as a poor analog for an impact because the velocity of the bullet is far too small relative to its mass, thus not enough energy is transferred to the target to simulate the damage of an impact. Typical impactors arrive at 10 to 20 km/sec (2.2×10^4 to 4.4×10^4 mi/hr). Melosh (1989, p. 53) reveals that impactors having velocities of more than a few km/sec impart to the target energies exceeding those in an equivalent volume of chemical explosives. Impactors moving at velocities in excess of 100 km/sec (2.2×10^5 mi/hr) impart energies that exceed nuclear explosives. Consequently, an impact is best viewed as the instantaneous deposition of an enormous amount of energy on the surface of the target body.

Cratering results from the rapid radial propagation of

energy into the target. Thus impactors with all but the most oblique incident angles, those from vertical down to about 10 degrees, leave circular craters. It is evident then that the theory of impacts is identical to the theory for explosions on surfaces. An excellent analog for the development of a complex crater is that of a liquid drop falling into a still pool of water.

An analysis of Arizona's Meteor crater by Shoemaker (1963) provides a useful scaling perspective. The crater is 1.1 km (0.7 mi) in diameter and was produced by a massive, but relatively small, nickel-iron meteorite. The energy required to blow out the crater was equal to what could be delivered by 10^5 ton object arriving at 20 km/sec (4.4×10^4 mi/hr). Such an object, only 30 m (100 ft) in diameter, could produce a crater 37 times its diameter.

Melosh (1989) has delineated three stages in the cratering process: (1) contact and compression, (2) excavation, and (3) modification. Evidence for all three is present in an uneroded crater, with the structures resulting from the later stages superimposed on the earlier. The job of sorting particular classes of structures out and assigning them to a stage relies on an analysis of cross-cutting relationships between the various classes of structures present in order to sequence them coupled with an analysis of stress indicators to assign them to the correct stage. The latter is facilitated by knowing approximately when specific classes of structures formed based on observations from explosions.

The contact and compression stage involves the transfer of kinetic energy from the projectile to the target. This stage is very brief and lasts only as long as it takes for the shock wave leaving the point of contact to travel through the impactor, reflect off its trailing surface and arrive back at the point of contact. At this moment, the projectile is unloaded and its remains simply go along for the ride as the crater opens around it. For a silicate projectile 10 m (33 ft) in diameter traveling at 10 km/sec (2.2×10^4 mi/hr), the contact and compression stage is over in 10^{-3} sec; for a projectile 1 km (0.6 mi) in diameter the elapsed time is 10^{-1} sec (Melosh, 1989, p. 46). Contact pressures are extreme, in the range of 10^2-10^3 GPa (10^{10}-10^{11} lbs/in^2) for geologically significant impacts.

A hemispheric shock wave propagates into the target during the excavation stage, so it and a trailing rarification wave set the target material into motion initiating a subsonic excavation flow that opens a transient crater. The target material under the point of impact is accelerated to a large fraction of the impactors velocity. Streamlines of the flowing rock radiate from the impact site and curve upward to the free surface of the target. By the time the excavation flow is underway, the shock wave has long since left the site of the impact. The excavation stage ends when the opening of a bowl-shaped transient crater ceases. The excavation stage is over in seconds to minutes even for large impacts. The material strength and gravity of the target become important only as this stage draws to a close. Arizona's small Meteor crater is a transient crater

Figure 5. Sandstone dike exposed on the east flank of the central peak of Upheaval Dome, Canyonlands, Utah, that was injected downsection from the White Rim Sandstone into the Organ Rock Shale during the earliest part of the excavation stage. The slightly overturned Organ Rock beds dip steeply to the left and their tops face toward the right. The White Rim Sandstone, folded to the vertical, lies just off the photo to the right. View is toward the north.

that was too small to undergo significant modification after the excavation stage was over.

The modification stage is gravity-driven. Intermediate-size craters collapse through large-scale slumping and a central peak rises as the compressed rocks below the crater rebound. The slumping and rebounding rocks fill and destroy the transient crater. The resulting ring structures are called complex craters and Upheaval Dome is a small example of this type.

STRAIN FEATURES

The primary evidence that Upheaval Dome is an impact structure includes: (1) a morphology that is consistent with proven impacts, and (2) the presence of subsidiary structures having sequencing, forms and stress indicators expected in an impact. Melosh's three stages for crater development provide a useful framework that can

be used to classify the various structures present because surviving features from at least the last two stages are preserved.

Earliest Excavation Structures

The rapid movement of the shock wave into the earth produces unambiguous diagnostic indicators in the form of highly shocked target rocks exhibiting shattercones, high pressure phases of quartz (coesite, stishovite), crystal planar deformation features, melts, etc. Unfortunately these near-surface indicators eroded from Upheaval Dome long ago. However, Shoemaker and others (1993) found samples of thin siltstone beds from the Moenkopi Formation inside the crater that are pervasively shattered and which yield pseudo-shattercones.

As the shock wave radiates into the earth, it expands and deteriorates into strong stress waves. Aquifers and petroleum reservoirs in the vicinity undergo a brief series of strong compressions and dilations as the stress waves pass. The fluids become acutely overpressured during the compressions resulting in hydraulic fracturing which propagates into surrounding strata. As the fractures open, mobilized rock fragments plucked from both the reservoir and fracture walls become entrained in the escaping fluids and move into the fracture. These natural proppants hold the fractures open, and are preserved as clastic dikes.

Huntoon and Shoemaker (1995) found two classes of clastic dikes that they associate with the Upheaval impact. The sharply domed Organ Rock, Moenkopi and Chinle strata in the central peak are riven with clastic dikes comprised of cataclastically broken sand grains derived from the White Rim Sandstone. The dikes range up to 0.6 m (2 ft) thick and extend both up- and down-section from the White Rim Sandstone (figure 5). The sands were mobilized as fluids flowed out of the compressed sandstone aquifer into opening hydraulic fractures. The shattering of the grains attests to the extreme pressures that developed as the strongest stress waves passed through the aquifer. It is possible that the fluids were locally vaporized.

Roberts rift is the second example of hydraulic fracturing attributed to the impact, but in this case not conclusively proven to be caused by it. The rift crops out northeast of the crater at a radial distance of between 22 and 32 km (14 and 20 mi). The fissure contains clasts derived from the Pennsylvanian Paradox Formation and younger rocks which have been injected as much as 1,000 m (3,300 ft) upward into the Mesozoic section (Hite, 1975). The origin proposed for the fissure is passage of strong stress waves through an highly localized, already overpressured fluid compartment in the Paradox Formation which triggered hydraulic fracturing. Petroleum fluids and hydrogen sulfide brines moving into the fissure entrained rock fragments torn from the reservoir and fissure walls. The clasts served as natural proppants which rendered the fissure permeable, allowing for upward circulation of the reducing fluids which caused bleaching that extends into the wall rocks as much as 15 m (50 ft).

Figure 6. Mechanical thickening of the stratigraphic section by imbricated thrust sheets comprised of beds of the Kayenta Formation at the top of the Wingate cliff, oppositely-dipping thrust sheets comprised of the lower Wingate Sandstone at the bottom of the cliff, and considerable ductile thickening of the Wingate Sandstone, Upheaval Dome, Canyonlands, Utah. Notice that the faults bounding the outward-dipping thrusts in the upper part of the cliff and inward-dipping thrusts in the lower part comprise a set of low-angle conjugate shears which yield a horizontal, radially oriented maximum principal stress at this stratigraphic level during deformation. This style of deformation appears to have occurred during the excavation stage as the transient crater opened and these rocks were flowing toward the left. View is of the north wall of Upheaval Canyon, on the west flank of the central peak which lies to the right.

Figure 7. Listric normal fault that carried Navajo and Kayenta strata toward the right into the transient crater as it collapsed during the modification stage, Upheaval Dome, Canyonlands, Utah. The center of the crater is to the right. Notice how the faulting cuts out the upper half of the Wingate section just to the right of center. The same fault passes under the Wingate Sandstone outcrop in the right foreground. This type of mechanical thinning produced the ring syncline around the crater. View is toward the northwest from Holeman basin.

Excavation Structures

There is rapid flow of rock from the point of impact as a transient crater opens. The maximum principal stresses are oriented radially away from the hypocenter. They are near-horizontal in the near-surface rocks, and produce outward thrusting there. Thrust plates having the form of flattened donuts with the impact at their centers expand outward and grow in circumference at near-surface levels as the crater opens. The rocks directly under the impact flow downward thus greatly depressing the floor of the opening transient crater.

Ductile and mechanical thickening structures are preserved in the near-surface strata at Upheaval Dome. Included are outward verging thrust faults, low-angle conjugate shears and ductile thickening of beds, all of which caused the rim of the transient crater to rise. Upheaval Canyon provides beautiful cross-sections through the thickened Kayenta and Wingate strata (figure 6). Conjugate shears and shortening folds of all scales in which the maximum principal stress orientations parallel the flow lines of the outwardly moving rock are common elsewhere in the core.

Modification Structures

Gravity forces dominate during the modification stage when the transient crater collapses and the depressed rocks below the impact flow upward into the transient crater. Projectile fragments and crater material are expelled from the closing transient crater and fall to earth leaving diagnostic, widely distributed residues.

The ejecta from the Upheaval impact eroded long ago (Koeberl and others, 1999) along with the highly shocked, near-surface rocks. In contrast, the structures produced when the crater collapsed and its floor rebounded are the best preserved of the structures because they were the last to be superimposed on the rocks.

Figure 4 is a snapshot of conditions at the end of the modification stage. The most revealing features on this section are the numerous listric normal faults which allowed the rocks along the perimeter of the transient crater to glide inward and upward on the rebounding central peak.

The outer limit of deformation is delimited by the most prominent listric normal faults found at Upheaval Dome. As shown on figure 7, these dip inward and displace younger rocks downward and inward toward the central peak. The stratigraphic section was mechanically thinned around the perimeter of the structure as the hanging wall rocks moved inward. This thinning produced the ring syncline (figure 8). The Navajo Sandstone, the youngest unit now remaining in the crater, is preserved in the syncline.

The inward continuation of the listric normal fault surfaces converge and ramp up on the central peak. The strata carried up onto the central peak dip steeply away from the center. Bedding in the central peak dips more steeply

Figure 8. Profile through the syncline that rings Upheaval Dome as exposed in a tributary on the south side of Upheaval Canyon, Canyonlands, Utah. The center of crater is to the right. The upper cliff is the Navajo Sandstone; the lower cliff the Wingate Sandstone. The right-dipping surfaces in the Wingate cliff to the left of photo center are faults; surfaces in the Kayenta and Navajo strata in the foreground are bedding. The syncline developed as the hanging wall blocks moved toward the right as the transient crater collapsed during the modification stage.

Figure 9. Outward-plunging radial synclines at the base of the Wingate cliff which are underlain by a listric normal fault that separates the Wingate Sandstone and some Chinle shales caught in the core of the fold from the almost flat-lying Chinle Formation below, Upheaval Dome, Canyonlands, Utah. The folds developed as the circumference of the hanging wall block - a donut-shaped ring - contracted as the rocks moved radially into the crater during the modification stage. View looking outward from the center of the crater toward the northwest.

than the faults so even there the faults cut down section. The central peak was simultaneously rising at the time these faults were active, so the dips of the fault surfaces on the central peak became progressively exaggerated as rebound continued.

The outward dips of the strata in the central peak increase toward the hypocenter, and stand vertical or even slightly overturned under it. The erosionally resistant White Rim Sandstone near the center of the crater juts almost vertically above its surroundings forming a discontinuous crown which surrounds the eroded core comprised of Organ Rock Shale.

The circular profile provided by the inward-facing Wingate cliff is deformed by a series of radiating, outwardly plunging anticlines (figure 9). The boundary between the folded Wingate Sandstone and the less deformed underlying Chinle shales is a listric normal fault along which the Wingate Sandstone moved toward the center. The radial anticlines in the Wingate Sandstone formed as space problems developed in the shrinking ring-shaped hanging wall block as it glided toward and contracted around the central peak. Shortening of its circumference was largely accommodated by the radial folds in the Wingate Sandstone. Additional shortening occurred along sets of minor conjugate thrust faults whose intersections also radiate from the center. The orientation of the maximum principal stress in the contracting donut, as deduced from the radial anticlines and accompanying minor conjugate thrusts, was horizontal and parallel to the circumference of the crater.

Figure 10. View toward the center of the crater of numerous listric normal faults (modification stage) and possibly some thrust faults (excavation stage) in the upper part of the Wingate cliff in the east wall of Syncline valley, Upheaval Dome, Canyonlands, Utah. Layering is bedding; numerous discontinuities are fault surfaces. The relative motion of the hanging wall rocks was either away from or toward the viewer depending on whether the fault was active during the modification or excavation stage.

Some of the listric normal faults on figure 4 first functioned during the excavation stage as thrust faults that allowed the hanging wall rocks to move out of the transient crater. They were reactivated in an opposite sense during the modification stage when the crater collapsed (figure 10).

AGE

The age of Upheaval Dome has not been determined definitively yet. The problem is that the crater is deeply eroded so crucial stratigraphic information is missing. One certainty is that the crater is younger than the Jurassic Navajo Sandstone which was deformed by the impact and is the youngest unit exposed in the vicinity.

Alvarez and others (1998) propose a cause and effect linkage between the impact and soft-sediment deformation in the Carmel Formation. The Carmel Formation exhibits strange region-wide wavy beds, internal shear discontinuities, sand-filled pipe-like liquefaction structures and other odd features leading to the conclusion that the unit experienced large-magnitude shaking before it became indurated. Thus the impact is viewed as a likely source for the required extreme seismicity giving it a Jurassic age. The nearest outcrops of the Carmel Formation lie 15.2 km (9.5 mi) west and 26.5 km (16.5 mi) north-northeast of the crater.

Accurate dating of the impact will help constrain the original size of the crater. If the impact occurred near the end of Carmel deposition, the 5.5 km (3.4 mi) diameter observed today is but slightly smaller than the original diameter. However, the deformed zone could be substantially larger if the impact occurred later when a considerable thickness of Mesozoic strata covered the site.

WHAT ABOUT SALT DIAPIRISM?

The greatest problem with the salt diapir interpretation for Upheaval Dome turns on the fact that there isn't another diapiric structure like it anywhere within the 40,000 km2 (15,000 mi2) part of the Paradox basin that is underlain by the Pennsylvanian Paradox salt section. To have a structure that is so totally unique defies plausibility because the causative environment is so widespread. There are salt diapirs in the Paradox basin, some rather close to the Upheaval impact, but their morphologies are radically different than that of Upheaval Dome, and their structures are consistent with salt domes found elsewhere in the world.

Eighty-five percent of the Paradox Formation in the Canyonlands area is comprised of thick beds of almost pure halite and potash separated by interbeds of gypsum, limestone, dolomite and shale which account for the remaining 15 percent. The unit reaches 16,000 ft (5,000 m) thick. The salts have been flowing at variable rates since shortly after they were deposited over 300 million years ago, and they are actively flowing today (Huntoon, 1988). The largest structures associated with the flowage are the grand salt anticlines which are the characteristic structure of the Paradox basin (Cater, 1970).

The largest population of salt diapirs in the Paradox basin are those that have risen off the salt bulges which core the salt anticlines. They cause refolding of the axes of the anticlines into strings of domes and basins. The biggest of these is the approximately 3 by 8 km (2 by 5 mi) elliptical Onion Creek diapir along the Cache Valley salt anticline 30 km (19 mi) northeast of Moab where the salt is actively extruding to the land surface (Coleman, 1983; Hudec, 1995). Smaller diapirs are exposed along the Cache Valley anticline north of the Colorado River, and along other salt anticlines such as the Spanish Valley collapsed anticline which trends through Moab.

An odd, second class of salt diapirs consisting of four examples is found where the Paradox salts have pierced the Honaker Trail Formation along the floor of Cataract Canyon. These are small, about 0.5 km (0.3 mi) in diameter or less. They breach the structurally thinned strata under the floor of the canyon where it has been arched up and eroded by the Colorado River during emplacement of the modern gravity tectonic Meander anticline-Needles fault zone complex (Huntoon, 1982).

Diapirs are otherwise uniformly missing in other settings within the Paradox basin; specifically, in the large expanses of rather flat-lying strata between the salt anticlines. Upheaval Dome occurs in one of these otherwise barren areas.

Both classes of proven diapirs exhibit commonalities. (1) Salt is present in the structures. (2) Caprock consisting of the Honaker Trail Formation and the Paradox gypsum, carbonates and clastics remain where the diapirs have breached the surface and been subjected to dissolution. Where dissolved, each cubic meter of caprock represents approximately 6 m^3 of intruded rock. (3) Remnants of the Paradox and Honaker Trail formations are commonly smeared along the diapir-wall rock contacts. (4) All stress indicators exhibit maximum principal stress orientations that are vertical including conjugate shears and kink folds in the domes above the diapirs, in the wall rocks adjacent to the diapirs, and in the salt cores. The stress indicators are most important because they reveal that the causative maximum principal stresses were vertical above and immediately surrounding the diapirs consistent with their gravity tectonic origin. Vertical maximum principal stresses in the diapirs contrast starkly to the sub-horizontal maximum principal stresses associated with the near-surface excavation and modification structures at Upheaval Dome.

Invoking a pinched-off diapir (one in which the salt totally evacuated the structure once it formed) to explain Upheaval Dome is particularly difficult because there is no evidence that salt moved through the core of the structure. Missing is an identifiable throat through which the salt passed even though the exposures of the entire core are exceptional. There are no allochthonous Paradox or Honaker Trail residuals anywhere in the core which would reveal that those rocks passed through. Lastly, there is no bleaching of the reddish-brown Organ Rock Shale in the core despite the fact that such bleaching is prevalent around the known salt diapirs. The bleaching agents are hydrogen-sulfide salt brines and petroleum fluids which are present in the salt section.

MODIFICATION BY SALT FLOWAGE

Has Upheaval Dome been modified by post-impact flowage of Paradox salts into the buried core of the structure? Particularly, has salt flowage caused additional doming within the structure? After all, there is a considerable thickness of Paradox salts in the region.

I have searched for evidence for deformation that could be attribute to post-impact salt flowage but have been unable to identify any. For example, there is no discernable refolding of impact-produced fault surfaces. More importantly, no high-angle conjugate faults have been imprinted on the rocks anywhere within or near the crater. High-angle conjugate faults, particularly ring faults, would reveal even minor amounts of subsequent diapirism.

DISCUSSION

The origin of Upheaval Dome has captured the imagination of every geoscientist who has observed it. Almost everyone who has worked in the area has felt obligated to comment in the literature on at least some aspect of its peculiar form and to speculate on its origin. Disagreement about its origin still prevails, but the list of plausible causative scenarios has converged over the years to two ideas now led by a wave of impactors and a dwindling but vocal core of salt diapirists.

I have come to embrace an impact origin based on the following objective criteria. (1) There isn't a salt diapir anyplace in the vast Paradox basin with a structure remotely similar to Upheaval Dome, although many classical diapirs are present. (2) The structural character of Upheaval Dome is identical to that of proven impact structures, whereas there is no known diapir with its structure. (3) The temporal relationship between different classes of strain features and the strain orientations that can be deduced from them at Upheaval Dome are consistent with the different stages of crater growth, whereas they are inconsistent with those of diapirs. (4) There are no remnants of Paradox or Hermosa strata, some of which are insoluble, either in the core or around Upheaval Dome to reveal that salt moved through the structure. (5) The energies required to produce many of the classes of structures observed in Upheaval Dome, to cause the shattering of sand gains in the clastic dikes in the core of the crater, and to possibly cause the hydraulic fracturing at Roberts rift and the soft-sediment deformation of the Carmel Formation far exceed those available in diapirism.

At this writing Upheaval Dome has not been conclusively proven to be an impact crater to the satisfaction of the last skeptic because the "smoking gun" in the form of an impactor fragment, true shattercone, impactite, melt rock, planar deformation feature, coesite, stishovite, or some such definitive feature remains to be discovered. Ironically, once it is, Upheaval Dome will become the archtype morphological example of a small complex impact crater both here on earth and on nearby solar bodies because it is so well exposed in the three dimensions.

REFERENCES

Alvarez, W., Staley, E., O'Connor, D., and Chan, M.A., 1998, Synsedimentary deformation in the Jurassic of southeastern Utah, a case of impact shaking?: Geology, v. 26, p. 579-582.

Boon, J.D., and Albritton, C.C., Jr., 1936, Meteorite craters and their possible relationship to cryptovolcanic structures: Field and Laboratory, v. 5, p. 1-9.

Bucher, W.H., 1936, Cryptovolcanic structures in the United States: Washington, International Geological Congress, Report of the 16th Session (1933), v. 2, p. 1055-1084.

Cater, F.W., 1970, Geology of the salt anticline region in southwestern Colorado: U.S. Geological Survey Professional Paper 637, 80 p.

Coleman, S.M., 1983, Influences of the Onion Creek diapir on the late Cenozoic history of Fisher valley, southeastern, Utah: Geology, v. 11, p. 240-243.

Fiero, G.W., 1958, Geology of Upheaval Dome, San Juan County, Utah: Laramie, University of Wyoming, M.S. thesis, 87 p.

French, B.M., 1990, Twenty-five years of the impact-volcanic controversy: EOS, v. 71, p. 411-414.

Hartmann, W.K., and Miller, R., 1991, The history of earth, an illustrated chronicle of an evolving planet: New York, Workman Publishing Company, 260 p.

Hite, R.J., 1975, An unusual northeast-trending fracture zone and its relation to basement wrench faulting in northern Paradox basin, Utah and Colorado: Four Corners Geological Society, 8th Field Conference Guidebook, p. 217-223.

Hudec, M.R., 1995, The Onion Creek diapir, an exposed diapir fall structure in the Paradox basin, Utah, *in* Travis, C.J., Harrison, H., Hudec, M.R., Vendeville, B.C., Peel, F.J., and Perkins, B.F., editors, Salt sediment and hydrocarbons: Houston, Gulf Coast Section of the Society of Economic Paleontologists and Mineralogists Foundation, 16th Annual Research Conference, p. 125-134.

Huntoon, P.W., 1982, The Meander anticline, Canyonlands, Utah, an unloading structure resulting from horizontal gliding on salt: Geological Society of America Bulletin, v. 93, p. 941-950.

—1988, Late Cenozoic gravity tectonic deformation related to the Paradox salts in the Canyonlands area of Utah, *in* Doelling, H.H., Oviatt, C.G., and Huntoon, P.W., editors, Salt deformation in the Paradox region: Utah Geological and Mineral Survey Bulletin 122, p. 79-93.

Huntoon, P.W., and Shoemaker, E.M., 1995, Roberts rift, Canyonlands, Utah, a natural hydraulic fracture caused by comet or asteroid impact: Ground Water, v. 33, p. 561-569.

Jackson, M.P.A., Schultz-Ela, D.D., Hudec, M.R., Watson,

I.A., and Porter, M.L., 1998, Structure and evolution of Upheaval Dome, a pinched-off salt diapir: Geological Society of America Bulletin, v. 110, p. 1547-1573.

Joesting, H.R., and Plouff, D., 1958, Geophysical studies of the Upheaval Dome area, San Juan County, Utah: Intermountain Association of Petroleum Geologists, 9th Annual Field Conference Guidebook, p. 86-92.

Kriens, B.J., Shoemaker, E.M., and Herkenhoff, K.E., 1999, Geology of the Upheaval Dome impact structure, southeast Utah: Journal of Geophysical Research, v. 104, p. 18867-18887.

Koeberl, C., Plescia, J.B., Hayward, C.L., and Reimold, W.U., 1999, A Petrographical and geochemical study of quartzose nodules, country rocks, and dike rocks from the Upheaval Dome structure, Utah: Meteoritics and Planetary Science, v. 34, p. 861-868.

Kopf, R.W., 1982, Hydrotectonics, principles and relevance: U.S. Geological Survey Open-File Report 82-307, 13 p.

Mattox, R.B., 1968, Upheaval Dome, a possible salt dome in the Paradox basin, Utah, *in* Mattox, R.B., editor, Saline deposits: Geological Society of America Special Paper 88, p. 331-347.

McKnight, E.T., 1940, Geology of area between Green and Colorado Rivers, Grand and San Juan Counties, Utah: U.S. Geological Survey Bulletin 908, 147 p.

Melosh, H.J., 1989, Impact cratering, a geologic process: New York, Oxford University Press, 245 p.

Shoemaker, E.M., 1963, Impact mechanics at Meteor crater, Arizona, *in* Middlehurst, B.M., and Kuiper, G.P., editors, The solar system, v. 4: Chicago, University of Chicago Press, p. 301-336.

Shoemaker, E.M., and Herkenhoff, K.E., 1984, Upheaval Dome impact structure [abs.]: Lunar and Planetary Science 15th Lunar and Planetary Science Conference, part 2, p. 778-779.

Shoemaker, E.M., Herkenhoff, K.E., and Gostin, V.A., 1993, Impact origin of Upheaval Dome, Utah [abs.]: EOS, v. 74, p. 388.

Woodward-Clyde Consultants, 1983, Overview of the regional geology of the Paradox basin study region: Columbus, Office of Nuclear Waste Isolation, Battelle Memorial Institute, consultants report ONWI-92, 433 p.

Geology of Utah's Parks and Monuments
2000 Utah Geological Association Publication 28
D.A. Sprinkel, T.C. Chidsey, Jr., and P.B. Anderson, editors

The Cockscomb Segment of the East Kaibab Monocline: Taking the Structural Plunge

Sarah E. Tindall[1]

ABSTRACT

The East Kaibab monocline in northern Arizona and southern Utah is a north- to northeast-trending fold in Paleozoic and Mesozoic sedimentary rocks on the eastern margin of the Kaibab uplift. The east-dipping monoclinal fold developed above a west-dipping fault in underlying Precambrian basement rocks between 80-50 million years ago (Ma). Erosion has since carved the monocline into a narrow series of ridges and valleys of colorful, candy-striped layers of rock, the most spectacular of which lie in Grand Staircase-Escalante National Monument.

A sequence of processes including folding, fault growth, uplift, and erosion formed the breathtaking and variable landscapes visible along this 'Cockscomb,' and left clues helpful to unraveling the three dimensional geometry and growth history of the monocline. The fold plunges gently to the north, exposing different stratigraphic levels, fault patterns, degrees of folding, and topographic and structural relief along its surface trace. Some of the changes in surface geology indicate variations in fault and fold geometry at depth, but some simply reflect the effects of erosion and exposure level. Analysis of these characteristics based on map relationships and field observations leads to the conclusion that the East Kaibab monocline formed by gradual upward propagation of a basement-rooted oblique-reverse fault, and its associated 'fault tip fracture zone,' within the core of the growing fold. This paper describes visualization techniques, conceptual models, and geological arguments that support an oblique-reverse fault-propagation-fold interpretation of the Cockscomb segment of the East Kaibab monocline.

INTRODUCTION

The Cockscomb in Grand Staircase-Escalante National Monument is one of the most spectacular geologic features of the Colorado Plateau, and the elegant details of its structural growth through time are exposed in outcrops stretching from the Grand Canyon in northern Arizona to Table Cliff Plateau in Utah. The steeply inclined, candy-striped layers of rock along the Cockscomb are part of an abrupt fold, the East Kaibab monocline, that interrupts the otherwise flat-lying sedimentary rock sequence (figure 1). Changes in the form of the fold and the surface fault pattern along its 60 km trace in southern Utah are evidence of the changing character of the underlying fault and fault-fold relationships. Subtle differences in the stratigraphy and structural geology exposed at the surface are clues to the complicated interactions among folding, faulting, uplift, and erosion that created this stunning geologic feature.

Early explorers in the Grand Canyon area described the region's monoclines and speculated that they formed by simple bending of sedimentary strata over differentially uplifted basement blocks (Dutton, 1882; Powell, 1873) (figure 2). This kinematically simple explanation is sufficient to describe the form of the Cockscomb at any one location, but differences in the surface expression of the monocline along its northeast-southwest trend are the result of more complicated processes. Tindall and Davis (1999) presented quantitative data and analyses to demonstrate that the Utah segment of the fold formed by oblique motion (a combination of strike-slip and reverse-slip offset) on the underlying basement fault, and propagation of oblique faulting into high structural and stratigraphic levels of the fold during its growth. In fact, the map pattern of the Cockscomb itself exposes equally compelling evidence for this interpretation when certain concepts of structural geology and geologic map interpretation are applied.

Because development of the Cockscomb involved interaction of many processes, understanding the structure's complexity requires incorporation of a number of tech-

[1]*Department of Geosciences, University of Arizona, Tucson, AZ 85721*

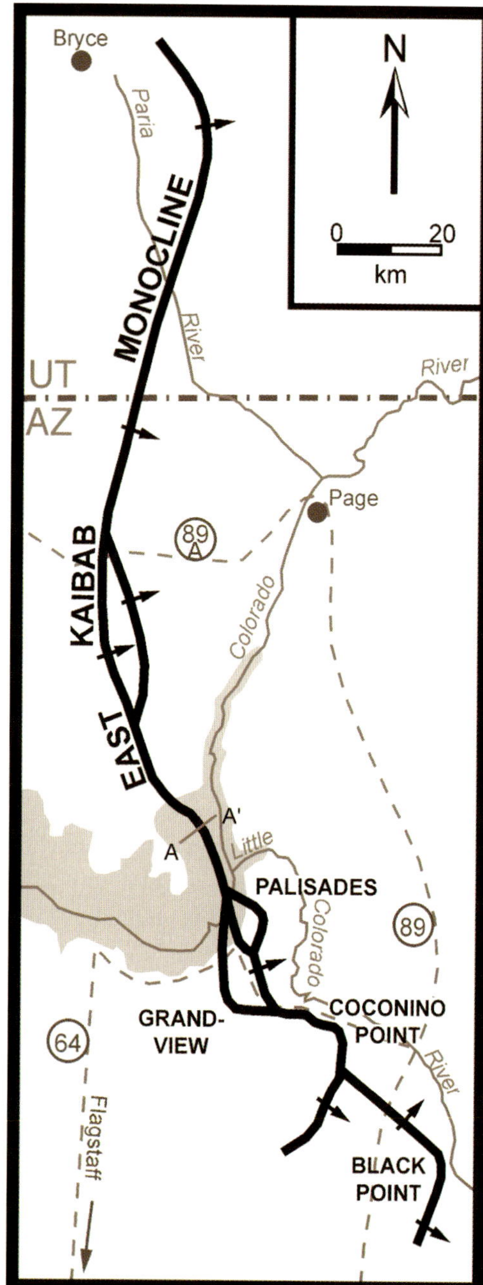

Figure 1. Location of the East Kaibab monocline and its branching segments (Palisades, Grandview, Coconino, Black Point) in northern Arizona and southern Utah. Shaded area is the Grand Canyon. Line A-A' shows the location of the cross section in figure 5.

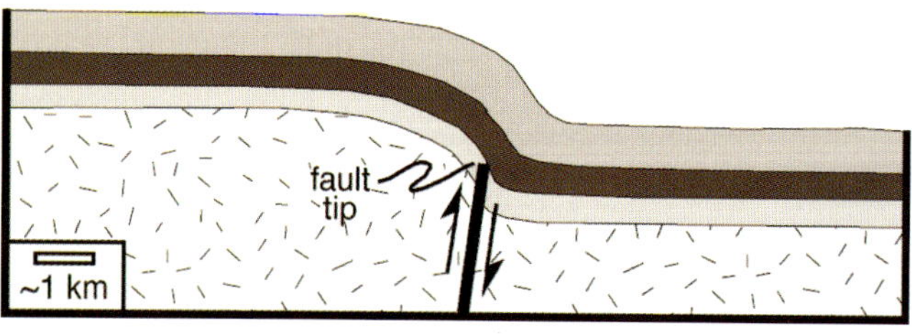

Figure 2. Simple cross section sketch of a Colorado Plateau monocline. Basement faulting at depth has caused folding of overlying sedimentary strata.

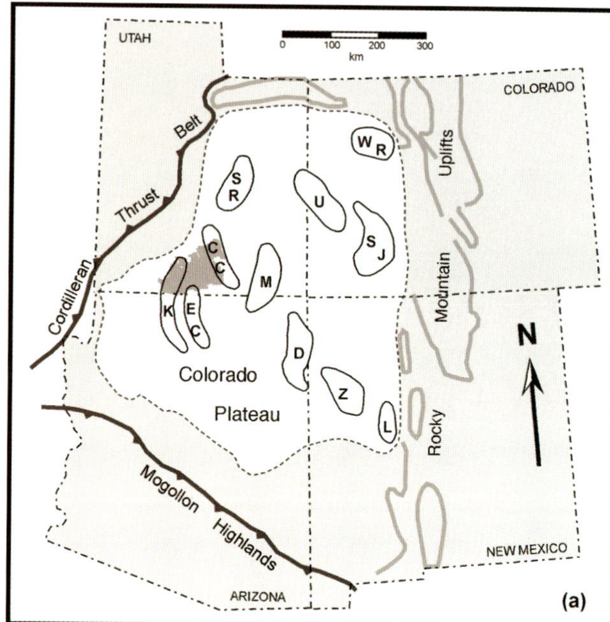

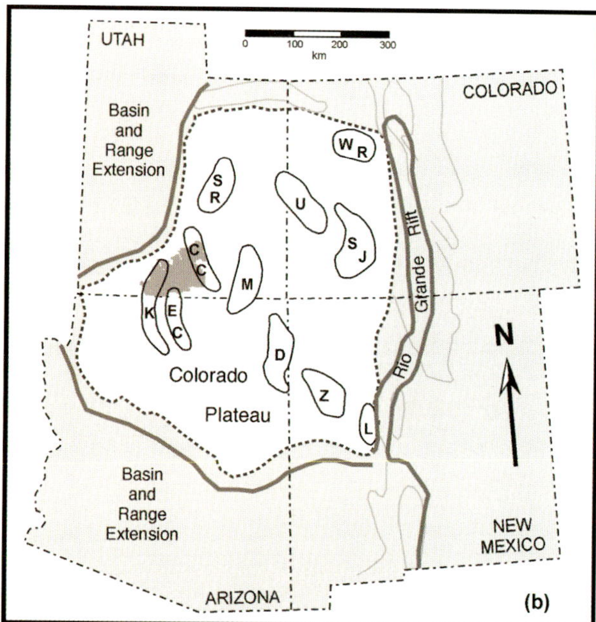

Figure 3. Regional maps of Mesozoic and Cenozoic structures of the Colorado Plateau and surrounding geographic provinces. Shaded area on the Colorado Plateau is Grand Staircase-Escalante National Monument. Deformation of the Plateau region has been minimal compared to that in surrounding areas throughout Phanerozoic time, for reasons that are still poorly understood. 3(a). Mesozoic and early Tertiary compressional tectonic events caused uplift of the Cordilleran thrust belt and Mogollon highlands on the west and southwest edges of the Colorado Plateau, and formation of enormous Rocky Mountain uplifts to the north and east. Deformation affected the Colorado Plateau region only mildly, resulting in broad, low uplifts bounded by monoclinal folds. Colorado Plateau uplifts include the Circle Cliffs (CC), Defiance (D), Echo Cliffs (EC), Kaibab (K), Lucero (L), Monument (M), San Juan (SJ), San Rafael (SR), Uncompahgre (U), White River (WR), and Zuni (Z). 3(b). More recently, Tertiary and Quaternary extension of the western United States has dissected the Cordilleran thrust belt, Mogollon highlands, and Rocky Mountain uplifts to form the modern Basin and Range and Rio Grande Rift. The Colorado Plateau remains largely unaffected by recent extensional tectonics.

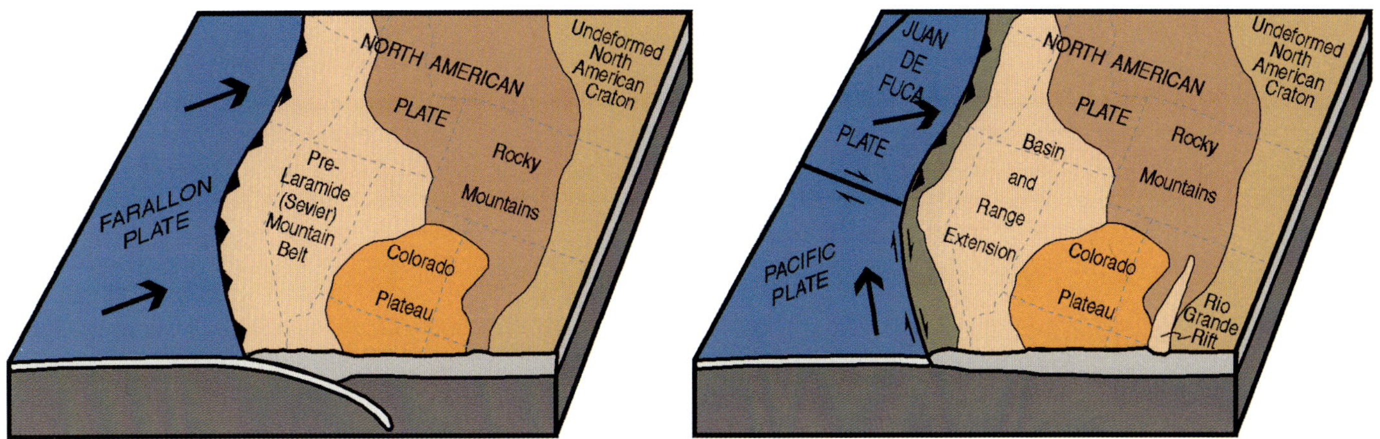

Figure 4. (a) Simple sketch of the plate tectonic setting of western North America during the Laramide orogeny (80-40 Ma). Shallow-angle subduction of the Farallon Plate beneath the North American plate transmitted horizontal compressive stress thousands of kilometers eastward into continental North America, forming the Rocky Mountain uplifts. The Colorado Plateau was only slightly affected by Laramide deformation. (b) After the end of Laramide subduction, a right-lateral transform boundary developed between the North American and Pacific plates (the San Andreas fault). Areas previously subjected to compressive stress began to collapse due to gravitational forces and crustal extension, forming the Basin and Range province and Rio Grande Rift, and dissecting the Rocky Mountain uplifts. The Colorado Plateau remains relatively unaffected by recent extensional tectonics. For the sake of simplicity, tectonic provinces far from the Colorado Plateau (for example the Cascade Mountains, Columbia Plateau, Coast Ranges) are not shown.

niques and ideas. Structural geologists use maps and measurements of folds, fractures and rock types exposed at the Earth's surface to build a thorough understanding of the three dimensional geometry of rock units both buried beneath the surface and removed by erosion from above. This task comes naturally to some geologists accustomed to filling in the missing puzzle pieces through application of concepts derived from simplified models of geologic structures. However, even under the best circumstances some important map clues are easy to overlook. This paper describes the changes in surface expression of the East Kaibab monocline north of the Grand Canyon, and presents models and diagrams of basic structural concepts as a tutorial for interpreting the three dimensional geometry of the Cockscomb in Grand Staircase-Escalante National Monument.

BACKGROUND

Regional Setting

The Colorado Plateau geographic province of the western United States occupies parts of Utah, Arizona, New Mexico, and Colorado. It is a region of relatively undeformed Phanerozoic sedimentary rocks surrounded by highly deformed rocks of adjacent tectonic provinces — the Rio Grande Rift on the east, Rocky Mountains on the east and north, and the Basin and Range province on the west and south (figure 3). The Rocky Mountains are an expression of the Laramide tectonic event that affected western North America approximately 80-40 Ma (Brown, 1988). This mountain building event was driven by east-directed subduction of the Farallon tectonic plate (ancient floor of

the Pacific ocean) beneath the western margin of North America (figure 4). Interaction of the Farallon and North American plates transmitted horizontal compressive stress thousands of kilometers eastward into the North American continent (Coney, 1976). Compression caused differential uplift of crystalline basement blocks and overlying sedimentary rocks on the east and north sides of the relatively rigid Colorado Plateau, and formed a belt of folded and thrusted sedimentary rocks to the west and south of the Plateau. More recently, extensional tectonics and crustal thinning affected the regions that were previously compressed and uplifted; tensional forces dissected the Rocky Mountain uplifts and formed the distinctive Rio Grande Rift and Basin and Range extensional provinces (Windley, 1995) (figure 4). Thinning of the crust began soon after the end of Laramide subduction and is still active in the Basin and Range and Rio Grande Rift today (Wernicke, 1992). Given the intense tectonic deformation expressed in rocks of these bordering regions, it is remarkable that the sedimentary rock layers of the Colorado Plateau have remained so undeformed. Within the Colorado Plateau, the effect of Laramide deformation is expressed in the landscape by broad, low uplifts separated from vast shallow basins by erosional cliffs or low-amplitude folds in Paleozoic and Mesozoic sedimentary rocks, and evidence of recent extension is almost entirely absent.

The Cockscomb

The Kaibab uplift in northern Arizona and southern Utah and its steep eastern limb, the East Kaibab monocline, are examples of Colorado Plateau structures formed during the Laramide orogeny. The landscape expression of the northern part of the East Kaibab monocline is often called the Cockscomb because erosion of the steep, east-dipping sedimentary layers has exposed strike-parallel ridges of near-vertical red and white rock that resemble a rooster's comb. The most visually stunning parts of the Cockscomb lie in Grand Staircase-Escalante National Monument, extending from near Kodachrome Basin State Park in Utah to the Arizona-Utah border. This stretch coincides with the area of greatest structural relief (vertical separation between anticlinal hinge and synclinal trough), ranging from 1,200 m to 1,600 m in most of the Monument. The East Kaibab monocline actually continues southward into Arizona and across the Grand Canyon to near Flagstaff, bifurcating in places to form several branching segments (for example the Grandview, Palisades, Coconino, and Black Point segments) (figure 1). Structural offset decreases southward from the Monument to 800 m in the Grand Canyon, 700 m at Coconino Point, and 150 - 300 m along the Black Point segment (Babenroth and Strahler, 1945). The total trace length of the monocline is approximately 240 km, making it one of the largest of the monoclines on the Colorado Plateau (Reches, 1978).

Structural Roots

The East Kaibab is one of the best studied of the Colorado Plateau monoclines, in part for its enormous trace length and considerable vertical offset. Perhaps more importantly, the Grand Canyon offers a deep cross-sectional exposure that reveals the nature of deformation in Paleozoic and underlying Precambrian rocks. This cross-sectional exposure reveals that a steep (60°-70°) west-dipping fault zone in Precambrian basement rocks, the Butte fault, underlies the folded Paleozoic and Mesozoic rocks that

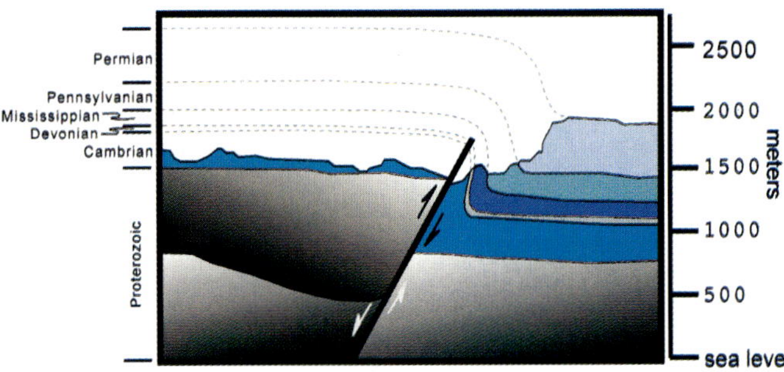

Figure 5. Cross section showing East Kaibab monocline fault-fold relationships in the Grand Canyon. A west-dipping fault in Precambrian and lower Paleozoic rocks underlies the east-dipping monoclinal fold in upper Paleozoic strata. Dashed lines represent Paleozoic rocks that have been removed by erosion. Overlying Mesozoic rocks also have been stripped away by erosion. Note that the lowest Precambrian layer shows normal (west side down) offset, indicated by white arrows. Normal faulting occurred before deposition of Paleozoic sedimentary rocks. After deposition of the Paleozoic and Mesozoic sedimentary section, reverse movement along the same fault (black arrows) formed the East Kaibab monocline. The magnitude of reverse offset must have been smaller than the magnitude of ancient normal offset, since normal separation is still preserved at the Precambrian level. Cross section location is shown on figure 1.

constitute the East Kaibab monocline (figure 5). West-side-down stratigraphic offsets in the Precambrian sedimentary sequence of the Grand Canyon Supergroup show that the Butte fault first became active in Precambrian time, long before the deposition of Paleozoic and Mesozoic sediments that now make up the Cockscomb (Walcott, 1890; Maxson, 1961; Huntoon, 1969, 1993; Huntoon and Sears, 1975). Beginning at ~600 Ma (Bond, 1997; Timmons and others, in press) Paleozoic and Mesozoic sediments accumulated to a thickness of at least 3,500-4,000 m during a time of tectonic quiescence (Hintze, 1988). Laramide compression initiated at about 80 Ma in this region and reactivated the ancient 'basement' fault, causing the west side to move up relative to the east. Over millions of years the gradual, earthquake-by-earthquake fault movement at depth formed the broad, asymmetrical Kaibab uplift and East Kaibab monocline in the overlying Paleozoic and Mesozoic cover (Huntoon and Sears, 1975; Huntoon, 1993). Although the Grand Canyon provides the only exposure of the basement fault underlying the East Kaibab monocline, the fault (or a network of similar faults) is assumed to underlie the fold for its entire length (Davis, 1978; Stern, 1992; Rosnovsky, 1998). This exposure and other Grand Canyon exposures of fault-cored monoclines (for example the Palisades Branch, Grandview, and Hurricane) are the basis for the widely accepted assumption that similar reactivated basement faults underlie other Colorado Plateau uplifts.

A VISUAL TOUR

Both early and more recent studies of the East Kaibab monocline have focused on outcrops in and near the Grand Canyon because of their spectacular exposure of the underlying basement fault. Although the Grand Canyon outcrops have helped build a basic understanding of the deep structure associated with the Kaibab uplift, they offer only a limited view of the changes in structural character along the trend of the East Kaibab monocline. That is, the deep Grand Canyon outcrops offer only one perspective in one location along the 240-km fold. Outside the walls of the Grand Canyon the gradual changes in rock types, topography, and scenery along the Cockscomb offer additional evidence for the changing structural geometry of the fold at the surface and at depth. This evidence does not contradict basic models of monocline development, but rather adds an appreciation for the complexity of these regionally significant features.

Systematic variations in stratigraphy and structural style along the Cockscomb in northern Arizona and southern Utah provide the observations necessary for interpreting the growth history of the East Kaibab monocline. Both obvious and subtle features in the photographs of figure 6 contain clues for deciphering underlying structural relationships. Figure 6a begins the visual tour at the bottom of the Grand Canyon where the steep, west-dipping Butte fault juxtaposes Proterozoic sedimentary rocks (right side) and volcanics (left side). At this location the folded Paleo-

Figure 6. North-directed photographs of the variable landscape, stratigraphy, and geologic exposures along the Cockscomb from the Grand Canyon to Table Cliff Plateau. Photographs 6a through 6h progress from south to north; locations are shown on an oblique perspective map of the Kaibab uplift. Interesting features of each photograph are discussed in the text.

zoic and Mesozoic rocks of the Cockscomb have been stripped away by erosion along the Colorado River (see figure 7 for stratigraphy). However, the overlying strata are preserved nearby in tributaries of the Grand Canyon, as shown in figure 6b. There the west-dipping fault terminates beneath the surface, but its west-side-up offset has generated an east-dipping monoclinal fold in Mississippian Redwall Limestone. Together, views 6a and 6b (figure 6) show that fault offset changes to fold-accommodated offset low in the Paleozoic stratigraphic section in the Grand Canyon. The point at which the discrete fault plane or fault zone disappears upward into folded strata is known as the fault tip (figure 2). At the location of photograph 6b, the tip of the Butte fault propagated upward through the stratigraphic section only to the level of Mississippian rocks before Laramide deformation ended.

At the stratigraphic level of upper Paleozoic rocks, House Rock Valley stretches from the north rim of the Grand Canyon northward toward the Arizona-Utah border (figure 6c). East-dipping Kaibab Limestone forms the western slope of the valley, and the flat-lying, red Moenave and Kayenta Formations compose the Vermilion Cliffs to the east. It is possible to imagine that folded, east-dipping Moenave and Kayenta Formations capped the east-dipping slope of the Kaibab uplift millions of years ago, as the Kaibab Limestone does today, but their folded and faulted layers along the crest and in the steep limb of the monocline have since been removed by erosion. The yellowish beds of Kaibab Limestone in the foreground dip gently to the east, parallel to the present edge of the Kaibab uplift in the background. Sediments on the floor of House Rock Valley obscure east-dipping Triassic strata in the synclinal hinge of the monocline.

Figure 6d is a view of the Cockscomb near the Arizona-Utah border. Brick red and grey strata (left center) belong to the Triassic Moenkopi Formation, and the brighter red rocks on the right side are Triassic-Jurassic Moenave and Kayenta Formations. Erosion has not dissected the monocline as deeply here, so that folded Kayenta and Moenave are preserved in the steep limb. The purplish unit in the right center is a narrow, fault-bounded sliver of Triassic Chinle Formation (faults are not obvious in this picture). From area 6c to 6d (figure 6), two obvious changes have occurred in the landscape. First, the steep limb of the fold is exposed in higher stratigraphic units at the location of figure 6d; that is, Moenave and Kayenta Formations are involved in the monoclinal fold at 6d (figure 6), but these were flat-lying on the east side of the fold at 6c (figure 6). Secondly, the dip of strata in the east-dipping monoclinal limb is much steeper at 6d than at 6c (figure 6); this reflects the gradual increase in structural relief between the two photo locations.

In figure 6e, just southeast of Paria, steeply dipping Jurassic Carmel and Entrada Formations mark the continued up-section exposure of deformation toward the north. To the northeast, in the right-hand background of the photograph, flat-lying Cretaceous rocks (Tropic and Straight

Cliffs formations) compose the high cliffs. The topographic expression of the cliffs is the result of erosion by the Paria River, which flows nearby in the synclinal trough of the East Kaibab monocline. Like the cliffs of flat-lying Moenave and Kayenta Formations in figure 6c, erosion has removed the folded and deformed portion of the Cretaceous strata from the crest of the monocline here, leaving eastward-receding cliffs of undeformed rock.

Where the Paria River crosses the steep limb of the Cockscomb, the canyon mouth exposes a west-dipping reverse fault in Navajo and Carmel Formations (figure 6f). Fault movement has placed a stratigraphically lower sandstone layer (white, left side) above stratigraphically higher Carmel Formation redbeds (right side). The fault is approximately parallel to the trend of the monocline, dips steeply west, and displays a west-side-up sense of offset, similar to but much smaller than the basement fault exposed in the Grand Canyon. Several west-dipping reverse faults are exposed along the monocline in the vicinity of figure 6f.

Still farther north, as shown by figure 6g, tan and grey stripes of Cretaceous Dakota, Tropic, and Straight Cliffs Formations are preserved in the steep fold limb. In the background, white Navajo Sandstone occupies the crest of the monocline, dipping less steeply than the Cretaceous rocks in the foreground. Finally, figure 6h is an oblique aerial photograph of the northern end of the East Kaibab monocline. Flat-lying, white Navajo Sandstone forms the crest of the monocline on the west, and flat-lying Cretaceous strata of the Kaiparowits basin make up the desolate landscape on the east. Northward along the fold, dips gradually die out until the monocline disappears near Table Cliff Plateau (barely visible in the left background).

The photographs in figure 6 offer a representative sample of the changes in scenery, stratigraphy, fold form, and fault expression visible in different areas along the Cockscomb. These changes present clues about the geometry of the Cockscomb at depth, and how this geometry changes both vertically (with depth) and horizontally (along the monocline). Surface evidence can be integrated through the use of geologic maps, visualization techniques, and conceptual models in order to decipher the three dimensional geometry and growth stages of the Cockscomb.

STRUCTURAL OBSERVATIONS

The northward changes in landscape along the Cockscomb in southern Utah correspond to structural patterns and stratigraphic clues in the geologic map (figure 7). Understanding the structural implications of the map-view expression of the Cockscomb requires several conceptual tools. These include geometry of plunging folds, down-plunge viewing, Riedel fracture development, fault-slip gradient, and fault-propagation folding. The following sections contain a general description of each concept, and application of the concepts to interpreting patterns of faulting and folding exposed along the Cockscomb.

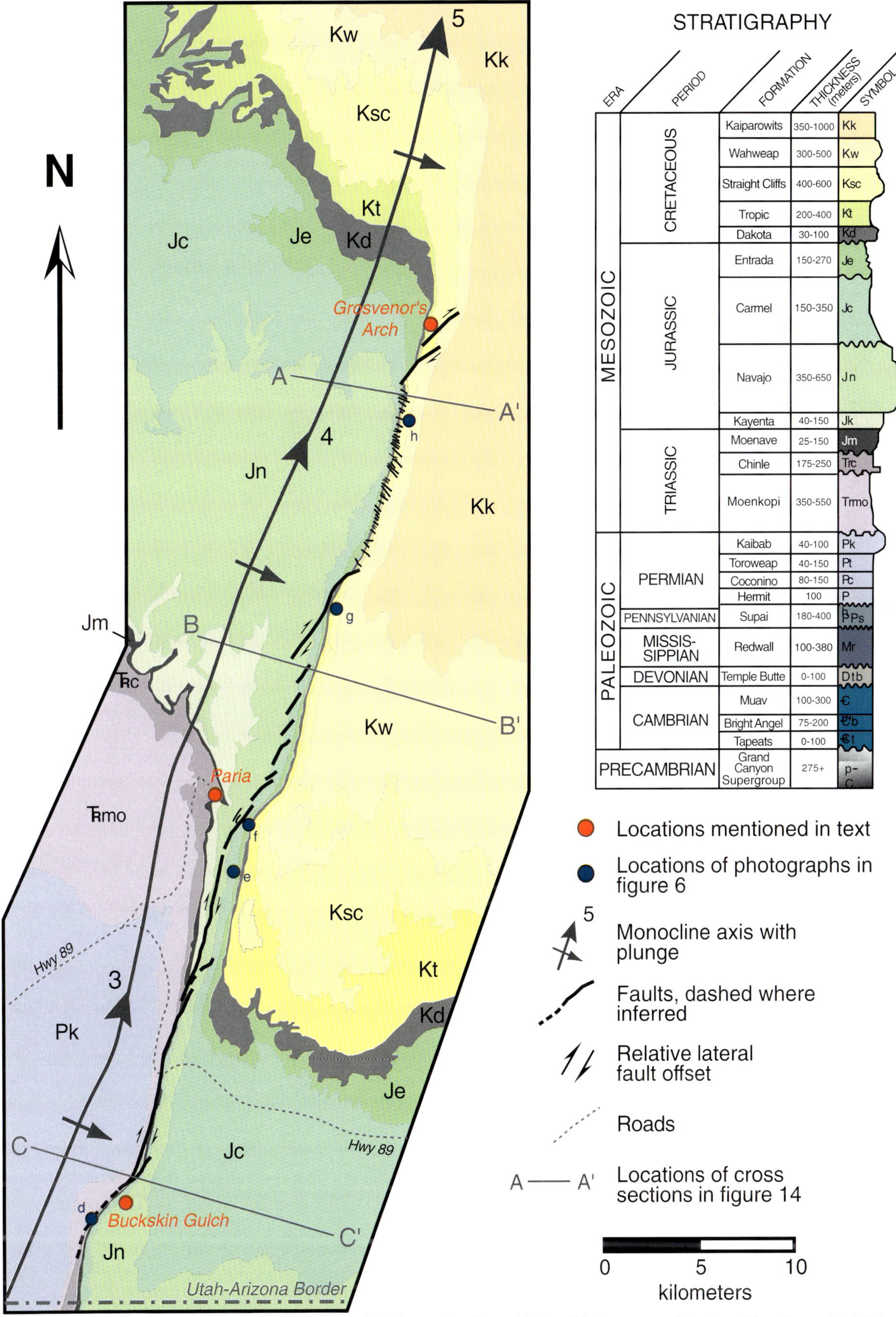

Figure 7. Geologic map of the East Kaibab monocline in Grand Staircase-Escalante National Monument. Stratigraphic column (right) includes Precambrian and Paleozoic rocks that are not exposed in the monument but are visible in the Grand Canyon. Cross sections A-A', B-B', and C-C' refer to figure 14.

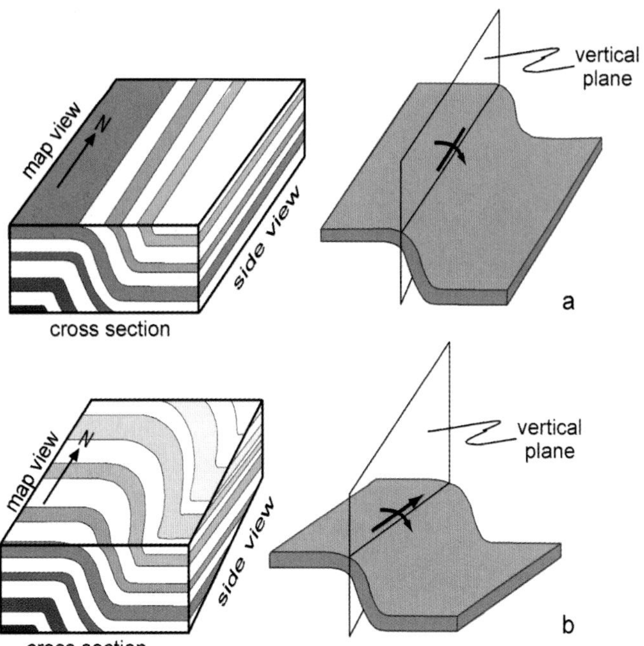

Figure 8. Diagrams of monoclinal folds with horizontal (a) and plunging (b) fold axes. Note that a monocline with a horizontal fold axis would expose the same stratigraphic units along its trend in a horizontal map view. In this non-plunging fold, a single bed intersects a hypothetical vertical plane along a horizontal line - - a horizontal fold axis. On the other hand, the plunging fold exposes progressively younger stratigraphic layers at the surface in the down-plunge direction. The stratigraphic sequence of layers can be seen in the front and side views of the block diagram. In this case, a single bed intersects an imaginary vertical plane along a line that plunges away from the viewer — a plunging fold axis.

Northward Plunge

When leveled off by erosion, the geometry of a plunging fold creates interesting geometric forms in horizontal map-view exposures. Figure 8 presents two schematic block diagrams of north-trending, east-vergent monoclinal flexures. The similarity in fold form is obvious in the cross-section view of each diagram. Note that in the side view of the block in figure 8a the sedimentary layers are flat-lying where not involved in the steep limb of the monoclinal flexure. This pattern is typical of folds that have horizontal fold axes. In figure 8b the side view shows that sedimentary layers dip toward the north, reflecting the fact that the fold axis plunges north. This northward plunge produces a very different pattern in horizontal map view (representing the eroded ground surface) compared with the pattern created by erosion of a non-plunging fold. In the map view of the plunging structure (figure 8b) older stratigraphic layers (lower in the vertical cross section) are exposed up-plunge, toward the south; in the non-plunging example (figure 8a) the same stratigraphic units are exposed along the entire length of the structure. As a result, the map view of a plunging fold (like figure 8b) resembles a distorted version of the cross section, and therefore contains information about structural geometry

at depth.

In southern Utah the East Kaibab monocline plunges gently (3°-5°) northward, exposing structural relationships in map view that relate to fold and fault geometry below the surface. The horizontal map view displays progressively lower stratigraphic and structural levels toward the south: Cretaceous rocks are folded in the steep limb near Grosvenor's Arch, giving way southward to Jurassic and Triassic rocks at Paria, and eventually Permian rocks near Buckskin Gulch (figure 7). This map pattern is a natural consequence of the northward plunge, and is ideal for down-plunge viewing.

Down-Plunge Viewing

Geologists use the down-plunge view technique to synthesize complicated map relationships into meaningful cross sections (Mackin, 1959). As described in the previous section, the map view of a plunging fold exposes an elongated but distorted view of fold geometry. Down-plunge viewing creates 'foreshortening' of the plunging map view, thus removing distortions imposed by the elongated horizontal perspective. The end product can be a properly scaled and accurate structural cross section based on map relationships rather than on speculation.

Figure 9 depicts application of the down-plunge viewing strategy to the map of the East Kaibab monocline. Map data from figure 7 indicate that the fold axis plunges about 5° to the north. Placing the map flat on a table and looking at it from 5° above the horizon creates a profile view of the structure (a cross section perpendicular to the fold axis). This perspective visually foreshortens the map view to create an apparent cross section of structural relationships at the level of strata shown on the map.

An accurate profile view of the Cockscomb results from applying the down-plunge viewing technique to the full map in figure 7. (Small irregularities of the lithologic contacts in the map view are caused by topography, and should be smoothed when visualizing the down-plunge cross section.) The down-plunge view reveals an abrupt monoclinal fold separating otherwise flat-lying strata, and a narrow zone of faults within the steep limb. However, an accurate cross section does not always provide the most informative view of a structure. Because the Kaibab uplift plunges at such a low angle, down-plunge viewing turns the 9-inch-long structural map into a cross section less than one inch high. The down-plunge view effectively blurs and obscures structural relationships that are only visible in the elongated and distorted map view. For example, the individual small fractures along the steep limb of the monocline visible in the plunging map view of figure 7 would not be evident in an actual vertical exposure like the Grand Canyon, or in a map view that exposed only a single structural level. With careful measurement and observation, and an understanding of shear fracture geometry, these details reveal more about lateral structural changes along the Cockscomb than does the down-plunge view.

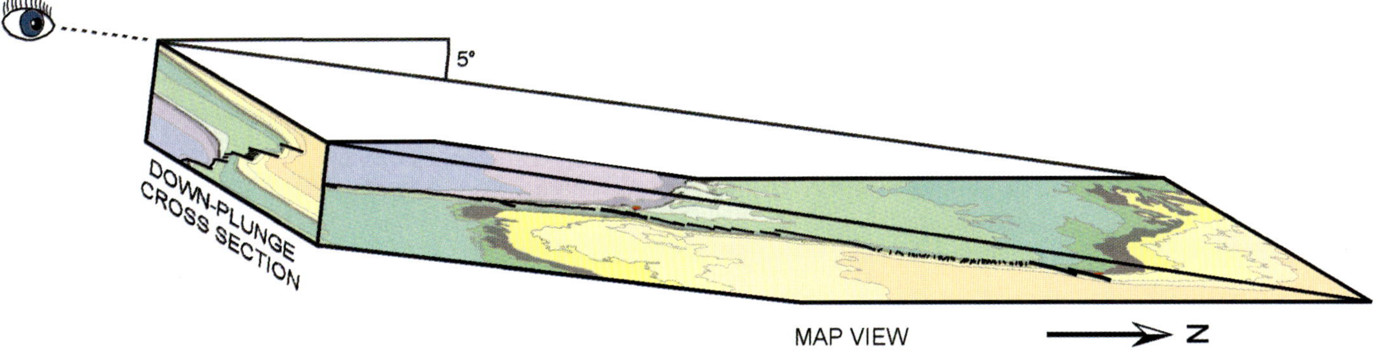

Figure 9. Down-plunge viewing involves looking at a geologic map of a plunging structure parallel to the plunge axis in order to see an accurate cross section view of structural relationships.

Fault-Tip Zone

Erosion of the Kaibab uplift to the level of the Mesozoic rocks in Grand Staircase-Escalante National Monument has exposed a monocline-parallel pattern of dense fracturing at the surface. Because the monocline plunges north the fault pattern, like the pattern of sedimentary rock layers, presents progressively deeper structural levels toward the south. Examination of the changes in fault orientations from south to north reveals a spatial and temporal sequence of fault development from deeper to shallower levels in the core of the monocline.

As shown in figure 7, faults south of Paria have long, continuous traces parallel to the surface trend of the fold. These faults accommodate apparent right lateral offset, shown by truncation and displacement of Chinle, Moenave, and Kayenta Formations. Between Paria and Pump Canyon Spring the continuous, monocline-parallel fault trace gives way to a disjointed series of faults that show right-lateral separation of Navajo and Carmel Formations. These are 'synthetic' faults because their apparent sense of offset is the same as that on the long, continuous faults farther south. The left-stepping, en-echelon synthetic faults strike about 20° clockwise from the trend of the monocline, but define a monocline-parallel zone of deformation. Between Pump Canyon Spring and Grosvenor's Arch the fault pattern consists of short, northwest-striking faults with apparent left-lateral offsets in Entrada, Dakota, and Tropic Formations. The left-lateral offset on these faults is antithetic to the sense of offset on the continuous fault surfaces south of Paria. North of Grosvenor's Arch the monocline-parallel fault zone disappears, indicating that deformation north of that location was accommodated entirely by folding rather than by a combination of folding and faulting.

The changing fault pattern along the East Kaibab monocline may represent the sequence of secondary fault development in a narrow zone of intense deformation directly ahead of the upward-propagating basement-rooted fault tip. A similar sequence of secondary fault growth has been observed in physical analog models of strike-slip (lateral offset) deformation. Models of strike-slip faulting typically develop a pattern of synthetic and/or antithetic faults on the upper surface preceding the appearance of long, continuous, shear zone-parallel faults (Tchalenko, 1970; Naylor and others, 1986; Sylvester, 1988; McKinnon and de la Barra, 1998). In such models the synthetic and antithetic faults, although discontinuous on the surface, link with the basement fault at depth. In effect, they accommodate strains that are slightly too great to be taken up by folding, but with continued deformation a discrete, shear zone-parallel fault is required to accommodate larger strains.

The same sequence of deformation took place along the developing East Kaibab monocline as Paleozoic and Mesozoic cover rocks folded and faulted in response to movement on the reactivated basement fault. The process of folding, development of discontinuous fractures, and eventual growth of a through-going fault began at depth near the basement-cover interface, and continued upward through the core of the East Kaibab monocline as the structure grew. The cross sections in figure 10 are exaggerated

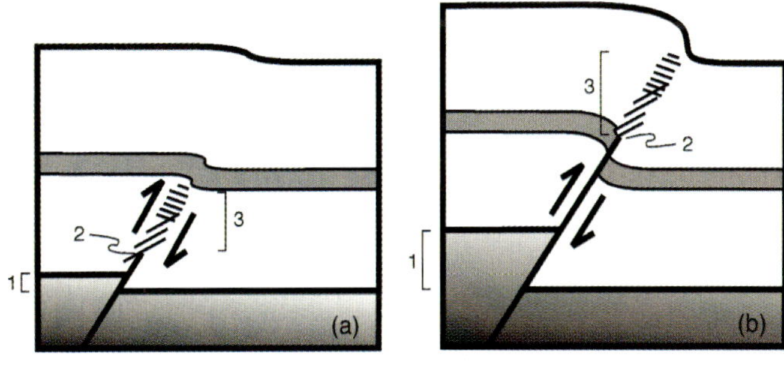

Figure 10. (a) Up-section migration of the basement-rooted fault and its fault tip deformation zone began near the basement-cover interface during initial increments of basement fault offset and overlying fold growth. (b) With continued deformation, the fault tip and associated fracture zone propagated upward through the core of the East Kaibab monocline as the fold grew. From diagram (a) to diagram (b); basement fault offset (1) increases, and the basement-rooted fault tip (2) and its fault tip deformation zone (3) migrate upward. The fracture pattern exposed along the north-plunging East Kaibab monocline in southern Utah preserves the final increment of this fault propagation and fault tip fracture formation in horizontal map view (figure 7).

sketches of fold development and simultaneous up-section migration of the fault tip deformation zone. The same structural relationships are visible in map view along the East Kaibab monocline because of the northward plunge of the fold axis. The small, discontinuous faults seen along the East Kaibab monocline represent synthetic and antithetic fractures that formed in higher structural and stratigraphic levels ahead of the upward-propagating tip of the basement fault.

Oblique Deformation

The orientations of fractures in the fault tip zone also contain clues about the vertical and lateral movements involved in growth of the East Kaibab monocline. It is simplest to imagine that movement on the basement fault was pure reverse-slip, with the west side moving up relative to the east. In fact, most early studies of Colorado Plateau monoclines assumed that the structures formed by this dip-slip reverse fault motion (Powell, 1873; Walcott, 1890; Stearns, 1971; Reches, 1978). However, the angular relationships between the monocline and the synthetic and antithetic faults in southern Utah suggest that right-lateral slip occurred in addition to reverse slip, causing the west side of the monocline and fault to move northward relative to the east side.

The angular relationships between synthetic and antithetic faults described in the previous section resemble a characteristic surface fault pattern recognized in physical modeling experiments and field studies of strike-slip fault systems (for example Riedel, 1929; Tchalenko, 1970; An and Sammis, 1996; Reading, 1980; Sylvester, 1988). This characteristic 'Riedel shear' pattern is easiest to describe using an example. Figure 11a shows the typical Riedel pattern that forms as a result of right-handed strike-slip offset. The shear fracture array that develops at the surface consists of Riedel or R-shears at an angle of 15° to the basement shear direction, Riedel-prime or R' shears at about 75° to the basement zone, and faults that are parallel to the shear zone (Y-shears). In a right-lateral shear zone the R and Y shears accommodate right-lateral offset, synthetic to the shear direction; R' fractures are antithetic to the shear zone, accommodating small left-lateral offsets. In physical models and in natural fault systems, synthetic and/or antithetic fractures can develop independently or together, producing map patterns similar to figure 11b, 11c, or 11d.

Note that in figure 7 the fault orientations in the fault-tip deformation zone strongly resemble Riedel fracture geometry. North of Paria, faulting in the steep limb takes the form of northeast-striking, left-stepping, en-echelon faults, and northwest-striking, right-stepping, en-echelon faults. These faults accommodate reverse-right-lateral and reverse-left-lateral offset, respectively. The fault pattern indicates that the steep limb of the East Kaibab acted as a shear zone during deformation, with small synthetic and antithetic faults accommodating reverse-right-lateral shear in the steep fold limb ahead of the advancing basement-rooted fault tip. The right-handed component of off-

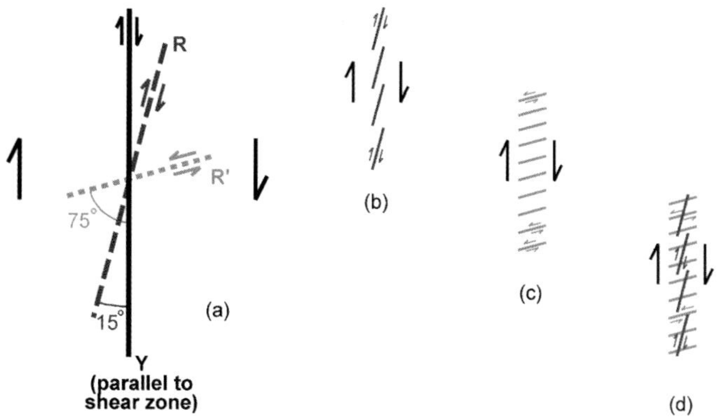

Figure 11. Riedel shear geometry. (a) In a right-handed system, synthetic faults at 15° to the shear zone accommodate right-lateral offset, and antithetic faults at 75° to the zone accommodate left-lateral offset. Synthetic and antithetic fractures can form independently or together, creating fault patterns that resemble (b), (c), or (d).

set within the shear zone in southern Utah is demonstrated by the orientations of striations on fault surfaces and by small right-handed offsets of stratigraphic layers. The reverse, west-side-up component of movement is expressed by the 1,600 m, west-side-up structural relief of the Kaibab uplift as a whole. The Mesozoic-level shear zone and its underlying cause, the reactivated basement fault, therefore resulted from reverse-right-lateral, oblique deformation.

The Riedel-type fault tip fracture pattern therefore provides two key pieces of information: it leads to recognition of the presence of an upward-propagating fault tip deformation zone, and permits interpretation of the oblique motions involved in fault and fold development. In this context, the disappearance of the shear zone north of Grosvenor's Arch represents the expected up-section transition from faulting to folding; that is, the dying out of the basement-rooted fault tip and associated Riedel fractures. However, the absence of the fault pattern south of the Arizona-Utah border raises other questions (see figures 6b, 6c, and 6d). Erosion has exposed the same rocks along the monocline in northern Arizona as in southern Utah, but evidence for basement-rooted faulting at the surface disappears to the south. In fact, in the Grand Canyon basement-rooted faulting has propagated only as high as the Mississippian Redwall Limestone (figure 5). If the Riedel type fracture pattern in southern Utah represents growth of basement-rooted faulting toward the surface, why is it not visible to the south, at lower structural and stratigraphic levels? Knowledge of the three dimensional nature of fault surfaces and fault offset can explain the discrepancy.

Fault Slip Gradient

Fault surfaces are often roughly elliptical, with offset decreasing from the center of the fault plane toward the lateral terminations of the elliptical fracture (Barnett and others, 1987). The block diagram in figure 12a contains a

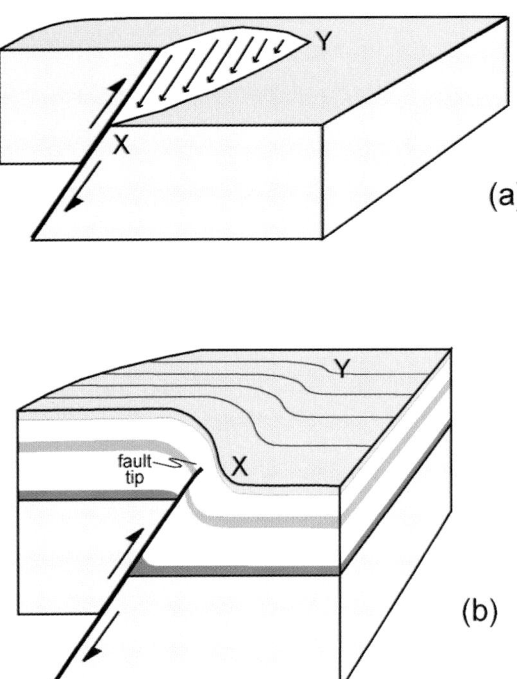

Figure 12. Faults and folds can accommodate different amounts of off-set at different locations. (a) Offset on a reverse fault diminishes from point X to point Y. (b) The fault dies out beneath the ground surface. Above the fault tip, fold offset diminishes from point X to point Y.

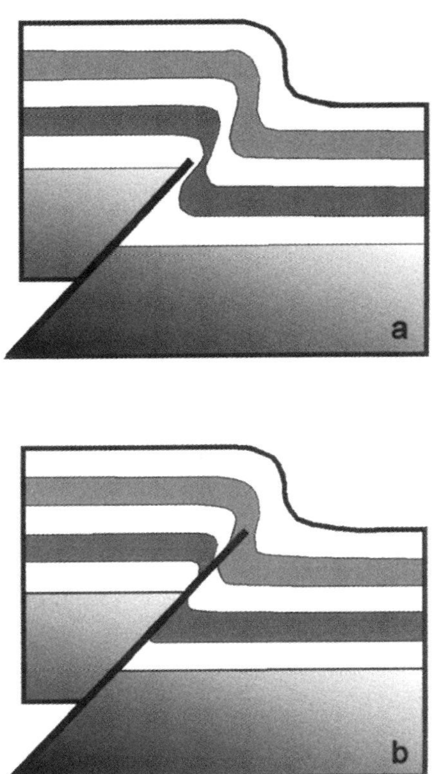

Figure 13. Schematic diagrams of drape folding (a) and fault-propagation folding (b). The drape fold model suggests that most deformation in the above-basement rocks is accommodated by stratigraphic thinning; faulting does not play a major role in above-basement deformation. In the fault-propagation fold model, increased fault offset in basement translates to increased fault development in sedimentary cover. Stratigraphic thinning may still take place during fold development, but the propagating fault accommodates increasing displacement in the sedimentary cover as the fault and fold grow.

segment of a reverse fault on which displacement gradually decreases. On the surface of the diagram, fault displacement is greatest at point X and decreases northward to zero at point Y. Gentle folding of the rock mass in the vicinity of the fault accommodates the change in fault slip along strike.

In reality not all faults propagate to the surface of the Earth. Often fault offset at depth gives way to fold-related offset toward the surface. Figure 12b presents the same geometric relationship shown in figure 12a, with fault displacement dying out from point X to point Y. However, cover strata in figure 12b are folded in response to the fault offset. Figure 12b clearly shows that fold displacement at the surface, like fault displacement, decreases from X to Y. In complex natural structures like the East Kaibab monocline, fold profiles can vary considerably along a structural trend, indicating changes in fault offset at depth.

The East Kaibab monocline obtains its maximum structural relief of 1,600 m in southern Utah (Gregory and Moore, 1931). This structural relief decreases gradually south of the Utah-Arizona border toward the Grand Canyon where offset is only 800 m, likely reflecting variations in fault offset at depth.

The magnitude of fault slip not only affects the fold form and degree of structural relief in overlying strata, but also determines the prevalence of faulting within the fold. Greater fault slip at depth results in more extensive faulting in the overlying rocks. The fault-propagation fold model describes the elegant interplay of faulting and folding.

Fault-Propagation Folding

Formation of monoclines traditionally has been explained by drape folding. In this conceptual model, fault displacement at depth gives way abruptly to fold-accommodated displacement in the sedimentary cover. The transition is accomplished by thinning and stretching of the lowest sedimentary rock layers over the displaced fault blocks, and as a result faulting does not play a major role in above-basement deformation (Stearns, 1971; Reches and Johnson, 1978) (figure 13a).

The drape fold model was applied to Colorado Plateau monoclines for good reasons. Firstly, the surface form of monoclines tends to support a drape fold origin. The monoclines are broad folds in above-basement sedimentary cover, and show little evidence for basement-rooted fault offset at the surface (as opposed to Rocky Mountain foreland uplifts, where faulting is of major importance; for example Schmidt and Perry, 1988; Schmidt

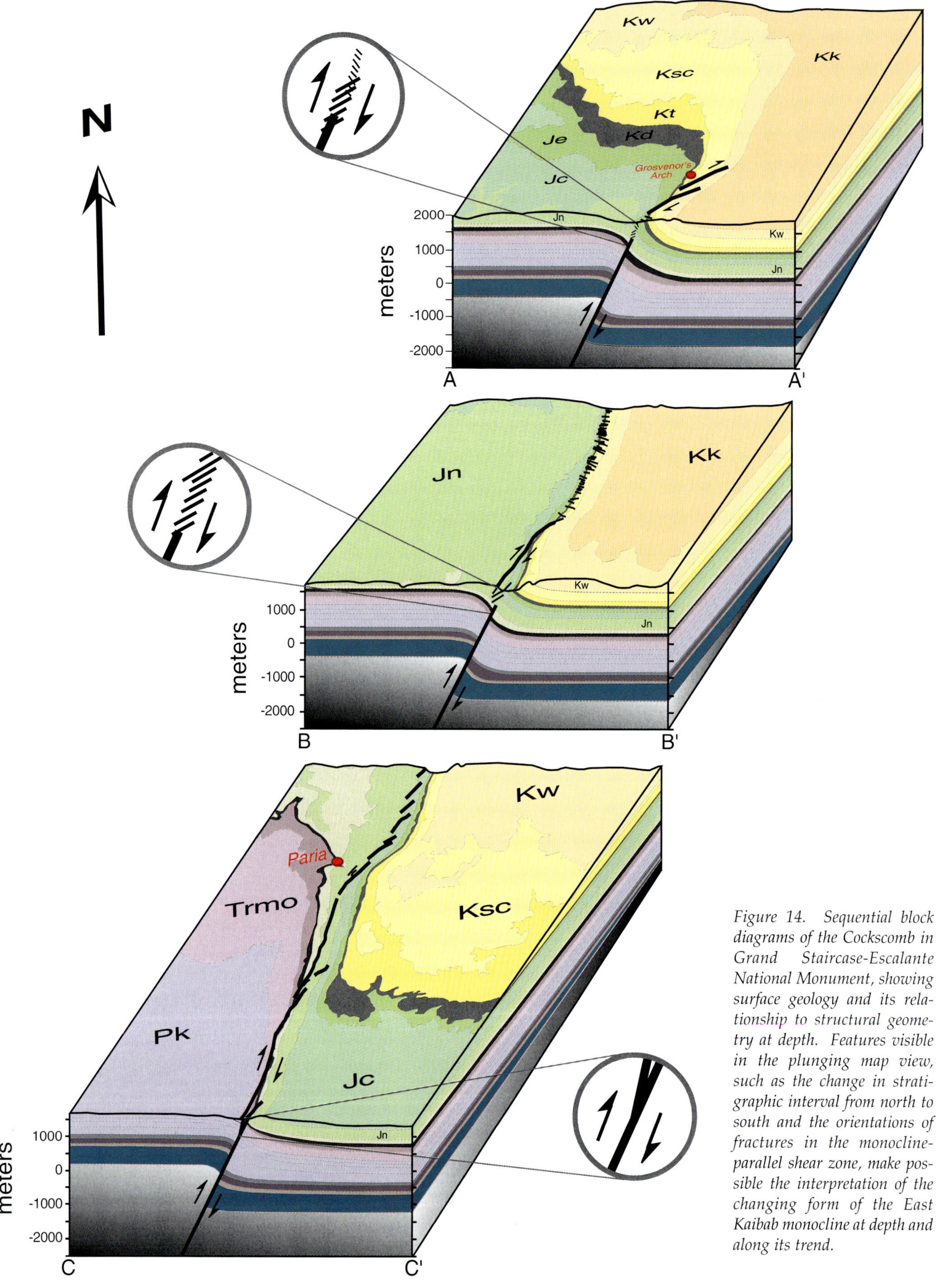

Figure 14. Sequential block diagrams of the Cockscomb in Grand Staircase-Escalante National Monument, showing surface geology and its relationship to structural geometry at depth. Features visible in the plunging map view, such as the change in stratigraphic interval from north to south and the orientations of fractures in the monocline-parallel shear zone, make possible the interpretation of the changing form of the East Kaibab monocline at depth and along its trend.

and others, 1993). Secondly, deep Grand Canyon exposures of monoclines show that fault offset changes to fold offset at very low levels in the post-Proterozoic sedimentary section (figures 2 and 5). Where the Grand Canyon incises the East Kaibab monocline the transition from fault to fold is accomplished by obvious thinning in the lower Paleozoic rocks, allowing higher stratigraphic units to fold without obvious faulting. Although fault-accommodated offset gives way to fold-accommodated offset very low in the above-basement section in the Grand Canyon, basement-rooted faulting is apparent at much higher structural and stratigraphic levels of the fold in southern Utah. The drape fold model fails to account for the prevalence of basement-rooted faulting along the East Kaibab monocline in Grand Staircase-Escalante National Monument.

The fault-propagation fold model proposes that a fault at depth progressively overtakes and displaces its overlying fold. Geologists have applied the term 'fault-propagation fold' to various structural settings because it describes succinctly the intimate relationship between faulting and fold growth. Despite some resulting confusion about the term's meaning (for example Mitra and Mount, 1999; Stone, 1999), one consistent feature of the model is that a fault tip at depth propagates upward, progressively offsetting higher levels in the overlying fold as displacement increases (Suppe, 1985; Davis and Reynolds, 1996) (figure 13b). The model implies that a fault with greater offset at depth will have propagated to higher levels in the overlying folded strata.

In the case of the East Kaibab monocline, the observation that faulting gives way to folding at a low stratigraphic level in the Grand Canyon simply reflects the relatively small amount of offset on the basement fault at that location. That is, if the East Kaibab monocline is a fault-propagation fold, greater vertical fault slip in the Grand Canyon would have resulted in propagation of faulting higher into the overlying strata. The Riedel shear pattern exposed in southern Utah represents initiation of basement-rooted faulting in the Mesozoic rocks in an area with twice as much structural relief as is present in the Grand Canyon (1,600 m versus 800 m). In a sense, the Cockscomb reached a more 'mature' stage of development in southern Utah than in the Grand Canyon.

Summary

The geologic concepts of plunging structure, down-plunge viewing, Riedel shear geometry, fault-slip gradient, and fault-propagation folding combine to illuminate the processes involved in the Laramide development of the East Kaibab monocline. The gentle northward plunge of the Cockscomb in southern Utah exposes structural relationships across several stratigraphic levels. Because of the northward plunge, lateral changes in landscape and map relationships along the structure correspond to different fold and fault geometry at depth. The down-plunge viewing technique offers a quick and accurate method for visualizing cross-sectional structural relationships at the

stratigraphic levels exposed on the map. Geometry of fractures exposed in the steep monoclinal limb indicates fault tip fracture propagation related to a basement-rooted oblique fault zone. The absence of the shear fracture pattern south of the Arizona-Utah border is explained by fault-propagation folding combined with a decrease in fault slip to the south.

The concepts described in the preceding sections allow interpretation of the East Kaibab monocline's oblique-slip fault-propagation fold origin and visualization of its resulting fault-fold geometry at depth. Figure 14 presents block diagrams of the Cockscomb that summarize key relationships exposed by or inferred from the relationships exposed in Grand Staircase-Escalante National Monument.

CONCLUSIONS

Interpreting the three dimensional geometry and mode of formation of the Cockscomb involves several conceptual steps. Firstly, reconnaissance of the structural changes along the East Kaibab monocline forms the basis for noticing clues to underlying structural relationships. Secondly, the special north-plunging map view provides the opportunity for down-plunge viewing of an accurate profile section. Distortions imposed by the elongated map pattern bring into view a deformation zone associated with the basement-rooted fault tip, and within this tip zone secondary fault orientations indicate oblique deformation. Changes in structural relief along the trend of the monocline indicate displacement variations along the basement fault at depth. These features together reveal the role of oblique fault-propagation folding in formation of the Cockscomb. Finally, simplified block diagrams can be constructed based on these essential techniques and concepts to summarize the three dimensional geometry created by faulting, folding, uplift and erosion.

The northward plunge of the East Kaibab monocline in Grand Staircase-Escalante National Monument provides all the necessary evidence for formulating an oblique-slip fault-propagation-fold interpretation of the Kaibab uplift (Tindall and Davis, 1999). The exposure of structural and stratigraphic relationships in the monument is unique, offering insight into the formation mechanisms of Colorado Plateau uplifts that can be found nowhere else. For this reason, the importance of oblique deformation and progressive fault-fold development in formation of this, and possibly other, Colorado Plateau uplifts merits further investigation.

ACKNOWLEDGMENTS

Many field assistants contributed to field work on the East Kaibab monocline, including Erin Colie, Scott Grasse, Nate Shotwell, Jessica Greybill, William Abbey, Pilar Garcia, Seth Gering, Shari Christofferson, and Danielle Vanderhorst. Thanks to Tom McCandless and George Davis for valuable reviews of the manuscript. Research was supported by National Science Foundation grant NSF#EAR-9406208 and the Dr. H. Wesley Peirce Scholarship, Department of Geosciences, University of Arizona.

REFERENCES

An, L.J., and Sammis, C.G., 1996, Development of strike-slip faults–shear experiments in granular materials and clay using a new technique: Journal of Structural Geology, v. 18, no. 8, p. 1061-1077.

Babenroth, D.L., and Strahler, A.N., 1945, Geomorphology and structure of the East Kaibab monocline, Arizona and Utah: Geological Society of America Bulletin, v. 56, p. 107-150.

Barnett, J.A.M., Mortimer, J., Rippen, J.H., Walsh, J.J., and Watterson, J., 1987, Displacement geometry in the volume containing a single normal fault: American Association of Petroleum Geologists Bulletin, v. 71, no. 8, p. 925-937.

Bond, G.C., 1997, New constraints on Rodinia break-up ages from revised tectonic subsidence curves [abs.]: Geological Society of America Abstracts with Programs, v. 29, no. 6, p. 280.

Brown, W.G., 1988, Deformational style of Laramide uplifts in the Wyoming foreland, *in* Schmidt, C.J., and Perry, W. J. Jr., editors, Interaction of the Rocky Mountain foreland and the Cordilleran thrust belt, Geological Society of America Memoir 171, p. 1-26.

Coney, P.J., 1976, Plate tectonics and the Laramide orogeny: New Mexico Geological Society Special Publication 6 – Tectonics and mineral resources of southwestern North America, p. 5-10.

Davis, G.H., 1978, Monocline fold pattern of the Colorado Plateau, *in* Matthews, V. III, editor, Laramide folding associated with basement block faulting in the western United States: Geological Society of America Memoir 151, p. 215-233.

Davis, G.H., and Reynolds, S.J., 1996, Structural geology of rocks and regions: New York, John Wiley & Sons Inc., 776 p.

Dutton, C.E., 1882, Tertiary history of the Grand Canyon district: U.S. Geological Survey Monograph 2, 264 p.

Gregory, H.E., and Moore, R.C., 1931, The Kaiparowits region - a geographic and geological reconnaissance of parts of Utah and Arizona: U.S. Geological Survey Professional Paper 164, 161 p.

Hintze, L.F., 1988, Geologic history of Utah: Brigham Young University Geology Studies Special Publication 7, 202 p.

Huntoon, P.W., 1969, Recurrent movements and contrary bending along the West Kaibab fault zone: Plateau, v. 42, p. 66-74.

Huntoon, P.W., 1993, Influence of inherited Precambrian basement structure on the localization and form of Laramide monoclines, Grand Canyon, Arizona, *in* Schmidt, C.J., Chase, R.B., and Erslev, E.A., editors, Laramide basement deformation in the Rocky Mountain foreland of the western United States: Geological Society of America Special Paper 280, p. 243-256.

Huntoon, P.W., and Sears, J.W., 1975, Bright Angel and Eminence Faults, eastern Grand Canyon, Arizona: Geological Society of America Bulletin, v. 86, no. 4, p. 465-472.

Mackin, J.H., 1959, The down-structure method of viewing geologic maps: Journal of Geology, v. 58, no. 1, p. 55-72.

Maxson, J.H., 1961, Geologic map of the Bright Angel quadrangle, Grand Canyon National Park, Arizona: Grand Canyon Natural History Association.

McKinnon, S.D., and de la Barra, I.G., 1998, Fracture initiation, growth, and effect on stress field–a numerical investigation: Journal of Structural Geology, v. 20, no. 12, p. 1673-1689.

Mitra, Shankar, and Mount, V.S., 1999, Foreland basement-involved structures–reply: American Association of Petroleum Geologists Bulletin, v. 83, no. 12, p. 2017-2023.

Naylor, M.A., Mandl, G., and Sijpesteijn, C.H.K., 1986, Fault geometries in basement-induced wrench faulting under different initial stress states: Journal of Structural Geology, v. 8, p. 737-752.

Powell, J.W., 1873, Exploration of the Colorado River of the West and its tributaries explored in 1869-1972: Washington, D.C, Smithsonian Institution, 291 p.

Reading, H.G., 1980, Characteristics and recognition of strike-slip fault systems: Special Publication of the International Association of Sedimentology, v. 4, p. 7-26.

Reches, Ze'ev, 1978, Development of monoclines: Part I, Structure of the Palisades Creek branch of the East Kaibab monocline, Grand Canyon, Arizona, *in* Matthews, V. III, editor, Laramide folding associated with basement block faulting in the western United States: Geological Society of America Memoir 151, p. 235-272.

Reches, Ze'ev, and Johnson, A.M., 1978, Development of monoclines: Part II, Theoretical analysis of monoclines, *in* Matthews, V. III, editor, Laramide folding associated with basement block faulting in the western United States: Geological Society of America Memoir 151, p. 273-311.

Riedel, W., 1929, Zur Mechanik geologischer Brucherscheinungen: Centralbl. F. Mineral. Geol. U. Pal., v. 1929 B, p. 354-368.

Rosnovsky, T.A., 1998, Variation in joint and fault patterns along the East Kaibab and Waterpocket monoclines, Colorado Plateau: Stanford University, M.S. thesis, 58 p.

Schmidt, C.J., Chase, R.B., and Erslev, E.A., editors, 1993, Laramide basement deformation in the Rocky Mountain foreland of the Western United States: Geological Society of America Special Paper 280, 365 p.

Schmidt, C.J., and Perry, W.J. Jr., editors, 1988, Interaction of the Rocky Mountain foreland and the Cordilleran thrust belt: Geological Society of America Memoir 171, 582 p.

Stearns, D.W., 1971, Mechanisms of drape folding in the Wyoming Province, *in* Renfro, A.R., editor, Symposium on Wyoming tectonics and their economic significance: Wyoming Geological Association 23rd Field Conference Guidebook, p. 125-143.

Stern, Sharon, 1992, Geometry of basement faults underlying the northern extent of the East Kaibab monocline, Utah: Chapel Hill, University of North Carolina, M.S. thesis.

Stone, D.S., 1999, Foreland basement-involved structures-discussion: American Association of Petroleum Geologists Bulletin, v. 83, no. 12, p. 2006-2016.

Suppe, John, 1985, Principles of structural geology: Inglewood Cliffs, New Jersey, Prentice-Hall, Inc., 537 p.

Sylvester, A.G., 1988, Strike-slip faults: Geological Society of America Bulletin, v. 100, no. 11, p. 1666-1703.

Tchalenko, J.S., 1970, Similarities between shear zones of different magnitudes: Geological Society of America Bulletin, v. 81, p. 1625-1640.

Timmons, M.J., Karlstrom, K.E., Dehler, C.M., Geissman, J.W., and Heizler, M.T., in press, Proterozoic multistage (~1.1 and ~0.8 Ga) extension in the Grand Canyon Supergroup and establishment of northwest and north-south tectonic grains in the southwestern United States: Geological Society of America Bulletin.

Tindall, S.E., and Davis, G.H., 1999, Monocline development by oblique-slip fault-propagation folding: the East Kaibab monocline, Colorado Plateau, Utah: Journal of Structural Geology, v. 21, no. 10, p. 1303-1320.

Walcott, C.D., 1890, Study of line displacement in the Grand Canyon of the Colorado in northern Arizona: Geological Society of America Bulletin, v. 1, p. 49-64.

Wernicke, Brian, 1992, Cenozoic extensional tectonics of the U.S. Cordillera, *in* Burchfiel, B.C., Lipman, P.W., and Zoback, M.L., editors, The geology of North America, the Cordilleran orogen–conterminous U.S.: Geological Society of America, v. C-2, p. 553-581.

Windley, B.F., 1995, The Evolving Continents: Chinchester, John Wiley and Sons, 526 p.

Bryce Canyon National Park
Photo courtesy of Utah Travel Council